DAY BY DAY
with the
BOSTON RED SOX

by Bill Nowlin

Published by Rounder Books

An imprint of
Rounder Records Corp.
One Camp Street
Cambridge, MA 02140

ISBN 1-57940-126-0

Cover design by Sarah Smith

Rounder Books
1 Camp Street
Cambridge, MA 02140

Nowlin, Bill, 1945–
Day by Day with the Boston Red Sox
1. Boston Red Sox (Baseball team). History I T.

First edition
2005910890

ISBN 1-57940-126-0

DAY BY DAY

with the

BOSTON RED SOX

This book is dedicated to Ed Walton, who wrote the groundbreaking *This Date in Red Sox History* back in 1978, and innumerable articles for the Red Sox Magazine for 30 years. Ed passed away as this manuscript came to completion. I wish Ed could have enjoyed reading this one. He was helpful right to the end, even having his wife Ruth send me a response to a question when (unbeknownst to me) he was unable to reply himself.

CONTENTS

ICON KEY

 Pitching event

 Hitting or slugging highlight

 Base running or Fielding feat or oddity

 Trade or business deal

 Unusual event

 High point/Low point (on the field or otherwise)

 An item about Fenway Park

 Statistical anomaly, or unusual statistical item

 Personal or civic triumph

 Tragedy or unfortunate event

 Interesting debut

JANUARY

January 1

2005 January 1, 2005 was the first day in 86 years that the Red Sox began a new year as reigning World Champions.

2003 Who knew the story this would become? The new year broke with the relatively 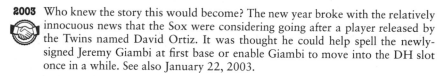innocuous news that the Sox were considering going after a player released by the Twins named David Ortiz. It was thought he could help spell the newly-signed Jeremy Giambi at first base or enable Giambi to move into the DH slot once in a while. See also January 22, 2003.

1920 Babe Ruth wanted his contract doubled, to $20,000, but declared that he would only play for Boston, and if Boston wouldn't pay it, he would not play in organized baseball. So reported the January 1, 1920 issue of *The Sporting News*. By the time of the report, Ruth had already been sold to New York, but it had not yet been announced. The article observed, "Here we have Frazee willing to trade Ruth or sell him to another club, and Ruth declaring himself that he wants to stick right in Boston."

1919 Fred Mitchell, president of the Chicago Cubs, opened negotiations with Red Sox owner Harry Frazee regarding holding joint spring training in Pasadena, California. It was not to be.

1917 Although the Players' Fraternity was attempting to organize baseball players and contemplated a strike to begin February 20, the first issue of the *Boston Globe* in 1917 reported that neither Braves president Percy Haughton nor Red Sox president Harry Frazee were fearful of a players strike.

BIRTHDATES
Frank Fuller 1893 (on Red Sox roster in 1923); Hack Miller 1894 (1918); Al Stokes 1900 (1925–1926); Lynn Jones 1953 (coach, 2004–2005)

DEATHS
None yet

January 2

1996 Free agent pitcher Jamie Moyer was one who got away. Signed by the Sox on the first business day of 1996, he compiled a 7–1 mark (and a high 4.50 ERA) and was traded to Seattle on July 30 for versatile outfielder Darren Bragg. Moyer went on to win over 100 games for Seattle, including a couple of 20-game seasons. Bragg had some good games but, with a lifetime average not much above .250, had moved from club to club.

1992 Free agent pitcher Frank "Sweet Music" Viola signed with the Red Sox, but the two-time 20-game winner only went 25–21 over three seasons with the team.

1927 Detroit owner Frank Navin admitted that Tigers pitchers had received "extra compensation from the management of the Chicago White Sox for their efforts to defeat the Boston team" back in 1917.

1917 "Well, what's the answer, Bill?" *Boston Globe* sportswriter Tim Murnane asked Bill Carrigan, in the day's column. President Harry Frazee had just returned from Lewiston, Maine where he had made Carrigan an extravagant offer to return as Red Sox manager for 1917. Murnane also noted that the Red Sox, as back-to-back World Champions (1915 and 1916), could demand more inducement from suitors seeking the Sox for spring training. Ultimately, Boston returned to Hot Springs, Arkansas.

1913 Pitcher George "Rube" Foster signed with the Red Sox, his signed contract being received in Boston on this date. However, according to a *Washington Post* story, "the officials of the club are in utter ignorance whether he won twenty and lost none or lost twenty and won none: only that, it is understood, he is the pick of [the Texas League]."

Jake Stahl declared himself ready to quit as soon as he could find someone to take his place at first base.

TRANSACTIONS
1908: Acquired Ed McFarland from the White Sox in trade for Al Shaw.
1992: Signed free agent Frank Viola.
1996: Signed free agent Jamie Moyer.

BIRTHDATES
Pop Rising 1872 (1905); David Cone 1963 (2001); Greg Swindell 1965 (1998); Jeff Suppan 1975 (1995–2003)

DEATHS
Curt Fullerton 1975; Eddie Smith 1994

January 3

1973 CBS sells the New York Yankees ball club, at a loss, to George Steinbrenner and a group of backers who put up $10 million for the purchase. Pocket change for Tom Yawkey; imagine the Red Sox owner financing the purchase through a proxy and running the franchise into the ground! Steinbrenner states that he will not be active in day-to-day operations, but will be an absentee owner sticking to shipbuilding. The only time this held true was between 1990 and 1993, when "he was serving a 'lifetime' ban from baseball. Even with this attention, his shipping company filed for bankruptcy in 1993." (Art McDonald, *This Date in New York Yankee Hating*)

1942 GM Eddie Collins is in Philadelphia for the wedding of son Eddie Jr. to Jane Pennock, daughter of pitcher Herb Pennock. Ted Williams telephoned and informed Collins that he had been reclassified in the military draft, and would be reporting for a physical on January 8.

1923 Trading with the enemy. The Yankees announce the acquisition of pitcher George Pipgras from the Red Sox in exchange for catcher Al DeVormer. In a separate deal announced the same day, the Yankees purchased infielder Harvey Hendrick for cash, also from the Red Sox.

1917   The *New York Tribune* reported that the sale of the Red Sox to Harry Frazee and Hugh Ward was contingent on Bill Carrigan returning to manage the team. The day before, Carrigan declined and on January 4, Carrigan reiterated his determination to retire to his business interests in Maine.

1911   Boston owner John I. Taylor announced the signing of both Hugh Bradley and Marty McHale, said he considered Fresno the best place on the West Coast to hold spring training, and offered the opinion "ballplayers make a great mistake in using too much hot water in bathing after their work in the field. His idea is a little hot water and then a cold plunge or a cold shower bath." (*Boston Globe*)

TRANSACTIONS
1913: Signed Hubert Benjamin "Dutch" Leonard.
1920: The official date of the sale of Babe Ruth to the New York Yankees.
1923: Traded Harvey Hendrick and George Pipgras to the New
       York Yankees for Al DeVormer and cash.
1946: Traded Eddie Lake to the Detroit Tigers for Rudy York.
1985: Drafted Daryl Irvine.
1996: Signed free agent Tim Van Egmond, just granted free agency on December 21, 1995.

BIRTHDATES
Herb Bradley 1903 (1927–1929); Bill Cissell 1904 (1934); Sid Hudson 1915 (1952–1954); Jim Dwyer 1950 (1979–1980); John Leister 1961 (1987–1990); Luis Rivera 1964 (1989–1993)

DEATHS
George Stone 1945; Al Smith 2002

January 4

1947   Workers began installing seven light towers at Fenway Park, to total 1,120 lights and enable night games to be played there.

1919   Larry McLean, a catcher who had the first pinch-hit in Red Sox franchise history in 1901, was found unconscious in a Turkish steam bath and hospitalized with severe burns on his back and legs. A worse fate awaited McLean, though. (See March 24, 1921.)

1912   Thirteen-year veteran outfielder Jimmy McAleer is named president of the Red Sox. McAleer played for Cleveland in 1889–1898, and managed the Cleveland and St. Louis American League franchises from 1901–1909. He had served as manager of Washington in 1910 and 1911. Jake Stahl became Boston's field manager. McAleer had been involved in the creation of the St. Louis franchise. There may have been concerns prompted by his nickname—"Loafer"—but, in fact, the Red Sox became World Champions during his very first year.

1910   In another embarrassing story of the Red Sox and race relations, manager Patsy Donovan was discussing a new league being organized that would accept players regardless of color and chose the moment to tell of a "colored club that once trounced a strong semiprofessional team. The colored boys looked so much alike that their opponents failed to realize that they were sending only five men to the bat, the five best batters doing the hitting for the whole team." Worse, perhaps, was that the *Boston Globe* simply reported the story as an amusing one. (For exculpatory information on Donovan, however, see January 9, 1910.)

1902 Bill Dinneen, star pitcher for Boston's National League franchise, jumped to the Americans, became a 20-game winner for three straight years, and won three games in the 1903 World Series.

TRANSACTIONS
1936: Traded Hank Johnson, Al Niemiec, and $75,000 cash to the
 Philadelphia Athletics for Doc Cramer and Eric McNair.
2000: Free agent Israel Alcantara was signed.

BIRTHDATES
Ossie Vitt 1890 (1919–1921); Don McMahon 1930 (1966–1967)

DEATHS
Hal Deviney 1933; Biff Schlitzer 1948

January 5

1997 Sox knuckleballer Tim Wakefield was struck by a car while jogging in Florida. Fortunately, the injuries are minor and did not require admission to a hospital.

1990 The Red Sox announced that their road uniforms would henceforth bear the name of the ballplayer over the numeral on the back of the jersey. This innovation was reportedly pushed through by GM Lou Gorman. A Red Sox fan was quoted as grumbling, "If you don't know who the player is without a name, you don't deserve to be a Red Sox fan."

1963 The Red Sox and the new AFL Boston Patriots agree to a two-year deal under **FP** which the Patriots will play their home games at Fenway Park. The Patriots, whose first game was played at Braves Field, ultimately played at Fenway through 1968. In earlier years, the pro football Boston Redskins played at Fenway in the 1930s and the Boston Yanks played at the park in the middle 1940s. The Redskins relocated to Washington, and the Yanks eventually became the Indianapolis Colts. The Patriots, of course, won several Super Bowls in the first years of the 21st century, sharing back-to-back wins in the year the Red Sox won the 2004 World Series.

1934 During a $500,000 renovation of Fenway Park, a spark from a cement mixing machine ignited a fire which swept through the new center field bleachers, then leapt across the street and consumed at least two neighboring buildings. Damage was estimated at $250,000.

1920 The New York Yankees finally announce their purchase of Babe Ruth; salary negotiations had delayed the confirming announcement. The purchase price was $100,000, accompanied by a loan of $300,000 to Red Sox owner Harry Frazee, secured by a mortgage on Fenway Park. Ruth was 89–46 as a Red Sox pitcher. For New York, he never lost a game, going 5–0 in appearances scattered over the next 14 years. He'd hit 49 homers for Boston, but poled out 659 for the Yankees. The next time the Red Sox team won more than half its games was 1935.

Frazee said that he'd sold Ruth because the Sox were "fast becoming a one-man team" and that he would use the money to purchase other players to build up the ball club. The following day, January 6, Frazee said, "I sold Ruth for the best interests of the club. The Babe was not an influence for good or for team play. He thought only of himself, whether the question was one of breaking contracts or of making long hits." (See also December 26, 1919.)

1918 This is the news story in its entirety as it ran in the February 5 edition of the *Washington Post*: "Harry Frazee, owner of the Red Sox, says he is going to get a star infielder for the club before long." (See January 13.)

1917 Bill "Rough" Carrigan, who managed the Sox to back-to-back championships in 1915 and 1916, was determined to retire in order to look after his business interests in Maine, and resigned from the team. The Red Sox name popular second baseman Jack Barry as player-manager. After posing for a "small army of snapshot men" while signing his contract, Barry quipped, "I had no idea of the hardships of managing a baseball club until this afternoon." (*Boston Globe*)

Barry set a sterling example in one regard: in 1917, he sacrificed 54 times during the course of the season. In 1918, Barry was called to military service, but returned for one final year of play in 1919. It was unfortunate that Barry missed the chance to serve with the Sox in 1918. He had already earned a World Series share for several ball clubs in six of the years in the decade: 1910, 1911, 1913, 1914, 1915, and 1916.

1913 The Red Sox planned to remove the seats set up on Duffy's cliff for the 1912 World Series, and the extra seats in front of the grandstand, but would otherwise retain the extra seating installed for the Series. Nonetheless, President McAleer said, "So far as 25-cent seats are concerned, there will be more of them at the Boston grounds than in any other." On January 13, it was announced that Fenway would have 8,000 seats priced at two bits apiece.

TRANSACTIONS
1988: Signed free agent Dennis Lamp.
1999: Signed both Rheal Cormier and Kip Gross as free agents.
2001: Signed free agent Kent Mercker.

BIRTHDATES
Rube Foster 1888 (1913–1917): Regis Leheny 1908 (1932); Jack Kramer 1918
(1948–1949); Jeff Fassero 1963 (2000); Chris Nabholz 1967 (1994)

DEATHS
Ben Beville 1937

January 6

2004 Dennis Eckersley, who pitched for the Red Sox from 1978 through 1984 and then in 1998, was elected to the National Baseball Hall of Fame.

2003 The Red Sox signed veteran pitcher Mike Timlin as a free agent. Timlin already owned two World Series rings (1992 and 1993, with the Blue Jays), and would add another for the Red Sox in 2004.

1992 A Houston judge dismissed charges filed against Roger Clemens after The Rocket was found not guilty of another charge "stemming from an alleged barroom brawl with an off-duty police officer." (See January 19, 1991.)

1944 "Jumpin' Joe" Dugan, briefly with the Red Sox but then a seven-year veteran infielder for the Yankees, had apparently lost a bit of the spring in his step and was injured some 13 years after retirement when he was hit by a car while crossing the street in Boston's Back Bay. He suffered a scalp laceration and brain concussion, but was not on the Boston City Hospital danger list.

1941 Foreshadowing an utterance that did GM Dan Duquette some damage some 60 years later, American League publicist Henry Edwards noted that the Red Sox had been in first place more days than the pennant-winning Detroit Tigers. The Sox were in first 57 days in 1940, 20 more than the Tigers and five more than the second-place finishers, the Indians. Edwards did acknowledge that "they pay off on the club that's first at the finish."

TRANSACTIONS
2003: Signed free agent Mike Timlin.

BIRTHDATES
Jack Slattery 1878 (1901); Billy Purtell 1886 (1910–1911); Lenny Green 1933 (1965–1966); Casey Fossum 1978 (2001–2003)

DEATHS
Frank Oberlin 1952; Hank Olmsted 1969

January 7

2000 Korean left-hander Sang-Hoon Lee made quite an impression when introduced to the media on a snowy field at Fenway Park. The Korean was known as "Samson" due to his long, flowing, orange-tinted hair, and he acknowledged his awareness of another Lee in the Sox family tree: "Bill Lee was crazy! So am I." The new Sox signing pantomimed pitching from the mound, then pretended to see a long home run drive sail out of the park off his pretend pitch. After another pitch, he grabbed his shoulder in mock pain. The Sox now had three Koreans on the roster (Jin Ho Cho and Sun Woo Kim being the others), but none of the three ever posted big numbers.

1937 Bobby Doerr recently shot a 446-pound bear on his place near the Rogue River in Oregon, and was having the skin made into a rug. Elsewhere, but reported the same day, Mel Almada bagged two deer in northwestern Mexico. After his playing days were over, Almada signed to manage a Mexican League team. In 1946, *The Sporting News* reported, "The first day he had an argument with his players. They wouldn't do as he said, so he quit and returned to Sacramento."

1924 The Red Sox acquired veteran Bill Wambsganss from the Indians as part of a seven-man trade. After 10 years with Cleveland, Wambsganss found himself busy at the keystone sack, setting Red Sox single-season records for putouts (463) and assists (494). They might have had Wamby a lot earlier, had it not been for a little deception by Cleveland's then-manager Lee Fohl back in 1916. Taking a player to be named later in the trade for Tris Speaker, the Sox had

10 days from the start of the season to choose between Wambsganss and Fred Thomas. Fohl declined to start Wamby (.195 in 1915) in the lineup until Boston had chosen Thomas.

1920 Babe Ruth signed with the Yankees, and the *Globe*'s James O'Leary reports that just a year earlier a frustrated Ruth supposedly told Frazee, "Why don't you trade me to the Yankees; they will give me what I am asking from you." *The Baseball Chronology* reports Ruth as having said, "Frazee is not good enough to own any ball club, especially one in Boston." It has not been possible to track down the latter comment.

1911 The Red Sox signed Boston English High School star Hal Janvrin to a contract for 1911. Janvrin stuck with the Sox through 1917.

TRANSACTIONS
1924: Traded George Burns, Chick Fewster, and Roxy Walters to the Cleveland Indians for Dan Boone, Joe Connolly, Steve O'Neill, and Bill Wambsganss.
1932: Selected Bernie Friberg off waivers from the Philadelphia Phillies.
1976: Drafted Dennis Burtt and John Tudor.

BIRTHDATES
Topper Rigney 1897 (1926–1927); Red Steiner 1915 (1945); Dick Schofield 1935 (1969–1970); Dave Gray 1943 (1964); Tony Conigliaro 1945 (1964–1975)

DEATHS
Dutch Lerchen 1962; Dud Lee 1971; Hal Rhyne 1971; George Burns 1978

January 8

1960 The Sox trade pitcher Leo Kiely (25–25 in six seasons with the Sox, but still in the Army) to Kansas City for Panama-born infielder Ray Webster, who first makes the majors in 1967 for…KC. Kiely was expected to be out of the Army in time for spring training.

1916 With the demise of the Federal League, the competitive bidding up of salaries in the "baseball wars" was a thing of the past. A number of new contracts for 1916 mailed to the defending World Champion Red Sox would contain "radical reductions in salaries," according to the *Chicago Tribune*.

1904 President Henry Killilea and the Boston Americans secured a seven-year lease on the Huntington Avenue Grounds from the Boston Elevated Railway Company.

TRANSACTIONS
1960: Traded Leo Kiely to the Indians for Ray Webster.

BIRTHDATES
Johnny Tobin 1921 (1945); Jim Busby 1927 (1959–1960); Willie Tasby 1933 (1960); Jeremi Gonzalez 1975 (2005)

DEATHS
Larry Pratt 1969

January 9

1998 Mo Vaughn is arrested in the early morning hours and charged with drunken driving when his Ford pickup truck collides with a car parked and abandoned in the breakdown lane. Mo's truck flipped over onto its roof. Vaughn failed a number of sobriety tests, according to state police, but pleaded not guilty to a charge of drunken driving at his arraignment. No one was injured, but Mo's reputation is the main casualty. (See March 11, 1998.)

1989 Carl Yastrzemski was elected to the Hall of Fame in his first year of eligibility. He is the first former Little League player elected to the Hall of Fame.

1982 After an interview for a broadcasting slot, Tony Conigliaro was being driven to Boston's Logan Airport by his brother Billy when he suffered a massive heart attack. He was in a coma for a considerable period of time, and in the hospital nearly two months. Though he lived for nearly eight years afterward, he never truly recovered.

1952 The U.S. Marine Corps announced it would recall aircraft pilots Ted Williams and the Yankees' Jerry Coleman to active duty. Ted was 33 years old at the time, had a wife and young daughter, and had not flown a plane since World War II.

1910 It's too bad the Red Sox didn't have the same management in 1945—when Jackie Robinson was accorded a sham tryout for the team—that they had in 1910. The Red Sox signed Native American pitcher Louis LeRoy, who had played well for St. Paul in 1909. Manager Patsy Donovan sized him up for a week, then signed him. When Donovan first scouted LeRoy in the summer of 1909, "LeRoy asked Donovan if his color would prevent him getting a trial in Boston, and was assured that Boston was looking for speed boys willing to hustle." (*Boston Globe*, January 9, 1910)

1903 Ban Johnson, architect of the American League, found two New York "businessmen" (Frank Farrell and Bill Devery) to buy the Baltimore franchise and move it to New York. The team, first known as the Highlanders, later became the New York Yankees. Three days earlier, the New York State Court of Appeals unanimously upheld Devery's removal as Chief of Police in New York City; Farrell owned a number of gambling houses in the city and was often in the news as a gambling czar.

TRANSACTIONS
1974: Drafted Bob Stanley, Chuck Rainey, and Steve Burke.
1976: Sold Terry Hughes to the St. Louis Cardinals.

BIRTHDATES
Bob Duliba 1935 (1965); Guido Grilli 1939 (1966); Otis Nixon 1959 (1994)

DEATHS
Ray Collins 1970; Lyn Lary 1973; Stan Spence 1983

January 10

2002 At the Boston Baseball Writers of America Dinner in Boston, GM Dan Duquette once again made the point that the 2001 Red Sox had done well by one standard: "We spent more days in first place than any year since '95." That may have been true—it's not clear that anybody even bothered to look it up—but the sour taste in every fan's mouth was the way the team fell apart over the last couple of months, and the final standings, which saw the the Sox a full 13½ games behind the New York Yankees, just three games over .500 at 82–79.

1950 The father pays for the sins of the son. When pitching prospect George Susce chooses to sign with the Sox, Cleveland fired his dad, longtime Indians coach George Susce.

1920 Bobby Roth was no Babe Ruth. He'd hit .256 without a homer in 63 games for the 1919 Red Sox. Like Ruth, Roth was apparently a difficult personality and when Boston traded him to Washington, the *Atlanta Constitution* noted that "he will become domesticated this year or his major league career will be abruptly terminated." Roth hit .291 (9 HR) in 138 games.

1918 The Red Sox acquired star infielder Stuffy McInnis from Connie Mack and the Philaelphia Athletics. Mack announced that had received no money in exchange and "practically made Boston a present of McInnis" and that (according to the *Chicago Tribune*) "while the men he will get later will help his team he does not consider them high class players." The transaction dated January 10 reportedly netted Mack the trio of Larry Gardner, Tillie Walker, and Hick Cady—actually quite a haul.

1908 A few weeks after owner John I. Taylor declared his team would be called the "Red Sox," *The Washington Post* wondered about the reaction in Chicago, home of the White Sox: "Shall they have to stop to slip in an adjective every time they refer to Comiskey's bunch?"

1906 American League president Ban Johnson denied that there was a movement afoot to oust John I. Taylor as president of the Boston ball club. He declared the Boston owners as "perfectly competent."

TRANSACTIONS
1918: Traded Hick Cady, Larry Gardner, and Tillie Walker to
   the Philadelphia Athletics for Stuffy McInnis.
1922: As part of a three-team trade, the Red Sox traded Roger Peckinpaugh to
   the Washington Senators. The Red Sox received Frank O'Rourke from
   the Senators and Joe Dugan from the Philadelphia Athletics. In addition,
   the Senators sent Jose Acosta and Bing Miller to the Athletics.
1978: Drafted Brian Denman in the 1978 amateur draft.
1983: Signed Josias Manzanillo as an amateur free agent.
1996: Acquired Wil Cordero and Bryan Eversgerd in trade from the Montreal
   Expos for Shayne Bennett, Rheal Cormier, and Ryan McGuire.

BIRTHDATES
Chick Stahl 1873 (1901–1906); Del Pratt 1888 (1921–1922); Johnny
Peacock 1910 (1937–1944); Ted Bowsfield 1935 (1958–1960)

DEATHS
Fred Bratschi 1962; Phil Marchildon 1997; Tommy Fine 2005

January 11

1930 The Red Sox planned a spring training in which they would not play any other major league clubs. "We have decided not to start in playing clubs that have been practicing two weeks before us, and neither do we want a heavy spring schedule," announced President Bob Quinn. After the team reached the north, they'd play two games each against Brooklyn and the Boston Braves.

1918 Is this the way a Red Sox prima donna is supposed to act? The very first Red Sox player to sign for 1918 was Babe Ruth.

1915 Col. Jacob Ruppert and Col. Tillinghast L'Hommedieu Huston complete the purchase of the New York Yankees from Frank Farrell for $460,000. After the sale, Farrell commented, "Money talks."

TRANSACTIONS
1983: Drafted Ellis Burks.
1999: Pat Rapp signed as a free agent.
2001: Signed free agents David Cone and Israel Alcantara.

BIRTHDATES
Ernie Andres 1918 (1946); Hank Fischer 1940 (1966–1967); Alex Delgado 1971 (1996)

DEATHS
Frank Quinn 1993

January 12

2001 After falling apart with a 4–14 (6.91 ERA) season with the Yankees in 2000, the Red Sox took a chance on former great (now free agent) David Cone. He performed acceptably (9–7, 4.31 ERA), but turned out to be a disappointment for the sum of money involved.

1946 Second Lieutenant Theodore S. Williams is discharged from the Marine Corps at Camp Miramar Air Depot near San Diego, five months after the end of World War II. He soon signs for the 1946 season and prepares to head for spring training, back in Florida after three years.

1924 Boston paid cash to purchase infielder Bobby Veach from the Tigers. Veach told newspapers that he would not go to the Red Sox, but he got over it, batted .298, and knocked in 99 runs in his one full season with the Sox.

1915 Manager Bill Carrigan admitted that several Red Sox pitchers had used emery paper to doctor the baseball, before it was banned in the fall of 1914. Joe Wood was particularly adept at doing so, actually having infielder Hal Janvrin be the one to hold onto the paper and rough up the ball's surface.

1913 The *Boston Globe* ran a feature in which 10 of the Red Sox explained how they spent the winter. Harry Hooper got married and motored to southern California, even visited Tijuana; he got in a lot of fishing and hunting as well. Charley Hall joined him and they bagged 67 ducks in one day, and caught 100 black bass on another. Joe Wood helped build a new house on his farm, and "succeeded in knocking off the end of my thumb with the hammer." Larry Gardner said he was leading the simple life in Vermont, and Ray Collins was home enjoying his family. Heinie Wagner took long walks to strengthen his legs, and pumped his player piano for an hour or so every day, again to strengthen those legs.

1910 The Red Sox had an option on Happy Jack Chesbro, but decided to let the veteran pitcher return to New York. Chesbro had appeared in just one game ever for the Sox, on the final day of 1909. It proved to be his last in the majors.

The Boston Nationals placed their order for new uniforms with Wright and Ditson, and specified that the team would once again wear red stockings. Once the team had given up the red hosiery after the 1907 season, however, the Boston Americans had seized on the opportunity to name their own team the Red Sox. (See December 18, 1907.)

TRANSACTIONS
1924: Purchased Bobby Veach from Detroit.
1973: Signed amateur free agent Luis Aponte.
1981: Drafted Mike Rochford and Charlie Mitchell.

BIRTHDATES
Gary Wilson 1877 (1902); William Matthews 1878 (1909); Hank Olmsted 1879 (1905); Mike Marshall 1960 (1990–1991); Mike Trujillo 1960 (1985–1986)

DEATHS
None yet

January 13

1983 It was really just a case of unloading pitcher Mike Torrez after five seasons with the Sox, when they traded him to New York (the Mets) for a minor leaguer.

1955 Bill Dinneen died; he'd been a star pitcher for the Boston Americans in the 1903 World Series and later served as an AL umpire for 28 years.

1954 The Sox re-sign Joe Dobson, who'd pitched eight years with the team, then gone to the White Sox for three years. Dobson proves to have less than three innings remaining in his major league career.

1926 Before mid-January, the Red Sox had already moved to bolster their 1926 ball club by making winter moves to acquire three new catchers, four flycatchers, and half a dozen pitchers, according to Burt Whitman, writing in *The Sporting News*. It was a case of "every man for himself." Looking over more than a few new prospects each year was unusual in the era.

1913 There were plenty of Red Sox allusions during the Majestic Theatre presentation of "Hanky-Panky" attended by members of the Winter League fan booster organization and by President McAleer. At the show's end, the entire company waved little red socks fastened to canes.

TRANSACTIONS
1981: Drafted Danny Sheaffer.
1983: Traded Mike Torrez to the New York Mets. Acquired, after
        he was named later, minor leaguer Mike Davis.

BIRTHDAYS
Emmett O'Neill 1918 (1943–1945); Kevin Mitchell 1962 (1996); Billy Jo Robidoux 1964 (1990)

DEATHS
Bill Dinneen 1955; Charlie Gelbert 1967; Bill Clowers 1978; Joe McCarthy 1978

January 14

2003 Red Sox GM Theo Epstein claimed Kevin Millar off waivers from the Florida Marlins. He had been placed on waivers for what the Marlins assumed was a formality in effecting Millar's transfer to the Chunichi Dragons of Japan. The Dragons had paid the Marlins $1.2 million for the rights to Millar, and negotiated at least an understanding toward a two year, $6.2 million contract with Millar himself. All seemed set until brand-new GM Epstein broke an unwritten code between clubs that they'd not interfere with the sale of players to overseas clubs. Millar's agents claimed that there was no "final agreement" with the Dragons, even though the Marlins had released him assuming there was. The waiver claim was rejected, but negotiations continued for several weeks and the Red Sox ultimately got their man.

2000 Carlton Fisk is elected to the Hall of Fame and says he will wear a Red Sox cap on his plaque; the New England-born catcher added, "this has always been my favorite cap." The Red Sox announced that his number would be retired at Fenway Park after his induction in Cooperstown.

1986 Pitching prospect Curt Schilling is selected by the Red Sox in the second round of the free-agent draft. Traded before he made the big league team, the first season Schilling would pitch for Boston would be 2004.

1959 Joe Cronin was recommended as the next president of the American League by a six-man screening committee.

1955 Though the Red Sox had mailed Ted Williams a contract for 1955, Ted announced mid-summer commitments to fish for marlin in Iquique, Peru, and for salmon in Nova Scotia. Ted lost his defense of the International Light Tackle Sailfish Tournament at West Palm Beach, but maintained that he did not intend to return to baseball.

1935 Bing Miller started the year as a coach. Boston bought him from the Athletics and he hit .304 in 138 at-bats, and was 13-for-45 as a pinch-hitter, driving in nine runs and winning five games.

 The Boston Braves are informed that Braves Field would not be available to them in 1935, since the field had been leased to the Boston Kennel Club. The Commonwealth Real Estate Company announced that the Braves were $11,000 in default under their lease, and declared it broken. Red Sox GM Eddie Collins announced that Fenway Park would not be made available, unless the Braves were homeless due to fire or accident. Tom Yawkey did not countenance dog racing and would not permit the Braves to play their home games at Fenway Park, should that be the reason they could not play at their home park. Yawkey also believed that each team should have its own park and separate identity.

TRANSACTIONS
1913: Larry Pape sold to Buffalo for cash.
1935: Purchased Bing Miller from the Philadelphia Athletics.
1978: Signed amateur free agent Jackie Gutierrez.
1985: Signed free agent Bruce Kison.
1986: Selected Curt Schilling in the second round of the draft.
2003: Claimed Kevin Millar off waivers from the Florida Marlins.

BIRTHDATES
Smead Jolley 1902 (1932–1933); Russ Scarritt 1903 (1929–1931); Pete Daley 1930 (1955–1959); Sonny Siebert 1937 (1969–1973)

DEATHS
Charlie Small 1953; Johnny Murphy 1970; Lloyd Brown 1974

January 15

2005 In six hours, the Red Sox sell out their entire 2005 spring training season, despite raising prices to $24 for regular box seats.

2003 The Yankees engineered a three-way trade that involved, one way or another, Orlando Hernandez, Bartolo Colon, and Javier Vasquez, who stayed in Montreal as a result of the trade. The machinations cost the Yanks $2 million and Hernandez, and all they appeared to get out of it was a minor leaguer and Antonio Osuna. Everyone assumed that the entire purpose of the trade was to prevent the Red Sox from acquiring either Colon or Vasquez from the Expos.

1969 Pinky Higgins was sentenced to four years at hard labor in the Louisiana State Prison after pleading guilty to negligent homicide when his car went out of control and killed a highway worker.

1959 Bucky Harris was appointed to take Joe Cronin's place as Red Sox GM, assuming that Cronin will become president of the American League; the day before, Cronin had been recommended for the presidency by a six-man search committee. Harris had served as Cronin's special assistant for two years.

1954 Babe Didrikson Zaharias edged out Ted Williams for the Comeback Athlete of the Year. Many years earlier, she once pitched against the Red Sox in an exhibition game. (See March 22, 1934.)

1942 Multilingual Moe Berg, it was said, could "out-talk a German professor and out-cuss an Argentine gaucho." (*The Sporting News,* January 1942) The Red Sox catcher was released by the team so he could join the staff of Nelson A. Rockefeller, coordinator of inter-American affairs. Berg's job was to serve as a "good-will ambassador" to Central and South America, thanks to his fluency in both Spanish and Portuguese and what the A.P. termed his "deep grasp of Pan-American problems." It was on this very day that President Franklin D. Roosevelt wrote to Commissioner Landis, giving the "green light" to play major league ball during the war. Hundreds of ballplayers served in the armed forces, however, and every major league baseball team was affected by the loss of many star players.

1935 News flash: Exercise good! Newly signed Red Sox trainer Roland Logan initiated a series of articles for the *Washington Post*, in which he advanced the argument that exercise was one of the most essential agents of body building.

1934 Sox again sign pitcher Herb Pennock, who served with the Sox from 1915 through 1922, before spending 11 very productive Hall of Fame quality years with the Yankees. In '34, he is undefeated (2–0), pitching 62 innings but with only two starts.

1917 Harry Hooper's new automobile backfired, and was totally consumed by flames at the Sutter Gun Club in Marysville, California. Hooper had purchased the car with some of his World Series bonus.

1913 The Chicago Cubs inserted a temperance clause in their player contracts. The club's prohibition policy applied to all associated with the team; only teetotalers would be allowed to travel with the Cubs. Red Sox president McAleer said there was no need for a similar policy: "The boys in the Boston club are the best behaved bunch in the business and there is no need of any temperance clause in their contracts."

TRANSACTIONS
1942: Released Moe Berg.
1934: Signed free agent Herb Pennock.

BIRTHDATES
Tom Oliver 1903 (1930–1933); Luis Alvarado 1949 (1968–1970); Wayne Gomes 1973 (2002)

DEATHS
Eddie Foster 1937; Fred Thomas 1986

January 16

2002 By a vote of 29–0, with only the New York Yankees abstaining, Major League Baseball approved the sale of the Red Sox to a group headed by John W. Henry, Tom Werner, and Larry Lucchino. Because the previous owner was a public charity, the JRY Trust, Massachusetts Attorney General Thomas F. Reilly had to give his stamp of approval as well. He did, but only after the Yawkey Trust was given an extra $10 million and the new ownership agreed to fund a Red Sox Foundation with assets of an additional $20 million. At the same time, baseball's owners agreed to permit John Henry to sell the team he owned, the Florida Marlins, which he did in mid-February. As it happens, Henry also owned a 1% stake in the New York Yankees, which he later disposed of. Perhaps for a moment in time, Mr. Henry owned parts of three major league franchises. (See February 27, 2005.)

1965 Former disc jockey Ed Penney, now a record promoter, announces that Tony Conigliaro has recorded his first 45 rpm single, "Why Don't They Understand" backed with "Playing the Field." See January 19.

1920 In a *New York Times* story, Babe Ruth said he had loved playing in Boston and loved the fans, but did not like Frazee. It particularly galled him that on "Babe Ruth Day," Frazee had required that Ruth buy a ticket if he wanted Mrs. Ruth to attend the game.

1905 "It seems simple enough on paper; the Red Sox buy OF George Stone from Washington. The Browns reclaim Frank Huelsman from the Senators, where he had been on loan, and send him along with OF Jesse Burkett to Boston for Stone. Boston then sends Huelsman back to Washington in payment for George Stone. This is Huelsman's fourth trade in eight months." (*The Baseball Chronology* at www.baseballlibrary.com)

TRANSACTIONS
1904: Sold both Jake Stahl and George Stone to the Washington Senators.
1905: Traded George Stone to the St. Louis Browns for Jesse Burkett and Frank Huelsman. Traded Frank Huelsman to the Washington Senators for George Stone. (See explanation above in text.)

BIRTHDATES
Jimmy Collins 1870 (1901–1907); Fred Bratschi 1892 (1926); Dave Stapleton 1954 (1980–1986)

DEATHS
Baby Doll Jacobson 1977; Ken Chase 1985

January 17

1970 The Yankees draft Fred Lynn, but the future Red Sox outfielder elects not to sign with New York. He went on to play major league ball for 17 years, the first seven of which were with Boston. He was on the All-Star team every full year he was with Boston, even leading the league in hitting in 1979.

1929 The January 17 issue of *The Sporting News* carried Bill Carrigan's comment that the Red Sox would wear the same uniform as in 1928. "Somebody suggested that we stick a miniature stocking on the front of the shirt, because it brought us luck in the old days. If I thought that would help, I'd plaster little stockings all over the uniforms, but I am afraid we will have to rely on other things to make us a better ball team."

1901 Connie Mack departed from Boston, having represented Ban Johnson and Charles Somers in obtaining a lease from the Boston Elevated Railway Company for grounds on Huntington Avenue which would be used to build an American League ballpark. Boston hence became the eighth and final team in the new American League, and the new park was scheduled to be built right across the tracks from Boston's NL park. Johnson, speaking from Washington on January 18th, said that "the hostile attitude of the National League...is responsible for our now adding Boston."

TRANSACTIONS
1910: Sold the contracts of Biff Schlitzer and Steve Yerkes
1919: Traded Hal Janvrin and cash to the Washington Senators for Eddie Ainsmith and George Dumont. Traded Eddie Ainsmith, Slim Love, and Chick Shorten to the Detroit Tigers for Ossie Vitt.

1970: Drafted Rick Burleson in the secondary phase of the 1970 amateur draft.
1992: Signed free agent Tom Barrett.

BIRTHDATES
Jack Merson 1922 (1953); Don Zimmer 1931 (manager, 1976–1980); Denny Doyle 1944 (1975–1977); Walt McKeel 1972 (1996–1997); Mark Malaska 1978 (2004)

DEATHS
Alex Mustaikis 1970; Nick Polly 1993; Hersh Freeman 2004;

January 18

1973 Orlando Cepeda signs with the Red Sox, making him the first player signed by a team to serve as a designated hitter. He plays just the one season for the Sox, but plays well, batting .289 with 86 RBIs. "Baby Bull" is now in the Hall of Fame.

1919 Indicative of the stormy relationship between Sox owner Harry Frazee and his star Babe Ruth was Ruth's declaration that, "I am going to ask for a figure in my contract for next season which may knock Mr. Frazee silly, but nevertheless I think I am deserving of everything I ask."

1917 Dave Fultz, a former ballplayer who led an early effort to organize a union (the Players' Fraternity), met at Boston's Hotel Touraine with Larry Gardner, Olaf Henriksen, Hal Janvrin, and Babe Ruth. Fultz said he'd been pledged their support.

1912 Former Red Sox pitcher Lefty Burchell became a "magnate," buying the Syracuse ball club of the New York League.

1909 Tek, Rice, Yaz, and Doc. Manager Eddie Lake appointed right fielder Harry "Doc" Gessler captain of the Red Sox for 1909.

TRANSACTIONS
1973: Signed free agent Orlando Cepeda.
1984: Drafted Dan Gakeler and John Leister.
1988: Signed free agent Mike Smithson.
1993: Signed free agent Tony Fossas.

BIRTHDATES
Danny Clark 1894 (1924); John Woods 1898 (1924); Bob Scherbarth 1926 (1950); Mike Fornieles 1932 (1957–1963); Brady Anderson 1964 (1988)

DEATHS
Pete Jablonowski (Appleton) 1974; Bob Barrett 1982; Johnny Tobin 1982; Leo Kiely 1984

January 19

1991 Roger Clemens' 39-year-old brother Randy was arrested around 1:30 A.M. at Houston's Bayou Mama's Swamp Bar; Roger was also arrested and charged with aggravated assault for hindering his brother's apprehension. The charge was a third-degree felony carrying up to 2-to-10 years in prison. Roger claimed he put his hands up in self-defense. Charges were downgraded to a misdemeanor in an April 17 grand jury proceeding and ultimately dismissed almost a year later (see January 6, 1992).

1965 Rookie of the Year Tony Conigliaro debuts as a recording artist, to mixed reviews of his single on the Penn Tone label. The two tracks were played over and over for 3½ hours at the preview party. (See a related story at July 13, 2005.)

1939 It must have been reassuring when GM Eddie Collins advised Sox players they could stop worrying about salary cuts. Not a single decrease and several increases, he said.

1937 The Baseball Writers Association of America votes Nap Lajoie and two former Sox stars—Tris Speaker and Cy Young—into the Hall of Fame.

1916 Following their World Championship in 1915, the Red Sox took advantage of the occasion to...*lower* their ticket prices. Box seats (the first five rows at Fenway) were cut from $1.50 to $1.00. The rest were considered grandstand seats, and cut to 75 cents apiece. The Sox also offered 50-cent seats and "more 25-cent seats than any park in either league," according to President Lannin. He said $1 was enough to pay to see a ball game in the regular season.

TRANSACTIONS
1979: Signed free agent Steve Renko.
2000: Free agent Marty Cordova signed.

BIRTHDATES
Merle Settlemire 1903 (1928); Dib Williams 1910 (1935); Ed Sadowski 1931 (1960); Rich Gale 1954 (1984); Brad Mills 1957 (coach, 2004–2005); Chris Stynes 1973 (2001); Wilton Veras 1978 (1999–2000)

DEATHS
None yet

January 20

1988 Ticket manager Arthur Moscato resigned after 40 years with the Red Sox. He admitted he "made a mistake" that cost the Sox some $18,000 and a good deal of embarrassment. The Massachusetts Attorney General's office ruled the Sox had tagged a $1 surcharge onto each credit-card ticket purchase during the 1987 season, a practice prohibited by state law. Team counsel John Donovan, a former batboy, said the resignation had "absolutely nothing" to do with the ruling. More likely, the resignation was due to the reported ready access of scalpers to tickets at the ballpark. Reporting that one scalper (Al Manditch) left off tickets at Window One to be picked up by his customers, the *Globe* noted, "wittingly or unwittingly, the Red Sox had served as a conduit in an illegal practice."

1966 Ted Williams was the only player elected to the National Baseball Hall of Fame in 1966; Casey Stengel was named later. Williams won on the first ballot, receiving a then-record 282 of a possible 302 votes.

TRANSACTIONS
1920: Traded Braggo Roth and Joe Shannon to the Washington Senators
for Eddie Foster, Harry Harper, and Mike Menosky.
1966: Drafted Dick Baney and Mark Schaeffer.
1994: Signed free agents Tony Fossas and Chris Howard.

BIRTHDATES
Bill James 1887 (1919); Joe Dobson 1917 (1941–1954); Gene Stephens 1933 (1952–1960)

DEATHS
Bunny Madden 1954; Nick Altrock 1965; George Hockette 1974

January 21

1996 Danny Monzon, the top Latin American scout for the Red Sox, was killed in a head-on automobile collision outside Santo Domingo, Dominican Republic.

1960 Birthdate of Yankees pitcher Andy Hawkins, who had a 162.00 ERA in starting three games at Fenway Park in 1989 and 1990. Total innings pitched in the three starts: one. Hawkins managed to surrender 18 runs on 13 hits and 6 walks.

1924 Perhaps hoping a new look would bring new fortunes, manager Lee Fohl selected new uniforms for the 1924 Red Sox. The "customary blue stripe" would be eliminated and team would wear all-white uniforms at home, with a special V-neck collar and trousers that would be "tight at the knees and full at the hips." The road uniform would be steel gray with pencil stripes. Did it work? In 1924, the team escaped the cellar for almost the only time during the Roaring Twenties, but only by a half-game (still leaving them 25 games out of first).

1913 When Everett Scott signed with the Red Sox, he was the fourth player to come to Boston from the Youngstown, Ohio ball club.

BIRTHDATES
Larry Boerner 1905 (1932); Sam Mele 1923 (1947–1955); Mike Smithson 1955 (1988–1989); Chris Hammond 1966 (1997); Keith Shepherd 1968 (1995); Byung-Hyun Kim 1979 (2003–2004)

DEATHS
Casper Asbjornson 1970; Gene Rye 1980

January 22

2003 The Red Sox signed David Ortiz off the scrap heap; he'd almost unaccountably been released by the Minnesota Twins, who had apparently simply not wanted to give him a raise from $950,000 despite his 20 homers and 75 RBIs. Gordon Edes of the *Globe* mentioned the Sox as wrapping up a winter (Jeremy Giambi, Bill Mueller, Todd Walker, and now Ortiz) of "shopping at Wal-Mart" but Theo Epstein saw Ortiz as having "a very high ceiling."

1962 For the final time, outfielder Jackie Jensen announces his retirement. (See also January 25, 1960.)

1947 Pitcher Lefty Grove is elected to the Hall of Fame.

1938 Eddie Collins announced the signing of righty pitcher Charlie Wagner. At the start of 2006, Charlie Wagner remains a Red Sox employee helping with scouting.

1917 Harry Frazee announced that he had nine Red Sox signed to contracts, thereby indicating that he was not troubled by the notion of players refusing to sign on for 1917 as union organizer Dave Fultz tries to build his Players' Fraternity.

1910 Red Sox President John I. Taylor called on his club's ballplayers to quit smoking cigarettes, and declared that if they quit, "I will agree to furnish the cigars for the team from April 14 to October 4." Taylor also wanted them to curb the all-night poker sessions, since "too much of the midnight oil hurts the eyesight." The health-conscious Taylor also suggested abstinence from alcohol: "Too much of even the light drinks will make a player logy and heavy and unfit to play ball."

TRANSACTIONS
1946: Sold Jim Tabor to the Philadelphia Phillies.
1938: Announced signing of Charlie Wagner.
1996: Signed free agents Esteban Beltre and Alex Cole.
1997: Signed free agent Steve Avery.
2003: Signed free agent David Ortiz.

BIRTHDATES
Bill O'Neill 1880 (1904); Amos Strunk 1889 (1918–1919); Ramon Aviles 1952 (1977); Jimmy Anderson 1976 (2004)

DEATHS
Ken Williams 1959

January 23

2001 Einar Gustafason dies; Gustafson was the original "Jimmy" of the Jimmy Fund, one of the first survivors of childhood cancer treated by Dr. Sidney Farber. The Jimmy Fund has been the primary charity of the Red Sox for over 50 years.

1996 Jerry Remy was named as television analyst for the games to be broadcast on Channel 68. He had already held the same position with NESN for some eight years, and would now be broadcasting the full Sox schedule. Remy took the place of Bob Montgomery.

1981 The Sox trade star center fielder Fred Lynn to the Angels (along with pitcher Steve Renko) for Frank Tanana, Joe Rudi, and Jim Dorsey. Because the Red Sox had mailed the contract extensions of both Lynn and Carlton Fisk two days after the deadline, the Sox might well have lost both to free agency. Lynn works out a deal with the Angels and so accepts the trade; Fisk will seek a ruling on his case from an arbitrator. (See March 9.)

1958 The Sox get shortstop Pete Runnels from the Senators. Runnels would win the AL batting title in 1960 (.320) and 1962 (.326), and come in among the top three in two other years. Boston gives up Norm Zauchin and Albie Pearson.

1954 Doris Williams filed for divorce from her husband Ted who, she alleged (among other things), used "obscene language" toward her. Imagine that!

1901 During two days in Boston, Ban Johnson met with the architect for the new American League ballpark, which became the Huntington Avenue Grounds. The ball club would be organized under the laws of the State of Maine, it was said.

TRANSACTIONS
1958: Acquired Pete Runnels from the Washington Senators in
    trade for Albie Pearson and Norm Zauchin.
1981: Acquired Frank Tanana, Joe Rudi, and Jim Dorsey in a trade with
    the California Angels for Fred Lynn and Steve Renko.
1985: Signed free agent Dave Sax.
1991: Signed free agents Mike Brumley and Tony Fossas.
2000: Free agent Andy Sheets signed.

BIRTHDATES
Ray Haley 1891 (1915); Bill Regan 1899 (1926–1930); Randy Gumpert 1918 (1952); Cot Deal 1923 (1947–1948); Frank Sullivan 1930 (1953–1960); Garry Hancock 1954 (1978–1982); Alan Embree 1970 (2002–2005)

DEATHS
William Matthews 1946; Walter Lonergan 1958

January 24

1989 On Boston's WCVB (Channel 5), Roger Clemens issued what was taken as a veiled threat to reporters, saying, "I don't appreciate reporters writing about my family. And somebody's going to get hurt one time doing that...somebody's going to get hurt and it's not gonna be me." Two days later, Clemens said he had been "misinterpreted."

1977 The Pawtucket Red Sox franchise was awarded to Lincoln, RI businessman Ben Mondor. The previous owner had discussed moving the club to Worcester or even New Jersey; his franchise was revoked by the International League a week earlier. The Pawsox became a well-run, successful minor league franchise.

1973 Mike Nagy broke in nicely, with a 12–2 (3.11 ERA) mark in 1969. He was 7–8 over the next three seasons, and ultimately traded on this day to the Cardinals for a player to be named later (PTBNL), who—come March 29—turned out to be named Lance Clemons.

1950 Former Red Sox pitcher (and current New Jersey State Labor Commissioner) Harry Harper was defeated in the Republican primary special election to fill the seat in Congress held by Rep. J. Parnell Thomas, in jail at the time of the election. William Widnall beat Harper 13,448 to 13,046. Harper was 5–14 in his one season (1920) with the Red Sox.

1910 In addition to baseball, both of Boston's major league ballparks would host other events. The National League Columbus Avenue grounds would be part of the "national hippodrome circuit," while the Huntington Avenue Grounds would offer "vaudeville engagements every evening." This, a *Washington Post* article indicated, means that both ball clubs would seek new grounds in two years when their respective leases expire.

TRANSACTIONS
1973: Traded Mike Nagy to the St. Louis Cardinals for a
  PTBNL (Lance Clemons, on March 29).

BIRTHDATES
Bunk Congalton 1875 (1907); Pinch Thomas 1888 (1912–1917); John Freeman 1901 (1927); Grant Gillis 1901 (1929); Clem Dreisewerd 1916 (1944–1946); Danny Doyle 1917 (1943); Dick Stigman 1936 (1966); Ted Cox 1955 (1977); Cory Bailey 1971 (1993–1994)

DEATHS
Ben Shields 1982

January 25

1960 Still a young 32, star outfielder Jackie Jensen retires from baseball, in part because of a serious fear of flying. There were family issues as well. "Looking back," he said, "it was foolish to quit. But I thought it would answer my problems." Jensen came back for one more season, 1961, which included transcontinental travel with the expansion of the league to include the Los Angeles Angels.

1956 Former Red Sox infielder and manager Joe Cronin is elected to Cooperstown.

1946 Ted Williams signs his contract to play again for Boston, after three years in the Navy and Marines.

1917 With the demise of the rival Federal League, there was less competition for ballplayers. The World War was also well underway. For both reasons, AL and NL owners began to cut costs. On this day, Harry Frazee hinted at salary cuts looming for the defending World Champion Red Sox. Dick Hoblitzell signed the same day for $5,000 rather than the $5,600 he made in 1916.

1910 Manager Patsy Donovan wrote to all the players he intended to invite to spring training, urging them to be vaccinated against smallpox and to send proof of vaccination to the Red Sox office, so they would be available if health authorities inquired. Hal Chase of the Yankees had recently contracted the disease.

BIRTHDATES
Les Nunamaker 1889 (1911–1914)

DEATHS
Hoot Evers 1991

January 26

2000 Tommy Harper is hired as a coach with the Red Sox. He had been fired following the 1985 season, after he had complained about a whites-only event held by the Elks Club in Winter Haven during spring training. Harper sued the Red Sox, charging discrimination, and the case was settled out of court. Bringing Harper back was one of many moves made by GM Dan Duquette to overcome the stain of a racist past.

1995 New GM Dan Duquette nearly pulled off a true coup. Both Sammy Sosa and relief ace John Wetteland visited Fenway Park, along with their mutual agent, Adam Katz. Within days, Wetteland agreed to a three-year, $15 million contract with the Red Sox and Sosa and the Sox came to tentative agreement as well. The National Labor Relations Board intervened in the ongoing baseball strike, however, and their ruling re-established the pre-existing system, dooming Duquette's dealings. (See January 31, 1995.)

1990 The Red Sox promoted associate counsel Elaine Weddington to assistant general manager, making her the first female assistant GM in baseball. She also became the highest ranking black female in baseball. Weddington had worked with Lou Gorman during his previous position with the New York Mets.

1957 Ty Cobb says that Ted Williams may be 38, but he could play for two or three more years with proper training, and notes that Williams often seemed to be out of shape in the spring, leading to early-season injuries. Ted went on to win the batting crown in both 1957 and 1958.

1951 "Double X"—Jimmie Foxx—is elected to the Baseball Hall of Fame.

1938 John I. Taylor died on this date. Taylor purchased the Boston AL franchise shortly after the World Championship of 1903 and owned the club through the 1911 season. The year after he sold it, the Red Sox won their second World Championship. It was Taylor, however, who provided the name "Red Sox" and the land on which Fenway Park was built.

1902 Lulu Ortman, a 21-year-old stenographer at a Fort Wayne, Indiana lumber company, was arrested as she was drawing a revolver to shoot Boston's Chick Stahl. She said he had jilted her for another woman and that she was going to kill him. Stahl claimed he had no idea why she would want to take his life.

TRANSACTIONS
1999: Rich Garces signed as a free agent.

BIRTHDATES
Tubby Spencer 1884 (1909); Hick Cady 1886 (1912–1917); Frank Owens 1886 (1905); Lefty Jamerson 1900 (1924); Charlie Gelbert 1906 (1940); Rip Russell 1915 (1946–1947)

DEATHS
Hugh Bradley 1949; Bill Barrett 1951; Steve O'Neill 1962

January 27

2005 In a trade noted for the number of letters in their surnames, Doug Mientkievich and Ian Bladegroen are traded, the Sox getting "The Blade" and the Mets getting "Minky." Mientkievich came to the Sox in the Garciaparra deal at the trading deadline in mid-2004. His catch of a flip from Keith Foulke recorded the last out of the 2004 World Series, but the Sox had two full-time first baseman in him and Kevin Millar and opted to keep Millar.

1997 Whenever a player hit a long drive, Sox radio broadcaster Jerry Trupiano would make the call, "Way back...way back..." The Sox acquire pitcher John Wasdin from Oakland in exchange for Jose Canseco and some money. Wasdin was known for giving up what appeared to be an unusual number of home runs, earning himself the nickname "Way Back" Wasdin.

1994 Dan Duquette became general manager of the Boston Red Sox. The 35-year-old native of Dalton, Massachusetts became the youngest GM in Red Sox history. His successor, Theo Epstein, took that honor for himself several years later. Duquette was reportedly the man the Sox wanted all along. Tommy Harper, who worked under Duquette in the Montreal Expos organization, praised Duquette as a good selection for the Sox.

On the same day, the Red Sox lost Sherm Feller, who had served for 26 years as the public address announcer for the hometown team. Feller, described by Bob Ryan as a "character with a capital C," was also a talented composer and songwriter; his best-known song is the classic "Summertime, Summertime."

1977 For the fifth year in succession, the Boston writers vote El Tiante as the Sox' most valuable pitcher.

1960 With the career of Ted Williams near its end, the January 25 retirement of Jackie Jensen, and the deterioration of Mike Higgins as manager, there'd been rumors that Ton Yawkey might be willing to entertain offers. In response to Leo Durocher's offer of $6 million, Yawkey said the Sox were not for sale.

1916 J. Garland "Jake" Stahl's Washington Park National Bank in Chicago was robbed by four masked and armed youths, one of whom held a revolver pointed at the former Boston ballplayer's face from just an inch away. The robbers escaped by automobile with about $12,000. A policeman who chased the getaway car got in a wreck with a truck, and so the bad guys escaped. They were arrested less than 36 hours later, and the confession of one was said likely to lead to the arrest of at least six Chicago police officers implicated in the plot.

1914 The Federal League hoped to become a third major league, tempting players away from the two existing leagues with offers of higher salaries. First baseman "Swat" Mundy accumulated 47 at-bats (.255) in the last six or seven weeks of 1913 with the Red Sox. He reported that the Indianapolis Federals had offered considerably more than Boston. It was maybe not the best career move—he didn't make either team.

1910 Fred Lake beat "Nuf-Ced" McGreevy at tenpins by...10 pins! McGreevy had challenged the recently-deposed Sox manager, but lost. In the meantime, Lake's replacement Patsy Donovan informed reporters that he didn't believe in pitchers having their arms looked after by professional trainers. "I know of great players going along for years without sore arms who never knew what a trainer was," he declared. "They simply took care of themselves and were better off for it."

1909 Most players traded to the St. Louis Browns would have regrets, but catcher Lou Criger (with Boston since the inaugural 1901 season) sent an open telegram to Boston fans expressing his regrets. "I want the Boston fans to know it was no wish of mine to leave Boston," he began.

TRANSACTIONS
1997: Acquired John Wasdin (and some cash) from Oakland in trade for Jose Canseco.

BIRTHDATES
Milt Gaston 1896 (1929–1931); Bob Barrett 1899 (1929); Fred Heimach 1901 (1926); Eric Wedge 1968 (1991–1994); Phil Plantier 1969 (1990–1992); Bry Nelson 1974 (2002)

DEATHS
Merv Shea 1953; Joe Vosmik 1962

January 28

1967 The Red Sox select New Hampshire's Carlton Fisk in the first round of this year's draft. Fisk is the #4 pick overall.

1959 Outfielder Marty Keough was injured in a head-on car crash when a 36-year-old woman pulled out of a market parking lot. Keough's left elbow and right knee were both cut, though not badly.

1948 A firestorm of controversy breaks out in Boston newspapers when Ted Williams is not present for the premature birth of his first daughter Barbara-Joyce (Bobby-Jo) Williams. Ted was fishing in Florida and took much longer to get to Boston than the newspapers deemed appropriate. (See February 2, 1948.)

1902 Henry J. Killilea and his brother Matt became effectively sole owners of the Boston AL ball club; Henry had secured a controlling interest in the club on August 10, 1901. Charles Somers retained a very few shares, so that he could remain as president. Ban Johnson commented that the Killileas were backed by a "wealthy man who may later appear as a baseball man." (*Boston Globe*)

1901 The magnates of the new American League met in Chicago and the league formally organized. Boston, Baltimore, and Philadelphia were admitted as franchises, replacing Buffalo, Indianapolis, and Minneapolis which had once been planned. The projected Kansas City franchise had been transferred to Washington at an earlier meeting. The Boston franchise was awarded to Charles W. Somers—who also owned the Cleveland franchise, and had an interest in the Phiadelphia and Chicago clubs, too. The league was just being built and some of the magnates played more than one role. Connie Mack of Philadelphia, as we have seen, represented the league in negotiating the lease of land for Boston's ballpark. Mack also made the initial salary offer to hire Jimmy Collins away from Boston's National League team to become manager (and third baseman) for Boston's new AL ball club. All of the leases and 51% of the capital stock of each franchise were placed in trust of league president Ban Johnson, who declared, "It's war with the National League." A constitution was adopted, and a 140-game schedule. The roster size for each ball club was to be just 14 players. The exact schedule had yet to be announced. (See also January 29.)

TRANSACTIONS
1967: Drafted Carlton Fisk and Don Newhauser.

BIRTHDATES
Frank Arellanes 1882 (1908–1910); Jack Coffey 1887 (1918); Guy Cooper 1893 (1914–1915); Lyn Lary 1906 (1934); Pete Runnels 1928 (1958–1962, 1966); Kevin Tolar 1971 (2003); Phil Seibel 1979 (2004)

DEATHS
Jake Thielman 1928; Pop Rising 1938; Stan Partenheimer 1989

January 29

1996 The Sox secured their target, Phillies relief pitcher Heathcliff Slocumb, as part of a six-player trade, replacing the disappointing Ken Ryan. Philadelphia got Lee Tinsley, Glenn Murray, and Ryan for Slocumb and two minor leaguers, Rick Holifield and Larry Wimberly. Slocumb would prove even more disappointing than Ryan, but was later dealt to Seattle for Derek Lowe and Jason Varitek.

1987 Three-time AL batting champ Wade Boggs had gone to salary arbitration two years in a row, but finally earns and signs a three-year contract.

1958 Mickey Vernon is placed on waivers, and claimed by the Cleveland Indians, where has one more very good year.

1936 Former Red Sox pitcher and slugger Babe Ruth is among the very first group of players voted into the Hall of Fame, and will later take part in the Hall's inaugural induction ceremonies.

1930 Obtained center fielder Tom Oliver on waivers. Oliver played in every game in 1930, led the American League in at-bats with 646, but struck out only 25 times, tying a league record for the fewest strikeouts by a rookie. Oliver batted .293 on the season. Oliver played in 514 games for the Red Sox from 1930 through 1933, with 1,931 at-bats. He never hit a single homer. Since the start of the 20th century, no ballplayer has as many at-bats without at least one home run.

The Yankees claim Ken Williams on waivers from the Red Sox, though he never plays another major league game. In 1922, Williams led the AL with 39 homers and 155 RBIs. He played outfield for the Red Sox in 1928 and 1929, and retired with a career .319 average.

1929 Secretary of the Boston Red Sox James R. Price committed suicide at Fenway Park, slashing his throat with a razor on one of the runways at the park. Not to trivialize the tragedy, but the 1920s could hardly have been worse years for the Red Sox. Two scraps of paper, on which Price had written in pencil, were accepted as a valid will by Suffolk Probate Court, despite lacking the required three witnesses. Price left all to his wife, sister, and two sons.

1901 Organization of the American League was completed, a significant element of the agreement regarding player contracts. Players would be asked to sign contracts for three, four, or five-year terms, but after five years would become, in effect, free agents and not bound by any reserve clause. Language stated, "No player shall be traded, farmed, or sold to any other club except with his consent." That didn't last long in practice, but combined with higher salaries that were offered, helped attract many former NL ballplayers to the fledgling league.

TRANSACTIONS
1958: The Cleveland Indians selected Mickey Vernon from the Red Sox off waivers.
1992: Signed free agent Herm Winningham.
1996: Acquired Heathcliff Slocumb, Rick Holyfield, and Larry Wimberly in trade from the Philadelphia Phillies for Glenn Murray, Ken Ryan, and Lee Tinsley.
2000: Free agent Shea Hillenbrand signed.

BIRTHDATES
Esty Chaney 1891 (1913); Elmer Eggert 1902 (1927); Bobby Bolin 1939 (1970–1973); Dick Mills 1945 (1970); Morgan Burkhart 1972 (2000–2001)

DEATHS
Del Gainer 1947

January 30

2005 That must have been some beach party! Rich Garces, the popular relief pitcher (1996–2002) known as "El Guapo," disappeared and was feared kidnapped in his native Venezuela. He'd often expressed his fears of being held for ransom and at the time of his disappearance it was tragically true that the mother of another Red Sox reliever—Ugueth Urbina—had in fact been kidnapped a month or so earlier and was still missing. Garces was due to be honored as "Comeback Player of the Year" by the Magallanes Navigators (Venezuela Winter League) but he didn't show for the final game of the season. His family filed a missing persons report. On this day, news broke back in Boston that Garces had turned up safe and sound after 10 days and had merely been away at a beach party on Venezuela's central coast.

2002 Though the Red Sox acquired infielder Pokey Reese in a trade with the Rockies, he was not offered a 2002 contract. Reese was later reacquired and played for the 2004 World Championship Red Sox, but then was not offered a 2005 contract.

1960 A former Sox player owned the Patriots. Dom DiMaggio is one of 10 owners of Boston's AFL football team, acting president Billy Sullivan announced.

1929 Boston's Mayor Malcolm E. Nichols signed a city ordinance permitting Sunday baseball to be played by the Boston Braves and Boston Red Sox. Both clubs agreed they would not increase prices for the Sunday games and both paid a special assessment for the season. In the case of the Red Sox, the assessment was $1000. (See also February 18.)

1923 The Yankees obtain Herb Pennock from the Red Sox, for three players and more cash. Players obtained by Boston were pitcher George Murray, infielder Norm McMillan, and outfielder Camp Skinner. Murray had hard luck. He broke his foot in spring training and was hampered throughout most of the year. In 1924, his mother died early in the season and his work suffered, so he was sent out to Mobile, where he broke his throwing arm at the elbow.

TRANSACTIONS
1908: Signed Gavvy Cravath from Los Angeles, Pacific Coast League.
1923: Traded Herb Pennock to the New York Yankees for Norm McMillan,
    George Murray, Camp Skinner, and $50,000 cash.
1978: Traded Steve Dillard to Detroit for two minor leaguers
    (Frank Harris and Michael Burns) and some cash.

BIRTHDATES
Mickey Harris 1917 (1940–1949); Walt Dropo 1923
(1949–1952); LaSchelle Tarver 1959 (1986)

DEATHS
Herb Pennock 1948; Duane Josephson 1997

January 31

2005 Awesome guys. The *Boston Globe* reported that CF Johnny Damon's new book contract specified that he not cut his hair until after the publicity tour for the book was over. Damon sported shoulder-length hair and a beard throughout the 2004 World Championship season, and was amused by all the comparisons between him and the popular image of Jesus Christ: "What more can you ask for? Even being mentioned in the same sentence as Jesus or God…I mean, those guys are awesome. I'm just a knucklehead." The name of the book is *Idiot…Or How I Stopped Thinking and Beat "The Curse."*

1995 The Major League Baseball Players Association voted to continue the freeze on player signings, thus putting the kibosh temporarily on tentative agreements the Red Sox had reached with pitchers John Wetteland and Kevin Appier, and nearly reached with slugger Sammy Sosa. "All we can do is wait and see what happens," shrugged GM Dan Duquette. Would the players be allowed to become free agents, in which case the deals would be done, or would they have to go back to their old clubs and go through arbitration? In the end, they were denied free agency, and never signed with the Sox.

1959 Joe Cronin signs on for seven years as president of the American League.

1956 Sam Snead beats Ted Williams by out-fishing him at the Silver Sailfish Derby in West Palm Beach, Florida.

1953 Marine Corps pilot Ted Williams arrived at the Naval Air Station at Barbers Point, Honolulu, on his way across the Pacific to enter the Korean War.

1916 Red Sox president Joseph Lannin received a telegram from pitcher George "Rube" Foster. The pitcher sent word from his ranch in Oklahoma that he had a new son, who was named Joseph Lannin Foster.

1914 The Indianapolis Federals made a strong play for two other Red Sox players—Boston responded with enough cash to hold onto shortstop Everett Scott, but it was a different story with pitcher Vic Moseley. Tim Murnane wrote in the

Boston Globe that "Red Sox management will make no effort to drag him away from the outlaws." Moseley won 19 and lost 18 with Indianapolis in 1914. The Red Sox had the highest payroll in baseball, according to the February 22 *Globe*, and still hadn't signed Tris Speaker (see March 6, 1914).

TRANSACTIONS
1986: Signed free agent Joe Sambito and released pitcher Jim Corsi.
1997: Signed free agent Mike Benjamin.

BIRTHDATES
Rip Williams 1882 (1911); Tim Hendryx 1891 (1920–1921); George Burns 1893 (1922–1923); Fred Kendall 1949 (1978); Jim Willoughby 1949 (1975–1977)

DEATHS
Beany Jacobson 1933; Charlie Chech 1938; Chick Maynard 1957; Ossie Vitt 1963; Pat Donahue 1966; Steve Yerkes 1971

FEBRUARY

February 1

1994 Sox infielder John Valentin blacked out at home in Braintree for three or four minutes. He was taken to Quincy City Hospital, kept overnight for observation, and released the following day. He thought it might have been due to eating shellfish the night before.

The same day, pitcher Jeff Gray announced that his comeback attempt was over. Gray had suffered a stroke in July 1991, and hoped to return to the game but finally decided it was time to move on.

1916 Sox owner Joe Lannin, asked by a St. Louis newspaper about the feasibility of 10-cent bleacher seats, wrote back, "You can't give grand opera for moving picture show prices." It cost about $1300 to $1400 to mount a first-class ballgame at this point in time.

TRANSACTIONS
1994: Damon Berryhill is signed as a free agent.
2005: Signed a minor league contract with Jeremi Gonzalez.
He would make the big league team in May.

BIRTHDATES
Joe Harris 1882 (1905–1907); Carl Reynolds 1903 (1934–1935); Bob Smith 1931 (1955); Tim Naehring 1967 (1990–1997); Kent Mercker 1968 (1999)

DEATHS
Tubby Spencer 1945; Greg Mulleavy 1980; Fred Walters 1980

February 2

1948 Ted Williams visits his daughter Barbara-Joyce for the first time, five days after she was born prematurely while he was fishing in Florida. He told newsmen asking why he'd waited so long to come north, "To hell with the public—they can't run my life." He said he would visit his wife and daughter briefly, then return to Miami. "This place is too cold for me and besides the fishing is great."

1943 Looking to bolster their depleted wartime roster, the Sox sign Al Simmons. The future Hall of Famer (born Aloys Szymanski) had 18 seasons under his belt, but was in the twilight of his career, batting .203 in 133 AB.

1933 Sox president Bob Quinn sent out questionnaires to his players asking what they thought they should be paid for 1933. After the first nine had been received back, five said they would leave the matter of pay up to Quinn, two asked for the same salary as in 1932, and only two sought increases. Quinn actually cut pay for some players, but there was not a single holdout.

1930 Irving Vaughan's *Chicago Tribune* column told how Sox pitcher Charlie Smith (1909–11) landed his first pitching job by replying to a "want ad" in a Cleveland newspaper. It wasn't a legitimate advertisement, but an ersatz want ad in an August 5, 1902 sportswriter's column. The next day, a Cleveland employee working the ballpark gate recommended his friend Smith, sitting in the bleachers, and Smith was summoned. With no professional experience at all, he pitched that very day and beat Rube Waddell and the Philadelphia Athletics, 5–4.

1918 Dutch Leonard joined the U. S. Navy on this date, according to press reports.

1910 The Red Sox purchased the contract of first baseman Hugh Bradley from Jesse Burkett's Worcester team. Bradley was the nephew of Foghorn Bradley, a pitcher with the 1876 Boston team in the first year of the National League. Hugh Bradley hit the first home run ever at Fenway Park.

TRANSACTIONS
1910: Purchased Hugh Bradley from Worcester and signed Duffy Lewis from Oakland.
1943: Signed Al Simmons.
2000: Free agent Julio Santana signed.

BIRTHDATES
Otto Miller 1901 (1930–1931); Wes Ferrell 1908 (1934–1937); John Tudor 1954 (1979–1983)

DEATHS
Jack Rothrock 1980; Al Van Camp 1981

February 3

1941 Pitcher Joe Heving is sold to the Indians, from whence he had come in mid-1938. His brother Johnnie had preceded him as a Red Sox player, and had been acquired 10 years earlier in January 1931.

1938 When prospect Lee Rogers received his contract for 1938, he was astounded at how large the figure was and so gladly began to sign—until he saw that the name under the signature line was Johnny Marcum. The veteran Marcum was presumably offered more, given his 13 wins the prior season. If he received Rogers' contract, Marcum may have been surprised, too.

1931 After seven years of service with the Red Sox, first baseman Phil "Hook" Todt is sold to the Athletics for a final season.

TRANSACTIONS
1931: Sold Phil Todt to the Philadelphia Athletics.
1941: Sold Joe Heving to the Cleveland Indians.
1997: Signed free agent Jim Corsi.
1999: Tim Young signed as a free agent.

BIRTHDATES
Lou Criger 1872 (1901–1908); Frank Barberich 1882 (1910); Fred Lynn 1952 (1974–1980)

DEATHS
Mike Herrera 1978

February 4

1923 The first Yankees team to win a World Series was the 1923 team. A good portion of the team was comprised of former Boston Red Sox, including Babe Ruth, Wally Schang, and Everett Scott, and four of the five World Series pitchers: Joe Bush, Waite Hoyt, Sam Jones, and Herb Pennock. Less attention has been paid to the fact that, at season's start, there were 14 former Yankees on the Red Sox roster (pitchers Ferguson, Murray, O'Doul, Piercy, Quinn, and Russell, and position players DeVormer, Fewster, McMillan, Miller, Mitchell, Ruel, Skinner, and Walters). That the Red Sox found themselves in last place in 1923 and five of the next six years might have something to do with the lack of celebration regarding their acquisitions from New York.

1917 Members of the 1916 World Champion Boston Red Sox received special watches engraved with the names of all the players. The players who had been fined $100.00 for barnstorming after the season, however, were informed that they would only receive their watches after they paid their fine. On March 16, it was reported that the watch that would have gone to 1916 owner Joseph Lannin had instead gone to new owner Harry Frazee, at Frazee's request. Lannin said he wouldn't even accept it if one were sent to him at such a late date.

TRANSACTIONS
1994: Signed free agent Andy Tomberlin.
2003: Claimed Bronson Arroyo off waivers from the Pittsburgh Pirates.
2004: Signed David Ortiz to a one-year contract.

BIRTHDATES
Rankin Johnson 1888 (1914); John Perrin 1898 (1921); Stan Papi 1951 (1979–1980); Gary Allenson 1955 (1979–1984)

DEATHS
Nemo Leibold 1977; Grant Gillis 1981

February 5

1933 Tom Yawkey purchases the Boston Red Sox from Bob Quinn for a reported sum of $1,500,000.

1918 Secretary of the Navy Josephus Daniels announced that ballplayers serving in the Navy would not be furloughed so they could play major league baseball during the summer, rejecting a plea by Rep. James A. Gallivan of Boston, who explained that most of the members of the Red Sox ball club were serving as yeomen in the Navy. If they are not stationed overseas come baseball season, they can form baseball teams in the Navy. Sox owner Frazee had gone on record a couple of months earlier that he did not seek furloughs. (See December 28, 1917.)

1910 The *Chicago Tribune* reported that Bullet Jack Thoney, "star outfielder of the Boston American baseball team," had slipped on a banana peel (!) and fallen while walking on the street at Fort Thomas, Kentucky. He broke his shoulder and dislocated the shoulder blade. Thoney was hardly a "star" in the majors, having batted just .125 in 40 at-bats in 1909, but physicians feared he would never play again. Thoney laughed and said "you don't know anything about baseball players' shoulders. I'll be back in harness next spring." It was the third year in a row that Thoney had been hurt. In 1908, just after he'd been secured by the Red Sox, he sprained his left hand while boxing. In 1909, he'd fallen ill during spring training; then, soon after the season opened, he broke his leg rounding third base in a ballgame, only returning at the very end of the year. (See also March 18, 1910.)

TRANSACTIONS
1916: Signed former Buffalo pitcher Lore Bader.
1951: Selected Al Evans off waivers from the Washington Senators.
2004: Signed free agent Ellis Burks.

BIRTHDATES
Jack O'Brien 1873 (1903); Al Worthington 1929 (1960); Lee Thomas 1936 (1964–1965); Vic Correll 1946 (1972)

DEATHS
Esty Chaney 1952; Rudy York 1970

February 6

1993 The Red Sox were due to open spring training on March 5, but Fort Myers homeowner Angela Grome was still refusing to move from her house, situated precisely where the Red Sox parking lot was planned to be. She was dissatisfied with the $55,000 price being offered by the city for taking her home. She was one of 173 families to be displaced by the construction of City of Palms Park. Grome was looking for $100,000, and was the only homeowner to take the city to court. The parking lot is there; how Grome made out is not clear.

1958 At $135,000, Ted Williams contracts to receive the largest salary ever paid to a major league player.

TRANSACTIONS
1912: Sold Jack Fournier to the White Sox.
1989: Signed free agent Danny Heep.

BIRTHDATES
Frank LaPorte 1880 (1908); Babe Ruth 1895 (1914–1919)

DEATHS
Hank Thormahlen 1955

February 7

1962 For the first time, the Red Sox hired a full-time scout to seek out "Negro talent." Hired was Ed Scott, a former outfielder with the Indianapolis Clowns of the old Negro leagues.

1950 Ted Williams signs his 1950 contract, which pays him $125,000—establishing a new record high.

1943 Ted Williams, denied the American League MVP despite winning the Triple Crown, was nonetheless feted as player of the year 1942 by the New York Baseball Writers Assocation at the banquet at the Commodore Hotel. Abbott and Costello entertained.

1917 Tim Murnane, baseball editor of the *Boston Globe* since 1888, died at age 65 while waiting for his wife to return from the powder room shortly after they both entered Boston's Schubert Theatre.

TRANSACTIONS
1990: Signed free agent Tommy Barrett.

BIRTHDATES
Dave Williams 1881 (1902); Mel Almada 1913 (1933–1937); Al Richter 1927 (1951–1953); Al Smith 1928 (1964); Juan Pizarro 1937 (1968–1969); Carney Lansford 1957 (1981–1982); Adrian Brown 1974 (2003)

DEATHS
Ollie Marquardt 1968

February 8

1999 After over 400 arbitration cases, the first female arbitrator hears the salary arbitration case of Boston ballplayer Midre Cummings. The decision goes against the native of the Virgin Islands. Boston's other Virgin Islander was 2001's Calvin Pickering.

1991 Roger Clemens rockets to the top of the payscale, agreeing to (who wouldn't have?) a four-year deal that makes him the highest-paid player in the game. His salary starts at $2,700,000 in 1991, and only increases from there: a guaranteed $21.521 million deal that begins in 1992, and contains a $6 million club option for 1996.

1940 The St. Louis Browns buy submarine pitcher Elden Auker from the Red Sox. Auker had one season with the Sox, a sub-par season at that. With the Browns, Auker wins 44 games before the war. His 2001 memoir, *Sleeper Cars and Flannel Uniforms*, presents an enjoyable look at the era.

1935 Tom Yawkey announced that his spending for players was over: "I am through buying." Yawkey had acquired Max Bishop, Joe Cronin, Rick Ferrell, Wes Ferrell, Lefty Grove, Fred Ostermueller, George Pipgras, Dick Porter, Carl Reynolds, Rube Walberg, Bill Weber, and maybe a few others, too. Before year's end, however, he added future Hall of Famers Jimmie Foxx and Al Simmons, and worked deals to acquire Eric McNair and Doc Cramer early in 1936.

1920 Babe Ruth hadn't stopped being a pain to Harry Frazee, even after Frazee sold him to the Yankees. Ruth announced that he wanted $15,000 of the $125,000 which he understood New York had paid Frazee to buy Ruth's contract.

TRANSACTIONS
1940: Sold Elden Auker to the St. Louis Browns.

BIRTHDATES
Hoot Evers 1921 (1952–1954); Steve Dillard 1951 (1975–1977)

DEATHS
Tom Hughes 1956; Alex Gaston 1979; Fabian Gaffke 1992

February 9

1994 The Ted Williams Retrospective Museum and Library opens in Hernando, Florida, with the opening gala attended by Joe DiMaggio, Muhammad Ali, and an unprecedented number of Hall of Fame players.

1953 Frank "Trader" Lane and the White Sox pried Vern Stephens away from the Red Sox, sending three pitchers (Hal "Skinny" Brown, Marv Grissom, and Bill Kennedy). The three-time RBI leader would bat only .186 and drive in 14 runs for Chicago before being sent to St. Louis. It was Lane's 155th transaction as Chicago GM.

1920 A day after Babe Ruth said he wanted $15,000 of the money Frazee got by selling him to the Yankees, former Red Sox owner Joseph Lannin's attorneys declared that they were putting Fenway Park up for auction on March 3. Lannin said when he sold the Sox to Frazee and Ward in November 1916, he had taken a note for $262,000 which was secured by the capital stock of the Fenway Realty Trust. The note had come due on November 1, 1919, and had not been paid. Accordingly, Lannin was prepared to sell the stock at auction.

1915 Red Glennan of Jamaica Plain signs on as the new Red Sox mascot.

TRANSACTIONS
1953: Traded Vern Stephens to the Chicago White Sox for Hal
    Brown, Bill Kennedy, and Marv Grissom.
1995: Signed amateur free agent Wilton Veras.

BIRTHDATES
Tex Hughson 1916 (1941–1949); Vic Wertz 1925 (1959–1961); Ted Wills 1934 (1959–1962)

DEATHS
None yet

February 10

1949 Ted Williams says he will retire after three more years. He doesn't.

1945 A one-sentence notice in the February 11 *Washington Post* states that George Digby had accepted a job as scout for the Boston Red Sox. Digby later signed such players as 2005 Hall of Fame inductee Wade Boggs. In 1949, Digby strongly recommended that the Red Sox sign a Birmingham ballplayer on whom they had first dibs—Willie Mays. Mr. Mays was apparently deemed the "wrong color" and the Red Sox declined to follow through.

 Earl Johnson's letter from Europe to Eddie Collins dated February 10 told the Sox GM: "I have been in combat for six months....I received a Bronze Star medal a couple of weeks ago. There was a jeep that was knocked out in front of our lines and only about 200 yards from the pill boxes on the Siegfried Line, and a couple of other fellows and I went out and towed it in." Johnson was a sergeant with an Army infantry platoon; he received a battlefield commission and some other medals as well.

1932 Because Babe Ruth had failed to hit a home run on May 19, 1929, two people were killed and 30 injured, according to a lawsuit filed against the New York Yankees. The stadium had inadequate numbers of exits and guards. May 19 had been a Yankees–Red Sox game day and both Gehrig and the Babe already had a homer apiece. As rains fell, the crowd lingered to see how Ruth would fare. He grounded out just as the shower turned into a deluge. In the resulting stampede, the deaths and injuries occurred. The defense of the Yankees was that the casualties occurred as the result of an act of God.

1930 "Red Sox Refuse to Deal with Yankees" (*The Sporting News*). Bob Quinn refused to sell Ed Morris and Red Ruffing, two pitchers for whom he had received handsome offers, particularly from the New York Yankees. Quinn allowed as how if the Yankees couldn't buy what they wanted—playing strength—then it was not money but playing strength that he was after for his club.

1923 Harry Frazee sent catcher Muddy Ruel and his batterymate Allan Russell to Washington, and obtained catcher Val Picinich and two utility players, Howard Shanks and Ed Goebel.

TRANSACTIONS
1923: Traded Muddy Ruel and Allan Russell to the Washington Senators
     for Ed Goebel, Val Picinich, and Howie Shanks.
1926: Sold Val Picinich to the Cincinnati Reds.
1994: Signed free agent Sergio Valdez.

BIRTHDATES
Herb Pennock 1894 (1915–1934); Johnny Lucas 1903 (1931); Lenny Webster 1965 (1999)

DEATHS
George Whiteman 1947; Rip Repulski 1993

February 11

2002 In order to enable John W. Henry to complete the purchase of the Red Sox, MLB owners vote to approve the sale of Henry's Florida Marlins to Jeffrey Loria. This means that Loria's team, the Montreal Expos, have to be sold, and it is: to a group set up by MLB itself.

1947 Pitcher Jim Bagby, Jr. is sold to Pittsburgh, after his second stint with the Sox.

1918 With Red Sox manager Jack Barry serving in the Navy, the team hired Ed Barrow to become manager of the 1918 Red Sox. Barrow consequently resigned as president of the International League. A "war tax" of 10 cents on regular seats and three cents on bleacher tickets was proposed by the National Commission. The *Chicago Tribune* noted that Barrow did not have a player's background: "his first experience in baseball was in handling peanuts and popcorn when he worked for Harry Stevens at Pittsburgh in the early days."

1916 Asked why he had not bid to acquire any of the players in the now-disbanded Federal League, owner Lannin said, "I doubt if they had a man who could help the Red Sox" and added "Harmony is everything in baseball and we had that in abundance in our team last season. We were also blessed with a class of men who played hardball without objectionable features of any kind. I could ask for no better ball team that the one we will have to start the season at Fenway Park on April 12."

1902 Owner Henry Killilea announced that he would make costly improvements to Boston's American League park, now only in its second year.

TRANSACTIONS
1947: Sold Jim Bagby to the Pittsburgh Pirates.
2000: Free agent Hipolito Pichardo signed.

BIRTHDATES
Ray Collins 1887 (1909–1915); Red Shannon 1897 (1919); Yank Terry 1911 (1940–1945); Ben Oglivie 1949 (1971–1973); Todd Benzinger 1963 (1987–1988); Brian Daubach 1972 (1999–2004)

DEATHS
Mike Fornieles 1998

February 12

1981 Carlton Fisk is declared a free agent by arbitrator Raymond Goetz. With the assistance of Marvin Miller and the Players' Association, Fisk contended that the club had mailed his contract for 1981 on December 22, and not on December 20, as required. The club argued, unsuccessfully, that it had signed him for a five-deal and that 1981 was the final year. The option needed to be exercised, ruled Goetz. Sullivan insisted it was not an error, but that he had mailed it late on the advice of the Players Relations Council. On March 9, Fisk said he had come to terms with the White Sox.

1963 Ed Walton reports that rookie first baseman Bobby Guindon said he would rather take spring training in the minors than with the Red Sox.

1940 With Ted Williams and Dom DiMaggio in the Red Sox outfield, the services of Joe Vosmik are no longer necessary, so he is sold to the Brooklyn Dodgers.

1911 In 289 fielding chances during 1910, Red Sox right fielder Harry Hooper had thrown out an even 30 opponents, for an assists percentage of more than 10%, reported the *Washington Exchange*.

TRANSACTIONS
1940: Sold Joe Vosmik to the Brooklyn Dodgers.
1981: Granted free agency to Carlton Fisk.

BIRTHDATES
George Cochran 1889 (1918); Dom DiMaggio 1917 (1940–1952);
Brian Denman 1956 (1982); Adam Stern 1980 (2005)

DEATHS
Haywood Sullivan 2003

February 13

1945 Sox GM Eddie Collins was married in Weston, Massachusetts, with his son Rev. Paul D. Collins performing the ceremony.

1918 Veteran Johnny Evers signed a contract to serve as Red Sox manager Ed Barrow's "right bower on the board of strategy." Barrow also signed George Whiteman to play right field. At age 35, he was not likely to be called into military service. Whiteman had played briefly for Boston in 1907, then next appeared in the majors five years later playing for New York in 1913. After a four-year absence, he was now set to play for Boston once more—and many credit him as the key man in the 1918 Red Sox World Series win. In a minor league career that ran to 1929, he reportedly rapped out 3,388 base hits.

1900 A new American baseball association is formed at Chicago's Great Northern Hotel. Boston is one of the founding seven teams; as of the announcement, the league is still seeking an eighth franchise. Just a few days later, plans for the association collapse. The team that became the Red Sox would not start until the American League is founded one year later.

TRANSACTIONS
2002: The Red Sox signed free agent Rickey Henderson.

BIRTHDATES
Eddie Foster 1887 (1920–1922); Herb Hash 1911 (1940–1941);
Mike Palm 1925 (1948); Brian Rose 1976 (1997–2000)

DEATHS
Happy Foreman 1953; Bill Humphrey 1992

February 14

1969 Ted Williams responded to what he termed a "the most fantastic offer I've ever received." It was apparently the proverbial offer he couldn't refuse, as Williams had previously declared, "You couldn't pay me enough to manage." Washington Senators owner Bob Short offered Williams a five-year contract that included stock in the ball club. It was reported on February 14 that Ted's agreement to come on board seemed certain. (See also February 21, 1969.)

BIRTHDATES
Jack Lewis 1884 (1911); Oscar Judd 1908 (1941–1945); Bill Marshall 1911 (1931); Tom Borland 1933 (1960–1961); John Marzano 1963 (1987–1992)

DEATHS
Jack Coffey 1966; Eusebio Gonzalez 1976

February 15

2000 Carl Everett agrees to a three-year contract with the Red Sox.

1990 The Red Sox signed free agent Bill Buckner for a second stint. He saw limited duty in 1990, hitting .186 in 43 at-bats, and was released on June 5. Buckner finished his 22-year major league career with a lifetime .289 average.

1957 Joe Cronin says that, yes, Ted Williams did pay the $5,000 fine assessed on him for his "salivary salutes" to Boston press and fans the previous season, denying a Boston newspaper column by Austen Lake that said the Red Sox "didn't collect a copper" of the fine from the "Splendid Spitter."

1946 The Red Sox announce that they will not play their scheduled home opener on April 19, because it falls on Good Friday, but will instead open the season the following day. As it happens, they open early instead, kicking things off on April 16. The Sox win 21 of their first 24 games.

TRANSACTIONS
1976: Signed free agent Gene Michael.
1990: Signed free agents Bill Buckner and Greg Harris.
2003: Acquired Kevin Millar from the Florida Marlins for cash considerations. He had been claimed on January 14 off unconditional release waivers. It's a complicated story.

BIRTHDATES
Candy LaChance 1870 (1902–1905); Bob Cremins 1906 (1927); Dee Miles 1909 (1943); Joe Hesketh 1959 (1990–1994); Ugueth Urbina 1974 (2001–2002)

DEATHS
Duke Farrell 1925

February 16

2004 The New York Yankees trade with the Texas Rangers and acquire Alex Rodriguez. Boston was trying to reach a deal for A-Rod two months earlier. The potential for dissatisfaction in the Red Sox clubhouse is great, given the preference that Sox ownership seemed to show for Rodriguez over Nomar Garciaparra, and given the placing of Manny Ramirez on waivers (no takers). In fact, the team comes together and has quite a good year.

1953 On a dive-bombing mission over North Korea, Marine Corps Captain Ted Williams is forced to crash-land his F-9F Panther jet after it is hit and badly damaged. Moments after he lands, the aircraft is engulfed in flame.

1920 Massachusetts Superior Court issued a temporary injunction forbidding Harry Frazee from selling the team or any stock in the Red Sox, or from drawing dividends from his ownership. The ruling followed former owner Joseph Lannin's petition claiming that Frazee and co-owner High Ward had failed to pay a note for $262,000 which had been due on November 1, 1919. The note had been secured by stock in the company that owns Fenway Park, and the court ruling explains why Frazee sold a mortgage on Fenway Park to the New York Yankees as part of the Babe Ruth deal. The Court later ruled that Fenway Park would be put up for sale auction to secure payment to Lannin. On March 5, a settlement was agreed upon.

1909 Coming off a 21–11 season (1.26 ERA), Cy Young was nearing his 42nd birthday and perhaps wanted to play closer to his Ohio home. The Sox sold him to Cleveland for two right-handed pitchers Charlie Chech and Jack Ryan, and also $12,500. Young won 19 games for Cleveland; between them, Cheech and Chong...rather, Chech (7) and Ryan (3) won 10. Though sorry to see him go, it was a transaction that provoked little rancor among Boston fans, detailed by a lengthy article in the February 18 *Globe*.

1900 Washington's baseball club sells home run hitter Buck Freeman, pitcher Bill Dinneen, and six other players to Boston's National League club, and winds down operations. Both Freeman and Dinneen would later hop to the new AL franchise in Boston.

TRANSACTIONS
1909: Traded Cy Young to the Cleveland Naps for Charlie Chech, Jack Ryan, and $12,500 cash.

BIRTHDATES
Alex Ferguson 1897 (1922–1925); Bobby Darwin 1943 (1976–1977);
Bob Didier 1949 (1974); Manny Delcarmen 1982 (2005)

DEATHS
Stuffy McInnis 1960; Cedric Durst 1971

February 17

1971 As this book goes to print, major league minimum wage is around $400,000. Carl Yastrzemski signed a three-year deal on this day for $500,000—said to be the largest amount of money paid any player in the history of the game.

1953 The day after he barely escaped death when crash-landing his Panther jet in Korea, Marine Capt. Ted Williams "bats again against Reds," up again on another mission to bomb supply routes south of Pyongyang.

1945 Lefty pitcher Earl Johnson, a rifle platoon sergeant serving with the Thirtieth Division, received a battlefield promotion to second lieutenant and was also awarded the Bronze Star medal for heroic action on the European front.

1943 In his fourth season with the Red Sox, Tom Carey batted 1.000. Over each of the four seasons, he played progressively fewer games, and in 1942 he appeared in one game, got one at-bat, got one hit, and drove in one run. He had one fielding chance and executed the play without an error for a 1.000 fielding percentage, too. Dubbed the "$5,000-a-Hit Player," Carey announced on this day that he would be joining the Army. After the war, back with the Bosox in 1946, Carey got into three games, but only had one more hit.

1937 Yet another Babe to New York. This time, it's Babe Dahlgren, sold to the Yanks by Tom Yawkey's Red Sox.

1919 An item in the *Atlanta Constitution* noted that Everett Scott (5' 9½") was the tallest member of the 1919 Sox infield, taller than Barry, McInnis, and Vitt.

1916 By arrangement with owner Lannin, motion pictures of the Red Sox at spring training in 1915 would be shown to inmates at Charlestown Prison on February 22. Sox players Henriksen and Janvrin were expected to be at the screening.

1909 The *Chicago Tribune* seemed to be out of touch with sentiment in Boston, reporting fans "up in arms" over the sale of Cy Young to Cleveland, and that Nuf-Ced McGreevy and others "were so indignant that they started an organized boycott of the American League grounds. Other fans talked of raising a purse to buy Cy back on their own hook."

TRANSACTIONS
1937: Sold Babe Dahlgren to the New York Yankees.
1978: Signed free agent Tom Burgmeier.

BIRTHDATES
Nemo Leibold 1892 (1921–1923); Ike Boone 1897 (1923–1925); Scott Williamson 1976 (2003–2004)

DEATHS
Kip Selbach 1956; Red Ruffing 1986

February 18

2005 In Caracas, Venezuela, 30 police stormed a remote mountain camp and rescued Maura Villareal, the mother of former Sox stopper Ugueth Urbina. She had been kidnapped more than five months earlier and held for ransom, but was unharmed. Two kidnappers were killed in a gun battle with police.

1999 Roger Clemens winds up in pinstripes, when the Blue Jays trade him to New York after he's won back-to-back Cy Youngs for Toronto. Was there an alleged secret (and prohibited) special understanding that Clemens could invoke a trade out of Toronto when he wished? We may never know.

1993 Reliever Jeff Russell signs an incentive-laden deal with the Sox, and saves 33 games in 1993.

1929 Because Fenway Park was located within 1000 feet of a religious edifice, Sunday baseball was not permitted, despite the recent statewide referendum. A delegation from the city of Revere, Massachusetts offered blueprints for a 41,000 seat stadium located in their city, in hopes that the Sox would relocate to Revere. The American League had already given Pres. Quinn approval to play Sunday games in Revere, but Quinn preferred to complete negotiations with Braves owner Emil Fuchs for use of Braves Field on Sundays.

1908 Nuf-Ced McGreevy was retained to help Deacon McGuire train the Red Sox during spring training. The saloonkeeper was a handball champion and active in many other sports as well, including winter swims with the L Street Brownies. (See also March 9, 1908.)

TRANSACTIONS
1994: Matt Stairs and Pete Young are both purchased from the Montreal Expos.

BIRTHDATES
Louis Leroy 1879 (1910); Bruce Kison 1950 (1985); John Valentin 1967 (1992–2001)

DEATHS
Marty McManus 1966

February 19

1999 "I think it's an unbelievable thing. I've always enjoyed Stephen King's work. My whole family is a fan of his," said Red Sox closer Tom Gordon on being asked about King's new novel published by Scribner's, *The Girl Who Loved Tom Gordon*. King is a lifelong Sox fan, since his first game in 1959.

1951 Center fielder Dom DiMaggio is almost lost at sea. Dominic and his brother Tom were out in the DiMaggio crabboat when the engine broke down, eight miles off the Golden Gate. Two fishing boats tried to tow them back, but both times the lines broke. A few days earlier in the same waters, another boat had capsized, with the loss of six lives. A Coast Guard vessel rescued the DiMaggios.

1947 Veteran catcher Frankie "Blimp" Hayes is signed as backup, but only hits .154 in 13 at-bats.

1929 The Red Sox and Braves came to agreement that the Sox would play their now-permissible Sunday games at Braves Field. They were not permitted to play at Fenway Park because a portion of the park was within 1000 feet of a church.

1918 The Baseball Players' Fraternity effectively won a victory over the Red Sox when, in a settlement, the Sox paid Fraternity president Dave Fultz some $2,385.19 in favor of former Red Sox player Kurt (Casey) Hageman, who contended a 1912 breach of contract on the part of the ball club. The settlement relieved current Red Sox owner Harry Frazee from showing cause why he should not be held in contempt of court.

BIRTHDATES
Weldon Wyckoff 1892 (1916–1918); Russ Nixon 1935 (1960–1968);
Bob Sadowski 1938 (1966); Juan Diaz 1974 (2002)

DEATHS
None yet

February 20

1957 *The Sporting News* quoted Jimmy Piersall about how his affection for newspaper writers differed from that of Ted Williams. "He knows I like the newspapermen and he gets on me about it. I give it to him back because I like to needle him. One time I was in the dugout in Baltimore talking with a bunch of writers and Ted came by and said to me, 'Why don't you kiss all those guys, you're so crazy about them.' So I did. I got up and kissed all the writers."

1945 Pitcher Rex Cecil's contract arrived in the mail on the very day his mother died. The contract was good news—satisfactory in every way—and he said he would leave for spring training right after the funeral.

1936 Red Sox players were not allowed to bring automobiles to spring training, according to a note in *The Sporting News*.

1917 Pitcher Carl Mays sent owner Frazee a telegram saying that he would head for spring training in one or two days and they could work out contractual details once he arrives. Frazee replied that if he showed up at spring training without having signed his contract, then his travel expenses were on him, and that he would not be allowed to work out with the team.

1912 The Red Sox Quartet which had formed during the 1911 cross-country spring training trip (see February 24, 1911), had that fall become a feature of the Keith's vaudeville circuit, playing to packed houses and reportedly earning at least six encores at every stop. The *Washington Post* singled out Hugh Bradley's rendition of "O, You Beautiful Doll" and added, "The second time you hear them you like them better than the first." Bill Lyons, coached on how to bow theatrically in appreciation of audience applause, grumbled in good humor, "Hold on there, I'm bowing so much now that my neck's lame."

TRANSACTIONS
1984: Signed free agent Rich Gale.
2003: Signed free agent Kevin Millar, though Millar had to get out of a deal he had signed with Japan's Chunichi Dragons. See February 15 transactions.

BIRTHDATES
Muddy Ruel 1896 (1921–1931); Jack Robinson 1921 (1949); Jim Wilson 1922 (1945–1946); Derek Lilliquist 1966 (1995)

DEATHS
None yet

February 21

1974 Today in Charles Schulz's syndicated cartoon strip "Peanuts," Snoopy declares, "I have a trivia question that will drive Woodstock up the wall." In the next frame: "Who played shortstop for St. Paul when they won the American Association pennant in 1938?" After Woodstock answers, Snoopy shakes his head in amazement: "How did he ever hear of Ollie Bejma?" Bejma, who played for Schultz's hometown team, was the co-MVP with teammate Whitlow Wyatt in 1938 (beating out Triple Crown winner Ted Williams) before playing for the White Sox. *(Source: The Baseball Chronology)*

1969 Out of the game since his retirement in 1960, Ted Williams signs a five-year contract to manage the Senators. After his first season, he is named Manager of the Year when the Senators finish five games above the Yankees in the standings. When the franchise relocates to Texas, Williams becomes the first manager of the Texas Rangers.

1959 Pumpsie Green, "first Negro to play for the Boston Red Sox," was denied accommodations at the team's headquarters hotel, the Safari Hotel in Scottsdale, Arizona. "Arrangements have been made for Green to stay in a plush hotel in Phoenix," explained traveling secretary Tom Dowd, who said that Pumpsie was also provided a car so he could commute.

1954 Jackie Jensen helped save the lives of Freddie Regacho, 6, and Joseph Calustre, 10, both of whom were floundering in the waters of the Oakland CA estuary, when the wake of a fireboat knocked them off their float. Later in the year, he drove in 117 runs for the Red Sox.

1947 Ted Williams is again denied the MVP award by the baseball writers, when one writer did not rank The Kid anywhere in his top 10. Williams had won the Triple Crown, but lost 202–201 to Joe DiMaggio, who trailed Ted in every category except triples (Ted had 9, DiMag had 10). A classier Yankee Clipper might have rejected the award.

1934 Dale Alexander, 1932 batting champion (.367), whose average had dropped off to .281 the following year, is sent to the Jersey City team for two pitching prospects, both of whom make the majors but only briefly.

1917 Sox spring training in Honolulu? Sox owner Harry Frazee said he was seriously considering the proposal of a group of Honolulu businessmen to have the Sox train there in the spring on 1918; the men offered to cover all expenses, including transportation to and from the island.

TRANSACTIONS
1934: Traded Dale Alexander to Jersey City for lefthanders
    James McCloskey and James Merena.
1968: Released Jackie Moore.

BIRTHDATES
Turkey Gross 1896 (1925); Dick McCabe 1896 (1918); Tom Yawkey 1903 (owner, 1933–1976); Jack Billingham 1943 (1980); Joe Foy 1943 (1966–1968)

DEATHS
Doc Adkins 1934; Tom Carey 1970

February 22

1989 Excerpts from a *Penthouse* magazine interview with Wade Boggs' mistress Margo Adams are received in the Red Sox spring traning clubhouse. "I didn't notice anyone distracted today," reported manager Joe Morgan.

1945 Fenway Park was due to host the 1945 All-Star Game, but with World War II still in progress, the game was canceled. A number of war benefit games are played in parks around the country instead. Fenway would host the first post-war game, the following year. Major league owners also adopted a rule requiring a minimum of 400 at-bats to win the batting title. This came back to bite Ted Williams a few years later, when he had so many bases on balls that he fell short of the requisite number of at-bats.

1911 The special train (complete with its own barber on board) carrying the Red Sox cross-country for spring training in California was delayed for several hours due to snows in Kansas and New Mexico. Hence, their scheduled stop in El Paso was too brief to allow the team time to visit the sights in Juarez, Mexico, though Nuf-Ced McGreevy and a few players piled into a couple of automobiles and drove over a bridge to squeeze in a quick visit.

BIRTHDATES
Chet Nichols 1931 (1960–1963); John Halama 1972 (2005)

DEATHS
Frank Morrissey 1939

February 23

1986 Wade Boggs lost his arbitration case, but the $1,350,000 salary he would receive from the Red Sox for 1986 is the largest salary any player had ever received in arbitration. Boggs had been seeking $1,850,000.

1928 Sox President Bob Quinn phoned the mother of 17-year-old prospect Joe Cicero, training with the big league club in Bradenton, suggesting that Joseph stay in high school instead. Mrs. Cicero said Joe was ambitious, but also conscientious, and would certainly return to school and finish up his high school work in the fall. Cicero made the big league club in late 1929 at age 18, and batted .313 in 32 at-bats.

1925 Though Boston Braves manager Bancroft planned two workouts a day for his team, his Red Sox counterpart Lee Fohl—ready to start spring training with the Sox in New Orleans—planned to stick to one session lasting maybe four hours.

BIRTHDATES
Roy Johnson 1903 (1932–1935); Elston Howard 1929 (1967–1968)

DEATHS
Pete Donohue 1988

February 24

1992 Carlos Quintana underwent five hours of surgery for a left arm and right toe both broken in a car crash that occurred while he was rushing to a Venezuelan hospital the day before, transporting two younger brothers who had been wounded by gunshots during a Carnival party. Quintana's wife suffered two broken legs in the accident when the car hit a bridge about 80 miles from Caracas.

In other hospital news, at Mass General, owner Jean Yawkey's condition had declined and she was downgraded from serious to very serious.

1990 Tony Conigliaro dies of pneumonia and kidney failure after nearly eight years as an invalid following his 1982 heart attack. He was just 45.

1928 In Bradenton, Florida, the Red Sox Spring training squad included three pitchers wearing eyeglasses. The bespectacled hurlers were Danny MacFayden and two prospects who didn't make the team: Charlie Small and Pete Traynor.

1917 Sox pitcher Smoky Joe Wood is sold to the Indians for $15,000; his arm never recovered from injury but he transformed himself into a good-hitting outfielder, batting as high as .366 in 194 AB in 1921. Wood had apparently requested a trade to Cleveland to rejoin friend Tris Speaker.

1911 The Red Sox took the train cross-country for spring training in California. To entertain themselves on the long trip, a Red Sox quartet was formed on board, featuring Hugh Bradley and Marty McHale as tenors, Tom O'Brien as baritone, and Larry Gardner as bass. Captain Heinie Wagner took exception to their barbershop harmonies and formed a rival quartet with Red Kleinow, Bill Carrigan, and Eddie Cicotte. The high-spirited trip included an attempt by the team to cross the border at El Paso and "take" the Mexican city of Juarez (surrounded at the time by Mexican revolutionaries), chasing jackrabbits (in vain), and a snowball fight outside Tucumcari.

When they arrived in California, a delegation of citizens presented them with baskets of oranges, some of which the Sox players proceeded to throw around to get a little workout.

TRANSACTIONS
1917: Sold Joe Wood to the Cleveland Indians.
1922: Selected Alex Ferguson off waivers from the New York Yankees.

BIRTHDATES
Pinky Pittinger 1899 (1921–1923); Bob Seeds 1907 (1933–1934); Del Wilber 1919 (1952–1954); Nick Esasky 1960 (1989); Bronson Arroyo 1977 (2003–2005)

DEATHS
Max Bishop 1962; Tony Conigliaro 1990

February 25

1982 "The Bird"—Mark Fidrych—signed with the Pawtucket Red Sox after seven years with the Tigers. "I'm not coming here as a star," Fidrych said. "I'm coming here as a pitcher with a history of a bad arm."

1946 Ted Williams serves notice. After three years serving Uncle Sam, he steps into the first pitch he sees in spring training and hits a home run.

1933 Four days after becoming immensely wealthy (through inheritance) at age 30, Tom Yawkey of 993 Fifth Avenue, New York City, bought the Boston Red Sox from Bob Quinn. Eddie Collins also purchased a share. The purchase ended rumors that a syndicate fronted by Walter Johnson would buy the Red Sox. Yawkey's foster father William Yawkey had owned the Detroit Tigers for four years, 1904–1907, and retained a half-interest in the Tigers until 1918—and it was reportedly Ty Cobb who first introduced Yawkey and Collins. After selling the team, Quinn announced, "The New York Yankees have not, and never have had, any financial interest in the Red Sox."

1929 Sox president Bob Quinn said he was thinking of closing Fenway Park and becoming co-tenants at Braves Field. The team had signed up to play 13 Sunday games at Braves Field, and three holiday games as well. Some saw it as only a matter of a few years before they moved all their games to Braves Field.

1916 Women will be given special privileges at Fenway Park, announced owner Lannin. They would be admitted to the grandstand for 50 cents instead of the usual 75, and there would be a "special reception room where ladies can wait for friends or enjoy half an hour in the reading rooms before the real battle begins." There would also be "special turnstiles for the women."

TRANSACTIONS
1982: Signed free agent Mark Fidrych.

BIRTHDATES
Danny Cater 1940 (1972–1974); Dana Kiecker 1961 (1990–1991); Rich Rowland 1964 (1994–1995)

DEATHS
Jack Lewis 1956

February 26

1992 Red Sox owner Jean R. Yawkey dies at the age of 83, leaving ownership of the team in a trust managed by John R. Harrington and other trustees. It would be a full decade before the trustees sold the team.

1990 With a possible lockout looming for the 1990 season, *Boston Globe* writer Michael Blowen suggested, "since most people go to Fenway Park because of what John Updike refers to as its bandbox quality, and not to see the Red Sox fail to hold a lead or a sore-armed pitching staff walk the winning run across in the 10th, why worry about fielding a team?" People could gather to watch the green lawn, for example. Why not transform the park into a "Family Fun, Art and Poetry Center" with John Kiley playing organ and Sherm Feller announcing the events? Perhaps the Green Monster could be converted into a drive-in theater screen, and Updike could read poetry from the mound. Other ideas from more creative minds would surely follow, Blowen allowed.

1989 The Fourth District Court of Appeals rules that Margo Adams cannot sue Wade Boggs for emotional distress, throwing out all but $500,000 of her claim in a lawsuit against Boggs, since Boggs' statements were made to FBI investigators and not to the public. She still seeks half a million for expenses and lost income during her four-year-long relationship with Boggs.

1950 Pitcher Jack Kramer was 6–8 (5.16 ERA) in 1949 and had been troubled with one ailment or another throughout the season. The Sox sold him to the New York Giants. Kramer was given the maximum 25% pay cut for 1950 and refused to sign. After the sale, he complained that the Red Sox "railroaded" him because he didn't get along with manager Joe McCarthy. Kramer went 3–6 for the Giants, then 1–3 for the Yankees the year after that.

1935 The Yankees let Babe Ruth go so he can sign with the Boston Braves for $20,000 and a share in the team's profits. It proves a disappointing return to the city where it all began for the Babe. (See April 16, 1935.)

1918 Harry Frazee took the strongest stand among baseball owners, declaring he would not countenance holdouts and any member of the Red Sox who had not signed would be denied reimbursement for travel expenses to spring training. If he wanted to talk contract with the ball club, he could pay his own way to the discussion. J. V. Fitzgerald of the *Washington Post* allowed that this might bring a number of disgruntled players around, since it was one thing to be cheated a bit on salary but quite another to have to fork out for their own car fare.

1914 It was moving day for the Red Sox front office, which moved from Fenway Park to 70 Devonshire Street, just a few yards from the Post Office.

At the Chelsea Football Grounds in England, an 18-year-old Cambridge, MA, native Tom Daly hit a home run in the 11th inning for a White Sox win in an exhibition game played for King George V and some 30,000 of his subjects. It was the final game of a world tour (using borrowed talent like Daly) between the Giants and White Sox. Daly was a coach for the Red Sox from 1933–1946.

1911 It was reported that the Red Sox would play in a new ballpark beginning in 1912. At public auction, for $120,000, General Charles H. Taylor purchased an estate known as the Dana lands, totaling some 365,203 square feet at Ipswich and Lansdowne Streets. The ballpark, when built in time for the 1912 season, was named Fenway Park.

TRANSACTIONS
1950: Sold Jack Kramer to the New York Giants.

BIRTHDATES
Rip Collins 1896 (1922); Stew Bowers 1915 (1935–1936): Bill Conroy 1915 (1942–1944); Jack Brohamer 1950 (1978–1980)

DEATHS
Tom Oliver 1988

February 27

2002 At 5:02 P.M., after 50 wire transfers were completed, John W. Henry became principal owner of the Red Sox, heading a group of investors which includes Tom Werner, Larry Lucchino, and The New York Times Company. The Yawkey Era (1933–2002) has come to its conclusion. On the same day, Henry sold his 1% share in the New York Yankees.

1966 Sox pitcher Earl Wilson said that he had been refused service at two different Winter Haven night clubs; the Red Sox responded that they had been in touch with city officials and regretted the racial discrimination.

1950 Sox management deny that pitcher Jack Kramer, traded the day before, was dealt due to differences with manager Joe McCarthy.

1919 A brief article in *The Sporting News* informed readers that both evangelist Billy Sunday and the Boston Red Sox planned use of Plant Field in Tampa the week beginning March 15. "It would be all right if they were not going to set up a great big tent spang on the clayed diamond right in front of the grandstand, but that is the case." Rev. Sunday, a former ballplayer, asked the Sox to step aside.

1911 The first Red Sox exhibition game of 1911 spring training took place at Redondo Beach, California, before 1500 fans. The Regulars beat the Yanigans, 3–2.

TRANSACTIONS
2002: The Red Sox signed free agent Rey Sanchez.

BIRTHDATES
Walter Moser 1881 (1911); Art McGovern 1882 (1905); Matt Stairs 1968 (1995); Willie Banks 1969 (2001–2002)

DEATHS
Howie Fitzgerald 1959

February 28

2002 The morning after taking ownership of the Red Sox, the new Henry–Werner–Lucchino group removed GM Dan Duquette from his position, naming Mike Port as interim general manager while they searched for a permanent replacement. No one, except Duquette, was surprised. Duquette will go down in history as having made a number of moves to heal rifts in Red Sox history, both in the area of race relations and with former players alienated from the team (though some may argue he alienated a few players himself, such as Clemens and Vaughn). At the same time, as the *Globe* put it, president Lucchino "had declined repeated opportunities to give [field manager Joe] Kerrigan a vote of confidence." (See March 5, 2005.)

2000 Newspaper readers learned that Tommy Harper had been named as coach for the Red Sox, a sign of "redemption" welcoming Harper back into the organization that had ostracized him in the middle-80s. Harper had sued the club for discrimination, and the case was settled out of court. "This is like night and day," said Harper, talking about the new, welcoming, and extremely diverse Red Sox organization. "This is a very different atmosphere altogether. It's refreshing."

1968 Former Sox manager and GM Mike "Pinky" Higgins was released from jail on $7500 bond. Higgins had killed one man and injured three others when his car drove into a work crew on I-20 in Louisiana. Higgins was convicted of negligent homicide and driving while intoxicated.

1946 A huge difference from today's "musical chairs" rosters; the February 28 *Sporting News* noted that every player on the Red Sox spring training roster (except Pete Fox, Hal Wagner, and Rudy York) are ones the Red Sox developed or purchased from a minor league ball club.

1944 Joe Wood, son of Howard Ellsworth (Smoky Joe) Wood, is signed by the Red Sox. No 34–5 season for Joe, he strikes out five in 9⅔ innings, but leaves the majors with a 6.52 ERA and a record of 0–1.

TRANSACTIONS
1919: Sold Wally Mayer to the St. Louis Browns.
1980: Signed free agent Luis Aponte.

BIRTHDATES
Homer Ezzell 1896 (1924–1925); Al Baker 1906 (1938); Frank Malzone 1930 (1955–1965)

DEATHS
Dizzy Trout 1972

February 29

1948 Joe McCarthy, strict manager of the Yankees from 1932–46 (winning nine pennants), is asked whether he will enforce a similar dress code on Sox star Ted Williams, known for his dislike of neckties. McCarthy shows up in Sarasota on the 29th, wearing a sports shirt and no necktie. "If I can't get along with a .400 hitter," he says, "I wouldn't be a very good manager."

No Red Sox player seems to have either been born or died on February 29.

MARCH

March 1

1954 Diving for a ball within an hour of suiting up for spring training, Ted Williams fell and broke his collarbone. He did not return until May 15. Though batting .345 at year's end, he only had 386 at-bats and lost the title to Bobby Avila (.341), since he was 14 at-bats short of the required 400. Ted walked a league-leading 136 times, however. A change was made, and later batting titles will be awarded based on plate appearances.

1948 Ted Williams shows up for the first day of spring training. This in itself is news.

1932 Big Ed Morris, Red Sox pitcher, was stabbed twice in the chest by gasoline station operator Joe White during a brawl at a Brewton, Alabama fish-fry intended to see him off to spring training. He died two days later. (See March 3 and March 28, 1932.)

1901 Future Hall of Famer Jimmy Collins, star third baseman with Boston's National League team, is hired to manage and play third for Boston's brand-new American League franchise.

BIRTHDATES
None yet

DEATHS
Hal Janvrin 1962; Rube Foster 1876; Johnny Watwood 1980

March 2

2005 A large Red Sox contingent visits the White House, where the 2004 World Champions are congratulated by President George W. Bush.

1946 A sucker born every minute. Dick Wakefield of the Tigers bets Ted Williams $1000 in each category that he would out-perform Williams in several stats. On this day, both deny it to the press, but in his autobiography, Williams admits it—and admits to having Commissioner Chandler cancel the bet by telegram. Wakefield hits .268 to Ted's .342, 12 HR to Ted's 38, and falls 64 short in RBI (59 to 123).

BIRTHDATES
Elmer Myers 1894 (1920–1922); Moe Berg 1902 (1935–1939); Babe Barna 1915 (1943); Don Schwall 1936 (1961–1962); Larry Wolfe 1953 (1979–1980)

DEATHS
Dale Alexander 1979

March 3

1976 Pitcher Dick Drago is traded to the Angels for John Balaz, Dave Machemer, and Dick Sharon. Drago later returns to the Sox for three more years, 1978–80.

1945 Sam Lacy of the *Afro-American* of Baltimore wrote Sox GM Eddie Collins (and the GMs of the Yankees and the Braves) with thoughts on how to facilitate integration in major league baseball. Collins replied on April 11, just five days before the team had finally consented to grant a tryout to three black players, one of whom was Jackie Robinson. The Red Sox could have been pioneers, to their everlasting credit. They chose not to take the opportunity, and paid a big price in opportunities (and probably pennants) lost.

1932 In Century, Florida, Ed Morris died from being stabbed two days earlier at a party in his honor. Morris was initially reported to be recovering, but may have succumbed to infection or pneumonia incurred as he swam across a river to flee his assailant. Owner Bob Quinn had reportedly been offered $80,000 cash for Morris at one point. Perhaps it was soon after his 19-win season for the 1928 Red Sox. In one 1931 incident, Morris apparently entered a hotel elevator and found the operator missing, so he starting running the elevator himself. The elevator boy sounded the alarm, and two house detectives responded and pursued Morris in another elevator. Morris, meanwhile, would open the door at each floor only long enough to give a loud rebel yell. Finally, the detectives sprang on him and wrestled him to the ground, wrenching his shoulder in the fracas. Morris was "practically useless" to the Sox for the rest of the year.

1923 Elmer Miller retires. After the Yankees traded him to Boston, the outfielder hit just .190 and so called it quits, joining instead the Fairbanks Morse industrial team in Beloit, Wisconsin. The position was a year-round one, covering the months outside the baseball season as well.

1919 Following the end of the World War, rather few Red Sox players had signed their 1919 contracts (see November 21, 1918), and the possibility of a collective holdout still lingered at the beginning of March. Babe Ruth said he wasn't part of the group; no matter what the others were doing, he definitely *was* holding out. Players did come around quickly; Ruth took longer.

1917 "When some of the Red Sox party observed that the train was leaving from Track 13, they winced a little," reported *The Boston Globe*. The Sox train departed Boston for spring training, with former championship boxer John L. Sullivan among those seeing them off. Was track 13 the reason the Red Sox won the World Series in 1915, 1916, and 1918—but fell short in 1917?

1911 Despite splitting into two teams to try to squeeze in more games (and revenue), both the Boston Red Sox teams in San Francisco and Los Angeles found their games rained out on March 3, 4, and 5. After another rainout in L.A. two days later, it was announced that 1911 rainfall had already exceeded a normal six months' total. Rain canceled most Sox games over a 10-day stretch.

TRANSACTIONS
1976: Traded Dick Drago to the California Angels in exchange for John Balaz, Dich Sharon, and Dave Machemer.

BIRTHDATES
Mike Remlinger 1966 (2005)

DEATHS
Ed Morris 1932; Hick Cady 1946; Jennings Poindexter 1983; Billy Jurges 1997

March 4

2005 The World Champion Red Sox won a 17–0 no-hitter in their second game of spring training. Their opponent was Northeastern University. In the day's night game, Boston College scored five times, but lost, 11–5.

2000 Cuban exile Juan Diaz was granted free agency in 1999 after the Dodgers signed him illegally. Now free once more, he signed with Boston, and in 2002 hit a double and a homer in seven AB. That was his major league career.

1984 Rick Ferrell is named to Cooperstown. Many think the Red Sox catcher's brother Wes was the more deserving of the two. Rick was an outstanding catcher, though, with 18 years of major league play.

1977 A portion of Jersey Street in Boston is renamed Yawkey Way, to honor the late Red Sox owner Tom Yawkey.

1944 GM Eddie Collins announced that the Red Sox would play exhibition games at 10 Army and Navy training camps during 1944.

1929 Rumors in Florida had boxing interests in New York talking to Bob Quinn about buying the Red Sox from him, but *The Sporting News* correspondent didn't believe Quinn would sell until he had fielded a championship team.

1927 Official starting date for 1927 Red Sox spring training at Heinemann Park, New Orleans is a late March 4 date, about two weeks behind that of many clubs. The park is a dog racing track and had to be readied for baseball. And, of course, everyone had to wait until Mardi Gras, which in 1927 fell on March 1. New manager Carrigan announced that no newspaper men, friends, or visitors of any kind—not even the police—would be allowed into the Red Sox clubhouse.

1921 After 12 years with the Red Sox, OF Harry Hooper went to the White Sox for Nemo Leibold and Shano Collins. A fair trade for both ball clubs. Leibold hit .306 for the Red Sox in 1921. He appeared in four World Series, but those came before and after his Red Sox stint. Hooper racked up 260 outfield assists for the Red Sox, more than any other Sox outfielder. He even pitched a couple of innings, in a 1913 game, and retired with a career ERA of 0.00. When he left as one of the last to have been sold or shipped out within a year and a half stretch, he said, "Frazee did me a favor. I was glad to get away from that graveyard."

1901 Both Bill Dinneen and Chick Stahl were reported to have "jumped" from the National League, and signed a contract for 1901 to play for the new Boston American League franchise. Manager–third baseman Jimmy Collins announced, "I have signed to play with the Bostons and shall have a team that will be first class in every particular. Boston is an ideal baseball town, and I know that the American League will have a complete success."

TRANSACTIONS
1921: Traded Harry Hooper to the Chicago White Sox for Shano Collins and Nemo Liebold.
2000: Free agent Juan Diaz signed.

BIRTHDATES
Charlie Hickman 1876 (1902); Lefty O'Doul 1897 (1923); Emmett McCann 1902 (1926); Mike Brown 1959 (1982–1986); Lee Tinsley 1969 (1994–1996)

DEATHS
None yet

March 5

2004 Nomar Garciaparra suffers a serious injury to his right Achilles tendon, and ultimately surrenders to the need to go on the disabled list on March 31. Nomar said he had been hit by a ball during batting practice. The odd thing about the injury, fueling any number of conspiracy theories, is that no one saw Nomar hit by a ball.

2002 Manager Joe Kerrigan was fired by new Red Sox ownership, with third base coach Mike Cubbage named as interim manager while the team sought a new field manager. Speculation indicated that Grady Little was the front runner. Little was hired on March 11.

1975 Tony Conigliaro, still trying to come back, signs on with the Pawtucket Red Sox. The Sox bring him up, but he only hits .123 in 57 AB.

1945 Doing their part to comply with war-time travel restrictions, the Red Sox again start training at Tufts College, then set up camp in Pleasantville, NJ. (Also see March 15, 1944.)

1928 NOTES OF GLADNESS and HEAT AND HAPPINESS RADIATE IN CAMP OF RED SOX—*The Sporting News* headlines on Burt Whitman's dispatch reported how pleased manager Bill Carrigan was with the first-time-in-Florida Red Sox spring training camp experience.

1924 The Red Sox held their first full spring training practice at their 1924 home, League Park in San Antonio. A welcoming party included a cake in the shape of a bat and ice cream scoops in the shape of baseballs complete with colored icing representing the stitching.

1901 The full lineup for Boston's first club in the brand-new American League was announced: Lou Criger and Ossee Schreckengost as catchers, Bill Dinneen as pitcher, Buck Freeman at first, Freddy Parent at second, Hobe Ferris at short, Jimmy Collins at third (and managing). Cozy Dolan, Chick Stahl, and Charlie Hemphill were all slated for the outfield—though Dolan never did play for Boston. In fact, there was a lot of uncertainty and waffling at first as players tried to decide whether or not to leave the National League and jump to the embryonic American. Some players indeed did jump back to the National League. (See, for instance, March 28, 1901.)

TRANSACTIONS
1975: Signed free agent Tony Conigliaro.
1976: Acquired Denny Doyle in trade with the California Angels, for Chuck Ross and cash.
2002: Dismissed Joe Kerrigan as manager of the Red Sox,
naming Mike Cubbage interim manager.

BIRTHDATES
Doug Bird 1950 (1983); Steve Ontiveros 1961 (2000); Chad Fonville 1971 (1999)

DEATHS
None yet

March 6

1987 Roger Clemens cleaned out his locker and left spring training when the Red Sox renewed his existing contract for 1987. Clemens had been seeking a major new contract; Sox GM Lou Gorman said that the team had made an offer, that it would have given Clemens the third-highest salary in the game, but that Clemens had rejected it.

1927 Sharing Heinemann Park for spring training, the New Orleans Pelicans worked out from 10 to 12 noon each day, then turned the park over to the Red Sox for their workout.

1923 Frank Chance seemed to be in effective charge of the Red Sox, reported *The Sporting News* under the subhead: "Whole American League United, It Is Said, In Movement to Get Frazee Out of Baseball." (See also July 11, 1923.)

1914 Tris Speaker finally signed up with the Red Sox again, becoming the most highly-paid player in history. Speaker had good leverage (aside from his .383 and .363 averages in 1912 and 1913): the Federal League had offered him $60,000 for three years, including a $15,000 signing bonus which was placed on the table in front of him in the form of 15 $1,000 bills. Lannin and the Boston Red Sox signed Speaker with a reported $40,000 for two years.

1912 If the March 7 game was called off due to rain, Jake Stahl said he'd take the team on a 24-mile hike. It was, but the hike was shortened to 15 miles.

BIRTHDATES
Bert Husting 1878 (1902); Cliff Brady 1897 (1920); Lefty Grove 1900
(1934–1941); Terry Adams 1973 (2004); James Lofton 1974 (2001);

DEATHS
Jimmy Collins 1943; Tex Pruiett 1953; Wally Schang 1965; Lou
Legett 1988; George Stumpf 1993; Frank Barrett 1998

March 7

2005 The intense rivalry between the Red Sox and Yankees is reflected by the hundreds of people in line for more than 36 hours outside Fort Myers' City of Palms Park waiting for day-of-game tickets for a split squad spring training exhibition.

2004 The hottest ticket in Florida is for the Red Sox–Yankees spring training game in Fort Myers, their first matchup since Game Seven of the 2003 League Championship Series, the game in which a steroids-enhanced Jason Giambi hit two home runs, but has yet to be re-played. At least one pair of tickets was seen on eBay at $500.00.

In Boston, the *Globe* reported the closing of the bowling alley under Fenway. It had been open for 15 years, but their string ran out back in October. There would be no more strikes under Fenway Park. New offices for Theo Epstein and the baseball operations staff were being constructed in place of the lanes.

2001 The bus for Bradenton was due to leave at 7:45 A.M. Manager Jimy Williams boarded the bus at 7:45. He decided to send a message to frequently-tardy star outfielder Carl Everett, who had just arrived at the clubhouse moments before, so at 7:46 the bus rolled out of the Fort Myers parking lot. The next day, Everett showed up 15 minutes early.

1999 Carlton Fisk was named special assistant to Red Sox general manager Dan Duquette, bringing Fisk back into the team for the first time since they let him get away. Duquette was particularly good about building bridges to Sox veterans who became estranged or drifted, and especially so with those he himself admired as a young fan. Having Fisk as a Sox employee set the stage for being able to retire his number after he was elected to the National Baseball Hall of Fame, so the Red Sox would not have to change their policy regarding number retirement: the player had to have played 10 years with the Red Sox, and finished his career with the Sox—and Fisk was now with the Red Sox. (See January 14, 2000.)

1964 U.S. Senator Edward M. Kennedy and the Red Sox announced proceeds from the season opener would be donated to the John F. Kennedy Memorial Library.

1941 It was an interesting boxscore for the Reds–Red Sox spring training game at Tampa. Pete Fox followed Jimmie Foxx in the Sox lineup. Heber (Dick) Newsome was the starting pitcher, and Lamar (Skeeter) Newsome helped on defense, spelling Cronin at short. The Reds had center fielder Mike McCormick batting second and first baseman Frank McCormick batting third. No relation. None of them.

1937 Pitcher Wes Ferrell spent six weeks in Hollywood over the winter and had passed a screen test with flying colors. He had studied dramatics and starred in a few amateur plays, and was reportedly mulling a move into the movies. It was later reported that his Southern drawl was too pronounced for filmdom.

1921 Trade one holdout for another? That was the idea—for the Sox to trade holdout Stuffy McInnis to Washington for holdout Joe Judge. It never happened; McInnis played with Boston in 1921. Another story of the day proved false: Del Pratt, obtained from the Yankees, emphatically denied he would play for Boston or any other team in 1921. Pratt hit .324 for the Red Sox, with 102 RBIs, in 1921 and had an excellent year in 1922 as well.

1917 Still among those in the "holdout league," Dutch Leonard and Duffy Lewis were playing for the Fresno Sunmaids and helped defeat the Chicago Cubs' second team at Fresno, 1–0, when Lewis was hit, stole second, and scored on a single in the bottom of the ninth. Earlier in the game, his throw cut down a Cubbie. Frazee allowed as how it was nice that they were training at their own expense.

Closer to home, Wolfie Jacobs, megaphone announcer at both Fenway Park and Braves Field, signed up for the 1917 season.

TRANSACTIONS
2003: Released Juan Pena.

BIRTHDATES
Galen Cisco 1936 (1961–1967)

DEATHS
Pee-Wee Wanninger 1981

March 8

1979 Bill Lee said, "I've never smoked the stuff," denying that he was a regular marijuana smoker. He added that caffeine, nicotine, and alcohol were more damaging to the body than marijuana. Earlier, Lee had said, "I've used it on my buckwheat pancakes"—but not that he had smoked it.

1952 Just prior to the first game of spring training, Sox manager Lou Boudreau was observing batting practice and put his face a little too close to the screen. A foul ball off the bat of catcher Gus Niarhos caught Boudreau flush in the face and knocked him out. He was treated at the local hospital in Sarasota.

1945 Boston City Councilor Isadore Muchnick announced he would file a motion at a March 12 council meeting to deny the annual license permitting the Red Sox to play baseball on Sundays unless they pledge to give all players equal treatment, regardless of race, color, or creed.

1920 Armando Marsans, star Cuban outfielder, signed a contract with a Red Sox agent in Havana, it was announced at the Sox spring training headquarters at Hot Springs. As it happens, Marsans never played in the majors again.

1911 An eighth-inning home run by third baseman Wallace gave Oakland's St. Mary's College a 1–0 victory over the Red Sox. The ball hit off Hugh Bedient was fair inside the right field foul line, but rolled through vehicles along the street. When Hooper fired the ball back in, the Red Sox infielders were not properly positioned and Wallace scored easily.

BIRTHDATES
Harry Lord 1882 (1907–1910); Ray Francis 1893 (1925); Pete Fox 1909 (1941–1945); Jim Rice 1953 (1974–1989); Win Remmerswaal 1954 (1979–1980); Joel Johnston 1967 (1995); Jesus Pena 1975 (2000)

DEATHS
None yet

March 9

1989 *The Boston Globe*'s Michael Madden reported from Winter Haven that the Red Sox spring training uniform surprised by lacking one element: the words "Red Sox" on the home jersey. Instead, the words had been replaced by "two cute little red socks over the left breast, sort of like pajamas for a cutesy infant."

1981 Newly-declared free agent Carlton Fisk agrees to terms with the White Sox, and will sign on March 18. Sox GM Haywood Sullivan neglected to pick up Fisk's option; the letter was postmarked a little too late.

1979 Ball clubs are notified by Commissioner Bowie Kuhn that reporters, regardless of sex, should be treated equally. Female reporters seeking to pursue their profession should not denied access to the clubhouse. A number of incidents in Boston and elsewhere prompted the notice.

1959 The Sox get Chuck Tanner from the Cubs for pitcher Bob W. "Riverboat" Smith (4–3, 3.78 ERA in 1958), but Tanner travels on to the Indians instead and never plays for the Sox.

1954 Surgeons in Cambridge, MA inserted a six-inch steel nail to help bind the pieces of Ted Williams' broken collarbone in place.

1949 In Sarasota, Joe McCarthy expected the 1949 Red Sox to be a better team, saying he liked the looks of new southpaws Frank McCall and Maurice McDermott. Fortunately, McDermott eventually made it to camp. Leaving Grand Central, McDermott took a train south, only realizing it when he entered the dining car and encountered Charlie Keller, Tommy Henrich, Joe DiMaggio, Specs Shea, and a number of other Yankees. "What in the hell were they doing here?" he wondered, before it dawned on him that he'd boarded the wrong train.

1946 In Havana to play exhibition games, Ted Williams was reportedly offered half a million dollars to sign with the Mexican League. The Sox defeated the Senators, 7–3, and Ted asked Bernardo Pasquel, "Will you give me four strikes, instead of three?" When Pasquel agreed, Ted added, "Well, I won't come anyhow."

1942 During spring training, Ted Williams explains why, as sole support of his mother, he has sought deferment from military service.

1914 Red Sox pitcher Fred Anderson signed a contract with the Buffalo team in the new rival Federal League, and won 13 games his first year and 19 the next. The Sox might not have missed him much, though; he'd been 0–6 with Boston in 1913. (In 1917, however, Anderson led the National League with a 1.44 ERA for the New York Giants.)

1908 The manager of the Natchez ball club of the Cotton State League saw Nuf-Ced McGreevy working out with the team, as the great Boston fan often did. After some negotiation, he approached Boston owner Taylor with an offer of $200 for McGreevy. Taylor saw the chance for some fun, so bargained up the price to $300 and then accepted the man's check for the higher amount. Taylor then introduced the Natchez owner to McGreevy. The Natchez man informed Nuf-Ced that he'd just bought his release from Boston, upon which McGreevy replied, "I guess you've been handed a good sized lemon." The man dug for his gun, but Taylor had already absented himself and, with everyone laughing, the Natchez man joined in as well—but had to buy a few rounds for his friends.

March 10

1998 After he'd played just one year in the majors, the Red Sox take a chance on star shortstop Nomar Garciaparra with a guaranteed $23,325,000 five-year contract, with two option years that push the final total another $21 million higher.

1987 Roger Clemens said he might elect to sit out the entire 1987 season; the day before, the Red Sox stated they might fine Roger Clemens $1,000 a day for every day he fails to return to spring training. (See March 6, 1987.)

1986 Bobby Doerr was selected by the Veterans Committee and will be inducted into the Hall of Fame.

1976 Because the Red Sox failed to sign Fred Lynn, Carlton Fisk, and Rick Burleson to new contracts by the March 10 deadline, all three had their contracts automatically renewed and entered their option year. They all worked it out eventually—this time around—but dragging out negotiations throughout the season probably hurt the team.

1960 Marty Keough and pitcher Dave Hillman were returning to Scottsdale's Safari Hotel, the spring training home of the Red Sox, 15 minutes after curfew when their car turned over five times.

1958 Joe Cronin spoke up in support of Ted Williams, who refused to wear a batting helmet at home plate. "We don't intend to make him wear one of those miner's hats if he doesn't want to do so," Cronin declared.

1908 Not wanting to be upstaged by the Red Sox laying claim to the color red, Boston's National League ball club decided to wear red socks and red caps and, it was suggested, may become known as the Red Caps rather than as the Beaneaters.

March 11

2002 Grady Little was named the 43rd manager of the Boston Red Sox. He was a veteran minor league manager, who had over 1,000 minor league wins to his credit and had four times been named Minor League Manager of the Year. He had also been manager of the Durham Bulls at the time the 1988 movie *Bull Durham* was filmed, and played a role training some of the actors. "I was in one of the scenes," he said, "but they cut it out of the movie." More recently, he had done a stint as a coach with the Red Sox (1997–1999). When the announcement was made to players inside a closed clubhouse, reporters outside could hear a "thunderous ovation" from the assembled Sox squad.

1999 Fostering brotherly love, the Sox sign free agent pitcher Ramon Martinez, bringing him together with his younger brother Pedro.

1998 In Fort Myers, Mo Vaughn blasted the Red Sox for what he called a "smear campaign" against him. Vaughn was seeking a five-year contract extension and $50 million, but his drunk driving arrest on January 9 had led to team management asking him to undergo alcohol evaluation. He replied he would if they would, but insisted that management was out to smear him.

1971 Rico Petrocelli and the Red Sox were both sued for $1,000,000 by Mrs. Susanne Mondlin, a United Air Lines stewardess who also worked as a model. She charged that on the team charter, Petrocelli had grabbed her indecently while she was serving coffee, then cursed her, made threatening gestures toward her, and kicked her in the leg.

1912 The Red Sox party arrived late to spring training when their train missed its connection at Memphis due to the wreck of a freight train between Cincinnati and Memphis. During a layover in Cincinnati, four of the Sox party went missing, but three turned up in the nick of time. Jack Lewis was the odd man out. Consulting the record book, we notice that—for whatever reason—he never played again for the Red Sox.

TRANSACTIONS
1969: Traded Mark Scheffer to the Astros for Hal King.
1999: Ramon Martinez signed as a free agent.

BIRTHDATES
Norwood Gibson 1877 (1903–1906); Buster Ross 1903 (1924–1926); Jim Bucher 1911 (1944–1945); Jack Spring 1933 (1957); Dwayne Hosey 1967 (1995–1996); Gar Finnvold 1968 (1994); Sang-Hoon Lee 1971 (2000)

DEATHS
Eric McNair 1949; Joe Judge 1963; Larry Gardner 1976

March 12

2003 Red Sox pitching coach Tony Cloninger was diagnosed with bladder cancer. The Red Sox lacked a closer on the pitching staff and were prepared to proceed with "closer by committee"—inserting the best pitcher for the occasion into each game situation, regardless of the new orthodoxy that deemed a closer a key role on the team. Cloninger had to leave the club for extensive treatment, but ultimately recovered. On June 9, however, the Red Sox hired Dave Wallace as their full-time pitching coach.

1993 Roger Clemens, cleared of charges in the Bayou Mama's incident back in December 1991, said that a civil suit filed against him on January 15 was a case of "somebody trying to get rich quick." The somebody was Houston police officer Luis Oviedo, whose attorneys said the sergeant had "sustained physical impairment, disability and disfigurement which he will have to endure for the balance of his natural life." Clemens had the officer in a headlock, the suit explained, and pain persisted despite many weeks off work and extensive physical therapy. Clemens countersued, claiming Oviedo was the aggressor, and his attorneys said he would not settle the case out of court.

1980 Thomas A. Yawkey is selected by the Veterans Committee for induction into the Hall of Fame. He's the first club owner chosen who had never held a position in the game other than as owner. Phillies player Chuck Klein was also picked by the Veterans Committee.

1975 In just his second appearance since his June 1974 knee injury, Carlton Fisk is hit by a pitch which breaks his arm during spring training, but still comes up big (.331) in half a season, helping lead the Sox to the World Series.

1945 The Boston City Council referred to the rules committee Councilor Isadore Muchnick's request to deny Sunday baseball licenses to both the Boston Braves and the Red Sox unless they agree not to discriminate against players. The presiding councilor said, "Whoever the baseball clubs hire is not the business of the Council, nor does it concern the matter of Sunday baseball licenses."

1937 The first-ever radio broadcast to New England from spring training camp featured Bill Cunningham interviewing players Jimmie Foxx, Wes Ferrell, Lefty Grove, and others, and transmitted over the Yankee Network. No relation to the team of similar name.

1902 It took the team just one year to first raise ticket prices. Grandstand ticket prices were increased from 50 cents to 75 cents, and the third base pavilion was increased from 25 to 50 cents, but bleachers still held at 25 cents, so a quarter could still get you into the Huntington Avenue Grounds.

1901 Ground-breaking is held for the construction of the Huntington Avenue Grounds, the first home field of the Boston Americans—the team now named the Boston Red Sox. Construction was quick; the first home game was on May 8.

BIRTHDATES
Alex Gaston 1893 (1926–1929)

DEATHS
None yet

March 13

1956 Ted Williams blasted "gutless politicians, gutless draft boards, and gutless sports writers" for not sticking up for Brooklyn Dodgers pitcher Johnny Podres, who was drafted and due to be inducted into the U. S. Army. The country was at peace, but Ted charged, "When Podres became a hero in the Series, some politicians said, 'Why isn't a big strong kid like that in the Army?'" Billy Martin of the Yankees spoke up in immediate agreement, joined the following day by Dave Sisler, Frank Baumann, and Frank Sullivan—all ex-military men like Williams and Martin.

1944 Cy Young tells the world that his middle name is True, as in Denton True Young, not Tecumseh. Newspapers and some baseball cards around 1939 often referred to Theodore Francis Williams, instead of using his real middle name: Samuel.

1935 Arthur "Skinny" Graham of Cambridge, Massachusetts, hit a seventh-inning grand slam off Al Smith to beat the New York Giants in a 7–5 exhibition game. The home run earned Graham a berth on the Red Sox. In 57 major league at-bats in 1934 and 1935, he never hit a homer and drove in just four runs.

BIRTHDATES
Ralph Glaze 1882 (1906–1908); Eddie Pellagrini 1918 (1946–1947); Dario Veras 1973 (1998)

DEATHS
Ira Flagstead 1940; Buddy Rosar 1994

March 14

2002 Luis Tiant was named Red Sox broadcaster for the 2002 season, working for Bill Kulik's Spanish Radio Network and helping broadcast all 162 Boston Red Sox games in Spanish.

2000 The Red Sox pitched a perfect game against the Toronto Blue Jays in a spring
STVT exhibition game in Fort Myers. Pedro Martinez started. It being spring, though, he was only meant to pitch a short stint. After three innings, a parade of pitchers kept the perfecto going: Fernando de la Cruz, Dan Smith, Rheal Cormier, Rich Garces, and Rod Beck all pitched in, while Garciaparra drove in four of Boston's five runs. Most of the fans were clueless; almost half the crowd was gone by the seventh inning.

1957 Michigan State Police announced the arrest of John Allyn Clawson, 26, of North
?! Manchester, Indiana, who had been posing as Red Sox pitcher Tom Brewer, giving away signed American League baseballs in taverns in and around White Pigeon, Michigan. After questioning, police decided he had committed no crime in giving away the baseballs, but they charged him with false registration at a motel since he had signed in as Brewer. He paid a $10 fine and $5 in court costs, and was asked to leave the state. It was 11-year-old Brian Muth, son of state police detective Andres Muth, who provided a baseball card with a facsimile signature that Clawson could not match.

1936 Tom Yawkey was frank in admitting he was trying to buy Boston a pennant, and felt that the Red Sox had every chance to become a pennant-winner.

1911 Red Sox minor league catcher Pinch Thomas was out sightseeing in San Francisco. A little after midnight, he was set upon by a "crowd of thugs and beaten into insensibility." It was thought he would lose the sight of one eye and confined to bed for a long time. In fact, he made his major league debut with the Red Sox on April 12 and played for 10 seasons in the big leagues.

BIRTHDATES
Marty McManus 1900 (1931–1933); Jack Rothrock 1905 (1925–1932); Bill Kennedy 1921 (1953); Mike Rochford 1963 (1988–1990)

DEATHS
Tracy Baker 1975

March 15

1944 With World War II still going, the Red Sox open training at Tufts College as they had in 1943, but will largely be based in Baltimore. (Also see 1943, below, and March 5, 1945.)

1943 It's the Frostbite League and not the Grapefruit League, as the Sox hold their 1943 spring training at Tufts College in Medford, Massachusetts, with much of the work done indoors out of necessity.

1942 Before an exhibition game against the Senators, several members of the Red Sox team went up into the stands to make a recording that would be broadcast to soldiers in overseas bases. So many fans pressed in to try for a Ted Williams autograph that it became uncomfortable for the Sox slugger.

1939 Former Cardinals manager Frankie Frisch signs on to broadcast home games of both the Boston Bees and the Boston Red Sox during the 1939 season.

1918 "Mr. Ellenberg; call for Mr. Ellenberg." The bellhops could not locate Mimos Ellenberg at the Majestic in Hot Springs. The 18-year-old Red Sox prospect, who Ed Barrow said "may be another Hornsby," impressed the team enough that they wanted to sign him. But they couldn't find him; he disappeared.

1906 Catcher Lou Criger collapsed at the Hot Springs hotel, in a comatose state for nearly two hours in the nighttime and in such excruciating pain when he awoke that he lapsed back into unconsciousness. He had been suffering serious ongoing medical problems for more than a month, with fears that he had spinal meningitis or some other condition. When Criger awoke with convulsions, his roommate Mike Regan had to call for help to hold him down. Three days later, Criger left Hot Springs, with his weight down to 119 pounds, almost 50 pounds below his usual playing weight.

TRANSACTIONS
1959: Traded Dean Stone to the St. Louis Cardinals for Nelson Chittum.

1979: Traded Mike Easler to the Pittsburgh Pirates for two minor leaguers (George Hill and Martin Rivas) and some cash. On the same day, perhaps using some of that cash, purchased Jim Dwyer from the Giants.

BIRTHDATES
Kevin Youkilis 1979 (2004–2005)

DEATHS
Bill Cissell 1949; Bob Cremins 2004; Chappie Geygan 1966

March 16

1967 It was a wild 18–13 game after eight innings, with the Mets beating the Red Sox in St. Petersburg. The Red Sox rallied with 10 runs in the top of the ninth to win, 23–18.

1963 Roman Mejias is reunited with his wife, two children, and two sisters from Cuba, thanks to efforts by the Red Sox. In 1975, Luis Tiant is able to welcome his father from Cuba, too, thanks to the Sox and U.S. Senator Ed Brooke.

1960 Catcher Sammy White and outfielder Jim Marshall are swapped to the Indians for catcher Russ Nixon. Three days later, White—with a brand new bowling alley in Brighton—chooses to retire instead and the trade is voided. The Sox get their man, though, on June 13. (See also March 25, 1960.) Sammy White made 79 double plays, the most of any Red Sox catcher.

TRANSACTIONS
1960: Traded Sammy White and Jim Marshall to the Indians for Russ Nixon. When White refused to report, the trade was voided and the players returned to their original teams.

BIRTHDATES
Patsy Donovan 1865 (manager, 1910–1911); Buddy Myer 1904 (1927–1928)

DEATHS
George Orme 1962; Bob Kline 1987; Jigger Statz 1988; Dick Radatz 2005

March 17

1991 The Red Sox were considering moving their spring training site from Winter Haven to Fort Myers, Florida. The small city had already lured the Minnesota Twins and the city council was prepared to build a $15 to $20 million complex for the Red Sox, to help renew an area where "until police initiated recent sweeps...had been the scene of the city's worst drug and prostitution problems" in the words of *Globe* staffer Steve Fainaru.

1962 On St. Patrick's Day in Mesa, Arizona, they became the Boston Green Sox for a day. Pete Runnels brought a Kelly green bat to the plate in the top of the first, and was thrown a green ball by Chicago Cubs pitcher Dick Ellsworth.

1943 Ted Williams undergoes a hernia operation at the Chelsea Naval Hospital, interrupting his training as an aviation cadet.

1911 Fire started by a plumber's blowtorch destroyed Washington's ballpark (and four adjacent buildings) and threatened the April opener hosting the Red Sox. (See April 12, 1911.)

BIRTHDATES
Hy Vandenberg 1906 (1935); Tim Lollar 1956 (1985–1986); Bill Mueller 1971 (2003–2005)

DEATHS
Rube Kroh 1944; Howard Ehmke 1959; Billy Purtell 1962

March 18

1957 After Herb Score's 20–9 season for the Indians, with a league-leading 263 strikeouts, the Red Sox wanted him. GM Joe Cronin reportedly offered one million dollars of cool cash. Cronin's counterpart GM Hank Greenberg declined the offer, seeing Score as a franchise player. Fifty days later, Score's brilliant career is altered forever as a result of a line drive that fells him on the mound.

1955 Ted Williams said "my mind is so filled with other things I can't think of returning to baseball right now." He and his wife had yet to agree on the financial terms of their divorce settlement.

1953 Owners of the National League ball clubs unanimously approved the move of Lou Perini's Boston Braves franchise to Wisconsin, where they became the Milwaukee Braves. From this day forward, Boston had but one major league ball club, the Boston Red Sox.

1938 Frederick Lieb wrote that Hobe Ferris was so upset by learning of Bob Fothergill's March 16 death of a heart attack that he suffered a fatal heart attack himself. Lieb may have mixed up the men; Ferris died on the 18th and Fothergill died two days later after suffering a "nervous ailment" and a stroke.

1919 Babe Ruth missed the boat. Intentionally. The star Red Sox pitcher–slugger did not join the Red Sox party which embarked for Jacksonville on the *Arapahoe* for 1919 spring training. Ruth was seeking $15,000 a year, or three years for $30,000. Sox president Harry Frazee said he was not worth that much as a drawing card; he was offering $8,500 for one year. Three days later, Ruth met with Frazee in New York and agreed on $27,000 for three years. Ruth had not expected to come to agreement, and had not even brought a suitcase with him, but immediately boarded a train for Tampa and asked a friend to send his baggage from Boston.

1910 Disregarding doctor's orders not to play ball, Jack Thoney started working out with the Red Sox in Hot Springs and snapped his shoulder joint while throwing a baseball before the game. (See also February 5, 1910.) Bullet Jack came back in 1911, and batted an even .250 (5-for-20) in limited action that constituted the end of his major league career.

TRANSACTIONS
1969: Purchased Bill Kelso from the Cincinnati Reds.

BIRTHDATES
Al Benton 1911 (1952); Eddie Lake 1916 (1943–1945); Fred Hatfield 1925 (1950–1952); Dick Littlefield 1926 (1950); Tomokazu Ohka 1976 (1999–2001)

DEATHS
Hobe Ferris 1938; Rudy Sommers 1949; Frank Bennett 1966; Tony Welzer 1971; Frank Bushey 1972; Paul Maloy 1976

March 19

1997 A 25-foot Coca-Cola "bottle" was unveiled atop Fenway's left-field Wall; the single bottle soon grew to a three-bottle cluster that now seems an accepted part of the park. At the time, traditionalists were understandably aghast.

1996 Red Sox righthander Vaughn Eshelman suffered one of those bizarre spring training accidents when, in the words of the A.P.'s Jimmy Golen, he "burned his hands trying to put out a fire in his hotel room that started when his wife used a candle to warm a bottle for their 10-week-old son." Eshelman quickly clarified that his son Evan drinks his bottles cold and that the story was false. His wife Julie had a candle lit in the bathroom and it started a fire. "Some people like candles, I guess." That was his explanation of how he had burned both of his hands. He'd heard his wife screaming, woke up, and found the towels on fire in the bathroom with flames licking up the walls. Eshelman used a washcloth to beat out the flames. His hands? "They looked cooked. Real charred. I'd never felt pain like that. It felt like my bones were on fire."

1986 After the Red Sox released Ed Jurak, he carped, "They never gave me a chance to show what I could do." He'd only been in the Red Sox system since he was drafted on June 3, 1975.

1967 Tony Conigliaro's left shoulder blade was broken as he was hit by a batting practice pitch. It was the fifth time he had suffered a broken bone after being hit by a pitch. Tony C. nevertheless remained aggressive, crowding the plate.

1951 Even in spring training! The A.P. reported that when Ted Williams was booed for not running out a grounder to the pitcher in an exhibition game, he spat toward the stands and spat again when crossing the plate after hitting a home run. Williams denied spitting at the fans, saying, "I had something in my mouth and I just got rid of it on the ground. I don't care whether they like me or not."

1941 Ted Williams slid into second base in Sarasota and hurt his ankle. It still prevented him from playing for two weeks, so the team finally had it x-rayed and learned there was a slight fracture. He was sent to Boston for treatment, but played on it all season long—possibly holding back on his swing just a hair and getting a better look at the ball in the process. The Kid had a pretty good year at the plate in 1941!

1937 Jack Russell pitched for Boston from his debut in 1926 until mid-1932, then appeared in a second stint briefly in 1936. He was released this day in 1937, then signed on with the Tigers. In his first seven years with the Red Sox, he posted a losing record each and every year. In his second stint, he went 0–3.

1917 Playing against Brooklyn on Sunday in Hot Springs, the first exhibition contest saw the Robins beat the Red Sox, 7–2, despite the combined efforts of Sox pitchers Mays, Ruth, and Shore. (See March 27, 1917.)

1914 An upset in the Ozarks? Playing in Hot Springs, the second-string Yanigans won their fifth spring training game in a row from the Regulars.

TRANSACTIONS
1937: Released Jack Russell.
1986: Released Ed Jurak.
1996: Acquired Luis Alicea on waivers from the St. Louis Cardinals.
1998: Midre Cummings was acquired on waivers from the Cincinnati Reds.

BIRTHDATES
Clyde Engle 1884 (1910–1914); Bill Wambsganss 1894 (1924–1925); Joe Gonzales 1915 (1937); Pete Smith 1940 (1962–1963); Ivan Calderon 1962 (1993)

DEATHS
Gordie Hinkle 1972

March 20

1978 Ted Williams returns to baseball, with the Red Sox, for the first time in over five years, as a special instructor working with rookies in spring training.

1972 Boston brings 1B Bob Burda on board, trading 1B Mike Fiore. Burda hits .164 and finishes his career. Fiore hits .100 for the Cardinals, then is sent to San Diego, where he hits .000.

1969 Pinky Higgins was paroled after serving just three months of a four-year sentence for the DWI death he dealt a Louisiana highway worker. Higgins was clearly ill and died the very next day.

1961 Sears, Roebuck & Co. bought a controlling interest in Ted Williams, Inc., the Miami-based fishing tackle company that belonged to the former Sox star.

1960 Red Sox in Vegas. The team lost a spring training game to the Cubs, 3–2, before 10,000 "gaudily attired spectators" in Las Vegas. The infield, according to the *Chicago Tribune*, was "pebbly" and "suited more to a rodeo than to major league baseball."

1957 *Fear Strikes Out* has its premiere; the film starring Anthony Perkins as Jimmy Piersall tells the story of Piersall's struggle with mental illness.

1947 John Michael Paveskovich petitioned Probate Court in Salem, Massachusetts to legally change his surname and that of his wife Ruth to Pesky.

1946 The Red Sox would meet the St. Louis Cardinals in the World Series, come October. Their springtime meetings did not go well for the Sox. The March 20 loss (9–6) in Sarasota was the fifth consecutive spring training loss to the Cardinals.

1920 Spring training in Hot Springs was a little cold, apparently. Umpire Von Sickel wore earmuffs during the Pittsburgh-Boston game.

TRANSACTIONS
1972: Acquired Bob Burda by trading Mike Fiore to the Cardinals. Purchased Bobby Pfeil from the Milwaukee Brewers.

BIRTHDATES
Stan Spence 1915 (1940–1949); Al Widmar 1925 (1947); Dana Williams 1963 (1989); Manny Alexander 1971 (2000)

DEATHS
Bob Fothergill 1938; Heinie Wagner 1943; Luis Alvarado 2001

March 21

1988 Bernard "Dick" Casey, a charter member of the Bosox Club, died in Boston at age 93. Casey was cited in 1971 by Mayor Kevin White as the city's "Ambassador to Baseball." He'd worked as an usher during the 1912 World Series.

1969 Pinky Higgins, who hated his nickname, died at a Dallas-area hospital the very day after he was released from prison in Louisiana. (See March 20.)

1938 Ted Williams was given the news that he was optioned to Minneapolis and would spend 1938 playing for the Minneapolis Millers, the top club in the Red Sox system. "Where you going, California?" one of the Red Sox outfielders taunted Ted. "I'll be back, and I'll be making more money than the three of you put together," Ted replied.

1931 The announcement was made that Graham McNamee would broadcast the Yankees–Red Sox opening day game at Yankee Stadium on April 14. He would kick off with a "half-hour preliminary description of the flag-raising and other ceremonies" and then go on to describe the game to NBC listeners.

BIRTHDATES
Bill Lamar 1897 (1919); Red Rollings 1904 (1927–1928); Owen Friend 1927 (1955)

DEATHS
Pinky Higgins 1969; Fritz Coumbe 1978

March 22

1974 Carl Yastrzemski is named captain of the Red Sox team.

1972 The trade may not have been made for baseball purposes. Relief specialist Sparky Lyle was maybe a little too rambunctious for the Red Sox; after five years with Boston, it was reportedly his penchant for sitting on birthday cakes with his bare butt that got him shown the door. If that's what it was, the Yankees lucked out. They sent Danny Cater to the Sox, where he mainly played first base and a few games at third. Lyle had 141 saves with the Yankees, and a 2.41 ERA over the next seven seasons. When Sparky won the Cy Young Award in 1977, whether they had a cake for him is unknown. There was a PTBNL—SS Mario Guerrero, who arrived on the last day of June.

1959 Ted Williams was unable to play in Arizona due to a "cold in his right shoulder." A week later, on March 30, he entered a Boston hospital for treatment.

1934 The starting pitcher facing the Red Sox was "girl Olympic star" Babe Didrikson, who threw the first inning of the day's exhibition game in Bradenton, Florida, for the St. Louis Cardinals. This particular Babe allowed three runs, but the Cardinals went on to win, 9–7.

1931 At Pensacola, the Red Sox beat the touring House of David baseball team, 14–4, ensuring victory with nine runs in the eighth. Earl Webb's home run was said to have traveled 550 feet.

1916 Tris Speaker had been a holdout, objecting to being offered a $9,000 salary, the same as he had been paid in 1913. Since signing for 1913, Speaker had hit .363, .338, and .322. It wasn't that Sox ownership was upset at his declining average; it was that major league teams no longer had to compete salary-wise with the upstart Federal League. That league had failed, but had driven up salaries for 1914 and 1915. Speaker had reportedly been offered $35,000 to jump leagues, and the Red Sox matched the offer to retain him. The way he looked at it in 1916, though, he was only being offered about half of what he'd been paid the last two years. On this date, Speaker wrote that he'd report to spring training at Hot Springs, and work out the salary matter once the team got to Boston. It was resolved, but only by shipping Speaker off to Cleveland, where he proceeded to win the batting title.

1912 A Philadelphia newspaper boxscore abbreviated the names of Red Sox players as follows: Hoo'r, Yer's, Spea'r, Stahl, Gar'r, Lewis, Krug, Nuna'r, Tho's, Hall, Bed't, Bush'n, Leo'd, Cady, Brad'y.

Sox Treasurer McBreen was happy to see a photograph in the Jersey City newspaper. It depicted Sox player Hal Janvrin in Bermuda with the Jersey City team. Last McBreen had heard, he was on the boat when it set sail for Bermuda, but had been reported as not seen since.

TRANSACTIONS
1972: Traded Sparky Lyle to the New York Yankees for Danny
        Cater and a PTBNL (Mario Guerrero, June 30).
1994: Acquired Lee Tinsley in trade from the Seattle Mariners, for a PTBNL (Jim Smith).
2005: Traded Adam Hyzdu to the San Diego Padres for pitcher
        Blaine Neal. See also the July 19, 2005 transaction.

BIRTHDATES
Marv Owen 1906 (1940); Moose Solters 1906 (1934–1935); Bill Butland 1918 (1940–1947); Billy Goodman 1926 (1947–1956); Al Schroll 1932 (1958–1959); Gene Oliver 1935 (1968); Dick Ellsworth 1940 (1968–1969); Sean Berry 1966 (2000); Ramon Martinez 1968 (1999–2000)

DEATHS
Gordon Rhodes 1960

March 23

1991 Late Saturday night, after dining at Christy's Sundown Restaurant in Sarasota and a visit to Christy's Lounge, Debbie Boggs pulled their Ford Explorer out of the parking lot—and Wade fell out of the car. He had bruises on his elbow and ankle and the elbow bruises were in a "tire-tread pattern, as if a tire ran over his right elbow," reported the *Boston Globe*'s Nick Cafardo. "I didn't have my seat belt on," Boggs commented, noting that he was glad to be alive. Apparently, the back tire of the car did run over his elbow. The story reminded Boggs-watchers of other stories, such as the time he bruised his ribs by falling over when trying to put on his cowboy boots in Toronto, or the time he said he had willed himself invisible to escape a knife-wielding man. (See March 25, 1989)

1967 Just four days after Tony Conigliaro's shoulder blade was broken, George Scott turned the wrong way on a fly ball and crashed into the concrete right-field wall of the Winter Haven home of the Red Sox, suffering a brain concussion. It was Scott's 23rd birthday, but he lost more than a minute of it while unconscious on the field. Two days earlier, Scott had been angered when manager Dick Williams had assigned him to play right field instead of first base.

1943 Joining in a wartime blood drive, 31 members of the Red Sox donated a pint of blood each to the effort. Joe Cronin organized the drive, after returning from a month of Red Cross service in the Pacific.

1929 Six members of the Portland Beavers were making their way from San Diego to training camp when their automobile was hit by another and driven down an embankment. Killed in the crash was Denny Williams, who played with the Sox in 1924, 1925, and 1928.

1926 Manager Lee Fohl had installed a system of bells to ring the bullpen and advise pitchers to warm up. One ring meant "get ready," two rings meant "warm up easy," and three meant "warm up hard." Mischievous players on the Boston bench began to fool around, and had pitchers warming up so quickly that they were sometimes all tired out by the time Fohl really wanted them. So readers were informed by the day's *Washington Post*.

1902 Boston ballplayers were all assembled for spring training in Augusta, Georgia, save for Cy Young, who was coaching at Harvard; Lou Criger, expected March 24; and newly-acquired pitcher Pete Husting (see April 4, 1902).

BIRTHDATES
Gavvy Cravath 1881 (1908); Lou Lucier 1918 (1943–1944); George Scott 1944 (1966–1979); Bo Diaz 1953 (1977)

DEATHS
Denny Williams 1929; Walter Murphy 1976

March 24

1962 In the expansion draft, the Houston Colt 45's select unprotected 17-year veteran Dave Philley from the Orioles. The Sox trade pitcher Tom "Spike" Borland to get him. Philley batted .143 for Boston in limited action (42 at-bats.) Borland was 0–4 with the Sox, but never played for Houston.

1921 One of the first players with Boston was catcher John Bannerman "Larry" McLean from Fredericton, New Brunswick, who appeared in the franchise's very first game, seeing limited action with the 1901 Boston Americans. He had last played major league ball in 1915, and then was said to have suffered "dissipation"—even becoming (this was apparently shocking in its day) a "Jamaica ginger addict." On this day in 1924, he was shot to death by saloon manager John J. Conner as McLean tried to climb over the bar of the near-beer saloon on Boston's Washington Street, to attack Conner. McLean made the first pinch-hit in American League history, batting for the pitcher in the ninth inning of the first game Boston ever played. Conner was sentenced to a year in jail, even though the D.A. had recommended a lighter sentence.

1916 Though still unsigned, Tris Speaker showed up at 10:00 A.M. at the Sox hotel just as the team was heading out to the ballfield. By 11:00 A.M., he was in uniform and jumped into an intrasquad game, Regulars vs. Yanigans (he played for the Regulars). Speaker hit a triple and a homer, 4-for-4 in all.

1911 Why would Red Sox players be so concerned about 25 crates of oranges shipped home from Pomona after their ballgames there? Because the "girls in the packing house learned of the plan and each fair maiden decided that it was a chance to give the little god of romance an opportunity." They slipped a heart throb note into each box. Unsuspecting, the Red Sox players had not eaten the oranges themselves. Each forwarded the crates home to waiting wives and sweethearts.

TRANSACTIONS
1962: Traded Tom Borland to the Houston Colt 45's for Dave Philley.
1978: Acquired Frank Duffy from the Indians in a trade for Rick Kreuger.
1984: Traded Luis Aponte to Cleveland for minor leaguers Paul Perry and Mike Poindexter.
1992: Josias Manzanillo was granted free agency. Thirteen years later, on January 5, 2005, he was signed to a minor league contract and invited to spring training. He was reassigned to minor league camp on March 30.
1993: Released John Marzano.

BIRTHDATES
Kip Selbach 1872 (1904–1906); Ernie Shore 1891 (1914–1917); Jud McLaughlin 1912 (1931–1933); Bob Tillman 1937 (1962–1967); Bruce Hurst 1958 (1980–1988)

DEATHS
Larry McLean 1921; Birdie Tebbetts 1999; Mace Brown 2002

March 25

2000 In 1999, Juan Pena pitched two games, winning both of them (May 14 and May 18), establishing an ERA of 0.69 before suffering some shoulder stiffness. He pitched some at Pawtucket, but didn't return to the majors. During a spring training game, Sean Casey hit a rocket off Pena's right wrist. He suffered a torn medial collateral ligament in his right elbow and had to undergo Tommy John surgery. Joe Sheehan, writing for Baseball Prospectus, commented: "Now, this would be a rather unusual way to suffer a torn elbow ligament, but the team's medical and front office staff have stood behind the explanation." To clear roster space for Bronson Arroyo, Pena was designated for assignment.

1989 bomb threat was called in to the Red Sox offices in Winter Haven. The caller said the bomb was directed at Wade Boggs and targeted the team's Piedmont Airlines flight from Tampa to Baltimore. The team called the FBI, then switched from a commercial flight to a charter. The story only broke several days later. Boggs joked, "I guess I'll have to be fitted for a bulletproof vest" and added, "I've already had my brush with death"—a reference to what the *Globe* termed "an off-season incident in which a man allegedly held a knife to his throat." Boggs claimed he escaped the man by willing himself invisible.

1983 George Steinbrenner is fined $50,000 for accusing NL umpires of favoring NL teams during spring training games. Other notable Steinbrenner fines:

- $300,000 for comments after the famous Pine Tar game
- $25,000 plus $200,000 in damages for tampering in Dave Winfield trade
- $25,000 for criticizing umpires' competence during the 1998 AL LCS
- numerous $5000 fines for tampering with unsigned players, questioning the integrity of an umpire and calling the co-owners of the White Sox "Abbott and Costello" (Art McDonald's *This Date in Yankee Hating*)

1978 Rookie southpaw Bobby Sprowl was shot in the right arm while sleeping in his Winter Haven hotel room; the gun was fired by a doctor in the next-door apartment who thought he heard prowlers. Sprowl was just grazed, and was quickly treated and released at the local hospital. In 12⅔ innings of late-season ball for the Sox in '78, he gave up three homers and nine earned runs.

1962 Did anyone check out The Splendid Splinter's alibi? A major fire destroys the Fenway Park press room.

1960 The Sammy White for Russ Nixon trade is voided by Commissioner Ford Frick. (See March 16.)

1953 The Cleveland Browns NFL football franchise traded Harry Agganis to the Baltimore Colts as one of 10 players they sent in exchange for five Colts. Of the 10 players sent to Baltimore, only four had ever worn a Browns uniform. It was recognized that Agganis was under contract to the Red Sox, who had a clause in their contract which prohibited Agganis from playing football. Baltimore was hoping he would "change his mind."

1946 Jimmie Foxx, retired as a ballplayer, began work as a sports reporter for WEEI in Boston, broadcasting daily on the CBS outlet from 6:15 to 6:30 P.M.

TRANSACTIONS
1978: Released Tommy Helms.
1984: Acquired Bill Buckner from the Chicago Cubs for Dennis Eckersley and Mike Brumley.
2003: San Diego claimed Lou Merloni, who had been placed on waivers by the Red Sox.

BIRTHDATES
Bill Evans 1919 (1951); Rudy Minarcin 1930 (1956–1957); Nelson
Chittum 1933 (1959–1960); Mike Nagy 1948 (1969–1972)

DEATHS
Al Shaw 1958; Red Morgan 1981

March 26

2002 The Red Sox announced that 400 new seats would be added to Fenway Park. Of these, 161 would be known as "dugout seats" attracting an initial price of $200 per seat per game, and installed in front of the existing front row seats. Other seats would be fit in here and there around the park, the first of several incremental expansions of capacity over the next several years. In addition, new concessions areas were to be installed as well as a new members-only dining room for season ticket holders.

1977 The Red Sox release SS Americo Petrocelli, after 13 years—all with Boston. Rico stays in New England and remains a fan favorite.

1974 Boston releases two future Hall of Famers—SS Luis Aparicio, who retires, and DH Orlando Cepeda, who signs on with the Kansas City Royals for one final season. Veteran pitcher Bobby Bolin was also released, after 13 years of major league service. After cleaning house, the team purchases catcher Bob Didier from the Tigers; he hits .071 over five games.

1965 The Sox played a game in Mexico and hit 10 homers, twice as many as in the first 12 games they played in the Cactus League exhibition season. The game was played against the Cleveland Indians in Nogales, Mexico. Boston won, 15–9.

1917 The Red Sox were on the eve of departing Hot Springs for Memphis, where they would meet the Brooklyn Robins for a a number of exhibition games. Brooklyn's owner Charles Ebbets suggested that the players on the tour be numbered, so that fans not familiar with the players will know who each is. The Red Sox were to wear red and white sleeve bands which would bear a number. The Robins were to wear blue and white bands. Numbers would be printed on score cards. This may be the first time that major league ballplayers wore numbers, and may have given birth to the sales cry, "You can't tell the players without a scorecard!"

TRANSACTIONS
1948: Sold Don Gutteridge to the Pittsburgh Pirates.
1950: Sold Jack Kramer to the New York Giants.
1974: Released Luis Aparicio, Bobby Bolin, and Orlando Cepeda. Traded
    Vic Correll to the Atlanta Braves for Chuck Goggin.
1977: Released Rico Petrocelli.
1997: Released Mike Maddux, Chris Donnels, and Greg
    Hansell, but sold Tim Spehr to Kansas City.
1998: Mark Lemke was signed as a free agent.
2000: Marty Cordova released.

BIRTHDATES
Alex Mustaikis 1909 (1940); Bill Zuber 1913 (1946–1947); Jesus Tavarez 1971 (1997)

DEATHS
Squanto Wilson 1967

March 27

1931 Hod Lisenbee and Jack Russell combined to no-hit the Birmingham Barons in an eight-inning spring training game curtailed by rain. The Red Sox won, 2–1.

1911 Spring training in California was such a washout due to unusually frequent March rains that manager Patsy Donovan said frankly that the team would probably not try it again. By contrast, when the team arrived in Yuma, Arizona, they found that the hotel even posted a sign, "No charge on cloudy days." The locals hosting the game couldn't find more than four players willing to take on the Red Sox, however, so Boston had to loan them Hugh Bedient as a pitcher, Duffy Lewis as shortstop, and several other players. The Red Sox collected 31 hits on the day—and that doesn't count the Red Sox who were playing for Yuma—scoring in every inning but the fifth, and winning 17–5.

TRANSACTIONS
1973: Traded Phil Gagliano and Andy Kosco to the Cincinnati
    Reds for Mel Behney. Released Lew Krausse.

BIRTHDATES
Joe Lucey 1897 (1925); Lynn McGlothen 1950 (1972–1973); Creighton Gubanich 1972 (1999)

DEATHS
Oscar Fuhr 1975; Chet Nichols 1995; Bob Cremins 2004

March 28

2003 Sister Sluggo, a 96-year-old nun living at Rose Manor in Watertown, still remembered the Sox winning it all in 1918 and still avidly rooted for the Red Sox. Her real name is Sister Rosita Colman but she acquired the nickname in the 1940s when playing for the Rosary sisters at the convent. So reported Emily Sweeney in a feature in a regional edition of the March 28 *Boston Globe*.

1986 The Red Sox and Yankees swapped their designated hitters: Mike Easler goes to New York for Don Baylor. Easler hit .302 for the Yankees, with 78 RBIs. Baylor hit only .238, but drove in 94 runs. Baylor was hit a record 35 times, one of eight times he led the league in hit-by-pitch.

1937 Trying to see if a new "dead ball" is better than the existing one, the new sphere is tried in a game between the Red Sox and the Senators. The Sox outslug the Nats, 13–12, as Cronin drives in six runs. Last week the ball was used in a game between the Giants and Bees with much the same result. On April 12, the White Sox and Pirates will test the new ball, with the Sox winning 9–6, though the longest hit is a double. (source: *The Baseball Chronology*)

1932 Alabama filling station operator Joe White was sentenced to three years in prison for the fatal knifing of Boston pitcher Big Ed Morris. Testimony indicated that White had initially tried to be a peacemaker in a fight between Morris and a Joe Nolan, but that Morris then pummeled White repeatedly until White grabbed a knife on the ground and stabbed the pitcher. (See March 1, 1932.)

1914 All the Red Sox players were underweight, because of being limited to manager Bill Carrigan's spring training regimen of two meals a day. Tim Murnane described them as having a "Weary-Willie look on their thin faces."

1913 Jerry McCarthy, the Red Sox mascot, now in high school and thought to be retiring after the 1912 season, returned for another year. "Jerry proved to be a high-grade mascot," in the assessment of the *Boston Globe*, and President McAleer met with a couple of players to agree on his return.

1911 With the Mexican Revolution expanding, and refugees flooding across the border into Texas, the Red Sox nevertheless did get in a game at El Paso. Despite the spectre of war, a news report said, "Locally there is more excitement over the visit of the regulars of the Boston Red Sox baseball team than there was over the war." Boston won the game, 9–1.

1907 Outfielder Chick Stahl committed suicide. He played with Boston's National League team for four years, then joined the Boston Americans in the first year of the franchise, hitting .303. After six seasons, Stahl was asked to take the reins as player-manager of the 1906 team in late season (August 29). The pressure may have been too great. He had apparently often mentioned that managing the team detracted from his ability to play on it. The team was barnstorming pre-season, and reached West Baden Springs, Indiana, when Stahl drank carbolic acid after breakfast after stepping into Jimmy Collins' adjoining room. The poison killed him. His suicide note read: "Boys, I just couldn't help it. You drove me to it." Several teammates recalled him talking about suicide for much of spring training. (See also January 25, 1902 and November 16, 1908.)

1901 Jimmy Collins and a number of players departed Boston for the very first spring training for the franchise, in Charlottesville, Virginia. Cy Young re-stated his commitment to honor his contract and play in the American League. He spoke out after Bill Dinneen had indicated that he would jump back to the National League. Both Jimmy Collins and Hugh Duffy spoke out harshly against Dinneen. Cy Young had a few words himself: "I have no respect for a contract jumper.... I can't understand how a man with any sense of honor can sign with the new league and then jump back into the National, where he claims to have been only a slave." Of Dinneen, Collins said, "Oh, I don't wish him any harm. I only told him that I hoped his arm would drop off the first ball he pitched."

TRANSACTIONS
1974: Purchased Bob Didier from the Detroit Tigers.
1978: Released Denny Doyle.
1986: Acquired Don Baylor from the New York Yankees in trade for Mike Easler.
2000: Tampa Bay returned Chris Reitsma to the Red Sox. They had claimed him in the 1999 Rule V draft on December 13, 1999. He would later be part of a trade to the Reds for Dante Bichette.

BIRTHDATES
Jimmy Barrett 1875 (1907–1908); Harry Gleason 1875 (1901–1903); Babe Martin 1920 (1948–1949)

DEATHS
Chick Stahl 1907; Hy Gunning 1975

March 29

1997 Three giant 25-foot-high fiberglass Coke bottles are strapped to a light tower and mounted atop Fenway's left-field Wall. The *Globe*'s Dan Shaughnessy labeled them "hideous" and added, "It's a shocker, like standing outside the Sistine Chapel and seeing a sign announcing, 'Thursday is Bingo Night.'" Not only were the bottles a source of revenue for the Red Sox, but Coca-Cola pledged to donate $100,000 a year to the Jimmy Fund as well. Sox PR man Dick Bresciani said they were within good taste, no neon, an "old-style bottle, one that's well-known." In truth, the bottles were well-accepted by fans nearly from the start.

1960 The Sox had just tried to trade outfielder Jim Marshall to the Indians in the Sammy White deal, but when it was voided, Marshall was available for another trade. Bags already packed, he was sent to the San Francisco Giants for pitcher Al Worthington. Marshall had been acquired from the Cubs on November 21, 1959, and never actually played with the Red Sox. Worthington did; he was 0–1 in 1960 before being traded to the White Sox.

1948 It's always been a rivalry, even when it doesn't really count. During spring training in St. Petersburg, the Yankees and the visiting Red Sox fight it out for 17 full innings. The Yankees came from behind in the ninth inning to tie the score. Tommy Byrne walked four batters in a row in the 10th to give the Sox the lead, but the Yankees tied it up yet again. In eight innings of relief, Byrne gave up just one hit. The game ends in seeming futility, a 2–2 tie, but in the process some 33 players got a bit of a workout.

1915 Ban Johnson's argument that spring training camps should be done away with and players should report in shape was the subject of much discussion at the Sox camp. Tim Murnane wrote that indeed they should report in shape, given their "very large salaries" but the free advertising the press gives teams while training was a boon. When the newspaper coverage stops, the trips would be curtailed. Should that occur, he noted, "while New York, Chicago, and Boston can afford to enjoy the spring luxury, it will become a real hardship for the smaller cities...."

1912 Pitcher Fred Anderson started a game in 1909, then retired to look after a business in North Carolina. He sold the business in the fall of 1911 and requested another shot at the Red Sox, who signed him up. Not in their plans for 1912, Boston did a deal to send him to Milwaukee, but Anderson balked; he wanted the Red Sox to make up the difference between the $2,000 he'd signed for in Boston and the $1,650 he'd be paid in Milwaukee. Unfortunately, Anderson played for the Red Sox in 1913. His record was 0–6.

1907 Caught without a manager in the wake of Stahl's suicide (see March 28 entry), Cy Young agreed to serve until a permanent manager could be hired. Young proved to be only the first of four more managers during the 1907 campaign. George Huff, Bob Unglaub, and Deacon McGuire all managed as well.

TRANSACTIONS

1960: Traded Jim Marshall to the San Francisco Giants for Al Worthington.
1969: Returned Bill Kelso to the Cincinnati Reds, after 11 days.
1975: Traded Danny Cater to the St. Louis Cardinals for Danny Godby.
1978: Acquired Leo Foster from the New York Mets in a trade for Jim Burton.
1988: Todd Pratt was returned by the Cleveland Indians; he had been selected
    by them on December 7, 1987 in the minor league draft.

2005: Acquired Mike Myers from the St. Louis Cardinals for Carlos de la Cruz and Kevin Ool. Myers was being reacquired; he had been on the 2004 World Championship team.

BIRTHDATES
Cy Young 1867 (1901–1908); Frank Oberlin 1876 (1906–1907); Squanto Wilson 1889 (1914); Eric Gunderson 1966 (1995–1996); Juan Bell 1968 (1995)

DEATHS
Wilcy Moore 1963

March 30

1978 In a six-player swap, the Indians provide pitcher Dennis Eckersley and catcher Fred Kendall to the Red Sox in exchange for pitchers Rick Wise and Mike Paxton, catcher Bo Diaz, and third baseman Ted Cox.

1971 Pitcher Vicente Romo and first baseman Tony Muser exchange red socks for white ones, as both players were traded to Chicago for pitcher Danny Murphy and backstop Duane Josephson.

1960 The segregationist South Louisiana Citizens Council urged a boycott of the Red Sox–Indians games planned for April 9 and 10 in New Orleans. "If fans do not attend these games, they will be doing an important part toward preserving the integrity of both races," the Council president declared.

1959 Ted Williams entered New England Baptist Hospital for treatment of what had proven to be a pinched nerve in his neck. The *New York Times* noted the irony that the man who hated neckties might now have to wear a neck brace.

1956 Not long after slamming the government for going after Johnny Podres (see March 13, 1956), Ted Williams was quoted by Harold Kaese as objecting to the tax deductions business executives can claim for company planes, boats, and automobiles, while ballplayers (with a much shorter career span) have few.

1941 A pitchers' battle in an exhibition game between Boston's Joe Dobson and Bucky Walters of Cincinnati ended in a 2–1 win for the Reds, and therefore a 2–1 edge in the three-game set the two teams played in Havana, Cuba.

1933 Faced with the end of Prohibition, the 16 major league ball clubs voted whether to sell beer or not. Eight declined to do so, while eight others (including the Boston Red Sox) wished to continue the practice. Though some clubs would begin to sell beer on April 12 Opening Day, both the Sox and the Braves had to await the drafting of beer-control legislation in the Commonwealth of Massachusetts. It proved a very long process. (See April 14, 1936.)

1923 From Hot Springs, the Red Sox announce they will file a claim of $15,000 against the Detroit Tigers because pitcher Carl Holling has failed to report. Holling was part of the October 30, 1922 trade involving Ehmke and Babe Herman. Holling says he'd rather stay in California and play independent baseball.

1920 Former Sox player Harry Lord (1907–1910) found his South Portland, Maine grocery store burglarized. Several cases of raisins and prunes were stolen.

1917 The Red Sox beat Brooklyn 10–4 in an Oklahoma City exhibition game held up for three hours by a "baby blizzard" of flying dirt, also described—likely inaccurately—as a "tornado."

1914 Shortstop Heinie Wagner was unable to play during spring training due to a sore arm. He believed he suffered from rheumatism, and missed the entire 1914 season, giving Everett Scott a chance to establish himself in the short field.

TRANSACTIONS

1971: Acquired Duane Josephson and Danny Murphy from the White
    Sox by trading Vicente Romo and Tony Muser.
1978: Acquired Dennis Eckersley and Fred Kendall from the Indians in a
    trade for Rick Wise, Mike Paxton, Ted Cox, and Bo Diaz.
1980: Acquired Dave Rader in trade from the Phillies for some cash
    and a PTBNL (Stan Papi was named on May 12).
1993: Released Matt Young.
1998: Signed free agent Billy Ashley and signed amateur free agent Jin Ho Cho.
1999: The Red Sox released Midre Cummings, and the Oakland
    Athletics took Ron Mahay on waivers.
2002: The Red Sox signed free agent Chris Haney.
2005: Traded Byung-Hyun Kim to the Colorado Rockies for Chris Narveson and cash. At the
    same time, the Red Sox acquired Charles Johnson from the Rockies and released him.

BIRTHDATES

Hal Rhyne 1899 (1929–1932); Grady Little 1950 (manager, 2002–2003)

DEATHS

Joe Connolly 1960; Charlie French 1962; Joe Cicero 1983

March 31

2003 The earliest regular season game the Sox have ever played was the March 31, 2003, Opening Day game at Tropicana Field; the Devil Rays won, 6–4, despite Pedro Martinez having thrown seven innings of one-run, three-hit ball, and reliever Ramiro Mendoza throwing a 1-2-3 eighth. The Rays scored five runs in the bottom of the ninth off the "closer by committee" Red Sox bullpen, embodied this day by Alan Embree and Chad Fox. The experiment of running a bullpen without a closer, throwing the best available pitcher on a given day in a given situation, sounded good in theory, but seemed not to work in practice.

2000 A Federal judge said he was not sure the Green Monster was a valid trademark. The Red Sox pressed for summary judgment in a case brought by Arthur D'Angelo of Twins Enterprises. He had been selling "Green Monster" T-shirts from 1986 to 1997 without a problem, until the Red Sox themselves starting selling similar shirts, wiping out his business in the shirts. The Sox countersued, arguing that they owned the trademark, which they registered in 1992. In the long run, the Sox bought out the D'Angelo interest in the souvenir stand across Yawkey Way and converted it into the Red Sox Team Store.

1932 Bob Quinn wanted to put his Red Sox on solid footing, so the team hired the president of the National Association of Chiropodists-Podiatrists, Dr. Joseph Lelyveld, to look after the feet of the Red Sox throughout the 1932 season, according to a news item in *The Sporting News*.

1922 Sox owner Harry Frazee was pleased with off-season trades and the team's progress in spring training. Optimistically, he declared, "I feel certain that the team will be in the first division during the entire season and it would not surprise me if they put up quite a battle for the pennant." He may have been surprised at season's end when the Red Sox finished dead last for only the second time in franchise history, 33 games out of first place.

TRANSACTIONS
1987: Released Tim Lollar.

DEBUTS
2003: Chad Fox, Jeremy Giambi, Ramiro Mendoza, Kevin Millar, Bill Mueller, Todd Walker

BIRTHDATES
Frank Truesdale 1884 (1918); Marv Grissom 1918 (1953); Ryan Rupe 1975 (2003); Jamie Brown 1977 (2004)

DEATHS
None yet

APRIL

April 1

Perhaps fearing possible repercussions, few trades of import have taken place on April Fool's Day.

2003 New acquisition Kevin Millar paid immediate dividends, cranking a 16th-inning home run out at Tropicana Field for a 9–8 win over the Devil Rays. The Sox experiment of "closer by committee" was spared embarrassment this day, as the final four of six relievers held the Rays scoreless during the final eight frames.

2002 The Red Sox open at home and host the Blue Jays, who command an early 7–1 lead after 1½ innings. Pedro Martinez lasts but three innings, leaving with an 8–3 deficit. Darren Oliver is tagged for 3 more, and the score is 11–11 after 4½. Another Darrin, name of Fletcher, has three RBIs in the game, then adds another with a game-winning sacrifice fly in the ninth. 12–11 final, Jays. The game was also marked by the Red Sox debut of slugger Tony Clark, who created a wonderful first impression, going 3-for-5 with a home run and three RBIs. In the whole rest of the season, he only hit two more homers and batted just above the Mendoza line, at .207.

1988 Mike Greenwell set up an April Fool's joke with the DJs at Framingham radio station WVBF, in which it was reported that Greenwell and San Horn were being traded to the Yankees for Dave Winfield. Greenwell then got on the air saying he'd heard the rumors and discussing what it would be like to report to Fort Lauderdale for spring training. Word spread that Greenwell was on the radio talking about being traded, and the Red Sox switchboard was inundated with calls. In an unrelated incident, which manager John McNamara said he was pushed into by Wade Boggs and Spike Owen, McNamara called rookie pitcher John Trautwein into his office along with pitching coach Bill Fischer. He said he and Fischer were impressed by Trautwein but had been outvoted by management and Trautwein was being sent back to Montreal. As Trautwein left the manager's office, the entire team shouted "April Fool" in unison.

1940 They thought it was an April Fool's joke at first, but it was true: the train bringing both the Red Sox and the Cincinnati Reds to Charleston, South Carolina ran out of coal six miles out of town.

1938 The Atlanta Black Crackers of the Negro American League changed its name to the Atlanta Red Sox after a contest seeking a new name for the team. Two weeks later, on April 15, they reverted to their original name to avoid confusion with the venerable Memphis Red Sox. Other Negro League teams of the era included the Los Angeles Red Sox and the Rosedale Red Sox, of Rosedale, Mississippi.

1936 Bill Cunningham of the *Boston Post* ran a story about the unsettled Red Sox spring training. The word was that newly-acquired Jimmie Foxx "is drunk all the time," and other players were undisciplined as well.

1932 Way out in Reno, Nevada, Dorothy P. Hoyt sued Waite Hoyt for divorce, seeking custody of their two children and $25 a week to support them.

1913 Through the carelessness of a messenger, 50 sets of Red Sox season tickets were left on a streetcar, but they had not been endorsed and so would be void.

1901 Jimmy Collins and 11 members of Boston's AL club began their first workout of their first spring training, at Charlottesville, Virginia, with two hours of light practice on the grounds of the local YMCA. Collins, Stahl, Freeman, Dowd, Hemphill, Schreckengost, Jones, McLean, Mitchell, Kane, McCarthy, and Connor joined in the session. Cuppy, Criger, Parent, Ferris, Kellum, and McKenna were all due to report the following day. Perhaps the first sign of exceptions for Red Sox superstars was set—Cy Young was training in Hot Springs and would report on Opening Day in Baltimore.

TRANSACTIONS
1985: Signed free agent Jim Corsi and released John Henry Johnson.
1991: Traded Rob Murphy to the Seattle Mariners for Mike Gardiner.
1994: Traded John Flaherty to the Detroit Tigers for Rich Rowland.

DEBUTS
1996: Wil Cordero, Mike Stanley
1998: Darren Lewis, Jim Leyritz, Pedro
    Martinez, Donnie Sadler
2002: Tony Clark, Johnny Damon,
    Rickey Henderson, Darren Oliver,
    Rey Sanchez

2003: Damian Jackson, Brandon Lyon,
    David Ortiz, Mike Timlin,
    Steve Woodard

BIRTHDATES
Jake Wade 1912 (1939); Frank Castillo 1969 (2001–2004)

DEATHS
Casey Hageman 1964

April 2

2002 Pitching for the Diamondbacks, Curt Schilling shuts out San Diego, 9–0. What does this have to do with the Red Sox? Schill's shutout made Arizona the first defending World Championship team to open the season with back-to-back shutouts since the Sox beat the Yankees 10–0 and the Senators 8–0 to kick off the 1919 season. In pre-game ceremonies, the D-Backs were presented their World Series rings, and Curt's young son Gehrig accepted on his behalf. Readers will recall that #38, Schilling, played a role in Boston's 2004 World Championship season.

2001 The Red Sox lost the first game of the year, 2–1, in 11 innings. The team played without star shortstop Nomar Garciaparra, who underwent surgery on Opening Day for a split tendon in his right wrist. He'd hoped it would heal during the off-season, but it had not and consequently, Nomar missed most of the season, not returning until late in July.

1993 A nice way to wind up the Grapefruit League, as two Sox pitchers (Frank Viola and Cory Bailey) throw a no-hitter, and the Red Sox beat the Phillies, 10–0.

1972 The Red Sox announce the first postponement of a season opener due to a players' strike. Opening Day had been set for April 6.

1968 Still suffering the effects of his 1967 beaning, Tony Conigliaro has to return to Boston and will miss the entire 1968 campaign.

1952 Ted and Jerry Coleman are both found physically fit to return to active duty, passing their physicals before a Marine Corps medical board at Yukon, Florida (near NAS Jacksonville). Neither has flown a plane for six years.

1951 Walt Dropo, 1950 Rookie of the Year with his 144 RBIs, breaks his wrist in spring training. He never reached 100 RBIs again.

1947 Farewell to "Catfish." After four years with the Red Sox, including the three war years and the 1946 pennant-winning season, George Metkovich is sold to the Indians. He'd been 1-for-2 with a double in the World Series.

1940 Just the day after their train had run out of fuel heading to Charleston, the Reds and Red Sox saw the left-field bleachers collapse just before their exhibition game, and more than 100 members of the Columbia, South Carolina, and Birmingham Barons ball clubs were thrown to the ground, fortunately without serious injuries.

1933 A major train wreck killed the engineer and fireman, but the Red Sox team escaped serious injury. The "Cavalier"—the Pennsylvania Railroad's Norfolk-to-New York express train carrying the Red Sox—crashed around 3:12 A.M. in the town of Wyoming, Delaware, derailing the engine and eight cars, including two of the three sleeper cars containing the Red Sox team, and tossing the players about. *Boston Globe* reporter Mel Webb was on board and provided a graphic account of the twisted wreckage. Doc Woods, the Red Sox trainer, helped administer to some of the wounded passengers on board. Tom Oliver tried to extricate the engineer, but gave up when he realized the man was dead. Only pitcher Bob Klein felt possible effects, to his shoulder, later in the day. Four of their trunks were destroyed, but not even one bat was cracked. Players were relieved at their narrow escape and reacted with some humor; Bob Seeds cracked that at first he had thought the crash was Fatty Fothergill sliding into home plate. The shaken-up Red Sox played an exhibition game against the Jersey City Skeeters later in the day, and won handily, 12–0. The following day, they shut out the Skeeters again, 6–0.

1913 Ray Collins started for the Red Sox, playing against George Huff's University of Illinois baseball team in Urbana. He allowed just one hit in five innings. In came Smoky Joe Wood in relief. He faced 12 batters and struck out every single one of them. The final score? 10–0. The Sox beat Illinois again on the third, 2–0. On April 5, Wood decided to pitch for Illinois to give the collegians a bit of a chance, coming into a game with the Sox on top, 9–1. He pitched the last five innings, holding the Red Sox to two more runs. The final was 11–2.

1911 In the first inning of a spring training game in Wichita, Tris Speaker hit a ball over the center field fence, but it bounced off the roof of a house there and back onto the field. When thrown back in, the umpire ruled Hooper out at home plate and Speaker out at third—two outs on a home run. The Red Sox still won the game, 5–4.

TRANSACTIONS
1947: Sold Catfish Metkovich to the Cleveland Indians.
1979: Seattle returned Keith McWhorter, who had been selected by
 Seattle on December 5 in the minor league draft.

1987: Released Jim Corsi.
2000: Free agents Gary Gaetti and Pete Schourek signed.

DEBUTS

1984: Mike Easler
1997: Butch Henry, Shane Mack
1998: Damon Buford,
    Midre Cummings

2001: Craig Grebeck,
    Shea Hillenbrand,
    Manny Ramirez,
    Chris Stynes

BIRTHDATES

Earl Johnson 1919 (1940–1950); Bobby Avila 1924 (1959); Dick Radatz
1937 (1962–1966); Reggie Smith 1945 (1966–1973); Al Nipper 1959
(1983–1987); Tom Barrett 1960 (1992); Curt Leskanic 1968 (2004)

DEATHS

Charlie Jones 1947; Dib Williams 1992

April 3

2005 The Red Sox begin their first defense of a World Championship since 1919, opening the 2005 campaign in the heart of the Evil Empire, Yankee Stadium. The Sox drew first blood, but were then battered and bloodied by the Yankees, 9–2. Edgar Renteria, the Red Sox' new shortstop, became the first player to make the last out in a World Series and then, the following year, join the team he'd opposed. His single to center in the 11th inning of Game Seven in the 1997 World Series helped establish him the only player to win a walkoff in one Series, and walk off after making the final out in another.

2002 A great deal was expected of new Sox starter Dustin Hermanson, but he was asked to pitch on a rainy evening in a game that was called after one full inning. Flawless in the first, Hermanson pulled a groin muscle while warming up on a slippery mound before the second, then seriously injured it in two pitches to Carlos Delgado. Hermanson had to leave the game. He missed most of the season, only starting one official game in 2002, and wound up 1–1 with a 7.77 ERA. Before the game began, in a gesture requested by new ownership, the Sox players (in uniform) greeted arriving patrons at the gates. Security was abysmal, because fans did not smoothly flow through as suggested but stopped to talk or simply gawk. Nice thought, though.

1997 Rookie Angel Jason Dickson throws a complete game five-hit shutout in Anaheim Stadium, blanking the Red Sox, 2–0. Tim Wakefield takes the loss, yielding single runs in the seventh and eighth.

1992 In their final game of spring training at Chain O' Lakes Park in Winter Haven, Florida, the Red Sox tame the Tigers, 14–4. City of Palms Park, Fort Myers, will become the team's new Grapefruit League home.

1989 Egyptian president Hosni Mubarak took in a Red Sox game in Baltimore, courtesy of U. S. President George Bush. It was Opening Day, but the presidents had departed before the Orioles won it in the 11th, 5–4.

1985 Wade Boggs opened the season going 2-for-4 with a double. By year's end, Boggs had banged out 205 hits with a league-leading 51 doubles. It was the seventh year in a row that Boggs had amassed 200 or more hits.

1968 The Red Sox release Dan Osinski. He'd thrown 78 innings in 1966 and 1967, winning three games with the Impossible Dream team.

1966 Felix "The Cat" Mantilla is traded for Houston's Eddie Kasko, who bats just .213 but will later manage the Red Sox, 1970–73.

1950 Mel Parnell won 25 games and lost only 7 in 1949, throwing 295⅓ innings with a 2.77 ERA. On this day he announced he had pitched the whole year with a sore arm. Trainers on other clubs may have been tempted to whack their pitchers throwing arm. Parnell won 18 games for the Sox in 1950 and again in 1951.

1920 The new mascot of the Red Sox was 13-year-old Francis Cadigan of Brookline, said to be so excited that "he can hardly multiply six by nine at his school desk." Francis knew Fenway well; Harry Hooper, his wife, and two children had stayed at the Cadigan house while in Boston, when Francis was younger.

1917 The Red Sox lost to Brooklyn, 13–5, in 12 innings in an exhibition game in Harry Frazee's hometown of Peoria. Enjoying the perks of ownership, Frazee had worked out in uniform, taking batting practice throughout spring training. Seeing his team give up eight runs in the top of the 12th inning did not convey the impression he had hoped. In an unrelated event, the United States Senate voted to declare war on Germany the following day.

TRANSACTIONS
1966: Traded Felix Mantilla to the Houston Astros for Eddie Kasko.
1968: Released Dan Osinski.

DEBUTS
1989: Nick Esasky, Rob Murphy
1996: Tom Gordon, Jamie Moyer,
    Brad Pennington
1997: Chris Hammond

2005: John Halama, Matt Mantei,
    Blaine Neal, Edgar Renteria,
    David Wells

BIRTHDATES
Gordie Hinkle 1905 (1934); Mike Lansing 1968 (2000–2001)

DEATHS
None yet

April 4

2001   In his first start for the Red Sox, Hideo Nomo pitched a no-hitter against the Orioles in Camden Yards, 3–0. It was the first no-hitter for the Sox since Dave Morehead threw one on September 16, 1965. With a first-inning walk, and a second-inning Red Sox error, and two more walks later in the game, there was no flirting with perfection, but Nomo became the fourth pitcher to throw a no-no in each league (he had thrown a no-hitter for the Dodgers against the Rockies on September 7, 1996). Daubach's two-run homer in the third was the game-winner. On May 25, Nomo threw a one-hitter.

2000 When Darren Lewis played right field in the year 2000 Opening Day, it represented the 13th year in a row that the Sox had a different man playing right. Working backward from Lewis, the players were Trot Nixon, Darren Bragg, Rudy Pemberton, Troy O'Leary, Mark Whiten, Billy Hatcher, Andre

Dawson, Phil Plantier, Tom Brunansky, Kevin Romine, Dwight Evans, and Mike Greenwell. Nixon played right in 2001 (and the next two years as well).

1994 Red Sox catcher Rich Rowland was 31 years old, not 28 as listed on the Red Sox roster. Rowland said it was his college coach Lefty Olgin who made the change, telling him, "You're not going to get drafted at the age that you are, so I changed it for you." The Tigers drafted him in the 17th round in June 1988.

1975 Mario Guerrero is traded by the Boston Red Sox to the Cardinals for a player to be named later. On July 4, the Cards send the Sox pitcher Jim Willoughby. Willoughby's record was a disappointing 3–12 in 1976 despite a fine 2.82 ERA.

1946 Two Pinkys on one team would have been one too many. Pitcher George "Pinky" Woods was sold to Indianapolis, clearing the way for the Sox to get Mike "Pinky" Higgins back from the Tigers on May 19.

1934 Purchased from Connie Mack's A's the preceding December, Lefty Grove is diagnosed with a sore arm. The 1934 season is a disappointing 8–8, but he bounced back to win 20 in 1935 and lead the league in ERA four more times.

1922 In dispatches from Dyersburg, TN, Del Pratt was named Red Sox captain, replacing Everett Scott who had been traded to the New York Yankees.

1921 Both first baseman Stuffy McInnis and owner Harry Frazee issued separate announcements that McInnis' holdout had been resolved and that he would be reporting to the ball club within a few days.

1902 Boston played an exhibition game inside the Augusta, GA armory against the Sacred Heart Cadets. In the background, St. Louis claimed that Bert Husting was under contract to them, even though he had signed with Boston. Since he was on Milwaukee's reserve list, he became property of St. Louis when the franchise was sold, argued the Browns.

TRANSACTIONS
1970: Sold Russ Gibson to the San Francisco Giants.
1975: Traded Mario Guerrero to the St. Louis Cardinals for a PTBNL. On July 4, 1975, the Cardinals sent Jim Willoughby to the Sox to complete the trade.

DEBUTS
1988: Brady Anderson, Lee Smith
1994: Damon Berryhill, Otis Nixon, Dave Valle
1996: Alex Delgado, John Doherty, Heathcliff Slocumb
2000: Carl Everett, Gary Gaetti
2001: Hideo Nomo
2004: Mark Bellhorn, Cesar Crespo, Pokey Reese

BIRTHDATES
Jake Volz 1878 (1901); Tris Speaker 1888 (1907–1915); Dutch Lerchen 1889 (1910); Joe Vosmik 1910 (1938–1939); Mickey Owen 1916 (1954); Gary Geiger 1937 (1959–1965); John Lickert 1960 (1981); Carlos Reyes 1969 (1998)

DEATHS
Les Wilson 1969; Carl Mays 1971

April 5

2005 When the Sox lost the first and second games of the season, it was the first time since April 9, 2000 that the team was two games below .500.

1999 After eight stellar seasons with the Red Sox (including the 1995 AL MVP award), Mo Vaughn plays his first regular season game for the Anaheim Angels, falls into the dugout chasing a foul ball and seriously sprains his ankle. He stills drives in more than 100 runs in both 1999 and 2000.

1988 Bill Lee appeared at Cambridge, MA's Nightstage as a candidate for President of the United States on the Rhinoceros Party ticket. His platform was an Earth-first one. "We believe like the old days—we all join hands and circle the Pentagon and levitate it. I believe in those concepts, group support and interaction, passive resistance a la Gandhi. Above all, poke fun at 'em any chance you get." He said that if the Rhinoceros Party effort fizzled, he would accept the VP slot for either of the two major parties provided it didn't interfere with playing baseball.

1977 The Yankees acquire Bucky Dent from the White Sox for outfielder Oscar Gamble and pitchers Bob Polinsky and Dewey Hoyt. This move has later repercussions.

1920 This day's scheduled exhibition game against the New York Giants in Asheville, North Carolina, was postponed due to snow.

1911 As the Red Sox made their way east from California, their 7–0 win over Topeka was the 17th consecutive win during the 1911 exhibition season. Red Sox trainer Doc Green was laid up with a lame back.

1902 Though most of the team was well underway with spring training, Cy Young was reportedly still working in the Boston area, training Harvard's baseball team.

1901 The team that would become the Boston Red Sox played its very first game as an organization on April 5, 1901, in Charlottesville, VA. Their opponent was the University of Virginia baseball team. The Bostons won handily, 13–0, behind the combined shutout pitching of Kane, Connor, and Mitchell, who held the U. Va. team to four hits, all off Kane. Boston played error-free ball. In an April 11 rematch, Boston beat Virginia by the score of 23–0.

TRANSACTIONS
1968: Returned Rule V draft pick George Spriggs to the Pirates.
1971: The St. Louis Cardinals returned former Rule V draft pick Cecil Cooper.
1978: Sold Ramon Aviles to the Phillies and Jim Willoughby to the White Sox.
1986: Signed free agent Jim Corsi.

DEBUTS
1974: Bernie Carbo, Diego Segui
1983: Tony Armas, John Henry Johnson
1993: Ivan Calderon, Andre Dawson, Scott Fletcher, Jeff Russell
1996: Esteban Beltre, Milt Cuyler, Kevin Mitchell
1997: Steve Avery
1999: Jose Offerman
2000: Manny Alexander
2001: Frank Castillo
2005: Matt Clement

BIRTHDATES
Bill Dinneen 1876 (1902–1907); Tony Welzer 1899 (1926–1927)

DEATHS
Wally Rehg 1946; Sam Dodge 1966

April 6

2003 Hitting a double, a triple, and a homer (and walking in the fifth), Nomar Garciaparra came up needing only a single to complete the cycle. He could have at least tried to lay down a bunt (the Sox were up 10–2 when he came to bat in the eighth), but instead he flied out to center. Only 19 Red Sox players have ever hit for the cycle.

1997 For reasons that remain unknown to this day, Red Sox legend Johnny Pesky was "banned from the bench," no longer allowed to sit in the Red Sox dugout during games. When John W. Henry took over ownership, one of his first calls was to welcome back the man known as "Mr. Red Sox."

1987 The Red Sox play errorless ball in the first game of the 1987 season. Adding this game to the final 10 games of the 1986 regular season, this is a stretch of 11 consecutive errorless games—longest in franchise history.

1973 The first use of a designated hitter in major league baseball was when Yankee Ron Blomberg stepped to the plate in this day's game at Fenway Park. Blomberg didn't hit the ball, as it turned out; he was walked by Luis Tiant in his first at-bat. Yanks lose 15–5, though Blomberg is 1-for-3 with one RBI. Fisk hit a grand slam and a two-run homer on this Opening Day. The Sox DH is Orlando Cepeda, and he didn't hit at all: Cepeda was 0-for-6 on the day.

1972 Opening Day 1972 is postponed due to a players strike. When the season ends, the Sox miss winning the pennant by a mere half-game. Had the April 6 game been played, who knows what the outcome might have been?

1971 The Red Sox scored single runs in the fourth, seventh, and eighth, and Ray Culp limited the Yankees to just five hits in a complete game win. Horace Clarke drove in one run in the top of the eighth and almost tied it, but Reggie Smith's throw to the plate nipped Jim Lyttle. Boston beat New York, 2–1, for its second consecutive Opening Day win against the Yankees.

1933 J. G. Taylor Spink of *The Sporting News* printed an open letter to Yankees owner Jacob Ruppert, suggesting it would be nice if the Yankees "repaid the baseball devotees of Boston for the loss of Ruth by selling a few men to Tom Yawkey and Eddie Collins." He suggested Myril Hoag and Dusty Cooke. He was quite serious about it, reminding Ruppert that "when the American League induced you and Colonel Huston to buy the Yankees, who were without a park or players, the various owners said they would help you strengthen the team."

1932 Boston scored twice in the top of the ninth to tie it, then twice more in the top of the 11th to win it. The opponent: the Newark Bears in an exhibition game held in Newark, NJ. Boston had 16 hits, and might have scored more runs than in the 10–8 victory but for a seventh-inning Newark triple play.

1926 Fred Parent, shortstop on the pennant-winning 1903 and 1904 teams, became an Ivy Leaguer, accepting the position of Harvard University baseball coach.

1916 RED SOX CRUEL TO PETS OF BROOKLYN read the headline in the *New York Times*, but the story did not evoke a call to the ASPCA. It referred to the exhibition game shutout posted by Boston over the Dodgers in Brooklyn, 6–0.

TRANSACTIONS
1916: Acquired Clarence "Tillie" Walker from the St. Louis Americans.
1966: Traded Russ Nixon and Chuck Schilling to the Minnesota Twins for a PTBNL (minor leaguer Jose Calero) and Dick Stigman.
1980: Sold Allen Ripley to the San Francisco Giants.
1981: Released Skip Lockwood.

DEBUTS
1971: Luis Aparicio, Doug Griffin, Duane Josephson
1973: Orlando Cepeda
1974: Reggie Cleveland, Terry Hughes, Dick McAuliffe
1988: Dennis Lamp
1994: Lee Tinsley, Ricky Trlicek
1997: John Wasdin
2000: Jeff Fassero
2004: Keith Foulke, Curt Schilling

BIRTHDATES
Marty Pattin 1943 (1972–1973); Lou Merloni 1971 (1998–2003); Blaine Neal 1978 (2005)

DEATHS
Al Evans 1979; Rudy Kallio 1979; John Wyatt 1998

April 7

1986 Dwight Evans set his stance in the Tiger Stadium batter's box, squared off against Jack Morris—and hit the very first pitch of the 1986 season for a home run. Jim Rice, Don Baylor, and Rich Gedman homered, too, but Detroit's Kirk Gibson knocked in five runs (four via his two HR) and the Tigers won, 6–5. "Big deal. We lost."—Evans, post-game.

1977 The Sox lost on Opening Day to the Indians, 5–4, in 11 innings. Yaz singled in the first and stole second, but had to leave the game after being hit by a pitch in the third. He made one putout in the game before he left. Between outfield and some time at first base, Yaz had 366 chances but never made even one error all season long.

1973 In George Steinbrenner's first two games as Yankees owner, the Red Sox scored 25 runs and won both games. In fact, the Sox won the third game as well, and then the fourth, after both teams had moved from Boston to Opening Day in New York. Maybe The Boss decided he had better get involved in day-to-day operations. Boston finished 1973 winning 14 of 18 from the Yankees.

1959 Pumpsie Green, expected to become the first African American to join the Red Sox, was instead optioned to Boston's Minneapolis farm club. The UPI report indicated that Green's play had tapered off in recent games and that "Red Sox officials feel that he needs further seasoning."

1936 Pitcher Johnny Marcum had his tonsils removed; the hope was that they were the cause of his ailing right arm. Maybe. He won 17 games in 1935 with Philadelphia, but only eight with Boston in '36, and Philadelphia was lower in the standings both years.

Now where the heck did I put those jewels? Mrs. Thomas Yawkey forgot jewels reported to be valued at $1,000,000 when she checked out of a hotel in Charlotte, NC. A maid later turned in a knitting bag that Mrs. Yawkey had left, and the gems were found in the unopened bag.

1919 In a Gainesville exhibition game, the Sox took their third in a row from the Giants, but McGraw's "overambitious" Giants took a measure of revenge on the Sox: both catchers (Wally Schang and Roxy Walters) were spiked in the 4–2 loss to the Red Sox. Boston won the fourth game, too, before the Giants won one.

1916 Talk that Tris Speaker might be traded is "all bosh," according to Red Sox owner Lannin. "If I sold Speaker to the Yankees, it would be just the same as selling them the American League pennant." Five days later, Speaker was traded to Cleveland.

TRANSACTIONS
1926: Purchased Topper Rigney from the Detroit Tigers.
1971: Released Tom Satriano, Jarvis Tatum, and Gary Wagner.
1976: Released Diego Segui.
1990: Signed free agent Jeff Gray.

DEBUTS
1970: Gary Peters
1977: Bill Campbell
1978: Jerry Remy, Mike Torrez
1979: Larry Wolfe
1986: Don Baylor, Joe Sambito, Sammy Stewart
1988: Steve Ellsworth, Mike Smithson, John Trautwein
1994: Rich Rowland
1999: Mark Guthrie
2002: Carlos Baerga
2004: Bobby Jones

BIRTHDATES
George Hockette 1908 (1934–1935); Bobby Doerr 1918 (1937–1951)

DEATHS
Si Rosenthal 1969

April 8

2004 On the eve of the home opener, the Red Sox wrapped up the four-game series in Baltimore with a 2–2 tie heading into the bottom of the 13th inning. Bobby Jones was the sixth pitcher of the game; he'd safely escaped the 12th, and never let up a hit for the rest of the game. But Jones started the 13th with a walk to Javy Lopez. After striking out Bautista, he then walked the bases loaded, issuing free passes to both Segui and Matos. And then walked Larry Bigbie, forcing in the winning run.

2001 In his first start, on April 4, Pedro Martinez let in just one run in seven innings, but the Sox lost in the 11th. This time, playing the Devil Rays at Fenway, Pedro completed a three-game sweep, striking out 16 and throwing eight innings of shutout ball.

1996 The Sox, coming off a horrid 1–5 opening road trip, are forced to postpone their home opener due to snow.

1991 In Skydome, Boston's new slugger Jack Clark hit a third-inning grand slam off Blue Jays ace Dave Stieb, giving Roger Clemens all the runs he needed for a 6–2 win. "All I saw was a trail of smoke," said Mike Greenwell, when asked how hard-hit the Clark homer had been. It was the first Opening Day slam for the Sox since Carlton Fisk delivered one in 1973.

1985 Phil Niekro is New York's starting pitcher on Opening Day 1985. He's lost six Opening Day games in a row, and gives up five runs in the first four innings, two of them on bases-loaded walks and the other three on home runs to Tony Armas and Dwight Evans. He's the second oldest player to ever start a game, but the 46-year-old knuckleballer goes on to win 16 games in '85. Boston's Oil Can Boyd beats him 9–2 on this day, and Niekro's now stretched his streak to seven. He loses his first start in 1986, too—Cleveland's home opener. Bill Buckner walks twice and has two official at-bats, but goes on to record 673 at-bats on the season, most ever for a Red Sox left-handed batter.

1975 Hank Aaron made his American League debut, as a Milwaukee Brewer, and Tony Conigliaro debuted again (he had made the team and was returning to major league ball after 3½ years away). Eight policemen climbed a fire department ladder to roust fans perched on the whiskey billboard overlooking the park from Lansdowne Street. Before the game, Captain Carl Yastrzemski called a clubhouse meeting and castigated his teammates for "the worst attitude I ever saw in spring training. If it keeps up," he said, "we'll finish in last place." Aaron was 0-for-3, the Sox won, 5–2. Bob Montgomery's double in the third drove in what proved to be the winning runs. Luis Tiant got the win.

1973 Orlando Cepeda's walk-off home run in the bottom of the ninth inning beats the Yankees, 4–3. It's the first hit ever recorded for a Red Sox designated hitter.

1969 THE DAY BELONGED TO TONY, headlined the *Boston Globe*. After his near-fatal beaning in August 1967, Tony Conigliaro had come back a long way to regain both his vision and his athleticism. The home opener was his first major league game in more than 18 months. Tony C. had hit a two-run homer in the 10th inning, to keep the Sox in the game, and then walked in the 12th, coming around to score the winning run on pinch-hitter Dalton Jones' bases-loaded sacrifice fly. Boston 5, Baltimore 4.

After pitching in both 1968 and 1969 for the Red Sox, righthander Fred Wenz still had not yielded even one fair ball, much less a hit. In his June 4, 1968 debut he struck out three of the four batters he faced; the other worked a walk. His second ML appearance was on April 8, 1969 and he was asked to walk Brooks Robinson intentionally to pitch to Davey Johnson, who he retired on a foul popup. Only in the 12th inning of the April 11 game did he allow a fair ball—one of them. After striking out the first two he faced, Tony Horton singled. Then Wenz pitched to four more batters before Lee Maye grounded back to him on the mound for another fair ball.

1937 Joe Cronin and his wife Mildred lost twins, both infants dying at birth. Eric McNair's wife had died a week after giving birth back in January, and Mildred was fortunate to survive. Just a day after the Cronins lost their children, Oscar Melillo learned that his wife's health was endangered a week after the birth of their child.

1934 Lefty Grove had two abscessed teeth extracted. A third was scheduled to be removed later. "I believe that will clear up the trouble," remarked Red Sox manager Bucky Harris, referring to pain that had affected Grove's pitching arm. "I'm going to be ready—let the teeth fall where they may," cracked Grove. (See also July 5, 1934.)

1930 WABC announced that it would mount a coast-to-coast radio broadcast of the first game of the new season, Boston vs. Washington in the nation's capitol on April 14. (See game account on April 14, 1930.)

1916 Tris Speaker was sold to the Cleveland Indians for a price reported to be around $50,000. Newspapermen assembled for the announcement by manager Bill Carrigan did not believe it. Only when Speaker came by to confirm it did the reality set in. Though he balked at first, Speaker soon said, "I'll go where the money is." Red Sox owner Joseph Lannin had proposed to cut the star's salary from $11,000 to $9,000, despite the Sox winning the World Series in 1915. Lannin had already moved to strengthen the Sox by signing Clarence "Tillie" Walker. Speaker had helped the Sox to win two world championships; as it would happen, they won again in 1916 without him.

1914 By a vote of 128–84, the Massachusetts House of Representatives votes against legalizing the playing of baseball on Sundays in the Commonwealth of Massachusetts.

1913 New pitcher Dutch Leonard held the Harvard team to one hit through six innings at Fenway Park, and another rookie, Rube Foster, pitched pretty well, too, giving up two hits in a 5–0 Red Sox shutout. Did those Harvard kids think they could beat the World Champions?

1911 The Red Sox refused to continue the exhibition game against the Kansas City Blues, charging that the umpire supplied new, solid baseballs when the local Blues were at bat, but gave Kansas City pitchers old and soft ones to throw to Red Sox hitters. The dispute was heated but when half a dozen policemen arrived, the game continued. Boston still won, 4–3.

TRANSACTIONS
1916: Traded Tris Speaker to the Cleveland Indians for Sad Sam
       Jones, Fred "Pinch" Thomas, and $55,000 cash.
1968: Signed free agent Russ Nixon.
1981: Traded Dick Drago to the Mariners for Manny Sarmiento.
1995: Signed free agent Mike Macfarlane.

DEBUTS

1971: Ken Tatum	1979: Gary Allenson, Jim Dwyer,
1973: Mario Guerrero	Mike O'Berry, Chuck Rainey
1978: Tom Burgmeier	1991: Jack Clark
	1993: Scott Bankhead, Bob Melvin

BIRTHDATES
Hap Myers 1888 (1910–1911); Frank Mulroney 1903 (1930); Andy Karl 1914 (1943); Charlie Maxwell 1927 (1950–1954)

DEATHS
Andy Karl 1989

April 9

2004 Opening Day 2004. The Red Sox sold 2,400,000 tickets before the season began. The Sox held a 5–4 lead after six, but the Blue Jays scored three times in the eighth and three more in the ninth, issuing a 10–5 defeat to the Red Sox. Position player David McCarty threw the final two-thirds of an inning in the ninth, the first time a non-pitcher had pitched since Mike Benjamin in 1997. McCarty was a legitimate backup pitcher, though, and by season's end had appeared in three games, acquitting himself reasonably well.

1990 Bill Buckner was back with the Sox for the first time since 1987. When introduced before the game to the Opening Day crowd, he received a standing ovation. Clearly, the fans forgave him for the one unfortunate fielding mishap of 1986, though media obsession with it made his life miserable in later years.

1985 Oil Can Boyd holds the Yankees to two runs, as the Sox beat New York 9–2 on Opening Day. When Butch Wynegar grounded to Buckner, and Buckner flipped to Boyd covering, it was the first of 42 putouts in 1985 for the Can. His 42 putouts set the Sox single-season record for a pitcher.

1976 Jim Palmer won 268 games for the Orioles, and Ferguson Jenkins won 284 for a number of teams. It was Fergie's Boston debut, on Opening Day, and the two squared off in a true pitcher's duel. Palmer won, 1–0.

1969 The Massachusetts Turnpike Authority proposed a three-pronged $325 million plan, which would include a third harbor tunnel and a new 50,000-seat stadium in the Fens, with provisions for a dome in the future "if necessary." The stadium would cost $91 million, part of which would pay for demolition of Fenway Park and construction of a 5,000-car parking garage over the Mass Pike. The third harbor tunnel eventually became part of the turn-of-the-century "Big Dig" (named the Ted Williams Tunnel). Fenway Park, yet to be demolished, looks toward its 100th anniversary in 2012.

1960 Ironically, given that the Red Sox were the last team to field a black player, they help integrate City Park Stadium in New Orleans during an exhibition game against the Cleveland Indians when an end is put to separate seating sections for black and white fans.

1936 The Red Sox just barely beat Holy Cross, 2–1, in a pre-season exhibition game in Worcester with a walk, error, and single in the ninth.

1927 Bill Carrigan, back for his second stint as manager of the Red Sox, had announced at the start of spring training that he would catch in any game when the Sox established a lead of eight of more. When the Sox scored two runs in the bottom of the seventh in a City Series game against the Boston Braves, and made the score 11–2, Carrigan kept his word and caught the final frame. The Red Sox won, 13–2. Carrigan never appeared in a regular season game, despite there being a handful where the Red Sox had eight-run leads.

1913 Completing their sweep of college teams in the pre-season, the Red Sox had it over Holy Cross, 8–1, on a biting cold day.

1912 The first ballgame played at brand new Fenway Park is an exhibition game played, in snow flurries, between Harvard University and the team that will become the 1912 World Champion Red Sox. The professionals barely squeaked out a 2–0 win over the Harvard squad—and that only because Sox pitcher Casey Hageman drove in the two runs with two singles. The game was called after seven innings on account of darkness, not snow.

TRANSACTIONS
1982: Acquired John Henry Johnson from the Texas Rangers in trade for Mike Smithson.
1995: Signed free agents Stan Belinda and Reggie Jefferson. Acquired Rheal Cormier and Mark Whiten in trade from the St. Louis Cardinals for Cory Bailey and Scott Cooper.

DEBUTS

1963: Jack Lamabe, Roman Mejias, Dick Stuart
1970: Mike Derrick, Ed Phillips
1975: Bob Heise
1976: Fergie Jenkins
1983: Doug Bird
1986: Ed Romero
1987: Danny Sheaffer

1989: John Dopson, Danny Heep
1990: Tony Pena, Billy Jo Robidoux
1991: Tony Fossas
1992: Frank Viola
1993: Jeff Richardson, Ernest Riles
1998: Brian Daubach, Mark Portugal
2004: Mark Malaska
2005: Ramon Vazquez

BIRTHDATES

Earl Caldwell 1905 (1948); Mike Brumley 1963 (1991)

DEATHS

Elmer Eggert 1971; Ed Morgan 1980; Bill Kennedy 1983

April 10

2000 Canton veterinarian Gary Lanier sold a surplus $18-dollar ticket for face value outside Fenway in July 1999 and was arrested on the spot. Lanier was handcuffed, fingerprinted, and held in a cell. Charges were dropped against him two days later, but he decided to fight back. U.S. District Court Judge Joseph L. Tauro ruled on April 10 that Boston police were barred for arresting individuals from selling tickets for face value or less. The anti-scalping law should only be enforced against those "in the business of reselling tickets." (See also August 1, 2000.)

1998 Good Friday and Passover both occurred on the same day, and in a vestige of Puritanism, the Red Sox decided not to serve beer at Fenway Park. It was the first beer-less game since Prohibition. For Kids Opening Day the following afternoon, all taps were open.

 Oh, the ballgame? Seattle's Randy Johnson had a two-hitter through eight innings, and the Sox were losing 7–2 when they came to bat in the bottom of the ninth in this day's home opener. The Mariners bullpen failed to hold the lead—in fact, the four pitchers asked to close the game never recorded a single out—as the Sox scored seven times, capped by Mo Vaughn's walkoff grand slam.

1990 It was only the second game of the season, but Sparky Anderson of the Tigers walked Wade Boggs intentionally three times in a row (in the second, third, and fifth innings), and every time it paid off. The Sox still won, though, 4–2—Boston beating Detroit for the 10th time in a row. Boggs shares this major league record (three IBBs) with Carl Yastrzemski. (See April 17, 1968.)

1982 The first two scheduled games are snowed out in Chicago, and the Red Sox returned to Winter Haven, but the season finally gets underway with a twin bill in Baltimore where The Eck throws a six-hit shutout for the Sox, but Bobby Ojeda takes the loss in the second game.

1981 Carlton Fisk, in his first appearance as a member of the White Sox, faced his old team—and did them in with a three-run, eighth-inning homer to beat the Red Sox at Fenway by a score of 5–3.

1978 It was a short season with the Sox for Reggie Cleveland, who came in to relive starter Allen Ripley in a tie game in the bottom of the ninth. He retired the first batter, but then had a ball hit back to him which went for a single. When the third batter reached on an error, Reggie was removed. The runner on second base scored and won the game, tagging Cleveland with the loss. One-third of an inning was all he pitched for Boston in 1978.

1977 All heck broke loose in the eighth inning of an otherwise-unremarkable game. Boston scored six times and Cleveland scored 13 times for a total of 19 runs all in the one inning. Final score: Indians, 19–9.

1969 A disputed Frank Robinson double in the bottom of the 13th set up the O's for 2–1 win over the Red Sox. Was it Emmett Ashford giving a makeup call for the previous game, when he called Tony C. safe on a pickoff play in the 12th inning? Conig scored the winning run in that one. Only Ashford knows for sure.

1932 Manager Shano Collins said he expected the Sox to perform better in 1932. The team had—for the first time in years—not finished last in 1931, and Collins declared "the boys have lost their inferiority complex" and would play more confidently. Perhaps they showed some confidence, but they did not play well. The team lost 111 games and finished an astonishing 64 games out of first.

1928 As was often the case, Opening Day in Washington preceded the rest of the season by one day, and the President, Calvin Coolidge, threw out the first ball. (His throw was wild, but umpire Owens snared it with a "lunging, one-handed catch.") Coolidge only lasted one inning, but he saw Washington score three times in the bottom of the first on just one hit off Boston's Danny MacFayden. Senators starter Milt Gaston lasted seven innings, but the Red Sox scored three times off him in his final frame and went on to beat the Senators, 7–5.

1919 Red Sox team secretary Larry Graver was arrested in Spartanburg, South Carolina for punching a local resident in the nose when the fan called him a "cheap Northerner" and raised his arm as if to strike Graver. Graver was a former ticket taker at the Cort Theater, given his job by Harry Frazee.

1916 Red Sox pitchers held the Harvard College baseball team to five hits, but
?! Harvard shut out the reigning World Champs, 1–0, helped by executing three double plays. Only one Red Sox runner reached third. Harvard scored on a two-out error by Larry Gardner, a single, and an infield roller when Sox pitcher Gregg failed to cover first. The Red Sox repeated as World Champions, and the Harvard nine did pretty well in 1916, too, rolling to a 22–3 season.

TRANSACTIONS
1959: Released Willard Nixon.

DEBUTS

1913: Rube Foster	1978: Allen Ripley
1928: Doug Taitt, Ken Williams	1980: Tony Perez, Dave Rader
1962: Eddie Bressoud, Dave Philley,	1981: Carney Lansford, Joe Rudi
Dick Radatz	1982: Wade Boggs
1968: Dick Ellsworth, Joe Lahoud	1991: Matt Young
1976: Tom House	1998: Mark Lemke

BIRTHDATES
Tex Pruiett 1883 (1907–1908); Bob McGraw 1895 (1919); Tom Jenkins 1898 (1925–1926); Bob Watson 1946 (1979); Jeff Gray 1963 (1990–1991)

DEATHS
None yet

April 11

2000 The Twins scored once in the top of the first, but Boston scored twice in the first and eight times in the second, beating the visiting Minnesotans, 13–4.

1999 The Red Sox lose to Tampa Bay, 5–4. Scott Aldred gets the win in relief. It was the first time in 50 consecutive appearances that Aldred had been credited with a win, a loss, or a save. That was a major league record.

1998 Pedro Martinez' first Fenway start with the Red Sox. Red Sox win 5–0 and Pedro strikes out Dan Wilson for his 1000th career K.

1987 A front-page *Boston Globe* article featured the BLOHARDS (Benevolent Loyal Order of Honorable Ancient Red Sox Diehard Sufferers) who travel each Opening Day from New York City to catch the first game of the year at Fenway Park. The BLOHARDS continue to meet in New York and in late 2004 one of the first stops of the Red Sox World Championship Trophy was at a special celebratory BLOHARDS luncheon.

1969 The Sox win in 16 innings, 2–1. It's their third game of the season and also their third extra inning game. Each game lasts longer than the one before. They won on Opening Day, beating Baltimore in 12 innings. 5–4. Bill Landis got the win, Juan Pizarro got the save. The next game, on April 10 and also in Baltimore, ran 13 innings, but the Sox lost, 2–1, Pizarro assigned the loss. On the 11th, a ground out by Lee Thomas scored Rico Petrocelli with the winning run in another road game against Cleveland. Landis got the win, Pizarro the save.

1962 Bill Monbouquette battled Cleveland rookie Ron Taylor through 11 scoreless innings, and Monbo retired the Indians in the top of the 12th. Finally, Taylor faltered, Yaz tripled to lead off the bottom of the 12th, so the Indians walked two to load the bases, and then gave up a walkoff grand slam to Carroll Hardy. Red Sox win, 4–0.

1961 The major league debut of Carl Yastrzemski saw Yaz go 1-for-5, and Boston lose to KC, 5–2. Yaz had his first major league hit, off Ray Herbert. He would add 3418 more before calling it a career. Yaz was trying to fill Ted Williams' shoes, a difficult task, and only hit .266 in his rookie season, with 11 HRs and 90 RBIs. Yaz played in a major league record 3,308 games, all in the uniform of the same ball club.

1959 The NAACP announced that it would request an investigation into the hiring practices of the Boston Red Sox when, after a superb spring training, the Red Sox sent "Jerry" Green (their first and only black player) to the minors. The head of the Massachusetts Commission Against Discrimination said they probably had no jurisdiction, since the infraction had occurred in Arizona, where the Sox trained, but that he might entertain a look at Red Sox practices overall. Pumpsie Green debuted on July 21.

1935 The Associated Press warned Fenway Park patrons that it might be illegal even to tell your wife, son, or neighbors who won the ballgame. New language on tickets read in part: "By the acceptance and use of this ticket, the holder agrees that he will not directly or indirectly transmit or aid in the transmission of any report, account, or result [either partial or complete] of the baseball game or exhibition." Apparently, the language was originally designed not to grant exclusivity to broadcasters but to provide "a weapon against tipsters employed by gamblers." (*The Sporting News*, April 16, 1936)

1932 President Hoover almost saw the Senators win a ballgame. He'd left the April 11 Opening Day game when it was still scoreless after seven innings; Washington scored once in the 10th to beat Boston, 1–0. Since taking office, the President had attended five games and seen the Senators lose every one.

1925 Burt Whitman termed it "Boston's first civil war in some time"—the Braves and the Red Sox met in exhibition matches, a two-game city series, for the first time in 15 years. Some 15,000 fans braved the cold to see the Braves beat the Red Sox, 4–3.

1920 The Red Sox and Giants took a different approach to spring training, planning to play almost all their exhibition games against each other, in various locales. Out of a planned 21 games, 15 were played, with the Giants winning 10. When the deal was struck, Babe Ruth was a Red Sox and large crowds were expected. "Minus Ruth, the tour was as sour as a dill pickle."—J. G. Taylor Spink.

1917 General Leonard Wood threw out the first ball, and the Yankees marched around the field for 15 minutes displaying their talents at military drill. "It was inspiring," reported the *Boston Globe*, "the crowd applauding the boys repeatedly, being agreeably surprised at the manner in which the players had applied themselves to this work." After the drill, the "Star Spangled Banner" was played. When the game got underway, Babe Ruth pitched a strong one for the Red Sox, granting just three singles. Dick Hoblitzell's three-run homer was the big blow that helped break a 3–3 tie in the seventh. Tillie Walker had a double and two triples, and two squeeze plays enlivened the action, and Yankees pitcher Ray Caldwell found himself the complete game 10–3 loser.

1916 Boston College lost to the Red Sox, 9–1, the only B.C. run scoring when first baseman Dick Hoblitzell lost hold of the ball when trying to tag a runner, and an Eagles runner scored from second on the play.

1912 The Yankees "presented a natty appearance in their new uniforms of white with black pin stripes" in the 1912 season opener at Hilltop Park. It was the first time they'd donned the pinstripes. A somewhat smaller than usual crowd turned out for bands, bunting, and baseball, but "the game itself was not of a nature to keep the several thousand fans keyed up to an enthusiastic pitch." (*New York Times*) In fact, the Red Sox won, 5–3, coming from behind with four runs in the top of the ninth. (See April 11, 1907 for another opener when Boston scored four runs in the final frame.)

1907 Boston was losing 3–2 with two outs in the ninth inning, when Athletics second baseman Danny Murphy blew an easy grounder and two runs scored. Philly managed to tie it back up off reliever Lee Tannehill. Neither team scored for the next four innings, until Boston scored four times in the top of the 14th.

TRANSACTIONS
1995: Signed free agent Erik Hanson.

DEBUTS

1907: Al Shaw, Denny Sullivan
1928: Charlie Berry, Ed Morris
1961: Chuck Schilling, Carl Yastrzemski
1969: Billy Conigliaro, Dick Schofield
1974: Dick Drago

1991: Danny Darwin
1992: Peter Hoy, Herm Winningham
1997: Jim Corsi
1999: Kip Gross, Pat Rapp
2000: Rob Stanifer

BIRTHDATES

Ossee Schreckengost 1875 (1901); Win Kellum 1876 (1901); Hal Deviney 1893
(1920); Bret Saberhagen 1964 (1997–2001); Bobby Jones 1972 (2004); Jason Varitek
1972 (1997–2005); Trot Nixon 1974 (1996–2005); Josh Hancock 1978 (2002)

DEATHS

Norm McNeil 1942; Dick McCabe 1950; Joe Heving 1970;
Clarence Blethen 1973; Mike Menosky 1983

April 12

2003 The home opener affords patrons the first opportunity to watch a ballgame from the newly-installed "Green Monster Seats" atop Fenway's famed left-field Wall. The old screen that used to top the fence is placed in storage, and the new seats become highly coveted commodities.

2000 Gary Gaetti had 1,341 major league RBIs, but only one of them as a member of the Red Sox. He hit a sacrifice fly in his last major league ballgame.

1994 Both teams had 15 hits, but the Red Sox scored twice as many runs in the 22–11 mauling of the Kansas City Royals. Fully one-third of Boston's hits came from third baseman Scott Cooper who hit for the cycle.

1992 Pitcher Matt Young walked Indians leadoff batter Kenny Lofton, who then stole **STVT** second. As Young struck out Glenallen Hill, Lofton proceeded to steal third. He scored when Luis Rivera committed an error on Carlos Baerga's grounder. The Indians had an early lead, 1–0. In the third inning, Cleveland got another run when Young walked the first two batters. The runner on second moved to third on one force out, and scored on the second. Young was losing the game 2–0, and he hadn't given up a hit. He never did. He threw eight full innings, never allowing the Indians a single hit. The game was in Cleveland, and the Indians had a 2–1 lead after 8½, so there was no need to pitch the bottom of the ninth. Young had thrown a no-hit game and lost. Some years later, Major League Baseball declared that it didn't count as a no-hitter because he only pitched eight innings. Regardless, he pitched the full game and never yielded a hit. Most people would agree that's a no-hitter. "The game's over and they don't have any hits," noted Young. Catcher John Flaherty had caught a no-hitter in his major league debut...except, well, MLB said it wasn't one. Even if it was.

Young's game was the first of the last regularly scheduled doubleheader in Red Sox history. Roger Clemens threw a two-hitter and won the second game, 3–0. On the day, Red Sox pitchers allowed just two hits in two full games.

1980 The Milwaukee Brewers welcomed the Red Sox to the 1980 season with three grand slams in the first two games. This day's game was the second of the young season, and the Brewers blasted two grand slams (Cecil Cooper and Don Money, off Mike Torrez and Chuck Rainey) in the second inning alone, en route to an 18–1 slaughter of the Sox.

1969 After back-to-back-to-back extra-inning contests, the fourth game of the 1969 season was a regulation nine innings, but Sox players wish it had never been played. In a chilly game by the Lake, the Indians overcome the 39-degree weather and three Red Sox runs, prevailing 5–3.

1967 Bundled against the 40-degree start-of-game temperature at Fenway, Boston fans are warmed when Rico Petrocelli hits a three-run blast to win the Opening Day game against the White Sox, 5–4. Jim Lonborg gets his first win of what will prove a Cy Young season. The Red Sox finished in ninth place, a half game ahead of the Yankees, in 1966 and fans expected similar results in 1967.

1966 Both Baltimore's Frank Robinson and Boston's George Scott debut; Earl Wilson hits Robinson in his first ML plate appearance, but Robinson homers later on in a game the O's win, when Jim Lonborg balks with the bases loaded in the top of the 13th. Scott tripled and earned his first RBI with a walk. By season's end, Scott holds a Red Sox rookie record, having earned 13 intentional walks. He also leads the major leagues in strikeouts (152) and GIDP (25). The day offered a tri-George debut, with George Smith and George Thomas also debuting for the Red Sox.

1965 President Lyndon B. Johnson threw out the first ball, but the Red Sox battered the Senators with five home runs, including the game-winner by Lee Thomas, playing his first full game, at first base. There were 12 hits in the game, and seven of them were homers, for a major league Opening Day record. It was Billy Herman's first game as manager, and the Red Sox won, 7–2.

1917 *Boston Globe* sportswriter Edward F. Martin complained that the day's game took too long—two hours and 20 minutes—and that the players should "quit this stalling out."

1916 Later, on June 23, 1917, Babe Ruth would be ejected from a game, and Ernie Shore come on in relief to pitch a perfect game. On Opening Day 1916, Shore was to start, but Babe Ruth took the ball instead, threw eight innings, and won, 2–1, beating Philadelphia. Ruth's error led to the sole A's run. *The Baseball Chronology* notes that Philly third baseman Charlie Pick made the first of his 42 errors, which left him at season's end with an .899 fielding average. That was a record that only Boston's Butch Hobson tied, in 1978. Starter Jack Nabors was on his way to a 1–20 record. Astonishingly, after compiling a 1–25 mark over two seasons, Philadelphia brought him back to try again in 1917.

1913 Dutch Leonard debuted with the Red Sox, entering the game in the second inning, in relief, and giving up just one run. Leonard, who led the league with a 0.96 ERA the following year, had forsaken a career in music to play baseball. The Leonard family of Fresno was a musical family, each playing different instruments. Hubert ("Dutch" to his baseball friends) "put over all the tricks of the trap drummer" according to the *Los Angeles Times*, and had been considering professional orchestra work when he hooked on as a ballplayer.

1911 A new concrete park was speedily constructed for the Washington Nationals, following the March 11 fire. Though not fully completed by the April 12 opener, it was in good enough shape to seat 16,000. President Taft threw out the first ball, and the Red Sox blew a 4–0 lead, losing 8–5.

1910 A crowd of 6,214 flocked to Huntington Avenue to see the Boston Red Sox regular lineup beat the Harvard University varsity nine, 4–1. What a boost!

1909 Babe Danzig debuted, got two singles in 13 at-bats, and then left major league ball. Five years later, another Babe made the Sox, and stuck.

1907 The Boston Americans hired George Huff, athletics director of the University of Illinois, to take over as manager. He had no professional baseball experience, but had developed seven championship baseball teams at Illinois in 10 years.

TRANSACTIONS
1994: Bob Melvin was released.

DEBUTS
1909: Babe Danzig, Jack Ryan
1911: Rip Williams
1913: Dutch Leonard
1916: Tillie Walker
1922: George Burns, Joe Dugan,
    Joe Harris, Frank O'Rourke,
    Jack Quinn, Elmer Smith
1927: Fred Hofmann,
    Pee-Wee Wanninger
1955: Eddie Joost

1959: Jim Busby, Gary Geiger
1965: Lenny Green
1966: Dan Osinski, George Scott,
    George Smith, George Thomas
1969: Guido Grillo
1970: Tom Matchick
1980: Glenn Hoffman, Bruce Hurst
1981: Mark Clear, Frank Tanana
1990: Dana Kiecker
1992: John Flaherty

BIRTHDATES
Harry Ostdiek 1881 (1908); Sam Agnew 1887 (1916–1918); Sammy Vick 1895 (1921); Eric McNair 1909 (1936–1938); Jack Wilson 1912 (1935–1941); Bill Wight 1922 (1951–1952); Vicente Romo 1943 (1969–1970); Mike Macfarlane 1964 (1995)

DEATHS
Joe Harris 1966; Red Shannon 1970; Johnny Reder 1990

April 13

2001 In the first meeting of the year, the Yankees scored once in the top of the 10th, but Boston banged out two runs in the bottom of the 10th to take a 3–2 win. When the Yankees grabbed the lead, they brought in their closer, Mariano Rivera, to face the Sox. An out, a single, an out, a single. Nixon and Everett moved up on a wild pitch. With first base open, Rivera had the choice: face Manny Ramirez, or walk him to set up a force at every base and face Troy O'Leary? He decided to face Ramirez, because Manny was 0-for-12 lifetime against Rivera, and six of those at-bats had been strikeouts. Not this time. Manny singled up the middle, drove in two, and won the game.

1997 At Boston's "Kids Opening Day," the Red Sox first introduce Wally the Green Monster, to loud boos from the crowd. Over time, thanks largely to TV broadcaster Jerry Remy's humorous accounts of Wally's antics, the Sox mascot became beloved. The April 13 game was also noted for two home runs: Wil Cordero hit the first homer off the large Coke bottle installed on a light tower over the real Green Monster, and Tim Naehring's grand slam sealed the 7–1 Sox win over Seattle.

1963 It's Dave Morehead's debut and he shut down the Senators, 3–0. The last time any Red Sox rookie debuted with a shutout was Dave Ferriss back in 1945.

1959 The Red Sox, responding to an inquiry from the Massachusetts Commission Against Discrimination, replied that players were used by the Red Sox "regardless of race, color or creed." The fact that not one African American player had ever made the Red Sox team, and that Pumpsie Green had been sent to the minors several days earlier on April 7, had nothing to do with bias, the team wrote MCAD. The next day, MCAD announced that it had invited owner Tom Yawkey to attend its next meeting "to answer charges of racial discrimination made by the Boston branch" of the NAACP. GM Stanley (Bucky) Harris was invited to attend as well.

1957 Pitcher "Rowdy" Russ Meyer, aka "The Mad Monk" is acquired from Cincinnati. His nicknames were better than his total performance for the Red Sox—five innings.

1943 Even though the Red Sox loaned B.C. both Yank Terry and Norman Brown as pitchers, the Eagles still got crushed by the Red Sox, 17–2, in an exhibition game at Fenway Park.

1933 NYC Mayor John L. O'Brien threw out the first pitch, Lou Gehrig hit a first-inning three-run homer (off Sox starter Ivy Andrews, not the Mayor) and the Yankees beat the Red Sox, 4–3. The Yankees had now played 212 consecutive games without being shut out; the Red Sox had played three. The one-run loss was the first of 33 one-run losses suffered by the Sox in 1933.

1931 The Yanks scored five times in the first and held a 6–0 lead, but the Sox crept back and tied it in the top of the ninth. A bases-loaded sacrifice fly for Babe Ruth won it for the Bombers in the bottom of the ninth. The best innings were the three innings of one-hit ball thrown by Boston's Jim Brillheart, who a Washington sportswriter had once playfully dubbed Jehoshaphat Besselievre Brillheart. J. B. had brought his younger brother Jerry to 1931 spring training, but Jerry was released to the Richmond ball club. Otherwise, the Sox could have boasted another brother combo.

1926 "If you're inclined to apoplexy, heart trouble, shocks or faints, don't spend your afternoons at Fenway Park." So began the *Globe*'s lead to the story of Opening Day, 1926. Against the Yankees, the Red Sox burned through a full nine pitchers and were down by 10 runs before they began to roar back. They even brought out Rudy Sommers, who had made the team but had last appeared (in the National League for just one inning) in 1912, pitching for the Cubs. They came to within a run, but nonetheless fell short, 12–11. Every run counted, and the third run the Yankees scored came on a first-inning double steal pulled off by Lou Gehrig and Babe Ruth. The game was the first Sox game broadcast on radio, with Gus Rooney working the microphone for WNAC.

1924 With new owner Bob Quinn at the helm, there was great optimism that the Red Sox could contend in '24. Over 25,000 fans turned out on Opening Day when Fenway hosted the world champion Yankees, a crowd larger than had attended the World Series games in 1918. Ehmke had a three-hit shutout going, and a 1–0 lead, when Babe Ruth hit safely to start off the ninth. Two errors by Wambsganss let two runs score, and the Red Sox lost, 2–1.

1921 U.S. President Warren G. Harding threw out the first ball and rooted for the Washington Nationals. General John J. Pershing raised the American flag. The Red Sox won, 6–3.

1912 Sox secretary McRoy, "wearied of the exorbitant demands made by hotel managers, and tired as well of the tipping system which drains the pockets of the players and officials," said that the ball club would plan to build their own clubhouse at Hot Springs, perhaps sharing the expense with as many as three other ball clubs. The players could eat, bathe, and sleep in the facility. This was deemed "a startling innovation" by the *Washington Post*. It also never came about.

TRANSACTIONS
1944: Tony Lupien was selected off waivers by the Philadelphia Blue Jays.
1957: Selected Russ Meyer off waivers from the Cincinnati Reds.

DEBUTS
1909: Charlie Chech
1916: Sam Agnew
1921: Shano Collins, Nemo Leibold, Muddy Ruel
1926: Fred Bratschi, Alex Gaston, Fred Haney, Sam Langford, Del Lundgren, Emmett McCann, Rudy Sommers, Tony Welzer, Hal Wiltse
1928: Merle Settlemire
1933: Bob Fothergill, Bernie Friberg, Johnny Hodapp, Greg Mulleavy, Bob Seeds, Merv Shea

1954: Harry Agganis, Tom Herrin, Jackie Jensen
1963: Dave Morehead
1966: Joe Christopher, Joe Foy, Pete Magrini, Ken Sanders
1974: Rick Wise
1977: Dave Coleman
1983: Jeff Newman
1986: Wes Gardner

BIRTHDATES
Jake Stahl 1879 (1903–1913); Vean Gregg 1885 (1914–1916); Wes Chamberlain 1966 (1994–1995)

DEATHS
Herb Welch 1967

April 14

1996 Red Sox fans are restless as the team lost its eighth game of the season's first 10, this time when Cleveland's Julio Franco homered in the 11th. The Red Sox hadn't suffered this bad a start to a new season since 1945.

1993 The Sox hit eight doubles, including two each by Mo Vaughn and Billy Hatcher, without even batting in the ninth. They beat the Indians, 12–7, at Fenway.

1978 With winds blowing in, preventing just about anything from going out to left, and fly balls dropping un-caught, Dennis Eckersley took the home opener into the 10th inning. Dick Drago got the final out in the 10th, and went home with a "W" as Jim Rice fought off a pitch that sailed an estimated 395 feet for a single, scoring Butch Hobson with the game-winner over the Rangers, 5–4.

1967 In his major league debut, rookie Billy Rohr sustains a no-hitter against the Yankees, in New York, for 8⅔ innings. Yankees catcher Elston Howard singles to right-center field to spoil the no-no, but Rohr still has himself a superb 3–0 one-hit shutout against Whitey Ford. Reggie Smith scored the only run needed with his leadoff home run. Rohr had lost a no-hitter on the final pitch of a June

24, 1965 seven-inning game, pitching for Boston's Toronto farm club. Rohr had thrown 10 no-hitters in high school and sandlot ball.

1965 Yaz hits for the cycle in a game against the Senators in Our Nation's Capitol, but the Sox lose, 6–4.

1955 Elston Howard became the first African-American to play for the Yankees. He entered the game in the top of the sixth inning after left fielder Irv Noren had been ejected for arguing a close play at the plate. Howard played left and came up to bat in the eighth, with the Yankees down, 6–2. Mantle and Skowron both walked, and Howard singled in his first at-bat, scoring a run. The *New York Times* reported that he "received a fine ovation." The Red Sox won, 8–4.

1947 Pitcher Johnny Murphy is released by the Yankees after 12 years, and snapped up by the Sox. He records a 2.80 ERA in 54⅔ innings.

1942 Johnny Pesky made his major league debut with a single and a triple in the Fenway home opener, on his way to a 205-hit rookie season. Ted Williams kicked off the year with a three-run homer in the first, and had himself a five-RBI day. The Red Sox beat Philadelphia, 8–3, on Opening Day.

1936 For the first time since Prohibition, and following three years of state and city licensing questions, beer is offered again at Fenway Park. At least that is the implication of a *New York Times* article on April 10, which read in part, "Fans will find several changes in the nation's ball parks this season. They will be able to buy a glass of beer in the Boston parks, for example." Oddly, none of the Boston dailies note the occasion.

1933 Former Red Sox pitcher Red Ruffing—now a New York Yankee—hit a grand slam in the bottom of the ninth off Boston's Bob Weiland and won the game at Yankee Stadium, 6–2.

1930 President Herbert Hoover threw out the ball for Opening Day in the District of Columbia with exceptional gusto, but his toss was "not entirely accurate"—in fact, it was a wild pitch and narrowly missed beaning a photographer before landing amongst the Red Sox players gathered for the ceremony. Hoover planned to stay just one inning, but sat through a full eight frames, stretching with the 23,000 in the seventh. The Red Sox won, 4–3.

1929 The Boston Braves shut out the Red Sox at Braves Field, 4–0, in the first Sunday baseball game ever played in the city of Boston. The exhibition game drew over 5,000 fans who froze in the stands, but found themselves part of history. Sox manager Carrigan pulled every one of his starting nine after five innings and put in a whole new team.

1925 The Red Sox had a 6–0 lead after Lefty Grove's major league debut disappointed Philadelphia fans, but the Athletics scored eight times in the final three frames, to tie the game, 8–8. The fourth Sox pitcher of the day, Rudy Kallio, gave up three hits, one run, and lost the game in the 10th. This same game also saw the debut of another future Hall of Fame ballplayer, Mickey Cochrane, who entered the game late and singled in place of catcher Cy Perkins.

1915 Herb Pennock had a no-hitter going for Philadelphia through 8⅔ innings, but then Boston's Harry Hooper hit a single right over his head. Forty-year-old second baseman Larry Lajoie made a "desperate try" for the ball but couldn't quite spear it and Pennock had to settle for a 2–0 shutout.

1914 Boston fans poured out en masse, the largest crowd in 10 years, to see Washington's Walter Johnson face their own Ray Collins. It was Johnson who was the draw, though, and he had a no-hitter going through five. When Bill Carrigan singled in the sixth, a "groan of disappointment arose." Johnson shut out the Red Sox, 3–0, and scored the winning run. After he singled to lead off the third, there was an out and then another single which moved Johnson to second base. With two outs, Milan singled to left and few thought Johnson would challenge Lewis' good arm, but he tore around third and caught Lewis by surprise. The throw was on the money, but Johnson crashed into catcher Carrigan, who dropped the ball and umpire Tom Connolly had to overrule his own call.

The game saw Everett Scott's debut. He might have been one of the lighter-weight Sox stars ever; in *The Sporting News* of October 29, 1942, he said, "I weighed 125 pounds when I started as a regular with the Red Sox in 1914, and I never tipped the scales at more than 138 pounds in the 13 years I played in the majors."

1910 Opening Day 1910 saw the largest crowd (25,000) to date for a New York American League ballgame jam Hilltop Park. The Red Sox and Yankees battled for 14 innings, and the game only ended on account of darkness, tied 4–4. They should have started it a little earlier than 3 o'clock; the game only lasted 2 hours and 45 minutes before darkness forced the end. *The Baseball Chronology* says that the 1910 Red Sox were the last major league team to wear a collar on their uniform. It adds that Hippo Vaughn had only needed three pitches to retire the Red Sox in the 10th, and only four pitches in both the fourth and 12th innings.

It was the first of five tie games for the Red Sox in 1910. In 1917, they also played five ties.

1908 Opening Day 1908 was the first time the team played a regular season ballgame as the Boston Red Sox. The winning pitcher was named Cy Young, and Young was old—the oldest pitcher ever to start an opener for Boston. He was 41 years and 16 days old when he started the first game of the 1908 season. After a playing of "The Star Spangled Banner," the Red Sox pleased the large crowd of home fans with a 3–1 win over the Washington Senators.

1906 Jack Chesbro faced Cy Young in the season opener at New York's Hilltop Park. Weather conditions were "anything but favorable" but the Highlanders only scored once in the second (on Chesbro's double) and Boston only scored once in the fifth, pushing the game into extra innings. New York won it in the bottom of the 12th on a double by Jimmy Williams and a two-out single by Hal Chase. 2–1, New York.

1904 New York's Happy Jack Chesbro earned his first win of season, 8–2, in NY, beating Boston and Cy Young. New York scored five runs in the first inning off Young. Chesbro finished the season with a record 41 wins. Chesbro had a homer; both Boston runs scored on inside-the-park homers (Buck Freeman and Freddy Parent).

Boston plays out the 1904 season with the fewest number of players of any team—using only 18 players.

TRANSACTIONS
1995: Acquired Troy O'Leary off waivers from the Milwaukee Brewers.

DEBUTS

1905: Jesse Burkett
1908: Doc Gessler, Frank LaPorte,
   Jim McHale, Jack Thoney
1914: Ed Kelly, Everett Scott
1921: Curt Fullerton
1922: Alex Ferguson
1925: Turkey Gross, Rudy Kallio,
   Doc Prothro, Billy Rogell
1928: Cliff Garrison
1930: Otto Miller, Tom Oliver,
   George Smith, Bill Sweeney

1931: Pat Creeden, Ollie Marquardt,
   Wilcy Moore, Tom Winsett
1933: Johnny Gooch
1936: Doc Cramer, Jimmie Foxx,
   Heinie Manush, Eric McNair
1942: Bill Conroy, Johnny Pesky
1958: Pete Runnels
1963: Jerry Stephenson
1967: Russ Gibson, Billy Rohr
1974: Juan Marichal
1985: Bruce Kison, Mike Trujillo

BIRTHDATES

Marty Keough 1935 (1957–1960); Joe Lahoud 1947 (1968–1971); Bobby Sprowl 1956 (1978); Brad Pennington 1969 (1996); Steve Avery 1970 (1997–1998)

DEATHS

John Freeman 1958; Al Benton 1968

April 15

2000 Pedro Martinez went to 3–0 on the young season as the Red Sox beat Oakland 14–2 at Fenway. Carl Everett was 3-for-4 with two doubles and four RBIs. Notable was the second-generation umpiring in the game, as three sons of former major-league umpires all worked this one game: Jerry (son of Shag) Crawford, Mike (son of Lou) DiMuro, and Brian (son of Tom) Gorman.

1997 It would have been Scott Hatteberg's first ML HR, and there was a visible dent on the center-field TV camera to prove it cleared the wall, but umpire Shulock didn't see it that way. In fact, he admitted later, he didn't see it at all. Two batters later, a Sox fan leaned over the fence and touched Nomar's fly ball that was then ruled a home run. The Sox won, 7–2.

1993 He'd hit 370 home runs in the National League, but Andre Dawson became one of a very few players to hit their 400th home run in a Red Sox uniform. He hit number 400 off Cleveland's Jose Mesa in the second inning of a 4–3 win made possible when Boston drove in two runs off Eric Plunk in the bottom of the 13th inning. They thereby overcame the run the Indians had scored in the top of the inning.

1978 A *Chicago Tribune* story headlined WILLOUGHBY CUTS LOOSE provided some candid comments by the former Red Sox pitcher. The story quoted Jim Willoughby passing on the word that "the Red Sox had private detectives on our tail all year" in 1976. That he didn't really mind, so much as he did the fact that the reports of the detectives were left lying around the locker room "where even a coach can see them."

1974 When Norm Cash hit a solo home run into the right-field stands in the top of the fifth inning, he won the game, a 1–0 shutout, with Detroit's Joe Coleman prevailing over Reggie Cleveland making his first start representing the Red Sox. The play of the game, though, was made by a pigeon, which was struck by Willie Horton's pop-up almost immediately over home plate. The ball fell foul, and the wounded bird fell at the feet of Bob Montgomery; it expired while being taken from the field.

1972 The strike-delayed '72 season finally gets underway, Boston losing to Detroit 3–2 in a one-game "series" at Tiger Stadium. The agreement was to play out the schedule, as originally constituted, regardless of the fact that teams might play a different number of games. As it turned out, had the Red Sox won this game, they would have won the pennant. They finished a half-game behind the Tigers.

Opening Day featured a moment right at the very start of the game that would be echoed later in the year. Tommy Harper singled to left to lead off, and Luis Aparicio singled, too, sending Harper to second. Yaz singled, loading the bases. After Reggie Smith struck out, Rico Petrocelli singled to left, scoring Harper. Aparicio rounded third but saw third base coach Eddie Popowski's stop sign and put on the brakes fast, stumbling but then scrambling back to the bag—just as Yastrzemski chugged in from the other direction. Yaz, faulted by the *Globe*'s Clif Keane, as being "overzealous," was ruled out. Danny Cater struck out for the third out. (See also October 2, 1972.)

1967 The drama of the first series between the rivals continued, as NY's Mel Stottlemyre pitched a 1–0 gem against Boston's Dennis Bennett.

1966 It takes three Cleveland pitchers and 12 innings, but they combine to issue 17 K's to the Red Sox in an 8–7 Cleveland Stadium loss to the Indians.

1964 This day was the scheduled season opener for the Red Sox, to be held at Yankee Stadium, but rains forced postponement. That was actually fortunate for Tony Conigliaro who, facing the biggest day of his life—his major league debut—overslept and was 45 minutes late to the Stadium. He was lucky to get off with a $10.00 fine.

1959 It was quite a 1959 debut for Red Sox rookie Jerry Casale, who held the Senators to three runs on seven hits, and in the bottom of the sixth inning hit a Russ Kemmerer curve ball for a three-run homer all the way over Fenway's left center-field wall and screen, landing atop a Lansdowne Street building. Casale had strong feelings about what he saw as the anti-Italian prejudice of Joe Cronin and Mike Higgins. About Higgins, he noted, "I don't like to say things like this, but the son of a bitch was always drunk. And he'd never talk to you." Casale felt that Frank Malzone would have come to the majors a lot earlier, Billy Consolo deserved more of a chance to play, and both Ken Aspromonte and himself never got the shot they merited. (See Casale's comments in *Red Sox Nation*.)

1918 With World War I going full bore in Europe, the baseball season opened with appeals to the crowd to buy Liberty Bonds, and with the Royal Rooters band in full swing. The season was planned to be 140 games long, a figure decided upon on October 24 the previous season by league president Ban Johnson, who declared that he always had thought 154 games to be too many. Babe Ruth pitched for Boston, driving in two runs while pitching the Red Sox to a four-hit win over Philadelphia, 7–1. Ed Barrow had won his first game as manager of the Red Sox.

1911 Walter Johnson struck out four Red Sox in the fifth inning, but it wasn't his best day. The victory went to Boston, 6–2

TRANSACTIONS
1935: Signed free agent Moe Berg.
1988: Signed free agent Rick Cerone.

DEBUTS

1904: Bob Unglaub
1915: Carl Mays, Bill Rodgers
1918: Stuffy McInnis, Dave Shean,
Amos Strunk
1920: Eddie Foster, Tim Hendryx,
Mike Menosky
1921: Pinky Pittinger, Del Pratt
1924: Dud Lee, Steve O'Neill, Bobby
Veach, Bill Wambsganss
1927: Grover Hartley
1930: Frank Mulroney
1931: Jim Brillheart, Johnny Lucas,
Al Van Camp
1941: Paul Campbell, Pete Fox,
Frankie Pytlak

1947: Harry Dorish, Sam Mele
1952: Don Lenhardt, Ted Lepcio,
Gus Niarhos, George Schmees,
Faye Throneberry
1955: George Susce
1961: Billy Harrell
1962: Bob Tillman
1966: Eddie Kasko
1969: Ray Jarvis, Syd O'Brien
1972: Danny Cater, Tommy Harper,
Marty Pattin
1978: Jim Wright
1985: Steve Lyons
2004: Phil Seibel

BIRTHDATES

Walt Lynch 1897 (1922); Ted Sizemore 1945 (1979–1980)

DEATHS

Emmett McCann 1937; Mickey Harris 1971

April 16

2005 Manny Ramirez passed Ted Williams on the all-time grand slam list when he hit his 18th grand slam; it was his second homer of the game. Manny drove in all six RBIs in the 6–2 win over the Devil Rays.

1995 Though the players had agreed to come back, major league umpires were still on strike. Eight umps showed up outside City of Palms Park in Fort Myers to mount a picket line and publicize their cause. They were surprised when Jose Canseco joined them in the line. John Hirschbeck had asked, and Jose had responded. "We've got to get the real umpires back." Canseco figured he'd go out, join the line in solidarity, get a photo taken to help the cause, and then head back into the Red Sox locker room. It took 15 minutes to find a lensman, prompting Jose to ask, "Where's a photographer when you need one?"

1990 "It was a very attractive game for us offensively," commented Brewers manager Tom Treblehorn, after their 18–0 blowout of the Red Sox in Boston. Sox fans even began to boo Sox fielders for making catches and slowing down the Milwaukee juggernaut. The Brewers hit nine doubles and one triple—20 hits in all—but not a single home run.

1977 Pitcher Bob Stanley breaks into the major leagues, and earns his first major league save throwing four innings in relief of Luis Tiant. The Steamer will appear in more games than any other Red Sox pitcher—637. It is a record that may never be beaten. Number 2 on the list is Tim Wakefield, who had 420 appearances through the 2005 season.

1973 Switch-hitter Reggie Smith hit homers in the sixth and eighth innings, one from each side of Fenway's home plate. The Red Sox still lose, to the Tigers, 9–7.

1969 In Tony Conigliaro's first Fenway start, Opening Day 1964, he hit a home run his first time up. Tony C. had been joined on the '69 Sox by brother Billy Conigliaro, and Billy filled in for Tony on April 16, since Tony was sidelined with a minor knee injury. Billy responded with not one, but two home runs in his first start, both into the screen in left-center field. Billy's father Sal was at work at a tool and dye plant in Lynn. George Scott hit a couple of homers, too, but the Sox lost, 11–8. Baltimore won, and took first place in the young season; the Orioles never once relinquished the lead in the standings.

1967 The Yankees beat the Red Sox 7–6 in 18 innings in a five-hour, 50-minute Stadium game. Yaz got five hits, Tony C. got five hits, but it was Joe Pepitone's single off Lee Stange (the 571st pitch of the game) with two outs in the bottom of the 18th that won it for New York.

1964 After being postponed twice, the Yankees and Red Sox finally get in Opening Day at Yankee Stadium, Yogi Berra's first game as a manager. Twice, the Yankees hit what looked like a walk-off homer in the 10th inning and a game-tying one in the 11th—but both hooked just foul. One 440-foot drive by Mantle was hauled in by Yastrzemski. In the 11th, Boston's Bob Tillman tripled even deeper to center—460 feet—and was on third with one out. Whitey Ford's sinker to Roman Mejias sunk too much and bounced off the plate, getting by Elston Howard and allowing Tillman to score.

1957 Because of an encounter with an enraged driver during spring training, in which Curt Gowdy twisted his back, the Red Sox broadcaster missed the entire 1957 season—arguably Ted Williams' best year ever.

1948 In pre-season City Series exhibition games, the Boston Braves and Red Sox played each other prior to the regular season. This day, the competition gets a little overheated when Earl Torgeson (Braves) and Billy Hitchcock (Sox) tangle and the two teams go at it.

1946 Opening Day for the first postwar season, with many veterans back in baseball uniforms. In the third inning, President Harry Truman and General Dwight Eisenhower saw Ted Williams bang Roger Wolff's 3–2 pitch deep into Washington's Griffith Stadium seats. Dom DiMaggio had a hit, Johnny Pesky had a hit, and Bobby Doerr had two. The boys were back! Tex Hughson and the Sox won the game, 6–3.

1945 The Red Sox at least appear to go through the motions of giving a tryout to three black players (Jackie Robinson, Sam Jethroe, and Marvin Williams), but claim not to see adequate talent in any one of the three. The *Globe*'s Arthur Siegel noted in 1963, "They weren't even invited to use the clubhouse facilities after the workout." Fifteen more years—and a tremendous opportunity—pass before the Red Sox have an African-American player on their major league roster. Robinson was named Rookie of the Year in 1947. Sam Jethroe was named N. L. Rookie of the Year in 1950.

1942 The day's *Sporting News* informed readers that Tom Yawkey donated five ambulances to the American Field Service, and that Ted Williams wears a special cap with a beak that was half an inch longer than the other players' caps.

1940 Dom DiMaggio breaks in with the Bosox. With Hall of Fame numbers, he was also one of the greatest center fielders in the game. In 1948, DiMaggio made 503 putouts, more in a single season than any other Red Sox outfielder. This day's game, the season opener, saw 40-year-old Lefty Grove throw just 93 pitches and beat Washington with a 1–0 two-hitter. Seven of his pitches resulted in foul balls on two-strike counts.

1937 Joe Cronin resumed the reins of the Red Sox again, after taking 10 days off due to his wife's illness. She had delivered still-born twins on April 7 and was in a precarious position herself.

1936 In just the second game of the season, Red Sox shortstop Joe Cronin broke his right thumb tagging out Pinky Higgins at second base. A few minutes later, Cronin initiates a double play to end the inning, then realizes how painful the thumb is and removes himself from the game. (Boston won, 10–4.) He's out a big chunk of the 1936 season.

1935 In his last professional appearance at Fenway Park (which hosted the Boston Braves for Opening Day while the Red Sox were playing at Yankee Stadium), and his first appearance as a member of the Boston Braves, Babe Ruth hit a home run off New York Giants pitcher Carl Hubbell.

The Red Sox were in New York; it was Joe Cronin's first game as Sox skipper. Lefty Gomez had beaten Boston 11 times in a row, and never lost to them. Billy Werber doubled to left. He took third when Lefty Gomez's pickoff throw to second went astray. Gomez struck out the next batter, Reynolds, but Bill Dickey dropped the third strike and had to fire to Gehrig at first to retire Reynolds. Werber seized the moment to streak home, just beating Gehrig's high return throw. Wes Ferrell threw a two-hit shutout, beating the Yankees, 1–0.

No one, including his biographer Nicholas Dawidoff, seems to quite know how Moe Berg ended up with the Red Sox, but come Opening Day 1935, there he was. Dawidoff's *The Catcher Was A Spy* details the mysterious life of this most unusual member of the Boston Red Sox. Berg was a backup catcher for the Sox from 1935 through 1939. Just a few months before signing with the Sox, Berg was touring in Japan with a visiting baseball team and, during a game on November 29, 1934, Berg dressed in Japanese clothing and made his way to the roof of St. Luke's Hospital in Tokyo, from which he shot movies looking down over Tokyo. In 1942, the OSS wrote Berg and thanked him for making available this film of "strategic importance."

1930 Washington beat the Red Sox, 4–3, for the first of 36 one-run games they would lose this year; they managed to win 17 such games.

1920 Neither recently-traded player Wally Schang nor recently-traded player Oscar Vitt reported to the Red Sox, so both were suspended.

DEBUTS

1906: Charlie Graham	1935: Joe Cronin, Babe Dahlgren	1967: Bill Landis
1909: Harry Hooper	1940: Dom DiMaggio	1968: Ray Culp
1910: Duffy Lewis, Hap Myers	1941: Tex Hughson, Oscar Judd	1975: Kim Andrew
1921: Hank Thormahlen	1946: Ernie Andres, Rudy York	1977: Bob Stanley
1925: Roy Carlyle, Tex Vache	1952: Dick Gernert, Randy Gumpert,	1988: Rick Cerone
1926: Topper Rigney	Len Okrie, Gene Stephens,	1996: Jim Tatum
1928: Cliff Garrison	Ken Wood	1999: Creighton Gubanich
1932: John Michaels, Johnny	1953: Hal Brown, Ken Holcombe,	2000: Andy Sheets
Reder, Bob Weiland	Tom Umphlett	2003: Kevin Tolar
	1964: Tony Conigliaro	
	1966: Dick Stigman	

BIRTHDATES
Dutch Leonard 1892 (1913–1918); Garry Roggenburk 1940 (1966–1969); Jim Lonborg
1942 (1965–1971); Bob Montgomery 1944 (1970–1979); Rick Jones 1955 (1976)

DEATHS
Chick Fewster 1945

April 17

2005 When Tim Wakefield struck out Tampa Bay's Aubrey Huff in the fourth inning, it was strikeout number 1,343 for Tim as a Red Sox pitcher, putting him one ahead of Cy Young. Wakefield only trailed Pedro Martinez (1,683) and Roger Clemens (2,590).

1999 Red Sox reliever Tom "Flash" Gordon had successfully saved 46 straight games, but walked off the field in the ninth inning after recording just one out. He had a strained right elbow and would miss more than half the season. Mark Portugal got the 8–5 win for the Red Sox, but no one got credit for the save.

1998 The Sox go 7–0 on the young season at home, and win the fifth of those games in their final at-bat. This time, it takes two runs in the bottom of the ninth to tie and Darren Bragg's bases-loaded single to win it, 3–2, over Cleveland. After Damon Buford ran for Hatteberg in the ninth, and scored, he started the 10th at second base, then switched positions with third baseman John Valentin after Cleveland's Manny Ramirez singled. After the first out, the two infielders switched positions once more. After the second out, they did it again. Buford's boxscore line reads: pr,2b,3b,2b,3b,2b.

1994 Greg Blosser had performed poorly late in 1993, batting a miserable 2-for-28 in late-season action (or inaction, if you prefer). He hit well in spring training, though, so had another look in April 1994. He made three errors in his first two games, and after going 0-for-3 this day with two strikeouts (a 1-for-11 start), the brass had seen enough. He never hooked on with any other team, either.

1969 Billy Conigliaro, who had two homers the day before, had his third major league hit—also a home run—in the fifth inning of another loss to Balitmore. Mike Greenwell later tied Billy's club record, late in 1985, when his first three hits were all home runs. (See September 25, 1985.)

1968 Carl Yastrzemski is walked intentionally three times in a row, after hitting an early home run. It paid off the first two times; the third time, the next batter singled in a run, but a few moments later Yaz was caught stealing third. Boston's Dick Ellsworth shuts out the White Sox, 2–0. (See also April 10, 1990.)

1964 It was a Fenway fundraiser for the John F. Kennedy Memorial Library, and also the major league debut for 19-year-old Tony Conigliaro. He pounced on the very first pitch he saw, a fastball from Chicago's Joel Horlen, and drove it over the Wall, over the screen, and out of the park. Manager Johnny Pesky was pleased, and so was 91-year-old John Dooley, witnessing his 71st Opening Day at a Boston baseball game, a record pre-dating the Red Sox back into the 19th century. Jack Lamabe pitched his first complete game, his third major league start, a 4–1 win.

1961 Boston beat California, 3–2, the first of five consecutive one-run games. In 1961, Boston played 59 games decided by just one run, winning 32 and losing 27.

1959 Tom beats Bob. Boston's Tommy Brewer turns the tables on New York's Bob Turley, and shuts out the Yankees, 4–0, on two hits. The loser this time around was Bob Turley; he'd beaten Brewer five days earlier on Opening Day. This was the first shutout of the Yankees by a Boston pitcher since Willard Nixon topped Don Larsen 1–0 on August 7, 1956—and 54 matchups in between. The Yanks had shut out the Sox four times.

1951 Mickey Mantle's major league debut comes at home in a 5–0 win against the visiting Red Sox. Mantle singles and drives in one run, going 1-for-4. The day also marked the debut of Yankees public address announcer Bob Sheppard.

1945 New York Mayor LaGuardia threw out the first ball at the Yankee Stadium opener. The Sox scored three times in the first, but it was the seventh inning that spelled doom for the Sox. Four errors and a grand slam by Russ Derry (his second home run of the game) led to seven Yankee runs. Three of the errors—two on one play—were charged to Boston first baseman George Metkovich—one for missing a tag, one for a wild throw, and one for booting a grounder.

The game was picketed by about 20 African Americans who carried signs reading, "If we can pay, why can't we play?" and "If we can stop bullets, why not balls?"

1936 Lou Gehrig was 2-for-3, but they were both singles and they were the only hits at all for the Yankees, as Lefty Grove shut out New York at the Stadium home opener, 8–0. Four different Yankees helped the Red Sox cause with errors, but the Sox collected 10 hits as well.

1935 The Red Sox beat the Yankees again, in another tight game. The Yankees were leading, 2–0, heading into the ninth inning, but Max Bishop hit a two-run homer off Red Ruffing, sending it into extra innings. Bing Miller drove in two in the top of the 10th, with a single to right field. Lou Gehrig homered in the bottom of the 10th, but there was no one on base and no further scoring. Boston won, 4–3. Joe Cronin said he thought the league was pretty balanced and the team that stayed intact through the summer could be the team to win it all. In other words, even the Red Sox had a shot at the pennant. It didn't quite work out that way.

1934 The first game played in the Yawkey-financed renovation of Fenway Park results—like the original opening in 1912—in another 11-inning game, this one a 6–5 loss to Washington.

1920 Wally Schang refuses to report to the Red Sox unless certain salary demands are met, and indicates he will work in the airplane business instead. Sox owner Harry Frazee declares that he will seek an injunction against Schang to prevent him from playing for the Lebanon club of the Bethlehem Steel League, or any other baseball club. Boston won its second game of the year without him, when Harry Hooper singled to deep center to drive in the winning run in a 2–1, 14-inning affair against Washington at Fenway. Also lacking Babe Ruth—now a New York Yankee—the Red Sox won their first five games of the 1920 season. Schang finally came to terms with Frazee on May 4.

1916 The sports page cartoon in the *Boston Globe* was titled RARELY HAS THE PEERLESS SIR WALTER BEEN SO COMPLETELY RIDDLED WITH SHOT. Walter Johnson was peppered for 13 hits and five runs, while Babe Ruth (the rains rendering the ball slick and slippery) allowed Washington one run in the eighth and final inning. The game was called after eight. Boston 5, Washington 1.

1912 Fenway Park's grand opening is rained out. So is the game of the 18th. So are the two games planned for the 19th.

1907 George Huff becomes manager, replacing acting manager Cy Young, who had replaced the late Chick Stahl.

1906 Opening Day 1906 was marked by "thousands in wild panic" as citizen John Farrell's horse was spooked by an automobile and streaked down the lane along the western side of the Huntington Avenue park just as the lane was filled with fans leaving the game (New York 4, Boston 3). About 20 people were knocked down and several were run over by the "swaying coupe" the horse dragged with it. "Women became hysterical and fainted, while hundreds fought their way to a place of safety, entirely regardless for the rights or loves of other equally imperiled," noted the *Boston Globe*. Several blocks from the ballpark, army veteran George Blake of Cambridge leapt onto the horse and covered its nostrils causing it to fall to the ground. Miraculously, no one was seriously injured. In the game, New York had broken a 2–2 tie with two in the ninth, and Boston came back with one, but fell one short of forcing extra innings. The next day's game ended in a tie.

TRANSACTIONS
1969: Released Jerry Stephenson.

DEBUTS
1908: Amby McConnell, Case Patten
1909: Tubby Spencer, Harry Wolter
1920: Mickey Devine, Hack Eibel
1927: Red Rollings
1933: Hank Johnson
1934: Max Bishop, Carl Reynolds,
    Moose Solters
1935: Bing Miller
1945: Otey Clark, Ben Steiner,
    Fred Walters
1951: Lou Boudreau, Bill Wight

1952: Ike Delock, Bill Henry
1955: Owen Friend, Billy Klaus
1956: Don Buddin, Mickey Vernon
1963: Felix Mantilla, Dick Williams
1964: Dalton Jones
1966: Bob Sadowski
1972: Bob Burda, Lew Krausse
1978: Jack Brohamer
1980: Skip Lockwood
1990: Jeff Reardon

BIRTHDATES
None yet

DEATHS
Jack Quinn 1946

April 18

2003 The Sox spotted the Blue Jays a 3–0 lead, but then started nibbling away, taking full advantage of beleaguered reliever Jeff Tam (who at one point threw 17 balls in 18 pitches, and got tagged with the 7–3 loss).

2001 Paxton Crawford pitched well, allowing Tampa Bay just one run in 6⅔ innings, but the Sox couldn't score at all off Albie Lopez and it was 1–0 for the Devil Rays after seven full innings. Lopez tired, though, and walked the first two batters of the eighth and the Red Sox went to work against two Tampa relievers, scoring nine runs in the top of the eighth. After the game, and after just two weeks into the young season, the Devil Rays fired manager Larry Rothschild.

1996 Coming off the worst start in the 96 years of the franchise (3–12), it was big news when the Sox secured a win, beating the Orioles 10–7 in Baltimore.

1995 Bob Ryan's column, "War is no game to Johnson," lauded Red Sox coach Tim Johnson's service with the Marines in Vietnam. "I don't talk much about it," said Johnson with modesty. Ryan added that Johnson "saw too many good people die. . . . A lot of people Tim Johnson knew in Vietnam either never came back or wish they hadn't." Manager Kevin Kennedy added, "Pressure is what you put on yourself, and that's pressure, living in rice paddies for eight months." The only problem was: Johnson never served in Vietnam, a fact he admitted some time after he'd left the Red Sox.

1985 The Sox won their first four games of 1985, then lost the following four. Game nine was at Kansas City, and the Red Sox won it with a two-out solo home run off Mike Jones in the top of the 14th inning.

1981 The Longest Game begins. The Pawtucket Red Sox and Rochester Red Wings play 32 innings of baseball before finally suspending the game at 4:07 A.M. The two teams completed the game on June 23.

1950 Shut out and down by nine runs in the sixth inning, the Yankees catch up and spoil Opening Day for Red Sox fans with a 15–10 win after a nine-run eighth inning. The Sox use five pitchers in the one inning, but still can't stop the rampaging Yankees. It's Billy Martin's debut game, and he marks it by becoming the first debuting player in major league history to get two hits in the same inning.

In 1950, the Red Sox scored the most runs of any year in franchise history: 1,027. That was an average of 6.67 runs per game. In 1906, they scored only 463 runs in the same number of games, averaging 3.00 runs per game.

Also on this day, Cleveland released 12-year veteran Ken Keltner. The Sox signed Keltner and he hit .321 in 28 at-bats, but was let go on June 6th.

1946 The train bearing the Red Sox pulled out of Albany without one key passenger: traveling secretary Tom Dowd. No one noticed that he'd failed to board until the players were presented their checks after dinner in the dining car. The April 18 *Sporting News* relieved readers by noting, "The club's credit was good and the players were spared the necessity of digging into their own pockets."

1940 As in 1919, the Sox kicked off the year with back-to-back shutouts, both in Washington, 1–0 (Grove) and 7–0 (Bagby). They then left the nation's capitol and took the train to Philadelphia, where they won again on the 19th but it took them seven runs to do so.

1938 Six runs in the bottom of the sixth routed Red Ruffing and gave the Red Sox an 8–4 triumph over the Yankees, behind the pitching of Jim Bagby's son Jim Bagby. Son Bagby won 15 games against 11 defeats in his rookie season.

1929 After back-to-back postponements, the Yankees open the season at home against the Red Sox. Babe Ruth, who married just two days earlier, homers his first time up and "doffed his cap with a great flourish" to his new bride as he rounded second base. "In the event any one needs the information, Babe Ruth is No. 3," reported the *New York Times*.

The Yankees were wearing numbers on their uniforms for the first time. Ruth, batting third in the lineup, was assigned number 3. (See also April 23, 1929.)

Rookie Russ Scarritt makes his Red Sox debut. He hits 17 triples in 1929, the Red Sox team record.

The 1929 Red Sox featured a full six former St. Louis Browns on their opening day roster: pitcher Billy Bayne, catchers Alex Gaston and Johnny Heving, and position players Wally Gerber, Phil Todt, and Kenny Williams.

1927 A jarring *Washington Post* headline read Ku Klux Klan Beats Red Sox, 5–3, in Opener. The box score showed the Knights of the Ku Klux Klan beating the Red Sox A. C., a Washington-area team of the era, on the Arlington, Virginia horseshow grounds. One assumes the K.K.K. team dispensed with the white robes and hoods, and one suspects that all the faces on both teams were white, just as they were in the major leagues for another 20 years.

1923 It was the grand opening of Yankee Stadium, with an announced attendance of 74,217 who see Babe Ruth hit a three-run homer to beat the Boston Red Sox, 4–1, behind the pitching of Bob Shawkey. Umpiring the game was Tom Connolly who had worked the very first American League game, held in Chicago in 1901. Connolly also worked the first World Series, and the inaugural games at Shibe Park, Comiskey Park, and Fenway Park.

1916 The Washington Nationals win against the Red Sox, 4–2. It's their first victory in Boston since the last day of the 1914 season. (See April 20, 1951 for an even longer winless streak by a Sox foe.)

1915 The day's *Washington Post* reported that Washington manager Griffith had provided five baseballs to umpire Evans to support his claim that Boston pitcher Ernie Shore had benefited from use of an emery board or other surface to doctor the balls. Sox manager Carrigan countered, "I caught Griffith in the act of rubbing one of these balls on the concrete wall after the game." He said he wouldn't be so foolish as to risk the prescribed $100 fine and 10 days suspension for such an offense.

1914 Harry Hooper and Larry Gardner, both Stutz automobile owners, led a group of players to the Indianapolis Speedway and had the opportunity to "ramble around the famous race-course as fast as gasoline could propel them"—they reached 65 miles-per-hour.

1912 The first game ever scheduled to be played at Boston's brand-new Fenway Park is rained out.

1907 The Boston Americans release Buck Freeman, who had played with the team since its very inception in 1901. Freeman led the AL in RBI in 1902 and 1903.

1906 Boston and New York battled hard, New York taking a 3–2 lead with two runs in the ninth, before Boston tied it up. The game was called a 3–3 tie after 11 innings on account of darkness.

1905 Throwing spitballs on a frigid day in Washington (before just 400 fans), Boston's George Winter threw a one-hitter, but lost the game, 1–0, when one run scored on back-to-back errors in the very first inning. Washington's William Wolfe won with a five-hit shutout.

1904 In an announcement made after Boston's 5–0 Opening Day victory over Washington, John I. Taylor purchased and became president of the Boston ball club for a price thought to be around $150,000. The game was a two-hitter for Jesse Tannehill, and was preceded by a ceremony at the center field flagpole where two banners were raised: the 1903 American League championship pennant and the flag celebrating Boston's win in the first World Series ever played.

TRANSACTIONS
1907: Released Buck Freeman.
1950: Signed free agent Ken Keltner.
1978: Sold Reggie Cleveland to the Texas Rangers.
1991: Signed free agent Steve Lyons.

DEBUTS
1904: Jesse Tannehill
1906: Bob Peterson
1908: Gavvy Cravath
1923: Al DeVormer, Norm McMillan,
    Howie Shanks, Camp Skinner
1925: John Bischoff
1928: Pat Simmons
1929: Bill Barrett, Elliott Bigelow,
    Milt Gaston, Bill Narleski, Bobby
    Reeves, Hal Rhyne, Russ Scarritt,
    Jerry Standaert
1931: Urbane Pickering
1938: Jim Bagby, Red Nonnenkamp,
    Joe Vosmik
1944: Bob Johnson

1945: Jim Wilson
1950: Al Papai, Charley Schanz
1954: Tom Brewer, Tex Clevenger,
    Mickey Owen
1956: Bob Porterfield
1960: Ron Jackson, Tom Sturdivant,
    Al Worthington
1964: Bill Spanswick
1968: Gene Oliver
1970: Don Pavletich
1974: Lance Clemmons
1976: Rick Jones
1978: Frank Duffy
1979: Steve Renko
2004: Earl Snyder

BIRTHDATES
Bill Rodgers 1887 (1915); Duffy Lewis 1888 (1910–1917); Bill Bayne 1899 (1929–1930); Ty LaForest 1917 (1945); Nick Polly 1917 (1945); Rico Brogna 1970 (2000)

DEATHS
Harry Niles 1953; Bill Sweeney 1957; Woody Rich 1983

April 19

1994 In the second inning of the annual Patriot's Day game, Mo Vaughn and Tim Naehring hit back-to-back homers off Bob Welch. In the sixth inning, they repeat the feat off Carlos Reyes. The Sox win, 13–5, over Oakland. Aaron Sele gets the win.

1986 That's power! The Sox were down, 2–1, entering the bottom of the eighth. Boggs doubled and Buckner walked, and then Jim Rice surprised everyone by bunting. It was an attempted sacrifice but blooped into just the right spot between the mound and first base, and Rice reached safely for a base hit. A Don Baylor grounder forced one out, but the tying run scored—and so did the go-ahead run on a throwing error. Sox win, 3–2.

1953 The whole Red Sox traveling party—29 players, five coaches, and two trainers, plus two radiomen and a photographer—flew by chartered airplane from

Washington to Boston's Logan Airport and had a bit of a scare when the inner glass layer of the plane's windshield shattered, showering the captain and the pilot with glass fragments. The plane landed at LaGuardia to effect repairs, then continued on to Boston.

1952 Harry Taylor's only win as a Red Sox pitcher in 1952 came courtesy of left-fielder Don Lenhardt's inside-the-park grand slam, kicking off a seven-run fourth inning in an 11–2 rout of the Philadelphia Athletics.

1948 Two war heroes started for Philadelphia in the day's doubleheader at Fenway. Phil Marchildon, a Canadian Air Force pilot shot down and captured during WWII, won 5–4 in the first game. Lou Brissie won the second game, 4–2. Brissie was the only survivor of his infantry unit; his leg was so badly damaged by German shrapnel that he had a metal plate in it. Ted Williams hit a "bullet-like line drive" off Brissie's leg for one of the seven Sox hits. Brissie collapsed on the mound but recovered and completed the game.

1945 Boston's Joe Cronin broke his leg when his spikes caught on second base during a game-tying seventh-inning Red Sox rally. The Yankees won, 4–3, in the bottom of the ninth when Boston pitcher Mike Ryba faced Johnny Lindell with the bases loaded and hit him on the left wrist. Completing the injury report, left fielder Lindell spiked Yankees center fielder Hershel Martin in the nose as they both chased a long fly ball in the second inning.

1944 After being shut out in the season opener by the Yankees, 3–0, the Sox took a Patriot's Day doubleheader from New York, 6–1 and 5–2.

1930 Expecting a larger turnout than Fenway Park could accommodate, the Red Sox leased Braves Field for the Patriots Day doubleheader opener against the Yankees. The Sox won the morning game, 4–3, after 15 innings of play, and took the afternoon game, 7–2. It was the high point of the season for the Red Sox, who posted a record of 50–102 and finished 50 games out of first place.

1926 Sox center fielder Ira Flagstead initiated three double plays in a nine-inning game. Two runners tried to tag and score from third, but he got both of them. The third one went 8-5-4-2. Flagstead's three assists helped preserve a slim 2–1 Red Sox win.

1924 The Red Sox won the annual Patriot's Day game, beating Philadelphia, 12–0, a score largely built around a 10-run bottom of the second. The crush of 26,000 fans trying to get into Fenway resulted in a gate to the bleachers giving way and four fans being treated at area hospitals, two with serious fractures from being trampled.

1920 Babe Ruth appeared at Fenway Park for the first time in a Yankees uniform, but the Red Sox swept both games of the day's doubleheader, and the game the following day to boot.

1914 The Red Sox were invited to attend a Sunday benefit show for Larry O'Connor, 10-year veteran piano player at the Keith theaters who had his fingers amputated due to frostbite.

1910 A dual-admission Patriots Day doubleheader brought a record 45,728 paying customers to Fenway. Boston beat Washington in two hard-fought games, 2–1 and 5–4, the latter game only won when the Red Sox scored three runs in the bottom of the ninth off Walter Johnson, Bill Carrigan driving in Harry Hooper with a walkoff single.

TRANSACTIONS

1969: Traded Ken Harrelson, Juan Pizarro, and Dick Ellsworth to the Cleveland Indians, acquiring Sonny Siebert, Joe Azcue, and Vicente Romo.
1976: Sold Tim Blackwell to the Phillies.

DEBUTS

1902: Patsy Dougherty, Charlie Hickman, Candy LaChance, John Warner
1904: Tom Doran
1923: George Murray, Lefty O'Doul
1928: Paul Hinson
1929: Ed Durham
1931: Walter Murphy
1934: Bill Cissell, Gordie Hinkle, Ed Morgan, Rube Walberg
1938: Charlie Wagner
1940: Herb Hash
1945: Billy Holm, Nick Polly
1947: Billy Goodman, Strick Shofner
1948: Johnny Ostrowski, Vern Stephens
1949: Walt Dropo, Tommy O'Brien
1950: Gordie Mueller
1953: Bill Werle
1960: Bobby Thomson
1964: Pete Charton, Ed Connolly
1966: Darrell Brandon, Jose Santiago
1971: Phil Gagliano
1974: Bob Didier
1996: Bill Selby
2003: Jason Shiell

BIRTHDATES

Dave Black 1892 (1923); Chick Shorten 1892 (1915–1917); John Donahue 1894 (1923); Bucky Walters 1909 (1933–1934); Don Gile 1935 (1959–1962); John Wyatt 1935 (1966–1968); Rick Miller 1948 (1971–1985); Frank Viola 1960 (1992–1994); Spike Owen 1961 (1986–1988); Jose Cruz 1980 (2005)

DEATHS

Charlie Hickman 1934; Jack Wilson 1995

April 20

2003 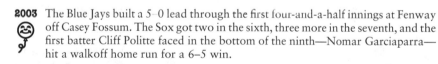 The Blue Jays built a 5–0 lead through the first four-and-a-half innings at Fenway off Casey Fossum. The Sox got two in the sixth, three more in the seventh, and the first batter Cliff Politte faced in the bottom of the ninth—Nomar Garciaparra— hit a walkoff home run for a 6–5 win.

1989 Jim Rice homered in the third inning, and Dwight Evans followed back-to-back. It was the 56th (and last) time that the two Sox sluggers would homer in the same ballgame.

1969 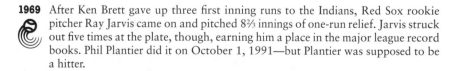 After Ken Brett gave up three first inning runs to the Indians, Red Sox rookie pitcher Ray Jarvis came on and pitched 8⅔ innings of one-run relief. Jarvis struck out five times at the plate, though, earning him a place in the major league record books. Phil Plantier did it on October 1, 1991—but Plantier was supposed to be a hitter.

1964 Bill Monbouquette shuts out the Yankees, 4–0, at Fenway. Bob Meyer pitches for New York; it was his major league debut.

1956 It is reported that Ted Williams suffered a broken blood vessel in the instep of his right foot. Though initially reported as "not serious," The Kid doesn't appear in another game until May 29.

1953 The earliest start time of any major league game since 1903 was this Patriots Day's 10:15 A.M. start at Fenway Park, where 5,385 early risers saw the Red Sox beat the Senators, 4–2. The following year, 1954, there was also a 10:15 A.M. start hosting the Yankees. Boston won that one, 2–1, before 18,682. Patriots Day games now typically begin at 11:05 AM, to theoretically conclude in time to see Boston Marathon runners pass through nearby Kenmore Square. (See April 20, 1903.)

1951 For the first time since September 12, 1948, the Philadelphia Athletics win a road game against Boston, 6–3, when they score three runs in the eighth inning to break open a tie game. Over the 19 intervening games, all Red Sox wins, Boston averaged 8.95 runs per game. Mel Parnell, stunned, absorbs the loss. Boston then takes the next five games.

1947 Mel Parnell's debut resulted in a 3–1 defeat, after Washington nicked him for three runs in the first inning. The southpaw would win 123 games for the Red Sox. Remarkably, when the Sox signed him as a pitcher in 1941, he was his New Orleans high school team's first baseman but had come in to pitch as scouts were evaluating his team's outfielder Red Lavigne. It was only the fifth game in his life in which Parnell had pitched, but despite Lavigne's two homers, it was Parnell's pitching that wowed the scouts.

1945 After Joe Cronin broke his leg in the third game of the year, Nick Polly came up from Louisville and filled in at third, making his first appearance in the majors since he was a September callup for the Brooklyn Dodgers back in 1937. Polly was 1-for-4. Making his major league debut was Jackie Tobin, who saw a lot of action at third base, but was apparently too heavy a drinker. Sox shortstop Eddie Lake told Peter Golenbock that after about six weeks, Tobin showed up "soused to the gills...in no condition to play." Lake says that Cronin called the commissioner's office and activated himself to play third base. If true that he was activated, the historical record does not reflect any time that Cronin actually played in a game after breaking his leg.

1943 Tex Hughson throws a 1–0 shutout of Philadelphia in an Opening Day starting later than usual, as the United States further mobilizes during World War II.

1939 At Yankee Stadium, rookie Ted Williams gets his first major league hit off the Yankees' Red Ruffing, doubling after striking out twice. Game features play by amazing number of future Hall of Famers: Cronin, Dickey, DiMaggio, Doerr, Foxx, Gehrig, Gordon, Grove, Ruffing, and Williams. Lefty Gomez was suited up and watched from the bench.

1933 Tom Yawkey officially assumes ownership of the Boston Red Sox.

1923 Dick Reichle hit his one and only major league homer off Waite Hoyt, a two-run bounce home run to left field, part of a three-run first inning for the Red Sox. Babe Ruth's double with the bases loaded in the ninth gave the Yankees the win. Reichle appeared in 122 games this year, but the next time he played major league ball it was in the NFL. He was an offensive end for the 1926 Milwaukee Badgers.

1916 Good thing the guy can pitch! Babe Ruth starts for the Red Sox and throws a five-hitter, winning his third game of the young season, over Philadelphia by a 7–1 score. At the plate, though, the Babe is 0-for-4. He wins his next start, too, on April 25—hitless again, but brings home a win.

1912 Opening Day 1912 was the first major league game ever played at Fenway Park. The Sox were 4–1 on the new season, and hosted the Yankees with Buck O'Brien going against New York's Jim Vaughn. The Yankees were 0–5 on the year, but spoiled the start of the game for the Red Sox, scoring three times in the very first inning. Boston got one back, but New York added two more in the third and led, 5–1. Then the Sox scored three times, making it a one-run game, and tied it in the sixth. Both teams scored once in the eighth, and the game went into extra innings, somewhat of a miracle for the Red Sox, given that they'd committed seven errors, three by second baseman Steve Yerkes. But Yerkes starred at the plate, going 5-for-7, and scored the winning run in the bottom of the 11th inning. 7–6, Boston.

On June 10, 2005, a baseball used in this very game, noted as such by umpire Tom Connolly, sold at a Sotheby's auction for $132,000.

1903 Boston's Huntington Avenue Grounds hosts two on a combined Opening Day– Patriots' Day twin bill. The 10:00 A.M. first game is the earliest start of any major league game since the start of the 20th century. Some 8,376 up-and-at-'em fans saw Cy Young and Boston beat Philadelphia's Rube Waddell, 9–4. Philly won the afternoon game, 10–7. A much larger audience of 27,658 saw Eddie Plank and Chief Bender combine to beat Long Tom Hughes and the Boston Americans.

1902 Rube Waddell may have shown up for Opening Day a little "under the weather" (that's a euphemism for being hungover). Nevertheless, he struck out the first four Boston players he faced, until they adopted the tactic of bunting repeatedly and forcing the portly, unsteady Waddell to field their bunts. Boston won, 9–4, but Philadelphia took the afternoon affair.

TRANSACTIONS
1923: Purchased Ira Flagstead from the Detroit Tigers.

DEBUTS
1903: Duke Farrell, Jake Stahl, George Stone
1910: Louis Leroy
1914: Rankin Johnson
1920: Benn Karr
1929: Bill Bayne
1937: Bobby Doerr, Pinky Higgins, Buster Mills
1939: Ted Williams
1941: Skeeter Newsome, Mike Ryba
1945: Loyd Christopher, Johnny Tobin
1947: Frankie Hayes, Mel Parnell
1951: Ray Scarborough
1953: Billy Consolo, Bill Kennedy
1958: Al Schroll
1960: Ed Sadowski

BIRTHDATES
Tommy Dowd 1869 (1901); Charlie Hemphill 1876 (1901); Charlie Smith 1880 (1909–1911); Harry Agganis 1929 (1954–1955); Mike O'Berry 1954 (1979); Randy Kutcher 1960 (1988–1990)

DEATHS
Chet Nourse 1958; Bucky Walters 1991; Pat Creeden 1992

April 21

1967 It looks like the Red Sox have a new Yankee-killer in Billy Rohr. In his second major league start, he again handcuffs New York allowing just one eighth-inning run, as Boston beats the Yankees, 6–1. Lionized in Boston, Rohr ran out of roar and never won another game for the Red Sox. He lost three, and finished out the season 2–3. In 1968, he was 1–0 for Cleveland. He never won another game in the major leagues.

1959 Dick O'Connell, VP and business manager of the Red Sox, told the Massachusetts Commission Against Discrimation that, as the *New York Times* noted in a headline, the ballclub would like to have a Negro. "If we had, I wouldn't be sitting here this morning," he said. Sounding confrontational, O'Connell continued: "The Boston Red Sox are entirely American. We have no discrimination against race, color or creed…We have the right to manage our own ball club. People from City Hall and the State House don't hire people for us. We hire them. We're not antagonistic, but we will be accused of it until we have a Negro on our roster."

When O'Connell later became General Manager, he is credited with finally opening up the Red Sox organization.

1958 The Sox keep putting men on the bases, but only score once as Ted Williams trots around on a solo home run. Fifteen others languish on base, though, to be fair, two of them were erased courtesy of the double play. Yankees 4, Boston 1.

1950 It was Connie Mack's 50th Opening Day, but the Red Sox ruled Philadelphia, 8–2, with Vern Stephens' ninth-inning grand slam putting the game out of sight. Stephens' grand slam gave him slams in seven consecutive years, more than any other player in American League history until Manny Ramirez did it for eight years through 2002.

Back in Boston, Sam Jethroe (one of three black players the Red Sox had rejected in the April 16, 1945 tryout) becomes the first black player for a Boston baseball team as he debuts with the Boston Braves. It will be more than nine years before the Red Sox field a black athlete.

1938 The Yankees outhit the Red Sox, 13–3, but lost the game by a 3–2 score, largely thanks to the eight bases on balls doled out by New York pitcher Atley Donald, in his first major league start. He also hit a batter, and was probably lucky the damage wasn't greater.

1933 A tradition of Ladies Day games each Friday had become established in Boston, and in 1933, Opening Day fell on Friday. The team didn't want to have to admit ladies for free when they might expect a large paying crowd so they announced that the first Ladies Day would be on the second home Friday game. The *Boston Post* reported that "over 200 women stormed the gates yesterday and demanded admission." The Red Sox reversed their ruling and let the ladies in.

Beer, now, that was another matter. Even though the repeal of Prohibition was still in the process of being ratified (both the Republican and Democratic party platforms had called for its repeal), local law said that there had to be seats where the brew was served and there were none at Fenway's refreshment stands. "So it is to be doubted that the beverage will be sold there," wrote the *Post*.

The Sox sported black caps and jackets. Babe Ruth hit a home run and the Yankees won, 7–5.

1917 Hurrah! For the home opener, Mayor James Michael Curley tosses out the first ball and pitcher Babe Ruth holds back the Yankees, helping Boston win by a score of 6–4. At the plate, the Bambino hits two doubles and a triple, for a perfect 3-for-3. With war declared, there was some military drilling on the field in pregame ceremonies.

1914 Sox center fielder Tris Speaker pulled off one of his patented unassisted double plays, against the A's. Philadelphia pitcher Bob Shawkey was on second base with one out in the top of the 13th inning. Tom Daley lined to Speaker, playing shallow as he usually did, and Speaker ran to second to double up Shawkey. The game ended in a 1–1 tie after 13 innings. (See also August 8, when Speaker made the play once more. See also April 22 for a follow-up to this day's tie game.)

1905 Boston captain Jimmy Collins raised the blue 1904 championship pennant on the flagpole, as the band played and thousands of fans shouted, waving flags, hats, and handkerchiefs. As the game progressed, Boston led by 4–0 after seven innings. Then came five Philadelphia runs and spirits were dampened, the final score a depressing 5–4.

DEBUTS

1905: Art McGovern	1946: Mel Deutsch,	1960: Dave Hillman
1915: Ray Haley,	Rip Russell	1969: Mike Nagy
Mike McNally	1951: Mike Guerra	1985: Dave Sax
1916: Sam Jones	1953: Marv Grissom	1998: Brian Shouse
1924: Danny Clark	1956: Marty Keough,	1999: Tim Harikkala
1934: Fritz Ostermueller	Dave Sisler	2002: John Burkett,
1941: Joe Dobson	1958: Bill Renna	Ray Webster
	1959: Herb Moford	

BIRTHDATES

Joe McCarthy 1887 (manager, 1948–1950); Gary Peters 1937 (1970–1972); Chris Donnels 1966 (1995); Kevin Brown 1973 (2002); Carlos Castillo 1975 (2001)

DEATHS

Ray Dobens 1980; Sam Dente 2002

April 22

1993 Pitching in the Kingdome, Chris Bosio walked the first two Boston batters, but never allowed a hit and won a 7–0 no-hitter against the Red Sox. The Seattle pitcher set down the last 26 Boston batters, including the final out—a barehanded grab behind the mound by shortstop Omar Vizquel, whose throw to first beat Ernest Riles by a couple of steps.

1978 Boston won eight in a row, drawing back-to-back crowds of over 36,000 to Fenway on the 22nd (which they lose, 13–4) and the 23rd (a twin bill split). In the game on the 22nd, Cleveland's Andre Thornton hit for the cycle, each hit off a different Red Sox pitcher.

1961 Boston lost 13 road games in a row when visiting Chicago's Comiskey Park, but Boston scored five times in the ninth inning and won this one on Pumpsie Green's leadoff 11th-inning homer.

1946 Local boy makes good. Boston's Eddie Pellagrini makes his major league debut game in the fifth inning after Johnny Pesky is beaned by a Sid Hudson fast ball. Pelly comes up in Pesky's slot in the lineup in the seventh inning and hits a game-winning home run over the left-field Wall in his first at-bat. The Red Sox beat Washington, 5–4.

1931 It was a battered Babe Ruth who featured frequently in a 7–5 Yankees win which spoiled the Fenway Park home opener. He had three hits, including an RBI single in the fourth and an RBI double in the sixth. In the sixth inning, he suffered not one, but three separate injuries. Running from second to third in the top of the sixth, he turned his instep. A few moments later, he crashed into catcher (and former football star) Charlie Berry, who was unsuccessfully blocking the plate for Boston. Ruth scored on a sacrifice fly. Taking the field in the bottom of the sixth, he tore a left thigh ligament chasing down a line drive down the foul line in left. Both runners on base scored, and Ruth had to be carried from the field.

1916 The humiliation. Jack Nabors and the A's beat the World Champion Red Sox, 6–2. Nabors ends the season with a 1–20 mark. Mack gave Nabors teammate Tom Sheehan a fair shot as well. Sheehan responded with a 1–16 record.

1915 Philadelphia's second baseman Nap Lajoie committed five errors in the Red Sox home opener, but the A's held the lead until the ninth inning when third baseman Danny Murphy dropped an easy two-out popup and two runners scored, giving the Sox the winning 7–6 margin. Some suggest that incessant playing of "Tessie" rattled Lajoie. Sox owner Joe Lannin went so far as to declare that "the Rooters and 'Tessie' won the game, and not the Red Sox. He also said that if the Sox win the pennant he would charter a special train for them." (*Boston Globe*)

1914 For the second day in a row, the Sox game ended in a tie against the Athletics, this one even at 9–9, but only because the Red Sox rallied with four runs in the bottom of the eighth to tie it. Tris Speaker's bases-loaded two-bagger was the big hit. There was no time to play the ninth, or any subsequent innings, since both teams had trains to catch to get on to their next games.

1909 In the bottom of the first, Tris Speaker hit a long drive to the flagpole in center, which would have kept rolling on a day not so damp. The slow grounds held up the ball, and Speaker had to settle for a triple. It was the only hit the Sox got off Jack Coombs. An eighth-inning error let an Athletic reach first, and "small ball" pushed him around to score for the 1–0 win.

1903 The Boston Americans watch AL President Ban Johnson present the 1902 pennant to the Philadelphia Athletics in pre-game ceremonies at the Philly home opener, then drop the game, 6–1. Athletics pitcher Rube Waddell had to face Boston's best three batters in the top of the ninth, but with bravado waved in all three outfielders and had them play in the infield, then (according to Jake Stahl's memory in the January 22, 1913 *Boston Globe*) struck out Buck Freeman, Chick Stahl, and Jimmy Collins without one of the three even fouling off a pitch.

A year later, Boston fans had the pleasure of watching the 1903 pennant raised at their home park.

TRANSACTIONS
1953: Sold Clyde Vollmer to the Washington Senators.
1995: Signed free agent Derek Lilliquist.

DEBUTS

1914: Fritz Coumbe,
    Squanto Wilson
1915: Ralph Comstock
1918: Wally Schang, Fred Thomas
1920: Harry Harper, Hob Hiller

1931: Gene Rye
1939: Woody Rich
1943: Garrison Ford, Eddie
    Lake, Johnny Lazor
1944: Joe Bowman
1946: Eddie Pellagrini

1956: Johnny Schmitz
1958: Bob Smith
1960: Lou Clinton
1962: Hal Kolstad
1996: Alex Cole

BIRTHDATES

Neal Ball 1881 (1912–1913); Mickey Vernon 1918 (1956–1957);
Terry Francona 1959 (manager, 2004–2005)

DEATHS

Lou Finney 1966

April 23

1991 Roger Clemens extends his scoreless innings streak to 30, and helps his own cause when he retires baserunner Joe Carter unassisted in the sixth. Did he pick him off first or catch him stealing second? Accounts differ. Does it really matter? Clemens wins the game, 3–0.

1985 The Sox win their first two games of the season, in New York, including a 5–4, 11-inning win on this date. The promising start to the Red Sox season continues when Boston sweeps the first three games the Yankees play at Fenway, on May 8, 10 & 11. Losing all six games to New York in August isn't helpful, though, and the Sox were never really in serious contention.

1975 What a showboat! Yankees left-fielder Roy White homers batting left-handed off Reggie Cleveland, then homers again batting righty against Rogelio Moret, but the Sox score five times in the eighth to take the lead and win, 11–7.

1969 Ted Williams returns to Fenway Park, in uniform. Trouble is, it's a Senators uniform for manager Williams. The Senators score five runs in the top of the third and win the game, 9–3.

1954 After Bill "Bugs" Werle threw nine balls in a row, manager Lou Boudreau made a decision—and replaced the man calling the pitches, Sox catcher Sammy White. It still wound up as a four-run inning, enough to make the difference in a 4–3 Senators win.

1939 The Kid, Ted Williams, made his first major league homer batting against Philadelphia's Bud Thomas, part of a 4-for-5 day. The A's win, though, 12–8.

1938 Jimmie Foxx hit his first homer of the year, in Shibe Park off Eddie Smith of the Athletics. Boston (and Lefty Grove) won, 10–4. By year's end, Foxx hit 50 homers for the Red Sox and drove in 175 runs. Both remain Red Sox records. Evidently, Fenway was Foxx's favorite—35 of his homers were hit at home and only 15 on the road.

1932 Johnny Reder doubled in a 5–0 loss to Washington, the only extra-base hit of his career. Reder holds two distinctions among Red Sox alumni: he is the only one born in Poland (Lublin, September 24, 1909) and the only one with a palindromic last name.

1929 Despite all the numbers on their uniforms, the visiting Yankees only put up two runs on the board. New York is the first team to wear numbers on their road uniforms. Morris beats Pipgras, 4–2.

1919 Always a nice way to start a season, the Red Sox played their opener in New York and shut out the Yankees, 10–0. The *New York Times* declared the Yankees "helpless against the queer pitching of Carl Mays." Babe Ruth drove in the winning runs in the first, with a two-run homer that bounced over the head of former Sox outfielder Duffy Lewis, stationed in center for New York. The *Times* said the best thing about the game for the Yankees was the first pitch of the game. It was a strike. There was a large and festive turnout, though, and so the paper noted, "Aside from the ball game, it was a lovely party."

1917 Over 1000 people from Worcester, including the mayor, turned out for "Jack Barry Day" at Fenway to honor native son Jack Barry, player-manager for the Red Sox. Boston lost to New York, 9–6. A dinner and dance that evening in Worcester drew quite a few locals but neither Barry nor other Red Sox players. Only team mascot "Red" appeared. The affair had been represented as a benefit for the Red Cross War Fund, but after meeting the promoter that day at Fenway Park, Barry concluded it was merely a private affair and declined.

1914 Johnson & Johnson. Rankin Johnson went head-to-head with Walter Johnson, and came out of top. Rankin got his first major league start and shut out the Washington Senators, winning 5–0, as this Johnson held the Senators to six safeties in the D.C. home opener.

1910 Tris Speaker earned two putouts as he executed another of his unassisted double plays early in a game that runs 11 innings; Boston loses, 5–3. He also had one assist in the game, one of 492 in his long career—the most assists of an outfielder in history.

TRANSACTIONS
1995: Signed free agent Alejandro Pena.

DEBUTS

1902: Bill Dinneen	1925: Joe Lucey	1950: Ken Keltner, Tom Wright
1903: Jack O'Brien	1936: Jim Henry	1950: Bob Scherbarth
1918: Joe Bush, Ossie Vitt	1939: Elden Auker,	1965: Jim Lonborg
1922: Rip Collins	Denny Galehouse	1969: Joe Azcue, Sonny Siebert
1923: Howard Ehmke	1940: Mickey Harris	1978: Fred Kendall
1924: Oscar Fuhr,	1943: Lou Lucier, Tom McBride,	2004: Lenny DiNardo
Denny Williams	Roy Partee	

BIRTHDATES
Dolph Camilli 1907 (1945); Tony Lupien 1917 (1940–1943); Rheal Cormier 1967 (1995–2000)

DEATHS
Jack Barry 1961; Harry Harper 1963; Freddie Moncewicz 1969; Deron Johnson 1992; Earl Wilson 2005

April 24

2004 Mark Bellhorn hits a sacrifice fly in the top of the 12th inning at Yankee Stadium for a 3–2 Red Sox win. It is one of three Sox sac flies in the game.

1977 Dave Coleman entered the game as a ninth-inning pinch-runner for Yaz (an honor in itself), and scored. He had just 12 at-bats in his major league career (all with the Red Sox) and never did get a hit.

1960 It wasn't exactly the shot heard 'round the world, but Bobby Thomson hit a two-run homer in the ninth inning for the Red Sox for the second day in a row, part of a 4-for-5 day. Alas, even Lou Clinton's solo shot which followed only brought the Sox to within one, and Boston lost to Washington, 11–10.

1954 Mickey McDermott, traded away from Boston, comes inside too much and his pitch breaks the arm of former teammate Mel Parnell. Pitcher Tommy Brewer ran for Parnell. Billy Goodman singled. When Karl Olson tried to sacrifice, he popped up to McDermott, who fired to second base for a 1-6-3 triple play. Boston won, 6–1.

1943 Mace Brown and the Red Sox lost in 12 innings, on a walk, fielder's choice, sacrifice, walk, and sacrifice fly. In 1943, the Sox played a major-league record 31 extra-inning games. They won 15, lost 14, and two ended in ties.

1937 Well, if you can't play college ball, you might as well play for the Red Sox. Red Daughters, 21, was ineligible to play another season for Holy Cross, so he signed with the Sox to go to spring training. He made the team, but only appeared in one game ever (April 24) and never even had an at-bat. It was Opening Day and the Yankees had broken the tie with two runs in the top of the 10th. Daughters entered the game as a pinch-runner, advanced around the bases and scored, but the Sox fell one run short and lost, 6–5.

1917 Southpaw George Mogridge wins a no-hitter at Fenway for the Yankees, 2–1. It will be 66 years before another Yankees lefthander (Dave Righetti) throws a no-hitter.

1913 Secretary of State Bryan was leaving for the West Coast on a 6:45 train, so President Woodrow Wilson was unable to stay much past the seventh-inning stretch (during which he remained seated, though smiling and waving at fans who shouted for him to stand). Due to his departure before the ninth inning, the President missed the four-run Red Sox rally that tipped the score in Boston's favor, 6–3. Boston's scoring was efficient; they only left one man on base in the game; Washington had 11 LOB.

1909 Home Run Baker only hit one grand slam in his career; it came off Boston pitcher Frank Arellanes on this day. Arellanes was a "California Mexican" personally scouted by Sox owner John I. Taylor, whose wife was from San Francisco. On visits west, Taylor scouted and signed Arellanes, Harry Hooper, and Duffy Lewis. Frederick Lieb says that Taylor secured Lewis "by using Western Union against the U.S. mails." The Indians expressed their interest through a letter, whereas Taylor sent a telegram.

1906 Boston annihilated the Washington Nationals, 19–2, in a year when scoring runs and winning games was difficult for Beantown.

TRANSACTIONS
1996: Traded Bryan Eversgerd to the Texas Rangers for a PTBNL (Rudy Pemberton).

DEBUTS

1912: Pinch Thomas	1939: Jake Wade,	1952: Hal Bevan
1924: Joe Connolly	Monte Weaver	1953: Jack Merson
1933: Mike Meola	1941: Odell Hale	1957: Russ Meyer
1937: Dom Dallessandro,	1943: Andy Karl, Dee Miles	1996: Rich Garces
Bob Daughters	1948: Mickey McDermott	
1938: Bill Humphrey,		
Dick Midkiff		

BIRTHDATES
Charlie Graham 1878 (1906); Howard Ehmke 1894 (1923–1926);
Harry Harper 1895 (1920); Todd Jones 1968 (2003)

DEATHS
Buster Ross 1982; Gary Geiger 1996

April 25

1995 Hoping to set things straight once and for all, Dan Shaughnessy wrote that he had taken a Stanley Steelmaster measuring tape, vaulted the rail at Fenway, and measured the distance from home plate to the left-field Wall. Though "315" was painted next to the foul pole in the left-field corner, Shaughnessy's measuring device came up with 309 feet, three inches. The original 1912 blueprints show it at 308 feet. The painted sign was soon changed to 310.

1990 Fans who observed Bill Buckner's permanent limp for a few years found it hard to believe when they heard that Buckner had an inside-the park homer in the fourth at Fenway. Right fielder Claudell Washington fell into the stands, enabling Buckner to huff and puff around the basepaths. It was the only run in the 3–1 Boston loss, and the last home run of Buckner's long career.

1979 Butch Hobson led off the fifth inning hitting a ball off a speaker inside Seattle's Kingdome 106 feet above the playing field; it goes for a triple and when Hobson scores on Dwight Evans' single, it proves the winning run in the 4–1 game.

1961 Gene Conley skipped the Boston Celtics celebration (they'd just won their third straight NBA title) so he could get a head start on his own spring training. In his first appearance for the Red Sox, he let up just one run in eight-plus innings of work. Boston (the Red Sox) won, 6–1, over Washington.

1946 The Sox beat the Yanks 12–5, commencing a 15-game win streak that will last until May 11, when the Yankees shut them out, 2–0. Even after the shutout, they have a record of 21–4.

1942 Bobby Doerr handled 15 chances at second base (seven putouts, eight assists), and was 3-for-4 at the plate (with two doubles), helping beat the Yankees, 4–2.

1924 Major league debut of first baseman Phil Todt. Todt had 8,676 putouts in his eight seasons with the Red Sox, more than any other Boston first baseman.

1916 Babe Ruth pitched a complete game (10 innings) 4–3 win over the Yankees. Ruth can't get himself a hit, but wins the game, 4–3.

1904 Cy Young loses a close one to Rube Waddell and the Athletics, 2–0. He retires the batters in the final two innings without giving up a hit. They are the first two innings of what becomes a 25⅓ hitless innings streak.

TRANSACTIONS
1928: Traded Hal Wiltse to the St. Louis Browns for Wally Gerber.
1964: Released Gene Conley.

DEBUTS
1902: Bert Husting	1937: Archie McKain	1947: Al Widmar
1905: Myron Grimshaw	1938: Lee Rogers	1948: Windy McCall
1910: Hugh Bradley	1939: Tom Carey	1961: Gene Conley
1923: Val Picinich	1941: Dick Newsome	1969: Vicente Romo
1924: Phil Todt	1942: Mace Brown	

BIRTHDATES
Fred Haney 1898 (1926–1927); John Wilson 1903 (1927–1928);
Lew Krausse 1943 (1972); Ken Tatum 1944 (1971–1973)

DEATHS
Dave Williams 1918

April 26

2002 Only what the *New York Times* dubbed a "questionable single in the seventh" stood between Hideo Nomo and his second no-hitter of the month, as he one-hits the Twins, and wins, 2–0.

1996 100-year-old pitcher Milt Gaston died. In 1929, he and his brother Alex were batterymates for the Boston Red Sox. Milt played for five different teams and it was said that he had more Hall of Famers as teammates than any other player.

1995 Baseball returned to the American stage with the Red Sox facing the Twins at Fenway Park. With the strike in August 1994 pushing back the start of the season in 1995, it had been 259 days since the Sox played an official major league ballgame at Fenway on August 10, 1994.

1983 Tony Armas hit his first and second home runs of the season. By the end of 1983, he hit 36 homers, drove in 107 runs, but had a batting average of only .218.

1947 Fireman! Fireman! Rudy York's hotel room in Boston's Myles Standish Hotel caught on fire. It wasn't the only time; York developed a bit of a reputation. After retiring from baseball, he—ironically—worked for a fire department in his home state of Georgia.

1936 The Yankees spot the Sox six runs in bottom of the first at Fenway, but rebound with seven of their own in top of second, and win game 12–9. Attempting to break up betting at the ballpark, Boston police arrested nine bookmakers in the right-field bleachers, while six others escaped. Cash confiscated totaled $5,000. Fans cheered both the police and the bookies who escaped.

1913 Despite abuse heaped on the Red Sox by Washington fans, Boston won easily, 8–3. Tim Murnane described "shameful scenes" in which "the vilest kind of language was hurled at the Boston players and umpires, and these tactics were encouraged by the members of the Washington team who delayed the game by half an hour in finding fault with strikes and decisions on the bases."

1912 When Fenway Park was opened, some writers said that no one would ever hit a ball over the tall green wall in left field. In the fifth game played at Fenway, first baseman Hugh "Corns" Bradley hit one over and out. It was the second, and last, home run of his career.

1909 The Red Sox beat the New York Highlanders, 1–0, when Harry Lord tripled in McConnell, who'd been walked. Chech threw a two-hitter.

1905 Washington beat Boston, in Boston! Why the exclamation point? The 2–1 loss to the D.C. franchise was the first loss to them in Boston since September 11, 1902! That merits an exclamation point or two!!

1902 Deadball era? Boston and Washington tangled at Washington's American League Park and combined for a record five home runs, six triples, and seven doubles— 18 extra-base hits in all. Half of the 18 were Boston hits, but Washington won the high-scoring game, 15–7.

1901 First game for the franchise, but a loss for Win. The Boston Americans play their first game ever, losing to Baltimore, in Baltimore, 10–6. Iron Joe McGinnity strikes out nine in the win, and Mike Donlin cracks two triples off losing pitcher Win Kellum. Jimmy Collins' double in the fourth inning is the team's first-ever hit; Collins scored, the first Boston run. Boston even has its first pinch-hitter, Larry McLean, and he gets a hit, too.

The first foreign-born player to ever play for Boston? He played in the very first inning of the very first game of the franchise: the pitcher, Win Kellum, who hailed from Waterford, Ontario, Canada.

TRANSACTIONS
1925: Traded Joe Harris to the Washington Senators for Roy Carlyle and Paul Zahniser.
1960: Released Jim Busby.
1995: Signed free agent Tim Wakefield.
1996: Signed free agent Adam Hyzdu.
2000: Curtis Pride joined the Sox from the Mets as "part of a conditional deal."

DEBUTS
1901: Jimmy Collins, Lou Criger,
Tommy Dowd, Hobe Ferris,
Buck Freeman, Charlie Hemphill,
Larry McLean, Freddy Parent,
Chick Stahl, Win Kellum
1902: Pep Deininger
1907: Tex Pruiett
1911: Judge Nagle
1912: Hugh Bedient, Hick Cady
1924: Homer Ezzell

1935: Moe Berg
1942: Ken Chase
1945: Bob Garbark
1946: Eddie McGah
1947: Tommy Fine, Johnny Murphy
1995: Luis Alicea, Jose Canseco,
Mike Macfarlane, Alejandro
Pena, Jeff Pierce, Frank
Rodriguez, Mark Whiten

BIRTHDATES
Jack Barry 1887 (1915–1919); Ray Caldwell 1888 (1919); Olaf Henriksen 1888 (1911–1916); Steve Slayton 1902 (1928); Dale Alexander 1903 (1932–1933); Sam Dente 1922 (1947); Ricky Trlicek 1969 (1994–1997); Alejandro Machado 1982 (2005)

DEATHS
Alex Ferguson 1976; Milt Gaston 1996

April 27

2002 Red Sox pitcher Derek Lowe throws his first complete game—the first of his career. It's a no-hitter, the first in Fenway since Dave Morehead's 1965 gem. D-Lowe shuts down the Devil Rays, 10–0. He'd had a no-hitter through seven against the O's earlier in his first start on April 5, and won with a two-hit shutout. Lowe had led the league in saves in 2000, and pitched well in relief for the Red Sox in 2001 as well. His conversion to starter sure was off to a good start.

1969 When Mike Andrews homers in the eighth inning of a 7–3 loss to the Tigers, it represents the 11th game in a row that has seen at least one Red Sox homer.

1968 Baltimore's Tom Phoebus walked two in the first inning, but settled down and no-hit the Red Sox, 6–0. There were some close calls but none closer than a third-inning high chopper that Mike Andrews hit to the mound. It glanced off the glove of the 5'8" Phoebus, but Mark Belanger grabbed it and fired off-balance to first. Brooks Robinson threw some leather at third, too. Calling the game was Curt Blefary, in one of his infrequent games behind the plate.

1963 **STVT** For at least a moment in the fourth inning, two NBA players (Gene Conley of the Celtics and Dave DeBusschere of the New York Knicks) each pitch for their respective Sox (Conley for the Red, and DeBusschere for the White). It's a 9–5 game, and Boston wins it.

1945 Today's loss to Philadelphia left the Red Sox 0–8 on the young season; it remains the longest losing streak at the start of a season for the Sox.

1919 The Sox started the season with two shutouts, first trouncing the Yankees 10–0 in New York, then (after a few days of rain) whitewashing Washington, 8–0. This time Sad Sam Jones won it for Boston. The only other year the Sox started with two shutouts was 1940.

1911 The squeeze failed, but the run scored. Wolter halted on the way home and headed back to third, but catcher Carrigan's throw pulled Engle out of position and allowed Wolter to reverse direction and score the go-ahead run in what proved a 4–3 win for the New York Highlanders.

1907 The Sox got two hits and two bases on balls, but Philadelphia committed five errors and Boston stole four bases. The "daring work on the bases" led Boston to a 5–2 win.

1905 Jesse Tannehill was busy coming off the mound, with an amazing 10 assists in a nine-inning game, "most of them on awkwardly rolling bunts." The defense paid off; Boston beat Washington, 2–1. (*Washington Post*)

1903 Boston catcher Duke Farrell, who'd been playing major league ball since 1888, broke his leg stealing second base. Cy Young's favorite backstop, Lou Criger, pretty much fills out the championship season.

DEBUTS

1901: Fred Mitchell,	1927: Elmer Eggert
Cy Young	1930: Earl Webb
1914: Matt Zeiser	1943: Al Simmons
1919: Roxy Walters	1996: Phil Clark

BIRTHDATES
George Winter 1878 (1901–1908); Lore Bader 1888 (1917–1918); Allen Sothoron 1893 (1921)

DEATHS
Ed Durham 1976; Ernie Neitzke 1977; Emerson Dickman
1981; Marty Karow 1986; Tommy Thomas 1988

April 28

2001 The Sox were tied for fewest errors in the league (10) before the game, but plunged down the list with five errors (by five players) leading to four earned runs in an 8–2 loss to the Royals at Fenway Park. "This was just one of those games," allowed manager Jimy Williams.

1990 Perhaps the plunging temperature gave the visiting A's a bit of a boost. They scored all three of their runs in the top of the ninth. Temperature at game time was a hot 95 degrees, but by the end of the game, it had fallen to a chilly 55. Boston won, 12–3.

1988 The Red Sox were glad to see another team take a record away from them. When Baltimore lost its 21st consecutive game, they earned sole possession of the dubious honor of the longest losing streak ever, taking Boston off the hook for their 20 straight defeats back in 1906.

On the same day, Sox farmhand pitcher Derek Livernois underwent uneventful surgery to correct a problem with his finger. Livernois later reported that he had been told he died during the operation, but been revived. Team physician Arthur Pappas, who conducted the operation, said nothing of the sort occurred, that in the medical record, "There is no indication that he was dead and then resuscitated." Livernois admits to being groggy at the time but recalled waking up with someone pounding on his chest. He was convinced that someone—perhaps an anaesthesiologist—told him he had died due to an overdose of morphine but been brought back. "You died for about a minute" is what he said he'd been told. Pappas did acknowledge that the medical chart indicated he had suffered some "respiratory distress" but not a heart attack and "from a factual point, he was not dead."

1987 The Coors beer company said that their beer was banned from Fenway Park because of a misunderstanding. Boston City Councilor David Scondras was wrong about their corporate stance on gay rights, said Peter Coors. An aide to Scondras suggested in the April 28 *Boston Globe* that if Coors wanted to find a way back into Fenway they should give its workers a union contract and stop supporting rightwing positions. He accused them of contributing funds to an anti-homosexual conference two months earlier, and referred to the 10-year long battle between Coors and the AFL-CIO over the union's decertification.

1969 After hitting 27 home runs in 11 consecutive games, Boston bats were nearly silenced as New York pitcher Fritz Peterson let them have just three hits, and shut them down, 1–0. The Red Sox squeaked out a win the next day, 2–1.

1964 Dick Stuart hits a grand slam in the 11th inning to bring Boston from behind and beat the Baltimore Orioles, 6–4.

1946 On the road, the Sox take two from the Athletics, and also take first place. They rang up 15 wins in a row, and remained in first place right to the last day of the season, winning their first pennant since 1918. Tex Hughson and Mickey Harris pitched 2–1 and 5–1 games, respectively.

Meanwhile, Fenway Park was far from idle. The Boston Braves played two games at Fenway and beat the Phillies twice, 6–1 and 2–1. Back on Opening Day at Braves Field, some 330 patrons complained that their clothing had been stained by green paint which had not yet dried. Tom Yawkey allowed the Braves the use of Fenway over the weekend while the Red Sox were out of town. The doubleheader drew 20,375.

1938 Boston had a comfortable 6–1 lead as the Yankees batted in the bottom of the ninth. The first two New York runners reached base safely. Was Lefty Grove tiring? Joe Glenn was up and lined a hard shot to Jimmie Foxx at first, who fired to Cronin starting a game-ending 3-6-3 triple play.

1930 Without even one hit, the Philadelphia Athletics scored four runs in the top of **STVT** the ninth, to win the game, 5–4. The visiting Quakers take advantage of walks by two Boston pitchers, and errors by two Boston infielders. The Athletics go on to win the 1930 pennant, and the Red Sox run last, exactly 50 games behind.

1929 The first pro baseball game on Sunday in Boston history is played by the Red Sox—at Braves Field. Voters had approved Sunday play in a 1928 referendum, but not within a certain distance of a house of worship; Fenway was too close to a neighboring church. The Sox lose the game to Philadelphia, 7–3, before 23,000 fans. The game also featured the first Gaston-Gaston battery: Milt on the mound and brother Alex catching for the Red Sox.

1920 They battled it out, but the Red Sox and Athletics remained tied 7–7 after a full 14 innings in Philadelphia. Darkness descended and the game was called.

1919 Figuring it was better to give Ruth one base on four pitches than four bases on one, Walter Johnson intentionally walked The Babe in the eighth. Ossie Vitt then tripled in three, and Boston won, 6–5.

That evening, patrons at Keith's Theatre were not only treated to Lew Pollock's whistling solo and some dance numbers, but motion pictures that include glimpses of the Red Sox in action.

1914 Game called on account of not enough fans? Apparently. A *New York Times* story reported the excuses offered, such as wet grounds and threatening skies, but described weather conditions as "fairly good" and reported some protests from the small crowd of fans outside the gates of the Polo Grounds. It must have been a small "crowd" because the paper reported, "It was said that the game was called off because the number of ball players on hand was greater than the number of spectators." The Red Sox lost the following day, 1–0.

1910 Washington Hall of Fame pitcher Walter Johnson gave up 16 hits to the Red Sox, but won the game. He struck out 12, and the game lasted 12 innings. After 28 hits by the two teams, the final score was a miserly 2–1.

The Red Sox visited the White House before the game, and President Taft unsuccessfully tried to get Eddie Cicotte to give up the secret of his famous knuckleball.

Though it was a little more expensive, the Sox took automobiles or taxicabs to and from the Washington ball grounds and not the "lumbering coaches used by the other clubs."

1909 Eight errors by the Highlanders, and 12 hits off Quinn and Ford, helped the Red Sox pile up an easy 12–2 win.

DEBUTS
1911: Les Nunamaker   1995: Rheal Cormier,
1944: Clem Hausmann   Derek Lilliquist,
1981: Dave Schmidt   Keith Shepherd
1990: Daryl Irvine

BIRTHDATES
Tom Sturdivant 1930 (1960)
DEATHS
Swede Carlstrom 1935; Bob Porterfield 1980

April 29

2005 He could hold the cup of coffee, but not take a sip. This is the sort of thing you don't tend to find in record books. Pitcher Tim Bausher was brought up to Boston and assigned a Boston Red Sox uniform for one day: April 29, 2005. He was available to play, but was not called upon to do so. He's still waiting for that first taste.

1997 Five different outfielders recorded assists in the ball game—all three of the Angels and two of the Red Sox. Sox center fielder Shane Mack is the odd man out. The Angels won the game, 5–4.

1986 Roger Clemens set a major league record, striking out 20 Seattle Mariners. Clemens won both the Cy Young Award and MVP in 1986, and had Boston fans eating out of his hand. He later became perhaps the most hated former Red Sox player, pitching for the Blue Jays and then the Yankees. In 2004, however, Clemens won his seventh Cy Young Award for the Houston Astros and won a new measure of respect from Red Sox fans—at the same time that a lot of Yankees fans in turn felt spurned.

1951 The score was tied, 6–6, after eight innings. Neither Philly nor Boston scored in the ninth or 10th, but Dom DiMaggio put the Sox up by one with a home run in the top of the 11th. The A's tied it back up. Tommy Wright put the Sox up by one—again—with a home run in the top of the 12th. The A's tied it back up. The Sox scored two more runs in the top of the 12th, and then Ted Williams homered to make it four. The A's folded. Three extra-inning homers set a Sox record.

1945 In his major league debut, Mississippi's Boo Ferriss of the Red Sox survives a horrific first inning. Every one of his first 10 pitches misses the strike zone. In all, he throws 17 first-inning balls and loads the bases, but escapes without surrendering a run, and then proceeds to whitewash the A's with a 2–0 shutout. He's no slouch at the plate, either, hitting 3-for-3. It's a doubleheader and Boston wins again, 6–3, though it takes 13 innings.

1903 Boston pitcher Norwood Gibson couldn't get the ball over the plate, and couldn't hold the runners that resulted. He walked nine Washington Nationals and they stole eight bases on him. It should be no surprise to learn that Boston lost the game, 9–5.

TRANSACTIONS
1932: Traded Charlie Berry to the Chicago White Sox for Smead Jolley, Bennie Tate, and Johnny Watwood. Sold Jack Rothrock to the Chicago White Sox on waivers.
1957: Traded Milt Bolling, Russ Kemmerer, and Faye Throneberry to the Washington Senators for Bob Chakales and Dean Stone.

DEBUTS
1901: Nig Cuppy
1903: Norwood Gibson
1919: George Dumont. George Winn
1932: Pete Donohue
1935: Doc Farrell, Jack Wilson

1945: Dave Ferriss
1955: Bob Smith, Joe Trimble
1995: Erik Hanson, Mike Hartley, Bill Haselman

BIRTHDATES
Amby McConnell 1883 (1908–1910); Johnnie Heving 1896 (1924–1930); Mickey McDermott 1929 (1948–1953); Luis Aparicio 1934 (1971–1973); Tom House 1947 (1976–1977); Rick Burleson 1951 (1974–1980); Steve Crawford 1958 (1980–1987); Wes Gardner 1961 (1986–1990); Kelly Shoppach 1980 (2005)

DEATHS
Dom Dallessandro 1988

April 30

1996 Al Nipper took one for the team; the Red Sox pitching coach was the sacrificial lamb after the Red Sox had posted a 6–19 record through April 29. Sammy Ellis took Nipper's place. Tim Wakefield held the Tigers to four runs as Boston batters drove in 13 runs.

1974 A Nolan Ryan fastball hits Doug Griffin in the head, and could well have killed him. As it is, Griffin is out a full two months. In 1975, Griffin batted .500 as a pinch-hitter, going 8-for-16.

1966 Getting two hits in an inning is rare enough; having them both homers is even more so. Rick Reichardt of the California Angels homered twice in a twelve-run eighth inning, giving the Angels all they need to beat Boston, 16–9. Teammate Bobby Knoop chips in with a double and home run in the same inning.

1961 After taking all of 1960 off, and frustrated by a poor '61 start, Jackie Jensen retired. Eight days later, he returned to the Red Sox and posted a decent but for him sub-par season.

1958 It was just a little 302 foot job out by the Pesky Pole, but it did the trick as Ted Williams hit the first pitch of the ninth inning for a home run, extra-base hit #1,000 of his career. He's just the 10th player to reach the mark.

 1952 It is dubbed "Ted Williams Day" at Fenway Park, the last before Williams has to depart to rejoin the Marines Corps. In what might well have proved to be his last at-bat in major league baseball, Williams hits a two-run homer off Dizzy Trout his very last time up, to break a 3–3 tie with the Tigers and win the game for the Red Sox, 5–3.

Boston sports columnist Dave Egan, no friend of Ted, suggested that rather than honor Williams, civic leaders should "officially horsewhip" him because of the "vicious influence that he had had on the childhood of America."

1950 Love those 19–0 shutouts! Boston scored 11 runs in the fourth inning, to make it 18–0, then added a single run in the eighth. Ted Williams hit two three-run homers, and drove in seven. Joe Dobson cruised the distance. The Red Sox edged out a win in the second game, 6–5.

1927 Facing a shutout, down 2–0 after 8½ innings, the Red Sox loaded the bases in the bottom of the ninth and pinch-hitter Jack Rothrock doubled down the right-field line, scoring two to tie. In came New York's Wilcy Moore in relief. He walked the first batter intentionally, then got a strikeout and a grounder for a force out at the plate—but then uncorked a wild pitch permitting the winning run to score. In 1931, Rothrock pinch-hit for a .500 on-base percentage: 9-for-19 and a walk.

1906 Boston piles up 23 hits and handily embarrassed the New York Highlanders in front of their home crowd, 13–4. The margin of difference is the nine runs scored by Boston in the top of the ninth inning.

1904 Guess you could call it a decent relief effort. Cy Young throws seven innings of hitless ball in relief, taking over for starter George Winter, who was getting himself in trouble in the third. Added to two prior scoreless innings, Young now had nine consecutive hitless innings. On May 5, his next appearance, he throws a perfect game. And doesn't stop there.

1901 The Boston Americans earned their first franchise win, but it wasn't easy. In front of 2,998 Columbus Park fans, the battery of Cy Young and Lou Criger survived Philadelphia's five-run third inning by pecking away with four one-run innings and Buck Freeman's two–run homer to tie it in the top of the ninth. Boston scored twice more in the 10th and won, 8–6. The game was the first extra-inning game in the American League. The losing pitcher was Billy Milligan. He appeared in 11 games over two seasons and never did win a game.

TRANSACTIONS

1930: Traded Bill Barrett to the Washington Senators for Earl Webb. Pitcher Bill "Beverly" Bayne is sent to Chattanooga. It proved the finale of his nine years in the majors.

1957: Purchased Karl Olson from the Washington Senators, then traded Olson to the Detroit Tigers for Jack Phillips.

DEBUTS

1928: Wally Gerber
1932: Smead Jolley, Bennie Tate, Johnny Watwood

1987: Ellis Burks
1995: Reggie Jefferson, Troy O'Leary, Steve Rodriguez, Terry Shumpert

BIRTHDATES

Babe Danzig 1887 (1909)

DEATHS

Patsy Dougherty 1940

MAY

May 1

1996 Roger Clemens was off to the worst start of his career (0–4) but he got a chance to pitch against the Detroit Tigers, who were 1–11. Clemens struck out 13 Tigers, got himself his first win, 5–1. He'd get even more Tigers in a game later in the year.

1987 Rich Gedman re-signed with the Red Sox. No other team had picked him up as a free agent. Coincidentally, Bob Boone, Ron Guidry, and Tim Raines all had the same experience, with the same result. Collusion was the conclusion come to in later legal proceedings.

1982 The Red Sox held their first Old-Timers' Day. Bob Montgomery homered, Bobby Doerr hit a two-run triple, Billy Goodman hit a two-run double, and Gary Geiger drove in three with a bases-loaded double. Ted Williams flew out, but threw some leather in left, with a shoe-top catch of a Mike Andrews fly ball.

1979 **STVT** Five runs on 17 hits; you won't see that too often. Leaving a club record 18 runners on base in nine innings, the Sox were just lucky they did it in Oakland and not in front of the home crowd. Not surprisingly, they lost, 7–5. The Sox left the bases loaded in the fourth, fifth, sixth, and ninth innings, with Jerry Remy striking out to close both the fourth and fifth.

1971 Boston scored three times in the bottom of the first off Twins pitcher Jim Perry. He gave up back-to-back leadoff homers to Luis Aparicio and Reggie Smith. Then a bunt single, two walks, and a double play brought in another run. All the scoring the rest of the game was by the Twins, and they won 7–3; Perry hit three singles himself, scored three times, and drove in one. The last time an AL pitcher had yielded back-to-back leadoff homers was in 1961—and it was the same pitcher (Jim Perry). The opponent was his current team, the Twins.

1966 **STVT** Double and nothing? In the first game of a Fenway doubleheader, the Red Sox are losing to the Angels 3–0 after three undistinguished innings of play. Dick Stigman started, but had already been relieved by Jim Lonborg, who induced Joe Adcock to ground into a double play. The Sox kept getting runners on base, but from the fourth inning through the bottom of the ninth—six innings in a row—they grounded out into an inning-ending double play. Five different batters shared the honors (George Scott doing it twice). 6–1 Angels, who hit into three DPs of their own. The nine DPs set a major league record. Boston won the second game behind Jerry Stephenson, 9–1. This game featured three more DPs, but only one by the Red Sox—George Scott in the first inning, making it seven innings in a row the Sox had made two outs on one at-bat. Scott's third double play of the day was with none out, and at least this time a run scored.

1965 Boston second baseman Chuck Schilling had some pop in his bat. He pinch-hit for Rico Petrocelli in the ninth inning and hit a home run. Just the day before, he hit for Jack Lamabe in the fifth and hit a home run then, too. With his second straight pinch-hit homer in back-to-back games, he tied a major league record. Also for the record: both games were in Detroit, and the Tigers won both contests.

1959 Pete Runnels singled in the first. That was the only hit the Red Sox got off White Sox pitcher Early Wynn. Wynn won the 1–0 game on the strength of his one-hit game, his 14 K's, and the solo homer he hit in the bottom of the eighth off Boston's Tom Brewer.

1955 The Indians scored four runs and won both halves of a doubleheader. Bob Feller only let the Red Sox have one hit in the opener—Sammy White's seventh-inning single—and Herb Score struck out 16 Red Sox in the nitecap, winning 2–1.

1950 First baseman Billy Goodman goes down with an injury, so the Sox call up Walt Dropo. All he does, despite missing the whole month of April, is hit 144 RBIs (one shy of the major league rookie record, set by Ted Williams in 1939), making his Rookie of the Year award a foregone conclusion.

1946 The Sox sent nine men to the plate in the first inning, and nine men to the plate in the second inning, winning their sixth straight game and tearing up the defending World Champion Detroit Tigers, 13–1, behind the four-hit pitching of Boo Ferriss.

1944 The Senators rack up 20 hits off Sox pitchers, and win 11–4. George Myatt has himself a 6-for-6 day, with four RBIs. Only Joe Wood, Jr., can stanch the Senators (one run in three innings).

1929 It was a May Day massacre, and with 29 hits for 44 total bases, it's not all that surprising that they scored a lot of runs. Philadelphia manhandled the Red Sox, 24–6. Future Red Sox pitcher Lefty Grove won the game, and future Sox slugger Jimmie Foxx hit two home runs. Future Sox sub Al Simmons (133 AB in 1943) had five hits and nine total bases for the Athletics.

1927 One-year wonder Hod Lisenbee, 28, blanks the Red Sox 6–0 for the Senators in his first ML start. He will be 18–9 with four shutouts for the third-place Senators and never have another winning season. (*The Baseball Chronology*)

1923 It's the top of the ninth inning at Fenway Park and Red Sox pitcher Howard Ehmke has two men on, nobody out, and a slim 5–4 lead. He struck out the side, and sent the fans home happy. Ehmke had 10 K's on the day.

1920 Babe Ruth got his first homer as a New York Yankee—the 50th of his career—and helps beat the Red Sox 6–0. His last home run for Boston against New York cleared the roof of the Polo Grounds. So did his first for the Yankees.

1912 Washington took a 1–0 lead in the bottom of the fifth, but Boston tied it in the eighth when Tris Speaker led off taking a walk on four pitches. When Hugh Bradley bunted to the pitcher, Dixie Walker, Speaker took second as Walker held the ball. Larry Gardner struck out, and Duffy Lewis grounded to Foster at third. Foster's throw across the diamond was errant and Speaker scored. Bradley would have scored as well, but the ball hit the Red Sox first base coach, Thomas, and so Bradley was held at third. The inning ended with the score tied, 1–1. It looked like it was headed for extra innings when, with two outs in the bottom of the ninth, Smoky Joe Wood struck out Danny Moeller. The ball hit home plate and got away, though, and Moeller ran to first—while John Flynn scored from third with the winning run.

1907 George Huff can't cut it, so he resigns as manager—a post he's only held since April 17—and Bob Unglaub takes the helm. Huff said the reason was that he "did not like professional baseball and that his heart was not in his work." (*Washington Post*) It may have been due to an "inability to get the measure of control he desired." (*Los Angeles Times*) Ed Grillo of the *Post* wrote that Huff was a bit of a "fall guy" and that owner John I. Taylor "did the managing." In the eight games Huff managed, he compiled a career record of 2–6. Huff did contribute to the Red Sox cause later in the year. He was kept on the payroll as a scout, and as such he signed both Tris Speaker and George Whiteman.

Unglaub won his first game as manager, with a bases-clearing triple in the bottom of the seventh boosting Boston to a 4–3 win over New York. Unglaub's tenure outlasted Huff—he managed 20 games (9–20) before being replaced on June 7 by Jim McGuire.

1906 New York pitcher Billy Hogg threw a one-hitter against Boston and beat Cy Young 8–0. In the seventh inning, Freddy Parent got the only Boston hit. It was the first of 20 consecutive losses, the worst losing streak in Boston AL history.

1902 NEARLY A RIOT—so read the *Globe* headline. Baltimore needed three runs to tie, in the bottom of the ninth. Umpire Sheridan ruled McGraw's drive down the right-field line a foul ball, and not a double. Then, when Dinneen hit McGraw with a pitch "right where he sits down," Sheridan ruled that McGraw hadn't sufficiently tried to get out of the way. McGraw blew up, getting himself ejected. After the game, as 13 officers surrounded the umpire to escort him off the field, Sgt. Joe Smith was hit in the face with a brick.

TRANSACTIONS
1935: Purchased Dib Williams from the Philadelphia Athletics.
1958: Traded Ken Aspromonte to the Washington Senators for Lou Berberet.
1987: Signed free agent Rich Gedman.

DEBUTS
1901: Ossee Schreckengost   1948: Jack Kramer
1920: Gary Fortune   1957: Bob Chakales
1929: Ed Carroll, Grant Gillis   1995: Joel Johnston
1944: Joe Wood

BIRTHDATES
Frank Foreman 1863 (1901); Al Zarilla 1919 (1949–1953)

DEATHS
Frank Barberich 1965; Gary Wilson 1969

May 2

1995 V for Victory. There had been times that a grand slam accounted for all the runs in a 4–0 win, but Boston's 8–0 defeat of the Yankees was the first time that two grand slams accounted for all the runs in a ballgame. Seton Hall teammates John Valentin (third inning) and Mo Vaughn (fourth inning) did the double deeds. All in all, a pleasant debut for Sox pitcher Vaughn Eshelman.

1947 It was his third straight shutout and his 10th one-hitter, as Bob Feller leads the Indians to a 2–0 win over the Red Sox. Johnny Pesky's first-inning single is the only safety the Sox can muster.

1946 A 10th-inning homer into the Red Sox bullpen wins the seventh game in a row for the early-surging Red Sox, 5–4. The day of the game, GM Eddie Collins announces the the Sox will install lights before the 1947 season.

1944 Theodore Samuel Williams "wins his wings" as he is appointed Second Lieutenant in the U.S. Marine Corps Reserve, over the signature of H. F. MacComsey, Captain, U.S. Navy.

1942 Ever heard of relief? Detroit starter Elden Auker, a 1939 teammate of Williams and Doerr, has already given up eight runs through eight innings. (To be fair, he'd kept them scoreless in the sixth, seventh, and eighth.) In the bottom of the ninth, though, with the Tigers winning 10–8, Johnny Pesky got on board and Ted Williams homered to tie the game. Paul Campbell got on, and Bobby Doerr doubled him home for the walk-off. Auker is charged with 10 runs on 17 hits, but at least he got credit for a complete game! In the top of the ninth, Johnny Pesky pulled off a hidden ball trick, but it doesn't count since Doerr—unaware of the unfolding drama—called time.

1938 The Sox score 13 runs on 13 hits in the first three frames, then cruise to a 13–1 victory, despite Pinky Higgins making four errors at third base. With the four misplays, Higgins ties an AL record set just two days earlier.

1927 Red Sox get infielder Charles Solomon "Buddy" Myer in exchange for SS Elmer Elmo "Topper" Rigney. They gave up the better nickname, but came out way ahead on the trade. And Washington had to trade five players to get Myer back after the 1928 season was over (see December 15, 1928).

1904 Leadoff batter Patsy Dougherty got the only hit off Philadelphia's Rube Waddell in a Boston benefit game for John L. Sullivan. Waddell put down the next 27 batters, beating Jesse Tannehill, 3–0. Waddell then apparently warned Cy Young that he'll suffer the same fate the next time the two meet. (See May 5, 1904.)

1902 George Pepper Wilson won one game in 1901 for the Boston Americans, in his September 23 debut. Come 1902, he decided to see how he'd fare with his name changed to George Pepper Prentiss. Not so well on this day; he gave up eight runs in relief of Cy Young (who yielded six in the first inning). Prentiss won two and lost two for Boston, and was then purchased by Baltimore, where he lost one game—and then died of illness at his father's Delaware home on September 8. Young tried again the next day and threw a four-hitter for a 10–1 win.

1901 Win and Loos? An early slugfest in Philadelphia, with Boston piling up the runs early on. Avenging their 14–1 defeat the day before (when Win Kellum lost his second straight game), Boston scored 23 runs, Philadelphia 12. The matchup pitted Ted Lewis against Pete Loos. With both teams giving up that many runs, was it coincidence that both surnames could be pronounced "lose"? Boston scored nine runs in the second inning, then topped that with 10 in the third. Before he managed an out in the second, though, Philly native Loos had walked four and was gone from the game. The record books show him as pitching just one inning of major league ball. Parson Lewis, born in Wales, was in the last year of a six-year career, though he did win 16 games in 1901. He surrendered 172 runs in 1901, though, an awful lot of runs to give up in this era. Maybe he'd be better as a college president? After the season, he quit baseball to teach full-time at Columbia University. Some 26 years later, he became president of the University of New Hampshire.

TRANSACTIONS
1927: Traded Topper Rigney to the Washington Senators for Buddy Myer.
1959: Traded Dave Sisler and Ted Lepcio to the Detroit Tigers for Billy Hoeft.
1994: Signed free agent Eric Wedge.

DEBUTS
1901: Charlie Jones, Ted Lewis
1914: Guy Cooper
1919: Ray Caldwell
1995: Vaughn Eshelman
2005: Jeremi Gonzalez

BIRTHDATES
Bill Piercy 1896 (1922–1924); Ralph Brickner 1925 (1952); Eddie Bressoud 1932 (1962–1965)

DEATHS
None yet

May 3

1999 Catcher Creighton Gubanich hits a grand slam for his first major league hit, in the very first inning, and the Red Sox lead Oakland 7–0 after two innings, but fritter the lead away and lose it on a bases-loaded walk in the 10th inning.

1996 At the end of the sixth inning, with the score Boston 5 and Toronto 1, the evening's game was suspended at 1:06 AM and completed the next day, May 4. The Blue Jays lost the resumed game, 8–7, and the regularly-scheduled one, 8–4. Heathcliff Slocumb got the save for the Sox in both games.

1982 Dave Stapleton's headfirst slide to home plate gave him an inside-the-park homer on a fly to right field which traveled less than 300 feet; it capped a four-run first inning in a 6–2 win over the Twins. The win brought the Sox to 16–7, for their best start since 1946.

1969 Fred Wenz picked up his only American League win, by throwing the last three innings of the day's game with Detroit. The Sox scored five times in the seventh and eighth, to take a 7–5 lead. Wenz walked and scored the penultimate (and winning) run.

1968 Boston scores twice in the bottom of the ninth, to take a little of the sting out of a 7–2 loss to Oakland. Ed Walton tells us that pitcher Jerry Stephenson lost his contact lens "touching off a hilarious scene on the mound while on his knees looking for the lost lens."

1952 Some unusual fan participation impinges on the game. The AP noted, "the game was delayed by a one-legged spectator who wandered onto the playing field to talk to Marty Marion, the Browns' veteran shortstop" in the third inning. Earlier, two college kids ran onto the field. Dressed in baseball uniforms, they started throwing a rubber ball back and forth. Ellis Kinder and the Red Sox kept their mind on the game and won, 5–2.

Third baseman Hal Bevan is sold to the Athletics. He only ever appeared in one game for Boston, and never batted. For Philadelphia, he had six hits in 17 AB.

He next resurfaced in 1955 for three at-bats in three games for KC, .000. Five years later, he made it back to The Show and got three at-bats with Cincinnati. He struck out twice, but the third time he got a home run.

1944 Hoping to snap a short Sox losing streak, manager Joe Cronin put himself into the game as the first baseman. He went 3-for-5, with a homer, and made both outs of a double play, the first one at first base and the second one across the diamond at third on a rundown play. His three RBIs help the Sox beat the Senators, 12–11.

1940 Jim Tabor's second home run of the game tied it in the bottom of the ninth, and his bases-loaded single in the 10th beat the Browns, 9–8.

1938 Lefty Grove beat the Tigers in 10 innings, 4–3. It was the first of 20 consecutive victories at Fenway Park. The next time Grove loses a game at Fenway is June 21, 1941. His winning percentage of .764 (55–17) is the highest of any Sox southpaw pitching at home. There were 15 walks in the game and 26 men left on base.

1920 Harry Frazee bought Fenway Park. Charles Taylor had never sold the park to the various owners who followed him since 1911, but had instead leased Fenway to them. Now that Frazee owned Fenway, he eliminated a threat from AL president Ban Johnson which might have led to the New York franchise moving to Boston and becoming the Boston Yankees. Mike Vaccaro provides a glimpse of the scheme's parameters in his excellent book *Emperors and Idiots*.

1919 The Red Sox won their first home game of the year on May 3, when Babe Ruth pitched a 3–2 win over the Yankees. Ruth's double was the only hit of the fourth inning as the Sox scored two runs.

TRANSACTIONS
1952: Hal Bevan was selected by the Philadelphia Athletics off waivers.
1965: John Sanders selected by the Red Sox off waivers.
1990: Signed free agent Jody Reed.

DEBUTS
1901: Frank Foreman
1925: Bud Connolly
1927: Buddy Myer
1944: Vic Johnson
1955: Pete Daley

BIRTHDATES
Del Baker 1892 (coach, 1945–48, 1953–60, manager 1960); Red Ruffing 1904 (1924–1930)

DEATHS
Tom Jenkins 1979; Darrell Johnson 2004

May 4

2002 A ninth-inning, two-out, pinch–hit slam by Shea Hillenbrand bumped the Sox to a 7–5 win over the Devil Rays. The Red Sox had come from behind in the ninth just the day before to win, 3–2. With an extra-inning loss to the Twins on May 2, it's three games in a row that Tampa Bay couldn't hold a ninth-inning lead.

1996 Former Red Sox third baseman and manager Butch Hobson was arrested at the Comfort Inn in Pawtucket for cocaine possession. He claimed he had no idea who had sent him the FedEx package, but took a leave from the Phillies' Red Barons club he was managing "until the situation clarifies." It clarified quite a bit when he fessed up later.

1982 It seemed funny at first, and Fenway bleacherites taunted Twins rookie Jim Eisenreich for his twitching and jerking as he played center field. They didn't realize that Eisenreich had Tourette's Syndrome; the game was one of five in a row from which Eisenreich (.310 at the time) had to remove himself.

1974 It wasn't quite as bad as Johnny Pesky making four errors in front of 8,000 fans at the first City Series exhibition game during his rookie year, but Rick Burleson made three errors in his major league debut. It tied a major league record.

1965 The only major league appearance of Bill "Rudy" Schlesinger came in a pinch-hitting role. Heading for the on-deck circle, he stumbled coming up the dugout steps, then couldn't get the doughnut off his bat, then dropped a little ball a few feet in front of the plate for an easy out: "It just went off home plate, and it went up real high and he got me by about a half a step at first base. And then that was it." He was waived three days later. Still, he had his moment in the sun.

1962 Pinch-hitter Russ Nixon batted for pitcher Mike Fornieles in the fifth inning—and got not just one, but two hits. It turned into a 12-run inning, and Nixon had two singles, drove in two, and scored twice. Nixon was an excellent pinch-hitter. In 1961, he was 10-for-18 (.555) and in 1962, he was 10-for-28 (.357).

1956 Mel Parnell gave up 14 hits but won, 6–4, over the Tigers, his first start since the previous August 15. One can only imagine the comments after the National Braille Press presented the 1956 Red Sox schedule to manager Pinky Higgins, the first time the schedule had been printed in Braille.

1949 The day after darkness forced the end of a 14–14 tie in 13 innings, the Tigers and the visiting Red Sox went at it again. This time, the Tigers got 14 more hits, but only three runs; that was sufficient, though, as Virgil Trucks held the Sox to three hits (one a Ted Williams homer), and won, 3–1.

1946 Ted Williams doubled, homered, and collected three RBIs, helping Jim Bagby beat Bob Feller and the Indians, 6–2, and running the Red Sox winning streak to nine in a row.

1941 With his aim on 300 wins, Boston's Lefty Grove won his 294th victory—his first of the season—going the distance in an 11–4 win over the St. Louis Browns. Fifteen hits by his Bosox teammates make a big difference.

1939 With fourth and fifth inning homers, rookie Ted Williams had his first two-homer game. He also racked up five RBIs, lifting the Sox to a 7–6 win over the Tigers. The second drive shot completely out of Briggs Stadium, the first ball ever hit over the right-field roof.

1934 Eddie Collins announced Tom Yawkey's plan, approved by AL President Harridge, for a bonus system by which a certain percentage of each player's salary would be given as a gift to the player if the team finished in third place, twice as much if the Sox finished second, and three times as much if Boston won the pennant. Yawkey paid no bonuses; the Red Sox finished in fourth place.

1931 Babe Ruth and Lou Gehrig switched positions, due to lingering effects of Ruth's injury. Ruth played first and Gehrig right field. They punched out five hits between them, but Gehrig's error figured in the 7–3 Red Sox victory.

1916 It took until the eighth inning before a Yankees batter reached second base off Sox pitcher Dutch Leonard. The baserunner was trapped in a rundown a few moments later. Leonard shut out New York, 3–0.

1911 Joe Wood struck out seven New York Highlanders and allowed only two hits, one of them a scratch hit at that. The Red Sox won in New York, 2–0.

1909 With two out and Washington's Clyde Milan on third, Cy Morgan balked in a run. It was the only run of the game as former Boston pitcher Jesse Tannehill shut out the Sox, 1–0.

TRANSACTIONS
1973: Sent Sonny Siebert to the Texas Rangers as part of a conditional deal.
1976: Released Gene Michael.
1990: Acquired Tom Brunansky from the St. Louis Cardinals in a trade for Lee Smith.

DEBUTS

1923: Dave Black	1963: Jim Gosger
1926: Boob Fowler	1965: Dennis Bennett, Rudy Schlesinger
1935: Dib Williams	1973: Craig Skok
1949: Jack Robinson	1974: Rick Burleson
1952: Ralph Brickner	1990: Jerry Reed
1958: Lou Berberet	1994: Todd Frohwirth

BIRTHDATES
Ralph Pond 1888 (1910); Jack Tobin 1892 (1926–1927); Jack Baker 1950 (1976–1977)

DEATHS
Vince Molyneaux 1950

May 5

1996 Those unearned runs can cost you; 10 of Toronto's 11 runs were unearned—more than enough for the 11–4 win over Tim Wakefield and the Red Sox.

1989 Dr. Arthur Pappas reported that the blood clot in Oil Can Boyd's shoulder had dissolved over the preceding 48 hours, but that he would not be able to continue as a pitcher using an overhand delivery. Boyd's future in baseball was understandably uncertain.

1972 Gopher ball drought. Rico Petrocelli's home run in the sixth inning is the first home run for the Red Sox in the last 378 at-bats. The last homer had been hit by Reggie Smith on September 28, 1971—220 days earlier (1972 was a leap year).

1949 Bob Feller got his first win of the year, thanks to Cleveland's six-run second inning which included Minnie Minoso's first major league homer and a three-run blast by Ken Keltner. Ted Williams hit his fifth, but Boston lost 7–3.

The Red Sox acquire outfielder Al Zarilla from the St. Louis Browns for Stan Spence and "cash considerations." Zarilla hit .329 for the Browns in 1948, and Spence had hit .255 for the Sox. Browns ownership indicated it was a move "to give the Browns some additional power." One suspects the cash—a cool hundred grand—might have had more to do with it; Spence only slugged .391 in '48 and Zarilla slugged .482.

1948 Ted Williams saved the game in the 10th, making a double play on a fly ball and a strong peg to Birdie Tebbetts at the plate; it was just one of three assists Teddy Ballgame had in the game. Vern Stephens took part in five double plays, also tying a club record. Pitcher Mel Parnell pitched well, but suffered the embarrassment of balking twice on successive pitches. Boston won, 4–3.

1938 It was said to be "the first fistic outbreak at Fenway Park a baseball crowd has witnessed in eighteen years" (Associated Press) The reference was to the May 27, 1920 game when umpire Hildebrand struck Shawkey with his mask. Boston scored four runs in the bottom of the fifth, but fiery Ben Chapman took exception to a called third strike—and even more exception to the taunting Tigers catcher Birdie Tebbetts tossed his way. The two grappled and were expelled, later drawing $25 fines and three-day suspensions. Detroit won the game, 7–5.

1934 Inauspicious beginnings. Coming off seven consecutive 20-win seasons with Philadelphia, newly-acquired pitcher Lefty Grove tested his sore arm, coming into a game in relief of Rube Walberg, with the Sox holding a comfortable 9–3 lead. He never recorded an out. A walk, a triple, a single, a double, and then another walk on four pitches—and Grove was out of there, tagged for five earned runs. The Browns tied it up, then went up by two runs the next innings, but Boston came back and won the game in the end, 13–12.

1931 Philadelphia kicks off a 17-game winning streak at the expense of the hapless Red Sox, who whiff 10 times and lose, 4–1. Earl Webb's solo homer in the seventh ended A's pitcher George Earnshaw's string of 16 scoreless innings.

1930 The Red Sox stopped Cleveland's six-game winning streak with a definitive 18–3 score, half their runs coming in a nine-run bottom of the fifth.

1923 After two outs in the top of the 12th, the Sox slapped out four successive singles and scored three runs for a 4–1 win over Washington.

1904 Coming just three days after Rube Waddell gave up one hit, then retired 27 Boston batters in a row, Cy Young pitched a perfect game against Philadelphia and mound rival Rube Waddell, who flied out as the 27th and final out. Young had now thrown 18 consecutive hitless innings, and his streak will continue. The score was 3–0, and Young reportedly shouted at Waddell, "How do you like that, you hayseed?" The game remains the only perfect game thrown by a Boston pitcher, though Ernie Shore couldn't have pitched any better to the 27 batters he faced and retired.

TRANSACTIONS
1925: Traded Alex Ferguson and Bobby Veach to the New York Yankees for Ray Francis and $9,000.
1969: Traded Bill (Rudy) Schlesinger to the Phillies for Don Lock.
1989: Signed free agent Joe Price.
1994: Bob Zupcic acquired off waivers from the White Sox.

DEBUTS
1926: Jack Russell
1934: Lefty Grove
1948: Ellis Kinder
1995: Brian Looney

BIRTHDATES
Frank Morrissey 1876 (1901); Jack Ryan 1905 (1929); Don Buddin
1934 (1956–1961); Tommy Helms 1941 (1977)

DEATHS
Ty LaForest 1947; John Godwin 1956; Eddie Cicotte 1969; Bill Marshall 1977

May 6

2002 Seventeen strikeouts are not good enough when your team can't get you even one run. Pedro Martinez posted 17 K's against the Devil Rays, but Steve Trachsel threw a shutout, and Tampa Bay beat Boston, 1–0.

1977 Pitching for the California Angels, Nolan Ryan struck out 15 Red Sox in 8⅔ innings before being relieved by Paul Hartzell, who got the final out—with a strikeout of George Scott. California won, 8–4. Jerry Remy had a 4-for-4 day, and walked, and stole two bases. He was playing for the Angels at the time.

1955 New York's Bob Turley two-hit the Red Sox in Boston. Boston's Frank Sullivan started, but had to leave the game early after swinging at a third strike, missing, and falling down and hurting his shoulder. New York 6, Boston 0.

1953 Del Wilber hit a pinch-hit homer in the seventh for Boston's only two runs in a 6–2 loss to Chicago. This is really only interesting in context; see also May 10 and May 21, 1953.

1948 Boston's Birdie Tebbetts and George Vico of the Tigers get into a fight on the field, which continues in the clubhouse afterward.

1946 Johnny Pesky had hit safely 11 times in a row. Twelve is the record. With Catfish Metkovich on first base, Pesky grounded out on a hit-and-run play. Cronin was criticized, but explained that Pesky called the play on his own. Boston won, 7–5, and won the second game of the doubleheader, too, on a ninth-inning single by Dom DiMaggio. It was one of Dom's 84 RBIs as a leadoff hitter in 1946.

1945 In his second start of the season, Boo Ferriss did what he did in his first major league start: pitch a shutout. First it was Philadelphia; this day it was the Yankees, 5–0, in the first game of a twin bill. Hank Borowy and the Yankees turned the tables in the nightcap, shutting out the Sox, 2–0.

1943 The Sox lost four games in a row at New York, every one of them by one run.

1934 Hoping to overcome a 2–1 deficit, the Sox scored 12 times in the fourth inning, driving the Tigers' Firpo Mayberry from the mound. Mayberry notably surrendered four consecutive triples to Boston's Carl Reynolds, Moose Solters, Rick Ferrell, and Bucky Walters. All were legit, none of the ground-rule variety. Boston won, 14–4.

1930 After he lost 25 games in 1928 and another 22 in 1929, it didn't seem a major loss when the Sox shipped Red Ruffing to the Yankees. They got $50,000 for him, and Cedric Durst, too. Ruffing went on to win 234 games for the Yankees and earn a plaque in Cooperstown.

1925 Pitcher Curt Fullerton (10–35 in four seasons with the Sox) is sent to St. Paul. After seven years in the minors, he comes back in 1933 and goes 0–2.

1919 Ray Caldwell struck out swinging at a second-inning wild pitch that advanced two baserunners. Both scored on Harry Hooper's subsequent single. Caldwell limited Washington to three hits and won the game, 2–0.

1918 "Ruth, 1b"—so read the boxscore. It was the first game in which Babe Ruth started at another position than pitcher. He went 2-for-4, opening the scoring with a two-run homer in the fourth inning. Yankees left fielder Ping Bodie one-upped the Babe, though, with five RBIs to win a 10–3 game.

1915 Babe Ruth was in his Red Sox uniform, pitching against the Yankees in New York. Boston had been leading when Daniel Boone drove in the tying run in the ninth, forcing extra innings. Ruth threw a full 13 innings, but lost the game, 4–3. Ruth also hit his first career home run, off NY's Jack Warhop.

Because Ruth's homer was hit in New York (into the upper deck, no less) the Massachusetts Woman Suffrage Association didn't have to pay off; that very day, the group announced they would send a $5.00 check to any Red Sox or Braves player who hit a home run in a Boston home game.

1911 Scoring five runs in the third inning helped put the Yankees on top. The Red Sox started to mount a rally in the ninth when Rip Williams and Les Nunamaker opened the inning with back-to-back singles. Bill Carrigan then hit a rocket—but it kicked off a 6-4-3 triple play, the first in Yankees history.

1910 Amby McConnell underwent surgery for appendicitis. The very next day, Hap Myers was in hospital with a slight case of scarlet fever. Harry Niles felt ill, too, and there was a bit of an uproar among the players, fearing that the scarlet fever was spreading by contagion, but fortunately Niles turned out to simply have a bad case of indigestion.

TRANSACTIONS
1930: Traded Red Ruffing to the New York Yankees for Cedric Durst and $50,000 cash.
1960: Traded Nelson Chittum and cash to the Dodgers for Rip Repulski.
1978: Signed amateur free agent Steve Crawford.

DEBUTS
1910: Frank Barberich   1990: Tom Brunansky
1920: Herb Hunter   1995: Stan Belinda
1936: Johnny Marcum

BIRTHDATES
Ed Karger 1883 (1909–1911); Ivy Andrews 1907 (1932–1933); Russ Gibson 1939 (1967–1969); Larry Andersen 1953 (1990); Tom Bolton 1962 (1987–1992); Phil Clark 1968 (1996); Israel Alcantara 1971 (2000–2001); Earl Snyder 1976 (2004)

DEATHS
Harry Ostdiek 1956; Joe Glenn 1985

May 7

1999 On a roll in a stellar season, Boston's Pedro Martinez struck out 15 Angels and beat Anaheim, 6–0, making him personally 6–1 as a starter.

1997 Scott Hatteberg got his first major league homer, and his second, in Boston's 11–3 win over the Minnesota Twins. Reggie Jefferson hit a pair, too.

1992 Despite working 15 walks off Chicago pitchers, the Sox still came up short, losing 7–6.

1983 Five plainclothes Boston policemen arrested infielder Julio Valdez in the clubhouse during the ballgame against the Seattle Mariners, removing him from Fenway Park in handcuffs. A 14-year-old girl had charged him with raping her on April 5 in a Boston hotel. The girl, missing from her Fall River home since March 28, had been found near Fenway on April 20 and taken into protective custody. On June 9, Valdez was bound over to a Suffolk County grand jury after a 2½ hour probable cause hearing. On July 13, however, the grand jury dropped the case, finding insufficient evidence and Valdez was a free man. Valdez, only batting .120 at the time of his arrest, never played in another major league game.

1960 The second Tiger he faced was Neil Chrisley, who doubled off the left-field Wall. After that, Boston's Bill Monbouquette didn't give up another hit and tamed the Tigers, 5–0.

1946 With two runs in the sixth and two more in the seventh, the Sox came from behind to tie St. Louis. The game went on and on until the bottom of the 14th, when Tex Shirley loaded the bases issuing a walk, a single, and an intentional walk. That brought up Leon Culberson, who swung at the first pitch he saw and put it into the left-field screen. It was Boston's 12th win in a row, and they were now 18–3 on the season.

1936 With Wes Ferrell pitching and Rick Ferrell catching, it was Double X (Jimmie Foxx) who was the big story, with two home runs helping deal the 11th straight defeat to the St. Louis Browns. Ferrell was pounded for 11 hits, but threw a complete game 9–6 win. He startled some of the hometown fans who'd been riding him by thumbing his nose at them, a very rude gesture in its day.

1934 The Tigers tied it with three in the top of the ninth, then won in it the 11th as pitcher Schoolboy Rowe, on for five innings of relief, hit a two-run homer over the Green Monster in left field. Boston lost, 8–6.

On the same day, John Kieran ran a story in the *New York Times* reporting that Sox GM Eddie Collins, believing the Red Sox were returning to the days of glory, had presented Postmaster General James A. Farley with designs for two commemorative postal stamps. One featured a tall left-handed figure wearing red socks and the motto "In Grove We Trust." The other showed the "valiant Red Sox conquering the Yankees in the drive for the American League pennant."

1917 It's a pitcher's duel between Boston's Babe Ruth and Washington's Walter Johnson. Johnson only allowed four hits, but Ruth was even stingier, only letting the Nationals get two singles. And it was Ruth's sac fly in the eighth inning that plated the only run of the game. Boston won, 1–0. It's the third time (the others were June 1 and August 15, 1916) that Ruth beat Johnson, 1–0.

1913 Blood was spilled and Tris Speaker was spiked three times in a free-for-all fight after the game, under the Cleveland grandstand. It all sprang out of Bill Carrigan's block of the plate, which nearly knocked Jack Graney unconscious early in the game. Boston won the game, 4–1. Boston's catcher Nunamaker turned up the next day with his eye swollen shut. Not one player spoke to another in the May 8 game, which Cleveland also lost, 3–2. Both clubs were to have been guests at a local theater on the 8th, but the Cleveland contingent declined to attend. Both Nunamaker and Cleveland third baseman Olson were hit with $25 fines for their role in the fray.

1903 The first game ever played between the Boston and New York American League clubs results in a Boston win (in Boston, at the Huntington Avenue Grounds) by the score of 6–2. Big Bill Dinneen beats New York's Hal Wiltse.

TRANSACTIONS
1944: Traded Ford Garrison to the Philadelphia Athletics for Hal Wagner.
1950: Traded Tommy O'Brien and Merl Combs to the Washington Senators for Clyde Vollmer.
1951: Sold Mike Guerra to the Washington Senators.
1958: Sold Bob Porterfield to the Pittsburgh Pirates.
1965: Bill (Rudy) Schlesinger was selected off waivers by the Kansas City Athletics.
1969: Sold Jose Tartabull to the Oakland Athletics.
1993: Signed free agent Steve Lyons.
1996: Signed free agents Reggie Harris and Jeff Manto.
2003: Claimed Bruce Chen off waivers from the Houston Astros.

DEBUTS
1904: Bill O'Neill
1994: Carlos Rodriguez

BIRTHDATES
Case Patten 1876 (1908); Al Papai 1917 (1950);
Dick Williams 1929 (1963–1964, manager 1967–1969)

DEATHS
Red Bluhm 1952; Bing Miller 1966; Marty McHale 1979

May 8

2005 The major league debut of pitcher Cla Meredith could have been worse, but not much worse. With a depleted pitching staff and a dual-admission doubleheader, the Sox called up Meredith and threw him into the seventh inning of a tie game with two outs and a runner on second. Meredith had risen incredibly fast in the Red Sox system, spending all of 72 hours at AAA. He had never given up a home run at any stage in all of his 42 prior pro appearances. He walked the first batter, and the second, then gave up a grand slam to Seattle's Richie Sexson, and gave up a double to straightaway center before finally getting an out on a fly to left-center. The Red Sox got two back, but lost, 6–2.

2004 Pokey Reese hit an inside-the-park home run in the fifth inning and a "conventional" home run in the sixth inning of the game against the Royals. It was only the seventh time in Red Sox history that a player had hit both types of homers in the same game, and the first since Tony Armas did it on September 24, 1983. Buck Freeman, Bill Regan, Jim Tabor, Dick Stuart, and Carl Yastrzemski were the others to pull this off. The Red Sox won, behind Curt Schilling's first complete game in the American League.

1978 The Red Sox were already up 5–4, but KC manager Whitey Herzog didn't want it to get any worse, so he walked Jim Rice intentionally and took his chances bringing in "The Mad Hungarian" Al Hrabosky to face Carl Yastrzemski. It got worse: a three-run homer.

1966 The Red Sox had lost 17 road games in a row against Minnesota, including games on May 6 and 7. Both Earl Wilson and Jose Santiago held the Twins to one run, and the Sox took both games of today's doubleheader, 8–1 and 4–1. Rico Petrocelli hit a grand slam in the first game.

1962 Ted Wills, a pitcher lacking the "iam" in his surname, is sold to Cincinnati. Wills was signed as a free agent by Boston in 1955, but never got much work with the big league club—just 42 innings over four seasons.

1957 Ted Williams hit three homers, all three off Chicago pitcher Bob Keegan, and drove in every run in the Red Sox 4–1 victory. He was walked his last time up. The night before, he'd singled to drive in a run, been walked three times, then hit a two-run homer to knock in three of the four Red Sox runs, that game being a 4–3 Boston win.

1953 For 13 games in a row, the Yankees beat the Red Sox. Boston really wanted this one. Each team scored a run in the second inning, but Skinny Brown shut down New York from that point forward, and Johnny Sain did the same to the Red Sox until Billy Goodman touched him for a walkoff home run in the 11th inning.

1946 Even though Boston pitcher Mickey Harris gave up 17 hits, he still won the game. That was because Boston had built up a 9–0 lead over the first three innings, and then added to it as the game progressed. The final was a 14–10 victory over the White Sox, and the 13th consecutive win for the Red Sox. Shortstop Johnny Pesky scored six times, setting a new American League record for runs scored in a game, and matching Mel Ott's NL mark. Spike Owen tied Pesky's record on August 21, 1986.

1939 Alabaman Lou Finney, a Philly first baseman, in purchased by the Sox and he is reborn, hitting .325 the rest of the season and .320 the following year.

1930 Pitcher Ed Carroll is sent to Newark. In 1929, he had a perfect 1–0 record for the Red Sox, but a 5.61 ERA in 67⅓ innings of work during his only time in major league ball.

1926 A grass fire caught a billboard on fire, and spread to the third base bleachers at Fenway Park, which were almost completely destroyed. Flaming embers threatened the grandstand. Ownership elects not to replace the seats. The Indians beat the Red Sox, 10–4. Glenn Stout has expressed that he believed the fire was deliberately set on the orders of Sox owner Bob Quinn for the insurance proceeds, noting that the very day before there had been three other fires at the ballpark, all doused by fans with buckets of water.

1915 It was, the *New York Times* wrote, "the biggest inning in captivity"—the fourth inning of this day's game at the Polo Grounds. The Yankees sent 16 men to the plate and scored 10 runs. They didn't score a run in any other inning, but had more than enough to beat the Sox, 10–3.

1911 In a game in New York called after six innings, due to rain, Smoky Joe Wood beat the Highlanders, 4–0. The only hit he allowed was a single by NY pitcher Ray Caldwell.

1906 A pitcher, put in as a late-inning defensive replacement, hits two home runs in one game. Entering the game in the sixth inning, Chief Bender had been asked to play left field against Boston, when injuries depleted Connie Mack's bench. The A's pitcher hit two inside-the-park homers, both of them off Boston's Jesse Tannehill, and helped Philadelphia win, 11–4. In 1,147 career at-bats, Bender had six home runs.

1903 It was only the second game—ever—between Boston and the New York franchise and already there was a physical clash when New York's Dave Fultz bowled over pitcher George Winter covering the bag at first, nearly knocking him out. New York beat Boston, 6–1, Jack Chesbro over George Winter. Boston's Hobe Ferris hits a home run for the second day in a row, this time in a losing cause.

1901 In the very first franchise home game, there was an innovation: a megaphone man (Charles Moore) as a public address announcer. Cy Young of Boston beat Bill Bernhard of Philadelphia, 12–4. Buck Freeman was the batting star with a homer, a triple, and a single.

Young led the league in 1901 with a 1.62 ERA, and (as *The Baseball Chronology* points out), his 33 wins are 41.8 percent of his team's 79 victories. A post-1900 record, it will stand until Steve Carlton wins 45.8 percent of the Phils' 59 wins in 1972. The Boston Nationals played on the same day, but the Americans outdrew the Nationals 11,000 to 2,000. Novelty was no doubt a factor, as well as lower ticket prices and the fact that the Americans had poached Jimmy Collins and some of the more popular local players.

TRANSACTIONS
1939: Purchased Lou Finney from the Philadelphia Athletics.
1949: Traded Stan Spence and cash to the St. Louis Browns for Al Zarilla.
1950: Sold Harry Dorish to the St. Louis Browns.
1962: Sold Ted Wills to the Cincinnati Reds.

DEBUTS
1908: Walter Carlisle 1957: Dean Stone
1926: Wally Shaner 1989: Joe Price
1930: Cedric Durst 1999: Juan Pena
1949: Al Zarilla 2005: Cla Meredith, Wade Miller

BIRTHDATES
None yet

DEATHS
Weldon Wyckoff 1961; Frankie Pytlak 1977

May 9

2001 In a game with five hit batsmen, Chris Stynes had the worst injury—a fractured cheekbone which sidelined him for a month and a half. Seattle scored five times in the eighth to double Boston's five runs, and won the game, 10–5.

1989 Rick Cerone dropped a foul ball in the eighth inning. Given new life, Minnesota's catcher Tim Laudner doubled and kicked off a three-run rally that helped the Twins. It was the first error for Cerone after a major league record 159 error-free games, comprising 896 chances.

1968 Washington's Ed Stroud bunted safely off Jerry Stephenson, then stole second. Stephenson might have been a bit rattled; he balked and Stroud strode to third. After inducing a ground out, with Stroud having to hold at third, Stephenson let loose a wild pitch and Stroud scampered home—all the way around the bases without a ball being hit safely more than 15 feet.

1965 Ten double plays in one doubleheader. Cleveland executed five double plays and Boston four; the nine double plays tied an American League record. There was just one double play, by the Red Sox, in the first game of the twin bill. The Indians won both games.

1964 Eddie Bressoud's double extends his hitting streak to 20 games; Steady Eddie hit in every one of the first 20 Sox games of '64, for the longest Sox streak ever.

1953 May 9 was Dom DiMaggio's final ballgame. He popped up in a pinch-hitting role, in a game the Sox lost, 6–4.

1948 Ted Williams hit a homer in each game, but Cleveland's Ken Keltner had three in the doubleheader and the Indians won both games, 4–1 (10 innings) and 9–5.

1946 The streak continued, now 14 wins in a row, as the Sox ran their record to 20–3 with a 7–5 win over the visiting White Sox. Mickey Harris won a game two days in a row, coming on in relief in this day's game.

1943 The Senators swept two from Boston, winning 3–2 in the 10th in the first game, and more handily, 8–2, in the second. The two catchers, Ellis Clary and Johnny Peacock, got into what the *Washington Post* called a "wild-cat melee," a real "snarling, clawing fist fight" in the first game.

1939 The Red Sox are air travel pioneers among ball clubs, chartering airplanes to fly from St. Louis to Chicago.

1938 Eleven hits was plenty, but the 12 bases on balls was the real killer. And Jimmie Foxx hit two home runs, batting in five runs. Jim Bagby won easily, 15–3, over the Indians.

1933 Depending on what use the cash was put to, the Sox came out ahead on a deal with the Browns, getting future Hall of Fame catcher Rick Ferrell and a pitcher named…Brown (Lloyd), in exchange for mediocre catcher Merv Shea and some cash. The A.P. wrote that the deal "generally was believed executed solely because of financial advantages offered the Browns." For the Sox, it was the first major transaction for new owner Tom Yawkey and his GM, Eddie Collins.

1927 Both teams used five pitchers, but the Tigers pounded out 17 runs on 22 hits, outdoing the Red Sox (11 runs on 12 hits). One of Detroit's hits was a homer by pitcher George Smith.

1918 Babe Ruth had a big day batting cleanup, 5-for-5 with 10 total bases—all without benefit of a home run—a single, three doubles, and a triple. He pitched, too, but was not as successful. The Red Sox lost to Washington, 4–3, when the Senators tied the game on a sac fly in the bottom of the ninth and won it on a sac fly in bottom of the 10th. No pitcher has ever had six hits in a major league game.

1916 Oops, wrong dugout. Tris Speaker had only ever played for the Red Sox, nine years in all, but this was his first visit to Boston as a Cleveland Indian. Speaker was cheered every time up, and no doubt felt quite at home, so it was perhaps not surprising that after one inning, he mistakenly went to the wrong dugout. Dutch Leonard beat Cleveland, 5–1.

1910 Six New York errors and some pretty poor pitching let the Red Sox beat the Yankees, 10–0.

1903 Unruly New York Players Out of the Game and Boston Won—so read the headline in the *New York Times*. Jesse Tannehill, pitcher for the brand-new franchise known as the Greater New Yorks, had the game under control and a 2–0 lead but was incensed when umpire Caruthers called a pitch a ball and then Chick Stahl doubled on the next pitch. Tannehill couldn't hold his tongue, but second baseman Jimmy Williams went even further and "assaulted the umpire." Both were ejected. Boston took advantage of Harry Howell, and Boston piled up a 12–5 win.

TRANSACTIONS
1932: Traded Merv Shea and cash to the St. Louis Browns for Rick Ferrell and Lloyd Brown.

DEBUTS
1925: Ray Francis, Paul Zahniser 1965: Jerry Moses
1927: Herb Bradley, John Wilson 1996: Brent Knackert
1959: Billy Hoeft 2000: Tim Young

BIRTHDATES
Buck O'Brien 1882 (1911–1913); Mickey Devine 1892 (1920); Paul Hinson 1904 (1928); Billy Jurges 1908 (1959–1960); Floyd Robinson 1936 (1968); Ron Jackson 1953 (2004–2005)

DEATHS
John Smith 1982; Ralph Brickner 1994

May 10

1999 It was a grand day for Nomar Garciaparra as he hit a grand slam in the first, a two-run homer in the third, and another grand slam in the fifth. Boston beat the Mariners, 12–4, and Nomar had 10 RBIs. Jim Tabor was the last to hit two grand slams in the same game for the Red Sox, back in 1939. Bill Mueller would do it next on July 29, 2003.

1997 Sox spectators were displeased when Texas overcame a 5–2 deficit with three runs in the seventh. Heathcliff Slocumb couldn't get an out in the ninth, giving up a grand slam to Juan Gonzalez, and keying an 11–5 defeat for the Red Sox.

1996 The V boys each homer (Mo Vaughn in the third and John Valentin to tie the game, 5–5, in the top of the ninth), but it was Troy O'Leary's homer in the 11th that wins the game at Skydome, 6–4. Tom Gordon started and struck out 12 Blue Jays; Mike Stanton and game-winner Heathcliff Slocumb K'd five more.

1979 The Angels won the game, 5–3, but at least the Red Sox enjoyed a triple play. After Rod Carew singled, leading off the seventh, Baylor singled, too. Then Joe Rudi hit into a 4-6-3 triple play to end the threat of further scoring.

1965 Yaz 3, Mantle 2. Mickey Mantle, out of action for about a week, returned to action with a vengeance and singled, doubled, and homered against the Sox at Fenway Park, accounting for two runs. But Carl Yastrzemski hit a run-scoring sac fly in the first, then banged out two home runs, accounting for all of Boston's runs in the 3–2 victory for Jim Lonborg, his first in the major leagues.

1961 Three Los Angeles Angels pitchers struck out 17 Sox but Boston beat them nonetheless, 3–2, when Chuck Schilling's RBI single and Yaz's two-run HR in the sixth put an end to Ron Moeller's five-inning no-hitter.

1960 Grand slams by two teammates—Vic Wertz and Eldon John "Rip" Repulski— win a 9–7 game for the Red Sox. It was Repulski's first at-bat in the American League after spending parts of seven seasons in the senior circuit. His eighth-inning slam won it for the Sox.

1953 Del Wilber pinch-hit a home run for the second straight at-bat (he'd also done it
?! on May 6), but it was in a losing battle against the Yankees, 7–4. When umpire Jim Duffy called Mickey Mantle safe at first on a play in the first, Sox second sacker Billy Goodman protested with such animation that—of all people—center fielder Jimmy Piersall had to physically restrain him. Goodman twisted and turned in Piersall's grip and strained some rib cartilage in the process, keeping him out of action for three weeks. (See also May 21.)

After the game there was another confrontation, when (in the words of the *Boston Globe*'s Harold Kaese), Sox pitcher Mickey McDermott "provoked a brief but angry fight with our colleague Bob Holbrook in the clubhouse." According to McDermott, in his autobiography *A Funny Thing Happened on the Way to Cooperstown*, when he struck Holbrook, Ted Williams applauded, saying, "Way to go. You're the first player to pop a writer in 20 years."

1952 The Yankees beat the Red Sox, 18–3, but it's a costly win as four Yanks go down with injuries: pitcher Tom Morgan (torn fingernail), Johnny Mize (bruised toe in batting practice), Joe Collins (charley horse), and Bob Cerv (bruised badly crashing into the left-field wall, trying in vain to prevent Mickey McDermott's three-run homer). The Sox dodged a few bullets in the sixth inning, throwing out three runners at the plate, but New York scored 11 times in the seventh.

1946 Another day, another win. More than 64,000 fans were present for Ladies' Day at Yankee Stadium, and Joe DiMaggio hit a grand slam in the fifth with nobody out, and starter Joe Dobson was shown to the showers. But Earl Johnson pitched four innings of scoreless relief and Rudy York's triple and Dom DiMaggio's single bumped the Sox up to a 5–4 win. The run of 15 straight victories constitutes the longest winning streak in more than a century of Red Sox baseball. The Sox streak was snapped the next day by New York's 2–0 win.

1935 Gordon "Dusty" Rhodes held the White Sox scoreless into the seventh, and won easily, 12–2, for his first decision of the year. He then lost his next 10 in a row, before finally winning one more on September 24. In 1936, he was pitching for another team.

1916 Tris Speaker vs. Babe Ruth. Now that Speaker was with the Indians, Ruth had to pitch to him. Scoring three runs, on two hits, Speaker led Cleveland to victory over the Red Sox, 6–2.

TRANSACTIONS
1955: Sold Hersh Freeman to the Cincinnati Redlegs.
1979: Released Luis Aponte.

DEBUTS
1925: Al Stokes

1937: Gene Desautels

1944: Hal Wagner

1960: Rip Repulski

1980: Keith MacWhorter

1994: Gar Finnvold

1998: Lou Merloni

BIRTHDATES
Ed Barrow 1868 (manager, 1918–1920); Ray Jarvis 1946 (1918–1920); Pete Schourek 1969 (1969–1970); Marino Santana 1972 (1998–2001)

DEATHS
Vic Johnson 2005

May 11

2005 For the second day in a row, the Red Sox entered the bottom of the ninth inning trailing by one. Within 18 hours (a night game followed by a day game), Oakland reliever Octavio Dotel walked David Ortiz in the ninth both on May 10 and May 11. Both times there was one out, and both times on a 1–1 count, Dotel served up a fastball that was hit out for a two-run walkoff home run. May 10's walkoff was hit by Kevin Millar; May 11's was hit by Jason Varitek. The only other time the Sox had won back-to-back on walkoff homers was in 1935, on July 21 and 22.

2004 When the Red Sox ran onto the field to take their positions and start the game, the first one out of the dugout was Manny Ramirez, waving a small American flag. He had become a naturalized American citizen in ceremonies in Miami on May 10. When he came up to bat, the team played the song "Proud To Be an American" and he received a standing ovation.

2002 During just the second inning of a game against the Mariners, third base coach Mike Cubbage waved Manny Ramirez around third base and too aggressively sent him home. Manny slid hard and headfirst into home plate trying to score on Shea Hillenbrand's double; there were no outs at the time. Manny fractured a finger and was out until June 25.

1981 It was the Allenson–Miller show. Gary Allenson drove in five runs, including the ninth-inning game-winner, but Rick Miller went 5-for-5 and tied a major league record with four doubles in the game. The Red Sox beat the Blue Jays, 7–6, when Miller doubled in the ninth and Allenson doubled him home with the tie-breaker.

1978 Subpar O's fielding, their failure to drive in runs with the bases-loaded, and Jim Rice's 11th homer all helped Bill Lee improve his record to 5–0 with a last-minute 5–4 win over Baltimore.

1970 Red Sox pitcher Ray Culp struck out the side in the first and again in the second, tying an American League record, but falling short of the ideal: 27 straight strikeouts. He threw seven innings, letting up just one run, and the game ran deep into extra innings until the Angels won it in the bottom of the 16th, 2–1.

1969 Despite an upset stomach due to Mexican food the night before, Rico Petrocelli hit two two-run homers to help give Sonny Siebert a 7–3 win over the California Angels. In the second inning, Siebert retired the side with just three pitches, perhaps the only time a Red Sox pitcher had ever accomplished the feat.

1953 Three swings, three home runs. It was just an exhibition game against the New
STVT York Giants in New York, but Del Wilber swing at the first pitch and hit it to the roof of the third deck in left field. The last two pitches he'd seen—one from Billy Pierce of Chicago and one from Vic Raschi of the Yankees—had both been hit out, too.

1950 The Sox were losing to the Tigers 13–0 when Ted Williams hit a grand slam in the eighth. In the second game of the day's doubleheader, Williams let a ball get through him, and three runs scored, providing the margin of victory in the 5–3 Detroit win. After an error in the first game, Ted made what the AP termed "a two-handed gesture…which some fans construed as insulting." After the second game error, resulting in three runs, "the boos were deafening" resulting in "a new gesture, thrice repeated toward different sections." The headline provided a better hint, terming Terrible Ted's gesture as a "finger salute." Ted apologized the next day.

Tom Yawkey further cements his reputation among players when he gives Chuck Koney a five-year contract. Koney was a prospect playing for the team's Louisville farm club when he lost his leg in an accident at home. Koney scouted for the Sox for years and in 1992 was named Midwest Scout of the Year by the Scout of the Year Foundation.

Denny Galehouse is let go, after just two innings of work in 1950.

1946 All good things come to an end. After 15 consecutive wins, the Red Sox lost, 2–0, as New York's Tiny Bonham shut out Boston. With Boston now 21–4 on the season, Boston sportswriter Dave Egan found a way to fan the flames of negativity: he blamed the loss on Ted Williams for taking a called third strike with two men on base and for misplaying a ball in the field (it was not ruled an error). Small wonder Williams disliked the "knights of the keyboard."

1930 Though he walked seven, Big Ed Morris threw a two-hitter the day after Milt Gaston had limited the same St. Louis Browns team to just a pair of hits. Regan's sixth-inning solo homer was the winning run in a 2–1 squeaker.

1917 A taste of his own medicine? Babe Ruth went to 7–0 on the young season with a 2–1 win over Detroit. Ty Cobb bunted safely to lead off the bottom of the ninth, then tried to go first-to-third on a grounder to third, but was tagged out so hard by Ruth, covering the bag at third, that he was down for a couple of minutes.

1904 Continuing his string of no-hit innings, which embraced his perfect game, Cy Young started the day's game against Detroit with six more no-hit frames. Finally, with one out in the seventh, Young falters and gives up a single to Sam Crawford. The streak had run to 24⅓ innings, a full 76 batters in a row who'd failed to get a hit. Crawford's hit doesn't shake Cy Young; he throws a 15-inning shutout! By the time he finally lets up a run, he'd thrown 45 scoreless innings. Over sixty years later, in 1968, Don Drysdale threw 58 shutout innings.

TRANSACTIONS
1911: Sold Frank Smith to the Cincinnati Reds, and Hap Myers to the St. Louis Browns.
1955: Released Hal Brown.
1956: Sold Grady Hatton to the St. Louis Cardinals.

DEBUTS
1933: Rick Ferrell
1939: Lou Finney
1945: Red Steiner
1950: Bob Gillespie, Clyde Vollmer
1969: Don Lock
1994: Andy Tomberlin
2003: Bruce Chen

BIRTHDATES
Jeff Sellers 1964 (1985–1988)

DEATHS
None yet

May 12

2001 He sneezed getting out of his car and hurt his back, but the Red Sox trainers worked wonders and Pedro Martinez struck out 12 and walked one, in seven innings. He allowed three earned runs (all on a Jason Giambi home run), but had strong Sox support with 19 hits and nine Red Sox runs. Trot Nixon was 4-for-5 from the leadoff spot, with a homer. Boston 9, Oakland 3.

1999 PEDRO PONCHA 15 MAS, wrote Tito Stevens in the *Boston Globe*. The newspaper always ran a Spanish-language story detailing Señor Martinez's starts. Seattle batters struck out 15 times—Pedro faced 29 batters in eight innings and threw 26 first-pitch strikes. It was the second game in a row in which he struck out 15 opponents. He'd done it on May 7 against the Angels. It was, at the time, his career high. Nomar Garciaparra was 4-for-5, with two doubles and three RBIs.

1991 The street signs get stolen time after time, but the Red Sox honored Ted Williams on the 50th anniversary of his great 1941 season, renaming Lansdowne Street as "Ted Williams Way." Ted tipped his cap to the fans, removing it from his back pocket where he'd tucked it away, saying, "Today I tip my cap to all the fans of New England—the greatest sports fans on Earth."

1979 Six doubles, two homers, and a 5-for-5 game by Jerry Remy help key a Mike Torrez 4–1 complete game over Oakland.

1964 After several ailments over the years, including a collapsed lung, this year serious ulcer problems compel talented outfielder Gary Geiger to retire. He returns in 1965 and fractures his skull. From 1966 on, he plays in the National League.

1963 The one hit he gave up was a home run by Chuck Hinton in the first inning, but that was all Dave Morehead allowed as Boston beat Washington, 4–1. Washington had won the first game on a 14th-inning homer by Don Lock, 3–2.

1961 Seventeen strikeouts by Bill Monbouquette set a new Red Sox team record, two more than Smoky Joe Wood's 15 K's a half-century earlier in 1911. The 17 established a league record for a night game, and Monbo lost his shot at tying the major league record when catcher Jim Pagliaroni dropped a foul tip for what would have been strike three. Washington's Peter Burnside only gave up two hits to the Bosox but lost, 2–1. Washington would have tied it, save for a great game-ending catch by Jackie Jensen.

1959 Ted Williams had a terrible year in 1959. He suffered a pinched-nerve in his neck during spring training, and didn't get into a game until this day. Ted went 0-for-5, and Chicago beat Boston, 4–2 (in 12 innings). He hit .254 for the year, a full 62 points below any other year's total in all his 19 seasons.

1958 The lights went out in Griffith Stadium, but power was restored and Jimmy Piersall couldn't blame darkness for the ball that bounced off his glove and into the stands in the bottom of the seventh, giving Neil Chrisley a homer and the Senators the final two runs of a 5–4 win.

1953 Those walks will come back to haunt you. In the top of the 10th inning, Ellis Kinder (who'd beaten the White Sox 18 times in a row—he hadn't lost to Chicago since July 22, 1948), walked two batters, and both scored. When the Sox couldn't match the two runs, they lost, 9–7.

"The Little Professor" retired, after just three pinch-hitting appearances (one single) in 1953. Dom DiMaggio had long maintained that when he was unable to play his regular position in center field, he would retire. When manager Lou Boudreau sat him out in favor of Tom Umphlett, Dom went to GM Cronin and asked to be traded or released. Cronin declined, so DiMaggio retired. He said he would have kept playing if he'd been traded or cut loose.

1951 Washington beat Boston, 5–4, but Dom DiMaggio had three hits, kicking off a 27-game hitting streak.

1950 The Red Sox front office issued a statement saying that Ted Williams apologized to Boston fans for "insulting gestures" which he offered in three directions to fans who booed after his two errors in the May 11 doubleheader against Detroit. Boston lost both games and Ted's error let the Tigers score what proved the second game's winning run.

1948 Ed Walton reports that station WBZ tries out televison cameras for the first time at Fenway Park. Was anyone watching? The station today has no records indicating its first broadcast.

1946 The largest crowd in Yankee Stadium history, and the second-largest in major league history (69,401—68,193 of whom paid) saw Spud Chandler hold the Sox to three hits. Trouble is, Mickey Harris held the Yanks to three hits, and New York committed three errors, permitting two unearned runs. Boston won, 3–1.

1941 Love that home cooking. Five runs in the first inning was all it took. Lefty Grove (BOS) out-pitched Lefty Gomez (NY), 6–4. It was Grove's 20th consecutive win at friendly Fenway Park. In the fifth inning, Boston's Johnny Peacock bunted to third, successfully sacrificing Jim Tabor to second. Tabor saw that third baseman Red Rolfe was nowhere near third, so he motored on to try and take an extra base, but was thrown out because alert Yankees catcher Buddy Rosar ran to third to take the throw.

1933 New Boston owner Tom Yawkey purchases infielder Billy Werber and pitcher George Pipgras from the Yankees for an even $100,000. Though a huge sum of money, Spink of *The Sporting News* said that Jacob Ruppert, flush with beer revenues now that Prohibition was over, didn't need the cash and congratulated Ruppert on his generosity helping out the Red Sox. "Ruppert really wanted to help Boston, for Boston had helped him so often." (*The Sporting News*, May 25) Really. He wrote that, and not tongue-in-cheek. Spink credited himself, too, pointing out that not long before he had written urging other teams, and the Yankees in particular, to help out the cellar-dwelling Sox.

1925 Even though first baseman Phil Todt went 4-for-4 (with 3 doubles), the Indians beat Boston, 9–4. Reportedly at one point in 1925, the Yankees offered a prospect named Lou Gehrig for Todt, but the Red Sox declined.

1920 Catcher Wally Schang, back on board (see May 5), had an astonishing eight assists in the game against Cleveland (one of which was as the middle man on a 1-2-3 double play), but Boston still lost 9–7.

TRANSACTIONS
1933: Purchased George Pipgras and Billy Werber from the New York Yankees.
1952: Purchased Del Wilber from the Philadelphia Phillies.
1953: Purchased Floyd Baker from the Washington Senators.
1954: Purchased Don Lenhardt from the Baltimore Orioles.
1958: George Susce was selected by the Detroit Tigers off waivers.
1966: Purchased Syd O'Brien from the Kansas City Athletics.
1980: Received Jack Billingham from the Detroit Tigers as part of a conditional deal.
1997: Acquired Toby Borland from the New York Mets in trade for Ricky Trlicek.

DEBUTS
1903: Aleck Smith
1911: Joe Riggert
1923: Ira Flagstead

BIRTHDATES
Casey Hageman 1887 (1911–1912); Hob Hiller 1893 (1920); Joe Dugan 1897 (1922); Archie McKain 1911 (1937–1938); Tom Umphlett 1930 (1953); Bob Heise 1947 (1975–1976)

DEATHS
Heinie Manush 1971

May 13

1991 Steve Lyons pulls off the hidden ball trick, getting Chicago's Ozzie Guillen in the fourth inning. But wait, that's not all. Lyons also stole a base, muffed a play, and drove in the tying run in the seventh. And that's not to mention the third inning, when Ellis Burks was at bat, the Sox down 2–0 and the count 2–2. It was 8:45 P.M. Then the lights went out in a power outage that last 59 minutes, due to a blown manhole cover on Comm. Ave. Backup systems provided meager lighting in the seating areas, but most of the park was dark, illuminated by lighters and flashbulbs. Sherm Feller, public address announcer, led the fans singing "Take Me Out to the Ballgame" and did his best to entertain those fans who could hear him in a vaudeville-type routine. Sox historians said that people had hardly noticed Fenway's last power failure because it was during a day game in April

1981. The Sox could have used a bit more power in the game, which they lost in 10 innings, 4–3.

1980 Fred Lynn doubled, homered, singled, and then tripled—hitting for the cycle as the Sox doubled up the Twins, 10–5.

1967 The Sox led the Tigers, 5–4, after seven innings at Fenway. Moose Korince came in to throw the eighth, the fourth pitcher of the day for Detroit. He walked one, but allowed neither hits nor runs. Then the Tigers mauled John Wyatt, scoring six runs in the top of the ninth. Pitcher Earl Wilson pinch-hit for Wyatt, homering for the fourth and fifth runs of the frame. Dave Wickersham took over mound duties, and the Sox surged back for three hits and three runs, but finally retired the side, preserving the win for Korince and preserving the Ottawa-born right-hander's claim to be the only undefeated Canadian pitcher in major league history. His record remains: 1–0.

1950 The first African American player the Red Sox ever signed was Piper Davis, who was assigned to the Scranton PA team. Had he stuck with the team until May 15, he would have been due an additional $7,500. Howard Bryant writes in *Shut Out*, "On May 13, with Davis leading the club in home runs, batting average, RBI, and stolen bases, manager Jack Burns told Davis the club was releasing him from his contract." Burns was apparently incensed about it, but powerless, says historian Jules Tygiel. Davis told Peter Golenbock, "Tom Yawkey had as much money as anyone on the East Coast. I don't talk about it that much. It wouldn't help. Sometimes I just sit here and a tear drops from my eye. I wonder why it all had to happen, why we have to have so much hate."

Birdie Tebbetts plays in his 1,000th game in the American League.

1948 Tex Hughson heads to Texas, to pitch for Austin, in hopes that the warm weather will help him overcome the soreness that has plagued him.

1947 Before the game, Ted Williams and Joe Dobson visited Glenny Brann, an 11-year-old boy who was in Malden Hospital, having both legs amputated after he was "burned at the stake" by playmates. The boy asked Ted to hit a home run for him. "I'll try, Glenny, and if I do you'll know I hit it for you," Ted told the kid. Ted hadn't hit a home run in Boston yet in 1947, but today he not only hit one homer, he hit two—both of them to left field. The Sox won, 19–6, helped in part by Bobby Doerr's second cycle. Doerr's single and double both came in the same inning—the eighth—as Ted's second homer.

1945 Boo Ferriss broke into the majors throwing 22 consecutive shutout innings before the Tigers scratched a run out of him in the fifth inning of today's game, which the Red Sox won, 8–2. He shut out the White Sox in his next start on May 18 and shut them out again on May 27. In between, he let the Browns have one run. By the first of June, the rookie was 6–0, only having yielded three runs over the six games. Rudy York managed one hit off Ferriss, but struck out the other four times—every one of them on a called third strike.

1934 Chicago's Milt Gaston walked the first three Red Sox batters he faced in the bottom of the second inning, and then Bucky Walters put the bat on the ball for a grand slam. After you, Gaston, said Chicago manager Dykes, showing him the door. Reliever Joe Heving retired the Red Sox in the second, but in the third inning gave up two singles, a walk, and a grand slam to Eddie Morgan. Bucky banged out a two-run homer in the seventh, too, and the Red Sox won, 14–2.

1912 A Western Union telegraph operator named Lou Proctor inserted his name as a pinch-hitter into the Browns–Red Sox box score (no at-bat, but Proctor did credit himself with a walk). *The Sporting News* published the box score and, years later, Proctor's name was dutifully included in the first editions of *The Baseball Encyclopedia* before the mistake was found and rectified. (Thanks to Jim Charlton and Lyle Spatz for help with this entry.)

1911 In Detroit, Ed "Loose" Karger, pitching for the Sox, is touched by Ty Cobb for a third inning grand slam, the first of Cobb's career. The game looks pretty hopeless, with the Tigers on top by 10–1 after five. After eight innings, it's 10–4 and Boston scores seven times—the big blow is Duffy Lewis's grand slam. The Tigers scored once in the bottom of the ninth, but Boston gets two more in the 10th, and wins it, 13–11.

1909 The Red Sox beat up on their former star pitcher, Cy Young, who threw a complete game despite being pounded for 17 hits and eight runs. His fellow Clevelanders let him down, with four errors committed behind him. Harry Hooper had four hits. The only Sox player without a hit was the pitcher, Cy Morgan, who threw a five-hit 8–1 victory.

1906 Sound familiar? They were the highest-paid club in baseball. As fans asked, "What's the matter with the Boston Americans?" a sign was placed on the clubhouse door reading "Positively no admittance. This means you."

1904 A group of firemen traveled from Reading, Pennsylvania to Pittsburgh to catch a Pirates game against Brooklyn, and they hired a band to march into the ballpark with them. A clever Brooklyn fan passed the unsuspecting bandleader a request to play a tune called "Tessie," and he was only too glad to accommodate. The first few notes ignited an immediate outburst of angry shouts of "Kill them!" and "Throw them out!" Some bleacherites left their seats and began to approach the band in a threatening manner before the band grasped that the musical selection somehow affected the crowd as a red flag affects a bull, and stopped in mid-performance. Brooklyn won, 2–0.

1901 Hobe Ferris made a team-record 10 putouts at second base. Max Bishop tied the mark on April 30, 1934.

TRANSACTIONS
1914: Sold Les Nunamaker to the New York Yankees.
1957: Released Russ Meyer.

DEBUTS
1911: Jack Killilay
1952: Del Wilber
1994: Chris Howard
1997: Toby Borland

BIRTHDATES
Larry Gardner 1886 (1908–1917); Hal Neubauer 1902 (1925); Boze Berger 1910 (1939); Lou Stringer 1917 (1948–1950); Bob Smith 1927 (1958); Billy Macleod 1942 (1962); Terry Hughes 1949 (1974); Juan Beniquez 1950 (1971–1975)

DEATHS
Urbane Pickering 1970

May 14

1996 Weren't baseball games supposed to be *nine* innings long? On May 11, the
STVT Sox beat the Blue Jays, 6–5 in 11 innings. On May 12, they lost, 9–8, also
in 11 innings. On May 13, they lost again, 8–7, this game going 10 innings.
And on May 14, for the fourth extra-inning game in a row—this time against
California—they won, 4–3, in 12 innings. On the 15th, they won 17–6 in a game
that was nowhere near tied after nine. But on the 16th and 17th, they again
played extra inning games, beating Oakland 5–3 (11 innings) and losing 6–5 to
Oakland (10 innings).

1986 Bill Buckner singled in the go-ahead run and the Red Sox scored three times in
the top of the ninth to beat the Angels, 8–5. Reggie Jackson hits home run #537
off Roger Clemens, passing Mickey Mantle on the all-time homer list.

1983 The Milwaukee Brewers tied it with two in the bottom of the ninth, thanks to
Ben Oglivie's third home run of the game (for five RBIs). Boston scored once in
the top of the 10th, but the Brewers came back with two in the bottom of the
10th, for an 8–7 win.

1967 Since Boston and Philadelphia slugged out 27 extra-base hits in a 1905
doubleheader, that total had stood as a league record. Detroit and Boston
combined for 50 hits, 28 of them extra-base hits, as the Red Sox beat the Tigers,
8–5 and 13–9.

1965 Yaz hit for the cycle, with a second home run as a bonus, but the eight Red
Sox runs weren't enough, as the game went into extra innings and Dick Radatz
uncustomarily gave up four runs to the Tigers and went down to defeat, 12–8.
Willie Horton hit two homers, too, for the second game in row.

1961 Washington took two from the Red Sox, 3–0 and 2–1. The score was tied 1–1
in the first game when Pete Daley tripled to lead off the ninth for the Senators.
Dale Long pinch-hit, but was walked intentionally. Billy Klaus pinch-hit and
was deliberately walked. Danny O'Connell bunted and fouled out. Throwing
two IBB's may have caused Mike Fornelies to lose track of the strike zone and he
quite unintentionally walked Marty Keough, the third pinch-hitter of the inning,
forcing in the winning run.

1946 The Red Sox won 17 out of 18 games, taking this one, 3–0, behind a Boo Ferriss
two-hitter. He wasn't on any pitch count, but it only took him 78 pitches to
dispatch the White Sox.

1940 The Red Sox blew a 4–0 lead, but Jimmie Foxx hit two home runs, including a
massive 10th inning homer that went clear over Comiskey Park's left-field roof.
Foxx's second homer won it, 7–6.

1922 Jack Quinn, born John Picus, whitewashed the White Sox, 12–0. Quinn, or Picus
(or maybe Pajkosz, said John Kieran of the *New York Times*), was listed in the
record book as 38, but admitted he was really 43. He pitched for a number of
teams over 23 years, finally retiring at an age that may or may not have been 50.
Kieran wrote that "the old spitball pitcher promised to give his right name and
his right age when he came to the end of his big league career, but apparently he
forgot his promise."

1919 Eddie Cicotte beat Carl Mays, 1–0, holding the Red Sox to four hits. The White Sox got five, with a Shoeless Joe Jackson double in the sixth (after a Red Sox error) scoring the only run of the game.

1914 Joseph Lannin bought out all the common stock holdings of the Taylor family, and became the sole owner of the Boston Red Sox.

1905 No, the Red Sox have never played a regularly scheduled game in Dayton, Ohio. The game scheduled for May 14, 1905 (transferred from Detroit to avoid conflict with a "race meeting") was rained out.

TRANSACTIONS
1934: Joe Judge was given his unconditional release.
1947: Sold Tom McBride to the Washington Senators.
1956: Sold Johnny Schmitz to the Baltimore Orioles.

DEBUTS
1910: Clyde Engle   1995: Zane Smith
1933: Billy Werber   2002: Bry Nelson
1953: Floyd Baker   2003: Robert Person

BIRTHDATES
Les Moss 1925 (1951); Tony Perez 1942 (1980–1982)

DEATHS
Lou Criger 1934; Frank O'Rourke 1986

May 15

2004 Kevin Youkilis had to leave the country to make his major league debut, flying into Toronto, but went 2-for-4 with an RBI (his fourth-inning home run) in a 4–0 Red Sox win.

2003 Some 33,801 attended Fenway Park—a sold-out house. They saw the Sox (and Pedro Martinez) beat the Texas Rangers, 12–3. It was the first sellout of a stretch that has continued without a break through the 2005 season, becoming the second-longest stretch of sold-out games in major league history on August 28, 2005 when the Fenway streak reached 204 games. That topped the Colorado Rockies' 203-game streak. (Cleveland's Jacobs Field holds the record, with 455 straight sold-out games from 1995 to early 2001.) On May 14, Fenway wasn't quite sold out: the figure was 32,485.

1999 The Red Sox announced grand plans for a new $545 million ballpark, to be built adjacent to the current Fenway Park and retain the same name. It would in many ways replicate the existing park, with a Green Monster and the same manual scoreboard moved to the new park. The Pesky Pole and other aspects of the Fenway field would be replicated. In effect, it would be a modern Fenway across the street from the old one, but seating 45,000 fans, and be newly constructed with additional luxury boxes for additional revenue. Preservationists asked, why have an ersatz Fenway next door when we already have the real thing? Would the Battle Green in Lexington be better across the street from the authentic one?

The issue was joined, with the Red Sox and much of the sports-oriented media on one side and a number of preservationist groups, including Save Fenway Park! on the other. (See also July 6, 1999.)

1998 Lou Merloni hit a home run in his first-ever Fenway Park at-bat. The second-inning solo home run off Jose Rosado was part of a five-run Red Sox rally that carried them to a 5–2 win over the Royals.

1996 Mo Vaughn homered twice and Troy O'Leary doubled thrice. The Red Sox scored in every inning but the eighth (winning 17–6, they didn't have to bat in the bottom of the ninth).

1991 Chicago took a 5–0 lead, but Boston fought back and ultimately won, 9–6. It took them a long time, though; the nine-inning game lasted four hours and 11 minutes, eclipsing the previous major-league record of 4:02.

1951 The American League's 50th anniversary was celebrated when Boston invited Harry Gleason, Charlie Hemphill, Fred Mitchell, Freddy Parent, and Cy Young from the original 1901 Boston Americans to ceremonies at Fenway Park. Another two dozen old-timers from other teams joined the festivities, driven onto the field in vintage automobiles.

 The game itself pitted the White Sox against the Red Sox, and featured Ted Williams' 300th career home run in the fourth inning. When Ted came up again in the eighth, manager Paul Richards moved his reliever, Harry Dorish, to third base and brought in lefty Billy Pierce to face Williams. Ted popped up and then Dorish, as one account put it, "relieved himself" on the mound, while Pierce took a seat in the dugout and Floyd Baker went to third. Interesting managerial moves, though one can't help but wonder about the image of Dorish relieving himself on the mound in front of all those fans and the old-timers, too. Nellie Fox's 11th-inning homer won the game, 9–7, and Dorish got the win.

1946 Here it was, May 15, before the Sox lost the fifth game of the season. Tex Hughson dropped a 3–2 loss in Chicago, but the Red Sox record was still a gaudy 23–5. They wouldn't lose their 10th game of the year until June 12.

1928 Former owner Joseph Lannin, who signed Babe Ruth to the Red Sox, fell from the ninth-floor window of a room he was said to be inspecting at Brooklyn's Hotel Granada, one of several properties he owned. He had suffered a number of heart attacks, but the former hotel bellhop had a net worth believed in excess of $7 million, making foul play a distinct possibility. The window he fell through was only 15 inches wide, but his attorney said he believed the death was accidental.

1923 The May 15 issue of *Library Life* announced that McGreevy's barroom was to be transformed into a Reading Room of the Boston Public Library. McGreevy presented a large number of photographs to the library. The April 28 *Boston Traveler* shows before and after photos of the saloon and the reading room.

1919 Babe Ruth wasn't due to appear in the game either as a hitter or a pitcher, but Joe Bush had to leave the game after one inning of no-hit ball, and Babe was brought on in relief. He was far from his best, allowing 13 hits and eight walks, but he labored through 11 innings of relief and held on to see the Red Sox beat the White Sox, 6–5, in 12 innings. He was 0-for-4 at the plate. See July 27, 1901 for the other Boston moundsman who threw 11 innings in relief.

1917 Though Dutch Leonard had to step in and pitch 3⅔ innings of relief, the Sox held on to beat Cleveland, 6–5, and give Babe Ruth his eighth win in a row.

1912 The Red Sox win a tight one, 2–1, putting across the winning run in the bottom of the ninth. Smoky Joe Wood was busy after the pitch, too, making five putouts.

1906 After Boston scored four runs to tie the game in the bottom of the fourth, an enthusiastic fan pulled the fire alarm. Within a minute, several pieces of fire-fighting apparatus appeared on the scene of the false alarm. One fan, recognizing the team's 6–18 record on the season, called out, "Don't worry; it isn't likely to happen often." By game's end, the record stood 6–19 and they lost their next eight games, too.

1903 Tom Hughes pitched a complete game, despite yielding 15 hits (including two homers and five triples) for 32 total bases. Patsy Dougherty had a rough day in the outfield, misjudging fly balls, as Detroit wins, 8–6.

1901 The first shutout in American League history unfortunately saw Boston on the short end, as Watty Lee of Washington beat Nig Cuppy, 4–0. Boston batters had just three hits.

TRANSACTIONS
1934: Traded Freddie Muller and $20,000 cash to the New York Yankees for Lyn Lary.
2004: Acquired Henri Stanley from the San Diego Padres for cash consideration.

DEBUTS
1951: Bill Evans
1960: Tom Borland
1980: Jack Billingham
1984: Roger Clemens
2004: Kevin Youkilis

BIRTHDATES
Steve Yerkes 1888 (1909–1914); Howie Storie 1911 (1931–1932); Steve Woodard 1975 (2003)

DEATHS
Johnny Gooch 1975

May 16

1970 Tied 2–2 in the bottom of the eighth, Carl Yastrzemski hit one of the longest home runs ever hit at Fenway Park. He pounded Dean Chance's pitch completely out of the ballpark over the center field wall to the right of the flagpole. Ray Culp got the 6–2 win over the Indians.

1969 Eleven runs in the 11th inning! It was 4–4 after nine, but reliever Vicente Romo allowed the Seattle Pilots to hit three homers and amass six runs in the top of the 11th. Fans who didn't slip out of Fenway in disgust saw their team battle back with five of their own until Yaz struck out to end the threat. Final score, 10–9.

1965 Earl Wilson shut out the Tigers, and Yaz drove in three runs in the second game, as the Sox took two from the Tigers, 5–0 and 4–3. Yaz wound up in the hospital, though, when he slammed too hard into second baseman Jake Wood trying to break up a double play. Not before he'd homered, though, in the third inning, followed back-to-back by Tony Conigliaro. The Yastrzemski–Congiliaro back-to-back surname combo ran 21 letters long, a major league record until Juan Encarnacion and Frank Catalanotto topped it with 22 on September 25, 1998.

1964 Idling at shortstop, Eddie Bressoud sits through an entire 10-inning game without recording a single assist or putout. He didn't even make an error. But he did hit a double and a homer, going 2-for-5. Singles by Russ Nixon, Dick Stuart, and pinch-hitter Dick Williams tied the game in the bottom of the ninth, and reliever Dick Radatz came through with a monstrous bases-loaded single to drive in the winning run in the bottom of the 10th.

1954 It was Ted Williams' first start since his collarbone was broken, and he had a metal pin holding his shoulder together, which hurt "like hell every time I swing." Ted singled three times in the first game, then hit two singles, a double, and two homers in the second. Ted went 8-for-9 with seven RBIs against the Tigers. Boston lost both games by one run, 7–6 in the first, and 9–8 (in 14 innings) in the second. Yankees manager Casey Stengel wondered out loud about maybe getting pins inserted in the shoulders of all his batters.

1949 With two outs in the top of the ninth, and the Senators up 3–2, two singles saw the Sox with men on first and second. To put in more speed, Joe McCarthy asked Lou Stringer to pinch-run for Tebbetts at first base. Sam Mele pinch-hit for Jack Kramer and singled to Buddy Lewis in right field. Lewis fired the ball to second in time to nab Stringer, who had overrun second base—a moment before O'Brien crossed the plate with what should have been the tying run. Game over.

1943 Albert Olsen, phantom ballplayer? What's the story here? American League records show Olsen pinch-hitting for Heber Newsome in the seventh inning. Olsen walked, then stole second, but never scored—and never appeared in another major league game. Olsen was a lefthanded pitcher who had been conditionally sold to the Red Sox by the San Diego Padres before the season began, and who appeared in some spring training games. It looked like he would be drafted by the Army, and two days before Opening Day both Norman Brown and Olsen were released. Olsen was returned to San Diego "because he was not in playing condition." On April 25, though, he gave the Padres a nice 7–1 win against Seattle. He was hit hard a couple of times, then inducted into the Army in early June. But was he in Boston on May 16 for the game in Chicago against the White Sox? The *Chicago Tribune* shows him in their boxscore; so does the AP in their boxscores printed in papers around the country. Through many editions of *The Baseball Encyclopedia* over 35 years, there was Olsen. But he wasn't in Boston. He was in the Pacific Coast League. Best guess? Despite him telling Ed Walton otherwise, the pinch-hitter was probably Leon Culberson, though it might have been Johnny Lazor. We'll likely never know.

1942 Jigger Statz had three at-bats for the Red Sox in 1920, without getting on base, but he was a bigger hit with his wife. On an NBC broadcast, she said, "Arnold is so perfect, I'm speechless. I know this is a good way to hint at a new dress, but he has been such a fine husband that, if I did spill any 'dirt' about him, I'd honestly have to make it up…And he can wash dishes, scrub floors and do housework with the best of them!"

1932 Left fielder Smead Jolley hit two home runs, the second one a two-run shot in the bottom of the ninth to tie the game. The visiting White Sox scored once in the top of the 10th, though, to beat Boston, 4–3.

1926 It was Sunday and baseball was not allowed in Boston. The Sox had just hosted the Tigers for three games in Boston, and on Tuesday would host St. Louis at Fenway. In between, though, they scooted out to Detroit to play a Sunday afternoon game. Boston came from behind to tie it with three in the ninth, but the Tigers won in the 11th, 6–5, when Roy Carlyle (his nickname was "Dizzy") lost Charlie Gehringer's two-out fly ball in the sun and it went for a double, driving in Johnny Bassler. Wally Shaner told Peter Golenbock that some of the Sox took advantage of the occasion to lug back suitcases filled with 24 bottles of illicit Black Label whiskey. (See also June 12, 1927.)

1915 In Cleveland, Smoky Joe Wood and "Alabama Blossom" Guy Morton stared each other down for nine innings of scoreless ball. Carl Mays relieved Wood, but Morton stuck with it. Morton faded in the 14th, when Mays dropped in a "sun hit" and an infield hit and two doubles followed. The Sox won in 14, 3–0.

TRANSACTIONS
1949: Signed Sammy White as an amateur free agent.

DEBUTS
1927: Cleo Carlyle
1933: Lloyd Brown
1943: Leon Culberson (but not Albert Olsen—see above)
1951: Paul Hinrichs

BIRTHDATES
Paddy Smith 1894 (1920); Howie Fitzgerald 1902 (1926); Dave Philley 1920 (1962)

DEATHS
None yet

May 17

2003 The Angels held a 3–2 lead at Fenway in the top of the ninth. With one out, the Angels singled twice. Bill Mueller couldn't handle David Eckstein's pop foul so Eckstein had another life. He flied out to Trot Nixon in right, who caught the ball and then flipped the ball to the fans. Nixon had thought there were two outs. Molina tagged at second and jogged all the way home on Nixon's blunder. Two more runs followed, and the Angels ultimately won, 6–2. (See also September 4, 2003.)

1992 Wade Boggs' single in the eighth inning was base hit #2,000 of his career. Only Doerr, Evans, Rice, Williams, and Yastrzemski had previously reached the plateau with the Red Sox. "Hopefully, it's just a stepping stone to 3,000. Three thousand is really the pinnacle." The Sox lost the game, 3–1, at Fenway.

1971 In the fourth transaction involving him in about a six-week stretch, Luis Tiant signed with the Red Sox. The Twins released Tiant on March 31, and the Braves signed him on April 16. The Braves released him on May 15, and the Sox snapped him up two days later. Tiant went 15–6 in 1971, then won 81 games over the four seasons that followed.

1967 It was a 10-homer game, three by the Red Sox (two by Yaz) and seven by the Orioles (four of them in the nine-run seventh inning). Every one of the Baltimore homers was by a different player. Not surprisingly, Baltimore won, 12–8.

1962 Mickey Mantle almost single-handedly won the game for the Yankees in the top of the ninth inning, by working a walk, stealing second, taking third on a bad peg to third by Boston catcher Jim Pagliaroni, and then scoring on an Elston Howard sacrifice fly. His was the winning run in a 2–1 game. The other Yankees run was set up by a Gene Conley wild pitch.

1947 It was Ellis Kinder's first start of the 1947 season. Pitching for St. Louis, he held the Red Sox to six hits and two runs, and won the game, 4–2, despite being bombed from on high. At one point in the game, a seagull flew over Fenway Park and lost its grip on a three-pound smelt which fell from the skies and landed near Kinder on the mound.

1944 After the Sox took the first game, 5–1, Bobby Doerr hit St. Louis for the cycle in the second game. When Doerr did it again on May 13, 1947, he became the only Red Sox player to cycle twice. The second game also featured infielder Eddie Lake pitching 2⅓ innings in a 13–8 losing effort.

1932 Boston out-hit Chicago, but the White Sox pulled off five double plays and won the game, 7–3. Chicago pitcher Milt Gaston initiated four of the five DPs, and three of them cut down a runner at home plate! The first twin killing was an unusual 1-6-2 play in Boston's fifth inning, followed by a 1-2-3 play in the eighth and another 1-2-3 in the ninth to end the game.

1925 George Sisler of the Browns extended his 32-game hitting streak, but it was just one of four St. Louis hits, yet they won, 11–6. How'd they do that? Well, Sox pitcher Buster Ross managed to hit a batter, walk eight Brownies, and personally commit a record four errors.

1917 With World War I underway, owner Frazee was seeking a drill instructor to travel with the Red Sox and conduct them in military drills as part of their preparedness program. It took over a month to locate one—the Red Sox were the last team to do so—but Corp. Arthur B. Hoffman, manager of the U.S. Army All-Star baseball team in 1914 and 1915, was promoted to sergeant and transferred from the Green Bay, Wisconsin recuiting station to Boston to serve as official military instructor for the Red Sox. The day before he commenced work, Hoffman revealed he had tried out for the Sox at Little Rock in 1908, but not made the team. On May 21, he conducted his first drill, explaining commands, movements, etc. for about an hour, despite the game itself being rained out.

1912 It was the formal "dedication day" for Boston's new $350,000 baseball edifice, Fenway Park. The huge crowd was disappointed when the White Sox scored four times in the top of the ninth, to pin a 5–2 defeat on pitcher Larry Pape.

TRANSACTIONS
1907: Acquired Bunk Congalton from Cleveland.
1951: Traded Matt Batts, Jim Suchecki, a PTBNL (Jim McDonald), and
    $100,000 cash to the St. Louis Browns, all for Les Moss.
1960: Traded Ron Jackson to the Milwaukee Braves for Ray Boone.
1961: Signed free agent Joe Ginsberg.
1971: Signed free agent Luis Tiant.
1989: Signed free agent Rick Lancellotti.

May 18

2002 Pedro Martinez was raring to go after a two-hour Fenway rain delay, and struck out Seattle on nine pitches in the first inning. Only 10 other AL pitchers ever had a nine-strike inning. Pedro ran his record to 10–0 lifetime against the Mariners.

1988 It was only game 39 of the season, but when Oakland's Dave Stewart balked in the fourth inning, he broke the major league record with his 12th balk. He was on a pace to more than quadruple the record, but got matters under control and wound up with "only" 16 balks. Oil Can Boyd got the 4–1 win.

1986 The Red Sox won, 5–4, in 10 innings, though Texas out-hit the Sox, 11–9. The difference must have been the 13 bases on balls served up by Rangers pitchers. Nope. Not one of the 13 batters walked ever scored. The Sox left 13 men on base—every single one of the ones who had drawn a base on balls. The Sox tied it in the ninth, but almost blew it in the 10th. The Rangers had scored once in the top of the 10th. Steve Lyons of the Red Sox then singled with one out. He wasn't having a very good game. As Dan Shaughnessy wrote in the *Globe*, he had "bobbled a single for an error, overthrew a cutoff man, botched a bunt attempt, and got picked off while going 0 for 3 in the first nine innings." Lyons took second when a pickoff attempt went astray. Then Marty Barrett dropped a ball down the right field line. It went into George Wright's glove, so Lyons ran back to second. Then it popped out of Wright's glove, and Fenway fans saw Lyons sliding into second from third base, and Barrett sliding into second steaming around from first. When Lyons started back for third, the startled Wright threw poorly and the ball went into the Rangers' dugout, allowing both runs to score.

1979 In the first contest between the Yankees and the Red Sox that followed the October 2 playoff game, the Yankees come to Fenway and win, 10–0.

1976 Carl Yastrzemski plays his 2,293rd game, eclipsing Ted Williams' record.

1975 Bernie Carbo led off with a single, and hit homers in the third and fifth innings off KC's Nelson Briles, driving in every Red Sox run in the 4–2 Fenway win.

1968 Yaz begins work in television, with a half-hour show every Saturday night on WNAC-TV, Boston.

1955 Just one of those days? The Indians dealt the Red Sox the worst shutout in franchise history, 19–0, behind the three-hit pitching of Herb Score. An 11-run fifth was the big one, with Vic Wertz driving in five runs in the frame, 80% of them with a grand slam.

1946 St. Louis pitchers dispensed 10 walks in the first three innings, and Ted Williams had already drawn three intentional walks (and one that wasn't) when he came to bat in the fifth inning. The bases were loaded, and the Browns were already far behind, so they decided to pitch to Ted. Big mistake. Grand slam. The Sox beat St. Louis, 18–8, and Mickey Harris won his seventh straight win.

1944 Ted Williams was signed by the Yanks! Yes, it was reported in the *Christian Science Monitor* that Gloucester native and Boston College fullback Ted Williams signed on with the Boston Yanks pro football team.

The Red Sox beat the Browns, 12–1, on 15 hits. Despite all the hitting, Bob Johnson walked four times in a row. Fifth time up, he finally collected a single. Johnson scored three times.

1939 Marcus Aurelius Roth, traveling secretary for the Yankees, told of a time when the railcar carrying the Yankees uniforms was sidetracked at 3:00 A.M., while the team itself continued on to Boston. Finding no uniforms, and with no idea where they were, the Yankees donned Red Sox road uniforms and prepared to play. At the last moment, the uniforms showed up, the Yanks put on the pinstripes and won the game. The story appeared in the May 18, 1939 *Sporting News*. The incident happened some time between 1906 and 1927, and researchers who might know the actual date are urged to send information to the author.

1932 For he's a Jolley good fellow. Smead Jolley's 5-for-5 day helped power the Sox to a 13–10 win over Chicago. The *Chicago Tribune* reported it was the first time the Red Sox had won at home all year long, but actually it was the third time they'd won in Boston. Perhaps it just seemed that way; the win was only their fifth of the year and lifted Boston to a 5–22 record. Actually, the paper was correct in the strictest sense—the two prior wins in Boston had been at Braves Field, not Fenway Park.

1930 The Yankees had 13 hits (including three doubles, two triples, and two homers) and beat up on Boston, 11–0, behind the shutout pitching of George Pipgras. The game stretched his string to 20 consecutive shutout innings. Babe Ruth's home run was described as the longest ever hit at Braves Field (another game played there rather than at Fenway, as was done from time to time), traveling to within two rows of the scoreboard behind the right-field bleachers.

1923 Howard Ehmke, who'd pitched for the Tigers in 1922, beat his old teammates, 6–2, as Boston scored twice to tie it in the ninth, and then scored four more runs off starter Hooks Dauss in the 10th. Ehmke hit both Fred Haney and Ty Cobb, and Cobb pursued the matter under the grandstand. Ehmke might not have purposely targeted Ty; he hit a Red Sox team-record 20 batsmen in 1923.

1914 Both pitchers hit a batter in the day's 2–0 Boston defeat of Detroit. After Dutch Leonard hit Ty Cobb, the Tiger center fielder stayed in character, bunting down the first base line and spiking Leonard when he came over to field the ball. One of Cobb's ribs was broken, so he apparently got the worst of it.

TRANSACTIONS
1905: Tom Doran selected off waivers by the Detroit Tigers.
1954: Hoot Evers was selected off waivers by the New York Giants.
1968: Sold John Wyatt to the New York Yankees.

DEBUTS
1930: Ben Shields
1951: Les Moss
1986: Mike Stenhouse

BIRTHDATES
Al Niemiec 1911 (1934); Carroll Hardy 1933 (1960–1962); Erik
Hanson 1965 (1995); Rich Garces 1971 (1996–2002)

DEATHS
Babe Barna 1972; Jack Kramer 1995

May 19

2003 When the Red Sox hosted the Yankees, it was the first meeting of a record 26 games between any two teams. The unbalanced schedule dictated 19 matchups, and the two teams then played seven games against each other in the American League Championship Series. In 2004, they played another 26. New York kicked off the 2003 season series with five runs in the top of the first, and won, 7–3. Astute fans will recall who won the last four of the 2004 games.

1993 Dave Stewart, long-time Red Sox nemesis, had won 13 out of 14 from the Sox, but doesn't even complete the second inning and is tagged for 10 earned runs, on seven hits and five walks. The Blue Jays scored five runs but simply had too big a hole to dig out of. 10–5 was the final.

1990 The Red Sox pile up 20 hits (with Tom Brunansky's 5-for-5 day accounting for a quarter of them). Brunansky knocked in seven runs. Roger Clemens struck out only two batters, but held the Twins to one run, and the Red Sox win, 13–1.

1986 Marc Sullivan had a less-than-distnguished career as a catcher for the Red Sox, with a lifetime average of .186 and a career total 28 RBIs over five seasons. That his father was GM Haywood Sullivan couldn't have had anything to do with his being on the team for such a long time, could it? As Leigh Grossman writes in *The Red Sox Fan Handbook*, Sullivan's "on-field highlight may have been [this game] when he provided the game-winning run by being hit in the rump with the bases loaded in the bottom of the ninth." The offending pitcher was Ron Davis of the Twins, who thereby lost, 8–7, as a presumably amused Wade Boggs (the 1986 batting champion) trotted home with the winning run.

1976 Yaz broke out of his deep .198 slump, going 4-for-4 with three homers and four RBIs. Jim Rice hit a three-run homer off Tiger pitching, and Boston won, 9–2. Boston's Metropolitan Cultural Alliance announced that attendance at museums in Boston outdrew the combined home attendance of the Red Sox, Celtics, Bruins, and Patriots over the prior two years. Museums, 8.9 million; sports teams, 6.1 million.

1962 Bob Tillman's first plate appearance was an April 15 walk, pinch-hitting for Mike Fornieles in the ninth inning. More than a month later, on May 19, he got his first official time at bat—and he hit a home run in the fourth inning of a game against the Angels.

1934 Lefty Grove held St. Louis to six hits and slugged a three-run homer to beat the Browns, 4–1.

1929 Two killed and 62 hurt at Yankees–Red Sox game. The Yankees were leading 3–0 after 4½ innings (hence an official game) when torrential downpours caused the over-capacity crowd to run for cover. A 17-year-old Hunter College sophomore and a 60-year-old truck driver were killed in the right-field bleachers crush.

1907 The game in Chicago was tied 0–0 after nine, but Cy Young swung at Doc White's first pitch in the top of the 10th and singled to left. Two batters later, manager Bob Unglaub came up and doubled to drive in two. Boston scored four, and won, 4–0.

TRANSACTIONS
1910: Sold Charlie French to the White Sox.
1946: Purchased Pinky Higgins from the Detroit Tigers.

DEBUTS
May 19 is the only date in the regular season which has never seen a player debut for the Boston Red Sox.

BIRTHDATES
Wally Snell 1889 (1913); Rick Cerone 1954 (1988–1989)

DEATHS
None yet

May 20

2005 When Jason Varitek hit a second-inning home run to left-center field, it marked the fifth year in a row that the new team captain had homered on May 20. Over those five games, Varitek now had a record of 11-for-18 (.611), with seven homers and 13 RBIs. Boston beat Atlanta, 4–3.

2002 One of the shortest home runs in many years was Shea Hillenbrand's three-run, third-inning poke to the Pesky Pole, estimated at 303 feet. Boston scored nine runs, and neither Derek Lowe nor Rich Garces let the White Sox score at all.

2001 Jason Varitek had himself a 4-for-4 day at Kauffman Stadium, with three homers and an RBI single, driving in seven runs, the margin of difference in Boston's 10–3 win.

1998 Pedro Martinez only let the White Sox have one run in seven full, as the Red Sox conquered the White Sox, 6–2. Jaime Navarro coughed up six earned runs in 4⅓ innings, and suffered his first defeat at the hands of the Red Sox since 1991. (See May 20, 1997.)

1997 After reaching base the first three times up, Chicago's Frank Thomas had made it 15 times in a row. Once more and he'd tie the major league record, held by Ted Williams. He just got under the ball too much, and flyed out against "El Guapo"—reliever Rich Garces. Jaime Navarro got credit for an easy win, 10–1, and he'd now won 10 in a row (spread over seven seasons) against the Red Sox.

That was as far as his streak would extend. On the very same date the following year, he lost. (See May 20, 1998.)

1996 After beating Oakland 12–2 on Sunday, the Sox beat up on them again, 16–4, on Monday night. Mo Vaughn and Jose Canseco hit homers in both games, Jose hitting two in this game. Bill Haselman had one, too, part of a 4-for-4 night.

1994 Where was Andy Tomberlin when they needed him? Red Sox pitchers Hesketh, Quantrill, Frohwirth, and Harris combined to give up 21 runs to the Twins (11 in the fifth inning alone). So the Sox called on outfielder Andy Tomberlin to throw the final two innings. Tomberlin walked one, struck out one, and gave up one hit, but blanked Minnesota, and consequently sports a lifetime ERA of 0.00.

1984 In his first start, Roger Clemens gives up four runs on seven hits, strikes out seven batters in seven innings, while walking just one. He bags his first big league win, 5–4, over the Twins.

1977 Both teams hit four homers, but the Brewers scored a lot more runs other than by the long ball, and won 15–7 over the Red Sox.

1976 It was the first meeting of the year between the two rivals, and the Yanks were ahead, 1–0. It was the bottom of the sixth at the Stadium, and there were two outs. Lou Piniella was on second when Oscar Velez hit to right field. Even though Dwight Evans had already cut down Fred Stanley at the plate in the third inning, Piniella decided to go for it. Evans cut him down, too, when Fisk held onto the ball (just as he had on August 1, 1973 when Munson tried to bowl him over). Piniella upended Fisk, who bounced up and onto Piniella. Both players got into it, and things seemed to be settling down again when Graig Nettles started punching Sox starter Bill Lee. The fight resumed with redoubled intensity. Nettles later said he'd thrown Lee on the ground, and apparently hurt his shoulder. Then, he said, Lee was yelling at him "until I couldn't take it any longer. I socked him in the eye, and he hit me." (*New York Times*) Lee had to leave the game—rushed to Lenox Hill Hospital—suffering a torn shoulder and some torn ligaments and looked to be through for the season. Though Ed Figueroa had kept the Sox scoreless until this time, Boston immediately exploded in the top of the seventh and went on an eight run rampage over the final three innings. The Sox had never hit a home run off Figueroa, but he gave up a two-run shot by The Rooster (Rick Burleson) in the seventh. Yaz hit homers in both the eighth and the ninth, and Boston won, 8–2.

1968 Anaheim Angels shortstop Jim Fregosi had a double, a triple, and a home run in the regulation nine innings. He'd hit for the cycle once before, and now he did it again, finally getting a single—which drove in the winning run in the bottom of the 11th inning, for a 5–4 Angels win.

1953 The St. Louis Browns were worried about catching the 6:00 P.M. train out of town, since the game had gone into the bottom of the 14th inning. When Del Wilber was announced as a pinch-hitter for Red Sox pitcher Ellis Kinder, a Boston sportswriter turned to Browns owner Bill Veeck and said, "Don't worry. You fellows can catch your six o'clock train to Cleveland. This guy always hits a home run when he comes in as a pinch-hitter." He took three balls, then a strike, and then Wilber hit it into the screen. It was his third pinch-hit homer in three weeks. This one was hit off Don Larsen and won the game for the Red Sox, giving Boston a 3–2 victory. (See also May 6 and May 10, 1953.)

1948 It took two pitchers to do it, but Boston served up 18 bases on balls to Cleveland batters. Mickey Harris gave out 7 passes, then handed the ball to Mickey McDermott, who doled out 11. The total set an AL record and, as McDermott once wrote, "Who else would want it?" Not surprisingly, Boston lost 13–4. Bob Lemon, Jim Hegan, and Ken Keltner all gained RBIs without even having to hit the ball.

1947 The Sox trade catchers with the Tigers, Hal Wagner heading to the Motor City and Birdie Tebbetts finding his way to Beantown. Offensively, the Sox got by far the better part of the deal—and you can look it up.

1943 Chief usher Joe Connolly was feted by his fellow workers at the Pennant Grill on the eve of his induction into the Army at Fort Devens. Connolly was chief usher at Fenway, at Braves Field, and also at the RKO theaters in Boston. He'd started a "new system of ushering" after Fenway was rebuilt in 1934; the guy sure knew how to show people to their seats.

1940 Detroit's Pinky Higgins hits homers in the fourth, fifth, and seventh innings, knocking in seven runs, and pretty much did everything he could to lift the Tigers to a 10–7 win over Lefty Grove, even though Grove hit a homer himself (and Jimmie Foxx hit a grand slam).

May 20 also saw the first issue of *Red Sox Ramblings*, a four-page free publication for fans edited by Sox publicity chief Ed Doherty. In WWII, Doherty piloted lighter-than-air blimps in the Pacific.

1938 Lefty Grove went 3-for-5 at the plate, his three singles driving in four runs. He needn't have exerted himself; the Red Sox beat St. Louis with ease, 16–2.

1925 Twenty walks reflects an awful lot of balls outside the strike zone. Three Sox pitchers from each team (White and Red) combined to walk 10 per team. Boston had the edge in hits, 10 to 9, but Chicago scored 10 times to Boston's 7.

1922 In the fifth inning, Boston's Bill Piercy served up Tris Speaker's first career grand slam. That put paid to the Red Sox, Cleveland winning the game, 5–2.

1919 With two runs across, and the bases loaded, Babe Ruth hit his first grand slam to help give the Sox six second-inning runs. Ruth pitched and batted cleanup, and got himself a W. Final score, Boston 6, Detroit 4.

1916 Pitching a no-hitter, but yanked after 5⅔ innings. Babe Ruth walked the first two hitters he faced. After the second walk, his catcher, Pinch Thomas, objected so strenuously he was ordered to depart. A sacrifice followed, and then a double steal, and St. Louis had one run. Ruth issued seven walks in all, and when he walked the bases loaded with two outs in the sixth inning, he was relieved by Carl Mays, who got him out of trouble. Final score, 3–1, Boston.

TRANSACTIONS
1907: Purchased Bunk Congalton from the Cleveland Naps.
1947: Traded Hal Wagner to the Detroit Tigers for Birdie Tebbetts.
1978: Signed amateur free agent Bobby Ojeda.

DEBUTS
1922: Bill Piercy
1940: Joe Glenn
1950: Jim Suchecki
1960: Ray Boone
2004: Jamie Brown

BIRTHDATES
Jake Thielman 1879 (1908); Paul Howard 1884 (1909); Joe Harris 1891 (1922–1925); Wilcy Moore 1897 (1931–1932); Pete Jablonowski (Appleton) 1904 (1932); Joe Wood 1916 (1944); Harry Taylor 1919 (1950–1952); David Wells 1963 (2005); Wayne Housie 1965 (1991)

DEATHS
Amby McConnell 1942; Hoge Workman 1972; Pete Runnels 1991

May 21

2004   Big news indeed, as Big Papi David Ortiz signed a two-year contract extension through the 2006 season, and granted the Red Sox a club option for 2007.

1995   Former replacement player Ron Mahay has his debut with the Red Sox, going 2-for-5 with an RBI two-bagger in his first at-bat. The Players' Association gave replacement players the cold shoulder, but Mahay credited Mike Greenwell with easing his acceptance in the Boston clubhouse.

1988   Bobby Doerr's #1 was retired in a ceremony at Fenway Park. Doerr had been voted into the Hall of Fame by the Veterans Committee in 1986.

1972   Chummy New York pitchers Fritz Peterson and Mike Kekich combined to beat Boston in a doubleheader, 6–3 and 3–2. Had either loss been swapped for a win, Boston would have won the pennant. In the strike-shortened '72 season, Boston won 85 games and lost 70, but the Detroit Tigers won 86 and lost 70. It had been decided that all teams would play out the season, even if it should end (as it did) with teams not having played an equivalent number of games.

1961   Don Schwall made his major league debut, and won, 4–1, over the White Sox. In 1961 he was 15–7 with a 3.22 ERA and was selected as American League Rookie of the Year.

1957   Boston baseball writers voted to continue to exclude women from the Fenway press box, keeping out Cleveland writer Doris O'Donnell. "'The vote here was close, because she's rather an attractive girl," smiled the *Globe*'s Bob Holbrook, head of the Boston chapter. Ms. O'Donnell informed this author that Ted Williams told her: "Well, you tell those guys to go screw themselves."

Billy Klaus made three errors at short, and spent the night in the hospital after he misplayed the third one and the ball hit him under the right eye. Cleveland pitcher Early Wynn walked seven Sox, but still won, 8–2.

1955   It was a 12-round fight and neither team had scored through the first 11. Tom Brewer started for the Sox and Mickey McDermott started for the Senators. Fisticuffs erupted on the field when McDermott picked Jackie Jensen off first and got him in a rundown, and Jensen knocked McDermott down, knocking the ball out of his glove. McDermott came up swinging, and both benches emptied. Jensen was called out for interference, then thrown out of the game for fighting. A leadoff walk to Pedro Ramos, in for the evicted McDermott, led off the bottom of the 12th for Washington. A dropped ball at third and a hit off Ellis Kinder's glove—neither of which were errors, but both of which might have stopped the winning run—led to the 1–0 Washington win.

1954 It was the Yankees' Whitey Ford against Red Sox rookie Frank Sullivan, who was making his first start in the majors, at the Stadium. It was Sullivan's first start since 1950, when he was drafted into the Army. Sullivan struck out Mickey Mantle the first three times he faced him, though The Mick finally got a bead on one and hit it out. A six-run sixth secured it for the Sox.

1940 For the second day in a row, Jimmie Foxx hit a grand slam. Three other Sox players hit homers, too. One of them was Doc Cramer, whose home run off Cotton Pippen was the only homer he hit in five seasons (and 3,111 at-bats) with the Sox. The Red Sox won the game, 11–8.

1928 A seven-game winning streak doesn't seem like anything THAT special, but this day's win is the first time since August 1919 that the Sox have won seven straight. They'll lose seven in a row from time to time, but the next time they'll win that many is in August 1937 when they actually play 13 games in a row without a loss (there was a 5–5 tie in there, though).

1926 White Sox first baseman Earl Sheely racked up 10 total bases, whacking three doubles and a home run at Boston. The day before, he'd hit three doubles in his final three times at bat, making it seven consecutive extra-base hits. The Red Sox rallied, though, for three runs in the bottom of the ninth, and got a win, 8–7.

1915 Tied 7–7 after seven, the White Sox and Red Sox battled it out for another 10 innings until the bottom of the 17th, when Chicago pinch-hitter Tommy Daly singled home Buck Weaver to pin a loss on Boston's Carl Mays. Mays had thrown nine-plus innings of relief.

1904 Over 100 years later, Bill O'Neill's mark is one to marvel at. Boston's shortstop managed to make a record six errors in one game. He got off to a quick start, making three errors in the first inning, on the first three balls hit to him, added another in the second (on his fourth chance of the game). He only had seven other chances throughout the game, but managed to flub two of them as well; the first time he fielded a ball cleanly was in the seventh inning. With six errors, four assists, and just one putout, well, the headlines describing his day as "ragged work" were kind. The game ran into 13 innings, when St. Louis scored two runs, set up by O'Neil's sixth error of the day. About six weeks later, O'Neil was traded to Washington.

TRANSACTIONS
1935: Traded Moose Solters and cash to the St. Louis Browns for Ski Melillo.
1947: Frankie "Blimp" Hayes is given his release.
1959: Selected Bobby Avila off waivers from the Baltimore Orioles.

DEBUTS
1907: Bunk Congalton   1961: Don Schwall   1997: Mike Benjamin
1932: Regis Leheny   1995: Ron Mahay   2003: Rudy Seanez

BIRTHDATES
Sam Langford 1899 (1926); Hank Johnson 1906 (1933–1935);
Mace Brown 1909 (1942–1946); Bryce Florie 1970 (1999–2001)

DEATHS
George Cochran 1960; Archie McKain 1985

May 22

1997 The Sox got 19 hits and left a full 16 men on base, but scored eight times and beat the Yankees, 8–2. Wil Cordero was 5-for-6 and Tim Naehring was 4-for-6. Tom Gordon started and won for the Red Sox.

1984 The quip is that Ed Jurak made the best play of his career in this game at Fenway. Bruce Hurst squared off against Rick Sutcliffe and neither team had scored, though the Indians had two men on and two out in the top of the third. At this point, a rat was spotted in the vicinity of the Red Sox on-deck circle. It headed straight toward the mound before veering left across the third base foul line, but not before Jurak came in and fielded the rat, scooping him up in his first baseman's mitt (which bore a couple of bite marks) and stuffed him in a trashcan in the dugout, which was then overturned, trapping the rodent inside. "I was sort of unnerved when the rat came out," said Hurst, "I didn't make a move because I knew Ed had him all the way." Hurst walked the next batter, Tony Bernazard, to load the bases but escaped the inning unscathed. The Sox scored three times in the bottom of the third and went on to a 7–1 victory.

1982 Bob Stanley threw 8⅓ innings in relief of Bobby Ojeda, and the Red Sox beat Oakland, 7–4.

1977 The Brewers and Red Sox hit 11 home runs in the first game of a doubleheader at Fenway. Boston won, 14–10. In the second game the Sox got only two hits and were shut out. Jim Willoughby broke his ankle, slipping on the outfield grass.

1960 The Sox left 22 runners on base (15 in the day's second game) and lost their eighth and ninth straight. The Tigers strand 18, but drove in more in both games.

1958 The 16th grand slam of Ted Williams' career gave the Sox the runs they needed to win 8–5 over the Kansas City Athletics. The slam put him one up on Jimmie Foxx, behind only Lou Gehrig and Babe Ruth.

1957 Tying their own 1940 record, four Red Sox hit homers in one inning—the sixth— as Boston beat Cleveland, 11–0. Gene Mauch, Ted Williams, Dick Gernert, and Frank Malzone all hit roundtrippers. Ted had been one of the 1940 crew, joining Jimmie Foxx, Joe Cronin, and Jim Tabor in the first four-homer inning. Jimmy Piersall doesn't play; it's his first game off in 294 games.

1953 The Red Sox win two games against Philadelphia, both by the same 3–2 score they won by on the 20th. They're closing in on the Yankees, until they lose (3–2) to New York the following day. The Red Sox won 35 one-run games in 1953.

1942 After several months of controversy over his deferment, and after standing up to those who would pressure him to register for the draft despite a valid deferment, Ted Williams quietly enlisted in the United States Navy at 150 Causeway Street in downtown Boston on the day off before a brief three-game home stand.

1937 One of the longest homers ever hit at Fenway was Hank Greenberg's blast off Wes Ferrell. The ball went over the center-field wall and "bounded off neighboring buildings more than 450 feet from the plate." The Sox hit three homers, though, and beat the Tigers, 11–9.

1933 George Pipgras threw a two-run game and Dusty Cooke's homer was the margin of the 3–2 Red Sox victory over visiting Chicago. The two Yankees alumni were joined by a White Sox alumnus, Johnny Hodapp, who drove in the other two Red Sox runs—hitting off the man for whom he'd been traded, Ed Durham.

1926 "Doing everything as it shouldn't be done" enabled the White Sox to lose to the Red Sox, 14–8. What they should not have done was to give up 14 hits, though Boston pitchers gave up 14, too. Chicago's moundsmen walked 13, though, and their teammates committed four errors. Three of the walks came with the bases full, all in the seventh inning. *Chicago Tribune* writer Irving Vaughn begged off providing detail, saying it was "too complicated and painful to bear narrating."

1915 A rough day for the rookie Babe Ruth. He gave up four runs in the first (he walked three batters, threw a wild pitch, and committed a throwing error—in addition to allowing three hits). At bat, he struck out on three straight pitches. Starting the second, he gave up back-to-back hits, and then was given the rest of the day off. The White Sox won, 11–3.

1914 "Youthful Red Sox twirler" (AP) George Foster shut out the White Sox on six hits, and ran his scoreless innings streak to 38 in a row! Cicotte pitched well, too, but Boston prevailed, 1–0.

1913 A moving picture firm that shot film without permission during the Red Sox–Giants matchup in the 1912 World Series was sued by the National Baseball Commission and the New York Baseball Club. A New York magistrate ruled that baseball players are "public characters" and photographers could take action shots of them without requiring their consent.

TRANSACTIONS
1979: Released Frank Duffy.

DEBUTS
1957: Jack Spring
1996: Jeff Manto
2004: Anastacio Martinez

BIRTHDATES
Al Simmons 1902 (1943); Ed Morgan 1904 (1934); Otey Clark 1915 (1945); Pinky Woods 1915 (1943–1945); Vaughn Eshelman 1969 (1995–1997)

DEATHS
Dave Shean 1963; Lefty Grove 1975; Bill Bayne 1981; Joe Cascarella 2002

May 23

2000 "I'm only a little man pitching out there and trying to do my job," said Pedro Martinez after a 3–2 defeat at the hands of the visiting Toronto Blue Jays. Had Pedro had a little more run support, he would have had a win, but Red Sox batters were 0-for-13 with runners in scoring position and left 10 men on base.

1999 Tom Gordon pitches one-third of an inning to close the game, earning him his 50th save in 50 consecutive chances. The Bosox beat the Blue Jays, 10–8.

1996 Ten years without a hit! Roger Clemens was on his way to an 11–4 complete game win over the Seattle Mariners, when Jose Canseco—who had been DH'ing for the Red Sox—moved to play left field. Since you can't bring in a new DH, the Canseco move brought up Clemens to the plate in the bottom of the eighth, facing Norm Charlton. The Rocket broke his bat on the first pitch, but then singled right through Charlton and up the middle. It was the first hit by a Red Sox pitcher since Tim Lollar in a pinch-hitting role in 1986.

1978 The American League unanimously approved the $15 million cash sale of the Boston Red Sox from the Thomas Yawkey estate to a group headed by Jean R. Yawkey and two other general partners—Haywood Sullivan, a former Red Sox catcher, and Buddy LeRoux, former Red Sox trainer—and nine limited partners. An earlier bid from just Sullivan and LeRoux had been rejected. With Mrs. Yawkey as partner and president, it took just five minutes to approve the sale.

1951 Mel Parnell had what you might call a double four-hitter. From the mound, Marvelous Mel shut out the St. Louis Browns, holding them to four hits. At the plate, Parnell peppered Browns pitching for four hits (three triples and a double). Ted Williams was 0-for-1 at the plate, but boosted his on-base percentage with five walks. Third baseman Vern Stephens had a shot at the record for assists, and shortstop Johnny Pesky knew it. The Sox were ahead 12–0 at the time, so when Ken Wood grounded to short on the last play of the game, Pesky fielded it and flipped to Stephens who earned an assist by firing to Walt Dropo at first.

1947 Allie Reynolds limited the Red Sox to two singles, one in the sixth and one in the eighth, as the Yankees beat Boston, 9–0. Exactly one month earlier, on April 23, Reynolds had also held the Sox to just two hits, in a 3–0 shutout.

1945 Pete Gray, the one-armed left fielder for the Browns, makes his Fenway Park debut, in the leadoff slot. The Browns are limited to five hits by Boo Ferriss; Gray goes 0-for-4. In 234 at-bats, he hits .218. The Browns hit .249 as a team in '45.

1944 The Red Sox were beaten 3–1 by the Great Lakes Bluejackets, behind the two-hit pitching of former Tiger Virgil Trucks now playing for the service team.

1934 Through eight innings, Lefty Grove had given up five runs. Left to bat for himself in the top of the ninth, he singled and scored to help his own cause, as the Red Sox rallied for three in the ninth for a come-from-behind 7–5 win.

1902 Cleveland's Charles Somers, who was also the president of the Boston club, met with second baseman Nap Lajoie in Philadelphia to induce him to jump leagues. Somers offered a four-year guaranteed contract at $7,000 per annum. Working hand in hand with Ban Johnson, Somers helped finance both ball clubs—Cleveland and Boston—and the rest of the league as well.

TRANSACTIONS
1929: Traded Doug Taitt to the Chicago White Sox for Bill Barrett.
1954: Traded George Kell to the Chicago White Sox for Grady Hatton and $100,000.

DEBUTS
1909: Charlie French	1991: Mike Brumley
1929: Bob Barrett	1996: Jose Malave
1946: Bob Klinger	1998: Keith Johns
1947: Birdie Tebbetts	

BIRTHDATES
Hugh Bradley 1885 (1910–1912); Pat Creeden 1906 (1931); Reggie
Cleveland 1948 (1974–1978); Kevin Romine 1961 (1985–1991);
Ricky Gutierrez 1970 (2004); Cesar Crespo 1979 (2004)

DEATHS
Danny Clark 1937; Gavvy Cravath 1963; Earl Webb 1965

May 24

2001 Pedro Martinez faced Mike Mussina. Both pitchers struck out 12, and both pitchers allowed only six hits, but the Yankees scored one more run and won the game, 2–1. Were the Yankees Pedro's daddy? Was Pedro cursed? The Sox had lost Pedro's last five starts against the Yankees, dating back to June 14, 2000.

2000 In a game delayed by rain at Fenway, and then extended into extra innings, things broke for the better when Brian Daubach launched an 11th-inning three-run homer off Toronto's John Frascatore and won the game, 6–3. It ended a stretch of 47 Boston at-bats with runners in scoring position, in which there were only four hits.

1995 Mike Blowers entered the game hitting .118. He connected for four extra-base hits, going 4-for-5 with two doubles, one triple, and a homer, responsible for eight runs batted in as the Mariners topped the Red Sox, 15–6. By game's end, he was hitting .179. By season's end, he had 96 RBIs and was hitting .257. Boston relief pitcher Jeff Pierce ran his record to 0–3 on the still young season, which was apparently all the Red Sox could take.

1987 In the seventh inning of a 4–1 loss to Chicago, Ellis Burks grounds into a double play off White Sox pitcher Jose Deleon. Not remarkable at the time, it turns out to be the only double play Burks hit into all season long, in 558 at-bats.

1973 In a game against Milwaukee, Bill Lee threw a pitch that hit catcher Ellie Rodriguez, a former amateur boxer and a player with whom Lee had a history from winter ball in Puerto Rico in 1972. When Lee had hit Rodriguez with a pitch in Mayaguez, the catcher and a couple of friends jumped him after the game and knocked out four of Lee's teeth. It looked like pure malice to observers when Lee picked Rodriguez off first, and then yelled to him, "That's once. I'm going to hit you again!" Reggie Smith saw it in racial terms and called out Lee, and the two of them got into a fight of their own in the Red Sox clubhouse. Lee said he was knocked unconscious by Smith, who hit from behind.

1957 Target practice: the *Boston Herald Traveler* reported that Ted Williams had shot 40 pigeons at Fenway Park.

1952 Barbs tossed during batting practice broke out into a fierce battle between two fiery competitors. The Yankees' Billy Martin had been swapping remarks with Boston's Jimmy Piersall all season long. Martin challenged Piersall to join him under the stands, and a fistfight broken out in the runway between the Red Sox dugout and dressing room. Martin reportedly drove Piersall to his knees. The two were separated, but then Piersall is said to have gotten into another fight with his own teammate, Mickey McDermott, when he was changing his bloodied shirt in the Red Sox clubhouse. Of secondary interest, the Red Sox won, 5–2. Piersall did not play.

1949 Ted Williams flipped his bat some 30 feet in the air, so disgusted was he at himself for striking out. Williams' strikeout to at-bats ratio was one of the smallest among major league players.

1947 On May 23, Allie Reynolds shut out the Sox on two hits. Now it was Spud Chandler's turn, throwing a two-hit, 5–0 whitewash, and the reigning AL champion Red Sox were halfway through being swept in four straight at the Stadium. The totals over the four games ran New York 40, Boston 5.

1911 A double in the first, followed by a bloop single, and the Browns had a run. At game's end, Joe Wood lost to Barney Pelty, 1–0.

1906 The season started with three straight losses. Then they managed a tie. And then they won a few, even approaching .500 with a 6–7 mark. Shut out in New York on the final game of a 9-game road trip, they came back to Boston and lost 19 games in a row! This game was consecutive loss number 20. It was the seventh start in a row for Cy Young without a win. Small wonder that the 1906 team would end up in last place, with a record of 49–105.

DEBUTS
1901: Ben Beville
1959: Bobby Avila, Ted Wills

BIRTHDATES
Jack Killilay 1887 (1911); Wally Shaner 1900 (1926–1927)

DEATHS
Ted Lewis 1936; Bill Lamar 1970; Bill Moore 1972

May 25

2004 "I love Fenway. I don't think you can replicate the magic you have here. It would never feel like Fenway."—principal owner John W. Henry. The Red Sox announced they were going to renovate Fenway Park, adding some 5,000 seats, and stay in the park for the foreseeable future.

2001 Hideo Nomo already had a no-hitter and a one-hitter to his credit in the young season. Facing the Blue Jays in Boston, the only hit he surrenders is a fourth-inning leadoff double by Shannon Stewart as the Sox beat the Blue Jays, 4–0.

1984 Dennis Eckersley was packaged with minor leaguer infielder–outfielder Mike Brumley and sent to the Cubs for 1980's NL batting champion Bill Buckner.

1981 It was the 3,000th major league ballgame for Carl Yastrzemski (only Cobb, Musial, and Aaron had played as many), and he slid across home plate with the winning run in the bottom of the ninth inning on Carney Lansford's bases-loaded high chopper to short. Boston had an 8–7 win over Cleveland.

1977 It was neither Tris Speaker nor Dom DiMaggio, but the Twins' Lyman Bostock, who made 12 putouts in the second game of the day. That tied the major league mark, as did the 17 total he recorded on the day. To make matters worse for the Red Sox, they lost both games.

1975 Made for the highlight films. Disgusted with the home plate umpiring, Yastrzemski bent down and used his hands to completely cover home plate with dirt. Umpire Lou DiMuro was not amused and gave Yaz the old heave-ho. Boston lost 6–1.

1965 One record was tied and one record was set in the day's 17–5 Twins win. Nine players hit homers (five Twins and four Sox); that tied a major league record. Jerry Moses became the youngest player ever to hit a pinch-hit homer, when he hit his first career home run off Mudcat Grant in the fifth inning. Moses was 18 years, 289 days old.

1953 Fourteen minutes longer than the 3:38 record, the Red Sox and Yankees played the longest nine-inning game to date. Casey Stengel used 19 players, including six pitchers, and the Red Sox used 13, with four pitchers. Boston out-hit New York, 20 to 13, and outscored them 14–10. Jimmy Piersall connected for an inside-the-park homer in the eighth.

1950 Walt Dropo's eighth-inning grand slam accounted for four of the six runs the Red Sox put across in the top of the eighth, giving them the lead for the first time in the game. It was a hitfest, with Boston outhitting the Browns, 19 hits to 15, and copping a 15–12 win. For the rookie Dropo, it was home run number 10 in the month of May.

1947 The Yankees out-hit the Red Sox 17–4, and outscored them by an even bigger margin, 17–2. In fact, Yankees pitcher Bill Bevens had a no-hitter going until Johnny Pesky connected for the first of his two hits in the seventh and had a shutout until Ted Williams hit a two-run ninth-inning homer to further spoil the fun. The *New York Times* termed it a "hollow victory" for Bevens, but one suspects he was glad to take it.

1945 Red Sox center fielder Leon Culberson recorded an unassisted double play, coming in to snag a short fly ball and, with momentum going for him, stepping on second base before St. Louis shortstop Vern Stephens could get back to the bag. Nels Potter, though, shut out the Sox, 5–0.

1941 Ted Williams had a 4-for-5 game, boosting his batting average to .404, as Lefty Grove and the Red Sox beat the Yankees, 10–3, for his 296th win. It was the first time since April 29 that Ted had batted above .400. One of the seven New York hits was a Joe DiMaggio single, part of his 56-game hitting streak.

1939 Bob Feller threw a one-hitter. Only Bobby Doerr's single to right field in the second inning spoiled the no-hitter; it was far from a perfect game as the 20-year-old Feller walked five and two other Red Sox reached on Cleveland errors. Not one of those seven baserunners scored, though, and Cleveland posted an 11–0 win, with Ken Keltner hitting three consecutive home runs off Red Sox reliever Emerson Dickman.

1935 Fritz Ostermueller was lucky to escape with only a badly-lacerated upper lip after St. Elizabeth's hospital X-rays revealed no broken bones. The Boston pitcher had been hit hard in the face by a Hank Greenberg line drive. Two innings later, Greenberg hit another hard one, for a home run—and put the Tigers up, 3–0. Final score: Detroit 3, Boston 2. Earlier in the year, Dick Thompson writes, Ostey had been hit hard on the kneecap and missed a few weeks. Later in the year, he was hit on the thigh and suffered a fractured leg.

Braves coach and traveling secretary Duffy Lewis saw Babe Ruth hit his last home run, his third of the day, at Forbes Field, Pittsburgh. Lewis had also seen Ruth hit his first, for the Red Sox, at the Polo Grounds, back on May 7, 1915.

1934 The Indians had suspended Wes Ferrell for refusing to report to spring training. On May 25, he was reinstated by Cleveland—but just for the purpose of getting rid of him, trading him to the Red Sox with Dick Porter, for Suitcase Bob Seeds, Bob Weiland, and $25,000.

1929 Double Barrett action. Both Bill Barrett and Jim Barrett played in the same game for the first time, as did Russ Scarritt and Charlie Berry. None of them were related, but that Sox team had the makings of a good law firm: Barrett, Barrett, Scarritt, and Berry. The Yankees still won, 8–3.

1924 The early season can sometimes be deceptive. When the Tigers came from behind to beat the Yankees, Boston and New York were tied atop the AL. They stayed neck-and-neck for more than two weeks, but by the end of the year all the Sox had managed to do was get out of the cellar for one season. They finished a half-game ahead of the Tigers, but still 25 games behind the league-leading Washington team.

1906 It was May 25 and Boston hadn't won a game since April. They were riding a 20-game losing streak (even worse, 19 of the 20 were played in front of their home fans). During the streak they had played every team in the league, and fallen short every time. The streak included five starts by Cy Young. Seemingly nothing could beat the hoodoo. It was the Curse of the...? Well, who knows? Finally, a Boston battery put it all together. Pitcher Jesse Tannehill threw a two-hitter against the White Sox, a double in the third, and an infield hit in the ninth. Catcher Bob Peterson singled twice, driving in all three Boston runs. The first run resulted from a throwing error by Jesse's brother Lee Tannehill, playing for Chicago. The final was 3–0, Boston. The efficient game lasted 79 minutes. The overall 20-game losing streak remained a league record until Baltimore topped it in 1988. The 19-game home losing streak endures. Not surprisingly, Boston finished in last place. So did Boston's 1906 National League team.

TRANSACTIONS
1929: Ira Flagstead was selected off waivers from the Washington Senators.
1934: Traded Bob Seeds, Bob Weiland, and $25,000 cash to the
    Cleveland Indians for Wes Ferrell and Dick Porter.
1984: Traded Dennis Eckersley and Mike Brumley to the Chicago Cubs for Bill Buckner.
1994: Peter Munro signed as an amateur free agent. Mario Diaz was released.

DEBUTS
1934: Dick Porter
1947: Leslie Aulds
1948: Babe Martin
1977: Mike Paxton
2004: Andy Dominique

BIRTHDATES
Doug Smith 1892 (1912); Joe Judge 1894 (1933–1934); Bud Connolly 1901 (1925); Bill Haselman 1966 (1995–2005); Dave Hollins 1966 (1995); Luis Ortiz 1970 (1993–1994); Todd Walker 1973 (2003)

DEATHS
Bill James 1942; Ray Grimes 1953

May 26

1978 It's not even the end of May, and Jim Rice already had 16 home runs (and 48 RBIs). Dwight Evans had two homers in the day's game, beating the Tigers, 6–3, behind Bill Lee's seven-hit pitching. Lee won his seventh game. Boston was doing exceptionally well in the young season.

1946 "Honest Abe" Wollick contacted the Red Sox. The fan had been trying to buy three tickets for the 1946 All-Star Game, but wound up being mailed 100 tickets to the Yankees-Red Sox doubleheader on May 27. The appreciative Sox gave him the three tickets he'd sought, two tickets to the doubleheader, and a season's pass. Wollick saw the Sox beat New York, 1–0, as Tex Hughson held the Yanks to just three hits. The second game was called off early, due to "almost impenetrable darkness" and rain "slanting down in a drenching downpour." The Yankees won, 4–1.

1945 Game-time temperature started at 86, but in a matter of minutes plunged to 64, exceeding even the 20-degree drop of April 25, 1962.

1944 St. Louis fans were on the brink of seeing perfection as their pitcher Nels Potter set down one Sox batter after another through 7⅓ innings. Alas, Nellie weakened and a run in the eighth robbed him of the perfect game, no-hitter, and shutout. Joe Cronin's sac fly tied it in the ninth, and then Potter lost the game in the 11th, 4–2, when Cronin drove in another run.

1941 Lefty Grove won his 296th game, and earned hearty applause from the Yankee Stadium crowd as the Red Sox beat New York, 10–3. All three Yankees runs were unearned, thanks to two Jimmie Foxx errors.

1917 Boston scored three times in the first, and St. Louis answered with four, but the real fireworks erupted in the top of the second. Umpire Brick Owens ruled that Everett Scott's ball had been caught on the short bounce in right field; the Browns thought that Baby Doll Jacobson had fielded it cleanly. Pop bottles flew and about 300 "irate bleacherites" became so incensed that they broke through gates out onto the field, and had to be restrained by police and players of both team—the Red Sox players wielding bats for a little extra protection. Scoring in every one of the first five innings, Boston built up enough of a lead to hold on and win, 11–7.

1916 Defending against the visiting World Champions, the Yankees took two from the Sox, 2–1 and 6–5, in 10 innings. In both games, they scored the go-ahead run in their final at-bat. Wally Pipp got the winning hit in game one, and pitcher Bob Shawkey (on in relief) singled in the winner in game two.

1914 Rube Foster's teammates let him down. He was riding a streak of 42 consecutive scoreless innings when Cleveland came to bat in top of the fifth inning. He retired the first two batters, but then shortstop Everett Scott misplayed a ball. Two singles followed, scoring the first run. Harry Hooper dropped a fly in right field and another run scored. Boston scored once each in the fifth and seventh, but in the top of the ninth, Nap Lajoie opened up with a triple and scored the winning run on the third Red Sox error, when catcher Bill Carrigan dropped relief pitcher Dutch Leonard's throw to the plate. 3–2, Indians.

1910 Red Sox purchase veteran catcher Red Kleinow from New York. Hopefully, he didn't cost too much, as he only hit .150 in 147 at-bats.

TRANSACTIONS
1910: Purchased Red Kleinow from New York.
1923: Nemo Leibold was selected off waivers by the Washington Senators.
1995: Acquired Tuffy Rhodes off waivers from the Cubs.

DEBUTS
1914: Del Gainer
1954: Grady Hatton
1984: Bill Buckner
1994: Greg Litton
2005: Shawn Wooten

BIRTHDATES
Jim Mahoney 1934 (1959); Chuck Hartenstein 1942 (1970); Rob Murphy 1960 (1989–1990)

DEATHS
George Winter 1951; Al Simmons 1956; Judge Nagle 1971; George Smith 1981

May 27

2005 STVT Ten consecutive hits made all the difference in the game. There was one out and Boston was leading, 2–1, when they closed the top of the sixth in the Stadium with five hits in a row and only managed one run; the last two hits resulted in runners being thrown out at home plate to end the inning—and left RBI machine Manny Ramirez in the on-deck circle. Then the Yankees went to town, knocking out five straight hits of their own, culminating in Gary Sheffield's three-run homer. The 10-hit spree gave the Red Sox one run, but gave the Yankees five, and therein lay the difference in a 6–3 New York win.

John Olerud joined the Red Sox; he was a 16-year veteran who had initially joined the Toronto Blue Jays without ever playing a game in the minor leagues. Coming off surgery, he appeared in two games with the Pawtucket Red Sox— finally, in 2005, making his first minor league appearance.

1988 With a single to center in the sixth, Red Sox right-fielder Dwight Evans had base hit number 2,000, though Oakland beat Boston, 3–2.

1985 Wade Boggs had a 4-for-4 day, the first of seven 1985 games in which he hit safely four times. By year's end, he amassed a total of 240 hits.

1977 Carlton Fisk and George Scott hit back-to-back homers in the game, the fifth time Pudge and Boomer have done so this year—and it's not even June yet.

1969 Rico Petrocelli has his 45th errorless game in a row at shortstop, setting a new team record while nudging Vern Stephens into second on the list.

1966 After Petrocelli flied out to left to lead off the game, and Jim Gosger walked, Washington pitcher Phil Ortega struck out seven Red Sox in a row. The feat tied an American League record. In the fourth and fifth innings, Ortega induced six consecutive ground outs. What would he try next? Well, nothing in particular. He did get one more K, though, and the 3–2 win.

1965 With the bases loaded in the ninth, Dick Radatz struck out back-to-back Twins pinch-hitters, and Dave Morehead's 2–0 shutout was saved. As it would happen, the game was the only one the Red Sox would win from Minnesota all season long; the final mark was 1–17.

1955 Norm Zauchin was one of those big sluggers the Red Sox seemed to favor in this era—6'5", 220 pounds, and he was batting .214 (with just one homer) entering the May 26 game against the Senators. He pounded a homer off Bob Porterfield in the first, and a grand slam in the second. In the fourth inning, his RBI double just barely missed going out, but in the fifth inning, his drive flew out of Fenway for a three-run homer. He had 10 RBIs and it was still just the fifth inning. That was it, though; Zauchin struck out in the seventh. Boston beat up on Washington, 16–0.

1945 Hitless wonders. Boston's Boo Ferriss held the visiting White Sox to just one second-inning single in the first game of a doubleheader, while pitcher Emmett O'Neill held them to two singles in the nightcap. 7–0 and 2–1 were the two scores, the run in O'Neill's game coming on three walks and a sacrifice fly in the Chicago second.

1939 Next time you look at the retired numbers at Fenway, think of this day when you see #1, #9, and #4: Doerr, Williams, and Cronin all hit home runs in the third inning of this day's game.

1932 Massachusetts Gov. Joseph Ely signed a new bill making Sunday baseball
FP possible at Fenway Park. Previous legislation had permitted baseball only if it was played 1000 feet or more from a house of worship. Fenway Park was 900 feet from the Church of the Redemption. The new bill changed the distance to 700—still further than any home run ball ever hit.

1920 Yankees pitcher Bob Shawkey walked home a run in the fourth inning and a number of New York players got on plate umpire George Hildebrand. With the bases still loaded, Shawkey got the next batter, pitcher Harry Harper, on a called third strike. Shawkey came off the mound, bowed toward Hildebrand, and doffed his cap. Hildebrand ejected Shawkey from the game, whereupon the pitcher charged the umpire who "defended himself with his mask and opened a wound on Shawkey's head." The walk produced the only run in the 6–1 Yankees win, wrapped up by former Sox pitcher Carl Mays.

1907 The St. Louis train crew forgot to furnish the gas needed to prepare food on board, so the Boston team went without food for over 15 hours, missing a connection along the way and forced into grabbing a little fruit from stands in the stations. When they arrived in Cleveland, the weather prevented play. That evening, they entrained for Philadelphia.

TRANSACTIONS
1914: Purchased Guy Cooper from the New York Yankees.

DEBUTS

1944: Stan Partenheimer	1995: Karl Rhodes,
1979: Stan Papi	Tim Wakefield
1982: Roger LaFrancois	2003: Matt White

BIRTHDATES
Pinky Higgins 1909 (1937–38, 1946, manager 1955–1962); Tom Hurd 1924 (1954–1956); Mark Clear 1956 (1981–1985)

DEATHS
Walter Carlisle 1945; Jesse Burkett 1953; Rip Collins 1968

May 28

2005 The Red Sox defeated the New York Yankees, winning by the most lopsided score in the history of the rivalry, 17–1. Relief pitcher Paul Quantrill gave up a grand slam, a three-run homer, and a two-run homer, in that order. Sad to say, the solo home run never occurred. (See also July 15, 2005.)

In his first plate appearance in the major leagues, Boston catcher Kelly Shoppach was hit by a Buddy Groom pitch. As the season wore on, Shoppach was up and down to Pawtucket, but accumulated 15 at-bats with Boston. After the final game on October 2, he was 0-for-15 as a major league hitter.

2000 A marvelous matchup saw both apostate Boston ace Roger Clemens pitching for the Yankees and Pedro Martinez, pitching for the forces of good, throw shutout ball through eight innings at Yankee Stadium. With two outs in the top of the ninth, Trot Nixon's two-run HR gave Boston the boost to win, as Pedro escaped a bases-loaded bottom of the ninth to hold on for a 2–0 victory.

1999 Boston had twice as many hits (18–9), but the oddity of the game revolved around Red Sox catcher Jason Varitek, who was charged with five passed balls (one short of the record), including three in the first inning alone. Knuckleballer Tim Wakefield was on the mound. Varitek doubled, though, and homered, going 3-for-5.

1997 Chicago White Sox manager Terry Bevington used four different pitchers, one each against the first four Red Sox batters in the seventh inning. Carlos Castillo, who had come in to pitch the sixth, gave up a triple to Nomar Garciaparra. Chuck McElroy walked Darren Bragg. Matt Karschner retired Wil Cordero on a grounder that scored Nomar. Tony Castillo struck out Vaughn and stayed in to strike out Stanley, too. Boston won, 5–3.

1992 Former Red Sox second baseman Marty Barrett filed a $15 million lawsuit against the Red Sox in Suffolk Superior Court, charging that the Red Sox and team physician–owner Dr. Arthur Pappas misdiagnosed his June 4, 1989 knee injury and failed to provided reconstructive surgery, which might have saved his major league career. (See October 25, 1995.)

1978 The Red Sox came from behind twice and took two games of a doubleheader by identical 4–3 scores, beating the Tigers at Fenway. The first game took 10 innings, but they wrapped up the second in regulation.

1970 The Sox trade .071-hitting infielder Tom Matchick to the Royals for .181-hitting first baseman Mike Fiore. Both improve—slightly—with a change of scenery.

1955 Sox batters were getting black and blue, hit five times by White Sox pitchers in two games. Camilo Pascual hit Sammy White twice, and White had to leave near the end of the game. The bigger story, though, was the return of Ted Williams to the lineup for the first time in 1955. He had "retired" until his divorce was finalized. Williams singled to center his first time up, but went 1-for-4 on the day (with one walk), and picked up a first-inning assist, too, playing a ball off the Wall and cutting down Senators leadoff batter Juan Delis.

1954 Those walks'll kill you. There were 20 walks issued in the game against the visiting Yankees, 12 served up by Sox pitchers, and 8 by New York's. And wouldn't you know it, the score stood 9–9 after eight innings. But Hec Brown walked Joe Collins, leading off the ninth. A bunt moved him to second and a single by Andy Carey made the score, 10–9 Yankees.

1932 Babe Ruth said he talked with friends about buying the Red Sox, but planned to play ball for another couple of years. Even if new Boston management offered him the position of manager, he planned to stick with New York "as long as Colonel Ruppert wants me." Had the timing been a bit different, though, perhaps Bob Quinn would have found a buyer in the Babe and not in Tom Yawkey.

1914 Boston's three outfielders, led by Harry Hooper and closed by Tris Speaker, featured Duffy Lewis as the middleman in a triple steal in the third inning. Cleveland catcher Fred Carisch protested too much and, with his manager, was among three Indians ejected. Even without their manager, though, Cleveland won, 5–2, scoring three runs in the ninth after there were two outs and nobody on base as Hooper let a bases-loaded ball scoot between his legs.

TRANSACTIONS
1962: Signed amateur free agent George Scott.
1970: Acquired Mike Fiore from Kansas City by trading Tom Matchick.
1978: Acquired Ramon Hernandez from the Chicago Cubs in
trade for Bobby Darwin. Sold Tom House to Seattle.

DEBUTS
1935: Ski Melillo   2005: John Olerud,
1987: John Leister   Kelly Shoppach
1999: Brian Barkley

BIRTHDATES
King Brady 1881 (1908); Bill Barrett 1900 (1929–1930); Marv Olson 1907 (1931–1933)

DEATHS
Charley Schanz 1992

May 29

2004 The Brockton Rox of the Northeast League held Grady Little Bobblehead Doll Night, although it was Little's right forearm that bobbed—as though he were making the signal to the bullpen to call in a right-handed reliever—as virtually everyone in the world knew he should have done before allowing Pedro Martinez to get hammered for not just one or two, but a full seven hits before he was removed in Game Seven of the 2003 LCS.

1993 After seven innings, the Red Sox led the Rangers, 12–1, so—well, why not? Texas manager Kevin Kennedy handed DH Jose Canseco the ball. Canseco got through the inning, but not before walking three and giving up a couple of singles. The Sox scored three earned runs and won, 15–1. As for Canseco, the stint cost him dearly. Not long afterward, he had ligament surgery in his right elbow and missed most of the rest of the season. Never again was he as effective an outfielder.

In pre-game events, 11 former Negro League players took part in an old-timers game against a team of Red Sox old-timers who included Jim Rice and Carl Yastrzemski. Mabry "Doc" Kountze, the first African-American issued a press pass by the Red Sox, was given a commemorative pass to the park and caught the first ball. The game ended in a 2–2 tie.

1990 Trying to hold the runner on first doesn't end up in the pitch count, but Roger Clemens and Charlie Hough threw 51 times to first base in a tight 2–1 win (Clemens winning and Hough taking the loss). Tony Pena homered for Boston in the fourth, then reached on a fielder's choice and scored on Carlos Quintana's double for the two Boston runs.

1984 Joe Cronin's #4 is officially retired in a Fenway Park ceremony. Although newspaper accounts the day after Ted Williams' last game said that Williams' number had been retired in 1960, it was (again?) retired in this day's ceremony.

1961 Three mistakes in a pitcher's duel between Whitey Ford and Ike Delock give the Red Sox a home win, 2–1. Ford made two mistakes and Delock only one.

1959 Jackie Jensen hit a three-run homer for the Red Sox in the top of the ninth to tie the game at 6–6, but Hal Naragon's bases-loaded single in the bottom of the ninth won it for Washington. Attending the game was President Dwight Eisenhower, who met Harmon Killebrew pre-game and told Hammerin' Harmon that he was grandson David Eisenhower's favorite player. When Killebrew homered in the third, the ball bounced back onto the field and was signed and presented to young David.

1956 Two weeks earlier, the Red Sox had tried in vain to put Willard Nixon on the disabled list with a sore arm. Lacking supporting medical information, their application was rejected by a skeptical Commissioner Ford Frick, who thought the Sox were trying to avoid cutting down their roster. Before a Yankee Stadium crowd, Nixon throws a perfect game until he suddenly walked Mickey Mantle on four straight pitches. He lost his no-hitter in the eighth, and lost the shutout in the bottom of the ninth when Mantle belted a three-run homer. Nixon and the Red Sox still won, 7–3.

1952 Mickey McDermott faced the minimum 27 batters, but a clean single by Mel Hoderlein spoiled any thought of a no-hitter. Hoderlein was erased when Jackie Jensen hit into a double play. Hoderlein had figured in an earlier play, after McDermott walked "The Walking Man" Eddie Yost, the leadoff batter. Hoderlein himself hit into a double play. Fred Hatfield's triple scored Clyde Vollmer in the sixth, and the resulting 1–0 score stood as the final.

1946 Boo Ferriss shuts out the A's, 2–0, as the Boston Red Sox launch another win streak; this one runs 12 games if you don't count the tie game in the middle.

1932 The last time the Red Sox called Braves Field home was a Sunday doubleheader against Connie Mack's A's. Boston won the first game, 6–4, but were shut out in the second, 3–0. After the minister of the church located near Fenway said he had no objection to the Red Sox playing down the street—no one had thought to ask—it was no longer necessary for Sox games to be scheduled at the Wigwam.

1927 Seeking some insurance runs, with their lead just 8–7, the Yankees scored seven times in the eighth inning and opened up some breathing room. The final was 15–7. It was a come-from-behind win, as Boston had led 6–1 after two and a half innings. Babe Ruth homered and later hit a bases-loaded single in the eighth.

1917 Playing at American League Park in Washington, the Red Sox scored twice in the ninth inning to give Dutch Leonard a 2–1 win, then exploded for seven runs in the fifth inning of the day's second game to give Babe Ruth another win, 9–0. Harry Hooper starred in game two, with two doubles and two stolen bases in a 3-for-5 nightcap.

1916 Boston's Carl Mays shut out the Yankees, 3–0, on just three hits. The win came after five straight losses to the New Yorkers.

1915 The Red Sox and Athletics split a doubleheader, and Connie Mack sells pitcher Herb Pennock to the Red Sox for $1,500. Herb Pennock ends up in the Hall of Fame, though not until the Sox passed him on to the Yankees.

1912 More than 50 baserunners crossed home plate before darkness forced an eighth-inning end to the second game. The Red Sox romped over Washington, 21–8 and 12–11. There were 59 hits in all, but only one homer (Heinie Wagner's). The twin bill saw an astonishing 17 errors in total, eight of them by Washington in the first game.

1908 Pat Donahue, catcher and occasional first baseman, debuted on this date. In 1910, he had the distinction of playing for four teams in one year: the Red Sox, Philadelphia Athletics, Cleveland Naps, and—again—the Philadelphia Athletics. This was topped only by Frank Huelsman, who played for five teams in 1904. Hitting .211 lifetime, Donahue played two games for BOS, 14 for PHI, three for CLE and one game (just one at-bat) for PHI again.

DEBUTS

1907: Jimmy Barrett	1940: Bill Butland
1908: Pat Donahue	1949: Frank Quinn
1912: Marty Krug	1993: Jose Melendez
1921: Allen Sothoron	

BIRTHDATES
John Kennedy 1941 (1970–1974); Mike Stenhouse 1958 (1986); Toby Borland 1969 (1997)

DEATHS
Mike McNally 1965; Carl Reynolds 1978

May 30

2001 Pedro's next start against New York was strong, allowing just four hits (to Mussina's five). Final score: 3–0 in Boston's favor. After the game, Pedro said, "I'm starting to hate talking about the Yankees. The questions are so stupid. They're wasting my time. It's getting kind of old. Maybe they should just wake up the Bambino, and have him face me and maybe I'll drill him in the ass." Maybe, also, Pedro shouldn't have said that. The Red Sox and Yankees matched up seven more times in 2001, and the Red Sox lost every one of them. Three of those seven games were Pedro starts, including the September 7 game at the Stadium where Pedro was bounced after three innings. It would be more than a year later (July 19, 2002) before he beat the Yanks once again.

2000 Fielding a routine grounder at third base, John Valentin's left knee crumpled and he fell to the ground writhing in pain as muscle had torn from bone. "My knee exploded," Val said. Valentin was coming back from knee surgery the previous November. The Red Sox won, 8–2, but every player's mind was on the loss of a teammate. A drama of doctors ensued. Dr. David Altchek operated on Val's ruptured patellar tendon on June 1, but on June 2 the Red Sox wrote Valentin's agent Dick Moss that his client had "ignored the terms and conditions" of his contract by using an unauthorized (albeit widely respected) surgeon, the same surgeon who had worked on Valentin in November. Valentin had told team doctor Arthur Pappas of his plans, but Moss argued that this was a case of GM Duquette asking, "Why didn't I get to make the decision?"

1997 Mo Vaughn hit three homers for the Red Sox, as Boston beat New York 10–4 at Fenway. New York pitchers gave up six HRs in all; reliever Danny Rios made his major league debut, only to surrender homers to the first two batters he faced.

1980 Dave Stapleton debuted for the Red Sox and hit a double during a 1-for-4 game. Stapleton holds the unusual distinction of playing seven seasons, all for (and only for) the same team, while seeing his batting average decline each and every year. From 1980 through 1986, his averages were: .321, .285, .264, .247, .231, .227, and .128. After the .128 season, the Sox had seen enough. But it's too bad he wasn't playing his usual first base to close out Game Six of the World Series.

1959 Ted Williams hit his first home run of the season (he'd missed more than a month with a pinched nerve in his neck), kicking off his 20th anniversary season with a 4-for-8 doubleheader. His two-run seventh-inning homer in the second game lifted the Sox to a 4–3 lead. Boston overcame Baltimore leads in both games.

1952 The Senators scored four runs in the top of the ninth to win the first game, 5–2, but Boston's Mel Parnell beat Washington for the 17th time in a row in the second game, 5–3, with a little relief help from Ike Delock. Parnell hadn't lost a game to the Senators since May 28, 1948. Oddly, Ellis Kinder was riding the record, too, with 17 consecutive wins against the White Sox, which he would extend to 18 with a June 1 win in relief.

1951 The whiffing man? The Red Sox take two from the Yankees, and New York rookie Mickey Mantle struck out five times in succession: three in game one and twice more to start the second game. He hardly made bat contact; there was only one foul ball amongst all those strikes. Manager Casey Stengel sent in Cliff Mapes to give Mantle the rest of the day off.

In the opener, the Yankees roared back from a 6–3 deficit, scoring seven runs in the bottom of the seventh to take the lead. The Sox got two back in the seventh, and Ted Williams tied the game at 10–10 with a two-run HR in the bottom of the eighth. With two out in the bottom of the 15th, Vern Stephens got a pitch he liked from Spec Shea and hit it into the screen in left, for an 11–10 win. He'd hit a first-inning homer to start the scoring. This was a game that even saw Williams (7-for-13 at the plate) score from second on a sacrifice bunt!

Williams doubled to tie the second game and Stephens came through again with a single to bring Ted home with what proved the winning run before the Red Sox ran the score up to 9–4. Ray Scarborough, with eight scoreless innings in the first game, and Bill Wight were the winning pitchers—the Sox now had 10 wins in a row, and the Yankees were knocked out of first place as the White Sox swept two games for their 13th and 14th straight wins.

1946 Overcoming a 4–1 deficit, tying and winning in the bottom of the ninth, the Sox took the first game from the visiting Senators, 6–5, and won the second, 7–2. Rudy York was 5-for-8 on the day, with three RBIs.

1943 Jim Tabor's solo home run off Virgil Trucks was the first home run of the season at Fenway Park. It won the game for the Red Sox, a 3–0 shutout for Dick Newsome. It was just the third homer of the year for Boston; major league totals were down since the baseballs being used were the so-called balata balls during World War II, used to conserve rubber for military purposes. Tony Lupien hit two triples in the 5–1 second-game win over the Tigers, pitched by Lou Lucier, the "Earl of Pawtucket."

1941 New York won the first game at Fenway, scoring three unearned runs after Jim Tabor's ninth-inning error. Joe DiMaggio made three errors all by himself in the second game and the Red Sox won, 13–0, as three other Yankees chipped in with their own miscues. In the fifth inning of game two, the Sox stole four bases in one inning. Skeeter Newsome stole second, and a couple of batters later found himself on third with the bases loaded and Dom DiMaggio at the plate. The Red Sox pulled off a triple steal, with Newsome stealing home, Frankie Pytlak taking third, and pitcher Mickey Harris taking second. Ted Williams has six hits in the doubleheader, helping him build up hit totals toward a .406 season.

1939 Ted Williams hit two homers, one in each game, as Boston hosted the Yankees in the Memorial Day doubleheader, from which over 10,000 fans were reportedly turned away. New York's Red Ruffing was chased early in the first game, which the Sox won, 8–4, but the Yankees seemingly scored at will in the second and took it easily, 17–9.

1938 Even the men's room lines must have been terrific as 83,533 fans somehow crammed into Yankee Stadium—the largest crowd in franchise history. They were rewarded; the Yankees took two from the Red Sox, 10–0 and 5–4. Red Ruffing shut out the Sox in game one; Lefty Grove had won eight games in a row, but just didn't have it. The second game was harder-fought, with the Yankees tying it in the eighth and winning in the ninth on Mike Higgins' throwing error.

The day is most noted for the fight between Jake Powell of the Yankees and Boston's manager Joe Cronin. When a pitch from Boston's Archie McKain hit Powell, the batter charged the mound. Protecting his pitcher, Cronin raced to intercede and absorbed Powell's blows. After the combatants were separated, and ejected, Cronin's only exit from the playing field in those days was through the New York dugout. Several Yankees followed him into the tunnel, prompting the three umpires to follow. "Presently all the other players also dashed from view," reported the *New York Times*, "leaving the record crowd to view in bewilderment nothing but the grass while Cronin and Powell renewed hostilities under the stands."

1937 Former Red Sox pitcher Pete Jablonowski (0–3, in 1932) changed his name to Pete Appleton, then won 14 games with the Senators in 1936. In this day's game in Boston, he got himself a win, throwing an 11–4 seven-hitter. He also drove in six of the runs, coming up with the bases loaded in both the second and third, and singling and tripling respectively for his first five RBIs. He had two singles later in the game, his eighth inning base hit driving in the sixth (and record-tying) RBI. Quite a few years later, Vic Raschi became the first pitcher to drive in seven.

1933 Philadelphia's Lefty Grove appeared in relief in both games of a Boston doubleheader. The Athletics won both games, the second one lasting 12 innings. The 1932 AL batting champion, Boston's Dale Alexander (.367), hurt his knee sliding into home plate during the second game. Boston's trainer tried a new heat therapy—diathermy—and burned Alexander's leg severely. "It was roasted like a leg of lamb," wrote newspaperman John Drohan. Alexander never recovered his batting stroke.

1931 The Fenway faithful saw quite a doubleheader. The first game pitted Philadelphia's Lefty Grove against Boston's Jack Russell, and neither team scored through 11 full frames. Suddenly, Mule Haas hit a homer into the right-field bleachers and Russell crumbled; before the inning was over, the Athletics scored five times and won game one, 5–0. In game two, the Athletics put together five more runs, scoring in the second through fifth innings, and the score stood 5–0 heading into the bottom of the ninth. Finally, Philadelphia's Roy Mahaffey tired, and neither he nor Eddie Rommel nor even Rube Walberg could stem the Sox, who poured on six runs to overcome and take the game.

1921 An eighth-inning muff of a pickoff throw was charged to Stuffy McInnis at first. Two plays later, the Athletics won the tight 2–1 game as Dykes—the runner who would have been retired had McInnis caught the ball cleanly—scored. It is the only error all year long by McInnis (in fact, the only error he'd made since June 23, 1919) and it is more than a full year (163 games) before he makes another one, 1,625 chances later. McInnis was pretty steady at the plate, too. In 1921, he had 584 at-bats, but only struck out nine times.

1919 At Philadelphia, during an Athletics rally, fans banged on the roof of the Red Sox dugout. Carl Mays, who'd pitched the day before, became incensed at the incessant pounding, grabbed a baseball and fired it hard into the stands, hitting Bryan Hayes of the Philadelphia customs office in the head and breaking his straw hat. Another Sox player punched the man sitting next to Hayes. Only the intercession of Connie Mack dissuaded Hayes from having Mays arrested. The Sox and Athletics split the day's doubleheader.

1913 Harry Hooper hit a leadoff home run in both games of a Memorial Day doubleheader in Our Nation's Capitol. Boston won the first game, 4–3. Hooper's homer made the difference. In the second game, Hooper's homer off Walter Johnson was the only scoring as the Sox win, 1–0. The twin homers were half of Hooper's home run output for all of 1913.

1911 Clarence DeMar, seven-time winner of the Boston Marathon, won his first in 1911. On this date, he won a "15-mile modified marathon" at the Red Sox home Huntington Avenue Grounds.

1910 Philadelphia beat the Sox 5–1 in the first of two, and the Red Sox were losing 5–1 in the second game heading into the bottom of the ninth. After making the first out, with large numbers of fans filing out, the Sox scored four runs to tie, and won it in the bottom of the 10th, 6–5.

1908 Cy Young throws a one-hitter, with Washington's first baseman Jerry Freeman making the only hit, a single, in the 6–0 win. Washington bats come alive, though, in the second game, and drive in 7 runs to Boston's 4.

1901 The Boston Americans play their first doubleheader ever, dropping both games to Chicago, in Chicago, 8–3 and 5–3.

TRANSACTIONS
1980: Released Ted Sizemore.
1995: Mike Maddux signed as a free agent.

DEBUTS

1910: Red Kleinow	1940: Marv Owen
1918: Dick McCabe,	1944: Jim Bucher
Vince Molyneaux	1965: Bob Duliba
1919: Bill James	1980: Dave Stapleton
1934: Wes Ferrell	

BIRTHDATES
Manny Ramirez 1972 (2001–2005)

DEATHS
None yet

May 31

1999 Tom Gordon's save of an 8–7 win over Detroit was his AL record 54th consecutive save dating back to April 19, 1998. He'd saved 43 games in 1998, and now his first 11 in 1999.

1998 The most runs ever scored in one inning against the Yankees: the Sox scored 11 runs in the third inning, jumping all over Andy Pettitte for eight earned runs, and his replacement Darren Holmes for three more. Sox won, 13–7.

1986 Wade Boggs had a 5-for-5 day, bumping his average to .402. Bruce Hurst started and got the win—but just barely. His very last pitch of the fifth inning resulted in a fly out, but Hurst himself fell to the ground with a groin injury. Boston won, 7–2. Hurst recovered in time to make his next scheduled start.

1980 Dave Stapleton shares an AL record with two home runs in his first two games. They both came in the second of the two games. The Sox hit six home runs in all, four of them in the fourth inning, but the Brewers cruised to a 19–8 victory.

1970 The Sox—White and Red—combined for 42 hits, but Chicago had 25 of them (including five each by their leadoff and #2 hitters—Walt "No Neck" Williams and Luis Aparicio). Williams scored five times, and the White Sox scored 22 times in all, beating Boston, 22–13. The total of 35 runs fell one short of the AL record game, a Red Sox 22–14 win over Philadelphia in 1950.

1969 Rico Petrocelli made an error, after 48 games without a miscue.

1961 Mantle and Maris homer again—a theme for 1961. After building up a 7–1 lead, the Sox kept chipping away, scoring in the seventh, eighth, and ninth—but New York's bullpen holds off a late Red Sox surge to win, 7- 6. Of note in the game: in the eighth inning, Carroll Hardy pinch-hit for Carl Yastrzemski and beat out a bunt single. Hardy thus assured himself immortality as a trivia answer; he'd now pinch-hit for both Ted Williams and Carl Yastrzemski. And Roger Maris.

1954 The Red Sox trounced Philadelphia in a Fenway doubleheader, winning 20–10 in the first game, and 9–0 (behind Bill Henry's mound work) in the second game. Harry Agganis was 0-for-6 in the opener, but had a double, a homer, and four RBIs in the second game. The first game saw Sox starter Tom Brewer banged out of the box in the second inning; rookie reliever Tom Herrin got the win. It would be his only major league win.

1944 Johnny Pesky was manager of the Atlanta Naval Air Station team. He singled and tripled, and helped beat the Bell Bombers, 7–1.

1943 Tex Hughson pitched for 13 innings and earned a 2–1 win over the Browns. Just 10 days earlier, on May 21, Hughson pitched for 13 innings and lost a 2–1 game against the Tigers. In between, he shut out the Indians, 2–0. The May 31 win came when Al Simmons, who had struck out three times with the bases loaded, finally got a runner home from third base with a single to center.

1942 Ted Williams knocked in his 41st run of May in a game against Buck Newsom of the Senators. It's the most runs batted in by a Red Sox player during a given month. Ted had two months when he drove in an even 40 runs—June 1950 and July 1951.

1938 Jimmie Foxx hits a grand slam off rookie Yankees pitcher Joe Beggs, his first of three 1938 grand slams. Foxx hit 50 HR for the Sox in '38 and led the league with 175 RBIs despite being walked a league-leading 119 times.

1924 What were the Red Sox doing in first place, anyhow? The Washington Nationals pummeled them, 12–0, and drove the Sox down from the heights. On June 4, with a 6–5 win over St. Louis, Boston climbed back on top. As late as June 14, the Red Sox held top rank, though by June 23rd they were already in fourth place and sinking.

1917 Larry Gardner's three-run homer in the sixth inning and Carl Mays' four-hit pitching were all the Red Sox needed to secure their 10th consecutive win, topping Cleveland, 5–1.

1907 With the bases loaded for New York in the top of the sixth in a scoreless game, Kid Elberfeld surprised Boston by sprinting for home the minute George Winter went into his windup. He executed a straight steal of home, sliding in under catcher Charlie Armbruster's tag. Taking advantage of the shock, Hal Chase and Wid Conroy stole as well, making it a successful triple steal. Then Chase tried his own steal of home, and almost made it. Elberfeld doubled in the eighth, stole third, and came home on Chase's grounder. Boston lost this game, 4–1.

TRANSACTIONS
1945: Oscar Judd was selected off waivers by the Philadelphia Phillies.
1994: Acquired Wes Chamberlain and Mike Sullivan in trade from
    the Phillies for Paul Quantrill and Billy Hatcher.
1999: Acquired Rob Stanifer in trade from the Florida Marlins
    for minor leaguer Brian Partenheimer.

DEBUTS
1924: Johnnie Heving, Red Ruffing
1970: Mike Fiore
1991: Mike Gardiner
1993: Jim Byrd
1995: Mike Maddux
2000: Hipolito Pichardo

BIRTHDATES
Tim Van Egmond 1969 (1994–1995); Jose Malave 1971
(1996–1997); Dave Roberts 1972 (2004)

DEATHS
Case Patten 1935; Rabbit Warstler 1964; Jerry Adair 1987

JUNE

June 1

2005 When Sammy Sosa homered at Fenway, it had been 5,824 days since the last time he'd homered there (June 21, 1989)—the longest stretch between homers in a given ballpark for any major league hitter.

2003 The 2003 Cy Young Award winner, Toronto's Roy Halladay, served up seven doubles to Red Sox batters (five of them in the third inning) at Skydome.

1987 Roger Clemens was 8–0 lifetime against the Minnesota Twins, but even Dwight Evans' 300th home run wasn't enough as the Twins hit four and won, 9–5.

1982 Rickey Henderson stole his 51st and 52nd bases, and hit a two-run homer in the fifth inning, to help Oakland beat Boston, 3–2. Henderson now had 52 steals in the season's first 51 games.

1971 Luis Aparicio batted .313 for the White Sox in 1970, but after 44 at-bats without a hit, the new Red Sox shortstop finally broke out of a prolonged slump.

1963 The Red Sox released their oldest player, who was the team's player rep—pitcher Ike Delock. In place of the 10-year Red Sox lifer, Boston called up local phenom Wilbur Wood; he'd been playing with the Sox farm team Seattle Rainiers.

1961 Bill Skowron hit homers in both the eighth and ninth, but with the Sox ahead, 7–1, he couldn't do it all by himself. Yaz hit the fourth homer of his young career—all four of them had been over Fenway's left-field Wall. Vic Wertz's triple helped drive Bob Turley from the game—it was Wertz's first three-base hit since June 14, 1955, almost six years earlier.

1952 Cousins from Chicago? In the seventh inning, Ellis Kinder came on to relieve Bill Henry in a tight 2–2 game. He got the Sox out of the inning, and Fred Hatfield's solo homer in the bottom of the frame gave Kinder the win. It was his 18th win in a row against the White Sox; he hadn't lost to them since 1948. (See May 30, 1952.) Saul Rogovin was the hard-luck loser.

1950 In the midst of the greatest start of a great career, and with the Red Sox in great position to contend once again, why would Ted Williams suddenly want to be traded to Detroit? Nonetheless, persistent press reports prompted him to issue a denial of Jimmy Cannon's story that he'd like to be traded. "I never said anything about being dissatisfied," Ted said. "There's nothing wrong with us that a few victories won't cure." Tigers manager Red Rolfe said, "I think we could find room for him," but doubted that Detroit could make a deal that would satisfy the Sox.

1942 Jimmie Foxx, out with a fractured rib, was placed on waivers and—not selected by any AL club—was picked up by the Chicago Cubs. It had been a tough year for Foxx; in spring training, he had broken a toe. Foxx had driven in 100 or more runs in 13 straight seasons.

1941 After a 4-for-9 doubleheader, Ted Williams was batting .430 on the season. People began to think he might have a shot at .400 for the year.

1930 Massachusetts native "Deacon Danny" MacFayden beats the Yankees 7–4. First baseman Phil Todt cuts down one New York threat with a triple play on a liner to first. Snaring the ball, he stepped on first base to get Dusty Cooke and then threw to short before Bill Dickey could get back to the bag. The drought is over; this win puts the finish to a 14-game losing streak.

1919 The reigning World Champion Red Sox were defeated in a Paterson, New Jersey exhibition game, 6–5, in 10 innings, despite Babe Ruth's three-run homer. The winning team: the Doherty Silk Sox.

1917 After 10 consecutive wins, the Sox streak ceased when Cleveland's Guy Morton shut them down with a one-hit (an eighth-inning Babe Ruth single up the middle) 3–0 game. Ruth was pitching well, too; he likewise only allowed one hit through eight innings. The Indians, though, scored twice in the fourth without a hit. The unusual inning featured *two* steals of home plate, one by Ray Chapman and one by Braggo Roth.

1916 The veteran Walter Johnson pitched against relative newcomer Babe Ruth, and both teams were scoreless through seven. Ruth won, 1–0, when Red Sox second sacker Mike McNally scored from second on an infield grounder to the shortstop. Neither Ruth nor Johnson had a hit, but Johnson struck Ruth out twice. McNally had 135 at-bats in 87 games in 1916, and never managed even one extra-base hit.

1914 Turning the tables, Rankin Johnson won a 1–0 game against Washington's Walter Johnson. Just two days before, on May 29, it was Walter who beat Rankin by the same 1–0 score. In their next matchup, on July 3, Rankin lost it, 12–0. He tried once more on July 6, but lost another close one, another 1–0 squeaker.

1909 A dead ball low-scoring affair in Philadelphia saw the Red Sox lose the first game 1–0, but win the second, also 1–0. Jack "Gulfport" Ryan pitched 11 innings for Boston in game one, before giving up a double and a two-out walkoff single to Danny Murphy. Hal Krause got the complete game win for Philly, but his fellow pitcher Eddie Plank lost the heartbreaker in the nightcap when he gave up a run in the eighth on a single, an error, and Tris Speaker's RBI single. Fred Burchell started, and Eddie Cicotte completed, the shutout win for Boston.

1901 Buck Freeman is the first player in franchise history to hit two home runs in one game, a 10–5 victory in Chicago. Though Chicago scored five runs in the first inning, courtesy of a little sloppy play by Freddy Parent and "Buttermilk Tommy" Dowd. Buck Freeman knocked in five runs all by himself with the two drives over the right-field fence, one in the fourth and one as part of a six-run uprising in Boston's half of the sixth.

TRANSACTIONS

1942: Jimmie Foxx selected off waivers by the Chicago Cubs.
1968: Sometime during the month of June, 1968, Bill (Rudy) Schlesinger was
received from the Chicago Cubs in an unknown transaction.
1988: Drafted John Valentin, Tim Naehring, John Flaherty, Scott Taylor, and Peter Hoy.
1992: Drafted Steve Rodriguez, Bill Selby, and Joe Hudson.
1995: Drafted Steve Lomasney, Matt Kinney, Cole Liniak, Paxton Crawford, and Juna Pena.

DEBUTS
1906: Ralph Glaze
1994: Wes Chamberlain
2003: Byung-Hyun Kim

BIRTHDATES
George Huff 1872 (manager, 1907); Lou Legett 1901 (1933–1934); Hal
Kolstad 1935 (1962–1963); Derek Lowe 1973 (1997–2004)

DEATHS
Fred Heimach 1973

June 2

1995 Scoring once in the seventh, once in the eighth, and once again in the ninth, the Sox beat Seattle, 6–5. The star of the day was John Valentin, 5-for-5, with three home runs. With a double and a single to boot, he was the first shortstop to hit 15 total bases in a single game.

1989 Junior Felix of the Toronto Blue Jays hit the only inside-the-park grand slam by an opposing player in Fenway history. It was hit off Bob Stanley, with two outs in the top of the ninth inning, taking the steam out of any hope for a Red Sox rally. Toronto won, 7–2.

1984 Jim Rice hit into two double plays; his 36 GIDPs in 1984 sets a major league record. Carl Yastrzemski holds the major league mark for a left-handed hitter (30), set in 1964.

1973 Mario Guerrero initiates four double plays and is the middle man in a fifth, but Oakland still scores two more runs than the Red Sox, and wins 3–1.

1966 The Monster has left the building. Perhaps befitting his size and stature, Dick Radatz is traded to Cleveland for two pitchers: Lee Stange and Don McMahon.

1959 With a double in the first inning off Kansas City's Ray Herbert, Ted Williams achieved his 2,500th major league hit. KC overcame Boston's 3–0 lead and won, 5–3, behind 7⅓ innings of stellar Tom Sturdivant relief.

1955 Today's game turned out to be the last game for Harry Agganis, who entered the hospital and died of complications from pneumonia on the 27th. In his final game, The Golden Greek was 2-for-4 with a double, but Boston lost.

1952 A 10th-inning grand slam by Don Lenhardt provides a grand ending to a 6–2 win over the White Sox. It wasn't looking good when the visiting White Sox took a 2–1 lead in the top of the 10th, but starter Ken Holcombe hit Fred Hatfield, yielded a single to Del Wilber (who'd failed twice to lay down a successful sacrifice), and Dom DiMaggio drove in Hatfield to tie it back up. An intentional walk later, Lenhardt hit the first pitch into the screen in left. It was his second slam of the season.

1945 The Tigers' Joe Orrell said, "I always have a good day after I buy a new suit" and headed out to shop, but only came back with a pair of new shoes. He lost the game to the Red Sox, leaving for a pinch-hitter in the seventh.

1944 The Tigers scored four times in the first three frames, and beat the Red Sox, 4–1. It was their seventh straight win, but got no help from Sox shortstop Eddie Lake, who pitched the seventh and eighth innings without surrendering a hit.

1943 In two days, the Sox and the Browns played four consecutive extra-inning games, working 45 innings in doubleheaders on May 31 and June 2. Boston won three of the four games. In the June 2 game, first baseman Tony Lupien turned two unassisted double plays, tying a record.

1940 The Sox split a pair with the Sox. Ted Lyons won his 225th game, shutting out the Red Sox in the first game, 6–0. Boston battled Chicago in the second game, with the lead changing five times. The White Sox tied it in the top of the ninth, but Jimmie Foxx hit a two-run homer into Fenway's left-field screen to win it in the bottom of the ninth.

1935 The *Chicago Tribune* headline read BABE RUTH QUITS, SO BOSTON FIRES HIM. Playing with the Braves, or not playing as the case may be, Ruth wanted to be excused to go to a party on the ocean liner *Normandie*. Braves owner Judge Emil Fuchs would not agree, so Ruth said he was retiring. On learning that the Braves had announced his unconditional release, Ruth un-retired and said he was taking a 60-day vacation to consider other offers. Ruth called Fuchs a "double-crosser" and Fuchs declared Ruth an "imbecile." It was not as gracious or as spectacular an exit as, for instance, that of Ted Williams. Ruth had made over one million dollars in salary from playing ball.

Yankees batters hit six solo homers and beat the Red Sox 7–2. The first Sox pitcher was George Pipgras, who took the loss and then was released after the game. The Sox' two runs came on a two-run shot by Mel Almada. Pipgras will later become an AL umpire.

1924 The Red Sox were contending for first place and drawing large crowds. Burt Whitman wrote in *The Sporting News*, "Boston rejoices that Frazee no longer has a finger in the Red Sox...Frazee radiated that he did not give a hoot for the fans." Whitman suggested that new owner Quinn put a second deck on the Fenway Park grandstand, to be able to seat all the fans. By mid-August, though, Whitman termed the Red Sox mound corps a "total wreck."

1922 Stuffy McInnis makes an error at first base for the first time in more than a year. His errorless streak started 163 games earlier, on May 31, 1921.

1915 Babe Ruth, described by the *New York Times* as "built like a bale of cotton," beat the Yankees, 7–1, in New York before about 500 frigid fans. Ruth limited the Yanks to five hits, and hit a two-run homer in the second off Jack Warhop. The next two times up, Ruth was walked. He reportedly kicked the bench in frustration, fracturing his toe, but he was able to start again on the 17th.

1903 Boston shut out New York for the first time ever, a 9–0 win with Bill Dinneen granting just five hits and not walking a batter, while Tannehill was pounded for nine runs in nine innings.

1901 Ahead in the game, 4–2, Boston is up in the top of the ninth with two outs and nobody on. Looking for some insurance runs, they get to Milwaukee's Bill Reidy for 10 consecutive hits and 9 more runs, all earned. It's a record. Five singles, four doubles, and a home run by Freddy Parent contributed to the piling-on. Cy Young pitched, but another pitcher, Ben Beville, took over at first base when both Jimmy Collins and Buck Freeman were ejected in the fifth inning. Beville had two doubles in the ninth—the only hits of his whole short career.

TRANSACTIONS

1914: Selected Del Gainer off waivers from the Detroit Tigers.
1966: Traded Dick Radatz to the Indians for Don McMahon and Lee Stange.
1967: Acquired Jerry Adair in trade with the Chicago White
Sox for Don McMahon and Bob Snow.
1986: Drafted Scott Cooper.
1987: Drafted Reggie Harris, Bob Zupcic, Jim Byrd, Jeff Plympton, and Phil Plantier.
1994: Drafted Nomar Garciaparra, Brian Rose, Donnie Sadler,
Carl Pavano, and Michael Coleman.
1998: Drafted Adam Everett, Mike Maroth, Josh Hancock, and Dennis Tankersley.
1999: Casey Fossum was selected in the first round (48th pick) of the amateur draft.

DEBUTS

1921: Ernie Neitzke, Sammy Vick
1926: Bill Regan

BIRTHDATES

Charlie Jones 1876 (1901); Mike Stanton 1967 (1995–1996, 2005)

DEATHS

Denny Sullivan 1956; Lore Bader 1973; Bob McGraw 1978

June 3

2002 Red Sox architect Janet Marie Smith revealed the possibility of adding around 500 on top of Fenway's "Green Monster." Preservation group Save Fenway Park! had floated the idea a couple of years earlier. When installed for the 2003 season, Green Monster seats became hugely-sought-after day-of-game real estate.

1990 After June 2, when catcher Tony Peña was flattened by a message pitch, Peña predicted, "Somebody go down tomorrow." The Indians' leadoff batter, Stan Jefferson, was hit by the second pitch thrown by Roger Clemens. Both benches emptied (see June 22, 1989) and manager Joe Morgan later crowed, "I loved it. We got even, didn't we?" He said the team had voted 34–0 "that it would be such." Tony Peña said it was the first time he'd thrown a punch in 10 years in the big leagues, but felt good about it: "We did something good as a team." The Red Sox won, too, 8–2. On June 5, Morgan was suspended three games for inflammatory comments.

1988 Margo Adams files suit against Wade Boggs for "palimony" after their four-year relationship broke up. The following year, they reached an out-of-court settlement. Adams could not file for emotional distress or fraud, and the amount Adams was seeking was reduced to "only" $500,000 (rather than the $12 million for which she had filed.)

Did all the attention distract Boggs in 1988? Hardly. He was hitting .310 on the season when the news broke. For the remainder of the season, he hit .380 and won his fifth batting championship.

1964   Tony Conigliaro hit a fifth-inning grand slam off Dan Osinski. Tony C. was 19 years and five months old, the youngest player who has ever hit a grand slam.

1963   In their fourth exhibition game for the Jimmy Fund since the Boston Braves decamped for Milwaukee, the Red Sox finally won one, 5–2. Dave Morehead gave up just two hits in his five innings of work—one to Hank Aaron and one to Hank's brother Tommy.

1952   Johnny Pesky and Walt Dropo were both traded to the Tigers, along with Fred Hatfield, Don Lenhardt, and Bill Wight. In exchange, the Sox secured George Kell, Hoot Evers, Johnny Lipon, and Dizzy Trout.

1946   They call it the keystone sack, but this is getting ridiculous. Bobby Doerr handles 28 balls at second base in back-to-back games, the second game of a May 30 doubleheader and the first game of this day's twin bill. He had 15 putouts and 13 assists.

1918   Just one first-inning walk away from a perfect game, Red Sox southpaw Hubert Benjamin "Dutch" Leonard threw his second no-hit game, taming the Tigers, 5–0. Babe Ruth played center field and got the game-winning hit, a home run in the top of the first.

1916   Manager Bill Carrigan announced he was playing the game under protest when umpire Ollie Chill kind of got in an argument with himself and Carrigan didn't like the outcome. In the third inning, Chill interfered with Cleveland's "Cotton Top" Turner reaching second base. The *Atlanta Constitution* reported that Chill "ruled Turner was entitled to the base, then reversed himself and called Turner out, and finally compromised by allowing the runner to remain on first base." As it happens, no runs scored in the third, but the Indians piled on later in the game to win, 11–2. Much of the offense came from former Sox star Tris Speaker, who had two triples, a single, and a sac fly, driving in five.

1913   In pre-game ceremonies, the Red Sox raised the 1912 American League pennant, then went on to beat Chicago, 3–2, Tris Speaker having a 3-for-4 day and extending his hit streak to 22 games. On June 25, the Sox will raise the World Championship banner.

TRANSACTIONS
1952: Traded Walt Dropo, Fred Hatfield, Don Lenhardt, Johnny Pesky, and Bill Wight to the Detroit Tigers for Hoot Evers, George Kell, Johnny Lipon, and Dizzy Trout.
1975: Drafted Dave Schmidt, Ed Jurak, Dave Stapleton, Mike O'Berry, and Mike Paxton.
1976: Traded Bernie Carbo to the Milwaukee Brewers for Bobby Darwin and Tom Murphy.
1980: Drafted Mike Brown, Pat Dodson, Al Nipper, Oil Can Boyd, and Tom Bolton.
1991: Drafted Aaron Sele, Scott Hatteberg, Luis Ortiz, Tony Rodriguez,
       Cory Bailey, Tim Van Egmond, Ron Mahay, and Joel Bennett.
1993: Drafted Trot Nixon, Jeff Suppan, Ryan McGuire, Lou Merloni,
       Andy Abad, and Shayne Bennett.
1997: Drafted Travis Harper, Angel Santos, Brian Barkley, and David Eckstein.

DEBUTS
1909: Bunny Madden
1966: Lee Stange
1977: Ramon Hernandez
2000: Dan Smith

BIRTHDATES
Urbane Pickering 1899 (1931–1932); Chappie Geygan 1903 (1924–1926);
Duane Josephson 1942 (1971–1972); Julio Valdez 1956 (1980–1983);
Steve Lyons 1960 (1985–1993); Carl Everett 1971 (2000–2001)

DEATHS
Roxy Walters 1956

June 4

2002 Carlos Baerga was 2-for-5, with four RBIs, his most productive day for the Red Sox. Baerga had left the majors in 2000 and 2001, and was owner of the Vaqueros, a baseball team in Bayamon, Puerto Rico. He joined the Red Sox for spring training 2002 as a non-roster invitee, and made the team. It was an unusual experience—the owner of one team vying to make another team as an invitee. When he joined the Red Sox, he then became—once again—a member of the player's association, thus being at the same time ownership (in Bayamon) and labor (in Boston). On top of that, one of his Red Sox teammates was Rey Sanchez, a player Carlos recruited and hired for Bayamon the previous winter.

1999 Gordon Edes of the *Boston Globe* suggested that Pedro Martinez was in a league of his own. Unfazed by interleague play, facing the NL East-leading Atlanta Braves, Pedro punched out 16 Braves batters, winning a 5–1 three-hitter. Pedro ran his record to 11–1. In 45 appearances for Boston, he already had 16 games with 10 or more strikeouts.

1995 Tim Wakefield kept Seattle scoreless for nine innings at Fenway. Trouble is, Tim Belcher shut out the Red Sox, too. Wakefield threw the 10th, but he let in a run. The Mariners turned it over to Bobby Ayala, and Troy O'Leary hit a two-run, walkoff home run.

1989 The Sox lost a 10–0 lead. Ahead of Toronto, 10–0, after six innings, everything fell apart. The Sox had been cruising behind the pitching of starter Mike Smithson, but when he had to leave with a foot blister in the seventh, Sox relievers yielded two runs in the seventh, four in the eighth, and five in the ninth. The Sox tied it up in the bottom of the ninth, but ultimately lost, 13–11, in 12 innings; it was the biggest blown lead in Fenway history.

1982 The California Angels made Anaheim fans happy, scoring three times in the bottom of the eighth to take a 4–2 lead. The Red Sox tied it with two in the top of the ninth. Come the 11th, and the Sox scored a full seven times (the most ever for the club in an extra inning), and won it, 11–4. (See also August 16, 2005.)

1977 Bill Lee only needed 78 pitches to throw a complete nine-inning game at Metropolitan Stadium, beating the Twins, 5–2. He never let a single batter even get to ball three.

1967 What a difference a change of scenery can make. Gary Bell had his good years and not so good years with the Indians. In 1967, he was having a bad one, going 1–5 for the Tribe. Traded to Boston, he won 12 games against 8 losses, and helped get the team into the World Series.

1952 Ted Williams had been recalled to the Marine Corps, and when replacement left-fielder Hoot Evers hit his first Fenway homer, fans cheered. Then Evers did something not seen at Fenway in years; the left fielder waved in acknowledgement. George Kell hit a homer, too, and Billy Goodman went 5-for-5 (all singles), scoring four times, as the Sox beat the Indians, 13–11. When the Indians' Larry Doby singled in the top of the ninth, he completed a cycle on the day.

1943 Al Simmons was ejected from the game by ump Bill Summers for being "overly noisy" (*The Sporting News*)

1936 Lefty Grove was pitching for Boston, and the bases were loaded with two outs in the top of the eighth. Cleveland's George Blaeholder struck out, but Moe Berg dropped the third strike. Berg picked up the ball and stepped on home plate for the force out. The umpire ruled a force out, but Blaeholder started running for first base anyhow. As he trotted across the field, Boston third baseman Billy Werber picked up the ball, which Berg had flipped to the mound, and threw it to Jimmie Foxx who tagged the bag at first. Thus, Grove picked up a strikeout. F}

1932 The Red Sox had managed five losing streaks of four or more games, but through June 3 had not yet managed to win two games in a row all season long. Their record stood at a horrendous 7–35. "Red Sox Amaze Own Boosters" read the *Los Angeles Times* article: the Sox had taken both games of a doubleheader against Washington, 4–2 and 9–8. It wasn't until more than a month later that they won another two in a row, games on July 12 and 13. The Sox got hot at the end of July and established a season-best *three*-game win streak, a mark they matched once more at the end of August.

1909 On June 2, down 5–0 to the Tigers after six full innings, the Red Sox rallied with two in the seventh and four in the eighth to take a 6–5 lead. The Tigers threatened, with runners on second and third with one out, but Sox pitching held and Boston won the game. On June 4, the Tigers got off to another 5–0 lead. This time Detroit won it, 5–0.

TRANSACTIONS
1964: Traded Lu Clinton to the Los Angeles Angels for Lee Thomas.
1967: Traded Tony Horton and Don Demeter to the Indians for Gary Bell.
1970: Drafted John LaRose and Tim Blackwell.
1976: Released Deron Johnson.
1984: Drafted John Marzano, Steve Curry, Jody Reed, and Zach Crouch.
1990: Drafted Frankie Rodriguez, Walt McKeel, Gar Finnvold, and Erik Plantenberg.
1995: Brian Bark signed as a free agent.
1996: Drafted Chris Reitsma, John Barnes, Robert Ramsay,
       Justin Duchscherer, and Shea Hillenbrand.

DEBUTS
1952: Hoot Evers, George Kell,	1968: Fred Wenz
Dizzy Trout	1976: Bobby Darwin
1961: Joe Ginsberg	1988: Zach Crouch
1966: Don McMahon	2003: Hector Almonte

BIRTHDATES
Paul Maloy 1892 (1913); Joe Connolly 1896 (1924); Bob Klinger 1908 (1946–1947); John McNamara 1932 (manager, 1985–1988); Arnold Earley 1933 (1960–1965); Doug Griffin 1947 (1971–1977); Tony Pena 1957 (1990–1993); Cla Meredith 1983 (2005)

DEATHS
Bobby Reeves 1993

June 5

2001 It took two games to do it—18 innings—but Shea Hillenbrand finally gave the Red Sox the win they'd been fighting for all night, 4–3, on a home run over the Wall in the bottom of the 18th inning. The Tigers weren't taking any chances with Manny Ramirez; he was given four intentional walks, tying the league record set by Roger Maris in 1962. The Red Sox used every position player they had before the game was over, some 5 hours and 51 minutes after it began.

1999 When Red Sox reliever Tom Gordon gave up two runs on three hits in the top of the ninth inning, he not only lost his first game of the year, 6–5, to Atlanta, but had failed to record a save for the first time all year. Gordon had converted a major league record 54 consecutive save opportunities. Two singles and a Javy Lopez double did the damage.

1996 Sox slugger Mo Vaughn had a 5-for-6 evening, but the Red and White Sox were tied 6–6 after nine. Red Sox reliever Heathcliff Slocumb let it get away, yielding a leadoff single, a walk, wild pitch (allowing the runners to move up), and a sacrifice fly to Frank Thomas for the go-ahead run. Final: Chicago 8, Boston 6.

1960 New York took two from Boston. The first saw the Yanks build up a 5–0 lead on homers by Mantle and Maris, and hold on despite a home run by Ted Williams to pull the Red Sox within one. 5–4, final. Art Ditmar and Bobby Schantz combined to hold back the Red Sox, 8–3, in the finale.

1958 Cleveland right fielder Rocky Colavito should have just let the ball drop. When he ran down an eighth-inning foul fly ball in right and made the catch, Gene Stephens tagged at third and came in to score the tie-breaking run for the Red Sox. Boston won.

1954 Ted Williams was diagnosed with viral pneumonia, and missed nearly three weeks, not returning until June 23.

1929 Every single member of the Red Sox collected at least one hit and drove in at least one run, as the Red Sox beat the White Sox, 17–2. Chicago scored first, but Boston racked up 23 hits and 39 total bases in a game that saw even Chisox manager Lena Blackburne take the rubber to get the final out. This was the most lopsided win of the 1920s, a decade in which the Red Sox lost far more games than they won.

1916 Babe Ruth threw a complete game six-hit shutout of the Indians. He had to work his way out of a bases-loaded sixth, but The Babe now had a string of 24 scoreless innings to his credit. Ruth went 2-for-3, but Boston's runs largely scored on Cleveland errors.

1911 Three of Chicago's five errors contributed to runs and helped Ed "Loose" Karger pick up a 5–4 win. Smoky Joe Wood came in to close out the seventh; in the ninth inning, he faced three consecutive pinch-hitters and struck out each one of them in turn.

1909 The Red Sox ship off pitcher Cy Morgan one day after he turns gunshy on a tag at the plate on Ty Cobb. The Sox get pitcher Biff Schlitzer in exchange. Cobb, on second base when Morgan tossed a wild pitch, never slowed rounding third and headed home. Morgan had the ball in plenty of time for the tag at home, but preferred to stand aside and execute a Veronica instead of blocking the plate. Cobb easily avoided the tag. (*The Baseball Chronology*)

1903 Boston held a 3–1 lead after two innings, but Chicago made a run for it, tying it in the fourth and coming up with four more runs in the top of the fifth. But Boston bounced back with five runs in the bottom of the fifth, the big blow being a grand slam inside-the-park home run to deep center by Hobe Ferris. Boston 10, Chicago 8.

TRANSACTIONS
1932: Traded Danny MacFayden to the New York Yankees for Ivy
    Andrews, Hank Johnson, and $50,000 cash.
1969: Drafted Rick Miller, Buddy Hunter, Jim Wright, Dwight Evans, and Steve Barr.
1973: Drafted Ted Cox, Fred Lynn, Rick Jones, and Butch Hobson.
1974: Drafted Sam Bowen and Joel Finch.
1979: Drafted Marty Barrett, Marc Sullivan, and Tom McCarthy.
1989: Drafted Greg Blosser, Mo Vaughn, Kevin Morton, Jeff McNeely,
    Eric Wedge, Jeff Bagwell, Paul Quantrill, and Greg Hansell.
1990: Released Bill Buckner.
1996: Signed free agent Jeff Frye.
2000: Drafted Freddy Sanchez in 11th round.

DEBUTS
1964: Lee Thomas
2002: Chris Haney

BIRTHDATES
Jack Chesbro 1874 (1909); Fred Mitchell 1878 (1901–1902);
Beany Jacobson 1881 (1907); Eddie Joost 1916 (1955)

DEATHS
Joe Mulligan 1986

June 6

2001 In a sign of changing times under GM Dan Duquette, the Red Sox (Medias Rojas, en Espanol) held their first-ever Latino Night at Fenway Park, complete with Latin music, special Latin foods for the evening, and more. Nine of the 25 Sox players were Latinos at the time. Unfortunately, just a day after the Sox took an 18-inning game from the Tigers, they allowed four unearned runs—the margin of Detroit's victory in a 7–3 loss to the same Tiger team, despite a quality start (two earned runs in seven innings) by Frank Castillo.

1998 In the top of the sixth, Tim Wakefield balked in Brian McRae, giving the Mets a 1–0 lead. It was the only run they got, but also the only one they needed. Bobby Jones (eight innings) and John Franco shut out the Red Sox on four hits.

1996 The last Sox cycle of the 20th century came from John Valentin, driving in two runs and scoring three times, to boost Boston to beat the White Sox, 7–4. *The Baseball Chronology* points out that the White Sox also pulled off a triple play in the game, "making it the first time since July 1, 1931 that a contest has featured both a triple play and a batter (Chuck Klein) hitting for the cycle."

1990 Yankee manager Bucky Dent was fired. His .404 win percentage was the worst of any Yankees manager since Babe Ruth was purchased from the Red Sox.

1983 The Tigers put a damper on Tony Conigliaro Night at Fenway, beating the Red Sox, 11–6. No one fully appreciated the big news of the day, however. In the June 6 draft, the Red Sox had the 19th pick overall and selected a 20-year-old pitcher from the University of Texas, Roger Clemens. Clemens was 9–4, 3.37 ERA, with 102 K and 15 BB. He'd been 12–1, 1.99 as a sophomore, but was not faring quite as well this year. Sox scouting director Eddie Kasko said he was surprised; the Sox had pegged Clemens at #5 overall nationally. "He's a legitimate power pitcher," said Joe Morgan, who had scouted Clemens along with Danny Doyle.

Also this day, Dick O'Connell was reappointed Red Sox GM by Buddy LeRoux, who had taken control of the ball club. It wasn't the last move in the saga involving LeRoux, Haywood Sullivan, and Jean Yawkey. (See June 7, 1983.)

1977 Luis Tiant wins his 100th game as a Red Sox, defeating Kansas City, 1–0. Boston's other 100+ winners include Cy Young (193), Mel Parnell (123), Joe Wood (112), Joe Dobson (106), and Lefty Grove (105) (Roger Clemens will join the group with 192). As of the end of 2005, Tim Wakefield had 130 Red Sox wins. Carl Yastrzemski walks in the game, his 1,452nd, tying him for 10th on the all-time list with Jimmie Foxx.

1950 Ken Keltner, the former Cleveland Indian, whose three-run homer broke open the 1948 playoff game and spelled defeat for the Red Sox, joined the Red Sox for his 13th season after a dozen with the Tribe. He was batting .321 in 28 at-bats, but was given his release.

1948 The Tigers used nine pitchers, but Boston took two, 5–4 and 12–4. Detroit held a 3–0 lead in the first game, but two-run homers by Stan Spence and Vern Stephens set it up for Stephens' bases-loaded single in the bottom of the ninth to secure a win. In the sixth inning of the second game, Ted Williams, Spence, and Stephens hit back-to-back-to-back homers off Fred Hutchinson. Spence, Stephens, and Bobby Doerr had done the same thing back on April 19.

1934 Myril Hoag, subbing for Babe Ruth, ties the AL record with six singles in six at-bats in the first game of a doubleheader with the Red Sox. The Yanks rout Lefty Grove and roll to a 15–3 win. Boston wins the nitecap, 7–3, to drop the Yanks to second place.

1917 "Stonewall" Jackson took over from Red Armstrong as announcer at Fenway. For reasons obscure to the researcher today, Jackson was reported by the *Boston Globe* to be "beloved by every umpire in both leagues."

1910 A tight 1–0 game in Chicago saw Big Ed Walsh threw a one-hitter (Duffy Lewis managed a single) and beat Sea Lion Hall (born Carlos Clolo), who'd only allowed four hits himself, two of them by Walsh. Unfortunately, he tried to pitch the next day, too. See June 7, 1910.

TRANSACTIONS
1950: Released Ken Keltner.
1966: Purchased Galen Cisco from the New York Mets.
1967: Drafted Mike Garman.
1972: Drafted Steve Dillard, Don Aase, Andy Merchant, and Ernie Whitt.

1978: Drafted John Lickert.
1983: Drafted Roger Clemens, Mike Brumley, John Mitchell, Dana Kiecker, and Mike Dalton.
1995: Willie McGee signed as a free agent.

DEBUTS
1923: Carl Stimson
1926: Howie Fitzgerald
1967: Jerry Adair
1989: Luis Rivera
1996: Jeff Frye

BIRTHDATES
Tony Graffanino 1972

DEATHS
Topper Rigney 1972

June 7

2003 In an interleague game at Miller Park, Kevin Millar entered the game, Boston down 10–5 in the seventh inning, and put them within a run with a pinch-hit grand slam. The Sox scored twice in the ninth to beat the Brewers, 11–10.

2001 It was the type of injury from which some players never recover. Jason Varitek was in the middle of his best offensive season when he broke his right elbow diving for a foul pop during a bunt attempt. The Sox beat the Tigers, 8–1, but losing Varitek hurt the team badly. Fortunately, Tek came back, as good as ever.

1983 Haywood Sullivan and Jean Yawkey filed in court for a temporary injunction to prevent a "reorganization of internal management" (i.e., a coup) of the ball club announced the day before by Buddy LeRoux. Ultimately, the courts forced LeRoux to sell his interest in the ball club.

1974 There was a 20-minute rain delay during the bottom of the first, a 37-minute rain delay in the bottom of the third, but there were fireworks galore when the White Sox erupted for seven runs in the bottom of the sixth inning at Comiskey. The grand finale was Ron Santo's grand slam, giving Chicago a 10–4 lead. It was 13–6 after seven, and already an official game, when play was stopped for 70 minutes in the eighth. This time, though, it was due to heavy smoke pouring from a fire in a popcorn machine in the right-field area. The smoke was so thick that between 2,000 and 3,000 fans were ushered onto the playing field. Not taking any chances, the city sent 25 pieces of equipment and approximately 125 firefighters to douse the blaze. Popcorn machine under control, the game resumed, but the scoring was over. 13–6 final.

1956
STVT Just two short of the maximum, the Red Sox left 13 runners on base over the first five innings. In all, they left 17 men on base—one short of the major league record. Not only that, but they also had three men thrown out at third base and one thrown out at the plate. Those, clearly, were not LOB. It's a good thing they didn't leave one more man on; in the bottom of the 10th, Mickey Vernon was on second base, but Ted Lepcio doubled him home with a walk-off that made the Red Sox 6–5 victors over the vanquished Tigers.

1950 Red Sox righthander Joe Dobson gave up two runs in the first, then saw St. Louis tie it back up 3–3 in the third. From that point on, he cruised, courtesy of seven Sox runs in the bottom of the third. Vollmer, Pesky, Williams, Stephens, Zarilla, and Doerr all had three or more hits. The Red Sox sent 10 men to the plate in the first, second, third, and sixth innings. Clyde Vollmer and Junior Stephens both had two homers. The only Red Sox batter not to hit safely was the 0-for-5 Dobson. Red Sox 20, Browns 4.

1938 "At Fenway, umpire Bill McGowan—who had tossed Johnny Allen on Opening Day—orders the Cleveland pitcher to cut off part of a shirt sleeve which is dangling as he pitches, distracting the batter. Allen refuses and walks off the mound. He is fined $250 by Cleveland manager Oscar Vitt, who makes a pitching change to avoid a forfeit. The Indians win the game, 7–5. Tribe owner Alva Bradley hurries to Boston and buys the shirt for $250; the shirt is then displayed at Higbee's Department Store, owned by Bradley's brother. The shirt later makes its way to the Hall of Fame museum in Cooperstown, NY."—*The Baseball Chronology*. Allen had been sent to the clubhouse to change his tattered shirt, but never emerged. After five minutes, Vitt went in to find him and Allen reportedly told his manager, "I've been pitching all season with this shirt on and if I can't pitch with it on, I won't pitch." Cleveland scored twice in the top of the ninth to break a 5–5 tie and take the game. A June 10 report in the *Washington Post* says that Allen sold the shirt to Higbee's "for more than my fine...got right close to $500 for it."

1921 The Red Sox returned pitcher Allen Sothoron to St. Louis. He'd been claimed on waivers from the Browns on May 20, made two starts for the Sox, with a total of just six innings, 15 hits, and an ERA of 13.50. Boston complained that full details of his contract were not made available to them at the time waivers were sought. Had he won both games...? Sothoron's contract apparently didn't prevent him from racking up a 12–4 record with Cleveland in what remained of the 1921 season.

1920 Was this guy the sort of player who would rig the lists of batting averages and the like? The Red Sox acquired outfielder Jigger Statz, late of the New York Giants. After two weeks with Boston, the team was ready to move him and gave him the choice of Los Angeles or Indianapolis. He chose L.A.

1910 The White Sox and Red Sox squared off again the day after Ed Walsh one-hit Boston. Jim Scott started for Chicago, and Irv Young closed out the sixth. It was 6–6 after six, and so Walsh was called on in relief. He pitched six scoreless innings, but in the 13th he walked Hugh Bradley, saw him steal second and then take third on a passed ball. A single drove him in with what proved the game-winner, 7–6. Chicago beat Boston the next day, in a 12-inning contest.

1908 After the first six batters reached first base for Boston, four runs had scored, and there was nobody out, Heinie Wagner hit into a triple play. It was the second day in a row that the Tigers turned a triple play against the Red Sox. Boston won both games, however, 10–5 and 9–5.

1907 Manager Bob Unglaub had some kind of serious row with Boston owner John I. Taylor and so Taylor sought another manager. Catcher Jim "Deacon" McGuire was named to become the fourth manager of the season for the 1907 team. It's certainly the only time an active player on New York's roster was hired away to manage Boston. Taylor had contacted New York's owner Frank Farrell, who was—in Taylor's words to the *Washington Post*—"delighted with the idea of giving his trusty player a chance, so we closed the bargain." Would George Steinbrenner let Boston hire away Jorge Posada to skipper the Sox? McGuire was born during the Civil War, in 1863, and 43 years old at the time. He was not intended to play, but got in a little playing time and was 3-for-4 at the plate. When he caught the 40-year-old Cy Young, the battery had a combined 83 years of life experience. McGuire, credited as the first catcher to use padding in his glove, had been in the majors since 1884 and Young since 1890.

On the same day, Boston traded away its former manager, Jimmy Collins, who'd been with the club since its inception in 1901. He was swapped for Jack "Schoolboy" Knight, "the brilliant youngster who has been reported as sulking under Connie Mack." (*Chicago Tribune*)

TRANSACTIONS

1907: Traded Jimmy Collins to the Philadelphia Athletics for John Knight. Hired Deacon McGuire from the New York American League club.
1911: Purchased pitcher Casey Hageman from Denver for the unprecedented sum of $5,000.
1968: Drafted John Curtis, Lynn McGlothen, Cecil Cooper, Ben Oglivie, and Bill Lee.
1977: Drafted Bobby Sprowl, Roger LaFrancois, Steve Shields, Pete Ladd, and Leo Graham.
1982: Drafted Sam Horn, Kevin Romine, Mike Greenwell, and Jeff Sellers.

DEBUTS

1906: Jack Hayden
1952: Johnny Lipon

BIRTHDATES

Heathcliff Slocumb 1966 (1996–1997); Jeff Pierce 1969 (1995); Roberto Petagine 1971 (2005)

DEATHS

Eddie Lake 1995

June 8

2004 The Red Sox were so popular, with every home game sold out, that several local Showcase Cinemas began to offer high-definition screenings of Red Sox games. Four cinemas showed the game, and they nearly sold out, too. For an extra touch, hot dogs vendors roamed the aisles in the dimmed theaters. Ticket prices were $5.00 per seat.

2002 The reigning World Champion Arizona Diamondbacks pulled into Fenway, and everyone was looking forward to the battle of Pedro Martinez (7–0) going up against Arizona's Curt Schilling (11–1). Boston scored once in the first, on Carlos Baerga's first home run in almost three years, and one more time in the eighth, but the game was Schilling's, 3–2, over Martinez. Pedro was suffering from a sore shoulder and said he didn't even know if he'd be able to pitch the second half of the season; it was, though, just his first loss of the year.

2000 Permitting just one hit in eight innings, with 10 strikeouts and only one walk, Pedro Martinez ran his record to 9–2 with a 3–0 Fenway win over the Indians, and a year-to-date ERA of just 0.95.

1999 Dan Smith made his pitching debut for the Montreal Expos and threw seven strong innings, only allowing three hits—all in the first inning. Jose Offerman,

Brian Daubach, and Nomar Garciaparra all singled, scoring one run. Then Smith retired 20 Boston batters in a row, before turning the game over to the bullpen. Final score, Montreal 5, Boston 1.

1993 Despite 47 appearances spanning two years, Matt Young had not won a game since May 20, 1991. Former Sox pitcher Young was due to pitch for the Cleveland Indians against the Red Sox, in Cleveland. Because the Red Sox were still paying $1.9 million of his salary...well, it's a great country, suggested Dan Shaughnessy. Instead, when the June 7 game was rained out, Jose Mesa got the start. Young did beat the Texas Rangers on June 12, his next appearance—and the last win he ever recorded.

1967 Yaz was 2-for-4 and 4-for-5, with three RBIs, but the Sox dropped the first game, and won the latter behind Gary Bell's Boston debut. Just 48 hours earlier, White Sox manager Eddie Stanky had characterized Yaz as "an All-Star, I suppose, but only from the neck down." When Yaz hit a sixth-inning homer in game two, he tipped his cap to Stanky.

1961 The hour was getting late. It was the bottom of the 11th inning in a game at Fenway against California, and the Angels had taken a 4–3 lead in the top of the inning. Chuck Schilling walked, and Gary Geiger promptly tripled to tie it up...but Geiger just kept on going—past third, back toward the Red Sox dugout. He was tagged out and, instead of the go-ahead run on third with nobody out, there was no one on and one out. Two outs later, the inning was over and the game was called at 1:18 A.M. due to rain. It's in the books: a 4–4 tie.

1951 Bob Feller ran his record to 8–1 on the season, granting the Red Sox just seven hits—none of them to Dom DiMaggio, whose 27 consecutive game streak was ended. 7–1, Indians. It was the Indians who'd halted Joe DiMaggio's 56-game hit streak back in 1941.

1950 In the most lopsided score in history, the Boston Red Sox annihilated the St. Louis Browns at Fenway Park, 29–4. Bobby Doerr had three home runs and eight RBIs; Walt Dropo, two home runs and seven RBIs, and Ted Williams, two home runs and five RBIs. Each one collected a round tripper in the eighth inning. Pitcher Chuck Stobbs walked four times in four innings. Al Zarilla hit four doubles, including two in one inning, and a single—without even one ribbie— as the Sox set a major-league record with 58 total bases. Other marks: most extra bases on long hits (32) in a game and the most extra bases on long hits in consecutive games (51). The Red Sox had 28 hits, with four players collecting four hits apiece, to total a record 51 for two days against the woeful Browns. Leadoff batter Clyde Vollmer went to the plate eight times in eight innings, the only time this has happened in history. Boston had now scored 104 runs in their last seven games and a record 49 in two straight games.

1944 When a walk was no walk at all. The Red Sox beat the Yankees, 8–7, in the bottom of the ninth, on catcher Roy Partee's solo home run. Partee's peg helped cut down a Yankee in the first inning. Boston pitcher Pinky Woods had two outs, but Bud Metheny was on second. Woods issued a base on balls to batter Nick Etten, but Etten had no chance to take the walk. He was still in the batter's box when Partee fired a shot to third base and caught Metheny trying to steal third. Then Etten stepped out of the box, and walked to his defensive position at first base. The Sox scored five runs in the bottom of the first.

1935 Again overcoming an injury to get back in the game, Lou Gehrig (3-for-3, with four RBIs) was run over by Carl Reynolds in the first inning of the first game, a 12–6 Yankees bashing. Gehrig, who had now played 1,559 games in a row, also played the second game, going 1-for-3 with an RBI, but Boston won, 4–2, largely thanks to Lefty Gomez, who walked eight and threw two wild pitches, both of which resulted in runs.

1911 In the fourth inning, four St. Louis Browns batters reached base on errors. It was an eight-run inning, and St. Louis scorched the Red Sox, 11–5.

1903 Boston won its 11th game in a row, 6–1 over Detroit. Long Tom Hughes started for Boston but was wild and after walking the first four batters in the third inning, manager Collins called in Cy Young in relief. Boston scored six times in the fourth inning, Buck O'Brien getting both a double and a home run. The game was called due to rain while Detroit was batting in the top of the sixth.

1902 Boston battered Jack Harper at St. Louis, with six runs in the top of the third. Cy Young got the 7–1 win; it was his 10th straight win.

TRANSACTIONS
1907: Traded Bill Dinneen to St. Louis for pitcher Beany Jacobson and $1,500.
1965: Drafted Billy Conigliaro, Ken Poulsen, Amos Otis, Jim Hutto, and Ray Jarvis.
1970: Purchased Cal Koonce from the New York Mets.
1971: Drafted Jim Burton, Jim Rice, Bill Moran, Mark Bomback, and Jack Baker.
1976: Drafted Bruce Hurst, Glenn Hoffman, Mike Smithson, Wade
        Boggs, Gary Allenson, Reid Nichols, and Chico Walker.
1981: Drafted Steve Ellsworth, Steve Lyons, Rob Woodward, and Todd Benzinger.
1990: Sent Rich Gedman to the Houston Astros as part of a conditional deal.

DEBUTS
1907: John Knight   1940: Stan Spence
1910: Ralph Pond   1967: Gary Bell
1935: Hy Vandenberg   1976: Tom Murphy

BIRTHDATES
Charley Schanz 1919 (1950); Pete Magrini 1942 (1966); Matt Perisho 1975 (2005)

DEATHS
None yet

June 9

2004 Jane Costa of Stoughton was hit by a foul ball at Fenway on September 11, 1998 and suffered serious injuries. She filed suit, arguing that the Red Sox should have issued more explicit warnings about the dangers of foul balls, not just some fine print on the back of the ticket stub. The state's three-judge Appeals Court sided with the Red Sox; it was the first case involving someone hit with a baseball in 54 years.

2003 Given that the 2003 Sox ended up mere outs away from making the World Series, it's sobering to remember that as of June 9, they had the second-worst ERA in the majors and were "on pace to post the worst ERA in franchise history" (*Boston*

Globe) with a 5.26 mark. Fortunately, they were leading the majors in batting with a .295 team mark. On June 9, the Red Sox hired Dave Wallace as pitching coach, taking over for Goose Gregson who had been handling the staff while Tony Cloninger was out for extended cancer treatment (see March 12, 2003).

1999 Pedro Martinez faced his old club, the Montreal Expos. He hadn't lost a game in two months and was sporting an 11–1 record. He was up against Mike Thurman. Pedro threw six innings, giving up four runs, but the Expos punished Mark Portugal and Mark Guthrie with eight runs in the eighth, and finally won, 13–1. Guillermo Mota hit a three-run homer in his first major league at-bat—and he was a relief pitcher for Montreal.

1977 Yaz hit a double in the first inning of a game against the Orioles; it was #500 of Captain Carl's career.

1975 Bernie Carbo's sixth-inning grand slam gave Boston four runs, but Texas Rangers batter Jim Sundberg slammed one of his own. Texas scored some other runs, too, and went home with the win, 12–4.

1967 Yaz hit two homers and made a couple of spectacular catches; Joe Foy entered the game as a pinch-hitter and hit a home run, stayed in the game and hit another one, which sealed the Red Sox 8–7 win over the Senators.

1963 Today belonged to Chuck Schilling. The Orioles were poised for a 2–1 victory, with two outs in the ninth inning in Baltimore, when pinch-hitter Mejias fouled out. Russ Nixon was on second base, Schilling, at the top of the order, was up. Schilling singled Nixon in for the tying run. With Radatz on the mound for the Red Sox, the game went into extra innings. In the 14th frame, Nixon got on base again, Radatz bunted him over to second, and Schilling singled Nixon home once again. Radatz pitched his sixth inning of scoreless relief, and the Red Sox traveled on happily to Detroit.

1961 Ryne Duren of the Los Angeles Angels struck out the last man up in the first, then struck out the side in the second and the third—seven consecutive K's, for a league record. It was a 5–1 win for the Angels.

1957 The Sox hit seven home runs in a twin bill at Kansas City; KC had four. Lepcio and Piersall each hit a pair. Boston won both games.

1950 Ned Garver, the Browns' best hurler, finally turns the tables on the Red Sox, winning 12–7. Despite the loss, the seven runs scored made it 111 total runs for Boston beginning with the June 2 game, a week ago, 56 of them in just the last three games.

1946 The Detroit Tigers were the reigning World Champions, but the 1946 Red Sox juggernaut swept them aside taking all three games when the champs came to Boston. At this point in the season, not a single western club had managed a win at Fenway Park all year long. Tigers Dizzy Trout and Hank Greenberg threw several punches at each other in the Detroit dugout during the first game of the day's doubleheader. Mickey Harris became 9–1 on the season, Boo Ferriss ran his record to 10–0, and Ted Williams hit home runs in both games, the latter one said to travel two-thirds of the way up into the right-field bleachers. That ball bounced off the head of one Joseph Bouchard, some 502 feet from home plate. Bouchard was sitting in section 42, row 37, seat 21—and displayed a straw hat with a hole in it after the game.

1934 The Washington Senators doubled six times (five in a row) in the eight-run eighth inning of an 8–1 victory over Boston's Lefty Grove.

1918 Dutch Leonard, following up on his June 3 no-hitter, shuts out the Indians 2–0 on eight hits. Leonard was 2-for-3 at the plate, with two singles, both of which moved a runner into scoring position from which Harry Hooper drove him in.

1915 Riding roughshod over the Red Sox, Detroit put up a 15–0 final. Ty Cobb stole three bases, including a third-inning steal of home. His first attempted steal, of second, spiked Sox shortstop Everett Scott, who had to leave the game.

1912 Tris Speaker showed why he was leading the league in hitting by going 4-for-5 and hitting for the cycle off Roy Mitchell, helping the Sox beat the Browns, 9–2. In his career, Speaker hit 792 doubles. No one has ever matched that mark.

TRANSACTIONS
1952: Traded Ken Wood to the Washington Senators for Archie Wilson.
1960: Traded Gene Stephens to the Baltimore Orioles for Willie Tasby.
1962: Signed amateur free agent Bob Montgomery.
1963: Released Ike Delock.
2003: Named Dave Wallace interim pitching coach to take the place
    of Tony Cloninger, undergoing cancer treatment.

DEBUTS
1910: Ed Hearn
1915: Herb Pennock
1926: Happy Foreman
1945: Randy Heflin

BIRTHDATES
Bill Narleski 1899 (1929–1930); Mike Ryba 1903 (1941–1946)

DEATHS
Odell Hale 1980

June 10

2005 The original contract that sold Babe Ruth to the Yankees transferred hands at a Sotheby's auction for a winning bid of $996,000—many times more than the price originally paid for The Babe himself. It was purchased by a Yankees fan, Pete Siegel. Fortunately, all of the proceeds from the sale went to a hunger-relief organization known as America's Second Harvest.

1996 Tim Wakefield was pitching on just two days' rest; he really took one for the team. He threw a complete eight-inning game in Chicago, didn't strike out a batter, walked three, and gave up 16 hits. He was charged with eight earned runs, and when it was all over, he'd thrown 162 pitches in an 8–2 loss to the White Sox. No pitcher in the 1990s gave up as many hits in one game.

1987 Ellis Burks hit a grand slam in the fourth inning off Eric Bell and Marty Barrett hit a grand slam in the seventh off Jack O'Connor. Not surprisingly, Boston beat Baltimore. After scoring four more runs in the ninth, two more of them on Burks' second homer, the game ended, 15–4.

1986 Wade Boggs said he injured his ribs taking off his cowboy boots; he was limited
STVT to pinch-hit duty. When he came up in the top of the 10th at Skydome with
runners on first and third, though, he was walked intentionally. Mark Eichhorn
preferred to take his chances with the .143 hitter Mike Stenhouse rather than
Boggs, who was batting .389 before the boots took him down. Stenhouse worked
a 3–2 count, then took the walk that forced in the winning run. It was the only
major league RBI of his Red Sox career. "If they don't throw strikes, I don't
swing at them," Stenhouse explained after the game. In his time with the Red
Sox, Stenhouse accumulated 21 at-bats in 21 games. He walked 12 times and
only struck out five. Five of the walks came in a four-game stretch on successive
days from July 20–23. And July 23 was his last game in major league ball.

1970 Jim Lonborg was put on the 21-day disabled list with right shoulder pain. In an
unusual move, the Sox requested permission from the Commissioner's office to
convert coach George Thomas to become an active player. Thomas played in 38
games, hitting .343. In 1971, he got in nine more games, but only hit 1-for-13.

1960 The Red Sox fire manager Billy Jurges. Though he had supposedly taken a leave
to get some rest, he reported feeling fine. The issue had been joined on May
26, when he'd told *Globe* writer Clif Keane, "I know what's wrong with this
club, but I can't do anything about it. My hands are tied." When the Sox hired
Mike Higgins for a second time as manager, Glenn Stout and Richard Johnson
commented in *Red Sox Century*, "Yawkey guaranteed more of the same by
bringing back old pal Pinky Higgins."

1953 Boston's Jimmy Piersall went 6-for-6 in the 11–2 first-game win over St. Louis,
but was then 0-for-5 in the second. The Sox took that one, too, though, dealing
defeat to the Browns for the ninth time in a row.

1950 With his 11th home run of the year, Ted Williams has now at least one RBI for
each of the last 11 games. Boston lost to Detroit, though, 18–8.

1945 Dave "Boo" Ferriss lost to New York, 3–2. It was the first loss of his career. He'd
won the previous eight, four of which were shutouts. When he first came up, all
the lockers were taken, and he'd hung his clothes on a pipe sticking out of the
wall. As long as he kept winning, he kept using the pipe. Now that he'd lost a
game, he accepted the locker the Red Sox had offered him.

1938 Lefty Lefebvre was a rookie Red Sox pitcher signed out of Holy Cross on June
9. He swung at the first major league pitch he ever saw and homered in his first
(and only) major league at-bat of the year in 1938. It was the only pitch he saw
all year long. His pitching wasn't as good that day; he gave up six earned runs
in the game's final four innings, surrendering two home runs. He played in 87
games over four seasons, but never hit another four-bagger.

1937 The Red Sox traded two brothers on the same day, sending both Wes and Rick
Ferrell to Washington together, receiving in return the wholly unrelated duo of
Bobo Newsom and Ben Chapman. The Mexican in the deal was Mel Almada,
who accompanied the Ferrells to D.C. Boston manager Joe Cronin was clear
about which Ferrell he preferred, "I sure hated to lose Rick—good ball player,
hard worker, easy to get along with."

1932 The Sox acquire Pete Jablonowski (later, after one game with the Yankees he
changed his last name to Appleton) for Jack Russell. Pete was reported in *The
Sporting News* to have studied law, and thought the name "Appleton" sounded

better on a shingle (though a couple of years later, *Sporting News* editor Spink wrote that Appleton had become a dentist.)

1926 Just a couple of weeks after the White Sox walked 13 Bosox, a couple of St. Louis Browns pitchers walked 10 and allowed 11 to hit safely, as Boston beat the Browns, 8–3.

1921 Babe Ruth set a new career home run mark, with his 120th roundtripper. The previous recordholder was another former Red Sox player, White Sox and Phillies slugger Gavvy Cravath (119 HR).

1916 Buffalo Bill Cody set up a tent city at the Huntington Avenue grounds for his Wild West show, staged for a full week at the old home of the Boston Red Sox.

1912 Boston beat the Browns, 3–2, in St. Louis, with runs in the eighth and ninth, and took over the league lead. They never looked back. By season's end, the second-place Senators were 14 games behind. New York finished last, 55 games behind the Red Sox.

1902 St. Louis shortstop Bobby Wallace was as busy as can be, handling 19 chances in a nine-inning game: 11 assists, six putouts, and two errors. He took part in four double plays, and twice he retired the side. Occasionally, other fielders helped, too, and the Browns beat the Bostons, 5–4.

TRANSACTIONS
1932: Traded Jack Russell to the Cleveland Indians for Pete Jabolonowski.
1937: Traded Rick Ferrell, Wes Ferrell, and Mel Almada to the Washington
     Senators. Received Ben Chapman and Bobo Newsom.
1952: Traded Walt Masterson and Randy Gumpert to the Washington Senators for Sid Hudson.

DEBUTS
1938: Bill Lefebvre   1988: Randy Kutcher
1970: Cal Koonce   1990: Jeff Gray
1975: Jim Burton   1995: Joe Hudson
1984: Rich Gale

BIRTHDATES
George Prentiss 1876 (1901–1902); Frank Gilhooley 1892 (1919); Fred Hofmann 1894 (1927–1928); Danny MacFayden 1905 (1926–1932); Pokey Reese 1973 (2004)

DEATHS
Jack O'Brien 1933; Matt Zeiser 1942

June 11

1997 Red Sox outfielder Wil Cordero was arrested in the early morning hours and charged with assaulting his wife Ana with a telephone receiver and trying to choke her. She withdrew the complaint and they walked out of court hand-in-hand. D.A. Thomas Reilly decried the quick release of Cordero, who didn't last long with the Red Sox after this incident. Sox players felt a little better after beating the Orioles in that night's game, 10–1.

1995 Visiting batter Mark McGwire hit home runs his first three times up, getting a standing ovation from Boston fans after the third one. He'd now hit five homers in two games, tying the major league mark. There wasn't much else for Sox fans to cheer about. Oakland won, 8–1.

1989 After losing the first game against the Yankees, manager Joe Morgan wanted to salvage a win in the second. In the eighth inning, the Red Sox had scored five times to come within a run. Now leading by just one run, 8–7, Dale Mohorcic threw three balls in a row to second baseman Ed Romero. The Yanks brought in another reliever, Scott Nielsen. Joe Morgan countered by sending in the left-handed hitting Rich Gedman for Romero. Understandably irritated at being removed when he'd worked a 3–0 count, Romero threw a cooler of Gatorade out of the dugout and onto the field. Told later he'd be fined for showing up his manager, the still-irate Romero replied, "He said he's going to fine me? Tell him to fine my ass." Romero found himself $500 poorer some 48 hours later.

1984 New York scored first, but the Red Sox never surrendered. After the Yankees batted in the top of the ninth, though, the Sox were looking at a 6–3 loss. Through a combination of singles and walks, the Sox scored one run—and then Bill Buckner singled in two to tie the game. Reid Nichols pinch-hit for Gedman and homered to win the game, 9–6.

1979 Bob Stanley pitched a very rare extra-inning shutout, throwing 10 innings in a 4–0 win over Kansas City.

1969 Red Sox right fielder Joe Lahoud had hit only four singles in 48 at-bats, therefore hitting just .083, and was riding a 1-for-24 stretch. Against the Twins, in Minneapolis, he suddenly exploded for three home runs in one game (off three different pitchers). The Sox beat Minnesota, 13–5.

Catcher Joe Azcue jumped the ball club, after complaining he was stuck behind first-string catcher Russ Gibson and wasn't being used enough.

1964 Bill Monbouquette, normally good against the Yankees, didn't have it, and gave up 13 hits, including two homers by Mantle and one by Maris. Jim Bouton was the beneficiary. NY 8, BOS 4.

1962 Neither team had scored, but the Indians had the bases loaded in the top of the third. Earl Wilson was pitching for the Red Sox, and just as he was about to throw, Tito Francona (the baserunner on first), shouted, "Hold it, Earl." Obligingly, Wilson held it—but balked in the only run the Indians needed. The next batter up, Willie Kirkland, hit a three-run homer. The Indians scored 10 and Jim Perry shut out the Red Sox, 10–0.

1960 At a Fenway day-night doubleheader, home runs (including Ted Williams HR #497) accounted for all five Red Sox runs, as they beat Chicago, 5–4. When Williams was walked his next time up, Vic Wertz hit a two-run homer. Don Buddin homered in the second game, but Boston lost, 8–4. The White Sox had only two assists in the day game, setting a league record, and just five in the night game, setting another record—fewest assists in back-to-back games.

1959 A confusing trade saw the Sox obtain P Dick Hyde and IF Herbie Plews from the Senators. They gave up P Murray Wall and IF Billy Consolo. Wall pitched a game for Washington, giving up a home run and a couple of other hits in 1⅓ innings—it's in the record books—but when Hyde turned out to have a sore shoulder and admitted he hadn't pitched for a couple of weeks, Boston sent him back to the Senators and Washington returned Wall.

1952 It was St. Louis 9, Boston 5, after 8½ innings. Satchel Paige was pitching well in relief, but Jimmy Piersall may have shaken him a bit. Not only did he cavort about flapping his arms and shouting, "Oink! Oink! Oink!" Piersall also told Paige he was going to bunt, and then did—beating out the bunt for a single. The Sox managed to load the bases, with one out, but Ol' Satch couldn't get Billy Goodman and walked in Piersall. Ted Lepcio singled home another run, and then Sammy White hit a grand slam to win it, 11–9. Showboating Sammy dropped to the ground after rounding third and crawled to the plate, where he planted a kiss.

1946 Bob Klinger, who would appear in Game Seven of the World Series, pitched well enough to beat the Indians as the Sox reeled off their 12th win in a row. The Sox were 41–9, and had won all 19 home games against visitors from "the West." Boston was losing 5–4 after 3½, but the big bats brought them from behind while Klinger settled in and threw five scoreless frames to close the game.

1934 Did they win a few cases of B&M baked beans to bring back to Beantown? The Red Sox traveled to Portland, Maine, and beat the Burnham and Morrill Company semi-pro nine, 7–1, before a crowd of 3,000 which included Maine's Gov. Louis J. Brann and Rudy Vallee, a member of the governor's staff.

1913 Cleveland's early 5–0 lead was matched by a five-run Boston sixth inning, and the game went through 14 innings, tied at five. With the bases loaded, Ivy Olson stole home in the top of the 15th to give Cleveland a 6–5 lead. His mates didn't stop there, though. Jack Graney walked, re-filling the bases. Grover Cleveland Land singled, driving in two, and took second on the throw to the plate. Then Graney stole home, as Boston's Dutch Leonard stood dumbfounded, holding the ball. Land took third, and moments later figured he'd try to steal home as well, but pitcher Vean Gregg, who'd gone the distance, swung and struck out, ending the inning. 9–5, Cleveland.

In the same game, second baseman Steve Yerkes stood around a lot, too. He never had a single fielding opportunity the whole 15 innings—no assists, no putouts, not even an error.

1910 Some fans may have been confused. The Boston Red Sox had just visited Chicago and dropped three out of four. On the 10th, they played in Cleveland and lost, but the morning papers on the 12th made it seems as though Boston was back in Chicago. The *Tribune* headline read RED SOX RALLY, BUT LOSE GAME. It turns out it was Jiggs Donahue's Red Sox playing the Cuban Stars.

TRANSACTIONS
1944: Sold Johnny Peacock to the Philadelphia Blue Jays.
1959: Traded Billy Consolo and Murray Wall to the Washington Senators for Herb Plews and Dick Hyde. Three days later, on the 14th, Wall was returned to the Red Sox and Hyde was returned to the Senators.

DEBUTS
1909: Biff Schlitzer	1937: Ben Chapman	1967: Gary Waslewski
1918: Frank Truesdale	1952: Archie Wilson	1971: Luis Tiant
1932: Ivy Andrews	1961: Galen Cisco	1995: Chris Donnels

BIRTHDATES
George Huff 1872 (manager, 1907); Chris Mahoney 1885 (1910);
John Doherty 1967 (1996); Bill Selby 1970 (1996)

DEATHS
Tex Vache 1953; Bill Regan 1968

June 12

2004 Position player David McCarty got his second chance to pitch in a ballgame, one in which the Red Sox lost to the Dodgers, 14–5. McCarty, who'd hoped to pitch since spring training, threw the top of the ninth, striking out one Dodger while not allowing even one hit.

2003 Not a record anyone would be proud of, but Trot Nixon left 12 men on base during the 13-inning interleague game against the Cardinals. He was 2-for-7 in the game, and had one RBI. The Red Sox could have used just one of those 12 runners; they lost, 8–7.

2002 The previous regime said a new ballpark was essential if the Red Sox were to be able to compete. New ownership gave strong hints in a radio interview that they valued Fenway Park, and that they had found nothing about Fenway that was "acute or dangerous or couldn't withstand another 30 to 40 years of use."

1927 The Red Sox interrupted a visit by the St. Louis Browns to go to Detroit, play the Tigers, and then come back and resume playing St. Louis. It wasn't a particularly great experience. Boston lost the Saturday game, 10–5, to the Browns, then took the train to Detroit so they could play a Sunday game (Lord's Day baseball was banned in Boston). They lost that one, 11–10 in 10 innings, despite shooting out to an early 8–1 lead. Back on the train, back to Boston, where the Browns were waiting to deal them a 2–0 loss on Monday. (See also May 16, 1926.)

1923 Red Faber pitched 20 years for the White Sox and won 254 games with a career 3.15 ERA. This was not one of his better outings; the Red Sox scored 10 runs off him and climbed out of the cellar—leapfrogging the struggling White Sox who sank to eighth place. No worries, though—the Red Sox finished last once again in 1923.

1919 Herb Pennock only faced 27 batters in the regulation nine innings, and won over the White Sox, 4–0. Pennock yielded three singles and one walk. Two baserunners were retired on double plays, and the other two were cut down trying to steal. Babe Ruth's two-run double off the cigarette sign on the left-field fence provided the winning runs.

1916 Inserted as a pinch-hitter in the top of the seventh, Babe Ruth hit a three-run homer into the Sportsman's Park center-field bleachers. It was Ruth's first pinch-hit homer. Ruth's drive tied the score, 3–3, but St. Louis won it with two outs in the bottom of the ninth when manager Bill Carrigan waved Red Sox right fielder Harry Hooper to reposition him and Jimmy Austin's double landed just where Hooper had been. Austin's drive drove in Eddie Plank.

1909 Cleveland's Heinie Berger held the Sox scoreless through eight, and Boston's knuckleballer Eddie Cicotte pitched equally well. With one out in the top of the ninth, though, first baseman Jake Stahl hurt his finger trying to catch Cicotte's errant throw to first. Wolter came in to replace Stahl and promptly committed two more errors, bracketed around a throwing error by third baseman Lord and a fielding error by French at second. Five errors total—and zero hits—resulted in four runs, and all Boston could come back with was Lord's single in the bottom of the ninth (just the third hit of the game for Boston) which was far from sufficient. 4–0, Indians.

TRANSACTIONS
1927: Sold Baby Doll Jacobson to the Cleveland Indians.
1932: Traded Earl Webb to the Detroit Tigers for Dale Alexander and Roy Johnson.
1962: Traded Tom Umphlett and cash to the New York Yankees for Billy Gardner.
2001: Received Doug Mirabelli from the Texas Rangers in trade for Justin Duchscherer.

DEBUTS
1920: Jigger Statz   1959: Herb Plews
1925: Hal Neubauer   1960: Willie Tasby
1932: Pete Jablonowksi 1979: Joel Finch
1937: Bobo Newsom   2002: Juan Diaz

BIRTHDATES
Damon Buford 1970 (1998–1999)

DEATHS
Bud Connolly 1964; Merle Settlemire 1988

June 13

2005 The right-field foul pole came to be known as the Pesky Pole over the years; on June 13, 2005, the left-field foul pole was officially dedicated as the Fisk Pole in honor of one of the great moments in Red Sox history, the early-morning October 22, 1975 game-winning homer in Game Six of that year's World Series.

1997 The Red Sox played their first interleague game ever, against the New York Mets, beating them 8–4. Boston won five of its first six interleague games, but fared poorly in others over the years until the 2005 season.

1989 John Dopson balked four times to tie an American League record, including balking in a Tiger for a run in the second inning. He also walked five, threw a wild pitch, and gave Rich Gedman another hard-to-handle pitch that was scored as a passed ball. Nonetheless, the Red Sox eked out an 8–7 win. He'd now run up a total of 11 balks on the season; no other pitcher on the Sox staff had issued even one. In Dopson's next time out, June 19, he only lasted 2⅓ innings, giving up six runs on six hits—perhaps concentrating too hard on not balking.

1988 Despite having four starting position players on the DL, the Yankees got 15 hits off Roger Clemens and ultimately won, 12–6. Jim Rice hit his 200th home run at home, behind just Ted Williams (248 Fenway homers) and Carl Yastrzemski (237 home homers).

1985 Wade Boggs hit 3-for-4, including a two-run homer, in the June 13, 1985 game. Over the next 162 games, the equivalent of a full season, Boggs hit the ball at a

.400 pace. His prolonged hot streak concluded on June 8, 1986, when he went hitless and dipped below the .400 mark.

1966 There had been an incident in spring training when Earl Wilson had joined Dave Morehead and Dennis Bennett at the Cloud 9 bar in Lakeland, Florida, and been refused service because of Wilson's presence. It became a news story, and Wilson's days with the Red Sox appeared numbered. When two more black players (Jose Tartabull and John Wyatt) were acquired on June 13, Wilson and his roommate Lenny Green both had the feeling there might have been "too many blacks on the team" (*Red Sox Nation*). The next day, Wilson was traded to the Tigers. He won 18 games in 1966 and his 22 wins in 1967 were more than any other pitcher in baseball.

1957 Ted Williams hit three homers in a 9–3 win over the Indians, two off Early Wynn and one off Bob Lemon. He'd hit three in a May 8 game against the White Sox. Doing it twice in one year made Ted the first American League hitter with two three-homer games in the same season; both Johnny Mize and Ralph Kiner had done it in the senior circuit.

1956 Jackie Jensen hit a bases-loaded triple in the bottom of the fourth inning to tie the game at Cleveland 8, Boston 8. The two teams played 11 innings, but rain forced umpire Ed Rommel to call the game, which went into the books as an 8–8 tie. All the individual records stand, though. The triple was one of Jensen's three bases-loaded triples in 1956, tied for a major league record. Jensen led the league with 11 triples.

1951 Boston took two games from the White Sox in Chicago, 3–2 and a 17-inning 5–4 win, with Ellis Kinder throwing 10 scoreless innings in relief in the nightcap, the longest night game in history.

1950 Bobby Doerr had himself a 4-for-4 day, with two homers, a triple, and a single. It all helped the Red Sox rout Bob Feller and win an 8–1 game behind the two-hit pitching of Chuck Stobbs. The four-hit game pushed Doerr's average to .306; at this point in the season, every Red Sox regular was hitting .300 or greater.

1947 A five-run fifth propelled the Red Sox past the White Sox for a 5–3 victory in the first night game ever played at Fenway Park. A capacity crowd of 34,510 "first nighters" enjoyed the evening.

1944 Joe Cronin had four plate appearances but not a single at-bat. He walked three times and laid down a sacrifice bunt another time, and scored two times in the 7–2 defeat of the Red Sox.

1940 In the Hall of Fame exhibition game at Doubleday Field, Cooperstown, Ted Williams hit homers in the second and seventh against the Chicago Cubs, but the Cubbies hit four homers and won the rain-shortened game, 10–9.

1932 Dale Alexander and Roy Johnson are traded by Detroit to Boston for Earl Webb. Alexander, batting only .250 at the time of the trade, went on a tear, hitting .372 with Boston and edging out Jimmie Foxx for the batting title by three points. Alexander was dubbed "the Nimrod of the Nollichucky" by the *New York Times*, referring to his roots in Greeneville, TN, and quoted him on his hitting philosophy: "Ah don't look foh anything except a good ball. If it looks good, Ah swing at it."

1927 St. Louis pitcher Elam Vangilder shut out the Red Sox, 2–0. His third-inning single started a rally that resulted in the first run. His fifth-inning homer over Fenway's left-field wall accounted for the second.

1916 Babe Ruth was 2-for-2, hitting a homer for the second day in a row, and the third of the month. He also singled in a run. This day, he was the pitcher, too, and held the Browns to one run through 5⅓ innings, before Ernie Shore took over. Boston won, 5–3, and Ruth never hit another home run in all of 1916.

1915 The Red Sox pick up Herb Pennock (3–6) on waivers from the A's. Following a strong 11–4 season with Philadelphia in 1914, and being Connie Mack's winner on Opening Day 1915, he became a subpar performer for years. In 1915–1917 combined, he was 5–7 for the Red Sox. In 1918, he was in the service, but in 1919 and 1920, he won 16 games per year.

1913 Down 6–2 after St. Louis scored five times in the top of the eighth, the Sox scored twice in the eighth and twice more in the ninth, then survived until the bottom of the 13th when they pushed across the winning run, 7–6.

1907 Going all out at a benefit game, the Boston Americans played the Providence Eastern League team to raise money for Chick Stahl's widow and ran the game to 16 innings, before Providence beat them, 3–2.

TRANSACTIONS
1915: Selected Herb Pennock off waivers from the Philadelphia Athletics.
1936: Traded Joe Cascarella to the Washington Senators for Jack Russell.
1949: Traded Sam Mele and Mickey Harris to the Washington Senators for Walt Masterson.
1960: Traded Marty Keough and Ted Bowsfield to the Cleveland
      Indians for Russ Nixon and Carroll Hardy.
1966: Acquired John Wyatt, Rollie Sheldon, and Jose Tartabull from the Kansas
      City Athletics by trading Jim Gosger, Ken Sanders, and Guido Grilli.
1972: Signed free agent Stan Williams.
1979: Acquired Bob Watson from the Astros in a trade for Peter Ladd, a PTBNL
      (Bobby Sprowl was named six days later), and some cash. On the same
      day, the Sox traded George Scott to Kansas City for Tom Poquette.
1995: Alejandro Pena was released.

DEBUTS
1979: Tom Poquette
1999: Kirk Bullinger
2001: Marcus Jensen
2003: Ryan Rupe

BIRTHDATES
Gene Desautels 1907 (1937–1940); Mel Parnell 1922 (1947–1956); Ernie Whitt 1952 (1976)

DEATHS
Dick Reichle 1967

June 14

2003 Hosting the Houston Astros, the game entered the bottom of the 14th tied 2–2. Houston was on its sixth pitcher, and Todd Walker singled to lead off the inning. Up came Nomar Garciaparra, who already had three doubles and a home run in the game. After the day's power display, Nomar stunned everyone by sacrificing Walker to second with a bunt back to the pitcher. Manny Ramirez, up next, singled and drove in Walker with the winning run.

1980 Jerry Remy stole second base in the first, fourth, and ninth innings—and then stole third base, too, in the ninth. The Sox beat the Angels, 7–3, and Remy's four stolen bases set a Red Sox record.

1976 Rick Wise had thrown a no-hitter for the Phillies in 1971, and a one-hitter in 1975. This evening in Minnesota, he had another one-hitter, the only safety being Jerry Terrell's third-inning single. Wise walked four, but shut out the Twins, 5–0. Fifteen days later, on June 29, Wise worked another one-hitter, beating the Orioles, 2–0.

1974 It took him 13 innings to do it, but Nolan Ryan nonetheless struck out 19 Red Sox. He got Boston first baseman Cecil Cooper six times in a row. Ryan also hit double figures in walks, doling out 10 bases on balls. A two-run homer by Yaz tied the Anaheim Stadium game in the top of the ninth, but California won it, 4–3, in the bottom of the 15th, when Denny Doyle doubled in Mickey Rivers. Tiant, who'd gone the distance, took the defeat.

1969 Reggie Jackson's 10 RBIs were just short of half Oakland's 21 runs, as they battered Boston, 21–7, embarrassing the Red Sox at Fenway. Reggie had two homers in a 5-for-6 day. Jarvis, Landis, and Roggenburk (not household names in Red Sox Nation) were the Boston pitchers each tagged with five earned runs.

1968 Ken Harrelson homered in the fifth, sixth, and eighth innings for Boston, driving in all seven runs in the 7–2 win over Cleveland. He was the first Red Sox batter to hit three home runs in succession.

1962 Join the club. The Orioles' Charlie Lau ties an American League record with three passed balls in the eighth inning, and a total of four, but Baltimore beats Boston 7–4. Lau now shares the team (and AL) record with Myron Ginsberg and Gus Triandos for most passed balls in an inning, all catching Hoyt Wilhelm. The 20th century mark is four in an inning, set by the Giants' Ray Katt in 1954. No surprise who was on the mound then—Wilhelm. (*The Baseball Chronology*)

1955 Not due to pitch until the 15th, and thinking the Red Sox were playing at night, Mel Parnell stayed in his hotel room and snoozed right through the game while his teammates helped Frank Sullivan win, 12–4. A well-rested Parnell won his game the following day.

1949 Joe Dobson was pitching for the Red Sox and Cleveland's Joe Gordon hit a first-inning grand slam off him. Predictably, the next Indian up, Lou Boudreau, got hit by Dobson. He was hit hard on the left elbow, took a couple of steps toward the mound, and both dugouts emptied. Nothing much eventuated, though, and as a courtesy the Sox allowed Ken Keltner to run for Boudreau. (Keltner was playing third base, and had just scored on the slam. He scored again a few minutes later.) Boston lost, 10–5. The courtesy runner was a practice that ended after the 1949 season. (See September 14, 2005 for an example of a mid-play runner).

1947 The Red Sox and White Sox traded first basemen, while Chicago was visiting Boston. Chicago wanted more power; Boston wanted more speed. Rudy York strolled over to the visitors' clubhouse, and the seven-years-younger Murrell "Jake" Jones took the reverse path.

1945 Clem Hausmann had his best start, throwing a three-hitter to beat the A's, 1–0. He did it again on June 19, against the Yankees: a 1–0 three-hitter. In the off-season, part of his work involved dropping nitoglycerin charges into dried-up oil wells to coax them back into production.

1940 It was the first 1940 night game in Chicago, but the Red Sox won it, 5–1. Denny Galehouse got the win. Ted Williams thought it an elaborate plot when the "sirens of dozens of pieces of apparatus went shrieking past the ball park" for fully 15 minutes. Sometime earlier, Williams had said that he was tired of baseball and wanted to be a fireman like his uncle in New York. Opposing teams razzed The Kid with fire helmets, sirens and the like, but this was a little much. The White Sox had already stashed fire helmets in their dugouts to put on when Ted came up to bat but, just before Boston came up to bat, a major fire broke out at a lumber yard not that far from Comiskey Park. All of a sudden, fire engines converged on the location.

1934 Buster Lucas couldn't quite make it with the Red Sox (three at-bats without a hit in four games in 1931 and 1932), so he signed with the House of David team. The Red Sox sold .216 hitter Bucky Walters to the Philadelphia Phillies. He decides to become a pitcher, making his first appearance later in the year—and goes on to win 198 major league ballgames.

1933 The Yankees rallied for five runs in the top of the seventh, knotting the score 5–5 with the Red Sox. Both Lou Gehrig and Yankees manager Joe McCarthy were tossed in the bottom of the seventh for complaining too vociferously that Boston catcher Rick Ferrell had run out of the baseline advancing from first to second. The Sox scored three times, and added five more in the eighth for a 13–5 win.

1913 The Jersey City ball club was required to pay the Red Sox $1,750 for the services of ballplayer Hugh Bradley (who'd coincidentally hit the first home run ever hit at Fenway Park, in 1912). Bradley had failed to make the Jersey City roster. The club claimed he was returned to Boston, which had refused him, but there was no record found of the transfer. Chairman Herrmann of the national baseball commission ordered Bradley to return to Jersey City.

1907 St. Louis banged three runs off Cy Young in the top of the first; he finished the inning but he was replaced by George Winter for eight scoreless frames. Boston scored three runs off Jack Powell in the second, and he left the game, too, but his replacement Fred Glade gave up a run in the fifth and Boston won, 4–3.

TRANSACTIONS
1934: Sold Bucky Walters to the Philadelphia Phillies.
1947: Traded Rudy York to the Chicago White Sox for Jake Jones.
1957: Traded Billy Goodman to the Baltimore Orioles for Mike Fornieles.
1963: Sold Mike Fornieles to the Minnesota Twins.
1966: Traded Earl Wilson and Joe Christopher to the Detroit Tigers
    for Don Demeter and a PTBNL (Julio Navarro).
1975: Acquired Denny Doyle from the California Angels for a PTBNL and
    some cash. The following year, on March 5, the Red Sox sent minor
    leaguer Chuck Ross to the Angels to complete the trade.

DEBUTS
1939: Boze Berger	1960: Russ Nixon	1966: John Wyatt
1944: Frank Barrett	1962: Billy Gardner	1975: Denny Doyle
1952: Sid Hudson	1964: Dave Gray	2001: Doug Mirabelli

BIRTHDATES
Herb Plews 1928 (1959); Luis Aponte 1953 (1980–1983)

DEATHS
Johnny Hodapp 1980; Monte Weaver 1994

June 15

1992 John Dopson was pitching so well through eight innings that most managers would have left him in. He bamboozled Yankees batters, allowing just five hits and no runs, and had thrown only 95 pitches. Still, manager Butch Hobson felt compelled to bring in Jeff Reardon for a save. "They'd have hung me if I hadn't brought Reardon in," he said after the game. The reason? Reardon was up for a record; if he could save the game, it would be his 342nd save, the most any pitcher had ever recorded. Reardon had to face two tough Yankees, both of whom had hit home runs off him within the last year. He retired the first two, gave up a single to Don Mattingly, then struck out Kevin Maas. Roger Clemens led the charge, and Reardon was hoisted on the shoulders of Frank Viola, Tom Brunansky, and Clemens, and transported over to where his wife was sitting.

The Sox won, 1–0, on three hits, with Phil Plantier's homer off Scott Sanderson practically representing the total offense. A Fenway employee retrieved the ball from the net for Plantier, and he had Reardon sign it for him.

1978 Jim Rice struck out twice early in the game, but then tied the game with a two-run homer in the bottom of the seventh. When he came up again in the eighth, he tripled in two more. The Red Sox won, 7–3, over the Oakland A's. The Sox were now 26–4 at home.

After the game, the Sox sold Bernie Carbo to Cleveland for cash. Carbo had been out with an ankle injury since May 21, but was one of the last of the "Buffalo Heads" banished from Boston. Ferguson Jenkins (December 1977), Rick Wise (March), Reggie Cleveland (April), and Jim Willoughby (April) were already gone. Bill Lee would be gone at the end of the year. (See also June 16, 1978.)

1976 The Sox made a big play, purchasing both Joe Rudi and Rollie Fingers from the A's for $1 million cash apiece. Then they found Charlie Finley was prepared to sell Vida Blue to the Yankees, so they said they'd take him, too. Finley's fire sale was voided by Commissioner Bowie Kuhn as not being in the best interests of baseball. Apparently, the initial deal had involved some combinations of players, such as one that included Rick Miller, Jim Willoughby, and Andy Merchant for the two A's, but Peter Gammons quotes Sox GM Dick O'Connell: "Finley says forget the damn players."

1965 After Detroit starter Dave Wickersham gave up four hits for three earned runs, while only recording one out, Denny McLain came on in relief—and shut the door he did. He struck out the first two batters he faced, struck out the side 1-2-3 in the second, and whiffed the first two Sox in the third. Seven straight strikeouts—to the first seven men he faced—set a major league record. His 14 K's was one short of the relief record (Walter Johnson struck out 15 in 11 innings of relief back in 1913). Four runs off Arnold Earley and Dick Radatz in the bottom of the eighth gave the Tigers the win, though it went to Fred Gladding, who'd taken over from McLain.

1947 Jake Jones, in his first game with his new team (the Red Sox) beat up on his old team (the White Sox). His first appearance for Boston came in a doubleheader. Jones homered in the first game, a solo shot that helped Boston beat Chicago, 7–3. In the second game, he came up with two outs and the bases loaded in the bottom of the ninth, the game a 4–4 tie. Bam! Slam! Thank you, Jake.

1944 Only 770 fans filed into Fenway, despite the Red Sox riding an eight-game win streak. Those who did were rewarded: Tex Hughson threw a 5–1 game against Philadelphia, and the Red Sox moved to within a half-game of first place. Maybe it was that war going on that held back attendance. D-Day was just nine days earlier. For Hughson, it was his fifth straight start in which he had given up just one run: 3–1, 11–1, 8–1, 2–1, and now 5–1.

1933 The Sox won four in a row from the visiting Yankees and, the story goes, Yankees owner Jacob Ruppert was so incensed he called the mortgage that he'd held on Fenway Park since 1920. Boston owner Tom Yawkey was by no means strapped for cash; he paid it in full the following day.

After the four-win streak, Sox trainer Doc Woods took note of the fact that the Sox infielders were throwing the same ball around before every inning, so he colored it with mercurochrome (so as to make it readily identifiable) and the team used it for infield practice the rest of the year.

1928 Danny MacFayden had a no-hitter going into the eighth inning; he lost the no-hitter and lost the shutout in the ninth, but still beat the White Sox, 3–1.

1926 It's too bad the Red Sox couldn't have kept Roy Carlyle on the team just a year longer. His brother Cleo joined Boston in 1927. Alas, the Sox put Roy on waivers and he was picked up by the Yankees. He hit .323 the remainder of the year for New York. In another transaction, Boston traded pitcher Howard Ehmke (3–10 on the season) to Philadelphia, where he ran up a record of 12–4 for the Athletics.

1924 Buster Ross, a chicken farmer from Kentucky, made his major league debut for the Red Sox. Over parts of three seasons, he was 7–12 with a 5.01 ERA.

1902 In an official game transferred from Cleveland to Canton, Ohio, Boston beat the "home team," Cleveland, 5–2. The overflow from the crowd of 6,000 patrons was placed, as was often the custom in those days, behind ropes in the outfield. Any ball hit into the crowd became a ground-rule double, and there were 10 in the day's game, seven by Boston and three by Cleveland. Boston won, 5–2.

1901 In Boston, the recently-acquired collegian George Winter debuted against Detroit, winning a five-hitter, 12–4 over the Tigers. Winter was 2-for-4 at the plate, involved in the scoring both times. It was the first of six straight wins for young Winter, typically dubbed "Winters" in early box scores.

TRANSACTIONS
1926: Roy Carlyle was selected off waivers by the New York Yankees. The
　　　Red Sox traded Howard Ehmke and Tom Jenkins to the Philadelphia
　　　Athletics for Slim Harriss, Fred Heimach, and Baby Doll Jacobson.
1959: Traded Billy Hoeft to the Baltimore Orioles for Jack Harshman.
1961: Sold Sammy White to the Milwaukee Brewers.
1969: Acquired Tom Satriano from the California Angels in trade for Joe Azcue.
1979: Andy Hassler was sold to the New York Mets.

DEBUTS

1901: George Winter	1947: Jake Jones	1972: Don Newhauser
1924: Buster Ross	1949: Walt Masterson	1979: Bob Watson
1932: Dale Alexander,	1952: Dick Brodowski	1991: Jeff Plympton
Roy Johnson	1960: Carroll Hardy	2001: Sun-Woo Kim

BIRTHDATES

Monte Weaver 1906 (1939); Babe Dahlgren 1912 (1935–1936); Ben Flowers 1927 (1951–1953); Wade Boggs 1958 (1982–1992); Tony Clark 1972 (2002); Ramiro Mendoza 1972 (2003–2004)

DEATHS

George Smith 1987

June 16

2002 The Braves vs. the Red Sox. It was another interleague matchup of "historic rivals," albeit ones who had only faced each other in exhibition play before interleague play began. The Red Sox fared poorly in the first years of interleague play, but Derek Lowe struck out 10 and beat the Braves, and Boston-area native Tom Glavine, 6–1.

1979 Dennis Eckersley got the win over the White Sox, 11–5, on the strength of a two-run inside-the-park homer by Rick Burleson, a two-run Jim Rice homer, and a two-run double by Carl Yastrzemski that was Yaz's 1,000th extra base hit.

1978 Before heading to Fenway, Bill Lee went to a cooking demonstration at a downtown department store. When he got to the park, though, he cleaned out his locker and said he was quitting. "Bill Lee, formerly of the Boston Red Sox," he said. Lee was angry that the Red Sox had traded Bernie Carbo and proclaimed, "Today just cost us the pennant." Manager Don Zimmer replied, "I don't like quitters." A day later, Lee returned. It may not have been coincidental that Lee was frustrated at his teammates for allowing 10 earned runs in his last two starts, but Lee was indeed a loyal friend and he also had his differences with Zim. Those differences were perhaps sharpened when Lee spoke from his home during the evening and called his manager "a gerbil, a no-good s.o.b." Of GM Haywood Sullivan, he fumed, "I'd like to punch his head off."

1975 Rookie Fred Lynn had a 20-game hitting streak come to its conclusion. He helped the Red Sox effort, though, by getting hit by a pitch in the 12th inning of a 2–2 tie. The Sox scored four times, and won 6–2, the final run coming when Rick Miller squeezed Lynn home from third.

1974 Carlton Fisk hit a solo homer in the third, but the Sox were losing 4–1 to the California Angels in the ninth, when Boston scored six times and won. Fisk's two-run double was the game-winner.

1961 Nine pitchers, 26 walks, and a score of 14–9 (Boston) resulted in a game just eight minutes shy of the existing record for a nine-inning game (3:52).

1950 For the second time in a six-day stretch, Hal Newhouser tamed the Red Sox, 4–1, doubling in the winning run in a heated fifth inning which saw Boston catcher Birdie Tebbetts ejected and (on another play) Newhouser called out for running out of the basepaths after his double.

1945 The Red Sox signed Dolph Camilli, who closed out his career with Boston. His son Doug was a coach for the Sox from 1970 through 1973.

1944 The Red Sox were making a run at it, but after winning nine in a row, they ran into Milo Candini. The Washington pitcher shut out the Sox, 4–0.

1938 Six plate appearances without an at-bat. Jimmie Foxx, with 19 homers on the season, gets six consecutive walks courtesy of the St. Louis Browns pitching staff. One is intentional and one appears semi-intentional. They were certainly pitching around him. Oh, yes—the Red Sox won, 12–8.

1936 Lefty Grove couldn't hold back the White Sox, and Jimmie Foxx's two solo homers were the only Red Sox runs, in a 4–2 loss at Comiskey. Foxx's first homer, in the fourth, went clear out over the left-field roof; it was the second time he'd hit one out. No other player had ever done it.

1928 The Red Sox scored enough runs in the fourth inning (eight) to win the game over Chicago (10–5). Bill Regan led off the fourth with a homer, and hit another one later on in the same frame, tying the major league record at the time of eight total bases in one inning.

1925 "Wind Helps Red Sox Win"—Ira Flagstead's fly ball in the fifth drifted away from the fielders and dropped in safely, giving Flaggy a double and what proved the game-winning RBI in a 2–1 win over the White Sox.

1917 What a riot! Near chaos broke out at Fenway, but somehow the game was never forfeited. The day started sunny, but when rain began falling in the fourth, all of the fans in the bleachers rushed for cover. They took advantage of there being no police present. Rather than just heading underneath the bleachers, they ran right across right field and into the grandstand. After a while, play resumed but the Red Sox stalled when they could, down 2–0 in the game and apparently not optimistic about their chances. With two outs in the top of the fifth, just before it would become an official game, a "tall man in a long rain coat" waved to others to follow him and "boldly leaped out upon the field. In ten seconds, he must have had 500 followers." They didn't approach the players, or the umpires, but made their way into the diamond and simply "stood around."

There were still no police present, but players and umpires talked to the men and somehow convinced them to go back in the stands, which they did, availing themselves of box seats with better views. Just as play was set to resume, more fans spilled out from right field, and they were joined with others from left field, and then the group which had taken box seats climbed back out onto the field as well. Five policemen arrived, but there was virtually nothing they could do. They also didn't try very hard, according to the *Chicago Tribune* report.

The players from both teams then rushed under the stands, and some pushing and shoving broke out, with White Sox players Buck Weaver and Fred McMullin accused of having slugged some of the fans. "They denied afterwards they had struck anyone more than was necessary to push their way through the mass to the exit," reported the *Tribune*. Under the stands, players, fans, umpires, owners, and police all had a heated discussion for about 35 minutes, with a lot of milling around. Sawdust had to be spread on the wet field, but play finally resumed. The whole affair was blamed on gamblers, who may have had money placed on the Red Sox to win. After the game, Buck Weaver was hit on the head by a pop bottle and a bit of a free-for-all erupted, but the police were able to break that up. One officer, accused of being "yellow" by Ray Schalk, almost arrested him but was apparently talked out of it. Chicago won the game, 7–2.

1913 Smoky Joe Wood and St. Louis' Tiny Leverens each yielded six hits over 12 innings. The fifth hit Leverens allowed was to Hack Engle, who singled in the bottom of the 12th. He advanced all the way to third when Wagner bunted and third baseman Wallace's throw to second went wild. The sixth hit was Wood's, scoring Engle on a walkoff single for a 3–2 victory.

1910 Even though pitcher Frank Arellanes hit a home run, the Red Sox played "football"—making nine errors—and lost 12–3 to the Tigers.

TRANSACTIONS
1986: Signed Ken Ryan as an amateur free agent.
1994: Acquired Tom Brunansky from the Milwaukee Brewers for Dave Valle.

DEBUTS
1919: Bill Lamar
1943: Babe Barna
1957: Mike Fornieles
1966: Rollie Sheldon, Jose Tartabull
1994: Sergio Valdez

BIRTHDATES
Johnnie Wittig 1914 (1949); Calvin Schiraldi 1962 (1986–1987)

DEATHS
George Dickey 1976

June 17

1978 In the bottom of the ninth, Carl Yastrzemski's bases-loaded single against a drawn-in infield drove in two and beat the Seattle Mariners, 5–4. It was the ninth win in a row for the Sox (and the 10th straight loss for Seattle). Bill Lee rejoined the club, sporting a T-shirt that read "Friendship first, competition second." Lee was fined one day's pay, the length of time he was AWOL (see June 16).

1977 A good start! At Fenway, the Sox banged out four home runs in the first inning against Catfish Hunter, and won 11–1. Rick Burleson and Fred Lynn led off, and Carlton Fisk and The Boomer (George Scott) homered as well. The Sox hit six homers in the 9–4 win and a total of 16 homers against New York in the three-game series, sweeping by a combined score of 30–9.

1964 Mickey Mantle hit the one homer he ever managed off Dick Radatz (who struck out The Mick in 12 of the 16 times they squared off), and it brought the Yanks to within a run, down 3–2. An unearned New York run tied it in the bottom of the ninth, but Russ Nixon's pinch single in the top of the 12th won it for Boston. "The Monster" (Radatz) had now won or saved five of the eight games the Red Sox had played against the 1964 Yankees.

1960 A two-run homer in the top of the third inning breaks a 1–1 tie and gives the Red Sox (and pitcher Frank Sullivan) a 3–1 win. Sullivan struck out 12 Indians. Cleveland's Wynn Hawkins surrendered the homer—#500 of Ted Williams' major league career. The only hitters preceding Williams in the 500 Home Run Club were Ruth, Foxx, and Ott. Williams was clearly pleased to have the ball returned from the left-field bullpen. UPI reported that he "gripped it in both hands when he received it from the attendant at the clubhouse."

1953 For Willard Nixon's 25th birthday, he held the Tigers to one run on five hits, made two hits himself, and drove in three. He had a little help from his friends, too, and Boston won big time, 17–1. Four Sox were injured in the game: Pitcher Mark Grissom took a shot off the ankle and had to leave the game. Floyd Baker hurt his back crashing into the third-base wall, but made the out. Dick Gernert hurt his elbow, and Gene Stephens pulled a muscle in his neck while running out a double in the seventh, the second of three hits Stephens made in the same inning. Will Cloney of the *Boston Herald* quipped that getting three safeties in one frame "made up for the times he couldn't get three hits in a week."

1943 Twice in the same day, Joe Cronin of the Red Sox hit a pinch-hit homer. Both were three-run blasts, one in each game of the doubleheader against St. Louis. Just two days earlier, he'd hit another pinch-hit three-run homer. By year's end, he had five pinch-hit four-baggers. As player-manager, he decided to put himself into games; in 42 pinch-hit at-bats, he racked up 18 hits and a major-league-leading 25 pinch-hit RBIs.

1936 Wes Ferrell pitched and won the game for himself with a two-run inside-the-park home run in the second inning, scoring his brother Rick before him in a 9–4 win over the White Sox in Comiskey. Later in the year, Rick had his own inside-the-park job. (See August 18, 1936.)

1925 Pitcher Ray Francis ran up a 7.71 ERA pitching for the Yankees and was traded to Boston on May 5. He then ran up an identical 7.71 ERA with Boston. On this day, he was waived to Cincinnati, but had pitched his last major league game.

1916 Shoeless Joe Jackson gets three hits off Boston pitcher Babe Ruth, and the White rack up 12 hits in all, helping lead to a 5–0 topping of the visiting Red Sox.

1915 The Red Sox kept on scoring from beginning to end, with five two-run innings, and it's good they did. St. Louis finally started to get to Sox starter Babe Ruth in the eighth, and scored seven runs off Ruth and reliever Mays. The final score was Boston 11, St. Louis 10.

1907 Recently-acquired Deacon McGuire was named manager, handed the reins by Bob Unglaub after just 29 games. McGuire was the fifth manager of 1907, and it was only June. After the suicide of Chick Stahl prior to spring training, Boston's managers had been George Huff (2–6), Cy Young (3–3), and Unglaub (9–20). McGuire went 45–61 and managed until Fred Lake took over in 1908. Despite managerial instability—which is putting it midly—Boston still finished ahead of Washington in the standings.

1903 Cleveland and Boston split a doubleheader. Norwood Gibson lost the morning game, 3–1. Tom Hughes, getting six runs in support, won the afternoon game, 6–1. Gunfire at the game? The *Boston Herald* reported a noisy holiday crowd (a state holiday officially termed Evacuation Day, but locally called Bunker Hill Day) "with revolvers, rattles and bells." One wanted to bring plenty of ammunition. The *Globe*'s Tim Murnane wrote, "Every time a good play was pulled off in favor of the home team, the rattle of small guns, firecrackers and the jingling of bells livened up matters until the whole affair reminded one of the Glorious Fourth in his boyhood days."

1902 There were four baseball games in Boston, played across the tracks from each other. The National League Boston Beaneaters took two from the New York Giants, 6–3 and 13–2, at the South End Grounds. On the other side of the railroad tracks, at the Huntington Avenue Grounds, the Boston Americans lost two to Cleveland, 7–3 and 4–3.

1901 Now it's a Chicago-Boston doubleheader in Boston, the first-ever AL twin bill in Beantown. It's Bunker Hill Day and Boston sweeps, 11–1 and 10–4, part of a five-game sweep of the White Sox. Boston nudges Chicago out of first place. Buck Freeman hit a rare home run; he drove in 114 runs in the franchise's first season. He had 12 homers on the team; the rest of the team had 25. For Boston, this makes four games in a row in which they had scored 10 or more runs (they beat Detroit 16–7 on the 14th and 12–4 on the 15th).

DEBUTS

1913: Earl Moseley   1969: Tom Satriano
1926: Baby Doll Jacobson   1997: Jesus Tavarez
1927: John Freeman   1999: Bob Wolcott
1966: Don Demeter

BIRTHDATES

Ben Shields 1903 (1930); Joe Bowman 1910 (1944–1945); Bill Humphrey 1911 (1938); Willard Nixon 1928 (1950–1958); Donnie Sadler 1975 (1998–2000)

DEATHS

Allen Sothoron 1939; Jim McHale 1959; Duffy Lewis 1979

June 18

1977 The Yankees fight amongst themselves; manager Billy Martin felt Reggie Jackson was loafing on a Jim Rice bloop to right. Martin stopped at the mound to relieve pitcher Mike Torrez, then embarrassed Reggie by walking out to right field and removing Jackson from the game. After both Martin and Jackson jaw at each other in the Fenway visitors' dugout, Martin has to be restrained from attacking Jackson. Boston wins,10–4, powered by five Sox home runs. Yaz and Carbo both hit a pair.

1976 Earlier in the week, Oakland owner Charlie Finley had sold off some of his better players: Joe Rudi and Rollie Fingers to the Red Sox, and Vida Blue to the Yankees, for a total of $3,500,000 cash. Baseball Commissioner Bowie Kuhn voided the transactions as "not in the best interest of baseball." Stripping a club of its better players would render it less competitive, and this was simply going too far. Finley threatened legal action, but the Commissioner's action held.

1975 All in a day's work. Fred Lynn had himself a day, going 5-for-6 and into double digits in RBIs. His 10 RBIs fell one short of the record. His 16 total bases tied an AL record. Luis Tiant's pitching held back the Tigers, but it was Lynn's three homers, one triple, and one single that almost single-handedly beat the Tigers, 15–1. Afterward, Lynn said, "I wasn't satisfied with the way I'd been swinging." He only slept three hours the night before and came to the park early for extra batting practice. It paid off.

1961 It was a day for comebacks that warmed the hearts of the Fenway faithful. Washington scored five times in the top of the ninth and led Boston, 12–5. After making the first out, Don Buddin singled. After the second out, the Sox scored eight runs (!) and won the first of two games. The eventful inning saw the Senators' Willie Tasby hit a grand slam in the top of the inning, and Boston's Jim Pagliaroni hit the game-tying grand slam in the bottom of the ninth. A walk followed, and a single, and then Russ Nixon singled home pinch-runner Pete Runnels to record a win. But that wasn't all. There was a second game and it lasted 13 innings. Washington tied up that second game in the eighth, but Boston put across a run in the bottom of the 13th to win another when—once again—Jim Pagliaroni homered, leading off against Tom Sturdivant.

A news story this day read MAGLIE SULKS AFTER 14–0 LOSS. In Bud Collins' account, Maglie was quoted as saying, "I don't understand it. I had good stuff." Nonetheless, he was pounded for 11 hits and 13 runs, 12 of them earned. Six batters hit homers off him, including Mark Runnels, Mike Buddin, Steve Nichols, Jimmy Malzone, Phil Crowley, Steve Dowd, and the oldest batter on the "Sox Sons" team, nine-year-old Gene Conley, Jr. It was the annual fathers-sons game and the Sox sons scored all their runs before Maglie retired even a single batter. Umpire Jim Honochick rebuked Maglie for brushing back a couple of batters, and eventually forfeited the game when Sal "The Barber" refused to behave.

1953 The Red Sox set 17 major league records in one ballgame, most of them built around the 17 runs they scored in the bottom of the seventh. Gene Stephens had three hits in the inning, and Boston sent 23 batters to the plate. The Tigers committed five errors in the game, but not one of them was in the seventh. The final was Boston 23, Detroit 3.

1947 A packed house at Fenway saw Billy Hitchcock homer to give St. Louis a 3–2 lead in the top of the 13th. The Red Sox tied it in the bottom of the 13th. Hitchcock singled with the bases loaded to drive in two in the top of the 14th, but the Red Sox came back and tied it again. Finally, in the bottom of the 15th, Johnny Pesky singled home pinch-runner Eddie Pellagrini and won the 6–5 game.

1946 The Red Sox scoured the waiver wire and picked up the only player ever to come from the Amana Colonies, Bill "Goober" Zuber, on waivers from the Yankees. Zuber's other distinction—last among major league pitchers in alphabetical order—was erased when the Indians called on George Zuverink in 1951.

1940 It was 7–7 in St. Louis and the Sox–Browns game was headed into extra innings. The Red Sox loaded the bases in the top of the 10th with one out, but catcher Johnny Peacock hit back to the pitcher for a 1-2-3 double play. The Browns loaded the bases in the bottom half of the inning, but St. Louis shortstop Johnny Berardino hit Jim Bagby's pitch out of the park for a game-winning grand slam.

1938 Lefty Grove and Chicago's Ted Lyons had been facing off for 14 years. Though Boston made three errors to Chicago's two, White Sox shortstop Boze Berger's throwing error in the top of the 12th was costly. Lyons himself made an error, his first since 1934. With the 4–3 win, Grove improved his record to 11–1.

1934 Browns pitcher Bump Hadley gave first baseman Ed Morgan a bump with a beanball, and when Morgan left to be treated, the Browns allowed Dusty Cooke to run for him. Cooke stole second and scored as part of a four-run Red Sox rally. Morgan re-entered the game, with Cooke being reinserted at center field for defensive purposes later in the game. Boston 6, St. Louis 5.

1933 In Cleveland, Indians pitcher Oral Hildebrand threw his fifth shutout of the season, 7–0; Mel Harder blanked Boston, too, 4–0 in the second game.

1932 Manager Shano Collins quits. The Indians beat Andrews and Jablonowski and won, 9–2. Collins sent a telegram to Boston owner Bob Quinn and said he was too discouraged to go on. He recommended second baseman Marty McManus as acting manager. While McManus was in church, Quinn's telegram arrived at his hotel. It read, "Beginning with today, you're the manager." McManus served the rest of 1932 and through 1933 as well. McManus (described in the *Chicago Tribune* as "one of the few Red Sox players still popular with Boston fans") seemed realistic in his ambitions, as reflected in a *Washington Post* headline: MCMANUS SETS SEVENTH PLACE AS THIS YEAR'S GOAL OF RED SOX. He didn't make it. But in 1933, under his leadership, the Sox finally did inch up to seventh.

1919 St. Louis held a 3–2 edge over the Red Sox, but Boston had Wally Schang on third base with one out. Ray Caldwell shot a rocket of a liner that was snared by George Sisler at first, in a spectacular play. In its aftermath, Schang didn't notice Browns third baseman Jimmy Austin tuck the ball under his arm. Moments later, Schang took a lead and was caught by the hidden ball trick, ending the game.

1917 On Bunker Hill Day, the Red Sox had to play without Ernie Shore and Heinie Wagner, both having been suspended for using "disrespectful language" in arguments during Chicago's June 15 8–0 shutout of the Red Sox. This day worked out, though, and the White Sox "lost two trenches" in their battle against the Red Sox as Boston swept two games, 6–4 and 8–7. Chicago was leading 7–4 in the second game, when the Red Sox combined three singles with two errors and one passed ball, coming from behind with four runs.

A Fenway fan, Augustin McNally, caused warrants to be served on Chicago ballplayers George "Buck" Weaver and Fred McMullin, charging them with assault and battery. The *Washington Post* reported that McNally "alleged that he was struck by the two players during an intermission caused by rain" in the June 16 game. He claimed he was attacked just because he gave three cheers for the Red Sox.

1912 The Sox take up residence on top of the American League and stay in first place for the remainder of the season. The second-place team finishes 14½ games out, and that rival team from New York ends up in last place, 55 games behind.

TRANSACTIONS
1904: Traded Patsy Dougherty to the New York Highlanders for Bob Unglaub.
1946: Purchased Bill Zuber from the New York Yankees.
1997: Rudy Pemberton granted free agency.

DEBUTS
1929: Jack Ryan
1959: Jack Harshman

BIRTHDATES
Tom McCarthy 1961 (1985)

DEATHS
None yet

June 19

2000 Sox fan extraordinaire Lib Dooley attended more than 4,000 consecutive Sox games at Fenway Park over 55 seasons. Ms. Dooley, 87, died hours before the Yankees dealt the Red Sox the worst defeat ever suffered at their hands, 22–1. "I do not consider myself a fan," she often said. "I am a friend of the Red Sox." Her grandnephew David Leary placed a game ball in her coffin. Nine runs in the eighth and seven more in the ninth, as New York piled on late. Winning pitcher for New York was Ramiro Mendoza, who allowed just six hits in seven innings. The two mop-up pitchers didn't allow a single hit in the last two frames.

1995 Did a frenzied mob of fans surround Jose Canseco's car after a rehab game in Pawtucket, pounding it with baseball bats because the Boston slugger refused to sign more autographs? Canseco signed generously before the game but when he declined after the game, he said around 200 fans crowded his vehicle and "my truck sustained quite a few dents. I'd never go back there. I don't care for what [expletive] reason." One of the fans said there were about 30 fans, none of whom carried bats and "there was no swearing or anything like that."

1991 After the *Boston Globe*'s Bella English drew attention to a number of incidents involving "perverts on parade" in Fenway's bleachers simulating sex acts with inflatable life-size dolls, the Red Sox announced plans to deal with such reprehensible behavior. Signs alluding to the incidents remain posted at Fenway Park in 2005.

1977 The Sox completed a sweep of the Yankees at Fenway, batting out a major league record 16 homers in the three games. "Guys were gettin' blisters shakin' hands," said Sox manager Don Zimmer. Not one of the homers belonged to Jim Rice, and no one on the Yankees team could claim one, either. Boston won, 11–1, and Yaz's homer hit the roof façade to the right of where the retired numbers are today. It was the closest any ball has ever come to going out of Fenway Park to right field. Boston had taken over the lead in the AL East by 2½ games.

1973 The Brewers had a 10-game winning streak until Boston took two. The first game was won with a four-run top of the ninth, the Red Sox on top, 8–4. In game two, Rick Miller's triple drove in two in the top of the 11th. Bob Montgomery drove home Miller, and the game ended with a 4–1 win.

1970 After eight full innings, Sonny Siebert had a no-hitter going against the Yankees, and a 5–0 lead to boot. Mike Andrews, Reggie Smith, and Yaz all had homers for the Sox, but the Fenway faithful were lusting for the no-hitter. It wasn't to be. After starting off with a 2–0 count on Horace Clarke, Siebert threw five pitches in the top of the ninth, and gave up four straight hits and four runs. The Sox had to send for Sparky Lyle to shut down the Yanks, which he did. 5–4, Boston.

1957 Mel Parnell, his arm worn out, calls it a career. As careers go, it was superb. He was 123–75 lifetime, all in service to the Red Sox. He has more wins for the Sox than any other Boston southpaw, and was inducted into the Red Sox Hall of Fame in 1997.

1942 Both Sox teams played at Comiskey under the lights, and it was a fine pitching duel between Boston's Charlie Wagner and Chicago's Edgar Smith. The Red Sox won it, 1–0, on a fifth-inning leadoff drive by Dom DiMaggio which landed fair but then rolled under the bench on which the Red Sox bullpen staff was sitting.

No one moved to make life easier for Chicago right fielder Wally Moses, but no one interfered either, and by the time Moses found the ball and fired it home, The Little Professor had an inside-the-park home run.

1940 Ted Williams cracks a 12th inning home run to give Boston a 4–3 win over the White Sox in game one. Ted thumps another in the 14–5 nitecap win. Winning pitcher Jack Wilson clubs a pair of homers, as does Joe Cronin. Jimmie Foxx homers as well as the Sox collect 20 hits.

1922 A former Red Sox player ejected the Yankees' Babe Ruth from a ballgame. Frustration boiled over, as the Yankees were on the brink of their eighth straight defeat, and left fielder Babe Ruth argued that Cleveland's runner was out at second base. Umpire Bill Dinneen, who had pitched for Boston from 1902 into 1907 (admittedly, before they were the Red Sox) tossed Ruth from the game.

1921 "Idleness not being good for any one, particularly ball players, Squire Ebbets and Harry Frazee arranged the garden party," wrote the *New York Times*. In a mid-season exhibition game in Flatbush, the Brooklyn Dodgers destroyed the Red Sox on 19 hits, 15–2. Ernie Neitzke started for the Red Sox, but was bombed. He only ever appeared in 7⅓ major league innings.

1905 Introduced to the New Bedford crowd as "Jesse Tannehill," Chick Stahl actually pitched three innings in an exhibition game. The crowd knew it was a joke, but Stahl struck out the side the first inning he threw. Boston won, 12–0.

1904 The fingers of AL founder Ban Johnson were almost certainly on this one. He wanted to make the New York franchise a contender. Why else would the World Champion Boston Americans trade one of their most popular players—Patsy Dougherty (.331 in 1903, he led the league with 195 hits and 103 runs)—for New York's untested infielder Bob Unglaub? Unglaub had only appeared in six games and was hitting .211; when he joined the Bostons, he hit .111. To be fair, he did improve—a bit—and even served as player-manager for a stretch in 1907. Dougherty was angry, and said he'd refuse to play for New York. "I'm good and sore and I won't stand it," he said—unless he was cut in on the proceeds of the sale. (See June 25, 1904.) If parity was Johnson's goal, he succeeded: the pennant was decided between Boston and New York on the final day of the season, and Doughtery played a role. (Also see October 10, 1904.)

TRANSACTIONS
1941: Odell Hale was sold to the New York Giants.

DEBUTS
1907: Beany Jacobson
1911: Tracy Baker
1928: Freddie Moncewicz
1963: Bob Heffner

BIRTHDATES
Eddie Cicotte 1884 (1908–1912); Casper Asbjornson 1909 (1928–1929); Don Gutteridge 1912 (1946–1947); Doug Mientkiewicz 1974 (2004); Bruce Chen 1977 (2003)

DEATHS
Ed Barry 1920; Wally Gerber 1951

June 20

2002 In a move that foreshadowed game-time closing of Yawkey Way to become a revenue source for the Red Sox during games, the team reached agreement with street vendors. (Vendors had sold their wares around Fenway since it first opened in 1912.) The Sox had tried to have street vendors banned, but their efforts ignited a firestorm of criticism. Now they worked out a compromise that allowed the vendors to sell around much of the park but not on a stretch of Yawkey Way itself.

1996 Roger Clemens labored hard, throwing 157 pitches, but still couldn't stem the tide of the Tribe, as the Indians came from behind to post a 5–4 win, their 13th consecutive defeat of the Red Sox.

1980 Frank Tanana held the Red Sox to five hits, while the rest of the Angels piled up 26 hits in a 20–2 drubbing of their hosts in Boston. The big surprise, though, was 5'4" Fred Patek. Over 12 major league seasons, he had hit 36 homers. This one day, Patek hit three homers and a double, too.

1977 Just after sweeping a weekend series with the Yankees, Boston welcomed in the Orioles. Rick Wise threw a two-hitter, shutting out the Orioles, 4–0. Butch Hobson's homer gave the Sox 22 four-baggers in their last six games, tying a major league record. Jim Rice had three hits, and a total of seven in a row, before striking out in the ninth inning.

1973 Opening in Milwaukee, leadoff batter Rick Miller hit a home run off Brewers starter Bill Parsons. Number two hitter Reggie Smith did the same. Carlton Fisk singled in another run in the fourth and Bill Lee held back the Brewers, 3–2.

1969 Faced with a little rain, umpire Hank Soar called off the game at Fenway in the first inning—and washed out Joe Pepitone's grand slam home run. Pepitone was livid, saying, "The infield, there wasn't a spot of water on it. Hell, it needed water!" Sorry, Joe.

1967 Tom Yawkey told the *Boston Globe*'s Will McDonough that Fenway Park was
[FP] deteriorating badly and that Milwaukee was appealing to him to move the Red Sox there. McDonough asked, "Can you see the Red Sox playing in Fenway in five years?" Yawkey said, "No. I don't intend to bankrupt myself."

Sox third baseman Joe Foy lived in The Bronx and when the Sox pulled in the night before, on June 19, he found his house on fire. After helping his parents get re-settled with his sister, and after losing almost all his possessions, he made his way back to the Red Sox team hotel for a few hours sleep of before breakfast. That evening, Foy hit a fifth-inning grand slam to beat the Yankees at the Stadium, 7–1.

1964 Dave Morehead, who would throw a no-hitter for Boston in September of 1965, let the Orioles score six runs in the bottom of the first inning in Baltimore before getting a single out. That was enough; the O's won, 10–5.

1951 Entering the game, Cleveland's Bobby Avila had one home run on the season. He hit three more, and a double, and a single, for four RBIs and 15 total bases, helping the Indians to a 14–8 win over the Red Sox. Avila's final homer was an inside-the-park job, hit in the ninth inning off the flagpole in deep center field.

1940 The Browns swept the Red Sox four straight at Sportsman's Park, and swept the Sox out of first place in the process. Harlond Clift's ninth-inning solo homer off Denny Galehouse won the first game, 2–1. In game two, the Browns came from behind three times, but then built up a convincing lead for an 11–4 victory.

1918 Sox pitcher Dutch Leonard was cruising along with eight wins in mid-June, including his June 3 no-hitter, and had an ERA of 2.72. Over the preceding five seasons, he'd won 14 or more games for the Sox. Hit on the thumb by a batted ball, he had to leave the game. Reclassified in the draft from Class 4 up to Class 1, he apparently decided to sign up with the Fore River Shipyard in Quincy, Massachusetts. If one were performing necessary defense work, one would not be conscripted into the Army. Leonard joined the Fore River Shipyard ball team. After the season, he was traded to the Yankees—but ended up on the Tigers instead (it's a long story). Later in life, he was head of one of California's largest wineries.

1916
STVT Tillie Walker, playing for the Browns at the time, hit a home run in a game at Fenway on September 24, 1915. He was then acquired by the Red Sox—and hit the only home homer by any member of the World Champion Red Sox during the entire 1916 season. The Yankees beat the Sox 4–1 and Walker's HR over the left-field Wall was their only score. There wouldn't be another Sox home run at Fenway until 1917.

Shortstop Everett Scott enters the game in the ninth inning for defensive purposes. Little could he have know this would be game #1 of a streak of 1,307 consecutive games—the longest streak of any player until Lou Gehrig passed him by.

TRANSACTIONS
1947: Purchased Denny Galehouse from the St. Louis Browns.
1955: Signed Bill Monbouquette after he graduated from high school.
1980: Sold Jack Brohamer to the Indians.
1998: Acquired Carlos Reyes, Mandy Romero, and Dario Veras from the San Diego Padres in trade for Jim Leyritz and Ethan Faggett.

DEBUTS
1906: Red Morgan
1926: Fred Heimach
1931: Bill Marshall
1943: Pinky Woods

BIRTHDATES
Billy Werber 1908 (1933–1936)

DEATHS
None yet

June 21

2003 Nomar Garciaparra was 6-for-6 (every hit a single) in a 13-inning game against Philadelphia in Veterans Stadium. Tied 2–2 after nine, both teams scored one run in the 12th. The Red Sox then scored twice in the top of the 13th, but the Phillies faced Jason Shiell and Rudy Seanez and came back with three runs to win the game. Three days later, Nomar had a 5-for-5 game.

2002 The Red Sox signed John-Henry Williams, the 33-year-old son of Sox slugger Ted Williams. The younger Williams, who never played past high school and reportedly couldn't make his college team, would be paid $850 a month to sign a minor league contract and be assigned to the Gulf Coast Red Sox. There was no signing bonus.

"Obviously, we're doing this out of respect for Ted Williams," acknowledged Sox assistant GM Theo Epstein.

1997 After employing four pitchers and still failing to tame the Tigers, manager Jimy Williams gave the ball to infielder Mike Benjamin to pitch the ninth. Benjamin set down Detroit 1-2-3, the only inning the Tigers went down in order. Detroit still won, 15–4.

1994 Scoring 10 runs before the Blue Jays ever got up to bat gave Boston enough of a boost to coast to an easy 13–1 win for Aaron Sele.

1977 Embarrassing Baltimore in their home park, after a two-hitter from Rick Wise and a three-hitter from Ferguson Jenkins, it was a near no-hitter for Luis Tiant over the Orioles. Burleson's bobble behind second base might have been ruled an error, but Pat Kelly's double off the right-field wall with two outs in the ninth made the matter moot. Homers by Jim Rice and George Scott ensured the 7–0 Red Sox win, and gave the Sox a record-tying 24 HRs in seven straight games.

1972 Rico Petrocelli earned six RBIs with just one hit in the game—the hit was a grand slam. He also drove in a pair with sacrifice flies. Rico and Yaz sparked an 11-inning Sox win, 10–9 Texas. Yaz was 5-for-6 and scored four runs. Luis Tiant got the win, his first of the year.

1969 Joe Pepitone had a grand slam rained out on the 20th, but things were looking up for the Yankees on the 21st when they scored three runs in the top of the 11th to take a 5–2 lead over the Sox at Fenway. They might have taken a larger lead, had not Boston first baseman George Thomas pulled the hidden ball trick and caught Jerry Kenney off first. Yankees reliever Ken Johnson, though, loaded the bases and then saw two runs score on a double by Joe Lahoud. After Dick Schofield walked, the aforementioned Thomas hit a little single to center off his fists and the Red Sox won, 6–5. In an evening game (it was a separate admission doubleheader), the Yankees were down 3–0 after two innings, but scored four runs in the top of the ninth to win, 6–3.

1967 A battle of beanballs erupts between the Red Sox and the Yankees at Yankee Stadium, as the New Yorkers lose their fifth straight game (and 10 of their last 13). The Red Sox scored four times in the first inning, and Yankees pitcher Thad Tillotson may have felt that Joe Foy had to pay the price for his fifth-inning grand slam the day before. In the second inning, Tillotson's pitch hit Foy on the helmet. This was back before the DH and Tillotson had to bat against Lonborg in the bottom of the second. He was hit in the back, between the shoulder blades and both benches emptied for five minutes. A few punches were thrown and Pepitone had to leave the game with a strained left wrist. No one was ejected, perhaps a mistake. The very next inning, Reggie Smith was floored, buzzed by a close one, and in the fifth inning, pinch-hitter Dick Howser was hit in the helmet by another one of Lonborg's throws. The Red Sox won, 8–1.

1961 Mantle and Maris each homer off pitcher Bill Monbouquette in the first inning, but it was Johnny Blanchard's ninth-inning pinch-hit grand slam that sinks the Red Sox, 11–8.

1960 The first six Kansas City Athletics batters hit safely, and scored five runs in the first inning off Jerry Casale, who never recorded an out. Even though Ted Williams had four RBIs on two homers and a single, the Sox lost 11–7.

1945 Boo Ferriss finally lost a game at Fenway, the inevitable result of letting the Yankees score nine runs off him in what became a 13-run fifth for New York. The nine runs matched the total Ferriss had allowed in his first 10 starts, all complete game efforts.

1941 Lefty Grove pitched well at Fenway in '40 and '41, so well in fact that he had won 21 games in a row at home. On June 21, he got pounded and had to leave in the second inning. The St. Louis Browns won, 13–9.

1938 Mike "Pinky" Higgins was 4-for-4 off Tigers' pitching in the first game of a doubleheader, and 4-for-4 in the second game. Two days before, he had a double and three singles. Mixed in were a couple of walks. Higgins now counted 12 hits in his last 12 at-bats, setting the still-standing record. On June 22, first time up, he struck out, ending his streak. Boston split, winning 8–3, then losing 5–4.

1927 The Sox lost a doubleheader to the Yankees, 7–3 and 7–1. On June 22, they lost two more to New York. It was the start of a stretch where they lost 15 consecutive games. In July, they had a seven-game losing streak and in August they had a 10-game losing streak. Small wonder that season's end had the Sox in last place, an astonishing 59 games out of first.

1916 The first no-hitter ever thrown at Fenway Park was by "little George Foster, the farmer boy from Oklahoma" (as the *New York Times* described him). The 5' 7½" Foster beat Bob Shawkey and the Yankees, 2–0. Foster walked three. The win earned Foster a $100 bonus from Red Sox President Lannin.

1903 A Boston batter hits for the cycle for the first time in franchise history—in a regular season game held in Canton, Ohio. In the Sunday game, Buck Freeman goes 5-for-6, with six RBIs, and helps Boston beat Cleveland, 12–7.

1902 It was the hot corner in Detroit today, for sure, with Boston third baseman Jimmy Collins fielding 15 balls at third base—nine assists, five putouts, and one error. Cy Young threw a complete 15-inning game, earning a 4–1 win when Boston combined three hits with a walk and took advantage of an error.

TRANSACTIONS
1911: Purchased Judge Nagle from the Pittsburgh Pirates.
1977: Signed free agent Tommy Helms. Released Doug Griffin.
1980: Released Jack Billingham.

DEBUTS

1919: Norm McNeil	1987: Todd Benzinger
1927: Marty Karow	1989: Dana Williams
1936: Ted Olson	

BIRTHDATES
None yet

DEATHS
None yet

June 22

1989 Sox starter Mike Smithson hits Texas' Rafael Palmeiro with a pitch and the Rangers bench empties. Coming to Smithson's defense was one Red Sox player—Joe Price. The rest, wrote Dan Shaughnessy the following year, "sat in the dugout like cigar-store Indians" as Price led the "charge up Joe Mooney Hill."

1982 Detroit led 4–2 into the ninth inning, but Dwight Evans tied it with a two-run homer and then Red Sox rookie Wade Boggs connected for his first major league homer in the bottom of the 11th, giving the Sox a 5–4 walkoff win over the Tigers. The very next day, regular third baseman Carney Lansford sprained his ankle going for an inside-the-park home run (he didn't make it), and Boggs took his place in the starting lineup. The rest is history, as Boggs batted at a .390 pace once he had the opportunity to play as a regular.

1977 Four times in six games, the Red Sox hit five or more home runs. It had never been done before. Sox manager Don Zimmer wanted to give Carlton Fisk the night off, but Fisk declined. Jim Palmer had won three Cy Young Awards in the previous four years, but Boston batters banged five home runs off him, with Fisk connecting for two, and Scott, Rice, and Hobson getting one each. The homer barrage beat Baltimore, 7–4, the tying and go-ahead runs coming in the top of the ninth on Fisk's second blow which ticked off left fielder Pat Kelly's glove into home run territory. "I was getting whiplash," cracked Orioles shortstop Mark Belanger about watching all five home run balls sail over his head to left field.

1916 Babe Ruth throws a three-hitter and holds New York scoreless, 1–0. It's one of his nine shutouts in 1916, the final one being his 3–0 win over the Yankees on September 29.

1912 Embarrassing the Yankees in front of the hometown fans with doubleheader wins of 13–2 and 10–3, the Red Sox complete a rout of the Yankees, scoring a total of 55 runs in the five-game series in New York. The *New York Times* writer, tongue in cheek, accused the Red Sox of "greed and avarice," complaining that "that's no way to make friends." Oddly, in the sixth inning of the first game, with the Red Sox at the plate, the Yankees fielders all came in from the field after recording two outs, and the Red Sox assumed their positions in the field before loud shouts from the crowd assisted the umpire in getting it right and giving the Sox their rightful third out.

The 23–5 margin in runs scored versus runs allowed was the biggest single-day margin of the year. For the full year, Boston scored 799 runs while only allowing 544, the largest difference in franchise history. (The worst year was 1932, when Boston allowed 915 runs but only scored 566, a difference of 349 runs. In 1950, Boston scored the most runs ever—1027—and that was when the season was just 154 games long. In 1958, the disparity was the closest, scoring 697 runs and allowing 691.)

1911 New York scored four times in the first and thrice more in the second. When rain started falling in the fourth—it not yet an official game—the Boston players "moped along like pallbearers" while the Yankees "hustled to beat the band," according to the *New York Times*) In the Yankees' fourth, Daniels swung wildly at three pitches, hardly intending to hit one. Fitzgerald got wood on one, a routine grounder, but Boston second baseman Engle "faded away from it scandalously" enabling Fitzgerald to reach second base. When Hartzell lofted an easy fly ball to left, Fitzgerald made no attempt to get back to second—he started running and never stopped, giving Boston no choice but to double him off the bag and end the inning. Umpire Connolly pushed the Red Sox to bat and move things along. The game was called after 4½. 7–0.

1902 Umpire Johnstone was attacked by 200–300 irate Detroit fans, but players from both teams surrounded the ump and got him safely to the dressing room outside the park. Even the Boston papers agreed he'd made a bad call ruling out a Tiger at the plate. Boston won, 7–5.

TRANSACTIONS
1907: Traded Bill Dinneen to the St. Louis Browns for Beany Jacobson and $1,000 cash.
1999: Jim Corsi was given his release.
2004: Signed Curtis Leskanic to a 2004 contract.

DEBUTS
1949: Johnnie Wittig
1998: Billy Ashley

BIRTHDATES
Walt Masterson 1920 (1949–1952); Faye Throneberry 1931 (1952–1956)

DEATHS
Tom Doran 1910; Charlie Hemphill 1953; Frankie Hayes 1955; Marv Owen 1991; Ron Kline 2002

June 23

2001 The ball was still rising when it hit the light tower above the Coke bottle and the Red Sox announced that Manny Ramirez's massive shot had a probable distance of 501 feet. Reporters immediately grasped the significance of the number, just one foot short of the June 9, 1946 home run Ted Williams hit to row 37 in the Section 42 bleachers. Manny hit another one estimated at 463 in the same game, but the Sox still lost, 9–6, on the basis of Toronto's seven-run top of the second. Both were solo shots; the two times Manny came up with the bases loaded later in the game, he made infield outs.

1990 Sox pitcher Jeff Gray recorded his first major league win, coming into the game and getting the last two Orioles in the top of the 10th. Bigger news, though, was ace closer Gregg Olson giving up the long ball. Dwight Evans tied the game in the bottom of the eighth. It went into extra innings and the Orioles scored once in the top of the 10th, but Evans hit another homer—a two-run blast—in the bottom of the inning, so the Sox (and Jeff Gray) got a 4–3 win. The very next day, Gray earned his first save. Greg Harris got credit for the June 24 2–0 win over the O's.

1981 The Pawtucket Red Sox won "the longest game"—it had started on April 19 and been suspended after 32 innings of play, at 4:07 A.M. After eight hours and seven minutes, it remained tied 2–2. The Rochester Red Wings had broken the 1–1 tie in the top of the 21st inning, but the Pawsox came back to tie it. The resumption of the game only added 18 minutes of playing time as the Pawsox loaded the bases in the bottom of the 33rd, and then won it on Dave Koza's bases-loaded single. Wade Boggs had gone 4-for-12 in the game. Dallas Williams of the Red Wings suffered personal frustration, going 0-for-12 in the April start, then missed the plane and only barely arrived in time to get another bat—and wind up with an 0-for-13 mark. Steve Grilli took the loss; he hadn't even been with Rochester at the time of the first game.

1977 On a seven-game winning roll powered by home runs, the Red Sox reached 30 homers in nine games for a new major-league record. Butch Hobson had the only homer in the June 23 game, but it helped in the 7–3 win over the Orioles.

1975 Carlton Fisk, out nearly a year with an injury to his leg, returns and hits .331 on the season, helping propel Boston into the 1975 World Series, for which he will always be remembered.

1973 Jesse Jefferson was pitching his first game in the majors, and only needed one more out to shut out the Red Sox. Rico Petrocelli ruined it for him, with a game-tying bottom-of-the-ninth home run. Baltimore won in the 10th, though, on back-to-back singles aggravated when Reggie Smith was slow fielding the first one, enabling Paul Blair to set up camp on second base. The day wasn't a total loss for Boston fans, as the Red Sox had won the first game, 5–1.

1954 The Orioles broke a nine-game losing streak , but it took them 17 innings to finally push across the winning run. Had the Orioles scored in the first inning, when they had the bases loaded and nobody out, it might have made a difference, but pinch-hitter Sam Mele hit into a triple play. The O's secured a 7–3 lead with three insurance runs in the bottom of the eighth, however, before Boston came right back with four in the top of the ninth to tie it. Before the game was over, the Red Sox had used 22 players and Baltimore had used 20, tying the major league total of 42. The game lasted 4:58, breaking the old record of 4:49. The Orioles won on a bases-loaded fielder's choice.

1952 You might say the Red Sox broke open a 1–1 tie when 12 consecutive Sox batters reached base in the fourth inning and the team scored 11 runs. Then they stopped scoring; the Red Sox beat Detroit, 12–6.

1950 After losing 11 of 13 games, Joe McCarthy resigned and coach Steve O'Neill was named to take the reins as Red Sox manager. McCarthy said he was "physically exhausted" following a bout with influenza and pleurisy. After the last-day elimination in the 1949 season, he'd left the ballclub for home without consulting GM Joe Cronin or owner Tom Yawkey, and taken fully two months to decide upon managing again in 1950. McCarthy's wife said his health would no longer permit him to continue as manager.

1940 Ted Williams rendered speechless. After an outfield collision with center fielder Doc Cramer, The Kid was knocked unconscious for several minutes and then hospitalized. An x-ray revealed a slight brain concussion. Ray Mack's eighth-inning fly ball went for an inside-the-park home run and helped the Indians build on a 2–1 lead; the final score was Cleveland 4, Boston 1. In game two, Jim Tabor hit two solo homers for all the scoring in Herb Hash's 2–0 shutout of the Tribe.

1927 Lou Gehrig put on a show at Fenway Park, hitting three home runs (the first time it had ever been done on the Red Sox home field) and sparking the Yankees' 11–4 triumph.

1919 Sox first baseman Stuffy McInnis hit a home run, but in the fourth inning, he also made his first error of the year, after 526 chances. It didn't matter, though: Washington won with ease, 12–3.

1917 Temper, temper. Ernie Shore pitches a perfect game for the Red Sox...or does he? In the second game of the day's doubleheader, Dutch Leonard shut out Walter Johnson and the Senators on four hits. But it was the first game that was the story. Babe Ruth was the Sox starter and he walked leadoff batter Ray Morgan, but he was so incensed by the call of ball four that he rushed to the plate to argue with umpire Brick Owens. Ruth was ordered back to the mound, and threw a punch that struck Owens on the ear. Ernie Shore was summoned to take Ruth's place. Immediately, Morgan tried to steal second but was thrown out, and Shore went on to retire every one of the 26 batters he faced. With Shore on the mound, the Red Sox recorded 27 outs without a single runner reaching base and for years it was considered a perfect game until later 20th century rulings declared it otherwise. The Red Sox won, 4–0. Ruth was suspended for nine days and had to pay a $100 fine. The *Washington Post* suggested that it was fortunate for Ruth that Owens showed restraint: "Brick has the reputation of being able to 'lick his weight in wild cats' and had he mixed with Ruth there is little question but what the pitcher would have finished second."

1916 Ekeing out a victory, Dick Hoblitzell walked, was sacrificed to second, took third on a fielder's choice, and scored on a wild pitch. The seventh-inning run was the only one of the ballgame as Ernie Shore shut out the Philadelphia Athletics, 1–0, before the Boston crowd. It was the third shutout in a row for Boston pitchers.

1911 A six-run fourth inning gave Boston a 7–3 win in game one, and a five-run fourth gave the Sox a 6–4 win over Philadelphia in the second.

1909 Doyle may have been slow, but it's doubtful Chesbro was happy. Red Sox batters feasted on Yankee pitching, collecting 11 hits off Slow Joe Doyle and 10 more off Happy Jack Chesbro. Final: Boston 14, New York 5.

1903 The Boston Americans take over first place. They never relinquish the lead and finish 14½ games ahead of the second-place Philadelphia Athletics and 47½ games ahead of last-place Washington.

TRANSACTIONS
1955: Sold Sam Mele to the Cincinnati Redlegs.
1969: Sold Garry Roggenburk to the Seattle Pilots.
1975: Released Tim McCarver
1994: Signed Jared Fernandez as an amateur free agent.
2002: Acquired Alan Embree and Andy Shibilo from the San Diego Padres for Brad Baker and Dan Giese.

DEBUTS
1931: Jud McLaughlin
1946: Bill Zuber
1977: Tommy Helms
1993: Aaron Sele
1995: Matt Stairs
1998: Carlos Reyes

BIRTHDATES
Bill Harris 1900 (1938); Dusty Cooke 1907 (1933–1936); Aaron Robinson 1915 (1951); Marty Barrett 1958 (1982–1990)

DEATHS
Joe Dobson 1994; Bob Smith 2003

June 24

2003 Three days after going 6-for-6, Nomar Garciaparra had himself a 5-for-5 day at the plate, helping beat the Tigers (who had seven hits as a team), 10–1. (See also June 21, 2003.)

1988 At 6:20 P.M., in a closed-door session, Wade Boggs apologized to his teammates for all the trouble caused by the $6 million palimony suit brought against him by mistress Margo Adams. Adams had caused several teammates to be called to provide depositions. Boggs told Channel 7 sports anchor John Dennis that he was able to blank it all out, but he realized some of the other Red Sox could not. A shouting match between Boggs and Dwight Evans had broken out on the team bus and in the hotel lobby back on June 19, and Evans and catcher Rick Cerone had to be separated by other players.

1977 Despite three Red Sox homers, extending their record by giving them 33 over 10 games, it was Roy White's game-tying two-run homer with two outs in bottom of the ninth which set up extra innings. The Yankees went on to win (6–5) the following inning on Reggie Jackson's bases-loaded single. This game is seen to be a major Yankees turning-point victory as NY wins its next two games as well, nearly erasing the Sox lead in standings.

1964 Boston won 9–0, the big blow being a Rico Petrocelli grand slam. Milwaukee relief pitcher Ed Rodriguez didn't do himself any favors when the first 12 pitches he threw in the seventh inning all missed the strike zone.

1942 During a road visit to Detroit, Joe Cronin and Ted Williams took time out to go to Flint, Michigan for a War Bond sales event with Tigers Charlie Gehringer and Birdie Tebbetts.

1931 In this day's game, 25 of the 27 outs recorded are infield putouts—two each by SS Rhyne and 2B Miller, but the lion's share are the 21 by Bill Reynolds at first base. It's one shy of the record Hal Chase set in 1906. Boston's catcher made the other two, one on a strikeout. The outfielders stood around all day and never did do anything in the field. In fact, they were 0-for-11 at the plate as well, but the Red Sox won the game, 7–3, scoring four times in the top of the ninth.

1926 The Yankees tied it in the top of the eighth, 4–4, then scored once in the ninth on Lazzeri's home run. Boston's Fritz Bratschi tied it back up with a pinch hit in the bottom of the ninth, and won it in the 11th when Lou Gehrig put his foot where his glove should have been and foozled a grounder that hopped over his head letting pinch-runner Smiley Bischoff scoot around and score from second base.

1922 George Burns executed the hidden ball trick on the Yankees' Chick Fewster.

1916 Mays saves one, wins one. Carl Mays took over late in the game and saved one for Dutch Leonard, though the "save" rule must have been different, since Boston came from behind to win in the bottom of the ninth. Mays just kept on pitching, and won the nightcap, 7–3, with a complete game effort.

1911 The A's and Red Sox were tied 1–1 after eight innings, when Boston pitcher Charley Hall stopped dueling. Touched for just four hits over the first eight and a run on a squeeze play in the second inning, he allowed double that number of hits (and six runs, four of them on a McInnis grand slam) in the top of the ninth. 7–1 final.

TRANSACTIONS
1958: Traded Jack Spring to the Washington Senators for Bud Byerly.
1967: Traded Dennis "The Menace" Bennett to the New York Mets for Al Yates and cash.

DEBUTS
1902: Doc Adkins
1908: Charlie Hartman

BIRTHDATES
Paul Musser 1889 (1919); Bobby Reeves 1904 (1929–1931); Mel
Hoderlein 1923 (1951); Charlie Mitchell 1962 (1984–1985)

DEATHS
John Perrin 1969

June 25

2000 Hopes of returning to the post-season were dashed by three consecutive extra-inning defeats, a 6–5 loss to the Blue Jays in 13, then back-to-back losses to Baltimore (6–3, in 10 innings, and 8–7, in 11). The Red Sox never saw first place again, except from below.

1977 The Yankees crept closer to the Sox in the standings, and a three-run homer by Graig Nettles was the damaging blow dealt Boston's Luis Tiant. Mike Torrez won it for New York, 5–1.

1975 The Sox lost, 8–5, and Fisk was just 0-for-2 in the game, replaced by Tim Blackwell after six innings, but it was good to have Fisk back. He'd been out for almost a full year dating back to a June 23, 1974 injury.

1970 The Sox were cruising, beating Baltimore 7–0 when the game became official in the fifth inning. They could have had more, given the five singles they collected off Mike Cuellar in the first inning, but Don Buford threw out two runners trying to go from first to third. The Orioles scored five runs in the sixth and tied it up with two more in the ninth, then pumped across a definitive six runs in the top of the 14th as both Jose Santiago and Cal Koonce collapsed. Boston's lone run in response was far from sufficient. Final, 13–8, Baltimore.

1950 Bobby Doerr and Walt Dropo participated in eight double plays in the day's doubleheader. Three of them, all in the second game, were of the 1-4-3 variety, with pitcher Walt Masterson kicking it off all three times.

1942 The war effort required real sacrifice from the Sox. Tom Yawkey told players they would have to carry their own uniforms in their own suitcases, sparing the need to ship the gear in equipment trunks. There was a practical aspect to it as well; should baggage cars be requisitioned on short notice, at least Sox players would have their uniforms at hand in the specially-constructed suitcases.

1937 As the Associated Press put it, Red Sox right fielder Ben Chapman had a field day in right, with nine putouts—seven of them in succession.

1924 Philadelphia scored three times in the top of the ninth to tie the game, 3–3. Ike Boone had two spectacular seasons, both for the Red Sox, in 1924 and 1925. He won this game pinch-hitting for the pitcher in the bottom of the ninth, driving in Phil Todt with the winning run.

1915 The third home run of pitcher Babe Ruth's career was a three-run job over the right-field fence. The second-inning homer off New York's Ray Caldwell gave the Sox a good lead. When Caldwell walked the first two batters in the third, Yankees manager Bill Donovan put himself in the game as pitcher. Ruth earned a 9–5 complete game win.

1913 The 1912 World Champion Red Sox raised the banner in ceremonies before the game, but the visiting New York team was inadequately impressed. Joe Wood only yielded four hits, but he was erratic, granting five walks (he was also undercut by three Boston errors). He also hit three batters, a lot of the wildness bunched in the eighth (which included Wolter's steal of home) and ninth, giving New York a 5–2 win.

1906 A tight pitcher's battle between Waddell and Dinneen saw Lord of the Athletics triple to lead off the bottom of the ninth and score moments later on Murphy's single, for a 1–0 win.

1904 A highly-anticipated battle between Jack Chesbro of the New York Highlanders and Cy Young, ends with New York on top, 5–3. Former Boston star Patsy Dougherty, apparently reconciled to the June 19 trade which sent him to New York, banged out three hits off Young. After Dougherty had crossed the plate, scoring in the first inning, "from force of habit...he turned to go to the Boston bench" and almost reached it before realizing his error. He then crossed the field to the New York bench with a smile on his face.

TRANSACTIONS
1952: Selected Paul Lehner off waivers from the Cleveland Indians.
1956: Purchased Harry Dorish from the Baltimore Orioles.

DEBUTS

1908: Larry Gardner	2000: Israel Alcantara
1960: Billy Muffett	2002: Alan Embree
1969: Bill Lee	2004: Curtis Leskanic
1972: Lynn McGlothen	

BIRTHDATES
Camp Skinner 1897 (1923); Don Demeter 1935 (1966–1967); Dick Drago 1945 (1974–1980); Alejandro Pena 1959 (1995); Mike Stanley 1963 (1996–2000); Aaron Sele 1970 (1993–1997)

DEATHS
Buck Freeman 1949

June 26

2005 At age 33, Manny Ramirez hit the 19th grand slam of his career, tying him for second all-time with Eddie Murray. Lou Gehrig still holds first place with 23. See also July 5, 2005. By a score of 12–8, the Red Sox completed a six-game road sweep beating both the Indians and the Phillies in back-to-back three-game sets. It was the first road sweep of six or more games since 1977, when the Sox won nine in a row on a West Coast road trip.

2001 The Devil Rays were at Fenway. Red Sox reliever Rolando Arrojo came in with the bases loaded in the top of the fifth. The first man he faced was Greg Vaughn. Bang! Grand slam. Tampa Bay reliever Travis Phelps came in with the bases loaded in the bottom of the seventh. The first man he faced was Trot Nixon. Bang! Grand slam. Nixon's homer tied the score, but Tampa Bay got another run in the top of the eighth. The Sox promptly re-took the lead on Daubach's RBI triple and three straight walks, and won, 7–6.

1999 Pedro Martinez picked up an easy win, departing after five innings; he felt free to leave after Red Sox batters scored 11 runs in the first inning, in a game they ultimately took, 17–1, from the White Sox.

1997 Busy on the basepaths was Brian Hunter of the Tigers, who stole four bases, helping stick it to the Red Sox in a 10–6 win. Scott Hatteberg was the catcher; Eshelman and Wasdin the two pitchers.

1987 The Red Sox built up a 9–0 lead early, with The Rocket on the mound—but the Yankees didn't wait long to respond. They scored 11 runs of their own in the third, and ultimately won the game 12–11 in 10 innings. Despite all the scoring, and Boston's 15 hits, not one of them was a Wade Boggs hit. His 25-game hitting streak had ended.

1977 On June 17–19, the Sox sweep three from the Yankees at Fenway. From June 24–26, the tables were turned as New York took three straight from Boston. The first was an 11-inning, 6–5 win. This day's game saw the Sox overcome a 4–1 deficit with three runs in the top of the ninth, but lose it in the bottom of the ninth when Bill Campbell loaded the bases, only got one out, and lost it on a ball that Paul Blair bounced over Butch Hobson's head into left field.

1962 Earl Wilson's first major league shutout was a Fenway Park no-hitter over the Angels, 2–0. Wilson hit a solo home run in the third inning, too—the only run the Red Sox truly needed.

1951 Ted Williams makes the putout on an unusual 4-2-7 double play (and has four RBIs) and Vern Stephens hits two homers, as the Sox win 13–5 over Philly.

1943 Which do you think he preferred to be called—Tex Hughson or Cecil Huntington Hughson? He was called a Yankee-killer at this point in his career. He beat the Yankees 4–1, for his eighth consecutive win over New York; they hadn't won from him since May 1942.

1939 Rookie Jim Tabor was suspended indefinitely by manager Joe Cronin (it proved a three-day suspension) because he "broke training rules" on the Sunday night train out of Boston. Leads one to wonder what transpired.

1922 Commissioner Landis visited Boston for the first time since 1889, lecturing players of both the Yankees and Red Sox "against betting on horse races and staying out to all hours of the morning." He also had a private talk with Babe Ruth before the game; Babe hit a three-run homer in the ballgame that followed.

1920 The rubber match of the Harvard-Yale baseball rivalry was held at Fenway Park, before 11,000 spectators, and Harvard won for the first time in years, 6–3. Boston Braves owner Grant was not pleased that the Red Sox rented Fenway for the occasion, as the game drew patrons away from a Braves home doubleheader. Grant planned to stage a number of Saturday afternoon boxing matches at

Braves Field while his team was out of town. Sportswriter Gus Rooney noted that a good card could outdraw a ballgame.

1913 The Red Sox chose this day to raise the 1912 World Championship banner for the first time. It was a small crowd of around 6,500 fans and Stout and Johnson report in *Red Sox Century* that "Mayor Fitzgerald and most of the Rooters were conspicuously absent." Not only that, the Sox lost to the Yankees, 5–2, in a dispirited game in which Smoky Joe Wood was off form and the Sox committed three errors behind him. New York's Wolter even stole home in the eighth.

1912 Though Washington's Walter Johnson struck out 10 Red Sox and only allowed four hits, Smoky Joe Wood threw a three-hitter and shut out Washington, 3–0.

1902 Doc Adkins won his only major league game, beating the Washington Senators, 4–2. The "fat boy" allowed the Nationals just four hits. The 5'10½" righthander weighed 220 pounds.

1901 Jimmy Collins and the Boston Americans showed up at Columbia Park in Philadelphia ready to play the day's game against the Athletics. Umpire Alfred Manassau was there, ready as well. But the Athletics were not. They were in Washington, playing the Senators. Meanwhile, the Baltimore Orioles were wondering where the Boston team was. As they were waiting for Boston, the Chicago White Sox showed up, coming into town early for their game the following day. Apparently, scheduling in the first year of a brand new league was less than flawless. No forfeit was assessed.

TRANSACTIONS
1919: Traded Jack Barry and Amos Strunk to the Philadelphia
     Athletics for Braggo Roth and Joe Shannon.
1961: Released Rip Repulski.
1970: Purchased John Kennedy from the Milwaukee Brewers.
1989: Purchased Jeff Stone from the Texas Rangers.
2002: The Red Sox acquired Alan Embree and Andy Shibilo from the
     Padres for two minor leaguers, Brad Baker and Dan Giese.

DEBUTS
1994: Tim Van Egmond

BIRTHDATES
Jim Henry 1910 (1936–1937); Mike Myers 1969 (2004–2005); Greg Blosser 1971 (1993–1994)

DEATHS
None yet

June 27

2003 Johnny Damon tied a major league record with three hits all in the same inning— the first—when the Red Sox scored 14 runs in the bottom of the first inning off the same Florida Marlins team that went on to win the World Series. Damon already had two hits before any Sox player made an out; neither of the first two Marlins pitchers ever retired a batter. Ten runs scored before the first out. Damon was going for the cycle, with a single, double, and triple all in the first frame. Final score, 25–8.

1994 Righthander Greg Harris—who was ambidextrous, but never given the chance to pitch lefthanded for the Red Sox—was released, about a month before he would become a 10/5 player and just a few incentive points shy of guaranteeing his $1.75 million salary for 1995. Apparently GM Lou Gorman felt it would be a "mockery" of the game if he were to pitch both ways. The ability to turn around to alternately face left-handed hitters or right-handed hitters provides interesting speculation, but as Jim Prime asked, "What happens if a switch-pitcher faces a switch-hitter? The at-bat might never end as the two keep alternating from one side to the other."

1991 When Mo Vaughn joined the Sox, wearing #42 in tribute to Jackie Robinson, he took a bit of the burden off Ellis Burks. Until the Hit Dog's arrival, Burks had been the only black player on the 1991 Red Sox, though not the only player "of color"—Carlos Quintana took over for Vaughn later in the day's game.

1986 Roger Clemens wins his 14th game with a 5–3 win over the Orioles; he hasn't lost a game all year. His 14–0 start is the best in Red Sox history.

1963 Chicago's Al Luplow made a terrific catch in the eighth inning of a 6–3 game, robbing Dick Williams of a three-run homer and preventing Boston from tying the score. Luplow leapt over the five-foot-high bullpen wall, then tumbled out of sight, reappearing with the ball moments later. It was ruled a catch (and a sacrifice fly as one runner tagged up and scored on the play). Boston manager Johnny Pesky played the rest of the game under protest, arguing that Luplow had left the field and made the catch in the bullpen.

1955 In a tragedy still remembered with sadness by older Sox fans, budding first baseman Harry Agganis died. He'd been hospitalized with pneumonia and died of complications.

1953 A stretch of bad fortune. Allowing the White Sox to score thrice in the top of the ninth, Ellis Kinder was tagged with the loss; he'd now lost a game three days in succession—pitching just 4⅔ innings total.

1951 Red Sox pitcher Ray Scarborough singled in the bottom of the third, but was hit near the right ear by a pickoff throw, knocked out, and then taken from the field to Cambridge Hospital, where he was kept overnight as a precaution. He was OK, but the win went to Willard Nixon when both Dom DiMaggio and Billy Goodman tripled in the seventh, sparking a three-run rally on the way to a 6–5 win over the Athletics.

1935 Conspiracy theorists could have had a field day with this one. The body of New York attorney Howard Carter Dickinson, 52, was found dumped in the Rouge Park section of Detroit, bullet holes in the head and chest. The attorney (who happened to be the nephew of Chief Justice Charles Evans Hughes of the United States Supreme Court) was in Detroit on behalf of Elizabeth Carmichael Witherspoon. Ms. Witherspoon claimed to be the natural daughter of the late William H. Yawkey and was seeking a share of the estimated $40 million that Yawkey had left to his adopted son Thomas A. Yawkey. First reports indicated that police discounted robbery as a motive since his gold watch and other gold items were left untouched.

1928 Senators manager Bucky Harris protested the first game of a doubleheader, arguing that Doug Taitt had batted out of turn in the fourth inning. Close inspection of the lineup card showed that Phil Todt had been listed twice, and

Taitt not listed at all. Harris complained that this allowed Boston manager Carrigan to bat Todt in whichever slot he preferred. Carrigan countered that history showed he always hit Todt third and Taitt sixth as indeed he had done in this game. Since Boston won with runs to spare, there was no need to re-play the game, ruled AL president E. S. Barnard in disallowing the protest. Boston won the second game, too.

1924 The Yankees overpowered the Sox, 12–7 and 10–5. Boston pitchers couldn't stop them, not even Hoge Workman in his major league debut. Workman walked one and surrendered three hits in 1⅓ innings and then was lifted for a pinch-hitter. He threw 18 innings in 11 appearances in 1924, but by season's end was playing in the National Football League for the Cleveland Indians.

1916 In a 7–2 win, Red Sox third baseman Larry Gardner was thrown out three times trying to steal. Things happen in threes? Gardner was one of three American Leaguers erased three times in a game—and all three were nabbed by alert Philadelphia players. After 1916, the next time an American Leaguer was caught three times in a game was Rickey Henderson in 1982.

1911 Boston fielders were still taking their positions, and Ed Karger was taking a couple of warmup throws before pitching the seventh. Philadelphia's Stuffy McInnis stepped into the box and hit the ball. With no outfielders yet in position, McInnis had himself an inside-the-park home run. The Sox protested, but given a recent (and short-lived) American League rule designed to speed up games, warmup pitches were not allowed when the batter was in the batter's box, so the home run stood.

1904 Patsy Dougherty, now playing for New York, helped beat Jesse Tannehill, now pitching for Boston. His three hits helped lead to an 8–4 New York win, trimming Boston's first-place lead to just a half a game.

TRANSACTIONS
1968: Sold Gene Oliver to the Chicago Cubs, and purchased
    Juan Pizarro from the Pittsburgh Pirates.
1992: Purchased Steve Lyons from the Montreal Expos.
1994: Greg Harris was released.
1997: Released Pat Mahomes.

DEBUTS

1907: Jack Hoey	1936: Emerson Dickman	1954: Russ Kemmerer
1916: Wyckoff Weldon	1945: Dolph Camilli	1991: Mo Vaughn
1922: Chick Maynard	1951: Leo Kiely	1995: Juan Bell
1924: Hoge Workman	1952: Paul Lehner	2000: Morgan Burkhart

BIRTHDATES
Red Bluhm 1894 (1918); Eddie Kasko 1932 (1966, manager 1970–1973); Rico Petrocelli 1943 (1963–1976); Jackie Gutierrez 1960 (1983–1985); Juan Pena 1977 (1999)

DEATHS
Harry Agganis 1955; Marty Krug 1966

June 28

2005 We'd really rather not remember this game; Keith Foulke coughed up five ninth-inning runs, four on Travis Hafner's grand slam, and the Indians won, 12–8. The boxscore reflects an unusual line worth noting, though, that of Indians leadoff man Grady Sizemore:

AB	R	H	RBI	BB
3	4	0	0	3

He was 0-for-3, but scored four times. Every time he walked, he scored, as well as a fourth time when he reached on a fielder's choice.

2003 Gabe Kapler had an impressive debut for the Red Sox. Fresh in from the Colorado Rockies, Kapler went 4-for-5 with three RBIs. The next day, June 29, he was 3-for-4 with two homers off Brad Penny and a total of four more RBIs.

2000 Baltimore's B.J. Surhoff went 5-for-6 and helped beat Boston, 8–7. He scored the tying run, after doubling in the ninth, and scored the winning run after doubling in the 11th. Surhoff was riding a 21-game hitting streak.

1997 Maybe he would have a future as a first baseman. After Brian Hunter stole four times against Scott Hatteberg on June 26, a couple of days later, the Tigers tested his arm again, and Damion Easley swiped four bases. Jimy Williams put in Bill Haselman to catch on the 29th, but he broke his finger and back in again came Hatteberg. The Tigers stole two bases off Haselman, but none off Hatteberg.

1990 The lead story in the *Boston Globe*'s Living/Arts section featured the Spanish language broadcast team for the Boston Red Sox. Hector Martinez and Bobby Serrano had begun broadcasting since earlier in the 1990 season on the Carter Radio Network. Sox VP Jim Healey noted the growing importance of the Hispanic market.

1984 Dwight Evans doubled, tripled, made three outs, then singled in the 10th, and lastly completed the cycle in style with a three-run walkoff homer in the bottom of the 11th off Edwin Nunez, for a 9–6 win over the Mariners.

1978 "Limit Imposed on Beer-Swilling Fenway Park Bleacherites"—subhead, Thomas Boswell's column as printed in the *Los Angeles Times*. The recent tripling of beer consumption led to rowdyness, and pot smoking was noticeable as well. A nearby liquor store sold more miniatures than any other store in Boston, a Sox official said, with people taping them to the inside of their arms before they entered the park. One man was nabbed with eight "nips" taped under each arm. "And he was coming in free on a clergyman's pass," noted the official. Boswell also noted the absence of black fans and those who might wear Yankees caps. This was years before Friendly Fenway.

1976 He had appeared in two road games in 1975, but Butch Hobson marked his Fenway Park debut with a double off the center-field wall and an inside-the-park home run, helping the Sox win, 12–8, over Baltimore.

1974 Batting .299 at the time, Red Sox catcher Carlton Fisk was bowled over by Cleveland's Leron Lee and his knee injury cost him the remainder of the season.

1966 In the Red Sox fourth, Don Demeter reached base on a Tom Tresh error and then scored on Lee Thomas's double to left when the relay by Yankees shortstop Dick Schofield hit Demeter in the back as he crossed home plate. In all, five Yankees errors gave the Red Sox three unearned runs and helped Boston win, 5–3.

1963 Al Downing was pitching a no-hitter through six, and held a 2–0 lead, but Boston put three across in the seventh, then went ahead in the eighth and The Monster—Radatz—held the 4–3 lead. In the very first inning, all three outs were recorded on grounders to Dick Stuart at first base, with Boston pitcher Bob Heffner covering all three times. Three assists for Stuart—of all people—and three putouts for the pitcher.

1952 Because of his "zany antics," the Red Sox sent Jimmy Piersall from Boston to Birmingham, "at Manager Lou Boudreau's pleading request." (A.P.) The move was said to be for the good of the club. The *Washington Post* indicated that Piersall was "in danger of being mangled by players on his own team." Piersall's increasingly bizarre behavior was not yet understood to be caused by mental illness. He hit a homer in his first game with the Birmingham Barons.

1949 Joe DiMaggio made his 1949 debut count, singling and scoring his first time up, and then hitting a two-run homer in the third inning. The Yankee Clipper had missed almost a full half-season with a heel injury. He received "a warm reception" from the full house at Fenway when he worked out pre-game. New York won, 6–4, and DiMaggio hit four homers in his first three games back, as the Yankees swept the Sox.

1928 The Red Sox lost the first game to the Senators, 4–3, but won the second one, 8–7, despite losing the services of manager Bill Carrigan and third baseman Buddy Myer, both ejected for disputing umpire Ormsby's call of a sixth-inning double play. Some hometown fans got involved, too, sending a shower of pop bottles onto the field to protest Myer's expulsion. Police positioned themselves in the seats behind first base, and escorted Ormsby to safety after the game. Carrigan received a three-day suspension.

1919 Clearly not on a tight pitch count, Red Sox pitcher Carl Mays throws two complete games in one day, shutting out the Yankees, 2–0, but losing the latter, 4–1. After winning the first game, he asked to pitch again, attempting what newspapers described as an "iron man" feat. The Yankees, though, scored single runs off him in each of the first three innings. Though he went the distance, too, NY's Bob Shawkey kept the Bosox to just one run.

1918 In a 3–1 loss, Babe Ruth hit his 10th home run of the year, the only hit the Red Sox managed off Washington's Harry Harper. Ruth became the only player to hit 10 home runs and win 10 games as a pitcher in the same year.

1911 Steve White said from his Dorchester home that although he'd sat on the New York Giants' bench on the 27th, he'd signed a contract with the Red Sox, and not with any other team. By year's end, he was off the Red Sox roster. He pitched two-thirds of an inning for Washington in 1912, and six innings for the other Boston team several weeks later, then was out of major league ball.

1903 Boston shut out St. Louis three games in a row, with 1–0 (Cy Young) and 3–0 (Tom Hughes) scores in a doubleheader. In the four-game series, St. Louis only scored one run. Young escaped a threat in the bottom of the ninth; with runners on second and third and no one out, he struck out the next batter. Hobe Ferris fielded a grounder at second base and fired home to Lou Criger who held the ball for the force despite being spiked, and Young induced a fly ball to center.

1902 With "Iron Man" McGinnity suddenly stripping his gears and giving up three singles, a double, a triple, and a homer in the sixth, Baltimore was losing, 9–4, when manager John McGraw lost it. The Orioles had begun to get to Cy Young in the bottom of the eighth, and a botched run-down play ended up with three Orioles on base with nobody out. Or maybe not. Freddy Parent yelled for the ball and tagged Seymour, standing on the bag at second base, claiming he had "cut" third base, as he retreated to second from having rounded the bag. Umpire Connolly called Seymour out. McGraw protested too much, was ejected, but refused to leave. Connolly then took away the four runs the Orioles had scored, by declaring the game a forfeit by the prescribed score of 9–0.

TRANSACTIONS
1911: Pittsburg releases Walter "Judge" Nagle to the Red Sox.
1971: Released George Thomas.
2003: Purchased Gabe Kapler from the Colorado Rockies.

DEBUTS
1919: Braggo Roth
1934: Joe Mulligan
2001: Bill Pulsipher
2003: Gabe Kapler

BIRTHDATES
Bill Mundy 1889 (1913); Ken Williams 1890 (1928–1929); Joe Cascarella 1907 (1935–1936); Gary Wagner 1940 (1969–1970); Don Baylor 1949 (1986–1987); Joe Sambito 1952 (1986–1987); Ron Mahay 1971 (1995–1998)

DEATHS
Cy Morgan 1962

June 29

1979 In the top of the 13th inning, Jerry Remy singled home Rick Burleson to provide a 3–2 Red Sox win in New York.

1977 Swapping sweeps, the Yankees completed a three-game sweep of the Red Sox in front of 55,039 fans, avenging the three losses suffered the previous week at Fenway. New York took a 4–1 lead into the ninth, but the Sox scored three runs to tie it up. In the bottom of the ninth, the Yankees' Paul Blair bounced a bases-loaded ball over the head of Butch Hobson at third base to pin the loss on reliever Bill Campbell.

1976 Just 16 days after shutting out the Twins on one hit at Metropolitan Stadium (see June 14), Rick Wise reprises the feat with another one-hitter, this time at Fenway. Paul Blair singled in the sixth, and the two runs the Red Sox collected off Mike Cuellar in the bottom of the eighth won it, 2–0.

1975 Back-to-back doubles by Bernie Carbo and Rick Burleson break the 2–2 tie with New York in the eighth, and the Sox dethrone the Yankees from first place; they won't vacate the top slot for the rest of the season.

1969 Throwing everyone into the game they could, the Red Sox employ five pitchers in the ninth inning, but can't stem the tide, and the Senators—managed by Ted Williams—win it, 5–4. They win the second game, too, 11–4.

1966 On June 28, Mickey Mantle hit two homers his last two times up in the game at Fenway. On the 29th, he did it again, kicking off the day with a three-run homer in the first and hitting another in the third, driving in four runs total to help New York build up a 6–0 lead. The Red Sox crept very close, though, losing only when a hard shot by Yaz glanced off Yankees reliever Hal Reniff to shortstop Dick Schofield, who started a game-ending double play. Final: Yankees 6, Red Sox 5. Mantle's four homers in two days were the last ones he ever hit at Fenway Park and tied him with George Herman Ruth for the most homers hit by an opposing batter.

1958 Jackie Jensen's home run off Paul Foytack is his 14th of the month, most ever by a Red Sox batter in a given month.

1950 The Red Sox scored 245 runs in the month of June. The 22–14 win over Philadelphia was the third time in the month the Sox had scored 20 or more runs in a game. The football-like score was an American League record for total runs in a single game. Nine members of the Red Sox scored two or more runs. The two pitching staffs contributed 21 walks, but there was only one home run in the whole affair (by Ted Williams). Had it not been for a brief letdown mid-month (the Sox scored only one run in consecutive games on the 15th, 16th, and 17th), the 1950 Red Sox might have reached 250 runs.

1949 Dom DiMaggio initiates what will stretch to a 34-game hitting streak, superseding Johnny Pesky's club-high 26 games.

1946 Eight Red Sox are named to the AL All-Star squad: pitchers Boo Ferriss and Mickey Harris, catcher Hal Wagner, 1B Rudy York, 2B Bobby Doerr, SS Johnny Pesky, LF Ted Williams, and CF Dom DiMaggio. Only third base and right field are not manned by Red Sox. The game was held at Fenway Park. What more could a Red Sox fan want? Oh, yes, the final score: AL 12, NL 0.

1934 Charles W. Somers died at Put-in-Bay, Ohio. His obituary in *The Sporting News* stated that he "not only financed the Boston club, of which he was president in 1901 and 1902, but owned the Cleveland franchise, was a partner with Connie Mack at Philadelphia, and is said to have advanced some money to Charles A. Comiskey, to get the Old Roman started in Chicago." In 1902, Somers' teams finished in first, third, fourth, and fifth place.

1915 As he would do in a more meaningful game during the 1916 World Series, Sheriff Gainer pinch-hit in the 10th inning to help give Babe Ruth and the Red Sox a 4–3 win. Tris Speaker was 5-for-5 on the day.

1912 It's always a nice day when the Red Sox can take two games in one day from the New York Yankees. Boston won the first, 13–6. The second game was a seven-inning game shortened by darkness, but nonetheless a convincing 6–0 shutout by Smoky Joe Wood. Dutch Sterrett was the only Yankee to get a hit off Joe. Boston catcher Hick Cady, though, got two hits in one at-bat, sort of. He singled in Jake Stahl from third base, but the plate umpire ruled that the pitcher had balked. Stahl still scored, but Cady was deprived of a run batted in—and he had to take the at-bat over. This time, he doubled.

1911 Yankees owner Frank Farrell accused John I. Taylor of the Red Sox of "welching" on a deal to sell Eddie Cicotte to New York. He said, "I...have sent my protest to President [Ban] Johnson and to the National Commission. I will fight this case through." Cicotte never pitched for the New York Yankees.

1910 Boston's 2–0 lead disappeared when Philadelphia tied it after two outs in the bottom of the ninth, but with two outs in the 15th, Gardner's triple down the right field line drove in two. The Sox scored four in all, enough to withstand an Athletics rally that scored one and left the bases loaded.

TRANSACTIONS

1907: Selected Deacon McGuire off waivers from the New York Highlanders.
1966: Drafted Ken Brett, Dick Mills, Mike Nagy, and Ed Phillips.
1970: Sold Lee Stange to the White Sox.
1986: Acquired Tom Seaver from the White Sox for Steve Lyons.

DEBUTS

1907: Deacon McGuire
1912: Neal Ball
1926: Slim Harriss
1968: Juan Pizarro
2000: Sang-Hoon Lee

BIRTHDATES

Bobby Veach 1888 (1924–1925); Dizzy Trout 1915 (1952);
Duane Wilson 1934 (1958); Peter Hoy 1966 (1992)

DEATHS

Clarence Winters 1945

June 30

2000 Thinking they were plugging a gap at third base, the Sox swapped with San Diego to get Ed Sprague. Sprague only hit .216 in 111 at-bats and, later in the season, was traded back to whence he had come, the Padres. On the same day, Red Sox batboy Carlos Cowart was arrested driving in Dorchester. It turned out he had no license, and was wanted on a prior charge of driving without a license. The car belonged to Red Sox backup infielder Manny Alexander, and was found to contain syringes and steroids in the glove compartment. The case was later dismissed for lack of evidence, in good part because so many people seem to have had access to Alexander's car.

1998 F. P. Santangelo was a switch hitter who was equally inadept at jumping out of the box. Steve Avery hit him early on, and then later in the game, batting from the other side of the plate, he was hit by Rich Garces. The Sox beat Montreal, though, 7–4.

1975 David Duncan apparently had Luis Tiant figured out, tagging El Tiante for four consecutive doubles. Two other Orioles doubled off Tiant, too. Duncan drove in one, and scored three times, and Baltimore beat Luis, 8–2. It wasn't a good day for the Red Sox. They'd won the first game, 5–2, but lost pitcher Dick Pole when Tony Muser's liner knocked him down, breaking his cheekbone in the ninth inning. At least Pole had the win as consolation during his recuperation.

1960 Overcoming the five-run lead that Detroit had built up, the Red Sox went ahead in the bottom of the eighth and had runners on second and third, thanks to Willie Tasby's sacrifice bunt. The Tigers pulled in the infield and the next batter—Pete Runnels—grounded to the shortstop, Chico Fernandez, who fired home to catcher Red Wilson to get Don Buddin, running in to score from third. With "one chance in a million" to elude Wilson's tag, Buddin ducked down, "so low that Wilson ran right past him and didn't even come close to tagging him." (*Boston Globe*) Buddin scored the go-ahead run, and Wilson tried to salvage an out by firing to third or even to second, but no one was covering either base. Wilson was ejected from the game for arguing with the umpire that Buddin had run out of the baseline, and he'd assumed that was an automatic out. The Sox scored three more and won the game, 11–7.

1954 Yankees pitcher Tom Morgan hits three Red Sox batters in one inning. With two outs and nobody on in the third, Morgan hit Billy Goodman, saw an error committed on the next play, then hit Ted Lepcio and Milt Bolling after that. The plunking of Bolling brought in a run, and the Red Sox scored two more, eventually winning 5–1.

1950 Two DiMaggios hit homers in the same game, as both Joe and Dominic go deep in a 10–2 Red Sox win. The last time two brothers had homered in the same American League game, it was 1935. (See July 5, 1935.)

1949 In one series, Joe DiMaggio hits four home runs against the Red Sox, and the visiting Yankees sweep the Sox. Had one of the three games gone the other way, the Red Sox would have been in the World Series.

1945 The June 30 *Chicago Defender* reported on the U.S. Army championship baseball game played in London, England. Former Boston Red Sox player Paul Campbell, now an Army sergeant, hit a ninth-inning bases-loaded game-winning double off former Kansas City Monarchs (Negro League) pitcher Lt. Donald Smith (his name with the Monarchs was Ford Smith). The final score was 7–5. Smith nonetheless won the MVP award.

1937 The battery of Rick Ferrell and Wes Ferrell was now working for Washington, and Wes extracted a little revenge on the Red Sox for trading both brothers on June 10. The pitcher he faced was Buck Newsom, with whom he'd switched uniforms. Newsom had been with the Senators but was part of the trade for Ferrell. When Newsom doubled off him in the fifth, Ferrell walked to second to shake Newsom's hand. They'd agreed whichever one gave up a hit to the other would extend the courtesy. Later in the game, though, it was Wesley at the plate with the bases loaded and he singled to center, driving in the tying run and the winning run in a 6–4 Washington win.

1932 The Red Sox lost to the Yankees, 14–5, completing two horrendous months. Through May and June, they compile a 9–44 record in 53 games.

1927 Handing the Red Sox their 12th straight defeat (the Sox would lose 15 in a row before salvaging a win, and were on their way to another last-place finish), Lou Gehrig hit home run #25 in the first, joined three innings later when Babe Ruth hit his 25th. Gehrig one-upped the Babe in one category, though—he stole home in the game, a 13–6 loss for the Red Sox.

1925 The Yanks lost their fifth in a row, a seesaw affair with the Red Sox until the Sox added three runs in the top of the 12th. John Picus Quinn, Boston's "bearded patriarch," continued his stretch of seven scoreless innings in relief to get the win, 9–6.

1920 Pitcher Allan Russell, who the Yankees had traded to Boston in 1919, suffered a minor stroke at his home in Baltimore and was "practically helpless" and "couldn't move his right side." The attending physician ascribed the slight cerebral hemorrhage to being overtaxed at having to face Babe Ruth several times with runners on the bases in a June 27 game against New York. Russell recovered and pitched five more major league seasons.

1919 Babe Ruth played first base for the Red Sox in game one, and hit a sixth-inning grand slam, but a four-run rally in the eighth inning keyed by Del Pratt's two-run single to center gave the Yankees a 7–4 victory. Ruth played left field in the second game (and "Flash" Gilhooley moved from left to play right field), but was 0-for-2 at the plate. Pratt, though, keyed another come-from-behind eighth-inning rally, again singling and driving in two, for a 4–2 New York win. The losing pitcher in game one was Bill James, no relation to Boston's Senior Baseball Operations Advisor initially hired in 2002.

1918 Said to be the longest homer ever hit in Washington, Babe Ruth blasted a two-run homer off Walter Johnson in the top of the 10th, his first hit of the day, giving Boston a 3–1 lead, held as Carl Mays completed his start, striking out three batters in the bottom of the inning. It was Ruth's 11th homer; when not pitching, he was playing center field. With the win, Boston climbed back into first place.

1916 Boston catcher Sam Agnew was arrested for assault and taken to Police Headquarters in Washington DC, as a result of a row in the third inning. After Agnew posted $60 bail, he was released to appear in court the following day. The fight broke out after Boston pitcher Carl Mays hit Washington Nationals captain George McBride with a pitch. McBride retaliated, flinging his bat at Mays. Players from both teams rushed onto the field and in the jostling that followed, Agnew punched manager Clark Griffith hard on the nose. Agnew said Griffith had used "vile language" and, furthermore, swung at him first. There was a background to the skirmish; players throughout the league contended that Boston pitchers were aggressively employing the beanball as a tactic. Both Mays and McBride had had strong words the day before. The first pitch McBride faced was "uncomfortably close" to his head; the second one hit him.

The next day, league president Ban Johnson indefinitely suspended Agnew, McBride, and both managers—Griffith and Bill Carrigan. In a crowded courtroom, Boston owner Joseph Lannin requested that a warrant be issued for McBride's arrest and one was granted, but after the parties conferred, Griffith declined to prefer charges and the case was referred to the United States Attorney's office for further investigation. The Sox won the June 30 game, 6–1, a two-hitter for Mays.

1908 Though not yet declared a state holiday in Massachusetts, Cy Young had the best day any Boston pitcher has ever had against the New York team. Young, 41, faced the minimum number of batters, with an 8–0 no-hitter. The only man to reach base was Harry Niles, who walked to lead off the game and was then cut down stealing. Young got himself three hits in the process. It was Young's third no-hitter, and the third no-hitter caught by Boston catcher Lou Criger. Bill Carrigan caught three in his tenure with the Sox.

1903 For southpaw Nick Altrock, this was his first (and, as it developed, last) start of the year for Boston. He could argue that he only had one bad inning—the first—but it was bad enough to cost the game. Chicago won 10–3, on the strength of their eight-run first inning. Altrock pitched the full game, though, and went 2-for-3 at the plate. But any time you walk the first three batters, you're asking for trouble. Chicago must have perceived something about Altrock that attracted them; they purchased his contracts just two days later. He went 4–3, with a good 2.15 ERA for the White Sox. After 16 years of major league ball, he retired with a 2.67 ERA.

TRANSACTIONS

1917: Released both Olaf Henriksen and J. Weldon Wyckoff.
1935: Purchased Joe Cascarella from the Philadelphia Athletics.
1941: Purchased Nels Potter from the Philadelphia Athletics.
1952: Selected George Schmees off waivers from the St. Louis Browns.
2000: Received Ed Sprague from the Padres for Dennis Tankersley and Cesar Saba.

DEBUTS

1911: Walter Moser	1932: Larry Boerner
1918: Jack Stansbury	1951: Karl Olson
1919: Red Shannon	1961: Wilbur Wood
1928: John Shea	1982: Ed Jurak

BIRTHDATES

None yet

DEATHS

Hap Myers 1967

JULY

July 1

2004 Manny Ramirez homered in the top of the 13th inning, but the Yankees come back with two runs to win the game in the bottom of the inning. The game highlight film shows Derek Sanderson Jeter (he was named after the famous Boston hockey player) diving headfirst into the stands to snare a foul ball, emerging bloodied and bruised moments later—with the ball. This was a hard-fought 5–4 loss, so packed with managerial moves that Boston's David McCarty gave full meaning to the term "utility player" by literally changing positions (and gloves) five times in the 12th inning, and Kevin Millar played first base, third base, and left field during the same half-inning.

1992 After Jean Yawkey died, the music began to change at Fenway Park. The *Globe*'s Dan Shaughnessy explored the initial changes in his July 1 column, noting a few oldies infiltrating the set lists, such as "I'm A Believer" by The Monkees and other tracks such as "Louie Louie" and "Summer in the City." John Kiley had played the organ at the park for 40 years. Hearing that rock music was coming in, Kiley said, "I never thought they'd go for it. I guess if the public wants it, you have to give it to 'em." Larry Cancro, Sox marketing VP, said the idea came from ownership. "Whoa. Ownership?" Shaughnessy wrote. "Don't tell us Haywood Sullivan came into a room, snapping his fingers and saying, 'How 'bout we play some Fine Young Cannibals between innings from now on?" "I think they did it because of me," said Steve Lyons, who had just begun his third stint with the Sox. "We've got to get out of the '40s," added Wade Boggs.

1988 Rich Gedman saw his eighth-inning longball hit the foul pole but get called a foul ball instead of a game-winning homer; moments later, Gedman hit into a double play. Boston lost, 9–8.

1979 Boston's Dennis Eckersley didn't have it this day, serving up five gopher balls to the Yankees at the Stadium, accounting for all the New York scoring in a 6–5 loss. The biggest loss of the game, though, was Jerry Remy. He tripled to lead off the game, but was cut down at home plate, trying to score on a ball Rick Burleson hit which turned into a double play. Remy hurt his knee badly, and never fully recovered. Here it was July 1, and he was hitting .304; he only played in seven more games in 1979. Worse, his base-running ability was compromised. In his first four seasons, he'd stolen 34, 35, 41, and 30 bases, but over the next six seasons he totaled just 68 more steals.

1973 In the sixth inning of a 9–5 loss to the Brewers, Luis Aparicio stole the 500th base of his long career.

1955 Ted Williams is out with back trouble first reported on June 24 after a stretch of home run hitting, and Vern Stephens goes 3-for-6 in left, but it's first baseman Norm Zauchin who wins the game with a 13th inning HR. Williams missed nine days in all, but returned on July 3.

1953 Mel Parnell shuts out the Yankees, 4–0, to win his 100th major league game, joining Cy Young, Smoky Joe Wood, Lefty Grove, and one other Red Sox pitcher who had accomplished this feat by 1953. Name the other pitcher. Joe Dobson.

Pitcher Marv Grissom was sold on waivers to the Giants, the team with which he'd first broken in.

1951 Bobby Doerr got the 2,000th hit of his career, and Johnny Pesky hit one of his infrequent home runs, off the glove of Cliff Mapes. Mel Parnell was not on his regular game, though, and the Yankees pleased the Stadium crowd, 5–2, propelling themselves into first place.

1950 The Sox beat New York 10–2 the day before, and thrashed them again, 13–4, on July 1. It was the major league debut of Charles Ford (called Eddye Ford in the *New York Times* game account)—later known as Whitey Ford—and an inauspicious one at that. Starter Tommy Byrne never got out of the second inning; Walt Dropo hit a grand slam off Byrne in the first inning and drove in two more in the second. Ford was banged around for five more runs, all earned.

1949 Beginning on July 1 and ending on September 27, Ted Williams reached base safely in every game he played, for a Consecutive Games on Base Safely (CGOBS) streak of 84 straight games. That's the major league record. In fact, in all of 1949, Ted only failed to reach base five times: June 3, 7, 26, 30, and September 28. For more than 10 years, Williams never had back-to-back games where he did not get on base safely, from July 14, 1940, through September 26, 1950.

1941 The 52,832 fans at Yankee Stadium hoped to see Joe DiMaggio tie Wee Willie Keeler's 44-game hitting streak, longest in major league history. His first two times up in the day's first game, he made outs—and the hit he was awarded his third time up may have been a generous gift from the official scorer. There was no cloud over Joe D.'s second hit of the game, though, and he had his 43rd straight game, a 7–2 win over the Red Sox (though brother Dom DiMaggio homered for Boston). The Yanks had no homers; they'd gone deep 25 games in a row. The homer streak was snapped. The second game was called after five innings, but fortunately The Yankee Clipper struck early with a "screaming single to center" his first time up. The Yankees won, 9–2, and Joe D had hit in 44 consecutive games.

1930 Milt Gaston, one of the handful of ballplayers who lived to be 100, pitched a three-hitter and had three hits himself off Cleveland's Mel Harder, all singles. Red Sox 3, Indians 1.

1926 Red Sox fans used to root for Boston pitchers to strike out Babe Ruth, but with so little for Bosox fans to cheer for by the mid-1920s, they nearly always rooted for Ruth to hit one out, according to Burt Whitman in the July 1 issue of *The Sporting News*. Only two of his 47 homers in 1926 were hit at Fenway Park.

1920 "Tell Walter he's got to pitch to me," Harry Hooper told Washington catcher Val Picinich, according to the *Washington Post*. It was the bottom of the ninth and Walter Johnson was pitching a no-hitter at Fenway Park. The score was 1–0. "This game is so close I'm going to bust it out of the park if I can," Hooper said. He hit it hard, a "vicious drive," but one that was speared by Joe Judge at first base, who threw to Johnson for the final out. Hooper had been the only Red Sox batter to reach base; Bucky Harris had fumbled his "easy grounder" in the seventh inning and cost Johnson a perfect game. Harris did provide the winning run, though. Unfortunately, after throwing this no-hitter, Johnson came up with a sore arm and performed poorly the rest of the year.

Boston Sox fans will be amused by a *Washington Post* column by veteran sportswriter Shirley Povich dated April 27, 1937. Povich writes that Sox fans have begun to boo Red Sox players, instead of (as heretofore) being uniformly loyal and forgiving. The newspapers, however, remained pure, not yet infected with this critical attitude. "Boston baseball writers are still the most loyal home-town scriveners in the league and the Red Sox, in their reports, can do no wrong." He reaches back and cites this July 1 game, where Boston writeups focused on Sox pitcher Harry Harper's brilliant game, only noting later in the story that the awful tough luck he suffered in losing was due—one learned by reading even further—to Johnson pitching a no-hitter.

1918 Ed Barrow and Babe Ruth had words, and Ruth threatened to punch Barrow in the nose. Barrow told Ruth he was going to fine him. And Ruth did two things he left the team and returned to his father's place in Baltimore, and he wrote a letter soliciting a job pitching for the Chester, PA shipyard ballteam. They offered to hire him to pitch the July 4 game. (See July 4, 1918.)

1916 Pitching a perfect start to the game, Babe Ruth retired the first 10 Washington Nationals—and drove in the first run for Boston with a third-inning sacrifice fly. Then he couldn't get anyone out, and after five Washingtonians in a row reached safely, Ruth was relieved. He took the 4–2 loss. Walter Johnson threw a two-hitter, and earned the win.

1903 Cy Young had the only RBI in the game, a 1–0 win in 10 innings against Chicago. Losing pitcher Patsy Flaherty also pitched a full nine innings of scoreless baseball. Each pitcher only struck out one batter, and Flaherty issued the only walk of the entire game. In the Boston 10th, with one out, Hobe Ferris singled, Lou Criger sacrificed him to second, and Cy Young won himself a ballgame with a double slashed hard down the third base line, nearly hopping the bag. Cy Young set a league record with this win—it was his third consecutive 1–0 shutout and (with his 7–0 win back on June 13) it was his fourth consecutive shutout overall.

1901 For failing to hold the lead, Ted Lewis was tagged with the loss. Boston was leading Baltimore, 5–2, when Boston starter Cuppy walked a man and gave up three hits. Jimmy Collins called on Ted Lewis to relieve Cuppy. The two inherited runners scored on a sacrifice bunt and a single. Baltimore won, 7–5, and it was Lewis who was deemed the loser.

TRANSACTIONS
1953: Marv Grissom was selected off waivers by the New York Giants.
1994: Acquired Steve Farr and Chris Nabholz in trade from
      the Cleveland Indians for Jeff Russell.
2003: Signed free agent Todd Jones.

DEBUTS

1941: Nels Potter	1986: Tom Seaver	1999: Wilton Veras
1952: Al Benton	1989: Eric Hetzel	2000: Paxton Crawford,
1971: Buddy Hunter	1998: Dario Veras	Ed Sprague

BIRTHDATES
Frank Barrett 1913 (1944–1945); Paul Lehner 1920 (1952); Ken Wood 1924 (1952); Hersh Freeman 1928 (1952–1955); Frank Baumann 1933 (1955–1959); Billy Rohr 1945 (1967)

DEATHS
Earl Moseley 1963; Walt Kinney 1971; Ray Scarborough 1982; Ed Connolly 1998

July 2

2002 During the latter innings of a day-night doubleheader at Fenway Park, the concessionaire Aramark ran out of bottled water. Julie Jordan, Aramark GM, said they'd had approximately 17,600 bottles before the day began. In an amazing display of self-reliance, hundreds of fans actually drank free water out of Fenway's water fountains!

2001 Hideo Nomo pitched well, giving up just one run in six innings, and benefited from terrific run support. The Sox scored five runs in the top of the first and six runs in the third. Manny Ramirez's three-run blast in the first was measured at 491 feet, the longest drive in Skydome (now Rogers Centre) history. Staked to an 11–0 lead after three, the Sox staff sewed it up for a 16–4 final.

1998 Pedro Martinez was a little stingy with his former Montreal Expos teammates, letting them get just two hits in six innings. Wasdin and Reyes in relief allowed just one more. Meanwhile, the Boston batsmen got to work, starting in on Carl Pavano and his compadres with 20 hits (just one homer by Nomar), and put together a nice, neat, tidy 15–0 triumph.

1986 Starting a season 14–0 saw Roger Clemens one game shy of the AL record, and the Blue Jays flew in the face of The Rocket's attempt at #15. The Jays came from behind with three runs in the eighth, and beat Boston, 4–2. Roger's record stood at 14–1.

1975 Rick Wise would have become only the second pitcher in major league history to throw a no-hitter in both leagues. (Only Jim Bunning had done it.) He had two outs in the bottom of the ninth inning in Milwaukee, and a 6–0 lead, facing the last batter he needed to retire—Bill Sharp. Wise walked Sharp on four straight pitches. Next up was George Scott. Home run. Up next, Bobby Darwin. Home run. That was the end of it, though, and the final score was 6–3. "I didn't have the steam anymore," Wise said. "Hell, it was hot out there." There was a second game and Scott was injured early, carried off the field in a stretcher. Jim Rice hit two homers for Boston in game one; Fred Lynn had a 38-game streak reaching base safely until the second game, in which he was retired every time.

1972 Red Sox center fielder Reggie Smith homered once in the sixth and once in the seventh, batting once left-handed and once right-handed. He helped maul Milwaukee, 15–4.

1958 The Sox will head to Scottsdale. After playing spring training in Sarasota since 1932 (save for the three wartime years), the team announced that beginning in 1959 they will train in Arizona, in the Cactus League.

In today's game, both Ted Williams and Jackie Jensen hit home runs; over five games, they've combined for nine homers and 20 RBIss.

1946 Yankees hurler Spud Chandler has a no-hitter going against Boston for 8⅓ innings until Bobby Doerr breaks it up with a single. Chandler had, incredibly, walked nine Sox batters in the first four innings, but got the win, 2–1.

1944 Lou Finney came in to play first base after Joe Cronin was tossed out of the game in the seventh inning. In the bottom of the ninth, Finney's first time up, he doubled in one run, and then was singled home with the tying run. Next time up, in the bottom of the 11th, there were two outs and Bobby Doerr on second. Finney singled in Doerr with the game-winner.

1941 Coming into the game with hits in 44 consecutive games, Joe DiMaggio was hoping to establish sole possession of the hitting-streak record by hitting in his 45th straight game. For some reason, less than 6,000 fans came to the well-publicized game at Yankee Stadium. Dick Newsome was pitching for Boston. First time up, right fielder Stan Spence speared DiMag's drive. In the third inning, third baseman Jim Tabor backed up on a ball hit hard behind third base, then gunned Joe out with a throw across the diamond. In the fifth inning, though, in the midst of a six-run rally that won the game for New York, DiMaggio hit one into the left-field seats for a home run and a new major league record.

1936 For the first time in recent baseball history, every regular on a baseball team (the 1936 Red Sox, including its manager and coaches) was comprised of players obtained from other major league ball clubs.

1934 Red Kellett made his major league debut, striking out as a ninth-inning pinch-hitter for Rube Walberg. The Penn graduate ('34) set a record in the Eastern Intercollegiate League with a .488 average, and stuck with the Red Sox all season, but only mustered nine at-bats, striking out five times and never getting a hit in his major league career.

1930 The Sox were losing 4–1 in the eighth, but scored three times to tie it. Starter Danny MacFayden had been taken out in the eighth for a pinch-hitter, and Big Ed Morris came on in relief, not only retiring the Indians but hammering a double off the left-field Wall to drive in the winning run, for a 5–4 victory.

1918 Babe Ruth struck out twice in key situations, and manager Ed Barrow fined him $500 and benched him, setting off an argument that resulted in Ruth leaving the ballpark. Word got out that Ruth was going to play on the Chester (PA) Shipbuilding Company team in the Delaware River Shipbuilding League. A day later, he sent owner Harry Frazee a telegram stating that he would return to the Red Sox. Ruth returned in time for the second game on July 4, and went 1-for-4 with two strikeouts.

1917 It was "Harry Hooper Day" at Fenway, and the Sox and Yankees squared off, ultimately playing to a 4–4 tie in a game called after 11 innings due to darkness. Mayor James Michael Curley presented Hooper with a diamond ring on behalf of Boston's fans.

1912 Larry Gardner hit an inside-the-park home run off New York's Russ Ford in the second inning, and he hit another inside-the-parker off Russ Ford in the eighth, but the Yankees scored three times in the top of the ninth and withstood the two that Boston came back with in the bottom of the ninth for a 9–7 win. It was New York's first win against the Red Sox since the previous year. Gardner only hit three home runs all year long, two of them in this one game.

1904 Washington swapped 10-year veteran Albert C. "Kip" Selbach to Boston for utility infielder O'Neill. Selbach was a good pickup to replace outfielder Patsy Dougherty. In his first game, he helped Boston win, both defensively and by scoring the winning run. The *Boston Herald* admitted it had perhaps protested too much and that Selbach was "in a class by himself in fielding."

TRANSACTIONS
1915: Purchased Jack Barry from the Philadelphia Athletics.
1933: Acquired Mel Almada and Freddie Muller from the Seattle Indians.
2004: Acquired Jimmy Anderson from the Chicago Cubs for Andrew Shipman.

DEBUTS
1902: Dave Williams
1934: Red Kellett

BIRTHDATES
Grover Hartley 1888 (1927); Hal Wagner 1915 (1944–1947); Chuck Stobbs 1929 (1947–1951); Tony Armas 1953 (1983–1986); Jose Canseco 1964 (1995–1996)

DEATHS
Tommy Dowd 1933; Frank Owens 1958; Rankin Johnson 1972

July 3

2001 Tomo Ohka couldn't hold back the Indians, and Boston lost, 9–1. Robby Alomar had a 5-for-5 day, and Jim Thome had three RBIs. Jake Westbrook held the Sox to five hits and the Cleveland bullpen didn't let up even one.

In Triple A action, batter Izzy Alcantara of the Pawtucket Red Sox charged the mound and administered a karate kick to pitcher Jeremy Salazar.

1997 It had been almost 90 years since the Sox were known as the "Speed Boys" but the Sox stole five bases in the day's game against the Toronto Blue Jays.

1978 The Red Sox increased their lead over the Yankees to eight full games with a 9–5 win at Fenway Park. Yaz had three hits, reaching and surpassing 2,800 hits in his long career.

1970 Ray Culp held the Indians to one run on five hits, and Carl Yastrzemski hit a tie-breaking homer in the bottom of the eighth for a 2–1 Boston win in the first of two. The Sox lucked out and won the second game, too, 5–4, when Dick Schofield reached on a little infield hit. Jerry Moses broke for home and was only safe when Graig Nettles' throw to the plate hit him on the hand.

1959 The Red Sox fired field manager Pinky Higgins, and appointed coach Rudy York as, in effect, manager for a day. The Sox lost to the Orioles, 6–1, with a three-run homer by former Red Soxer Walt Dropo doing the most damage in Baltimore's five-run first inning. Billy Jurges would take over the reins the following day.

1943 Leon Culberson hit for the cycle—and picked up another RBI by walking with the bases loaded in the sixth inning—as Boston beat Cleveland, 12–4. They hadn't needed the seven runs they scored in the top of the ninth, but they didn't hurt, either.

1940 Giving Philadelphia a head start of 8–0, the Red Sox scored three in the fifth and three in the eighth. They were down 11–6 heading into the ninth inning but scored five times to tie it, and then Jimmie Foxx won it with a solo home run of the walkoff kind. Williams and Tabor had homers and three RBIs each, and Cronin had one HR and two RBIs.

1938 About 75 picketers set up outside Yankee Stadium before the game against the Red Sox, and six were arrested—four were affiliated with the Building Service Employees Union and two were members of the Theatrical Treasurers, Managers and Press Agents Union and the Ushers and Ticket Takers Union. All were charged with disorderly conduct and held in $500 bail each. Most fans were unaware of the arrests; the Yankees won the game, 9–3.

1935 Al Schacht's black eye was not the stuff of comedy; he earned it fair and square, as the Red Sox coach got into a five-minute fistfight after the game with Washington pitcher Ed Linke. The two had exchanged bitter words on at least a couple of previous occasions dating back to the previous season. Schacht had been riding Linke during the July 3 game, and Linke sent word he'd meet Schacht under the stands after the game. Schacht sent word back he'd see him there. When the game was over, both teams rushed to watch. "It was more of a wrestling match than a fight, and Linke's superior bulk gave him the advantage," wrote the *Washington Post*. The battle was broken up when Washington's secretary arrived on the scene. Boston had won the game, though, 14–7. Schacht was presumably riding Linke about his performance in the July 2 game, when the Red Sox hit three homers and scored five times in the seventh to beat Washington, 6–5.

1932 The Yankees prevailed, 13–2, in the first Sunday game ever played at Fenway. Earle Combs hit two doubles in the same inning—as did teammate Lyn Lary.

1929 Red Ruffing was pitching well for the Red Sox, and had a 5–0 lead over the Yankees—in part thanks to a two-run homer of his own. But in the seventh, he let in a run and loaded the bases, then Babe Ruth hit a grand slam into the right-field bleachers to tie the score. Fred Heimach hit another homer the next inning to give the Yankees a 6–5 win.

1919 Their July 1 loss to Philadelphia dropped the Red Sox to 24–32 on the season and inspired a Hugh Fullerton article penned the following day, which appeared on July 3 under the *Atlanta Constitution* headline BOSTON'S BOYS HAVE GIVEN UP HOPE FOR YEAR'S CHAMPIONSHIP. He reported dissension on the ball club, with the 1918 World Champions wanting Jack Barry back as manager. Fullerton ranked the trade sending Barry back to Philadelphia a "corker for both teams" and went on to admit that he hadn't thought Ed Barrow would make a good manager, but that Barrow was indeed "showing a lot of stuff." (See July 19, 1919 for more.)

1914 Boston pitchers Rankin Johnson and Guy Cooper were over-matched by Washington's Walter Johnson, 12–0. It was the worst defeat of the year for the Red Sox, a year when—remarkably—the team ERA was 2.36 and three pitchers (Foster, Leonard, and Shore) each had ERAs of 2.00 or lower.

1913 The Red Sox got 15 hits in 15 innings off Walter Johnson, but Ray Collins took a 1–0 loss when two doubles scored one run for Washington. The Sox had the bases loaded with nobody out in the bottom of the ninth, but Johnson escaped unscathed. Fifteen hits by a team being shut out is a major league record.

DEBUTS

1915: Jack Barry	1967: Ken Poulsen
1918: Walter Barbare,	1974: Tim Blackwell
Red Bluhm	1994: Chris Nabholz
1958: Duane Wilson	2002: Wayne Gomes

July 4

2003 Switch-hitting third baseman Bill Mueller hit homers from both sides of the plate, off Yankees D. Wells and D. Miceli. Jason Varitek hit two homers in the game as well, but both were from the same side of the plate.

1998 At least his on-base percentage benefited. The Sox were shut out, 3–0, and Nomar Garciaparra's 24-game hit streak was ended, but Nomar drew two bases on balls. The game was Jin Ho Cho's debut, who pitched well, but without any run support this first effort by a Korean pitcher for the Red Sox was in vain.

1984 Jim Rice was riding a 4-for-5 day with two RBIs, but Oakland tied the game (9–9) with two runs in the bottom of the ninth. Rice had more work to do. In the bottom of the 10th, Oakland reliever Gorman Heimueller gave up a single, suffered seeing his second baseman commit an error, bore a sacrifice bunt, and was told to walk Dwight Evans intentionally. That brought up Rice with one out and the bases loaded. The last pitch Heimueller ever threw in the major leagues was hit for a grand slam. Sox win, 13–9.

1983 Dave Righetti pitched a 4–0 no-hitter against the Red Sox in Yankee Stadium. Rice walked in the first, Nichols walked in the fifth. Two men left on base. An excellent performance, and the first Yankees no-hitter since Don Larsen's 1956 perfect game.

1977 The Sox served notice that they were coming back, hitting eight home runs in one game—four of them in the eighth inning. Fred Lynn hit two and George Scott hit two; Carbo, Hobson, Rice, and Yaz all hit one. The eight homers set a major league record, but with eight homers the Sox only scored nine runs. That was enough to beat Toronto, in Boston, 9–6.

1970 All the Sox and Sonny Siebert needed were the hometown home runs by brothers Tony Conigliaro and Billy Conigliaro in this 5–1 win over the Indians. The two brothers also homered in the same game on September 19.

1964 Ending a four-game losing streak by taking decisive action, 13 Red Sox batters came to the plate and nine scored in the bottom of the first. The Angels were doomed from the first, and went down to a 13–5 defeat. Lee Thomas's grand slam accounted for the first four runs.

1963 In Cleveland, CF Gary Geiger had 15 putouts on the day, as the first game against the Indians went 14 innings; Geiger only played eight innings in the second game since the Indians won that one, too.

1962 Lu Clinton had seven consecutive hits all on the same day, in the twin bill against the Twins: 3-for-4 in the first game with a double and a homer, and 4-for-4 in the second with another double and another homer. He scored five times and had four RBIs on the day to boot.

1958 Two pitchers had mini-streaks going. For Frank Sullivan, the first game 5–1 win was the seventh game in a row he'd won from Baltimore; he hadn't lost to them since 1956. In the second game, Arnie Portocarrero won his fourth game in a row from the Red Sox, 5–3.

1955 Sox pitcher Willard Nixon drove in two to help the Sox win the Yankee Stadium opener, 4–2. The Yankees sent four pinch-hitters to the plate and Boston pitchers struck out all four. Cerv, Robinson, Byrne, and Howard all whiffed in the fifth, seventh, ninth, and ninth, respectively. Prime Minister Nu of Burma arrived between games and was able to stay for the first three innings of the second game. He saw the Yankees tie it up, overcoming a 5–1 deficit. Had he stayed to the end, he would have seen Jackie Jensen's ninth-inning grand slam which sealed the 10–5 win and the day's Sox sweep.

1951 Clyde Vollmer homered off Morrie Martin of the Athletics in the top of the ninth, capping a 9–0 shutout for Mickey McDermott. It was the first of 13 home runs that Vollmer hit in the month of July, an astonishing burst of power from someone with 797 at-bats and just 23 home runs in the years before 1951. After July was over, he hit four more homers the rest of the year, and just 24 in the 775 at-bats in the years that followed.

1948 Ted Williams batted three times in a 14-run inning, but got a hit. The game was tied going into the bottom of the seventh, 5–5, when the Red Sox decided to resolve the matter. Ted led off and walked. By the time he came up the second time, rookie reliever Charlie Harris still hadn't recorded an out. Ted walked again. Manager Mack finally took out Harris—after the Sox had scored 12 runs. Even the pitcher, Ellis Kinder, had two hits in the inning. When Williams came up the third time, he grounded out to the shortstop for the third and final out.

1939 Philadelphia scored 19 runs, but still lost two games. The reason? The Red Sox scored 34 runs on 65 hits, and Jim Tabor hit four homers as Boston beat Philadelphia twice, 17–7 and 18–12. Tabor hit two grand slams in the second game (one of them an inside-the-park slam) and when he turned off the light that night, he'd added 19 total bases and 11 RBIs to his personal stats.

1937 After hosting the Athletics over the Fourth of July (and sweeping four games), the Red Sox were off to New York for a pair against the Yankees and the Athletics were heading back to Philadelphia to host the Senators. Red Sox infielders Boob McNair and Ski Melillo inadvertently boarded the wrong train out of Boston's South Station and found themselves surrounded by the opposition. They hopped off at Providence, and waited for the train carrying their teammates to arrive.

1933 The Sox took two from Philadelphia at Shibe Park, the 14–4 win in the first game helped along a bit by eight Athletics errors (four by the shortstop), but knocked out 14 hits as well. They won the second game with 15 hits, 9–1.

1914 An error decided each game of a doubleheader in Washington. Boston won the first game, 1–0, on a fourth-inning error by Ray Morgan. With runners on first and third and two outs, Larry Gardner hit the ball to second baseman Morgan who booted the ball as Tris Speaker scored. In the second game, the error was a Sox one, committed by Everett Scott at shortstop. He misplayed a ground ball and Chick Gandil scored the tie-breaking, go-ahead run in the bottom of the sixth for a 3–2 Washington win.

1913 Joe Wood wasn't throwing smoke, but he doubled twice in the bottom of the fourth inning, when the Sox scored seven times. Steve Yerkes hit three doubles in the game. The Sox won, 13–6, in a game shortened to eight innings. In a separate afternoon game, which lasted nine innings, Boston lost a 3–1 lead as Philadelphia scored four times in the last two frames. OK, so he wasn't perfect as a fielder; Harry Hooper dropped a line drive and the error resulted in three of those four runs. Hooper hit a homer earlier in the day.

1912 Eddie Plank of the A's beat Smoky Joe Wood, 4–3, but Wood beat the Browns, 5–1, four days later. That July 8th win was the first of 16 consecutive victories for the fireballing Red Sox pitcher.

Elsewhere in Greater Boston, there was an aviation meet and Johnny Murphy of the Red Sox caught a few baseballs dropped from an airplane by aviator Glenn L. Martin. It's unclear what position Murphy held with the team, as he does not appear on the roster of players who have served the Sox.

1911 Starter Eddie Cicotte was overcome by heat after eight, and Joe Wood took his place. Washington tied it in the ninth, but then Hooper, Gardner, and Speaker all singled for the Red Sox. Duffy Lewis flied out to left field, but Jack Lelivelt fired a perfect strike to the plate and would have had Hooper—but catcher John Henry dropped the ball, and Boston won, 4–3.

1905 It was a morning–afternoon doubleheader, and Philadelphia took the first one, 5–2, on three tie-breaking runs in the bottom of the eighth. The second game went on and on. Boston got two runs off starter Rube Waddell in the first inning (Waddell had pitched briefly in the first game), and the Athletics got two runs off Cy Young in the top of the sixth. It was tied from that time on, and the two pitchers just kept on pitching. In the 20th inning, an error (one of five by Boston), a hit by pitch which knocked out Jack Knight, and two singles enabled the A's to get two runs. Waddell threw his 19th straight scoreless inning and earned the 4–2 win. After 20 innings, Young hadn't walked even one batter, but still lost the game. The 29 innings of baseball in a doubleheader still stands as the Red Sox record.

1903 Boston celebrated the "Glorious Fourth"—Independence Day—by winning both games of their A.M.–P.M. doubleheader with St. Louis, 4–1 (Hughes) and 2–0 (Dinneen). It was a loud crowd and "about every play of more than usual excellence was accompanied by a salvo of reports of cannon crackers and the discharge of firearms." The presence of firearms at the game was no isolated matter of a few cranks; the *Boston Post* reported "hundreds of firearms" being discharged and both the *Post* and *Globe* had editorial cartoons depicting numerous men firing pistols into the air. Perhaps worried about firearms in the hands of rabid baseball fans, umpire Connolly never showed up for the morning game, and umpire Hassett showed up late, so Boston pitcher Cy Young served as the sole umpire for the first inning, yielding to Hassett when he arrived. Connolly made it in time to begin umpiring during the second inning of the second game.

Boston fans are first reported as indulging in what has since become the time-honored practice of scoreboard watching. "A fine large score board is in operation at each game and the scores of the games away are bulletined as they are received," reported the *Herald*.

TRANSACTIONS
1904: Traded Bill O'Neill to the Washington Senators for Kip Selbach.
1960: Released Bobby Thomson.

DEBUTS
1904: Kip Selbach   2000: Bernard Gilkey
1935: Joe Cascarella   2003: Todd Jones
1967: Sparky Lyle   2004: Jimmy Anderson
1994: Jin Ho Cho

BIRTHDATES
None yet

DEATHS
None yet

July 5

2005 Just eight games after hitting his 19th grand slam, Manny Ramirez hit #20, placing him second all-time to Gehrig at 23. It was Manny's third granny of 2005, the first on April 16 and the second on June 26.

2002 Number 9 passed away at age 83. Red Sox great Ted Williams succumbed in Florida after a long stretch of declining health. Both the *Herald* and *Globe* ran special editions, which were snapped up by the thousands. ADIEU, KID read the large headline in the *Globe*'s July 6 edition. The less said about the tawdry aftermath, the better.

1998 Talk about a slugfest. Battering each other back and forth, the White Sox scored 14 runs on 12 hits, but the Red Sox scored 15 runs on 20 hits and prevailed. Chicago had six extra-base hits and Boston had nine. Chicago employed six pitchers to try and stop the Red Sox, and the Red Sox used seven pitchers.

1991 Kevin Morton threw a five-hitter in his major league debut, benefiting from seven runs driven in by Jack Clark in a 10–1 drubbing of Detroit. Morton and Mo Vaughn had known each other since Little League days in Norwalk, Connecticut, both played on the same American Legion team, both had played for Seton Hall, and both had been drafted by the Red Sox on the same day in the same round. Both debuted within two weeks of each other. Vaughn contributed a two-run double in the Red Sox rout.

1971 The Yankees scored five times in the top of the first, depressing Boston's loyal rooters, but the Sox replied with three in the first (on Reggie Smith's three-run homer) and two in the second (on a Yaz single). Each team scored one more run, and then the Yankees took a 7–6 lead in the top of the sixth. Putting an end to this seesaw affair, the Red Sox scored six times in the sixth—Rico hit a triple with the bases full and both Boomer and Lahoud homered. Both teams had exactly 16 hits at game's end, but the Red Sox had more runs, 12–7.

1970 John Kennedy, just acquired from Milwaukee, entered his first major league game as a pinch-hitter in the fifth inning of a game the Sox were trailing, 3–2. He hit a drive to right field off Rich Austin that got by Roy Foster and rolled to the wall. Kennedy circled the bases for a game-tying inside-the-park home run. The Sox went on to win, 8–4.

1967 The Red Sox scored twice in the top of the ninth to take a 3–2 lead over the California Angels, but Don Mincher hit a two-run homer off Jose Santiago in the bottom half for a 4–3 victory. It was the last game Santiago lost in the regular season; he won the next eight, helping make the Impossible Dream possible.

1948 Ted Williams was 0-for-7 in the doubleheader with the Yankees, but Bobby Doerr hit one homer in the first game and two in the second, helping beat New York twice, 6–5 and 8–7. Denny Galehouse got a save in the first game and a win in the second, when the Sox scored the tie-breaking run in the bottom of the ninth. Galehouse helped advance the cause in the final frame, but fell over first base and hurt himself, and had to go on the disabled list.

1937 Joe DiMaggio's first career grand slam came off Boston pitcher George Elvin "Rube" Walberg. The sixth-inning shot made all the difference, breaking a 4–4 tie and establishing the final 8–4 score.

1936 There's just nothing like an 11-run inning to get a game off to a good start. Wes Ferrell was the beneficiary of an 11-run second inning, as the Sox exploded on their way to a 16–2 win, the 11th win of the year for Wesley. Brother Rick Ferrell, Wes's batterymate, was 4-for-5 on the day, but it was Johnny Kroner's five RBIs that led the way. Boston beat the Athletics in the second game, too, 8–2. Moe Berg spelled Rick Ferrell and drove in a pair.

1935 Two uncles of Sam Mele—Tony Cuccinello of the Dodgers and Al Cuccinello of the Giants—both hit home runs in the same game at New York's Polo Grounds. Dom and Joe DiMaggio are the next set of brothers to perform the feat. (See June 30, 1950.)

1934 Billy Werber singled twice and stole his 20th base of the year, helping beat the Yankees, 8–5, in the first of two. Boston lost the second game, despite a Werber triple. Werber was one of only six Sox players to lead the league in stolen bases, and the only one to do so twice (1934 and 1935). In 1934, he stole 40 bases. In 1935, 29 was enough for the title.

In the ongoing saga of Lefty Grove's mouth (he had abscessed teeth removed on April 8), Grove had a set of badly infected tonsils removed at St. Elizabeth's Hospital in Brighton. It was again hoped that oral surgery would help his pitching; he was only 4–4 on the season at this point. He finished up 8–8, but reverted to form the following year.

1927 Philadelphia got two to tie it in the top of the ninth, 5–5, but Phil Todt got his fourth hit of the day and drove in a sixth run to win it for Boston. Todt made headlines another way, too—he broke umpire Tom Connolly's nose with a thrown ball in the seventh.

1921 Nothing much good happened in the 1920s for the Red Sox. On this day, they lost their fourth consecutive doubleheader.

1915 The Sox set out to play the Senators six times in three days. The string of back-to-back-to-back doubleheaders began with back-to-back shutouts, 4–0 (Rube Foster) and 6–0 (Babe Ruth, in a game shortened to five-and-a-half innings). Boston swept all six games, and swept into first place in the process.

1906 It was, the *New York Times* wrote, "a very bad game of baseball...Some of [manager Jimmy] Collins' men played like schoolboys." Catcher Bob Peterson led the way with two wild throws in the first inning, and three errors on the day. In all, the Bostons committed nine errors (and it is clear that there were at least one or two errors of omission as well, during the five-run fifth inning that was all New York needed to sail to an 8–3 win).

TRANSACTIONS
1952: Released Pahl Lehner.
1969: Purchased Ron Kline from the San Francisco Giants.

DEBUTS

1920: Gene Bailey	1985: Tom McCarthy
1933: Lou Legett	1991: Kevin Morton
1970: John Kennedy	1995: Willie McGee

BIRTHDATES
Jack Quinn 1883 (1922–1925); Hank Thormahlen 1896 (1921); Rick Lancellotti 1956 (1990)

DEATHS
Pete Fox 1966; Joe Kiefer 1975; Ted Williams 2002

July 6

2000 During the course of a four-day visit to the Hubert H. Humphrey Metrodome, the Sox drubbed out 53 hits, scored 44 runs, and won four ballgames. Morgan Burkhart drove in seven of the runs.

1999 After weeks in which sports talk radio jocks, particularly on radio station WEEI, mocked preservationists fighting to save Fenway Park, the Red Sox released a poll showing that 83% of those surveyed favored the proposed plan for a replacement park. The survey was commissioned by the Red Sox. Release of polling data was timed to be the day before the group Save Fenway Park! had planned to reveal cost estimates for a renovation of Fenway. The Red Sox had not yet specified how much public money they were seeking for the new ballpark.

1978 Yaz kicked things off with a three-run homer in top of the first inning, but the White Sox picked up one run each in the seventh, eighth, and ninth to send it into extra innings, a 6–6 tie. Why didn't they take out Willoughby? The former Red Sox reliever had given Chicago two good innings, but in the top of the 10th, Fred Lynn hit Willoughby's first pitch for a home run and Soup Campbell savored the Red Sox victory, finishing up his 2⅔ innings in relief.

1966 The Red Sox swept New York, 5–3 and 5–4. Dalton Jones provided the power **STVT** to win the first game with a pinch-hit, tie-breaking, two-run homer in the ninth, batting for the pitcher, Don McMahon. John Wyatt earned the save. In the second game, Yaz hit an inside-the-park two-run homer off Jim Bouton, but it was later in the game—with Don McMahon on the mound again—that the Sox took the lead. Once again, John Wyatt saved it. According to *The Baseball Chronology*, the only other pitcher to beat the Yankees in both games of a doubleheader was Dave Davenport of the Browns back in 1916. Those were both complete game efforts. These dual defeats came back to haunt the Yankees at year's end; Boston finished just a half-game ahead of the last-place 1966 Yankees.

1951 Follow this thread throughout July. Clyde Vollmer tripled to clinch a 6–2 win over the Yankees. It was the first of many key hits in one of the best months any Red Sox player has ever had.

1944 "Indian Bob" Johnson hit Tigers pitching for the cycle and was so exhausted from all that hoofing it that he let Tom McBride take over his left-field position in the seventh. Bobby Doerr had a triple, a double, two singles, and five RBIs. As one can imagine, the Sox won this game. Hughson got the win, 13–3.

1933 Bill Dickey and Mickey Cochrane were both hurt, so Rick Ferrell ended up working the full game in the very first All-Star Game ever held. Ferrell was 0-for-3 at the plate, but the American League won the "game of the century," 4–2.

1918 Babe Ruth's sixth-inning triple knocked in two runs. He over-ran third base, but Bill Wambsganss's throw to nip him went wild, and Ruth scored. The three runs boosted the Sox to a 5-4 lead which they maintained. The win put the Sox in first place, and they maintained that lead, too, till season's end.

1914 Washington's Walter Johnson won a 1–0 ballgame for the 16th time in his career. It was the fifth time Walter had squared off against Red Sox pitcher Rankin Johnson. In the Johnson vs. Johnson matchups, each man had won two, each counting one 1–0 win, and Rankin lost this one to Walter by the narrowest of margins—when Washington's captain, George McBride, stole home in the fourth inning while Walter Johnson was batting. It was a straight steal of home, with Walter stepping aside only at the very last second to let McBride slide across.

1912 A rather confident Jake Stahl made an early prediction: "We expect to win the pennant...We have no old, worn-out men who are likely to go to pieces. Our team is rounded into a good organization." Admitting that any number of things could go wrong, Stahl nonetheless thought his Red Sox would be the team to win it all. He was right.

1909 Red Sox rookie Larry Pape makes his debut with a 2–0 win over the crippled Washington Nationals, in the second game of a doubleheader sweep. Of the eight Sox pitchers who threw shutouts in their first start, Pape was the only one to do so at home (in this case, Boston's Huntington Avenue Grounds). No one has ever done it at Fenway Park.

TRANSACTIONS
1995: Acquired Rick Aguilera in trade from the Minnesota Twins in trade for Frankie Rodriguez and a PTBNL (J. J. Johnson).

DEBUTS
1909: Larry Pape	1995: Rick Aguilera
1920: Paddy Smith	1996: Tony Rodriguez
1975: Jim Willoughby	

BIRTHDATES
Walter Carlisle 1883 (1908); Steve O'Neill 1891 (1924, manager 1950–1951); Karl Olson 1930 (1951–1955); Lance Clemons 1947 (1974)

DEATHS
Ray Francis 1934; Sam Jones 1966; Bob Johnson 1982

July 7

1985 Boston second baseman Marty Barrett puts the ball on Bobby Grich, tagging him out with a hidden ball trick. Barrett executes the trick just two weeks later, on July 21, and again on September 5, 1988.

1972 In a game at Anaheim, the Red Sox win 5–3 in 10 innings, though the most fun was Boston skipper Eddie Kasko pretending to faint while protesting home plate umpire Hank Morgenweck's ninth-inning out call on Ben Ogilvie at the plate. Several towels were thrown from the dugout and both Kasko and Phil Gagliano were ejected. The Sox played the game under protest, though they didn't protest the final 5–3 win when Ogilvie hit a two-run homer his next time up.

1966 The Yankees were being shut out, 2–0, by the Red Sox at Yankee Stadium, with Don McMahon on the mound. McMahon had won two games the previous day, and was being asked to save this one. Starter Roland Sheldon had walked two batters, but McMahon couldn't hold back New York. First, they tied it on a pinch-hit single and a sac fly, and then Mickey Mantle (one hit in his last 17 at-bats) pulled one into the right-field seats for a 5–2 win.

1951 The six runs the Red Sox scored in the bottom of the first, four of them thanks to Clyde Vollmer's grand slam, provided the margin of difference in a 10–4 defeat of the visiting New York Yankees. Ted W. and Dom D. each hit homers for Boston, too.

1949 Washington Senators owner Clark Griffith was negatively impressed when pitcher Mickey Haefner walked five Boston batters in the first inning and gave up five runs. In particular, he cited Haefner's "indifference" fielding Boston pitcher Chuck Stobbs' easy tap back to the mound; the irritated owner gave Haefner his walking papers. In all, the Sox walked 13 times—and this was in a game ended after six innings so they could catch a train. The game was resumed on August 20, and the Washington pitcher walked two more, for a club record 15 walks in one nine-inning game.

1943 Not so hot at the hot corner. It wasn't a matter of fumbling the ball; he simply never got a chance. Jim Tabor played third base through 14 innings of a game against the White Sox in Chicago, but never had a ball hit to him. No putouts, no assists. Johnny Lazor in left was idle thoroughout the game, too. One thing Tabor might have done to help, as long as he was out there, would have been to hold Wally Moses a little closer to the bag on third; Chicago won the game when Moses stole home in the bottom of the 14th. Lazor wore #82, the highest uniform number ever worn by a member of the Red Sox. He also might have won the batting title in 1943, hitting .310 and appearing in the required minimum 100 games. However, in 17 of them he'd only appeared as a pinch-hitter so league president Will Harridge awarded the title to Yankee Stuffy McInnis.

1936 Boston pitcher Lefty Grove started the All-Star Game for the AL, and was charged with the loss in the game played at Braves Field. Almost the entire Red Sox team turned out for the game, sitting together, except as the *Boston Globe* explained: "Notable absentees were Wes Ferrell and Moe Berg. Wes allowed as how if he wasn't good enough to play in the game, he didn't want to see it, while the professor was deep in the Modern Language Library in Ogunquit, Maine."

1935 Sensational baserunning by Billy Werber earned the Red Sox a win over the Athletics in the bottom of the 13th inning. With one out, Werber walked, stole second, and then sprinted all the way from second base to home on a grounder hit to the second baseman.

1933 "Roly-poly Rob Roy Fothergill" was given his release by the Red Sox. A crowd favorite in Boston, the *Washington Post* wrote, "Whenever a game became dull and the Sox were runs behind, as they were mighty often up to a short time ago, the cry would be raised, 'We want the people's choice—Fatty Fothergill.' And usually the stout one would oblige with an appearance at the plate."

1925 Pitcher Joe "Scootch" Lucey only threw 11 innings of major league ball, but he walked 14 batters and gave up 18 hits. Maybe he just wasn't right for the Red Sox, even in the 1920s. The team released him to Buffalo.

1923 Cleveland scores in every inning (3-2-3-1-2-13-1-2), but since they were the home team they don't get a chance to fatten their averages by batting in the ninth. The 27 runs is a league record. Boston pitcher Lefty O'Doul is in the Hall of Fame, but not for this performance; in just the third inning, he yielded a major league record 13 runs. When he came in—to relieve Bill Piercy—there were already two outs. Why didn't manager Frank Chance pull O'Doul for a reliever? It seems that O'Doul was in the doghouse and Chance was determined to leave him in until he could get that third out. O'Doul faced 16 batters before he could record the final out; he walked six of them. Both are Red Sox records. O'Doul quit pitching after 1923—perhaps understandably—but returned to the majors as an outfielder in 1928. The Red Sox made four errors; of Cleveland's 27 runs in the game, 18 of them were unearned. The Tribe won the second game, too, 8–5.

1920 In an automobile accident in Wawa, Pennsylvania, Babe Ruth, his wife, and three New York Yankees players were pinned under the automobile that Ruth was driving at 2:00 A.M., which overturned on a sharp curve. A news report said that Ruth was able to lift the car sufficiently so the others could crawl out from under, and they then held it up so he could get out.

1917 A flurry of excitement occurred midgame, as somehow a fire started inside the rolled tarpaulin near the stands, but the first aid crew doused it with a bucket of water from the ice tank.

1916 Cleveland scored once in the top of the first, but Red Sox pitcher Babe Ruth only allowed one more hit through the seventh. The Sox loaded the bases in the bottom of the seventh, and put in light-hitting Olaf Henriksen to pinch-hit for Babe Ruth. He walked, and the score was tied. Jack Barry hit the first pitch of the eighth for a single. Duffy Lewis sacrificed him to second, he took third on a sacrifice fly, and scored on Tillie Walker's single for a 2–1 win, won by reliever Carl Mays.

1914 Suffering heavy losses from Federal League competition in Baltimore, the Orioles' (International League) owner Jack Dunn offers Babe Ruth (plus Ernie Shore and catcher Ben Egan) for $10,000 to old friend Connie Mack, who refuses, pleading poverty. Cincinnati, which has a working agreement giving them the choice of two players, ignores Ruth and takes OF George Twombley and SS Claud Derrick. Dunn finally peddles his threesome to new owner Joe Lannin of the Red Sox for a reported $25,000.

1911 At St. Louis, Smoky Joe Wood had a no-hitter through eight, but Burt Shotton singled off him in the ninth. Boston won the one-hitter, 6–1. Wood struck out 15 batters, the most by any Red Sox pitcher for decades.

1904 Jack Chesbro suffered the "rather strong and opportune batting" of the reigning champions, as Boston beat New York's Happy Jack, snuffing out his 14-game winning streak with a 4–1 Boston victory.

TRANSACTIONS
1933: Fatty Fothergill released by the Red Sox.
2005: Acquired INF Alex Cora from the Cleveland Indians in exchange for INF Ramon Vazquez

DEBUTS
1906: Bill Carrigan
1929: Ray Dobens
1930: Charlie Small
1940: Alex Mustaikis
1950: Dick Littlefield,
Willard Nixon
1999: Chad Fonville
2005: Alex Cora,
Adam Stern

BIRTHDATES
Billy Herman 1909 (1964–1966); Red Nonnenkamp 1910 (1938–1939); Sammy White 1928 (1951–1959); George Smith 1937 (1966); Chuck Goggin 1945 (1974); Bob Gallagher 1948 (1972); Glenn Hoffman 1958 (1980–1987); Matt Mantei 1973 (2005)

DEATHS
Norwood Gibson 1959; Harry Wolter 1970; Paul Musser 1973; Joe Dugan 1982; Vic Wertz 1983; Ben Chapman 1993

July 8

1999 One of the most famous baseballs in World Series history was Carlton Fisk's Game Six homer from the 1975 World Series. At auction, the baseball sold for $113,273.

1994 With runners at first and second and nobody out, everyone's thinking triple play, right? Not everyone. Seattle DH Marc Newfield lined right to Sox shortstop John Valentin, who stepped on second, doubling off the baserunner, and then "trotted a few steps to tag the runner (Keith Mitchell) coming from first—all very nonchalantly," wrote Nick Cafardo in the next morning's *Globe*. EASY AS 1-2-3 headlined the paper's sports section. John Trainer (another *Globe* writer) said that it unfolded rather slowly, and looked so routine, that "it took the Fenway fans a full two minutes" to realize what they'd just witnessed—an unassisted triple play. Valentin was trotting toward the dugout when he came across Mitchell, who had "slowed to a walk, and Valentin tagged him as he jogged by." Valentin himself admitted, a little sheepishly, after the game, that he thought there was already one out. "Mitchell wasn't really running. I looked over at the scoreboard and saw that there was one out [the liner having already been registered] and my teammates reminded me to tag him." In the bottom of the second, Valentin followed the example of Neal Ball, who he'd probably never heard of before, homering to lead off the inning. (See July 19, 1909.)

1973 Chicago won the first of two, 6–1, but fans at Comiskey left the park dazed when the Red Sox broke open a 2–2 tie in the top of the 10th with a staggering nine runs. Boston 11, Chicago 2. Sox second baseman Buddy Hunter had been hit by a pitch, walked, hit a sacrifice fly, and walked. Four plate appearances, but not one official at-bat. His RBI single in the 10th scored Dwight Evans and the

Sox batted around. Second time up, Hunter doubled, and he scored run #9 a few moments later when Tommy Harper singled.

1956 Ted Williams drove in five runs, one of which was the 1,500th RBI of his career, as Boston beat Baltimore, 9–0 and 8–4. In the first game, he hit a home run, giving him 399, just one away from the 400 mark. RBI #1,500 came in the second game, on a fly to left that fell in between three fielders. They all count.

1951 Vic Raschi couldn't hold a 3–0 lead, and both Clyde Vollmer and Lou Boudreau hit two-run homers for the Red Sox to win, 6–3, and complete a three-game sweep of the Yankees. Some papers made much of a "feud" between Joe DiMaggio and manager Casey Stengel, occasioned when DiMaggio was replaced in center after taking his position in the field (he'd pulled a muscle) but John Drebinger of the *Times* dubbed the whole hoo-hah a misunderstanding.

1947 The All-Star Game was tied 1–1 in the seventh inning when Bobby Doerr singled, stole second, and took third when Johnny Sain's pickoff hit him and caromed into the outfield. He then scored the winning run on Stan Spence's single.

1941 The moment Ted Williams always said was his greatest thrill in baseball came in the ninth inning of the July 8, 1941 All-Star Game. Playing at a time when league rivalries really were heartfelt, Ted came to bat with two outs and two men on, and the American League down by one run, 5–4. Ted's dramatic home run won the game for the AL, 7–5, and he galloped and leapt around the bases in film footage still frequently shown today, more than 60 years later.

1934 The original walking man: Max "Camera Eye" Bishop walked eight times in one day's doubleheader, four times in each game. The first game, a 7–4 win for the Red Sox, featured RBIs by three Johnsons: one by Philadelphia's left fielder Bob Johnson, one by Boston pitcher Hank Johnson, and three by Boston's left fielder Roy Johnson. The two left fielders were brothers, but no relation to Hank. There was also an all-Johnson play: one of Hank's pitches was hit by Bob to Roy. As it happened, the first five batters in this day's Athletics lineup would all find themselves on the Red Sox within the next few years.

1924 The Red Sox led 7–0 after two innings, but lost the game as St. Louis crept closer, and closer, and closer, then added single runs in the seventh, eighth, and the unanswered go-ahead run in the ninth.

1918 Cleveland's Stan Coveleskie threw nine shutout innings; Sad Sam Jones threw 10. The Red Sox were batting in the bottom of the 10th, when Amos Strunk singled. The next batter was Babe Ruth. Ruth got ahold of one and blasted the ball into the right field bleachers. The Sox won the game, but the score was only 1–0. Under the rules of the day, only the run needed to make the difference counted, so only Strunk scored. How to account for Ruth's home run? Score it a triple, and so it reads in the box score. Ruth ended the season tied for the AL title with former teammate Tillie Walker; they both had 11 homers.

1912 Smoky Joe Wood gave up a first-inning run to St. Louis, but his teammates put three across in the bottom of the first and won the game, 5–1. It was the first of 16 consecutive wins for Joe Wood.

1905 Doubles galore. Boston hit 12 doubles and Philadelphia hit 14 in a double-filled doubleheader. Boston second baseman Hobe Ferris had the most, with five two-baggers on the day.

1903 For the second time in four days, Cy Young served as umpire—and Patsy Flaherty of Chicago umpired for the second time in two days! Chicago had moved on to Boston from New York but no umpires showed up at all, so the two served as arbiters in a game Boston won 6–1. Chicago scored their one run in the first off Winter, but he gave up no more runs. Nick Altrock pitched in his first game with the White Sox, against the team that had recently discarded him, but fared little better than he had for Boston. Both Freddy Parent and Jimmy Collins hit home runs, Collins also tripling.

1902 Boston pitcher Doc Adkins gives up 12 hits while facing a record 16 batters (both major league records) in the sixth inning of a 22–9 loss to Philadelphia. The A's score 12 runs in the inning, but Lefty O'Doul spared Adkins having to retain that record, too. (See July 7, 1923.) One would think that facing 16 batters in one inning would be a uniquely horrible experience, but Adkins shares the shame with O'Doul and with Howard Ehmke (September 28, 1923). In all three instances, the disaster occurred in the sixth inning.

TRANSACTIONS
2000: Curtis Pride was released.

DEBUTS
1922: Walt Lynch   1933: Freddie Muller
1931: Bill McWilliams   2001: Carlos Castillo
1932: Ed Gallagher

BIRTHDATES
Wally Mayer 1890 (1917–1918); Bill Spanswick 1938 (1964); Darrell Brandon 1940 (1966–1968); Ken Sanders 1941 (1966)

DEATHS
Bill Carrigan 1969; Merl Combs 1981; Jim Busby 1996

July 9

2002 Derek Lowe was the first of nine AL pitchers to take part in this year's All-Star Game, the game that ended in a 7–7 tie after 11 innings, simply because there were no more pitchers to be had.

1979 Not one member of the Yankees was elected to the All-Star team. The starting outfield will be all Red Sox—Carl Yastrzemski, Jim Rice, and Fred Lynn. It was a first that the players of just one team comprised the whole starting outfield.

1976 On this day, Boston Red Sox owner and president Tom Yawkey passed away.

1972 Angels pitcher Nolan Ryan struck out the side in the first inning, in the second inning, and in the third inning—the last eight in succession. By the fourth inning, the Red Sox figured out other ways to make outs and all three batters flied out or popped up. By game's end, Ryan had 16 K's and a 3–0 one-hitter.

1970 It was a "grand slam single" when Dalton Jones of the Detroit Tigers pinch-hit and banged Vicente Romo's offering into the upper deck for a bases-loaded grand slam. Jones didn't go into his home run trot early enough, apparently, and passed Don Wert between first base and second. He was therefore ruled out, and his hit had to be scored a three-run single. But it was enough to propel the Tigers to a 7–3 win.

1965 The Red Sox lost a tight 2–1 game when Washington's Ed Brinkman singled to break the tie in the bottom of the ninth; in the day's second game, Earl Wilson and Jim Gosger both homered and Wilson got the 10–1 win. Frank Howard of the Senators struck out seven times that day.

1960 New York's Jim Coates hadn't lost since the previous season, winning 14 games without a loss, until he ran into Vic Wertz. The Sox first baseman singled, doubled, and homered, driving in four runs. The Red Sox won, 6–5.

1959 Bobby Avila homered twice and drove in four runs. Ted Williams homered and drove in three, and Vic Wertz hit a solo homer. They all helped the Sox score 14 times and overpower the Yankees, who scored but thrice.

1948 Ted Williams and Sam Mele were rough-housing on the train to Philadelphia and Ted tore some rib cartilage, costing him 15 games. Mele found himself in the doghouse. Had the Sox won one more game in 1948, there'd not have been a playoff for the pennant. Had Ted not missed so many games . . . ?

1946 Playing in the All-Star Game in Boston, Ted Williams had himself a field day—Teddy Ballgame hit two home runs, singled twice, and walked. The American League swamped the NL, 12–0. Five of the runs were driven in by The Kid, whose second home run took Rip Sewell's famous blooper ball, the eephus, and deposited it in the bullpen. This All-Star Game was held at Fenway Park, but it was the stellar performance of so many individuals on the '46 Sox team that resulted in an astonishing eight of them making the squad: Dom DiMaggio, Bobby Doerr, Boo Ferriss, Mickey Harris, Johnny Pesky, Hal Wagner, Ted Williams, and Rudy York.

The Sox purchased Don Gutteridge, the player-manager of the Toledo Mudhens, leaving the Mudhens without one of their infielders and without a skipper.

1944 Tex Hughson won his 18th game in his final start before reporting for induction in the Navy. He threw a four-hitter, winning 9–1. Hughson was 2-for-3 at the plate. Anchors aweigh!

1940 Joe Cronin of the Red Sox managed the AL All-Star squad, at the suggestion of New York's Ed Barrow, the first time the manager of the league's entrant in the preceding year's World Series was not named manager. The NL held the Americans to three hits and administered a 4–0 shutout.

1939 Winning two games, 4–3 and 5–3, the Red Sox completed what was thought to be the first five-game sweep of New York in Yankee Stadium history. In both games, the Sox scored the deciding runs in the eighth inning on two-run homers—Joe Cronin's in the first game and Jimmie Foxx's in the second.

1937 A see-saw affair: Philadelphia and Boston kicked off a five-game series in Philly. Boston had a 4–2 lead after 7½, but the A's scored six times in the bottom of the eighth to go on top, 8–4. Boston batters struck back with four runs in the top of the ninth to send the game into extra innings. The Red Sox looked to win it in the 10th, by scoring three times, but the Athletics weren't ready to call it quits just yet and they matched Boston with three of their own. In the 11th, Ben Chapman tripled and Joe Cronin doubled him in, and this time Rube Walberg—Boston's fifth pitcher of the game—held the A's scoreless. 12–11, Red Sox.

1920 Two runs in the bottom of the seventh gave Bullet Joe Bush and the Sox a 2–1 win over the visiting Browns. Mike Menosky stole one base but was caught stealing once, too; it was one of 19 times he was caught stealing in 1920—a Red Sox record for "Leaping Mike."

1918 The Red Sox bought the release of outfielder Hugh High from the Yankees, and he consented to join the Red Sox—but never showed up. His explanation: "My wife won't let me."

1915 Babe Ruth lasted only one-third of an inning, giving up two hits, two walks, and suffering three errors. Four runs scored, and Ruth was relieved. It got worse as the game wore on, and Detroit dominated the Red Sox, 15–4.

1914 Boston Red Sox owner Joseph Lannin made a couple of good pickups, purchasing catcher Ben Egan and pitchers George Herman Ruth and Ernest Grady Shore from Jack Dunn of the Baltimore Orioles, for around $25,000. Egan never played for the Red Sox, but the other two certainly made contributions.

1913 Club president James McAleer and owner-manager Jake Stahl were reported at odds, both vying for control of the ball club. It seemed certain that one or the other would have to leave. Stahl apparently felt McAleer did not deserve his big salary as somewhat of a figurehead leader, and McAleer faulted Stahl for the poor performance of the Sox on the field and for trying to undermine his position. (See July 15, 1913.) Troy Soos suggests the rift had roots in the sixth game of the 1912 World Series, when McAleer ordered field manager Stahl to start Buck O'Brien on the mound. (See October 14, 1912.)

Both the Red Sox and the White Sox were claiming rights to the services of catcher Tom Daly, who was playing for Lowell in the New England League. Chicago won. Daly later achieved off-season fame by hitting a home run in front of the King of England.

1911 Ted Sullivan of Tioga, Texas, visits the Red Sox and says the town will offer training grounds and provide free equipment if Boston will schedule spring training in Tioga.

Hal Janvrin debuts, playing first base, and has himself a 2-for-4 day, with one RBI (his only RBI of 1911, it turns out). The 18-year-old is the first major leaguer to come directly from high school right to the big leagues.

1902 In an early classic pitchers duel, the A's pitted Rube Waddell against Boston's Big Bill Dinneen. Along about the 15th inning, Waddell may have revived any flagging energy by doing a number of handsprings on the field. The battle was joined for 16 full innings before the visiting Philadelphians pushed across a pair of runs in the 17th to win, 4–2, on shortstop Monte Cross's two-run homer. In the marathon game, Freddy Parent fielded 17 balls at short.

TRANSACTIONS

1914: Bought Babe Ruth and Ernie Shore from Baltimore for around $25.000.
1992: Acquired Billy Hatcher from Cincinnati for Tom Bolton.

DEBUTS

1911: Hal Janvrin
1933: Bucky Walters
1969: Ron Kline

1992: Billy Hatcher
2005: Scott Cassidy

BIRTHDATES
Dave Shean 1883 (1918–1919); Tex Clevenger 1932 (1954); Mike Andrews 1943 (1966–1970)

DEATHS
Ossee Schreckengost 1914; Aleck Smith 1919; Tony Lupien 2004

July 10

1992 Bob Zupcic's eighth-inning grand slam off Bobby Thigpen makes the difference in Boston's 6–5 win over the White Sox. It's Zupcic's second slam in his rookie year (his ninth inning slam on June 30 was a walk-off game-winner). Ellis Burks had two grand slams in his own rookie year, 1987. The two share the major league record.

1986 BURNED-UP BOYD TAKES A WALK, RED SOX DEFEAT ANGELS ON A BALK—the poor attempt at headline poetry in the *Washington Post* told readers that Oil Can Boyd was so incensed that he'd not been named to the All-Star squad that he ripped off his uniform before the game, threw clothing around the clubhouse, and stormed out of Fenway Park. He later tangled with police and was briefly hospitalized for psychiatric testing.

The July 10 game was pretty exciting, too. The Angels and Red Sox were tied 4–4, and there were two outs in the top of the 12th, when Mike Brown was brought in to get the last out. Instead, Wally Joyner hit a triple, Brown threw a wild pitch, walked the next two batters, and gave up a single and a double—all before he was pulled. 7–4, Angels. But when the Angels called on Mike Cook to close it out, Jim Rice hit a two-out homer with Marty Barrett on base and then—error, walk, single, error, and finally (score tied) the Angels decided to take their chances bringing in Todd Fischer. Before throwing his first pitch, Fischer promptly balked home Dwight Evans with the winning run!

1977 Against the Milwaukee Brewers, the Red Sox posted a mark of 28 men left on base. Well, OK, it was a doubleheader and eight of the stranded runners were in the second game, but they tied a major league mark with 20 LOB in game one (it ran 11 innings). All's well that ends well, though. The Sox won both games. One Boston player not left on base was Ramon Aviles. It was his major league debut. He pinch-hit for Bernie Carbo—there's a switch—in the seventh, with men on first and second and nobody out. Aviles grounded out to first, advancing the runners. Hobson was walked intentionally, and Tommy Helms sent in to pinch-hit for Denny Doyle. The Brewers changed pitchers, so Rick Miller was sent in to pinch-hit for the pinch-hitting Helms and he grounded into a double play. Aviles played second base in the seventh and eighth, but Dwight Evans batted for him in the ninth. That was the only appearance Aviles ever had in the American League. Two years later, he hooked on with the Phillies and appeared in 116 games over three seasons.

1971 At a 5:00 A.M. (!) press conference, Tony Conigliaro says he will have to quit baseball because of ongoing vision problems. He had gone 0-for-8 in his last couple of games. Brother Billy unloads, complaining that a conspiracy of Carl Yastrzemski, Reggie Smith, and the team's equipment manager was behind

Boston's trade of Tony to the Angels on October 11, 1970. "You can quote me—because I don't care. I know I'm next," he tells the Associated Press. Tony C. had called Yaz out for loafing on a grounder in a 1970 game in Milwaukee. After the season, on October 11, 1971, Billy was traded to Milwaukee.

1966 The Red Sox were going for a five-game sweep of the White Sox at Fenway, but Chicago took the game into extra innings, tied 6–6. The Sox put three men on base in the bottom of the 10th, though, and then second baseman George Smith swept the bases clean with a game-winning, series-sweeping grand slam.

1960 Vic Wertz hit the first of two 1960 grand slams. By year's end, he had 103 RBIs, the third team for which he'd driven in 100 or more runs in a season.

1956 Ted Williams hits another All-Star Game homer in Washington.

1945 The All-Star Game—scheduled for Fenway Park—was canceled because of wartime travel restrictions. Seven inter-league games are played throughout baseball, raising large sums for the war effort. In the "All-Star replacement game" at Fenway, the Braves and Red Sox squared off in a sort of City Series reprise. The Sox pummeled the Braves, 8–1, before more than 22,000 spectators.

1936 Tom Yawkey and his first wife, Elise (described by the *New York Times* as "the former Miss Bliss Sparrow"), adopted a nine-week-old girl from The Cradle in Evanston, Illinois. When Mrs. Yawkey was asked why she selected a girl to adopt, she told the *Chicago Tribune*, "I was afraid that Tom might make a ballplayer of a boy and trade him off." Sparrow was the daughter of a Birmingham, Alabama fire captain who later became a magazine cover girl in many portraits by artist James Montgomery Flagg.

1933 Bucky Walters was purchased from the Pacific Coast League Missions by the Red Sox on July 2, but when he arrived in Boston, he found that the Boston Braves had "entered a defensive claim for Walters' services with Baseball Commissioner K. M. Landis." Walters had played for the Braves in 1931 and 1932. Landis told Walters he could play for the Red Sox while he studied "the obscure agreement the Braves have with the Missions regarding his services." (A.P.) Walters played out the season with the Red Sox, though he did play once more for the Boston Braves 17 years later—one game in 1950, his final game as a major league ballplayer.

1926 Boston outfielder Ira Flagstead was suspended indefinitely as a result of comments made during the ballgame to umpire Geisel, but the comments were apparently so understated that Burt Whitman wrote "no one else besides Flaggy and Geisel knew that anything had been said."

1916 The world champion Red Sox were humbled by White Sox moundsmen Lefty Williams and Reb Russell—shut out twice, 4–0 and 3–0, in Fenway.

1912 Just two weeks earlier, the Red Sox signed Turners Falls, Massachusetts high school pitcher Doug Smith, who averaged 15 strikeouts per game in the 13 games of his senior year, with three no-hitters to his credit. In his debut, Smith was brought into a game the Sox were losing 8–2 to the visiting St. Louis Browns, and threw the last three innings, giving up one run. It would be his only major league appearance. The Philadelphia Phillies contested Smith's signing, arguing that they had signed him. On July 17, the National Commission ruled in favor of the Red Sox, noting that the Phillies claim was based on an unsigned contract that had a statement by Smith's brother and guardian written on its back. On August 13, Smith was released to the Lowell ball club. The only other time he appeared in the *Boston Globe* was as an author of a February 11, 1913 piece on the greatest play he'd ever seen on a ballfield. He named Hooper's catch in the final game of the 1912 World Series.

The big news of the day was that the Red Sox denied admittance to some 30 fans known as "knockers." They had bunched in the first-base bleachers and yelled insulting remarks to Sox pitcher Buck O'Brien earlier in the week. Whether there was a direct connection to the habitual gambling in this same part of the park is unknown, but club president James McAleer said the goal was "to prevent gambling on our grounds, and for the protection of the players from the abuse of the spectators."

The Red Sox sell pitcher Eddie Cicotte to the White Sox. Unfortunately, Cicotte's name crops up as one of the 1919 Chicago "Black Sox," and is later banned from baseball for life.

1909 Jake Stahl hit his fourth home run in 10 days (he had six on the year), winning the game for the Red Sox, 2–1.

1908 The Red Sox purchase first baseman Jake Stahl from the Highlanders. He will star for the Sox and even manage them to a World Series win in 1912. As soon as Cleveland manager Lajoie heard of the deal, he claimed that *his* club had signed Stahl. President Farrell of the Highlanders responded, "Boston is the only club that has any claim on the services of Jake Stahl, and the player will leave on the midnight train for Boston."

TRANSACTIONS
1908: Purchased Jake Stahl from the New York Highlanders, selling
     Bob Unglaub to Washington immediately afterward.
1925: Jack Quinn was selected off waivers by the Philadelphia Athletics.

DEBUTS

1912: Doug Smith	1988: Steve Curry
1947: Sam Dente	1994: Steve Farr
1977: Ramon Aviles	2004: Joe Nelson

BIRTHDATES
John Michaels 1907 (1932); George Dickey 1915 (1935–1936);
Andre Dawson 1954 (1993–1994)

DEATHS
Skinny Graham 1967

July 11

1976 "With the kind of talent we have on this team, playing .500 baseball is a disgrace," said an emotional Carl Yastrzemski before the game. The Red Sox won, 6–4, with a good 8⅔ innings from Ferguson Jenkins and a little offense, Yaz's two-run double the key. Captain Carl had a little help from some snack food; Twins center fielder Lyman Bostock missed the catch as he raced back to take it against the wall in center. "I lost the ball," he said, adding, "then I looked up and all I saw was popcorn falling down out of the stands."

1972 Marty Pattin has a no-hitter through eight innings in Oakland, working with a 4–0 lead. He got the first out in the bottom of the ninth, but Reggie Jackson singled cleanly to right center. A one-hit shutout just isn't the same thing.

1971 Responding to Billy Conigliaro's charges of a conspiracy to get his brother Tony C., Yaz says that Billy is just "alibiing for a lack of ability." Meanwhile, Reggie Smith, Yaz's alleged co-conspirator, added of Billy, "I don't want to play with him anymore. The club should take disciplinary action." On July 14, Billy C. apologizes to Yaz in an attempt to end the feud.

1969 Yaz hit one home run in each of two games, with one RBI in the first and four in the second game. Reggie Smith had four RBIs and was 7-for-9 on the day. With 22 hits in the nightcap, the Sox won, 12–3. They'd taken the first game, 7–4.

1960 Bill Monbouquette started the All-Star Game, surrenders four runs, and was pinned with the loss.

1959 With the Yanks ahead 3–1 after 7½ innings, the Sox scored three runs and went ahead in the bottom of the eighth, on Tony Kubek's throwing error, which let in two of the three runs. Kubek, batting in the ninth, tied it on a home run. In the bottom of the 10th, the Yankees battery of Ryne Duren and Yogi Berra were both ejected in an argument over a pitch called a ball. Jim Bronstad (who would finish the season 0–3) couldn't get either of the next batters out, and so Bob Turley was trotted in. His first pitch was blasted over the Green Monster just down the line for a grand slam. The batter? An unlikely hero—Don Buddin.

1954 Talk about competitive imbalance. The Red Sox pummeled the Athletics 18–0 in the first game and 11–1 in the second. On top of that, A's slugger Gus Zernial broke his collarbone and would be out for weeks to come, and 1B Lou Limmer was out with contusions from a Billy Goodman liner. Jackie Jensen led with six RBIs; Ted Williams led with six runs scored.

1950 In the first inning at the 1950 All-Star Game, he caught the ball, robbing Ralph Kiner of extra bases, but slammed into the left-field wall at Comiskey Park and hurt his elbow badly. Ted Williams played in pain for eight full innings, and even singled in the fifth to give the AL a one-run lead. After the game, Ted learned he'd broken his elbow. He had been off to the best start of his career, and said felt he was never quite the same again—though check out his stats for 1957!

1937 The Red Sox took two games in Philadelphia, but right fielder Ben Chapman was so incensed by umpire John Quinn calling him out on a delayed steal play that after he took his position in the field, he fired a baseball "apparently aiming at Quinn." (A.P.) When ejected, he rushed at Quinn and had to be restrained, but only after throwing his glove at Quinn and hitting him. He received a $50 fine and three days' suspension.

1925 The Red Sox sent 20 men to the plate in the fifth and sixth innings, scoring five runs per frame, and beat the Indians by the score of 14–7.

1923 Yankees center fielder Babe Ruth singled four times and scored two runs, as New York beat Boston, 3–1.

At virtually the same time, Red Sox owner Harry Frazee sold the team to a Columbus, Ohio syndicate for a little over $1,000,000. Palmer Winslow was the money man, almost certainly prompted by Ban Johnson. Bob Quinn became the new president. Wild celebrations akin to those attendant on the end of the World War did not engulf Boston, but Red Sox loyalists were very pleased. *The Sporting News* suggested in a subhead: "Hub May Make Date of Red Sox Sale New Holiday." Even the *New York Times* recognized in its story on the sale that Frazee had sold off Boston's stars one by one, and the "Yankees have been the chief gainers in strength since Frazee began to place his stars on the market." (See also July 26, 1923.)

1917 Babe Ruth of the Boston Red Sox almost had himself a no-hitter. Only Donie Bush's eighth-inning hit that caromed off Ruth himself spoiled the no-hit bid. Ruth did walk four and hit two batters, so it was far from a perfect game, but the one-hitter held up for a win when Chick Shorten pinch-hit a triple in the top of ninth to score Tillie Walker for the 1–0 final. Boston 1, Detroit 0. The next day, Ruth said he thought he should have been charged with an error.

1916 Manager Bill Carrigan announced Babe Ruth to start the first game of the doubleheader against the White Sox, and Ruth did indeed pitch to Felsch, the first Chicago batter. The White Sox had constructed their lineup to face the lefthander, Ruth, but after getting the first out, Carrigan replaced Ruth with Rube Foster, a righthander. Foster got the 5–3 win, courtesy of five singles in the fourth and then two bases-loaded walks doled out by Chicago's reliever, Eddie Cicotte. Ruth started and won the second game, a 3–1 six-hit performance.

1914 "Ruth, formerly of Baltimore, made his debut..." The Babe held the Indians to eight hits in seven innings before he was relieved by Dutch Leonard; the Red Sox won, 4–3. Ruth struck out his first time up, and was 0-for-2 on the day. With the score tied in the seventh, Duffy Lewis pinch-hit for Ruth, singled, and scored the fourth Red Sox run.

TRANSACTIONS
1925: Purchased Jack Bischoff from the Chicago White Sox.

DEBUTS
1913: Paul Maloy
1914: Babe Ruth
1921: John Perrin
1948: Mike Palm

BIRTHDATES
Harry Wolter 1884 (1909); Clarence Blethen 1893 (1923); Billy Ashley 1970 (1998)

DEATHS
Dutch Leonard 1952; Frank Gilhooley 1959

July 12

1997 Aaron Sele struck out 13 Blue Jays, but was touched for three runs. He was up against Roger Clemens, now pitching for Toronto, who whiffed 16 Red Sox—and then gestured to GM Dan Duquette's suite. Duquette had elected not to re-sign Clemens, who had been sub-par four years in a row. The 29 K's was one shy of the record for two teams facing each other.

1975 Though he'd pitched the whole game, and was leading, 10–4, after seven and a half innings, Luis Tiant had not batted. Neither had any other Red Sox pitcher since the designated hitter was implemented in the AL. Yaz came out of the game, and Cecil Cooper took his place at first base. It's confusing, but Retrosheet phrased it thus: "Tiant replaced Yastrzemski (pitching)"—since he'd actually been pitching all along. In any event, Tiant came to bat in the bottom of the eighth, made contact, but flied out to right. End of game: still 10–4 Red Sox.

1970 In the first inning of the only start of his major league career, Indians pitcher Fred Lasher hit Tony Conigliaro on the left forearm. Conig didn't take kindly to it and, in the words of David Cataneo, "dashed to the mound, let out a small yell, and karate-kicked Lasher on the left thigh and hacked him in the face with a left-handed karate chop." After Tony was ejected, brother Billy moved over from left to take Tony's place in right field. Leading off the second inning, Billy homered off Lasher, who bore the loss in the 8–2 game.

1959 During NBC's game-of-the-week telecast of the Red Sox–Yankees game from Fenway Park, the center-field camera employed a special 80-inch lens which clearly showed close-up shots of catchers Yogi Berra and Sammy White flashing signs. Announcers Mel Allen and Phil Rizzuto interpreted the signs for viewers, and were invariably correct. Although neither the Red Sox nor the Yankees filed a protest, Commissioner Ford Frick requested that NBC voluntarily cease use at future games and NBC acquiesced. The Red Sox won the game, 7–3, the fourth of five games the Sox took as they swept a five-game series from the Yankees.

1951 The Red Sox (winning 15 of their last 19) climbed into first place with two wins over the White Sox, in Chicago, 3–2 and 5–4. The latter game ran a full 17 innings, the longest night game in history to that point, and it might have been a mistake for the White Sox to let Saul Rogovin pitch all 17 innings. He was maybe a bit fatigued. Two singles and Clyde Vollmer's sacrifice fly (he hit a two-run homer in the first game) brought home the go-ahead run. Ellis Kinder pitched scoreless ball from the eighth through 17th innings. (See the next day's game, July 13, 1951.)

1945 Two former batboys were welcomed back by the Sox. Joe Kelly was a POW in a German prison camp, freed by Russian troops on April 29. Freddy Stack earned six battle stars serving in both the European and the China–Burma theatres.

1943 To raise money for war bonds, both Ted Williams and Joe DiMaggio played on the same team, managed by Babe Ruth, in an exhibition game against the Boston Braves at Braves Field. Ted's home run wins it for the Ruth All-Stars, 9–8.

1933 Lefthander Lloyd Brown threw an 11-inning shutout, beating the Tigers, 1–0. He is one of just nine Red Sox pitchers to throw an extra-inning shutout since 1918. And not only that—*The Sporting News* informed readers that his left leg was a full 1½ inches shorter than his right leg.

1920 With Harry Hooper in the hospital, the Sox were lacking Foster, Hendryx, Hooper, Hoyt, McNally, Menosky, and Russell. The *Globe* called the 1920 Sox at mid-season just a "shell of a team."

1919 It only took him until July 12 to do it, but Babe Ruth's home run—his first ever in Chicago—tied his own league-leading mark of 1918 with his 11th home run of the year. Ruth helped Boston beat the White Sox, 12–4.

1912 Ray Collins struck out Ty Cobb when a hit would have meant a couple of runs, Jake Stahl doubled twice, and a four-run sixth won the first game for the Red Sox, 4–1. Joe Wood was invincible in the second, striking out 10 Tigers and winning 1–0 in 11 innings.

1901 Cy Young spotted Connie Mack's Athletics a couple of runs in the first, but Boston won the game, 5–3. It was Young's 11th straight win and #300 of his major-league career.

TRANSACTIONS
1905: Acquire rights to Charlie Armbruster from New London.
1927: Sold Fred Haney to the Chicago Cubs.

DEBUTS
1910: Chris Mahoney
1986: LaSchelle Tarver

BIRTHDATES
Jack Harshman 1927 (1959)

DEATHS
None yet

July 13

2005 Over 2,000 people crowded a Lansdowne Street nightclub celebrated the release of pitcher Bronson Arroyo's new CD, *Covering the Bases*. Arroyo was joined on stage by teammates Johnny Damon, Kevin Youkilis, and Lenny DiNardo, and Standells front-man Dick Dodd, to perform the Standells' classic "Dirty Water." It had been more than four decades since the last Red Sox player held a record release party; that was Tony Conigliaro on January 19, 1965.

2004 Manny Ramirez hit a two-run homer in the All-Star Game off former Red Sox pitcher Roger Clemens. Later in the game, David Ortiz hit a homer off former Red Sox pitching prospect Carl Pavano.

2000 In the bottom of the first inning as the Sox hosted the Mets in interleague play, Jose Offerman led off with a walk but was caught stealing. It was the eighth time in 2000 that he'd been gunned down, without even one successful steal. Though "Awfulman" (as he was known in Boston) played most of the games the rest of the season, he quit trying to steal bases. Only one player in major league history (Pete Runnels, Washington, 1952, caught stealing 10 times) attempted more steals in a season without ever succeeding.

1999 In the All-Star Game, held at Fenway Park, Pedro Martinez struck out the first four batters he faced: Barry Larkin, Larry Walker, Sammy Sosa, and Mark McGwire. Pedro was later named MVP. This was the first real All-Star extravanganza, with three days of home-run hitting contests and a number of fan fest features. What everyone most remembers, though, is the unscripted moment when Ted Williams was driven out onto the field and all of the Hall of Famers and current players flocked around him, delaying the proceedings for a good 10 or 15 minutes.

1988 The Red Sox named third base coach Joe Morgan their new manager, after firing John McNamara. McNamara had managed for 3½ years, and came as close as one could get without winning it to getting the Red Sox a world championship. Boston was 297–273 under McNamara, and one game above .500 (43–42) at the time he was let go.

1962 In Kansas City, Lu Clinton hit for the cycle, then added another single in the top of the 15th inning, to top the Kansas City A's, 11–10. Clinton was 5-for-7.

1959 The Sox completed a five-game sweep from New York, winning 13–3. Gene Stephens came in to run for Ted Williams in the sixth, and the Red Sox batted around, bringing Stephens up to bat later in the inning with the bases loaded. Stephens hit a grand slam to punctuate the nine-run inning.

1951 From the fifth inning on, the game was deadlocked, 2–2. The evening before, the two teams had played 17 innings for the longest night game in history. They improved on that record by heading into the 19th still locked up. 36 innings in two games. Mickey McDermott threw 17 full innings for the Red Sox, before letting Harry Taylor take over. The Red Sox thought they had it, scoring twice in the top of the 19th, but Taylor let the White Sox load the bases in the bottom of the 19th. A single by pinch-hitter Ed Stewart tied the score, and Don Lenhardt's sacrifice fly brought in the 5–4 game-winner.

1950 Between seven and fifteen bone fragments were surgically removed from Ted Williams' elbow in a 75-minute operation. "I never had quite the extension on an outside pitch that I had before," Ted told Ed Linn. "And I lost a little power." You'd hardly know it. He hit .336 for the rest of his career, and won a couple more batting titles.

1945 It was bad enough that Tigers pitcher Stubby Overmire had to face red-hot Boo Ferriss, but he had to do so on Friday the 13th. Catcher Hack Miller told him not to worry: "I was born on February 13, 1913, and I've had plenty of good luck. There's nothing to this jinx business." Overmire was driven from the game by the third inning, losing 5–1 to Ferriss, who notched his 15th victory.

1942 Naval aviation cadets Ted Williams and Johnny Pesky began taking evening classes at Boston's Mechanic Arts High School three nights a week while the Red Sox were in town, as part of their preparation for full-time training that would begin after the season concluded.

1939 The Red Sox play their very first night game and, wouldn't you know, it goes into extra innings. Playing in Cleveland, the Sox knocked out Bob Feller in the fourth inning with five runs and held the 5–0 lead until the bottom of the ninth when the Indians tied it up with five last-minute runs of their own. In the top of the 10th, Joe Cronin walked, stole second, and then moved up to third base as Mel Harder walked the next two batters. Pinch-hitter Lou Finney singled him in, and the Sox won, 6–5, for their ninth straight victory.

Earlier in the day, members of the Massachusetts Senate each contributed 10 cents to send a telegram to the team congratulating them for sweeping the Yankees five games in a row.

1934 Pitcher Wes Ferrell hit two homers off Dick Coffman of the Browns, keying a 7–2 victory for the Sox and himself. On August 22, he had another two-home run game. In 1934, during Ferrell's 23 starts, the Red Sox supported him with nine home runs—but four of them were Ferrell's and only five hit by the rest of the team combined.

1933 The Red Sox lost 3–2 to the Tigers. This was the first of 20 consecutive losses
STVT in one-run games for the Red Sox. In the next 19 games they played which were decided by one run, the Red Sox lost every one of them. This remains the longest such streak, topping the 16 straight lost by the Philadelphia Athletics in 1916. When Boston beat Cleveland 4–3 on September 19, the streak was snapped.

1925 There were 35 hits in the game, but pinch-hitter Roy Carlyle's two-run homer in the top of the ninth supplied the final two runs (and the slim margin of victory) in a 12–11 squeaker over the Indians, in Cleveland.

1922 While the Red Sox were losing their third straight at Fenway to the Indians, divine intervention prevented the Yankees–Browns game from being played. At approximately 3:00 pm, while the Browns were taking batting practice, lightning struck at the Polo Grounds. A special dispatch to the *Boston Globe* reported that the crash "carried the Yankees' treasured American League pennant to the ground as it splintered that flagpole in center field."

1919 In a move reminiscent of Dutch Leonard deserting the Sox in the summer of
?! 1918, another Sox starter—this time, Carl Mays—walked off the team between innings, due to shoddy Sox fielding. Shortly afterward, Red Sox owner Harry Frazee traded Mays to the Yankees for two pitchers and $40,000. The trade set off a dispute with AL President Ban Johnson, who forbade the Yankees to pitch Mays. They pitched him nonetheless, and obtained a court order allowing them to do so. The battle raged on for some time, even after the season was over. (See July 29, 1919.) There are indications that Mays was suffering more than pique; James C. O'Leary writes that Mays had been hit in the back of the head by a ball thrown by one of his fielders, but played out that inning. When he failed to reappear, Barrow sent someone to find him and he was found "weeping" in the clubhouse. He was despondent, perhaps troubled, and may have lost face with his teammates when word got around.

1913 Sox President James McAleer denied he was feuding with manager Jake Stahl. He told the press that "Manager Stahl and I are in perfect accord and the best of friends." (See July 14, 1913 on how McAleer fired Stahl 24 hours later.)

1908 Fans threw bottles on the field in Boston in protest of some umpiring decisions, occasioning a *Globe* correspondent to describe the act as "thoughtless and unbecoming," and out of line with Boston's fine reputation for fair play.

TRANSACTIONS
2005: Acquired RHP Chad Bradford from the Oakland Athletics for OF Jay Payton.

DEBUTS
1901: Frank Morrissey
1980: Bob Ojeda

BIRTHDATES
Eusebio Gonzalez 1892 (1918); Harry Dorish 1921 (1947–1956); Don Pavletich 1938 (1970–1971); Greg Litton 1964 (1994); Pat Rapp 1967 (1999)

DEATHS
Mickey Owen 2005

July 14

2003 Sox owner John Henry sided with stars Manny Ramirez and Pedro Martinez, both of whom left the team a day early before the All-Star Break. Manny said his mother was sick. Pedro had not been scheduled to start and was given permission to leave early.

1997 "Apparently, it's a lot easier to forgive and forget when you're circling the bases," wrote Larry Whiteside in the next morning's *Globe*. The last-place Red Sox pummeled the Tigers, 18–4, but Whiteside was referring to the crowd reaction to Sox left fielder Wil Cordero, who received a standing ovation when he homered in the seventh inning. Cordero had heard nothing but boos since June 11, when he was arrested for assaulting his wife. He'd not played for 11 games after the incident, and been booed for his first 14 at-bats after returning. The reaction was largely temporary, though, and Cordero's tenure in Boston was limited.

1995 Mo Vaughn sat out the game, his left eye swollen shut with bruises sustained during an early morning scuffle at The Roxy on Boston's Tremont Street. A Dorchester man claimed that Vaughn attacked him; Mo blamed Theron Davis, characterized as a street gang member who had approached Vaughn's lady friend and licked her on the face. Vaughn was back on the field by July 16.

1977 Yaz homered to lead off the fourth, and then singled in the fifth inning. The homer tied Ted Williams for the most hits recorded by any player in a Red Sox uniform, and the single established him as the all-time leader in hits. Butch Hobson homered, too. It was not nearly as momentous an occasion, but Hobson triggered a rally that led to the 7–4 Red Sox win over the Indians.

1972 For the second game in a row, Juan Beniquez made three errors at shortstop. Two, in the fifth inning, led to two Twins runs. The third set up the first run in the bottom of the ninth as the Twins scored three times (winning it, 7–6, when Harmon Killebrew walked with the sacks full). John Kennedy took over at shortstop for the Red Sox in games to come.

1970 Yaz was 4-for-6 (three singles and a double, with one RBI and one run scored) at the 1970 All-Star Game, played at Riverfront Stadium, Cincinnati. He played very well at both CF and 1B, but the NL won it in 12 innings, 5–4.

1958 Ted Lepcio's pinch-hit bases on balls forced in the winning run in the bottom of the 10th inning in a 4–3 win over the Indians. Writer Ed Walton says the earlier Red Sox runs scored on two passed balls, two sacrifice bunts, and a wild pitch.

1956 Mel Parnell no-hit the White Sox before a fortunate 14,542 at Fenway, the first no-hitter in Boston's ballpark since August 21, 1926, when Ted Lyons of the same White Sox humbled the hometown team. It had been even longer since any Red Sox pitcher had thrown a no-hitter; Howard Ehmke did it on September 7, 1923, in Philadelphia. The win was especially nice for Marvelous Mel, since he'd lost eight straight starts to Chicago, dating back to May 1953. He was also glad just to get the game in; rains delayed the start for 68 minutes. Final score, 4–0. The final out came when pinch-hitter Walt Dropo bounced one right back to Parnell, who ran to the first base bag and became the only pitcher to make the final out of his own no-hitter.

1953 Ted Williams, just back from flying 39 combat missions in the Korean War, is named an honorary member of the AL team at the All-Star Game in Cincinnati.

Capt. Williams throws out the first ball, and is permitted to sit on the AL bench throughout the game.

1951 Clyde Vollmer was one of the most dramatic single-season run producers the Sox have ever had. He helped win another, singling in two ninth-inning runs to help Boston beat Chicago, 3–2, in Comiskey Park.

1950 For the second time in 1950, the Sox scored 11 times in one inning—the second inning of the day's game against the visiting White Sox. It was only mid-July, but Vern Stephens's three RBIs (with homer #19) vaulted him just over Walt Dropo and Ted Williams. The three sluggers had 84, 83, and 83 RBIs, respectively. The Red Sox won, 13–1. Ellis Kinder won with ease.

1947 Ted Williams recorded the 1,000th hit of his major league career with a solid single off Don Black of the Cleveland Indians.

1946 The Boudreau Shift (aka the Williams shift) was first implemented by Cleveland's player–manager Lou Boudreau in the second game of a doubleheader. Ted had three homers (one a grand slam) and eight RBIs in the first game, which Boston won, 11–10. The Shift couldn't stop a ball hit out of the park, but Boudreau moved all the fielders, except the third baseman and left fielder, to the right side of the diamond to defend against the pull-hitting lefty Williams. First time up, Ted looked at the shift, then at four straight balls. He dropped his bat and walked to first. He walked once more, his 96th of the season, and grounded out twice.

1945 Player-manager Joe Cronin puts himself on the inactive list, so he can activate Lou Finney, returning from an injury.

1938 Lefty Grove hurts his arm throwing to first while fielding Charlie Gehringer's first-inning bunt. Red Sox team physician Edward O'Brien is mystified; Grove has no pulse at all in his left arm and is unable to grip objects firmly. The arm weakened progressively during the game and he had to leave in the fifth, but had stuck in there long enough to pick up his 14th win of the season. He does not win another game all season long, but it's one of nine seasons Grove leads the league in ERA.

1937 Buster Mills' true first name was Colonel, which makes one wonder what his life would have been like had he become a career man in the military. He had himself a good day, driving in five runs as the Red Sox rolled over St. Louis, 15–6. It was right-fielder Fabian Gaffke, though, who made the record books, with five runs scored in the game.

1922 Though books on the Red Sox typically cite 409 as the lowest paid attendance at a home Red Sox game (September 29, 1965), the July 15, 1922 *Chicago Tribune* reports that only 68 fans attended Fenway Park on July 14. "Exactly sixty-eight people, and the figures are not exaggerated, sat in the grand stand this afternoon...the turnout was the smallest of the season. This small attendance was approached other days during the year." The paper also reported that a committee of players formed on July 13 to appeal to owner Harry Frazee to sell the team. Not one of five daily papers in Boston indicates any less than 2,800 in attendance, nor does any other newspaper note such a committee.

1916 No one ever did score. In a game called on account of darkness after 17 scoreless innings, St. Louis left hander Ernie Koob blanked Boston—though the Sox had 14 hits off him—he walked three, and hit Jack Barry twice. Carl Mays pitched even more effectively for Boston, but it looked like he'd given up a run in the 15th when Koob came around third base and barreled over Mays at home plate. Koob failed to touch third, though, and third baseman McNally retrieved the ball and tagged him out. Mays wasn't hurt badly, but was replaced by Leonard.

1913 The Red Sox weren't going anywhere, with a 39–39 record before the game on the 14th. Jim McAleer fired Jake Stahl as manager and named catcher Bill Carrigan to the post. They lost the next two, but finished with a winning record, albeit 15½ games out of first place. AL President Ban Johnson was angered, saying that Stahl had been "publicly humiliated" and "we don't do things like that in the American League." Carrigan apparently came by his nickname "Rough" the hard way. Umpire Bill Evans once heard quite a commotion coming out of the Red Sox clubhouse and later asked a player about it. He was told, "Bill just grabbed one of the boys who wouldn't listen to reason and shook him up a bit. He'll behave from now on."

TRANSACTIONS
1970: Received Chuck Hartenstein from the St. Louis Cardinals as part of a conditional deal.

DEBUTS
1914: Ernie Shore
2005: Chad Bradford

BIRTHDATES
Jesse Tannehill 1874 (1904–1908); Fred Burchell 1879 (1907–1909); Johnny Murphy 1908 (1947); Chuck Rainey 1954 (1979–1982); John Dopson 1963 (1989–1993); Mark Brandenburg 1970 (1996–1997)

DEATHS
Babe Danzig 1931; Al Kellett 1960; Jackie Jensen 1982

July 15

2005 The Red Sox clobbered the Yankees, 17–1, matching the greatest margin of defeat they had ever administered to the Evil Empire. Oddly, the previous pounding was their 17–1 win on May 28, 2005, in Yankee Stadium. The July 15 win was just the third game they faced New York since May 28. This evening's win at Fenway featured an inside-the-park home run by Trot Nixon and a grand slam by David Ortiz.

2004 Trot Nixon called it "an absolute joke, and you can quote me" regarding a directive from Major League Baseball that fined him for having too much pine tar on his batting helmet, obscuring the "B" team logo, and instructed him to wipe off the obscuring substance. One of Boston's original "Dirt Dogs," Trot speculated that Commissioner Selig was bored one day and decided to drum up some controversy. It would be another matter if the fans cared, or his own team had come to him with the request. "I don't care what they say. I'm not paying any fine."

2001 The Red Sox drew more fans on the road than any other team in baseball in 2005, but the building trend was noted early. More than four times the usual number of fans packed Montreal's Stade Olympique for a series against the Red Sox—and both the crowd inside and that outside on the streets of Montreal was overwhelmingly Sox supporters. Red Sox Nation had crossed the border into Quebec. When Hideo Nomo singled in the fifth, he got a standing ovation. Unison shouts of "Let's go, Red Sox. Red Sox, let's go" echoed in the Metro after the game. You felt bad for Expos fans.

2000 Outfielder Carl Everett, who once said he didn't believe in dinosaurs because he had never seen one, went too far in an argument with umpire Ron Kulpa. Everett blew up when umpire Kulpa drew a line in the batter's box to show Everett he meant business, enforcing the rule where the batter must stand. Everett bumped Kulpa and the two literally butted heads in anger. Everett was later suspended for 10 days and fined.

1999 Doug Glanville hit a leadoff homer off Boston's Brian Rose to kick off the game; perhaps Jose Offerman figured he'd try the same thing. Offerman hit a leadoff homer off the Phillies' Paul Byrd. Boston went on to win, 6–4.

1998 DH Midre Cummings, one of the few major leaguers from the Virgin Islands, hit a fifth-inning homer off Cleveland's Bartolo Colon. The solo shot provided the only run in Pedro Martinez's 1–0 win, the first complete game 1–0 win for Boston since Roger Clemens won one on May 27, 1987.

1988 It seemed like magic when Joe Morgan took over from John McNamara as manager of the Red Sox. The Sox took two from the Royals, 3–1 and 7–4. On May 9, Roger Clemens had struck out 16 Royals in a game, and now he did it again. Dwight Evans hit a two-run homer. The second game featured doubles by Greenwell and Burks to give them the lead in the first inning, a homer by Boggs in the third and, though the Royals scored four times, the Sox never relinquished the lead.

1986 Roger Clemens pitched three no-hit innings to kick off the All-Star Game in Houston, and get the win. He is the only Red Sox pitcher to record an All-Star Game victory. Seven have taken the loss: Lefty Grove, Tex Hughson, Frank Sullivan, Monbouquette, Radatz, Tiant, and Eckersley—which is a pretty good collection of pitchers.

1975 In eight All-Star Games, Yaz had only driven in one run, so he was pleased with his pinch-hit three-run homer on the first pitch he saw from Tom Seaver. The National League won, 6–3.

1973 Worth the wait. After an incredibly long 2:50 rain delay, the Sox and Rangers got the game underway. The Red Sox were leading in the bottom of the sixth when the rains fell again and the game was called. Since the Sox were up 3–1, the score stood.

1935 With brothers Wes and Rick already playing for the Red Sox, George Ferrell asked, "Why in the world doesn't some enterprising big league mogul make room for that other deserving Ferrell boy, George, who can hit like nobody's business?" George's 15 home runs led the Piedmont League at the time, and his .407 average led all minor leaguers nationally except for Oscar Eckhardt of the PCL Missions. He never made the majors.

1927 Roy Carlyle played for the Red Sox in 1925–26 and, after being traded to the Yankees in the middle of 1926, passed the Boston baton to his brother Cleo, who played in 1927. Cleo hit his only home run this day, unfortunately a solo shot, as Boston lost its 10th game in a row to St. Louis, 3–2.

1926 In a busy doubleheader, shortstop Topper Rigney made 24 plays without an error, 15 in the second game alone.

1916 It was their fourth doubleheader in a six-day period, with a 17-inning 0–0 tie in between. When Boston scored one run on Tillie Walker's double in the eighth, the Red Sox had scored for the first time in 28 innings. Unfortunately, that was the only run they scored and St. Louis already had two. In the second game, though, Boston bats cracked out 17 hits and 17 runs, winning 17–4.

1914 Dutch Leonard didn't let up a hit for four innings, and threw a 4–0 shutout against the Cleveland Naps. The Red Sox starting nine emerged unscathed, but umpire Tom Connolly was irritated by "loud coaching from the dugout" (*Globe*) and ejected four or five players from the Boston bench.

A proposed Sunday benefit game between the Red Sox and Detroit Tigers in Lynn, Massachusetts for the city's firefighters was opposed by Mayor Newhall and other city councilors. No admission was to be charged, but contributions would be accepted. At a municipal council session, 10 ministers appeared to oppose baseball on the Sabbath.

1912 Historian Ed Walton brought about a correction in Hall of Fame records when he discovered a "missing" home run that Tris Speaker hit on July 15, 1912. The HOF had recorded a triple for Speaker, and thus nine on the season. Crediting Speaker with a 10th home run gave him a tie for the league's lead, with Home Run Baker of Philadelphia. The blow in question came in the eighth inning of a 6–4 loss to the Tigers, and is correctly reflected in game accounts in *The Sporting News, Sporting Life, Boston Globe, New York Times, Washington Post*, etc.— but the official scorer had noted it down as a triple, and so it stood until Walton uncovered the error in 1978.

1903 Tom Hughes started, and was given a 2–0 lead to work with when Boston scored twice in the first, but he was hit so hard in the second that Cy Young was brought in to relieve. It became a hard-fought battle with Addie Joss and went into extra innings, until Young took matters into his own hands and hit the ball into the roped-off crowd for a ground-rule triple, driving in Lou Criger in the bottom of the 10th to win the game, 4–3. It was said that George Winter pitched the finest game of his life in the second game (five hits, one walk, and one hit batsman) but Boston only scored two runs, committed three errors, and lost, 4–2

DEBUTS
1905: Hank Olmsted
1911: Les Wilson
1927: Frank Welch
1990: Tim Naehring

BIRTHDATES
Red Kellett 1909 (1934); Tim Harikkala 1971 (1999)

DEATHS
Tully Sparks 1937; Chris Mahoney 1954

July 16

2002 Manny Ramirez went 5-for-6, with a double, a homer, and three RBIs, helping power the Red Sox to a 9–4 win over the Tigers at Comerica Park. Three Red Sox batters were hit by pitches, but Detroit's Damion Easley was himself hit three times.

1998 Troy O'Leary hit a grand slam and had five RBIs, while Nomar Garciaparra matched O'Leary in RBIs on the strength of a 4-for-4 day, including two doubles and a homer. The first three men in the order—Darren Lewis, Darren Bragg, and Nomar Garciaparra—all scored three times apiece. Boston 15, Cleveland 5.

1978 Fred Lynn drove in all three runs in the 3–2 night game win over the Twins, completing a doubleheader sweep for the day.

1970 Boston scored early, Milwaukee scored late, and the teams were tied 5–5 after regulation. In the 10th, with nobody out, Yaz singled and Tony C. doubled. Brewers manager Dave Bristol walked Rico Petrocelli to load the bases and set up a force. Then he brought outfielder Tommy Harper in from left field to play between shortstop and third base and try to help cut down the run at the plate. Goerge Scott boomed a fly ball to right field, though, and it was deep enough to allow Yaz to tag up and score the winning run.

1958 Ike Delock ran his record to 9–0 (and 12 in a row, going back into 1957), with a 5–2 win over the Kansas City Athletics. Billy Consolo's triple in the sixth sparked a four-run rally. Ted Williams, disgusted at going hitless and striking out once, flung his bat into the dugout as he reached the steps.

1950 Dom DiMaggio, Vern Stephens, and Walt Dropo each hit home runs in the first inning, and Dropo hit two more in the game, a 13–10 clobbering of Cleveland. Despite scoring three times in the bottom of the ninth, Boston lost the second game, 8–4. By year's end, Dropo hit 34 homers, most ever for a Sox rookie.

1941 In the last day of his 56-game hit streak, Joe D. manages three hits off two pitchers. After failing to hit successfully on the 17th, DiMaggio went on and hit for another streak of 16 games in a row. Because he walked on the 17th, and walked in the game before the hitting streak began, all told DiMaggio had crafted a stretch of 74 straight games in which he reached base. SABR researcher Herm Krabbenhoft terms this statistic CGOBS (Consecutive Games On Base Safely). Ted Williams had a stretch of 69 CGOBS in 1941, and then in 1949, Ted exceeded Joe D.'s CGOBS mark during the 1949 season. (See July 1, 1949.)

1939 Joe Cronin completed his 25th consecutive game (142 chances) without an error, as the Red Sox won their 12th game in a row—at the time, the longest winning streak in Red Sox history.

1914 When the Red Sox announced they had obtained first baseman Dick Hoblitzell from Cincinnati on waivers, Yankees owner Frank Farrell was indignant. Earlier in the day, he'd announced that *he* had purchased Hoblitzell and that the first baseman would be reporting to the Yankees on July 17. Hobby finished his career with the Red Sox.

1909 Biff Schlitzer pitched the game of his life on July 16, a 10-inning complete game that the Red Sox won, 2–1. St. Louis lost when Harry Niles was hit by a pitch, moved up on a sacrifice, took third on an out, and scored on a hit by Gessler. Schlitzer was one of 18 starters the Red Sox employed in 1909, trying to make up for the trade of Cy Young. Pitchers who started for the Sox were: Anderson, Arellanes, Burchell, Chech, Chesbro, Cicotte, Collins, Hall, Karger, Matthews, Morgan, Pape, Ryan, Schlitzer, Smith, Steele, Wolter, and Wood.

1903 Boston kicked off the contest with seven runs in the first and put the game away early. Rains threatened, and Cleveland's player-manager Lajoie took himself out of the game in the third inning with Boston up 9–0. And Cleveland, having to catch an early train, simply quit after 7½ innings, despite the fact that the game was only an hour and 33 minutes old. Dougherty was 4-for-5, but all told Boston only out-hit Cleveland 12 hits to 10. Four of Boston's first-inning runs scored after Collins and company were given new life; Cleveland had made the third out, but it was disallowed because the umpire had turned away to get some replacement balls. 11–4 final.

1901 Cy Young recorded his 12th win in succession, but it wasn't a pretty one. Cleveland scored four times in the bottom of the ninth to pull within two; fortunately for Young, Boston had rung up five more runs in the top of the ninth. The Cleveland crowd was so incensed over several decisions by umpire Al Manassau that they pursued him after the game, and "pelted him with cushions and pop bottles" until the Cleveland players escorted him to safety. Final: Boston 10, Cleveland 8.

TRANSACTIONS
1914: Selected Dick Hoblitzell off waivers from the Cincinnati Reds.
1959: Released Jerry Zimmerman.
1967: Purchased Norm Siebern from the San Francisco Giants.
1988: Signed free agent Larry Parrish.
1995: Released Derek Lilliquist.

DEBUTS
1924: Chappie Geygan   1978: Garry Hancock
1943: Catfish Metkovich   1994: Stan Royer
1950: Phil Marchildon

BIRTHDATES
Bob Peterson 1884 (1906–1907); Doc Prothro 1893 (1925);
Len Okrie 1923 (1952); Bob Burda 1938 (1972)

DEATHS
Les Howe 1976

July 17

2002 The Red Sox unveil plans for a new large exterior concourse which during games will make Yawkey Way an extension of Fenway Park itself, allowing fans to spill out onto the sidewalk, and consume. The Sox did their homework with the community and built adequate support for the measure to be approved. The new concourse first opened for business on September 5.

1996 Boston was at home, ahead 9–2 after six. The Yankees scored three in the seventh, two in the eighth, and four in the ninth to take an 11–9 lead. Yankee reliever John Wetteland had saved 27 straight games, but after getting one out in the bottom of the ninth, he walked Tim Naehring on four pitches and then gave up a double off the Wall to former Yankee Mike Stanley. He struck out Kevin Mitchell, and walked Reggie Jefferson to load the bases. Pinch-hitter Troy O'Leary doubled off the Wall to tie the score, and Jeff Frye (0-for-5 on the day) finally connected, singling to right field to win the game.

1995 Jeff Suppan's first major league appearance was a start, and Keith Lockhart of the Kansas City Royals was the first batter he faced. Lockhart took him long, for a leadoff home run. Suppan joined Charlie Mitchell (August 9, 1984) as the only other Red Sox pitcher to give up a home run to the very first man to step into the box against him. Kansas City won, 4–3.

1990 In the fourth inning, Tom Brunansky grounded to Gary Gaetti, who initiated a round-the-horn 5-4-3 triple play. Boston scratched out one unearned run in the fifth. With the score just 1–0, the Red Sox were looking for an insurance run or two in the eighth when the same triple-play situation presented itself: runners on first and second with nobody out. Jody Reed grounded to Gaetti, and there it was again, another 5-4-3 triple play. It was the first time in major league history that a team had executed two triple killings in one game. In total, Gaetti had started five triple plays for the Twins. The Red Sox, stunned, still won, 1–0.

1987 Mike Greenwell caught the 10th inning of the day's ballgame, after the Sox had scored three runs in the bottom of the ninth to tie the game. He took Danny Sheaffer's place, who'd taken Marc Sullivan's place. Greenie may not have called that good a game—four Red Sox pitchers combined to give Oakland seven runs in the top of the 10th. Boston got back two, but lost, 11–6.

1959 Cleveland's Joe Gordon was ejected from the game for too energetically protesting umpire Jim Honochick's ruling that Vic Power was out due to interference. The next Indians batter due up, Minnie Minoso, refused to enter the batter's box, and home plate umpire Frank Umont signaled to Red Sox reliever Leo Kiely to throw to the plate. Three throws, three strikes, and Minoso was called out. Flinging his bat in Umont's direction, Minoso was also tossed out of the game. A three-run Red Sox rally in the ninth almost got them the game, but they fell short by one, 8–7.

1956 Red Sox pitchers Tom Brewer and Bob Porterfield both stymie the Athletics, 10–0 and 1–0. The lone run in the nightcap was scored on Ted Williams' 400th career home run, hit in the sixth inning. As he crosses the plate, Williams makes a spitting gesture toward the press box. The next time the Sox shut out an opponent twice in the same day would be September 26, 1975. Boston was shut twice on September 30, 1964 and May 30, 1966, but we definitely don't want to dwell on those.

1938 Boston beat St. Louis twice, 11–5 and 14–4. Jimmie Foxx homered once in each game, and so did Joe Vosmik.

1935 Billy Werber tied a major-league record with four doubles in the first game of the day's doubleheader with the Indians. Al Zarilla, Orlando Cepeda, and Rick Miller all share the record of four doubles in a game, but Werber was the only Red Sox player to hit them in consecutive at-bats. In the second game, Werber couldn't get a hit, but Moe Berg went 1-for-3, driving in every one of Boston's three runs with a second-inning sac fly and a bases-loaded single in the fourth. Berg ensured that batterymate Lefty Grove got the win.

1926 The Red Sox beat the White Sox in both games of a doubleheader, scoring the go-ahead runs in each game courtesy of a Chicago error and choking off a ninth-inning White Sox rally in each game, too, squeaking by, 3–2 and 4–3. There were 13 sacrifices recorded in the twin bill.

1923 Col. Jacob Ruppert of the New York Yankees asserted, "There is absolutely nothing to the report that Harry H. Frazee has purchased or is about to purchase an interest in the New York American League club."

1911 "In a business proposition, if I were offered enough money I might be expected to sell almost anything." John I. Taylor went on record as willing to sell the Red Sox. The *Washington Post* correspondent noted that "both the Taylors are extremely disgusted over the poor showing of the club."

1909 After the Red Sox scored five times in the sixth to take the lead, Red Sox reliever Smoky Joe Wood pitched the last four innings at Cleveland and struck out 10 of the 17 batters he faced. Boston won, 6–4.

1903 Norwood Gibson was locked in a scoreless pitchers' duel with Detroit's Bill Donovan until the bottom of the 10th, when the first man up, Buck Freeman, slammed a ball that hit off the right-field fence, not far from leaving the park. He ran for a triple, but was able to trot home when Tigers second baseman Smith fired the ball wide to third base hoping to catch him.

TRANSACTIONS
1908: Traded Frank LaPorte to the New York Highlanders for Harry Niles.

DEBUTS
1905: Charlie Armbruster
1929: Hod Lisenbee
1939: Bill Sayles. Sayles had previously pitched for the
    American Olympic team in Berlin in 1936.
1995: Jeff Suppan

BIRTHDATES
Les Wilson 1885 (1911); Hank Patterson 1907 (1932); Ed Connolly 1908 (1929–1932); Lou Boudreau 1917 (1951–1954); Deron Johnson 1938 (1974–1976)

DEATHS
Jack Slattery 1949

July 18

1998 The Red Sox clawed the Tigers, 9–4. Donnie Sadler, Darren Lewis, Nomar Garciaparra, and Mo Vaughn all hit home runs after there were two outs in the seven-run fourth inning.

1990 The Red Sox won the game at Fenway, 5–4, and didn't bat in the bottom of the ninth. That reduced the number of half-innings played from 18 to 17, but it was still enough for the Sox and Twins to hit into a record-setting 10 double plays. In six of its eight at-bats, Boston hit into DPs. And Boston turned four against the Twins. This all occurred just the day after the Twins turned two triple plays against the Red Sox.

1989 Former Angels pitcher Donnie Moore inflicted multiple gunshot wounds on his wife, who survived, but was more accurate taking his own life. The two had separated a month before, the same month in which Moore was released by the Kansas City Royals' minor league affiliate in Omaha. Some felt Moore had never gotten over being one strike away from taking the Angels to the World Series in 1986, when he was instead taken deep by Dave Henderson of the Red Sox.

1980 Mike Torrez did win some games for the Red Sox. On this day, he threw a 10-inning complete game shutout, beating the Twins, 1–0.

1975 Watching their team win their ninth home game in a row, Boston's bleacherites were still stunned when Jim Rice's third-inning homer cleared the wall in center field some 20 feet to the right of the flagpole. Kansas City pitcher Steve Busby reckoned the ball landed "on the New Hampshire tollroad somewhere." Clif Keane said in the *Globe* that the ball rolled out to Ipswich Street (not Lansdowne—check a map of Fenway) and bounced under an automobile. Only five other players had actually hit one out in center: Jimmie Foxx (August 12, 1937) and Carl Yastrzemski (May 16, 1970) for the Red Sox, and Hank Greenberg, Bill Skowron, and Bob Mitchell for the visitors.

1970 Ted Kubiak 7, Red Sox 5. Actually, the final was 10–5, but Milwaukee second baseman Kubiak's seven RBIs would have been sufficient. The Brewers were down, 5–1, after five innings, but then Kubiak went to town. He had 15 RBIs for the year to date, but drove in three with a double and a couple of singles, and then hit a grand slam in the ninth for good measure.

1969 Red Sox pitcher Ray Jarvis won it by himself, first pitching a six-hitter against the Orioles. Their only run came on a Don Buford homer, hit with pinch-hitter Dave May on first base. Wait. Doesn't that mean two runs scored? No, May held up, unsure if it was a home run as Tony Conigliaro dove and fell into the right-field stands going after the ball—and Buford passed him on the basepaths. So, it wasn't really a homer, after all, but only because Buford didn't see May in time. Buford was credited with a single, and was ruled out. May "scored"— even though in the confusion of the argument that followed, he never actually rounded the bases. The wrong man was called out—it was Buford who should have been out, and the umpire later said it was Buford he'd ruled out, but the game continued. Back to Jarvis: he drove in one run with a single and another with a sacrifice fly. The final was 6–1.

1954 Russ Kemmerer throws a one-hitter against the Orioles, in his first major league start. Only Sam Mele's single off the Wall in left spoiled the outing for the 22-year-old rookie.

1947 Ted Williams hit two home runs and batted in five runs in the first 5-for-5 game of his career. The Sox had 17 hits in all, but the lead changed four times, and three errors and five walks helped permit the Browns to beat Boston, 9–8.

1926 Winds estimated at 100 miles per hour wreaked havoc across New England, uprooting trees, destroying property, and causing the loss of a few lives. The winds also did a number at Fenway Park, demolishing the last three rows of grandstand seating.

1919 Babe to the rescue. The Red Sox were riding a nine-game losing streak, and were down by four coming into the ninth inning. The Sox scored once in the top of the ninth to get the gap down to 7–4, and then Babe Ruth hit a grand slam off Fritz

Coumbe to win it 8–7. It was Ruth's second homer of the day. Indians manager Lee Fohl resigned and Tris Speaker took over as skipper.

1916 Babe Ruth tripled and scored in the third inning, crashing into Browns backstop Hank Severeid, knocking the ball out of his hand, and rendering him unconscious. The Babe's aggressive play tied the game, 2–2. Ruth held the Browns to just one more run, while the Red Sox scored two more, and Ruth had himself a 4–3 win over St. Louis.

1913 Fielding a fourth-inning grounder, Joe Wood fell and injured his right thumb. He had to leave the game, later learning that the thumb was broken. The only time he started again in 1913 was a September 8 exhibition game in Manchester, New Hampshire. Smoky Joe thus followed up his 34–5 season (1912) with but an 11–5 one. He was never the same pitcher again.

1912 Scoring 10 runs in the bottom of the first was a great start for the Red Sox, yet the inning never ended. With two outs, the rains came, the field became a lake, and the game was postponed—all those hits and all those runs washed away. The game was made up the following day, and the Red Sox beat Chicago, 8–0, but that took nine innings. Boston won the second game on the 19th, too, 2–1.

1901 George Winter was "hit hard throughout the game, but sensational fielding cut off many runs." (*Washington Post*) Both Boston and Cleveland had 10 hits (one of Boston's hits was a home run by Winter), but the Red Sox committed four errors and the Indians took advantage by bunching their hits. Lou Criger had to take over at first when Buck Freeman injured himself. Cleveland won, 6–5.

TRANSACTIONS
1954: Floyd Baker was selected off waivers by the Philadelphia Phillies.

DEBUTS
1902: Tom Hughes
1958: Bill Monbouquette
1988: Larry Parrish

BIRTHDATES
Larry McLean 1881 (1901); Carl Stimson 1894 (1923); Marty Karow 1904 (1927); Andy Gilbert 1914 (1942–1946); Windy McCall 1925 (1948–1949); Billy Harrell 1928 (1961); Mike Greenwell 1963 (1985–1996); Rolando Arrojo 1968 (2000–2002)

DEATHS
Ted Wingfield 1975; Del Wilber 2002

July 19

1997 In another incident, a Cleveland man said that Mo Vaughn punched him in the mouth outside an area strip club at 2:30 A.M. This was two years after a fight at Boston's Roxy.

1983 The seven-day trial to determine who would run the Red Sox ended in Suffolk Superior Court. Some of the words used in a *Boston Globe* summary were: squeeze play, power play, bad faith, shabby, vindictive, conspiracy, and greed. The goal of the proceedings was to remove Buddy LeRoux from ownership, and a central complaint was LeRoux's announcement that he was taking over the ball club on the night of the June 6 benefit for the stricken Tony Conigliaro. The group bringing the complaint was comprised of Jean R. Yawkey, Haywood Sullivan, and John Harrington. They prevailed.

1978 In Milwaukee, the Sox came from behind late in the game, with eight runs evenly split between the seventh and eighth innings. They tied it in the seventh, and went ahead when Frank Duffy singled in former Brewer George Scott from second. Ben Oglivie's relay home was up the line and Scott scored, though he went back to touch the plate to be sure. Milwaukee catcher Charlie Moore thought he had Scott and argued his case, but did not prevail. Meanwhile, Butch Hobson, who'd been on first when Duffy singled, just kept coming. "I slowed down when I got to third," he said. "But when I saw that nobody had called time, I just kept on going." Duffy tried to reach third on the play, but by that time, Moore had reawakened and fired to Sal Bando to cut him down. Boston won, 8–2.

1958 The Red Sox scored twice in the bottom of the ninth, but Ted Williams grounded out with the winning run on third. The Sox had tied the Tigers, though, 5–5. Detroit scored once in the top of the 12th. Jimmy Piersall pinch-hit a single in the bottom of the 12th. With two outs, Williams hit a two-run homer into the seats in right for a 7–6 win.

1954 Mickey Owen came in to pinch-run for Sammy White in the eighth inning of a game the Sox were losing to the Orioles, 7–3. He was left stranded on the basepaths, but when it came to be his time to bat in the ninth, Owen hit a grand slam that capped a six-run Red Sox rally. The hometown folks were even happier when the Sox swept the second game of the doubleheader as well.

1953 Al Smith singled in the fourth inning of the first game, but that was the only hit the Indians registered off Mickey McDermott and Ellis Kinder. Boston won, 2–0. The Tribe assembled 11 hits in the second game, but their five runs were two less than the Red Sox, who won the second game, 7–5. The story behind the story: Al Hirshberg says that reliever Kinder was so drunk that he had to be helped to the stadium and helped into his uniform. Once in the bullpen, he fell asleep in the 103-degree heat. When manager Lou Boudreau called to the pen to get Kinder warming up, he was told that Kinder was asleep. "I don't care if he's dead," Boudreau snapped. "Get him up." Kinder came out and pitched hitless ball. Boudreau told him to take the rest of the day off, but Kinder went back out to the pen, fell asleep again, got the call, was awakened and closed the second game, too. Hirshberg does not provide the exact date, and some of what he says doesn't quite match, but these were the only two games in a doubleheader in Cleveland where Kinder appeared in both games, so it's our educated guess that this is when it all occurred.

1946 Umpire Red Jones "berated" White Sox pitcher Joe Haynes for "an alleged effort to hit Ted Williams with a bean ball" in the third inning, according to the *Chicago Tribune*. Haynes was furious, and the White Sox bench jockeys started chirping that Jones was playing to Fenway's Ladies' Day crowd "by electing himself as guardian of Ted's safety." Ralph Hodgin was the first Chicago player to be chased, followed in succession by Dario Lodigiani, Edgar Smith, and coach Bing Miller. Next came Leo Wells. "The attack on Jones was said not to be profane or obscene," wrote the *Tribune*. The worst word used was reportedly "meat head," but Jones walked over to the visitors' dugout and banished Mike Tresh, Johnny Rigney, Hal Trosky, Guy Curtright, Eddie Lopat, Whitey Platt, Frank Whitman, Wally Moses, and Glen Liebhardt.

1942 Pitcher Mike Ryba strapped on the "tools of ignorance" and caught both halves of a doubleheader against Cleveland, appearing at the end of the first game but catching the whole second game. As it happened, Boston lost both games, 10–7 and 4–0.

1933 Wes Ferrell was pitching for Cleveland. Rick Ferrell was catching for Boston. Wes hit a homer off Sox starter Hank Johnson, and Rick hit one, too. It was the first time two brothers on opposing teams had homered in the same game—and Rick's homer came off his brother Wes. The Indians won the game in the 13th inning, when Sox first baseman "Suitcase Bob" Seeds threw the ball wildly, allowing a run to score.

1932 Sox left fielder Smead Jolley misjudged Cleveland pitcher Wes Ferrell's fly ball to left, and ran all the way up the grassy incline known as Duffy's Cliff, which used to serve as warning track at Fenway. He realized then that he'd gone too far, turned to come back, but tripped and tumbled back down as the ball dropped in safely. Boston's offense was inept as well; Ferrell held the Sox to four hits and won, 7–0.

1919 The reigning champions of the world were mired in seventh place. The team issued a statement over the signatures of "virtually every member of the team" denying that it was due to dissension or mismanagement. Manager Ed Barrow was said to have "treated his players in a manner that could not be improved upon." Owner Frazee said he would trade away Carl Mays, who was not amongst the signers, having quit the team on July 13.

1918 A busy man at first base was Stuffy McInnis, with 21 putouts and one assist; Bill Sweeney tied McInnis's record on June 24, 1931.

Secretary of War Newton D. Baker declared that baseball was a "non-essential occupation." Consequently, a large number of Red Sox and other players would serve in the service or enroll to work in shipyards, and the 1918 season would be brought to an end by September 1.

1917 The second-place Red Sox were pressing league-leading Chicago, and crept closer with Babe Ruth's 3–2 win. First baseman Del Gainer "took all the joy out of life," hitting a two-run homer in the top of the first into Comiskey's left-field bleachers. Boston added a third run on a bloop double by Larry Gardner and Harry Hooper's single.

1909 Though he had a league-leading 81 errors the year before, Cleveland Naps shortstop Neal Ball pulled off the first unassisted triple play in modern baseball in the top of the second inning against the visiting Red Sox. Boston had Heinie Wagner on second and Jake Stahl on first. Cy Young was pitching for Cleveland. Batting with a 3–2 count, it was a hit-and-run play when Sox second baseman Amby McConnell hit a line drive right to Ball, who stepped on second and tagged the oncoming Stahl. In the bottom half of the inning, Ball drove a ball to deep center for an inside-the-park home run, his first AL roundtripper. With nine putouts on the day, he had three more than either the first baseman or the catcher. Cleveland won 6–1, but Boston took the day's second game, 3–2.

1906 With a record of 19–61 at the time of the announcement, the team might have wanted to try anything to bring people to the ballpark. Any boy 18 or younger wearing a baseball uniform of any sort was offered free admission to the Huntington Avenue Grounds for the July 19 game. Nearly 4,000 boys turned out, and even those without uniforms were admitted. Three turned up in bathing costumes. Boston (and Cy Young) lost to Detroit, 6–1.

TRANSACTIONS
1927: Released southpaw Rudy Sommers.
2005: Acquired Adam Hyzdu back from the Padres (see March 22, 2005) in exchange for Scott Cassidy. It was Hyzdu's fourth stint with the Red Sox organization dating back to Trenton (1996) and Pawtucket (1997). Acquired Tony Graffanino from the Kansas City Royals for nonroster OF Chip Ambres and LHP Juan Cedeno.

DEBUTS
1909: Ray Collins
1937: Tommy Thomas
1958: Bud Byerly
1998: Keith Mitchell
1999: Tomokazu Ohka, Marino Santana

BIRTHDATES
Joe Kiefer 1899 (1925–1926); Billy Gardner 1927 (1962–1963); Keith Johns 1971 (1998)

DEATHS
Sam Agnew 1951; Len Swormstedt 1964

July 20

2000 Pursuant to his July 15 bumping of umpire Ron Kulpa, Carl Everett is handed a 10-game suspension. Rather than be contrite, Everett instead attempts to assign blame to the media.

1991 Such symmetry. The Twins scored twice in the first, once in the fifth, and twice in the ninth. The Red Sox posted zeroes across the board, despite nine hits, and lost to Scott Erickson, 5–0.

1987 Tommy Harper wished he could go back to work in baseball. In December 1985, Harper was fired by the Red Sox. He had been serving as a minor league hitting instructor. He argued that he was fired for speaking out against discriminatory practices by the Red Sox, after he was interviewed by the *Boston Globe* in the springtime about how the Red Sox handed out passes to the whites-only Elks Club in Winter Haven, Florida. In July 1986, the U.S. Equal Opportunity Commission agreed with Harper that his firing had been retaliatory. A December 1986 settlement was reached, but Harper was still working at an auto body shop near Fenway, for UPS, and running summer baseball clincs for the Parks Department of the City of Boston. Many years later, Harper was rehired by the Red Sox.

1966 Darrell "Bucky" Brandon wins the first game of the day's doubleheader, a complete game two-hitter, but in striking out to close the second inning has now whiffed in seven consecutive at-bats.

1965 The Yankees took a slim 2–1 lead in the bottom of the fourth when Tony Kubek hit a two-run homer. In the fifth, Yankees pitcher Mel Stottlemyre came up with the bases loaded and nobody out. Bill Monbouquette was on the mound and had walked two batters, sandwiched around a safe bunt. Stottlemyre swung at Monbo's very first pitch and stroked the ball all the way to the fence in left-center for an inside-the-park grand slam, the first in over half a century (Deacon Phillippe hit one for the Pirates in 1910). New York won, 6–3.

1958 Jim Bunning struck out 12 Red Sox, and induced Ted Williams to fly out routinely to right for the final out in a 3–0 no-hitter. The Tigers and Red Sox played a second game, and this one pleased the Fenway fans more. Ike Delock improved his record to 10–0, with a 5–2 defeat of Detroit. After the game, Bunning received a note from Sox starter Frank Sullivan: "You were terrific all the way. I knew if I couldn't hit you, no one could hit you." Sullivan's lifetime average was .144. Bunning's feat marks the last time an opponent no-hit the Red Sox at Fenway. It had only been done four times in the park's nearly 100 year long history. The three earlier times were: August 21, 1926 (by Chicago's Ted Lyons), July 1, 1920 (by Washington's Walter Johnson), and April 24, 1917 (by New York's George Mogridge).

1956 The Red Sox sort of ruined Joe Cronin Hall of Fame Recognition Night by giving up 9 runs on 15 hits and losing to the Tigers, 9–6. Ted Williams further marred the evening after catching a fly to end the seventh, by throwing the ball high in the air, throwing his glove in the air, and spitting toward the press box. Cronin got a new car out of it, though, and a bunch of cash which he donated to the Jimmy Fund.

1955 Rookie pitcher George Susce Jr. gave up a single to the first batter he faced—Vic Power—but allowed no hits for the rest of the game, a 6–0 Sox shutout.

1913 Joe Jackson's long drive in the first inning bounced off the top of the fence and landed back in the field for a double, driving in the only run of the game for Cleveland. Had it bounded out, it would have meant two runs. The Red Sox won in the ninth, breaking a 1–1 tie after Ray Chapman fumbled an easy grounder by Boston's pitcher Ray Collins, who took second on a sacrifice and scored on Tris Speaker's single.

1904 Cy Young was hit hard and driven from the mound, as Cleveland routed Boston, 9–0. Young started 41 games in 1904 and pitched 40 complete games. This was the only start he failed to see through to completion. Relief pitching was not in vogue for Boston in 1904. Of 157 games played, 148 of them were complete games. The team only carried five pitchers all year long. They didn't need more; this squad posted a 2.12 earned run average.

TRANSACTIONS
1991: Released Mike Marshall.

DEBUTS
1914: Dick Hoblitzell
1926: Bill Clowers
1940: Earl Johnson
1958: Ted Bowsfield
1986: Calvin Schiraldi
1992: Paul Quantrill
2002: Dustin Hermanson
2005: Tony Graffanino

BIRTHDATES
Red Kleinow 1879 (1910–1911); Happy Foreman 1897 (1926); Heinie Manush 1901 (1936)

DEATHS
Bill O'Neill 1920; Tom Winsett 1987

July 21

2005 In the top of the ninth, Manny Ramirez fouled out to White Sox third baseman Joe Crede, who dropped the ball. On the very next pitch from Luis Vizcaino, Manny hit a solo home run that broke the 5–5 tie and gave the Red Sox the win. How often does a "second life" result in a game-winning homer? Not very. The Elias Sports Bureau said that the last time it happened was August 28, 1992, when Dan Gladden of the Tigers took advantage and beat the Angels, 4–2.

1991 It was clearly a lost cause, with the Twins humiliating the Red Sox, 14–1, after just six innings at Fenway Park. Manager Joe Morgan had a good sense of humor, and enjoys baseball trivia immensely, and he would have known that Steve Lyons had pitched a couple of innings for the White Sox in 1990. So he sent Ellis Burks out to play center field and asked "Psycho" Lyons to pitch the ninth. Psycho pitched better than Bolton, Morton, Lamp, or Fossas. He didn't let in a run, giving up two hits, and striking out Chuck Knoblauch. It was the eighth position Lyons had played in 1991; the only role he'd not yet played was behind the plate, though he had caught against the Cubs in spring training.

1988 Manager Joe Morgan asked Spike Owen to pinch-hit for slugger Jim Rice. Spike laid down a sacrifice bunt in the eighth to advance the baserunner, Ellis Burks. Rice got into it with Morgan and shoved him, but Morgan was not intimidated. The incident resulted in a three-game suspension for Boston's superstar Rice, and served notice that Morgan was in charge. The Twins tied the game with single runs in the eighth and ninth, and scored twice in the top of the 10th, but the Rice-less Red Sox scored four times in the bottom of the 10th, the last three on Todd Benzinger's home run scoring Owen and Reed. 9–7, Red Sox. Dan Shaughnessy snuck in a column, asking, "Why stop now? Why not bite the bullet and send Big Jim Ed packing?"

1985 Just two weeks to the day after catching Bobby Grich napping, Marty Barrett pulls off another hidden ball trick—the time with a twist. Maybe Doug DeCinces cast a wary eye on Barrett, but Marty wasn't near second base. Glenn Hoffman was, though, and Barrett flipped the hidden ball to Hoffman and DeCinces was tagged out.

1977 Luis Tiant recorded strikeout number 2,000 by getting Indians DH Rico Carty in the fourth inning. Butch Hobson lost the chance at a two-home run inning when the first ball he hit out was ruled to have bounced off the wall, though replays made it clear it had first hit the left-center field screen. He hit a three-run homer his second time up in the nine-run inning. It was the second time in 1977 that a Hobson homer was ruled a double; the same thing happened on May 28.

1961 Mickey Mantle and Roger Maris went back-to-back in the top of the first to give the Yankees an early 2–0 lead, but the Sox scored eight times and held an 8–6 lead heading into the ninth. Neither Whitey Ford nor Bill Monbouquette were pitching well at all. In the ninth, New York got one run, and then backup catcher Johnny Blanchard hit a pinch-hit grand slam to subdue the Sox, 11–8.

1959 The Red Sox lost the game, 2–1, to Chicago, but finally accomplished something long, long overdue. When Vic Wertz singled in the bottom of the eighth, Pumpsie Green was sent in to run for him. Green, who had just been called up earlier in the day from Boston's Minneapolis farm club, became—in the words of the *New York Times*—the "first Negro ever to play for the Red Sox, the last major league team to get a Negro on its roster." Pumpsie played shortstop in the ninth, and started at short the following day.

1954 After playing a 5–5 tie in 16 innings the day before (called due to curfew), the July 21 started off as a promising one for the Red Sox as they leapt out to a 6–0 lead after three innings. The Indians came back with seven runs. Boston scored once in the sixth to tie it up, but it was still knotted 7–7 in the ninth when the rains came and washed it out. It was the second tie for the Sox in two days.

1946 Williams was 3-for-4 with a double in the first game, but his first time up in the second game, Ted Williams hit a home run into the right field stands. Next time up, it was a triple off the bullpen wall in right. Adding a single and a double, it was Teddy Ballgame hitting for the cycle while Boo Ferriss shut out St. Louis. Ted struck out in the ninth inning, but Dobson and Klinger combined on a 7–4 Bosox win.

1935 One of the best-hitting pitchers ever, Wes Ferrell was sent up to pinch-hit for Lefty Grove with two outs in the ninth inning and the Red Sox trailing Tommy Bridges and the Tigers, 6–4. The Tigers seemed to put the game away with three runs off Grove in the top of the ninth, but—playing the percentages—the right-hander Ferrell was sent up to hit for Grove. Ferrell had already pitched against Bridges three times, and helped win each game with a homer off Bridges, so Mickey Cochrane called on Bridges to walk Wes. Bridges argued the point in a mound conference, and Cochrane relented. Wes hit Bridges' first pitch for a long home run over the left-field Wall to win the game. Grove got the W, but somehow it seems like it should have been Ferrell.

1932 After his professional career saw him the subject of 26 transactions in an eight-year stretch, the Red Sox signed Larry Boerner in June 1932. In his start against the Yankees, he threw two-hit ball through seven innings, but the Sox only scored the tying and winning runs in their 3–2 win after he'd left the game. In limited action, Boerner compiled a record of 0–4.

1928 It was "Ira Flagstead Day" at Fenway Park. Flaggy, in his sixth season with the Red Sox, was presented "$1,000 in gold and other presents" but went 1-for-8 on the day as Boston split a twin bill with Cleveland before 17,000 fans.

1925 Roy Carlyle hit for the cycle when the Red Sox visited Chicago. Carlyle tripled in a run in the first, doubled in the sixth, singled home another run in the seventh, and then homered off Chief Bender in the ninth, the ball carrying all the way to the top row of the right-field bleachers. Boston won, 6–3. Four of the runs were knocked in by Carlyle.

1917 Boston took a 5–4 lead over the White Sox in the top of the 14th, as Sox center fielder Jimmy Walsh tripled in Ruth, colliding hard with Buck Weaver at third on the play. Chicago fans nearly caused a forfeit after showering Walsh with pop bottles when he took the field for the bottom of the inning. After the debris was cleared, play resumed and the White Sox tied it back up. The game was called after 15 innings on account of darkness.

1915 RUTH HITS BETTER THAN HE PITCHES read the headline on the game story in the *Washington Post*. Ruth threw a five-hitter and won the game, 5–2, relieved by Joe Wood who came in to get the last two outs. Both runs were unearned, coming on errors by second baseman Heinie Wagner. At the plate, though, Ruth went 4-for-4, hitting "the longest home run ever witnessed" at the park in St. Louis, and doubling twice after that. He drove in three of Boston's five runs.

1913 Ty Cobb said it would "tickle him to death" if he had the chance to join the Red Sox. There had been rumors of Speaker-for-Cobb trade. Cobb said, "I wrote to a Boston newspaper man that I would like to be traded to the Red Sox, or to one of two other clubs."

1909 Red Sox catcher Ed "Tubby" Spencer deserted the team about two weeks earlier, saying he was going to California to join the outlaws' league. The *Washington Post* supposed he went home to Scranton instead, and that his father talked him into rejoining the Red Sox.

TRANSACTIONS
1959: Bobby Avila was selected by the Milwaukee Braves off waivers.
2004: Acquired Ricky Gutierrez from the Chicago Cubs for a PTBNL or cash considerations.

DEBUTS
1928: Steve Slayton   1967: Norm Siebern
1951: Al Evans   1970: Carmen Fanzone
1959: Pumpsie Green

BIRTHDATES
Larry Pape 1883 (1909–1912); Howie Shanks 1890 (1923–1924); Billy Holm 1912 (1945); Gary Waslewski 1941 (1967–1968); Dave Henderson 1958 (1986–1987)

DEATHS
Larry Pape 1918; Hugh Bedient 1965; Jimmie Foxx 1967

July 22

2005 The Boston Red Sox filed the first part of an application with the National Park Service to have Fenway Park granted landmark status on the National Register of Historic Places. The status would help the Red Sox benefit from significant tax advantages as they pour up to $200 million into a decade-long renovation to Fenway Park and the surrounding area. The move was ironic because preservationist groups had sought landmark status for Fenway as a defensive move, to prevent the park from being sold or demolished when previous ownership had announced plans to leave Fenway and build another facility.

2004 Left-handed pitcher Abe Alvarez started the day's game, and became the only left-hander to start any one of the 162 regular-season games played by the 2004 World Champion Red Sox. Alvarez has a further distinction: he is legally blind in his left eye. He didn't pitch well and the Sox lost, 8–3, but he had a taste of The Show and remained a top prospect.

2002 A celebration of the life of Ted Williams was held at Fenway Park, attended by some 20,000. On his way home from the event, longtime but retired broadcaster Ned Martin passed away.

1994 An unscheduled, unexpected four-game series with the Seattle Mariners began at Fenway Park. The games would have been played in Seattle, but structural problems at the Kingdome resulted in that facility being closed for repairs and the game moved to Fenway by mutual consent. The Sox put the last-minute tickets on sale at old-fashioned prices: $10 for a grandstand seat. Home field advantage may not have counted for much; Boston lost the first game, 6–3, with Seattle's Randy Johnson out-pitching Aaron Sele.

1972 There's something about these day-night doubleheaders, once called "Branch Rickey specials." By having two admissions, the Red Sox were able to accommodate 59,346 paying customers. Those who came to the first game saw the Sox lose, 5–3, but they did see Yaz hit his first home run of the season—it had been an 85-game drought! Those who attended the second game saw Sonny Siebert shut out Oakland, 3–0.

1962 Chicago White Sox batter Floyd Robinson had a record-tying 6-for-6 day—every hit a single "slashed, tolled, and blooped to all sectors of Fenway Park." (*Chicago Tribune*) The other White Sox added 11 more hits, and out-scored Boston, 7–3.

1961 For the second time in less than 24 hours, New York's Johnny Blanchard was called on to pinch-hit in the ninth inning. With two outs, he jumped on Gene Conley's first pitch and drove it into the seats in right, tying the score, 9–9. Luis Arroyo, New York's pitcher, also swung at the first pitch, and doubled. Bobby Richardson singled and Tony Kubek doubled—both of them connecting on Conley's first pitches as well. Four pitches, three runs, and the Yankees had an 11–9 lead they retained.

1960 There it is, in the boxscore: SB—Williams. Ted homered in the game, though Vic Wertz's three-run homer and four RBIs were a bigger part of the 6–4 Boston victory. It was when Ted stole second base in the seventh inning, though, that he created another piece of baseball trivia: the only ballplayer to steal at least one base in each of four decades. It wasn't until 40 years later that Ted had to share the record, with Rickey Henderson and Tim Raines.

1950 Citing illness, manager Joe McCarthy left the team, replaced by Steve O'Neill. The Red Sox got a complete game win from Mickey McDermott, 11–2. It was their 12th win in the last 13 outings with St. Louis. Ted Williams sat on the bench and cheered on his teammates, after having five of the 10 stitches in his arm removed in the clubhouse. Ed Walton reports that McDermott fielded a passed ball which nonetheless struck out a St. Louis batter, and threw to first base to get the out, earning himself an assist in the process.

1948 Boston won the first game, 3–0, behind Denny Galehouse. Red Jones got into it again (see July 19, 1946) with Chicago; the umpire tossed four players from the ballgame which was tied at the time, 3–3. Irving Vaughan of the *Chicago Tribune* said that Jones had made "an obviously bum decision" and summarily tossed out the Chicagoans before umpire Bill Summers interceded, "shoving his associate back to where he belonged." Vaughan was offended by Jones, and this was reflected in the *Tribune*'s headline on the jump: UMPIRE AND BOSTON BEAT SOX TWICE. Boston scored two more runs, and won, 5–3. Vern Stephens hit home runs in both games. Ellis Kinder won the second game, and also his next 17 decisions against the White Sox.

1945 The war in Europe over, the Sox game sells out as fans see Boo Ferriss win #17 on the season, 3–2 over the Browns.

1942 Ted Williams was assessed a $250.00 fine for "loafing" by manager Joe Cronin.

1935 Wes Ferrell had a pinch-hit home run the day before, winning the game for the Red Sox. Today he did it again—another walkoff, high over Fenway's left-field Wall. This time it broke a 1–1 tie, and this time Ferrell got the win. The Red Sox would not win back-to-back games on walkoff homers again until May 10 and 11, 2005. And those weren't by the same player. Nor were they by a pitcher.

1924 The old Picinich–Wambsganss combo did the trick. After losing nine games in a row, the Red Sox were lucky to tie this one in the bottom of the ninth scoring twice on Val Picinich's home run to make it 3–3. They won it in the 11th when Wambsganss poked an infield single with two outs and the bases loaded.

1918 Bullet Joe Bush won his league-record fifth 1–0 shutout of the season, beating the Tigers. He also lost two 1–0 games. In all, the Red Sox won seven 1–0 games in 1918, and 23 one-run games in all.

1915 In an era when even one relief pitcher was not an everyday occurrence, the Sox used three pitchers and the Browns used four, despite the score only running 7–3 in favor of the Red Sox. Foster started, but Carl Mays pitched from the second through the eighth for the Red Sox. Boston scored three times in the top of the ninth, and even faced first baseman George Sisler who came in to get the final out—though Smoky Joe Wood stroked a single off him before he could do so.

1913 Recently-fired manager Jake Stahl was more of a martyr than a scapegoat, as rumors about the Red Sox continued. The team was still losing, always a bad sign, and word was that the Taylors were ready to wrest leadership from club president McAleer.

1909 Mexican-American pitcher Frank Arellanes started for Boston, but the Tigers were getting to him too easily, so Wolter was installed instead. The Tigers won handily, 6–0, but the most interesting feature of the game was the Georgia Peach, Ty Cobb, who stole four bases in the game—and, in the seventh inning, stole second base, third base, and home plate. It was the first time he'd ever stolen home, but three more times he completed the hat trick, stealing all three bases in one inning.

1902 Here it was still July, and Cy Young won his 20th game of the season, beating Chicago, 4–1, almost half of Boston's 41 wins on the year.

TRANSACTIONS
2003: Traded Brandon Lyon and Anastacio Martinez to the Pittsburgh Pirates
    for Scott Sauerbeck and Mike Gonzalez. See also July 31, 2003.
1972: The Sox signed another player named Williams. Stan.
1930: Purchased Harold "Rabbit" Warstler from Indianapolis
    for a combination of players and cash.

DEBUTS
1918: Paul Musser
1985: Tim Lollar
2004: Abe Alvarez, Ricky Gutierrez

BIRTHDATES
Doc Cramer 1905 (1936–1940); Sparky Lyle 1944 (1967–1971)

DEATHS
Bill Narleski 1964; Amos Strunk 1979; Don McMahon 1987

July 23

2002 The Tampa Bay pitching staff gave Nomar Garciaparra three gifts for his 29th birthday in the form of two two-run homers in the 10-run third inning (off Sturtze and Backe) and a third one in the fourth (again off Backe). Nomar tied a major league record with five homers in two games. The Red Sox took the gift-wrapped game, 22–4. After a 2:13 rain delay held up the day's second game, the atmosphere had changed. It was looking good, with the Sox hold a 4–0 lead heading into the ninth, but Chris Haney and Ugueth Urbina combined to give up five runs and the game.

2000 Behind Pedro Martinez, the Red Sox defeat the White Sox, 1–0. Martinez goes the distance, striking out 15 and not walking a batter.

Carlton Fisk is inducted into the National Baseball Hall of Fame in Cooperstown. Fisk caught more games than any other Red Sox catcher (990) and had more putouts than any other (5,111).

1994 The first single-admission doubleheader since July 16, 1978 was brought about because of the last-minute scheduling of a series with Seattle at Fenway (see July 22, 1994). The whole affair lasted over nine hours, complete with three rain delays. Boston won the first game, 6–5, but lost the second (in 11 innings), 6–3. The Sox won the July 24 game, 8–2, for a split of the four games.

1991 What was it about #308? *The Baseball Chronology* notes that Nolan Ryan notched win #308 and Rich Gossage garnered career save #308, both in the same 5–4 defeat of the Red Sox.

1979 It was already Angels 9, Red Sox 0— but the Sox salvaged some sense of dignity with a triple play in the eighth, when The Rooster (Rick Burleson) converted Willie Mays Aikens' liner into a trio of outs. Burleson's .980 fielding average led all shortstops, and the Gold Glove he won in 1979 is the last ever won by any Red Sox infielder.

1977 Reggie Cleveland took Fenway's mound against the Cleveland Indians and faced four batters: Duane Kuiper singled, Buddy Bell tripled, Larvell Blanks doubled, and Andre Thornton homered. Cleveland the team had cycled against Cleveland the pitcher and the game was only four batters old. The game was over for Cleveland the pitcher, though. He was replaced by Mike Paxton. Final: Cleveland the team 9, Red Sox 8.

1967 During a doubleheader in Cleveland, Tony Conigliaro hit two home runs—#100 and #101 of his career. At age 22, he was the youngest player in history to reach the 100-homer mark. The Sox swept the doubleheader, and completed a 10-game road winning streak. Heading home, just one-half game out of first place, the team was met by an estimated 10,000 fans at Boston's Logan Airport.

1960 Ted Williams had homered off Jim Perry earlier in the game, as had Willie Tasby, and Cleveland was clinging to a 4–2 lead after four innings. When Ted Williams came up to bat in the eighth, Indians center fielder Jimmy Piersall took it upon himself to try and distract Ted by "dashing back and forth in the outfield while Williams was batting" (UPI). Umpire Ed Hurley ejected him, and Piersall erupted, having to be restrained by Vic Power. He argued that he had a right to change his position. Apparently, he changed his position repeatedly, and in rapid succession. The Red Sox won, and Piersall was later assessed a $100 fine by AL president Joe Cronin.

1957 In what many consider his greatest season, 39-year-old Ted Williams began a 17-game hitting streak over which he would average .533.

1948 The Red Sox followed back-to-back doubleheaders with a 13–1 fifth game victory for a five-game sweep of the White Sox. Ted Williams, back after being out 15 days with torn cartilage, singled and doubled (and walked, too) in five trips to the plate. The Sox won 13 of the 15 games that Williams missed.

1947 In the third straight extra-inning game between the two Sox teams, Chicago was visiting Boston and trying to hold the line in the bottom of the 14th inning. Doerr singled and stole second without drawing a throw. He moved up to third on a fielder's choice. The White Sox then issued two intentional walks to load the bases. Don Gutteridge came up to pinch-hit for Hughson, and Chicago countered with Earl Caldwell on the mound. The one thing the White Sox weren't expecting was the squeeze bunt, but Gutteridge executed it so perfectly that no White Sox player even touched the ball before Doerr crossed the plate.

1941 Whe first reported deployment of a "Williams Shift" occurred at Fenway, when White Sox manager Jimmy Dykes shifted his fielders to the right side of the field. Ted went 2-for-5, with a double to left as one of his two hits.

1933 Alejandro V. Martinez, the Mexican consul in Los Angeles, helped host "Melo Almada Day" at Wrigley Field, Los Angeles, to celebrate the signing of Almada to the Red Sox. September 8, 1933 became the date of Almada's debut. Almada traced his ancestry back to Don Alvaro Vaz de Almada, Count of Abranches, who died in 1449. Descended from conquistadors, his father was offered an ambassadorship to France but declined, accepting the post of consul in Los Angeles in 1914. His son Melo thus moved to southern California at the age of one, and learned baseball as a child.

The Red Sox installed a buffet lunch area in the press room, with draught beer and sandwiches for the hard-working writers, who immediately rated the Red Sox as champions in the American League.

1922 Another trade with the Yankees brought forth comment from the Boston press, with Burt Whitman of the *Herald* writing, "Apparently whenever the Yanks find themselves up against it...all they need to do is make an offer to the Red Sox and presto, a good player, or several, comes from Boston and an inferior man joins the Red Sox." Sox fans were beaten down by "Big Hearted Harry" [Frazee], wrote W. C. Spargo in the *Traveler*, saying the common reaction had become, "What difference does it make?" (See also July 26.)

1912 Smoky Joe improved to 20–4 on the season by beating Cleveland, 6–3; although he was hit hard, he "tightened in the pinches." (*Chicago Tribune*) Red Sox catcher Hick Cady frustrated an attempted steal of home plate by leaping out in front of the batter to grab the pitch; the umpire sent the baserunner back to third and awarded first base to the batter.

1905 A team from Michigan (Detroit) played a team from Massachusetts (Boston), but what was unusual was that they played the regular season game in Columbus, Ohio. Boston won 6–1. There were two games played in Ohio's capitol; the games were deemed home games for Detroit, but Boston won them both. News accounts indicate nothing by way of brushbacks, though Detroit's catcher was named Drill.

1903 Boston played two in New York, winning the first one 6–1 but losing the second, 4–2. Cy Young won the first game, letting up seven hits without a walk. New York scored its one run in the fifth, but the run was bracketed by four goose eggs on both sides of the line score. Dougherty and Collins each had a brace of doubles, and while Boston scored, it wasn't until late in the game—one run to tie in the sixth, another to go ahead in the seventh, and four insurance runs in the ninth. Deering had departed Detroit and was now pitching for the Highlanders, only letting Boston have four hits. Boston held a 1–0 lead until the bottom of the sixth, when New York tied it. New York got three more runs in the eighth, which came in handy as Boston bounced back with one (but only one) in the top of the ninth.

1902 Bill Dinneen threw a complete 13-inning game against Frank Donahue and the St. Louis Browns, a 3–2 Boston win on a Collins single, sacrifice, and a line-hugging ball hit by Buck Freeman between the Browns' first baseman and the bag.

TRANSACTIONS

1922: Traded Joe Dugan and Elmer Smith to the New York Yankees for Chick Fewster, Elmer Miller, Johnny Mitchell, Lefty O'Doul, and $50,000 cash.
1946: Purchased Wally Moses from the Chicago White Sox.
1987: Released Bill Buckner.
1996: Acquired Arquimedez Pozo from Seattle for Jeff Manto.
2000: Signed free agent Sean Berry; he was released on August 10.

DEBUTS

1972: Stan Williams
2003: Scott Sauerbeck

BIRTHDATES

Ray Scarborough 1917 (1951–1952); Strick Shofner 1919
(1947); Nomar Garciaparra 1973 (1996–2004)

DEATHS

Rip Williams 1933; Wally Snell 1980

July 24

2004 Mariano Rivera had successfully converted 23 consecutive save opportunities, but Boston third baseman Bill Mueller hit a three-run homer off Rivera in the bottom of the ninth inning and won the game for the Red Sox, 11–10. Earlier in the game, both benches emptied and punches were thrown, after Boston's Bronson Arroyo hit Alex Rodriguez with a pitch and A-Rod took offence, leading to a little jostling with Jason Varitek, who wound up shoving his glove into Rodriguez's face. Some argue that this was the moment the Red Sox became energized and began to turn the season around.

2001 David Cone won his sixth, for a 6–1 record, and Derek Lowe saved his 20th, as the Sox scored early and held on for a 6–4 win over the Blue Jays at Fenway.

2000 Sean Berry had some good years, but was a short-lived bust for Boston. He only appeared in one game, went 0-for-3—and then was called out on strikes to end the ballgame.

1999 Mark Portugal started and got the win, greatly helped by Trot Nixon, who hit home runs in the second, fourth, and eighth innings, and drove in five RBIs. Nomar hit two homers, and Daubach and O'Leary each hit one, too. 11–4, Boston beat the Tigers.

1995 Though sporting a 10–1 record with a miniscule 1.63 ERA, Tim Wakefield disputed any notion that he'd taken over from Roger Clemens as the ace of the Red Sox pitching staff. "I just don't think you can put a knuckleballer as the ace of any staff," Wake averred. "I've been at both ends of the spectrum, and I'm just trying to stay in the middle and stay humble."

1979 Boston and Oakland were tied 3–3, when Carl Yastrzemski hit a two-run homer in the seventh inning. It was the 400th home run of Yaz's career. He drove in another run with a first-inning single, and needed just 40 more hits to become the first player in major league history to record both 400 homers and 3,000 hits. Eckersley got the win, 7–3.

1961 Jackie Jensen tied a 4–2 game with a two-run homer in the sixth, then won it 5–4 with a solo home run in the 10th. After the game, though, the Red Sox were set to fly to Los Angeles and Jensen's fear of flying caused him to ground himself. Instead he took the train to join the team once they arrived in Kansas City from L.A. Jensen was not paid for the games he missed.

1953 Bill Henry shut out the Browns, 8–0, and Mickey McDermott shut them out again, 6–0. With the twin shutouts, St. Louis had now not recorded a run for 25 innings—and had only gotten two runners as close as third base in that whole stretch. Bill Henry drove in two runs with a triple in the first game.

1943 Red Sox pitcher Oscar Judd slammed a line drive off Browns pitcher Bobo Newsom's forehead, but Newsom kept pitching after brief treatment in the St. Louis dugout. That was maybe not a good idea. When he returned to the mound, it was a Bobo-Skeeter matchup as Newsom faced Newsome. Newsome singled, and then Catfish Metkovich homered. After the inning, Newsom left the game; he also took the loss.

1930 Outfielder Earl Webb goes 4-for-4, with a double and a homer, three RBIs, and makes two double plays from the outfield. A subhead in *The Sporting News* once proclaimed that Webb "took up baseball to regain health he lost as 12-year-old miner." Young Earl started full-time in the Ravenscroft, Tennessee mine at age 11, working 10 hours a day for five cents per hour. After more than a year working in the mine as a trapper, the mine doctors urged him to get some outdoors exercise.

1926 The Red Sox routed the Browns, 14–8, in the first game, but the Browns really didn't want to miss the train to Cleveland, so the second game was stopped, 5–5, when the Red Sox managed to score two runs and tie it at the very last minute, in the bottom of the ninth.

1922 Red Sox trade premier third baseman Joe Dugan and outfielder Elmer Smith to the Yankees for pitcher Frank "Lefty" O'Doul, shortstop John Mitchell and outfielders Elmer Miller and Chick Fewster. Other teams are upset by the Red

Sox supplying the Yankees with such a big boost in the midst of a competitive pennant race, and this trade prompts Commissioner Landis to institute a trading deadline for earlier in the season (June 15).

1909 Fred Burchell (3–3 on the season with the Red Sox) was sold to Buffalo, but vowed he would not report. In 1903, he'd similarly refused to report when the Phillies sold him, but he'd come back for parts of three seasons with Boston (starting 19 games in '08). He said he didn't need the money, and this time he apparently meant it.

1906 In a year when they won 49 and lost 105, to sweep a doubleheader was pretty astonishing. They did it once against New York in April, and then again on July 24, Young and Tannehill beating third-place Cleveland handily, 5–1 and 9–2.

1905 Playing the rare major league games in Columbus, Ohio, Boston beat Detroit behind Cy Young on July 23, and Bill Dinneen, 7–1, on the 24th. Hobe Ferris hit a homer, but most of the runs came in the five-run third inning; Detroit's defense made four or five errors (boxscores differ) in the game.

1901 They got in a full nine innings, though newspaper reports said that by the sixth inning "it was so dark that the players could hardly see the ball." That may be part of why Lou Criger was beaned and unconscious for several minutes. The umpire, Mr. Sheridan, insisted on continuing. Boston right fielder Charlie "Eagle Eye" Hemphill muffed a ball in the third, and two Milwaukee runs scored. Boston lost, 4–3.

TRANSACTIONS
1952: Signed free agent Ken Holcombe.
1963: Signed free agent Bob Turley.
1978: Purchased Andy Hassler from the Kansas City Royals.
1995: Acquired Dave Hollins from the Phillies in trade for Mark Whiten.
1996: Signed Jack Cressend as an amateur free agent.
2004: Acquired Terry Adams from the Toronto Blue Jays for minor leaguer John Hatti and cash consideration.

DEBUTS
1930: Rabbit Warstler   1998: David West
1978: Andy Hassler   2000: Sean Berry

BIRTHDATES
Bob Adams 1901 (1925); Al Flair 1916 (1941); Joe Oliver 1965 (2001); Shawn Wooten 1972 (2005)

DEATHS
None yet

July 25

2005 The Red Sox set a major league record by playing the first 98 games of the season without getting into an extra-inning game. In game 99, the Tampa Bay Devil Rays tied it up in the bottom of the seventh. The Sox had scoring opportunities in the top of the ninth, but couldn't get a run across. Worse, they lost the game in the bottom of the 10th. Their last extra-inning game had also been against Tampa Bay, at Tropicana Field, on September 28, 2004, with 103 contests in between the 10–8 win in 2004 and the 4–3 loss in 2005.

1999 Why can't the Red Sox get players like this? Tony the Detroit Tiger Clark hit a three-run homer batting left-handed in the sixth inning. When he came up again the next inning, he turned around and batted right-handed and hit another homer. It was the second time in 1999 that the switch-hitting Clark homered from both sides of the plate. Brian Rose took the loss, final score 9–1. Oh, wait... the Red Sox did a player like that? The Sox signed Tony Clark himself in 2002; unfortunately, he only hit .207, with just three home runs.

1990 They say it's a game of inches. Carlos Quintana hit a two-run homer off the County Stadium right-field foul pole and that's all that Roger Clemens needed. He threw a three-hit shutout, beating Milwaukee, 2–0.

1988 The Red Sox won their first 12 games under new manager Joe Morgan. It was "Morgan Magic"—but tonight's 2–0 three-hitter by Roger Clemens marked the last win. The Rangers won the next night, but it took them 11 innings to do so. The Sox then won their next seven. Losing one out of 19 ain't bad.

1969 Russ Gibson's three-run pinch-hit homer in the eighth inning gave the Sox sufficient edge for a 7–6 win over the Seattle Pilots. There was a Red Sox homer that was painful for the home team, though. Tony Conigliaro hit his 14th home run of the year in the third inning, and wrenched his back in the process. *The Baseball Chronology* reported, "The injury forces him to walk slowly around the bases before being replaced."

1966 Ted Williams is inducted into the Hall of Fame and gives a moving speech from his own handwritten notes. The speech is most noted for its appeal that the great Negro League players such as Josh Gibson and Satchel Paige also be honored with induction into the Hall of Fame.

1954 Edward Prell of the *Chicago Tribune* termed it "the most brilliant White Sox pitching performance since 1920, when Charley Robertson hurled the last perfect game." Jack Harshman struck out 16 Boston batters, and won, 5–2. He had 15 K's after seven innings, but only threw four pitches in the eighth as the Red Sox grounded out three times on infield rollers. Chicago took both games at Fenway, winning the second game, 4–2.

1948 In Boston, the "other DiMaggio" made two spectacular catches against the Indians and homered off Satchel Paige. Bobby Doerr drove in the other two with a long triple to right center, as the Red Sox beat Cleveland, 3–0. They'd now won 15 of their last 16 games, and sat atop the standings, percentage points ahead of three other teams.

1941 Robert Moses "Lefty" Grove, age 41, stayed the course, pitching a complete game while the Red Sox offense overcame a 6–4 deficit with two runs in the seventh and four more in the eighth. It was Grove's 300th win. "The thrill of a lifetime? This is it!," he declared after the game. It was also Grove's last win. He started six more games, but couldn't get another "W."

1936 Two innings made all the difference, as the Red Sox scored six times in the second inning, then doubled that with 12 runs in the fifth. With 20 hits in all, the Red Sox shredded the Tigers, 18–3.

The head of the American League filed a complaint with the FCC against radio station WMCA in New York, alleging that the practice of broadcasting "off-scene" versions of Red Sox, Yankees, and Athletics baseball games was "piracy" and that the station should have its license revoked. WMCA's attorney claimed the FCC had no jurisdiction because the station was broadcasting "versions" of the games in effect dramatized recreations of the game as read by an announcer who typically ran about one inning behind actual play.

1916 Tris Speaker teed off on former Boston teammate Babe Ruth, with three hits, driving in three runs. Ruth had a couple of hits, too, and drove in a pair. Cleveland won, 5–4, on the strength of three eighth-inning runs. Speaker figured in all five Tribe tallies.

1915 The first game was a high-scoring 9–8 win for the Browns, who scored four unearned runs off starter Babe Ruth and a number of runs off reliever Carl Mays as well. The day's second game ended in a 1–1 tie after nine innings, the game called due to darkness. George Sisler pitched yet again, as he had on the 22nd, this time throwing two scoreless innings.

1908 Future Red Sox pitcher Hugh Bedient (1912–1914) struck out 42 (!) batters in a July 25 ballgame. Clearly, the game lasted more than nine innings. In fact, it ran 23 innings. Bedient went the distance, pitching for a Falconer, New York, semipro team, winning the game, 3–1, over valiant opponent Charles Bickford, who also threw a complete game for the Corry, Pennsylvania, team (striking out 16). Corry only marshaled six hits, and Falconer only had 10.

1907 Boston out-hit Detroit twice, but the Tigers won both games in Boston, 2–1 and 3–2. Boston manager Deacon McGuire sent in a pinch-hitter for his starter, Tex Pruiett; he sent in himself. McGuire hit a home run off Detroit starter Ed Siever, tying the game in the bottom of the ninth. The Tigers took it in 11. McGuire hit his first major league home run for the Toledo Blue Stockings of the National League back in 1884, some 23 years earlier. The 43-year-old McGuire, who played for a record 12 teams, became the oldest player to hit a pinch home run.

1903 This game looked like it was over in the second inning when New York posted a "5" off Winter. Boston battled back with one in the third, another in the fifth and when they scored four times off Tannehill in the sixth, Collins asked Cy Young to close out the game for them, holding them scoreless in the final four frames. Buck Freeman and Freddy Parent each had a pair of two-baggers.

TRANSACTIONS
2005: Signed pitcher Craig Hansen to a four-year contract.

DEBUTS
1902: Tully Sparks   1987: Sam Horn
1922: Johnny Mitchell   1996: Arquimedez Pozo
1928: Marty Griffin   1997: Brian Rose
1946: Don Gutteridge   2004: Terry Adams
1970: Chuck Hartenstein

BIRTHDATES
Marc Sullivan 1958 (1982–1987); Ed Sprague 1967 (2000)

DEATHS
Frank Welch 1957; Buck O'Brien 1959; Herb Hunter 1970; Al Flair 1988

July 26

2005 The day after their first extra-inning game of the year, center fielder Johnny Damon leapt and caught a ball in the bottom of the ninth to prevent a Tampa Bay win, then homered on the very first pitch he saw in the top of the 10th, which proved the game-winner. The game was packed full of unusual plays and oddities, but Boston prevailed, 10–8.

1998 Nomar Garciaparra's seventh-inning three-run inside-the-park homer into the right-field corner keyed the Sox to a 6–3 win over the Blue Jays. Jose Canseco homered off Derek Lowe in the top of the eighth, giving him home run #380, tops at the time among foreign-born hitters. Soon Sammy Sosa would far outpace Canseco.

1996 These were aces? Brad Radke was pitching for the Twins, with a record of 5–13, and Roger Clemens was not having a good year for the Red Sox (4–9). The Twins scored three times off Clemens and dealt him the loss in a 5–1 game. Clemens sank to a 4–10 record and seemed to be in the twilight of a great career.

1993 Tom Brunansky, with the Brewers after nearly three seasons with the Red Sox, was not faring well, batting just .175, but entered the game as a last-chance pinch-hitter with two outs in the bottom of the ninth. He was facing Jeff Russell of the Red Sox, who was riding an eight-game save streak. The Sox themselves had a 10-game winning streak going. Brunansky hit an 0–1 pitch out of the park, winning the game, 3–2, and driving the Red Sox out of first place.

1987 Sam Horn joins Dave Stapleton as the only Sox to have two home runs in his first two games.

1985 Wade Boggs struck out twice, walked once, and flied out deep, but his 0-for-3 day put an end to his 28-game hitting streak, the longest one in major league ball for five years. Halted halfway to Joe DiMaggio's record, Boggs had hit in every game from June 24 to July 26. "It's not the end of the world, thank God," Boggs said. Meanwhile, in Cooperstown, Armand LaMontagne's statue of Ted Williams was unveiled.

1964 Tony Conigliaro hit a homer in Boston's 6–1 win over the Indians, then had his arm broken in the second game. He got in Dutch a little with manager Johnny Pesky, too, as reflected in the *Los Angeles Times* headline: CONIGLIARO BREAKS ARM, CURFEW—FINED $250. It was Tony's third curfew violation. Hit by a Pedro Ramos pitch, his right forearm was fractured.

1962 The Yankees scored eight runs in the third inning as they beat Boston, 13–3, at Yankee Stadium. Knocked out of the box was starting pitcher Gene Conley, charged with all eight earned runs in 2⅔ innings. Two of them were runs he walked in. It'd be enough to drive a man to drink.

The story continues. Later in the day, Conley and Pumpsie Green got thirsty as the team bus was stuck in traffic waiting to go through the tunnel out of Manhattan, disembarked to use a rest room—and didn't come back. Green showed up sheepishly a day later. Conley turned up at the airport, wanting to fly to Israel, but was denied boarding since he had no visa. Conley was suspended without pay, and finally showed up at his trailer home in Foxboro on the 30th, saying, "I'm mostly tired and have other plans." His plans changed yet again, though, and he rejoined the Red Sox.

1951 Neither team scored after the sixth, but Clyde Vollmer's three-run homer in the bottom of the sixth pulled the Red Sox up 13–10 over visiting Chicago. Vollmer helped get them to the sixth, with earlier home runs in the first and fifth.

1948 The Red Sox are in first place and so are the Braves. It's the first time since 1916. Except for one October playoff game, they would have played each other in the '48 World Series.

1936 Both brothers doubled. Rick and Wes Ferrell each have a double, Rick driving in a run, but it wasn't one of Wes's better games; he gave up 13 hits, walked five, and hit a batter. Still, the Tigers left 14 men on base. The more efficient Red Sox, despite the same hit total, greatly outscored Detroit, 10–3. Two Jimmie Foxx homers helped, as did Mel Almada's.

At one point in the game, Heinie Manush was so angered at being robbed of a seemingly sure base hit that he flung his bat in front of the dugout. Unfortunately, it hopped into the box seats and struck his daughter. She likely forgave him, but league president Harridge fined Manush $25 (though told him he would refund the money if Manush was good for the rest of the season).

1933 Under rules not changed until the late 1940s (see details of how Johnny Pesky's ejection brought about the change, in the book *Mr. Red Sox*), if one was ejected in the first game of a doubleheader, one was ejected for the day. The Yankees won the first game, 2–0, but lost big-time in the second, 9–4. As the Red Sox rolled up five runs, umpire Bill Summers banished Lou Gehrig for "haranguing too much" on one of his calls. Had Gehrig been tossed in game one, his consecutive games streak would have been snapped.

1926 The 1926 season was such a poor one that the headline over Burt Whitman's column read Wait Till Next Year—with several games left to play in July. The Red Sox were 28–66 after the July 26 game. They only won 18 more games all season long, for a grand total of 46.

1923 An editorial in *The Sporting News* reported, then challenged as spurious, a published story that Bob Quinn and the new owners of the Red Sox had issued an appeal to the other ball clubs to help out the Red Sox by sending them surplus players to help Boston become more competitive. It might have helped. Financial angel Palmer Winslow died soon after buying the team, leaving a man of modest means in Quinn in charge. The Red Sox wouldn't have enough money to seriously compete until 10 years later when Tom Yawkey bought the ball club.

1922 Reacting to Boston's trade of Joe Dugan and Elmer Smith to the Yankees, the St. Louis Chamber of Commerce protested it as "unsportsmanlike" in a letter sent to Commissioner Landis and the presidents of the two leagues. With obvious reference to the recent Black Sox scandal, the Chamber argued, "If the dollar mark is to be the emblem of victory in the baseball world, the American people will have to take more seriously the detrimental disclosures of the past and fairly judge that baseball has sold its birthright." About 10 days later, Landis responded that the protest was well taken and (using a gambling metaphor) noted the trade was "like removing or adding a handicap when the horses are coming down the stretch." He suggested advancing the inter-league trading deadline from August 1 to July 1—though, of course, that wouldn't affect intra-league trades.

1920 The Red Sox held an 8–0 lead after 3½ innings in The Bronx, but Sam Jones didn't want to take any chances, so he kept on walking Babe Ruth. The Bambino was 4-for-4 in the bases on balls category. It wasn't as though Jones didn't have it; only three Yankees got to him for singles. Fans booed, particularly so in the eighth inning when Ruth was walked with no one on base and Boston up, 9–0. Jones got his shutout.

1919 Babe Ruth was knocked unconscious after slamming into Boston's left-field wall in the seventh, but the Sox held a 5–4 lead over the Yanks until an error, a walk, and four singles in the top of the ninth scored four runs for New York, and wiped out the Red Sox.

1914 Both teams scored once in the fourth, but Boston broke the tie in the top of the ninth when Cleveland's Guy Morton walked the first two batters, and then gave up singles to Henriksen and Hoblitzell, and a sac fly to Cady. The final was a 4–1 Boston win. Morton was 1–13 in 1914. Ernie Shore got the win.

TRANSACTIONS
1999: Acquired Butch Huskey from Seattle in trade for Robert Ramsay.

DEBUTS
1918: Eusebio Gonzalez,   1963: Bob Turley
      Walt Kinney   1977: Don Aase
1922: Elmer Miller   1995: Dave Hollins
1932: Johnny Welch   2005: Manny Delcarmen
1946: Wally Moses

BIRTHDATES
Sam Jones 1892 (1916–1921); Ellis Kinder 1914 (1948–1955); Mel Deutsch 1915 (1946); Dick Brodowski 1932 (1952–1955); Norm Siebern 1933 (1967–1968); Jody Reed 1962 (1987–1992)

DEATHS
Otto Miller 1959

July 27

1999 A six-run fifth helped the Sox overcome a 7–3 deficit and beat the Blue Jays in a wild 11–9 game, in which newcomer Butch Huskey had his Red Sox debut with three hits, including a phantom home run ruled a single. Replays clearly showed the ball had hit in the bullpen and bounced back onto the field. Huskey got two shots in the following day—a sixth-inning grand slam and a ninth-inning solo shot in an 8–0 shutout of the Jays.

1975 Bill Lee shut out the Yankees, 1–0, the sole Sox run coming in the top of the ninth after Fred Lynn reached on an error. With two out, Lynn stole second and then scored on a single by Rick Miller and an error by Alomar. He also made what he considered his best catch in the bottom of the ninth, snagging a drive to left-center off the bat of Graig Nettles. Roger Moret and the Sox won the far less suspenseful second game of the day, 6–0. The Red Sox won the pennant, too.

1969 It was 1–1 after eight. And after nine. And even after 19. Joe Lahoud (1-for-7 to that point in the game), hit a two-run homer in the top of the 20th, and the Sox scored another one, too. Seattle's Tommy Harper hit a homer in the bottom of the 20th, but the final score was 5–3 in Boston's favor. Boston's sixth pitcher of the night, Jim Lonborg, collected the win.

1962 The AWOL Gene Conley and Pumpsie Green may not have made a difference, but the Senators slaughtered the Red Sox in a doubleheader on the 27th, 11–2 and 14–1. In the latter game, manager Mike Higgins left Galen Cisco in until he'd been beaten to the tune of 13 runs on 16 hits through 5⅓ innings.

1947 A 60-foot triple on a foul ball? Yes. Boston's Jake Jones had already extended **STVT** his nine-game hitting streak, but it was still a treat that he was awarded a triple by umpire Cal Hubbard because St. Louis pitcher Fred Sanford threw his glove at a batted ball (to prevent it rolling fair). The rule wasn't changed until 1954; a glove thrown at a batted ball was to be ruled an automatic triple. The Sox took two games from St. Louis.

1946 First baseman Rudy York hit a grand slam in the second inning and then repeated the feat in the fifth inning. Tex Shirley of St. Louis served up both slams. Double X (Jimmie Foxx) had also hit a first inning double, driving in two, so his total was 10 RBIs on the day. Boston's Jim Tabor had also hit two slams in a game, on July 4, 1936. With four RBIs the day before, York had 14 RBIs in two days.

1935 Boston's Lefty Grove hit a grand slam in the second inning but lost the game in the 15th when two former teammates—Boob McNair and Doc Cramer, still with the Athletics—combine to score the winning run in a 7–6 game. The following year, all three will be playing on the same team once more—the Boston Red Sox. Grove only had five RBIs in all of 1935; 80% of them came on this one blow.

1918 The original schedule for 1918 had the Red Sox ending the season on October 5, hosting Washington for a doubleheader. On July 26, though, Secretary of War Newton D. Baker proclaimed that organized baseball would have until September 1 to conform to the "work-or-fight" principle that able-bodied men should either be in the armed services or performing essential wartime work. Accordingly, the season would end over a month earlier than usual.

1914 Boston's Tris Speaker had a sac fly, two singles, and a triple. He also made eight putouts in center field. By year's end, he had a record 423. Dutch Leonard blanked Cleveland, 3–0.

1907 Shortstop Heinie Wagner made 10 putouts in a regulation game. Vern Stephens earned a share of the club record on June 25, 1950.

1906 The 1906 Boston Americans only won 45 games all season long, but this was a great one. Jack Powell, pitching for St. Louis, threw a five-hitter, only giving up one run to Boston in the top of the ninth inning. Boston pitcher Bill Dinneen, however, only gave up one hit—a single—and beat the Browns, 1–0.

1904 The New York Giants already looked to be likely winners of the National League pennant. Both manager John McGraw and owner John T. Brush announced they would not play in a "world series" with the AL champions, as the Pittsburg Pirates had done with the Boston Americans in 1903. "When we clinch the National League pennant, we'll be champions of the only real major league," McGraw declared. Clearly, National League magnates were still angry with the upstart American League. By 1905, under rules promulgated by Brush, the World Series became the annual fall classic.

1901 Chicago knocked around Fred Mitchell for five runs in the first, and manager Jimmy Collins called on Ted Lewis to take over. Lewis threw 11 innings in relief, holding Chicago to just two more unearned runs, while Boston put across seven to tie it up. In the bottom of the 13th inning, though, Lewis threw away his masterful effort. Dutch Hartman was the first batter up for Chicago and he bounced a ball between third base and the mound which Lewis scooped up and fired to first. The throw was about as wild as a throw can be; the *Chicago Tribune* said it "flew on out to the bleachers and just as it reached them took a high bound over the screen and disappeared under the seats." Hartman raced around the bases but scored easily. Babe Ruth also threw 11 innings of relief, in a May 15, 1919 game.

TRANSACTIONS

1933: Acquired Joe Judge to fill in for injured Dale Alexander. Judge had initially
    signed with the Red Sox in 1914, but never appeared for them until 1933.
1945: Sold Lou Finney to the St. Louis Browns.
1990: Acquired Mike Marshall from the Mets in exchange for Greg
    Hansell and Ed Perozo, plus a PTBNL (Paul Williams).
2000: Received Rolando Arrojo, Rich Croushore, Mike Lansing, and even some cash from
    the Rockies, for Jeff Frye, Brian Rose, John Wasdin, and minor-leaguer Jeff Taglienti.

DEBUTS

1909: Chet Nourse
1950: Jim McDonald
1992: John Valentin
1999: Butch Huskey

BIRTHDATES

Charley Hall 1885 (1909–1913); Rube Walberg 1896 (1934–1937); Ed
Carroll 1907 (1929); Bill Sayles 1917 (1939); Ray Boone 1923 (1960);
Don Lock 1936 (1969); Shea Hillenbrand 1975 (2001–2003)

DEATHS

Nig Cuppy 1922; Howie Storie 1968; Billy Holm 1977; Joe Wood 1985; Rick Ferrell 1995

July 28

1998 An arbitrator rules that the Red Sox (47%) and the Boston Bruins (31%), co-owners of the New England Sports Network, are entitled to full revenue shares from NESN whether or not viewers receive NESN on basic cable or as premium programming. The loser is Viacom, owner of 19% of NESN shares.

1982 Red Sox GM Haywood Sullivan had the Blue Jays remove a television they were watching in the bullpen. Boston won, 9–7, thanks to homers by Evans and Lansford in a six-run fifth inning. Meanwhile, in a reversal of roles down in Texas, Rangers manager Don Zimmer was fired and Darrell Johnson handed the reins. Six years earlier, it was Zimmer who had taken Johnson's spot at the helm for the Red Sox.

1979 At Arlington, Texas, Boston's Dennis Eckersley out-pitched Ferguson Jenkins, 1–0. The Sox may have needed the triple play they pulled off in the bottom of the first inning. Johnny Grubb singled to lead off, and took third on Buddy Bell's single to center. Al Oliver blooped one to short right field, but second baseman Jack Brohamer ran out, dove, and caught it. Rising to his feet, he fired to first and doubled up Bell. Bob Watson threw across the diamond and tripled up Grubb. The 4-3-5 triple play was the third of the year for the Red Sox (May 10, and just five days earlier on July 23 were the other two).

1965 Again, Tony Conigliaro is seriously injured when hit by a pitch. His left wrist is broken in the fifth inning of a 6–0 shutout of Kansas City by Bill Monbouquette. Wes Stock's pitch does the damage, and Tony C.—riding a 10-game hitting streak—misses about a month.

1957 Ted Williams, 4-for-4 on the day, reached the 2,300 hit mark. Had he not missed nearly five full seasons in military service, he'd already be closing in on 3,000.

1953 Ted Williams turned up at Fenway Park and took some swings. According to 19-year-old reporter George Sullivan, writing for the *Cambridge Chronicle*, The Kid had Paul Schreiber throw him some batting practice—and he hit nine in a row out of the park! Then Ted grumbled to Joe Cronin that home plate was out of alignment. Everyone thought he was pulling their leg, but they took measurements to humor him and found out that Ted was right—after more than a year away from baseball, within a few minutes he'd noticed something no ballplayers had noticed all year, that the plate was very slightly off. Home plate was repositioned.

1951 The surprising Clyde Vollmer keeps surprising. (See July 6, 7, 8, 12, 13, 14, 18, 21, and 26!) In Boston, Mickey McDermott kept the Red Sox in the game, through 16 innings. It was 2–2 after nine. The Indians scored once in the top of the 15th, but clutch-hitter Clyde drove in a run for the Red Sox to tie it back up. Doggedly, Cleveland went right back ahead by a run in the top of the 16th. In the bottom of the 16th, Ted Williams doubled to drive in Johnny Pesky, the bases filled up and here came Clyde, facing Rapid Robert Feller in relief—home run! Grand slam! Sox win, 8–4!

1950 The Indians hit five homers and Early Wynn carried a 13–0 shutout through 8⅔ innings, before Vern Stephens doubled and Tom Wright singled. OK, so it ended 13–1 instead of 13–0.

1945 A B-25 bomber crashed into the Empire State Building at 9:49 A.M., at a point 915 feet above street level. Thirteen people were killed in the crash. The New York Yankees were spared major front office losses; the crash hit almost exactly where they had planned their private offices—but the lease was rejected by Del Webb who didn't really want a 10-minute elevator ride to the 78th floor.

1924 The game that never was. Did you ever hear of a game being protested, and the protest succeeded? The Sox beat St. Louis, 10–5, in 10 innings. Or did they? St. Louis manager George Sisler protested the game when the umpire forced the Browns' Tony Rego to bat out of turn, possibly killing a ninth-inning rally. The Sox scored five times in the 10th. AL President Ban Johnson upheld the protest on August 17, and the game was replayed after the regularly-scheduled game on September 13. The Red Sox won it again, this time, 13–11.

1917 The Sox swept St. Louis, 3–2 and 3–2. The first game ran 12 innings and the Sox won it on a single and a sacrifice, followed by another single and another sacrifice. Continuing the theme of duplication, in the second game Sox pitcher Ernie Shore was twice called out for being hit by batted balls. In the combined 20 innings, not a single Red Sox player struck out. Earlier in the day, manager Jack Barry enrolled as a third-class yeoman at the Charlestown Navy Yard; his number had come up right near the top of those chosen for conscription.

1916 When Rube Oldring of the Yankees homered in the ninth inning and beat the White Sox in Chicago, it cost Red Sox ownership $1250. He had promised Sox players $50 apiece if they reached first place, and the defeat of the White Sox let Boston back into first, so Lannin passed out the checks.

1915 Chicago's Jim Scott held the Red Sox scoreless in Boston, and the White Sox prevailed, 1–0. It was a nerve-wracking contest with several chances to score, but both teams executed three double plays. Twice Boston had two men on with no outs, but neither time could they push a run across. One fan, W. E. Coman of Everett, Massachusetts, could not stand the strain and died of a heart attack during one of the tenser moments.

1911 Pitcher Walter "Judge" Nagle's arm had been bothering him ever since coming to the Red Sox from Pittsburgh (he hurt it before the season working out in a gym), and he sought to better it by "taking Christian Science treatment," visiting an "one of the most eminent Christian Science practioners" on a daily basis. Whatever the treatment, his arm didn't take him very far. He finished the season with a 1–1 record, and that was it for his career in the majors.

1905 There were still 74 games remaining on the schedule, but if the Boston Americans failed to finish first the third year in a row, they were prepared to play the Boston National League club in post-season exhibition games, said President Taylor.

TRANSACTIONS
1914: Traded Fritz Coumbe, Ben Egan, and Rankin Johnson
      to the Cleveland Naps for Vean Gregg.
2000: Signed free agent Lou Merloni.

DEBUTS
1908: Frank Arellanes   1959: Jim Mahoney,
1918: Jean Dubuc   Earl Wilson
1925: Jack Rothrock   2001: Casey Fossum
1928: Carl Sumner

BIRTHDATES
Elmer Miller 1890 (1922); Ray Dobens 1906 (1929); Ben Steiner
1921 (1945–1946); Ted Lepcio 1930 (1952–1959)

DEATHS
None yet

July 29

2005 John Olerud's grand slam provided enough to win a game against the Twins, 8–3. It was the 250th home run of his career, and the 10th grand slam of the season, setting a new Red Sox club record—with two months to go in the season.

2003 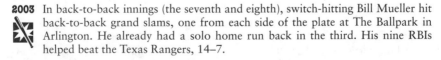 In back-to-back innings (the seventh and eighth), switch-hitting Bill Mueller hit back-to-back grand slams, one from each side of the plate at The Ballpark in Arlington. He already had a solo home run back in the third. His nine RBIs helped beat the Texas Rangers, 14–7.

2001 Nomar Garciaparra returned to the Red Sox lineup; he had been out since Opening Day surgery. He homered, leading off the sixth, to tie the White Sox, 2–2. After Chicago scored once in the top of the seventh, he came up with two outs and the bases loaded and singled to drive in two and put the Sox ahead to stay, 4–3.

1997 Mo Vaughn hit a two-run homer off Seattle's Randy Johnson, and Nomar Garciaparra doubled twice. Tim Wakefield pitched a complete game five-hit shutout and added a win, 4–0.

1990 The Red Sox broke a 56-year-old record, for the most doubles in a game. The Tigers had hit 11 against New York on July 14, 1934. This day, Wade Boggs hit three; Ellis Burks, and Tim Naehring, and Jody Reed each hit two; and Mike Greenwell, Randy Kutcher, and Carlos Quintana each hit one, for a grand total of 12 doubles—all of which made life easy on starter Greg Harris (who won his first game in his last six starts, 13–3).

1976 It's a great story, but not verified: George Sullivan wrote that in 1976, Rick Wise was facing the Indians at Fenway when a line drive hit him on the leg, dropped into the hole dug by pitchers toeing the rubber, and Wise couldn't find it because he was standing on the hole. There was only one date in 1976 when Wise faced Cleveland in Boston, July 29, but game accounts don't mention the event.

1975 Diego Segui struck out 12 Milwaukee Brewers, but only started with the strikeouts after the first two batters had homered. His strikeout of Gorman Thomas in the fourth inning was Thomas' eighth consecutive strikeout, tying the league record. Thomas finally broke the string in the sixth inning—by grounding into a double play. Meanwhile, Milwaukee's Jim Colborn kept Boston's bats at bay with a seven-hit, 4–0 shutout.

1974 On the 27th, Bob Montgomery singled off Sparky Lyle in the bottom of the ninth to win the game for the Red Sox, 5–4. On the 29th, a Dwight Evans homer tied the game 1–1 in the bottom of the eighth, and it went into extra innings. Lyle walked Yaz, then threw wide of first when Montgomery laid down a bunt. With two on and no one out, he walked Burleson intentionally. With a force at every base, and the Yankees infield in, Doug Griffin was up. He bunted and Lyle couldn't handle it, but plate umpire ruled that the ball had struck Griffin while he was still in the batter's box. Foul ball. Griffin then grounded to short and Yaz was thrown out at the plate. Terry Hughes got one of his six RBIs of the season with a sacrifice fly to center. It won the game for the Red Sox, 2–1.

1967 Joe Foy's two-run double in the bottom of the eighth capped the four-run eighth inning and gave the Sox a 6–3 edge over the Twins. Yaz cut down not one, but two Twins with throws on the money to home plate. In the second inning of the second game, George Scott boomed an inside-the-park home run to right, but the Twins homered five times and won, 10–3.

1962 The AWOL Gene Conley, suspended without pay, sends a telegram to manager Pinky Higgins which reads, "I am sorry for the way I have handled things, but I'm mostly tired and have other plans. Thank you for everything, Mike." Contacted at home, Conley told a reporter, "It's a personal matter and I don't think it's anyone's business. I'm very tired. I just want to go to sleep." When he decided to rejoin the Red Sox a day later, he was fined a reported $2000.

The Red Sox won the day's ballgame, 4–2 over the Senators, with Dick Radatz striking out five men in two innings of hitless relief.

1958 Ted Williams hit the 17th (and last) grand slam of his career. At the time, only Lou Gehrig, with 23, had more.

1953 Ted Williams signed his contract for 1953 and started to try to get back in shape. The first day Ted was back in Boston after missing most of two seasons while serving in the Marines, the Sox seemed poised to win a tight 1–0 game over the visiting White Sox. It was the top of the ninth and Mickey McDermott was pitching a two-hitter. Then he imploded. When the Chicago half of the inning was over, they had an 8–1 lead. Now faced with the need to bat in the bottom of the ninth, the Red Sox scored a couple of runs, but it was far too great a gap to overcome and they lost, 8–3.

1948 The Sox scored once in the second, and then started hitting homers to help Big Jack Kramer win his 10th game in a row. Kramer himself had the game-winner, a third-inning solo home run. Bobby Doerr hit a two-run job in the sixth, and Billy Goodman upped the ante with a grand slam in the top of the seventh. Red Sox 8, Tigers 1.

1945 Bob Johnson broke a bat making his 2,000th hit in the fourth inning of the game against Washington. He planned to install the bat in the trophy room of his ranch in Washington state—which already bore the name Broken Bat Ranch. He was 4-for-4 in the Sox win.

1919 Babe Ruth had already hit two doubles off Tigers hurler Dutch Leonard, and now here he was up again in the ninth inning with Braggo Roth on first base. Ruth already had eight HR in July, but Leonard had a four-run lead, so he pitched to the Babe, who pounded the first pitch into the center-field bleachers. Roth and Ruth both scored. The Tigers still won.

On the same day, Carl Mays was traded to the Yankees, a couple of weeks after he'd walked off the field—and the Red Sox—during a ballgame. (See July 13.) The Sox got Allan "Rubberarm" Russell and Robert Emmett McGraw (whose nickname was "Bob"), a minor league PTBNL, and a sizable sum of money. League president Ban Johnson tried to block the deal, and ordered umpires not to let Mays pitch, but after some injunctions, some lawsuits, and some negotiations, Johnson had to cave in. See October 29, however.

1914 Boston scored once in the eighth and once in the ninth, tying the game. Manager Bill Carrigan inserted himself into the game in the 10th inning, and drove in the go-ahead run. Harry Hooper then tripled and drove in a couple more. The "Speed Boys"—as they were known in this era—put four runs across, and beat Chicago, 8–4.

1911 On July 7, in St. Louis, Smoky Joe Wood had a no-hitter going through 8⅓ innings, ultimately winning a one-hitter, 6–1. On July 29, he faced the Browns when they visited Boston's Huntington Avenue Grounds—and was even better. He struck out 12, walked two, and hit one batter—but not a single Brownie could get a hit. Joe Wood had a no-hitter. Boston won, 5–0.

1903 Cy Young gives up 15 runs on 19 hits, but keeps on pitching, no doubt a little peeved at the eight errors by the Boston defense. He only walked one. What was a miracle was that the game was so close. New York's ace Jack Chesbro was chased in the sixth. It was 15–10 after 8½, and Boston scored four times in the bottom of the ninth, but fell just short. Boston LF Patsy Dougherty hit for the cycle—and stole a base, too.

TRANSACTIONS
1919: Traded Carl Mays to the New York Yankees for Bob
      McGraw, Allan Russell, and $40,000 cash.
1954: Selected Sam Mele off waivers from the Baltimore Orioles.
1988: Acquired Mike Boddicker from the Baltimore Orioles in
      trade for Brady Anderson and Curt Schilling.
2003: Traded minor leaguer Phil Dumatrait, a PTBNL, and cash
      considerations to the Cincinnati Reds for Scott Williamson.

DEBUTS
1909: Ed Karger
1914: Vean Gregg
1918: George Cochran
2000: Mike Lansing
2003: Lou Collier

BIRTHDATES
Felix Mantilla 1934 (1963–1965); Luis Alicea 1965 (1995)

DEATHS
Vean Gregg 1964; Elmer Myers 1976

July 30

2002 The Red Sox traded the wonderfully-named Seung Song and another Korean pitcher, Sun Woo Kim, to obtain power hitter Cliff Floyd from the Montreal Expos. Floyd had been traded from the Marlins to the Expos at the beginning of the month. The Marlins had belonged to new Sox owner John W. Henry. The Yankees were angry that the Sox scooped up Floyd. Conspiracy theories abounded, so much so that Gordon Edes wrote a column on the subject in the August 1 *Globe*.

1999 Yankees second baseman Chuck Knoblauch went 5-for-6, with a double and a homer, and drove in four RBIs. Jeter and Posada hit homers, too, and the Yankees scored 13 runs, beating Boston by 10 full runs.

1997 Pinch-hitting in the 10th inning, Steve Avery grounds out, but goes in the books at the first Red Sox pitcher to pinch-hit since Tim Lollar did it on August 12, 1986. Despite the out, the Sox scored a run and beat Seattle, 8–7.

Nomar Garciaparra's seven at-bats help boost him toward the year's total of 684, the most ever by any Red Sox batter. Only walking 37 times had a lot to do with it, but it's hard to complain about a .306 average and 98 RBIs from a leadoff hitter.

1996 Boston gets a leadoff hitter when the Mariners trade OF Darren Bragg to the Red Sox in exchange for pitcher Jamie Moyer. Moyer, in a portent of his success with the M's, is 7–1.

1991 Red Sox reliever Jeff Gray was a bright light for Boston, having a breakthrough season with a 2.34 ERA in 61⅔ innings of work. After a morning workout before the game with the Texas Rangers, Gray suffered a stroke in the Red Sox home clubhouse. The Red Sox had lost nine consecutive home games, their worst losing streak since 1927. Carlos Quintana helped break the streak in the third inning with a grand slam off Dennis Boyd (yes, The Can was pitching for the Rangers) and a two-run double in the same 10-run inning. The six RBIs in one inning tied the major league record.

Later reports on Gray's stroke indicated that it had taken a fair amount of time to get an ambulance for Gray. By August 8, it was announced that Gray would almost certainly miss the rest of the season. As it transpired, he never played major league ball again.

1990 "In a decision almost certain to bring jubilation to Yankee fans, baseball commissioner Fay Vincent...liberated the storied franchise from George Steinbrenner [causing him] to resign as the club's general partner by August 20th and bans him from day-to-day [operations], forcing the owner to permanently relinquish all day-to-day operations of the team because of his payments to a known gambler." So wrote Steve Fainaru in the front page story in the *Boston Globe*. "He can no longer be involved in the management of the team. Ever." So declared Vincent. Steinbrenner had paid $40,000 to "confessed gambler" Howie Spira, a former employee of Yankees outfielder Dave Winfield. George was looking for dirt on Dave. Vincent's supposedly permanent ban lasted but a short time, and Steinbrenner financed a succession of championships for New York, winning him back the fan support he had lost in the 1980s.

1973 The Yanks and the Sox were battling for first place. Kicking off a series at Fenway, pinch-hitter Jim Ray Hart homered in the ninth inning to drive in two runs for New York and tie the score. The Yankees lost it when Boston batted in the bottom of the ninth. Sparky Lyle came in to pitch for the Yankees. Rico Petrocelli singled. A wild pitch and a couple of grounders got him to third, and Rick Miller singled him in.

1965 Few friends were made when the Angels and the Red Sox tangled at Dodger Stadium. Dean Chance almost hit Felix Mantilla in the top of the sixth, and that's what seems to have set the stage. Dave Morehead hit the first batter up for the Angels, Jose Cardenal. Two batters later, Jim Fregosi homered to tie the game 2–2. Morehead was up second in the seventh, and he got hit by Chance. After a home run drove Morehead from the game in the eighth, and the Angels were up 5–2, Arnold Earley came on in relief, and his very first pitch plunked Bob Rodgers, who charged the mound as the dugouts emptied. It was Earley's last pitch, too. He was ejected, as was Rodgers. 9–2 final.

1962 Pete Runnels hits a homer in the All-Star Game at Wrigley Field.

1959 Five Boston Red Sox pitchers gave up an average of one hit each—but they combined to issue 15 bases on balls. Starter Earl Wilson walked nine, and not one of them scored, since he never did let up a hit before being relieved in the fourth innings. Fortunately, Detroit left 15 men on base, and lost by one run to the Red Sox, 6–5. Leading Boston's offense was Pumpsie Green, with three hits and three runs scored.

1950 In a game in Cleveland, Bobby Doerr hit his 200th major league home run.

1948 Was this the game that stuck in Joe McCarthy's mind, when he determined to pitch Denny Galehouse in 1948's single-game playoff against this same Cleveland Indians club? Mel Parnell walked three and yielded four hits to the Indians in just one-third of an inning. Galehouse took over and pitched 8⅔ innings of two-hit relief. The Red Sox came from being down 6–3 to an 8–7 win. It was the 25th win for Boston in the month of July, a record hard to top.

1936 For the first time ever, a major league ball club all flew from one city to another in the same plane (two years earlier, three planes had transported the Cincinnati Reds to play the Cubs). Though five players chose to travel by train, the rest of the team—and owner Tom Yawkey—flew the 260 miles from St. Louis to Chicago in 90 minutes, and dined while aloft. Getting a good night's rest might have helped, as they won the next day—but they dropped the three after that.

1917 All the scoring was done by the second inning, and the Red Sox beat the visiting Chicagoans, 3–1. Babe Ruth won on a four-hitter.

1916 The Red Sox dealt a 9–3 defeat to Detroit, behind Carl Mays, and moved into first place.

1914 Ernest Shore shutout the White Sox, 4–0. His career won-lost record now stood at 4–0, too. The *Chicago Tribune's* James Crusinberry attributed the Boston win—despite having fewer hits—to their hurling themselves "into the fray with reckless abandon while the [White] Sox were compelled to play things safe and skimp along..."

TRANSACTIONS
1996: Acquired Darren Bragg from Seattle for Jamie Moyer. Traded Kevin
    Mitchell to Cincinnati for Roberto Mejia and Brad Tweedie.
1998: Acquired Mike Stanley from the Toronto Blue Jays for Peter Munro and Jay Yennaco.
2001: Released Bryce Florie.
2002: The Red Sox acquired Cliff Floyd from the Montreal Expos in a trade
    for two Korean pitchers: Sun-Woo Kim and Seung Song.
2005: Acquired OF Jose Cruz Jr. and cash considerations from the Arizona
    Diamondbacks in exchange for minor league INF Kenny Perez and minor
    league RHP Kyle Bono. On August 9, Cruz was traded away.

DEBUTS
1920: Hal Deviney   1999: Lenny Webster
1922: Chick Fewster   2000: Rolando Arrojo
1954: Tom Hurd

BIRTHDATES
Frankie Pytlak 1908 (1941–1946); Scott Fletcher 1958
(1993–1994); Steve Ellsworth 1960 (1988)

DEATHS
Howie Shanks 1941; Joe Lucey 1980

July 31

2004 Red Sox GM Theo Epstein traded minor league outfielder Henri Stanley to the Dodgers for the versatile (and swift) Dave Roberts. (See October 17, 2004.)

2003 When both Ortiz and Nixon hit homers in the game in Texas, the Sox had a record 55 home runs, the most for the ball club in any given month.

2001 The Red Sox obtain closer Ugueth Urbina from the Expos for pitchers Tomo Ohka and Rich Rundles. The Expos even threw in $1,000,000. Urbina's name was one of the most widely mentioned in trading deadline rumors. Urbina had apparently failed a late June physical with the New York Yankees.

1997 The best trade in Red Sox history? The Sox sent struggling reliever Heathcliff Slocumb to Seattle for two minor leaguers: Jason Varitek and Derek Lowe. Slocumb was 0–5 for the Red Sox; he improved his record with Seattle (0–4 in 1997, 2–5 the following year). Lowe spent seven full seasons with the Sox, and won the final game of the 2004 World Series. Varitek became a key member of the Sox, so much so that he was named team captain after re-signing with the team in early 2005.

1991 For the 47th time, Rickey Henderson hit a leadoff homer, building on his existing major league record, and Oakland took a 1–0 lead. Both teams scored often; Wade Boggs had a 5-for-7 night with three doubles. Boston's Jack Clark hit a grand slam and a solo homer—and then a third solo home run that won the game, 11–10, in the bottom of the 14th inning.

1985 Had they called it after six innings, the White Sox would have won 1–0, but the Red Sox tied it (on a Dave Sax sacrifice fly) in the bottom of the seventh and the umpires motioned for the tarp at 10:16, finally calling the game at 11:34. Over a foot of water was reported in the visitors' clubhouse. The individual records stand in the record books, but the game itself was replayed in its entirety at 5:00 P.M. the next day, as part of a doubleheader. Boston lost that game, 7–2.

1978 The slumping Sox had won just two of their last 12, and only scored five runs over the last six of those games. They broke out of it, at least for a day, as George Scott emerged from an 0-for-25 slump and Jim Rice from a 1-for-21 stretch. The Eck got the win, 9–2, to run his record to 12–4. Rick Burleson doubled with three on, and had three hits.

1973 The Yankees scored three runs in the ninth and won their first game at Fenway Park since August 2, 1972. Bill Lee yielded a homer, a single, and then the mound to reliever Bob Veale, who whiffed Horace Clarke but then yielded three singles to give the Yankees the 5–4 advantage.

1970 Mike Andrews hit a solo homer. Carl Yastrzemski hit a solo homer. And Red Sox starter Sonny Siebert subdued the Angels with a one-hitter (a third inning single by Jay Johnstone), as the Red Sox beat California, in California, 2–0.

1968 Outfielder Floyd Robinson was purchased from Oakland. Jackie might have been better, even at age 58. Floyd hit .125 in 24 AB.

1959 Earl Wilson, making his first start for the Red Sox, pitched and left the game with a 4–0 lead, without the Tigers getting a hit off him. He did, however, walk nine batters. He was replaced in the fourth inning and a parade of Red Sox pitchers walked six more Detroiters. They only gave up five hits, though, and managed to win—in good part due to Pumpsie Green, who had three hits and scored three times.

1955 In an attempt to distract Ted Williams at the plate, Tigers shortstop Harvey Kuenn played what Williams biographer Michael Seidel called a "roving shift." In other words, "he simply ran like a mad man from one side of second base to the other while Williams stood at the plate." Manager Pinky Higgins ran out and complained about the "bush-league crap" to umpire Ed Rommel, who instructed Kuenn to cease and desist.

The Sox won both games. Ted Williams hit a grand slam to clinch the 8–3 opener and Jimmy Piersall's homer in the bottom of the ninth broke a 2–2 tie to win the second game.

1951   Clyde Vollmer doubled and drove in two. The Red Sox lost, 8–6, to St. Louis, with Satchel Paige getting the win. Vollmer's remarkable July included 40 RBIs on 31 hits, including 13 homers.

1946   Bob Feller would have had another no-hitter but for Bobby Doerr's single in the second inning. This was the second time Doerr had done Feller in; see also May 25, 1939.

1941   Though it would seem a reasonably short game by today's standards, the 16–11 win of a nine-inning game was, at 3:11, the longest game in league history.

1940   Jimmie Foxx was ready to return to the lineup, but Lou Finney had hit so well that manager Joe Cronin wasn't entirely sure how to proceed. Foxx offered to catch, so Finney played first and Foxx squatted behind the plate as Denny Galehouse's batterymate. Galehouse was long gone by game's end, as both teams used five pitchers and the Indians beat the Red Sox, 12–11, with a four-run rally in the eighth. Foxx was 2-for-4 and drove in two (Finney drove in three). Ken Keltner of Cleveland drove in five.

1936   Jimmie Foxx lacked only a single as he doubled, tripled, and homered to help Lefty Grove beat the White Sox, 7–3. He was walked intentionally in the seventh inning, so he didn't even get a sporting chance. Moe Berg lacked only the homer, as he singled, doubled, and tripled. The next Berg hit a home run came on August 30, 1939.

1935   Slugging pitcher Wes Ferrell hit two home runs off Buck Newsom, a three-run homer in the fourth and a solo shot in the seventh, and won the Griffith Stadium game against Washington, 6–4. It wasn't easy to hit homers that year; Dick Thompson in his biography of the Ferrell brothers says that only four members of the Senators hit home runs in Griffith Stadium in all of 1935—just one apiece. Wes hit two in one day.

1933   The Red Sox bought a new ball club, the Reading (PA) franchise in the New York–Pennsylvania League. It was seen at the time as the start of the modern Red Sox farm system under new owner Tom Yawkey and his GM, Eddie Collins.

1919   With Carl Mays gone, the Sox bring in Waite Hoyt to take his place. Not a bad substitution, given that Hoyt proved to be a Hall of Fame pitcher. The battle over Mays continued, with Boston's sale of the troublesome pitcher to New York and league president Ban Johnson's ban of Mays, which kicked off a "baseball war" with the other six clubs protesting the deal between New York and Boston. (See also August 6.)

1916   No Tiger ever reached third base, though two were cut down trying to advance from second to third in the very first inning. Babe Ruth settled down and threw a two-hit, 6–0 shutout. The game was a quick one hour and 33 minutes long.

1914   Why was International League president Ed Barrow prolonging his stay in Detroit? On July 31, the answer became evident as the announcement was made that Boston Red Sox owner Joseph Lannin had purchased the Providence Grays from Detroit, converting the I.L. franchise back again to a Boston farm club. *The Baseball Chronology* reports that Detroit was granted the right to pick one player from the Providence roster. They picked Red Oldham, overlooking Carl Mays who made the Red Sox in 1915, and became a 20-game winner for them in 1917 and 1918.

1904 Jake Volz started and won the last game of the year for the Boston Americans in 1901, despite giving up nine runs. He played the next several years in the New England League and on July 31, 1904, threw two complete games for Manchester, allowing Nashua just five hits in the two contests, and winning 3–0 and 3–1. His next, and final, win in major league ball came nearly seven years after his first, pitching a 5–1 victory for Cincinnati over Brooklyn.

TRANSACTIONS

1926: Purchased Jack Tobin from the Washington Senators.

1959: Jack Harshman was selected off waivers by the Cleveland Indians.

1968: Purchased Floyd Robinson from the Oakland Athletics.

1990: Signed free agent Joe Hesketh.

1995: Acquired Mike Stanton and a PTBNL (Matt Murray) from the Atlanta Braves for some players to be named later (minor leaguers Mike Jacobs and Marc Lewis).

1996: Acquired Mark Brandeburg and Kerry Lacy in trade from the Texas Rangers for Mike Stanton and a PTBNL (Dwayne Hosey). The deal was made at five minutes before midnight.

1997: Acquired Derek Lowe and Jason Varitek in trade with the Seattle Mariners for Heathcliff Slocumb.

1998: Acquired Orlando Merced and Greg Swindell from the Minnesota Twins in trade for Josh Barnes, Matt Kinney, and Joe Thomas. Also, received Eddy Diaz from Milwaukee for Joe Hudson.

1999: Acquired Bryce Florie from the Detroit Tigers for Mike Maroth.

2000: Released Mike Stanley.

2001: Received Ugueth Urbina from Montreal for Tomokazu Okha and Rich Rundles.

2002: The Red Sox receive Bobby Howry from the White Sox in trade for Frankie Francisco and Byeong Hak An.

2003: Traded Freddy Sanchez, Mike Gonzalez, and cash considerations to the Pittsburgh Pirates for Jeff Suppan, Brandon Lyon, and Anastacio Martinez.

2004: In a complicated set of deals, Nomar Garciaparra went to the Chicago Cubs with Matt Murton and some cash considerations. Orlando Cabrera arrived in Boston from the Montreal Expos and Doug Mientkiewicz arrived from the Minnesota Twins. Dave Roberts arrived from Los Angeles for minor leaguer Henri Stanley.

DEBUTS

1919: Waite Hoyt	1987: John Marzano
1948: Earl Caldwell	1988: Mike Boddicker
1953: Frank Sullivan	1996: Darren Bragg
1955: Frank Baumann	2005: Jonathan Papelbon
1964: Tony Horton	

BIRTHDATES

Bob Unglaub 1881 (1904–1908); Allan Russell 1893 (1919–1922); Gordon McNaughton 1910 (1932); Bill Fleming 1913 (1940–1941); Joe Mulligan 1913 (1934); Billy Hitchcock 1916 (1948–1949); Scott Bankhead 1963 (1993–1994)

DEATHS

Sam Langford 1993; Hy Vandenberg 1994

AUGUST

August 1

2004 Newly-acquired shortstop Orlando Cabrera, replacing fan favorite Nomar Garciaparra, didn't waste time attracting the attention of Fenway fandom as he hit a home run in the first inning of his first game at Fenway Park. The victim was 2004 Cy Young winner Johan Santana of the Minnesota Twins.

2002 Happy to strike back at his former employers, the Red Sox, Texas center fielder Carl Everett hit a three-run homer in the first and helped drive John Burkett from the game (charged with eight earned runs in 1⅓ innings). Everett followed with a grand slam in the second. The Rangers scored six runs in each inning, but Frank Castillo was left in to absorb 10 earned runs over 3⅔ innings. Everett's seven RBIs matched those of the whole Red Sox team, and the Rangers won—in Texas—19–7.

2000 Sleepless… in Boston, staying up to watch the Seattle ballgame. The Sox scored four runs in the third, but the Mariners tied it with two in the fifth and two in the sixth. For the next 12 innings, no one scored. Neither did the Red Sox in the top of the 19th at Safeco Field. The Red Sox called on their seventh pitcher of the night, Jeff Fassero. The first batter he faced was Mike Cameron, who homered for a 5–4 Seattle win.

In courtroom action, three men sued the City of Boston for being arrested on the charge of selling Red Sox tickets outside Fenway Park; all sold tickets for less than face value. All sued for false arrest and imprisonment, revisiting their arrests in 1998 and 1999, before Judge Tauro's April 10, 2000 court decision voiding similar arrests.

1996 Roger Clemens only struck out four, while walking three and serving up 11 hits (and seven earned runs). His record declined to 4–11, as Kansas City beat the Red Sox, 9–4, at Kauffman Stadium. Was this the twilight of a great career?

1993 Around 6:00 A.M., Roger Clemens was bitten by an injured dog lying beside an exit road along a Baltimore expressway. Clemens tried to lift the dog to help it, but the mixed terrier bit the Rocket, breaking the skin on his right thumb and requiring a tetanus shot at Johns Hopkins University Hospital. Baltimore health department manager Earl C. Watson said he didn't anticipate a rabid Roger since there had not been cases of rabies among Baltimore dogs for several years. The dog paid for the incident with its life; it was destroyed. Inquiring reporters wanted to know if Clemens was out early, or still out from the night before. GM Lou Gorman said it was too early to determine if Clemens was guilty of any curfew violation.

1973 This was the date of the famous Thurman Munson–Carlton Fisk brawl. It was the top of the ninth, in a tie game, and Munson doubled to lead off. He moved up to third on a Graig Nettles grounder and Yankee Gene Michael was supposed to bring him home with a bunt, but Michael missed and Munson had no choice other than to barrel through, upend Fisk, and try to dislodge the ball. Fisk was flattened but held the ball for the out. Fisk then "flipped Munson over to get rid of him. Munson threw a punch, they clinched and then Michael (ball one, strike one) jumped over Munson to throw a few for the visitors." (*New York Times*)

"There's no question I threw the first punch," Munson admitted later, but argued, "Fisk was lucky he didn't get into a fight last night after the way he blocked the plate on Roy White."

Munson and Fisk clinched, and when Michael launched himself onto Fisk, a donnybrook erupted. Both catchers were ejected, but Michael was not—which prompted another round of upset. Bob Montgomery filled in for Fisk, and singled with two out in the bottom of the ninth, moved up on a walk, then scored the winning run on Mario Guerrero's single to center. Sparky Lyle lost his fifth straight game to Boston since being traded in 1972. Guerrero had been the player to be named later in the Lyle-for-Cater trade.

1969 Yastrzemki drove in the first Red Sox run, but was erased at home plate two batters later, when George Scott topped a slow roller off the mound toward first base. Blue Moon Odom threw home and bagged Yaz. Manager Dick Williams was not impressed with Yaz's hustle, so he told his left fielder to grab some bench, and put Joe Lahoud in left. Jim Lonborg had a three-run lead into Oakland's bottom of the ninth, when the A's scored three times and won, 4–3. Yaz was reportedly fined $500, too.

1968 The Yankees scored their lone run off Dave Morehead in classic old-time baseball style: a drag bunt by Tom Tresh, a stolen base, and Bill Robinson's clean single to center. Yankees rookie Stan Bahnsen struck out 12 Red Sox, grudgingly doled out just three hits, and won the 1–0 shutout.

1962 Only one second-inning walk to Al Smith stood between Bill Monbouquette and a 1–0 perfect game over the White Sox. Early Wynn was pitching for Chicago and helped keep it scoreless until the eighth; he got the first two outs but then three straight singles broke the ice for the sole Red Sox run. The no-hitter came just five weeks after Earl Wilson threw one for Boston. The final batter was Luis Aparicio and Monbo had two strikes on him, but ump Bill McKinley said that Luis checked his swing on the next pitch. He called it a ball. A Red Sox fan at Comiskey shouted, clear as day, "They shot the wrong McKinley!" Monbo said it was hard to keep his focus, but he got Luis swinging on the next pitch.

1953 In the ninth inning of a 3–1 game, Detroit had runners on first and second with just one out. Sox pitcher Skinny Brown threw three balls to Matt Batts, and on the 3–0 count, manager Lou Boudreau called in Ben Flowers to relieve. Flowers threw one pitch—a ball, loading the bases. It was the eighth straight game in which Flowers had appeared, still a major-league record. Kinder was called on next. Two inherited runs scored, and the game was tied. The Tigers won it in the 10th, 4–3.

1948 In the 1948 race, teams were bunched together so tightly that when the Indians took two from the Red Sox, it dropped the Sox from first place to fourth place in one day. Boston could only get one run in each loss, 12–1 and 6–1. Cleveland's Lou Boudreau stole home early in the second game, and Boston players kicked because they thought the pitch should have been ruled strike three.

1923 Harry Frazee sold the Red Sox to a group headed by Bob Quinn. The weakened Red Sox limped through the 1920s, while the Yankees prospered. Donald Honig quotes Ernie Shore as later summing up: "When they talk about a Yankee dynasty, I say it was really a Red Sox dynasty, in a Yankee uniform."

1921 Red Sox pitcher Bullet Joe Bush gave up a single to George Sisler in the first inning, and not another hit the rest of the game, beating the Browns, 2–0. Both Sox runs scored in the first.

Even though the world war had ended in November 1918, Harry Frazee's Red Sox continued to assess a 10% "war tax" on tickets to Fenway Park; the Braves did not. Grandstand prices at Braves Field were $1.00, but at Fenway they were $1.10. It may have finally come to hurt the Sox, as attendance in late July games were "only a few hundred persons each day." (*Boston Globe*) Boston Mayor Peters wrote a letter to Frazee asking for an explanation.

1907 Every Boston batter had two or more hits, except the center fielders (they were changed mid-game), and every Boston batter scored at least one run. Even the pitcher, Ralph Glaze, had three hits and scored a run. Boston's 22 hits were more than three times as many as the seven given up by Glaze, but Boston beat Cleveland by a much larger margin, 14–1.

1905 One reason the Red Sox played nine doubleheaders in a 16-day stretch in September was due to the unusual number of rainouts earlier in the year. After the August 1 rainout in Boston, there had already been eight rainouts on the road and eight more at home.

1903 Highball Wilson was the winner in the first game, giving Boston but five hits and walking just one—in the process beating the similarly stingy Cy Young 1–0. Young's weakness—such as it was—came in the fifth when he let up a run on back-to-back-to-back singles. After the tie game the day before, both teams may have been hustling this game along—the entire game was over in 1:05. That's right, a 65-minute ball game!

Both games combined were played in less than three hours, the second game being 1:45 long. Neither team scored in the first four innings, but then Boston scored one run in the fifth, keyed by a Jake Stahl triple, and four more runs in the sixth. This was the first game in which both Stahls started. Only Jake got a hit—two in fact, one a three-bagger. Chick was hitless. Buck Freeman's drive hit the top of the fence in right and dropped over for a two-run homer—said to be the longest ball yet hit in Washington. It was his seventh of the season, and Boston lead the league with 27 homers. Boston 5, Washington 1.

TRANSACTIONS
1907: Purchased Cy Morgan from the St. Louis Browns.
1932: Sold Wilcy Moore to the Yankees on waivers. Purchased
    Dusty Rhodes from the Yankees on waivers.
1944: Purchased Rex Cecil from San Diego.
1957: Purchased Murray Wall from Dallas.

DEBUTS

1913: Wally Snell	2002: Cliff Floyd,
1959: Nelson Chittum	Bobby Howry
1995: Mike Stanton	2003: Scott Williamson
1996: Mark Brandenburg	2004: Orlando Cabrera
2001: Ugueth Urbina	

BIRTHDATES
Frank Bushey 1906 (1927–1930); Tony Muser 1947 (1969); Brent Knackert 1969 (1996)

DEATHS
Ike Boone 1958

August 2

1995 The Tigers' Sean Bergman shut out the Sox, 5–0. It was the only time the Sox were shut out during the 1995 season. (In 1906, they were shut out 28 times.)

1987 Kansas City rookie Kevin Seitzer learned he'd only tied a league record with a 6-for-6 day. "I guess I should try for seven next time," Seitzer laughed. The two homers, a double, and two singles, driving in seven RBIs, was the best day he ever had. He helped the Royals roll the Red Sox, 13–5, on a 102-degree day which staffers say measured 154 on the artificial turf.

1978 The Red Sox began to come back to life. After sporting a 14-game lead over the Yankees in mid-July, Boston had lost 11 of their last 14 games, while the Yankees had won 12 of 16. And the Yankees got off to a 5–0 lead in this evening's game in New York. The Red Sox put together five to tie it in the middle innings. After two rain delays, and 14 innings, the score remained tied at 1:16 A.M. The curfew took effect, and the game would be played out the following evening, weather permitting. (See August 3, 1978.)

1972 The Red Sox lost the first game of a home doubleheader against New York. They won the second game and then, with the exception of one loss on July 31, 1973, they won every time they hosted the Yankees until September 9, 1974.

1971 The Sox pulled the plug on Luis Tiant after the Orioles scored four runs off him in the bottom of the first. Bill Lee came on in relief and got the final out in the first, then limited the Birds to two hits over the following eight. He also beat out three infield hits; his second-inning bunt came with two outs in the top of the second and scored Bob Montgomery from third. Final score: Boston 7, Baltimore 4.

1959 Detroit's Jim Bunning pitched the first "perfect inning" since Lefty Grove in 1928, as he struck out the Red Sox on nine pitches in the ninth inning. Jackie Jensen's three-run homer in the eighth, off Paul Foytack, pinned the 5–4 loss on the Detroit starter. Bunning's job was to keep it close in the ninth, so the Tigers would have a chance. He succeeded admirably. But Ike Delock held the Tigers at bay, and when Bobo Osborne pinch-hit for Bunning, he flied out.

1956 The record for a game is 11 RBIs, but Boston's Jackie Jensen banged in nine, more than sufficient to help tame the Tigers, 18–3. Jensen had a three-run homer in the first, drove in one with a sacrifice fly in the fifth, cleared the bases with a triple in the sixth inning, and then singled in two more in the seventh.

1947 It's Bobby Doerr Night at Fenway Park. Eleven years with the Red Sox, at age 29 he had the most seniority among current players. He really cleaned up: a sedan, a truck for his mink farm in Oregon, a powerboat given him by Ted Williams, a tractor, a juke box, another dozen assorted gifts (including ones for his wife and son), and even a portable bowling alley. In the ballgame that followed, he went 0-for-4, but at least the team won.

1940 The visiting Red Sox out-slugged the Tigers, 12–9, with four of the 14 hits coming off the bat of shortstop Joe Cronin. He hit a single, a double, a triple, and—in the eighth inning—a home run, for his second cycle (the first time was with the Senators in 1929). The Tigers used four pitchers, but it didn't matter—Cronin, and the Sox, kept hitting.

1938 Jim Tabor doubled twice in his major league debut with the Red Sox. He'd signed with the Athletics, but was underage at the time and so ruled a free agent. Meanwhile, the Red Sox did a deal with his father. That one was legal.

1933 The Red Sox had two outs in the seventh inning but had scored one run and had runners on first and third. Lefty Weiland hit a ball up the middle which would have easily driven in Johnny Hodapp with a second run—except that the ball hit off the leg of umpire Bill McGowan. The ump ruled it a dead ball and sent Hodapp (who had already crossed home plate) back to the third-base bag, though permitting Weiland to take first (which prompted the runner on first to advance to second). Bases loaded, but a fly ball retired the side and the run never scored. Boston lost the game, 2–1.

1931 Playing a Sunday doubleheader against the Yankees at Braves Field (before mid-1932 any Sunday Sox home games had to be played at Braves Field, since Fenway was situated too close to a house of worship), former Sox pitcher Red Ruffing won the first game for New York (4–1), and former Yankees pitcher Wilcy Moore won the second game for Boston (beating future Red Sox pitcher George Pipgras, 1–0). 39,700 fans turned out.

1923 Bob Quinn's group assumes ownership of the Red Sox. The Frazee era is finis.

1922 Five Cambridge boys broke into Fenway Park and stole 10 pairs of spikes, 12 caps, six bats, 10 gloves, and other items. They were caught the next day wearing various items and "cavorting about the field"—one had on Muddy Ruel's chest protector, another was wearing manager Hugh Duffy's stockings, etc. The 15-year-olds all pleaded guilty to breaking and entering and larceny.

1920 Pitcher Elmer Myers was obtained from the Indians. This was a good pickup; he went 9–1 for the Red Sox before the season was out.

1914 Don't you just hate when that happens? George Foster was locked in a pitchers' duel with Carl Weilman of the St. Louis Browns through 12 innings at Sportsman's Park. Then shortstop Doc Lavan dropped down a perfect squeeze bunt, fielded by Foster, bringing home the lone run of the game in the bottom of the 13th inning. Browns 1, Red Sox 0.

1913 Esty Chaney made his major league debut for the Red Sox, throwing the ninth inning of the second game against Cleveland. At 6–0, it was the fifth loss in a row to Cleveland. Chaney walked two, gave up a hit, but allowed just one run, making the final score 7–0. The only other major league appearance of his career was in the short-lived Federal League, throwing four innings in a game for the Brooklyn Tip Tops.

1906 The White Sox beat Boston, 3–0, the first of four consecutive shutouts suffered by Boston.

1904 Four Boston ballplayers arrived back at the Hotel Euclid after beating Cleveland at League Park. They discovered a fire on the fifth floor and put it out. The four—Bill Dinneen, Hobe Ferris, Norwood Gibson, and Freddy Parent—were recommended for medals.

1901 Cy Young came to the ballpark, hoping to win his 20th game of the year. There was never any suspense. Boston scored five times in the first, four more times in the second, and banged out 22 hits, while Philadelphia's fielding was so wretched (eight errors) that it's surprising Boston only scored 16 times. Young won with a shutout, 16–0.

TRANSACTIONS
2001: Released Pete Schourek.

DEBUTS
1913: Esty Chaney
1919: Bob McGraw, Allan Russell
1938: Jim Tabor
1998: Greg Swindell

BIRTHDATES
Tom Burgmeier 1943 (1978–1982); Roger LaFrancois 1954 (1982);
Jim Dorsey 1955 (1984–1985); Danny Sheaffer 1961 (1987); Tim
Wakefield 1966 (1995–2005); Scott Taylor 1967 (1992–1993)

DEATHS
Guy Cooper 1951

August 3

2000 *Boston Globe* columnist Diane White suggested the Red Sox relocate to Hartford, Connecticut, saying the plan for a replacement Fenway was a disastrous one. Since the Sox are supposed to be New England's team, why not Hartford?

1995 Axed hitting coach Mike Easler and the Red Sox reached an out-of-court settlement on the wrongful dismissal lawsuit Easler had filed against his former employer. Easler had refused to coach replacement players if he received a salary that was less than the $109,000 offered the replacement men. Jim Rice took over as hitting coach. The NLRB ruled that Easler had a case, supporting his claim that he was part of the union, since he paid dues, and not part of management.

1992 Boston's Billy Hatcher stole home in the third inning of a 7–1 Red Sox win over Toronto. It was the first time a Red Sox player had stolen home since Joe Foy in August of 1968. Jays catcher Pat Borders made it easy, instinctively bounding out in front of the plate to grab the ball when he saw Hatcher breaking for home out of the corner of his eye. Having left the catcher's box to take the ball, Hatcher was automatically safe due to catcher interference, but home plate umpire Rocky Roe said he would have been safe in any event. He had the plate stolen. Roe apparently erred, however, in not awarding first base to Brunansky; the pitch should have been called a balk, but that would have taken some of the romance out of Hatcher's steal.

1980 Relief pitcher Tom Burgmeier became the last Red Sox pitcher to play another position in the field, when he was shifted to take Jim Rice's spot in left field for the final out of the ninth inning in Boston. Skip Lockwood came on in relief of Burgmeier, whose defensive skills weren't tested as Lockwood got shortstop Dave Roberts to pop up to catcher Carlton Fisk and preserve the 6–4 win over the Rangers. No other Red Sox pitcher had played in the field since Mike Ryba caught three games behind the plate back in 1942.

1978 Resuming the 14-inning affair begun the previous evening, neither team had a hit until the 17th inning, when four Sox singles plated two runs, and Bob Stanley held the Yanks hitless again. Boston 7, New York 5 was the final. The evening's regularly-scheduled game started later, due to the continuation of the August 2 game, and the teams were unable to complete it, again due to late-evening rains. This time, though, the Sox had a 4–1 lead after six innings. They started playing the seventh and Fred Lynn hit a three-run homer and Bob Bailey homered, making it 8–1. That was it. After a 1:29 rain delay, the game was finally called at 12:51 A.M. That made it two partial games in one evening, and both went into the books as Red Sox wins.

1967 The Red Sox secure the services of catcher Elston Howard from the Yankees. New York gets some cash and two players to be named. Howard hit only .147 for Boston but called a good game and helped stabilize the Impossible Dream team. One player named rather quickly is Pete Magrini; the other, named just five days later, is Ron Klimkowski.

1949 Ellis Kinder struck out 14 Browns—the most strikeouts recorded by a Red Sox pitcher since Smoky Joe Wood's 15 on July 7, 1911.

1948 The Red Sox scored early and late, but only once in the middle innings. Boston beat the St. Louis Browns, 15–8. Jack Kramer had to leave early, and Earl Johnson finished up. The oddest moment was when three of the five eighth-inning Red Sox runs scored on a wild throw by third baseman Bob Dillinger—that must have been some throw!

1945 In absentia, since he was serving in the Coast Guard, Bobby Doerr was awarded the MVP award for 1944 by *The Sporting News* in ceremonies held to celebrate the 155th anniversary of the Coast Guard. Joe Cronin accepted on his behalf. Washington beat Boston in two games, 7–3 and 3–1.

1944 Bobby Doerr went for a second physical and was again rejected because of a punctured eardrum, but the finding was overruled and Doerr was scheduled for induction. Losing Doerr (and Tex Hughson) to military service late in the season may well have cost the Red Sox the pennant in 1944.

No cheering in the press box—but it's OK if you're about 9,000 miles away. Sgt. Hy Hurwitz, former *Boston Globe* sportswriter now serving with the Second Marine Division, wrote to Joe Cronin from Saipan and said he'd formed a local chapter of the Red Sox Marching and Chowder Society, organizing fellow servicemen from a number of cities to root for the Red Sox to win the pennant— the idea being that the last time the Red Sox won the pennant was in 1918, the year the U.S. won World War I.

1930 Washington won the first game, beating the visitors from Boston, 11–2. Red Sox pitcher Jack Russell held the Senators to five hits in the second game, and hit a home run, too. Boston won, 7–1.

1929 Thirteen of Chicago's 15 runs were unearned, as Boston fielders committed five errors in the first three innings, though Red Ruffing could hardly complain as he yielded 10 hits in 2⅔ innings. The final score was 15–4.

1914 Sox owner Joseph Lannin offered the Boston Braves the use of the larger facility, Fenway Park, for the rest of the 1914 season, free of charge. The South End Grounds, where the Braves played, was simply too small to accommodate the large crowds the pennant-contending Braves were attracting.

1909 The novelty of having 13 college men on a baseball team was the subject of Wallace Goldsmith's sports page cartoon in the *Boston Globe*, terming them all "summa cum laude in batting and fielding" and "a natural product of cultured Boston." There was a crowd so huge that an estimated 10,000 people had to stand on the field itself, forcing many people in the seats to stand as well, some standing on their seats. Thousands more were denied entrance, simply because there was no room. Fans even sat on the benches in the dugouts, as a newsphoto depicted. Mel Webb said that it was impossible to see from the press box "except the backs of the catchers' heads and the caps of the men at bat." The crowd was good-natured, though it was a constant struggle to keep them from encroaching on the field of play; Arellanes used a broom and a sense of humor to keep the fans back. Somehow Tim Murnane wrote the story, though, of the twin defeats doled out to Detroit, 2–1 and 8–7, the latter a come-from-behind win with two runs in the bottom of the ninth.

1906 Chicago's Big Ed Walsh would have had a no-hitter, but Boston right fielder Jack Hayden spoiled it with a single in the ninth inning.

TRANSACTIONS
1967: Acquired Elston Howard from the New York Yankees in trade
    for Pete Magrini and a PTBNL (Ron Klimkowski).
2000: Rico Brogna was obtained through the waivers process from the Phillies.

DEBUTS

1926: Jack Tobin	1943: Emmett O'Neill	1998: Orlando Merced
1933: Joe Judge	1968: Floyd Robinson	1999: Bryce Florie
1938: Bill Harris,	1973: Dick Pole	2004: Doug Mientkiewicz,
Joe Heving	1979: Win Remmerswaal	Dave Roberts
1940: Yank Terry	1990: Joe Hesketh	2005: Jose Cruz Jr.

BIRTHDATES
Ed McFarland 1874 (1908); Doug Taitt 1902 (1928–1929); Vic Johnson 1920 (1944–1945); Rod Beck 1968 (1999–2001); Kevin Morton 1968 (1991)

DEATHS
Jack Hayden 1942; Homer Ezzell 1976; Elmer Smith 1984

August 4

2001 Only two Red Sox have hit multiple home runs on their birthday. Nomar Garciaparra is the only major leaguer to have hit three (July 23, 2002). Troy O'Leary hit a pair on August 4, 2001. Both came in the first game, a 10–4 Sox win over Cleveland, hit off two different pitchers. O'Leary was 3-for-4 in the game, but didn't take part in the night game, a 6–2 Bosox win.

1992 In a Leland's auction, actor Charlie Sheen placed the winning bid by telephone for the baseball hit by Mookie Wilson which had skittered through Bill Buckner's legs and won Game Six of the 1986 World Series for the New York Mets. The price, with the premium, was $93,500.

1991 The *Boston Globe* published the first of a three-part series by Steve Fainaru on "Blacks at Fenway," noting that the BoSox Club fan group had never had a single black member, that the crowd at Fenway still "resembles a rugby match in

Pretoria" (in the words of one outspoken fan), and interviewing black employees at Fenway while noting that before Mo Vaughn arrived, Ellis Burks had been the only black player on the 1991 team. Montreal's Tim Raines had vetoed a trade to the Red Sox because of the perception of racism. A *Globe* tally found just 71 black patrons among the 34,032 attending the August 2 game.

1988 "It wasn't our night," said Joe Morgan after an 11–6 loss to the Tigers brought an end to Morgan Magic. The Red Sox had won 18 of Morgan's first 19 games as manager.

1986 White Sox pitchers held the Red Sox to three hits, and starter Jose DeLeon got the 1–0 win. Now 2–0 on the season, DeLeon's two wins had both come at the expense of Roger Clemens and the Red Sox; he'd won the July 30 game, 7–2. Clemens, instead of being 19–2, was but a mere 17–4, but it was his throwing error that set up a sac fly producing the lone Chicago run.

1983 Bob Mackin reports a bizarre attempt to halt a slump, apparently the idea of first-base coach Rich Donnelly's wife Peggy. She painted "TR"—for Texas Rangers—on the coach's bottom. During a team meeting, he emerged from the manager's office and mooned the team. Rangers pitcher Danny Darwin may have been shaken; the Red Sox scored four runs off him in the top of the first. Texas tied it in the bottom of the ninth, but lost in the 10th, 5–4, on doubles by Jim Rice and Dwight Evans. Go Sox!

1975 Denny Doyle went 2-for-4, extending his hitting streak to 22 games. "When I signed my first pro conrtact," he said, "I thought I'd be hitting in front of Mickey Mantle and Babe Ruth, I guess. The World Series every year. Of course, it didn't work out that way." But he was enjoying the ride. The Red Sox lost the game, though, 12–8, to the Orioles.

1968 Bill Harrelson picked up the ball for the California Angels, continuing a 1–1 tie game which had started on June 13 but was suspended in the middle of the sixth. He got them to the ninth, but then Mike Andrews singled, Joy Foy walked, and Carl Yastrzemski walked. Sox first baseman Ken Harrelson (no relation) was due up. Rather than risk a Harrelson-Harrelson faceoff, the Angels beckoned Andy Messersmith to deal with the no-out, bases-loaded jam. Oops. The Hawk hit a grand slam into the left-field screen. Red Sox 5, Angels 1. There was a regularly-scheduled game on August 4, and California fared much better in that one, beating Boston, 12–6.

1959 Pumpsie Green's first hit at Fenway Park is a truly rare triple off the left-field Wall. Later the same season, on September 12, future Sox manager Joe Morgan hit a triple off the Wall, too. Morgan was playing at the time for Kansas City.

1948 Before St. Louis even got up to bat, Boston scored six first-inning runs. Not sufficiently discouraged, the Browns scored seven times in the bottom of the first. The Red Sox tied it in the third, went ahead by one run in the sixth, but after getting two outs in the ninth, Red Sox relief pitcher Ellis Kinder gave up two singles which drove in the tying and winning runs, 9–8.

1945 An unusual day: Wally Holborow's 4–0 shutout of the Red Sox was a win for Washington. It was his first major league start—and a two-hitter. Havana, Cuba's Carlos Santiago Ullrich started for the Senators in the second game. Boston's Tom McBride came up twice in the fourth inning, with the bases loaded both times. Both times he cleared the bases, with a double and a triple, first off the

Cuban native and the second time off Joe Cleary, a native of Cork City, Ireland.

It was Cleary's only major league appearance—he walked three and gave up five hits, while retiring just one batter. His career ERA was 189.00. Cleary didn't seem too effective, so the Senators turned to a one-legged pitcher instead. That's worse than it sounds; Bert Shepard was a war hero who wore an artificial leg and showed tremendous determination to play major league ball. He acquitted himself well in what proved to be his only major league appearance, throwing 5⅓ innings to close out the game while only giving up three hits and one run. His lifetime ERA stands at 1.69. McBride's two hits were a double and a triple, and his six RBIs in one inning (half of the 12 runs scored in the fourth frame) tied the major league record at the time. Final score, 15–4.

1940 The win made Lefty Grove 59–16 lifetime against the Detroit Tigers. His catcher for the day was Jimmie Foxx, who homered and (like Grove) drove in a run; Ted Williams tripled in three, the blow that did in Hal Newhouser. Sox 7, Tigers 3.

1937 Cleveland second baseman Roy Hughes made 11 putouts in the first game of a doubleheader. That tied a record held by three other modern era second basemen. With four assists, he fell short of the record of 18 chances. He did go 2-for-5 at the plate. Despite all that, the Red Sox won, 8–6.

1917 Pitcher Carl Mays bought a tonic at Fenway and then, with a Sunday fishing trip planned, went to digging worms under the grandstand. He lost his purse containing $70 and believed he lost it while exploring. Who found it remains unknown. Dutch Leonard handled mound duties and saw the Sox beat the Indians, 3–2, in 11 innings, largely through "scientific sacrificing"—Boston batters bunted seven times, one of them a successful squeeze.

1916 Despite winning 14 games in a row, including this day's 6–1 defeat of Babe Ruth and the Red Sox, the St. Louis Browns remain mired in seventh place. Eddie Plank did the honors, holding Boston to just two hits.

1904 The reigning World Champions had been in first place since the fifth day of the year, but fell out of first on this day with an 11–1 loss to Cleveland.

DEBUTS

1932: Gordon Rhodes	1964: Jay Ritchie
1945: Ty LaForest	2000: Rico Brogna
1950: Buddy Rosar	2005: Roberto Petagine
1957: Murray Wall	

BIRTHDATES

Ski Melillo 1899 (1935–1937); Ken Poulsen 1947 (1967); Roger Clemens 1962 (1984–1996); Troy O'Leary 1969 (1995–2001); Bobby Howry 1973 (2002–2003); Paxton Crawford 1977 (2000–2001)

DEATHS

Camp Skinner 1944; Jerry Standaert 1964; Lefty Jamerson 1980

August 5

2000 Returning to the Red Sox following his 10-game suspension, outfielder Carl Everett kicked things off with what Bob Hohler called "a high-decibel shouting match behind closed doors with manager Jimy Williams." Profanities were uttered. Everett went 3-for-5 in the game, with a solo homer in the bottom of the ninth, but the Sox fell just short to the Royals, 7–5.

1997 Troy O'Leary hit two long home runs, Nomar Garciaparra was 4-for-7 with a homer and two doubles, and John Valentin hit a pair of doubles, too. Boston had 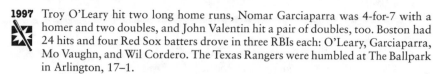 24 hits and four Red Sox batters drove in three RBIs each: O'Leary, Garciaparra, Mo Vaughn, and Wil Cordero. The Texas Rangers were humbled at The Ballpark in Arlington, 17–1.

1979 The Sox beat the Brewers in County Stadium, 7–2, in the first game—and then piled on in the second, 19–5, with 27 hits, and runs in every single inning but the fourth (despite Rice singling and Watson walking to lead off the inning). Win Remmerswaal got the win (his first major league win), by virtue of being the man on the mound at the end of the fifth when the game became official. It was, at that time, 13–3.

1975 Scheduled starting Red Sox pitcher Rogelio (Roger) Moret figured in the day's news earlier than he had planned, when he crashed his car into a parked trailer on I-95 in North Stonington, Connecticut, at 4:30 A.M. Management wasn't sure why Moret was (still?) out at that hour, or why he was in southern Connecticut in the first place, and said Moret was still groggy when they had spoken.

1953 After setting his consecutive-games-in-relief record the previous week, Boston's Ben Flowers got his first major league start and shut out the Browns, 5–0. The Sox made three errors, jeopardizing the shutout, but also executed five double-plays to atone. The losing pitcher was Don Larsen.

1935 It may have been just as well that the game ended in the sixth, a barely-official 10–2 Yankees win at washed-out Fenway. There were several injuries, and even Lou Gehrig had to play, after "hobbling about the field for four innings, a victim of lumbago, which had him crippled and playing under difficulties." The Sox tried to kill time, hoping to have the game canceled. When Myril Hoag stole home, he did so standing up; the Red Sox didn't want to record another out. Yankees runners were less than swift on the basepaths. On August 12, both managers were fined $100.00 for "highly reprehensible" stalling.

1934 Bill Werber stole three bases in a doubleheader when he went 5-for-8. Still, Boston could only manage a split with the Senators.

1927 Two triples by Ira Flagstead sparked a 4–1 Red Sox win over the visiting White Sox. Slim Harriss got the win.

1922 Beloved 19th century Boston ballplayer Tommy McCarthy died in Boston. On August 14th, an all-star team played the Red Sox and prevailed in a benefit game that raised more than $5,000 for McCarthy's family. He was voted into the Hall of Fame in 1946. (See also August 14, 1922.)

1916 St. Louis made all the errors (three) in the first game, and the Red Sox won, with Ernie Shore pitching, 4–1. In the second game, Boston out-erred the Browns, with four to St. Louis's one. Worse, three of the errors were bunched in the fifth inning. Combined with a walk, three singles, and a double steal, the Browns scored five times, to win 6–3.

1915 Tim Murnane wrote in *The Sporting News* that "no player ever received such abuse from a Boston crowd as did [Buck] Weaver in this series." Among the incidents mentioned, regarding three recently-completed White Sox visit to Boston, was Weaver thumping Jack Barry in the head with a baseball as Barry was going into second base.

1910 Reflecting estrangement, Boston owner John I. Taylor made the unusual announcement that team captain Harry Lord was on the market to be traded. By August 10, the *Chicago Tribune* reported that Lord was at his home in Maine and that the White Sox had tried to trade for him, but Boston had asked for ace pitcher Big Ed Walsh. "I'll give you this ballpark before I'll trade Walsh," Comiskey said he told Taylor. "I'll let him go when shuffleboard becomes the national game."

1904 For the first time in American League history, New York reached first place, .614 to Cleveland's .613 and Boston's .611.

1901 Cy Young got the 3–1 win, courtesy of Baltimore third baseman Jack Dunn's error in the eighth. There was a second game, and Baltimore won that one easily, 9–0. Baltimore's Burt Hart doubled in the second but was thrown out trying to stretch it to a triple; he was so angry with umpire John Haskell that he struck him in the face. Baltimore manager John McGraw was the peacemaker this time; Hart was, of course, ejected.

TRANSACTIONS
1946: Released Frankie Pytlak.
1964: Signed free agent Al "Fuzzy" Smith.
1977: Signed amateur free agent Rich Gedman.
1989: Released Ed Romero.
2003: Signed David McCarty off waivers from the Oakland Athletics.

DEBUTS
1935: Stew Bowers
1964: Al Smith
1967: Elston Howard
2003: David McCarty

BIRTHDATES
Doc Adkins 1872 (1902); Fabian Gaffke 1913 (1936–1938); Bob Daughters 1914 (1937); Bernie Carbo 1947 (1974–1978); Reid Nichols 1958 (1980–1985); John Olerud 1968 (2005); John Wasdin 1972 (1997–2000)

DEATHS
Sammy White 1991

August 6

2001 As the saying goes, it was from the outhouse to the penthouse. Red Sox catcher Scott Hatteberg lined into a triple play in the fourth inning. In his next at-bat, after the Rangers scored five runs to take a 7–5 lead, Hatteberg came up with three batters on base—and hit a grand slam off reliever Juan Moreno to give the Red Sox a lead they would never relinquish. Final: Red Sox 10, Rangers 7.

1989 Carl Yastrzemski's #8 was retired before the game at Fenway Park, joining Ted Williams, Joe Cronin, and Bobby Doerr as the only player numbers retired by the Red Sox. When the game began, Roger Clemens started and got the first out, but then was removed from the game after two singles and a walk loaded the bases. Dennis Lamp relieved and all three inherited runners scored. The Red Sox scored six times, though, and Rob Murphy got the win in relief.

1984 Marty Barrett got four hits in the first game, but the Red Sox lost to Detroit, 9–7. Wade Boggs got four hits in the second game, two of them were homers, and the Sox had Roger Clemens on the mound. Boston won the second game, 10–2.

1967 Dean Chance of the Twins retired every Red Sox batter he faced—all 15 of them. The game was an official game, a 2–0 win for the Twins. But because the game was called after 4½ innings, Chance was denied credit for a perfect game and didn't even get credit for a no-hitter as a consolation prize. He was credited with a complete game, though. And glad to get the win.

1950 Ellis Kinder really wanted this one; the Red Sox pitcher limited the White Sox to five hits, and helped his own cause with a sixth-inning grand slam off Billy Pierce. Kinder was the fourth Sox pitcher to hit a grand slam, and drove in six runs total. It was Kinder's only home run in 484 major league at-bats.

1942 Former Red Sox pitcher Gordon McNaughton, working as a postal clerk in Chicago, was enjoying the company of Mrs. Dorothy Moos in a hotel room when his jilted girlfriend, Mrs. Eleanor Williams, entered and shot and killed him. Williams used the service pistol of policeman Barney Towey, who was left sleeping in the hotel room to which he and Mrs. Williams had repaired after nightclubbing. Mrs. Williams was a "dice girl in a roadside tavern" and said she shot McNaughton because "he tried to dust me off." Both Williams and Moos said they had left their husbands to be with McNaughton. Though she could have received the death penalty, Williams was sentenced to just 1 to 14 years imprisonment and, upon losing her appeal for a new trial, said she would remarry her former husband—telegrapher Clarence Williams—in her jail cell. Towey shot himself to death after he was discharged from the police force for negligence in the care of his weapon. Exculpatory testimony on Eleanor's behalf came from other dice girls who said she "was a good girl" until McNaughton came on the scene and "gave her the old pitch."

1932 The ball took a "trick bounce" and hopped over second baseman Bill Cissell's outstretched hand, a fourth-inning single for Dale Alexander that proved to be the only hit of the game the Red Sox managed off Cleveland's Wes Ferrell.

1922 After the first inning, Boston held a 2–1 lead until Tris Speaker's solo homer tied it up for Cleveland. Despite 25 hits, it remained 2–2 until the bottom of the 12th when two bases on balls and two walks gave the Indians a 3–2 win.

1919 The New York Yankees obtained a temporary injunction from Justice Robert L. Luce of the New York Supreme Court, restraining Ban Johnson from interfering with the sale of Carl Mays from the Red Sox to the Yankees or canceling any games that New York would play with other league teams.

1917 Sox right-hander Rube Foster walked two Cleveland batters and then Joe Harris hit a double, giving the Indians a 2–0 lead. Boston never scored off Jim Bagby, and Cleveland never got another hit. Foster lost the one-hitter, 2–0.

1916 The game at St. Louis was a tight 1–0 win for Rube Foster and the Red Sox, a three-hitter, but the most excitement came in the sixth inning when words were spoken. The *New York Times* reported that after Jimmy Austin of the Browns had two strikes on him, Red Sox catcher Pinch Thomas "was heard making a remark." Austin struck out on the next pitch, and apparently took exception to the remark, for he "immediately tore off Thomas's mask, and the two came to blows. Players and police rushed to separate them." That was it for the two of them, of course. The game continued.

1912 There was just no beating Joe Wood. Cleveland knocked out 13 hits off him, and pushed the game into extra innings, but Wood still won, 5–4, and improved his won-loss record to 23–4.

1911 A nice Sunday outing on Lake Winnipesaukee for eight of the Red Sox took a turn for the worse when their chartered power boat sprang a leak and was beached on Governers Island. Carrigan, Hall, Karger, Nunamaker, Speaker, Wagner, Rip Williams, and Joe Wood were all rescued by another boat sent out to fetch them.

1910 Harry Lord was disappointed that his plan to have the Sox play an exhibition game the day after Labor Day (he would have pocketed a healthy share of the proceeds) was rejected by owner John I. Taylor, and Lord was clearly out of sorts. Taylor felt compelled to award the team's captaincy to Heinie Wagner instead, but sat down with Lord and talked it out. Lord's request for a trade was thought shelved but in fact he was traded within three days.

1909 Señor Frank Arellanes held the White Sox to five hits, in an 8–1 Red Sox win the *Chicago Tribune* dubbed "an alleged baseball contest." Four Chicago errors greased the skids, starting with pitcher Bill Burns mishandling a leadoff bunt in the first inning.

TRANSACTIONS
1951: Selected Aaron Robinson off waivers from the Detroit Tigers.
1998: Purchased Pete Schourek from the Houston Astros.
2004: Acquired Mike Myers from the Seattle Mariners for cash or
    a PTBNL, leaving some to wonder which it was.

DEBUTS
1907: Cy Morgan
1920: Elmer Myers

BIRTHDATES
Hy Gunning 1888 (1911); Hal Wiltse 1903 (1926–1928); Leon Culberson 1919 (1943–1947); Herb Moford 1928 (1959); Ray Culp 1941 (1968–1973); Jim Pankovits 1955 (1990); Stan Belinda 1966 (1995–1996); Keith Mitchell 1969 (1998)

DEATHS
Gordon McNaughton 1942; Tex Hughson 1993

August 7

2005 With eight innings of work (two earned runs, 11 strikeouts, and one walk), Tim Wakefield joined pretty select company—Cy Young and Roger Clemens—as the only three pitchers to throw at least 2,000 innings for the Red Sox. Wake reached 2,001 in the day's game against the Twins.

David Ortiz homered twice in the game, completing a stretch of 12 hits dating back to July 27 in which every hit was an extra-base hit. There were three games in which he had no hits at all, but if he made a hit, it was of the extra-base variety (including five doubles, two triples, and five home runs.)

1992 Sox DH Jack Clark doubled, going 1-for-4 with two RBIs, which might have made him feel better. Earlier in the day, Clark, who was making $8,700,000 under a three-year deal with the Red Sox, filed for bankruptcy. Newspaper accounts reported that he owned 18 automobiles. The vintage 1934 Ford must have had an appeal, and the two Ferraris, but did he really need three 1992 GM vans and three 1992 Mercedes? And what about the $37,000 he'd run up on his Nordstrom's charge card? The filing said he owed over $11 million in debts and had assets of under $5 million. Sure, blame it on Saddam Hussein. Clark said he was a victim of the Gulf War and the recession.

1990 Dave Winfield singled to second base in the bottom of the first inning off Boston starter Tom Bolton. It was the 2,500th hit of his career. The Red Sox beat the California Angels, 6–3, but there was a cloud hanging over Winfield's head as a result of a *Sports Illustrated* story alleging Winfield had bet on non-baseball sporting events. He denied the report, which appeared to emanate from allegations by gambler Howard Spira, currently under Federal indictment. Yankees owner George Steinbrenner was mixed up in all this, and was ultimately banned from baseball for life—clearly, the Boss had more than one life.

1988 Bruce Hurst threw 10 innings and a complete-game shutout, beating the Tigers, 3–0. He did so on the 31st anniversary of Willard Nixon's similar feat.

1984 Bill Buckner hit a grand slam in the bottom of the first, and Tony Armas hit a grand slam in the bottom of the second. Jack Morris served them both up, and another solo homer to Buckner in the second, too. This made Boston's Bruce Hurst happy, though he might have relaxed too much; Hurst gave up seven earned runs of his own, but got the win: Boston 12, Detroit 7. There was another game, and Detroit scored seven times in that one, too—the last two in the top of the 11th on Lance Parrish's second home run of the game. Boston only scored five times. Consequently, the Tigers won. Aurelio Lopez went to 9–0 on the season.

1977 A rare West Coast road trip where everything went right. Boston completed the road sweep, beating Oakland for their ninth straight road win, 5–2. Boston had now won 10 in a row, and Oakland had lost nine straight.

1972 In an interview with Massachusetts' *Springfield Union*, Carlton Fisk criticized both Yaz and Reggie Smith for failing to provide good leadership by example. He issued an unconvincing denial the following day. Smith and Yastrzemski had both been taken to task a year earlier by Billy Conigliaro, though in a different fashion. (See also July 10, 1971.)

1956 Yankees pitcher Don Larsen started and threw 10 innings, scattering just four hits. Willard Nixon was pitching a gem for the Red Sox, and after 10½ innings, neither team had scored. Larsen had some bad luck and, thanks to two Yankees errors and a walk, found the bases loaded in the bottom of the 11th with nobody out and Ted Williams in the on-deck circle. Stengel called on Tommy Byrne to relieve Larsen, but Byrne promptly walked Williams, forcing in the winning run, and the Sox won, 1–0. It was reported to be the largest crowd in Fenway history. Williams flipped his bat in the air—in a foul mood on the day and a little disgusted, since he always loved to hit—and started walking to the dugout until coach Del Baker reminded him he had to touch first base. Earlier in the same inning, Terrible Ted had spit at the fans who booed him loudly after he dropped a Mantle fly ball. It wasn't an easy crowd; earlier in the day, Jackie Jensen had to be held back by some of his teammates to prevent him from charging into the stands after a heckler over in right field. It was reported that Williams was assessed a $5,000 fine for his actions. Willard Nixon had earned an 11-inning complete game shutout.

1942 The first Red Sox batting champion, Dale Alexander (in 1932), was now a tobacco farmer in Greene County, Tennessee. He came up short in his campaign as the Democratic candidate for county sheriff, losing 5,196 to 4,876.

1941 Though Ted Williams often seemed to attract negative press coverage, Victor O. Jones of the *Boston Globe* devoted his column to The Kid's visit to Peter Gill, an amputee at Massachusetts General Hospital. As was always the case with Ted, his visits were neither publicized nor promoted. Jones learned of this one, though, and wrote it up.

1919 Everett Scott set an American League record by playing in 479 consecutive games. After four more games, he broke Fred Luderus's major league record.

1916 Boston's Dutch Leonard had a bad day and the White Sox outscored the Red ones, 7–1. Even pitcher Reb Russell got into the act, scoring the winning run with a third-inning single, moving up to second on a ground out, to third on a single by Eddie Collins, and scoring on a delayed double steal. It was the only time an opposing pitcher ever stole home against the Red Sox.

1915 Smoky Joe Wood "should have had a no-hit game in the first contest, Cleveland's only safe rap being a scratch hit [by Bill Wambsganss] made possible by Janvrin's slow fielding," wrote the *Washington Post*. Wood's one-hitter frustrated Cleveland, 2–0. It was Smoky Joe's fifth one-hitter.

1913 Fred "Spitball" Anderson joined the Red Sox again (he'd appeared in one game at the end of 1909 and done quite well) and got off to a decent start, but was bombed in the seventh. The Sox beat St. Louis, 9–8, but Anderson was gone by the time the Sox rallied. In 1913, Anderson posted a disappointing 0–6 record. The following year, he tried his luck in the Federal League.

1907 Heinie Wagner had a busy day at shortstop, fielding 16 balls behind Cy Young's complete game 14-inning 2–1 victory, but it was when he finally got his first hit his sixth time up that he singled in Hobe Ferris with the winning run.

1902 St. Louis bombed Cy Young for six runs in the bottom of the first inning, and added another six during the game, beating Boston, 12–4. It was the second time in 1902 that Young had allowed six runs in the first. Of 43 starts, Young pitched 41 complete games. This was not one of them. Both teams made four errors.

1901 The Bostons beat the Baltimores, 10–5, in the first game, out-hitting them 18–14. A seven-run sixth inning did Cuppy in, and Baltimore won, 10–4 in the latter game. There were another 23 hits in game two, for a day's total of 55 hits—and yet, the two games together lasted just three hours and 10 minutes. One inning ended suddenly, with a triple play, in the first contest, the play going 1-5-2-4-6.

TRANSACTIONS
1913: Purchased Mike McNally from Utica.
1968: Released Norm Siebern.
1989: Selected Greg Harris off waivers from the Phillies.

DEBUTS
1911: Joe Giannini
1918: Hack Miller, Bill Pertica
1989: Jeff Stone

BIRTHDATES
Chet Nourse 1887 (1909); Ted Wingfield 1899 (1924–1927); John Trautwein 1962 (1988); Rich Croushore 1970 (2000); Greg Pirkl 1970 (1996); Kerry Lacy 1972 (1996–1997); Edgar Renteria 1975 (2005)

DEATHS
Bobby Veach 1945; Tony Tonneman 1951; Hal Wagner 1979; Jimmy Cooney 1991; Mickey McDermott 2003

August 8

2005 The Red Sox activated Kevin Youkilis, calling him back up from Pawtucket in one of the ongoing flurry of roster moves that seems to characterize the early 21st century Red Sox. The Red Sox had activated Gabe Kapler on July 30, back from a partial season in Japan. When Youkilis joined Kapler and Adam Stern, they became the first team to ever have three Jews on the 25-man roster all at the same time. Coincidentally, after the Sox had designated Jay Payton for assignment in early July (at his request), they did not have a single African-American on the roster. Nothing nefarious, not like the old days.

2004 Tim Wakefield allowed a record six home runs in the game, the first Sox pitcher to throw as many gopher balls in one game, and the first major leaguer to do so since George Caster on September 24, 1940. The Sox scored six runs in the fourth inning, though, and supplied enough offense to ensure that Wakefield even walked away with the win! Boston 11, Detroit 9.

1989 Flash Gordon held the Red Sox to four hits and one run, 8–1. Late in the game, Rich Gedman pinch-hit (unsuccessfully) for Randy Kutcher, and stayed in the game, with Rick Cerone shedding the shinguards and taking over for Kutcher in right field.

1982 A line drive off the bat of Dave Stapleton fractured the skull of five-year-old Jonathan Keane of Greenland, New Hampshire. The child was carried to the first-aid station by none other than Sox slugger Jim Rice. The Red Sox beat Chicago, 12–6.

1976 An accomplishment destined to be broken, but the approximate $1,000,000 deal between Fred Lynn and the Red Sox was the richest in major league history.

1973 Boston's original designated hitter, Orlando Cepeda, did what he was designated to do: hit. He hammered four doubles off three Kansas City Royals pitchers, tying the major league record for two-baggers in a ballgame, and driving in six runs in Boston's 9–4 win at Royals Stadium.

1966 Billowing fog was so heavy in Boston that play was stopped a full four times, but the Boomer—rookie George Scott—banged a two-run tater out of sight over the left-field screen, to give the Red Sox a 3–1 win.

1961 Buddin and Geiger vs. Camilo Pascual, and Pascual came out on top. Gary Geiger thrilled the Fenway crowd with an inside-the-park grand slam in the third inning, the first in Red Sox history. It was looking dour for the Twins. Pascual was no great hitter—he hadn't driven in a single run all year—but he doubled in two runs in the fifth and singled in the Twins' sixth run in the sixth. Even though Don Buddin hit a homer in the seventh, Pascual prevailed, 6–5.

1945 Hank Greenberg's hard line drive hit 22-year-old rookie pitcher Jim Wilson behind the left ear. Young Wilson (with six wins to his credit) had to be carried from the field on a stretcher, and apparently had a plate put in his head. He went on to play 12 years of major league ball. It would take him until 1951 before he won another game, though—and then it was for the Boston Braves. The accident came in the second inning of a 12-frame Red Sox 7–4 win, giving the Sox a split on the day. Detroit's Walter Wilson was the loser.

1944 Tex Hughson won #18, but then had to enter military service to try and help win a war.

1940 It was Dom DiMaggio who did the damage, with a 4-for-5 day that included driving in the ninth-inning tying run, while pushing the ultimate winning run into scoring position. The Sox took four out of five from the visiting Yankees, and Dominic was 11-for-18 at the plate.

1937 Well, that was definitive! The White Sox blanked the Bosox, 13–0. The loss, though, is the first one for Boston in a couple of weeks. They've just enjoyed a 12-game winning streak, the longest streak in their history at the time. Actually, it was more like a non-losing streak since there was a tie game in the middle of it, but a non-loss is a non-loss. They did have 11-game streaks in 1903 and 1909.

1934 After 2½ innings, the Red Sox had a 10–1 lead over Philadelphia and it looked like an easy win for Wes Ferrell. He coughed up six runs in the bottom of the third, though, on two home runs. He was so angry he walked off the mound toward shortstop. Manager Bucky Harris managed to get the ball from him, and hand it to Lefty Grove to relieve. Ferrell was so angry at himself that as Billy Werber wrote in his autobiography, "Ferrell struck himself in the jaw with his fist and slammed his head into the concrete wall." He had to be restrained to prevent further damage. Grove recalled another time when Ferrell hit himself so hard on the jaw that he fell to the ground, having knocked himself out. The Sox did win this day's game, 11–9.

1931 Washington's Bobby Burke walked four Sox in the first four innings, but got his delivery under control and managed to throw a complete game no-hitter, blanking the Red Sox, 5–0. Only Walter Johnson had ever thrown a no-hitter for

Washington. The left-hander Burke pitched for 10 seasons, but never won more than the eight he won this year. "Burke didn't throw more than a half dozen curves all afternoon," said the plate umpire, George Moriarty.

1914 This guy could hit pretty well, too. Center fielder Tris Speaker executed an unassisted double play and started another DP, too. It was his second unassisted one of the season, pretty much a carbon copy of the April 21 twin killing. Three Tigers errors gave the Red Sox the margin of victory in a 5–2 home win.

1913 Hosting the Tigers, Red Sox pitcher Earl Moseley came up to bat in a tie game with one out in the bottom of the ninth. The *Boston Globe*'s James O'Leary wrote of Moseley: "As a rule, he misses the ball altogether, swinging on about everything served up, and the best he has got since he joined the team has been two or three fouls." Moseley drew a walk and was sacrificed to second. Speaker was walked, and Duffy Lewis hit one over the heads of the outfielders, scoring Moseley and winning the game.

TRANSACTIONS
1905: Percy Sumner "Pop" Rising purchased from New London.
1967: Sold Bob Tillman to the New York Yankees.
2002: Traded Jose Offerman to the Seattle Mariners for cash considerations.

DEBUTS
1911: Hy Gunning
1920: Cliff Brady
1951: Aaron Robinson
1996: Ken Grundt, Greg Pirkl

BIRTHDATES
None yet

DEATHS
Gene Mauch 2005

August 9

2003 Kevin Millar hit Fenway Park's 10,000th home run over the Wall during the eighth inning of a 6–4 victory over the Orioles.

1992 Sam Militello debuted for the Yankees and was staked to three runs in the bottom of the first. He shut out the Red Sox, with only Tony Pena squirting out a "chopper in the hole"—a second-inning hit through the shortstop hole. In the seven innings Militello pitched, before rain forced a 33-minute rain delay, he gave up just that one hit. Steve Farr got the save, when play resumed, retiring all six Sox batters he faced. New York scored three more times in the bottom of the eighth, and won, 6–0.

1984 Pitcher Charlie Mitchell made his major league debut with the Red Sox, coming in to pitch the eighth in a game the Sox were trailing, 6–3, against the Texas Rangers. The first batter he faced was first baseman Pete O'Brien. Oops, 7–3. Mitchell is one of only two Sox pitchers to have given up a home run to the first batter he faced in the big leagues. (See July 17, 1995.) Mitchell threw 16⅓ innings in 1984 and posted a 2.76 ERA. In 1985, he appeared in just two games.

The first batter he faced doubled. Andre Thornton hit a home run off him in the next inning. It was a short career.

1971 Bill Freehan's third home run of the game tied the score 11–11 in the top of the ninth. Detroit had six homers in the game. Boston's offense included a grand slam and a two-run double by Bob Montgomery. But it was a single that won it, in the bottom of the ninth. John Kennedy's double would have scored Billy Conigliaro, but Billy C. fell down rounding third and was thrown out at the plate. Rico Petrocelli pinch-hit for Sparky Lyle and singled to left, scoring Kennedy with the go-ahead run.

1960 With his home run over the right-field fence in Cleveland, Ted Williams tied Mel Ott for #3 on the all-time home run list at 511 home runs. *The Baseball Chronology* describes another, bizarre home run from the same game (a 6–3 win by the Indians): Vic Power hit a ball which ricocheted off the top of the same right-field fence to Sox right fielder Lu Clinton. "The ball hits Clinton's foot and is 'kicked' over the fence. Umpire Hal Smith ruled the hit a home run, since the ball never touched the ground."

1953 In his second at-bat since returning from Korea, Ted Williams drilled a pinch-hit home run off Mike Garcia in the seventh inning to cap a brief three-run rally in a 9–3 Fenway loss to the Indians.

1949 Dom DiMaggio was riding a 34-game hitting streak—the longest in Red Sox annals. Ted Williams and Birdie Tebbetts each hit two-run homers and the Red Sox had an early 5–0 lead. As the game progressed, the Red Sox had 10 hits off New York's Vic Raschi, but none of them were Dominic's. As Boston's leadoff batter, The Little Professor got one more at-bat (in the eighth) than some of the players further down in the order, but he failed to get a hit each of his first four times to the plate. Then he hit a line drive to center that was sinking—until Joe DiMaggio made a shoestring catch, ending the streak. Boston won, 6–3. There was no ninth-inning rally that might have given Dom one more at-bat. "I'm glad it's over," he said after the game. "There's a certain pressure in a batting streak that's distracting."

1946 Rudy York's three-run homer into the left-field Yankee Stadium stands provided all the needed runs to overcome a 3–1 deficit. Boo Ferriss won the game, 4–3. Ted Williams still didn't have a hit all year in Yankee Stadium. He was 0-for-17—but his 1946 Stadium on-base percentage was .452 thanks to the 14 walks he'd earned. On this day (actually, evening) every game in the major leagues was played at night. It was the first time that occurred.

1921 After a nine-year wait and more than 750 consecutive games in a Red Sox uniform, Everett Scott, captain of the Red Sox, finally hit his first home run at Fenway Park. It was an inside-the-park drive off Detroit's Dutch Leonard (a former teammate) that rolled all the way to the wall in right-center field. It was also the last home run he hit at Fenway or for the Red Sox.

1909 Charley Hall got his first start for the Red Sox, and threw a three-hitter, beating the White Sox, 2–1, when Boston scored the winning run in the ninth. Hall, born as Carlos Clolo, joined Frank Arellanes on Boston's pitching staff, which thereby boasted two Mexican-Americans at the same time. The name change may have been designed to mask Hall's ethnicity. If so, it may have worked. The August 25 *Chicago Tribune* referred to "Señor Arellanes" taking over from the starter, Hall, and commented on "Hall and the Mexican."

1901 Manager John McGraw took over for Baltimore third baseman Jack Dunn in the top of the fifth inning of the game in Boston. Dunn fouled off a pitch which hit him in the nose, knocking himself out (and breaking his nose). Baltimore won, 11–9, helped by five Boston errors. Boston scored five times in the fourth inning of the second game, and won that one, 6–2.

TRANSACTIONS
1991: Released Kevin Romine.
2005: Acquired LHP Mike Remlinger and cash considerations from the Chicago Cubs for minor league RHP Olivo Astacio. Traded OF Jose Cruz Jr. to the Los Angeles Dodgers for a player to be named later.

DEBUTS
1908: Jake Thielman
1909: Charley Hall
1982: Brian Denman
2005: Mike Remlinger

BIRTHDATES
Johnny Mitchell 1894 (1922–1923); Phil Todt 1901 (1924–1930); Billy Jurges 1908 (manager, 1959–1960); Ralph Houk 1919 (manager, 1981–1984); Milt Bolling 1930 (1952–1956); Roman Mejias 1930 (1963–1964); Jerry Moses 1946 (1968–1970); Buddy Hunter 1947 (1971–1975); Bill Campbell 1948 (1977–1981); Matt Young 1958 (1991–1992); Pat Mahomes 1970 (1996–1997)

DEATHS
Harry Lord 1948; Billy Rogell 2003

August 10

2005 When Gabe Kapler's ball hit off the top of the Green Monster and fell back on the field, the umps ruled it a double. Trot Nixon was on the disabled list and watching on television in the Red Sox clubhouse. He saw that it was a home run, raced out to protest, and found himself ejected from a game he wasn't in and (on the DL) *couldn't* be in.

1999
STVT Tim Wakefield tied a major league record by striking out four Kansas City batters in one inning (there's never been five, even with a knuckleballer pitching.) It was the bottom of the ninth inning, and the four K's came while the Royals were scoring twice, to tie the game 5–5. The Red Sox scored four times in the top of the 10th, and Wake needed a little help from El Guapo (Rich Garces) to close it out. KC scored once in the bottom of the 10th. Final: Boston 9, KC 6.

1994 In the final game of 1994, the year a work stoppage canceled the season with the Montreal Expos in first place, Kirby Puckett led the Twins to a 17–7 beating of Boston. Puckett had seven RBIs on a grand slam and a two-run homer. He earned two intentional walks as well. The game was also the last appearance of left-handed relief specialist Tony Fossas for the Red Sox. He pitched two innings and gave up an uncharacteristic six hits. Remarkably, in the four seasons Fossas pitched for Boston, he appeared in 239 games, but only threw a total of 160⅔ innings.

1986 The Tigers had just taken a 6–4 lead, scoring four runs in the bottom of the seventh. Rich Gedman entered the game as a pinch-hitter, and banged a grand slam off Willie Hernandez to give the Sox a lead and, as it turned out, the game.

1978 The Indians took a 5–4 lead in the top of the 13th on a Rick Burleson error, a sacrifice bunt, a groundout which advanced the runner to third, and a single by Andre Thornton. In the bottom of the 13th, leadoff batter Butch Hobson hit a fly ball behind second, but never stopped running—and there's a lesson in Hobson's hustle. Duane Kuiper lost the ball in the sun and it dropped in as first baseman Andre Thornton bumped into Kuiper (Thornton was charged with an error) and the ball rolled toward first base where catcher Bo Diaz was backing up the play. Diaz attracted an error, too, throwing the ball wildly toward third base. Hobson ran home. The throw in from the outfield was on time, but Diaz couldn't make the play and Hobson scored, re-tying the game. George Scott doubled and Rick Burleson singled in pinchrunner Garry Hancock for the win.

1977 Don Zimmer was no fan favorite at the time. He removed Reggie Cleveland from the game, after Reggie got the first two outs in the top of the seventh. Zimmer was booed loudly as he came out to the mound, and Cleveland was given such a huge ovation he was forced to tip his cap. Zimmer signaled for the left-hander Ramon Hernandez and must have thought it was defiance when Bill Lee came in from the bullpen instead. In fact, the phone rang and bullpen coach Walt Hriniak explained to pitching coach Al Jackson that Hernandez had a sore arm. Lee was asked to come in; he retired the one batter he faced and the Red Sox scored three runs in the seventh and three more in the eighth (two on a Bernie Carbo pinch-hit homer) to eke out an 11–10 win. Asked later if it bothered him to come in without time to warm up, Lee shrugged it off: "No, I had to get up to answer the phone anyway."

1969 Billy Conigliaro, sent down to Triple A Louisville, said that he thought Dick Williams was a dishonest manager and that he didn't want to play for Boston under Williams.

1965 Manager Billy Herman had an emergency appendectomy at Sancta Maria Hospital, so Pete Runnels was asked to serve as interim manager in Herman's absence. Taken to the same hospital at almost the same time, Sox coach Len Okrie was operated on for a broken jaw; he was hit by a Jim Gosger batting-practice line drive. The Red Sox helped Runnels by posting a "12" in the fifth inning of the first game, to beat Baltimore, 15–5. Lonborg got the win. Baltimore got 12 runs in the second game, though, and beat Boston, 12–4. Runnels jokingly claimed that coach Mace Brown had managed the second game.

1960 Ted Williams surpassed Mel Ott's mark of 511 homers, with #512 and #513 (off Barry Latman and Johnny Klipstein, respectively), helping pace Boston to a 6–1 win over the Indians. Ted was 3-for-5, with 10 total bases on the day, and scored three times. After the game, he declared his intention to retire after the season was over.

1950 After Boston lost 11–2 in the first game, Walt Masterson threw a six-hitter and stole the first base of any Red Sox pitcher all year, to help hold the Senators to three runs as the Red Sox scored four.

1942 It was a particularly mortifying moment when Ted Williams was picked off third base in the top of the ninth, with one out and the Red Sox losing a 1–0 game to the Senators. What helped make Williams dub it his most embarrassing moment in baseball was that he'd been picked off by quick-throwing catcher Jake Early back in the first inning as well.

1935 Red Sox third baseman Billy Werber slugged teammate Babe Dahlgren and bloodied his nose. His objection was to first baseman Dahlgren's lack of hustle, or what he called his "slovenly" play, which allowed Washington to tie up the game. Manager Joe Cronin chalked it up to both players' desire to win and removed neither of them from the game. The two players shook hands after the game, a 9–8 Red Sox win.

1934 Babe Ruth announced he would retire at the end of the 1934 season and declared, envisioning a future role as field manager, "There is nothing I would like better than to finish my career in Boston where I started." He added that he hoped to play out the current season with the Yankees and get into another World Series.

In the day's game, the Yankees batted out of turn several times in a 10–3 victory, but the Red Sox failed to protest. From Retrosheet: "Manager Joe McCarthy had revised his lineup and the players did not bat in the order on the official lineup handed to the umpires. In the top of the first inning there were two outs when both Babe Ruth and Lou Gehrig walked. Ben Chapman then batted ahead of Bill Dickey and loaded the bases with an infield single. Dickey then came to the plate out of turn and singled to center scoring Ruth and Gehrig. Pitcher Rube Walberg then threw the ball into center field trying to pick off Chapman at second and both runners advanced one bag. Tony Lazzeri then singled to center scoring both runners. If the Red Sox had protested when either Chapman or Dickey hit out of turn, none of the four runs would have scored in the inning. Chapman and Dickey again batted out of turn the second time through the lineup but without any damage done. In the fifth inning, Gehrig walked and Chapman, again out of turn, struck out. Then Dickey batted out of turn and singled. Finally the Red Sox noticed and protested the batting order. The Yankees then followed the official lineup through the end of the game."

1933 The Dodgers signed Arthur "Skinny" Graham, a .409 hitter recently released by Woonsocket. But then the Red Sox stepped in, arguing that they had rights to Graham. He'd been signed to play for the Lawrence ball club, and Lawrence had a working relationship with the Red Sox that they could not dispose of any player without permission. Lawrence moved the franchise to Woonsocket, but the Sox argued that the obligation remained. Graham never played for Brooklyn, but did debut in September 1934 for the Bosox. In 57 at-bats, over parts of two seasons, he batted .246 and drove in a total of four runs.

1924 Ty Cobb was active on the basepaths, stealing second base once, third base twice, and stealing home once as his Detroit Tigers beat Boston, 13–7.

1917 How things would change in just a couple of years. Babe Ruth hit his first home run of the year, in mid-August. The Babe pitched and beat the Tigers, 5–4, behind a four-hitter. His home run was reportedly the first ever hit into the center field bleachers at Fenway Park, and the longest one hit in Fenway's first five seasons. Rube Foster beat the Tigers, 5–1, in the day's second game.

1915 Babe Ruth went 2-for-4 with a double and won his 10th game, pitching a seven-hitter—while striking out seven—to help Boston to a 10–3 win over St. Louis in a Fenway doubleheader (St. Louis won, 3–2, in the first game). The Sox were victim of an unusual triple play in game two. Said to be the first triple play in Boston within the memory of even the oldest fan, it was a 7-3-2 triple killing:

Shotton ran in hard from left field and grabbed Dick Hoblitzell's fly ball, fired to Sisler at first base doubling up Tris Speaker, and then Sisler threw home, nipping Hal Janvrin trying to score.

1903 A 7–2 win, Cy Young over Eddie Plank. Young set down the first 21 in succession. Two triples and two singles scored three in the fourth and Boston got three more the next inning, the crowd giddy as Cy Young showed craftiness on the basepaths. Young singled to center. Patsy Dougherty hit a grounder that went right through Murphy at second and big Cy Young pounded his way around second heading for third. "Twenty feet from the base Young ran in zigzag manner" and center fielder Pickering's throw struck him in the leg, ensuring his safe arrival at third and giving Dougherty the chance to take second. He scored—as did Dougherty behind him—when Jimmy Collins grounded to Murphy, whose throw home was low and then was "intentionally or accidentally kicked" by Young, letting Dougherty come around and score as well. Young had a single in the sixth as well, and it was said he wielded the bat as well as anyone this day.

1902 The weather was poor, and Comiskey offered "a diamond fit for nothing but pigs" (in the measured words of the *Chicago Tribune*, which described mud "several inches deep" on the baselines and "real lakes of water" in the outfield). Given the descriptions offered, there were relatively few errors by the standards of the day, and the game was tied 4–4 through 10 innings. Boston scored once in the 11th to win it when Ferris hit a long double driving in Freddy Parent. The win was Cy Young's 25th victory of 1902.

TRANSACTIONS
1995: Selected Eric Gunderson off waivers from the Seattle Mariners.

DEBUTS
1905: Pop Rising
1990: Rick Lancellotti
2004: Mike Myers

BIRTHDATES
Charlie Hartman 1888 (1908); Frank Welch 1897 (1927); Odell Hale 1908 (1941); Bob Porterfield 1923 (1956–1958); Bob Chakales 1927 (1957); Brandon Lyon 1979 (2003)

DEATHS
Elliot Bigelow 1933; Win Kellum 1951; Lou Boudreau 2001

August 11

1994 The scene was Camden Yards. It was the third inning and the Red Sox were winning, 1–0. Then the rains came. After a 2:16 rain delay, the game was called off. So was the season. There would be no more baseball—no World Series, nothing—until a slightly-delayed start in 1995, due to the players' strike. The Sox were spared the ignominy of finishing in last place, but only barely. They were one game ahead of the Tigers in the AL East. Not that anyone really cared.

1989 Pitcher Wes Gardner was arrested in Room 326 at the Cross Keys Inn in Baltimore on charges that he assaulted his wife by pushing her against the wall of their hotel room. Three hours after being placed in a holding cell, Gardner was released on $2,500 bond at 6:15 A.M. Gardner's wife said she did not want to press charges, but under Maryland law the officer was permitted to make an arrest if s/he believed an assault had occurred. Joy Gardner had bruises and told the arresting officer that it wasn't the first time. Mrs. Gardner was on the trip along with several Sox wives, a result of Roger Clemens pushing to have a more family-friendly atmosphere. As Sox player rep, Gardner had helped push Clemens' argument.

1979 Jim Rice hit homer #30 in the first inning off of Milwaukee's Moose Haas. It was the third year in a row Rice hit 30-plus, making him only the third Red Sox player to have done so. Foxx did it five years in a row, and Williams did it four. Milwaukee still won, 9–6, in extra innings.

1962 When Ike Delock limited the visiting Orioles to five hits without a run, he'd thrown the third straight shutout for the Red Sox staff. Boston won, 3–0. And Don Schwall held the O's scoreless through five in the separate-admission night game. When right fielder Whitey Herzog homered in the sixth, it ended a run of more than 32 scoreless innings rung up by Red Sox pitchers. Schwall got the complete game win, 7–3.

1957 Ted Williams was hitting .387 and being pitched to cautiously. He'd long since topped his own American League record of 17 intentional walks, but in the first of two games the Sox won from the Senators, he tied Duke Snider's major league mark (26) and, pinch-hitting in the second, took his 27th IBB to set a new record. Ted was walked intentionally six more times before the year was over, for a total of 33.

1955 Ted Williams was looking for his 2,000th hit, but had failed to hit for two games against the Yankees. In the third game of the set, he finally found it, in the very first inning. Nothing dramatic, just a little pop fly off the bat that plopped into left-center field amongst three Yankees fielders. The Kid had a ground-rule double later in the game, but the day was a 5–3 loss to the Yanks.

1947 Newspapers, seat cushions, sandwiches, beer cans, and even shoes were thrown on the field in protest when umpire Rue called Bobby Doerr out on a steal of third. "It rivaled any rhubarb seen in Brooklyn," wrote the *Washington Post*'s Shirley Povich, "and was first page stuff in the Boston newspapers." Doerr, coach Del Baker, and manager Joe Cronin were all evicted, and Rue was given a police escort from the field after the game. Only two scratch hits prevented Earl Johnson from throwing a no-hitter and the Red Sox beat the Senators, 1–0.

1934 Babe Ruth hit an eighth-inning homer giving the Yankees a 1–0 lead, but Boston tied it in the bottom of the ninth. New York scored again in the top of the 13th, but Boston tied it and Wes Ferrell's pinch-hit single to center won the game.

1917 Plainclothes policemen arrested five gamblers in Fenway's right-field bleachers. The crackdown was said to have been prompted by pressure brought by A. L. president Ban Johnson. An active campaign followed at Braves Field.

1911 The Red Sox pioneered once more, fielding the first Danish-born ballplayer in major league history, Olaf "Swede" Henriksen, who'd born in Kirkeup, Denmark. He hit .366 his first season in the majors, in 93 at-bats. He remains the only native Dane to make the majors.

1904 Hobe Ferris had a 5-for-5 day, and drove in five runs as the Boston Red Sox beat the St. Louis Browns, 12–5.

1903 After this game, Boston took a 6:00 P.M. train to Detroit to begin a long road trip that lasted until September 3, but the team left contented with a 5–1 win over Rube Waddell and the Athletics, having taken five of six from the challengers. Scoring early and often enough (two in the first, one in the second, and another in the foutth), only Ferris's three errors at second marred this game, though none resulted in a run. It was a day to forget for Ferris—he was also the only one on his team not to have a hit. For the third day in a row, the attendance exceeded 10,000 patrons—each crowd an "immense throng" by the standards of the time.

TRANSACTIONS
1907: Sold Frank Oberlin to the Washington Senators.
1910: Traded Harry Lord and Amby McConnell to the Chicago
    White Sox for Billy Purtell and Frank Smith.

DEBUTS
1911: Olaf Henriksen

BIRTHDATES
Walter Barbare 1891 (1918); Jim Galvin 1907 (1930); Bobo Newsom 1907 (1937);
Gordon Rhodes 1907 (1932–1935); Bill Monbouquette 1936 (1958–1965)

DEATHS
Jake Volz 1962

August 12

2004 In the bottom of the fifth inning, Jason Varitek singled and third base coach Dale Sveum waved Kevin Millar in from second, hoping to score a run. Tampa Bay center fielder Rocco Baldelli threw a strike to catcher Toby Hall and Millar was erased. Varitek took second on the play. Orlando Cabrera singled, and Sveum sent Varitek around third to home. Same play, Baldelli to Hall. Same result. Two outfield assists by the same fielder in the same inning. It was quite a stretch; Sveum sent six runners home and had six runners cut down in a 12-day period.

1997 Former President George H. W. Bush took a front row seat near the Rangers dugout (the team partly owned through a blind trust by his son, George W., then governor of Texas), and received a warm response from the crowd, as did acting Massachusetts Gov. Paul Cellucci, who accompanied him. Aaron Sele was not welcomed graciously, though. Texas scored two runs in the top of the first and five more in the second. Texas won, 12–2.

1989 It was tied after seven, but not resolved until the 13th, when Rich Gedman doubled in one run and Dwight Evans singled in Gedman. By that time, the Red Sox had left 19 men on base. The final score was 10–8 over the Orioles, who left on 10 of their own.

1988 The Sox beat the Tigers at team-friendly Fenway, 9–4, behind the combined efforts of Bruce Hurst and Bob Stanley, and on the strength of a six-run third inning. It was their 23rd consecutive win at home, and it eclipsed the long-standing American League record of 22 set by the 1931 Philadelphia Athletics. The last time the Sox lost at home was the first game of a short homestand on June 24, when Roger Clemens lost 6–2 to Baltimore and Jose Bautista. They swept an 11-game homestand in July and a short six-game stand that spread from late July into early August. (See August 13 and 14, 1988.) It's a good thing they did win this game; at year's end, Boston finished in first place, just one game ahead of Detroit.

1986 When Bud Black hit Boston pinch-hitter Don Baylor in the day's second game, it was the 25th time Baylor had been hit, breaking the AL single-season record—and there were still seven weeks to go. Baylor wound up the season with 35 black and blue marks. Ron Hunt (50) holds the major-league record.

Pitcher Tim Lollar pinch-hit and singled in the ninth inning of the game, a 6–5 loss. With the single in his only at-bat of the year, he posted a 1.000 batting average. With his 2–0 record on the mound (with wins on April 13 and July 10), he ended the season with a 1.000 winning percentage, too.

1975 The Red Sox built up an early 5–0 lead, encouraging news for pitcher Rick Wise, who went on to beat California, 8–2, and record his 16th victory of the year, and his ninth straight win. The last time he'd lost was June 22. He lost his next start and never did get the coveted 20, but he led his team in wins, helped get them to the World Series, and even got the win in the Game Six classic.

1974 Before Roger Clemens struck out 20 in 1986 (and again in 1996), the record for K's in a nine-inning American League game was held by Nolan Ryan. Both Steve Carlton and Tom Seaver had 19 in NL games. Ryan struck out 19 Red Sox batters at Anaheim Stadium on August 12, 1974, getting Rico Petrocelli four times and whiffing Dwight Evans, Rick Miller, and Bob Montgomery three times apiece. Both teams had the same number of hits, and the Sox did manage a couple of runs, but Red Sox moundsman Roger Moret allowed four (he struck out five but walked seven).

1969 As the Red Sox visited Chicago for three games, pitcher Vicente Romo was reported missing for more than 36 hours and a search of hospitals, jails, and the morgue failed to turn him up. "Then he returned to the Red Sox hotel, looking scared and disheveled," reported Arthur Daley in the *New York Times*. Romo, who spoke little English, had gone out with some Mexican friends and had too much to drink. "Strictly an amateur drinker," he was too ill to cope, and then, the morning after, too scared and confused to know what to do. "Manager Dick Williams was so relieved he didn't even fine him," Daley wrote.

1962 Coming off three straight shutouts, Red Sox pitchers had only allowed four runs in five games.

1949 Scoring 28 runs will eat up some time. The 13–11 Red Sox win in the second game of a twin bill lasts 3:14 and is the longest game in AL history after nearly half a century of play. Boston won the first game, 15–7, but it only lasted 2:25.

1936 Wes Ferrell wasn't at his best on the mound, giving up four runs on nine hits to Philadelphia. He won the game in the batter's box, though. In the third inning, he hit a home run over the left-field Wall, driving in brother (and batterymate) Rick Ferrell ahead of him; the two-run homer tied the game. In the next inning, Wes was up again, this time with the bases loaded. He did it again—a home run over the left-field Wall, this time a grand slam. Sox win, 6–4. Wes drove in all six runs. Too bad he didn't bat in the day's second game; the Sox were shut out. (See July 27, 1935 for another Wes Ferrell slam.)

1934 Over 46,000 fans packed Fenway for Babe Ruth's last AL game in Boston, and between 15,000 and 20,000 more had to be turned away. All cheered Ruth as he hit safely twice in the first game. During the second game, he left mid-game to a tremendous ovation, stopping to shake hands with the umpires while leaving the field. Wes Ferrell and the Red Sox beat the Yankees, 6–4.

1916 Walter Johnson blew a save in relief. Washington's Harry Harper had out-dueled Babe Ruth and the Red Sox were losing 1–0 in the bottom of the ninth, but Johnson walked one and the Sox got three singles and beat the Big Train, 2–1.

1911 Jack Killilay won his first four games for the Red Sox, but lost on this day, lost his next start, too, and he never appeared in the record book again.

TRANSACTIONS
1908: The Red Sox purchase Howard Wood from Kansas City. His
      fastball soon earns him a nickname: Smoky Joe Wood.
1981: Placed Tom Poquette on waivers; he was selected by the Texas Rangers.
1990: Released Jerry Reed.

DEBUTS
1995: Matt Murray

BIRTHDATES
Skinny Graham 1909 (1934–1935); Reggie Harris 1968 (1996); Matt Clement 1974 (2005)

DEATHS
None yet

August 13

1997 Boston traded Mike Stanley—a catcher and DH—back to New York after a year and a half with the Red Sox. Stanley would later return to coaching work with the Red Sox.

1988 The Red Sox tacked another onto the longest home winning streak in league history, making it 24 in a row. Dwight Evans almost made it happen all by himself; Dewey drove in seven in the 16–4 clobbering of the Tigers.

1977 Yaz hit a homer in the second, but in the sixth, after two men were out, George Scott, Butch Hobson, and Dwight Evans hit three consecutive homers. Before the inning was over, Boston scored seven times on the way to securing a 13–6 win over the Mariners of Seattle.

1955 Jim Pagliaroni made his major league debut at age 17, the youngest player to ever appear for the Red Sox. When the Senators built up a 17–6 lead over the Sox, he was put in to spell Sammy White behind the plate and caught a couple of innings. He never did get an at-bat, but he picked up an RBI with a sacrifice fly. It was more than five years later before he appeared in another major league game, but ended up playing 11 years in major league ball.

1949 Always a nice way to close a game—Vern Stephens (0-for-5 on the day) stroked a grand slam home run in the bottom of the 12th inning to give Ellis Kinder a complete-game win and send the Fenway faithful home in a happy mood.

1947 Always a nice way to kick off a game. The Sox got five runs in the first, largely due to home runs by Sam Mele and (on back-to-back pitches) Bobby Doerr and Jake Jones.

1944 27-year-old rookie pitcher Rex Cecil flew all the way cross-country from San Diego—a bit of an ordeal in those days—and stepped right into his major league debut. He'd never seen a major league game, and never even been in a major league ballpark. Boston scored a run in the bottom of the ninth and tied the game 6–6. Cecil arrived at Fenway Park, was fitted for a uniform, and shown to the mound. He got out of a bases-loaded jam and kept the Browns scoreless for four innings until Bobby Doerr hit a homer to win it in the bottom of the 13th.

1940 Ted Williams popped off, saying he didn't like Boston, didn't like the fans, didn't like the streets, and didn't even like the trees. He demanded a trade, preferably to the Tigers or the Yankees. Tom Yawkey said "Williams isn't bigger than baseball."

1933 The Red Sox scored 11 runs in the bottom of the first inning off three Philadelphia pitchers, just enough to ultimately beat the Athletics, 19–10. Despite 29 combined runs on 30 hits, the game only took 2:01 to complete.

1931 After Earl Webb mistakenly treated his own eyes with iodine, Sox owner Quinn decided the team's medicine cabinet should be placed under lock and key.

1924 Only one assist was made by Boston, and that was pitcher Howard Ehmke's. There were 11 unassisted putouts made by infielders in the game, and Steve O'Neill the catcher made one, too. The 6–0 win catapulted the Red Sox into the seventh place slot they'd had their eyes on.

1914 Dutch Leonard had won 12 straight, and only let the Yankees score one time— but lost the game, 1–0. Fenway fans cheered the scoreboard each time the Braves scored against the New York Giants in a 5–3 win for Boston's other team at the Polo Grounds.

1910 Umpire Billy Evans ordered Jake Stahl off the field, telling him to sit on the bench. Stahl said he would not go, but Evans said, "All right, then, you can now go to Winthrop," banishing Stahl from the ballpark to his home in Winthrop.

1908 It was "Cy Young Day" and nearly 20,000 fans came out to an exhibition game to honor Boston's veteran ace. Young dressed up in a farmer's outfit, with luxurious whiskers, to lead the processional, Doc Gessler dressed as a "country dentist," while others affected cowboy gear, dressed like "Chinamen" etc. A good time was had by all, with even the umpires making Cy a presentation on behalf of all the AL umps. Young pitched early in the game, but was long gone when the Sox were beaten in the ninth, 3–2, by an All-Star team that included Hal Chase, Jack Chesbro, Harry Davis, Fielder Jones, Willie Keeler, and George Mullin, plus a number of former teammates.

TRANSACTIONS

1997: Traded Mike Stanley and minor league Randy Brown to the New York
    Yankees, and received Tony Armas Jr. and a PTBNL (Jim Mecir).

DEBUTS

1910: Billy Purtell	1955: Jim Pagliaroni
1932: Gordon McNaughton	1970: John Curtis
1944: Rex Cecil	1998: Pete Schourek

BIRTHDATES

Cliff Garrison 1906 (1928); Lou Finney 1910 (1939–1944); Mark Lemke 1965 (1998)

DEATHS

Mel Almada 1988

August 14

2000 "A son of Massachusetts, Rico Brogna, rose from semi-exile on the bench and saved the night with a two-out, two-strike grand slam in the bottom of the ninth that hoisted the Sox to a 7–3 victory," wrote Bob Hohler in the *Boston Globe*. Pretty much sums up the hitting. Pedro Martinez left the game in the third, with shoulder problems, which cast a pall over the night before Brogna's punch put Devil Ray Billy Taylor's pitch into the Tampa Bay bullpen. Brogna had grown up in New England, and fantasized being Fisk or Yaz—and now he'd won a game for the Red Sox with a walk-off grand slam.

1999 Red Sox DH Brian Daubach's brightest spot in a strong rookie season was the 5-for-5 day he had against John Halama and other Seattle pitchers. Dauber hit a three-run homer and had six RBIs on the day. He'd knocked in five RBIs, also against Seattle, just the night before. That's 11 RBIs in about 18 hours.

A bigger story in the media, though, was that scheduled starter Pedro Martinez strolled into work very late, so late that manager Jimy Williams gave Bryce Florie the game ball. Pedro was sent to the bullpen, and indeed was used in relief, throwing the final four innings and getting the win.

1998 The Red Sox scored 13 runs, but only won by one. The day before, on the 13th, they had scored eight runs, but only won by one. On both days the Twins came up just short.

1996 Otis Nixon stole four times off Jeff Suppan and Mike Stanley, and the Blue Jays scored five times off Suppan (Nixon had three runs scored). Toronto led, 5–1, after five at Skydome. The Sox scored three times in the eighth and three more times in the ninth and were a happier team as they passed through Customs/ Douanes on the way back to Fenway with an 8–6 win in their pocket.

1991 On the same day that Lee Smith saved his 30th game for the St. Louis Cardinals, so did Massachusetts native Jeff Reardon for the Red Sox, saving a 2–1 game against the Indians for Joe Hesketh. Both now had six seasons of 30 or more saves. Some of those saves were at the expense of the Red Sox, though; 1991 was Reardon's second season with Boston.

1989 Red Sox right fielder Danny Heep reached to catch a Rance Mulliniks fly ball by the Pesky Pole when a fan jumped up and knocked the ball away from Heep's glove; the umpires ruled it a two-run homer, which gave the Blue Jays the lead. Victimized pitcher Mike Boddicker said all the fan needed to do was ask for a ball "and I would have signed it for him, too." The Blue Jays won, 4–2.

1988 Riding a 24-game home winning streak, looking to get to 26 to tie the major league mark set by the 1916 New York Giants, the Red Sox had Roger Clemens on the mound, but were definitively denied an extension, as the Tigers scored 18 runs to beat Boston, 18–6. Clemens only lasted 1⅓ innings, charged with eight runs. Master of the understatement, manager Joe Morgan explained the reason in post-game remarks: "Roger just didn't have it, I guess." Clemens had book-ended the streak. It was his June 24 loss that was the last game Boston had lost at home before today's.

1982 In the fourth inning of a scoreless game, Baltimore's Ken Singleton hit a ball that ricocheted off Boston pitcher Mike Torrez's head so hard that it was fielded by center fielder Reid Nichols. No error was assessed. Torrez finished the inning, but then had to be rushed to the hospital for examination. The game remained scoreless until right after the seventh-inning stretch when the Red Sox scored eight times—and would have had two more except that a freak blast of wind blew back Gary Allenson's drive that seemed certain to hit the Wall. As the inning unfolded, Gary Allenson, Jerry Remy, and Jim Rice were all walked intentionally. The three IBB in one inning tied the AL record. Boston 8, Baltimore 0.

1977 Helping beat Seattle for the 10th time in a row, and winning 14 out of 15 on the schedule, Carl Yastrzemski doubled in the second inning for the 506th double of his career, tying him with Babe Ruth. Yaz ended up with 646 career doubles. The score was 11–1.

1961 Frank Malzone hit two of Boston's five bases-empty home runs. Pitcher Gene Conley hit one, too—and shut out the Indians on six hits, 8–0.

1959 The Yankee Stadium crowd was stunned in the top of the eighth. Cruising with a 6–2 lead, Whitey Ford faded. He retired Ted Williams, but then surrendered three straight singles. Ryne Duren replaced Ford, and Vic Wertz pinch-hit for Don Buddin. Wertz knocked a grand slam into the right-field bleachers. That tied the game. Boston kept batting, and posted nine runs for an 11–6 triumph.

1951 Ted Williams reached two milestones on the season: 25 homers and 100 RBIs. And the Red Sox pulled off a triple play to keep some Athletics off the bases. Boston beat Philly, 7–4.

1942 Ted Williams' two-run homer won the first game, 2–0, as Tex Hughson shut out the Senators. George Case stole home in the first inning to give Washington a one-run lead, but Bobby Doerr's two-run homer topped that. The lead went back and forth a bit; Washington took a one-run lead in the top of the ninth, but Lou Finney's triple scored Boston's tying and winning runs in the bottom of the inning for a 7–6 win.

1922 Lizzie Murphy played the first inning at first base for a team of all-stars in an exhibition game staged at Fenway Park as a benefit for the family of recently-deceased former Boston ballplayer Tommy McCarthy. Murphy played for the Providence All-Stars, and thus became the first female to play for a major league team, albeit one assembled for an exhibition contest. Names in the game included

Nick Altrock, Jim Bagby, Donie Bush, Chick Shorten, and Tillie Walker. The All-Stars won it in the 10th, on a Doc Johnson triple. The Red Sox claimed they lost because they'd been jinxed when former Mayor John F. Fitzgerald sang "Sweet Adeline" before the game.

1919 Joe Bush issued a demand that the Red Sox either give him his release or pay him his salary due him through the end of the year. He had been suspended for the rest of the season because of his inability to get in condition. If he was not given his immediate release, he said he would report daily to Fenway Park to work out. He contended that a reaggravated spring training arm injury had prevented his pitching. Bush reverted to form in 1920 and for several seasons thereafter.

1915 Babe Ruth squared off against Walter Johnson for the first of several classic matchups. Ruth had two hits and scored once, but Olaf Henriksen was apparently a nemesis for Johnson and his pinch-hit in the eighth started a two-run rally. Ruth, up next, singled him to third. Another hit and a sac fly brought the Sox to a 4–3 victory.

1913 0–0 in the top of the 11th, in St. Louis, when a ball slipped through the shortstop, and four hits followed, for four runs. Hugh Bedient kept the Browns scoreless and the Sox won, 4–0.

1912 Tris Speaker got a hit in both games of the doubleheader with St. Louis, giving him a 21-game hitting streak. Already this year, he had a 20-gamer and a 30-gamer. No other major leaguer has had three streaks of 20-plus games in a single season. Smoky Joe Wood reached a landmark of his own, winning his 25th game with an 8–0 shutout.

1903 Cy Young recorded his 20th win of the season, beating Detroit, 6–3. Young finished the season 28–9, with a 2.08 ERA.

TRANSACTIONS
1962: Released Dave Philley.
1963: Signed amateur free agent Jim Lonborg.
1968: Sold Galen Cisco to the Kansas City Royals.
1995: Acquired Chris James from Kansas City in trade for Wes Chamberlain.

DEBUTS
1905: John Godwin   1992: Tom Barrett
1910: Dutch Lerchen   2001: Allen McDill
1918: Jack Coffey

BIRTHDATES
Bill Clowers 1898 (1926); Angel Santos 1979 (2001)

DEATHS
Tim Hendryx 1957; Lynn McGlothen 1984

August 15

1990 Mark McGwire hit his 30th home run of 1990, a game-winning grand slam in the bottom of the 10th inning off reliever Rob Murphy, who had come in with the bases loaded and just one out. Oakland won, 6–2. McGwire became the first player who'd hit 30 or more homers in every one of his first four seasons.

1984 Tony Armas hit his 33rd home run of the year, on his way to a league-leading 43. When the season was over, Tony would only have 32 walks, so this was the day he hit more homers than he would need to surpass his walk total for the year. The differential of 11 more homers than bases on balls is the largest in history.

1979 Jim Rice went 2-for-4 with a three-run homer in the fifth; he singled and scored the winning run on Yaz's homer in the bottom of the eighth. It was the sixth multi-hit game in a row for Jim Ed (14-for-26 in the six games). Dick Bresciani points out that Rice is the only player in major league history to have hit 200 or more hits and 35 or more home runs in three consecutive seasons (1977–1979).

1977 Jim Rice doubled and became the first Sox player since Ted Williams (1939) to have 20 homers, 20 doubles, and 10 triples in a single season. The only other post-WWII players to have done this were all Yankees—Charlie Keller, Joe D., and Mickey Mantle.

1966 Pitcher Bill Short is purchased from the Orioles, and before the season is out, he contributes 8⅓ innings of pretty average work. The Sox also picked up pitcher Hank Fischer, who won two games (and lost three). Without one of those two wins, though, it would have been the Red Sox and not the Yankees who finished in last place in 1966.

1961 Frank Malzone hit two home runs, and had a 5-for-5 day with three RBIs. Gene Conley threw a six-hit shutout and, maybe just for fun, hit a solo homer himself off Gary Bell in the top of the fifth, on his way to an 8–0 cruise over Cleveland.

1955 It was State of Maine Day at Fenway. Whoever hit the first home run for the Red Sox would win a Maine bear named "Homer." Norm Zauchin hit two, drove in five RBIs, and keyed a 9–6 win over Washington. Boston won the second game, too, 2–1. Zauchin had the bear shipped to a zoo in Birmingham, Alabama, where Homer lived to a ripe old age.

1950 The season seemed a lost cause for the Sox, but twin bill triumphs over the Philadelphia Athletics kick off a stretch where Boston wins 27 of 30 games and makes a real run for the flag. The scores were 8–3 and 9–4, though Sox fans worried about Walt Dropo, beaned and hospitalized. He would be OK.

1942 A two-run homer by Ted Williams gave Tex Hughson all he needed to spin a 2–1 win over Washington's Sid Hudson. Broadway Charlie Wagner got the 7–6 win in the second game, when Lou Finney hit a two-run triple in the bottom of the ninth. Wagner's last six wins have all been by one-run margins, two of them 1–0 wins on June 19 and June 24.

1941 The game was reported in all the next day's newspapers as a 6–3 home win for the Washintgon Senators. Boston had a 3–1 lead when heavy rain began to fall; the Sox gave up three runs in the fifth and solo runs in both the sixth and seventh, and then the umpires called the game. *Boston Globe* writer Gerry Moore commented, "Any chance of continuing had been cagily prevented by the Griffith Stadium ground help, who at no time made an effort to put a covering of any kind on the diamond." Cronin protested the game on the basis of "the negligence of the Washington baseball club" to cover the field. By the time the game was called, the rains had already stopped and the game could easily have continued, except for the fact that the grounds were now in unplayable condition. When they'd ordered Senators manager Bucky Harris to cover the infield, the umpires had been told that there wasn't a sufficient crew to comply with their request. The Senators outsmarted themselves; American League President Harridge later forfeited the game to Boston. The score in the permanent books is 6–3 in favor of the Red Sox. Appropriately, no pitcher was credited with a win nor tagged with a loss.

1937 The Red Sox lost two games to Washington and dropped to fourth place; for the Senators, they'd now won eight in a row, but some hometown fans missed the moment as they'd been escorted from the park by police for showering umpire Cal Hubbard with pop bottles after he'd ejected second baseman Buddy Myer for arguing a call too strenuously.

1922 A singular affair. The White Sox make 21 singles (of 25 total hits), the Red Sox make 14 (of 18 hits). The 35 singles are an American League record. Chicago wins the game, 19–11.

1916 For the third time in 1916, Walter Johnson ("Goliath of American League pitchers") met an unkind fate—seeing his team shut out at the hands of his David, aka George Herman Ruth. The final score was 1–0, but this time Johnson held the Sox scoreless until the bottom of the 13th inning. Jack Barry's ball deflected off Johnson's glove for an infield hit, but Johnson got the next two batters. Tillie Walker singled Barry to third, and Larry Gardner drove him home.

1914 An advertised pitchers duel at Fenway Park proved to be just that, as Vean Gregg and Ernie Shore combined to beat New York's McHale, 1–0, the lone run coming in the bottom of the eighth as Cady doubled and Hooper drove him in.

1912 "If Tris Speaker quits baseball it will be because he loved his mother more than the game at which he is considered one of the best in the world." (*Washington Post*) Mrs. Speaker applauded her son during the day's doubleheader, and enjoyed hearing the Boston fans do the same, but her visit to the Hub was to try and persuade him to come back home to Texas. If those were the choices, it would appear Speaker loved baseball more.

TRANSACTIONS
1914: Chick Shorten purchased from the Worcester ball club for $1,500.
1922: Eddie Foster was selected off waivers by the St. Louis Browns.
1966: Purchased Bill Short from the Baltimore Orioles.
1972: Acquired Andy Kosco from the California Angels by trading them Chris Coletta.
1989: Signed Jose Malave as an amateur free agent.

DEBUTS
1947: Eddie Smith

BIRTHDATES
John Warner 1872 (1902); Ben Van Dyke 1888 (1912); Jose Santiago 1940 (1966–1970); Billy Conigliaro 1947 (1969–1971); Tony Rodriguez 1970 (1996)

DEATHS
Jim Henry 1976; Ed Chaplin 1978; Bob Garbark 1990

August 16

2005 **STVT** Though a veteran of 13 seasons in the majors, in his first two appearances for the Red Sox, Mike Remlinger never recorded an out. Five batters up, five batters reached base, and every one of them ultimately scored. Finally, on August 16, he was brought into a game in which the Red Sox built up a 10–3 lead. The Sox were losing 3–2 heading into the ninth, and only had two hits on the night. David Ortiz tied it up with a solo homer with one out in the ninth, and then the Sox scored seven runs in the top of the 10th—tying the team record for the most runs ever scored in an extra inning (June 4, 1982). Not surprisingly, the Sox won that game.

Remlinger struck out the first Detroit batter he faced in the bottom of the 10th (after the Red Sox had tied the game up in the bottom of the ninth, then scored seven times in the top of the 10th). Even that wasn't easy. The pitch was a little off, and Jason Varitek couldn't hold onto it; he had to throw to first to record the out. Remlinger got the first two outs, then walked a batter and gave up an infield hit. Both runners moved up on a wild pitch. He walked the fifth batter, and then gave up a grand slam to Craig Monroe. Finally, he induced a fly ball to right field and the Sox took away a win, but not by much, 10–7. Monroe's slam appears to be the only instance in AL history in which a team hit a grand slam in extra innings, but lost the game.

2004 The Red Sox were, at this juncture, 10½ games behind the Yankees in the AL East. The team had been in a doldrums for a couple of months, and the only faint hope that Red Sox rooters could muster was for a "reverse 1978"—the season in which the Sox had a seemingly insurmountable 14-game lead, only to see the Yankees surmount it. The Sox started something with an 8–4 win over the Blue Jays and won 16 of their next 17 games.

2002 The Twins down the Red Sox, 5–0. The first run that scored, in the bottom of the fifth, terminated Pedro Martinez's scoreless inning streak at 35, a pretty good stretch and the longest in a couple of seasons.

2001 The Red Sox "promote" pitching coach Joe Kerrigan to manager, to replace the just-released Jimy Williams. The last Sox manager named Carrigan spelled his name differently but managed the team to two World Championships.

1999 Daubach would not be denied. Batting with the bases loaded, the Red Sox down 5–3 with two outs in the bottom of the ninth, he hit a long foul ball that was just a foot or two foul by the Pesky Pole in right. He'd just barely missed a game-winning grand slam. Daubach hung in there, fouling off five pitches one after the other. Oakland catcher A. J. Hinch missed catching one foul pop-up by a mere six inches. Daubach then doubled to left field off Todd Worrell, driving in three runs, winning the game, and running his total to 15 RBIs in the last four games. Pretty good for a guy who couldn't even be depicted on a baseball card, because he'd been a replacement player in the 1994–95 player strike.

1978   Luis Tiant wins major league game #200, and he'd been up against Nolan Ryan of the Angels. Ryan walked eight, but that wasn't what hurt him. It was Jim Rice's two-run homer in the fourth, and then—tied 2–2 in the ninth—the Angels defense imploded, committing three errors and permitting two unearned runs. Boston 4, California 2.

1968   Denny McLain of Detroit won his 25th game, at the expense of the Red Sox. McLain was 16–0 in road games, and shut out the Sox, 4–0. Jim Lonborg only allowed two hits in his seven innings of work, but somehow managed to hit Tigers catcher Bill Freehan in three consecutive at-bats.

1954   The Red Sox won a Fenway-based exhibition game against the New York Giants, 6–5, in the bottom of the ninth, when Ted Lepcio doubled in Sam Mele. Unfortunately, hyper-competitive Jimmy Piersall hyper-extended his arm in a pre-game throwing contest (they wisely don't hold these any more) and suffered a sore arm that he says hampered him from throwing as well ever again.

1952   Boston loses to New York, 5–4. The Red Sox lose 12 games in a row to the Yankees, before next winning on May 8, 1953.

1940   Neither Monteagudo nor Krakauskas could stop Double X. Sox catcher Jimmie Foxx homered off Rene Monteagudo in the first inning to give the Red Sox a 2–0 lead over the Senators; the home run was #30 of the year and tied him with Lou Gehrig for 494 career home runs. Washington went ahead, 6–5, in the top of the ninth, but the Sox scored once to tie it. In the 10th inning, Foxx homered again—this time off Joe Krakauskas—to win the game and to pass Gehrig with home run #495. That guy named Ruth only had 219 more.

1926   Sox catcher Alex Gaston hit a bases-loaded triple off his brother Milt Gaston, pitching for St. Louis. That was the big blow of the second inning. In the third, Milt was still on the mound and Alex was in the on-deck circle with the bases loaded, but before he could get up, Boston third baseman Fred Haney hit another bases-loaded triple. Milt retired Alex, but it was now 7–1 in favor the Red Sox and that was all it took to win a rain-shortened second game, 7–1, after 6½.

1916   Now playing left field: Duffy Lewis. And Chick Shorten, and even two pitchers: Sad Sam Jones and Rube Foster. For Foster, it was the only time he ever played outfield; Jones played part of one game for the Yankees, too, in 1925. The White Sox–Red Sox game in Boston ran 16 innings, after the Pale Sox tied it 4–4 in the eighth. During the course of the game, the Red Sox used three pitchers (not unusual), seven pinch-hitters or pinchrunners (pretty unusual), and four left fielders (extremely unusual). Every member of the Red Sox, other than Bill Carrigan and Vean Gregg, played in the game. With two outs in the bottom of the 16th, Hooper walked and then stole second. Jack Barry hit a grounder to third baseman Fred McMullin, who committed his second error of the game with a bad throw to first that allowed Hooper to score. That was just the first game; darkness halted the second after 5½, but Boston was ahead, 2–1, and so had a sweep.

Between the games, the Red Sox raised the World's Championship pennant before the largest crowd of the year, around 25,000 fans. Why it took them so long to get around to it is unknown.

1915   Harry Hooper hit the first ball pitched to the Red Sox in the bottom of the first. Everett Scott, up next, brought Hooper home with a sac fly to center field. That was the only scoring in the whole game. Smoky Joe Wood shut out Washington, and Bert Gallia nearly did the same to Boston, throwing a two-hitter—but the first-inning run counted and the Nationals lost their 11th and final game of the year at Fenway Park—every game all year long.

1912 You can't win 'em all. Last-place St. Louis beat the league-leading Red Sox, 3–2. Earl Hamilton held the Sox to six hits.

1909 NEW ENGLANDERS EXPECT RED SOX TO WIN PENNANT (*Washington Post*). The Red Sox were in the midst of an 11-game winning streak, and things were looking rosy. The Tigers, though, proved the better team and Boston finished third, 9½ games back.

TRANSACTIONS
1991: Acquired Dan Petry from the Altanta Braves for a PTBNL (Mickey Pina).
2000: David Eckstein was acquired on waivers by the Anaheim Angels.

DEBUTS
1924: Lefty Jamerson
1951: Mel Hoderlein
1979: John Tudor
1995: Chris James
1996: Kerry Lacy

BIRTHDATES
Baby Doll Jacobson 1890 (1926–1927); Bob Fothergill 1897 (1933); Terry Shumpert 1966 (1995); Damian Jackson 1973 (2003); Jin Ho Cho 1975 (1998–1999); Michael Coleman 1975 (1997–1999)

DEATHS
Bunk Congalton 1937; Babe Ruth 1948

August 17

1999 Mike Stanley hit a solo home run for the Red Sox, but Bret Saberhagen, Tim Wakefield, and John Wasdin were all hit for four runs apiece, as Oakland beat Boston, 12–1. Gil Heredia scattered 10 Sox hits, but Oakland's eight-run seventh inning put the game beyond reach.

1998 A *Boston Globe* article celebrated the many nuns who attend games as Red Sox fans, and recalled when Richard Cardinal Cushing talked the team into an annual "Nuns at Fenway Day." The Sisters of St. Joseph were the most active fans, and Sox CEO John Harrington, VP John Buckley, and GM Dan Duquette had all attended schools run by the order. They readily admit to offering prayers for the team, and vow to break out the champagne when the team wins the World Series.

1997 Nomar Garciaparra singled twice, stole a base, and hit a sacrifice fly. The two safeties gave him a 20-game hitting streak, the longest by a Red Sox rookie (tied with Fred Lynn). Boston won, 10–5, over the Twins. Nomar was two-thirds of the way to his ultimate 30-game streak.

1996 Roger Clemens pitched a little like the Clemens of old, shutting out the California Angels, 6–0, at Fenway Park. Though it was his 37th shutout for the Sox, it was his first in 2½ years, stretching back to April 20, 1994.

1984 Jackie Gutierrez tags out Tim Teufel at second, successfully executing the hidden ball trick.

1974 Right fielder Dwight Evans has nine putouts in nine innings. He was also 2-for-4 at the plate, but the Sox lost, 7–4.

1966 The Orioles scored five runs in the top of the ninth, and even though the Sox scored twice, the O's had an 8–4 win. Stunned Sox fans taking in the three-game series had seen it happen two days in a row; just the day before, Baltimore scored five times in the top of the ninth, for a 6–4 win. On the 15th, it had been two runs in the top of the 11th, as the Orioles won that one in extra innings.

1960 Ted Williams is named "Player of the Decade" by *The Sporting News*.

1950 At what was reportedly the first Ladies Night Game in the league, the 7,146 hometown ladies who attended as guests of a paying customer saw the Red Sox get out to a 7–0 lead in the first three innings, spoiling Joe Murray's major league debut. Ellis Kinder went the distance for Boston, but Philadelphia scored five times off him in the last two innings. Not enough. 10–6 final.

1947 Denny Galehouse pitched 11 innings against the Yankees and didn't allow any runs. It was a 3–0 shutout.

1940 By homering in five consecutive games, Jimmie Foxx set a club record. The Sox got 18 hits and 37 total bases and beat the Senators, 12–9. Boston batters who later homered in five consecutive games include Ted Williams, Dick Stuart, George Scott, and Jose Canseco.

It was revealed that Lefty Grove had broken a bone in his foot by fouling a ball off himself while batting in a game against Washington on August 11. He was expected to be out for the season, though he did manage to return, win one, and lose one.

1926 The Sox swept a doubleheader from St. Louis, 5–1 and 4–0. They won a game the next day and another the day after that. From that point on, Boston won only four more games until the season was over, losing 28 of their final 32 games.

1914 Nearly 2,500 fans came out to see the Red Sox play an exhibition game against Manchester of the New England League. Babe Ruth pitched a 4–2 win against Manchester's King, who helped his own cause with three hits. Ruth was hitless. The next day Ruth was sent down to the Providence Grays. He'll be back.

Meanwhile, back at Fenway Park, Col. Theodore Roosevelt gave a speech as part of his advance campaign to run for President again, this team as a Progressive Party candidate. The event drew the same attendance: 2,500.

1913 The "wreck of the Red Sox" was attributed to a number of "player scribes"— players who had newspaper columns appearing under their name. The players were paid for the use of their name, but the columns were, of course, written by newspapermen. An article that appeared in a number of papers on August 17 decried the "fad of printing alleged opinions of ball players under their alleged signatures" and said charges were made that the practice "was largely responsible for the wrecking of a team of world's champions so shortly after its triumph as to cause considerable wonder." Some of the Boston men writing the columns were said to be inexperienced, not checking with the players in question, and exacerbating existing tensions with the comments that were printed.

1904 Jesse Tannehill hit the first batter he faced and walked another batter in the first inning, but got control of himself and from that point on "not another Comiskeyite lived to hobnob with LaChance at first." (*Chicago Tribune*) Translation: Tannehill retired every White Sox batter he faced. Candy LaChance was Boston's first baseman. Not one White Sox batter collected a hit all day long, not even younger brother Lee Tannehill, who played third base for Chicago. It was the second no-hitter of the year for Boston (Cy Young threw a perfect game on May 5).

TRANSACTIONS
1908: Traded Frank LaPorte back to the New York Highlanders for Harry Niles.
1971: Released Cal Koonce.
1972: Signed amateur free agent Allen Ripley.
1979: Acquired Ted Sizemore from the Cubs in a trade for a PTBNL (Mike O'Berry) and cash.
1986: Acquired Dave Henderson and Spike Owen from Seattle in trade for Rey Quinones, some PTBNL and some cash. The players named later were Mike Brown and Mike Trujillo (named on August 22) and John Christensen, named on September 25.
1993: Released Ivan Calderon.

DEBUTS
1911: Walter Lonergan   1935: Walt Ripley
1913: Bill Mundy   1972: Andy Kosco
1927: Bob Cremins

BIRTHDATES
Vince Molyneaux 1888 (1918); Bill Pertica 1898 (1918); Johnny Watwood 1905 (1932–1933); Ed Durham 1907 (1929–1932); Rudy York 1913 (1946–1947, 1959); Clem Hausmann 1919 (1944–1945); Diego Segui 1937 (1974–1975); Skip Lockwood 1946 (1980); Butch Hobson 1951 (1975–80, 1992–1994); Alex Cole 1965 (1996)

DEATHS
Ray Caldwell 1967; Sammy Vick 1986

August 18

1993 Danny Darwin had a no-hitter into the eighth inning, but Dan Pasqua's triple off Fenway's center-field fence "just inches over the glove of 5-foot-10-inch Billy Hatcher" (AP) prevented the feat. The Red Sox beat the White Sox, 5–0.

1990 Rick Lancellotti hit 276 minor league home runs, but appeared in just four games for Boston. His only Red Sox RBI came when he pinch-hit in the seventh inning of this game, and drove in a run with a sacrifice fly.

1967 Tony Conigliaro liked to establish coverage of home plate, but it had already resulted in two fractures when he was hit with pitches. In the fourth inning of the evening's game, a Jack Hamilton fastball struck Tony C. on his left cheekbone and Tony went down, carried unconscious from the field. He missed the remainder of the 1967 season—the injury arguably cost the Red Sox a World Series win—and the entire 1968 season, too. The 22-year-old was a Greater Boston native and already had more than 100 home runs to his credit, one of Boston's most popular players ever. The Red Sox won, 3–2, but not a fan went home happy. Boston took the next three from the Angels, too.

1936 Catcher Rick Ferrell hits an inside-the-park home run to help Lefty Grove win a 6–2 game against Philadelphia. Rick's brother Wes Ferrell had an inside-the-park homer for the Red Sox earlier in the same year, on June 17.

1932 The Sox beat St. Louis, 7–6, in 15 innings. It was a see-saw game which saw St. Louis tie it 2–2 in the top of the ninth, then take a 3–2 lead in the 11th. Boston tied it back up with one in the bottom of the 11th. In the 14th, the Browns bid to end it, scoring three times—only to see Boston come back with three of their own. Finally, George Stumpf tripled to lead off the bottom of the 15th. After two intentional walks, with one out, Hal Rhyne hit a fly ball deep enough to left to enable Stumpf to tag up and score the winning run.

1920 Mike McNally streaked from second base to score on pitcher Elmer Myers' infield hit which eluded Tigers first baseman Harry Heilmann. It was the bottom of the 11th, and the Sox won the game, 6–5.

1917 Umpire Brick Owens may have caused the Red Sox to drop out of first place, with a 2–1 win by Cleveland, earned by the Tribe after Owens had ejected manager Jack Barry, Dick Hoblitzell, and Dutch Leonard.

1913 Bill Carrigan caught a terrific game for the Red Sox, correctly sniffing out at least two stolen base attempts and retiring the runners by signaling Boston's Hugh Bedient for a pitchout. He retired Hal Chase, attempting to come home on a double steal, when Carrigan's throw went back to his pitcher instead of all the way to second. But Chicago's Tex Russell outpitched Bedient, allowing only two runners to second and none further. The lone run the White Sox scored came on another double steal, when Carrigan's throw rolled into center field.

1911 In a game featuring seven stolen bases, Ty Cobb's first-inning steal of home was the most dramatic. There were seven errors, too. Detroit won for their home crowd, 9–4.

1907 Boston's Rube Kroh won one game in 1906 and one in 1907. This was his 1907 win. After Cy Morgan shut out St. Louis in the first game, 1–0, Kroh pitched a seven-hit 2–1 complete game win.

TRANSACTIONS
1937: Purchased pitcher Charlie Wagner from Minnesota of the American Association.

DEBUTS
1923: Les Howe
1979: Ted Sizemore

BIRTHDATES
Wally Gerber 1891 (1928–1929); Bernie Friberg 1899 (1933); Billy Consolo 1934 (1953–1959); Joe Azcue 1939 (1969); Bob Zupcic 1966 (1991–1994)

DEATHS
Candy LaChance 1932

August 19

2001 The Red Sox scored six runs in the bottom of the second to stake Hideo Nomo to a 6–1 lead, but he was battered for four more runs, and replacement Hipolito Pichardo coughed up four himself. Nomo (and Scott Hatteberg) allowed four stolen bases, and the O's grabbed another one off El Guapo later in the game. Baltimore beat Boston, 13–7.

1978 After a bad outing, giving up five runs in an 8–4 loss to Oakland, Bill Lee (with 10 wins) was never given another start by manager Don Zimmer. One more win for the Red Sox and there never would have been a single-game playoff.

1939 Ted Williams hit the first grand slam of his career, in the ninth inning of a home game, lifting the Red Sox to an 8–6 triumph over the Senators. Serving up the pitch was reliever Pete Appleton (born Jablonowski), who'd worn the Red Sox uniform for part of the 1932 season.

1934 Sox rookie Moose Solters hit for the cycle; the victim was the "General," Alvin Crowder, pitching for Detroit, and he did it before the largest crowd in Boston baseball history: paid attendance was—somehow—46,995. Back in 1927, when a July 1 telegram arrived asking for "the Solters boy" to come play ball with the Fairmount club of the Middle Atlantic League, Moose's older brother Frank went instead. Frank hit a homer off Chief Bender of Jonestown, but then struck out three times in a row—and a few more in later games, too. It became clear he wasn't the Solters they had sought. They soon tracked down the right man.

1921 Ty Cobb was 5-for-10 in a Detroit doubleheader. In the second game, the 34-year-old recorded his 3,000th hit, with years to go for his final total of 4,189. Cobb's victim of the day was Elmer Myers, who was doling out hits left and right. Myers pitched a complete game 19-hitter, and lost 10–0 since his counterpart Bert Cole only gave up four. At least Boston won the first game, 12–8.

1915 The White Sox scored once in the second. The Red Sox scored an unearned run in the top of the sixth, but Chicago countered with one more in the bottom of the inning. That was it, as Red Sox pitcher Rube Foster lost to Chicago's Red Faber. It was unclear how long the 1915 season would run. The August 19 issue of *The Sporting News* said that owner Frazee understood that many of his players "were not inclined to take part in any games in September unless assured their draft status would not be affected."

TRANSACTIONS
1910: Purchased Buck O'Brien from the Hartford ball club.
1940: Purchased Charlie Gilbert from Washington.
1969: Signed free agent Craig Skok.

DEBUTS
1974: Jim Rice
1986: Dave Henderson, Spike Owen

BIRTHDATES
Al DeVormer 1891 (1923); Tim Blackwell 1952 (1974–1975);
Gary Gaetti 1958 (2000); Matt White 1977 (2003)

DEATHS
Bob Klinger 1977

August 20

2004 News reports state that the Houston Astros put Roger Clemens on waivers and that he was immediately claimed by the Boston Red Sox. The Astros then pulled him back. Wouldn't that have been something?

2003 After their third loss in a row, in which reliever Byun-Hyung Kim got tagged for four runs in the top of the eighth inning, Red Sox first baseman Kevin Millar expressed anger at the media and the fans, calling on folks to "cowboy up and stand behind this team one time and quit worrying about all the negative stuff and talking about last year's team and 10 years ago and 1986." The phrase "Cowboy Up!" became a Red Sox watchword for a team that went on a run that seemed destined to land them in the World Series.

1997 Garciaparra hit safely twice in both games of a doubleheader at the Oakland-Alameda County Coliseum. He thereby set a new major league rookie record by hitting in 22 consecutive games. Boston took both games, 7–5 in the opener (all seven runs scored in the top of the fifth), and 5–4, in the latter game, after 13 innings. Oakland had a 4–1 lead after three, but could only make one hit from the fourth through the 13th innings.

1976 Jean R. Yawkey becomes President of the Boston Red Sox.

1967 Offensively, it was the Reggie Smith–Carl Yastrzemski show as Boston took two from the Angels, 12-2 and 9-8. Yaz hit a three-run homer in the first game and a three-run homer in the second game. Reggie Smith hit two homers in the first game, one from each side of the plate, and another homer in the second game. That second game win was particularly sweet because California had an 8-0 lead before Boston batted in the bottom of the fourth. The Sox rallied to tie it, and Jerry Adair won it with a home run in the bottom of the eighth.

1962 Scoring three unearned runs off Don Schwall (the error was Frank Malzone's) in the first got the game off to a bad start, but Boston had taken a 4–3 lead in the top of the sixth. Harmon Killebrew's two-run homer in the bottom of the inning put an end to that, and the Twins won, 6–4.

1960 Babe Ruth had been the only player patient enough and feared enough to draw 2,000 bases on balls, until Ted Williams took walk #2,000 in the first inning of the first game of the twi-night doubleheader. Ted hit two three-run homers, too (#514 and #515), the second one being the come-from-behind game-winner. Boston won, 8–6, but went scoreless in the 6–0 night game.

1959 The Red Sox out-performed the Athletics in Kansas City, 11–10, a high-scoring affair in which KC's Bob Cerv had the only three home runs. Red Sox pitcher Earl Wilson was 2-for-3 with a double and drove in three runs, getting his first major league win, in relief.

1933 Red Sox pitcher Bob Kline already had a single in the game, and was up at bat again in the sixth inning. The ump called strike two and he stepped out of the box to argue, but hadn't been granted time. The Indians' pitcher threw a quick one over the plate and Kline dashed back to the box to try to swing at it, but missed and struck out. He was so upset that he gave up four runs in the bottom of the inning turning a close 5–4 deficit into the 9–4 final.

1917 After passing his Army physical, John J. Curnan was asked if he had a claim for exemption. He requested that he be deferred for a couple of months so he could see the Red Sox in the World Series. He was informed that it was impossible to stop the war for the Series, and was inducted into military service.

1910 Pitcher Benjamin Franklin Hunt arrived from Sacramento, and the *Boston Globe* said he "looks every inch a baseball player." Hunt debuted on the 24th, winning a four-hitter 5–2. The *Globe* headlined HUNT PITCHES LIKE A VETERAN and in the "Echoes of the Outing" section led by saying, HUNT LOOKS GOOD. He may have looked great, but his nickname was better than he was. "High Pockets" Hunt started seven games in all (2–3, 4.05 ERA). The next time he appeared in a major league game was in 1913 for the Cardinals.

1903 Nick Altrock, released by Boston to Chicago earlier in the season, earned a 9–5 win over his former teammates. Tom Hughes, the Chicago native pitching for Boston, gave up seven runs and bore the loss. Buck Freeman's home run was reported as the first ball ever hit over Chicago's right-field scoreboard.

1901 CY TAKES IT EASY…COLLINS AND THE REST OF THE TEAM GIVE THE FARMER GREAT SUPPORT—so read the *Boston Globe* headline. It only took an hour and 20 minutes, and Cy shut out Milwaukee, 6–0, hitting a triple in his own cause.

TRANSACTIONS
1977: Released Ramon Hernandez.

DEBUTS
1938: Al Baker
1990: Mike Marshall
2001: Todd Erdos

BIRTHDATES
Eddie Popowski 1913 (manager 1969, 1973); Joel Finch 1956 (1979); Tom Brunansky 1960 (1990–1994)

DEATHS
Hank Johnson 1982

August 21

2005 Fenway was packed for opening night of the 2005–06 tour by the Rolling Stones. Mick Jagger was glad to appear in Boston, a "championship city" and said, "We want to hit one over the Green Monster." By all accounts, they hit a grand slam.

2000 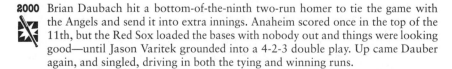 Brian Daubach hit a bottom-of-the-ninth two-run homer to tie the game with the Angels and send it into extra innings. Anaheim scored once in the top of the 11th, but the Red Sox loaded the bases with nobody out and things were looking good—until Jason Varitek grounded into a 4-2-3 double play. Up came Dauber again, and singled, driving in both the tying and winning runs.

1986 The Sox traded for Spike Owen on August 21, and two days later he scored six runs as the Red Sox dismembered the Cleveland Indians, 24–5. The Sox scored 12 runs in the sixth inning, 11 of them after there were two outs.

1984 Rookie Roger Clemens ran his record to 8–4 by fanning 15 Kansas City Royals batters. He didn't walk a soul. Not since Bill Monbouquette struck out 17 Senators in 1961 had a Boston moundsman reached the 15-K mark. Boston scored 11 times, and won 11–1.

1975 Tony Conigliaro retires from baseball for the second time, and takes a job as a sportscaster with a Providence TV station.

The Red Sox sign Dick McAuliffe, manager of the Bristol Red Sox farm team, as an infielder for the big league club. He contributes one RBI in the 1975 pennant-winning campaign.

1974 For the second time in two weeks, Red Sox pitcher Roger Moret just missed a no-hitter. On August 7, a two-out single in the eighth spoiled his bid; this day, it was a one-out infield single in the seventh by Dick Allen. Boston 4, Chicago 0.

1961 Returning to Boston for a Jimmy Fund benefit game, the former Boston Braves beat the Red Sox, 4–1, behind the combined work of seven Milwaukee pitchers. Warren Spahn pitched the first inning, and struck out rookie Chuck Schilling, got defending AL batting champion Pete Runnels to ground out, and then whiffed rookie Carl Yastrzemski. The veteran Spahn had won his 302nd major league victory just the day before.

1937 It was a "lost home run" when Jimmie Foxx led off the bottom of the second, homering off Jimmy DeShong. Retrosheet reports that the ball "cleared the left field wall and the street behind Fenway Park. It was the only run that the Red Sox scored in four innings as the Senators were winning, 5–1, when umpire George Moriarty called the game due to a torrential downpour."

1936 Joe Cronin was furious when Sox pitcher Wes Ferrell walked off the mound in the midst of a three-run sixth-inning rally by the New York Yankees. With two outs, Ferrell just left. It had been a tight 1–1 game—the sole Red Sox run being a homer hit by Rick Ferrell, Boston's catcher and Wes's brother. Wes walked Gehrig after Joe DiMaggio had popped out. Bill Dickey singled Gehrig to third, but Selkirk fouled out. Then things went wrong. Jake Powell's ball hit off Boob McNair's glove (it was not scored an error), and Lazzeri walked. Monte Pearson banged the ball right through the box, driving in two. And Ferrell took a walk. The incensed Cronin said he fined Ferrell $1,000 and suspended him for the rest of the year. Ferrell had made another unauthorized exit earlier in the week.

Ferrell offered more than one explanation. He said it "was just another one of those mistakes." He was angry at McNair for not playing where Ferrell had motioned him to before the pitch. After Pearson's hit, he said, "I looked over to the bench and Cronin was making signs with his hands. The signs were horizontal…I thought I was out of the ball game and walked straight to the Yankee dugout, which is on the way to the clubhouse." He faulted himself for not turning around to realize that Cronin had not been removing him from the game. However, Ferrell also was quoted as saying that he would punch Cronin in the nose when he saw him, and that he would refuse to pay any fine: "They can suspend me or trade me, but they're not getting any dough from me." The threat to punch Cronin notwithstanding, Ferrell also tried to assess some blame to Cronin, declaring, "My only criticism of Cronin is that he's too lenient." A good punch in the nose might shake him out of his leniency?

The Red Sox lifted Ferrell's suspension four days later, but traded Ferrell away after the season was over.

1934 That's hustle! Billy Werber is issued a base on balls and notices no one paying much attention to him as he trots to first base, so he rounds the bag and tears for second, reaching the base safely. Schoolboy Rowe, though, wins his 15th straight game for the Tigers.

1933 Desperate for pitching after an injury-ridden road trip, the Red Sox signed a pitcher out of Boston's semi-pro Twilight League. He was righty Curtis Fullerton, who'd appeared for the Sox from 1921–25, but not in the majors for eight years. Eddie Collins saw him win three games in seven days and signed him. He was bombed by the White Sox, 12–1, on his first start (August 23), and threw another complete game, losing 5–3 to the Browns. He appeared four times in relief, racking up an 8.53 ERA but stuck with the team until being released January 13, 1934.

1927 The Red Sox were the team to beat throughout the 1920s—the team easily beaten, that is. The St. Louis Browns took two, 5–0 and 4–3.

1926 Ted Lyons only struck out two batters, but he threw a no-hit 6–0 game, shaming the Red Sox in front of the fans at Fenway.

1920 Two future Hall of Famers (and future Yankees), Waite Hoyt and Herb Pennock, shut out the Cleveland Indians, 12–0 and 4–0, both throwing three-hitters.

1917 Chicago's first baseman Chick Gandil claimed that his counterpart, Boston's Del Gainer, tried to spike him as Gainer was doubled off first base in the fourth inning. In the ninth, on a play that wasn't close at all, Gandil slid into first showing his spikes. No harm was done in either case, but the players got into it a bit. Boston pitcher Lore Bader wasn't in the game, but he stuck up for Gainer with a few words of his own. After the game, Gandil lingered on the way to the dressing room and confronted Bader. It was, the *Chicago Tribune* subhead said, a "one punch fight"—Gandil knocked Bader unconscious. The White Sox had won the game, too, 2–0. Bader, incidentally, joined Slim Love as the only Red Sox players who were born in a town that was the same as their surname. Those towns were Bader, Illinois and Love, Mississippi.

1916 Boston beat the Indians, 4–0, at Cleveland, in what the *Washington Post* called a "loosely-played game." Cleveland committed five errors, three of them by pitcher Guy Morton. Jack Barry was 0-for-0 in the box score, tying a major league record with four sacrifices in the game.

1915 Burt Shotton stole home in the first inning, but that was the only run scored off Babe Ruth as the Red Sox beat St. Louis, 4–1.

TRANSACTIONS
1975: Signed free agent Dick McAuliffe.
1987: Acquired a PTBNL in trade from the Los Angeles Dodgers for Glenn Hoffman. On December 8, minor leaguer Billy Bartels was sent to Boston.
1993: Rob Deer arrived from the Tigers as part of a conditional deal.

DEBUTS
1905: Ed Barry
1940: Charlie Gelbert, Bill Fleming
1966: Hank Fischer, Bill Short
1990: Phil Plantier
1991: Dan Petry

BIRTHDATES
John Henry Johnson 1956 (1983–1984); Karl Rhodes 1968 (1995);
Lou Collier 1973 (2003); Ramon Vazquez 1976 (2005)

DEATHS
Blaine Thomas 1915; King Brady 1947; Bill Harris 1965

August 22

1993 Recently-acquired right fielder Rob Deer hit a second-inning solo home run in his first plate appearance for Boston, part of a 3-for-6 debut.

1992 John Valentin's first major league homer was a sixth-inning grand slam, greeting Seattle's Mike Schooler, who had just entered the game. Val's blast tied the game at 7–7. Tom Brunansky's two-run homer in the eighth won it for the Boston Red Sox, 10–8.

1976 Boston erased a 6–1 deficit with five runs in the sixth inning, when Oakland reliever Rollie Fingers couldn't stop the Sox. Bert Campaneris had a 5-for-6 day with two RBIs and his hit in the top of the 11th moved Phil Garner over to third base, from where he scored the winning run on a totally unanticipated suicide squeeze bunt by big slugger Don Baylor. Oakland won, 7–6.

1971 Bookends. After losing to Oakland, 9–3, the Red Sox started the second game with Sonny Siebert giving up a leadoff homer to Bert Campaneris. The Red Sox scored once mid-game with a run in the fifth. Reggie Jackson came up with two outs in the bottom of the ninth and hit the last Sonny Siebert pitch of the game over center fielder Billy Conigliaro, and sped around the bases for an inside-the-park game-winning home run.

1964 In the daytime, the Yankees lost their sixth game in a row, when the Red Sox scored three runs in the bottom of the eighth for a 5–3 win. Under cover of darkness, the Yankees broke through with a 6–0 shutout behind Mel Stottlemyre and three Roger Maris RBIs. Jack Lamabe gave up homers to Mantle, Maris, and Johnny Blanchard.

1951 Browns pitcher Tommy Byrne walked 16 Red Sox but Boston left 22 men on base, leaving the bases loaded four times and three times leaving two men on base. The Sox only managed one lone run through the first nine innings. The game ran 13 innings, and Boston finally won, with two runs in the top of the 13th as Ted Williams singled, Billy Goodman popped out—and then Byrne walked four batters in a row.

1934 Pitcher Wes Ferrell tied the game against Chicago at two each with a home run in the bottom of the eighth inning. His next time at bat was the bottom of the 10th. Again, he faced Les Tietje and again he hit one out. The *Chicago Tribune* noted, "Both sailed over the left center field wall, the final one being such a long drive that the Chicago outfielders were on their way off the field before it disappeared from view." It was the second time this year that the slugging pitcher hit a pair of homers in a game; he would do it six times in his career.

1922 Herb Pennock, showing no flashes of greatness, allowed 16 hits, walked three, hit a batter, and saw his defense make four errors. St. Louis beat Boston, 9–4.

1919 Left fielder Babe Ruth was incensed at umpire Brick Owens' call of a third strike and threatened to hit Owens, but was physically restrained by players of both the Red Sox and the Indians. Cleveland won a sloppy contest, 10–7.

1918 Secretary of War Newton Baker decided not to cancel the 1918 World Series and announced that it could be held if concluded by September 15 (the season had already been cut short, to conclude by September 1, as part of the war effort). It was already evident that the Series would be the Cubs vs. the Red Sox, and so the temporary exemption from the government's "work or fight" policy would affect a relatively small number of men. Baker's main rationale: "American soldiers in France are intensely interested in the results." In other words, it would be good for morale.

On the field of play, only a month after setting the Red Sox record of putouts in a nine-inning game (21, on July 19), Stuffy McInnis was again busy at first base setting another record that endures into the 21st century: he had six assists in nine innings. Bill Buckner had six assists, too, in the June 14, 1986 game, just four months before the World Series game where he rather famously failed to record an assist.

1910 Had he only stopped at second one time, he could have hit for the cycle. Harry Hooper had a single, a homer, and two triples, sparking seven late-inning runs for an 8–2 Boston home win over St. Louis.

1907 Heinie Wagner only hit two home runs in all of 1907. They were the first two homers of his career and they were hit on the same day off the same pitcher, Bill Donovan. Both were inside-the-park home runs, both hit to the identical spot in deep left-center. Alas, both were solo shots and the Tigers won the game, 8–7.

TRANSACTIONS
1952: Sold Ray Scarborough to the New York Yankees.
1967: Signed free agent Jim Landis.

DEBUTS
1908: Harry Niles
1993: Rob Deer
1997: Bret Saberhagen

BIRTHDATES
Wally Schang 1889 (1918–1920); Oscar Fuhr 1893 (1924–1925); Dud Lee 1899 (1924–1926); Carl Yastrzemski 1939 (1961–1983); Hipolito Pichardo 1969 (2000–2001)

DEATHS
Jim Tabor 1953; Bob Daughters 1988

August 23

1982 Home plate umpire Dave Phillips threw Gaylord Perry out of the game in the seventh inning for "doctoring the baseball." The following inning, Reid Nichols hit a two-run homer which won it for the Sox, 4–3, over Seattle. Perry was an acknowledged spitballer, but this was the first time in 21 years that he'd been bounced for messing with the ball.

1974 El Tiante wins his 20th game of the season, a 3–0 shutout over Vida Blue and the Oakland A's. Boston held a seven-game lead in the division, as the *New York Times* reported: "the Red Sox are on their way to the title in the American League's Eastern Division."

1968 Carl Yastrzemski plays his first game at first base. He handles himself well in the field, and goes 2-for-4 at the plate.

1942 In between games of the doubleheader in Philadelphia, the 28,000 fans saw "a parade of America's military might" by the 104th U.S. Cavalry, which included "armored scout cars with two-way radio, jeeps, peeps and motorcycles." (*New York Times*) Tex Hughson shut out the A's, 2–0 in the first game, and Joe Dobson continued the whitewash, 7–0, in the second. The game raised money for the Army-Navy Relief Fund, though the main battle occurred when frustrated Philly fans got on a frustrated (0-for-7) Ted Williams, who fired back some choice words and was then pelted with fruit, scorecards, and newspapers until a police detail was dispatched to the bleachers.

1940 Boston GM Eddie Collins appeared on the CBS radio quiz show *Choose Up Sides*, teamed with sportswriter Arthur Mann, and the two shared the $50 prize for answering more questions than the opposing pair.

1938 Love those ninth-inning grand slams. Playing in front of the home crowd, the Bosox won the first game easily, 13–3, on 21 hits, but the Indians gave them more of a run for their money in the nightcap. In fact, it was 10–6 Indians after 7½, but the Red Sox scored four times in the bottom of the eighth to tie it up. Cleveland immediately doused the hopes of the locals by scoring twice in the top of the ninth, but Jimmie Foxx found himself at the plate with the bases loaded and two outs in the bottom of the ninth. Relief pitcher Willis Hudlin was brought in and threw one pitch—grand slam!

It was Foxx's second homer of the game, for a total of six RBIs. In 1938, Foxx knocked in over 100 RBIs—in Fenway Park alone! His home total was 104 RBIs, with another 71 on the road.

1910 It's listed in the books as a "bounce home run"—the only homer Billy Purtell ever hit for the Red Sox. The story is a little more interesting. Purtell had only recently been traded to Boston by the White Sox and was facing his former teammate Barney Pelty in the bottom of the sixth, with two runners on base at Boston's Huntington Avenue Grounds. He punched a hard grounder to Art Griggs at third base. The ball took an unexpected hop, bounced off Griggs' forehead and sailed into the seats for a home run. The game itself was won by an eighth-inning home run hit by relief pitcher Joe Wood for a 13–11 final score.

1903 Cyclone Hughes and Cy Young combined to take two in a twin bill, 5–3 and 4–2. St. Louis scored three times off Hughes in the first inning, on a single, two doubles and a throw to third by right fielder Freeman—with no one there to receive the throw. The Browns were blanked from that inning onward, as Hughes struck out 10. Twice runners were cut down at the plate. Boston came back for two in the fourth, a third in the fifth on Jake Stahl's home run into the seats in left, and won the game when Hughes doubled in the eighth, Dougherty bunted, and Freeman singled him in.

Cy Young only let up one hit for the first five frames in the second game. Boston scored twice in the top of the first and once more in the fourth. The Browns got two in the sixth and after Boston bumped their lead up to 4–2 in the top of the seventh, St. Louis responded with a threat. The first two batters singled and the third beat out a bunt to load the bases with nobody out. St. Louis pitcher Wee Willie Sudhoff was allowed to bat for himself and he banged a ball "like a cannon shot to right center" that looked like a sure double. The runners took off but Boston second baseman Hobe Ferris raced out and snagged the ball, fired to Parent covering short, who in turn relayed to LaChance at first. Triple play.

TRANSACTIONS
2000: Released Ed Sprague, who had just been acquired on June 30.
2001: Signed free agent Willie Banks and picked up Bill
    Pulsipher off waivers from the White Sox.

DEBUTS
1910: Doc Moskiman
1967: Jim Landis

BIRTHDATES
Cedric Durst 1896 (1930); Nels Potter 1911 (1941); Ken Holcombe 1918 (1953); George Kell 1922 (1952–1954); Mike Boddicker 1957 (1988–1990); Jeff Manto 1964 (1996); Allen McDill 1971 (2001); Mark Bellhorn 1974 (2004–2005)

DEATHS
None yet

August 24

2002 Manny Ramirez had reached base 12 times in a row. He reached safely on an infield single in the first inning and doubled in the fourth, making it 14 times in a row, just two shy of the record set by Ted Williams. Flying out to center field his next time up, in the sixth inning, Manny's streak was snapped. Angels pitchers only allowed five hits all afternoon, and won the game 2–0.

1991 Mo Vaughn and Mike Greenwell's shouts escalated into a fight at the batting cage in Anaheim, to the surprise of fans watching batting practice. Both exchanged punches and Greenwell left with three visible bruises on his face. Others intervened, and the batting cage was nearly knocked down during the scuffle. It apparently started with Vaughn playfully tapping Greenwell, and not knocking it off when Gator asked him to. Videotape shot by a fan showed that Greenwell struck first. The next day's club blackboard bore a coach's message: "Hitting: 11:35. No infield. No fighting."

1988 Leigh Montville noted in the *Globe* that the billboard above the right-field bleachers read, "Hit One Up Here and Win A Pair of Thom McAn Shoes" was, if nothing else, confusing. Spike Owen thought it meant all you had to do was hit a ball into the bleachers to win a pair of shoes. Most players thought you had to hit the actual sign—positioned some 600 feet from home plate. Sox marketing head Larry Cancro said the team had informed Thom McAn's ad agency that it was impossible, that no one would ever win a pair of shoes. They said they knew that and it was a joke. Confusion reigned; it was all good publicity.

1977 The game ended at 2:26 A.M., the latest ending of any game the Red Sox ever played. Of the 31,784 there before the rain delays, only an estimated 4,000 remained. And they saw the Rangers beat the Red Sox, 6–3. The latest they ever played was at Tiger Stadium on August 5, 1988. That game went until 2:32 A.M., and Boston lost that one, too, 3–2.

1974 Riding a five-game winning streak, and atop the American League by eight games, the Sox get a head start on their traditional September swoon when Carl Yastrzemski made a throwing error in the ninth that saw one run score and the runners move up. Two more scored on succeeding plays. First man up for Boston in the bottom of the ninth was Yastrzemski, but he struck out. The Angels had a 4–1 win. The Sox lost 11 of their next 13 games, and were 14–23 after this loss, winding up in third place, seven games out.

1973 Outfielder Reggie Smith demands a trade, blasting Boston as a racist city.

1961 In the bottom of the 10th inning, Jackie Jensen hit a bases-empty homer to give the Red Sox a 5–4 win over Washington. This was the same day that the Red Sox said that when Jensen missed ballgames because of his fear of flying, he would not be paid for the days he missed.

1950 With Walt Masterson locked in against Cleveland's Ned Garver, it was a 2–1 game when the Red Sox came to bat in the bottom of the ninth. They loaded the bases, but Johnny Pesky's fly to right was too shallow to score the tying run. With two outs, an error on Billy Goodman's grounder let Boston tie it up, and then Vern Stephens ran the winning streak to nine with a grand slam off Ned Garver, who had won the only previous 1950 game the Sox lost to St. Louis. They were 18–1 versus the Browns.

1948 The late innings seesawed as the Red Sox tied it 6–6 in the bottom of the eighth, and Cleveland took an 8–6 lead in the top of the ninth. The Sox scored once on a sacrifice fly by Ted Williams, and finally Vern Stephens hit the first pitch he saw for a two-run homer—his 15th game-winning hit of the season.

1944 Tex Hughson is drafted into the United States Army, unfortunately leaving the Sox at a crucial time in a year when they had a real shot at the pennant; Hughson was a spectacular 18–5 at the time.

1940 With Detroit winning 11–1, Joe Cronin turned the mound over to Ted Williams, who came in from left field to pitch the final two innings. Pitcher Jim Bagby took Ted's place in left. Though 0-for-4 at the plate, Ted threw pretty well, allowing just three hits and one run, and (he was always proud to remember) striking out Rudy York on three pitches. A great trivia question emerged, the answer being Joe Glenn, who had caught Babe Ruth the last time he pitched, back in 1933, and now caught Ted Williams the last (and first) time he pitched.

1939 Four K's for Double X. Jimmie Foxx struck out four times during a 3–1 night game loss to the White Sox.

1922 It was all over but the shouting after St. Louis scored nine runs in the first two innings. Three Red Sox pitchers combined on a 20-hitter and, not surprisingly, lost. The final was 13–2. Neither side had a homer.

1918 The Sox scored all three runs in the second inning of a 3–1 win over St. Louis, the third run coming when Boston pitcher Babe Ruth stole home on the front half of a double steal. He's the only Sox pitcher to ever steal home.

1916 On his way to a 23–12 season, in which he posted a league-leading 1.75 ERA, Babe Ruth shut out the opposition for the seventh time, with a three-hitter over the Tigers, 3–0.

1909 The 1909 Sox were known as the "Speed Boys" and by year's end boasted Harry Lord with 36 stolen bases, Tris Speaker with 35, while both Harry Niles and Amby McConnell had more than 25. Boston beat the White Sox, 5–2, this day with just one stolen base (Niles) but the Sox scampered around the field and on the basepaths enough for the *Chicago Tribune* to comment on their "new style of baseball."

1901 Boston players rescue umpire Joe Cantillon from incensed Boston rooters, who called him a "robber" and "thief." The *Chicago Tribune* reported, "There was much stupid playing from both teams today and there were also many close decisions against Boston. The crowd started for Cantillon at the close of the game, but the home team kept them back and hurried the umpire off the field." Chick Stahl and Parson Lewis apparently played important roles in the rescue. Cantillon did not umpire after the 1901 season.

TRANSACTIONS
1999: Kent Mercker acquired from the St. Louis Cardinals in
        trade for Mike Matthews and David Benham.

DEBUTS
1908: Joe Wood
1910: Ben Hunt

BIRTHDATES
Harry Hooper 1887 (1909–1920); Jimmy Cooney 1894 (1917); Les Howe 1895 (1923–1924); Kip Gross 1964 (1999); Arquimedez Pozo 1973 (1996–1997)

DEATHS
None yet

August 25

2001 In the first nine innings, both the Rangers and Red Sox scored seven times each. In the second nine innings of the 6:35 game (believed the longest ballgame the Red Sox ever played), only one run was scored. Probably the Sox were simply worn out. There were two walks, an error, a wild pitch, a steal of third, and then Chad Curtis scored on a ground ball. The Red Sox used nine pitchers and Texas used eight. Derek Lowe was the losing pitcher, giving up one unearned run on zero hits. It was the first loss in what became a nine-game Sox losing streak.

1996 The Sox were leading the Mariners, 8–1, heading into the eighth. Alex Rodriguez hit a three-run homer off Joe Hudson, and then Ken Griffey, Jr. went back-to-back. It was the 17th time in the '96 season that the M's had back-to-backed, setting a new major league record. Hudson's personal stats were messed up, but the Sox still won, 8–5.

1995 Jose Canseco's homer with two outs in the top of the ninth was the only run, and one of just three hits, for the Red Sox. It was the fifth game in a row in which Canseco had homered.

1972 One month on, one month off. Outfielder Bob Burda is released, only to be signed again on September 24, and ultimately released yet again on October 27. The man all this back and forth was about hit .164 on the season.

1970 Three bombs had exploded in the previous two weeks in Minneapolis and St. Paul, so authorities took it seriously when they received a bomb threat during the fourth inning of a scoreless game at Metropolitan Stadium. A trace of the call indicated it had been made from inside the stadium. Most of the 17,697 fans were evacuated, though about 2,000 congregated in center field. After a 45-minute search was completed, the game resumed. The only run scored in the game was Tony Conigliaro's eighth-inning solo home run. With one out and runners at first and second in the bottom of the ninth, pinch-hitter Jim Holt grounded into a 4-6-5-2-5 double play.

1968 After almost five and a half hours of play, Boog Powell doubled with two outs in the bottom of the 18th and Brooks Robinson singled him home. 3–2 Orioles.

1965 There were five Red Sox homers and three by the Senators, but Earl Wilson's 13 strikeouts made a big difference in Boston's 8–3 win.

1963 Boston won the first game easily, 8–3, but Cleveland and Boston were still 0–0 after nine innings. The Sox got a run in the top of the 10th after starting pitcher Bob Heffner doubled and came around to score. Tito Francona evened it back up with a home run. It was 1–1 after 14, until the Indians singled twice in the bottom of the 15th and then Francona singled in the winning run. The two games featured 27 Cleveland strikeouts and 17 Red Sox strikeouts. Both the 27 and combined 44 set league records.

1960 Bill Monbouquette was struggling, so Vic Wertz was sent in to pinch-hit for him in the bottom of the fourth. The move paid off; he hit Don Newcombe's first pitch for a grand slam, his third of the season. Ted's two-run homer also helped beat Cleveland, 10–7.

1950 An 11-game win streak is always good news, and Mel Parnell won his 12th while Boston beat the first-place Tigers, 6–2, to close the gap to 3½.

1946 A Gardner, Massachusetts, furniture company transported the world's largest chair to Fenway Park and had Ted Williams pose for photographs sitting on the chair. Every Sox player and coach was given a chair before the game; Williams was also given a huge baseball bat which remains on display today at the Hall of Fame in Cooperstown.

  This seemed to be a weekend of gimmickry. Between games of the doubleheader, Johnny Price, described as the "Cleveland Indians stunt man," used a sling to heave a baseball out of the ballpark. Unfortunately, this time his aim was off and the ball knocked out one Red Sox fan sitting in the right-field bleachers and gave a head contusion to his companion.

1940 Johnny Niggeling's knuckler stymied the Red Sox, 7–2, in the first game. Even though enjoying a 5–2 lead in the second game, they cut loose for 11 runs in the bottom of the sixth, with Jimmie Foxx's third grand slam of the season the big blow. The game had to end early, due to Boston's Sunday law, but the Sox won after seven, 17–3.

1937 Bob Feller struck out 16 for the second time in a year, one short of his league record. Three times each, he fanned Foxx, Higgins, and Gene Desautels, and won handily, 8–1.

1925 After scoring nine times in the bottom of the first inning, the Tigers were running away with the game, but Boston catcher Al Stokes got in a little playing time later in the game and made a nice little play—tagging out two Detroit runners with one sweep of his arm. It was the seventh inning and Johnny Bassler was on second, with Fred Haney on first. Topper Rigney hit a long fly to center. Ira Flagstead ran it down but dropped it. Bassler had held up, but Haney had not, and so was hard on Bassler's heels as both men ran to home plate. Flagstead picked up the ball, threw to the cutoff man, Rothrock, who fired the ball home to Stokes. Bassler slid to the inside of the plate while Haney slid to the outside. Both Tigers "hit the dust simultaneously. Stokes stood his ground, and with one sweep of his arm, tagged them both before their spikes hit the rubber. Not to be outdone, the umpire shot both arms upward, indicating the double play." (*Washington Post*) Stokes recorded the two outs, but also made two errors in the same game. Boston lost, 14–4.

1918 Harry Frazee rejected Ban Johnson's call for the first three games of the 1918 World Series to be held in Chicago, then transferring to Boston. Frazee said it was unfair and "I will refuse to abide by the schedule." In the end, he acquiesced and the Red Sox won two of the three Chicago games.

1915 Having failed to win the pennant two years in a row, the Red Sox won 19 of 21 and strong outfield defense helped them complete a road sweep of the Tigers with a 2–1 win in 13 innings.

1911 On their final swing out west, the Red Sox took two from St. Louis. Each team scored once in the ninth in the opener, but Smoky Joe Wood earned win #20, 3–2. The Sox won the second game, 6–2.

1910 Down 4–1 heading into the bottom of the eighth, the Red Sox scored six runs off a suddenly-wild Willie Mitchell, and beat Cleveland, 7–4. They didn't have to bat in the bottom of the ninth.

TRANSACTIONS
1972: Released Bob Burda.

DEBUTS
1911: Blaine Thomas
1926: Danny MacFayden
1977: Sam Bowen
1995: Eric Gunderson
2003: Bronson Arroyo

BIRTHDATES
Rube Kroh 1886 (1906–1907); Jim Suchecki 1926 (1950); Darrell Johnson 1928 (manager, 1974–1976); Andy Abad 1972 (2003)

DEATHS
Waite Hoyt 1984; Cliff Garrison 1994

August 26

2002 Manny Ramirez had a 5-for-5 day, with two solo homers and four RBIs. Johnny Damon's homer off the Angels' Scot Shields in the bottom of the 10th inning is the one that made the day. Boston 10, Anaheim 9 (10 innings).

1995 Catcher Mike Macfarlane's fourth-inning grand slam gave the Red Sox, obviously, four runs, but Oakland already had nine, and added two more in the middle innings. The final was 11–4, Athletics.

1990 For the first time since August 1962, the Sox won three straight shutouts. All three were against the Toronto Blue Jays, and all in SkyDome. The Jays led the league in runs scored, but these were "Deadball Era" scores: 2–0, 1–0, and 1–0. Dana Kiecker, Roger Clemens, and Greg Harris were the winning pitchers. Jeff Gray got two saves; Clemens pitched a complete game in between.

1978 Jerry Remy was hit by a pitch that cracked a wrist bone, keeping him out of the lineup for a couple of weeks, though he still helped out—notably scoring the winning run in the game the very next day. Just three days later, during the same homestand, Dwight Evans was hit on the head by a pitch and was woozy for weeks, sub-par for the rest of the season. In one stretch, the Gold Glove outfielder dropped four fly balls in one week. Given that one more win would have secured the pennant for the Red Sox...

1972 The Sox scored five runs in the bottom of the ninth to come from behind and steal one from the Texas Rangers, 7–6. Phil Gagliano's two-run double pushed across the tying and winning runs. Rangers manager Ted Williams, Texas owner Bob Short, and a number of old Red Sox hands such as Johnny Pesky and Dom DiMaggio held a surprise testimonial dinner for Tom Yawkey that evening.

1966 A game that took a sudden turn for the worse: Baltimore was losing 2–0 with nobody on in the bottom of the ninth, when pinch-hitter Vic Roznovsky homered and Boog Powell pinch-hit and homered, too. It was the first time there had been back-to-back pinch-hit homers in the AL. Three extra innings were played, and the Orioles won in the 12th, 3–2, on a bases-loaded single by Russ Snyder.

1962 Dick Donovan of the Indians won his 100th game convincingly: a 4–0, two-hit shutout. By definition, the shutout meant no Sox homers; they homered in each of their previous 13 games (including a game they lost 10–5 earlier this day).

1957 Adding to the 4–0 lead they'd staked Sox starter Willard Nixon, the Bosox hit four homers and scored 10 runs in the seventh inning on the way to a 16–0 shellacking of the Kansas City Athletics, in Kansas City.

1948 Sox prospect George Washington Wilson, playing for Birmingham, had declared, "I'm going to be a better hitter than Williams ever was." He picked up the nickname "Teddy" and made it to the majors, all but 19 of his 145 major league at-bats came with the New York Mets. Wilson hit .191 with three home runs.

1946 The day after Ted Williams sat on the world's largest chair, and an Indians stunt man knocked a Fenway bleacherite unconscious while flinging a baseball from his sling, yet another incident occurs. When the Indians used the "Shift" against Ted, effectively abandoning third base defensively, a three-foot-tall dwarf ran on the field, grabbed a glove, and pretended to play third base. Marco Songini was a local vaudeville performer who said he was "seized with an irresistible urge to help out the losing Indians." The umpires were not amused and had him removed from the field.

1945 Boo Ferriss pitched a complete game for his 20th win, after the Sox sent it into extra innings with a game-tying run in the bottom of the ninth. He won it for himself with a double driving home Catfish Metkovich in the 10th. Boston took the second game, too, 4–3.

1933 Brown beats Browns. Pitcher Lloyd Brown held St. Louis to one run on seven hits, and nearly hit for the cycle—with a single, double, and a home run to his credit. His five RBIs were more than enough for the 8–1 win.

1930 Eighteen members of the Red Sox played an exhibition game in St. John, New Brunswick against the St. John team of the Greater Boston Twi League. A little farflung, St. John; the other teams in the league were: Roslindale, Dorchester, Malden, Portland, and Quincy. Big Ed Morris pitched for the Red Sox and won, 7–5, despite a three-run rally in the bottom of the ninth off reliever George Smith, who had come into the game pinch-hitting for Morris in the seventh.

1926 Harry Frazee was sentenced to 10 days in a New York City jail. Harry, Jr., that is, sentenced to 10 days in The Tombs for speeding (34 miles per hour) at Broadway and 184th Street.

1920 Cleveland's players circulated a petition appealing to all American League players to refuse to play in any game when New York pitched Carl Mays. Ray Chapman, Cleveland's popular shortstop, had been killed by a Mays pitch on August 16. Though Boston players were angry about the incident, manager Ed Barrow indicated that the boycott was Cleveland's issue and not Boston's. The boycott did not succeed and Mays was able to keep to his regular rotation.

1916 Carl Mays makes a club-record 10 assists in a game against the Tigers.

1915 The Red Sox overtook the Tigers with four runs in the top of the ninth, for a 6–5 lead, but Sam Crawford drove in a run to tie it in the bottom of the inning. In the bottom of the 12th, Cobb singled, moved to second on a sacrifice, and scored the game-winner easily when Veach banged one all the way to the wall in left.

1908 Catcher Bill Carrigan takes ill with appendicitis and club physician Dr. Theodore Erb said there was "no chance of Carrigan getting back into the game this year even with the best of luck."

TRANSACTIONS
1936: Papers reported that the Red Sox had purchased the contract of Bobby
Doerr from the San Diego Padres of the Pacific Coast League.

DEBUTS
1908: Ed McFarland
1913: Wally Rehg

BIRTHDATES
Fred Wenz 1941 (1968–1969); Carlos Quintana 1965 (1988–1993); Jeff Richardson
1965 (1993); Brian Bark 1968 (1995); Ken Grundt 1969 (1996–1997)

DEATHS
John Kroner 1968; Danny MacFayden 1972

August 27

1990 Ellis Burks homered twice in the fourth inning of a 12–4 win over Cleveland, at Cleveland. He homered off starter Tom Candiotti to lead off the inning, then was the first batter to face Candiotti's replacement, Colby Ward. He homered off Ward as well.

1978 Jerry Remy, despite having a wrist bone cracked by a pitch the night before, returned as a pinch-runner and scored the tying run in the bottom of the 12th inning. Yaz singled to lead off, and Remy was put in to run. With one out, Fred Lynn walked, advancing Remy to second. After a second out, George Scott hit a grounder to Carney Lansford who threw wildly for a two-base error while Remy streaked for home. California had scored once in the top of the 12th to take the lead. With the score re-tied, Butch Hobson singled to drive in Lynn with the winning run and a 4–3 finale.

1977 With four homers, the Sox beat the Twins, 7–5. Tommy Helms and Butch Hobson went back-to-back; it was the 15th time in 1977 that there had been consecutive Sox home runs.

1969 Hard liquor was banned on team flights, per order of GM Dick O'Connell. A notice posted in the clubhouse mentioned "serious instances aboard planes, especially with crew personnel. Obscene language and poor conduct directed toward stewardesses have caused this and other ball clubs considerable embarrassment."

1967 Yaz hit two homers and right-fielder Jose Tartabull cut down Ken Berry's potential tying run in the ninth inning, preserving a 4–3 Red Sox victory. Elston Howard blocked the plate expertly, and made the tag. Stout and Johnson term it "the signature moment of the season" in *Red Sox Century*. In the second game, Darrell Brandon's walk to pinch-hitter Rocky Colavito forced in the winning run, 1–0, in the bottom of the 11th inning.

Dick O'Connell said the Red Sox were looking for a new stadium, paid for by state funds, because the team "firmly believes it cannot be privately financed." Gov. John Volpe submitted a bill to supply up to $50 million in funds from the Massachusetts Turnpike Authority.

1963 New York swept a pair from the Boston Red Sox, 5–0 (Jim Bouton) and 3–0 (Ralph Terry).

1950 Bob Feller had a seven-run lead after 2½ innings, but the Red Sox came right back with five runs in the bottom of the third, centered around Walt Dropo's three-run homer. In the seventh inning, the Sox scored six times—with Clyde Vollmer's pinch-hit grand slam as the centerpiece. Boston won, 11–9.

1949 Chuck Davis, writing in the August 27 *Chicago Defender*, noted the Red Sox purchase of Piper Davis of the Birmingham Black Barons. Piper Davis, it was said, would "bring a near .400 batting average to the lineup of the Beantowners." Added to the one-two punch of Ted Williams and Vern Stephens, the Sox would be a stronger team. "He will also bring the first colored face to the Red Sox squad," the writer noted. Not so fast. A full decade would pass before that first "colored face" made the major league Red Sox squad.

1946 Ted Williams is involved in an automobile accident in Holliston, Massachusetts. Fortunately, his good friend John Blake of the Massachusetts State Police was a passenger in Ted's car at the time.

1911 Big Ed Walsh of the White Sox no-hits the Red Sox, 5–0.

1910 The only Cleveland batter who got a hit off Charley "Sea Lion" Hall was relief pitcher Elmer Koestner, with a single. The hit came on a high popup right in front of home plate. Shortstop Wagner shouted, "Take it, Bill"—but both Bills (third baseman Purtell and catcher Carrigan) looked at each other, the ball hit the ground and bounced foul, but nicked Purtell's foot on the way, making it a fair ball. Hall won his one-hitter, 7–1.

1907 Cy Young and the Bostons beat Cleveland, 2–1, both runs coming on Cleveland errors. The second run came when Young unexpectedly bunted to third base, and reached on third baseman Bradley's error. A couple of plays later, catcher Clark pounced on Denny Sullivan's bunt and threw it into the first base bleachers.

1903 Tom Hughes was the hero of the day. He let the Athletics take a one-run lead in the first (they scored one more in the seventh when neither shortstop nor second baseman covered the bag and Criger's throw to cut down the stealing Lave Cross sailed into center) but held them to five hits on the day. Eddie Plank had only given Boston three hits through eight innings. The score was tied heading into the ninth, with the bottom of the order coming up for both teams. In the top of the ninth, with two out, a runner on, and having worked a 3–2 count, Hughes homered over the liquor sign into the middle of Columbia Avenue. Hoffman tripled in the bottom of the inning but was cut down at the plate, trying to stretch it into an inside-the-park job. Final score: Boston 4, Philadelphia 2. The *Lawrence American* wrote that only a train wreck or a smallpox epidemic could stop Collins' team from winning the pennant.

1901 Detroit scored once in the top of the first and Boston matched that with one in the second. The next run scored was the game-winner when starter Cy Young drove in a run in the bottom of the 15th inning, winning his 25th game of the year, 2–1, and making a hard-luck loser out of Detroit's Roscoe Miller (who won 23 games in 1901).

TRANSACTIONS
1909: Selected Jack Chesbro off waivers from the New York Highlanders.

DEBUTS
1999: Kent Mercker

BIRTHDATES
Hal Janvrin 1892 (1911–1917); Ted Olson 1912 (1936–1938); Mike Maddux 1961 (1995–1996)

DEATHS
Frank Truesdale 1943; John Wilson 1980

August 28

2002 The Yankees beat Boston, 7–0, as Pedro Martinez didn't have it and Mike Mussina did, throwing a three-hitter. NY's David Wells had shut out the Red Sox the day before, 6–0. It was the first time Boston had suffered back-to-back shutout home losses to New York since September 11 and 12, 1943.

1999 Knuckleballer Tim Wakefield faced knuckleballer Steve Sparks (Anaheim). Both teams scored four runs in the third, and the Angels added two in the eighth. Boston scored a run in the first, another in the sixth, and plated the go-ahead run in the bottom of the eighth, Derek Lowe got the win as he closed out the ninth.

1982 The Angels took a 5–0 lead, but the Sox scored five times in the seventh to tie it up and then pulled ahead by one in the eighth. The Angels tied it, 6–6, in the top of the ninth. With one out in the bottom of the ninth, Carney Lansford singled off Bruce Kison. Unexpectedly, he stole second—his first stolen base since June 17 and just his seventh on the season. After an intentional walk to Boggs, Lansford stole third while Boggs stole second. After a K and another IBB, the slow-footed (three stolen bases in a seven-year career) Gary Allenson was up with two outs and the bases loaded. Acting on his own, Allenson surprised every one of the Angels by dropping down a perfect bunt to third to push across the winning run. "I wish I could say I thought of it," said manager Ralph Houk, "but I'm not that smart." It was thought that the last time the Sox bunted across the winning run was on a Tony Conigliaro bunt back in 1966.

1978 Butch Hobson's two-run double off Fenway's center field wall capped a three-run ninth-inning Red Sox rally that converted a 9–7 deficit to a 10–9 triumph over Seattle. Fred Lynn had five hits in the game, Jack Brohamer had four. Bob Stanley had come in to get the last two outs in the top of the ninth, and picked up the win. He thereby raised his won-loss record to 12–1, but bore the good-natured moniker of "The Vulture" for some of the easy wins along the way.

1967 The Red Sox kept up the pace with a 3–0 shutout of the Yankees in Yankee Stadium, as Dave Morehead held New York to four hits. Yaz was given a color TV and a Chrysler convertible by well-wishers from Bridgehampton, Long Island, and his sacrifice fly in the first was the only run needed. Reggie Smith homered, too, for good measure.

The Red Sox signed free agent Ken Harrelson. In his book, *Hawk*, Harrelson recounts how he was hoping to get $100,000 but couldn't bring himself to utter a figure that high. With a little bargaining back and forth, never quite naming a figure, the Red Sox wound up out-bidding a couple of other teams, and paying him $150,000 per year. He homered his first time up with the Red Sox, but averaged only .200 during his time with Boston. The stylish Hawk nonetheless was a true fan favorite, achieving cult status in a very short time.

1950 After 2½ innings, you wouldn't have blamed fans who left early. Mickey McDermott had started the game and given up six runs on one hit (he hit the first batter and walked six or seven—accounts differ). The Indians built a 10–0 lead, with 20-game-winner Bob Lemon on the mound. The Indians, though, had blown a seven-run lead the day before; Boston won that one, 11–9. And the 1950 Red Sox could hit! Hit they did, with a big eight runs in the fourth closing much of the gap. Even bringing in Bob Feller in the eighth didn't stem the tide, and Boston won, 15–14.

1948 Everyone in the lineup had a hit, except for Ellis Kinder—but he held the White Sox to seven hits and two late-inning runs. Vern Stephens had four of Boston's 13 hits, including two doubles, for two RBIs. Boston won, 6–2.

1944 The Red Sox battery of Tex Hughson and Hal Wagner were both set to enter the Navy on the very same day, August 28. Hughson threw a two-hitter in his last game before departing for service. Shortly beforehand, Hughson changed his mind and signed up for the Army Air Corps instead, reporting on the 28th.

1932 Jim Charlton described this day's Red Sox action: "The Red Sox 'eclipse' the Indians in the second game of a doubleheader, 4–3, in 11 innings, as light-hitting Bennie Tate poles a one-out HR to end it. The game was previously scheduled for August 31, but a solar eclipse was due that would blacken the ballpark for 20 minutes, so the game is played today instead. The Indians take the opener, 10–1, scoring seven runs in the first inning to drive Bob Weiland to the showers."

1926 Deja-vu? Cleveland's Emil Levsen pitched two complete game wins against the Red Sox, in Boston. Without a single strikeout and with the exact same lineup behind him in both games, Levsen limited the Red Sox to four hits and one run in the first game and four hits and one run in the second game. Si Rosenthal scored the Red Sox run in both games. The scores? 6–1 and 5–1. Levsen, the AP reported, "was going as strong at the finish as at the start."

1914 Dutch Leonard makes his last start of the season, but winds up with a 19–5 record and 224⅔ innings. His 0.96 ERA is the lowest in major league history; he gave up only 24 earned runs all year long. Second in the league in ERA was Rube Foster, with a 1.70 ERA. It was the first time two AL pitchers on the same team finished 1–2 in ERA. In 2002, Pedro Martinez (2.26) and teammate Derek Lowe (2.58) also finished 1–2.

1913 Coming off a string of 14 straight wins, Walter Johnson allowed just one hit for the first nine, in all pitching a brilliant game: 10-plus innings of three-hit ball, striking out 10 and walking not a one. Trouble is: he lost. Second baseman Steve Yerkes singled in the second and the Red Sox were hitless until the bottom of the 11th when Yerkes singled once more—and center fielder Clyde Milan let the ball get through him. Yerkes wound up on third. Wagner grounded to short, but the throw home nipped Yerkes. Wagner took second on the play and, with two strikes on him, Bill Carrigan singled home Wagner with the winner, 1–0. Credit Boston's Ray Collins with a great game, as well, a six-hit shutout.

1912 In just three hours and 18 minutes of play, the Red Sox won two games from Chicago, 5–3 and 3–0. Smoky Joe Wood won the shutout for his 27th win of the year, on a bases-clearing double by Larry Gardner.

1908 In a surprise announcement, Red Sox field manager Jim "Deacon" McGuire resigned, at the request of club president John I. Taylor who named Fred Lake in his place. Lake had been a Sox scout for the preceding two years. The reason given was simply the hope for "better results by a change."

1907 "Highlander pitcher John 'Tacks' Neuer, begins baseball's most successful short career by besting the Red Sox 1–0 in his first start, the nitecap of a DH. In one month he will pitch six complete games, win 4, including three shutouts, and then disappear from the major league scene. In the first game, Boston's Cy Young wins his 20th game, defeating the Highlanders, 5–3." Couldn't have written it better than this version online at www.baseballlibrary.com. New York's only run in the second game came in the first inning, and grew out of a throwing error by Boston pitcher Rube Kroh.

1906 Manager Jimmy Collins was suspended "for absenting himself from the team without leave." The *Washington Post* reported that Collins had, for a period of "several weeks...declined to take any part in the management." The *Boston Globe* noted his AWOL status two days running, and that there were "several" similar instances in the season. Collins was apparently depressed at the quality of play and the lack of incoming talent. He apparently also neglected to stay in condition to play himself at third base. Outfielder Chick Stahl became acting manager. (See also August 29, 1906.)

TRANSACTIONS
1967: Signed free agent Ken Harrelson.
2003: Acquired Lou Merloni from the San Diego Padres in trade for minor leaguer Rene Miniel.

DEBUTS
1909: William Matthews
1924: Clarence Winters
1937: Joe Gonzales

BIRTHDATES
Ben Beville 1877 (1901); Braggo Roth 1892 (1919); Tom Satriano 1940 (1969–1970); Mike Torrez 1946 (1978–1982); Darren Lewis 1967 (1998–2001); Shane Andrews 1971 (2002)

DEATHS
Bill Piercy 1951; Jean Dubuc 1958; Al Zarilla 1996

August 29

2005 Tony Graffanino hit safely in the first 12 home games he played at Fenway Park, but his streak ran out on August 30.

2000 Pedro Martinez almost had himself a perfect game, putting down the first 24 Devil Rays in order. The first batter in the bottom of the ninth, though, was Tampa Bay's catcher, John Flaherty. As Pedro faced him, the chain holding Pedro's crucifix broke after a pitch. He removed it and tucked it in his back pocket; Flaherty stroked the next pitch for a clean single. Flaherty, a former Red Sox player, was the only Devil Ray to reach base. Pedro struck out 13 and walked none. During the course of the game, eight Devil Rays were thrown out of the ballgame.

1986 Three Joe Carter homers and his two singles (he was 5-for-5, with four RBIs) did a number on the Red Sox, and the Indians prevailed at Fenway, 7–3.

1977 Jim Rice hit three homers and a single for 13 total bases, but Oakland's Mitchell Page hit two homers and a triple, matching Jim Ed's RBI total at four, and Page's ninth-inning homer off Bill Campbell was the one that won the game for Oakland, 8–7. The last player to hit three homers in a game for the Sox had been Norm Zauchin on State of Maine Day in 1957: May 27.

1972 In 1968, Luis Tiant was 21–9 for the Indians. Then his win totals dropped to 9, 7, and just one win in 1971. Signed by the Red Sox, he was having himself a comeback and this day's 3–0 triumph of the White Sox was his third successive shutout. Reggie Smith had two doubles, each of which drove in a run. Luis finished the year 15–9, and led the league in ERA (1.91). Three of the next four years, he won 20 or more games.

1967 A Yankee Stadium doubleheader sees Boston win the first game 2–1, but lose a 20-inning nightcap 4–3 as sixth Sox pitcher Darrell Brandon yielded a single to John Kennedy, then hit Jim Bouton, moving Kennedy into scoring position. Jose Santiago was brought in, but Horace Clarke slapped a single through the infield into right, driving in Kennedy to end the game at 1:57 A.M. Earlier on, Ken Harrelson hit a home run in his very first plate appearance for the Red Sox.

1965 Chicago's Ron Hansen was busy at shortstop, handling 29 chances with nary an error. He had seven putouts and 12 assists in the first game, and three putouts and seven assists in the second. The first game ran 14 innings and it was Hansen who doubled Gene Freese to third base, where he scored on a sac fly. Both games were won by Chicago, 3–2 and 3–2. White Sox rookie Bob Locker got a win in game one, and a save in game two.

1964 It was officially Elston Howard Night, but one could argue that it was Joe Pepitone's, too. Pepitone is the one who hit three home runs, including a grand slam in the first inning of the first game. For Roger Maris, it was a singles night— six singles in eight at-bats. New York won both games, 10–2 and 6–1.

1936 The *Chicago Defender* of August 29 reprinted a *Sunday Worker* story in which National League president Ford Frick said there was no written rule barring Negroes from organized baseball. Ed Barrow of the Yankees would not comment. Tom Yawkey replied by wire as follows: "Have never given any thought to the matter. This would be something for the big leagues as a whole to decide, therefore, feel that any expression should come from baseball in general and not from individuals like myself."

1932 Any pitching staff that walks 12 batters faces difficulty. Dusty Rhodes (7) and Gordon McNaughton (5) just kept giving out free passes to first base. With just five hits, Cleveland beat Boston, 6–3.

1921 Commissioner Landis ruled that the Red Sox must pay their share of the proceeds from an April exhibition game against Vanderbilt University. The game was held on the same day that the Nashville team was to play an American Association team, and therefore violated the territorial rights of the Nashville ball club.

1919 Captain Roger Peckinpaugh of the New York Yankees says the team had offered the Red Sox a record $75,000 cash and a couple of players in a trade for "the Tarzan of baseball," Babe Ruth. The trade was seen in the offing.

1916 Is a broken hand sufficient evidence? Umpire Owens was skeptical whether Jack Barry has truly been hit by the pitch, but awarded him first base. Barry was out for the rest of the year. The Browns "took the measure of three of the leading Boston boxmen," with a 5–3 win over the combined efforts of Dutch Leonard, Babe Ruth, and Carl Mays. Clyde Davenport doled out but three hits to the reigning World Champions, one of them to Ruth, but Ruth struck out the time he was up with the bases loaded. There was a second game, and Ernie Shore got pounded, too, losing 8–2.

1906 Cy Young threw an excellent game, not allowing a single Clevelander to reach first base until after 7⅔ innings. Young tired and let two runs score in the ninth, but Boston won, 6–2, and Chick Stahl collected his first win as acting manager of the Bostons. AL President Ban Johnson acknowledged the suspension of Jimmy Collins—it being understood that it was likely he had truly been dismissed. Further details emerged, including the fact that the absence of Collins for a full week during the late July western road trip had been unauthorized and that he had left no word at all where he could be reached.

1904 Boston earned first place honors once again with a 1–0 win over Detroit, Dinneen over Killian. Dinneen had yielded but two hits, then won the game for himself in the bottom of the ninth with a single to right, scoring Hobe Ferris.

1903 Tied 2–2 in the 10th, Cy Young was glad to grab another W when Patsy Dougherty doubled to lead off the bottom of the inning, singled home moments later by Jimmy Collins. The day's second game against Washington was an extra-inning affair, too, knotted 1–1 (Winters vs. Orth) after 11, when the game had to be called due to darkness.

TRANSACTIONS
1974: Signed amateur free agent Juan Agosto—in August!
1996: Acquired Jeff Manto from Seattle on waivers. It had only been
       on July 22 that Manto had been sent to Seattle.
2005: Claimed RHP Chad Harville off waivers from the Houston Astros.

DEBUTS
1928: George Loepp
1944: Clem Dreisewerd
1967: Ken Harrelson

BIRTHDATES
Jack Bushelman 1885 (1911–1912); Ford Garrison 1915
(1943–1944); Steve Lomasney 1977 (1999)

DEATHS
Charlie Graham 1948; Al DeVormer 1966; Paul Howard
1968; Clem Hausmann 1972; Andy Gilbert 1992

August 30

2003 With yet another home run, David Ortiz had homered in six straight starts. (The only game he'd not homered in was August 26, when he failed to homer in a pinch-hit appearance.) Near the end of July at one point, he had banged out 12 consecutive extra-base hits.

1999 Jose Offerman stole home in the fifth inning, as Jeff Frye stole second. It was the last time in the 20th century that a Sox player stole home.

1997 Rookie shortstop Nomar Garciaparra went 0-for-3, ending his 30-game hitting streak, four more games than the previous league record set in 1943. Nomar did drive in a run with a sacrifice fly, but it was one of just two as the Red Sox bowed to superior batting (19 hits) by the Atlanta Braves, 15–2.

1996 Oakland shut out the Red Sox, 7–0, and two names stand out in the win. The most recognizable is Mark McGwire, who hit his 45th homer and drove in three runs, Less-known is Dave Telgheder, who pitched the first eight. The Red Sox, who had been 17 games out of first place at the beginning of the month, were (despite the loss) now just six games back.

1990 Perhaps determined to help Roger Clemens win #20, on this date against the Indians, the Red Sox scored once in the top of the eighth to tie the game, 2–2, and then scored seven times in the ninth to nail it down, 9–2.

1986 Roger Clemens won 7–3 over the Indians and rolled his record up to 20–4, the first pitcher to win 20 games in 1986. (See also August 30, 1990, when he also won his 20th game, once more against the Indians.)

1984 Like Mark Bellhorn setting a new record for strikeouts in 2004, this was not a record anyone would want: Jim Rice put his name in the books by grounding into his 33rd double play of the year, breaking the old mark set by Jackie Jensen back in 1954. Rice still had a full month to go, and would add three more to his total. Other news from the game was good: Wade Boggs got three hits, drove in three runs, and helped administer a 9–3 Red Sox defeat of the Twins.

1980 Yaz got a couple of hits, and finished the season with an even 100—he is the first player in history to have 100 or more hits in his first 20 seasons. Hit #99 was a homer, and Yaz cracked his rib crashing into the scoreboard a couple of innings later. He stayed in the game and singled in the ninth for hit #100.

1970 The Red Sox really embarrassed the White Sox at Comiskey, with a 22–11 win in the first game, then got better pitching (from Mike Nagy) and were able to relax a bit more in the 4–1 finale.

1967 The day after the 20-inning marathon, Boston beat New York, 2–1. Yaz won it with a solo shot off Al Downing with two outs in the top of the 11th. John Wyatt pitched four scoreless innings in relief of Jerry Stephenson.

1960 Pete Runnels had nine hits (9-for-11) in the twilight–night doubleheader, both games going into extra innings. Runnels played both second base and first base in the first game, which ran 15 innings until Runnels doubled to center, driving in the winning run. It was his sixth hit—and he stole a base. In the second game, he was 3-for-4 with two doubles. The Sox won on an error in the bottom of the 10th. Don Buddin was 3-for-10, but was beaned in the seventh inning of the second game.

1958 Baltimore's Dick Williams played center field, then right field, then left field—all in the same game. He didn't have an assist or make a putout in any of the positions, but may have kept the Sox coaches guessing. The Orioles won, 7–2.

1957 Ted Williams turns 38. Some say that 1957 was his best year—batting .388, only five hits shy of another .400 season, and drawing an American League record 33 intentional walks. In the second half of the season, Williams batted .453.

1945 Bill Bevens was perfect through six, and the Yankees had a 3–0 lead over 20-game-winner Boo Ferriss. Bevens walked the first batter in the top of the seventh, Eddie Lake, and then—with two outs—lost the no-hitter and the shutout when Bob Johnson doubled Lake home. The Yankees avenged Bevens with four more runs in the bottom of the seventh, to win with ease, 7–1.

1942 Kept busy fielding, pitcher Bill Butland made five putouts and had two assists in a 12–6 win over St. Louis.

1938 After starter Joe Heving and reliever Dick Midkiff are both kicked around by the Browns, manager Joe Cronin lets right-fielder Doc Cramer take the mound. He didn't do any worse; he did better. He only allowed three hits over the four innings, though he had a little trouble finding the plate (four walks) and holding men on base (three runners stole bases). Boston lost, 9–5, but at least that was better than the 15–1 loss the day before.

1918 Let's play two! Ernie Banks wouldn't be born until 1931, but Carl Mays whitewashed Philadelphia, 12–0, in the first game, and threw a 4–1 complete game in the second. Mays was also 5-for-6 at the plate in the twin bill. In six 1918 starts against Philadelphia, Mays gave up a total of four runs.

1916 On August 29, Red Sox starting pitcher Dutch Leonard lasted just one-third of an inning before he was pulled. Catcher–manager Bill Carrigan gave him another shot 24 hours later—and Leonard threw a no-hitter against the very same St. Louis Browns. The only two Browns to reach base were on walks in the eighth and ninth. Boston won, 4–0. The next day, Leonard received a $100 bonus for his no-hitter. Carrigan had also caught Foster's no-hitter on June 21.

1910 Ray Collins one-hit the White Sox at Boston's Huntington Avenue Grounds. The game lasted 97 minutes and was a 4–0 shutout. The lone safety was a third-inning single by right fielder Paul "Molly" Meloan. Collins walked no one, and there were no Red Sox errors. Meloan was the only Chicagoan to reach first base. The game was the second one-hitter for the Red Sox staff in a four-day stretch; Sea Lion Hall had thrown one on August 27. The fielding for both teams was rated exceptional, and Tris Speaker robbed Amby McConnell of a homer at one point.

1904 Was winning the previous day's game, 1–0, at the very last minute, on a hit by the pitcher Dinneen, too much of a nail-biter? Boston piled up a baker's dozen of runs the next day, on 18 hits, and Cy Young benefited from a 13–0 laugher. Young himself was 3-for-4 at the plate, with two singles and a triple. The seven-run seventh was superfluous, given the 6–0 lead after 6 ½. Detroit chipped in with five errors, too.

TRANSACTIONS
1916: Boston acquired outfielder Jimmy Walsh from Philadelphia,
    in partial payment for catcher Ray Haley.
1990: Acquired Larry Andersen from the Houston Astros in trade for Jeff Bagwell.
1992: Traded Jeff Reardon to the Atlanta Braves for Nate Minchey and Sean Ross.
1997: Signed free agent Curtis Pride.

DEBUTS
1924: Al Kellett
1996: Reggie Harris, Pat Mahomes

BIRTHDATES
Charlie Armbruster 1880 (1905–1907); Bing Miller 1894 (1935–1936); Ted Williams 1918 (1939–1960); Carmen Fanzone 1943 (1970); Andy Merchant 1950 (1975–1976)

DEATHS
None yet

August 31

2003 Manny Ramirez never turned up at Fenway Park, because he was too ill, reportedly with pharyngitis, but he had been spotted in the bar at the Ritz-Carlton (where he lives) with Yankees player Enrique Wilson on the night of August 30. This was fodder for radio talk shows for days on end. Pedro Martinez had been scratched from an August 21 start for the same disease, one no listener had ever heard of before that time. Red Sox officials uttered a lot of "no comment" comments, as they looked into reports of the Manny sighting.

2002 Johnny Damon made an error. Normally, that might not be so remarkable, but a week earlier Damon had set a new American League record by handling 576 consecutive chances without an error. From May 4, 2001 through August 30, 2002, Damon played 250 games without committing an error.

1980 With his save of a 5–1 win over Oakland, Bob Stanley established a team-record 12 saves in a given month.

1971 Rico Petrocelli completes his 77th consecutive error-free game at third base.

1965 Dave Morehead (6 IP, two hits) and Dick Radatz (3 IP, one hit) combined to blank Washington, 4–0, in the first game, and the Red Sox won the second, 8–5. Russ Nixon had three run-scoring sacrifice flies (off three different pitchers) in the second game, and Tony Horton's three-run homer (after an IBB to Mantilla) won it in the 10th.

1952 When the Red Sox purchased Al Zarilla from the St. Louis Browns, it was the second time they'd acquired the same player from the same team. Earlier, they had traded for Zarilla on May 8, 1949.

1948 Johnny Pesky and Ted Williams pull off a double steal, with Ted drawing the throw to second as Johnny scampered home. Parnell got the 8–4 win, to go to 11–6 on the year.

1946 With two hits, Johnny Pesky had 53 in one month, the most ever for a Red Sox hitter. Outfielder Dom DiMaggio replicated the number in the same month, August, in 1950.

1933 The worst home loss ever dealt to the Yankees in the first 50 years of play between the Sox and Yanks was the 15–2 drubbing Boston administered on this day. It wasn't until September 1, 1990 that the Bosox beat New York by a bigger margin (15–1), only to top that with their 17–1 domination on May 28, 2005. In the 1933 game, Herb Pennock gave up six runs, leaving before getting an out in the third. It was a double Dusty day for Boston: Dusty Rhodes pitched a six-hitter and Dusty Cooke singled twice, doubled, and tripled, scoring three times and driving in two.

1927 The Murderers' Row team had three homers (two by Lazzeri, one by Ruth) and opened up a 17-game lead over their nearest rival, the A's. The *New York Times* took a ho-hum attitude about the 10–3 rout of the Red Sox, noting that it would really be something if the Sox beat the Yanks, but the result as it was "is to be taken as a matter of course"—which was just about right. Boston finished last, 59 games behind New York.

1920 Did the Red Sox win a tainted game? A day or two after the news broke that several Chicago White Sox players had thrown the World Series, *Boston Globe* sportswriter James C. O'Leary recalled a three-game set in Boston during the 1920 season. Chicago lost all three games, but it was the middle game in particular that O'Leary recalled. Starting for Chicago was Eddie Cicotte, one of the Black Sox, and there was a story going around Boston late in September that gamblers had been holding something over Cicotte's head and he had been coerced into throwing the game. Once the grand jury revelations spilled out, there seemed to perhaps be some substance to all the talk. O'Leary even recalled one Boston newspaperman, observing play during Chicago's 7–3 loss to the Red Sox thus: "They are playing just like they did in the World Series." At the time, there was no insinuation of any wrongdoing attached to the observation, but it took on more ominous overtones when recalled in light of the revelations regarding the fix.

1918 By winning the first game of a doubleheader against the visiting Athletics, 6–1, the Red Sox clinch their fourth pennant in seven years. Babe Ruth was the winning pitcher, holding the A's to three hits, and going 2-for-4 at the plate with one run scored. His double to deep center just missed going out. The losing pitcher was Mule Watson, who stubbornly decided to pitch the second game, too, and threw a one-hitter (holding center fielder Ruth hitless in two at-bats), winning a tight 1–0 game against Joe Bush. The decision was interesting in that this was the seventh start during 1918 in which Bush was involved in a 1–0 ballgame. He won the first five of them, and lost the last two. Bush is tied with seven other pitchers for the most starts in a season involving a 1–0 score; Bush's accomplishment is greater in some ways in that the war-shortened 1918 season was but 126 games long.

1916 Babe Ruth doubled and scored a run, but it was the only run and St. Louis scored twice to beat him, 2–1; two Sox pinch-hitters failed in the ninth, and Ruth popped up to end the game.

1912 It was still August, the Red Sox juggernaut rolled over Philadelphia for the third game in a row, and the venerable Connie Mack acknowledged that Boston (87–37) was the near-certain pennant winner. More than 30,000 thronged Fenway.

1902 Boston once played an official game on meadows previously used for public hangings and known as Jailhouse Flats, in Fort Wayne, Indiana? Yes, it's true. 3,500 fans attended what proved to be an exciting 11-inning game between the Boston and Cleveland clubs, Cy Young beating Addie Joss, 3–1. Cleveland was the "home team."

TRANSACTIONS
1931: Traded Muddy Ruel to the Detroit Tigers for Marty McManus.
1952: Purchased Al Zarilla from the St. Louis Browns.
1988: Returned John Trautwein (earlier draft pick) to the Montreal Expos.
Then received Trautwein from the Expos for John Rosario.
1995: Acquired Dwayne Hosey from Kansas City off waivers. Received Jack Voigt from the Texas Rangers in trade for Chris Howard.
1998: Acquired Chris Snopek from the White Sox for Corey Jenkins.
1999: Rod Beck was acquired from the Chicago Cubs for Mark Guthrie and a PTBNL (who is Cole Liniak, named just the very next day).
2000: Acquired Dante Bichette from Cincinnati for Chris Reitsma and John Curtice, and acquired Midre Cummings from the Minnesota Twins for minor leaguer Hector De Los Santos.

DEBUTS
1910: Frank "Piano Mover" Smith
1950: Fred Hatfield
1992: Ken Ryan
1993: Luis Ortiz
1996: Nomar Garciaparra

BIRTHDATES
Duke Farrell 1866 (1903–1905); Wally Rehg 1888 (1913–1915); Paul Hinrichs 1925 (1951); Tracy Stallard 1937 (1960–1962); Ramon Hernandez 1940 (1977); Mike Hartley 1961 (1995); Jeff Frye 1966 (1996–2000); Stan Royer 1967 (1994); Hideo Nomo 1968 (2001); Nate Minchey 1969 (1993–1996); Gabe Kapler 1975 (2003–2004)

DEATHS
Skeeter Newsome 1989

SEPTEMBER

September 1

2004 In a story reflecting how absurd talk of the Curse of the Bambino had become, it became front-page news in the *Boston Globe*'s City and Region section. Lee Gavin, 16, was hit in the face by a foul ball during the August 31 game at Fenway. A bit of blood was drawn. Gavin had lived his entire life in the farmhouse in Sudbury where Babe Ruth had lived while he played for the Red Sox. Gavin's blood was somehow supposed to expunge the Curse. Maybe it did?

2002 Tim Wakefield was "on" at The Jake, beating the Indians, 7–1, allowing just three hits and one run in seven innings before turning it over to the bullpen. Manny Ramirez and Brian Daubach hit back-to-back homers in the first inning.

1996 In his first major-league starting role, Nomar Garciaparra whacked a home run off future teammate John Wasdin, as the Red Sox beat Oakland, 8–3.

1990 Mike Greenwell hit an inside-the-park grand slam in the fifth inning, and helped the Sox crush New York, 15–1. It's not as though the Yankees didn't try; two outfielders were injured, both having to leave the game, in the same seven-run Red Sox fifth inning. Greenwell hit one other inside-the-park home run, too. It was also in a game against the Yankees, a solo homer on July 7, 1989. The pitcher in both games was the same one: Greg Cadaret.

The Yankees starter in the game was Andy Hawkins; he was gone after one-third of an inning. Hawkins had a hard time getting started at Fenway. On September 26, 1989, he'd pitched just one-third of an inning, and been tagged for eight earned runs. His next start at Fenway also lasted one-third of an inning; on June 5, 1990, he gave up five earned runs before being removed. Now, on September 1, for the third time in a row, he started and was chased after one-third of an inning. He finally got the third out! The three one-third innings produced a total of 18 runs, for a combined ERA of 162.00. (See May 28, 2005 for an even bigger margin of victory for the Sox at the Stadium.)

1986 Steve Crawford was on in relief of Bruce Hurst, entrusted with the final three innings, with the Sox up, 6–2, over the Rangers at Fenway. He done good— he only let up two hits. But not that good—they were back-to-back pinch-hit homers in the top of the ninth to Oddibe McDowell and Darrell Porter. The final? 6–4, Boston.

1976 Ferguson Jenkins was cruising through 4⅓ innings of shutout ball when he tore his Achilles tendon covering the bag at first base, going off-stride to avoid a potentially serious collision with Lenny Randle. The tear might have been worse; but he was lost for the season. Tom Murphy came on in relief and continued to shut out the Rangers, 3–0, collecting the win. Jenkins was one of just five Hall of Famers who also played (during the off-season) with the Harlem Globetrotters.

1967 Well, that was quick. Jim Landis was signed on August 22, appeared in his first Sox game on August 23, homered in his one at-bat on the 24th, played on the 25th and 27th, and then was released on September 1. The homer was his only hit, as he went 1-for-7 in his short stint with the Red Sox. It was also the end of his major league career.

In the day's game, Ken Harrelson tripled in the first, homered in the fifth, and doubled in the seventh. If he'd gotten up once more and hit another homer, he said, "I would have stopped at first base."

1935 Buck Newsom and Lefty Grove squared off for 14 rounds. The score was tied 1–1 after both teams scored in the fourth. Ten innings later, in the bottom of the 14th, Washington's center fielder Jake Powell stole home with what would have been the winning run—except that Newsom's swing ticked the ball, the foul forcing Powell to return to third. From goat to glad-handing within seconds, Newsom connected two pitches later for a single to win it.

1931 Lou Gehrig hit a homer (his 39th) in the first game and another (his 40th) in the second. He'd thus homered six games in a row. His three RBIs in game one aided the 11–3 pasting of the Red Sox, and his grand slam (the third slam he had hit in four days) made all the difference in the 5–1 final game.

1926 In what the *Washington Post* termed a "test as to which team's pitchers were the least ineffective," sportswriter Frank H. Young said "the Red Sox won the argument and the Nationals won the game." Nine pitchers were put to the test. Since Boston lost the game, 14–12, did the typesetter make a mistake or did the writer's prose become too convoluted?

1912 Major F. C. Blanchard of Brockton had a dog named Buster, noted the September 1 *Boston Globe*. Buster walks to the newspaper offices with his master every afternoon and looks at the baseball bulletin, then "invariably barks when the Red Sox or Brocktons win a game."

1906 Tied 1–1 from the sixth inning on, the Philadelphia–Boston game just kept on ticking. Jack Coombs was pitching for the Athletics and Joe Harris was pitching for the Boston ball club, and both of them went the distance—24 innings! Neither of the two young pitchers had much major league experience. Harris gave up one run in the third, then threw 20 innings of scoreless baseball until the top of the 24th. The notion of anyone today pitching 20 innings of scoreless ball in one game is so off the charts that it will almost certainly never be approached. But Harris lost. Both teams requested a halt to the game after 23 full, due to darkness, but the umpire told them to play on. Harris got the first batter in the 24th, striking out Coombs. There followed a single by Hartsel, a stolen base, and another strikeout. When Schreckengost ducked out of the way of a pitch, the ball struck his bat and bounced over second base, scoring the tie-breaker. Back-to-back triples followed and Philadelphia had scored three times. Coombs retired the Boston side in the bottom of the 24th and got the win.

There was supposed to be a doubleheader played but, needless to say, the second game never got underway.

Harris finished the abysmal 1906 season with a record of 2–21. He got as far as 0–7 the following year before they give up on him, and he finished his major league career with a 3–30 record—despite a decent 3.35 lifetime ERA.

TRANSACTIONS

1907: Sold Charlie Armbruster to the Chicago White Sox.
1960: Sent Al Worthington to the Chicago White Sox as part of a conditional deal.
1967: Released Pete Charton and Jim Landis.
1974: Purchased Tim McCarver from the St. Louis Cardinals.
1987: Dave Henderson was traded to the Giants for a PTBNL (Randy Kutcher). Don Baylor
    traded to Minnesota for a PTBNL, which proved to be minor leaguer Enrique Rios.
1994: Scott Bankhead was sold to the New York Yankees.
1998: Released Orlando Merced.

DEBUTS

1916: Jimmy Walsh	1997: Michael Coleman, Derek Lowe
1931: Marty McManus	1998: Mandy Romero
1993: Cory Bailey	1999: Rod Beck
1995: Dwayne Hosey	2000: Dante Bichette

BIRTHDATES

Freddie Moncewicz 1903 (1928); Paul Campbell 1917 (1942–1946); Bob DiPietro 1927 (1951); Dean Stone 1930 (1957); Merlin Nippert 1938 (1962); Craig Skok 1947 (1973); David West 1964 (1998)

DEATHS

Mike Meola 1976

September 2

2005 The Red Sox only scored three runs in a home game, losing 7–3 to the visiting Orioles. The power outage ended a string of 14 home games in a row in which Boston had scored seven or more runs. Fans looking over their shoulder at the 2005 Yankees were glad to see them remain 3½ games out of first, blanked by Oakland, 12–0. This game featured the only Red Sox appearance of pitcher Matt Perisho, acquired July 19 from the Padres. Perisho faced only one batter, allowed one run on one hit without recording an out. He was given his release on September 15.

2001 Mike Mussina had a perfect game going through 8⅔ innings at Fenway Park, and the Yankees were leading the Red Sox by a razor-thin 1–0 score (the lone run was scored off Sox pitcher David Cone in the top of the ninth). Cone had pitched a perfect game for the Yankees two years earlier. With two outs in the bottom of the ninth, no runner had reached first base and Mussina needed just one more strike. He had a 1–2 count on pinch-hitter Carl Everett. Mussina had struck out Everett four times back on May 24, every time on a high fastball. He tried it again, but Everett was ready and banged a clean single to left-center field. It was the third time Mussina had taken a perfect game into the ninth, and the third time he'd failed to get 27 consecutive outs. The next batter was Nixon; he grounded out to end the game. The Yankees completed a sweep of the Sox, despite not having scored in the first seven innings in any game in the series.

1996 Mike Greenwell was 4-for-5 on the day, with a two-run homer in the fifth inning and a grand slam in the seventh. And that wasn't all. He drove in three more runs, too. In fact, he drove in every run the Red Sox scored—just enough, as it turned out—sparking a 9–8 win over the Seattle Mariners at the Kingdome.

1974 You could call it a lack of run support. Luis Tiant threw a three-hitter, but lost to Baltimore's Ross Grimsley, 1–0. Mike Cuellar's was a three-hitter as well. In the second game of the doubleheader, Bill Lee also held the Birds to one run, but Mike Cuellar shut out the Red Sox, for a matching 1–0 score. The two Orioles runs were scored on a solo homer (first game) and sacrifice fly (second game).

1971 Sonny Siebert was the story. He threw a three-hit 3–0 shutout of Baltimore, and drove in all the runs in the game with two homers into Fenway's left-field screen. He remains the last American League pitcher to hit two home runs in a game.

1970 Weak-hitting pitcher Cal Koonce had 239 major league at-bats over 10 seasons, but only batted .100 and only drove in eight runs in those 10 years. He threw a complete game three-hitter, and his sixth-inning bases-loaded single drove in 25% of his career RBI—two runs—beating the Tigers, 10–1.

1960 In his last year playing major league ball, Ted Williams homered off Washington's Don Lee, the only run in a 5–1 loss to the Senators. Williams had also homered off Lee's father, Thornton Lee, on September 17, 1939—during his first year in baseball. The Sox lost the second game, too, 3–2. Washington's Jim Lemon hit a home run in both games, including the game-winner in the second matchup. Lemon saved a couple of runs with his fielding and throwing as well.

1958 Two successive sixth-inning pitches served up by Dick Sisler were sent out of the Stadium by Messrs. Mantle and Berra, breaking the 0–0 tie. New York's pitcher Zack Monroe (0-for-12 at the plate) finally cracked his first hit, a seventh-inning ground rule double, and prevailed, 6–1, for his first complete game in the majors. Only Dick Gernert's two-out solo homer in the ninth spoiled his bid for a shutout.

1957 Jimmy Piersall hit his 15th and 16th home runs of the year, but it was #15 that earned him an unusual distinction: for seven years in a row, beginning in 1950, Piersall had hit more home runs each year than the year before. It's a record he shares with four other players. Piersall hit 19 in '57, but unfortunately only eight in 1958.

1950 It was the game in which Boston "shattered the A's one-game winning streak over the Red Sox." (*Los Angeles Times*) Boston jumped out to a 5–0 lead and Mel Parnell won his ninth straight victory against Philly, 9–3.

1944 The Red Sox finished the day just 1½ games out of first place. Bobby Doerr had been exempted from military service due to a punctured eardrum, but his exemption was overruled and September 3 would be his last game before reporting for induction into the United States Army. Despite leaving baseball a month before the season ended, *The Sporting News* voted Doerr the American League MVP for 1944. On September 2, Doerr was 2-for-5 with a triple and one RBI in a one-run game, a 6–5 ninth-inning triumph over the Athletics concluded by Roy Partee's bases-loaded walkoff single.

It was an interesting game. Boston scored five runs in the first inning; it looked like manager Joe Cronin was able to read pitcher Russ Christopher's every pitch. When Connie Mack pulled catcher Frankie Hayes, though, Christopher pitched excellent ball until the final frame. He even hit a homer. The November 2 *Sporting News* said that Mack believed Cronin was stealing signs from Hayes, not Christopher.

1941 Eddie Collins hired receptionist Helen Robinson, who served the Red Sox until October 2, 2001. "I was the only non-uniformed personnel that Mr. Collins ever hired," she said. She worked right up to the very end.

1935 Starter Wes Ferrell was knocked out of the box in the third, and Jack Wilson took over mound duties for the Red Sox. Though down 7–0, the Sox kept coming back and finally tied it, 8–8, with a five-run rally in the bottom of the eighth (Joe Cronin's grand slam providing the bulk of those runs). In the bottom of the 11th, Wilson took matters into his own hands and hit a home run into the center field bleachers for a 9–8 win. Boston came from behind to tie the second game in the bottom of the ninth, but Washington won it in 13 innings, 3–2.

1932 Benefitting from seven home runs, the Athletics beat Boston 7–3 and 15–0. Lew Krausse, Sr. won the second game. *The Baseball Chronology* provides a follow-up: "Five days later Krausse will injure his arm in an exhibition game against the Stroudsburg Poconos and though only 20 years old, his big league career is over. As historian Lyle Spatz notes, in 1961, Lew Krausse, Jr. pitches a shutout for the KC A's in his major league debut, giving the Krausses (father and son) back-to-back shutouts twenty-nine years apart."

1922 Behind Alex Ferguson and Bill Piercy, the cellar-dwelling Red Sox twice shut out the "lowly Griffmen" (the Washington Senators) winning 3–0 and 1–0. Walter Johnson lost yet another 1–0 heartbreaker to Boston when the Sox scored their lone run in the top of the ninth on a walk, force play, single, and sacrifice fly.

1918 The 1918 season ended on this day, the year shortened due to war. Boston already had the pennant in its pocket, and split the day's doubleheader with New York. If one excludes Eusebio Gonzales, who only had five at-bats, there was only one player on the whole Red Sox team who hit as high as .300—Babe Ruth, whose average was right on the mark, an even .300. Ruth's 11 homers led the league; adding up all the homers hit by the rest of the Red Sox, one finds a total of four.

1912 Boston won two nail-biters at New York's Polo Grounds, scoring twice in the eighth for a 2–1 opener; the tying and winning runs came on a single, a triple by Yerkes, and a balk by Russell Ford. Hugh Bedient, throwing a two-hitter, collected the win. Boston scored in the first inning of the nightcap, and Smoky Joe Wood out-dueled George McConnell—five times pitching himself out of jams with a Yankees runner on third base. Not one scored and Wood had his 30th win, a 1–0 shutout (his eighth shutout of the season). The two wins completed the year's road sweep of the Yanks; the Red Sox won every one of the 10 games in New York. (See September 29, 1913.)

TRANSACTIONS
1916: Traded Ray Haley to the Philadelphia Athletics for Jimmy Walsh.
1972: Purchased Bob Veale from the Pittsburgh Pirates.
1975: Released Tony Conigliaro.

DEBUTS
1914: Bill Swanson
1932: Andy Spognardi
1957: Ken Aspromonte
1960: Marlan Coughtry,
    Chet Nichols
1980: Steve Crawford, Julio
    Valdez, Chico Walker

1990: Larry Andersen
1996: Rudy Pemberton
1998: Chris Snopek
1999: Ramon Martinez, Jon Nunnally
2001: Joe Oliver
2005: Chad Harville, Alejandro
    Machado, Matt Perisho

BIRTHDATES
Joe Heving 1900 (1938–1940); Marty Griffin 1901 (1928); Jeff Russell 1961 (1993–1994); Jose Melendez 1965 (1993–1994)

DEATHS
Johnny Welch 1940; Jack Ryan 1967; Jim Brillheart 1972; Jim Wilson 1986; Jim Bagby 1988

September 3

2005 When Mike Timlin came in from the bullpen to pitch the ninth inning, in relief of starter Matt Clement, it was Timlin's 70th appearance of the year. He became the first pitcher in Red Sox history to appear in 70 games for three years in a row. Timlin earned the save.

2003 David Ortiz hit not one, but two go-ahead homers (including the game-winner) in a 5–4, 10-inning win over the White Sox at Chicago. Big Papi's first homer came in the eighth with Manny Ramirez on base.

2000 Paul Abbott pitched seven innings of no-hit ball. The only Red Sox batter to get a hit this Sunday afternoon was Rico Brogna, with one out in the eighth inning. Alex Rodriguez hit a two-run homer in the ninth, but it was just icing on their cake as the Mariners won, 5–0.

1997 Mike Lansing, playing for the Montreal Expos, had the only hit of the ballgame off Boston's Aaron Sele—a third-inning homer. Sele and Tom Gordon combined on a one-hitter, but lost the game. Lansing's homer was the game-clincher, for a 1–0 win at Stade Olympique, as Expos pitcher Carlos Perez limited the Red Sox to just two hits. Expos mascot Youpi would have been biting his nails if he had nails to bite.

1956 Tommy Brewer breezed to a 16–0 win over Washington. Jimmy Piersall was the star of the day; he had five RBIs in the first game and three more in the game Brewer won.

1947 The Yankees go on a hitting spree at Fenway, with 18 hits—but every one of the hits is a single. No matter: they win handily, 11–2. They sock the Sox for 16 more hits in the second game, and take that one, 9–6, albeit with a few extra-base hits included.

1939 The Red Sox win the first game of Fenway twin bill by a score of 12–11, but in the second game the score was tied 5–5 in the top of the eighth when the Yankees scored two runs with nobody out. In those days, the Red Sox played under a 6:30 P.M. Sunday curfew and the Yankees runs scored at 6:19. If the inning was not played to completion, the runs would not count so the Red Sox took their time walking Dahlgren. Meanwhile, the Yankees for their part sent George Selkirk running from third on a supposed steal of home (really, to be tagged out so they could close out their half of the inning and get the Red Sox up to bat). Dahlgren refused to be walked by swinging to miss on what would have been ball three and ball four. At this point, Joe Gordon "stole home" and was easily thrown out. Boston manager Cronin complained that the Yankees were deliberately making outs, but umpire Cal Hubbard found no rule against it. Boston fans threw so much garbage on the field that the umpires declared a forfeit and awarded the game to New York. Five days later, AL President Will Harridge overruled Hubbard and ruled the game a tie, to be replayed later in the month.

1934 In an eighth-inning collision at first base with Red Sox pitcher Wes Ferrell covering the bag, Washington's Joe Cronin broke a bone in his right arm and was finished as a player for the year. The Red Sox won, then played Washington to a 4–4 tie after eight in the day's second game.

1933 With two outs in the bottom of the ninth, it looked like Ivy Andrews of the Red Sox was locked in a 2–2 ballgame against Washington's Monte Weaver. Ossie Bluege singled and stole second, so Andrews walked the next batter, Luke Sewell. Weaver was due up next, but rookie catcher Cliff Bolton was summoned from the bullpen to pinch-hit, and he singled in the tiebreaker.

1918 The Red Sox arrived in Chicago too late to get in a workout this day before the opening of the World Series, but they were pleased at the news that Fred "Jackie" Thomas would be able to play third base. The third base slot was a real weakness for Boston since Thomas had enlisted in the Navy a number of weeks earlier, but Thomas had remained on the eligible list, stayed in baseball shape playing for the service team at the Great Lakes Naval Training Station, and was granted a furlough to play in the World Series. Thomas played throughout the Series, anchoring the infield at third, though only batting .118 (2-for-17), without a single RBI. His lack of run production didn't matter; this was a very low-scoring Series. (See September 11, 1918.)

1915 When Ernie Shore left after six, the Sox had a 10–0 lead over the A's; only a two-run homer in the bottom of the ninth off reliever Slyveanus Augustus Gregg spoiled the shutout.

1903 Another extra inning game, but this one was a win at home, 6–5, in 12 innings. Even though doling out just seven hits in the first seven innings, Cy Young let the Athletics run up a 5–1 lead. Boston rebounded with four runs in the bottom of the seventh to tie the game. Young's double drove in the first run. Once Boston pulled even, Young didn't let up another hit for the final five frames. Lou Criger threw out four of five would-be base-stealers. Boston left 11 men on base to Philadelphia's four; there were scoring opportunities galore which were unrealized. Chick Stahl cost Boston two runs on a strange interference call against him as a baserunner in the first. In the 12th, Buck Freeman led off with a double and Freddy Parent's sacrifice moved him to third, but he was out at the plate on Candy LaChance's grounder to the second baseman. Hobe Ferris singled to center. With Ferris on first, Jake Stahl pinch-hit for Criger and drove a grounder that barely eluded the shortshop, while the speedy LaChance rounded the bases on a tear and scored the winning run.

1901 Billy Cristall, pitching for Cleveland? Just up from Albany, Bill Cristall debuted with a very impressive five-hitter, shutting out Boston, 4–0. September 3 was the first day that one American League team administered a double whitewash to another. Cristall's teammate Earl Moore and Boston's Ted Lewis both threw two-hitters in the first game, but Cleveland scored a run on two Boston errors, and won the first game, 1–0. It was Cristall's only win; he finished the season (and his career) with a 1–5 record.

DEBUTS
1983: Lee Graham
1988: Mike Rochford
2004: Adam Hyzdu

BIRTHDATES
George Stone 1877 (1903); Tom Brewer 1931 (1954–1961);
Mike Paxton 1953 (1977); Chad Fox 1970 (2003)

DEATHS
Bert Husting 1948

September 4

2003 Just Manny being Manny. The Red Sox held an 8–0 lead after three innings at Yankee Stadium, so it was no big deal when Manny Ramirez made a spectacular catch of Bernie Williams' fly ball to right, tossed the ball into the stands, and ran in towards the Red Sox dugout on the third base side. Trouble was: that was just the second out. No damage done; there wasn't anyone on base. The Red Sox won, 9–3.

2000 The Red Sox retired #27, the uniform number belonging to catcher Carlton Fisk. His is just the fifth number of a former Red Sox player to be retired. Carl Everett's RBI in the game which followed (a 5–1 win over Seattle) gave him 100 on the year, and he thereby became just the sixth switch-hitter in major league history to drive in 100 runs in one league, switch leagues, and knock in 100 or more in the other.

1999 Pedro Martinez improved his record to 20–4, allowing just two hits in eight innings, while striking out 15 Mariners. Rod Beck closed the 4–0 shutout.

1992 Frankie Rodriguez, 19, was booked for statutory rape in Lynchburg, Virginia where he played for the Carolina League team in the Red Sox system. The young pitching prospect admitted having sex but had not realized the young woman in question was only 14 years old.

1988 Marty Barrett executed the third hidden ball trick of his career, tying him with Johnny Pesky for the most HBTs. Barrett flipped to Jody Reed, who caught Jim Traber off the second base bag.

1981 There had been the 24-inning game on September 1, 1906, at Boston's Huntington Avenue Grounds, but the September 4, 1981 20-inning affair was the longest in Fenway Park history. The game had been suspended after 19 innings in the wee hours of the morning, but quickly came to conclusion when Seattle's Dave Henderson singled and Joe Simpson tripled. Despite a couple of singles in the bottom of the 20th, the Sox could not score. 8–7, Seattle. Julio Cruz hit a three-run homer for the Mariners, and they won the regularly-scheduled game of the evening, 5–2.

1978 Single, double, homer. It was 3–0 Red Sox after three batters. Then Scott McGregor buckled down and retired the next 22 Bosox batters, as his Orioles teammates got to Dennis Eckersley sufficiently for a 5–3 win.

There were two tragic (and fatal) footnotes to the game. Two men, 58 and 75, both collapsed at Memorial Stadium during the game. Both were pronounced dead on arrival at Union Memorial Hospital, one following the other by just some 30 minutes.

1974 The Orioles knocked off the Red Sox, shutting out Boston for the third game in a row (1–0, 1–0, and today's 6–0). Over the three games, the Red Sox made just six hits (3-2-3). As a result of six straight losses, the league-leading Sox now shared the lead with the surging Yankees—and Boston went on to lose their next two games as well—but Baltimore was the team on a roll and won the division.

1972 With a 2–0 shutout of the Brewers in Milwaukee, Luis Tiant had pitched his fourth consecutive shutout; Luis had won August 19, August 25, August 29, and now September 4—without giving up a single run. Later in the season, after two games in which the other team scored runs, he would throw two more shutouts. The two runs came on a third inning homer by Carl Yastrzemski off a former teammate, Jim Lonborg.

1971 Rico Petrocelli pops off, saying that manager Eddie Kasko plays favorites, that there is no unity on the ball club, and that there's a lack of communication. One thing Rico expected to have communicated as a result was his departure from the ball club. "I'm unhappy," he said. "I don't expect to be here next year and I don't know if I want to be." In fact, Rico served five more seasons with the Sox, and Kasko served a couple more, too.

1965 The Yankees held "Date Night" at Yankee Stadium. It was, Joseph Durso of the *New York Times* wrote, a "rock 'n' roll session and ballad recital"—suggesting that Durso might know sports but not music. He did note that Joe Pepitone got more applause for doing The Twist in the dugout than anything he did on the field. He was 1-for-7 with a triple. The Yankees lost both games, 1–0 and 7–2. Dave Morehead beat Jim Bouton in the first game, allowing just three hits; the Sox scored just the one run, on three singles in the top of the eighth, despite getting 12 hits off Yankees pitching. Jack Cullen was tagged with the loss in the second game.

1948 Ted Williams makes 10 putouts in the game and Dom DiMaggio makes five. Not a single putout for the Red Sox right-fielders, though. The Sox score three times in the eighth to beat the Athletics, 5–3. The AL record is 11 putouts for a given outfielder. Ted's 10 is the Red Sox record, though, shared by Fred Lynn, Lee Tinsley, and Tommy Umphlett.

1946 The 16½ game lead the Red Sox had built by September 4 tied the longest lead they have ever enjoyed, the September 14 and 15 lead back in 1912.

1941 Other than the war-shortened 1918 season, when the Red Sox clinched the pennant on August 31, the earliest clinch occurred on this day in 1941, as the Yankees beat Boston, 6–3.

1930 It was 4–4 after nine in Philadelphia. Bobby Reeves of the Red Sox homered in the top of the 10th, but Bing Miller of the Athletics matched that with a solo home run of his own. The Sox scored twice in the top of the 13th, but Mickey Cochrane doubled and Al Simmons homered, tying it up for a third time. Ed Durham came on to pitch for Danny MacFayden and closed out the inning, but in the 15th, leadoff batter Lefty Grove singled, as did Dykes. Cochrane walked, and Simmons singled all the way to the center-field wall to win it for the Athletics.

1927 Phil Todt hit two home runs off Sloppy Thurston; the second one won the game in the 11th inning, 5–3, over Washington. The homers were the fifth and sixth of the year for Todt. Hardly any "Murderer's Row," Todt's six homers led the 1927 Red Sox, who only managed 28 home runs all year long—less than half of those hit by alumnus Babe Ruth that season.

1920 Former Red Sox star Babe Ruth hit his 45th and 46th home runs for New York, one in each game, as the rival teams split two in Boston. Ruth was greeted by ovations from the Boston fans. Former Red Sox star Carl Mays pitched for the Yankees in the second game and was also welcomed by the large crowd. The Yankees scored two runs off Joe Bush in the top of the ninth, but Mays gave up four hits in the bottom of the ninth. Fielding one ball, Mays failed to touch the bag at first base, resulting in an early run for the Red Sox. Bodie's throw from center to Ruel at the plate was off the mark, and Joe Bush scored with the winning run—perhaps because Mays had not properly backed up the play.

1911 Catcher Bill Carrigan broke his leg sliding into second base in a game against New York.

1908 Boston's Frank Arellanes fired a one-hitter—it was a sixth-inning homer to Athletics shortstop Simon Nicholls—and the Red Sox won, 10–1.

1906 The New York Highlanders swept their fifth doubleheader in six days with 7–0 (Walter Clarkson) and 1–0 (Al Orth) shutouts of the Boston Americans.

DEBUTS
1905: Ed Hughes
1920: Ed Chaplin
1971: Juan Beniquez, Rick Miller, Ben Oglivie
1974: Tim McCarver
1980: Luis Aponte

BIRTHDATES
Tillie Walker 1887 (1916–1917); Fred Walters 1912 (1945); Ken Harrelson 1941 (1967–1969); Bobby Guindon 1943 (1964); Sun-Woo Kim 1977 (2001–2002)

DEATHS
George Loepp 1967; Babe Dahlgren 1996

September 5

2001 Boston's 10–7 win over Cleveland was the only win in a stretch of 13 losses, ranging from August 26 into mid-September, and including the Mike Mussina near-perfecto on September 2.

1985 Cleveland got a couple of runs off Oil Can in the top of the first, but leadoff batter Dwight Evans homered and Wade Boggs, batting in the #2 hole, also homered—so the Sox were right back in it. They scored four in the third and four in the fourth, on their way to a 13–6 win. An umpiring decision that even the Indians' left fielder agreed was wrong cost Boston's Mike Easler what should have been his third grand slam in five days. Marc Sullivan hit one of his five major league homers in the second game, which Cleveland took, 9–5. The second game finally ended at 2:17 A.M.

1977 Reggie Cleveland allowed five hits; rookie Don Aase only allowed three. Between them, the two Sox pitchers shut out the Toronto Blue Jays in both games of a doubleheader in Toronto.

1957 In New York, Sox starter Willard Nixon faced Yankees reliever Bob Grim in a 2–2 tie, with two outs in the bottom of the ninth. There were two Yankees on base, but Grim had not had a hit all season long. On Nixon's very first pitch, Grim hit a home run into the first row of the right-field grandstand to administer a 5–2 defeat to the Red Sox.

1956 Sliding into third base in the very first inning, Don Buddin broke a bone in his right hand. It may have been a precursor of unfortunate events for the evening. In the eighth inning, Yogi Berra broke a 2–2 tie with a home run that was the first earned run the Yankees had scored off Red Sox pitcher Willard Nixon in 27⅓ innings. New York won, 5–3.

1936 Sox won 3–2 in the first game; in game two, the Yankees not only hit into a triple play but commited four errors and were lucky to hold onto a 7–7 tie in a game called after 12 innings because of darkness. The triple play was initiated by Sox shortstop Joe Cronin, the third triple play in which he had been involved (once as a victim).

1935 In the first game, Lefty Grove lost to Cleveland, 8–1. Cleveland hurler Hudlin's two-run homer in the second inning proved adequate as the game-winner. In the second game, the one-run score was on the other foot, as Wes Ferrell won his 21st game of the year, beating his former teammates, 6–1.

1931 For the second time in 1931, George Earnshaw lost a no-hitter. The A's pitcher took his no-hitter into the eighth when shortstop Dib Williams got a bad jump on Marty McManus's grounder—dubbed "an easy chance" by the *New York Times*—and the ball went off his hands. Why it was not ruled an error by the scorer is a mystery. Philadelphia won, 8–0, but lost 6–3 in the second game.

1927 Opening Day to Labor Day. In an 18-inning game, Boston beat New York 12–11—reversing the Opening Day defeat by the identical score. The Yankees had tied it (8–8) in the ninth, and the game went on through 16 innings. New York scored three times in the top of the 17th, but the Red Sox tied it back up with three of their own. Boston finally won it in the 18th on doubles by Buddy Myer and Ira Flagstead. Red Ruffing had pitched the first 15 for Boston and the Yankees must have liked what they saw, since they later acquired Ruffing from the Red Sox. The Yankees won the second game of the day's doubleheader, 5–0, ended after five innings. Shortest-ever Red Sox game? It might have been this one; according to the *Globe*, it was 52 minutes long.

1922 In 1923, the Yankees began playing at Yankee Stadium. The last home run Babe Ruth ever hit at the Polo Grounds came on this day off Boston pitcher Herb Pennock. As it would happen, it was Pennock who gave up Ruth's first home run as a Yankee, on May 1, 1920, at the Polo Grounds. As of the 1923 season, Pennock wasn't in any position to give up any more home runs to Ruth, because they became teammates when Pennock joined the Yankees. The Yankees lost two one-run games to the Red Sox, though, and dropped out of first place.

1921 The Yankees' Bob Meusel had four outfield assists in one game, and the Yankees set a record with five. Despite having all those runners cut down, the Red Sox won 8–2.

1918 Because of the ongoing war effort, the season ended early and the Cubs–Red Sox World Series began on September 5. The first three games were held in Chicago, to minimize the need for rail transportation, and were played in the larger Comiskey Park. Babe Ruth continued to build his scoreless innings streak, shutting out the Cubbies on six singles, while Hippo Vaughn allowed a walk and two singles to all occur in the fourth innings, giving the Red Sox a 1–0 Game One win. Dave Shean walked, George Whiteman singled him to second, and Stuffy McInnis singled him home, Shean just beating the throw from left field by a matter of inches.

1916 Tigers president Frank Navin promises each player a $50 suit of clothes if they can pass the Red Sox in the standings and take first place.

1905 Rube Waddell had a streak of 44 scoreless innings going when his defense fell apart behind him and Boston scored twice in the nick of time, tying the game 2–2 in the bottom of the ninth. He'd allowed just two hits to that point; he struck out 17 on the day. A walk, sacrifice, and a single by Jimmy Collins (the third Boston hit of the game) beat Waddell and Philadelphia in the bottom of the 13th.

1903 The Americans crush the visiting Philadelphia Athletics, 12–1. Patsy Dougherty has two singles and three triples. In over 100 years, no player has ever hit four triples in a game. The Boston team knocked out a still-record total of 113 triples during 1903. Part of the reason there were so many triples in this era was due to the practice of letting overflow crowds onto the outfield, behind ropes. Balls hit into the crowd were often deemed ground rule triples.

DEBUTS

1932: Hank Patterson	1986: Pat Dodson
1974: Fred Lynn	1990: Scott Cooper
1978: Bobby Sprowl	1993: Greg Blosser, Jeff McNeely
1985: Mike Greenwell, Kevin Romine, Rob Woodward	2003: Andy Abad

BIRTHDATES

Max Bishop 1899 (1934–1935); Merv Shea 1900 (1933); Dave Morehead 1942 (1963–1968)

DEATHS

Tom Hurd 1982; Loyd Christopher 1991; Billy Herman 1992

September 6

2003 Bruce Springsteen and the E Street Band rock 35,000 at sold-out Fenway Park, in shows on September 6 and 7. Unlike George Steinbrenner, this "Boss" is very welcome at the ballpark and leads the crowd in the singalong "Take Me Out to the Ballgame" and a full evening of rock and roll. The following year, on September 10 and 12, Jimmy Buffett and the Coral Reefer Band played two evenings at the park, releasing a live CD in late 2005.

1975 You can't always count on 24 hits to help you win a game, but Roger Moret had no complaints as he improved his record to 12–3, thanks to 20 runs scored against Milwaukee. The final was 20–6, and Moret felt it was OK to take the rest of the day off after seven innings.

1971 The Red Sox lost the first game, 5–3, to the Yankees, and Eddie Kasko figured he'd try something different in the second game. He put in four September callups from Louisville and, in fact, every single player in the second-game lineup was different. The Yankees won again, 3–0.

1964 Twice in one week, Zoilo Versalles spoiled a no-hitter for an opposing pitcher. On September 2, it was his eighth-inning hit off Milt Pappas of Baltimore. With two outs in the sixth inning, the Twins shortstop hit a two-run homer—the only hit off Boston's Bill Monbouquette. Worse for Monbo, it cost him the game. The Red Sox only scored once, on five hits, and so Versalles won the game, 2–1.

1960 Mickey Mantle's homer gave the Yankees one run in a 7–1 loss to the Red Sox at the Stadium. It was the last game Ted Williams would ever play there, and he homered as well (#518).

1954 The Yankees pull out all the stops to win a pair. They used nine pinch-hitters on the day, and won the first game in the bottom of the ninth, 6–5, but the Red Sox came back to erase a 7–0 deficit and Jimmy Piersall's two-run homer won the second. The Yankees threw 18 players into the fray, but still fell short, 8–7.

1941 Former umpire Billy Evans had been hired in 1937 to build up a farm system for the Red Sox. He built an excellent one, and on August 10, 1941, Sox owner Tom Yawkey asked Evans to move to Louisville to oversee the new franchise he had helped the Sox acquire. The Louisville team owned the contract of shortstop Pee Wee Reese. Shortstop Joe Cronin, currently player-manager with the Boston club, did not welcome the possibility of a threat to his position at short. Only a few weeks later, on September 6, Yawkey called Evans and asked for his resignation. Evans claimed Yawkey was drunk at the time and it was just his misfortune to have been home at the time of the call.

1927 Ruth hit five home runs in three games over two days. Was there a little skullduggery here? Red Sox catcher Fred Hofmann had been Ruth's teammate with the Yankees the preceding six years. Years later, Sox left fielder Wally Shaner told Peter Golenbock, "In '27, when Ruth hit all those home runs, if we were a lot of runs behind, no chance to win the ballgame, in the later innings, Freddie would tell Ruth what was coming. He hit a couple a mile over the fence. I know, 'cause Freddie told me afterwards. But we didn't mind because Ruth used to fill up the ballparks." The first game on September 6 saw Ruth hit two off Tony Welzer, in a game that Boston lost, 14–2. He hit another in the second game, a solo home run, in the ninth inning of a game the Sox were winning, 5–0. Of the 60 homers Ruth hit in 1927, 11 were hit off Red Sox pitching.

1922 Moments of glory. The lowly cellar-dwelling Red Sox knocked the Yankees out of first place by taking a pair of close games in New York, 4–3 and 6–5.

1919 Harry Hooper had a big day against Philadelphia. He was 3-for-5 with a homer and a double in the 11–3 first game, then won the second game with a triple in the 11th inning. He hit a single in the first game, too, for a cycle on the day.

1918 World Series Game Two: Cubs southpaw George Tyler "made himself the Babe Ruth of the Cubs" (*Chicago Tribune*) by holding the Red Sox to one run on six hits, while driving in two of Chicago's three second-inning runs with a hot grounder through the drawn-in infield. The lone Red Sox run came on back-to-back triples by Amos Strunk and George Whiteman to lead off the ninth; there have been nine times in World Series history that a team has tripled twice in the same inning. The Red Sox have done it five times, this being the last of those five times. Cubs 3, Red Sox 1. The Series was even 1–1.

Jean Joseph Octave Arthur Dubuc forever after could boast that he'd played in the 1918 World Series—and hope no one ever asked what he did. Dubuc, who went by the nickname "Chauncey," pinch-hit for Thomas in the ninth with one out, and swung his bat three times, missing each time.

1915 In a morning–afternoon doubleheader, the Sox were shut out by Ray Fisher and the Yankees in the first game, 4–0. Babe Ruth pitched even better in the afternoon affair, not giving New York a hit through seven. In the top of the eighth, he gave up three. Dutch Leonard came in to relieve, but New York scored three runs and ultimately won, 5–2.

1913 Taking advantage of Boston pitcher Fred Anderson's deliberate delivery, Philadelphia pull off three double steals in a game. That wasn't Anderson's only problem, though. He yielded 13 hits and walked three. Philadelphia won, 9–2.

1912 A huge crowd flocked to Fenway to see Smoky Joe Wood join in battle with Walter Johnson. Wood was going for his 14th win in a row and his 30th win of the year; Johnson had won 16 in a row but dropped his last two decisions. Wood got strikeouts when it counted, nine in all. Tris Speaker hit a ball into the overflow crowd standing in left field for a ground-rule double. Duffy Lewis followed with another double, off the fingertips of right fielder Moeller. 1–0 Boston was the final score.

1910 Harry Lord, traded to Chicago by Boston, issued a challenge to John I. Taylor's Red Sox. After the season, Lord declared, he would assemble a team of players cast off by Taylor, for a stake of $2000. The team would include Amby McConnell, Patsy Dougherty, Freddy Parent, and Lord himself—all currently with the White Sox. In addition, Lord would add Lou Criger; pitchers Young, Morgan, Altrock, and Arellanes; infielders Unglaub, LaPorte, and Knight; outfielders Stone, Gessler, and Wolter. "They can play all the games on Boston grounds if they want to," he offered. "We are not particular, but just want to show Boston that it has traded off a better team than it has now."

1909 In a separate admission double header, the Red Sox played to 35,000 fans. The 14,000 who attended the morning game saw the Sox tie it 9–9 with two runs in the bottom of the ninth, and win in the 10th. New York had a 5–0 lead at the midpoint, but "wild, weird fielding" turned the tide—despite eight of the game's 11 errors being Boston's. The second game saw Boston with a 6–3 lead, but a ninth-inning collapse granted five runs (and a 9–6 win) to the Yankees.

1904 With a 4–1 win in the first game, Boston beat Washington for the 22nd consecutive game, stretching all the way back to August 31, 1903. At home, Boston won 20 in a row hosting Washington and didn't lose until April 26, 1905.

1902 Pitcher Cy Young gave up 11 hits but won his 30th game of the year, beating the St. Louis Browns, 6–5.

TRANSACTIONS
1964: Sold Wilbur Wood to the Pittsburgh Pirates.
1969: Traded Mike Jackson to the Philadelphia Phillies and acquired Gary Wagner.

DEBUTS
1941: Al Flair	1982: Marty Barrett
1970: Bob Montgomery	1983: Jackie Gutierrez,
1975: Rick Kreuger	Al Nipper
1977: Bo Diaz	2002: Benny Agbayani

BIRTHDATES
Paul Zahniser 1896 (1925–1926); George Schmees 1924 (1952)

DEATHS
Charlie Berry 1972

September 7

1994 Major league ballplayers had been on strike for nearly a month, but someone nevertheless managed to steal home plate at Fenway Park. Both the Boston Police and the Red Sox were seeking suspects in the thefts of home plate and also of three flags from outside the park. Despite 24-hour security, someone managed to get onto the field and dig up the plate, and climb onto the roof and make off with the flags.

1984 The Yankees, heading for a season where they end up 17 games out of first place, enjoy one moment of glory, when they score three runs in the top of the ninth to come from behind for a 4–2 win over the Red Sox in Boston. At year's end, New York finishes one game ahead of the Red Sox.

1978 The so-called "Boston Massacre" begins. The Bosox lead had eroded and the Yankees arrived in Boston four games behind. New York battered Boston, 15–3, on 21 hits.

1972 Winning their 13th of 16 games, the Red Sox took first place over the Tigers on the strength of three-run homers by Tommy Harper and Rico Petrocelli. Pitcher Sonny Siebert hit one, too, and Boston beat New York, 10–4.

1966 The Sox picked up Garry Roggenburk from the Twins. He pitched one-third of an inning in 1966, 8⅓ innings in 1967, and 9⅔ innings in 1968 before being sent to Seattle.

1959 In a concerted burst of power from an unlikely trio, Don Buddin, pitcher Jerry
STVT Casale, and Pumpsie Green hit consecutive home runs in the second inning of a 12–4 drubbing of the Yankees. Buddin hit 41 homers in his career, Casale hit four, and this was Pumpsie Green's first of 13 lifetime.

1951 Ellis Kinder threw five innings in relief of Bill Wight in the first game of a twin bill with Philadelphia, and got the win when the Sox scored three times in the last two innings for an 8–5 win. It was Kinder's 54th appearance of the year, setting a new Red Sox record (since eclipsed).

The day was Bobby Doerr's final game with the Red Sox. He left the first game after one unfruitful at-bat. In 1,865 games, Doerr batted .288 with 223 HR and 1,247 RBI. Doerr made 4,928 putouts at second base, more than double that of runner-up Hobe Ferris (2,411). His 5,710 assists far outpaced Ferris's 3,064, and his 1,507 double plays almost tripled Marty Barrett's second-place 578.

1944 A Boston Red Sox fan group called "We the People Speak" held its third annual gathering at the Parker House in Boston, with guests Pete Fox, Bob Johnson, and Mike Ryba. The group was decribed as "an organization of bleacherites at Fenway Park."

1938 It's officially designated "Joe Cronin Day" at Fenway Park, but it's really Jimmie Foxx's day. Cronin had a good day, 1-for-3 with an RBI in a 11–4 whomping of the New York Yankees. But Foxx had two home runs and a double in his three trips to the plate, and earned eight RBI. All that in a game that was called on account of rain before the Red Sox even finished batting in the sixth inning. Cronin did get a $1,000 silver service in pre-game ceremonies.

1935 The Red Sox were down, 5–3, but had a rally going in the bottom of the ninth. Two runs were in and the bases were loaded. There was nobody out. The Indians called in reliever Oral Hidebrand, but Joe Cronin hit a wicked smash that third baseman Odell Hale couldn't get a glove on. He used his head, though inadvertently. The hard-hit ball ricocheted off Hale's head to shortstop Bill Knickerbocker, who caught it in mid-air for the first out, then flipped to second baseman Roy Hughes, who tagged second and threw to Hal Trosky at first, twice catching the Red Sox runner before he could get back to the bag. It was a 5-6-4-3 triple play and ended the game. Hale was both hale and hearty, and went 2-for-4 in the second game, also won by the Indians, 5–4.

1927 The Red Sox tallied 10 runs off Yankees pitching, but Babe Ruth hit two homers (#48 and #49), doubled, and singled for five RBIs in a 12-run Yankees assault. Ruth had five homers in two days, and New York won again, 12–10.

1926 New York's Babe Ruth doubled in two of the three third-inning runs, as the Yanks dealt Boston their 17th straight loss, 4–2.

1923 Howard Ehmke's 4–0 no-hitter was preserved, even after the opposing Athletics' pitcher hit a long drive in the sixth inning that landed fair and made second base on the play. Trouble is, Slim Harriss failed to touch first base on his way to second and was ruled out. Red Sox catcher Val Picinich had now caught three no-hitters for three different teams. (See also September 28, 1923 when Ehmke had a much worse day.)

1918 Game Three of the World Series. He probably shouldn't have come back on one day's rest, but Hippo Vaughn still held the Red Sox to just two runs, on a hit batsman, two singles, and Everett Scott's squeeze bunt. Both Vaughn and Boston's Carl Mays threw seven-hitters, but Mays only allowed one run. The game had a thrilling—though for the hometown Cubs fans, deflating—finale. With two outs, down by one in the bottom of the ninth, Charlie Pick singled. Turner Barber pinch-hit and had the count 2–1 when Pick successfully stole second, putting himself in scoring position. A passed ball got away from Red Sox catcher Wally Schang and Pick took third as Schang's throw to Thomas was just late—and ticked off Thomas's glove, rolling about 30 feet away. Pick picked himself up and raced for the plate, but a perfect throw had him by a step. Boston led the Series two games to one.

1914 Braves Field was not big enough to handle the crowds the team was beginning to draw as the "Miracle Braves" headed into the homestretch of their pennant drive. Beginning with Labor Day on September 7, they played in Fenway Park— and it immediately paid off as the team drew an estimated 73,000 fans for the morning–afternoon doubleheader. The Braves played the rest of their home games at Fenway, and the home World Series games as well.

TRANSACTIONS

1962: Placed Galen Cisco on waivers and he was claimed by the New York Mets.
1966: Purchased Garry Roggenburk from the Minnesota Twins.
1974: Purchased Deron Johnson from the Milwaukee Brewers.

DEBUTS

1926: Bill Moore	1975: Butch Hobson
1931: Howie Storie	1980: Rich Gedman
1950: Jim Piersall	1991: Bob Zupcic
1970: Dick Mills	2002: Shane Andrews

BIRTHDATES
Earl Moseley 1884 (1913); Clarence Winters 1898 (1924); Cleo Carlyle 1902
(1927); Al Van Camp 1903 (1931–1932); Roy Partee 1917 (1943–1947); Tom
Matchick 1943 (1970); Joe Rudi 1946 (1981); Dave Wallace 1947 (coach,
2003–2005); Sergio Valdez 1964 (1994); Darren Bragg 1969 (1996–1998)

DEATHS
Joe Cronin 1984; Al Papai 1995

September 8

2002 As Fenway's organist became further relegated to just brief interludes, the Red
Sox tried to honor ballplayers who liked to have a favorite song played over
the park's sound system as they strode to the plate or came in from the bullpen.
Manny Ramirez requested "I Get High" by the group Styles, and it was indeed
played when he approached home plate during the game hosting the Blue Jays.
Trouble is, there was a 12-letter expletive uttered early in the song. First, the
artist discussed how he needed drugs, then he came out with the word. Second
base umpire Angel Hernandez called upstairs after Manny's fly out, and said he
would report it to the commissioner's office. "I think we'll have a CD burning
ceremony," said Sox VP Dr. Charles Steinberg. "Whatever that song was, you
won't hear it again at Fenway Park."

2000 Yankees Roger Clemens and Mariano Rivera combined to shut out Roger's
former teammates, 4–0, on five hits. Boston's Bryce Florie, pitching in the ninth,
was hit flush in the face by a line drive hit by Ryan Thompson. "Is my eye still
there?" he asked trainer Jim Rowe. Florie suffered a couple of broken bones,
including the eye socket. He was finished for the year, and did not attempt to
pitch again until June 28 of the following year. He was, not surprisingly, rather
ineffective, with an 11.42 ERA in seven appearances in 2001, his last in major
league ball.

1995 Sox players Scott Hatteberg, Lee Tinsley, Carlos Rodriguez, and Chris Donnels
all hit consecutive pinch-hits against the Yankees; it ties the Red Sox for an
America League record. Boston only mustered seven hits in the game, though,
and lost 8–4.

1984 The Yankees out-double the Red Sox, with eight doubles to Boston's four. As
one might imagine, they scored more runs as well, and won, 12–6, though it was
only the five-run top of the ninth that really put the game out of reach.

1978 Part two of the Boston Massacre saw the Yankees win, 13–2, as the Yanks
accumulated 17 more hits and are helped by seven Red Sox errors. The Yankees
are now just two games behind.

1977 When Carlton Fisk hit a two-run homer off Jesse Jefferson and George Scott
went back-to-back with (obviously) a solo shot, it set a new major league record:
this was the 16th time that Sox batters had gone back-to-back. The old record
was held by the Twins (set in 1964). Fisk helped his pitcher, Mike Paxton, win a
complete game effort, 7–2.

1966 The Red Sox fired manager Billy Herman and offered the job through 1967 to
Pete Runnels. Runnels agreed to serve as interim manager through the end of the

1966 season but elected not to take the job for '67. He had ulcers at the time, and was shepherding a team that only missed last place by a half-game. Who knew that 1967 would offer such possibilities? Of course, one might wonder how the Sox might have fared had Runnels skippered the team rather than Dick Williams.

1961 A "Vic Wertz Night" was planned at Fenway on September 24, but the date was switched to September 19 when local committee organizers learned that Wertz was traded back to the Tigers. The venue was switched as well—to Detroit.

1960 Detroit holds a "Ted Williams Night" as Ted made his final circuit around the major leagues. Generous of them, but Ted didn't let up. He went 3-for-3, one of the hits being the 519th home run of his long career.

1953 Infielder Johnny Lipon was sold to the Browns. Whatever the Red Sox got in exchange, it was a good deal.

1937 Darn! Almost had 'em, too. The Sox and Yankees squared off in a doubleheader at Yankee Stadium. New York won the first game with a run in the bottom of the ninth, breaking a 2–2 tie. Newsom was the hard-luck loser. Pitcher Jackie Wilson held the Yanks to just two hits through eight innings, and the Red Sox had an 8–1 lead going into the ninth, but the Yankees scored eight times to win it, the final runs coming with a little help from two Joe Cronin errors, and a Lou Gehrig home run off reliever Tommy Thomas.

1933 Baldomero Melo Almada Quiros made his major league debut with the Red Sox. He batted .341 in 14 games late in 1933. The *Los Angeles Times* noted that Almada was the third Mexican ballplayer to play in the majors. One fact it did not note: all three played for the Boston Red Sox. The Sox had previously fielded pitchers Frank Arellanes (debut July 28, 1908) and Charley Hall (born Carlos Clolo, who pitched for the Red Sox from 1909 through 1913). Would that the Red Sox had pioneered in the signing of African American ballplayers as well!

1930 An "old-timers' game" was held in Boston, and the "Boston Americans" beat "The All Stars," 8–4. Cy Young got the win with a no-hitter of sorts (he only pitched one inning). Big Ed Walsh was the losing pitcher. The Americans featured the golden outfield of Duffy Lewis, Tris Speaker, and Harry Hooper, and Lewis even ran to the left-field Wall to haul in a drive off the bat of Home Run Baker. Patsy Donovan, who'd played back in 1890, pinch-hit for Bill Dinneen, and singled. Ty Cobb played for both teams, but went 0-for-4.

1929 Milt Gaston pitches a 10-inning complete game shutout against the St. Louis Browns. It would have been a win, except for the inconvenient fact that the Browns' George Blaeholder also pitched 10 scoreless innings. The game ended in a 0–0 tie, called because of the Sunday law in Boston, which required games to be wrapped up by a certain time. The tie was the second game of a doubleheader. Boston pitcher Joe Heving won the first game with a bases-loaded single in the bottom of the ninth.

1928 Some 25,000 Fenway fans cheered Connie Mack and Philadelphia as the A's swept two games from the Sox, 7–6 (10 innings) and 7–4. The reason? The rivalry with New York. The sweep catapulted Philadelphia into first place, by a half-game. Boston had lost both games the day before as well, eliciting even more local glee.

1926 They won one! After 17 consecutive losses stretching back to August 20, the Red Sox scored more runs than the Yankees (5–2) and that's what's called a win. The next day, though, the Yankees shut out the Red Sox, 10–0.

1925 The Yanks took two in Boston, 5–4 and 7–4. Ben Paschal hit two homers for the Yanks in the second game, but it was Babe Ruth's 300th career homer (served up by Chester Ross) which thrilled the crowd. Though he'd been gone nearly six years, the Boston fans gave him a loud and heartfelt ovation.

1921 Boston owner Harry Frazee had failed to answer his wife Elise's court complaint and thus was ruled in default during her proceedings for divorce. Mrs. Frazee had sued for divorce saying that they had been living apart for four years "on account of his fondness for Elizabeth Nelson and other young women."

1919 Boston's Babe Ruth broke the all-time home run record, hammering #26 high into New York's right-field grandstand off Jack Quinn. The record was Buck Freeman's 1899 mark with Washington. Boston won, 3–1, and also won the second game of the day, 3–0, a Waite Hoyt three-hitter in which Ruth scored two runs and drove in the third. One oddity: the second game was played under protest—by the Detroit Tigers. It had originally been scheduled for Boston, but both Boston and New York agreed to play it in New York instead. Detroit objected. It remains in the record books, though.

1915 Even though Larry Gardner had a 4-for-4 first game, the rest of the Red Sox lineup was ineffective and the infield committed three errors. Philadelphia won, 1–0. Shaking up the lineup for the second game might have made a difference, but Ray Caldwell also granted the Sox 12 walks and 11 hits, and the Red Sox won, 13–2.

1914 Boston scored three times in the top of the first, and the Yankees got all five of their runs in the bottom of the first. Then Yankees pitcher Ray Fisher—"he has a heart as big and as generous as Santa Claus"(*New York Times*)—did the Red Sox a favor in the top of the eighth, walking Harry Hooper with the bases loaded to force in the go-ahead run in a 6–5 victory.

1908 Though one run scored on his wild pitch, Cy Young beat Washington yet again, winning #20, by a 3–1 score. All three runs came in when right fielder Otis Clymer let Doc Gessler's bases-loaded single get through him and roll all the way to the fence.

1903 With two outs in the top of the ninth inning, frustrated by being down to New York, 1–0, Buck Freeman tried to tie it with one swing. Some 10 swings all resulted in long foul balls, a few of which would clearly have gone out of the park had they been straightened out. Finally, with "the hardest swipe of all" (*Globe*), he hit the ball fair—a dribbler to first baseman Ganzel. Game over.

1901 Though most Eastern cities prohibited Sunday baseball until the 1920s and, in the case of Boston, the 1930s, the less-civilized Western locales like Chicago and St. Louis permitted play on the Lord's Day—and drew huge crowds in an era when the six-day workweek was common, and there were no night ballgames. The largest crowd in American League history (this was the first year for the junior circuit), some 20,000 fans, saw a thrilling game in which Chicago scored one run in the bottom of the fourth, and Boston tied it in the top of the fifth. Chicago scored once more in the fifth, and Boston tied it yet again in the top of the sixth. It was Cy Young for Boston against "Boy Wonder" Patterson. In the bottom of the ninth, Jimmy Collins booted a ball at third. A sacrifice failed as the runner was thrown out at second. Callahan batted for Patterson and singled. With runners on first and third, Callahan stole second when Boston quickly threw to third to prevent the double steal. Then Dummy Hoy hit a single into the overflow crowd in left field, and Cy Young was defeated, 4–3.

TRANSACTIONS
1953: Sold Johnny Lipon to the St. Louis Browns.
1961: The Detroit Tigers claimed Vic Wertz from the Red Sox off waivers.
1982: Signed amateur free agent Rey Quinones.

DEBUTS
1925: Si Rosenthal
1933: Mel Almada
1971: Cecil Cooper
1995: Scott Hatteberg
2001: Angel Santos
2004: Pedro Astacio, Sandy Martinez

BIRTHDATES
Joe Giannini 1888 (1911); Val Picinich 1896 (1923–1925); Jim Bagby 1916 (1938–1946); Steve Barr 1951 (1974–1975); Don Aase 1954 (1977); Bob Wolcott 1973 (1999)

DEATHS
George Prentiss 1902; Ralph Pond 1947; Ed Hearn 1952

September 9

2003 The Red Sox hit three homers and handily won, 9–2, over the Orioles at Camden Yards. David Ortiz's two-run homer in the top of the third was #214 of the season for the Sox (and his 26th), setting a new club record for home runs, topping the '77 Sox. By season's end, the Sox had obliterated the old record and boasted 238 dingers, ranging from 37 for Manny Ramirez and 31 for Ortiz to one each by David McCarty and Damian Jackson.

2001 Swept in Yankee Stadium, the Sox had lost 12 of their last 13 games and were effectively knocked out of the race. Buster Olney of the *New York Times* declared them "ready for an autopsy."

1997 Nomar Garciaparra was just 1-for-5 but drove in two RBIs in a losing effort, as the Yankees beat the Red Sox, 8–6. The two runs batted in were his 85th and 86th of the year, which tied and exceeded Harvey Kuenn's old 1956 record, though, for most RBI by a leadoff batter. Nomar would drive in 12 more before he was done, finishing with 98. (See September 27, 1997.)

1990 What a way to start a game. Matt Young, pitching for the Mariners, struck out the side—and then some—in the first inning. He struck out Jody Reed and Carlos Quintana, and then struck out Wade Boggs, too, but the ball got away from the catcher so Boggs took first. Ellis Burks singled, but then Young fanned Mike Greenwell for his fourth K of the inning. He won the game, too, 3–1.

1979 Captain Carl singled in the eighth inning for his 2999th major league hit. It took him a while to get to number 3000. Unfortunately, Boston rooters weren't nearly as pleased to see the Orioles whip the Red Sox, 16–4. Every single Oriole had a hit and every single Oriole scored a run. Only one, Mark Belanger, had an RBI. The game proved to be the last one for Bob Montgomery. Grandfathered in, he was the last major league ballplayer to play without a batting helmet.

1978 With 11 more hits, and a seven-run fourth inning, the Yankees win again (7–0) as the massacre continues; the Yankees are now just one game behind Boston.

1977 Jim Rice hit homers #36 and #37, and Bill Campbell recorded saves #25 and #26, as Boston took two from the Tigers, 5–1 and 8–6, even though the Tigers put a scare in the Sox in game two, coming back from a 5–0 deficit. Notable only in retrospect: the second game featured the debuts of two Tiger rookies: Alan Trammell and Lou Whitaker. For nearly 20 years, they were the shortstop–second base combination for Detroit.

1974 The Yankees beat the Red Sox at Fenway Park, 6–3. They hadn't won in Boston for over a year, since July 21, 1973—and that one was their only Boston victory in all of 1973.

1973 Highly-regarded prospect Tom Maggard, the #1 draft pick for the Sox in 1968, died of a staph infection following an insect bite he'd contracted a couple of weeks earlier while catching for Pawtucket.

1962 The Yankees were swept for the ninth time in a doubleheader loss to the Red Sox, 9–3 and 5–4. The second game lasted a full 16 innings, with Dick Radatz pitching nine innings of relief for the Red Sox. With a man on third and one out in the top of the 16th, Radatz was up to bat and Sox manager Pinky Higgins put in Billy Gardner, who bunted hard to the charging pitcher Marshall Bridges. Bridges "went sprawling head first" and Bob Tillman scored easily. Chet Nichols, on in relief of Radatz, held off the Yanks in the bottom of the 16th.

1950 It was quite a race in September 1950. By winning two from Philadelphia, 8–3 and 11–3, the Sox pulled to within a game and a half of the Tigers and a half-game of the Yankees. The two beatings given the A's ran the record up to 21 wins in a row over Philly at Fenway; the last time an Athletics team had won a game in Boston was in September 1948. There were four Philly errors in the first game and every single one of the eight Red Sox runs was unearned. Seven runs in the second inning of the second game sealed that one. Dom DiMaggio stole his 15th base of the season—and 15 was all it took to lead the entire league in stolen bases in 1950.

1939 Jimmie Foxx had an appendectomy in Philadelphia. Losing his appendix would cause the Red Sox to lose Foxx for the rest of the season. With 35 homers already in the books, he still won the title—two ahead of Hank Greenberg and four ahead of rookie teammate Ted Williams. Foxx had been experiencing symptoms since June and even had to bow out of the lineup after the June 26 game. Even after diagnosis, he refused to stay in the hospital until after playing the six scheduled September games against the Yankees.

1938 A suspended player got in the game nonetheless, hit a home run, and beat the Red Sox. Philadelphia's Billy Werber, a former Red Sox infielder, had gotten in a fight with Washington's Buddy Myer and was suspended for three days by AL President Will Harridge, who sent a telegram to manager Connie Mack of the Athletics. Mack knew what the telegram would say, and stuck it unopened in his pocket until after the game. Werber's two-run homer in the eighth inning at

Fenway off Boston's Jim Bagby was the margin of difference in a 4–3 win for the Athletics. The Red Sox elected not to protest.

1937 The day after the Yankees took two from Boston, *Times* writer John Kieran ran into Moe Berg at Grand Central Station. The Sox catcher greeted him in Japanese and joined Kieran for lunch, ordering nothing but a bowl of applesauce. Berg was reading *An Enquiry Concerning Human Understanding* by David Hume, but declined to comment on the literary taste of his teammates. He asked, "Know what I would like to do?" and then proceeded to say he'd like to catch a no-hitter and win it with a home run. Also, he'd like to own the *New York Times*. "What a marvelous instrument of power…" Berg then talked about a British restaurant that refused to take his order for roast beef because it was too close to 9:00 P.M. and the cooked beef would not arrive at his table until after then, about the need the Red Sox had for more hitting from their outfield, and about his conversation at Meiji University with then Secretary of State Stimson about the Japanese incursion into Manchukuo. The Red Sox took the next two games from New York. Backup catcher Berg was 0-for-1 in the first one and didn't play in the second.

1925 G. Herman Ruth hit two singles, two doubles, and drove in three—but "was the perfect picture of a man not in a hurry" chasing down a ninth-inning ball in the outfield. By the time his throw came in, Boston's Si Rosenthal made it home to score the winning run. 5–4, Red Sox.

1923 Babe Ruth hit an inside-the-park home run, a fourth-inning fly ball that was "grossly mismanaged" by Boston center fielder Reichle. The ball was hit so high that by the time it came down, Ruth was already at third. It then landed behind the center fielder, and Ruth ran home, beating the throw by a step. New York won, 4–0, in the day's second game (they'd already won the first one, 6–2). (See also September 10, 1923.)

The same game also saw Boston right fielder Ira Flagstead throw out three Yankees baserunners, recording two putouts and three assists on three batted balls. In the day's second game, Flagstead had no putouts, no assists, and was 0-for-3 at the plate.

1918 In Game Four of the 1918 World Series, Ruth knocked in two runs on a "lusty" fourth-inning triple and he pitched seven scoreless innings before the Cubs knotted it up in the eighth with two runs that ended the 29⅔ scoreless innings Ruth had thrown in World Series play. On in relief, "Shufflin' Phil" Douglas and his catcher got crossed up on signs and one Douglas offering went for a wild pitch, which he then compounded with an error on a subsequent throw to first base. A run scored, and Boston had the lead, but had starting pitcher Tyler not tried to challenge Ruth with a fast ball back in the fourth, the Cubs might have come out on top. Ruth got the win, but only after Bullet Joe Bush came on in ninth-inning relief with two on and nobody out and squeaked out a save. To keep Ruth in the lineup, Barrow moved him from the mound to take over left field from George Whiteman.

Before the game at Fenway Park, a band played "The Star-Spangled Banner" to the crowd. It is the first reported pre-game playing of the song which became the National Anthem some 13 years later, in 1931. The tune had previously been noted as played occasionally during the seventh-inning stretch, e.g., in the game of June 5, 1917.

1916 Babe Ruth seemed to have the Big Train's number. In a Washington game, Ruth out-pitched Walter Johnson and the Senators, 2–1, allowing just four hits. It was the fifth game in a row, and the fourth of the 1916 season, in which Ruth faced down Johnson. The Senators run was the first they had scored off Ruth in the four 1916 games. The scores of the preceding three games had been 4–0, 1–0, and 1–0. It took them 10 innings, but the Senators salvaged a win in the second game, 4–3.

1914 With the score still 0–0 heading into the 11th inning, Eddie Plank vs. Boston's Ray Collins, an error in right and a grounder that took a bad hop gave the visiting Red Sox two men on base. Plank walked Duffy Lewis intentionally, and ran the count to Dick Hoblitzell to 3–2. The next pitch was called a ball, forcing in a run. Hal Janvrin's grounder resulted in Speaker being forced at home, but the bases remained loaded. Another 3–2 count to Larry Gardner resulted in another walk, and another run, and the Sox retired the Athletics to win the game, 2–0.

1913 Keeping the ball on the ground, Boston had 18 assists (including three by the catcher and four by starting pitcher Vic Moseley) in a game that ended with a pinch-hit RBI single by Wally Rehg of the Red Sox in the bottom of the 11th inning.

1912 While the Red Sox take their final road swing of 1912, some 8,000 seats were to be added to brand new Fenway Park to boost capacity to 30,000 in anticipation of the World Series.

It's not a new phenomenon: in Boston, souvenirs were being manufactured for the coming World Series: pennants, dolls dressed in Red Sox uniforms, badges, neckties with red socks on them, and a number of souvenir pins.

1911 It was Buck O'Brien's first major league start, and the 19-year-old from Brockton shut out the A's, 2–0. O'Brien got in several more starts in September and finished the season 5–1, with an amazing 0.38 ERA. He was a 20-game winner in 1912 (20–13, with a 2.58 ERA), but declined distinctly in 1913 and after he was sold to the White Sox, he declared, "they might just as well have shipped me to Hawaii." And after a few starts there, he quit.

1909 Just before the game against the Nationals, team captain Doc Gessler was traded to Washington. He was already Washington's property, but manager Joe Cantillon loaned him to the Red Sox for the afternoon. Gessler came into the game (for Boston) in the ninth, and singled in Speaker with the go-ahead run in the top of the 10th. It was truly the case that a member of the Washington Nationals, wearing a Boston uniform, drove in the winning run for the Sox.

1907 Now that's control. Cy Young and Philadelphia's ace Rube Waddell both pitched 13 scoreless innings in a game that goes in the books as a 0–0 tie. Neither pitcher walked even one batter.

1901 Even though Buck Freeman hit a triple and his 12th home run of the year (Lajoie would hit 14 for the league lead), Chicago beat Boston, 4–3, in the first game and took the second, 6–4, completing a four-game sweep of the visiting Bostons. Though Boston took all three games when Chicago visited a couple of weeks later, at year's end, Chicago held a four-game lead over second-place Boston.

TRANSACTIONS
1902: Signed Nick Altrock
1909: Traded team captain Doc Gessler to the Washington
      Nationals for Charley Smith and $2,500.
1959: Sold Chuck Tanner to the Cleveland Indians.
2000: Acquired Hector Carrasco from the Twins for prospect Lew Ford.

DEBUTS
1911: Buck O'Brien
1936: Fabian Gaffke
1974: Deron Johnson
2001: Calvin Pickering

BIRTHDATES
Frank Chance 1877 (manager, 1923); Mike McNally 1892 (1915–1920); Walt Kinney 1893
(1918); Waite Hoyt 1899 (1919–1920); Johnny Marcum 1909 (1936–1938); Johnny Lazor
1912 (1943–1946); Jim Corsi 1961 (1997–1999); Robinson Checo 1971 (1997–1998)

DEATHS
Hal Neubauer 1949; Ed Karger 1957; Doc Cramer 1990

September 10

1999 At Yankee Stadium, Pedro Martinez threw a complete game one-hitter, 3–0.
Martinez faced only one batter over the minimum, and racked up 17 strikeouts—
the most Yankees ever to strike out in a single game. Getting stronger as the
game progressed, he struck out the side in the fifth, seventh, and ninth innings.
New York only hit one ball in fair territory after the fourth.

Ironically, it was in this game that Pedro's string of 40 consecutive innings with
a strikeout came to an end. The old record was 25 consecutive innings—until
Pedro posted 33 innings in a row earlier in 1999. Now, he pushed the record to
yet another high. It's not often that a number would increase by 60% in one year.
Imagine Ted Williams' improving by 60% on his .406 average—the equivalent
increase would give him a .649 batting average.

1989 Reliever Joe Price was suspended for four days without pay for swearing at
manager Joe Morgan in the dugout runway the day before. Several days earlier,
Price had complained he was "embarrassed as a professional" to pitch in a game
the Sox lost, 13–1. Price said Bob Stanley hadn't been given enough time to
warm up and wondered out loud why Morgan was playing the infield in with the
score 10–1. He was brought into the Saturday night game with a 5–2 lead but
gave up three hits, had four bases stolen against him—including steals of second,
third, and home by Devon White—and lost the lead. Price first denied he swore,
but the following day charged that Morgan baited him into it.

1978 The Yankees won the fourth and final game of the "Boston Massacre," 7–4.
Eighteen more hits. They outscored Boston 42 runs to 9 over the four-game
series, courtesy of 67 hits and 12 Sox errors. The 19 bases on balls doled out by
Red Sox pitchers didn't hurt the Yankees cause. The Yankees took the lead in the
standings on the 13th.

1976 The shortest ever Red Sox game, just 57 minutes long. With one out in the first, Ben Oglivie homered for the Tigers. Reggie Cleveland only allowed two other hits, but got tagged for the 1–0 loss in a game rained out after five full innings.

1974 The Yankees purchased designated hitter Alex Johnson from the Texas Rangers, and Johnson flew to Boston. He arrived in the middle of a tied game, put on the pinstripes, and hit a homer to give New York a 2–1 victory.

1950 The Red Sox win their 22nd in a row at home from the Athletics, 6–2. Eleven wins in 1949 and 11 more in 1950. Tom Wright won this one with a pinch-hit double in the bottom of the eighth, breaking a 2–2 tie. He scored shortly afterward on a Dom DiMaggio double.

1944 George Metkovich got hits in both halves of the doubleheader and extended his hitting streak to 25 games, a new club record. There were no games until the 15th—a gap of open dates in the schedule left for makeup games, but there had been very few rainouts and hence no need to fill in. When the Sox next played, Metkovich went 0-for-4.

1938 With 15 runs on 19 hits, the Athletics prevailed, 15–7, but Jimmie Foxx cracked the headlines hitting two home runs in the game for his record-breaking ninth "circuit couplet" of the year. Babe Ruth and Hack Wilson had each held the previous record with eight two-homer games.

1933 When Bob Weiland lost to the Browns, 3–2, in the first game of a doubleheader, it was the 20th consecutive loss for the Red Sox in games decided by one run, establishing a major league record that still stands today. The next Red Sox game decided by one run was a Weiland win, 4–3, against the Indians on September 19. The streak of losses ran from July 13 through September 10. The actual doubleheader saw the first game 1–0 St. Louis, heading into the ninth. Both teams scored two runs, for the 3–2 final. In the nightcap, it was still 0–0 after 10 innings, but Boston starter Welch weakened (well, fell apart) and the Browns scored four unanswered runs for a 4–0 final. Which was, of course, not a one-run game.

1923 For the second day in a row, Babe Ruth hit an inside-the-park home run, this one being HR #35 on the year. The *New York Times* called it "slightly tainted" reporting that it "started out in life as an ordinary single, but…Joe Harris, while running over from left field to meet the ball, let it carom off his ankle and roll to the outskirts of the field." Though Boston scored first, with one run in the top of the second, the Yanks replied with eight unanswered runs.

1918 Finances reared their ugly heads, with players on both the Cubs and the Red Sox unhappy with pay for the Series in progress. They threatened to not play unless guarantees of compensation were made. They wanted $2,500 each for the victors and $1,000 each for the losers. The owners backed them down by convincing them that they would look too greedy at a time when so many other young men were fighting and dying in the World War. So the owners kept more for themselves. On the field, Sad Sam Jones became even sadder when Hippo Vaughn shut out the Sox, pitching a 3–0 five-hitter on just two day's rest.

1917 Offering a bonus to players as an inducement to win was against league rules, but President Frazee acknowledged in an interview that he had been planning to give each player a present of $1,000 apiece if they won the pennant for the third year in a row.

1912 Smoky Joe Wood won his 15th game in a row, beating Chicago, 5–4. Sea Lion Hall helped by closing out the game.

1909 Team president John I. Taylor suggested a split-admission triple-header (two afternoon games, one evening game) for September 11. Connie Mack declined.

1904 Cy Young struck out 12 Athletics, and spread out seven hits over 13 innings, while his team played error-free ball, but Boston bowed to Eddie Plank (who struck out only one) in a 1–0 defeat in Philadelphia. In one inning, Young struck out all three batters on nine straight pitches, not a foul ball among them.

TRANSACTIONS
1924: Purchased Ted Wingfield from the Washington Senators.
1956: Signed Gene Mauch as a free agent.
1970: Selected Bobby Bolin off waivers from the Milwaukee Brewers.
2000: Signed free agent Steve Ontiveros.

DEBUTS
1947: Matt Batts
1952: Dick Bolling, Hersh Freeman
1969: Gary Wagner
1972: Bob Veale
2002: Kevin Brown, Jeff Hancock, Freddy Sanchez

BIRTHDATES
Harry Niles 1880 (1908–1910); Tony Tonneman 1881 (1911); Marty Krug 1888 (1912); Arlie Tarbert 1904 (1927–1928)

DEATHS
Shano Collins 1955; Roy Johnson 1973; Johnny Marcum 1984

September 11

2005 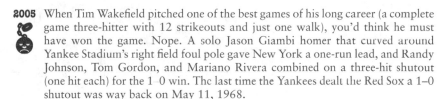 When Tim Wakefield pitched one of the best games of his long career (a complete game three-hitter with 12 strikeouts and just one walk), you'd think he must have won the game. Nope. A solo Jason Giambi homer that curved around Yankee Stadium's right field foul pole gave New York a one-run lead, and Randy Johnson, Tom Gordon, and Mariano Rivera combined on a three-hit shutout (one hit each) for the 1–0 win. The last time the Yankees dealt the Red Sox a 1–0 shutout was way back on May 11, 1968.

1999 With five home runs, two by Nomar and the game-winner by Butch Huskey, the Red Sox out-slug the Yankees at the Stadium, 11–10.

1971 Ray Culp struck out three times in a row. Though not unusual for a pitcher to have a weak bat, Culp had now managed to strike out eight times in succession. Joe Coleman was pitching for the Tigers and he had a no-hitter through seven, racking up 11 K's by game's end. Culp took the 1–0 loss.

1955 Frank Sullivan wins the first game of a doubleheader with the Yankees, for his 18th win of the season. There were no 20-game winners in 1955; Sullivan has three more starts, but the Sox lose all three games. Eighteen wins is enough to lead the league, though, tied with Whitey Ford and Bob Lemon. Ted Williams get his 2,000th hit in the second-game 5–3 loss to NY.

1923 Howard Ehmke, coming off a no-hitter on September 7, pitched against the Yankees in New York. The first batter he faced, Whitey Witt, was credited with a hit on a ball which bounced off third baseman Howie Shanks' chest and rolled toward second base before he could retrieve it. Some observers called it an obvious error, but others disagreed, and the man whose "vote" counted—Frederick Lieb, the official scorer—refused to change it. It was the only hit Ehmke allowed in a 3–0 Sox win. The *New York Times* called Ehmke's 18 innings of one-hit ball "the greatest exhibition of box-work in the history of baseball."

1919 A gang of gunmen had come from New York to Boston, with plans to rob the Fenway Park ticket office while the till was bulging with receipts from the game, according to underground sources cited by police. There was also a plan to stick up certain fans known to carry a lot of money on their person. Captain Thomas Goode called on two companies of the State Guard and 100 volunteer policemen armed with pistols and clubs, to supplement a detail of "loyal policemen." The *Chicago Tribune* reported, "They formed lanes from the grandstand exits near the box office to Jersey Street, Brookline Avenue and the Kenmore subway station and forced all the spectators to march between the guards." At first glance, this seems like an extreme over-reaction, but there has been a spreading lawlessness around Boston since the Boston Patrolmen's Union went on strike on September 9 (hence the reference to "loyal policemen"). Seven were killed and one was dying, with dozens more injured, as 5,000 troops of the State Guard were called out to attempt to maintain order. Machine guns and bayonets were used to combat "gamblers, thugs, and thieves" operating almost around the city. It's probably good that on the field of play, the Sox won two shutouts against St. Louis, 4–0 and 6–0. (See also September 14.)

On a New York witness stand in the case of Carl Mays, traded from the Red Sox to the Yankees, AL president Ban Johnson testified that he advanced the money which Robert McRoy put into helping purchase the Red Sox in 1911. James McAleer and Robert McRoy were listed as co-owners of the ball club. Johnson withdrew his interest while McAleer was on a baseball world tour in 1914, and it was sold to Joseph Lannin. Both current owner Harry Frazee and Yankees owners Ruppert and Huston said that Johnson's admission proved their contention that Johnson "had the entire league under his domination."

Arthur Duffey wrote in the *Boston Post*, "Harry Frazee bought Babe Ruth for $2700 six years ago but it is a safe bet that Frazee would not sell Babe for 127,000 cold iron men [dollars] now."

1918 The boys of September—the 1918 Red Sox, playing the World Series in early September after a war-shortened season—won the World Series in Game Six, on the strength of Carl Mays' 2–1 three-hitter. In the third inning, the Red Sox scored both runs off Lefty Tyler on two walks and George Whiteman's liner to right field, which was dropped by Max Flack. The same Flack singled and scored for the Cubs in the top of the fourth, but the Sox' two unearned runs held up, thanks to Mays' mound magic and solid Red Sox defense. This was their third World Championship in a four-year stretch—1915, 1916, and now 1918. The Sox staff ERA for the Series was 1.70, but the Cubs pitchers were better yet: 1.04. Not one of the games lasted as long as two hours. Over the six games, the Red Sox scored only a total of nine runs, but those nine runs were enough to win the requisite four games.

1911 John Bushelman had one at-bat for the Cincinnati Reds in 1909. Two years later, he was issued a Red Sox uniform and given the game ball, to pitch against the Washington Nationals. With Walter Johnson going for Washington, no one expected a pitcher's duel. Bushelman managed something a little different, though, giving up five runs in the first—without allowing a hit. In fact, only three players even registered official at-bats. He walked four and hit one batter, but had Larry Gardner executed the double play at second base, Bushelman would have been out of the inning with just one run. Had Hal Janvrin not made a throwing error, he'd have only seen two runs score. Bushelman only had himself to blame for an errant pickoff throw. Over the next six innings he steadied and gave up but two hits. The final score was 7–1.

1909 In a doubleheader that epitomized the "deadball era," Philadelphia hosted the Red Sox and took the first game behind Eddie Plank, 1–0. Eddie Cicotte was the loser, despite giving up just four hits. In the nightcap, both Harry Krause and Smoky Joe Wood gave up four hits apiece, but two doubles brought home one run for the Red Sox, and they won. Two games, two runs total.

Jack Chesbro (0–4) was picked up on waivers from the Highlanders. Chesbro pitched and lost one game for Boston—a sad ending to his Hall of Fame career.

1907 The first night game at the Huntington Avenue Grounds was arranged by John I. Taylor, and pitted the Cherokee Indians against the Dorchesters. About 1,000 fans turned up and 20 electric lights on poles, providing approximately 50,000 candle power, illuminated the infield (a smaller, softer ball was used, designed to keep the ball from really leaving the infield). Dorchester won. The following day, two boys from Fall River aged 10 and 11, were sent home. They had become entranced by baseball under the lights several days earlier and had been following the Indians, earning money with songs and dances on trains they took.

1906 Two Boston players were ejected for fighting—with each other! It was a frustrating game for "the Stahlwarts" (Jake Stahl's Boston ball club) as New York built up an 11–2 lead through six innings. Right fielder Jack Hayden was slow to chase down Frank LaPorte's fly ball to short right in the sixth, allowing LaPorte an inside-the-park home run. After the inning, as Hayden was leaving the field, he grumbled to second baseman Hobe Ferris that he hadn't tried for the ball, endeavoring to make Hayden look bad. Ferris came back with some remark and after reaching the Boston bench, Hayden struck Ferris four blows to the head. After Hayden was set down, Ferris rushed back and kicked him hard in the mouth. Twelve policemen rushed to restore order, and 500 fans poured onto the field. By the time umpire O'Loughlin threw Ferris out of the game, he'd already been arrested by New York City police. Both were charged with disorderly conduct, but neither would press charges against the other. The Highlanders won the game.

1905 In the most lopsided defeat in the young franchise's short history, Boston lost 14–0 to the Washington nine. They'd won the first game, but couldn't do a thing in the second.

DEBUTS
1905: Frank Owens
1911: Jack Bushelman
1947: Cot Deal
1976: Jack Baker

BIRTHDATES
Ray Grimes 1893 (1920); George Loepp 1901 (1928); Randy Heflin 1918 (1945–1946); Marlan
Coughtry 1934 (1960); Jeff Newman 1948 (1983–1984); Ellis Burks 1964 (1987–2004)

DEATHS
Braggo Roth 1936; Del Baker 1973; Clem Dreisewerd 2001

September 12

2005 When David Ortiz hit his 40th home run of the season in the top of the 11th
inning of the game in Toronto (he'd hit #39 in the fourth inning), it gave him
back-to-back seasons of 40 or more home runs. Only one other Sox slugger had
ever done it—not Williams, not Foxx, not Rice, and not Manny Ramirez. Yaz
hit an even 40 in both 1969 and 1970. The extra-innings shot won the game for
Boston, 6–5.

2003 Four White Sox pitchers kindly combined to provide 12 bases on balls to Red
Sox batters, helping enable Boston to a 7–4 win. Five of the batters who were
walked score. Three of the walks forced in runs.

1999 For the first time since their pennant-winning year of 1986, the Red Sox sweep
the Yanks at Yankee Stadium, with a 4–1 win behind the five-hit pitching of Bret
Saberhagen and four relievers. Rheal Cormier gets credit for the win, since he
was the pitcher of record when the Sox scored three times in the top of the eighth
to break the 1–1 tie.

1992 Wade Boggs handled a ground ball hit to him at third base by Detroit's Tony
Phillips; official scorer Chas Scoggins ruled it an error. But Boggs questioned
the call after the game, and Scoggins reviewed the play and changed his scoring
to make it a hit. This gave Boggs one less error, but resulted in two earned runs
being tagged onto Roger Clemens. It raised Clemens' ERA from 2.24 to 2.31, in
the final weeks of his fight for his fourth Cy Young Award. Had Boggs simply
absorbed the error, it would hardly have mattered to him. Pitcher Danny Darwin
said, "Wade isn't going for a batting title or a Gold Glove. Roger is going for a
Cy Young." Boggs said he hadn't appealed to Scoggins to change the ruling, and
he told Sox publicist Jim Samia to ask Scoggins to change it back if it was going
to cause controversy. That didn't happen.

1979 Carl Yastrzemski got his hit 3,000th hit, off Yankees pitcher Jim Beatttie. Yaz
became the first AL player with 3,000 hits and 400 home runs. As a bonus,
Boston beat New York, 9–2.

1965 The Red Sox played 18 games against the Twins in 1965, and lost all but one
of them, the final defeat coming on this date, 2–0. The only one they won was a
May 27 four-hit shutout thrown by Dave Morehead.

1959 Sox-skipper-to-be Joe Morgan hit a triple off the left-center field wall in a pinch-
hitting appearance for Kansas City. It was his only extra-base hit for KC.

1948 Philadelphia wins a game at Fenway Park. This is noteworthy, because they
won't win another one until April 20, 1951. Not one in 1949, not one in 1950.

1946 Paid not to play. The day's *Boston Globe* reported that owner Tom Yawkey paid Ted Williams $10,000 not to participate in any exhibition or barnstorming games after the season was over. Bob Feller had organized a national tour of stars, and Ted was part of the entourage, but Yawkey didn't want The Kid to risk getting hurt. Feller claimed he had no problem with the payment, but suggested that the deal would scuttle the tour and deprive Dom DiMaggio, Bobby Doerr, and other players of their opportunity to make some extra cash. "Why don't they get some money, too?" he asked. Yawkey's rejoinder: "Why doesn't Feller stay on his own ball club?"

1942 The Croatian connection. Cleveland fans of Croatian ancestry held "Johnny Pesky Day" in Cleveland to honor Mr. Paveskovich before he entered the U.S. Navy after the season was over.

1937 Athletics fans were disappointed as the Red Sox came back from a 5–0 deficit to tie it with three in the sixth and two more in the eighth, but they were crushed when Boston then scored eight times in the top of the ninth and Philadelphia could only come back with one run of their own. 13–6, Red Sox.

1933 Dusty Cooke had a busy day in right field, recording eight putouts and getting an assist on a 7-6-5 double play. The Sox beat St. Louis, 4–1.

1931 Both starters threw 13 innings. Eddie Durham of the Red Sox and "Red" Herring of the Tigers combined to put up 25 zeroes on the scoreboard, until Bill Sweeney doubled in the bottom of the 13th (and moved on to third when Harvey Walker's throw was off). Tom Oliver's sacrifice fly to right field scored the only run in the 1–0 Red Sox win. Boston had beaten Detroit, 5–0, the day before, and been shut out by them the day before that, 3–0.

1916 Babe Ruth and Walter Johnson had squared off on September 9, with Boston and the Babe winning the game, 2–1. It was Ruth's fourth win over Walter Johnson in 1916. Just two days later, on the 12th, the two went at it again. Boston had a 2–0 lead heading into the bottom of the ninth, but the Nationals sent it into extra innings when John Henry drove in two to tie it. The Sox got a run in the top of the 10th on three singles, but Washington scored two more runs to win it for Walter, 4–3. Ernie Shore was the loser, though. Ruth had been taken out of the game after 8⅔.

Bill Carrigan says he will probably retire after the season. The *Washington Post* guesses he will not, both because of his love of the game and the "healthy stipend" he is paid by the Red Sox: "It's dollars to doughnuts" he'd be back, because baseball is "mighty lucrative" for him. He is "well fixed and not dependent on the game," but the lure of "diamond gold" was thought to be too much. It was not. Carrigan helped win the World Series, and then retired.

1911 League president Ban Johnson set out by train to Boston to observe the sale of a 50% share in the Red Sox to James McAleer, recently manager for the Washington club. As soon as the sale was consummated, construction would begin on a new ballpark in the Fenway area of the city, for which the ground had already been cleared and graded. John I. Taylor and his father would rent the completed park to the ball club. McAleer, who had unsuccessfully sought to buy into the St. Louis or Washington clubs, was understood to be purchasing a one-sixth interest. Ban Johnson's secretary, Robert McRoy, was expected to move to Boston to become secretary of the Red Sox. (See also September 14.)

1909 A datelined story in *The Sporting News* reported that 4,000 new seats had been added to the Huntington Avenue grounds, a combination of bleacher seats and private boxes in front of the grandstand. The press box was placed on the roof of the grandstand, so sportswriters no longer needed to sit in grandstand seats with the "rabid rooters" of the day.

1907 Philadelphia beat Boston, 7–1, the first of 18 games in a row that Boston couldn't win. In fact, they didn't win another game until October 3, the last game they would win all year. There were, however, two moments of moral victory: tie games on September 13 and 30. The season even ended with a 3–3 tie against New York.

1903 Boston didn't score once in their last 25 innings in New York, but they did big time when the Highlanders came to visit them: 10–1 was the final score. Boston built up a 7–0 lead before New York plated its sole run in the seventh. Hughes went 2-for-4 at the plate, singling and tripling, one of four Boston triples. Play was not as one-sided as the final score would imply; New York had nine hits to Boston's 13. Ground rules cost Buck Freeman; a triple he'd hit in the fifth would have been a home run had there not been an overflow crowd. Any ball hit into the crowd was ruled a triple. Long Tom Hughes got the win, #20 of the year.

TRANSACTIONS
1977: Signed free agent Keith MacWhorter.

DEBUTS

1907: Elmer Steele	1976: Ernie Whitt
1940: Tony Lupien	1987: Jody Reed
1947: Merl Combs	1993: Nate Minchey
1962: Merlin Nippert	2000: Hector Carrasco
1970: Bobby Bolin	

BIRTHDATES
Tom Herrin 1929 (1954)

DEATHS
None yet

September 13

1983 Al Nipper made his first start, losing to the Orioles, 7–1. In his 113 starts for the Red Sox, he never registered a shutout. Of all the pitchers who ever played major league ball, only Roy Mahaffey had more career starts (128) without a single shutout than Nipper's 124.

1982 Nothing went their way. A safety squeeze turned into a double play when a sign was missed, and Reid Nichols popped up to the pitcher. On other plays, what looked like a Cleveland foul ball was ruled a double, and Boston's Carney Lansford was called for obstruction at third base. It just wasn't their day, and the Sox lost two games to the Indians, 3–1 and 4–3 (in 11 innings).

1973 Thurman Munson extracted some revenge for the August 1 melee, singling in a run in the bottom of the eighth to give the Yankees a 1–0 lead. The Sox tied it in the ninth on a Rick Miller homer. Munson walked in the 10th, but didn't score.

In the bottom of the 12th, Clarke and White singled, and Munson singled to center to break the tie and win the game. Bob Veale took the loss.

1953 The Red Sox won, 7–6, on an eighth-inning walk and Frank Sullivan, who had just joined the team after serving in Korea, won his first major league game, though it wasn't the sort of win to write home about. He'd entered in relief of Parnell, who'd left with two on and one out. Sullivan walked the first man he faced, struck out the second, and then yielded a bases-clearing triple, giving the Indians a 6–5 lead. The first two runs were, of course, charged to Parnell, but the third and go-ahead run was Sullivan's. He got out of the inning without further scoring and remained pitcher of record. The Sox scored two in the eighth and Sid Hudson came on to get the save. During the game, Sox catcher Sammy White pulled off an unassisted double play.

1946 Coming off an eight-game winning streak, all the Sox had to do was win one more game to clinch the 1946 pennant. Instead, they lost six games in a row. In the very first inning, Ted Williams took unusual measures to win it. With the "Williams Shift" on, he hit the ball hard to left field. Cleveland left fielder Pat Seerey had no chance to get it, playing as he was behind shortstop. Ted ran all the way around the bases and scored, for the only inside-the-park home run of his career. Tex Hughson threw a three-hit shutout, and the first-inning score stood after nine: 1–0 Red Sox. Clinch.

1942 Ted Williams hit a homer in the seventh inning of the first game, making it a record-tying 12 games in a row that he'd had a run batted in (the mark he tied had been set by Joe Cronin). In the second game, Ted went 1-for-2, and scored two. He was walked twice in the game, once intentionally. Boston won both games, keeping their '42 pennant hopes mathematically alive.

1920 Boston beat St. Louis, in St. Louis, by the score of 5–4 in a 14-inning game that featured only one strikeout, by a Browns pitcher. Boston backstop Wally Schang didn't record a single putout.

1918 The Red Sox had just won their fifth World Series. The Braves had won in 1914. Boston teams were 6–0, but the *Boston Herald* alerted readers in an editorial: "Of course, it is possible that some year will yet see a Boston team losing a world's championship."

DEBUTS

1907: George Whiteman
1909: Charlie Smith
1913: Swede Carlstrom
1920: Ben Paschal
1924: Ted Wingfield
1931: Marv Olson

1962: Billy Macleod, Pete Smith
1968: Luis Alvarado
1970: Roger Moret
1982: Oil Can Boyd
2000: Rich Croushore

BIRTHDATES

Curt Fullerton 1898 (1921–1933); Rabbit Warstler 1903 (1930–1933); George Susce 1931 (1955–1958); Bob Heffner 1938 (1963–1965); Rick Wise 1945 (1974–1977); Steve Curry 1965 (1988)

DEATHS

Ralph Comstock 1966

September 14

2005 Gabe Kapler blew out his Achilles tendon rounding second on what he hadn't yet realized was a home run by Tony Graffanino. Unable to continue, Kapler was removed from the game. Fortunately, Graffanino held up and did not pass him on the base paths. Inserted as a courtesy runner, Alejandro Machado scored his first major league run trotting home in front of Graffanino who may have set a major league record for the time it took to complete the circuit around the bases. (Also see September 16, 2005.)

In the eighth inning, David Ortiz hit his second game-winning homer in three days against the Blue Jays. It was Ortiz's 38th homer as a designated hitter in 2005, topping Edgar Martinez (37) for the most home runs hit in a single season by a DH.

2002 Manny Ramirez hit two solo homers, and Trot Nixon drove in two, to help Boston beat Baltimore, 6–4. Derek Lowe started and got the win, number 20 on the year. Ugueth Urbina recorded his 35th save. With the win, Lowe became the first pitcher to save 20 games in one season (2001) and then win 20 the following year.

2001 The Red Sox arrived home after a 28-hour journey by bus, rail, and air. The team had been in St. Petersburg when terrorists hijacked four airplanes and struck New York's World Trade Center and the Pentagon. After a Delta charter from BWI to Warwick, RI, they re-boarded buses for the final leg into Boston. On the 15th, they held a four-hour workout at Fenway Park, but one that was closed to reporters for "security reasons."

1990 Peter Gammons profiled Sox fan Testa Lane, who had once pitched to Babe Ruth in the summer of 1915 when the young Ruth and the Red Sox visited a girls camp in Guilford, New Hampshire, where 8-year-old Testa was enrolled. She was the pitcher on the team, so threw one to the Babe that was hit so far that "we scoured the woods the rest of the summer looking for that ball." Tris Speaker always caller her "Blondie" at Fenway, but she didn't like that. She'd attended all the 1912 World Series games at age five. When Duffy Lewis passed away, he left her $500 in his will "for ice cream." The article mentioned her taking "kids like Sam and Jamie Kennedy of Brookline to games." Sam Kennedy is currently Senior Vice President of Sales and Marketing for the Red Sox.

1988 Mike Greenwell hit for the cycle, homering in the second and going 4-for-4 while scoring three of the four Red Sox runs in Mike Boddicker's 4–3 win over the Baltimore Orioles.

1975 After trailing at one point, 5–1, the Sox tied it and Yaz broke the 6–6 tie with a two-run double in the three-run seventh, giving Boston an 8–6 victory over the visiting Milwaukee Brewers. Hank Aaron hit his last homer of the year, #745, off Bill Lee in the fifth; it was the only homer he ever hit at Fenway Park. And Robin Yount—still a teenager—played in his 242nd game, breaking Mel Ott's record for most major league games by a player still in his teens.

1951 The Browns' Mickey McDermott brought a couple of gopher balls to the mound, and St. Louis rookie Bob Nieman hit a solo shot in the second and a two-run homer in the third—homering in his first two major league at-bats. He couldn't keep that up forever, but did have a 3-for-5 debut. Browns fans were disappointed that Walt Dropo, Dom DiMaggio, and Ted Williams all hit homers for the Red Sox, and won the game, 9–6.

1949 Ted Williams hit a long home run in the sixth inning, into Fenway's left-field screen, for the only run in Boston's 1–0 victory. Hal Newhouser was pitching for the Tigers, a four-hitter, but all it took was the one hit to give Boston's Ellis Kinder the win—his 20th of the season. The Tigers had put on the "Williams Shift," but when you hit a ball over the Green Monster, there's no shift that's going to hold you down. It was Williams' 145th RBI.

1941 Jimmie Foxx's grand slam pushed his year-to-date RBI total to 102, the 13th straight year that he'd batted in 100 or more runs.

Ted Williams walked in the same game (his 143rd of the season), marking the 19th consecutive game in which he worked a walk. Not surprisingly, this was the year Ted set the all-time 20th century mark for on-base percentage, .553.

1923 In the second inning of what proved a 12-inning game, Boston first baseman George Burns erased a rally by the Indians when Frank Bowser hit a liner to first. Burns tagged out Rube Lutzke before he got back to first and then ran to second, sliding into the bag "a few feet ahead" of the returning Riggs Stephenson. It was the fourth unassisted triple play in baseball history. The Indians scored once and might have won it in the 12th, but for the two Red Sox runs driven in by Ira Flagstead's bases-loaded single to left that tipped the balance back in Boston's favor for the 4–3 win.

1919 With the general concern over lawlessness in Boston during the ongoing police strike, there was discussion regarding the possibility of the Red Sox playing their home games in Brooklyn providing use of the field could be obtained from President Ebbets and the American League would consent.

1917 Carl Mays pitched Boston to a 6–5 win over the Yankees, while going 4-for-4 at the plate and driving in three runs, including the go-ahead run in the top of the eighth inning.

1915 Chicago's first baseman John Collins doubled to drive in Eddie Murphy, who'd reached on an error. With Babe Ruth tossing a two-hitter, it was the only run the White Sox got. Collins made two errors in the bottom of the seventh, on which one run scored and Ruth's double scored the second. Boston won, 2–1.

1912 At the close of play on September 14, 1912, Boston held a 16½ game lead over the second-place Philadelphia Athletics. They held it one more day, through September 15. It is the largest lead the Red Sox have held at any time, matched only by the 16½ game lead they maintained from September 4–6, 1946.

1908 Boston pitcher Elmer Steele speared Queenie O'Rourke's liner in the top of the ninth, enabling himself to win the game against New York, 2–1. It was one of Steele's five putouts on the day.

1907 What did I get myself into here? Tris Speaker debuted with Boston, and the team lost both halves of a doubleheader against Philadelphia, the first two losses of a 13-game losing streak. Speaker accomplished little (batting .158) in his first stint with the Sox, but hit .600 in a post-season exhibition series against the New York Giants. Frederick Lieb, though, says the Sox were not impressed enough and forgot to send Speaker a contract after the season.

1905 Just as Fenway Park served as a venue for a number of sporting events from boxing matches to pro football games, so the Huntington Avenue Grounds on this day hosted a track and field event with footraces and discus. Placing second in discus was Ellery H. Clark of the Boston Athletic Association, and later an author of a couple of early and engaging books on the Red Sox.

1904 In a tight pennant race, with Boston just a half-game in the lead, New York and Boston played back-to-back doubleheaders, in Boston. The four games could hardly be better balanced: Boston lost the first game on the 14th, 3–1, but won the first one next day, 3–2. The second game each day ended in identical 1–1 tie scores.

1901 Cy Young won his 30th game of the season with ease (he finished 33–10, with a 1.62 ERA). Limiting the visiting Washington Nationals to four hits, while his teammates got 12 (and benefited from six Washington errors), Young won the game, 12–1.

TRANSACTIONS
1914: Purchased Carl Mays and outfielder Guy Tutwiler from the Providence
      Grays. This was easier to accomplish in that Red Sox owner Lannin
      had also bought the Providence team several weeks earlier.
1960: Released Ray Boone.
1965: Traded Jack Lamabe to the Houston Astros for Darrell Brandon.

DEBUTS

1907: Tris Speaker	1942: Andy Gilbert	1958: Jerry Casale
1920: George Orme	1943: Danny Doyle	1969: Tony Muser
1934: Skinny Graham	1956: Gene Mauch	1996: Walt McKeel

BIRTHDATES
Bunny Madden 1882 (1909–1911); Dave Hillman 1927 (1960–1961);
Stan Williams 1936 (1972); Chad Bradford 1974 (2005)

DEATHS
None yet

September 15

2000 It was only a nine-inning game, but the Red Sox were in a pennant race and so they threw 24 players into the fray, out-manning the Tigers, who used 18 players. They outscored the Tigers, too, 7–6, with a run in the top of the ninth. The Sox used four pinch-hitters, three pinch-runners, five relief pitchers, and made two defensive substitutions.

1999 Rookie Trot Nixon tied it in the top of the ninth with a sac fly, and after 12 innings it was Boston 4, Cleveland 4. Jason Varitek led off the 13th with a home run to right and Trot Nixon hit a homer, too, giving the Red Sox a 6–4 win, the save going to John Wasdin, who'd pitched the 12th and 13th frames.

1996 Tim Wakefield gave up five home runs (three by Chicago first baseman Frank Thomas) but Mo Vaughn and John Valentin each hit a pair, and the Sox win, 9–8. On the season, Wakefield allows a team-record 38 homers, letting Earl Wilson off the hook (Wilson let up 37 HRs in 1964).

1979 Hitting for the cycle is one thing, but doing it in order is something else. Bob Watson hit a single in the second, a double in the fourth, a triple in the eighth, and a homer in the ninth. Completing the cycle made Watson the first player to cycle in both leagues.

1978 The Boston Massacre continued. After being swept four games in a row in Fenway, the Sox visited New York and lost this day's game to Ron Guidry who threw a 4–0 two-hitter. It was his second two-hitter in a row against the Red Sox; he'd thrown one on September 9 as well. The Sox lost the next day, too. Boston had been 52–19 earlier in the season, then gone 26–33. Had they just played .500 ball…

1975 Roger Moret won his 14th game of the year. Working with an 8–0 lead after two innings, he let the Brewers nibble away but was relieved in time and, with relief help from Pole, Burton, and Drago (each of whom let Milwaukee gain one run), the final score stood 9–7.

1974 Though Fred Lynn had appeared in an earlier game, this was his first start, and he hit a home run in the second inning, his first at-bat in his first start. Milwaukee's Gorman Thomas hit a grand slam, though, and Tim Johnson tripled home two more. Luis Tiant sought his 21st win, but in vain, as the Brewers won, 9–5.

1950 In his first start since breaking his elbow in the All-Star Game, Ted Williams hit a three-run homer atop Sportsman's Park's right-field pavilion roof; he also hit three singles, and the Red Sox outscored St. Louis, 12–9. With Ted back in the lineup, Johnny Pesky—despite a .313 average—was benched in favor of Billy Goodman. Goodman had a shot at the batting title and Pesky volunteered to step aside so he could accumulate the requisite at-bats. It worked—Goodman won the AL batting crown. This was even more remarkable in that Goodman never played a regular position, but was a utilityman who played every infield position and the outfield as well.

1935 St. Louis scored five times in the top of the first, but Lefty Grove buckled down until the Sox' sixth. Wes Ferrell pinch-hit for Grove in the sixth and drove in one of six runs that gave the Red Sox the lead and Grove the win.

1928 The Red Sox outhit the White Sox, 14–8, but came up short where it really counts, losing the game, 4–3. Red Ruffing's double was #13 of the season tying Smoky Joe Wood (1912) for the most doubles ever hit in any season by any pitcher in major league history.

1922 The Browns kept the pressure on the Yankees (they finished the season just one game behind New York) by responding to Boston's lone run with five of their own in the seventh, then adding a pair in the next inning. It was a 7–1 final.

1917 How many home runs did Babe Ruth hit in 1917? Two. The second came in the day's 8–3 win, a complete game three-hitter for pitcher Ruth at the Polo Grounds in front of thousands of soldiers who marched back and forth across the field before the game, with military bands playing and flags flying.

1912 Smoky Joe tied Walter Johnson's American League record by winning his 16th consecutive game, 2–1, in the second game of a doubleheader. St. Louis won the first game, 5–4. With darkness approaching, the Browns tied the game 1–1 in the bottom of the seventh. Wood walked in the eighth, moved to second on Harry Hooper's single. Earl Hamilton did not want to pitch to Tris Speaker, so he was walked intentionally. As Hamilton pitched to Duffy Lewis, he uncorked a wild pitch and Wood ran home with the go-ahead run. He shut down St. Louis in the bottom of the inning and earned his 33rd win of 1912.

1911 A 50% interest in the Boston American League baseball club was purchased by James McAleer, immediately after he resigned as manager of the Washington ball club, and Robert McRoy of Chicago. It was assumed that John I. Taylor would no longer be active in running the Red Sox.

1904 Boston swapped first-place status with New York, thanks to a 2–1 win. New York scored first, twice, off Tannehill, but Boston got to Orth more as the game wore on and Tannehill won it both by tripling in the seventh and then beating the throw home when Parent grounded to the third baseman Conroy. Both teams played nine innings in a second game, too, but it had to be called on account of darkness, tied 1–1.

1903 Boston beat New York, 15–3, in the final game of the season between the two franchises. In head-to-head competition, Boston won 13 games and New York won 7. Boston would go on to win the pennant, and proceed to win the very first World Series.

DEBUTS

1912: Ben Van Dyke	1947: Chuck Stobbs
1925: Tom Jenkins,	1956: Rudy Minarcin
Herb Welch	1985: Jeff Sellers
1936: Jennings Poindexter	2003: Adrian Brown

BIRTHDATES
Nick Altrock 1876 (1902–1903); Jean Dubuc 1888 (1918); Fritz Ostermueller 1907 (1934–1940); Dan Smith 1975 (2000)

DEATHS
Frank Chance 1924; Earl Caldwell 1981

September 16

2005 Machado had scored his first major league run just two days earlier. Now Manny Ramirez was up with the bases loaded and Machado on third. The A's positioned five infielders to cut down on the chance of a groundball getting through, but Ramirez was hit by a pitch, forcing in Machado with the winning run.

1978 New York builds up a 3½ game lead over the Red Sox, with a bottom of the ninth 3–2 win. Boston then comes back to life and wins 12 of its next 14 games.

1975 The Red Sox increased their AL East lead to 5½ games over the Orioles as El Tiante shut out the Birds, 2–0. Boston's magic number became 7. Jim Palmer bore the loss, the result of two solo homers by Rico Petrocelli and Carlton Fisk. It was Tiant's 36th shutout but, oddly, the only one so far this year (he would throw one more later in the month).

1972 Luis Tiant threw a three-hit shutout for the Red Sox and Yaz drove in four of Boston's 10 runs. It was Tiant's fifth shutout in his last nine decisions, a stretch in which he had gone 8–1. The Tigers won, too, keeping pace with the Red Sox, just a half-game behind.

1965 It was a strange day. Before Fenway's smallest crowd of the year—1,247 fans, including author Bill Nowlin -- Dave Morehead threw a no-hitter, beating the Indians, 2–0. The only batter to reach base in the entire game was Rocky Colavito, the beneficiary of a second-inning walk. Morehead struck out eight, three less than Cleveland's pitcher, Luis Tiant. The winning run scored in the sixth when Jim Gosger singled and Dalton Jones tripled. Red Sox owner Tom Yawkey visited the clubhouse and told Morehead he would rip up his contract and replace it with another one that paid $1,000 more (the league forbade bonuses). But then Yawkey clumsily stole some of the headlines by firing general manager Mike Higgins, a long-overdue move but one that could have waited another day or two.

1949 The Red Sox won handily, beating the Browns 12–4 as Parnell racked up his 23rd win. Lou Stringer had himself a good day, going 4-for-4 with a home run and a double. After a second-inning double, he took third when Tebbetts reached on a misplayed grounder. Parnell then fouled out to the catcher—and Stringer tagged and scored on the play! Catcher Moss had thrown down to second base to try and get Tebbetts, and Stringer scored when shortstop Sullivan "mishandled the ball." The play was ruled a double steal, with no error pinned on Sullivan.

1948 Bobby Doerr ran up a spectacular errorless streak, and in this game completed his 386th consecutive chance without a miscue.

1931 Sox Recapture Cellar! Lose to Boston, 2 to 1—a sarcastic *Chicago Daily Tribune* article by Westbrook Pegler bore the subhead "Frasier Gets Credit for Defeat." The piece claimed the Chisox had achieved lowest honors once more, but this time were confident of defending the cellar to the bitter end. They traveled to Philadelphia "fully aware they must keep constantly on their hands and keep their heads down if they are to lose." The game against the Red Sox "aroused the disinterest of the customers as no other sporting event" and concessionaire Harry M. Stevens was said to have had a "no hot dog, no bag of peanut game." Marv Olson of the Red Sox made a bid to play worse ball, dropping a pop fly in the eighth, but to no avail— try as he might, he couldn't make his team play any worse than Chicago.

1930 Outfielder Gene Rye is obtained from the Waco, Texas ball club. Born with the surname Mercantelli, Rye was known as "Half-Pint." He caught the attention of the Red Sox in an August 6 Texas League game against Beaumont. Waco was down by four runs in the eighth inning, but scored 18 runs to win the game. Rye homered three times in the one inning—first a solo homer, then a three-run job, and finally a grand slam. He was a holdout before signing for 1931, then broke his wrist on February 27, in the first few days of spring training. He appeared in 17 big league games, batting .179, and completed the season—but never made the majors again.

1916 Don't believe everything you read in the newspaper. So said the *Boston Globe*, issuing a statement that Sox manager Bill Carrigan was neither the author or, nor in any way responsible for, the September 3 column published under his name. The syndicate that supplied columns by various sports figures had been "imposed upon," explained the *Globe*. Carrigan might have taken exception to the description of Sportsman's Park, St. Louis, as "like a hay field. The grass in the outfield was knee high. The infield was shaggy and uncut." The Browns had a team that could run to advantage, and even kept the soil loose, according to the unauthorized ghostwriter.

1915 Both the Red Sox and Tigers had 90 wins under their belt (though Detroit had lost four more games) when they met for four at Fenway. Hooks Dauss held the Red Sox to one run on five hits, while Detroit scored five times before Boston got that one run. The crowd was surly, shouting, booing, and hissing at Ty Cobb from the start. In the eighth inning, Sox reliever Carl Mays, no shrinking violet himself, threw two balls that Cobb thought were intended as beanballs, so Cobb threw his bat at Mays. Mays then hit Cobb on the wrist; an aggressive baserunner as always, Cobb came around to score. At game's end (6–1, Detroit) the bleacher fans rushed Cobb, throwing wads of paper at him, and only a wedge of policemen diving into the crowd rescued the embattled Georgia Peach.

1911 Cleveland got 12 hits in two games, but zero runs. Smoky Joe shut them out, 6–0, in the first game on four hits, and Buck O'Brien shut them down, 3–0, despite yielding eight hits, in the second. O'Brien struck out 12.

1904 On September 14, Boston hosted a doubleheader against New York, losing 3–1 and tying the second game, 1–1. On the 15th, the two teams squared off again, and Boston won, 3–2, and tied another time, 1–1. The third twin bill was a classic matchup—Jack Chesbro won his 35th game against Bill Dinneen in the first game, and Cy Young beat Ned Garvin in the second.

1903 Boston clinched a tie for the pennant, beating up on Cleveland, scoring at least once in each one of the eight innings they bat, to win 14–7. Boston almost doubles Cleveland's 12 hits with 23 of their own.

Boston and Pittsburg sign the agreement that will see them play each other in head-to-head post-season play in the very first World Series.

DEBUTS

1909: Paul Howard	1972: Dwight Evans	1990: Jim Pankovits
1916: Jack Lewis	1980: Reid Nichols	1997: Robinson Checo
1924: John Woods	1982: Mike Brown	2000: Steve Ontiveros
1934: Spike Merena	1988: Carlos Quintana	

BIRTHDATES
George Orme 1891 (1920); Buster Mills 1908 (1937); Mike Garman 1949 (1969–1973); Roger Moret 1949 (1970–1975); Chad Harville 1976 (2005)

DEATHS
None yet

September 17

2004 Yankees ace reliever Mariano Rivera blows another save, yielding ninth-inning homers to both Orlando Cabrera and Johnny Damon in a 3–2 Red Sox victory.

2001 Carl Everett had turned up late for a workout, and new manager Joe Kerrigan **?!** sent him home, to make a point. Everett replied with loud obscenities, calling Kerrigan a racist and a drunk. Everett was suspended for four days, but in fact never played for the Red Sox again.

1998 The Red Sox edge Baltimore, 3–2, with two runs in the top of the 10th, giving Eckersley the win and thanks to Flash Gordon, who registered his 39th consecutive save, setting an American League record.

1997 Mo Vaughn got Ron Mahay a win with a two-run homer in the bottom of the eighth, giving the Red Sox a 4–2 lead (the final was 4–3). Vaughn had been booed when the lineups were announced, and was booed every time up, in response to his comments that he didn't want to play for the Red Sox after '97.

1983 When Rick Miller pinch-hit and singled in the seventh of a 3–2 win over Detroit, it was his final pinch-hit of an extraordinary year in which he batted 16-for-35 as a pinch-hitter, a .457 average. The only American Leaguers to ever do better were Smead Jolley of the 1931 White Sox and Gates Brown of the 1968 Tigers.

1978 The Red Sox finally won one against the Yankees, after dropping six straight games to New York (and nine of their last 10 overall). The 7–3 win over New York seemed too little, too late, but kept them in the race. George Scott was suffering an 0-for-36 stretch, but his key double in the eighth helped in the three-run inning. Yaz had only hit three homers since July 15, but came through with one this night. There were signs the team still had a little life left.

1970 All it took was one Baltimore win or one Yankees loss, and the Orioles would clinch the AL East. Baltimore lost its game, 2–0, to last-place Washington, but the Yankees fumbled in the field and bumbled on the basepaths. Jack Aker, pitching for New York, hit Billy Conigliaro after George Scott had singled; pinch-hitter Tom Satriano singled in Scott for a 5–4 lead that Bobby Bolin held. The Orioles backed into the pennant.

1960 Ted Williams won the game, 2–1, with his two-run homer in the sixth off Pedro Ramos. It was the next-to-last home run of Teddy Ballgame's long career. The game ran exactly 100 minutes long.

1953 Ellis Kinder broke the AL record, set in 1908 by Chicago's Big Ed Walsh, for most appearances when he threw the ninth inning in relief of Sid Hudson. It was his 67th appearance of the season, and he helped the Sox hold the 2–1 lead over the Detroit Tigers.

1952 The Red Sox asked an outfielder to start the game, but he lost. It was one of two pitching performances for George Schmees in his career, both with Boston. His lifetime ERA was 3.00, better than the team average.

1939 Ted Williams hit his 28th homer of his rookie year off Thornton Lee. On September 2, 1960, Ted hit one off Don Lee, Thornton's son, who was just five years old in 1939.

1938 Jimmie Foxx hit home run #45, but the Indians beat Boston, 5–4, as Big Jeff Heath hit a homer and three singles, and Hal Trosky's seventh-inning double drove in Heath with the winner.

1934 George Edward "Lefty" Hockette made his major league debut a memorable one, pitching a no-hitter through seven innings in St. Louis, as the Red Sox built up a 3–0 lead. A single by Grube in the eighth and another by Bejma in the ninth proved the only hits, and Hockette had himself a two-hit 3–0 shutout. He was one of just six Sox starters to shut out an opponent in their debut game. The others were: Rube Kroh, Larry Pape, Buck O'Brien, Dave Ferriss, Dave Morehead, and Billy Rohr.

1931 Right fielder Earl Webb hit his 64th double in the first game, tying the major league mark set by George Burns in 1926. In the second game, Webb doubled again, to set a new single-season doubles mark at 65. It was Webb's birthday, the day he turned 34. He hit two more before the end of the year; Webb's record of 67 still stands. The Sox won the first game, 9–3, after scoring seven times in the first inning, but a bases-loaded single in the second game scored a run for Cleveland in the top of the ninth to give them a 2–1 lead. The Red Sox loaded the bases in the bottom of the ninth, but couldn't push a run across.

1925 The Wingfield–Zahniser combo pull off a rarity for the Red Sox in the 1920s—a double shutout. Hosting St. Louis, Ted Wingfield shut out the Browns, 2–0, on a four-hitter. Paul Zahniser yielded twice as many hits, but still no runs, and the Red Sox scored twice as many runs in the first game, for a 4–0 win.

1920 For a game that ended 14–13 in the 12th inning to be described as a "slow, listless game" seems surprising, but that is how precisely the *Atlanta Constitution* portrayed it. Detroit used five "recruit pitchers" but the Sox only mustered nine hits in the game, while the Tigers got 19 hits. The Red Sox collected 20 walks, however. Tiger Bobby Veach was 6-for-6, with a cycle. It was, as the *Constitution* headlined its account, a "weird game."

1916 Boston took Chicago's second-place slot by topping the White Sox, 6–2, at Comiskey before a crowd of 40,000, said to be the largest crowd in South Side baseball. Babe Ruth allowed two runs to Chicago in the first, but not one more in the following eight innings. For Ruth, it was his 20th win, making him the youngest pitcher ever to win 20 games. Ruth was 21 years, 7 months old. In 1939, the 20-year-old Bob Feller pushed Ruth down to #2 on the list.

Though Boston had won, Sox President Lannin lamented the handling of the crowd in Chicago, and the umpiring. "We are getting the worst of everything," he complained, adding, "If we are robbed of the American League championship— and it looks as if we might be—I will get out of baseball at the end of the year." The Red Sox won the pennant, and the World Series, but Lannin quit anyway. (See November 1, 1916.)

1910 Though the White Sox got only three hits in the game, they scored four times in the bottom of the first, the fourth run coming on a triple steal which surprised batterymates Ed Karger and Bill Carrigan. Chicago held on for a 4–3 win.

1915 There was worry about how Ty Cobb would be received after he had to be rushed off the field by police the day before, but the boos were drowned out by thousands of Red Sox fans clapping for the Tigers star. Cobb doffed his hat. Dutch Leonard tamed the Tigers with a one-hitter through eight, just a "dinky hit" by Oscar Vitt, while Boston rolled up a seven-run lead that only shrunk marginally with Cobb's two-run homer in the top of the ninth.

1903 Boston had scored in every inning the day before, and did it again every inning in this game, too—except the seventh and final one when Dusty Rhoads, who went the distance, somehow retired the side without a run. Boston had scored in each of the last three innings of the September 15 game against New York and then for 14 consecutive innings against Cleveland, for a total of 17 straight innings. No one had more than two hits for Boston, but in fact everyone for Boston got two hits with the exception of Hobe Ferris, who had to be content with his second home run in as many games, and pitcher George Winter, who was 0-for-4. As a courtesy, Cleveland captain Larry Lajoie allowed Cy Young to run for Farrell both times he hit safely. 14–3 was the final score.

DEBUTS

1902: Nick Altrock
1906: Chet Chadbourne
1923: Clarence Blethen
1927: Frank Bennett,
Frank Bushey

1928: Casper Asbjornson
1930: Bob Kline
1931: John Smith
1934: George Hockette

1954: Guy Morton
1955: Frank Malzone
1991: Wayne Housie
1992: Scott Taylor

BIRTHDATES

Ed Hearn 1888 (1910); Earl Webb 1897 (1930–1932); Orlando Cepeda 1937 (1973)

DEATHS

Hack Miller 1971; Leon Culberson 1989

September 18

2001 In a game played under unprecedented security following the September 11 terrorist attacks, the Red Sox won the first game after baseball resumed, 7–2, as Manny Ramirez hit his 40th home run. Everyone from ballplayers to vendors to fans joined in singing a rousing "America the Beautiful" during the seventh-inning stretch.

1998 There were 32 hits and 20 runs; unfortunately, the White Sox had 11 of the 20. Boston had nine extra-base hits, three more than Chicago, but the 11–9 score did not mirror the extra-base hit totals.

1996 Reenacting his 20-K game 10 years ago, Roger Clemens of the Red Sox struck out 20 Tigers in Detroit without walking anyone. With a little help from catcher Bill Haselman (two RBI), The Rocket won, 4–0. Two games: 40 K, 0 BB.

1993 The Yankees were down to their last out. They were behind, 3–1, with two outs in the bottom of the ninth. There was a man on first, but Greg Harris got Mike Stanley to fly out to left field. Mike Greenwell caught it for the final out—but it was ruled invalid. A young fan had run on the field and third base umpire Tim Welke had called time, so Stanley was given new life. Seeing another pitch that looked good to him, he swung again and this time he singled. So did Wade Boggs. Dion James walked, and Don Mattingly singled to both tie the game and win it, 4–3. Roger Clemens issued a threat to fans that "it could get ugly" if security brought another fan through the Red Sox dugout. The following day, another "nitwit du jour" frolicked on the field, but the Red Sox won.

1990 The Sox lost undisputed control of first place, when Tom Bolton lost his no-hitter and the game. After 6⅔ innings, Bolton finally surrendered a single to Cal Ripken, but on the next batter, Jody Reed's seemingly-sure double play throw hit Ripken and the inning continued. Bolton gave up three singles in all—and a three-run homer to Diego Segui. Baltimore won, 4–1.

1985 With Al Nipper giving up just one run on six hits in a complete game effort, he didn't really need all seven of the runs batted in by his catcher, Rich Gedman. Geddy was on fire, and hit for the cycle as the Red Sox rolled over the Toronto Blue Jays, 13–1.

1977 The Red Sox beat Baltimore 10–4, and part of the reason was Ted Cox. It was the 22-year-old's debut, in which he not only went 4-for-4 but was in the on-deck circle with a shot at a fifth hit, when Rick Burleson grounded out to end the game. (See September 19, 1977 for how Cox picked up where he'd left off.)

By striking out twice in the game, Butch Hobson struck out his 153rd time and broke Goerge Scott's club record. He extended his record the very next day, and wound up the season with 162. Hobson's record was surpassed by Mark Bellhorn's 177 K's in 2004.

1967 With just 11 games to go, every win counts. The Red Sox scored three times in the first but couldn't crow for long, since the Tigers tied it in the second. Each team scored once more, and the game was tied 4–4 after seven. The Tigers took a one-run lead in the eighth, but Yaz hit homer #40 to tie it back up in the ninth. Dalton Jones homered in the 10th for a 6–5 win; Jones had a 4-for-5 day. At day's end, the Red Sox, the Tigers, and the Twins were in a three-way tie for first place with identical 85–66 records and 10 games left on the schedule.

1963 In the third inning, Earl Wilson threw a wild pitch—his 21st WP of the season, setting a new club record. The 21 also led the league in '63. It didn't lead to a run, though. The Red Sox lost the game, 4–3 to Chicago, but the loss was reliever Arnold Earley's.

1960 Bill Monbouquette gave up just one run, in the first. Willie Tasby's solo home run in the fourth tied it for the Red Sox and Lou Clinton's single in the sixth won it, driving in two for the 3–1 win.

1958 The first two Kansas City batters homered off Red Sox pitcher Ted Bowsfield. Pete Runnels goes 0-for-4 while Ted Williams gets a hit in three at-bats; the two are contending for the batting championship and Runnels dropped from .322 to .319, just one point ahead of Ted at .318.

1938 The Yankees won the pennant despite losing bath halves of a doubleheader, because the Red Sox were rained out of theirs. In this era, games which were rained out were not made up. The Yankees clinched, but imagine the clubhouse celebration after dropping two games to the St. Louis Browns.

1934 St. Louis Browns pitcher Buck Newsom walked seven Sox, but threw a nine-inning no-hitter. Boston scored once in the second on two walks, an error, and a fielder's choice. Wes Ferrell objected to umpire Lou Kolls calling him out on a called third strike, and "unleashed a wordy barrage in more than one language," according to a brief story in the *Globe* a couple of days later. Rick "covered his brother's retreat with a vocal drumfire" and was routed as well. Mound duties were assigned to Rube Walberg, who gave up just one run in the sixth. With the score tied, the game went into extra innings. Newsom walked Max Bishop and Billy Werber, and then gave up his first hit of the game, a single to Bob Johnson, who drove in the go-ahead run. Walberg closed it out.

1916 The White Sox seemed to forego several chances to score, and errors resulted in three unearned runs, giving the 4–3 win to the Red Sox, though to be fair, Boston out-hit Chicago 10–6. Ernie Shore pitched well enough to get the win, and Boston edged into first place by .003 over Detroit. After the win, Boston took the train to Detroit and won all three games there.

1915 As the pennant race neared its conclusion, the Tigers and Red Sox battled through 11 innings of scoreless ball, Stan Coveleskie pitching for Detroit and Ernie Shore for Boston. The game was reported as played brilliantly, both in the field and tactically, and both pitchers seemed to get better as the game grew longer. In the bottom of the 12th, the Sox filled the bases with one out and manager Bill Carrigan called on himself to pinch-hit for Shore. He hit a tailor-made double play ball to Donie Bush at shortstop, but the second baseman, Ralph Young, dropped the ball and Duffy Lewis scored with the winning run. 1–0.

1912 Looking out the window at the rains in Cleveland, the Red Sox win the pennant. When Philadelphia lost, the Red Sox were in a position that even if they lost every one of the remaining 15 games, they would still have the pennant. Accordingly, the Sox informed New York that they would not make up a rainout from earlier in the season.

United States President William Howard Taft did not adopt any false impartiality. He said he'd be "down among the fans" and rooting for the Red Sox at the first World Series game in Boston. A Washington fan, Taft transferred his allegiance to the American League contender.

1908 He came within one out of throwing a no-hitter against the Sox in 1904 (September 27), but this time pulled it off. Bob Rhoads pitched a no-hitter for Cleveland, beating Boston, 2–1. His opposition was Frank Arellanes of the Red Sox, who'd only doled out five hits. "Dusty" Rhoads walked two, hit one, and his teammates committed two errors.

1903 Bill Dinneen won his 20th game of the season, but it wasn't at all easy. He gave up five runs in the first two innings, and was losing 6–0 in the fifth, but Boston scored three in the fifth, one in the seventh, and one in the eighth. Meanwhile, Dinneen had settled down, allowing just three hits after the second inning. In the last-chance last of the ninth, Jimmy Collins singled between third and short, but Chick Stahl (3-for-3 in the game at this point) fouled out. Buck Freeman reached safely on a hard-hit ball that took a bad bounce on the shortstop. Freeman tried to steal second but was ruled out. Freddy Parent, who'd tripled the inning before, then hit a deep fly ball to center that just escaped Iott's effort to catch it. With his cap clutched in his hand, Parent raced around the bases and scored, winning the game on an inside-the-park home run. Boston 7, Cleveland 6.

DEBUTS

1911: Casey Hageman   1966: Mike Andrews, Reggie Smith
1919: Joe Wilhoit   1969: Carlton Fisk
1923: Ike Boone   1977: Ted Cox
1966: Garry Roggenburk

BIRTHDATES

Jerry Mallett 1935 (1959); Ken Brett 1948 (1967–1971); Sam Bowen 1952 (1977–1980)

DEATHS

Jake Stahl 1922; Doug Smith 1973; Marv Grissom 2005

September 19

2005 Craig Hansen made it all the way to the major leagues without ever having even one run scored off him in professional baseball. Signed soon after graduating college, Hansen had only appeared in 11 games at the professional level before being asked to pitch in the final two weeks of the 2005 season, with the pennant on the line. His debut game saw him throw one inning, and set down the Devil Rays 1-2-3, with two strikeouts.

1997 The Red Sox scored once in the first inning. Butch Henry pitched 7⅔ innings and never did let up a run. Tom Gordon closed out the eighth, but before he could record an out in the ninth, Chicago loaded the bases, and Albert Belle hit a grand slam. The Red Sox responded, though, with three runs in the bottom of the ninth, on pinch-hit home runs by Curtis Pride (solo) and Scott Hatteberg (one on, three batters later), for a 4–4 tie that sent the game into extra innings. In the 10th, Frank Thomas singled home a run, and Boston couldn't match it. Chicago 5, Boston 4. Nomar Garciaparra was 2-for-5 with two doubles, giving him 348 total bases, breaking the Red Sox rookie record set by Ted Williams in 1939. Nomar would add 17 more TB's by the end of the year. Pride, who is deaf, hit his home run in his first-ever plate appearance for the Red Sox.

1996 Roger Clemens shut out the Tigers, 4–0, for his 38th Red Sox shutout. The Rocket is tied with Cy Young for the most shutouts by a Red Sox pitcher, just as he is tied at 192 with Young for the most wins by a Red Sox pitcher. Clemens started more games than any other Sox starter—382 to Young's 297. He walked more batters than any Red Sox pitcher, with 856. Young walked much less than half that number, 299. Clemens struck out 2,590 opponents, almost double the mark of any other Boston pitcher.

1991 Mike Barnicle devoted his column in today's *Globe* to expressing his shock at hearing female fans at Fenway call out to Phil Plantier, "Nice buns, Phil!" His column was crafted as a bit of a weak (not to mention insensitive) rejoinder to colleague Bella English's earlier column decrying boorish bleacherites handling inflatable life-size nude female dolls earlier in the summer.

1977 Rookie Ted Cox was 4-for-4 in his debut in Baltimore on the 18th. The Sox hosted the Yankees at Fenway on September 19. Cox was the second batter in the bottom of the first, and singled off New York's Ed Figueroa. He was second up in the third and singled again—six hits in his first six major league at-bats.

1970 The Sox won two from the Senators, 7–3 and 11–3. Washington manager Ted Williams watched both Billy Conigliaro (#17, in the fourth) and Tony Conigliaro (#31, in the seventh) homer in the second game. Senators slugger Frank Howard struck out five times in the first game, and was 0-for-3 in the second.

1967 The Red Sox scored three runs in the top of the ninth to come from behind and beat the Tigers, in Detroit, 4–2. The win dropped the Tigers all the way to fourth place. The Red Sox and Twins remained tied for first. A second-inning Sox run had been set up by a wild pitch, and it was former Boston pitcher Earl Wilson's bases-loaded wild pitch that permitted the go-ahead run to score in the ninth.

1961 Ted Williams and Lee Howard were married in a quiet ceremony in Cambridge, Massachusetts. Tongue in cheek? Ted listed his occupation as "public relations." It was the second marriage for both, and it didn't last long.

1953 Scoring three times in late innings, the Sox beat the Yankees, 3–0, but most of the credit goes to southpaw Mel Parnell, who held New York scoreless for the fourth time in 1953. Only Walter Johnson had shut out another team four times in one season—and that was back in 1908. And Parnell did this to the Yankees!

1951 Early Wynn beat the Red Sox and won his 20th game of the year with ease, 15–2. Larry Doby was 0-for-0 at the plate, but scored four runs (he was walked five times—half of Cleveland's 10 bases on balls).

1948 One day after setting the major league record for consecutive games by a second baseman without an error, Doerr made an error in the first inning of the second game against the Tigers. Over 73 games, he had rung up 182 putouts plus 229 assists—411 chances without an error.

The Red Sox announced the purchase of Lou Stringer, manager of the Hollywood Stars of the Pacific Coast League. The PCL season had just ended, and Stringer joined the Sox as a backup infielder in time to get into four games. He stuck with Boston in 1949 and 1950, too.

1945 Pigeons played a role in a wild first game against the Athletics. In the top of the third, Red Sox center fielder Tom McBride mistook a pigeon for the ball and chased after it. Sam Chapman's double hit off the center field wall "at least thirty feet away from the pursuing outfielder." (Associated Press) In the bottom of the third, Philadelphia right fielder Hal Peck ran down Skeeter Newsome's hit to right and fired the ball in toward second base and hit a pigeon, killing it. This, too, may have helped Philadephia. Frederick Lieb wrote in *The Sporting News* that the throw was wild and yet when it struck the pigeon, it fell in such a way that Newsome was thrown out at second. The A.P. story reports the fatality, but credits Newsome with a double. The Red Sox scored four times in the bottom of the eighth for an 11–10 win. The second game was less eventful, as Otey Clark shut out the Athletics, 3–0. It was the only shutout of his short career.

1940 When Jimmie Foxx played third base against the Browns, it was the third position he'd played in six days. Double X had caught on the 14th and played first base on the 15th. The only position he'd not played in his 15-season career at that point was second base, the position he'd played in high school.

1933 The Indians had runners on first and second with only one out, and good-hitting Wes Ferrell at the plate. Rick Ferrell of the Red Sox was catching Bob Kline. Wes ducked to get out of the way of Kline's pitch and the ball caught his bat, landing fair in front on the plate. Rick jumped on the ball and fired to third base to get one out, and Bucky Walters threw to first to wipe out Wes. Later in the game, Wes drove in two, but Boston won, 4–3.

1923 Sox pitcher Howard Ehmke is lifted in the bottom of the ninth inning for a pinch-hitter, Al DeVormer, who jumps on the first pitch he sees and singles to left field to win the game for the Red Sox, 2–1. DeVormer also won the game for Ehmke, who now has 20 wins on the year. He's a 20-game winner on a team that only wins 61 games all season long: the last-place Red Sox (61–91).

1912 The rain may have helped Cleveland twice, though both games were likely lost causes from the Red Sox perspective. Boston trailed 9–3 when rain caused the game to be called after five innings. Both teams waited an hour, and when the rains let up, they decided to play the second game. Cleveland built up a 6–0 lead through six, when this game, too, was called—though on account of darkness.

1903 The first official announcement of the dates and arrangements for the post-season games between Pittsburg and Boston was made this day. Many American League managers picked Boston to win. Cy Young won his 28th (and final) game of the season. A 13–3 win over the White Sox brought the Boston run total for the week to 63 runs in six games; Boston had 18 doubles, 13 triples, and nine home runs, with a team batting average of .388. Though Boston jumped out to a 4–0 lead, Chicago came back with two and after 6½ the score was 5–3, in no way a guaranteed win. Boston had 16 hits, with Young contributed two himself. Six of them came in the Boston seventh—three singles, two triples, and a Hobe Ferris home run resulted in six runs. Freeman hit a homer in the eighth.

1902 Cy Young makes his 43rd start of the 1902 season, but he lost to Rube Waddell, 6–4. In 1902, Young threw 41 complete games and finished with a record of 32–11, down one win from the year before.

TRANSACTIONS
1977: Acquired Bob Bailey from the Cincinnati Reds in trade for minor leaguer Frank Newcomer and cash. Bailey got two at-bats before season's end, then hit .191 the following year. In 1984, a sportswriter cast one vote for Bailey in Hall of Fame polling.

DEBUTS

1911: Tony Tonneman	1934: Al Niemiec	1997: Curtis Pride
1914: Larry Pratt	1948: Neill Sheridan	1998: Carlos Valdez
1922: Dick Reichle	1959: Jerry Mallett	2001: James Lofton
1925: Joe Kiefer	1964: Bobby Guindon	2005: Craig Hansen
1931: George Stumpf	1981: John Lickert	

BIRTHDATES
Jack Ryan 1884 (1909); Stuffy McInnis 1890 (1918–1921); Murray Wall 1926 (1957–1959); Bob Turley 1930 (1963); Mike Derrick 1943 (1970); Lenny DiNardo 1979 (2004–2005)

DEATHS
Slim Harriss 1963; Bill Butland 1997

September 20

2005 Boston batters tied a league record when four batters each had four hits—David Ortiz, Manny Ramirez, Trot Nixon, and Jason Varitek. Both Ortiz and Ramirez hit a pair of home runs, and for Ortiz they were his 45th and 46th of the season, tying him with Jim Rice for second-most homers ever in a single season for the Red Sox (Foxx, with 50, still ranks #1). The second blast was #27 on the road for Ortiz, eclipsing the old mark of 26 hit by Ted Williams in 1957. The Red Sox won the game in Tampa, 15–2.

2003 The Red Sox were invoved in discussions that might result in playing regular season games in Europe, perhaps Italy or England, according to president Larry Lucchino. MLB was planning both for what became the World Baseball Classic, and the possible visit of a couple of teams to play in Europe. MLBPA head Donald Fehr was also in favor of more international play.

2001 Calvin Pickering had a 3-for-4 game with a home run to win a tight 2–1 game over Tampa Bay. The supersized Virgin Islands native first baseman (listed at 290 pounds) slugged the first pitch he saw from Ryan Rupe, and hit it a ton.

1995 With a 3–2 win over Milwaukee, the Red Sox clinched the AL East, holding a 10½ game lead over second-place New York. Mo Vaughn celebrated by riding a police horse on the field at Fenway. He said Roger Clemens goaded him into it. Clemens was the first to ride, but another eight Sox took their turns as well.

1994 He hadn't been managing anyone, anyhow, since the players' strike ended the 1994 season back on August 11, but Butch Hobson was fired as manager of the Red Sox. Red Sox CEO John Harrington would now oversee the hiring of a new field manager, his first. Hobson, Peter Gammons wrote, "was always Haywood Sullivan's guy."

1988 With three hits (he was 3-for-3 and walked the other two times he was up), Wade Boggs passed the 200-hit mark for the sixth straight year. He was the first player to do so in the 20th century. In 1989, he did it again. Boggs walked 125 times, too, the third straight year he'd made 200 hits and also collected 100 walks; only Lou Gehrig before him had done that.

1976 They never did it at Navin Field, they never did it at Briggs Stadium. The venue was the same; only the name changed. Detroit's 1912 ballpark was Tiger Stadium when the Sox visited in 1976—and won every single game of the year as the visitors. Boston took all nine games from the Tigers.

1968 Carl Yastrzemski had three hits (a home run and two singles) in his quest to retain the batting title he'd won in '67. Jim Lonborg had a complete game win, and drove in one run—the margin of victory in Boston's 4–3 win over New York. One of the Yankees' runs was a home run by Mickey Mantle, the last one he would ever hit—#536.

1967 Yaz was 4-for-5 (including homer #41 in the sixth) and was leading the AL in average, RBI, and home runs. In the top of the ninth, with two outs, he singled, then took second on a wild pitch, and scored the go-ahead run on Reggie Smith's single. Rico Petrocelli had a two-run homer in the sixth, too.

Rooting against the Red Sox was Jackie Robinson. "Because of Boston owner Tom Yawkey, I'd like to see them lose," Robinson said. "He is probably one of the most bigoted guys in organized baseball." (*Chicago Defender*)

1960 Ted Williams had to leave the game in the first inning, after he fouled a ball off his ankle. Carroll Hardy pinch-hit for Ted—the only time Ted was pinch-hit for. Hardy hit into a double play. In his time in the majors, Hardy also pinch-hit for Roger Maris and Carl Yastrzemski. The Orioles won the game, by mistake—Brooks Robinson was trying to get out of the way of a pitch and his bat plopped the ball into play for a run-scoring single.

1955 Frank Malzone got his feet wet on the 17th, running for Grady Hatton in the ninth. But his first start came in this day's doubleheader, and he went 6-for-10. Despite his bat, Boston dropped both games to the visiting Orioles.

Ted Williams homered on the day and finished the season with 28 homers. He only struck out 24 times. It was the fourth year in which Ted had more homers than strikeouts.

1952 Mel Parnell lost to the Senators. That sort of thing happens from time to time—losing a game—but it had been a while. The last time the Senators beat Marvelous Mel was May 28, 1948. He'd beaten them 17 times in a row.

1949 Mel Parnell tied Babe Ruth's team record by winning his 24th game of the season. Ruth was the last lefty who had won 24 games for the Red Sox, when he was 24–13 in 1917. Parnell topped the mark on the 25th, with his 25th.

1947 Johnny Pesky was 2-for-4 and 2-for-4, in the two games of the day's doubleheader. He finished the day with 202 hits, surpassing the 200-hit mark for the third year in a row. Pesky did it despite missing three years while serving in the Navy during World War II. No other American League player had ever hit 200 hits his first three years in baseball.

1927 Can I get a little help here? Red Sox fielders had 41 assists in the doubleheader against Detroit, but still lost both games.

1926 The Red Sox won their final game of the year, #46, breaking up a string of what otherwise would have been 11 straight losses to close out the season. They were last in the league (46–107), last in batting average, last in slugging, last in stolen bases, last in ERA, and just missed being last in attendance (the Browns drew 1,169 fewer patrons.)

1919 It was Babe Ruth Day at Fenway Park, and as it turned out his last day in town as a Boston Red Sox. Ruth hit his 27th homer of the season, tying the 1884 record held by Ned Williamson, and won the game for Boston. The following year, Ruth complained that Harry Frazee had made him "buy my wife's ticket to the game," adding, "Fifteen thousand fans show up and all I got was a cigar."

1915 The Tigers and the Red Sox were running neck and neck in the race for the pennant, until Detroit arrived in Boston on the 16th for a four-game set. The Tigers trailed the Sox by two games. By the time Babe Ruth led the Red Sox to a 3–2 win on the 20th, taking three out of four, the Tigers were four games behind. Ruth was 1-for-3 at the plate. Boston would win the pennant by 2½ games.

1912 Joe Wood finally lost a game, for the first time in 78 days. After winning 16 straight, tying Walter Johnson's record, Smoky Joe lost to the Tigers, 6–4. He walked four Detroiters in a row in the fourth, gave up seven hits, and just wasn't his usual self. Tim Murnane of the *Boston Globe* acknowledged that Wood "labored under a great strain, and has evidently been creeping up to a nervous break." When the Tigers loaded the bases, shortstop Marty Krug let Ty Cobb's routine fly ball bounce off his chest, and two runs scored. Did Krug thereby help the Sox win the World Series? The *Washington Post* later wrote Wood "would probably have been a wreck" by the start of the Series had he kept winning.

TRANSACTIONS
2000: Acquired Jesus Pena from the White Sox for a PTBNL (who was named on March 19, 2001, and turned out to be Mike Rupp).

DEBUTS
1906: Frank Oberlin	1948: Lou Stringer	1978: John LaRose
1929: Joe Cicero,	1950: Charlie Maxwell	1984: Jim Dorsey
Ed Connolly	1955: Haywood Sullivan	2005: Hanley Ramirez

BIRTHDATES
Ed Phillips 1944 (1970); Chris Snopek 1970 (1998)

DEATHS
Tillie Walker 1959

September 21

2000 Showing a stunning lack of support for his manager, GM Dan Duquette threw his support behind outfielder Carl Everett, despite Everett's 10-game suspension for bumping umpire Ron Kulpa, his profane shouting match with manager Jimy Williams, and assorted run-ins with coaches, teammates, and reporters. Everett had turned up late for practice in late September—while the team was trying to make the playoffs—but Duquette would not discipline him. "I think the bottom line is how you perform on the field," said Duquette. Williams might normally have quit, but said he would not walk out on his players. Two days later, on the 23rd, Williams rebuked the Duke, saying, "If I was general manager, I certainly would back the manager. If you can't back the manager, you probably need to get rid of him."

1999 Pedro Martinez struck out 12 Blue Jays and accomplished a couple of marks in doing so (in addition to winning his 22nd game of the season, against just four losses). He reached the 300-strikeout mark on the year, topping Roger Clemens' 291-K Red Sox record. In so doing, Pedro joined Randy Johnson as the only two active pitchers who had struck out at least 300 batters in both leagues. Pedro finished the year with 313 K's.

1985 Wade Boggs tied and broke Tris Speaker's club record by hitting his 222nd and 223rd hits in the 7–6 Boston win over the Tigers. Mostly a singles hitter, the 223rd hit was Boggs' 185th single, breaking the since-eclipsed American League record for singles set in 1980 by Willie Wilson.

1984 Rookie Jim Traber made his major league debut twice—once before the game, singing the National Anthem, then during the game as the DH for the Orioles. He hit all the notes in the Anthem, but just one single in his 1-for-4 debut against Oil Can Boyd. That wasn't so bad, really, as the rest of the Orioles only mustered four other hits while The Can shut them out, 8–0, striking out nine.

1975 The Red Sox reduced their magic number to five when Denny Doyle hit a bases-loaded double in the top of the ninth, driving in two runs against Detroit to win the game, but suffered damage that probably cost them the World Series when Vern Ruhle's second-inning fastball hit and broke Jim Rice's left hand.

1972 The AL East pennant race couldn't get much tighter without being a draw. Boston bowed to the Tigers, 10–3, leaving the Red Sox with a winning percentage of .54545 and the Tigers just a bit more than half a point lower at .54482. Pitcher Joe Coleman helped his own cause, driving in three of the 10 runs. Detroit scored four runs in the very first inning, and it was off to the races.

1968 Yankee Stadium fooled with minor-league attractions like an egg-throwing contest and wheelbarrow races before the game, but it paid off with a large crowd, who were largely disappointed when Red Sox righty Ray Culp held the Yankees hitless through six. The 1–0 shutout concluded as a no-hitter only wrecked by Roy White's single in the seventh. It was the third shutout in a row racked up by Ray. The *New York Times* intoned afterward that "the egg-throwing contest was, without question, the greatest ever held in Yankee Stadium." The *Times* devoted seven paragraphs to its coverage of this important competition, won by Russ Nixon and Garry Roggenburk of the Red Sox. You could look it up.

1967 The Sox were tied for the lead in the standings as they amassed a 6–1 lead in Cleveland, then barely held on as the Indians made it 6–5 before a one-hour rain delay in the ninth and a perfect inning by reliever John Wyatt closed the game.

1963 Hammerin' Harmon Killebrew of the Twins tied the AL record by homering four times in a doubleheader, three in the 13–4 Twins-won first game and once in their 11–2 loss in the second. Yaz walked twice, giving him 93 walks on the season. He'd walk two more times, but 93 was enough to give him the league lead at season's end. Yaz finished the season leading the league with 183 hits. One would think the hits leader would often be first in walks as well, but apparently Yaz in 1963 was the only American Leaguer to ever lead the league in both categories in the same season.

1958 The Red Sox beat the Senators, in Boston, by 2–0, the same 2–0 score as the day before and the day before that. Ted Williams was called out on a third strike, and was so angry at himself that he flung a bat carelessly. It sailed 75 feet and into the stands where it hit a woman on the head. The bat hit Joe Cronin's housekeeper, Gladys Heffernan. Williams apologized profusely. As she was being taken to the hospital for precautionary X-rays, Heffernan said she knew he didn't mean to hit anyone. From the hospital, the generous Gladys added, "I don't see why they had to boo Ted. I felt awfully sorry for him after it happened." Williams played out the game, 1-for-3 with a double. He was fined, and also gave Ms. Heffernan an expensive gift by way of further apology.

1956 The Yankees left 20 runners on base. Three times, they left the bases loaded. And Boston made five errors. But the Red Sox still won, 13–7.

1937 Nothing like a little 10-run rally to brighten Lefty Grove's day. And it was by no means his best day, giving up seven runs to the Detroit Tigers (five from a pair of Hank Greenberg homers). It was 1–1, with two outs and nobody on, when Joe Cronin needled opposing starter Boots Poffenberger. Before the game, Poffenberger had called Cronin "Showboat" for reasons no one could determine, mystifying him. Taken aback and speechless, Cronin later asked Poffenberger if he could play well under artificial light and that he'd better get used to it because he'd be playing night games in lower level Texas League ball before too long. The count was 0–2 against him when Cronin started it up again, yelling that the electric lights might hurt the pitcher's eyes. Poffenberger fell apart, hitting Cronin, then giving up seven runs, including a Ben Chapman grand slam. Cronin hit a bases-loaded double, just a few inches shy of a second grand slam. The Sox scored 10 times in the fifth, all they needed in the 12–7 win.

1931 Dutch Leonard's wife Sibyl (a former vaudeville dancer known as Muriel Worth) sued him for divorce in Fresno Superior Court, alleging that he "has been cold and indifferent" to her. It was further charged that he wouldn't go places with her and didn't treat her visiting guests hospitably.

1930 In the bottom of the ninth, Cleveland's Wes Ferrell scored the tying run to keep himself and the Indians in the game, but then gave up five runs to the Red Sox in the top of the 10th, and Boston won, 9–4.

1928 Red Sox pitcher Red Ruffing hit a three-run homer in the seventh to convert the 3–2 St. Louis lead to the 5–3 deficit that proved the final score.

1922 He only appeared in one major league game, but it was a day to forget. Cleveland pitcher Doc Hamann entered the game in the ninth inning, with his team down, 9–5. He walked the first two Red Sox batters, hit the next batter, and then walked in a run. A triple by Boston center fielder Elmer Miller drove in three more. Hamann took a deep breath, then gave up a single, a wild pitch, and another single. After failing to get out even one batter and being charged with six earned runs, Hamann was sent packing. His career ERA is infinity.

1917 The Chicago White Sox clinched the pennant, eliminating the Red Sox by virtue of a 2–1, 10th inning victory at Fenway Park. The last batter for Boston was pinch-hitter Babe Ruth who hit into a double play that spelt the end of the Red Sox' chances.

1914 Commissioner Ban Johnson indicated that stiff fines would be doled out to any pitcher caught using sandpaper to doctor the ball. Both Ray Keating of the Yankees and Joe Wood of the Red Sox were said to be using the technique to rough up the surface of the ball to afford a better grip.

1912 Both Tris Speaker (BOS) and Sam Crawford (DET) had inside-the-park home runs, in a lopsided 11–4 Boston triumph, but third baseman Larry Gardner broke his finger fielding a Donie Bush grounder and was out for the remainder of the season. Fortunately, he was able to come back in time for the World Series.

1906 Cy Young pinch-hit for Chick Stahl in the ninth inning of the first game, but in vain. Boston lost, 5–1. Young threw a five-hitter to win the second game, but was 0-for-4 at the plate.

1903 The Huntington Avenue Grounds were home to a 12-inning battle between Boston and Chicago, with Norwood Gibson pitching for the home team. Tied 3–3 with two outs in the bottom of the 12th, Buck Freeman hit an inside-the-park home run off Roy Patterson to win the game. It was Freeman's 12th homer, and the third of four consecutive inside-the-park homers. Freeman hit 13 HRs in all, winning the home run crown; seven of them were IPHRs.

TRANSACTIONS
1978: Released Juan Agosto.

DEBUTS

1923: Frank Fuller	1974: Chuck Goggin
1935: George Dickey	1996: Trot Nixon
1963: Rico Petrocelli	2000: Jesus Pena

BIRTHDATES
Elmer Smith 1892 (1922); Del Lundgren 1899 (1926–1927); Elden Auker 1910 (1939); Billy Muffett 1930 (1960–1962)

DEATHS
None yet

September 22

2004 When David Ortiz hit his 40th home run, and maintained his average over .300 through the end of the year, it helped create another Red Sox milestone. At season's end, Ortiz and Manny Ramirez each had more than 40 homers, more than 100 RBI, and an average over .300. They are the only pair to ever accomplish this in the American League, except for two players named Ruth and Gehrig some 73 years earlier.

2003 When Kevin Millar hit his 30th double off Kerry Ligtenberg, he became the eighth Red Sox player with 30 or more doubles on the season, a major league record.

Jockeying for position in the race for the Democratic nomination for President, Massachusetts Senator John Kerry charged that opponent Howard Dean was a New York Yankees fan. Dean had grown up in New York City before moving to Vermont and becoming governor. Kerry hoped to take the steam out of a rally Dean planned for Boston on the 23rd. Dean admitted to rooting for the Yankees in the past but said he converted to Red Sox Nation when Yankees pitcher Roger Clemens beaned Mets catcher Mike Piazza. Presumably it was hard to stomach rooting for the Evil Empire with Clemens on the roster, so Dean chose to favor New England's team.

2002 Once Pedro settled down (he allowed two runs in the first), Sr. Martinez and associates didn't allow another run, while the Red Sox hit Sidney Ponson hard (Johnny Damon hit two homers and Trot Nixon's ninth-inning grand slam furnished a fine finale). The Sox piled up a 13–2 win over the Orioles at Camden Yards. Pedro won his 20th game of the year. Derek Lowe also had 20; it was the first time since 1949 that the usually competitive Red Sox had two 20-game winners. And Pedro's victory made him the first pitcher in the majors to win 20 games while throwing less than 200 innings.

1987 With a 2-for-4 day, Wade Boggs accumulated 200 hits for the fifth year in row. Only two players from each league had accomplished this previously. Boggs also became the first to combine 200 hits with 100 walks in back-to-back seasons since Lou Gehrig in 1936–37.

1975 The Sox beat Ron Guidry and the Yanks, 6–4, to extend their lead to four games. For the second year in a row, the Red Sox turned to veteran player Deron Johnson. In 1974, they acquired him from the Brewers. This year, it was from the White Sox. In 35 at-bats, over the two short stretches, he hit .257.

1974 Almost every Red Sox fan knows that Roger Clemens struck out 20 batters in a game, and did it twice, 10 years apart. Far fewer know that Diego Segui holds the team mark for the most strikeouts thrown in a relief effort. Segui came on in relief of Reggie Cleveland and struck out 12 Orioles in 7⅔ innings. Boston lost nonetheless.

1957 With a fourth-inning homer, following a first-inning walk, Ted Williams had hit home runs in four consecutive official at-bats over a four-game stretch. The first two were in pinch-hit roles. The third was a grand slam. Williams was walked 11 times during the stretch. Later in the game, Ted singled and drew another walk, reaching base four times in a row. In the game, both teams had five hits, but the Yankees beat the Sox, 5–1.

1951 Bobby Doerr announced his retirement, due to a spinal condition that had bothered him the last two years. The 1,865 games he played are more than any other player at this point in Red Sox history. Only today's 5–0 shutout of the Yankees, through the work of Mel Parnell, prevented the Sox from losing their last 13 games of the year. As it was, this was the last win of the year and they dropped the last nine.

1947 A tribute to Duffy Lewis at the Statler drew 1,000 guests and reunited the stellar Sox outfield of Lewis, Tris Speaker, and Harry Hooper for the first time since 1915. Other guests included Hoblitzell, Barry, Scott, Cady, Nunamaker, Thomas, Foster, Shore, Mays, and Babe Ruth. Lewis said that it had cost less than $5,000 to buy the rights to Lewis, Speaker, and Hooper, and that in 1910 the combined salaries for the trio totaled less $10,000.

1936 AP report: "A new dahlia, 13 inches in diameter and winner of three gold medals at last week's Pennsylvania flower shows, was named today for Jimmy Foxx, Boston Red Sox outfielder, at the twenty-second annual flower show of the American Dahlia Society"

1935 Except for the take at the turnstiles, it was a loser of a day. The fans poured into Fenway—some 47,627—which included maybe 5,000 on the field itself with another 10,000 reportedly turned away. There were two attractions: a doubleheader with the Yankees and a Field Day beforehand. The Yankees won everything—sweeping the games, 6–4 and 9–0, and four of the five Field Day events. There were 15 doubles, resulting from balls hit into the roped-off crowd on the field. The only Red Sox winner in Field Day festivities was catcher Rick Ferrell, who successfully sunk the third of his three throws to second base into a barrel set up as a target. Sox center fielder Mel Almada spiked a fan while trying to grab one fly ball and suffered a stomach wound when he fell onto one of the stakes that were driven into the ground to hold the ropes that contained the overflow crowd.

1928 First baseman Phil Todt hit a seventh-inning homer to start the scoring. Two other runs followed, and then Todt hit a two-run homer in the eighth for a 5–0 Red Sox lead, and what proved to be the winning runs in the 5–3 final in St. Louis.

1925 Havana native Ramon "Mike" Herrera debuted with the Red Sox as a backup infielder. Herrera hit .275 in 276 major league at-bats with the Red Sox. Was he the first black player in the majors, 22 years before Jackie Robinson? Herrera had indeed played in the Negro leagues. The answer seems to be that the Negro leagues did not discriminate on racial grounds, the way that the major leagues did.

1915 Returning the favor, the Boston Braves announced that they would loan the Red Sox the use of Braves Field for the 1915 World Series. In 1914, the Braves had used Fenway, bigger than their own ballpark, but in the meantime completed construction of the new larger-than-Fenway Braves Field. During the day's action, at Braves Field, the Sox took two from Cleveland.

1914 Ray Collins was a 20-game winner for the Red Sox, and he got 10% of his wins this day, throwing two complete games against the Tigers. And he got stronger as the day wore on. After getting tagged for 12 hits and three runs in the 5–3 first game win, he held those Tigers to four hits and shut them out 5–0 in the second. The second game was called after eight innings on account of darkness, but that was still 17 straight innings all in one day, and two more in the "W" column.

1911   Sox pitchers walked eight, and saw four bases stolen (one of which was Ty Cobb's record-breaking 82nd steal of the season). Cobb already had 232 hits and was batting .417 at the time. Detroit won the game, 8–3.

1906   A little lack of run support. When Joe Harris lost 7–0 to the Indians, it was the eighth shutout he'd lost in 1906. None were close-scoring affairs.

TRANSACTIONS
1975: Acquired Deron Johnson in trade with the White Sox, for a PTBNL (minor leaguer Chuck Erickson, named on November 7, 1975) and cash.

DEBUTS
1905: Joe Harris
1915: Chick Shorten
1917: Jimmy Cooney
1925: Bob Adams, Mike Herrera
1969: Mike Garman

BIRTHDATES
Walter Lonergan 1885 (1911); Jimmy Walsh 1885 (1916–1917); Ira Flagstead 1893 (1923–1929); Ollie Marquardt 1902 (1931); Tom Wright 1923 (1950–1951); Ken Aspromonte 1931 (1957–1958); Dave Sax 1958 (1985–1987); Lee Graham 1959 (1983); Mark Guthrie 1965 (1999)

DEATHS
Jesse Tannehill 1956

September 23

2002   Baltimore tied it, 3–3, at the last minute and sent the game into extra innings. Boston scored once in the top of the 14th on Jeff Conine's error, but Conine tied it right back up with a homer in the bottom of the inning. Finally, in the 15th, Oriole Willis Roberts literally threw the game away: he walked Johnny Damon. Damon ran all the way to third on a wild pickoff throw to first base, and then scored on a wild pitch.

1969   The Red Sox released manager Dick Williams, because of "a communications breakdown between the managerial staff and the players." GM Dick O'Connell agreed that there had been disharmony between Williams and some Sox stars. "There is a great deal of difference between being a crown prince and a king, between bidding for success and then attaining it," he said, and then posed the question: "After you attain success, what do you do with it?" One player who got along fine with Williams was Bill Lee, who said of Williams, "I liked him. He was surly and mean, but he was honest." Eddie Popowski was appointed acting manager. The team won 5–4 as Pop saw the Sox through season's end. Popowski also managed for the final day of the 1973 season, and won that game

1957   Ted Williams singled, worked three walks, and got hit by a pitch, extending his streak to 16 consecutive times reaching base. As a bonus, the Sox won the game. His streak was broken on the 24th when he grounded out in the first inning. Next time up, though, he slammed his 38th home run. Between September 17 and 23, 1957, soon after he turned 39 on August 30, Williams reached base in 16 consecutive plate appearances, the final 13 against the Yankees:

Sept. 17 vs. KC: Pinch-hit home run
Sept. 18 vs. KC: Pinch-hit walk
Sept. 20 at NY: Pinch-hit home run
Sept. 21 at NY: Home run, three walks
Sept. 22 at NY: Home run, single, two walks
Sept. 23 at NY: Single, three walks, hit by pitch

1955 Needing just one win to clinch the flag, New York fell to the Red Sox in the first game of a day-night twin bill, and had to wait something like seven more hours until they defeated the Sox, 3–2, in the night game.

1945 The final home game of 1945 is dubbed Dave Ferriss Day at Fenway Park. He received an automobile and several other gifts, and even had a pinch-hitting role in the first game of the day; the Sox beat the Yankees, 6–5, in the bottom of the 14th. He started the second game, which had to be played quickly, given the Sunday law that prohibited baseball after 6:29 P.M. on Sundays. The two teams took one hour and two minutes, and just barely completed five innings, but the Sox were on the short end, 2–1, and the one thing Ferriss did not get was his 22nd win of the year.

1941 Jimmie Foxx, acting captain, filled out his lineup card incorrectly. So even though Joe Dobson had been announced as the starting pitcher and had taken all his warmup throws, he was not permitted to pitch. The rules require that the man on the lineup card face at least one batter, so Heber Newsome strolled out of Fenway's dugout to face leadoff batter George Case—who bounced the ball back to Newsome. The unexpected starter threw the ball to first for the out, then left the game in favor of Dobson. Newsome pitched in his regular slot the following day, and won, 5–4, despite giving up 12 hits. Dobson never made it through this day's game. Facing Case in the seventh inning, he pulled a muscle in his side and had to motion to the dugout for another pitcher to take his place. Washington scored twice off Jack Wilson in the bottom of the ninth to win it, 4–3.

1937 The Boston Red Sox hand the Yankees the pennant by beating the Tigers, 4–3. Detroit's loss eliminated them from the race, so even though the Yankees lost to the Browns, they backed into the title for their ninth pennant.

1933 A lot of action in one nine-inning game. There were 39 hits, as the Yankees beat the Red Sox—in Boston—16–12. Ruth and Gehrig hit homers. Melo Almada replaced Smead Jolley mid-game and hit a homer and scored three times. Frank Crosetti committed three errors of NY's seven. There were two wild pitches, and one hit-by-pitch.

1912 When the Red Sox returned from their West Coast road trip, the Red Sox found what the *Globe* estimated to be 220,000 fans lining the one-mile route from South Station to a gathering on the Boston Common that had been set up to welcome the pennant-winners. Business stopped, streetcar traffic was held up, and the area flooded with fans. Mayor John F. Fitzgerald presented keys to the city to each of the players.

1905 Second baseman Hobe Ferris had a record 11 assists in a nine-inning game.

1902 Cy Young won his 32nd game of the year (his final record was 32–11, 2.15 ERA), and won it easily, 14–1 over Washington. At the plate, Young had a 3-for-5 day. Boston hit four homers, two doubles, and two triples, all off "Doughnut Bill" Carrick, who pitched a complete game. And—just in case that wasn't enough—Washington committed six errors, too.

TRANSACTIONS
1972: Released Stan Williams.

DEBUTS
1901: George Prentiss
1937: Johnnie Peacock
1950: Harry Taylor
1951: Bob DiPietro, Al Richter, Norm Zauchin

BIRTHDATES
Heinie Wagner 1880 (1906–1918, 1930); Hod Lisenbee 1898 (1929–1932); George Murray 1898 (1923–1924); Dennis Lamp 1952 (1988–1991); Tony Fossas 1957 (1991–1994)

DEATHS
Gary Fortune 1955; Bill Mundy 1958; Paul Hinson 1960

September 24

2002 Frank Thomas hit a home run, and so did Joe Crede, but they were the only two runs that "The Blade" (Casey Fossum) allowed, as four Boston batters got an RBI apiece in the fourth, and beat the White Sox, 4–2. Fossum even pulled off an unassisted double play in the bottom of the first, catching a pop-up bunt attempt and continuing on to first base to double off the runner.

2001 Former Sox player Tuffy Rhodes hit his 55th home run of the season. Tuffy was playing for the Kintetsu Dragons, however. The homer tied Tuffy with Sadaharu Oh for the Japanese single season home run record. For the rest of the year, he never got another pitch he could hit out.

1998 Tom Gordon saved his 45th game for the Red Sox, ensuring that Pedro Martinez would win his 19th game despite giving up five runs. Clearly, the offense helped, and Nomar Garciaparra was a big part of that, batting 3-for-4, with three RBIs (on two home runs) and four runs scored. For Gordon, it was his 42nd save in a row without a loss or blown save. That set a major league record, and clinched a wild card berth for Boston.

1997 Jason Varitek made his first appearance for the Red Sox, pinch-hitting a single and batting 1.000 in his first season. With his appearance in the 2004 World Series, Varitek became the only player other than Ed Vosberg to appear in the Little League World Series, the College World Series, and Major League Baseball's World Series.

1996 Boston's Mo Vaughn blasted three home runs and drove in five runs with a 4-for-5 night. The Red Sox won by five runs, outscoring the Orioles, 13–8. Tom Gordon started and got the win.

1992 Father Guido Sarducci conducted an exorcism at Fenway Park, at the behest of local radio station WBCN personality Charles Laquidara. Not permitted entry to the park, the good father and the "WBCN Rock Babe" climbed into a cherry picker and sprinkled some holy water on the outside of the park. "The curse is gone," promised Father Guido. "Next year the Red Sox will win the World Series." Asked years later what went wrong, Father Guido said the Red Sox never expressed any appreciation, never greased his palm, never offered him even a single Boston baked bean.

1983 Tony Armas hit two two-run homers off Detroit's Dan Petry, the second an inside-the-park one. They were his last two homers of the year, #35 and #36. At season's end, Armas had 107 RBI, but a batting average of only .218, the lowest average of any player to drive in 100 or more runs.

1978 Boston kept pace with New York, still one game behind, with a 7–6 win in 14 innings at Exhibition Stadium, Toronto, on three singles and an error by the Blue Jays' third baseman. Ron Guidry, meanwhile, threw his third two-hit shutout of September for New York.

1969 Brett vs. Klimkowski, in Boston. Both went the full nine, with neither team scoring a run in support. After 13 innings, the score was still knotted 0–0, Sonny Siebert in relief of Brett, with four New York pitchers having spelled Klimkowski. George Scott reached first on an infield hit (how often did that happen?) and was sacrificed to second by Satriano. Siebert was taken out and Dalton Jones walked. Mike Andrews swung on the first pitch and doubled about 10 feet up on the left-field Wall to score Scott. 1–0 Boston.

1960 The Yankees employed 20 players, and the Red Sox the same, for a battle resolved by Mickey Mantle's solo home run in the top of the 10th off Ted Wills. Gil McDougald had started the scoring in the first, hitting Monbouquette's third pitch for a home run. Roger Maris tripled and Mantle brought Maris in with a drag bunt. Final: New York 6, Boston 5.

1959 Lolly Hopkins, one of the most devoted Red Sox fans, died in Providence, RI.

1958 The Red Sox lost their last home game of the year, 7–5 to the Yankees. Teammates Pete Runnels and Ted Williams were still competing for the batting title. Ted was 2-for-3, moving up from .317 to .320, while Runnels dropped from .325 to .324 with a 1-for-4 afternoon.

1957 Ted Williams had reached first base 16 times in a row, setting an all-time record (see September 23, 1957). Third man up in the first inning, Ted's streak ran out as Washington's Hal Griggs finally retired him, forcing a ground out. In the fourth inning, though, up for the second time, Ted homered. The solo home run won the 2–1 game for Frank Sullivan. Ted was 1-for-3 on the day.

A busy day at the hot corner: Frank Malzone had 10 assists at third base, while Billy Klaus had just two at short. Ken Aspromonte had one at second, Frank Sullivan had two on the mound, but Mickey Vernon didn't have any at first.

1949 New York's Ralph Houk took Boston starter Ellis Kinder out drinking the night before and they both got hammered. Mike Vaccaro quotes Casey Stengel years later as saying, "Mr. Houk did his part for the cause." It didn't faze Kinder in the least. He granted the Yankees five singles and a double, but no runs and no more than one hit per inning. It was his 23rd victory of the year, and 13th in a row. Ted Williams hit his 42nd home run of the year, and the Red Sox won, 3–0. The Sox stood just one game behind New York in the standings.

1948 Issuing an intentional walk with the bases loaded is the ultimate tribute one
STVT can pay to a batter, and Joe Page of the Yankees had already been stung by Ted Williams' two-RBI bases-loaded double in the third inning. When Ted came up again with the bases full in the eighth, Page walked him, conceding the run he forced in, then retiring Vern Stephens on a pop-up to escape further damage. Though the at-bat was not recorded as an official IBB since it was a five-pitch walk, *Epic Season* author David Kaiser writes, "Technically it wasn't intentional, but everyone at the park seems to have understood what he was doing." John Drebinger in the next day's *New York Times* seems to agree: "Page solved the problem by walking Williams to force in one. Perhaps it was the smartest move he could have made for Stephens ended the round with a foul pop-up to Henrich." New York won, 9–6.

1943 A good-fielding pitcher, Joe Dobson made his first error after 156 games without one. But...he won the game, 1–0, a complete game 10-inning shutout.

1940 The AL record for extra base hits (7) and total bases in one inning (25) are both set by the Bosox in the sixth inning of the day's first game. Pitcher George Caster of Philadelphia allowed home runs by Ted Williams, Jimmie Foxx (#500 of his career), Joe Cronin, and Jim Tabor, and news reports suggest that Bobby Doerr might have had an inside-the-park homer, but settled for a triple instead. The Sox got to Caster for six homers in all.

1934 The Yankees were denied the pennant when Boston scored five times and John "Spike" Merena shut out New York on four hits. It was the last New York home game for Babe Ruth. He walked, but had to hobble to first and requested a pinchrunner to take over for him.

1932 Charley Devens, a Milton native and star pitcher for Harvard, crossed the Charles River and beat the Red Sox, 8–2, in his major league debut, for the New York Yankees. The losing pitcher was another local college star, Ed "Lefty" Gallagher of Boston College. Both Gehrig and Ruth homered to help Devens.

1931 Biographer Jim Kaplan pointed out that when Lefty Grove won the day's game, 9–4, he not only won his 31st game of the year, but since July 25, 1930, had rung up a record of 46–4, the best "50-decision streak" of the 20th century.

1928 The last meeting of the year between sixth-place Detroit and eighth-place Boston only attracted 404 Motor City fans. Sam Gibson threw a five-hit, 8–0 shutout for the Tigers. Their fourth-inning run was enough, but three consecutive triples in the seventh provided one interesting feature, as did the Red Sox' Jack Rothrock, who played the outfield (LF), the infield (SS), and pitched the final inning of the game (without letting a runner reach base). (See also September 29, 1928.)

1921 Dixie Davis pitched two complete nine-inning games, just barely losing the first game when the Red Sox scored once in the ninth to beat the Browns, 2–1. Davis only struck out two Sox all day, both in the second game. He won that one with ease, 11–0.

1919 In the ninth inning of the second game of the day's doubleheader, left fielder Babe Ruth hit "the longest drive ever made at the Polo Grounds" to tie up the game, 1–1. The ball went completely over the roof and landed in weeds in the next lot. It was The Babe's 28th home run of 1919, setting a new record for the most homers in a single season.

The Yankees had scored their first run before the first out in the second inning. Boston pitcher Waite Hoyt then went 1-2-3 to close the second, and pitched perfect baseball for more than 10 innings, retiring 34 batters in a row. Finally, in the bottom of the 13th, Wally Pipp tripled to right and then scored the winning run on Del Pratt's sacrifice fly. Hoyt bore the defeat.

Three days later, Ruth played what proved to be his final game for the Red Sox—on the very day Johnny Pesky was born.

1917 Babe Ruth gave up nine hits, walked four White Sox, threw two wild pitches, and was 0-for-3 at the plate—but struck out eight and shut out Chicago, 3–0.

1916 With the bases loaded in Cleveland, in the fifth inning, Marty Kavanagh came up to pinch-hit for Cleveland starter Joe Boehling, facing Boston's Dutch Leonard. He hit a ball that rolled to the fence in left—and kept going, right through a hole in the fence. It was a grand slam—the first pinch-hit grand slam in American League history. Cleveland won, 5–3.

1913 Weldon Wyckoff walked 12 Red Sox batters. He hit one, too. And the Sox got 11 hits off him, scoring nine runs. Nonetheless, he pitched a complete game, and got the win. The Athletics collected 17 hits off four Boston pitchers, and won 10–9, thanks to four runs in the eighth.

TRANSACTIONS
1972: Signed free agent Bob Burda.

DEBUTS
1920: Ray Grimes
1921: Sam Dodge
1960: Tracy Stallard
1997: Jason Varitek

BIRTHDATES
Johnny Reder 1909 (1932); Clyde Vollmer 1921 (1950–1952); Bernard Gilkey 1966 (2000); Kevin Millar 1971 (2003–2005)

DEATHS
Dick Porter 1974; Ernie Shore 1980

September 25

2003 Derek Lowe was flawless in the field in his last appearance of the regular season. He handled 65 balls without making an error all season long (20 PO and 45 A). The last pitcher to complete 50 or more chances without muffing one was Rick Wise back in 1976. The 14–3 win clinched a post-season berth for the Sox, and four other players joined Lowe in a sprint down Yawkey Way to the nearby Baseball Tavern where they took over the bar, handing out beers and partying.

1997 Steve Avery started for the Red Sox and pitched very well against the Tigers, giving up just two hits in five innings. It was his first start since August 31, and his 18th of the season. Avery had a contract providing that if he made 18 starts, his contract would be renewed for another full year. There is no way the Red Sox organization wanted that to happen (his ERA was 6.42 at year's end, and he had only won six games), but manager Jimy Williams—who had worked with Avery when they both were in Atlanta—gave him the assignment and $3,900,000 of additional guaranteed Red Sox money. In 1998, Avery did win 10 games and brought his ERA down but it was a still very disappointing 5.02.

1996 Mike Greenwell started packing his locker to leave the team, at season's end— but the season wasn't over yet. The Sox were still mathematically in the wild card hunt. On the 26th, he announced he would not be returning to the Red Sox. His nameplate was gone from above his locker. So was that of Roger Clemens. GM Duquette had offered Greenie a 13th season as a role player, but Greenwell only wanted to be a starter. To play part-time, he said, "would be degrading...I want to go where I'm respected."

1989 Wade Boggs collected a hit in each of his first three times at bat, and thus became the first player in major league history with 200 hits and 100 walks in four consecutive years. For Boggs, it was the seventh year in a row he made 200 or more hits, itself a modern record. The hits helped the Red Sox (and Roger Clemens) beat Yankees rookie Kevin Mmahat, 7–4.

In consecutive afternoon meetings, the Red Sox announced they would not be inviting Jim Rice back for 1990 and Bob Stanley announced his retirement. The team held a $2.5 million option on Rice and a $1 million one on The Steamer.

1985 After going 0-for-6 since joining the Red Sox, Mike Greenwell finally gets his first major league hit—a home run—in the top of the 13th inning, which boosted Boston to a 4–2 win over the Blue Jays. The very next day he hit another two-run homer, and Boston beat Toronto, 4–1. His third major league hit was also a home run, on October 4, in the bottom of the 12th inning at Fenway, but it was a solo shot and the Brewers had a two-run lead.

1984 It wasn't a pretty win, a 14–6 complete game win over Toronto, but Al Nipper got the win, improving his record to 11–6. It's the last time through 2005 that a Red Sox pitcher won 10 or more games in his rookie year.

1977 How many times does a starting pitcher give up 18 hits without being yanked? Reggie Cleveland threw a complete game against Detroit. The Tigers got 18 hits off the struggling Cleveland, but left 12 men on base and only scored five runs. Fisk, Yaz, and Hobson all homered for Boston, and helped earn Cleveland a 12–5 complete game victory.

1968 Another day, another shutout. Ray Culp throws his fourth straight shutout, beating the Senators, 1–0. He was on a roll, but he wouldn't get his next chance until early April 1969. He won his first four starts, but none were shutouts.

1965 It was clearly just done for the publicity value, but Satchel Paige acquitted himself well with his first major league pitching appearance since 1953. A reputed 59 years of age (he might have been older), Paige started for the Kansas City Athletics and was exceptional. He threw the first three innings, didn't walk a batter, and only gave up one hit: Carl Yastrzemski's double in the first inning. Long after Paige had departed the mound, the Sox scored five runs for the 5–2 win. What might be the oldest batter versus pitcher matchup ever took place when Frank Malzone, 35, faced Satchel Paige, 59.

1960 The Yankees clinched the 1960 pennant with a 4–3 cliffhanger win over the Red Sox. Boston had pulled within a run of the Yankees and had runners at first and third. Stengel called on Luis Arroyo in relief of Ralph Terry. Arroyo was facing Pete Runnels, the 1960 batting champion. Arroyo threw one pitch, and Runnels popped up foul to the third baseman. Game over. Season over. The Yankees had their 10th pennant in 12 years.

1956 The Massachusetts House of Representatives approved the measure dubbed the "Ted Williams Bill," despite a committee report that recommended against the bill. The bill would fine persons $50 if they uttered "profane or slanderous statements at participants in sporting events." United Press said that it "resulted from jibes at the Red Sox slugger." It did not ultimately pass, but one wonders if it would equally have applied to Williams himself uttering profane statements at fans or sportswriters.

During the afternoon's game, Ted Williams drove in four, with a three-run homer and a bases-loaded walk. Boston wiped out Washington, 10–4. Williams was only 1-for-4, however, and dropped another point in his batting race with Mickey Mantle.

1950 Philadelphia came up empty twice, squelched 8–0 in a three-hitter by Mel Parnell in the first game, and rendered scoreless in a two-hitter, 3–0, crafted by recent Red Sox acquisition Harry Taylor.

1949 Mel Parnell won his 25th game of the year, breaking the record set by Babe Ruth for most wins by a Red Sox left-hander. The win over the Yankees brought the Sox into a dead heat with them for first place; New York had seen a 12-game Independence Day lead evaporate. The Red Sox set a new team record by executing their 199th double play. Despite winning 25 games, Parnell walked 134 batters, the most ever by a Red Sox pitcher.

1936 Historian Dick Thompson reports that Sox pitcher Jim Henry was so flustered during a double steal attempt (of second and home) in the third inning that he threw the resin bag toward second base and dropped the ball to the ground. After that was resolved, Henry went into a full windup for his next pitch, and the man on second stole third. He'd already walked two, hit a batter, and yielded a two-run single. And Cronin had seen enough. That was it for Henry that day.

1932 Dale Alexander was 2-for-4 with a double and two RBI, helping the Red Sox to an 8–3 defeat of the Yankees. Alexander led the AL with a .367 average, one of only three American Leaguers to lead the league in average while playing for a last-place team. Because he only had 392 at-bats, some sources do not credit Alexander with winning the batting title.

It was the depths of the Depression, after all, but the pathetic Red Sox (43–111) only drew 182,150 paying customers, an average of 2,365 per game. It might not have been reasonable to expect more for a team that finished a stunning 64 games behind the league-leading New York Yankees.

1923 In the third inning, Homer Ezzell of the St. Louis Browns had his shoe torn while being spiked. The Red Sox allowed Pat Collins to come in as a courtesy runner while Ezzell changed shoes. Collins came in to score, and Ezzell came back in the game.

1914 The Red Sox drafted two infielders who were twin brothers, Joseph and Maurice Shannon, from the Asbury Park team of the Atlantic League. Imagine the possibilities!

1912 Smoky Joe Wood beat New York, 6–0, for his 34th win of the season (and his 10th shutout). The two-hitter was win #100 for the 1912 Red Sox—the first time the team reached the century mark. Over the course of his career, Wood started 158 games and recorded 28 shutouts. The 17.72% ratio is second only to Chicago's Big Ed Walsh, who earned shutouts in 18% of the games he started.

1907 Jake Stahl said he would sue the National Commission and the Washington, Boston, and Chicago ball clubs, alleging he had lost about $4,000 by virtue of the commission's decision that prevented him from playing in 1907, despite Boston having offered him that sum. Stahl had refused to play again for Washington after he was replaced as manager by Joe Cantillon. He was sold to Chicago, and also refused to play there.

1906 Hobe Ferris was suspended by the American League for the rest of the 1906 season because of a fight with teammate left fielder Jack Hayden. "It was the most cowardly attack I have ever witnessed upon the ball field," said umpire Silk O'Loughlin. "I understand that even Ferris' wife upbraided him for kicking Hayden in the face." Hayden lost several teeth when Ferris, swinging his spikes from the top of the dugout, kicked him in the mouth. Interestingly, Hayden was a dental student at the University of Pennsylvania.

1901 Cy Young finished the season 33–10, with a win over Nixey Callahan and the White Sox. Callahan lost to Boston the following day as well, but the White Sox edged Boston by four games to win the pennant.

DEBUTS
1907: Harry Lord
1909: Fred Anderson
1923: John Donahue
1959: Don Gile
2001: Willie Banks

BIRTHDATES
Matt Zeiser 1888 (1914); Ed Chaplin 1893 (1920–1922); Hoge Workman 1899 (1924); Greg Mulleavy 1905 (1933); Eric Hetzel 1963 (1989–1990); Reggie Jefferson 1968 (1995–1999)

DEATHS
Joe Wilhoit 1930; Frank LaPorte 1939; Pep Deininger 1950; Cliff Brady 1974

September 26

2000 Pedro Martinez pitches just five innings in his last start of the year, and allows just one hit. Pedro closes out the season with opposing batters only managing a collective .167 batting average against him. It's the lowest season mark ever posted by a Boston pitcher. Martinez finishes the season with an 18–6 mark. He is the unanimous winner of the 2000 Cy Young Award.

1991 Was Don Zimmer the subject of FBI scrutiny for possibly making bets while manager of the Boston Red Sox? In the issue of *Penthouse* magazine released the previous day, an article stated that Zim regularly bet $3,000 to $5,000 a week on football and basketball while he was manager of the Chicago Cubs. MLB would neither confirm nor deny rumors of FBI involvement.

1982 Prof. Emily Vermeule's classic "Odysseus At Fenway" ran in the September 26 *New York Times Magazine*. The article by Harvard's Professor of Classics and Fine Arts related Fenway Park to the sophisticated intricacies of Knossos and noted, in 1982, "some growing feeling of compassion for Polyphemos" amongst patrons of the game. She likened Haywood Sullivan and Buddy LeRoux to Scylla and Charybdis, and labeled Ned Martin "our resident Milton," while suggesting that Jerry Remy's smile would have looked well on Alexander the Great.

1978 Dennis Eckersley shut out the Tigers, 6–0, winning his 19th game. He was 10–1 at Fenway, and 9–7 on the road. Jim Rice hit home run #44. New York clung onto a one-game lead, with but five games on the schedule.

1975 Luis Tiant blanked the Indians, 4–0, on four hits in the first game. Reggie Cleveland blanked the Indians, 4–0, on five hits in the second game. The last time the Sox had back-to-back shutouts in a doubleheader was July 17, 1956. Reggie Cleveland did it again on September 5, 1977, winning 6–0 after Don Aase beat the Blue Jays in the first game, 8–0. It hasn't happened since.

1973 With his 52nd steal of the season, Tommy Harper tied Tris Speaker's club record, set in 1912. Speaker stole 25 or more bases for seven straight seasons with the Red Sox. Harper ultimately stole 54 bases in 1973. (See September 29, 1973.)

1972 The last time a pitcher wearing a Red Sox uniform hit a home run during a game, it was Marty Pattin, on September 26, 1972. Pattin had a 15–12 record going into the game, and the Red Sox held a very slim lead over the Tigers in the race for the pennant. There were nine games to go. Yaz hit a two-run homer in the first and Boston jumped out to an early 2–0 lead over Milwaukee. Pattin made it 4–0 with a two-run homer in the second inning. The Brewers got a run in the fifth, another in the sixth, and three unearned runs in the eighth, and Pattin lost the game, reducing the Sox lead to just .003 over Detroit.

1958 The Sox swept the Senators in both games of a doubleheader, 6–4 and 3–1. Ted Williams only played the first game and had a 2-for-3 day, with a homer. Pete Runnels, competing with Ted for the AL batting title, was 2-for-9 on the day. Astonishingly, both players were tied with averages of .322580645161.

1954 Ted Williams had announced his retirement from baseball to follow the 1954 season. He'd announced it in the springtime in an article he had written for the *Saturday Evening Post*, and at this day's game against the Senators, he reiterated his intention, "I've had enough. This is the end of it." He came up in the seventh inning of the game facing Constantine Keriakazos with a chance to hit a home run in what looked to be his final time at bat in the major leagues. Bang! Home run! As it happened, though, the Sox scored five runs in the seventh and that brought Ted up again in the eighth. Rather than pull him for a pinch-hitter, Joe Cronin let him hit and Ted popped up. Cronin noted that there was a lot of time between the end of the season and the start of spring training in 1955. Williams finished the year with more walks (136, leading the league) than hits (133). He'd missed the first 37 games after breaking his collarbone, but was only three homers shy of Larry Doby's league-leading 32

1950 From July 14, 1940, through this date more than 10 years later, Williams never had back-to-back games without reaching safely, if a pinch-hit appearance in 1941 and another in 1948 are discounted.

1949 Tempers blazed after Johnny Pesky was declared safe at home plate by umpire Bill Grieve, scoring on Bobby Doerr's squeeze bunt in the eighth inning. Johnny scored the deciding run in a tense 7–6 Red Sox win at Yankee Stadium, as both teams battled for the pennant with only a handful of games to go. Catcher Ralph Houk received the ball in time, and claimed he had the plate blocked. Neither Pesky nor (fortunately) Grieve saw it that way. Grieve said he would have tossed Houk in the ensuing argument, which involved a little pushing by both Stengel and Houk, but for the fact that Houk was the only catcher the Yankees had.

After the game, under the stands and out of public view, Yankees outfielder Cliff Mapes screamed, "How much did you bet on the game, you ------?" The ump lunged at Mapes, and the two had to be separated by Grieve's colleagues, Charlie Berry and Cal Hubbard. Hubbard, incensed as well, asked reporters rhetorically, "How can a team that walks two men, makes an error, and then fails to cover first base on a play blame the umpires for losing?"

The four runs the Sox scored in the eighth might never have scored. With no one out and two slow runners on first and second, Dom DiMaggio scorched the ball directly at shortstop Phil Rizzuto. It was a tailor-made triple play—but the ball was hit so hard it ripped the webbing right out of the Scooter's glove.

1940 Jim Bagby threw some leather on the field, making three putouts—all in the fourth inning and having himself a couple of assists, but he also threw some unfortunate pitches. A single, triple, and single in the top of the ninth drove in two, allowing the Senators to eke out a 6–5 win.

1927 The Sox had 41 assists in the day's twin bill. Boston lost the first game to Washington, 4–2, despite pulling off a triple play and playing error-free ball in the field. In the second game, though, the Sox fell just two short of the record 12 errors held by the White Sox in 1903, but 10 errors was more than enough to lose the game, 11–1. Catcher Bill Moore did his part, with four miscues; it was the last major league game he was ever asked to play. His batterymate John Wilson probably wasn't too thrilled, either. He'd just been recalled from the minors. Wilson was allowed back in '28, though only for five innings of work.

1913 The Boston Braves canceled plans for a post-season city series with the Red Sox, citing the absence of Maranville (spiked) and Connolly (broken leg), two of their best players. Sox president McAleer did not object, saying he had no desire to send the Sox against a crippled team.

1912 ALL PENNANT WINNERS DRINK BEER AND SMOKE—headline, *Los Angeles Times*. The newspaper further informed readers in the subhead, "Boston Red Sox Freely Indulge in Drinks and Cigarettes." Neither the Red Sox nor their upcoming World Series rivals, the New York Giants, believed in prohibition, according to writer John Robinson.

In the final home game of the championship season, it looked like the Sox were going through the motions, losing 12–7 after 7½ innings, but in the bottom of the eighth they scored eight times off New York pitching. First, two triples knocked out rookie starter Ray Keating. One run was in, but there were two outs. Then followed a single and a double—and six consecutive bases on balls, four by Ray Caldwell and two more by his replacement, Tommy Thompson. Tris

Speaker deliberately swung and missed at three bad pitches to end the farce. By the time the inning finally ended, it was too dark to play any more and the game was called. The score at the end was Red Sox 15, Yankees 12.

1905 Doc White was the starting pitcher for the White Sox, but the first two Bostons reached base as White realized he had a sore arm. He had to leave before retiring even one batter. Ed Walsh was pressed into duty and, lacking time to warm up, allowed five runs in the first, but his teammates picked him up with 15 hits (Walsh added one of his own) and 10 runs. Walsh was to be the pitcher in the day's second game, so he forged ahead and won that one, too, 3–1, holding the Red Sox to just three hits. (See also September 29, 1908, when Walsh effectively re-enacted his feat.)

1901 Ted Lewis pitches his final game in major league ball, and goes out in style—with a two-hitter, beating the Chicago White Sox, 3–2.

DEBUTS
1906: Heinie Wagner
1907: Fred Burchell
1951: Sammy White

BIRTHDATES
Johnny Hodapp 1905 (1933); Kevin Kennedy 1954 (manager, 1995–1996); Rich Gedman 1959 (1995–1996); Brian Shouse 1968 (1980–1990); Brian Looney 1969 (1995); Matt Murray 1970 (1995)

DEATHS
Joe Giannini 1942; Paul Zahniser 1964; Rip Russell 1976

September 27

1999 Making his last start of the year, Pedro Martinez struck out 12 Orioles. It was the 19th game in which Pedro registered 10 or more K's. He'd improved his record to 23–4, and his league-leading 313 strikeouts gave him an average of 13.20 strikeouts per nine innings, the highest of any pitcher in league history. Boston's ace only walked 37 batters all year long, giving him an 8.46 to 1 strikeout to walk ratio, the best ever in the American League. Of the eight seasons in which a pitcher struck out more than 200 batters while walking less than 40, Cy Young has one year (1901) and Pedro has four (1999, 2000, 2002, and 2003). Pedro's 24 wins and 2.07 ERA also led the league, giving him pitching's triple crown.

1998 Does a team finishing 22 games out of first place deserve to make the playoffs? The Yankees won their 114th game on September 27, and the Red Sox won their 92nd. Those 92 wins were enough to win the Wild Card slot for the Red Sox, despite finishing 22 games behind the Yankees. The 92 wins placed them ahead of even the winners in the other two divisions.

1997 Nomar Garciaparra's leadoff home run off Pat Hentgen was his 30th of the season, and his team-record seventh leadoff homer. It was also his 98th RBI as a leadoff hitter, far exceeding the old record of 85 set by Harvey Kuenn. Nomar was 3-for-4 on the day, thereby breaking the Red Sox rookie record for hits set by Johnny Pesky in 1942. Nomar now had 207 hits on the year. Pesky hit 205.

1978 Though the Yankees won and ensured that they would remain at least one game ahead of the surging Red Sox, Boston scored three runs in the first (Fisk hit a two-run triple) and kept pace with a 5–2 Luis Tiant win over Detroit at Fenway Park. George Scott homered for the first time since August 29, for his 1,000th career RBI.

1977 Bill Campbell saved his 30th game in relief, breaking Dick Radatz's old 1964 team record. A few other marks noted by Ed Walton in this day's game: Jim Rice had his 200th hit of the season; he was the first Sox batter to get 200 hits since Johnny Pesky in 1947. Yaz knocked in his 100th run, the fifth year he'd driven in 100 or more. He was also the fifth oldest player to drive in 100; the other four were Ty Cobb, Babe Ruth, Ernie Banks, and Honus Wagner.

1975 The New York Yankees secured the 1975 pennant for the Red Sox—thank you very much—by sweeping Baltimore in a doubleheader in the Bronx, even though the Sox dropped their game to the Indians. The Sox clinched their first-ever title in the AL East, a division that had not existed in the years before expansion.

1970 The Red Sox hit their 200th homer of the year, when George Scott hit his second of the game in the eighth. Tony Conigliaro had one in the sixth, and Red Sox starting pitcher Gary Peters knocked out a three-run homer for #201. It set a new club record, topping the 197 they had hit in 1969.

1968 Mickey Mantle was given a first-inning standing ovation by Fenway fans, who believed it would be his last ballgame in Boston. Mantle goes 0-for-3, and Sox win 12–2. His actual last game was the following day: September 28, 1968.

1966 The Red Sox beat the White Sox, 2–1, in the last game of the year. The Yankees won two of their last three games against the White Sox (the Yankees' season extended five days after the Red Sox had wrapped up theirs.) The season ended with the Red Sox 26 games out of first place, in ninth place—but the Yankees were in 10th place, 26½ games out.

1959 Ted Williams finished with a flourish, 2-for-4 with a double, but wound up the season batting a miserable .254. Jackie Jensen said he wanted to spend more time with his family and got a head start, leaving for home a few hours before the final game of the season. He still won the RBI crown, but only by one run over Rocky Colavito, 112 to 111. Despite the bad year, Ted Williams still outhit everyone else in baseball for the decade of the 1950s, with a .336 average. It was the second decade in a row he had earned this distinction—the only player who has ever led for two decades. In the 1940s, Williams hit .356.

1958 Locked to the 12th decimal point with identical league-leading averages, Ted Williams and Pete Runnels had three hits, but Runnels had a 3-for-6 day, while Ted's was 3-for-4, with a walk. The fact that both hit back-to-back home runs in the fourth inning was irrelevant to the race, but not to Boston's 9–5 win over Washington.

1949 Heading into the final five games of a tight pennant race with the Yankees, the Red Sox were fortunate to have the first three against the Senators before facing New York for the last two. With a 6–4 win, Boston "flattened the already well-flattened cellar occupants" (*New York Times*) to win their 11th consecutive game.

1947 On his 28th birthday, Johnny Pesky went 3-for-4 with two doubles and two RBI. The Red Sox beat Washington, 8–1. Johnny finished the season with 207 hits but only 35 of them were extra-base hits.

1944 The Red Sox had lost 10 in a row, and the St. Louis Browns were riding a seven-game winning streak, currently tied for first place with the Tigers. They'd shut out Boston the two previous games. Despite five hours of rain and a muddy field, the Browns pressured to play the game. Boston scored first and last, both times aided by errors, and won the game, 4–1. This Browns loss was the only one in their last 12 games, and they just barely won the pennant, by one game over the Tigers. The Browns tried very hard to get this game in—and almost blew the pennant by losing it. The game was originally set for 2:30, but heavy rain caused it to be called off at 3:30. The Sox had checked out of their hotel to head out of town, but agreed to reschedule as a night game at 8:00. The game got underway at 9:05 and, despite another rain delay, was completed at 11:09.

The Red Sox had now gone 26 long years (all the way since 1918) without a pennant; no team in the American League had suffered a longer drought.

1942 Tony Lupien Day at Fenway is also the last day before Ted Williams, Johnny Pesky, and Dom DiMaggio enter military service. Tex Hughson helps Boston win, 7–6. His one strikeout gives him 113 on the season, but that's enough to lead the league, tied with Buck Newsom. It was the first time a Red Sox pitcher had led the league in strikeouts since Cy Young in 1901. Hughson's 22 wins give him the league lead, too, and he goes down as one of only eight pitchers who led the league in wins without recording a shutout. Johnny Pesky ended the season leading the league with 205 hits, and would clearly have been "rookie of the year" if the award had been instituted. Ted Williams won the Triple Crown.

As part of the war effort, 4,293 people brought some 29,000 pounds of scrap metal to the park, thereby earning free admission.

1941 The day dawned with Ted Williams batting .40099 and only three exceptionally meaningless games left on the schedule, all against Philadelphia. Neither wins nor losses could alter their status in the standings for either team. Manager Joe Cronin suggested to Ted Williams that he might sit and preserve his average. Ted would not, and went 1-for-3, dropping down under .400 to .3996, with just the following day's doubleheader to go.

1924 At the close of the 1924 pennant race, Washington clinched the AL pennant by defeating the Red Sox at Fenway Park, 4–2. Boston fans cheered the Senators, as their victory meant the New York Yankees were denied the pennant.

1923 Frank Chance would finish the season but retire as Red Sox manager, announced Red Sox owner Robert Quinn. It was perhaps mixed praise when the *Atlanta Constitution* wrote that Chance had "instilled his fighting spirit into a weak team with such results that its won and lost percentage is over .400."

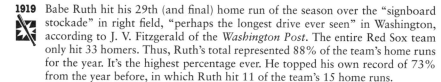 **1919** Babe Ruth hit his 29th (and final) home run of the season over the "signboard stockade" in right field, "perhaps the longest drive ever seen" in Washington, according to J. V. Fitzgerald of the *Washington Post*. The entire Red Sox team only hit 33 homers. Thus, Ruth's total represented 88% of the team's home runs for the year. It's the highest percentage ever. He topped his own record of 73% from the year before, in which Ruth hit 11 of the team's 15 home runs.

Demonstrating that the interest in sports memorabilia is not new, it was reported in the day's *Atlanta Constitution* that one Baltimore fan had offered Ruth $2,500 for the bat he used, and that the Babe was being "pestered to death" by souvenir hunters and that he might have to hire a private secretary to look after his correspondence. Many letters were from "admirers among the fair sex." Unlike Tillie Schafer, who said he quit baseball because he was receiving so many perfumed notes, the prospect may not have displeased Mr. Ruth.

1915 Sore loser? In a signed article in the *New York Evening World*, Ty Cobb charged that the Red Sox had won the pennant by "unfair methods." He blamed two baseball reporters for inciting a riot ("and I am calling things by their right name"). He added an allegation about the 1912 pennant as well: "It is baseball history that Boston won the pennant from the Athletics in 1912 by 'pegging' at batters. The pitchers would keep throwing the ball at the heads of the Philadelphia players, especially the two stars, Collins and Baker, so that they would have to drop flat to avoid being hit."

1905 Chisox bats, useless in the first game, broke out big-time in the second. Big Bill Dinneen, who hadn't started since August 31 due to a lame arm, fired it up today and threw a no-hitter, winning 2–0. There were no Boston errors, and just two first-inning walks stood between Bill and perfection. The second game was called after six innings, not under any mercy rule, but simply because it was too dark to continue. The White Sox knocked Cy Young out early and rolled up a 15–1 lead before the game was called. Boston had now played doubleheaders five days in a row, with no games on Sunday the 24th. As an umpire after he finished as a player, Dinneen officiated during six no-hitters.

1904 Boston took the lead in the top of the fourth without a hit—on a walk, a stolen base, and a wild throw by the catcher, with the runner coming home from third on an out. Cleveland tied it up immediately. Bob Rhoad was pitching well—very well—and held the Bostons hitless into the ninth. After 8⅔ innings, Chick Stahl broke up the no-hitter with a single, but Lajoie's two-run homer in the eighth won the game, 3–1.

1902 Bill Dinneen won 4–2, and had won each of his last four starts, giving him 21 wins and improving his record to an even 21–21, one of only seven AL pitchers to both win and lose 20 games in the same year.

1901 What was it with these Wilsons? George Pepper Wilson won his first game, beating Ned Garvin of Milwaukee, 7–2. You'll find him in the boxscores of the day's game, but not in most record books. Reason being, he changed his name to George Pepper Prentiss for 1902 and was 2–2 for Boston, then 0–1 for Baltimore, and then died at his father's Wilmington, Delaware home of illness before the season was over.

In the 1960s, Red Sox pitcher Earl Wilson, we learn, changed his name from Earl Lawrence Wilson to Robert Earl Wilson. He was still known as Earl. They must have had their reasons.

TRANSACTIONS
1999: Mark Portugal was given his release.

DEBUTS

1901: Harry Gleason   1960: Arnold Earley
1902: Gary Wilson   1967: Ken Brett
1930: Jim Galvin

BIRTHDATES

John Smith 1906 (1931); Walter Murphy 1907 (1931); Johnny Pesky 1919 (1942–1952, manager 1963–1964 and 1980); Jerry Casale 1933 (1958–1960)

DEATHS

Ben Hunt 1927; Jud McLaughlin 1964

September 28

2005 Edgar Renteria scored two runs, #99 and #100 of his season. The 2005 Red Sox were the first team to have four players (Damon, Ortiz, and Ramirez were the others) to score 100 or more runs in a season since 1950.

2003 Kevin Millar's 28th home run was #238 for the Red Sox, a club record for HRs in one season. Hit at Tropicana Field, it was their 127th road home run, also a club record. Six Sox had 20 or more homers, and nine had 10 or more. Millar's HR was extra-base hit #649 on the season, a major league record. The game's six singles and Millar's homer completed the total of 2,832 total bases, also setting a new major league mark. The team had the highest slugging average of any team ever, .491, topping the 1927 Yankees despite a season that was eight games longer. Eight Red Sox players had 80 or more RBI, tying a major league mark; another mark was tied when nine players had 100 or more hits. The team also set a club record with 64 sacrifice flies.

2001 Nervous he was apparently not. It was Jeff Weaver Bobblehead Night at Comerica Park, Detroit, but Weaver was steady as can be, striking out six, not walking a Red Sox batter, and throwing eight innings of scoreless baseball, for his 13th win of the year and a 4–1 win over the Red Sox. Lou Merloni hit a pinch-hit homer in the top of the ninth off reliever Matt Perisho.

1996 The last game Roger Clemens pitched for the Red Sox was a 4–2 loss to the New York Yankees and sophomore southpaw Andy Pettitte. Clemens was looking ahead to a four-year contract with the Red Sox, but the Red Sox were looking back and saw that Clemens had been 10–13 (3.63 ERA) in 1996, and 11–14, 9–7, and 10–5 for the three prior years—a total of 40–39. It didn't look like the best investment. Woken from his doldrums by the effective rejection, Clemens put together back-to-back 20-win Cy Young seasons for the Toronto Blue Jays.

1990 Jeff Stone, inserted as a pinch-runner in the eighth, got his only hit of the year, and it was a game-winner. Stone singled in the bottom of the ninth against the Blue Jays, driving in Wade Boggs from third, and winning the game for the Red Sox, 7–6.

1986 The Red Sox clinched a berth in the World Series with a convincing 12–3 effort over the Blue Jays, earning Roger Clemens his 24th win and a victory ride around Fenway on horseback, courtesy of a Boston Police Department mounted policeman. News services suggested that the Sox had thereby "exorcised some demons" and laid to rest "the curse of Bucky Dent." Before October was over, the notion of another curse—of longer standing—the Curse of the Bambino—would be born.

1978 Pope John Paul I died of a heart attack and Boston radio station WBCN disk jockey Charles Laquidara uttered his locally famous quote on his early morning show: "Pope dead, Sox still alive. Details at 11." Thomas Boswell of the *Washington Post* put it thus: "The multimillion-dollar disappointment of the Boston Red Sox, Mike Torrez, ended his 40 days in the wilderness last night." With his first win since August 18, Torrez terminated a 0–6 skid, squeaking out a 1–0 win. The lone Sox run was provided by a fourth-inning Jim Rice homer, #45, hit hours after working in the cage with Ted Williams. Rice's home run total was more than any Red Sox player since Jimmie Foxx in 1938.

1977 For the first time, Red Sox home attendance passed the 2,000,000 mark.

1973 With his 53nd steal of the season, Tommy Harper topped Tris Speaker's club record, set back in 1912.

1968 Mantle's actual last game. He flied out in the first, and was removed with a sore ankle. Overcoming a 3–0 deficit, the Yankees tied the score in the eighth inning on Andy Kosko's homer. Kosko had been the one to take Mantle's place. A Joe Pepitone homer won it for New York in the top of the ninth, 4–3.

1966 The Red Sox appointed Dick Williams as manager. He had taken Boston's Toronto ball club to the championship two years running. The move paid off big-time the following year.

1960 At Fenway, in his final major league plate appearance, against Baltimore's Jack Fisher (12–11), Ted Williams picks out a 1–1 pitch and drives it 450 feet onto the roof over the Boston bullpen bench. It is Williams' 521st and last home run, putting him third on the all-time list. Williams stays in the dugout, ignoring the crowd's cheers, but when he trots out to left field in the ninth, he is replaced immediately by Carroll Hardy. The Splendid Splinter retires as a standing crowd roars. The Sox rally for two runs in the ninth, featuring a double by Vic Wertz, to give the seventh-place Red Sox a 5–4 victory.

1958 Forty-year-old Ted Williams wrapped up a win of his seventh (and final) batting title, with a 2-for-4 day, while teammate Pete Runnels went hitless in four at-bats. Williams had been batting under .300 in June, but hit over .400 in his last 55 games and finished with a flourish, with seven hits in his last 11 at-bats.

1951 The Yankees clinched the pennant, by taking two from the Red Sox in Yankee Stadium, 8–0 and 11–3. The first game set up the clinch, as Allie Reynolds threw his second no-hitter of the season. He nearly lost it when Ted Williams, batting with two outs in the ninth, hit a towering foul popup for the final out—and Yogi Berra dropped the ball. Granted new life, Ted…fouled out again, and Berra held onto this one. The 11–3 second-game win featured the last home run of Joe DiMaggio's career.

1949 With every game a "must-win," the Red Sox lost, 2–1, but it was a loss accompanied by exceptional ninth-inning dramatics. Three singles, a sacrifice, a runner erased at home on a squeeze foiled by a pitchout, and then Mel Parnell's two-out wild pitch that bounced in front of the plate allowed Al Kozar to score the winning run from third. The Sox remained one game ahead of the Yankees. The race was so tight that the league announced a coin-tossing ceremony would be held on the 29th to determine where the venue would be if a single-game playoff was necessary to break a tie.

1947 Ted Williams won his second Triple Crown. No player has ever won three. Again, he falls short in the MVP voting.

1941 In a doubleheader season finale in Philadelphia, Ted Williams goes 6-for-8 and boosts his average well over the .400 mark to a spectacular .406. Had the sacrifice fly rule not been eliminated the previous December, he would have hit .411 on the season (and not faced the need for the final day's drama). Williams ended the season with an on-base percentage of .553, the best ever until Barry Bonds obliterated the mark in 2003 and upped the ante again in 2004. Ted still holds the highest career on-base percentage of any player, ever.

Dom DiMaggio had a good day, too, going 4-for-9. He finished the season batting .283. Remarkably, this was the lowest average The Little Professor ever posted in 11 major league seasons.

1940 Some managers are just plain sadistic. He wasn't a rookie; this was his fourth season with the Athletics, though he'd thrown less than 100 innings over the four years, but you could say that Philadelphia pitcher Chubby Dean was struggling as he gave up 19 hits, and 5 walks, and 16 runs, but was left in to pitch a complete game, as the Red Sox romped 16–4.

1930 In the final game of the season, Babe Ruth won a 9–3 complete game pitching against Boston, in Boston, years after he'd been converted to a full time position player. He hadn't pitched since 1921. Gehrig asked if he could play left field, when he heard Ruth was pitching. Seeing The Babe on the mound may have shaken the Sox. He struck out three, and initiated two double plays. Until the sixth inning, not a single Sox player reached second base. It wasn't until he tired in the eighth that Boston scored its first earned run. Ruth contributed two singles and drove in one run.

1928 Only 200 cash customers witnessed the tight match between the Red Sox and the Indians, in Cleveland. Red Sox rookie George Loepp tripled to lead off the top of the first and scored on an infield out. It was one of just six runs he scored in his Red Sox career, but it was enough to win the game as Jack Russell shut out Cleveland, 1–0.

1923 The Yankees beat the Red Sox 24–4 in one of their most lopsided victories against the longtime rivals. Boston pitcher Howard Ehmke, who had thrown a no-hitter against the Athletics three weeks earlier to the day, was left in to face 16 batters in the sixth inning, giving up 17 runs and 21 hits in the six innings he pitched. All told, Yankees batters racked up an AL record 30 hits. The winning pitcher was Sam Jones, who had thrown a no-hitter against the Athletics just three days before Ehmke.

1919 It was the last game of the year, and not a meaningful one for either ball club, so when Washington coach (and comedian) Nick Altrock (0–1 with Boston in 1903) put himself on the mound to pitch again, it was all in good fun. Altrock did this often at the end of a year, but this time he got lit up for four straight hits and was relieved. It nearly cost Washington the game, but they held on to win, 8–7. Altrock subbed for future baseball comic Al Schacht, who was in just his second major league game.

1917 In the day's ballgame, just 356 fans turned out, the lowest reported attendance ever at Fenway Park. The *Boston Globe* called it the "smallest crowd in years" leading today's readers to wonder if there had been yet smaller "crowds" in earlier times.

1908 Cy Young made his last start (of 325 starts) for the Red Sox, and it ended in a 2–2 tie with Chicago. Young ended his final season with Boston's AL club with a record of 21–11 and a stellar ERA of 1.26, the best of his long career (and Young turned 41 years old before the season began).

1903 St. Louis and Boston decided to end the season a day early, advancing the Tuesday September 29 game to Monday, creating a final doubleheader. Boston took the two contests, 8–7 (Gibson) and 6–0 (Dinneen winning his 21st game and his sixth shutout). It was the 20th shutout of the season for the Boston team. Despite a lot of back and forth about whether or not the winners in each league would play each other after the regular season, Pittsburg Pirates owner Barney Dreyfuss said the World Series was on.

1901 Boston wrapped up the first year of the franchise win two high-scoring wins over Milwaukee, 8–3 and 10–9. Jack Slattery, making his major league debut as Boston's catcher, went 1-for-3, and then got injured in the eighth. In 1903, he caught on with Cleveland. Buttermilk Dowd homered for Boston in the first game. The second game was perhaps not the best. "Both pitchers worked wretchedly," wrote the *Washington Post*. Manager Jimmy Collins hit two homers for Boston, but it was Hobe Ferris who won the game in the bottom of the seventh with a two-run triple. Then the umpire (games in this era often had just one), Tommy Connolly, called the game due to darkness. Boston wound up the year with a six-game winning streak but finished four games behind the first-place White Sox. They drew three times as many fans as the Boston Nationals. The team that would become the Red Sox was here to stay.

TRANSACTIONS
1936: Released Bing Miller as player, but named him as third base coach
     for 1937, replacing Al Schacht who was also released.
1997: Released Wil Cordero.

DEBUTS
1901: Jack Slattery, Jake Volz
1906: Len Swormstedt
1910: Marty McHale
1917: Wally Mayer
1975: Steve Dillard, Andy Merchant
1977: Bob Bailey

BIRTHDATES
Denny Sullivan 1882 (1907–1908); Jim Brillheart 1903 (1931); Carl Sumner 1908 (1928); Dick Midkiff 1914 (1938); Al Evans 1916 (1951); Dick Gernert 1928 (1952–1959); Mario Guerrero 1949 (1973–1974); Todd Frohwirth 1962 (1994); Rob Woodward 1962 (1985–1988)

DEATHS
Norm McMillan 1969; Moose Solters 1975

September 29

2005 David Ortiz tied the game in the bottom of the eighth with his 47th home run of the season, and won it in the ninth with a single. It was his 10th walkoff hit in three seasons with the Sox. The home run placed him second only to Jimmie Foxx's 50 for the most home runs in a single season by a Red Sox batter. Jim Rice hit 46 in 1978.

2000 Nomar Garciaparra goes 2-for-5 in his last game of the year, for a season total of .372. It's more than enough to win the AL batting championship and is the highest single season average for any Red Sox right-handed hitter ever.

1999 Nomar Garciaparra was 2-for-4, with a double and a two-run homer—and he ended the game turning an unassisted double play. The 6–2 win over the White Sox clinched the wild card. That they lost the second game of the evening no longer really mattered. It was the first time since 1915–1916 that the Red Sox had clinched back-to-back post-season berths.

1998 After losing 13 consecutive post-season games, the Sox finally won one, beating the Indians by a convincing 11–3 margin. They promptly lost the next three, and the Division Series as well, but at least Sox fans had this game to remember. Two players produced all 11 runs: Mo Vaughn was the star with two homers and seven RBI, and Nomar Garciaparra knocked in the other four runs. Pedro Martinez got the win; Jaret Wright took the loss.

1995 John Valentin had a 3-for-5 night, with four RBI, his bases-clearing double in the second boosting his total for the year to 101. He was the first Sox shortstop to drive in 100 since Rico Petrocelli did it in 1970. Only Joe Cronin and Vern Stephens had reached the plateau before Rico. Boston won the game, 11–9.

1993 Ted Williams lost sole possession of the single-season record for intentional walks (which he set in 1957) when John Olerud of the Toronto Blue Jays earned his 33rd IBB in a game against Milwaukee. The two remain tied for the AL record, but the major league mark was set by Barry Bonds in 2004, with a staggering 120 intentional walks.

1989 Wade Boggs was 1-for-3, the hit being his 205th of the year. For the seventh year in a row, Boggsie had hit 200 or more hits (in 1987 it was an even 200). No one before him had done this in six straight seasons.

1988 Mike Greenwell's third-inning single drove in the winning run, the 23rd time in 1988 that Greenwell had the game-winning hit. He holds the AL record. For the record, that's a full 25% of the 89 Red Sox wins in 1988.

1978 The Red Sox knew they were going to win, with an 8–0 lead after just three innings. They knew the Yankees were behind in their game with the Indians, but just a few moments after savoring their ultimate 11–0 thrashing of the Blue Jays, the news filtered into the clubhouse: New York had tied it. Then, New York added two more and won, and the battle for the pennant would continue.

Bob Stanley got the win for Boston, improving his record to 15–2. And Jim Rice had two hits—a single and a double. The three total bases brought him to an even 400—the first American League batter with 400 total bases since Joe DiMaggio in 1937.

1977 Haywood Sullivan, Buddy LeRoux, and Jean Yawkey are principals in a 13-person ownership group selected by the Thomas A. Yawkey estate to assume the reins of the Boston Red Sox.

1973 Bobby Mitchell of the Brewers drove a home run all the way out of Fenway Park to the right of the flagpole in center field, only the fifth ball ever hit out in that area. The Sox won, though, 9–4. Tommy Harper stole his 54th base of the year and Roger Moret improved his record to 13–2.

1969 Rico Petrocelli set a new record for home runs in a season by a shortstop, hitting #40 in the seventh inning and thereby eclipsing Vern Stephens' 1949 mark.

1968 Despite a disappointing 0-for-5 day at the plate, last year's Triple Crown winner Carl Yastrzemski nevertheless won the American League batting crown. Remarkably, his average was the only one in the entire American League over .300—and it was just barely that, at .3005565, which translates to .301. Ken Harrelson did not drive in a run, but he won the RBI title with 109. The Red Sox lost the game to the Yankees, 4–3. Ray Culp was charged with all four runs, and the loss, a comedown after 39 successive scoreless innings. The loss dropped the Sox from third place to fourth. NY finished fifth.

1965 Successfully beating the record low attendance of 461 fans, set just the day before, even more stayed away—consequently, only 409 saw Tony Conigliaro homer to break a 1–1 tie in the fourth inning. Earl Wilson and Dick Radatz combined to win, 2–1. The all-time low yet found by Sox historians seems to be the 356 fans attending the September 28, 1917 ballgame.

1956 Battling right to the finish, the Yankees used 26 players in the game, but lost (in 13 innings) to the Red Sox, who used 18—for a total of 44 players. Both the 26 by one team and 44 for two were new records. Imagine what the lineup cards looked like. Boston won the match, 7–5.

1949 Ellis Kinder wins his 18th straight game as a starter (though he did get tagged with a loss in a relief stint in late July).

1947 Former Yankees manager Joe McCarthy is brought out of the retirement, hired to manage the 1948 Red Sox. McCarthy had led the Yankees to nine pennants, and came as close as one can (without succeeding) to winning two more for Boston. The Sox would fall short on the final day in both 1948 and 1949.

1938 With a convincing 13–5 win over Washington, the Red Sox clinched second place in the American League, the highest they had finished since 1918. Joe Vosmik went 3-for-5 and reached 201 hits on the year, to lead the league. Teammate Doc Cramer managed 198 hits to finish second. It's the only time Red Sox batters have finished 1–2 in the hits department.

1928 Jack Rothrock strapped on the "tools of ignorance" and caught an inning in the game, playing his ninth field position of the season—he'd pitched, now caught, and played every infield and outfield slot. The Sox hit 12 doubles in the game, and won it 6–5 with three runs in the ninth, but starting pitcher Merle Settlemire still couldn't get himself a win. He only threw the first four innings and finished the season—his only one in major league ball—with a record of 0–6. Settlemire was also known for getting in a knife fight with fellow pitcher Big Ed Morris and stabbing him. This was the same Ed Morris fatally stabbed just a few years later on the eve of his departure to spring training. (See March 1, 1932.)

1924 In the Hub, some 15,000 fans at Fenway stood and cheered enthusiastically when the game was over and the Red Sox had lost. The reason was that Washington's 4–2 win clinched the pennant for the Senators, and the Yankees were eliminated.

1920 It happened the very day that banner front-page headlines broke the news about the fix of the 1919 World Series, following confessions by Lefty Williams before a Chicago grand jury.

This happened the very day that banner front page headlines broke the news about the fix of the 1919 World Series, following confessions by Lefty Williams before a Chicago grand jury.

1917 Tillie Walker went 4-for-4 and scored three runs. Gainer scored thrice as well. The Red Sox beat St. Louis with ease, 13–5, in the first game. Babe Ruth went to work in the second, throwing a six-hit shutout and going 3-for-3 at the plate, scoring three times, and winning, 11–0. It was Ruth's 24th win of the year, one more than in 1916 and the most of his career. Ruth's ERA was 2.01.

1916 Beating the Yankees, 3–0, pitcher Babe Ruth recorded his AL single-season record 10th shutout. Ron Guidry came close, with nine, in 1978. In 1916, Ruth won 23 games and didn't give up even one home run all season long. His ERA was a league-leading 1.75.

1913 For the first time in more than two years—since June 22, 1911—the Yankees actually beat the Red Sox in New York! They did it twice, 3–1 and 5–1. The very next day, however, the Red Sox started a new streak, taking both halves of a doubleheader. The new streak only lasted those two games, since Boston lost their first New York road game of 1914—but Boston had won a record 18 consecutive road games against the Yankees, in Gotham.

Free agents after 10 years in the majors? Sox President James McAleer, responding to the players fraternity suggestion, said, "I am with the boys heart and soul on that proposition." The suggestion was not one of pure free agency, even after 10 years of service; the proposal would have ensured that should a big league club decide it no longer wanted to keep a veteran player, the player would be given his outright release and not simply sold to the minors.

1912 The first woman in baseball? The official Red Sox team photo shows Smoky Joe Wood's young sister perched on his shoulder.

1911 Charles H. Taylor and two others purchased the Fenway park grounds on Ipswich and Lansdowne Streets, and served as trustees of the Fenway Realty Trust "to develop the property, build grandstand pavilions and otherwise grade and improve the grounds" for a new facility for the Boston Red Sox. The Charles Logue building company began work on the foundation.

1910 Cleveland lost a tight one to the Red Sox, 2–1. Cleveland might have fared better had they blundered a little less on the base paths. The Naps had a total of four runners thrown out at home plate.

1908 Big Ed Walsh didn't even have to extend himself in two games against the Red Sox, granting three hits in the first and (perhaps having tired a tad) four hits in the second. The White Sox won, 3–1 and 2–0. (See also September 26, 1905.)

TRANSACTIONS
2005: Acquired from LHP Mike Stanton from the Washington Nationals
in exchange for RHP Rhys Taylor and RHP Yader Peralta.

DEBUTS
1909: Steve Yerkes
1935: John Kroner
1950: James Atkins
1951: Ben Flowers

BIRTHDATES
Rob Deer 1960 (1993); Joe Hudson 1970 (1995–1997); Calvin Pickering 1976 (2001)

DEATHS
None yet

September 30

2005 Reggie Jackson had a candy bar named after him, and Yaz had Yaz Bread, but David Ortiz had a Boeing 757 named after him—one of Delta's Song Airlines jets was christened "Big Papi" in ceremonies at Boston's Logan Airport.

1998 It didn't take long for the the fireworks to start. The Red Sox scored twice in the top of the first, and both starting pitcher Dwight Gooden and Indians manager Mike Hargrove were tossed from the game before the Indians even retired the side. Sox starter Tim Wakefield didn't last much longer, but in his case it was because he let up six runs, departing after 1⅓ innings. Cleveland won the second game of the Division Series, 9–5.

1996 The Red Sox fired manager Kevin Kennedy. Without having to work too hard to read between the lines, GM Duquette's explanation was that he'd given Kennedy the players, but Kennedy had not done his job. Jose Canseco said Kennedy was being made a scapegoat and that he would demand a trade. Just over seven weeks later, Jimy Williams was named (see November 19) as Kennedy's replacement.

1992 Frank Viola almost no-hits the pennant-contending Toronto Blue Jays; Viola throws a no-hitter for eight full innings, until Devon White singles to lead the ninth. It remains the only hit, and Boston wins, 1–0.

1988 The Indians beat Roger Clemens and the Red Sox, 4–2, but Boston backed into a clinch of the AL East title hours later as Oakland eliminates Milwaukee, 7–1.

1978 The Red Sox won their seventh game in a row, kicking off the scoring with four runs in the first inning. Fenway had long had dedicated scoreboard watchers, though, and depression descended on the Faithful, just moments later, as a "5" was posted next to New York. The Yankees rolled to a win, clinching at least a tie. The Red Sox won, too, 5–1, behind Dennis "Home Eck" Eckersley. Eck was 11–1 at Fenway, and the win was his 20th of 1978. But even to have a shot at the pennant, the next day's results had to see Boston win and New York lose.

1977 The Red Sox kept themselves alive, but eliminated the Orioles from the pennant race with an 11–10 win. Carlton Fisk earned his 100th RBI of the year, becoming one of only five catchers with 100–100 seasons (100 runs scored and 100 RBI). He was one of four Red Sox (Hobson, Rice, and Yaz were the others) to have 100 or more RBI. They were the first team since the 1940 Red Sox to have four players reach the 100 mark.

With three putouts in the game, Carl Yastrzemski had played a full season of error-free baseball. He made 287 putouts in the outfield, and 57 while playing first base. He had six assists at first, and his 16 outfield assists led the league. Ken Harrelson played error-free as an outfielder in 1968 (241 putouts), but made three errors as a first baseman.

1973 The brass apparently couldn't wait one more day, and manager Eddie Kasko is fired just before the last game of the year. Eddie Popowski assumes the reins as manager-for-a-day, and the Sox win, 3–2, when two runs score on a Ben Oglivie eight-inning sacrifice fly to center on which Brewers catcher Charlie Moore is assessed an error at the plate. Darrell Johnson is hired to lead the Sox in '74; Kasko will stay with the team as an executive scout and watches the game from Tom Yawkey's box.

1972 Knowing that the Tigers had already won their game, the Red Sox worked a win over the O's in Baltimore, 3–1. With four games to play, the Red Sox had a 1½ game lead over the second-place Tigers.

Ted Williams had had enough. He'd been the last manager of the Washington Senators (and, as the franchise moved to Texas, the first manager of the Texas Rangers) but, after four years, it was enough.

1970 It took him until the last game of the season, but New York's Fritz Peterson won his 20th game of the year, holding the Red Sox to eight hits and three runs, by the score of 4–3. Billy Conigliaro hit a homer, as did Sox shortstop Luis Alvarado; for Luis, it was his first major league home run, after 233 at-bats.

And Yaz lost his chance at another batting title. After his second at-bat in the game, Yaz was at .3297872. "I legged out an infield single. I twisted my ankle and should have came out of the ballgame. It's your back leg, where all the weight is. But I stayed in." He stayed in and made two more outs, reducing his average to .3286219. Alex Johnson of the Angels went 2-for-3, and ended his day with an average of .32899. Had Yaz come out of a game that meant nothing in the standings...

1969 Dalton Jones singled to center in the seventh. It was his 55th and final pinch-hit for the Red Sox, a team record.

1967 The Red Sox and the Twins met head-to-head in the next-to-last game of the year, and Boston thrilled the fans at Fenway with a 6–4 win, putting the two teams into a dead tie for first place. Both teams had identical records of 91–70, and the stage was set for an October 1 showdown, the winner to take the pennant. Detroit split two with the Angels but could still hope to take two the following day, which would give them a tie with the winner of the Twins–Red Sox game. Yastrzemski and Killebrew were both vying for the home run title. Yaz went one up over Killebrew when he hit #44 in the seventh inning, but Killebrew responded with his 44th in the ninth.

1966 YANKEES LOSE, 6–5, CLINCH 10TH SPOT—so read the headline in the *New York Times*. The White Sox scored two in the bottom of the 11th to beat the Yankees 6–5, and ensure that even should New York win its last two games of the year—

which they did—they were stuck in last place for the first time since 1912. This year—1966—offered a new low, however, in that there were only eight teams in the league in 1912. The Yankees, last in the league, were only in eighth place. In 1966, they wound up in 10th place, one-half game behind the Boston Red Sox.

Two former Red Sox players took different job offers. Bobby Doerr accepted a position for the 1967 campaign as a coach under manager Dick Williams, and would help coach the team to the World Series. Former Boston batting champ Pete Runnels was named vice president of Camp Champions, a new venture near Austin, Texas, described as an executive boys' camp.

1964 Two Cleveland pitchers, Luis Tiant and Sam McDowell, shut out the Sox, 5–0 and 3–0.

1962 Pete Runnels won his second AL batting crown, batting .326, despite not playing in the two final games, the day's doubleheader with Washington. The Senators won the first game, 3–1, then the teams flipped scores and the Red Sox took the second, 3–1. Don Gile played both games. He'd had one hit the first game of the year, but not had another one since; he entered the day batting 1-for-34 on the season. Gile had a single in the first game, and hit a two-run, game-winning home run in the bottom of the ninth, to break a 1–1 tie. Just like Ted Williams, Don Gile hit a home run in his last at-bat in the major leagues.

1960 In a double-axing, both GM Bucky Harris and Farm Director Johnny Murphy are let go.

1959 Johnny Orlando is fired as clubhouse head; he had served the Sox since 1925, when he'd been batboy for the team.

1956 The New York Yankees win another pennant—no surprise there—and Mickey Mantle wins the Triple Crown, leading both leagues in homers, RBI, and average. His .353 beats out Ted Williams at .345. Williams had only batted .196 against Yankees pitching.

1953 Observing the 50th anniversary of the first World Series, 86-year-old Cy Young—the first pitcher to throw a ball in a World Series, threw out the first pitch of the 1953 Series. Also attending were 1903 alumni Fred Parent and Bill Dinneen, umpire Tommy Connolly, and former Pirates Fred Clarke, Tommy Leech, and Art Krueger.

1951 With "one more brisk, businesslike performance" (*New York Times*), the Yankees took the final game of the 1951 season, from the Red Sox, 3–0. The Yankees ended the year sweeping five straight from the Red Sox, the last three games all being shutouts. Over the final five, New York outscored Boston, 29–4.

1949 With an 11–9 win against the Washington Senators, Boston travels to New York for the two final games of the '49 season. Winning either game will give the Red Sox the pennant.

1939 Ted Williams plays the final games of his rookie year. He still holds the major league rookie records for most runs batted in (145) and walks (107), the American League record for slugging percentage (.609), and Red Sox team records for extra-base hits (86) and runs (131).

1924 Having already clinched and letting down a bit, the Washington Senators lost

13–1 to the Red Sox. Nick Altrock, a 48-year-old coach with Washington, was activated for the game and scored the only Senators run when he tripled and then scored on Leibold's grounder. Altrock became the oldest player ever to hit a triple. He also pitched the last two innings, giving up just one final run to the Red Sox. Altrock would match his 1.000 average by again going 1-for-1 five years later in 1929, but apparently couldn't leave well enough alone, and ended on a down note, going 0-for-1 in his final at-bat, in 1933—matching the .000 average he had recorded for Boston back in 1902.

Later, in 1927, Frank H. Young of the *Washington Post* suggested that Washington hadn't tried very hard to win the game. They'd clinched the pennant the day before and at least one Boston newspaper had facetiously written the next morning that since the Red Sox "had let Washington win the pennant, the least the Harrismen could do was to lose and thus enable the Beaneaters to beat the White Sox out for seventh." Bucky Harris's team did in fact lose, spectacularly so. Harris himself was out of town at the time, as was Walter Johnson. And the Red Sox ended the season a half-game ahead of the White Sox. There were seven Washington errors, and Altrock several times "tossed his glove to the batter instead of the ball." Numerous players took up unfamiliar defensive positions, such as pitcher "Oyster Joe" Martina playing shortstop. It was a mockery, but notable as the only year from 1922 through 1930 that the Red Sox escaped the cellar.

1916 In a pennant race that was not to be decided until October 1, the Red Sox clinched at least a tie by winning a hard-fought 10-inning battle with the Yankees. Both Dutch Leonard and Nick Cullop had pitched nine innings of shutout baseball. Tillie Walker had helped cut off one potential rally with an unassisted double play in the fifth, running in from center to catch a short fly ball and reaching second base before the baserunner could retreat. Sox manager Bill Carrigan assigned himself the role of catcher for the day and, after Everett Scott singled to kick off the bottom of the 10th, he bunted to sacrifice Scott to second, but reached safely when no one covered first on the play. The next batter bunted, too, and he also reached base safely. Harry Hooper was up with the bases loaded and hit a weak fly to right field, but pinch-runner McNally gambled and scored the winning run as Hendryx's throw to the plate was off the mark.

1915 Boston clinched the American League pennant, but the headline in the *New York Times* read RED SOX NOT EXCITED. Word arrived as the Sox were boarding a train for Washington that St. Louis had beaten Detroit, guaranteeing the Red Sox win. The World Series would once more put Philadelphia against Boston, but this time it was Philly (NL) vs. Boston (AL).

1913 The Red Sox took two from the Yankees, 3–2 and 3–0, behind the pitching of Dutch Leonard and Vic Moseley. The two losses pushed the Yankees back into last place. So sad.

1912 Tris Speaker hit an inside-the-park home run off Joe Engel. He only hit 10 homers in 1912, and eight of them were of the inside-the-park variety.

1909 The Red Sox and New York Giants announce a six-game post-season exhibition series, to begin October 8 in New York.

1906 Boston American pitcher Floyd Myron "Rube" Kroh shut out St. Louis, 2–0, allowing just two hits in his major league debut. He won one game the next year, too, but lost four, despite a good 2.62 ERA.

1905 Wrapping up a busy month by splitting a doubleheader with the Tigers, Boston had played 11 doubleheaders in September (and a total of 35 September games which, given that they did not play on Sundays, kept them fully occupied otherwise. Of the doubleheaders played, they won two, lost two, and split the remaining seven.

1903 Two days after the season concluded, so did the contracts of Boston's ballplayers. Consquently, they were under no agreement that would pay them for post-season play. Boston owner Killilea offered to extend the contracts by two weeks to pay them for participating in the World Series, but the players seek more and state their refusal to play without adequate compensation.

DEBUTS
1906: Rube Kroh
1951: Harley Hisner

BIRTHDATES
Jennings Poindexter 1910 (1936); Eddie McGah 1921 (1946–1947); Jeremy Giambi 1974 (2003)

DEATHS
Jim Galvin 1969; Hank Patterson 1970; Del Pratt 1977; Nels Potter 1990; Eddie McGah 2002

OCTOBER

October 1

2005 The Red Sox reacquired Mike Stanton for the pennant stretch; he pitched just one inning—against the Yankees—allowing one hit, but no runs, in a game the Sox lost to NY, 8–4.

2003 The Wild Card entry Red Sox lose the first game of the American League Division Series, a 12-inning heartbreaker in Oakland, 5–4. Todd Walker's first-inning homer started the scoring, but it was bookended in the bottom of the ninth when Erubiel Durazo singled home the tying run for the A's. With the bases loaded and two outs in the bottom of the 12th, Ramon Hernandez dropped down a perfect bunt and caught Derek Lowe and the Sox sufficiently off-guard.

1995 Chris Donnels took over at second base for Luis Alicea late in the game, and had one at-bat, in the ninth inning. Donnels hit a home run off Milwaukee's Scott Karl, in a game the Sox dropped, 8–1. It looked like he would join Chick Stahl, Ted Williams, and Don Gile as having hit a home run in his last major league at-bat, but five years later, Donnels hooked on with the Dodgers and Diamondbacks for another 202 at-bats (which included 10 more homers), and his last at-bat was a fly out to center.

1991 Wade Boggs hit two doubles in an 8–5 loss to the Tigers, and finished the year with 42. It was the seventh year in a row that he'd hit 40 or more, the first American Leaguer to do so. Joe Medwick had earned this distinction in the NL

Phil Plantier struck out five times in nine innings, and shares the major league record with Ray Jarvis (April 20, 1969).

1988 Jeff Sellers of the Red Sox had a no-hitter going into the eighth. Cleveland's John Farrell was throwing scoreless baseball, too. First baseman Luis Medina (who had seven RBIs on the year) hit a solo home run—and that proved the difference in a 1–0 loss for the Red Sox. Medina finished the year with eight RBIs and six home runs.

1983 After playing in 3,308 major league ball games—the most ever—Yaz calls it quits. He had a 23-year career. Yastrzemski concluded pre-game ceremonies with an emotional run around the field, shaking hands with fans in the front seats as he circled the park.

1980 Manager Don Zimmer was released. The team asked coach (and former manager) Johnny Pesky to serve as interim field manager for the remaining four games.

1978 The Yankees lost their final game of year, 9–2, to Cleveland, while Boston won theirs over the Blue Jays—the 5–0 shutout by Tiant was the eighth straight win for the Sox. The result is a dead tie for first place at the end of the regular season, setting the stage for a single-game playoff in Boston the following day.

1977 Baltimore beat Boston at Fenway, thus handing the '77 pennant to New York, who won it while watching TV in the clubhouse, in the midst of a nearly three-hour long rain delay. Carlton Fisk went 3-for-4 and scored two runs; he was the first catcher in major league history to both score (106) and drive in (102) runs in one season.

1967 The Red Sox won the pennant on the final day of the season, beating the Twins, 5–3. Yaz was 4-for-4; he'd put on a terrific close to the season, with 10 hits in his last 13 at-bats. Yaz won the Triple Crown—and no one in either league has won it since. He finished with a .326 average, 44 homers, and 121 RBI. Spared last place only because Kansas City was much, much worse, the Yankees still ended the season a full 20 games behind the league-leading Red Sox.

1964 Fans at Fenway saw ace reliever Dick Radatz appear in his 78th game of the season, and hold the lead as the Sox won, 4–2. There weren't many fans, though: the attendance was just 306 fans. It was reportedly the smallest crowd in years, less than half the low point of 674 reached just a year earlier, on September 24.

1961 In the last game of the year, in Yankee Stadium, Roger Maris hit his 61st home run, off Bosox pitcher Tracy Stallard, on a fourth-inning waist-high fastball. Stallard struck Maris out his next time up. The Yankees won a well-pitched game, 1–0. Obviously, #61 was the game-winner.

1960 The Yankees won their 14th game in a row, beating the Red Sox, 3–1. Pete Runnels was 1-for-2, closing the season with a league-leading .320 average. He stands as the only player in American League history to win a batting title but drive in less than 40 RBIs (he drove in only 35 runs all season long).

1950 Despite breaking his elbow in the All-Star Game, and missing a total of 65 games, Ted Williams racked up 97 RBIs in just 89 games. He had four hits and three RBIs in the final game of the year, a 7–3 win over the Yankees.

Catcher Birdie Tebbetts spoke to 250 friends at a bachelor dinner thrown for him at Boston's Parker House, a few weeks before he was to get married. Looking back on the season just completed, he described two of the Red Sox pitchers as "moronic malcontents" and "juvenile delinquents"—but tantalized us all by not mentioning any names.

1949 Had the Red Sox won either of the final two games of the season, both against the Yankees (and both in New York), they would have won the 1949 pennant. New York caught league-leading Boston (and Mel Parnell) with a win this day, bringing the two teams to a first-place tie. The Yanks had been down 4–0, but come back to take the game, 5–4. Joe Page earned the win, firing five innings of strong relief, and Johnny Lindell's homer made the difference.

1946 The Red Sox wanted to keep up their skills while waiting for the National League playoff to wind up, so they worked out at Fenway in an exhibition game against a group of American League All-Stars (including Joe DiMaggio). Senators pitcher Mickey Haefner had a pitch get away from him in the fifth inning and it hit Ted Williams on the right elbow. It was the first time in his career that Ted had been forced out of the lineup after being hit with a ball, but it immediately raised a knot "about the size of an egg." (AP) The injury was a serious one and raised doubts as to whether Williams could play in the World Series. He did, but was sub-par throughout.

1944 Do you suppose they were in a hurry to get it over with? The *Chicago Tribune* noted that, "Showing hustle which was conspicuously absent during most of the campaign," the White Sox and the Red Sox played a season-ending doubleheader and wrapped up both games in just two hours and 42 minutes. The first game was 1:38 and the second game just 1:04. They split...and then they split.

1939 Both the Red Sox and the Yankees dropped their last two games of the 1939 season; the scheduled doubleheader between the two teams was washed out, not to be made up. Even without the final two games, Ted Williams set a rookie record of 145 RBIs which has never been topped.

1938 How grand! Jimmie Foxx hit two home runs: a three-run homer in the third inning and a grand slam in the sixth off Johnny Murphy. It was his third grand slam of the 1938 campaign, but the two roundtrippers were #49 and #50 of the season. No Sox player has ever matched Foxx's total. David Ortiz's 47 in 2005 comes the closest. The 9–2 win over the Yankees (courtesy of Foxx's seven RBI) guaranteed that the Yankees would win no more than 99 games in '38. Foxx's 175 RBIs also stand as the all-time Red Sox record.

1933 He gave up a lot of fly balls (the Yankees recorded 18 outfield putouts), but Babe Ruth pitched the final game of his career, on the last day of the season. He threw a complete game and beat the Bosox, 6–5, batting in the cleanup spot and even hitting a home run in his own behalf.

1915 Rumors had the Red Sox trading Tris Speaker to the Yankees for three players, but Bill Carrigan said the rumor was too absurd to discuss: "I would not trade Speaker for the whole New York club."

1912 How many Red Sox fans survive to still savor this day, when New York lost its 100th game of the season? 1912 saw the biggest gap ever between the two teams. New York finished the season a full 55 games behind Boston, with a 50–102 record. Boston's final record was 105–47.

Joe Wood also beat Walter Johnson in "Cupid's Game," winning the hand of Miss Laura O'Shea of Kansas City away from his rival suitor.

1903 The first game of the first modern World Series was played at the Huntington Avenue Grounds between the Boston Americans and the Pittsburg Pirates. Cy Young started for Boston, but Deacon Phillippe pitched a better game, striking out 10 and walking not one Boston batter. Young yielded four runs in the top of the first, which made all the difference in the 7–3 Pirates win. The first home run in World Series play was hit by Pittsburg right fielder Jimmy Sebring in the seventh; Sebring had a 3-for-5 day, and Tommy Leach was 4-for-5 with two triples. Candy LaChance drove in two of Boston's three runs, but without benefit of even one hit.

TRANSACTIONS
1968: Signed amateur free agent Juan Beniquez.

DEBUTS
1974: Steve Barr
1982: Marc Sullivan

BIRTHDATES
Jeff Reardon 1955 (1990–1992)

DEATHS
George Huff 1936; Mickey Devine 1937; Billy Goodman 1984

October 2

2005 Some of the spectre of October 2 as one of the worst dates in Red Sox history was removed by the 10–1 Fenway victory over the Yankees, in the final game of the season. On the very first play of the game, Manny Ramirez gunned down Derek Jeter trying to reach second base, and recorded his league-leading 17th outfield assist. Despite the lopsided score, manager Terry Francona inserted Mike Timlin to get the final out, giving Timlin a club-record 81 appearances (50% of the season's games), eclipsing Greg Harris's 80. More importantly, the win gave the Red Sox the AL Wild Card, placing them in postseason play for the third straight season—the first time any Sox team has accomplished that feat. The sold-out home game ranked Fenway with Cleveland's Jacobs Field as the only two ballparks to totally sell out the season two years in a row. Fenway, at 226 consecutive sellouts, still trailed Jacobs at 455, but tallykeepers look forward to 2008 when the Red Sox should surpass the Cleveland mark. The Red Sox led the majors in runs scored (with 910, 292 of them driven in by the Ortiz-Ramirez 3–4 punch) for the third consecutive season, the first time that's been done since the 1951–1954 Brooklyn Dodgers. Both Ortiz and Ramirez hit more than 40 homers and drove in more than 140 runs; they're the first duo to have done that since Ruth and Gehrig did it in 1927. As a team, the Red Sox once again led the majors in batting average (.281) and on-base percentage (.357).

2003 Oakland took a demoralizing two-games-to-zero lead in the best-of-five ALDS by winning their second straight, all thanks to five runs in the bottom of the second off Boston's Tim Wakefield.

1998 Four solo homers gave the Indians four runs in Game Three of the Division Series, but the Red Sox came within a run in the bottom of the ninth. But only within a run; they lost, 4–3. Garciaparra drove in all three Red Sox runs. Boston now trailed 2–1 in the best-of-three series.

1992 After broadcasting Red Sox games since 1961, Ned Martin was dismissed by NESN, the television station owned in part by the last-place Red Sox. "The Sox can't improve their ball club, so now they're going to try to improve their image by giving you club propaganda from the broadcast booth," wrote an angry Dan Shaughnessy. "Martin never was afraid to say the emperor has no clothes. And we can't have that when so many Sox officials are walking around buck naked." Jack Craig offered a nice tribute in his October 9 *Boston Globe* column.

1988 Despite dropping six of their last seven games, the Red Sox won the AL East, 3½ games ahead of the fifth-place Yankees. Wade Boggs reached 200 hits for the sixth year in a row. The Oakland A's swept the Sox in the ALCS, 4 games to 0.

1986 Don Mattingly went 2-for-4 playing in a 6–1 Yankees defeat of the Red Sox. In the process, he broke a 59-year-old record for the most hits in a season. He finished the year with 238 hits, but came in second to (and five points behind) Boston's Wade Boggs for the batting title.

1983 Carl Yastrzemski played in a record 3,308 American League games. He had 13,990 plate appearances. In his final game, he played left field and improved his lifetime batting average, going 1-for-3 as the Sox topped Cleveland 3–1.

1982 New York Yankees manager Clyde King said something uncharacteristic of Yankees managers, that he had really hoped to finish the season at .500: "That was a goal for me. You have to have a goal to look forward to." He fell short, as Red Sox rookie Brian Denman shut out New York, 5–0. He didn't know it at the time, but the win was Denman's last major league appearance. It was the equivalent of hitting a home run in your last at-bat, but even rarer: Denman was only the fifth pitcher ever to throw a shutout in his last appearance.

1981 On the final weekend of the season, the Sox faced elimination with the loss of any one of their last three games. Ahead 4–3 after six, the Indians tied it and then Mark Clear walked Pat Kelly in with the go-ahead run. Before it was over, the Indians rolled up an 11–4 margin and ended Boston's chances. The Red Sox finished 1½ games out of first.

1978 In the single-game playoff for all the marbles, the Yankees were losing 2–0 after six innings, but scored four times in the top of the seventh with the infamous Bucky Dent three-run home run being the big blow. The less said about that, the better, in the view of most Boston fans. The Yankees brought back Bucky Dent to throw out the first pitch in a 2004 ALCS game, hoping to fend off a Boston comeback. It didn't work.

1977 The Sox end the season in second place with a 97–64 record. Baltimore ends the season with an identical record. The two teams had been scheduled to play in Fenway, but the final game of the season is rained out and so they remain tied. Both teams were just 2½ games behind first-place New York.

1972 It was a play that may have cost the Red Sox the 1972 American League pennant. In the third inning, the Sox had runners on first and third with just one out, when Yaz hit a double to center field. One run scored, but Luis Aparicio—running from first base—tripped rounding third base and so headed back to the safety of third rather than running home. Unfortunately, Yaz had his head down and just kept motoring, and both of the baserunners wound up on third base. Yaz was tagged out. Just one run scored and there were now two outs. Reggie Smith then struck out. Mickey Lolich held the Red Sox to just the one run and won his 22nd game, 4–1. The Tigers took over first place, dropping the Red Sox to second place, with only two games to go. Aparicio's fall was like deja-vu, dating back to the Opening Day game, also against the Tigers. (See April 15, 1967.)

1964 GM Mike Higgins fired manager Johnny Pesky and all of his coaches with just two games remaining in the season. Billy Herman took over as manager, but he had to manage the final two games without a coaching staff. The Sox won both games. Hall of Famer Frankie Frisch said that Pesky "should get the manager of the year award for all he's put up with…No team can win with a bunch of Humpty Dumpties."

1950 Again, two Sox tie for the RBI crown: this year both Vern Stephens and Walt Dropo have 144 RBI. Stephens and Williams had both driven in 159 the previous year. Dropo fell one short of Williams' rookie record 145 RBIs in 1939. Dropo's 34 homers, though, remains a Red Sox rookie record.

1949 For the second year in a row, the Red Sox face sudden-death elimination on the final day of the season. They lose, 5–3, Kinder bowing to Vic Raschi. After a four-run eighth, the Yankees carried a 5–0 lead into the ninth. Boston scored three runs and had the tying run at the plate before it was over. Dramatic, but the Yankees prevailed. It is the third time in four years that the Sox faced sudden death, and died. Joe McCarthy managed the Red Sox for just two full seasons. In both years (1948 and 1949) the team lost the pennant on the final day.

George Kell of the Tigers went 2-for-3 while Ted Williams was hitless in two official trips. Kell's final mark is .3429 and Williams' is .3427. Ted did draw a walk, though, reaching base 358 times (194 hits, 162 walks, and 2 HBP), most by any Red Sox player. Williams reached base more than 300 times in seven different seasons.

1948 Boston beat the Yankees, 5–1 and 10–5, on the final two days of the season (October 2 and October 3), placing the Sox in a tie with the Cleveland Indians, and forcing a single-game playoff which a coin toss determined would be at Fenway Park. Ted Williams never hit in the clutch? In the last three games of 1948, he was 6-for-8 with three doubles, a home run, and four RBI.

1938 The Red Sox finished the season with the best team average in baseball, a very high .299. They finished 9½ games behind the first-place Yankees, though.

1933 Marty McManus is let go as manager of the Red Sox.

1921 The Yankees closed out their first pennant-winning season with a 7–6 victory over Boston. The New York Giants beat the Yankees in the World Series, with every one of the games played at the Polo Grounds—home to both teams.

1915 Walter Johnson won 3–1, over Joe Wood and Babe Ruth. The second game of the day was a 3–3 tie, called on account of darkness after 10 innings.

1914 This young 21-year-old pitcher Babe Ruth had debuted earlier in 1914, but was then sent to the minor-league Providence Grays. Ruth helped the Grays win the International League pennant, and was then recalled to Boston. He started his third major league game, pitching against the New York Yankees. Ruth held them to six hits and earned the 11–5 win. Ruth also got his first major league hit, doubling (and scoring) off Yankees pitcher Leonard "King" Cole.

1909 Jack Chesbro, who'd won 41 games for New York in 1904, was placed on waivers by them late in 1909 and picked up by the Red Sox. He only appeared in one game, a start, on this date, but was (despite throwing just six innings) charged with the 6–5 extra-inning loss. It was his last major league game.

1903 Bill Dinneen blanks Pittsburg 3–0 on three hits and 11 strikeouts to even the World Series. His four starts will give him three victories, making this the only Series to produce two three-game winners. Boston left fielder Patsy Dougherty hits two home runs; in 14 World Series games they are the only home runs he will hit. In fact, no one hit a home run in another World Series game until five years later, in 1908. With Boston electing to bat first, Patsy's first homer is a leadoff blast against Sam Leever. It stands as Boston's first home run in World Series history and one of the more unusual, in that it was an inside-the-park home run. His second homer came in the sixth, off Bucky Veil.

TRANSACTIONS
1937: Traded Red Kress, Bobo Newsom, and Buster Mills
to the St. Louis Browns for Joe Vosmik.
1952: Selected Bill Werle off waivers from the St. Louis Cardinals.
1963: Released Billy Gardner.
2002: Claimed Jason Shiell off waivers from the San Diego Padres.

DEBUTS
1909: Jack Chesbro

BIRTHDATES
Ed Barry 1882 (1905–1907); Earl Wilson 1934 (1959–1966); Ernest Riles 1960 (1993)

DEATHS
None yet

October 3

1999 Steve Lomasney appeared in his only major league game, for the Red Sox, but struck out twice in his only two at-bats. A series of hard-luck injuries held him back from future appearances in future years.

1998 Needing a win to even up the Division Series at two games apiece, the Red Sox scored first in a tightly pitched contest. Pete Schourek was pressed into service for the Sox, and held the Indians to two hits and no runs in 5⅓ innings. Garciaparra's solo homer in the fourth was the only run in the game until the Indians got two on a double by Dave Justice off ace reliever Tom Gordon in the eighth inning. The Red Sox didn't get the win they needed, and Cleveland eliminated the Sox, 2–1.

1995 The first game of the AL Division Series against the Indians was a beauty. Boston got two runs in the third, gave up three in the sixth, and tied it in the eighth. Tim Naehring's homer gave the Sox the go-ahead run in the top of the 11th, but Albert Belle of the Indians matched that with a leadoff homer in the bottom of the inning. Employing perhaps a bit of gamesmanship, Red Sox manager Kevin Kennedy asked plate umpire Tim Welke to check whether the bat was corked. The bat was confiscated, sawn open, and found to be legal. Cleveland catcher Tony Pena (ex-Red Sox) ended the game in the 13th, a little after 2:00 A.M., with a two-out homer off Zane Smith. Cleveland 5, Boston 4.

1993 Greg Harris pitched one-third of an inning, appearing in his club-record 80th game of the year. Manager Butch Hobson apparently lacked a flair for the record books. Had he put Harris in one more game, say the game on October 2, Harris would have appeared in exactly half the season's games. Even worse, Harris was ambidextrous and he said that, while he always pitched right-handed, he really wanted one chance to throw both ways in a game. He was denied the opportunity. (On October 2, 2005, Mike Timlin eclipsed Harris' record.)

1992 The 1992 Red Sox finished in last place, only winning 45% of their games. They also homered only 84 times all year long, the lowest total for a full season since World War II. Boston beat the Yankees in a far-from-meaningful match at Fenway, 7–5. The win went to Scott Taylor, who threw 6⅓ innings of one-hit relief. It also turned out to be his only major league win.

1990 When Mike Greenwell hit into a double play in the eighth inning, it was #174 of the 1990 season. That total is the most committed by any major league team. Nevertheless, the Red Sox finished first in the AL East, and the Yankees finished last. The Red Sox won on Tom Brunansky's dramatic sliding catch by the Pesky Pole, preserving the slim 3–1 Sox lead. Come the ALCS, though, and just as in 1988, the Oakland A's won four games and swept. Boston scored a total of four runs in the four games, one run per game.

1982 Not that it really mattered, given that the Sox were in third place and the Yankees were in fifth, but on the final game of the season, Boston beat New York, 5–3, in 11 innings. The first Sox hit during the final frame was by Roger LaFrancois, who was 2-for-5 on the day. Three batters later, he scored the winning run. LaFrancois had been with the team for the entire year, and finished the season batting an even .400. LaFrancois remains the last player in baseball to have played with a team for an entire season and batted .400. Trouble is, he was only 4-for-10, some 492.2 plate appearances short of qualifying for the batting title.

1972 The Tigers beat the Red Sox 3–1 and thereby won the pennant, though the teams played an uneven number of games due to the players' strike early in the season. Boston played one less game than Detroit, and they ended the season with the same number of losses but the Sox had one less win. Had Boston had a chance to play one more game—the same number as the Tigers—and won it, they'd have finished tied with the Tigers and the two teams would have to meet in a playoff. But the agreement at the beginning of the season was just to play out the schedule, regardless of the number of games. That proved to Boston's disadvantage. You'd think the team was cursed or something.

1964 Billy Herman managed the final game of the 1964 season, after GM Pinky Higgins fired Johnny Pesky with two games remaining on the schedule. Herman's Sox won both games, just as Pesky's Sox had won the game before.

1948 Joe DiMaggio was 4-for-5 and drove in three, but the Red Sox still overwhelmed the Yankees, 10–5, with home runs by Dom DiMaggio and Vern Stephens, two doubles by Ted Williams, and both offensive and defensive work by Billy Goodman. When the Fenway crowd saw a "4" posted next to Detroit on the scoreboard, they knew that the Indians were losing. The 7–1 Indians loss, and the Red Sox victory, saw the two teams locked at 96–58, requiring a single-game playoff at Fenway on October 4.

1937 Joe DiMaggio's 46th home run of the year was a grand slam off Boston pitcher Joe "Smoky" Gonzales, ending the season (and Gonzales' brief stint in major league ball) with a 6–1 victory.

1917 Walter Johnson had a hard time in pitching matchups with Babe Ruth, including three 1–0 losses. Ruth didn't have it this day, yielding 11 hits—including the bases-clearing double that Johnson hit off him in the eighth. Washington won, 6–0. Before the ninth inning, only two Red Sox runners got as far as second base. Boston's share of the gate receipts went to benefit the 101st Regiment.

1914 It was called a "sleepy game" with "neither club showing much ginger until the finish." (*New York Times*) Ernie Shore only gave up one unearned first-inning run, and turned it over to reliever Guy Cooper after seven. The Yankees scored twice in the top of the ninth, but had to hold off the resurgent Red Sox in the bottom of the ninth as they scored two of their own—but one too few to tie. The Red Sox committed seven errors, four of them by Hal Janvrin at short. The *Globe* added that several Boston players "seemed to take very little interest in the game."

1912 Philadelphia's Boardwalk Brown held the Red Sox scoreless through four, but Boston got to him and scored eight times in the fifth (attributable to five Brown walks and Duffy Lewis's grand slam) and at least once in every inning thereafter—though Herb Pennock was responsible for all the later runs. The Sox won, 17–5.

1911 The Red Sox swept the October 3 doubleheader in New York, and then won the next day's game, too. Opening Day 1912 is in New York, and the Red Sox sweep a three-game series to kick off the season. In June, they sweep five games in New York and then take both halves of a twin bill on September 2. In fact, from October 3, 1911 until September 29, 1913, the Sox under manager Jake Stahl don't lose a single game in the Big Apple. There was one tie on May 24, 1913; that must have felt like a moral victory for the hapless Yankees.

In a curious Lewis–Lewis–Lewis–Lewis play, Jack Lewis stole second, drawing a throw, and Duffy Lewis stole home. Jack Lewis was shaken up on the play, so—despite having just stolen home and scored, Duffy Lewis took Jack's place on second base as a courtesy runner. Unfortunately, he didn't steal third and then home; that would have made for a better story. Nor did he score. Jack was OK and got back in the game.

1907 Cy Morgan (a three-hitter) out-pitched St. Louis' Harry Howell (a four-hitter), and Boston won the game, 1–0. It was the only win of the 1907 season between September 11 and the final game on October 5.

1906 Hard luck Joe Harris loses his 14th game in a row, and ends the season 2–21, despite pitching another terrific game (see his September 1 outing when he gave up only one run in 23 (!) innings, but lost). Harris pitched nine shutout innings. Boston got a run in the top of the 10th, but the Washington Nationals got to Harris for one in the bottom of the 10th to tie it up when his catcher Charlie Armbruster threw the ball back badly to him; it got away and a run scored. In the 11th, Harris walked two and let up a single, and lost another close one.

1903 Deacon Phillippe came back on one day's rest to beat Boston again, 4–2, before 18,801, the largest crowd of the Series. Jimmy Collins had half the Boston hits with a single and double, while Long Tom Hughes and Cy Young (who relieved Hughes after two innings) allowed five doubles (out of seven hits total). The 3–0 lead the Pirates built after three innings held, and the two teams headed off to Pittsburg with Boston down 1–2 in the Series.

DEBUTS
1964: Mike Ryan
1999: Steve Lomasney

BIRTHDATES
Al Shaw 1874 (1907); Dom Dallessandro 1913 (1937); Jack Lamabe 1936 (1963–1965); Dennis Eckersley 1954 (1978–1998); Jim Byrd 1968 (1993); Wil Cordero 1971 (1996–1997); Scott Cassidy 1975 (2005)

DEATHS
John Donahue 1949

October 4

2003 Facing elimination in the Division Series, the Sox were at least back home in Fenway, but it was a battle that stretched into extra innings. Derek Lowe, Mike Timlin, and Scott Williamson held the A's to just one run, and Oakland kept the Sox to just one run, too. In the bottom of the 11th inning, Doug Mirabelli singled with one out and Trot Nixon slammed a pinch-hit, two-run, game-winning, walk-off home run into the center-field seats off relief pitcher Rich Harden for the 3–1 Sox triumph.

2001 When the lineups were read at Camden Yards, Tim Raines Jr. was starting in center field and his father Tim Raines Sr. was starting beside him in left. It was only the second time that a father-son combination had played in the same game. The Griffeys—Senior and Junior—were the first. Raines the elder had just joined the Orioles the day before.

1995 Having lost Game One of the ALDS at 2:08 in the morning, the Red Sox got such sleep as they could and gathered again for this evening's game against the Indians. They had to face Orel Hershiser, though, and he shut out the Red Sox on just three hits. Erik Hanson started for the Sox and pitched scoreless ball until Omar Vizquel's two-run double in the bottom of the sixth; Boston lost, 4–0.

1987 On the last possible day, Roger Clemens won his 20th game of the year, a two-hit shutout of Milwaukee, 4–0. Roger had 12 K's and no walks. It was his league-leading seventh shutout of the season. Later in the year, Clemens won his second straight Cy Young Award.

1986 The Yankees beat the Red Sox twice in a doubleheader on the penultimate day of the 1986 season. Dave Righetti earned saves in both games, 5–3 and 3–1. With 46 saves in '86, he'd set a new record. Don Mattingly had four hits on the day and raised his average to .35119, but that left him nearly six points behind league-leading Wade Boggs, who was resting an injured hamstring to get ready for the World Series. If Mattingly had a 6-for-6 day on October 5, he could take the batting title from Boggs. It was, unsurprisingly, too tall an order.

1975 The ALCS opened in Boston and the Red Sox scored twice in the bottom of the first. Though they added five runs in the bottom of the seventh, they needn't have. Luis Tiant threw a three-hitter and the Sox beat the Oakland A's, 7–1.

1967 In the first game of the 1967 World Series, St. Louis Cardinal Lou Brock's four hits and two stolen bases were key offensive contributions. He singled and scored in the third, but Boston pitcher Jose Santiago evened the score by homering off Bob Gibson in his first World Series at-bat. Brock hit Santiago's first pitch in the seventh and then stole on Santiago's first pitch to the subsequent batter, moved to third on a ground out, and scored when Roger Maris grounded out to the second baseman. Maris had two RBI, both scoring Brock, and both coming on infield grounders. Gibson struck out 10, the only Boston run coming on Santiago's homer. St. Louis 2, Boston 1.

1948 Boston manager Joe McCarthy unexpectedly handed the ball to Denny Galehouse (8–7 on the season) as starting pitcher in the first playoff game in AL history. Cleveland player–manager Lou Boudreau started 19-game winner Gene Bearden. Boudreau hit safely four times, including two homers. The Sox lose the sudden-death game, just as in Game Seven of the '46 Series. Final score: 8–3.

1946 Norfolk, VA police chief John Woods, Red Sox pitcher from 1924 to 1926, was killed when his car collided with a wrecking truck that was hauling another car out of a ditch.

1945 A few days after the season ended, Boo Ferriss was shopping in Malden, Massachusetts when fire broke out in a store where he was buying seat covers for his car—the car fans had presented him late in the year. He helped maintain order while employees and customers were evacuated from the building.

1922 Litigation was not only a late 20th century plague. John F. Talbot of Somerville filed a suit seeking $10,000 from the Boston American League Baseball Club for injuries suffered when hit by a baseball in a July 8 game. He argued that the Red Sox were careless and negligent in failing to protect patrons at the park.

1918 For the second Series in a row, the champion Red Sox were to be disciplined for engaging in post-Series play. Word was that the National Baseball Commission would deprive several Boston players of the emblems usually presented to World Series winners.

1916 The Red Sox divided into two teams and played 10 innings at Braves Field, to accustom themselves to the venue that would serve as their home park for the 1916 World Series. After the workout, Duffy Lewis drove himself, Heinie Wagner, and George Foster to the State Prison in Charlestown where they presented the prison baseball team with several bats and balls for use in prison games. They also toured the death house and inspected the electric chair. On October 5, they were due to travel to Worcester to play the Philadelphia Athletics in a benefit game for former National League umpire John Gaffney.

1913 The final Boston Red Sox game of the season was termed a "weird exhibition" by the *Los Angeles Times*. The game, played in D.C., featured several role reversals, but mostly among the Washington players. Moeller played right field, then pitched, then played center. Gedeon played third and pitched. Walter Johnson played center and pitched, while Rip Williams played first, then catcher. Ainsmith started at second but took a stint on the mound as well. It went on and on. In all, eight players pitched, three caught, three played first, three played third, two played second, etc., etc. Even the "Old Fox," manager Clark Griffith, got into the act, playing three positions. During most of the day, the Nationals had no right fielder. Hal Janvrin hit two inside-the-park homers. The Sox lineup was pretty straightforward, though with Duffy Lewis playing third, a number of Nationals bunted in his direction. Despite it all, Washington actually won the game, 10–9, though Boston made it close with six runs in the top of the ninth.

1912 A small fire broke out in John I. Taylor's office on Washington Street. No World Series tickets or applications were destroyed, since all were at Fenway Park.

TRANSACTIONS
1963: Released Chet Nichols.
1965: Traded Bill Monbouquette to the Detroit Tigers for George Smith,
    George Thomas, and a PTBNL. The player—Jackie Moore—was
    named more than one year later, on October 13, 1966.
1999: Kirk Bullinger, Kip Gross, and Tim Harikkala are all granted free agency.

DEBUTS
1972: Vic Correll

BIRTHDATES
Don Lenhardt 1922 (1952–1954); Rip Repulski 1927 (1960–1961); Jimy Williams 1943 (manager, 1997–2001); Billy Hatcher 1960 (1992–1994); Chris James 1962 (1995)

DEATHS
John Woods 1946

October 5

2005 The Buckner that wasn't. Maybe the surest sign of a difference in Boston, a year after winning the World Series, came when second baseman Tony Graffanino booted a ready-made inning-ending double play in the top of the fifth. Almost immediately, the White Sox' Tadahito Iguchi slammed a three-run homer to give Chicago a 5–4 lead. Graffanino remained a favorite, and never had to endure the burden of a Bill Buckner. Boston lost the League Division Series, swept in three straight games by the dominant White Sox who went on to win the World Series in four straight. The Red Sox, decimated by injuries, were lucky to get into the playoffs but only lasted the minimum number of games.

2004 The visiting Red Sox beat the Anaheim Angels handily, 9–3, in the first game of the Division Series. Ramirez doubled, Ortiz singled, and the Sox got a run in the first. They broke the backs of the Angels, though, with a seven-run fourth inning, when Millar hit a two-run homer and Manny upped the ante with a three-run bomb, off starter Jarrod Washburn and reliever Scot Shields.

2003 The Red Sox evened the ALDS at two games apiece with a 5–4 come-from-behind win over Oakland, when a struggling (0–16) David Ortiz slammed Oakland reliever Keith Foulke's 3–2 pitch for a two-run double in the bottom of the eighth. Scott Williamson held the A's at bay, and the two teams traveled back to the Bay Area for the fifth and final game. Foulke would end up on the Red Sox in 2004 and threw the final pitch of that year's World Series.

2001 Calvin Pickering homered in his last at-bat in the major leagues…but wait! After a couple of years out of the bigs, he played with Kansas City for 32 games in 2004 and erased his name from the record books.

1988 Just two years after the disheartening loss in the 1986 World Series, the Red Sox were back in the post-season, facing off against the Oakland Athletics. Game One was held at Fenway Park, Bruce Hurst pitching for Boston against Dave Stewart. Oakland scored first when Jose Canseco hit a leadoff homer in the fourth. The Red Sox tied it in the bottom of the seventh on a walk, HBP, single, and sacrifice fly. In the top of the eighth, Oakland's Carney Lansford doubled and 1986 Sox star Dave Henderson singled him in, for what proved to be the winning run. Oakland 2, Boston 1.

1975 It was Reggie Cleveland against Oakland's Vida Blue in the second game of the League Championship Series. Reggie Jackson's two-run homer in the top of the first inning was an ominous beginning, and after Joe Rudi and Claudell Washington hit back-to-back doubles in the fourth, it stood 3–0 Oakland. Yaz hit a two-run homer in the bottom of the fourth. A Fisk double followed, then a Lynn single. Petrocelli grounded into a double play, which nonetheless brought in the tying third run. Rico hit a homer later, one of three more runs the Sox scored, while keeping Oakland scoreless. Boston 6, Oakland 3.

1967 The Sox want to win once in Boston, after Jose Santiago lost the tight 2–1 game the day before. Jim Lonborg rose to the occasion and even had a no-hitter going deep into the eighth inning. Julian Javier's two-out double was the only hit of the game for the Cardinals. Yaz hit a solo home run in the bottom of the fourth off St. Louis starter Dick Hughes. After two walks and an error loaded the bases with one out in the sixth, Ron Willis took over for Hughes, and only one inherited runner scored, on Rico Petrocelli's sac fly. Then Yaz sealed it with a three-run homer in the seventh, to greet Joe Hoerner, who had taken Willis's spot to pitch to Yastrzemski. Boston 5, St. Louis 0.

1923 It wasn't a big year for strikeouts. Washington's Walter Johnson led the league with 130, and got almost 10% of them in the last game of the year. Johnson struck out 12 Red Sox, winning his 17th game by a 4–2 margin.

1914 Walter Johnson, batting sixth in the Washington lineup, doubled and homered in his 9–3 win at Fenway, the win being his 28th of the year. Johnson's home run in the fourth broke a 2–2 tie and was the first ball ever hit into Fenway Park's center-field bleachers. His double paid off, too—it won him an extra $25.00, hitting a sign on the left-field wall that promised the sum for hitting the sign. He struck out Boston's young rookie, Babe Ruth, on three pitches. Ruth had entered to pinch hit for Ray Collins in the seventh.

1912 The Red Sox defeated the A's 3–0 behind the shutout pitching of Buck O'Brien, winning his 20th game of the year. It was the 105th win of the season for the team, an AL record until the 1927 Yankees reached 110. Boston's batting champ was Tris Speaker (.383); even with that average, he came in third in the league. Speaker led the league in homers (10) and doubles (53)—and he stole 52 bases. O'Brien had won five games in 1911. He won four games in 1913. Twenty of his 29 career wins were all concentrated in 1912.

Interest in the World Series against the Giants was intense, with over 3,000 people estimated taking the train from Boston to New York. Baseball in the days before radio saw a reported 10,000 telegraph operators expected to convey game play-by-play around the country. Hundreds of electric bulletin boards had been erected to display the results, and thousands of theaters were expected to seat patrons wanting to hear updates as they happened.

1906 October 5 and 6: New York won the last two games of the season, in Boston, and finished ahead of Boston in the standings. New York had also won the first three games of the year. In all, New York won 17 games and only lost four (there was one tie) in its battles against Boston. New York finished the season just three games out, but Boston was in last place 45½ games behind the pennant-winning White Sox.

TRANSACTIONS
1990: Tom Brunansky was granted free agency.

DEBUTS
1908: King Brady
1991: Josias Manzanillo, Eric Wedge

BIRTHDATES
Ed Hughes 1880 (1905–1906); Norm McMillan 1895 (1923); Dennis Bennett 1939 (1965–1967); Andy Kosco 1941 (1972); Rey Sanchez 1967 (2002)

DEATHS
Hal Bevan 1968

October 6

2004 Pedro Martinez pitched against Bartolo Colon. For a few minutes, the Angels took a 3–1 lead in the bottom of the fifth, but Jason Varitek's two-run homer in the top of the sixth evened it back up. A Ramirez sac fly in the seventh proved the winning run, but the Sox took out some insurance with four runs in the top of the ninth—the main blow a bases-clearing double by Cabrera—beating the Angels, 8–3. Now it was back to Fenway, only needing to win one more game for the Division title.

2003 Back in Oakland for the deciding game of the American League Division Series, Manny Ramirez's three-run homer was the big blow in the four-run Red Sox sixth, and the Sox held on to win—just barely. With two outs in the bottom of the seventh, Jermaine Dye hit a looper and a terrible collision between Johnny Damon's head and Damian Jackson's head rendered Damon unconscious on the field for quite some time. An ambulance drove onto the field and bore him away. Heads-up play caught Dye trying to take second before time was called. With a slim one-run lead, Scott Williamson walked the first two men he faced in the bottom of the ninth. Derek Lowe was brought on, and got one out but it was on a sacrifice bunt that moved the runners up. Lowe pitched to pinch-hitter Adam Melhuse, and struck him out, but then walked the next batter. Bases loaded, two outs, he fooled the pinch-hitting Terrence Long on a called third strike, and the Red Sox were set to travel to New York and face the Yankees for the pennant.

2000 Red Sox CEO John Harrington announced that the team would take bids from prospective buyers of the ball club, with the Yawkey Trust controlling interest being up for sale. Though having planned to build a new ballpark first, and then sell the club, it was proving impossible to attract private funding for a new stadium to replace Fenway Park, despite pledges of over $100 million in state infrastructure "improvements" and a commitment of another $212 million in city funds. The sale ultimately saved taxpayers a ton of money, and saved Fenway Park.

1999 Bartolo Colon faced Pedro Martinez in Game One of the 1999 Division Series. Nomar Garciaparra and Mike Stanley each drove in an early run, but Pedro had to leave the game after the fourth inning with a pulled muscle in his upper back, and Jim Thome took advantage of John Valentin's error with a two-run homer on the next pitch. Travis Fryman hit a bases-loaded single off reliever Rich Garces in the bottom of the ninth, for a 3–2 Cleveland victory.

1995 As in 1988 and 1990, the Red Sox had again won the AL East. As in 1988 and 1990, the Red Sox couldn't win a single game in the 1995 post-season. Tim Wakefield's knuckler was seriously hampered by the strong winds that swirled around Fenway Park this evening. The Sox were swept by the Indians, losing 8–2. The two Sox sluggers—Jose Canseco and Mo Vaughn—were a combined 0-for-27 (leaving 17 baserunners stranded) in the three games. The 1995 sweep made 13 straight defeats in post-season play.

1990 Roger Clemens and Oakland's Dave Stewart went head-to-head a number of times, and it seemed like Stewart always came out on top. The Rocket threw six shutout innings in Game One of the 1990 AL Championship Series, clinging to a 1–0 lead after Wade Boggs' homer into the screen in left. The A's tied it in the seventh, went ahead in the eighth, and then dumped a post-season record seven runs on the reeling Red Sox in the top of the ninth. 9–1, Oakland.

1988 Game Two, ALCS. Storm Davis pitching for Oakland, and Roger Clemens for the Red Sox. Boston scored first, in the bottom of the sixth, two times, on a walk, walk, error, and single. Faced with two runs on the board, though, Oakland one-upped the Red Sox with three runs in the top of the seventh. Henderson singled and Canseco homered for the first two. A single, a balk, and a Clemens wild pitch set the stage for Mark McGwire to single home the third run. Gedman homered to tie it in the bottom of the seventh, but in the ninth three straight singles—including the game-winner from Walt Weiss—scored a fourth, unanswered run. Athletics 4, Red Sox 3. Boston was down 2–0 in the best-of-seven series.

1985 Wade Boggs went 3-for-4, with a double, for a team-record total of 240 hits in 1985. He hit safely in 135 games, tying a major league record. Boggs had 758 plate appearances, an American League mark. Bill Buckner had a 2-for-5 day, giving him 201 hits on the year, becoming one of only five players who reached the 200-hit mark in both leagues.

1962 The Red Sox name Johnny Pesky to replace Pinky Higgins as field manager. Unfortunately, Higgins is bumped upstairs rather than shown the door and his disinclination to do anything to help Pesky proves destructive.

1946 The first World Series appearance by the Red Sox since 1918 opened with a second-inning Boston run when Rudy York was hit by a pitch, advanced to second when Doerr walked, then scored when Mike Higgins singled to center. St. Louis tied it in the bottom of the sixth on a Schoendienst single and Musial double. The Cardinals went ahead by one in the eighth, but the Sox tied it up again in the top of the ninth. Howie Pollet was still pitching in the 10th when York hit a two-out homer out of Sportsman's Park. 3–2, Red Sox.

1923 Suffolk County District Attorney Thomas C. O'Brien announced an investigation into the ownership of both Boston baseball teams, questioning why there seemed to have been so many one-sided trades to the detriment of the Boston clubs. Two days later, having studied the incorporation papers, the D.A. suggested it was not a matter he would look into any more deeply.

1915 It was, in effect, a dress rehearsal for the World Series. Manager Bill Carrigan used pitchers Shore, Leonard, Wood, and Mays in the first game against New York; the combination shut out the Yankees, 2–0. Babe Ruth pitched the whole second game and won that one, 4–2. Ruth finished the season with an 18–8 (2.44 ERA) mark, starting 1–5 but then winning 17 of his last 20 decisions. Despite that stellar season, he was never asked to pitch in the 1915 World Series. Sportswriter Joe Cashman suggested that manager Bill Carrigan wanted to teach him a lesson, that the team could succeed without him.

1906 Not realizing it was to be his last at-bat, Chick Stahl hit a two-run home run in the eighth inning of a game against former teammate and now New York pitcher Long Tom Hughes. Stahl took his life before the next season began (see March 28, 1907), so like Ted Williams and Don Gile, he is among Boston players who homered in their last at-bat.

1903 The Pirates led the World Series three games to one, when a travel day and rainout enabled Deacon Phillippe to pitch and win again, 5–4, before 7,600 at Pittsburg. Boston rallied for three runs in the ninth but it was not enough. Ginger Beaumont and Honus Wagner had three hits, but Honus will manage just .222 for the World Series. Even though Boston lost, the day is noted for the first rendition of "Tessie" by the Royal Rooters. Once they got it down right, its incessant use began to rattle the Pirates. Just a half-year later, the *Boston Globe* reported that "Baseball fans look upon it as the biggest hoodoo ever fastened to a club." (See May 13, 1904.)

TRANSACTIONS
1994: Andy Tomberlin granted free agency.
1995: Acquired Brent Cookson off waivers from Kansas City. Granted free agency to Juan Bell and Terry Shumpert.

DEBUTS
1908: Doc McMahon

BIRTHDATES
Len Swormstedt 1878 (1906); Red Morgan 1883 (1906); John Knight 1885 (1907); Ken Chase 1913 (1942–1943); Jerry Stephenson 1943 (1963–1968); Oil Can Boyd 1959 (1982–1989); Robert Person 1969 (2003); Darren Oliver 1970 (2002)

DEATHS
None yet

October 7

2005 Papi (Ortiz) hit a home run and Manny hit two, but all three were solo shots, and the Red Sox lost to the other Sox, 5–3, swept in the AL Division Series in three straight games. Given all they suffered throughout the season, effectively losing their ace (Schilling) and closer (Foulke) for most of the year, it was surprising they made it to the post-season for an unprecedented (for a Boston ball club) three straight years. As Johnny Damon said, "We didn't really have a No. 1 starter all year. Or even a No. 2."

1999 Though Boston scored one run in the third, the Indians slaughtered Bret Sagerhagen and the Red Sox, 11–1, to take a 2–0 lead in the ALDS. Jim Thome homered for the second day in a row, this one a grand slam. Harold Baines had a three-run dinger. Charles Nagy pitched well. The margin of loss made this the worst defeat in Red Sox post-season history.

1990 As in Game One of the L.C.S., the Sox scored first—with one run. As in Game One, that was the only run they scored. Harold Baines knocked in three runs and Oakland won 4–1, taking a 2–0 lead in the playoffs.

1986 The first game of the American League Championship Series pitted California's Mike Witt (18–10, 2.84 ERA) against Roger Clemens (24–4, 2.48 ERA), but the results weren't even close. Witt threw a complete game, giving up one run on five hits. After striking out the first two Angels in the second, Clemens got banged around for four runs on three hits. By the time he left the game in the eighth, Clemens had struck out five, but he'd walked three, yielded 10 hits and eight runs (seven earned). "Roger was throwing the ball down the middle of the plate," said Rich Gedman. "He never throws the ball down the middle of the plate." Final score: California 8, Boston 1.

1975 The Red Sox swept the Oakland A's in three straight games with a 5–3 win at Alameda County Coliseum, jumping out to a 4–0 lead over Ken Holtzman, starting (on two days' rest) for the second time in the best-of-five short series. Rick Wise got the win, relieved by Dick Drago.

1967 Game Three of the World Series saw the Cardinals score three times in the first couple of innings off Gary Bell. St. Louis pitcher Nelson Briles scattered six singles and a solo home run by Reggie Smith, but the Red Sox never fully came alive and Briles had himself a complete game 5–2 win, and the Cardinals had a 2–1 edge in the Series.

1960 A little over a week after retiring from baseball, Ted Williams joked that he might have to return so he could get some peace and quiet. Williams was being deluged with job offers. "It's become a real rat race," he said. He was being offered money for his life's story, both in a book and a film. Baseball clubs mentioned executive positions, among them the Yomiuru Giants of Japan. A hotel in Key West even wanted him to take over their establishment.

1946 Harry Brecheen handled the Red Sox in Game Two of the World Series, scattering just four singles, shutting out Boston, 3–0. Del Rice led off the St. Louis third with a double, and Brecheen singled him home. The Cards added a pair more in the fifth, but Boston never could get to Brecheen.

1923 The Red Sox finished in last place, and the Yankees finished in first place. New York went on to win their first World Championship—with 11 former Red Sox players on their roster.

1916 Playing again in Braves Field, Rube Marquard of the Brooklyn Robins battled Ernie Shore of the Sox, and the two pitchers were evenly matched, the Sox holding just a 2–1 advantage after six (and that only because of a brilliant catch and throw to the plate by Hooper in the fourth). Janvrin doubled off Marquard to lead the Sox seventh, and errors on back-to-back plays had the Robins reeling. A throw home failed to choke off another run, and the Red Sox added three more, plus another in the eighth. Brooklyn mounted a four-run rally in the top of the ninth but Carl Mays finally got the last out, and it was a 6–5 Boston win.

After the game, an argument in a Brooklyn barroom with a rabid Brooklyn booster resulted in the death William Sickles, a 39-year-old letter carrier and fervent Red Sox fan. Sickles should be a hero in Red Sox Nation; he lost his life defending the Sox.

1914 It became obvious early on that the Red Sox were not going to prevent the Senators from claiming third place, so the game morphed into "purely a burlesque." (*Washington Post*) Bedient started for Boston, threw three innings, and then turned the ball over to Ruth. Ruth threw three and handed it to Guy Cooper, who pitched two and gave the ball to Tris Speaker. It was Speaker's one and only stint on the mound and he retired the side in the ninth, touched only for a couple of hits and one run. Not to be outdone, Senators skipper Clark Griffith decided to pitch an inning, too; it was like an annual appearance for him, the fourth time he'd appeared in one single ballgame. He struck out one, gave up one hit, and set the Sox down scoreless. Washington won, 11–4.

1911 The last ballgame played at the Huntington Avenue Grounds is a good one for Boston; the Red Sox rout the Senators, 8–1.

SHATTERING OF HER ROMANCE IS DUE TO CLUB PRESIDENT—Miss Eleanor Keane, engaged to marry Sox left-fielder Duffy Lewis this week, was heartbroken. She claimed that Lewis told her that "the wedding could not take place on account of the advice he had received from [Red Sox] President Taylor." The *Washington Post* also carried her acknowledgement that hers was the third engagement Lewis had broken. (See also October 24.)

1905 Boston closes an otherwise undistinguished season with four straight wins over the Highlanders, capped by a doubleheader sweep on this day. In fact, Boston won its last eight games of the year, winning all seven scheduled October games. The team batting average for the season, though, was a pathetic .234. Cy Young posted a stellar 1.82 ERA—his third-best season—but lost 19 games while only winning 18.

1904 Parity seemingly achieved, New York took a half-game lead in the pennant race as Chesbro beat Gibson 3–2, with four games to play—every one of them head-to-head matchups with Boston. It was Chesbro's 41st win (!) of the season.

1903 Cy Young stops the Pirates 11–2 on six hits. Pittsburg's Brickyard Kennedy, pitching on his 35th birthday, is ahead 4–2 in the sixth when Honus Wagner makes two errors, and Boston scores six runs. After giving up another four runs in the seventh, Kennedy is gone, and will not pitch in the majors again. Patsy Dougherty has a single and two triples, while Chick Stahl and Jimmy Collins add three baggers. The 36-year-old Cy Young drives in three Boston runs.

TRANSACTIONS
1975: Released Dick McAuliffe.
1997: Jesus Tavarez was granted free agency.

DEBUTS
1908: Harry Ostdiek

BIRTHDATES
Grady Hatton 1922 (1954–1955); Milt Cuyler 1968 (1996); Butch Henry 1968 (1997–1998)

DEATHS
Charlie Armbruster 1964; Walt Ripley 1990

October 8

2004 Bronson Arroyo was pitching well, and the Red Sox hitters piled up a lead of 6–1. It looked like the Sox would sweep the ALDS from Anaheim, when all of a sudden, the lead was completely wiped out by a five-run Angels seventh inning. Tied after regulation, the Sox had one on but two outs in the bottom of the 10th when Angels manager Mike Scioscia summoned Game One starter Jarrod Washburn to face the lefty, David Ortiz. One pitch. Boom! Home run! An extra-inning walk-off home run before a delirious Fenway, to propel the Sox to the next stage: facing the Yankees in the League Championship Series.

2003 New York and Boston meet again in post-season play. After losing four games to one in 1999, the Red Sox wanted to win it all this time. At Yankee Stadium, Boston took Game One behind Tim Wakefield's two-hit, six-inning stint, while Mike Mussina yielded home runs to David Ortiz, Todd Walker, and Manny Ramirez. Boston 5, New York 3.

1988 After the Athletics won the first two games at Fenway, Game Three of the 1988 ALCS moved to the Oakland–Alameda County Coliseum. The Red Sox roared off to a good start, driving Bob Welch out of the box and amassing a 5–0 lead after just 1½ innings. Mike Greenwell doubled in two in the first, and hit a solo homer in the second. Boston's Mike Boddicker didn't last much longer, though. The A's figured him out for four in the bottom of the second and took the lead with two more in the third. McGwire, Lansford, and Ron Hassey all homered off Boddicker before he was pulled. By the time the game was over, Oakland had a commanding 3–0 lead in the series. Score: Oakland 10, Boston 6.

1986 Bruce Hurst started Game Two of the ALCS and only gave up two runs—one unearned. Meanwhile, Sox second baseman Marty Barrett drove in a run in the bottom of the first and a run in the bottom of the second. The Angels tied it, but Dwight Evans drove in Bill Buckner to re-take the lead in the fifth. The Sox added three runs in the seventh and three more in the eighth. Boston 9, California 3.

1967 Game Four of the World Series had Bob Gibson on the mound for St. Louis, and Jose Santiago again throwing for Boston. Gibson was the man. Santiago got tagged for six hits and four runs and was removed in the bottom of the first inning so that Gary Bell could retire the last Cardinal in the inning: Gibson. Jerry Stephenson came in to pitch the third and he was lit up for another two runs. Gibson, meanwhile, was unperturbed by Red Sox batters. Yaz was 2-for-4 with a double, Jose Tartabull was 2-for-4, but the only other player to have a hit was George Scott, and no one drove in or scored a run. It was a 6–0 shutout and the Cardinals were up three games to one. Ken Brett pitched a hitless eighth inning. At age 19 years, 20 days, he remains the youngest American League player to appear in a World Series game.

1915 Baker Bowl was the venue for Game One of the World Series, the Phillies hosting the Red Sox. Two singles off Ernie Shore in the bottom of the fourth scored the only run in the game until Boston tied it in the eighth on a walk, fielder's choice, and single by Lewis. The Phillies came right back, scoring twice without getting the ball out of the infield (and without an error) on a couple of walks and a couple of infield singles. Only one Phils hit (a Texas Leaguer) made it out of the infield, yet they won, 3–1, behind Grover Cleveland Alexander.

1912 It had been nine long years since the 1903 World Series. It was Jeff Tesreau for the Giants against 22-year-old Smoky Joe Wood for the Red Sox, with Game One set at the Polo Grounds in New York. The Giants had a substantial edge on paper, outhitting Boston by 50 points and with an ERA lower by one full run. And they scored first, two runs in the third, when Red Murray singled, before making the third out himself trying to stretch it to a double (8-2-6). Boston got one in the sixth after Speaker tripled, and a big three runs in the top of the seventh when Hooper doubled in Wagner and Yerkes drove in two more. Chief Meyers drove in one and the Giants had runners on second and third with one out. Wood settled down and struck out the two final batters (for a total of 11 K's) and saved his own 4–3 victory.

1904 Boston had traveled to New York to play one game on October 7, and they were beaten, 3–2, losing their lead in the standings to the New York team. Both teams hopped on the train to travel to Boston to play two on October 8. Jack Chesbro, the October 7 winner, tried to pitch again on zero days' rest. That wasn't a good idea; Boston won behind Dinneen, 13–2. And Cy Young shut out New York, 1–0, in the second game. Then both teams entrained back to New York to play the final two games of the season there on Monday the 10th. Why the back and forth? It seems that New York's owner Frank Farrell was trying to make a little more money and had rented out the ballpark to Columbia University for football games on the 8th. He easily obtained Boston's consent to play the one game that had been scheduled for the 8th in Boston. Since the two teams were to be back in The Hub, it provided an opportunity to make up a rained-out game from June 29, so a doubleheader was ordered. Thank you, Mr. Farrell.

1903 Bill Dinneen evens the Series with a 6–3 win over Pittsburgh's Sam Leever, who was 25–7 during the season. Ginger Beaumont leads the offense with four hits and two steals, but Boston scores more runs.

TRANSACTIONS
1949: Traded Billy Hitchcock to the Philadelphia Athletics for Buddy Rosar.
1996: Obtained Bob Milacki from the Mariners on waivers,
and granted Jeff Manto his free agency.

BIRTHDATES
Larry Pratt 1886 (1914); Wally Moses 1910 (1946–1948); Lee Rogers 1913 (1938); Rex Cecil 1916 (1944–1945); Bob Gillespie 1919 (1950); Catfish Metkovich 1920 (1943–1946); Bill Landis 1942 (1967–1969); Jerry Reed 1955 (1990); Sandy Martinez 1970 (2004)

DEATHS
Murray Wall 1971; Ray Haley 1973; Boob Fowler 1988

October 9

2003 In Game Two of the League Championship Series, the Yankees evened it up with a win. Andy Pettitte struggled in the first two innings, allowing six hits and walking a batter, but was bailed out by a couple of key double plays. He out-pitched Derek Lowe, though. Lowe was throwing on short rest and yielded all six Yankees runs. New York 6, Boston 2.

1999 Facing sudden defeat in the best-of-five AL Division Series, the Sox started Pedro's brother Ramon Martinez against Cleveland's Jaret Wright. Twice the Sox took one-run leads, only to have Cleveland go ahead or re-tie the score. Brian Daubach's three-run homer followed John Valentin's tie-breaking two-run double, and the Sox scored six runs in the seventh. Derek Lowe got the 9–3 win in relief.

1990 As in Game One and Game Two of the best-of-seven Championship Series, Boston scored first, with one run. For the third time, they could neither hold nor build on their lead. Three Boston errors were not helpful, either. Oakland won, 4–1, and now held a 3–0 lead in the best-of-seven series.

1988 Bruce Hurst tried to stave off a four-game Oakland sweep of the League Championship Series, but the Athletics would not be denied. Canseco homered in the first and they got another run in the third. That was enough in itself, since the Red Sox only ever scored once, on a Jim Rice groundout. Dennis Eckersley saved the 4–1 win—in fact, Eckersley saved every one of the four games and was named the MVP. All four games were well-contested, but the Red Sox came up short every time and had now lost six straight post-season games.

1967 A loss in Game Five meant elimination, but the Red Sox had Jim Lonborg going for them. Lonborg was 22–9 in the regular season and had thrown a one-hitter in Game Two. He was masterful again. Ken Harrelson singled home an unearned run in the third for the Red Sox, but Steve Carlton got through six innings giving up just three hits. The game was 1–0 Red Sox, heading into the ninth. Ron Willis toed the rubber, but loaded the bases with a walk, a double, and an intentional walk, and then departed, saying "Good luck" to a former Sox pitcher, Jack Lamabe. Elston Howard's single scored two, which was good for the Red Sox because Roger Maris hit a solo homer with two outs in the bottom of the ninth. Lonborg's shutout was spoiled, but he had a 3–1 three-hitter, and the Series was headed back to Boston. "I didn't even knock anyone down," Lonborg said with a grin after the game.

1946 Boo Ferriss against Murry Dickson in Game Three. Rudy York homered again, and again it was the game-winner. This time, it came not in the 10th inning, but in the bottom of the first inning, at Fenway Park. The Red Sox added an insurance run in the bottom of the eighth, but they didn't need it. Ferriss faced down St. Louis, shutting them out 4–0 on just six hits, and the Red Sox took a lead in the Series, 2–1.

1940 Herb Pennock was appointed the new head of the Red Sox farm system, the former Sox (and Yankees) pitcher taking over from Billy Evans, who had built the system after Tom Yawkey bought the ball club.

1916 Babe Ruth got his first World Series start; his counterpart was Brooklyn's Sherry Smith. Both pitched complete games—through 14 innings. In fact, the *Boston Traveler* reported that both starters threw 148 pitches. The third batter in the top of the first was Hy Myers, and he hit a drive to deep right-center that neither Tillie Walker nor Harry Hooper could corral. Myers had himself an inside-the-park home run and a quick 1–0 lead for the Robins. After 323.2 innings, it was the only home run that Babe Ruth surrendered in all of 1916. In the bottom of the third, Everett Scott led off with a triple. He had to hold at third when Thomas grounded to second, but when Ruth grounded to second again, Cutshaw didn't field as cleanly, so, though he got Ruth at first, Scott scored the tying run. Inning after inning passed, and neither team scored. Finally, in the bottom of the 14th inning, Hoblitzell walked (for the fourth time in the game—no one has topped this Series record), and Lewis sacrificed him to second. Larry Gardner was only 3-for-17 in the Series. Carrigan decided to send up a pinch-hitter, Del Gainer, for his first at bat of the Series. McNally was in to run for Hoblitzell. On the second pitch he saw, Gainer singled to left field and McNally wheeled around third and scored easily—winning the game, 2–1. Ruth had thrown 13 scoreless innings. It was the start of his streak of scoreless World Series innings that would run to more than 29⅔ innings. The 14 innings were the most of any Series game until 2005's Game Three matched it. Hooper's assist in the third inning gave him five in Series play; only Ross Youngs of the Yankees has matched the total.

More than 15 years later, the quaintly-named Jim Nasium wrote a piece in *The Sporting News* (December 3, 1931) in which he definitively stated that McNally missed home plate by a full six inches. But catcher Otto Miller still hadn't tagged him out, so the win remained uncontested.

There was some confusion attendant on the playing of "Tessie," when the band suddenly started up playing as the Sox were at bat in the top of the 11th. Not even the most ardent Royal Rooter would have wanted the band to play while Boston was batting, and the group could not determine who ordered it up. It was immediately stopped when an emissary of Brooklyn president Ebbets shouted, "Cut that out!" It was reported to be "the first time in the history of a World's Series that the musicians were forbidden to play whenever they chose." Some Boston fans wondered why the ban did not apply to Brooklyn fans who "beat their dish-pan accompaniment while Boston was at bat" on other occasions.

1915 World Series, Game Two. Philadelphia's Erksine Mayer walked Harry Hooper to lead off the game. With one out, Speaker singled Hooper to third on a hit-and-run, and then the two tried a delayed double steal. Speaker was out at second, but Ed Burns dropped the return throw to home plate and the Red Sox had a 1–0 lead that held to the bottom of the fifth when the Phils tied it up on back-to-back doubles by Cravath and Luderus. Bancroft singled in the sixth, but those were the only three hits off Boston's Rube Foster. President Woodrow Wilson was watching quite a game, tied 1–1 after eight full. Larry Gardner singled to open the ninth and, after one out, advanced to second on Janvrin's grounder. Manager Bill Carrigan wasn't about to take out Foster, so he let him hit for himself (he was a .277 hitter in 1915)—and Foster lofted one that fell in right-center, driving in what proved the winning run, as he retired the side 1-2-3 in the bottom of the ninth. Foster was 3-for-4 at the plate. Boston 2, Philadelphia 1, and the Series was tied one game apiece as it moved on to Boston.

1912 Boston rooters were thrilled when the Sox scored three times in the bottom of the first inning (two unearned). The Giants nibbled back with one in the second and one in the fourth, though the Sox added another in the fifth. The top of the eighth saw New York get to starter Ray Collins and reliever Charley Hall for three runs, and a 5–4 lead, but shortstop Fletcher's third error of the day set up the tying run for Boston in the bottom of the eighth. In the 10th, Merkle tripled and a sacrifice fly brought him home. Backs against the wall, Tris Speaker drove one far to center field and looked to have tied it back up on an inside-the-park home run when the throw beat him to the plate. But catcher Art Wilson couldn't hold the ball; Speaker was credited with a triple and scored on the error, and the game was re-tied at 6–6. (The *New York Times* suggested that Wilson's error may have been fortuitous, preventing a scandal, since Speaker had been interfered with three times as he raced around the bases.) After 11 innings, with Christy Mathewson still on the mound for the Giants, the still-tied game was called due to darkness. It is one of just three tie games in Series history.

1905 The first "city series" game between the Boston Americans and the Boston Nationals resulted in a 5–2 win for the Nationals, Bill Dinneen losing to Vic Willis. According to Troy Soos, the Americans then swept the next six games to win the 1905 series. When the two teams matched up again in the 1907 postseason, the Americans won another six in a row. Fans lost interest and it was years before the idea was revived.

TRANSACTIONS
1956: Released Harry Dorish.
1995: Luis Aquino signed as free agent.
2002: Claimed Brandon Lyon off waivers from the Toronto Blue Jays.

BIRTHDATES
Jim Tatum 1967 (1996); Bill Pulsipher 1973 (2001)

DEATHS
Red Kleinow 1929; Mike Guerra 1992

October 10

1999 Down two games to one in the best-of-five ALDS., the Sox were forced to start Kent Mercker against Indians ace Bartolo Colon. Cleveland got a run in the top of the first, but Boston brought their bats to this game and scored 23 runs on 24 hits (both new post-season records). Final score, 23–7. Other records set or tied occurred when Jason Varitek scored five runs and when Mike Stanley had five hits. John Valentin had a pair of homers.

1990 The Red Sox had lost to Oakland in the first three games of the American League Championship Series. No team in the history of baseball had ever come back from being down 3–0 to win a best-of-seven set. It was another Dave Stewart–Roger Clemens pairing, but in the second inning Clemens started jawing with plate umpire Terry Cooney, matters escalated, and Clemens got himself thrown out of the game. Tom Bolton warmed up quickly, came on to relieve Clemens, and promptly surrendered a two-run double to Mike Gallego. Boston lost the game, 3–1, swept in four games, having scored just one lone run in each of the four losses. With two losses to close the 1986 World Series, and having been swept in four in 1988, also by Oakland, the Red Sox had now lost 10 consecutive post-season ballgames.

1986 Candelaria against The Can at Anaheim Stadium, with the ALCS. tied after two games. The Angels scored once in the sixth, to match the one the Sox had scored in the second. Both Dick Schofield and Gary Pettis homered off Oil Can Boyd in the seventh, and California batters gave Candelaria the win, as Donnie Moore got the save.

1946 Tex Hughson didn't have it. The Cardinals scored three in the second and three in the third, and Hughson was shown to the showers. His fielding error cost the final two runs. But St. Louis wasn't through. They scored a run in the fifth, a run in the seventh, and four more runs in the top of the ninth. The Red Sox ran through six pitchers, and the Cardinals had 20 hits and four walks, while Red Sox fielders committed four errors. Maybe they were lucky the score wasn't higher. St. Louis 12, Boston 3.

1916 Game Three of the 1916 World Series was the first game in Brooklyn. The Robins scored in the third and fourth, and added two runs in the fifth when Ivy Olson tripled in two men Carl Mays had walked, to build up a 4–0 lead. Jack Coombs gave up a couple of hits and a couple of runs in the sixth, and was replaced after Larry Gardner homered in the seventh, but Jeff Pfeffer shut the door (as did Rube Foster for the Red Sox after the fifth), and Brooklyn won, 4–3.

1912 Game Three, in Boston, sees Buck O'Brien limit the Giants to one run in the second and one in the fourth. New York's Rube Marquard held the Red Sox scoreless all the way until the bottom of the ninth inning. A one-out single by Duffy Lewis and a double by Larry Gardner drove in one. Heinie Wagner, coaching at third, tried to hold up Lewis, but Tris Speaker shoved Wagner aside and Lewis scored! Fans argued that Gardner could easily have made second, but for Wagner's conservative coaching. Then Stahl reached on a fielder's choice, and the fielder (Marquard himself) made the right choice, nipping Gardner as he was trying to reach third. Tension built as Merkle made an error and Wagner reached first, sending pinch-runner Olaf Henriksen to third—and then Wagner stole second. But Marquard's focus was on Hick Cady at the plate. Cady drove the ball very deep to right-center, both runners raced to score, and the Boston crowd erupted in celebration with fans flocking to the exits—but 5'6" right-fielder Josh Devore made the catch of his life, running back at top speed and reaching up to make the catch. Giants 2, Red Sox 1. Some Sox fans who rushed out prematurely only learned later that their team had lost.

Neal Ball's only role in the Series was an eighth-inning pinch-hit appearance which saw him swing three times and strike out—but still earn a World Series share. A *Washington Post* writer noted that he did more than infielder Marty Krug, who "merely sat on the bench and looked wise." (For a theory regarding Krug's impact on the Series, see September 20, 1912.)

1911   In competition at Comiskey Park, Harry Hooper took first place in an "accurate throwing" contest, placed second in the 100-yard dash, and came in third in the long-distance throw.

1910   More than 4,000 people came to Centennial Field in Burlington, Vermont to see two graduates of the University of Vermont field teams drawn from the Boston Red Sox. Larry Gardner's team beat Ray Collins' team, 4–1.

1904   Back in New York yet again (see October 8, 1904), the Highlanders and the Boston Americans were set to play a season-ending doubleheader at Hilltop Park. If Boston won either game, they won the pennant. New York's ace pitcher Chesbro threw a wild pitch in the top of the ninth, and Boston's Lou Criger scored from third, to give Boston a 3–2 lead. Dinneen kept NY from scoring in the bottom of the ninth, and Boston won its second straight pennant. It was Dinneen's 37th complete game of the year. Boston would win four more pennants for a total of six, before the team that became the Yankees finally won their first pennant 17 years later. New York second baseman Jimmy Williams (no relation to Jimy Williams) committed an error earlier in the game which let in the first two Boston runs.

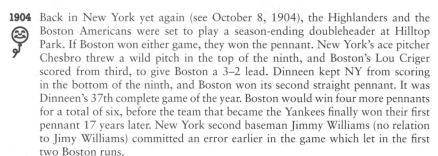

Giants president John T. Brush had proclaimed, "We are content to rest on our laurels." *The Baseball Chronology* advises that John McGraw let it be known that "he, not president John Brush, was responsible for refusing to play the AL winner in a post season series." *The Sporting News* will declare Boston champions by default.

1903   Do things sometimes come in threes? Three days' rest are apparently too much for Phillippe, who gives up first-inning triples to Boston's Jimmy Collins and Chick Stahl for a 2–0 lead. Five of the first 11 hits are triples, as the ground rules call for any balls hit into the crowds to be three baggers. In all, there were seven triples hit in the game, five by Boston. The Pirates made three errors and Cy Young won fairly easily, 7–3.

TRANSACTIONS
1996: Milt Cuyler was granted free agency.

BIRTHDATES
Pep Deininger 1877 (1902); Tommy Fine 1914 (1947); Floyd Baker 1916 (1953–1954)

DEATHS
Louis Leroy 1944; Wally Moses 1990; Joe Wood 2002

October 11

2003 At Fenway Park, the Yankees and Red Sox grappled in a classic Roger Clemens–Pedro Martinez matchup, with New York coming back to overcome an early 2–0 Sox lead. Manny Ramirez took exception to a Clemens pitch, and both benches cleared. Seemingly out of nowhere, Yanks bench coach (and former Sox skipper Don Zimmer) charged Martinez, who sidestepped Zim, grabbed his head, and flipped him to the ground; after the game, Zimmer tearfully apologizes. In the ninth inning, blood is drawn as Yankees reliever Jeff Nelson suddenly assaults groundskeeper Paul Williams, objecting to Williams' rooting for the Red Sox. Yankees outfielder Karim Garcia leaps over bullpen walls and joins the attack on the groundskeeper. Both Yankees players are charged by police, and ultimately sentenced to perform community service. New York 4, Boston 3.

1999 Bret Saberhagen (BOS) against Charles Nagy (CLE) in the deciding game of the 1999 ALDS. It was a see-saw affair, which saw the Sox score twice in the first, but the Indians counter with three—and add two more in the second. Cleveland manager Mike Hargrove walked Nomar Garciaparra to load the bases in the top of the third, to get to Troy O'Leary. On the first pitch, O'Leary hit a grand slam—the first ever in Red Sox post-season play. It was 8–8 before Boston finished batting in the fourth, and stayed that way until the seventh, when Hargrove tried to play the percentages again. Once more, he walked Nomar to get to O'Leary. Once more, O'Leary made him pay, again hitting the first pitch, this time for a three-run homer. The seven RBIs by the hero of the day tied a post-season record. Pedro Martinez, meanwhile, was heroic as well, throwing six innings of no-hit baseball in relief and it was lights-out for the Indians, while the Sox were set to go to New York and face the Yankees for the pennant.

1986 It was Game Four in the best-of-seven ALCS and Roger Clemens fended off the Angels for eight innings. Buckner doubled in one run for the Red Sox in the sixth, and Marty Barrett singled in Spike Owen, then scored a second run in the two-run eighth. Clemens took a 3–0 lead into the ninth. Doug DeCinces cracked the armor with a leadoff homer. After getting one out, Clemens gave up two singles and manager John McNamara summoned Calvin Schiraldi. This was never a good move in the 1986 post-season. Pettis doubled, scoring one. After an intentional walk, and a strikeout, Schiraldi hit Brian Downing, giving him an RBI and, worse, tying the score. The game went into extra innings. Doug Corbett got the Red Sox to make six straight outs. Schiraldi did not; coming on in relief, he let in two runs and California tied the game in the bottom of the ninth. Jerry Narron singled to lead the 11th, and was sacrificed to second. Ruppert Jones was walked, but Bobby Grich singled in the game winner. California won, 4–3, and led in the Series, three games to one.

1975 The Red Sox hosted the "Big Red Machine," the Cincinnati Reds, in Game One of the World Series. It was a year in which neither team had a 20-game winner. Don Gullett and Luis Tiant both pitched six scoreless innings, but in the bottom of the second, Tiant hit a solid single to left. Dwight Evans tried to bunt Luis over, and reached base safely himself. Denny Doyle singled, then Yaz singled to drive in Tiant, and the Red Sox were on the board. Before the inning was over, the Red Sox had rolled up six runs. Tiant pitched a complete game five-hit shutout, 6–0.

1970 The trade included one Jarvis for another, saw two unrelated Tatums come to Boston, broke up the brother duo of Tony and Billy Conigliaro, and even involved Moses! The Sox traded the immensely popular Tony Conigliaro, along with Ray Jarvis and Jerry Moses to the California Angels for two unrelated Tatums (Ken and Jarvis) and Doug Griffin. Sox GM Dick O'Connell said, of breaking up Tony C. and Billy C., "You trade when you can trade to help your club. The boys are better off separated. I think it's been a liability having them on the same club."

1967 The Red Sox still had their backs against the wall, down three games to two and ready to enter Game Six in the World Series. They couldn't start Jim Lonborg again on one day's rest. Instead, they pinned their hopes on a rookie, Gary Waslewski, 2–2 on the season, with only eight major league starts in his brief career. Playing on the same team as Yastrzemski, Waslewski was sometimes called "the utility Pole." Waslewski had thrown three perfect innings in the Saturday 5–2 loss. Manager Dick Williams said he had complete faith in Waslewski, but admitted, "With enough rain, Jim [Lonborg] would pitch every game." Rico Petrocelli gave the Red Sox an early lead with a second-inning solo homer off Dick Hughes, but the Cardinals got two runs on four hits in the top of the third. In the bottom of the fourth, the Sox did something that had never been done before in World Series history, all thanks to Hughes: Yastrzemski homered, Reggie Smith homered, and Rico homered. Three homers in one inning established a still-unmatched World Series record. John Wyatt took over pitching for the Red Sox in the sixth, and the Cardinals tied it in the seventh on Lou Brock's two-run homer, but then a flurry of singles mixed in with a double and a sacrifice fly scored four runs for Boston in the bottom of the seventh, and the 8–4 Red Sox win sent it to Game Seven.

1954 Lou Boudreau was fired as Red Sox manager, despite having a year remaining on his contract, and was replaced as skipper by Mike "Pinky" Higgins.

1946 Alternating victories, the Red Sox won Game Five, the final game in Boston, with a 6–3 win behind the four-hit pitching of Joe Dobson. The Red Sox made three more errors and the first-inning run and the two ninth-inning Cardinals tallies were all unearned. Ted Williams drove in his only run of the World Series with a single in the first, a run scored in the second, and Leon Culberson homered in the sixth. The Red Sox added three more in the seventh on two hits, an error, and a couple of walks. Boston 6, St. Louis 3. If the Red Sox could win either Game Six or Game Seven, they'd win their first World Championship in 28 long years.

1916 Looking for the chance to even up the Series at two-all, Rube Marquard was back on the mound, and after he effortlessly disposed of the Red Sox in top of the first. Brooklyn scored two runs with a leadoff triple by Jimmy Johnston, a single, a walk, Dutch Leonard's wild pitch, and an error. Leonard got out of the inning when Zack Wheat was cut down trying to steal home and Mike Mowrey struck out. It took only minutes for the Red Sox to strike back. Dick Hoblitzell walked, Lewis doubled to right, and Larry Gardner hit a drive far over Myers' head that rolled all the way to the back wall for an inside-the-park home run and three big RBI. Brooklyn got a double in the fourth and two singles in the fifth, but those were the only three hits Leonard let them have for the rest of the game. The Red Sox added three more runs, one per inning in the fourth, fifth, and seventh. Boston 6, Brooklyn 2—and the Red Sox held a 3–1 advantage in the Series.

1915 Back in Boston, and playing at Braves Field—the brand-new and larger facility loaned to the Red Sox in appreciation for the use of Fenway Park by the Braves in the 1914 World Series—Game Three matched the Game One winner, Grover Cleveland Alexander, against Boston's Dutch Leonard. The Phillies scored when Burns led off the third with a single and first baseman Hoblitzell flubbed Alexander's sacrifice bunt. Stock sacrificed, moving up both runners and Bancroft singled one home. From that point on, Leonard was perfect, setting down every one of the next 20 Phillies batters. The Red Sox tied it when Speaker tripled in the fourth and Hobby hit a sac fly. It stayed 1–1 until the bottom of the ninth, when Harry Hooper hit a single to right and, four batters later, with two out, was singled home by Duffy Lewis. The game ended Boston 2, Philadelphia 1—and Boston led in the Series, 2–1, too.

1912 Game Four starting pitchers were, once again, Joe Wood for the Red Sox and Jeff Tesreau for the Giants. Once again, the game was at the Polo Grounds. A triple and then Tesreau's wild pitch gave the Sox one in the second. Boston eked out one run in the fourth (set up when Jake Stahl stole one of two bases) and another in the ninth, while the Giants only scored once off Wood, in the seventh, when Fletcher doubled in Herzog from first. Boston 3, New York 1.

Hoodlums attacked the Red Sox party after the game. On Tuesday, October 8, the automobiles of the Royal Rooters were "stoned and deluged with dirt by the urchins lined up along the street and avenues leading from the ballpark" to downtown. On the 11th, it was the players themselves who were "bombarded" with dirt and stones; Buck O'Brien was hit in the face and cut by a sharp stone. A few players decried the inaction of New Yorks' finest in "no unmistakable terms." The *Boston Globe* report indicated that police made no effort to stop the rowdyism.

TRANSACTIONS
1970: Traded Tony Conigliaro, Ray Jarvis, and Jerry Moses to the California Angels for two unrelated Tatums (Ken and Jarvis) and Doug Griffin.
1971: Traded Jim Lonborg, Ken Brett, Billy Conigliaro, Joe Lahoud, George Scott, and Don Pavletich to the Milwaukee Brewers for Marty Pattin, Lew Krausse, Tommy Harper, and minor leaguer Pat Skrable.
1996: Acquired Greg Hansell off waivers from Minnesota.
Granted free agency to Nate Minchey.

BIRTHDATES
Gary Fortune 1894 (1920); Tom Carey 1906 (1939–1946); Mike Guerra 1912 (1951); Joe Ginsberg 1926 (1961); Mike Fiore 1944 (1970–1971); Pat Dodson 1959 (1986–1988)

DEATHS
Emmett O'Neill 1993

October 12

2004 The first game of the League Championship Series presented the opportunity to pick up where the 2003 LCS left off—another battle royale between Boston and New York. Game One saw Boston's ace, an obviously sub-par Curt Schilling, get banged around for six runs in the first three frames. Six more Sox pitchers saw service, but the Yankees built an 8–0 lead after six innings. The Red Sox put a scare into them with five runs in the seventh and two more in the eighth, but New York won in the end, 10–7. There was worry that the Sox ace, Schilling, was injured and unable to pitch again.

1986 Few teams ever come back from a three-game deficit in a best-of-seven post-season series, so on entering the game, the Red Sox were staring elimination in the face with little prospects for hope. The situation was even more hopeless when Bill Buckner came up to bat in the top of the ninth. The Red Sox were losing, 5–2. Buckner singled to center. Dave Stapleton pinch-ran for Buckner, and stayed in the game as he usually did for late-inning replacement purposes. There wasn't going to be any bottom of the ninth, though, unless the Red Sox somehow scored three or more runs—and the only scoring off Mike Witt was way back in the top of the second, when he made one mistake and Rich Gedman took him deep for a two-run home run. After Jim Rice struck out, Don Baylor homered and it was 5–4, Angels. Evans popped up for the second out. To get the last out—the left-handed hitting Rich Gedman—Angels manager Gene Mauch pulled Witt and put in lefty Gary Lucas. Lucas hit Gedman. Mauch summoned Donnie Moore to get Dave Henderson, already the goat of the game after Bobby Grich's two-run homer in the sixth had glanced off Hendu's glove into the stands. To the ever-lasting joy of Red Sox Nation, Henderson homered and even gave the Red Sox a 6–5 lead in the process. The Angels tied it back up in the ninth, off Steve Crawford, and Henderson made his second installment of redemption with a sacrifice fly in the 11th. The Red Sox won, 7–6, in 11 innings.

1975 The Sox started the scoring in World Series Game Two, with one run in the bottom of the first. Each team scored another single run, but Sox starter Bill Lee held the Big Red Machine to one run through eight innings. The Sox led, 2–1, but the ninth-inning leadoff batter, Johnny Bench, doubled off Lee, and Darrell Johnson brought in Dick Drago to relieve. One more out would have saved the Red Sox win, but Dave Concepcion singled Bench in to tie and Ken Griffey doubled Concepcion in to give Cincinnati a 3–2 lead. Rawley Eastwick had seemed vulnerable in the eighth, but in his second inning of relief he retired the Red Sox in order and picked up the win.

1967 Before Game Seven of the World Series, Bob Gibson had one more day of rest between starts than Jim Lonborg, and it may have shown. Lonnie was just tired. A triple, two singles, and a wild pitch gave St. Louis a 2–0 lead in the top of third. They added two more in the fifth. Bob Gibson homered. Lou Brock singled, then stole second, and then stole third, and scampered home on a Roger Maris sacrifice fly. Brock had seven stolen bases in the Series. The Red Sox got one back, but the Cardinals upped the ante even more when Julian Javier hit a three-run bomb to put St. Louis ahead, 7–2. Lonborg had yielded seven runs (six earned) on 10 hits, and by the time he finished the sixth, the Red Sox were finished, too. Gibson threw a three-hitter and won his third game of the Series. It was another loss at the final moment, following in the tradition of 1946, 1948, and 1949. Soon other years would join the litany, long before deliverance finally came in the early 21st century.

1916 For Game Five, the Series came back to Boston. A win would give the Red Sox another championship. Brooklyn scored first, though, with a run in the top of the second scored without benefit of a hit: there was a walk, sacrifice, fielder's choice, and passed ball. Immediately, the Red Sox responded with one of their own when Lewis tripled off Fred Pfeffer and Larry Gardner lofted a sac fly. It was the sixth triple of the Series for the Sox, still a Series record. Boston added two more runs in the third, both runs unearned. The lead increased to 4–1 when Hal Janvrin doubled home Hooper in the bottom of the fifth. Ernie Shore only yielded three hits, all singles, in the fifth, seventh, and ninth innings. The 4–1 score stood at the finale, and the Red Sox won the World Series for the second year in a row. The 1916 Series was so lacking in drama that Hugh Fullerton of the *New York Times* suggested that the World Series simply be abandoned in the years to come.

After the Series, Mike McNally returned to his hometown of Minooka, Pennsylvania, where a congratulatory banquet was held to honor him and fellow major leaguer Steve O'Neill. Loyal friend NcNally had attended so many events honoring O'Neill over the years that he knew O'Neill's stock speech by heart, so he pulled a fast one on his friend by delivering O'Neill's speech when asked to talk, thereby rendering O'Neill speechless.

1915 Game Four, with Boston leading two games to one. First game starter Ernie Shore was slated for the Sox, but the Phillies countered with George Chalmers, a surprise in that his season record was 8–9. Chalmers performed very well indeed, though, and Boston only scored twice off him—once in the third on a walk, single, sacrifice bunt, and Hooper's single, and once in the sixth on Hoblitzell's single and Lewis's double. Shore pitched slightly better—seven hits to the eight Chalmers gave up and, more to the point, one less run. Philadelphia scored just once, in the top of the eighth, when Gavvy Cravath tripled when an apparent routine single to center took a huge high hop over Speaker's head. Fred Luderus singled him home. That was it. 2–1, Boston—for the third game in a row. And the Red Sox now held a three-games-to-one edge.

1912 In foggy Boston, it's Game Five, and the Red Sox led off the third by banging back-to-back triples off Christy Mathewson (Hooper and Yerkes, and Yerkes scored on the next play, an error by second-baseman Doyle). That was it, though. The Sox never got another hit. Fortunately, two was sufficient, as the Giants only scored one uncarned run off Hugh Bedient, in the seventh. Red Sox 2, Giants 1—and the Red Sox just needed one more win to wrap up the World Series.

A few fans had trouble making their way to Fenway Park. Two boys from Holyoke were caught riding a freight train through Ware and were hauled off at 4:00 in the morning. John Wilson from New York drove up to see the game in Boston, but was halted in the Milton Woods by two thugs who pointed a revolver at him and took his car. Wilson made his way to the game, and saw his Giants lose that, too.

1905 Boston's post-season city series competed for attention in The Hub with baseball's World Series, with headlines like GIANTS WIN 9–0, BOSTON AL 12–0; MATHEWSON AND WINTER EACH SCORE A SHUTOUT. After the Boston Nationals took the first game, the Americans came back with four straight wins, taking the best-of-seven set.

TRANSACTIONS
1933: Traded Lloyd Brown to the Cleveland Indians for Bill Cissell.
1989: Released Jeff Stone.

BIRTHDATES
Charlie French 1883 (1909–1910); Bill Swanson 1888 (1914); Rick Ferrell 1905 (1933–1937); Joe Cronin 1906 (1935–1947); Joe Trimble 1930 (1955)

DEATHS
Joe Foy 1989

October 13

2004 It is up to Pedro Martinez to be the stopper, and he bears up well under relentless taunting from 55,000 Yankees fans chanting, "Who's your daddy?" (a reference to his ill-advised comment in frustration after a September loss, acknowledging that he just couldn't seem to beat New York). Pedro scatters four hits in six innings, but uncharacteristically walks four, and yields three runs, the big hit being a two-run home run by NY's John Olerud in the sixth. It's a close 3–1 win for the Yankees and, to make matters worse, Boston fans learn that 21-game winner Schilling is most likely lost for the rest of the post-season due to a crippling tendon problem in his right ankle.

2003 Tim Wakefield again outdueled New York's Mike Mussina, and the Red Sox pulled even in the League Championship Series at two games each. Todd Walker's fourth-inning homer is his fifth of the 2003 post-season, and sets a Red Sox record. Boston 3, New York 2.

1999 For the first time, the Sox and Yankees face each other in post-season competition. Two runs on two hits and an error, and Kent Mercker (BOS) had a lead against New York's El Duque (Orlando Hernandez). Adding another in the second gave the Sox a 3–0 lead, but New York got two in the second and tied it up in the seventh off El Guapo (Rich Garces). Bernie Williams won it for NY with a walk-off home run off Rod Beck in the bottom of the 10th. Final score: 4–3.

1970 Pitcher Fred Mitchell, an original player in the 1901 franchise that became the Red Sox, died in Newton, Massachusetts at age 92. Mitchell served as a coach for the Boston Braves in their "miracle" season where they rose from last place in mid-July to become the first team to sweep the 1914 World Series in four games.

1966 Lee Howard, a fashion model who had been the second wife of Ted Williams, won a divorce and settlement from Williams. Like Ted's first wife, she charged him with making her life unbearable with "constant obscene criticism."

1946 Back in St. Louis, Mickey Harris couldn't get through the third inning as the Cardinals scored three times on five hits, before Tex Hughson took the ball. Rudy York tripled to lead off the seventh, and scored on Doerr's fly to left. That was the only run the Red Sox scored, as Harry Brecheen won his second game of the World Series. The 4–1 win evened it up at three games each.

1915 The Series moved back to Philly, but the home team was in trouble. Lose today, and the Red Sox would be the champions. Erskine Mayer opposed Rube Foster of the Red Sox. Phillies fans had their hopes raised when the bases were loaded in the bottom of the first with nobody out, but then deflated when Cravath hit into a 1-2-3 double play. Luderus doubled, though, bringing home two, and all seemed right. Jack Barry singled in a run for Boston in the second and Hooper hit a solo homer in the third, to tie it up, 2–2. Two batters later, Eppa Rixey relieved Mayer. The Phils got a homer of their own in the bottom of the fourth, from Luderus—looking like a hero with his third RBI—and got another run on back-to-back two-out singles by Niehoff and Burns, when Hooper's throw went way past Gardner and then Gardner's throw to Thomas at the plate skipped away. The two-run Philly lead was restored, and stood until the top of the eighth.

Del Gainer beat out an infield single, and Lewis homered, re-tying the score, 4–4. The Phils got two men on base in the bottom of the eighth, but manager

Carrigan stuck with Foster. He had Carl Mays in the bullpen and Babe Ruth (18–8), but neither were called on in the Series. Foster bore down and got out of the inning—and then Harry Hooper, who hit two home runs in all of the regular season, hit his second solo homer of the game! Foster, with his first lead of the game, retired Philadelphia 1-2-3, and the Red Sox won the World Series for the second time in four years.

1903 An overworked Deacon Phillippe pitched his fifth complete game of the Series, losing to Bill Dinneen, 3–0. Only 7,455, the smallest crowd of the Series, saw Boston win the championship. Phillippe's five decisions and 44 IP are still World Series records, as are his starting two straight World Series games, not once but twice. Hobe Ferris's fourth-inning single drove in the first of two runs in the inning. The team that became the Red Sox had won the first-ever World Series.

TRANSACTIONS
1907: In a three-way trade, the Sox acquire Freddy Parent from
        the White Sox and send Jake Stahl to New York.
1995: Acquired Butch Henry on waivers from Montreal.
2000: Midre Cummings and Andy Sheets were both released.

BIRTHDATES
Ben Paschal 1895 (1920); Elliot Bigelow 1897 (1929); Frankie Hayes
1914 (1947); Lou Clinton 1937 (1960–1964); Bob Bailey 1942 (1978);
Dick Pole 1950 (1973–1976); Scott Cooper 1967 (1991–1994)

DEATHS
George Dumont 1956; Fred Mitchell 1970; Ed Carroll 1984; Leslie Aulds 1999

October 14

2003 It was another close game as the "other Boomer"—David Wells—held the Sox to just one run in seven innings, while Derek Lowe yielded three runs in the top of the second. New York won, 4–2, and took a 3–2 lead in the ALCS.

1999 David Cone's only big mistake was the two-run homer that Garciaparra hit in the top of the fifth, though both Varitek and O'Leary missed homers by inches. Ramon Martinez pitched nicely for the Red Sox, but the Yankees won Game Two of the ALCS, 3–2.

1986 The Red Sox and the Angels went back to Boston for Game Six of the ALCS. Starting pitchers were Oil Can Boyd for Boston and Kirk McCaskill for California. Each team scored twice in the first. But then the Sox broke the game open, scoring five runs in the bottom of the third, all of them off McCaskill. The Angels added one in the seventh, but Spike Owen tripled in two more for the Red Sox. The game ended 10–4, and Boston had won two in a row to even the series at three games apiece, setting up the deciding game of the Series. One team would win the 1986 pennant. The other team would pack up and disperse.

1975 Game Three of the World Series was at Cincinnati's Riverfront Stadium. Carlton Fisk hit a homer off Gary Nolan to lead off the second, but the Reds scored five runs on a two-run homer by Bench (in the fourth) and homers from Concepcion and Geronimo in the fifth. It was 5–1 Cincinnati after five. The Sox got one back in the sixth, Bernie Carbo pinch-hit a homer in the seventh, and when

Dwight Evans greeted Rawley Eastwick with a two-run homer in the top of the ninth, the game was tied. Unfortunately, it ended on a sour note in the 10th. It wasn't the seventh home run of the game. It was a sacrifice bunt by pinch-hitter Ed Armbrister that set up the sad finish. Jim Willoughby was pitching. Geronimo beat out a single over second base. Armbrister laid down a bunt, hesitated running to first, and then collided with Fisk as he was fielding the ball and throwing down to second base. Fisk's throw went wild, and the Reds had runners on second and third with nobody out. The Sox argued that even unintentional interference was still interference. Plate umpire Larry Barnett said, "It is interference only when the batter intentionally gets in the way of the fielder." Roger Moret replaced Willoughby and walked Pete Rose. After Moret struck out Rettenmund, Joe Morgan singled in the winning run, 6–5.

1964 Infielder Dick Williams is released; the Sox will see him soon, but as their field manager. Another, less memorable, infielder—Al Smith—is released as well.

1915 A planned post-World Series exhibition tour of the West Coast by the two respective pennant-winners (the Red Sox and the Phillies) was called off when financial guarantees were deemed unsatisfactory, or because the Phillies insisted on keeping a banquet commitment back home, depending on who you believe.

1912 Game Six was just about all over in the first inning as the Giants scored five times off Buck O'Brien in a wild inning that featured a balk which produced the first run, a steal of home by Buck Herzog, four singles, two doubles, and ended with the runner on first being picked off. Rube Marquard's error let the first Red Sox reach base in the second. After a single and a couple of outs, Hack Engle pinch-hit a double and drove in two unearned runs. That was it. Ray Collins in relief pitched extremely well, but Marquard kept mowing them down, and the game ended, 5–2 Giants.

1909 The Red Sox won Game Five and beat the Giants, four games to one. Huh? In post-season play, the Red Sox were battled to a 4–4 tie in 11 innings, trying to beat the Berkeley team in the Woonsocket mill league on October 3. Then, while the Detroit Tigers were pushing the Pirates to a seventh game in the World Series, the New York Giants and the Red Sox (both finished in third place in their respective leagues) held an exhibition series. New York took the first game, but Boston then won four in a row. The series was not a financial success, and cold weather limited attendance at the final game to 769 or 789 people (accounts differ). In the fourth inning, the Red Sox pulled off an unusual 8-5-3 double play on what started with a base hit by Murray of the Giants. Two Red Sox sixth-inning runs gave Boston the 5–4 edge.

TRANSACTIONS
1963: Released Bob Turley.
1964: Released Dick Williams and Al Smith.
1994: Scott Fletcher and Greg Litton were both granted free agency.
1995: Chris James and Matt Stairs were both granted free agency.
1996: Stan Belinda was granted free agency, and selected
    Ricky Trlicek off waivers from the Mets.

BIRTHDATES
Bill Renna 1924 (1958–1959); Tommy Harper 1940 (1972–1974); Frank Duffy 1946 (1978–1979); Midre Cummings 1971 (1998–2000)

DEATHS
Ed Hughes 1927; Bill Swanson 1954; Doc Prothro 1971; Denny Galehouse 1998

October 15

2003 Back at the Stadium, without a day off and facing elimination, the Red Sox took an early 4–1 lead but an inning later give up five runs to fall behind, 5–4. Garciaparra, Ramirez, and Ortiz all hit reliever Jose Contreras safely in the seventh and the Sox tied it up. The call went to the bullpen; Felix Heredia came in and threw a wild pitch, moving the runners to second and third. He walked Trot Nixon intentionally—then walked Johnny Damon quite unintentionally, forcing in the go-ahead run. Yankee killer Trot Nixon's two-run homer in the top of the ninth was just the icing on the cake. The ALCS is now tied at three games each, forcing a deciding Game Seven the following day. Boston 9, New York 6.

1986 Game Seven, ALCS. The Red Sox had come back from a 3–2 deficit to tie the Series at three games apiece. They led with Roger Clemens and the Angels started John Candelaria. On a combination of walks, singles, and an error, Boston scored three times in the second. The first Sox batter reached on an error in the fourth, too, and four more runs followed. Candelaria was tagged for seven runs—all unearned. Both teams scored a single run late in the game, but it was a walk in the park, and Roger and the Red Sox won the game, 8–1. In an improbable comeback, topped only in 2004, the Red Sox had recovered from a 3–1 deficit—and traveled to Shea Stadium to face the Mets in the World Series.

1975 Tiant started again in Game Four, but Pete Rose singled, Griffey doubled, and— after a couple of outs—Johnny Bench doubled. The Reds had a 2–0 lead. In the top of the fourth, though, Cincinnati's Fred Norman gave up singles to Fisk and Lynn, and then a triple to Evans. Burleson doubled and drove in Evans. Borbon replaced Norman, and Luis Tiant singled off Borbon. Three batters later, the Sox had five runs and a lead they wouldn't give up. The Reds got back two in the bottom of the fourth, but Tiant threw another complete game, a 5–4 win.

1968 The second-ever major league expansion draft results in the Red Sox losing the services of six players. Infielders Jerry Adair and Joe Foy went to the Kansas City Royals, along with pitcher Dave Morehead, and three other pitchers (Dick Baney, Gary Bell, and Darrell Brandon) all went to the Seattle Pilots.

1946 With the Series tied at three wins each, it's sudden death in St. Louis. Boston scored first, in the first, but was down 3–1 after six innings. The Red Sox then scored two more runs off Murry Dickson in the eighth, to tie the game. Harry Brecheen relieved Dickson and closed out the inning. After Bob Klinger took the mound for Boston to pitch the eighth, Enos Slaughter singled. Slaughter stayed stuck on first, as both the first out and then the second out were recorded. A second or two before Harry Walker singled to left-center (the official scorer ruled it a double, but it was clearly a single), Slaughter was off and running before contact. On a ball that fell in front of Leon Culberson in left-center field, Slaughter unexpectedly churned all the way around third base and streaked to the plate as Culberson lofted a routine return throw to cutoff man Johnny Pesky. Pesky's throw to the plate was inevitably late, given Slaughter's unexpected "mad dash." Despite back-to-back singles by York and Doerr, Brecheen held the line in the ninth and won his third World Series game—and the Series itself. Pesky allowed himself to be portrayed as the goat for "holding the ball," although none of the players fault him, and existing film shows no clear hesitation. Ted Williams always blamed himself, having hit just 5-for-25, with only one RBI (he was visibly hampered by the elbow injury suffered on October 1), though Stan Musial also had a sub-standard 6-for-27 Series.

1912 It was Game Seven, and Boston held a three-games-to-two lead in the World Series (there had been one tie). It was a cold day in Boston, and the fans never recovered from the top of the first inning. For late arrivals, it was all over before they were seated. The Giants evened the Series, scoring six runs (on seven hits) off Joe Wood in the very first frame. Charley Hall relieved, starting in the second, and he let in five more—even though he was 3-for-3 at the plate, tied for the record number of hits by a pitcher in a World Series game. The final score was 11–4, with the deciding contest the next day, pitting Christy Mathewson against Hugh Bedient. Baseball aficionados appreciate one element in Boston's game, however—the unassisted double play Tris Speaker pulled off in the eighth. It's the only one there's ever been in a World Series game.

Before the game, there had been a great commotion and near riot when Boston's booster club the Royal Rooters paraded into the park behind a band, to find that their accustomed seats had not only not been held for them, but had been sold to others. The police had to be called to restrain the Rooters, and the game held up for quite some time before the whole matter was brought under control. The club paid the price for the final and deciding game on October 16, when some 15,000 fans boycotted the game, attendance not much more than half of every other 1912 Series game.

After the game, Buck O'Brien was welcomed in his native Brockton, mobbed by many thousands of fans as he disembarked the train to try and head for a waiting automobile. The crowd was frantic in their enthusiasm and "his clothing was almost torn from him."

1903 The winners earned less than the losers. Pirates owner Barney Dreyfuss offered 100% of his club's World Series gate receipts, and each Pirate received $1,316.25. The Boston players received $1,182 apiece, some $134 less.

TRANSACTIONS

1965: Purchased Jose Santiago from the Kansas City Athletics.
1968: Joe Foy, Dave Morehead, and Jerry Adair are all selected from Boston by the Kansas City Royals in the 1968 expansion draft. The Sox also lose Gary Bell, Dick Baney, and Darrell Brandon to the Seattle Pilots in the same draft.
1984 Free agency granted to Dennis Burtt and Chico Walker.
1986: Free agency granted to Mike Stenhouse.
1987: Signed Alex Delgado as an amateur free agent.
1988: Granted free agency to both Pat Dodson and Danny Sheaffer.
1990: Mike Dalton and Rick Lancellotti were both granted free agency.
1991: Tom Barrett and Todd Pratt were both granted free agency.
1992: Tom Barrett, Bob Geren, and Wayne Housie are all granted free agency.
1993: Free agency granted to Steve Mintz, Jeff Richardson, and Franklin Stubbs.
1994: Free agency granted to Todd Frohwirth, Jose Melendez, Jose Munoz, and Sergio Valdez.
1996: Granted free agency to: Alex Cole, Alex Delgado, Ken Grundt, Brent Knackert, Tom McGraw, and Alan Zinter.
1997: Vaughn Eshelman was acquired on waivers from the Oakland Athletics. The Red Sox granted free agency to: Gary Bennett, Ken Grundt, Adam Hyzdu, Rusty Meacham, Curtis Pride, and Carlos Valdez.
1999: Free agency was granted to Andy Abad, Israel Alcantara, Raul Gonzalez, and Creighton Gubanich.

BIRTHDATES

Bill Henry 1927 (1952–1955); Tim Young 1973 (2000)

DEATHS

Neal Ball 1957; Al Widmar 2005

October 16

2004 Game Three of the ALCS is back in Fenway, and though both aces, Schilling and Martinez, failed to win a game in New York, there is hope that coming home will help the Red Sox. The Yanks score three times in the top of the first, though. The Sox come back with four in the second. New York takes a 6–4 lead in the third, but the Sox immediately tie it back up. In the fourth, facing Leskanic and Wakefield, the Yankees begin to tee off, and it's 17–6 at the seventh-inning stretch. The humiliating final score of 19–8 deals a crushing and seemingly fatal blow to Boston's pennant hopes for 2004 as the hated Yankees win their third straight game of the LCS. Never in baseball history has a team faced a 3–0 deficit in a seven-game series, and come back to win the series.

Almost the only thing good about Game Three was Jason Varitek's seventh-inning homer, his ninth in Red Sox post-season play; he has two more than David Ortiz and Nomar Garciaparra.

2003 Game Seven of the ALCS. It was the first game seven played at Yankee Stadium since 1957. With the Red Sox taking a 4–0 lead early in the game, Boston's hopes soar. This would be their first World Series appearance since 1986, and it would be so sweet to step on New York to get there. Any dedicated fan knew that Pedro Martinez tired dramatically after 100 pitches, but Boston manager Grady Little chose to stick with his tiring ace way too long. Pedro squeaked out of the seventh, only allowing one run, which David Ortiz promptly got back with a home run in the top of the eighth. Boston led in the game, 5–2, with only six outs standing in the way of the pennant. Despite Pedro accepting congratulations from his teammates for making it through the rocky seventh, and despite the Sox having a lights-out and rested bullpen ready to rock, Little unaccountably sent Pedro back out to pitch the eighth. Three quick runs and the Sox lead evaporated. The game went into extra innings. After midnight, it became October 17 and New York ultimately won the game (and the 2003 pennant), 6–5, in the bottom of the 11th inning on Aaron Boone's walk-off home run.

1999 The Yankees held a 2–0 lead in the ALCS, but the venue shifted back to Fenway Park and the game was a much-hyped matchup between New York's (ex-Red Sox) Roger Clemens against Boston's new ace Pedro Martinez. Clemens was chased early, to hoots and hollers from the Boston fans. Pedro gave up two hits in seven innings, and the Sox gave him what you could call strong run support (John Valentin drove in five). The final score was Red Sox 13, New York 1. The Sox had 21 hits; the Yankees had just three.

1975 Reggie Cleveland became the first Canadian pitcher to start a World Series game. In the top of the first in Game Five, Denny Doyle tripled and Yaz hit a sac fly to bring him home, but the Reds' Tony Perez hit homers in the fourth and again in the sixth, and his four RBIs helped give Cincinnati a 5–1 lead. The final was Reds 6, Red Sox 2.

1960 Red Sox pitcher Mike Fornieles pitched a three-hit, 4–0 shutout for Marianao against Cienfuegos in the opening day of Cuba's Winter Baseball League. Premier Fidel Castro threw out the first ball. Fornieles appeared in 70 games for the 1960 Sox, led the league with 14 saves, and had 10 wins in relief, with a 2.46 ERA.

1945 In a hallway at his Macon, Georgia office, Hack Eibel was found shot to death, a bullet hole in his temple and a pistol nearby. The former Sox player, manager of the Macon Sports Palace, had been ill for some time.

1912 The day started with the Mayor of Boston denouncing McRoy, the secretary of the Red Sox club, because of the brouhaha the day before when the devoted fan group, the Royal Rooters, had found their tickets sold to the public. Rumors of a fix were in the air as well, and thousands boycotted the game in protest. Attendance was only somewhat more than half that of the day before.

  The deciding game of the 1912 World Series pitted Boston's Hugh Bedient against the Giants' legendary Christy Mathewson. After six innings, it was 1–0 New York, when Red Murray doubled in Josh Devore, who had walked to lead off the third. Boston tied it in the bottom of the seventh when Jake Stahl singled, Wagner walked, and Olaf Henriksen, pinch-hitting for Bedient, doubled in Stahl. Smoky Joe took over for Bedient. The game was tied after nine, but Red Murray doubled and Fred Merkle singled him in. Wood was due up first in the bottom of the 10th and, though an excellent hitter, player–manager Stahl put in Hack Engle to hit. He hit an easy fly to center—but Fred Snodgrass dropped it. It was the 31st error of the World Series. Snodgrass partially atoned for his muff with a spectacular catch of Hooper's drive, which was so deep that Engle tagged and took second. Tris Speaker's pop foul unaccountably landed where it easily could have been caught. Given second life, Speaker singled in the tying run. After an intentional walk to set up a force, Larry Gardner hit a deep fly ball to right, and Yerkes scored easily. Great joy swept Boston. They say there's no cheering in the press box, but Frederick Lieb reports that one of the New York writers, Sid Mercer, was "so overcome with emotion that tears of chagrin coursed down his handsome cheeks as he dictated the tenth inning to his telegraph operator."

TRANSACTIONS
1992: Mike Brumley granted free agency.
1995: Tuffy Rhodes, Rich Rowland, and Jack Voigt are all granted free agency.

BIRTHDATES
Fred Lake 1866 (manager, 1908–1909); Mike Menosky 1894 (1920–1923); Matt Batts 1921 (1947–1951); Dave Sisler 1931 (1956–1959); Tim McCarver 1941 (1974–1975); Josias Manzanillo 1967 (1991)

DEATHS
Hack Eibel 1945; Jack Ryan 1949; Herb Bradley 1959; Ellis Kinder 1968; Larry Boerner 1969

October 17

2004 The Red Sox take a deep breath, down three-games-to-none in the LCS, and try 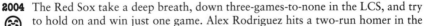 to hold on and win just one game. Alex Rodriguez hits a two-run homer in the third to test the faith of the Fenway faithful. Boston gets three in the fifth for a momentary lead, but New York takes a 4–3 lead in the top of the sixth. The Sox score in neither the sixth nor the seventh and one of the greatest closers of all time, Mariano Rivera, handles them easily in the eighth. The Sox are down, as deep in the depths as a team could possibly be, three outs away from elimination. No team had ever come back from a 3–0 deficit, and they were losing this one. Kevin Millar worked a walk. Dave Roberts was put in as a pinch-runner and although everyone in the park knew he was going to try to steal second, he pulled it off. Bill Mueller promptly singled him home, to tie the game. Rivera's blown save was his third against the Sox in 2004. The game rolled on until the bottom of the 12th inning, when David Ortiz won it well after midnight on a walk-off home run into the Yankees' bullpen in right field.

1999 The Yanks built a commanding 3–1 lead in the League Championship Series, when a tight game got completely out of hand. New York got one in the second, matched by the Red Sox, who took a one-run lead of their own in the third. Pettitte (NYY) and Saberhagen (BOS) were both pitching pretty good baseball. The Yankees went back to being one run on top in the fourth, and their 3–2 margin held up until the ninth, when they put the game out of sight with six runs for a 9–2 win. Extremely poor umpiring (and the refusal of the umpires to consult with each other) led to Red Sox fans throwing plastic bottles and other debris on the field, and play was halted for a few minutes. It was a game marred by four Red Sox errors, and the pinch-hit grand slam by Ricky Ledee was the most demoralizing blow. After the game, umpire Tim Tschida admitted he blew the call, but while the game was still in play, he had refused Sox skipper Jimy Williams' requests that he ask for help. Williams was still upset about another admitted blown call, by Rick Reed back in Game One.

1913 Tris Speaker agreed to play with the White Sox, for a late November tour of the U.S. In a separate story, Sox pitcher Ray Collins was elected VP of the Players' Fraternity to represent his fellow ballplayers.

1910 Mayor Fitzgerald stood on the steps of City Hall and threw a baseball to Tris Speaker, who then climbed into his new automobile to make the long drive to Austin, Texas and present the ball to the governor of the Lone Star State before motoring on to his ranch in Hubbard City, Texas. He planned to present the car to his mother. Speaker reached Hubbard City on the evening of November 15.

TRANSACTIONS
1966: Sold Bill Short to the Pittsburgh Pirates.
1997: Toby Borland and Pete Walker granted free agency.

BIRTHDATES
Johnny Ostrowski 1917 (1948); Hector Almonte 1975 (2003); Abe Alvarez 1982 (2004)

DEATHS
Olaf Henriksen 1962; Johnny Peacock 1981; Bob Adams 1996; Ray Boone 2004

October 18

 2004 Deja-vu all over again? This game lasts just under six hours. It ran 47 minutes longer than the one which had only ended about 19 hours earlier on this very same October 18. Again, the Yankees held a lead, and again the game extended into extra innings, courtesy of another blown save by Rivera. This one drags into the 14th, thanks to eight scoreless innings of work out of the Red Sox bullpen, the last three innings thrown by Tim Wakefield. Jason Varitek stayed in as catcher, though Doug Mirabelli routinely caught knuckleballer Wakefield. Varitek (and the Red Sox) survived three passed balls in the top of the 13th. Then, in the bottom of the 14th, Boston took two walks—and David Ortiz singled to center for his second walk-off hit in a 24-hour period, winning back-to-back post-season games against the Yankees and keeping Red Sox hopes alive. Ortiz had his third game-winning hit of the five Sox post-season victories so far in 2004. (See October 8 and see October 17.) Boston 5, New York 4. Everyone who follows the game is reminded a dozen times that no team has ever won even a sixth game, when down three-games-to-none. The Red Sox keep to the mantra "all we have to do is win one game"—and pressure mounts on the Yankees.

Later that night, in Massachusetts, a fan named Jose Rivera was shot and killed in an argument over the ballgame. A source familiar with the investigation told a *Boston Herald* reporter, "They were arguing over the Red Sox game. The shooter was a Yankees fan." It was the second time a Red Sox fan had been killed in a post-game argument; see also October 7, 1916.

1999 The Yankees scored early and late, and easily beat Boston, 6–1, to take the ALCS in five games and earn their 36th American League pennant in the process. Orlando "El Duque" Hernandez pitched seven shutout innings, won the game, and won the honor of being named Series MVP. New York 6, Boston 1. The Yankees took the series four games to one, thereby claiming the pennant and advancing to the World Series. The Sox had just the one win, the 13–1 thrashing of Clemens. In the Series, the Yankees swept the Braves in four straight.

1994 The Boston Red Sox name Kevin Kennedy, fired the week before by Texas, as their new manager.

1986 Game One of the World Series was an old-fashioned 1–0 pitchers duel between Boston's Bruce Hurst and Ron Darling of the Mets. After six innings, neither team had scored and both teams had just three hits. Jim Rice walked to lead off the seventh, and advanced to second when Darling uncorked a wild pitch. Mets second baseman Tim Teufel flubbed a routine Rich Gedman grounder and Rice ran around to score. It was the game's only run. Calvin Schiraldi closed it out, combining with Hurst on the four-hit shutout.

1920 The National League's directors met in New York, joined by Jacob Ruppert, Cap Huston, Charles Comiskey, and Harry Frazee of the AL. They named a committee to draw up an agreement along the lines of Albert Lasker's proposal, and give the five AL clubs still backing Ban Johnson an ultimatum: come in by November 1st or the Yankees, White Sox, and Red Sox will pull out of the AL and join a 12-team NL (with a team in Detroit to complete the roster). The AL five turns it down, and bluff and counterbluff blow through the autumn air.

1917 The U.S. Navy called up five members of the Red Sox on the same day. All five were enlisted as first class yeomen in the naval reserve: Duffy Lewis, Mike McNally, Ernie Shore, Chick Shorten, and Red Sox manager Jack Barry.

TRANSACTIONS
1996: Mike Greenwell was granted free agency.
2000: Carlos Castillo, Kevin Foster, and Dan Smith were all granted free agency.
Nine days later, on October 27, the Red Sox signed Carlos Castillo again.

BIRTHDATES
Charlie Berry 1902 (1928–1932); Andy Spognardi 1908 (1932); Skeeter Newsome 1910 (1941–1945); Andy Hassler 1951 (1978–1979); Allen Ripley 1952 (1978–1979); Jeff McNeely 1969 (1993); Doug Mirabelli 1970 (2001–2005); Alex Cora 1975 (2005)

DEATHS
George Murray 1955

October 19

2004 Back in the Bronx, the Yanks are up three games to two, but it feels like they're the ones with their backs to the wall. Curt Schilling takes the mound after pioneering surgery to temporarily bind his loose ankle tendon in place, and pitches a courageous game while blood visibly seeps through the sock on his right foot. Mark Bellhorn's three-run homer in the top of the inning sees the Sox up 4–0 right through Ronan Tynan singing "God Bless America" during the seventh-inning stretch. Bernie Williams hits a solo homer to put New York on the board, and the Yankees mount a rally when (with one out) Cairo doubles and Jeter singles him home. Alex Rodriguez weakly grounds out to Arroyo, who runs to tag A-Rod as he motors toward first. The Yankee superstar slaps the ball out of Arroyo's glove, and then scampers to second as the ball rolls away; Jeter runs all the way around to score. It is one of those moments that seems to turn the tide—until the umpires confer and call A-Rod out for interference. All runners must return to their original bases so Jeter has to emerge from the dugout and reassume his place on first base, with there now being two outs. It is the second time in the game the umpires conferred and reversed a call. Bellhorn's homer was originally not ruled as such and would have stood as a double had not the umpires talked and gotten it right. Game Six becomes a 4–2 Sox win that—almost incredibly—ties the Series at three games each and sets up a Game Seven showdown between the two rivals for the second year in a row.

1994 Kevin Kennedy was hired as new manager of the Boston Red Sox, assuming that there will indeed be baseball in 1995. If he lasts four years, Dan Shaughnessy notes, he'll have held the job longer than anyone in the last half-century. Kennedy described himself as a "disciplinarian, but I'm also a players' manager."

1986 In Game Two of the World Series, the Red Sox won again, despite facing Dwight "Doc" Gooden (17–6, 2.84 ERA). It was 6–3 after five innings, when the good doctor departed. Boston bats popped 18 hits off five Mets pitchers, while Steve Crawford and Bob Stanley threw 4⅔ innings of scoreless ball in relief of Clemens. The Sox added some runs in the late innings, and won, 9–3. The Series headed back to Boston with the Red Sox having won both games on the road and the Mets having won no games at all.

1975 The *Boston Globe* uses aerial photography to measure the distance from Fenway's left-field to home plate: 304.779 feet. Art Keefe and writer George Sullivan measure it this month at 309 feet, four inches. (*The Baseball Chronology*)

1919 Seeking to save his marriage, Sox shortstop Everett Scott said he would not play for the Red Sox in 1920, and that he wanted to play for a Western club, in order to be closer to his wife and child. As it happened, he played in 1920 and 1921 for Boston, then became a New York Yankee for the next 3½ seasons.

TRANSACTIONS
1993: Tony Pena was granted free agency.

BIRTHDATES
Herb Welch 1898 (1925); Mike Meola 1905 (1933–1936); Mike Gardiner 1965 (1991–1992); Keith Foulke 1972 (2004–2005); Jason Shiell 1976 (2003)

DEATHS
Hugh Duffy 1954; Grover Hartley 1964; Del Lundgren 1984; George Pipgras 1986

October 20

2004 Game Seven. The pennant was on the line for the second year in a row. Should the Yankees lose, they would go down as guilty of the biggest choke in baseball history, blowing a 3–0 lead in a playoff series, something no team had ever done. The pressure was on the Yankees, and they wasted no time in losing the game. Kevin Brown, a real bust as a $15,000,000 starter, who'd broken his own (non-pitching) hand punching a clubhouse wall in frustration just a few weeks before, gave up a two-run homer to David Ortiz in the first inning. After Brown loaded the bases in the top of the second, NY manager Joe Torre called on Javier Vazquez in relief. Vazquez served one up and Johnny Damon hit it for a grand slam. It was 6–0, Red Sox. Derek Lowe's strong pitching limited the Yankees to one run through six innings. Surprising everyone, Pedro Martinez took the mound and quickly gave up two runs, but Mark Bellhorn hit a homer off the right-field foul pole and Cabrera drove in another run in the ninth. It was a blowout, the Red Sox cruising to a 10–3 win, the pennant, and the trip to the World Series that had been snatched from them in Game Seven of 2003. For the first time since 1981, a visiting team savored champagne at the Stadium. The game had been won at the very stroke of midnight on October 20. The corks were popped moments later, on October 21.

1999 After MLB umpires Rick Reed and Tim Tschida both admitted they had blown key calls during the 1999 ALCS between the Red Sox and the Yankees, Dr. Carmen Puliafito (chair of ophthalmology at Tufts University School of Medicine) said he suspects both some umpires are secretly nearsighted. "That's the only explanation I have for these three horrible calls." Puliafito said his clinic had confidentially treated a number of sports officials and offered free eye exams and (if indicated) free prescription lenses or laser surgery for major league umpires during the postseason. Being confidential, we do not know if any umps accepted the good doctor's offer.

1975 Fans waiting for Game Six of the 1975 World Series have to wait another day, as rain forces postponement for the third day in row. Meanwhile, umpire Larry Barnett reports that his life was threatened and he was placed under police guard, as were his wife and daughter. Barnett's refusal to call interference on a controversial play in the 10th inning of Game Three of the World Series probably cost Boston the game. FBI agents were stationed in the stands at Fenway Park for the remaining two games of the Series. The death threat may have represented mixed motives; the letter (addressed to "Dear Jerk Larry Barnett") explained that the writer had lost $10,000 betting on the game; he demanded repayment of the $10,000 or else a ".38 bullet in your head" would be Barnett's fate. Barnett continued to umpire in the Series, and for many years afterward. He was consistently greeted with boos at Fenway.

1951 In Tokyo's Korakuen Stadium, some 50,000 fans watched Dom DiMaggio hit a double and a single and score three runs in a 7–0 victory for the American baseball All-Stars against the Yomiuri Giants. Mel Parnell was the winning pitcher. Dom was better than his brother Joe, 1-for-3 on the day.

1916 The National Commission voted to deny World Series emblems to several members of the 1916 team because they participated in a barnstorming exhibition in New Haven on October 15. The purpose of the rule, a newspaper report explained, was "to keep the heroes of the diamond from dragging their laurels out on the prairies and letting them trail in the mud for a few extra dollars."

1912 Pitcher Casey Hageman wanted the World Series share he was denied when cut by the Red Sox in June. Hageman was farmed out to Jersey City, recalled, then sent to Denver. He objected to the pay cut and instead reported for duty every day at Fenway Park beginning June 22, though no longer on the Red Sox payroll.

TRANSACTIONS
1961: Battery discharged: pitcher Tom Brewer and catcher Joe Ginsberg are both released.
1994: Tom Brunansky and Frank Viola are both granted free agency.

BIRTHDATES
Jigger Statz 1897 (1920); Juan Marichal 1937 (1974); Rudy Seanez 1968 (2003)

DEATHS
Allan Russell 1972; Freddie Muller 1976

October 21

2004 After taking the American League Championship Series from the Yankees, a large crowd of fans celebrated wildly outside Fenway Park, early in the morning of October 21. Boston police overreacted, firing pepper-powder bullets into the crowd. One young fan, 21-year-old Victoria Snelgrove, was killed by police bullets. In 2005, the Snelgrove family received the largest wrongful-death financial settlement in City of Boston history.

1986 Game Three, World Series. The Mets win the first Fenway first, 7–1. Lenny Dykstra homered to lead off. The first four Mets batters hit safely and, before the Red Sox even got up to bat, the Mets had scored four runs. Oil Can Boyd was their victim, but he survived to pitch seven innings. After the Mets grabbed a couple more in the seventh, The Can was done. Former Red Sox pitcher Bobby Ojeda held the Sox to one run in the third inning.

1975 It was the first World Series night game at Fenway, and what a game it was. Pushed back and pushed back by three days of rain, the Sox were facing sudden death. A Sox loss would give Cincinnati the World Championship. Fred Lynn's three-run first-inning home run roused Sox fans until the Reds tied it in the fifth, and built up a 6–3 lead over Boston after 7 ½. The home crowd had all but given up hope, when Bernie Carbo hit a dramatic pinch-hit homer into the center-field bleachers in the bottom of the eighth to tie the game, 6–6. It was Carbo's second pinch-hit homer of the Series. Boston looked to have victory in hand when they loaded the bases with nobody out in the bottom of the ninth, but they couldn't push the winning run across. In the bottom of the 12th inning—already October 22—Carlton Fisk hit his famous homer off the left-field foul pole to send ecstatic Sox fans home with a 7–6 win, and a memory of having witnessed one of the defining moments of modern baseball.

1968 Elston Howard, the first African American to play for the New York Yankees, announced his retirement after completing his career with two seasons on the Red Sox.

1916 Baseball's National Commission reiterated that any ballplayers engaging in post-season barnstorming games would be disciplined. For most of the Red Sox, this meant that their championship emblems (the equivalent of today's rings) would be denied them, because they defied the rule by playing a game in New Haven on October 4. Three days later, the Baseball Players' Fraternity objected, saying that baseball can't discipline players for exhibitions after the season was over and after player contracts had expired. (See December 8.)

1912 After the World Series, the Boston players departed for various off-season diversions, from hunting to vaudeville. Joe Wood and Tris Speaker were each offered $1,000 a week to go into vaudeville. Wood declined, to head back to his farm via Kansas City, but Speaker was reportedly intrigued by the offer. Speaker had won a Chalmers automobile as the best player in the American League.

TRANSACTIONS
1961: Released Tom Brewer and Joe Ginsberg.
1966: Released both Lenny Green and Eddie Kasko.
1970: Traded Dick Schofield to the St. Louis Cardinals for Jim Campbell.
1994: Danny Darwin and Andre Dawson are both granted free agency.

BIRTHDATES
Jack Hayden 1880 (1906); Stan Partenheimer 1922 (1944); John Flaherty 1967 (1992–1993)

DEATHS
Harry Gleason 1961; Jack Killilay 1968; Dolph Camilli 1997; Jim Bucher 2004

October 22

1986 Al Nipper started for the Red Sox and Ron Darling started for the Mets. It was Game Four of the World Series. Darling left after seven innings of scoreless pitching. The Sox picked up a couple of runs off Roger McDowell in the eighth. Gary Carter pretty much won the game, with a two-run homer off Nipper in the fourth and a solo shot off Crawford in the seventh. The Mets won, 6–2, and the Series was even, two wins for the Red Sox (both at Shea Stadium) and two wins for the Mets (both at Fenway Park).

1975 In Game Seven at Fenway Park, with most of the Fenway faithful exhausted after the exhilaration of the early-morning Carlton Fisk home run, excitement mounted when Boston scored three times in the bottom of the third inning off Don Gullett. Bill Lee was the starter for the Red Sox, and with just four innings to go, it was 3–0, Red Sox. Tony Perez golfed another home run off of a modified eephus pitch, a two-run shot, in the top of the sixth. Griffey walked in the seventh, and Roger Moret relieved the Spaceman. Griffey stole second, then scored on Pete Rose's single and the game was tied, 3–3. Jim Willoughby came on to pitch the eighth, but was taken out for pinch-hitter Cecil Cooper with two outs in the bottom of the eighth. Rookie Jim Burton was given the ball; he had a 2.89 ERA through 53 innings. He walked Griffey. Geronimo bunted Griffey to second. After a walk to Pete Rose, Joe Morgan singled in Griffey. The Reds had taken a 6–5 lead in the ninth, having come from behind, as they had in each of their four wins. Yes, they won Game Seven, too; the Red Sox failed to get a baserunner off Will McEnaney in the bottom of the ninth.

1951 Lou Boudreau is named new Red Sox skipper, replacing Steve O'Neill. "We'll trade anybody," Boudreau said, in order to strengthen the team. Even Ted

Williams? "Yes. Everybody…you don't give away a player who drives in 126 runs, but we'll trade Ted if we can get what we need."

1926 Lee Fohl resigned after losing 87, 105, and 107 games in his three seasons as skipper of the Red Sox.

1919 Babe Ruth announced his departure for Los Angeles. Though he had just signed a three-year contract with the Red Sox in late March, he now pronounced himself dissatisfied and required a considerable increase or he would forego baseball for motion pictures. Two days later, he turned in his uniforms to the Red Sox and was out of the game unless the Red Sox "comes through good." He wanted at least $20,000 a year.

TRANSACTIONS
1980: Granted free agency to Jim Dwyer.
1996: Bob Milacki was released.
1998: Released Butch Henry.

BIRTHDATES
Bill Carrigan 1883 (1906–16, 1927–1929); Norm McNeil 1892 (1919); Jimmie Foxx 1907 (1936–1942); Ron Jackson 1933 (1960); Wilbur Wood 1941 (1961–1964); Hector Carrasco 1969 (2000); Jay Payton 1972 (2005)

DEATHS
Charlie Hartman 1960; Ben Van Dyke 1973

October 23

2004 Game One of the 2004 World Series. David Ortiz hit a three-run first-inning home run in the first World Series at-bat of his career. Despite Boston taking a 7–2 lead, the St. Louis Cardinals fought back to tie it in the top of the eighth, 9–9. The Sox made four errors but still won the game in the bottom of the eighth as Mark Bellhorn hit a tie-breaking two-run shot off the Pesky Pole. Boston 11, St. Louis 9.

1986 Bruce Hurst was back on the mound for Boston, just in time to get the Sox back on track, after losing Games Three and Four to the Mets. Game Five matched up Hurst with Doc Gooden. The Mets managed 10 hits off Hurst, but they were scattered and New York only scored once in the eighth and once in the ninth. The Red Sox, on the other hand, built up a four-run cushion—one each in the second and third and two in the fifth. The Red Sox took a three-games-to-two lead in the Series. Boston 4, NY 2.

1945 Branch Rickey announced that the Brooklyn Dodgers had signed Jackie Robinson. He coulda been a Red Sox, had the Red Sox signed him at the April 16, 1945 tryout.

1916 The front page of *The Sporting News* discussed a story circulating that Connie Mack was coming to Boston as the new manager and part-owner of the Red Sox. Never happened.

TRANSACTIONS
1973: Acquired Dick McAuliffe from the Detroit Tigers by trading Ben Oglivie.
1981: Sold Manny Sarmiento to the Pirates.
1998: Pete Schourek and Mo Vaughn were both granted free agency.

BIRTHDATES
Hugh Bedient 1889 (1912–1914); Vern Stephens 1920 (1948–1952)

DEATHS
Chick Shorten 1965

October 24

2004 In Game Two of the World Series, Curt Schilling, his ankle tendons sutured once more, takes the mound and holds the St. Louis Cardinals back (despite four more Red Sox errors). Schilling earns himself a permanent place in the hearts of Red Sox Nation. Boston 6, St. Louis 2.

1990 Faced with the choice of exercising a $1.6 million option to extend the contract of popular right fielder Dwight Evans, or pay a $200,000 buyout, the Sox take the less expensive route. The 19-year Red Sox veteran will play one last year in major league ball, but wearing a Baltimore uniform.

1977 After 31 years with the Red Sox, Dick O'Connell is let go by the executors of the Yawkey estate, as a new leadership group headed by Haywood Sullivan and Buddy LeRoux are expected to take control. A substantially larger offer by a Cleveland firm holds up the sale to Sullivan and partners. On March 4, 1978, Jean Yawkey joins in as a partner with Sullivan and LeRoux, and that makes all the difference.

1968 Johnny Pesky was brought back into the Red Sox organization, this time to stay, after a few years coaching and managing with the Pirates. Pesky joined Boston's broadcast team of Ken Coleman and Ned Martin, replacing Mel Parnell.

1911 Duffy Lewis's engagement was reportedly back on, but the marriage would now take place in California. Apropos of nothing, when Lewis retired after the 1921 season, his career batting average was the same as his average in three years of World Series play, .284.

TRANSACTIONS
1951: Buddy Rosar is released.
1973: Traded Marty Pattin to Kansas City for Dick Drago.
1974: Released John Kennedy, Juan Marichal, Dick McAuliffe, and Bob Veale.
1990: Released Dwight Evans.
1994: Joe Hesketh granted free agency.

BIRTHDATES
Jack Russell 1905 (1926–1936); Charlie Small 1905 (1930); Ed Jurak 1957 (1982–1985); Ken Ryan 1968 (1992–1995)

DEATHS
Jimmy Barrett 1921; Jack Thoney 1948

October 25

2001 After the terrorist attack on the United States, which resulted in the destruction of the twin towers of New York's World Trade Center and the killing of more people than the 1941 attack on Pearl Harbor, a great many baseball fans—including some Red Sox fans—began to root for the Yankees to win the 2001 playoffs and World Series. A TRUCE: LEGIONS OF YANKEE HATERS ARE TEMPORARY ROOTERS headlined a story in the day's *New York Times*. The 2001 Series was one of the most exciting ones in history, but it's safe to say that most Sox fans came around and were rooting for the Arizona Diamondbacks as the Series progressed.

1995 Marty Barrett was awarded $1.7 million in lost wages by a jury in U. S. District Court. The jury ruled that Dr. Arthur Pappas, Red Sox team surgeon, must pay for his misdiagnosis of Barrett's condition. Barrett did not get the $15 million he was seeking, but proclaimed himself content and said he felt vindicated, hoping that future players would seek second opinions and not simply accept the diagnosis of the team doctor.

1986 One strike away from a World Series victory for the first time in 68 years, the Red Sox had started Roger Clemens (and the Mets had started his former teammate of just the year before, Bobby Ojeda.) Hardly anyone remembers the starters in this game, since all the action seemed to take place in the 10th inning. The Sox scored single runs in the first and second innings, but the Mets tied it with two in the bottom of the fifth. Boston took a 3–2 lead in the seventh; Gary Carter's sacrifice fly tied it back up in the bottom of the eighth. Tied 3–3, the game went into the 10th, and the Red Sox got two runs off Rick Aguilera. The first was hit by leadoff batter Dave Henderson, and it looked like Hendu was going to go down as the Series hero—a World Series in which the Red Sox only appeared thanks to his home run heroics in the American League Championship Series. The Red Sox led, 5–3, and Calvin Schiraldi retired the first two batters in the bottom of the 10th inning. One more out, and the Red Sox would have the World Championship. But then Gary Carter singled, and Kevin Mitchell singled (batting for Aguilera), and Ray Knight singled, scoring Carter. It was a one-run game, with men on first and third—though still two outs. Bill Buckner, even though he was typically replaced in later innings for defensive purposes, and even though he'd been hit by a pitch in the top of the 10th, was playing first base. Bob Stanley was summoned to replace Schiraldi and nail it down. Stanley then threw a wild pitch (as it has been scored, though some feel Rich Gedman should have been charged with a passed ball). Whatever the call, it allowed the Mets to tie up the game. Mookie Wilson then hit a grounder directly to Buckner at first. The game seemed set to head to the 11th...until the ball scooted right *through* Buckner and out into right field. The Series was tied 3–3. Both teams had a chance to win it all in Game Seven.

1960 Ted Williams was named Comeback Player of the Year by UPI.

1941 A match made in baseball heaven? Herb Pennock's daughter (Jane) and Eddie Collins' son (Eddie Jr.) announced plans to wed. Pennock was head of the Red Sox farm system at the time, and Collins Sr. was VP and business manager.

1934 Manager Bucky Harris is fired.

1919 Harry Frazee's sale of Carl Mays to the Yankees, in effect, becomes final when the New York Supreme Court enjoined AL President Ban Johnson from suspending

Mays. Frazee charged that Johnson continued to try to drive him out of baseball. It's a long story....

TRANSACTIONS
1922: Frank O'Rourke is sold to Toronto.
1973: Released Ray Culp and Bob Veale.
1974: Released Deron Johnson.
1993: Ernest Riles and Luis Rivera were both granted free agency.
1994: Steve Farr granted free agency.

BIRTHDATES
Joe Wood 1889 (1908–1915); Phil Marchildon 1913 (1950); Russ Meyer 1923 (1957); Bobby Thomson 1923 (1960); Chuck Schilling 1937 (1961–1965); John LaRose 1951 (1978); Danny Darwin 1955 (1991–1994); Pedro Martinez 1971 (1998–2004); Joe Nelson 1974 (2004)

DEATHS
None yet

October 26

2004 The Series shifts to St. Louis and the Cardinals hope to win at home, but their offense remains anemic and Pedro Martinez is in fine form. Manny Ramirez drives in two, and the Red Sox win, 4–1. No one has ever come back from a deficit of 3–0 in a seven-game series—well, that is, until the previous week. It doesn't look good for the winningest team in 2004, the 105-win Cardinals. Pedro's win is his sixth post-season win for the Red Sox, a club record. He strikes out 26 in the 2004 playoffs, for a club-record 80 total playoff K's.

1992 Dottie Green died of cancer in Natick, Massachusetts. She had been catcher for the Rockford Peaches, and was portrayed by Geena Davis in *A League of Their Own*. She later worked at Framingham State Prison for Women. She only became a fan of men's baseball late in life, when she started rooting for the Red Sox. "She thought the men were too slow," said longtime friend Mary Bond. "She said she didn't care to watch them."

1934 Tom Yawkey pays more than twice as much for Washington's player-manager Joe Cronin than Col. Ruppert paid for Babe Ruth. Washington owner Clark Griffith sold his son-in-law to the Red Sox for $225,000—and the Sox had to throw in Lyn Lary, too. Cronin was married to Griffith's adopted daughter Mildred.

Accompanying stories to the Cronin purchase indicate that Yawkey's expenditure on the Red Sox, including renovation of Fenway Park, has already totaled around $3,000,000.

1933 Tom Yawkey began to spend some of his considerable fortune to improve the Red Sox. And Philadelphia was still without Sunday baseball, which limited the income the Athletics could attract. Word broke on this day that Connie Mack had sold star pitcher Lefty Grove to Boston, along with infielder Max Bishop, for a cash sum thought to be around $200,000.

1920 Ed Barrow resigns as manager of the World Champion Boston Red Sox.

TRANSACTIONS
1934: Traded Lyn Lary and $225,000 cash to the Washington Senators for Joe Cronin.
1973: Acquired Rick Wise and Bernie Carbo from the Cardinals
in a trade for Reggie Smith and Ken Tatum.
1992: Wade Boggs is granted free agency.
1995: Chris Donnels released.
1998: Mike Benjamin and Mark Lemke were both granted free agency.

BIRTHDATES
Swede Carlstrom 1886 (1911); Dick Hoblitzell 1888 (1914–1918); George Winn 1897
(1919); Bud Byerly 1920 (1958); Dave Coleman 1950 (1977); Zach Crouch 1965 (1988)

DEATHS
Jack Bushelman 1955; Bobby Avila 2004

October 27

2004 For the first time in 86 years, the Boston Red Sox win the World Series. The Sox
scored first, as they had in every game of the Series, and Derek Lowe never let the
Cardinals score at all, nor did the Boston bullpen. Boston took the game early,
3–0. The Sox had swept the Angels. The Yankees pushed them right to the brink,
but Boston won four in a row to win the pennant—and then won four more in a
row, sweeping the World Series. For Lowe, it was his 17th appearance in a post-
season game for the Red Sox, a club record for pitchers. A couple of dozen books
have been written on the 2004 World Series win; we won't dwell on it here.

2003 Choosing not to pick up the option on Grady Little's contract for 2004, the
manager was not technically fired—but he certainly wasn't coming back to work
for the Red Sox.

1986 The deciding Game Seven of the World Series had been postponed a day due to
rain, which enabled the Sox to pitch Bruce Hurst for a third time, and for the
Mets to counter with Ron Darling. Hurst could have used another day's rest, but
it was what it was. In any event, the Red Sox jumped out to a 3–0 lead in the
top of the second inning when Dwight Evans led with a homer and then Rich
Gedman went back-to-back with another home run. Henderson walked, moved
to second on Hurst's bunt, and scored on Wade Boggs' single. That was it for the
early scoring, though Marty Barrett singled later in the inning, his 13th hit of the
Series. Barrett is tied with Bobby Richardson and Lou Brock for the most hits
obtained in a given World Series. Neither team scored again until the Mets tied it
in the sixth with three runs on three hits. Then the scales tipped in favor of New
York when they scored three more runs in the seventh. Hurst had left after six,
replaced by Calvin Schiraldi. The first man up, Ray Knight, homered. A single,
a wild pitch, a single, a sacrifice. Joe Sambito replaced Schiraldi: an intentional
walk, another walk, and a sacrifice fly. Stanley replaced Sambito, and finally got
the third out. Mets 6, Red Sox 3.

The Red Sox got two back right away, in the eighth, when Buckner singled,
Rice singled, and Evans doubled them both in. The Mets weren't content with
a one-run lead and, with Al Nipper now on the mound, Darryl Strawberry
homered, another run scored, and it was 8–5 Mets. That was the final score,
Mets 8, Red Sox 5. The World Series was over. The Red Sox had been one out
away in Game Six—in effect, one pitch away—and fell short. For the second

game in a row, Schiraldi took the loss, charged with losing both Game Six and Game Seven.

1980 Falling deeply behind New York in the standings, the Sox turn to another former Yankees manager (they'd hired Joe McCarthy in the 1940s), seeking salvation. They hire "The Major," Ralph Houk. Though the Sox got back to within four games of the lead in 1981, just hiring a former Yankee was no guarantee of success.

1972 Pitchers Ray Culp and Gary Peters are released. Bob Burda is released for the second time in '72. He was released back on August 25 as well, but re-signed.

1933 The *Boston Traveler* reported that Red Sox owner Tom Yawkey was enthusiastic about hiring Babe Ruth as manager of the team. Eddie Collins "was said to be hesitant." Wiser counsel prevailed. (See October 29, 1923.)

TRANSACTIONS
1972: Released Bob Burda, Ray Culp, and Gary Peters.
1978: Purchased Mike Easler from the Pittsburgh Pirates.
1995: Luis Aquino released.
1997: Mike Benjamin granted free agency.
1998: Greg Swindell granted free agency.

BIRTHDATES
Patsy Dougherty 1876 (1902–1904); George Smith 1901 (1930); Frank Bennett 1904 (1927–1928); Pumpsie Green 1933 (1959–1962); Lee Stange 1936 (1966–1970); Jim Burton 1949 (1975–1977)

DEATHS
Dave Black 1936; Bennie Tate 1973; Rube Walberg 1978; Ben Steiner 1988

October 28

1975 Fred Lynn was the near-unanimous choice for AL Rookie of the Year, missing unanimity by only a half-vote.

1958 Pete Runnels is named "Comeback Player of the Year." He'd hit .301 with Washington in 1956, but then slumped to .230. The Red Sox acquired him, and he came back all right—all the way back to .322, second only to Ted Williams (.328) in the American League.

1920 Two days after he resigned as field manager for the Red Sox, Ed Barrow is hired as business manager of the New York Yankees. Barrow had managed the Red Sox to a World Series win in 1918. While serving as Yankees GM until 1945, he oversaw 14 Yankees pennants and 10 World Championships.

TRANSACTIONS
1988: Released Larry Parrish.
1991: Joe Hesketh is granted free agency.
1992: Tom Brunansky is granted free agency.
1997: Jim Corsi and Shane Mack granted free agency. Brian Shouse was signed as a free agent.
1998: Steve Avery granted free agency. In a separate transaction, the Red Sox purchased the contract of Morgan Burkhart from Richmond of the Frontier League.

BIRTHDATES
Frank Smith 1879 (1910–1911); Chet Chadbourne 1884 (1906–1907); John Bischoff 1894 (1925–1926); Bob Veale 1935 (1972–1974); Sammy Stewart 1954 (1986); Bob Melvin 1961 (1993); Kirk Bullinger 1969 (1999)

DEATHS
Walter Barbare 1965; Cal Koonce 1993; Bob Seeds 1993

October 29

2003 The Sox placed Manny Ramirez on irrevocable waivers. Any team that wanted to could claim him and pick him up for the negligible waiver price. At first glance, this seems an insupportable way to treat a man who had hit 37 homers, driven in 104 runs, and led the league in on-base percentage, and was established as one of the greatest hitters in baseball history. Manny had spoken out several times about being unhappy in Boston, so GM Theo Epstein did him the courtesy of offering him more or less freely to any other team. No one claimed him; Epstein probably figured no one would. It wasn't collusion; it was the nearly $100 million still due Ramirez under his long-term contract with the team. After the 48-hour period expired, Manny's agent thanked the Red Sox, Manny became reconciled to life in Boston and seemed to embrace it, and went on to become World Series MVP in 2004. Had anyone claimed him, the Sox would have had that extra money with which to work. It simply wasn't that much of a gamble.

1991 A top executive with the Red Sox, John Donovan, said the team would be open to move from Fenway Park to a domed stadium. Mayor Raymond Flynn and the Boston Redevelopment Authority were discussing plans prior to a "sports summit" to be convened on the 30th by Gov. William Weld. The summit would look at financing for a new Boston Garden and the needs of the New England Patriots as well. A multipurpose domed facility was one option to be discussed.

1933 Bucky Harris was announced as the new manager of the Red Sox. Harris agreed to a one-year contract. New owner Tom Yawkey did the hiring, without checking with his GM, Eddie Collins. Apparently Yawkey had not known that Collins and Harris were enemies, and Collins immediately set to work trying to figure out how to get rid of Harris. The book *Red Sox Nation* goes into the machinations in some depth, and how the purchase of Joe Cronin from Washington was engineered to supplant Harris's position as manager of the Sox.

1919 The Yankees were officially deprived of their third-place finish for reinstating banned pitcher Carl Mays. Players did not receive their third place money, but if you look in the record books, the team is listed in third place. (See July 29.)

TRANSACTIONS
1946: Mace Brown is released.
1968: Released Elston Howard and Floyd Robinson.
1993: John Dopson was granted free agency.

BIRTHDATES
Mandy Romero 1967 (1998)

DEATHS
Frank Fuller 1965; Al Niemiec 1995

October 30

2004 An estimated 3 million people (about five times the population of the city) jammed Boston streets to see the 2004 World Champions on parade. The parade route even included a river ride as the amphibious "duck boats" conveyed the champions up and down the Charles River. The only moment of concern came when a baseball flew through the air and beaned Pedro Martinez before plopping into the dirty water of the River Charles.

1929 Back in the days when players had to work in the off-season, Red Sox pitcher Ray Dobens set sail on the liner *President Garfield*, not as a tourist but as an ordinary seaman.

1922 Rip Collins and Del Pratt are traded to the Tigers for Danny Clark, Howard Ehmke, Babe Herman, Carl Holling, and $25,000 in cash. Holling never reports (see March 30, 1923). Collins had been the only pitcher on the 1922 Red Sox to post a winning record (14–11, 3.76 ERA).

TRANSACTIONS
1922: Traded Rip Collins and Del Pratt to the Detroit Tigers for Danny Clark,
      Howard Ehmke, Babe Herman, Carl Holling, and $25,000 cash.
1933: Johnny Hodapp and Tom Oliver are both released.
1946: Tom Carey, Mike Ryba, and Charlie Wagner are all released.
1995: Jose Canseco granted free agency.
1997: Chris Hammond granted free agency.

BIRTHDATES
Buck Freeman 1871 (1901–1907); Marty McHale 1886 (1910–1916); Rudy Sommers 1886 (1926–1927); Al Kellett 1901 (1924); Grady Little 1950 (manager, 2002–2003); Tom Poquette 1951 (1979–1981); Dave Valle 1960 (1994); Mark Portugal 1962 (1999); Andy Dominique 1975 (2004)

DEATHS
Dick Midkiff 1956; Lee Fohl 1965; Rex Cecil 1966; Pinky Woods 1982

October 31

2005 At the 11th hour and just about the 59th minute of a protracted negotiation, Red Sox GM Theo Epstein stunned media watchers by suddenly resigning his position, despite being offered nearly quadruple his existing salary. Clearly, there were other issues that meant much more to him than the money itself. To leave Fenway without being accosted by the media, Epstein took advantage of Halloween. He donned a gorilla costume and simply walked down the street, incognito, away from the park.

2004 Halloween would have been Game Seven of the 2004 World Series; the mere prospect would have spooked Sox fans haunted by the ghosts of years past. The media overkill would have been nearly too much to bear. Fortunately for the sanity of current and future generations, the 2004 Red Sox hadn't wasted a moment wrapping up the Series in four straight games.

TRANSACTIONS

1994: Damon Berryhill granted free agency.
1995: Rick Aguilera granted free agency.
1997: Bret Saberhagen granted free agency.
2002: Declined to exercise the club option on Dustin Hermanson.

BIRTHDATES

Ken Keltner 1916 (1950)

DEATHS

Deacon McGuire 1936; Ralph Glaze 1968; Johnny Lucas 1970; Buddy Myer 1974

NOVEMBER

November 1

2005 Jason Varitek was awarded a Gold Glove for his play in 2005, the first time any Red Sox player at any position had won a Gold Glove since Tony Pena won it in 1991. Dwight Evans, with eight Gold Gloves, leads all Red Sox players. Yaz won seven Gold Gloves.

1995 The Red Sox inaugurated the Red Sox Hall of Fame. Automatically included were all those previously honored by induction at Cooperstown: Eddie Collins, Jimmy Collins, Joe Cronin, Bobby Doerr, Jimmie Foxx, Curt Gowdy, Lefty Grove, Harry Hooper, Rick Ferrell, Babe Ruth, Tris Speaker, Ted Williams, Carl Yastrzemski, Tom Yawkey, and Cy Young. Charter members of the Red Sox Hall of Fame were: Tony Conigliaro, Dominic DiMaggio, Frank Malzone, Johnny Pesky, Jim Rice, Smoky Joe Wood, and Jean Yawkey.

1967 Dick Williams is named Manager of the Year (AL) by UPI, with 23 of a possible 24 votes. He'd brought the Sox from ninth place in the standings in 1966 to the seventh game of the World Series in 1967.

1949 "Joe didn't lose the pennant, we lost it for him," said the players. Joe McCarthy agreed to take up the Red Sox on their standing offer and to serve two more years as manager, despite being so disheartened at losing on the final day of the season for two years in a row.

1944 Bobby Doerr was named American League MVP, even though he was in the U.S. Army before the season was over.

1916 After winning back-to-back World Championships, Joseph Lannin sold the Boston Red Sox to two New York theater men, Harry Frazee and Hugh Ward, for a reported $675,000. Manager Bill Carrigan announced his retirement to Lewiston, Maine.

1909 Fred Lake did a decent job with the 1909 Sox, and he sought a significant raise from owner John I. Taylor. The two could not come to terms, so the Sox let Lake go. The very next day, Taylor hired veteran manager Patsy Donovan to run the Red Sox. Lake didn't have to travel far to find a new position; he managed Boston's National League team in 1910.

TRANSACTIONS

1946: Virgil Stallcup was drafted by the Cincinnati Reds in the Rule V draft.
1979: Granted free agency to Bob Montgomery and Bob Watson.
1982: Released Tony Perez.
1984: Signed free agent Eduardo Zambrano.
1991: Dan Petry granted free agency.
1993: Rob Deer granted free agency.
1995: Signed free agent Jim Tatum, and granted free agency to Erik Hanson and Zane Smith.
1996: Mike Maddux granted free agency.
2000: The Red Sox granted free agency to: Manny Alexander, Rico Brogna, Hector Carrasco, Rheal Cormier, Bernard Gilkey, Tom Gordon, Ramon Martinez, Steve Ontiveros, Pete Schourek, and Tim Wakefield.

BIRTHDATES
Russ Kemmerer 1931 (1954–1957); Carlos Rodriguez 1967 (1994–1995)

DEATHS
George Winn 1969; Joe Bush 1974

November 2

1972 Fred Parent, 96, died in a Sanford, Maine nursing home. Parent was the last survivor of the first World Series, when Boston beat Pittsburg.

1964 CBS became the first corporation to own a baseball team, buying the Yankees for $11.2 million. They later sold the team at a loss to a group headed by George Steinbrenner. Too bad Tom Yawkey didn't have a "ringer" buy the team and sell off all the best players. Then again, it was a few years before the Yankees developed into a good team again, anyhow.

1938 With 305 of a possible 336 points, Jimmie Foxx was voted MVP of the American League for the third time, the first player in either league to be so honored thrice. Foxx had also been the 1932 and 1933 MVP.

1912 Pleased with his ball club and its World Championship, Red Sox president James McAleer made the unusual announcement that he would neither make any trades nor purchase any other players: "We have all the players we want for 1913."

TRANSACTIONS
1909: Patsy Donovan named manager of the Red Sox.
1977: Rick Miller granted free agency.
1978: Fred Kendall and Luis Tiant were both granted free agency.
1992: Billy Hatcher granted free agency.
1999: Pat Rapp is granted free agency.
2004: Declined the club option on Curtis Leskanic, making him a free agent.

BIRTHDATES
Chick Maynard 1896 (1922); Jerry Standaert 1901 (1929); Tom McBride 1914 (1943–1947); Greg Harris 1955 (1989–1994); Willie McGee 1958 (1995); Sam Horn 1963 (1987–1989); Orlando Merced 1966 (1998); Orlando Cabrera 1974 (2004)

DEATHS
Everett Scott 1960; Freddy Parent 1972; Regis Leheny 1976; Dee Miles 1976; Bill Zuber 1982; Hal Wiltse 1983

November 3

2005 More honors come the way of David Ortiz as he is named the Outstanding Player of the Year (AL) by a vote of his fellow major leaguers in the Players Choice Awards. During the World Series, he was given the Hank Aaron Award as the best overall hitter in the league.

1997 Former Red Sox outfielder Wil Cordero was given a 90-day suspended sentence in the Middlesex House of Correction, after he pleaded guilty to domestic assault in the beating of his wife on June 11. He was required to take a 40-week course for convicted batterers. He had faced a prison term of up to eight years. Ana Cordero had wanted the charges dropped, but DA Thomas Reilly declined. (See also December 11, 1997.)

In happier news, a unanimous vote awarded the AL Rookie of the Year honor to Nomar Garciaparra. He was a multi-tool player, and the first rookie in history to bat over .300, hit 30 homers, more than 90 RBI, and more than 20 stolen bases. Nomar led the American League in hits (209) and his 98 RBIs set a record for a leadoff batter. He was the first Red Sox player to win the honor since Fred Lynn won, also by unanimous vote, in 1975.

1967 Winning 18 of 20 first-place votes, Jim Lonborg (22–9) is named the Cy Young Award winner in the American League "I'm pleased, but not surprised," was his honest reaction.

1953 The National Playing Rules Committee decided not to charge a batter with an at-bat on a sacrifice fly. The committee also required players to take their gloves off the field between innings. Strange as it may seem, the committee also felt compelled to rule that a runner will be declared out if he runs the bases backwards or if he takes a lead off the base in the wrong direction. Had the sacrifice fly rule been in effect in 1941, as it was when Ted Williams first broke in, The Kid would have batted .411 in 1941.

1942 New York's Joe Gordon wins the AL MVP award despite leading the league in just three categories: strikeouts, hitting into double plays, and errors by second basemen. Ted Williams had 137 RBIs to Joe Gordon's 103. Ted had 36 HR and Joe had 18, only half as many. Ted had 34 doubles and Joe had 29; Ted had 5 triples and Joe had 4. Ted scored 141 runs and Joe scored 88 runs. Ted batted .356 and Joe averaged .322. Ted's on-base percentage was .499 and Joe's was .409. Ted's slugging percentage was .648 and Joe's was .491. For what it's worth, Ted's fielding average was .988 and Joe's was .966.

TRANSACTIONS
1959: Traded Frank Baumann to the White Sox for Ron Jackson.
1995: Willie McGee was granted free agency.
1998: Both Dennis Eckersley and Darren Lewis were granted free agency.

BIRTHDATES
Rick Kreuger 1948 (1975–1977); Dwight Evans 1951 (1972–1990); Paul Quantrill 1968 (1992–1994); Anastacio Martinez 1978 (2004)

DEATHS
Frank Smith 1952; Vern Stephens 1968; Red Kellett 1970; Jack Russell 1990; Boze Berger 1992

November 4

2000 Ted Williams is taken to the hospital with congestive heart failure. Though he does not die until July 2002, this is really the beginning of the end.

1990 Kevin B. Winn, 24, was arrested in Farmington CT, and charged with passing bad checks, forgery, and impersonating Red Sox catcher John Marzano in order to pick up women who he later jilted. When arrested, Winn was parked in a stolen car outside a restaurant.

1986 John McNamara is named Manager of the Year for bringing the Red Sox from fifth place in 1985 to Game Seven of the World Series in 1986.

1975 The Red Sox announce they will install padding on the outfield wall and a new electronic scoreboard over the center-field bleachers.

1948 Former Yankees outfielder Jake Powell shot and killed himself in a police station in Washington, D.C. On May 30, 1938, Powell had been involved in a fight with Joe Cronin. Later that same year, in a July 29 radio interview with Bob Elson, Powell talked about "beating up niggers and then throwing them in jail" as part of his off-season duties as a policeman. Powell was suspended for 10 days by the commissioner for his statements. It is perhaps ironic that Powell ultimately took his own life in a police station.

1944 An overflow Fenway Park crowd estimated at 45,000 greeted President Franklin D. Roosevelt for the final rally of the 1944 campaign for President. As it turned out, it was the last major political rally of FDR's career.

1910 Sometimes you can believe what you read in the press. In a statement said to be released with his authorization, Jake Stahl said he will retire from baseball and enter the banking business in Chicago. "This is the first I have heard about it," declared Sox president John I. Taylor.

1908 Former Red Sox scout Fred Lake's contract as manager was renewed for the 1909 season; Lake had taken over for Deacon McGuire during the 1908 campaign. Sliding scale salaries were planned for every position.

TRANSACTIONS
1988: Bruce Hurst, Dennis Lamp, and Mike Smithson are all granted free agency.
1990: Mike Boddicker and Danny Heep are both granted free agency.
1991: Dennis Lamp granted free agency.
1992: Steve Lyons granted free agency.
1993: Steve Lyons granted free agency, on the anniversary of
    his grant of free agency the year before.
1996: Roger Clemens was granted free agency. The Red Sox also acquired
    Mark Brandenburg and Kerry Lacy from the Texas Rangers in
    trade for Mike Stanton and a PTBNL (Dwayne Hosey).
1999: Reggie Jefferson is granted free agency.
1998: Creighton Gubanich was signed as a free agent.

BIRTHDATES
Guy Morton 1930 (1954); Carlos Baerga 1968 (2002)

DEATHS
Ed Kelly 1928; Cy Young 1955; Johnny Mitchell 1965; Pinky Pittinger 1977; Yank Terry 1979

November 5

1976 In the expansion draft, the Red Sox lose several players: pitchers Steve Burke, Rick Jones, and Dick Pole, catcher Ernie Whitt, and outfielder Luis Delgado.

1944 Red Sox players were practicing their skills, despite the war. On November 5, under team manager Dom DiMaggio, Charlie Wagner threw a seven-inning one-hitter to help the Navy All-Stars beat an Army team, 17–0, in front of 12,000 in Brisbane, Australia. Al Flair pitched for the Guinea Chicks on the remains of a Japanese airstrip "somewhere in New Guinea" and hit two doubles and a single. Mickey Harris was pitching for an air base in the Canal Zone.

1941 Former Red Sox player Billy Rogell is elected to the Detroit City Council. Rogell broke in with Boston, but played 10 seasons in Detroit. He served nearly 40 years on the City Council, from 1942 to 1980.

1920 Hugh Duffy is named manager of the Red Sox, replacing Ed Barrow who defected to the Yankees.

TRANSACTIONS
1976: Lost Dick Pole, Rick Jones, Steve Burke, and Puchy Delgado to Seattle in the expansion draft, and lost Ernie Whitt to the Toronto Blue Jays in the same draft.
1991: Steve Lyons granted free agency.
2001: Players granted free agency on this date include: Rod Beck, Dante Bichette, Darren Lewis, Hideo Nomo, Troy O'Leary, Joe Oliver, Hipolito Pichardo, Bret Saberhagen, and John Valentin.
1998: Darren Lewis signed as a free agent.
2002: Signed free agent Alan Embree.

BIRTHDATES
Roxy Walters 1892 (1919–1923); Pete Donohue 1900 (1932); Jim Tabor 1916 (1938–1944); Rudy Schlesinger 1941 (1965); Johnny Damon 1973 (2002–2005)

DEATHS
Tommy O'Brien 1978; Gene Desautels 1994

November 6

2002 "We think it's a minor coup," said Red Sox president Larry Lucchino on the hiring of Bill James ("the godfather of modern statistical analysis in baseball"— Bob Hohler, *Boston Globe*) as a consultant. James became Senior Baseball Operations Advisor when the official hiring took place on November 15.

1976 Five days after being granted free agency, former Twins reliever Bill Campbell signed a million-dollar contract to pitch for the Red Sox, inking a four-year deal. Campbell was the first free agent to sign with a new team.

1939 Ted Williams pled guilty in Red Wing, Minnesota Municipal Court to duck hunting after the designated 4:00 P.M. closing time. He was fined $15 and lost his $30 shotgun.

1936 Tom Yawkey and guests Eddie Collins, Mickey Cochrane, Tris Speaker, Rube Walberg, and other players wrap up a month-long hunting trip in Wyoming.

1928 In a statewide referendum, Massachusetts voters permit professional baseball on Sundays in the Commonwealth, by a landslide margin. The vote in Boston was 172,574 to 53,990. Pennsylvania then stood alone as the only state where a major league team is based that does not permit Sunday ball. The referendum prohibits ball within 1,000 feet of a house of worship, which will forbid games at Fenway until later amended.

1926 Reports are persistent that Roger Peckinpaugh will manage the Red Sox in 1927. Nine days later, reports said that Eddie Collins would take the reins. (See also November 22, 1926.)

1922 The Red Sox were ordered to pay $534.05 to Henry Molliter of the Jonestown PA independent baseball club. An exhibition game had been planned for September 8, 1921, but the Red Sox never showed. The ball club said that the game had been called off when two of Jonestown's players were ineligible; it turned out they actually were eligible. No damages were assessed, but the Red Sox were ordered to cover Jonestown's expenses.

On the same day, Smoky Joe Wood took a position as assistant baseball coach at Yale University. In 1926, Fred Parent became Harvard's coach and, in 1930, Harry Hooper became Princeton's.

1911 Jake Stahl, President of Woodlawn State Bank of Chicago, is said to be hired to manage the 1912 Red Sox, and play first base. Stahl issued a denial. (See November 10.)

TRANSACTIONS
1953: Pitcher Leo Kiely is discharged from the U. S. Army and will be free to rejoin the Red Sox.
1976: Signed free agent Bill Campbell.
1992: Herm Winningham granted free agency.
1995: Mike Macfarlane and Mike Maddux were both granted free agency.
1997: Damon Buford and Jim Leyritz were acquired from the Texas Rangers
    for Mark Brandenburg, Bill Haselman, and Aaron Sele.
2001: David Cone granted free agency.

BIRTHDATES
Harley Hisner 1926 (1951); Jim Gosger 1942 (1963–1966)

DEATHS
Jack Chesbro 1931; Al Baker 1982; Ed Sadowski 1993

November 7

1978 Jim Rice received 20 of the 28 first-place votes and won the MVP award in the American League. Rice's season produced 406 total bases. It was the first time any AL batter had reached 400 since Joe DiMaggio had in 1937. Rice led the league in RBIs (139), homers (46), and hits (213), slugging percentage (.600), and triples (15). The runner-up was Ron Guidry, who had 291 points to Rice's 352. Larry Hisle of Milwaukee was third with 201. Guidry was the hands-down winner of the Cy Young Award.

1950 Walt Dropo was voted AL rookie of the year, with 15 of the 24 votes. Coming in second was Whitey Ford of the Yankees, who earned six votes.

1921 At the newly-opened Red Sox offices at the corner of Beacon and Tremont Streets, Hugh Duffy strongly denied that Stuffy McInnis was to be traded to the Yankees. He said that Frazee wanted to build up the team and "not tear down what he has to build on." A month later, McInnis was traded to Cleveland, while a number of other players were sent to New York.

1915 During the first week of November, Boston pitcher Babe Ruth visited the Baltimore orphanage where he had lived as a youth, but it was a costly visit. While showing his pitching form to the youngsters at St. Mary's Industrial School, Ruth managed to lose a 2½-carat diamond ring.

TRANSACTIONS
1969: Signed amateur free agent Ramon Aviles.
1983: Free agency granted to Doug Bird.
1994: Juan Bell and Bill Haselman were both signed as free agents.

BIRTHDATES
Tracy Baker 1891 (1911); Dick Stuart 1932 (1963–1964); Don Newhauser 1947 (1972–1974); Andy Tomberlin 1966 (1994)

DEATHS
None yet

November 8

2005 Former Sox reliever Ugueth Urbina was arrested and charged with attempted murder in Venezuela after he and four other men allegedly attacked workers at his home with machetes and then also tried to set them afire. His attorney denied the charges, saying Ugie was asleep at the time.

1957 Reserved grandstand seats hit the $2.00 mark at Fenway Park, as prices were hiked 10 cents. Bleacher tickets stayed at 75 cents.

1920 AMERICAN LEAGUE PLANS BOSTON CLUB read the headline in the *Boston Globe*. Huh? Didn't they already have the Red Sox? In a proposal that was described by the *New York Times* as a "declaration of war" on Ban Johnson, both the Boston Red Sox and Boston Braves announced their intent to become members of the New National League, according to plans hatched to form a new 12-team league. The Yankees and Giants and Dodgers from New York, and the Cubs and White Sox from Chicago would all be in the league as well, with the chairmanship offered to Judge Kenesaw Mountain Landis. An effort to bring all 16 existing clubs together in a joint session had failed. Johnson and his five teams determined to also put another Boston team into the American League, and ones in Chicago and New York as well. A joint meeting was agreed upon and, in the end, as we know, the new league did not form. (See November 12, 1920.)

TRANSACTIONS
1955: Traded Karl Olson, Dick Brodowski, Tex Clevenger, Neil Chrisley, and minor leaguer Al Curtis to the Washington Senators for Mickey Vernon, Bob Porterfield, Johnny Schmitz, and Tom Umphlett.
1984: Granted free agency to Gary Allenson and Rich Gale.
1999: Kent Mercker is granted free agency.

BIRTHDATES
Pat Donahue 1884 (1908–1910); Bucky Harris 1896 (manager, 1934);
Jerry Remy 1952 (1978–1984); Jose Offerman 1968 (1999–2002)

DEATHS
Fred Anderson 1957; Bucky Harris 1977

November 9

So far as can be determined, this is the one day of the year when almost nothing of great interest ever happened in more than 100 years of Red Sox history.
But, over in Germany in 1989, the Berlin Wall came down.

TRANSACTIONS
1987: Steve Crawford and Joe Sambito were both granted free agency.

BIRTHDATES
Johnny Gooch 1897 (1933); Jon Nunnally 1971 (1999); Scott Sauerbeck 1971 (2003)

DEATHS
Carl Stimson 1936; Fred Haney 1977; Bob Weiland 1988

November 10

2002 Just a day after it appeared that the Red Sox had landed Billy Beane as their new GM, Beane announced that he had changed his mind and would stay put in Oakland, citing personal and family reasons. Beane had told John Henry and Larry Lucchino the day before that he would accept the position. Apparently, having slept on it, he had second thoughts. On November 25, the Red Sox promoted Theo Epstein to the GM slot. Less than 24 months later, the Red Sox won their first World Series since 1918.

1997 Roger Clemens was named American League Cy Young Award winner for the fourth time; this time he was pitching for the Toronto Blue Jays.

1932 Yankees owner Jacob Ruppert was said to be amused at the suggestion of some that the Yankees were too strong and that "some of their players should be handed over to the Boston Red Sox, for instance." He ridiculed the idea, noting, "There is no charity in baseball." (*The Sporting News*) See also May 12, 1933.

1912 The *Chicago Tribune* published a long story of how Red Sox ace pitcher Smoky Joe Wood had broken into baseball as "Lucy Tolton" of the Bloomer Girls, and recounted the time that Lucy's wig fell off during the middle of a ballgame.

1911 Jake Stahl was officially announced as the new manager of the Red Sox, under a two-year deal which also provided that Stahl will play first base. Player-manager Stahl also becomes a part-owner of the ball club, the only time the Red Sox have had a player-owner. The return of the popular Stahl saw him lead the 1912 Sox to a World Championship the very first season in their new digs: Fenway Park.

1908 Red Sox President Taylor was a busy man, selling off 10 players in one day to a number of clubs for a total of $17,000.

TRANSACTIONS
1947: Drafted Babe Martin (from the St. Louis Browns) and Johnny Ostrowski
    (from the Chicago Cubs) in the Rule V draft. The Cleveland Indians
    drafted Bill Kennedy from the Red Sox in the same draft.
1948: Irv Medlinger drafted by St. Louis Browns in the Rule V draft.
1982: Granted free agency to Tom Burgmeier.

BIRTHDATES
Cy Morgan 1878 (1907–1909); Jack Hoey 1881 (1906–1908); Del Gainer 1886 (1914–1919);
Ben Hunt 1888 (1910); Chick Fewster 1895 (1922–1923); Birdie Tebbetts 1912 (1947–1950);
Johnny Lipon 1922 (1952–1953); Gene Conley 1930 (1961–1963); Larry Parrish 1953 (1988);
Bob Stanley 1954 (1977–1989); Jack Clark 1955 (1991–1992); Butch Huskey 1971 (1999)

DEATHS
Ben Paschal 1974

November 11

1999 With 20 of a possible 28 first-place votes, Boston's Jimy Williams was named Manager of the Year in the American League for shepherding his team into the Wild Card spot in the 1999 playoffs.

1987 Roger Clemens won the Cy Young Award (AL) for the second year in a row. (See also November 12, 1986.) He out-pointed Jimmy Key, 124 to 64, and was the only player in either league named on all the ballots. Jim Palmer had won back-to-back Cy Youngs in 1975 and 1976, the last pitcher before Clemens to do so.

1975 Umpire Larry Barnett says he holds TV announcers Tony Kubek and Curt Gowdy responsible for the death threats he and his family received after his controversial World Series call (see October 20, 1975). Barnett said that 95% of the negative mail he received mentioned the television announcers and the views they had expressed. He praised the Boston Police for protection accorded him in Games Six and Seven.

1903 Jimmy Collins signs a contract to manage the Boston Americans for three years. They will be called the Americans during his years at the helm.

BIRTHDATES
Boob Fowler 1900 (1926); Bill Lefebvre 1915 (1938–1939); Ike
Delock 1929 (1952–1963); Rey Quinones 1963 (1986)

DEATHS
Frank Mulroney 1985

November 12

1986 Roger Clemens was the unanimous selection for the American League Cy Young Award. Only Denny McLain (in 1968) had won it unanimously before Rocket Roger. Clemens also won the 1986 MPV award. Clemens was 24–4 (2.48 ERA) and had 245 K's. He'd struck out 20 Mariners in April, beaten every AL team at least once, and helped lead the Sox to the World Series.

1978 Radical fugitive Abbie Hoffman, writing while underground, said he "almost threw up" when the Red Sox lost the October 2 playoff game to the Yankees.

1939 Center fielders ran in the family. The San Francisco Seals Pacific Coast League club sold Dominic DiMaggio, younger brother to Vince and Joe, to the Red Sox for a reported $40,000.

1920 Baseball magnates met in joint session and worked out a new plan for baseball, preserving the two eight-team leagues and scuttling thoughts of a single 12-team league. Judge Landis accepted their offer to become commissioner of baseball, or what the *Chicago Tribune* headline dubbed, the "Big Umpire." His duties would begin on January 12, 1921. He will remain a sitting judge on the bench.

1918 November 11 was Armistice Day. The war was over. And the very next morning's newspapers assured readers that major league baseball would be back in 1919. The 1918 season was truncated as of September 1, 1918, so there was some discussion as to whether contracts were terminated as well, but not even Dave Fultz of the Players Fraternity (the closest to a players union in its day) claimed that contracts had been abrogated.

TRANSACTIONS
1939: Purchased Dominic DiMaggio and pitcher Larry Powell from the San Francisco Seals. The Red Sox later gave an option on outfielder John Barrett to the Seals.
1985: Bruce Kison and Rick Miller were both granted free agency.
1986: Free agency granted to: Tony Armas, Rich Gedman, Glenn Hoffman, Joe Sambito, Tom Seaver, Dave Stapleton, and Sammy Stewart.

BIRTHDATES
Carl Mays 1891 (1915–1919); Emerson Dickman 1914 (1936–1941)

DEATHS
Ed Connolly 1963; Cleo Carlyle 1967

November 13

2000 For the second year in a row, Pedro Martinez was the unanimous winner of the American League Cy Young Award. With his NL Cy in 1997, Pedro had won three of the last four years. He'd been 23–4 in 1999, but Buster Olney of the *New York Times* rated Pedro's 18–6 record better in 2000 because his 1.74 ERA was almost a full two runs lower than his closest rival, Roger Clemens (3.70). Martinez had held opponents to a .167 batting average, and he had a 9-to-1 strikeout to walks average. We could go on and on citing other stellar stats; it was a superlative season.

1991 Roger Clemens won his third Cy Young Award for the Red Sox.

1978 Luis Tiant signed with the Yankees, taking the reverse route of Mike Torrez the year before. Torrez had left the New York team to sign with the Red Sox. Tiant signed a two-year deal to pitch; his contract reportedly had him serve as the Yankees' director of Latin Affairs for 10 years after that. The Red Sox had offered one year, but the Yankees offer was clearly superior. Tiant posted a 13–8 year for New York in 1979, same as he had for the Red Sox in '78.

1944 Elise Sparrow Yawkey (residing at the Tumbling D-W dude ranch to establish Nevada residency) was granted a divorce from her husband Tom, on grounds of three years of separation. At last word, Tom was hunting on his South Carolina estate with Ed Barrow.

TRANSACTIONS
1951: Traded Mel Hoderlein and Chuck Stobbs to the Chicago
    White Sox for Randy Gumpert and Don Lenhardt.
1981: Granted free agency to Bill Campbell, Jerry Remy, Joe Rudi, and Frank Tanana.
1985: Acquired Calvin Schiraldi, Wes Gardner, John Christensen, and
    LaSchelle Tarver from the New York Mets for Tom McCarthy, Bobby
    Ojeda, John Mitchell, and minor leaguer Chris Bayer.
1989: Oil Can Boyd, Nick Esasky, Greg Harris, Dennis Lamp, Joe Price, and Mike
    Smithson were all granted free agency. Jim Rice was given his release.
1998: Signed free agent Jose Offerman to a four-year contract.
2001: Mike Lansing granted free agency.

BIRTHDATES
Ernie Neitzke 1894 (1921); George Dumont 1895 (1919); Si Rosenthal 1903 (1925–1926);
John Kroner 1908 (1935–1936); Bob Garbark 1909 (1945); Dan Petry 1958 (1991)

DEATHS
Muddy Ruel 1963; Johnny Ostrowski 1992; Wally Shaner 1992

November 14

2005 Former Red Sox pitcher Dennis "Oil Can" Boyd surrendered to Federal authorities in Tupelo, Mississippi after being indicted on charges that, in five telephone calls, he threatened a former girlfriend who was also a business associate.

1967 The Major League Executive of the Year Award was won by Red Sox GM Dick O'Connell, perhaps no surprise in the year of the "Impossible Dream" team. Two other Sox execs received votes, too—Haywood Sullivan got two and Tom Yawkey got one.

TRANSACTIONS
2003: Signed Mike Timlin to a one-year contract.

BIRTHDATES
Jim Piersall 1929 (1950–1958); Kim Andrew 1953 (1975); Curt Schilling 1966 (2004–2005)

DEATHS
Art McGovern 1915; Les Nunamaker 1938; Jack Hoey 1947; Dick Hoblitzell
1962; Ski Melillo 1963; Gene Bailey 1973; Hod Lisenbee 1987

November 15

1967 Carl Yastrzemski won the AL Triple Crown (no player in either league has won it since) and was the near-unanimous MVP. Yaz led the Sox to their first pennant since 1946, won the batting title, the home run crown, and had more RBIs than anyone else. For some reason, one vote was given to Cesar Tovar (.267, six home runs, 47 RBI). Yaz batted .326, had 44 homers, and 121 RBI.

1955 Red Sox manager Pinky Higgins is voted AL Manager of the Year. Though the Boston finished fourth both years, the club improved from 1954's 69–85 record to 84–70.

1949 Ted Williams and party were lost in the wilds of Minnesota overnight. The full story is detailed by John Smrekar in *Ted Williams: The Pursuit of Perfection.*

1946 Ted Williams handily beat out Hal Newhouser in the voting for AL MVP. Bobby Doerr came in third, and Johnny Pesky came in fourth. Boo Ferriss ranked seventh and Dom DiMaggio ninth.

1945 Johnny Pesky was serving as business manager of the Air Service football team in Honolulu, awaiting his discharge from the Navy. On the same day, it was reported that Ted Williams had put on weight, from 173 to an even 200 pounds, during his three years in the service.

1934 The November 15 *Sporting News* said that new manager Joe Cronin was not going to tolerate any "play boys" on the 1935 Red Sox. One of his first moves was to release Ed Morgan, who context indicates may have been involved in an April 1934 fracas resulting in a broken arm for a Red Sox teammate.

1917 Four Red Sox players—Jack Barry, Chick Shorten, Mike McNally, and Ernie Shore—all reported for duty in the United States Navy at the Charlestown Navy Yard. In courtroom activity, Louis Bennett "well known in sporting circles" (*Boston Globe*) lost a lawsuit in which he sought $750 from Boston pitcher Carl Mays for money he claimed he gave Mays via Joseph J. Sullivan in October 1915. Mays denied he ever asked Bennett to give the money to Sullivan in the first place.

1911 James McAleer, designated the new president of the Boston Red Sox as of the new year, arrived in town to consult with Robert McRoy, slated to become team secretary. McRoy left almost immediately to begin preparations for spring training in Hot Springs.

TRANSACTIONS
1948: Released Wally Moses.
2002: Announced the hiring of Bill James as senior baseball operations advisor.

BIRTHDATES
Gene Rye 1906 (1931); Hal Bevan 1930 (1952); Ray Webster 1937 (1960);
Daryl Irvine 1964 (1990–1992); Craig Hansen 1983 (2005)

DEATHS
Phil Todt 1973

November 16

1999 Pedro Martinez had earned pitching's Triple Crown, leading the league in wins, strikeouts, and earned run average, and it was a foregone conclusion that he would win the 1999 Cy Young Award. He did so unanimously. Having previously won a National League Cy Young, he became just the third pitcher to win a Cy Young in both leagues.

1995 Mo Vaughn was selected the AL's Most Valuable Player, by a 308–300 vote, despite Cleveland's Albert Belle hitting 50 home runs and 50 doubles for the AL championship Indians. Belle was a bit of a pariah, while Vaughn was fairly popular with the writers.

1971 Carl Yastrzemski denied that he had faked a back injury to avoid the final week of the 1970 season. Billy Conigliaro had made the allegation, which Yaz said was "ridiculous" given that manager Eddie Kasko had told him to take off the last 10 days so Kasko could get a better look at some of the team's prospects. Of Billy C., Yaz declared, "In all my years I've never seen a player who's done so little pop off so much."

1950 "Ted isn't bigger than baseball," Bosox manager Steve O'Neill said, when asked about Ted Williams' statement that he might or might not play in any spring training games in 1951. "If I do not feel right," Williams had said, "I won't play in any." O'Neill said Ted would play if he was fit.

1918 The National Commission voted to assess fines against three players (Amos Strunk, Joe Bush, and Walter Schang) who played post-Series exhibition games while billed as the Boston Red Sox. The commission also voted to withhold the world championship emblems (the equivalent of today's rings) from all Series participants, because of their role in threatening to strike during the Series itself. The commission envisioned reduced 18-man rosters for the 1919 season.

1908 The medical examiner found that Chick Stahl's widow, Julia Stahl, had died of natural causes. She had been found dead in a South Boston doorway late on November 15. Chick Stahl had committed suicide during spring training 1907. Julia's family, however, was convinced that she was the victim of foul play. Her brother-in-law said he believed she had been "drugged, murdered, and then robbed of her jewels." He called for police to search for the three rings she had been wearing, worth an estimated $2,000. More news about Chick Stahl's suicide indicated that he had been engaged to a woman named Barnett while he was in Buffalo, and then also engaged to Julia Harmon. On a return visit to Buffalo, at the New York Central rail depot, Barnett caused a "dramatic scene in the waiting rooms…took carbolic acid, with the intention of committing suicide." She was rushed to the hospital and survived. Stahl was said to brood over the scandal. When Stahl successfully committed suicide, he chose the same medium: carbolic acid. (See also March 28, 1907.)

TRANSACTIONS
1950: Drafted Paul Hinrichs from the New York Yankees in the Rule V draft. Joe DeMaestri was drafted by the Chicago White Sox in the Rule V draft.
1979: Signed free agent Tony Perez.
1998: Jose Offerman and Raul Gonzalez both signed as free agents.
2000: Received Chris Stynes from Cincinnati for Michael Coleman and Donnie Sadler.

BIRTHDATES
Chris Haney 1968 (2002)

DEATHS
Joe Gonzales 1996; Russ Meyer 1998

November 17

1992 The fourth major league expansion draft sees the Sox lose two players, both to the Colorado Rockies: catcher Eric Wedge and infielder Jody Reed.

1975 The Rangers trade seven-time 20-game winner and future Hall of Famer Ferguson Jenkins to the Red Sox for OF Juan Beniquez, two pitchers, and cash.

1947 In a major deal that helps the Red Sox, Boston ships Roy Partee, Jim Wilson, Al Widmar, Eddie Pellagrini, Pete Layden, Joe Ostrowski, and $310,000 to the Browns for Jack Kramer and Vern Stephens. Stephens would lead the AL in RBI in two of the next three seasons while averaging 33 HRs each year.

1934 Joe Cronin's first official act when installed as manager of the Red Sox was to appoint a clown to coach the Red Sox! He named noted baseball clown Al Schacht to handle third base duties.

TRANSACTIONS
1947: Acquired Vern Stephens and Jack Kramer from the St. Louis Browns in trade for six players and some dough. See also November 18, 1947.
1949: Sid Schacht (St. Louis Browns) and George Strickland (Pittsburgh Pirates) were both selected in the Rule V draft.
1975: Acquired Ferguson Jenkins in a trade with the Texas Rangers for Juan Beniquez, Steve Barr, and a PTBNL (Craig Skok).
1992: Jody Reed and Eric Wedge were both selected by the Colorado Rockies in the 1992 expansion draft.
1997: Bret Saberhagen signed as a free agent.

BIRTHDATES
Tex Vache 1894 (1925); Norm Zauchin 1929 (1951–1957); Dan Osinski 1933 (1966–1967); Gary Bell 1936 (1967–1968); Tom Seaver 1944 (1986)

DEATHS
Smead Jolley 1991; Floyd Baker 2004

November 18

1999 Pedro Martinez comes in second in MVP voting as two writers decide on their own that pitchers should not be the MVP, despite clear instructions accompanying the voting process that pitchers are to be considered. The newspapers in question continued to employ the writers.

1997 In one of their best swaps ever, the Red Sox obtain Cy Young Award winner Pedro Martinez from the Expos in exchange for pitcher Carl Pavano and a player to be named.

In the major league expansion draft on this date, the Red Sox lost pitcher Jeff Suppan to the Arizona Diamondbacks and pitcher Jim Mecir to the Tampa Bay Devil Rays.

1986 Roger Clemens won 19 of 28 first-place votes, easily out-pointing Don Mattingly as the choice for the 1986 Most Valuable Player Award in the American League. The last starting pitcher who had won the MVP was Vida Blue in 1971.

1947 The Red Sox add Ellis Kinder to their roster by trading for him and IF Billy Hitchcock. They send St. Louis one pitcher (Clem Dreisewerd), two infielders (Sam Dente and Bill Summers), and a bunch of money, said to be $65,000.

1942 Pitcher Broadway Charlie Wagner, Ted Williams' roommate with the Red Sox, joined the many major leaguers heading off to military service when he enlisted in the United States Navy.

TRANSACTIONS
1947: One day after an eight-player trade with the St. Louis Browns, the Red Sox traded Sam Dente, Clem Dreisewerd, Bill Summers, and $65,000 cash for Ellis Kinder and Billy Hitchcock.
1997: Pedro Martinez was acquired from the Montreal Expos for Carl Pavano and a PTBNL, who was Tony Armas, Jr. On the same date, the Sox lost pitchers Jeff Suppan (selected by Arizona as their third pick in the 1997 expansion draft) and Jim Mecir (selected by Tampa Bay).

BIRTHDATES
Deacon McGuire 1863 (1907–1908); Spike Merena 1909 (1934); Joe Cicero 1910 (1929–1930); Gene Mauch 1925 (1956–1957); Cal Koonce 1940 (1970–1971); Jamie Moyer 1962 (1996); Dante Bichette 1963 (2000–2001); Chris Howard 1965 (1994); Tom Gordon 1967 (1996–1999); David Ortiz 1975 (2003–2005)

DEATHS
Wally Mayer 1951; John Michaels 1996; Ken Brett 2003

November 19

1996 Jimy Williams is named new manager of the Red Sox, replacing the fired Kevin Kennedy. The former Blue Jays skipper was somewhat of an unknown to the players. Mo Vaughn said, "I'm not really aware of what kind of manager he is or anything. I'm sure he'll do a good job."

1965 35-year-old Frank Malzone was given his unconditional release after nine seasons with the Boston Red Sox. Sox GM Dick O'Connell told reporters that the release was to let the seven-time All-Star Malzone try to find a place as a player with another club, but further explained that a position would be waiting for him in the Red Sox organization if he were unable to find a slot elsewhere. Their assessment seems correct, as Malzone signs with the California Angels but only hits .206 in 155 at-bats. And Frank came back later to work with the Red Sox organization.

1949 Keeping busy in the off-season, Ted Williams traveled to Stuttgart, Arkansas to serve as one of five judges in the national duck calling contest.

1928 Sox president Bob Quinn admitted that he had passed up some opportunities to work trades with the Yankees, because of enduring fan negativity at "the way the Frazee Red Sox built up the New York Yankees from the nowhere class to contendership and championships." (Burt Whitman, *The Sporting News*) Quinn deferred to fan passions, but passed on at least one opportunity a few years earlier to make a deal for a player the Yankees were offering who proved to truly become a star pitcher. He vowed never again to decline the chance to strengthen the Red Sox. (See also February 10, 1930.)

TRANSACTIONS

1951: Drafted Hal Bevan from the Pittsburgh Pirates in the Rule V draft. George Wilson
was drafted from the Red Sox by the Chicago White Sox in the Rule V draft.
1965: Released Frank Malzone.

BIRTHDATES

Everett Scott 1892 (1914–1921); Joe Glenn 1908 (1940); Joe Morgan
1930 (manager, 1988–1991); Andy Sheets 1971 (2000)

DEATHS

Marty Griffin 1951; Frank Foreman 1957; Fred Hofmann 1964

November 20

2001 Sox fans celebrated the signing of Detroit slugger Tony Clark. It was hoped the switch-hitting Clark would fill the slot vacated by effectively-expelled Carl Everett. Clark batted .207 with three home runs, but everyone agreed he was a "good guy" and a "positive force in the clubhouse." Bob Hohler of the *Globe* noted at the time of his signing that he had been "hampered by injuries and inconsistency the last two years."

1990 For his actions that resulted in his ejection from Game Four of the 1990 ALCS, pitcher Roger Clemens was suspended for five games and fined $10,000. It meant he would miss his first start in 1991 and be docked about $77,000 in pay. The penalty was assessed for "making significant physical contact with an umpire; for threatening umpire Terry Cooney; for personally abusing Cooney with personal obscenities; and for not leaving the dugout immediately after the ejection." Clemens had not been issued a warning on the field, and some felt the punishment was therefore too stiff. First base umpire Vic Voltaggio reported that Clemens had said to Cooney in the heat of the moment, "I'm going to find out where you live and come after you this winter."

1972 For the first time ever, there was a unanimous choice for the American League's Rookie of the Year. It was Boston's Carlton Fisk. The catcher batted .293 and hit 22 homers, not to mention leading the league in triples with nine.

1958 Jackie Jensen is named the AL MVP.

1918 Red Sox owner Harry Frazee recommended that the existing three-man National Commission (in which the NL had two votes and the AL only had one) be replaced with an independent commissioner of baseball. Frazee and AL president Ban Johnson, one of three members of the then-current National Commission, were at odds on a number of issues, this among them. (See also December 10.)

TRANSACTIONS

1962: Traded Jim Pagliaroni and Don Schwall to the Pittsburgh
  Pirates for Dick Stuart and Jack Lamabe.
1988: Signed free agent Dennis Lamp.
1990: Released Jeff Stone.
1998: Purchased Tomokazu Okha from the Yokohama Bay Stars of Japan's Central League.
2001: Tony Clark was picked up from the Detroit Tigers, on waivers.
2003: Claimed Phil Seibel and Edwin Almonte off waivers from the New York
  Mets. Declined option on Bobby Howry, making him a free agent.

BIRTHDATES

Neill Sheridan 1921 (1948); Lou Berberet 1929 (1958); Jay Ritchie 1936 (1964–1965)

DEATHS

Fred Burchell 1951; Bill Sayles 1996; Dick Littlefield 1997

November 21

1959 In the first trade during a newly-implemented three-week interleague trading period, the Cubs sent pitcher Dave Hillman and infielder Jim Marshall to the Red Sox for first baseman Dick Gernert.

1927 Manager Bill Carrigan of the Red Sox is reported to have selected Bradenton, Florida for their spring training home in 1928. He wanted his charges to play as many exhibition games as they could against big league opponents. President Quinn was glad to back his manager in this regard. Quinn was reportedly feeling better, too, after his partner in the Red Sox, Columbus physician Robert Drury, removed "a growth as big as a baseball" from Quinn's right knee.

1922 BILL PIERCY IN TROUBLE AGAIN—*Boston Globe* headline. Pitcher Piercy was found to be playing winter ball on the Pacific coast with Joe Pirrone's All-Stars, a violation of the anti-barnstorming regulation promulgated by the baseball commissioner's office.

1918 Ball club owners acted quickly to renew contracts with their players. Virtually all players had been released from their contracts when the War Department closed major league parks effective September 1 (the World Series was allowed to play itself out). With the Armistice on November 11, clubs suddenly realized that they had very few players signed, and worried that all the unsigned players would suddenly become free agents.

TRANSACTIONS

1959: Traded Dick Gernert to the Chicago Cubs for Jim Marshall and Dave Hillman.
1997: Signed free agent Mike Benjamin. Signed Sun-Woo Kim as an amateur free agent.
2001: Michael "Prime Time" Coleman signed as a free agent.

BIRTHDATES

Todd Erdos 1973 (2001)

DEATHS

Dusty Cooke 1987

November 22

1957 Mickey Mantle edges Ted Williams 233 to 209 votes to win the American League MVP. Roy Sievers was a close third with 205. Williams just missed hitting .400 again, at age 39 years of age, with a .388 average. He hit 38 home runs and led the league in OBP (.528) and slugging average (.731), for an OPS of 1.259, at the time the fifth highest ever (only Babe Ruth topped Ted). Yet one Chicago voter ranked Ted 10th and another ranked him ninth. Sox owner Tom Yawkey remarked, "I do not think anyone who lets personalities interfere with his judgment is qualified or competent to vote on such a ballot."

1928 Boston buys pitcher Bill "Beverly" Bayne from the Indians. He won five games for the Red Sox in 1929.

1926 Francis J. Powers reported in *The Sporting News* that "Old Lady Rumor"in Cleveland was saying that Ty Cobb was on the verge of buying the Red Sox and installing Tris Speaker as manager.

TRANSACTIONS
1928: Purchased Bill Bayne from the Cleveland Indians.
1954: Ben Flowers drafted from the Detroit Tigers via the Rule V draft. Joe
     Trimble drafted from the Pittsburgh Pirates in the Rule V draft.
1974: Signed amateur free agent Win Remmerswaal.
1999: Lou Merloni was sold to the Yokohama Bay Stars of Japan's Central League.

BIRTHDATES
Mike Benjamin 1965 (1997–1998); Jay Payton 1972 (2005)

DEATHS
Roy Carlyle 1956; Joe Bowman 1990

November 23

1993 Haywood Sullivan was bought out of his ownership in the Red Sox by the JRY Corp. with a payment of a reported $12 million. Later reports said the amount was greater yet. Sullivan had initially bought into the Red Sox with $1 million loaned to him by Jean R. Yawkey and now her estate had to buy back his shares for 12 times the amount he could never have paid in the first place had she not loaned him the funds. After Jean Yawkey passed in February 1992, John Harrington said he would run the team for "two or three more years" and then effect its sale.

1990 Former Red Sox catcher Bo Diaz, 37, was crushed to death by a television satellite dish which fell on him while he was trying to adjust it on the roof of his home in Caracas, Venezuela.

1939 A "speed meter" device which was a precursor to today's radar gun had ballplayers fire a ball into a carriage containing two "light curtains"—when the two beams were broken, the time between the two was calculated. The two fastest Sox throwers were Jim Tabor and Doc Cramer, tied at 128 feet per second. Bob Feller only hit 119. The highest score of all was 139, by Atley Donald of New York (matched by Rudy York of the Tigers.)

TRANSACTIONS
1977: Signed free agent Mike Torrez.
1980: Granted free agency to Dave Rader.
1988: Released Rich Garces and Billy Ahsley.

BIRTHDATES
Dick Reichle 1896 (1922–1923); Jake Jones 1920 (1947–1948); Luis
Tiant 1940 (1971–1978); Dale Sveum 1963 (2004–2005); David
McCarty 1969 (2003–2005); Jonathan Papelbon 1980 (2005)

DEATHS
Bo Diaz 1990; Lee Rogers 1995

November 24

2005 A big trade with the Marlins became official, Boston acquiring three established major leaguers—pitchers Josh Beckett and Guillermo Mota, and three-time All-Star third baseman Mike Lowell for four prospects (Hanley Ramirez, Anibal Sanchez, Jesus Delgado, and Harvey Garcia).

1949 Ted Williams led the league in RBI and tied for the lead in homers, but he fell less than two-ten-thousandths of a point short of George Kell for the batting title. He won the MVP voting with ease, though, with 272 votes to second-place Phil Rizzuto's 175 votes. Ironically, in the two years Ted did win the Triple Crown, he wasn't deemed good enough to get the MVP. New York bookies, out $500,000, claimed foul, alleging that New Jersey bookies had been tipped in advance that Williams was the winner.

1931 Fred Lake died of heart trouble in Boston. Lake had managed both the Red Sox (1908) and the Boston Braves, coached baseball at both Tufts and Harvard, and all in all was known as the "tourist of American baseball," having worked in baseball in more than 20 cities.

1925 It was a rude surprise to the new Red Sox owners when Harry Frazee's sale of Babe Ruth cost them an extra $27,575.09. The Sox were assessed additional income tax for the sales of Carl Mays and Babe Ruth to the Yankees. Because the $140,000 for the two was paid over three years, the ball club had paid when the income was realized, thus spreading and reducing the net tax. The government felt otherwise, and the United States Board of Tax Appeals upheld the Internal Revenue Bureau. Whether Harry Frazee kicked in anything is not known.

TRANSACTIONS
2005: Traded top prospect Hanley Ramirez, plus pitching prospects Anibal
     Sanchez, Jesus Delgado, and Harvey Garcia, for Florida's ace Josh Beckett,
     setup man Guillermo Mota, and three-time All-Star Mike Lowell.

BIRTHDATES
Ralph Comstock 1890 (1915); Billy Rogell 1904 (1925–1928); Tom
Winsett 1909 (1931–1933); Jeff Plympton 1965 (1991)

DEATHS
Fred Lake 1931; Ivy Andrews 1970

November 25

2003 The Red Sox announced that Terry Francona would become the next manager of the Red Sox. (See December 4, 2003.)

2002 The Red Sox introduced 28-year–old Theo Epstein as the team's new GM and, as it happens, the youngest GM in ML history. "This is no longer your father's Oldsmobile," declared Sox President Larry Lucchino.

1967 Capitalizing on winning the pennant, the Red Sox raised ticket prices. Reserved seats leapt from $2.25 to $2.50. General admission remained $1.50, and bleacher seats stayed at an even $1.00.

1962 It's not often that a team will trade the reigning batting champion, but the Boston Red Sox traded Pete Runnels to the Houston Colt 45's for promising outfielder Roman Mejias. Runnels was a Texan and had won the title both in 1960 and 1962. Mejias had banged out 24 homers in 1962, and was five years younger than Runnels, but it was more that Runnels was superfluous at first base, thanks to Boston's acquisition of slugger Dick Stuart.

1936 It's no crime to use profanity in a police station, per ruling of Judge George B. Merrick of Hyattsville MD, as he dismissed a charge of disorderly conduct against Sox third baseman and College Heights resident Billy Werber. Werber had been charged with speeding and fined $10; after paying the fine, he challenged the policeman to come see him some time when he (the cop) wasn't wearing a uniform. Some expletives accompanied the challenge, and the officer cited Werber. Two days later, the judge let Werber off the hook.

TRANSACTIONS
1969: Sold Fred Wenz to the Philadelphia Phillies.
2002: Named Theo Epstein general manager.

BIRTHDATES
Freddy Parent 1875 (1901–1907); Gene Bailey 1893 (1920); Archie Wilson 1923 (1952); Mike Ryan 1941 (1964–1967); Chico Walker 1957 (1980–1984); Mark Whiten 1966 (1995)

DEATHS
None yet

November 26

2000 There was no "curse of the Bambino," argued historian Glenn Stout in an interview with Gordon Edes of the *Boston Globe*, drawing on the book *Red Sox Century* which Stout had written with Dick Johnson of the New England Sports Museum. It was really race, not Ruth, that cursed the Red Sox—the refusal of the club to sign black players from Jackie Robinson to Willie Mays and more. Stout suspects that it was Yawkey who may have shouted the notorious "Get those niggers off the field" while Robinson and two other African-American players were given a sham tryout at Fenway to appease integration advocates. In any event, Stout points out, ultimately "the buck stopped at the top." (Jackie Robinson may have known it to be Yawkey; see September 20, 1967.)

1975 Already recognized as Rookie of the Year, in a landslide vote Fred Lynn becomes the first rookie to also win the MVP. Lynn hit .331 with 21 homers and 105 RBI. He led the league in slugging (.566), runs (103), and doubles (47). He also won a Gold Glove for his play in the field.

1958 The American League MVP is Boston slugger Jackie Jensen, winning over New York's Bob Turley and Cleveland's Rocky Colavito.

1938 His car skidded on icy pavement and Billy Evans, head of the Red Sox farm system, struck and killed Anthony Salvatore who was changing a tire on his car. Both drivers were exonerated by a coroner's jury but Salvatore's heirs filed suit in Cleveland against Evans.

1920 Evidence that the Yankees owners held more than just a mortgage on Fenway Park "percolated into the offices of President Johnson of the American League, according to the *New York Times*, which stated that the "mortgage covers the real estate holdings as well as the baseball franchise" itself. (See December 1.)

1917 Just-enlisted yeoman first class Del Gainer, sometimes called "the sheriff" by his teammates, was assigned to the chaplain's office at the Navy Yard. He joined Barry, Lewis, McNally, Shore, and Shorten in Naval service.

1915 Joe Wood saved a man's sight by rushing lumberman Charles Wells to a hospital for treatment when Wells was hooked in the forehead just above his left eye by a canthook. Joe's personal physician, Dr. F. E. Gessner, treated Wells, and it was said he likely would have lost the sight of his eye but for the prompt treatment.

TRANSACTIONS
1961: Traded Don Buddin to the Houston Colt 45's for Eddie Bressoud.
1962: Traded Pete Runnels to the Houston Colt 45's for Ramon Mejias. Bob Heffner
(to Cincinnati) and Ted Schreiber (New York Mets) were both taken in the Rule
V draft. Glenn Beckert was selected by the Cubs in the first-year draft.
1984: Signed amateur free agent Carlos Quintana.

BIRTHDATES
Hugh Duffy 1866 (manager, 1921–1922); Bob Johnson
1905 (1944–1945); Walt Ripley 1916 (1935)

DEATHS
None yet

November 27

2003 Red Sox GM Theo Epstein enjoys Thanksgiving dinner at free agent pitcher Curt Schilling's Arizona home. Presenting the pitcher with statistical evidence that Fenway Park is not necessarily death to the hopes of right-handed fly-ball pitchers, Epstein persuades Schilling to give the Sox a shot and come to Boston where he can truly make a difference.

1966 Three AL managers were all injured as the taxi in which they were riding was involved in an accident on its way from the Columbus OH airport to the downtown site of baseball's winter meetings. Dick Williams (Boston), Hank

Bauer (Baltimore), and Ralph Houk (New York) were all slightly injured ("just a few scratches and bruises and some torn clothes"—Houk); the cab driver was taken to the hospital.

1950 The Red Sox sign "deposed Cleveland manager" Lou Boudreau as a player for the 1951 team. A year later, Boudreau supplanted Steve O'Neill as skipper.

1947 Joe DiMaggio gets one more vote for AL MVP than does Ted Williams, despite the fact that Williams won the Triple Crown, 202–201. Ted hit .343 to Joe's .315, hit 32 HR to Joe's 20, and knocked in 114 runs to Joe's 97. Ted also led the league in runs scored, walks, on-base percentage, and slugging. Joe did not lead the league in a single offensive category. *The Sporting News* named Williams "Player of the Year."

1941 By a vote of 291 to 254, voters chose Joe DiMaggio and his 56-game hitting streak over Ted Williams and his .406 batting average in AL MVP voting.

1922 Former manager Bill Carrigan said he wanted to buy the Sox from Harry Frazee or become his partner, but wasn't interested in returning as a salaried manager.

1913 John I. Taylor was said set to re-purchase control of the Red Sox from James McAleer and company; he already owned 50% of the shares but had agreed not to involve himself with players or finances. New Yorker Joseph Lannin purchased the remaining half instead. (See November 30.)

1911 Buck O'Brien and the Red Sox Quartet performed at Keith's Theater. O'Brien was joined by Hugh Bradley, Marty McHale, and pitcher Bill Lyons. "They can sing, and sing well. They compare favorably with any quartet in vaudeville," commented the *Boston Globe* a couple of days before the show. After a quartet number, each one soloed, Lyons leading off with "Any Old Port in a Storm." O'Brien then sang "The Garden of my Heart," followed by McHale's "When You and I Were Young, Maggie." Bradley contributed "O, You Beautiful Doll."

TRANSACTIONS
1950: Signed free agent Lou Boudreau.
1961: Lost Marlan Coughtry to Los Angeles Angels in the Rule V draft.
    Jim Hannan was selected by the Washington Senators and Frank
    Kreutzer was selected by the White Sox in the first-year draft.
1972: Drafted Bob Gallagher from the Houston Astros in the Rule V draft.
1979: Signed free agent Skip Lockwood.
1989: Signed free agent Tony Pena.
1992: Signed free agent Billy Hatcher.

BIRTHDATES
Joe Bush 1892 (1918–1921); Johnny Schmitz 1920 (1956); Frank Quinn 1927 (1949–1950); Bill Short 1937 (1966); Jose Tartabull 1938 (1966–1968)

DEATHS
Arlie Tarbert 1946; Bob Peterson 1962

November 28

2003 RED SOX HIT JACKPOT, LAND SCHILLING read the front page headline in the *Boston Globe*. Schilling, who had originally signed with the Sox back in '86, was acquired from the Arizona Diamondbacks in exchange for Casey Fossum, Brandon Lyon, Jorge DeLaRosa, and Michael Goss. He also signed a three-year contract with the Red Sox.

1965 Haywood Sullivan resigned as A's manager to become Vice President and Director of Player Personnel for the Red Sox.

1958 Carl Yastrzemski paid is first visit to Fenway Park, while his father and Sox scout Bots Nekola talked turkey about a contract for the young Yaz. He walked around the park, looking it over, then told Nekola, "I can hit in this park."

1955 It is announced in Hollywood that Tony Perkins will play the role of Red Sox outfielder Jimmy Piersall in the forthcoming movie *Fear Strikes Out*.

1951 The Sox traded with the Browns: catcher Les Moss for catcher Gus Niarhos and outfielder Tom Wright for outfielder Ken Wood. Or was it Moss for Wood and Wright for Niarhos? Moss had been traded *to* Boston on May 17.

1940 The November 28 issue of *The Sporting News* told of a pitcher the Red Sox lost—Jimmy Cooney. Offered a $500 signing bonus by the Red Sox back in 1920 by Ed Barrow, Cooney's manager over-reacted when told he'd be paid by check, and demanded cash. Barrow got his back up, too, shouting, "So, you don't think our check is any good, eh! Cash! Get out of here, both of you—and stay out!" The Red Sox could have used a pitcher like Cooney during the 1920s; he won 34 games for the Braves.

TRANSACTIONS
1951: Traded Les Moss and Tom Wright to the St. Louis
    Browns for Gus Niarhos and Ken Wood.
1960: Drafted Billy Harrell from the St. Louis Cardinals in the Rule V draft.
1966: The Red Sox drafted Bill Landis from Kansas City in the Rule V draft,
    but had Amos Otis drafted from them by the New York Mets.
1967: Drafted George Spriggs from the Pirates in the Rule V draft.
2003: Traded Casey Fossum, Brandon Lyon, Jorge de la Rosa, and a
    PTBNL to the Arizona Diamondbacks for Curt Schilling.

BIRTHDATES
Lee Fohl 1876 (manager, 1924–1926); Benn Karr 1893 (1920–1922); Frank O'Rourke 1894 (1922); Ed Gallagher 1910 (1932); Bill McWilliams 1910 (1931); John Burkett 1964 (2002–2003); Pedro Astacio 1969 (2004)

DEATHS
Elmer Miller 1944; Ed McFarland 1959

November 29

Rather little of note seems to have happened on this day in Red Sox history. There is this one story, though...

1932 The Red Sox have performed so poorly for so many years that columnist Westbrook Pegler suggests they be allowed to field 15 players instead of the standard nine.

TRANSACTIONS
1958: Signed Carl Yastrzemski as an amateur free agent.
1964: Traded Dick Stuart to the Philadelphia Phillies for Dennis Bennett.
1965: Three players were drafted from the Red Sox in the Rule V draft: Gary
       Geiger (by the Atlanta Braves), Bob Heffner (by the Cleveland Indians),
       and Jimy Williams (by the St. Louis Cardinals). The Red Sox selected
       Ken Sanders from the Kansas City Athletics in the Rule V draft.
1971: Drafted Vic Correll from the White Sox and Bob Gallagher
       from the Dodgers in the Rule V draft.

BIRTHDATES
Tom Hughes 1878 (1902–1903); Pat Simmons 1908 (1928–1929); George
Thomas 1937 (1966–1971); Dick McAuliffe 1939 (1974–1975); Mike Easler
1950 (1984–1985); Joe Price 1956 (1989); Steve Rodriguez 1970 (1995)

DEATHS
Bob Unglaub 1916

November 30

2005 The Red Sox filed a lawsuit in Boston's Suffolk Superior Court, seeking a ruling that would restore to the team the World Series-clinching baseball that first baseman Doug Mientkiewicz gloved and took home in 2004. The case went to arbitration.

2000 Dashing the hopes of Dan Duquette, and all of Red Sox Nation, free-agent pitcher Mike Mussina chose to sign with the New York Yankees instead of the Red Sox. The talented pitcher passed up the chance to sign with a team where he could truly stand out and make a difference, to sign with the Yankees in hopes of winning a World Series ring. Quite a few seasons later, Mussina is still waiting for that ring; the Yankees haven't won a World Series in the 21st century. Duquette may have felt compelled to offer slugger Manny Ramirez more than necessary, in order to come out of the off-season with one stellar signing.

1967 Bill Schlesinger had had his one moment in the sun for the Sox. The Sox sent him to the Cubs, along with some money, to buy pitcher Ray Culp.

1926 Bill Carrigan is lured out of retirement to manage the Red Sox again. (A 1928 article in *The Sporting News* estimated he was paid three times the average manager's salary.) Carrigan had led the team to World Championships in both 1915 and 1916, but then retired to lucrative business interests in Maine. He was thought to have been one of the wealthiest players in the game, and his fortunes had only expanded since. He was not as active any more in running his banking and theatre ventures, though only age 42, and his wife reportedly agreed it might "keep him young and happy" to return to baseball. In retrospect, one wonders if managing the 1927 and 1928 Red Sox was more likely to have taken years off his life.

1913 New Yorker Joseph Lannin bought the 50% of Red Sox shares owned by McAleer, McRoy, and Jake Stahl. General Charles H. Taylor and his son John retained ownership of their half. The sale was—no surprise—more or less dictated by AL architect Ban Johnson, angry that McAleer had dismissed Jake Stahl as manager in mid-season. Canadian-born, Lannin had been a bellhop in a Boston hotel, rose in the ranks, and eventually came to own three New York hotels. Lannin became President of the Red Sox. An indication of Johnson's involvement was how McAleer learned of the sale. Joe Cashman told Peter Golenbock that McAleer received a telegram reading, "You have just sold the Red Sox to Joseph Lannin. Ban Johnson." Interestingly, Lannin ultimately sold the Sox to another former bellhop, from Peoria: Harry Frazee.

TRANSACTIONS

1964: Drafted Mike Jackson, Sparky Lyle, and Pete Magrini
from the Phillies, Orioles, and Twins.
1965: Traded Eddie Bressoud to the New York Mets for Joe
Christopher. Released Frank Malzone.
1967: Traded Bill (Rudy) Schlesinger to the Chicago Cubs for Ray Culp.
1970: Lost Cecil Cooper to the St. Louis Cardinals in the Rule V draft.
1977: Signed free agent Jack Brohamer.

BIRTHDATES

Myron Grimshaw 1875 (1905–1907); Leo Kiely 1929 (1951–
1959); Joe Kerrigan 1954 (manager, 2001)

DEATHS

John Shea 1956; Bill Evans 1983

DECEMBER

December 1

1997 The Red Sox signed 18-year-old outfielder Kenichiro Kawabata, the first Japanese player other than a pitcher to sign for an American major league club.

1961 Red Sox pitcher Don Schwall, a 15-game winner, was named Rookie of the Year in the American League. He'd started the season in the minor leagues with the Seattle Rainiers, but did so well early in the season that he made the mid-season MLB All-Star Game, one of only three major league players to make the squad despite being in the minors on Opening Day.

1959 Bobby Thomson, who hit the "shot heard 'round the world," becomes a member of the Red Sox, thanks to the Chicago Cubs. The Sox send pitcher Al Schroll to Chicago. Thomson hit five homers for the Red Sox.

1953 The Sox sent Mickey McDermott and Tommy Umphlett to Washington for former Yankee and current Senator Jackie Jensen. In Boston, Jensen bloomed as a hitter, jumping from a career-high 10 homers to an average of more than 25 in his first six seasons with the Sox. He averaged over 111 RBIs in the same period, leading the league three times, and even won the MVP in 1958. Umphlett hit three home runs, total, in the remainder of his major league career, and never reached .220. McDermott was 17–25 for the Senators. Not a bad trade!

1949 The Sox get pitcher Al Papai from the Browns on waivers. Papai is no relation to Stan Papi, nor is Stan Papi related at all to David Ortiz.

1942 After completing the first two weeks of Navy flight school at Amherst, Massachusetts, Ted Williams said he wasn't batting .400 in the course yet, but he liked flying so much he might quit baseball to be a pilot.

1930 Bob Quinn named Shano Collins to replace Heinie Wagner as manager of the Red Sox. Collins had originally joined the Red Sox when traded by the White Sox for Harry Hooper; he played from 1921 into 1925.

1924 The Red Sox selected New Orleans as spring training home for the 1925 season, and spent the next three springs training in the Crescent City.

1920 The mortgage on Fenway Park was with the Fenway Realty Trust, separate and distinct from the Boston ball club, said counsel for the Red Sox. The franchise is not part of the mortgage, further explained team counsel.

1910 Sox president John I. Taylor wants no country club atmosphere. "Discipline is to prevail," he announces, singling out pitchers for not running out balls they had hit. "There will be no loafing by ball players in my employ next summer," he stated.

TRANSACTIONS
1949: Selected Al Papai off waivers from the St. Louis Browns.
1952: Drafted Jack Merson from the Pittsburgh Pirates in the Rule V draft.

1959: Traded Al Schroll to the Chicago Cubs for Bobby Thomson.
1969: Acquired Mike Derrick from Detroit in the Rule V draft. Both Hal King and
    Ken Wright were drafted from the Red Sox in the same Rule V draft.
1970: Acquired Luis Aparicio from the White Sox by trading Mike Andrews and Luis Alvarado.
1992: Signed free agent Scott Fletcher.
2005: Acquired RHP Jermaine Van Buren from the Chicago Cubs
    for a player to be named or a cash consideration.

BIRTHDATES
Herm Winningham 1961 (1992)

DEATHS
Buster Mills 1991

December 2

1998 Mo Vaughn hit the jackpot. Having initially sought a five-year, $50 million deal
with the Red Sox, he is offered $80 million for six years with the Anaheim
Angels. He wastes no time signing that deal, and says he was glad to sign with a
team that wasn't so concerned with trying to spin the news. In Boston, he says,
"I just heard so much negativity for the past few years."

1974 Tom Yawkey said he might quit baseball if the players continued to pursue their
demand for 20 percent of all gross income. "Over the years, more ball players
have been overpaid than underpaid," Yawkey grumbled, while noting that his
players were already receiving the equivalent of 29 percent of revenues.

1951 An impatient fan. The AP reported: "Tired of waiting for the Boston Red Sox
to win the American League pennant once more, Calvin J. Hubbard observed
his 100th birthday today by switching to the New York Yankees for the 1952
baseball season. 'I've been a Red Sox rooter all my life,' explained Hubbard to
200 well-wishers, 'but I'm tired of waiting for them to win again. It's the New
York Yankees for me from now on.'"

1937 Joe Vosmik comes to the Sox (from St. Louis) in exchange for P Bobo Newsom,
SS Ralph Kress, and OF Colonel Mills.

TRANSACTIONS
1932: Traded Milt Gaston to the Chicago White Sox for Bob Weiland.
1957: Drafted Chuck Churn from the Pittsburgh Pirates in the Rule V draft.
1958: Traded Jimmy Piersall to the Indians for Vic Wertz and Gary Geiger.
    Traded Lou Berberet to the Tigers for Herb Moford.
1963: Drafted Billy Rohr from the Pirated and Reggie Smith from the Twins in the first
    year draft. Luke Walker was selected by Pittsburgh Pirates in the same draft.
1968: Acquired Dick Schofield from the Cardinals, trading them Gary
    Waslewski. Lost Bobby Mitchell to the Yankees in the Rule V draft,
    and lost Russ Nixon to the White Sox in the same draft.
1974: Traded Tommy Harper to the California Angels for Bob Heise. Drafted
    Kim Andrew from the Baltimore Orioles in the Rule V draft.

BIRTHDATES
Tom Doran 1880 (1904–1906); Johnny Welch 1906 (1932–1936)

DEATHS
Paddy Smith 1990

December 3

1932 Now there's an idea! After training in Savannah, GA, in 1932, the Red Sox announced they would hold spring training in Sarasota, FL, beginning in 1933 so the team could play against other major league teams in pre-season games.

1916 The secret purchase of the Red Sox by Harry Frazee (from Joe Lannin) is exposed by the Boston press. The deal is officially announced the next day.

1903 The first annual ball of the "Boston baseball rooters" was convened at the Odd Fellows Hall, some 500 strong, including Mike McGreevy and a number of local political figures. The evening was graced by Tom Hughes, Duke Farrell, and Hobe Ferris of the World Champion Boston Americans. After a small boy led the crowd in the singing of "Tessie," the party kicked into full swing.

TRANSACTIONS
1940: Sold Denny Galehouse and Fritz Ostermueller to the St. Louis Browns.
1943: Purchased Indian Bob Johnson from Washington.
1956: Drafted Jack Spring from the Philadelphia Phillies in the Rule V draft. Bob
    Smith was drafted by the St. Louis Cardinals in the Rule V draft.
1959: A catcher for a pitcher. Received Tom Sturdivant from
    the Kansas City Athletics for Pete Daley.
1970: Purchased Don Bryant from the Houston Astros. Traded
    Carmen Fanzone to the Cubs for Phil Gagliano.
1973: Drafted Bill Moran from the White Sox in the Rule V draft.
1984: Acquired Mike Trujillo from the San Francisco Giants in the Rule V draft.
1997: Jim Corsi signed as a free agent.

BIRTHDATES
Bennie Tate 1901 (1932); Charlie Wagner 1912 (1938–1946); Ed
Connolly 1939 (1964); Damon Berryhill 1963 (1994)

DEATHS
Earl Johnson 1994; Herb Moford 2005

December 4

2003 The Red Sox signed Terry Francona as the 44th manager in Red Sox club history. Asked if it was going to be difficult for him to manage in Boston's intense atmosphere, Francona replied, "Think about it a second. I've been released from six teams. I've been fired as manager. I've got no hair. I've got a nose that's three sizes too big for my face, and I grew up in a major league clubhouse. My skin's pretty thick. I'll be OK." He was.

1955 "I don't care if he's 82 as long as he can pitch," declared Frank Lane as he selected 42-year-old Ellis Kinder, the oldest player in the majors, off waivers from the Red Sox.

1954 Ted Williams flew out of Miami to "try for some big ones" at the Deep Sea Fishing Club near Talara, Peru.

1943 The Washington Senators sold outfielder Bob Johnson (.265 in 1943) to the Red Sox, where he hit .324 in 1944. The Senators' Griffith termed it the worst trade he ever made.

1918 Ban Johnson of the American League received a letter from General Peyton March, Chief of Staff for the War Department, informing him that baseball could resume normal scheduling in 1919. The general wrote, "The wholesome effect of a clean and honest game like baseball is very marked and its discontinuance would be a great misfortune." Hope was expressed that all players currently in the service would be discharged in sufficient time to make spring training.

1916 The official announcement is made that Harry Frazee and Hugh Ward have purchased the Boston Red Sox from Joseph Lannin.

1910 Boston's owner John I. Taylor, a bit of a publicity hound, suggested the *Atlanta Constitution*, his most recent headlines prompted by saying he'd be willing to trade his three biggest stars: Bill Carrigan, Joe Wood, and Clyde Engle.

1906 Chick Stahl was named manager of the Boston Americans for 1907, converting his status as interim manager to a permanent one. He killed himself 114 days later.

TRANSACTIONS
1943: Purchased Bob Johnson from the Washington Senators.
1955: Ellis Kinder was selected off waivers by the St. Louis Cardinals.
1989: Selected Reggie Harris from Oakland in the Rule V draft.
1990: Signed free agent Matt Young, and released Billy Jo Robidoux.
2003: Signed Terry Francona as field manager.

BIRTHDATES
Jesse Burkett 1868 (1905); Biff Schlitzer 1884 (1909); Shano Collins 1885 (1921–1925, player-manager 1931–1932); Lee Smith 1957 (1988–1990)

DEATHS
Russ Scarritt 1994; Eddie Popowski 2001

December 5

2002 The Red Sox received the official go-ahead enabling them to install Green Monster seats at Fenway Park for 2003, and another set of seats atop the right-field roof, which would be installed in time for the 2004 season.

1991 The Red Sox and the city of Ft. Myers reached a tentative agreement on a 15-year lease for a facility (now known as City of Palms Park) to be constructed in time for Red Sox spring training to open in Fort Myers in February 1993.

1944 The Sox announce that spring training 1945 would be held at Pleasantville High School, in Pleasantville, New Jersey. The team would be quartered in Atlantic City. How pleasant.

1906 Outfielder Jack Hayden was hurt badly playing football for Canton, and it was thought he would never play baseball again. He did make it back, though briefly, playing in 11 games for the Cubs in 1908.

1905 Jerry Watson, prominent among Boston's Royal Rooters, spoke at campaign rallies in both Dorchester and Charlestown in his fight against Mayor John F. Fitzgerald. As a reform candidate, one of his pledges was to cut the mayor's salary by at least 25%. Watson was the Municipal Ownership candidate. Though predictions had him collecting 1,500 to 5,000 votes, in the December 12 election, he came in a distant last among the field of four candidates, earning only 502 votes to Fitzgerald's 44,174.

TRANSACTIONS
1986: Signed free agent Joe Sambito.
1994: Vaughn Eshelman was drafted as a Rule V player from the Baltimore
    Orioles. Both Carlos Rodriguez and Ricky Trlicek were released.
1996: Reggie Harris was released.

BIRTHDATES
Dave Ferriss 1921 (1945–1950); Cliff Floyd 1972 (2002)

DEATHS
Val Picinich 1942

December 6

1991 It was 15 degrees Fahrenheit outside with a wind chill of 10 below, and the Sox hadn't fared all that well in 1991, but fans had begun to line up outside Fenway since 1:00 P.M. on December 4 waiting for 1992 regular season tickets to go on sale three days later, at 9:00 A.M. on Saturday, December 7.

1973 Yaz playing for the Nippon Ham Fighters? Reports come out of Japan that Carl Yastrzemski is visiting there, and discussing the possibility of playing for a Japanese team.

1937 Former Red Sox pitcher Bill Dinneen resigned his post as dean of American League umpires after 15 years as a player and 28 years of service as an umpire.

1921 Think of the ready lines afforded the pundits. Comedian Fred Stone stated that he had offered Harry Frazee the sum of $750,000 to buy the Boston Red Sox. Frazee said he didn't know of any offer.

1917 FRAZEE FROWNS ON CALAMITY HOWLERS—so read the *Boston Globe* headline. Harry Frazee deplored those who sought exemptions for baseball players, adding, "You would think that baseball was the biggest thing in the world and that the war came after it." Ban Johnson was among those seeking exemptions. Frazee said he would swing a pickax for Uncle Sam for $1 a day, if asked. Apparently no one did ask.

1916 Tillie Walker wrote the Red Sox from Limestone, Tennessee that his piano and organ business was doing so well that he might have to quit baseball, regardless of how much he loved the game. "We are selling them faster than we can get them," he wrote. As it happens, Walker played seven more seasons of major league ball.

TRANSACTIONS

1938: Traded Johnny Marcum to the St. Louis Browns for Tom Carey.
1976: Acquired George Scott and Bernie Carbo from the Milwaukee Brewers in trade for Cecil Cooper. Sold Bob Heise to the Kansas City Royals.
1982: Acquired Tony Armas and Jeff Newman from the Oakland Athletics in trade for Carney Lansford, Garry Hancock, and minor leaguer Jerry King.
1983: Acquired Mike Easler from the Pirates in trade for John Tudor.
1989: Signed free agents Dennis Lamp and Jeff Reardon.
1995: Signed free agent Jose Canseco.
1996: Signed free agent Robinson Checo.
2004: Claimed Tim Bausher off waivers from the Colorado Rockies.

BIRTHDATES

Jack Stansbury 1885 (1918); Hack Eibel 1893 (1920); Gus Niarhos 1920 (1952–1953); Tony Horton 1944 (1964–1967); Adam Hyzdu 1971 (2004)

DEATHS

Charley Hall 1943; Lou Clinton 1997

December 7

1957 The AP votes Tony Kubek of the Yanks as the Rookie of the Year. Frank Malzone of the Red Sox, who was declared ineligible, receives one vote. Malzone, with better offensive numbers, will later claim that he was robbed by New York writers, when the BBWA changes the minimum number of at-bats during the season, thus excluding him. (*The Baseball Chronology*)

1937 Eddie Collins signs The Kid. Bill Lane of the San Diego Padres trades Ted Williams to the Boston Red Sox for Dom Dallessandro, Al Niemiec, Spencer Harris, and cash variously reported as either $25,000 or $35,000.

1933 By December 7, only three members of the 1931 Red Sox remained with the ball club: Bob Kline, Marty McManus, and Rabbit Warstler. Kline and Warstler were traded to Philadelphia on December 12. McManus had already been let go as manager in early October, though remained on the roster a bit longer. The initial makeover of the team under the new Yawkey–Collins regime was nearly complete.

1925 Although the Red Sox ended the season in the cellar once again, owner Bob Quinn denied rumors he was planning to dump manager Lee Fohl. He said "of course" he was going to keep Fohl; "it would be the act of a coward to even think of doing anything else." Look at the 1925 team's batting average, Quinn said. "The team did not have players of a high caliber...he did not have the men with which to win many ballgames. Accordingly, why make a grandstand play, by blaming him for the poor showing of the team?"

TRANSACTIONS

1973: Acquired Reggie Cleveland, Diego Segui, and Terry Hughes from the Cardinals in a trade for Lynn McGlothen, John Curtis, and Mike Garman.
1978: Acquired Stan Papi from the Montreal Expos in trade for Bill Lee.
1987: John Trautwein was drafted as a Rule V player from the Montreal Expos.
   Todd Pratt was selected by Cleveland in the 1987 minor league draft.
1990: Larry Andersen was granted free agency.

1993: Otis Nixon signed a free agent.
1994: Acquired Luis Alicea from the Cardinals for Jeff McNeely and Nate Minchey.
1996: Signed free agent Mike Maddux and, in an unrelated
     move, granted Tim Naehring his free agency.
2000: Signed free agents Frank Castillo, Pete Schourek, and Tim Wakefield.
2005: Traded backup catcher Doug Mirabelli to San Diego for second baseman Mark Loretta.

BIRTHDATES
Hobe Ferris 1877 (1901–1907); Ed Morris 1899 (1928–1931); Denny
Galehouse 1911 (1939–1949); Shane Mack 1963 (1997)

DEATHS
Bobo Newsom 1962; Lefty O'Doul 1969

December 8

2004 In another of those public relations moves that have won the Henry–Werner–Lucchino Red Sox fan favor throughout Red Sox Nation, the team committed to taking the 2004 World Championship trophy to every one of the 351 cities and towns in the Commonwealth of Massachusetts. The trophy also visited locations in all the other New England states, the Dominican Republic, a meeting of the BLOHARDS fan club in New York City, Sonny McLean's Boston sports bar in Santa Monica, and locations in Georgia, Florida, and other states.

1988 Pitcher Bruce Hurst, considered the cream of this year's free-agent crop, signs a three-year contract with the Padres.

1977 The Red Sox really wanted to get Jerry Remy, so they gave the Angels $175,000 and the very promising pitching prospect Don Aase. Now the Angels, too, can boast the #1 pitcher in major league history (alphabetically).

The proposed sale of the Red Sox to a group headed by Haywood Sullivan and Buddy LeRoux is rejected by the American League. The group is then reconfigured and expanded to include Jean Yawkey as the principal.

1973 Sox purchase Juan Marichal from the Giants; at the time, Marichal (with 238 wins) is the leader among active pitchers.

1916 Ten members of the Red Sox were fined $100 each by the National Commission for participating in post-season exhibitions.

1910 Sox President John I. Taylor said he would only make trades if they would improve the team. Presumably this meant as opposed to trades which would weaken the team. Seriously, though, he said he was "not looking for money, but ball players to strengthen my team."

In what was clearly a completely separate story, the *Washington Post* reported that Taylor was rumored being ready to buy the Boston Nationals during the coming week's meetings, adding another Boston team to his portfolio. Though there were objections to one owner holding two teams in the same league, there had never been protest against a man owning a team in two leagues.

TRANSACTIONS

1939: Purchased Marv Owen from the Chicago White Sox.
1973: Purchased Juan Marichal from the San Francisco Giants.
1977: Acquired Jerry Remy from the California Angels in trade for Don Aase and cash.
1981: Signed free agent Jerry Remy.
1987: Acquired Lee Smith from the Chicago Cubs for Al Nipper and Calvin Schiraldi.
1988: Acquired John Dopson and Luis Rivera in trade with the
      Montreal Expos for Spike Owen and Dan Gakeler.
1992: Signed free agent Scott Bankhead. Received Ivan Calderon in trade from the
      Montreal Expos for Mike Gardiner and minor leaguer Terry Powers.
2003: Claimed Mark Malaska off waivers from the Tampa Bay Devil Rays.
2005: The Sox traded disappointing shortstop Edgar Renteria and maybe $11
      million to the Braves for Atlanta's top prospect, Andy Marte.

BIRTHDATES

Jack Thoney 1879 (1908–1909); Jim Pagliaroni 1937 (1955–1962); Brian Barkley 1975 (1998)

DEATHS

Bernie Friberg 1958; Tris Speaker 1958; Benn Karr 1968; Bill Wambsganss 1985

December 9

1953 At the baseball meetings at Washington's Hotel Commodore, the Sox get "the golden boy"—Jackie Jensen—from the Senators for Tommy Umphlett and Mickey McDermott.

1936 When the Red Sox acquired Pinky Higgins in trade for Billy Werber, Higgins became the 10th member of the Philadelphia Athletics to come to the Red Sox since the end of the 1933 season, including the entire 1933 A's infield. Other former Mackmen were: Max Bishop, Doc Cramer, Jimmie Foxx, Lefty Grove, Johnny Marcum, Boob McNair, Bing Miller, Rube Walberg, and Dib Williams.

1925 The Sox got Fred Haney from the Tigers for Homer and Tex. It sounded like the Sox had traded away the makings of a western or hillbilly music act. Homer Ezzell and Tex Vache. You couldn't have more cowboy of a name than Tex Vache. The trade had been effected at the request of the Texas League ball club based in Fort Worth; the Tigers immediately moved Homer and Tex to Fort Worth in exchange for pitcher Augustus Johns and Bill Mullen.

1910 On December 8, it was rumored that John I. Taylor would buy the Boston Nationals. On December 9, word was that the Mayor of Boston, John F. Fitzgerald, was "slated to take the reins."

1909 Fred Lake moved from being manager of Boston's American League team to becoming manager of Boston's National League team. Lake managed the Sox for part of 1908 and all of 1909, but the reported $6,500 he sought was too much for Sox ownership. Boston's Nationals wasted little time, signing him on December 9.

1902 Both the National League and American League owners were meeting in separate locations in New York. On December 9, AL President Ban Johnson announced that the league had secured a site in Manhattan and that they would field a first-class franchise beginning in 1903. Furthermore, he personally had signed Wee Willie Keeler away from Brooklyn to play for the new New York team. The very next day, NL owners unanimously passed a resolution appointing a committee of three to work out a peace plan with the American League.

TRANSACTIONS

1925: Traded Homer Ezzell and Tex Vache to the Detroit Tigers for Fred Haney.
1936: Traded Billy Werber to the Philadelphia Athletics for Pinky Higgins.
1953: Traded Mickey McDermott and Tom Umphlett to the
   Washington Senators for Jackie Jensen.
1974: Traded Bob Didier to the Houston Astros for Roe Skidmore.
1977: Acquired Garry Hancock from the Cleveland Indians in trade for Jack Baker.
1992: Signed free agent Andre Dawson. Received Jose Melendez
   from the San Diego Padres in trade for Phil Plantier.
1994: Acquired Jose Canseco from the Texas Rangers in trade for Otis Nixon and Luis Ortiz.
1996: Signed free agent Bret Saberhagen.
1997: Dennis Eckersley is signed as a free agent.
2004: Signed free agent Matt Mantei.

BIRTHDATES

Sam Dodge 1889 (1921–1922); Bob Kline 1909 (1930–1933); Billy Klaus 1928 (1955–1958); Ed Romero 1957 (1986–1989)

DEATHS

Wes Ferrell 1976; Ted Olson 1980; Johnny Lazor 2002

December 10

1998 Dennis Eckersley of the Red Sox retired after appearing in 1,071 games—more than any other pitcher in history. His 24-year career ended with a lifetime 3.50 ERA and set the stage for an early election to baseball's Hall of Fame.

1997 Pedro Martinez came to agreement on a six-year, $75,000,000 contract with the Red Sox. (See also December 12, 1997.)

1991 Roger Clemens appeared in a Houston courtroom and heard testimony regarding an incident when Roger, 28, and his older brother Randy, 39, had been arrested outside Bayou Mama's Swamp Bar in Houston. Randy had tangled with a salesman; when an off-duty policeman intervened, Roger pulled him off and was charged with hindering apprehension of his brother. It was suspected that alcohol was involved. (See also January 6, 1992.)

1940 The sacrifice fly rule was eliminated for the 1941 season. Even with the six sac flies Ted Williams hit in 1941, which counted as outs and hurt his average, The Kid still batted .406. He would have hit .411 under the rules as they stood before and as they have stood since.

1935 Tom Yawkey continues to stock the Red Sox with the best players he can buy. Jimmie Foxx and Johnny Marcum are sold to the Red Sox for $150,000; the Sox also send Philadelphia batterymates Dusty Rhodes and George Savino.

Former Red Sox owner Bob Quinn became owner, president, and GM of the Boston Braves.

1924 The Yankees return infielder Mike McNally to Boston in trade for infielder-outfielder Howie Shanks. McNally had been sent to New York in the earlier December 15, 1920 trade. Boston is just a stop on the way to Washington for McNally, though; 24 hours later, he is traded to Washington for Doc Prothro, who will be released 364 days later. McNally made his way back to the Yankees, though, in a deal in mid-June 1925 as part of the transaction by which Washington acquired Everett Scott.

1919 The Red Sox and Yankees owners combined with Comiskey of the White Sox to form a solid faction in the fight to wrest control of the American League from Ban Johnson. The retiring board of directors passed a number of resolutions stating that, among other things, Johnson had "not only performed, but has broken" the conditions of his employment by the league and "forfeited all right to compensation." The new board, installed in meetings at the Biltmore, allowed Johnson to consolidate his power and more firmly grasp the reins.

1918 Harry Frazee proposed a one-man Commissioner of Baseball, recommending former U.S. President William H. Taft for the slot. Frazee had begun to campaign for the removal of Ban Johnson from the current Commission, and said, "I would rather lose the World Championship than to be downed by Ban Johnson." Some owners speculated about the possibility of Judge K. M. Landis of Chicago becoming such a one-man commissioner. (See also December 14.)

1908 The Red Sox traded catcher Lou Criger to the St. Louis Browns for Tubby Spencer. Criger was a charter member of the Red Sox, jumping from the NL to the fledgling franchise before the 1901 season. Criger served as batterymate for Cy Young during the pitcher's unparalleled years in Boston.

TRANSACTIONS

1908: Traded Lou Criger to the St. Louis Browns for Tubby Spencer.
1924: Traded Howie Shanks to the New York Yankees for Mike McNally.
1925: Released Bud Connolly, Johnnie Heving, Doc Prothro, and Bill
    Wambsganss. Acquired Alex Gaston and Emmett McCann.
1935: Traded George Rhodes, minor leaguer George Savino, and $150,000 cash
    to the Philadelphia Athletics for Jimmie Foxx and Johnny Marcum.
1941: Purchased Mace Brown from the Brooklyn Dodgers.
1947: Traded Leon Culberson and Al Kozar to the Washington Senators for Stan Spence.
1950: Traded Joe Dobson, Dick Littlefield, and Al Zarilla to the Chicago
    White Sox for Ray Scarborough and Bill Wight.
1962: Acquired Dick Williams from the Houston Colt 45's in trade for Carroll Hardy.
1973: Sold Buddy Hunter to the Kansas City Royals.
1980: Acquired Carney Lansford, Rick Miller, and Mark Clear from the
    California Angels in trade for Rick Burleson and Butch Hobson.
1982: Acquired Doug Bird in trade with the Chicago Cubs for Chuck Rainey.
1985: Released Jerry Remy.

BIRTHDATES

Ed Kelly 1888 (1914); Roy Carlyle 1900 (1925–1926); Gordie Mueller 1922
(1950); Dalton Jones 1943 (1964–1969); Steve Renko 1944 (1979–1980)

DEATHS

Walter Moser 1946; Joe Harris 1959; Jack Tobin 1969; Joe Riggert 1973

December 11

2002 There never had been a plot to kidnap Pedro Martinez's father, said Sox spokesman Kevin Shea. Major League Baseball officials followed up on a police investigation in the Dominican Republic, which concluded that the alleged plot was either "kidding or very loose discussion" and was never a serious situation.

2000 Tox GM Dan Duquette signed free agent outfielder Manny Ramirez to an eight-year $160 million contract. The same day, the Texas Rangers signed Alex Rodriguez to a deal slightly in excess of $252 million. The *Boston Globe*'s Bob Ryan wrote to fervently loyal Red Sox fans, "Duquette was just the negotiator. He didn't bring Ramirez here. You did."

1997 Former Sox OF Wil Cordero was served with a restraining order after police in Puerto Rico responded to a call from Ana Cordero that her husband had threatened her. "He told her he was going to rip off her head and shut the door," said Mayaguez Police Captain David Ortiz (yes, that was his name). "But later she called the district attorney's office and said she didn't want to file charges." Cordero was on probation for assaulting his wife in June. Ana was expecting a second child in April 1998, though the couple had separated.

1963 Gene Conley was detained and interrogated by the FBI after telling a New York airport baggage agent, "We're going to bomb Boston." Conley was working his other job, as center for the New York Knicks, and was predicting the Knicks would beat the Celtics. They did not; the Celtics won, 132–113.

1953 Ted Williams won the West Palm Beach international sailfish tournament.

1922 Frank Chance (former Cubs and Yankees manager) signed as field manager with the Red Sox, according to team president Harry Frazee. It was the first step in the reconstruction of the Red Sox, Frazee declared.

1910 In his letter dated December 11, Jake Stahl finally notified the Red Sox that he was retiring to go into the banking business.

1908 Cy Young was "downcast" over the sale of catcher Lou Criger to the St. Louis Browns, and "all but refuses to believe that the trade was made." Young told the *Washington Post* that Criger was "one of the greatest catchers that ever donned a mask. I've pitched to him so long that he seems a part of me...So confident am I of his judgment that I never shake my head."

TRANSACTIONS
1924: Traded Mike McNally to the Washington Senators for Doc Prothro.
1962: Acquired Felix Mantilla from the New York Mets in trade for
 Tracy Stallard, Pumpsie Green, and a PTBNL (Al Moran).
1985: Acquired Ed Romero from the Milwaukee Brewers in a trade for Mark Clear.
1992: Tony Fossas was released.
1998: Mark Portugal was signed as a free agent.
2000: Signed Manny Ramirez to an eight-year $160 million contract.

BIRTHDATES
Fred Anderson 1885 (1909–1913); Joe Riggert 1886 (1911); Slim Harriss 1896 (1926–1928);
Merl Combs 1919 (1947–1949); Hal Brown 1924 (1953–1955); Frank Rodriguez 1972 (1995)

DEATHS
Doc McMahon 1929; Myron Grimshaw 1936

December 12

2005 In a saga that seemed to continue to unfold, the Red Sox hired from within and announced the appointment of Ben Cherington and Jed Hoyer as co-general managers. Everyone at the press conference spoke in such a way that left the door open for the possible return in some capacity of recently-resigned general manager Theo Epstein.

2002 Acquired second baseman Todd Walker from the Cincinnati Reds in exchange for two minor leaguers to be named later.

1997 Pedro Martinez signed a contract that would net him more than $92 million, at the time the richest contract in baseball history. GM Dan Duquette termed the deal a bargain.

1944 Detroit traded light-hitting but versatile utility infielder Joe Orengo to Boston for Skeeter Webb. The *Washington Post* murmured that the trade "savors a bit of nepotism" as Webb was the son-in-law of Steve O'Neill, the Tigers manager. O'Neill's comment: "I read about it in the morning paper."

1933 Connie Mack is still selling. First he sells Lefty Grove, the A's top winner in each of the past five seasons, along with Max Bishop and George Walberg, to the Boston Red Sox for $125,000 and two players, pitcher Bob Kline and infielder Rabbit Warstler. Then George Earnshaw and recently-acquired backstop Johnny Pasek go to the White Sox for $20,000 and catcher Charlie Berry. Berry once led the NFL in scoring and will become a major league umpire in the 1940s.

1924 The New York Yankees obtained catcher Steve O'Neill from the Red Sox on waivers. O'Neill will later serve as Red Sox manager.

1923 Boston purchased shortstop Dud Lee from Tulsa. He'd played for the Browns in 1920–1921 where he was known as Ernest Dudley. Now he was known as Ernest Dudley Lee. Statistically, the Dud part was pretty much on the mark.

TRANSACTIONS

1924: Steve O'Neill was selected off waivers by the New York Yankees.

1933: Traded Bob Kline, Rabbit Warstler, and $125,000 cash to the Philadelphia Athletics for Max Bishop, Lefty Grove, and Rube Walberg.

1940: Purchased Pete Fox from the Detroit Tigers. Traded Doc Cramer to the Washington Senators for Gee Walker. Traded Jim Bagby, Gene Desautels, and Gee Walker to the Cleveland Indians for Frankie Pytlak, Odell Hale, and Joe Dobson.

1944: Boston traded Skeeter Webb to Detroit for Joe Orengo.

1945: Traded Vic Johnson and cash to the Cleveland Indians for Jim Bagby. Sold Skeeter Newsome to the Philadelphia Phillies.

1975: Traded Roger Moret to the Atlanta Braves for Tom House. Signed amateur free agent Julio Valdez.

1985: Acquired Mike Stenhouse from the Minnesota Twins in a trade for Charlie Mitchell.

1999: Acquired Manny Alexander from the Chicago Cubs by trading Damon Buford.

2002: Acquired Todd Walker from the Cincinnati Reds for two minor league players to be named later.

BIRTHDATES

Tully Sparks 1874 (1902); Pee-Wee Wanninger 1902 (1927); Bill Moore 1903 (1926–1927); Steve Farr 1956 (1994)

DEATHS

Doug Taitt 1970; Ken Keltner 1991

December 13

2003 Red Sox sign free agent reliever, 2003 Fireman of the Year Keith Foulke.

1996 The Blue Jays sign free agent pitcher Roger Clemens (10–13) to a three-year contract worth $24.75 million. The Red Sox' last minute offer falls short and The Rocket's flirtation with the Yankees comes to naught. The Sox are successful in retaining Tim Naehring, who was minutes away from signing with Cleveland.

1950 Bye bye Birdie. Birdie Tebbetts was sold to the Cleveland Indians.

1933 To get Carl Reynolds from the St. Louis Browns (astute readers will note that the early Red Sox seem to have traded with the Browns as frequently as with all the other teams in baseball combined), the Sox sent pitcher Ivy Andrews and outfielder Smead Jolley.

1906 Jimmy Collins had his suspension revoked and he signed to play third base again in 1907, though Chick Stahl would remain as manager.

TRANSACTIONS

1933: Traded Ivy Andrews, Smead Jolley, and cash to the St. Louis Browns for Carl Reynolds.
1941: Traded Stan Spence and Jack Wilson to the Washington
    Senators for Ken Case and Johnny Welaj.
1950: Sold Birdie Tebbetts to the Cleveland Indians.
1969: Traded Dalton Jones to the Tigers for Tom Matchick. Also traded to
    acquire Gary Peters and Don Pavletich from the White Sox, sending them
    Syd O'Brien and minor leaguer Billy Farmer. On March 9, 1970, the Red
    Sox sent Jerry Janeski to the White Sox to complete the trade.
1988: Acquired Nick Esasky and Rob Murphy from the Cincinnati
    Reds in trade for Todd Benzinger and Jeff Sellers.
1989: Signed free agents Billy Jo Robidoux and Jeff Stone.
1994: Acquired Terry Shumpert from the Royals in exchange for a PTBNL.
1996: The Red Sox signed free agent Tim Naehring.
2000: The Red Sox signed free agent Manny Ramirez.
2001: Carl Everett was traded to the Texas Rangers for Darren Oliver.
2003: Signed free agent Keith Foulke.
2004: Selected Adam Stern from the Atlanta Braves in the Rule V draft.

BIRTHDATES

Fritz Coumbe 1889 (1914); Denny Williams 1899 (1924–1928); Dick Newsome 1909 (1941–1943); Joe Christopher 1935 (1966); Fergie Jenkins 1942 (1976–1977)

DEATHS

Frank Arellanes 1918; Mike Ryba 1971

December 14

1977 The Red Sox trade future Hall of Fame pitcher Ferguson Jenkins to the Rangers for John Poloni and cash. Jenkins, who supposedly had to be awakened in the bullpen on September 17 and never pitched after that, will partially regain his form in Texas, averaging 15 wins a year for the next three seasons.

1976 A double funeral was held for Luis and Isabel Tiant, parents of Red Sox pitcher Luis Tiant. His mother had died less than three days after Luis, Sr. passed away. "My father was a better pitcher than me," the younger Tiant stated.

1967 Cy Young Award winner Jim Lonborg signs a new contract for 1968; 10 days later, he severely injures his knee in a Lake Tahoe skiing accident.

1963 For the fifth time in seven years, a Red Sox player won the batting title when it was officially announced that Carl Yastrzemski was the 1963 champion.

1918 Warring with Boston owner Harry Frazee, AL president Ban Johnson said he was in possession of "certified information" that gambling existed in Boston's ballpark. Under the league's constitution, that could constitute grounds for terminating the membership of a ball club in the league. Johnson said there were "several groups of men" who wanted to buy the Boston Red Sox.

In a separate story, a man named Yawkey was named in a lawsuit. The suit alleged that $2,500 of the Red Sox World Series earnings was paid to William H. Yawkey and Frank J. Navin, owners of the Providence, Rhode Island, ballpark, as payment for player Walter Mayer, sold to the Red Sox. The plaintiff, B. P. Moulton, was owner of the Providence club and said the money should have been paid to him and not the owners of the park. Yawkey and Navin later became owners of the Detroit Tigers. Wally Mayer did appear in an undistinguished 30 games for the Sox in 1917 and 1918.

1917 First it was Smoky Joe, then Bullet Joe. Connie Mack's Athletics needed money, so he sold pitcher Bullet Joe Bush, catcher Wally Schang, and outfielder Amos Strunk to the Red Sox for sore–armed pitcher Vean Gregg, outfielder Merlin Kopp, catcher Pinch Thomas, and $60,000. Bush must have been happy, as he had lost 14 straight games to the Red Sox (June 2, 1914–July 5, 1917). Rumors persist that Sox owner Frazee is trying to sign Ed Barrow to manage the team.

1916 Meeting in Chicago, the American League owners unanimously voted to accept New Yorkers Harry Frazee and Hugh Ward as the new owners of the Boston Red Sox.

TRANSACTIONS
1917: Traded Vean Gregg, Merlin Kopp, Pinch Thomas, and $60,000 cash to the Philadelphia Athletics for Joe Bush, Wally Schang, and Amos Strunk.
1954: Traded Del Wilber to the New York Giants for Billy Klaus.
1960: Jerry Casale, Jim Fregosi, Fred Newman, and Ed Sadowski were all selected by the Los Angeles Angels in the first-ever major league expansion draft. Jim Mahoney, Tom Sturdivant, Haywood Sullivan, and Willie Tasby were all selected by the Washington Senators in the same draft.
1977: Acquired John Poloni and cash from the Texas Rangers in a trade for Ferguson Jenkins.
1987: Acquired minor leaguer Randy Randle from the Houston Astros for Marc Sullivan.
1990: Marty Barrett was released.
1992: Signed free agent Bob Melvin.
1995: Signed both Rich Garces and Mike Stanley as free agents.
1996: Shane Mack signed as a free agent.
1999: Carl Everett was acquired by trading a different Everett (Adam) and minor-leaguer Greg Miller to the Houston Astros.
1998: Several free agents were signed: Israel Alcantara, Kirk Bullinger, Brad Clontz, and Tim Harikkala. The team also drafted Joel Adamson from the Oakland A's in the Rule V draft, and released Carlos Reyes.
2004: Signed free agent David Wells.

BIRTHDATES
Rudy Kallio 1892 (1925); Bob Weiland 1905 (1932–1934); Eddie Smith 1913 (1947); Bill Buckner 1949 (1984–1990); Scott Hatteberg 1969 (1995–2001); Marcus Jensen 1972 (2001)

DEATHS
Elston Howard 1980; Danny Doyle 2004; Stewart Bowers 2005

December 15

1997 Thomas Sneed, an African-American former executive with the Red Sox, filed a complaint with the Massachusetts Commission Against Discrimation alleging a number of racially-based incidents in which he was targeted, such as the defacement of a photograph of himself and his fiancée on his desk at the ballpark. Sneed felt the ball club's investigation was half-hearted at best. At a MCAD hearing in February 1998, the Red Sox said they had hired a private investigator, installed surveillance cameras, and used a private fingerprint laboratory to try and catch the perpetrator. The case continued until a settlement, believed to be in six figures, was finally reached in February 1999.

1995 Ted Williams has a tunnel named after him. In ceremonies this day, the third harbor tunnel in Boston, a $2 billion key component of "The Big Dig" is named after Ted Williams in ceremonies the 77-year-old slugger attends.

1992 Wade Boggs, five-time American League batting champion for the Red Sox, signed with the Yankees as a free agent. He'd only hit .259 for the Sox in 1992, but he did a Clemens and recovered to post four more over-.300 seasons with New York.

1960 "The biggest trade in history? The Phils lose more than 2½ inches when they acquire pitcher Frank Sullivan from the Red Sox for 6' 9" Gene Conley." (*The Baseball Chronology*). Conley, a member of the 1952 Boston Braves, went with the Braves to Milwaukee but also played several seasons with the championship Boston Celtics basketball team. The trade, prompted by clashes with Phils manager Gene Mauch, set the stage for Conley to play for his third Boston pro sports team.

1953 Golfer Sam Snead bought a "substantial interest" in Ted Williams, Inc., a fishing tackle manufacturing company.

1950 Graham Treadway of the Horton Bristol Manufacturing Company of Connecticut, a firm specializing in fishing equipment, announced the signing of baseball star Ted Williams to a long-term contract as a "fish professional." Williams, the AP story noted, was known among fishermen not just as a "proficient fly and bait caster, but as a technical expert in the design of equipment."

1930 On the 10th anniversary of the date he'd first been acquired by the Red Sox, they again picked up Muddy Ruel, this time from Washington. This time he was Harold Ruel, Esq., having earned a law degree from St. Louis' Washington University earlier in the year.

1928 The Red Sox traded their best player of 1928, Buddy Myer, to the Senators, for not one...not two...but five players. It's a shame they lost Myer—look it up.

1920 The Yankees acquire another nice batch of players from Boston: pitchers Waite Hoyt and Harry Harper, catcher Wally Schang, and infielder Mike McNally in exchange for 10 Boston subway tokens. Actually, Boston obtained third baseman Del Pratt, catcher Muddy Ruel, outfielder Sam Vick, and pitcher Herb Thormahlen.

1919 Harry Frazee serves notice that everyone on the Red Sox is fair game for trade, except one: Harry Hooper. To be precise: "I will deal any player except Harry Hooper." Though not yet revealed, he had sold Babe Ruth the day before.

1917 Both Lore Bader and Herb Pennock, Boston starting pitchers, enlisted in the U.S. Navy, increasing the number of Red Sox serving in the military to 11. (See October 18.) Del Gainer, Dick Hoblitzell, Harry Hooper, and Dutch Leonard were among those serving. George Huff, briefly manager of the Red Sox in 1907 and now at the University of Illinois, suggested hand grenade throwing became an intercollegiate sport, presenting the recommendation of the Big Ten coaches.

1911 Jake Stahl had refused to report to the Red Sox in the spring of 1911, and was suspended. Hired as manager of the Sox for 1912, and given an ownership share as well, he had to apply to the National Commission for reinstatement. Taking an advance look at the Red Sox roster, though, he was a bit startled on two accounts. First of all, Fournier—carried on the roster as a pitcher acquired from Vancouver—turned out to be a catcher instead. The Red Sox didn't really need seven catchers, so the Sox sold him to the White Sox in February 1912. Too bad—Jack Fournier played 15 seasons with a career .313 average. Secondly, there was Lockwood. Boston also acquired him from Vancouver, but then sold him to Sacramento, only to learn that he had died in the interval.

TRANSACTIONS

1920: Traded Harry Harper, Waite Hoyt, Mike McNally, and Wally Schang to New York Yankees for Del Pratt, Muddy Ruel, Hank Thormahlen, and Sammy Vick.

1927: Purchased home-run hitter Ken Williams, 38, from the St. Louis Browns. He hits eight for Boston.

1928: Traded Buddy Myer to the Washington Senators for Elliot Bigelow, Milt Gaston, Grant Gillis, Hod Lisenbee, and Bobby Reeves. Word is that Washington offered Joe Cronin instead of Reeves, but no go.

1930: Purchased Muddy Ruel from the Washington Senators.

1932: Traded Ed Durham and Hal Rhyne to the Chicago White Sox for Bob Fothergill, Johnny Hodapp, Greg Mulleavy, and Bob Seeds.

1938: Traded Pinky Higgins and Archie McKain to the Detroit Tigers for Elden Auker, Chet Morgan, and Jake Wade. Traded Ben Chapman to the Cleveland Indians for Denny Galehouse and Tommy Irwin.

1949: Sold Tex Hughson to the New York Giants.

1958: Traded Billy Klaus to the Orioles for Jim Busby.

1960: Traded Frank Sullivan to the Philadelphia Phillies for Gene Conley.

1965: Traded Lee Thomas, Arnold Earley, and a PTBNL (Jay Ritchie) to the Atlanta Braves for Bob Sadowski and Dan Osinski.

1966: Traded Dick Stigman and Rollie Sheldon to the Cincinnati Reds, along with some cash, to obtain Hank Fischer.

1967: Acquired Dick Ellsworth and Gene Oliver from the Philadelphia Phillies in trade for Mike Ryan and cash.

1988: Released Glenn Hoffman.

1990: Signed free agent Jack Clark. Wes Gardner was traded to San Diego for minor leaguers Brad Hoyer and Steve Hendricks.

1995: Signed free agent Mike Maddux.

2000: The Red Sox signed free agent Hideo Nomo.

2001: The Red Sox acquired pitcher Dustin Hermanson from St. Louis for three minor leaguers: Rick Asadoorian, Dustin Brisson, and Luis Garcia.

2002: Acquired Jeremy Giambi from the Phillies for Josh Hancock. For Giambi, it is his third uniform this year, and we don't mean because of human growth hormone.

2004: Signed free agent John Halama.

BIRTHDATES

George Stumpf 1910 (1931–1933); Haywood Sullivan 1930 (1955–1960); Mo Vaughn 1967 (1991–1998)

DEATHS

Ed Barrow 1953 executive; Dick Newsome 1965; Dick Stuart 2002

December 16

2003 The Major League Baseball Players Association rules that its most highly-paid member will not be allowed to do what he wants: take a $28 million pay cut to play for the Boston Red Sox. They would only approve a $13 million pay cut. The Red Sox are not willing to make up the difference, and therefore decline to move forward in their attempts to work out a deal to sign Alex Rodriguez. Later, the Yankees do work out a deal with the Texas Rangers and A-Rod. In the end, Sox fans are not at all upset.

Something else happened this day, hardly noticed at the time: the Minnesota Twins released a player named David Ortiz. One person who did notice was a general manager named Theo Epstein. (See January 22, 2003.)

1998 Several Boston City Councilors blasted the Boston Red Sox for trying to prevent pushcart vendors from selling their wares on Yawkey Way and the streets around Fenway Park. The team had announced that it would decline to sign the customary permits whereby abutters allow vendors to sell outside their property. Efforts to broker a compromise had failed. Some of the vendors had sold peanuts and other items for decades. (See also December 24, 1998.)

1967 Yaz officially is named as AL batting champion (not that it was any secret), and also the winner of the Triple Crown, only the 11th player in history to lead his league in average, HR, and RBI.

1965 Boston had finished the season in last place, but led the league in slugging percentage. The prime reason was Carl Yastrzemski, who won the 1965 slugging crown. The Sox set a new record for men left on base in a single season: 1,183.

1964 After seven seasons in Scottsdale, Arizona, the Red Sox will leave the Cactus League and return to Florida, setting up spring training HQ in Winter Haven, beginning in 1966.

1946 Johnny Pesky said he was neither interested in a $45,000 offer to play in the Mexican Baseball League, nor in an invitation to visit on vacation. He'd received a written offer, but said it was not clear whether the $45,000 covered one year or three. In any event, gracias but no thanks.

1929 Catcher Alex Gaston was released to the San Francisco club of the Pacific Coast League. No longer would pitcher Milt Gaston have his brother as a batterymate.

1918 Harry Frazee, escalating his war of words with AL head Ban Johnson, declared that Johnson was conducting a "war of extermination" against him and trying to drive him out of baseball.

TRANSACTIONS
1924: Steve O'Neill is claimed by the Yankees off waivers.
    Johnny Kerr was released to Salt Lake.
2003: Acquired Mark Bellhorn from the Colorado Rockies for a PTBNL. Also, selected both Lenny DiNardo and Randall Bean in the Rule V draft.

BIRTHDATES
None yet

DEATHS
None yet

December 17

1996 Red Sox veteran Mike Greenwell signs a one-year contract to play for the Hanshin Tigers. The Sox had designated him for assignment on October 15, so his leaving Boston after 10 years was inevitable.

1994 The *New York Times* reported that the Boston Celtics were interested in buying the Boston Red Sox. Sox GM John Harrington said it was news to him, but if there were interest on the part of the Celtics, it was not reciprocal: "The shares of the Yawkey estate are not for sale." Harrington believed the value of the shares would increase significantly once baseball solved its labor problems—and the team started winning. Dan Shaughnessy had a field day, talking about a new Green Monster and noting that Buddy LeRoux had been the trainer for both teams. Then there was Gene Conley, who played for both teams.

1959 After an extremely disappointing 1959 season in which Ted Williams batted only .254, he said he doubted he would play in 1960 and, regardless of press reports that his Sox salary was $100,000 or more, it was just $60,000. He made $23,000 from other work, he said, in contesting a court motion by his ex-wife Doris Tradico for an increase in child support for their daughter Barbara Joyce.

On the same day, Ted announced that both he and Sam Snead would enter the "World Series of Sport Fishing" in Florida on January 15, 1960.

1957 Gene Mauch is released and begins his long managerial career, starting as player-manager for Minneapolis.

1917 A special dispatch to the *Globe* claimed that 21-year major league veteran Napoleon Lajoie had signed with the Red Sox. If so, nothing ever came of it.

1910 Early groundwork building "Red Sox Nation"? The Red Sox announced the longest exhibition road trip ever, breaking into two touring teams and beginning March 27 in Yuma, Arizona, and Reno, Nevada, and running through Texas, Oklahoma, Kansas, Missouri, Utah, Colorado, Iowa, and Nebraska. The ambitious trip was planned to include a full 40 exhibition games, and to be a real money-maker. After the trip was completed, Boston Red Sox historians can record games played in Ogden, Sioux City, Amarillo, and a number of other unlikely locales.

TRANSACTIONS
1935: Traded Carl Reynolds and Roy Johnson to the Washington Senators for Heinie Manush.
1957: Released Gene Mauch.
1985: Acquired Sammy Stewart from Baltimore for Jackie Gutierrez.
1995: Signed free agent Nate Minchey.
1996: Chris Hammond signed as a free agent. The Red Sox also acquired
        Pat Mahomes from the Twins for a PTBNL (Brian Looney).
2004: Signed Edgar Renteria as a free agent.

BIRTHDATES
Jim McHale 1875 (1908); Jerry Adair 1936 (1967–1968); Rollie Sheldon 1936 (1966); Bob Ojeda (1980–1985); Curtis Pride 1968 (2000); Rudy Pemberton 1969 (1996–1997)

DEATHS
Fritz Ostermueller 1957

December 18

1955 Sox GM Joe Cronin denies that the recent purchase of the San Francisco Seals ball club presages the move of the Red Sox franchise to San Francisco. "That's silly," Cronin said.

1918 The *Boston Post* wrote that "it will take a lot to convince Boston fans that they got the best of this one." Dutch Leonard, Duffy Lewis, and Ernie Shore were all sent to the New York Yankees for under-performing pitchers Ray Caldwell, Frank Gilhooley, Slim Love, and young catcher Al "Roxy" Walters. Sox fans remain unconvinced.

1914 The Red Sox hired Tom McCarthy, chief scout of the Boston Braves, to work for them, at the same time retaining the services of Patsy Donovan, who'd been their top scout in 1914.

1907 Owner John I. Taylor decides his team will adopt red stockings and call themselves the Red Sox. Taylor selected the uniform style personally, selecting red stockings because the original Boston team wore them. It was predicted that the name "Red Sox" would be a popular choice.

TRANSACTIONS
1918: Traded Duffy Lewis and Ernie Shore to the New York Yankees for Ray Caldwell, Frank Gilhooley, Slim Love, Roxy Walters, and $15,000 cash.
1950: This means war! Purchased Mike Guerra from the Philadelphia Athletics.
1998: Brian Daubach signed as a free agent.
2001: Carlos Baerga was signed as a free agent.
2002: Mike Timlin was signed as a free agent.

BIRTHDATES
Syd O'Brien 1944 (1969)

DEATHS
Harry Hooper 1974

December 19

2001 John Burkett was signed as a free agent. That was the simple deal. The Cincinnati Reds, who tried to sign Pokey Reese in April to a four-year, $21 million contract, ship the second baseman and pitcher Dennys Reyes to the Rockies for pitchers Gabe White and Luke Hudson. In turn, Colorado sends Reese to the Red Sox on the 19th for catcher Scott Hatteberg. The Sox don't tender Pokey a contract and he hence becomes a free agent two days later, on December 21. The A's don't tender Hatteberg a contract and he becomes a free agent. Pokey signs in January—with Pittsburgh. Hatteberg eventually does sign with the A's.

TRANSACTIONS
1988: Signed free agent Mike Smithson.
1989: Released Rick Cerone.
1990: Signed free agents Tom Brunansky and Danny Darwin.
1991: Signed free agent Joe Hesketh.
1992: Ellis Burks granted free agency.

1995: Signed free agent Juan Bell.
1998: Mark Guthrie signed as a free agent.
2001: Signed free agent John Burkett. Traded Scott Hatteberg
    to the Colorado Rockies for Pokey Reese.

BIRTHDATES
Doc McMahon 1886 (1908); Fred Thomas 1892 (1918); Mike Herrera
1897 (1925–1926); Tommy O'Brien 1918 (1949–1950)

DEATHS
John Knight 1965; Al Stokes 1986

December 20

2001 In a unanimous vote, after a nine-hour meeting, the team's majority owner
Yawkey Trust and the limited partners of the Red Sox determined to sell the
Sox (and their 80% share in the NESN cable network) to a group led by Florida
Marlins owner John W. Henry and former San Diego Padres managing partner
Tom Werner. The price was $660 million and the assumption of $40 million in
debt, double the price of any previous baseball franchise.

1996 In lieu of serving jail time for cocaine possession, former manager Butch Hobson
says he will enter a program where he will counsel others not to use drugs.

1980 The deadline to mail Carlton Fisk an offer tendering his 1981 contract was
December 20. When the offer arrived, it was postmarked December 22. Historian
Glenn Stout calls it "the biggest front office error in the history of baseball." As
a consequence of Haywood Sullivan and Buddy LeRoux's failure to meet the
deadline, Fisk became a free agent. (See February 12, 1981.)

1957 The official results were announced: Ted Williams, age 39, won the AL batting
title (and led the league in slugging for the ninth time, with a .731 percentage).
Ted's .388 was five hits short of .400. Though denied the MVP award, the
Associated Press poll named Williams the Outstanding Male Athlete of 1957.

1929 After three years managing the Red Sox to a last place finish, Bill Carrigan elects
to retire. Heinie Wagner was expected to succeed him. The *New York Times*
reported that "the spirit in which the players performed so pleased the local fans
that they were loyal in support of the club. Attendance figures show that while
Carrigan handled the Red Sox they drew more than any other last-place team."

1921 The Yankees raid Boston again and come away with pitcher Bullet Joe Bush,
shortstop Everett Scott, and pitcher Sad Sam Jones in exchange for shortstop
Roger Peckinpaugh (who goes on to Washington), pitchers Jack Quinn, Rip
Collins, Bill Piercy, and $50,000. On the same day, the Sox got three for the
price of one. The Sox send Stuffy McInnis to Cleveland, and get back George
Burns, Joe Harris, and Elmer Smith. (See December 22, 1921.)

The following day's *Boston Post* headlined FRAZEE JUNKS HIS BALL CLUB and
Paul Shannon noted that the members of the 1916 and 1918 championship
teams fell into two categories: those sold or traded by Frazee (Lewis, Shore,
Leonard, Walker, Hooper, Hoblitzell, Gainer, Barry, Gardner, Janvrin, McNally,

Shorten, Thomas, Ruth, Mays, Bush, Jones, Schang, Scott) and those still with the Red Sox (Pennock). He could not have yet known that Pennock's trade to the Yankees was just 13 months in the future, but he might have guessed. He snarled, "They might as well hang crepe next season on the doors of Fenway Park."

1918 The Sox could not locate Lt. Hal Janvrin, their infielder serving in the Army. Harry Frazee hoped to trade him to Clark Griffith's Washington Nationals.

1908 Team secretary Hugh McBreen announced that the Red Sox would try out 27 men at spring training at Hot Springs. Among them would be "Outfielder Hooper, the second Ty Cobb."

1903 Boston traded "Long Tom" Hughes to New York for Jesse Tannehill, despite the popular Hughes having won 21 games in 1903 (21–7). With New York in 1904, Long Tom would only win seven while losing 11. Tannehill turns out to be the much better pitcher in '04 (21–11) and in the years to come.

TRANSACTIONS

1903: Traded Tom Hughes to New York for Jesse Tannehill.
1921: Traded Joe Bush, Sam Jones, and Everettt Scott to the New York Yankees for Rip Collins, Roger Peckinpaugh, Bill Piercy, and Jack Quinn. On the same day, Boston's Harry Frazee traded Stuffy McInnis to the Cleveland Indians for George Burns, Joe Harris, and Elmer Smith.
1939: Boze Berger is picked up off waivers by the Brooklyn Dodgers.
1986: Signed free agent Glenn Hoffman.
1989: Released Sam Horn and Bob Stanley.
1993: Granted free agency to Tony Fossas.
1995: Granted free agency to Dave Hollins.
2004: Traded Dave Roberts to San Diego for Jay Payton, Ramon Vazquez, David Pauley, and cash considerations.
2005: Signed relief pitcher Rudy Seanez and saw free agent Johnny Damon sign with the Yankees.

December 21

2001 The John W. Henry–Tom Werner–Larry Lucchino group formally took ownership of the Red Sox. President Larry Lucchino pledged, "This isn't so much a wish as it is a commitment. We will extinguish the curse of the Bambino." They did.

1951 The Pennsylvania Senate resolved unanimously that native son Steve O'Neill was not to blame for the failure of the Red Sox to win the 1951 pennant.

1944 Boston Red Sox Owner Tom Yawkey indicates a commitment to diversity—or at least better ticket sales? "I'm in the market for a good Jewish ball player. I'm now convinced that's the only way I'm ever going to win over the South Boston trade." (*The Sporting News*)

1938 A Boob for a Boze. The Sox get Boze Berger for Boob McNair, thanks to a trade with the White Sox.

1936 The Boston Red Sox were voted the biggest sports "floperoo" of 1936, by a margin of more than 2-to-1 over their nearest rival, Joe Louis (knocked out by Max Schmeling), in a poll of 83 "experts."

1929 Heinie Wagner was named to manage the Red Sox in place of Bill Carrigan, who had retired the day before. Wagner had played 11 years with the Red Sox and had been serving as Carrigan's right-hand man.

1921 Sportswriter A. J. Rooney of the *Boston Traveler* was incensed at Frazee's December 20 trade of three Red Sox stars to the Yankees. "Frazee could not help sending Scott, Jones and Bush to New York," Rooney wrote. "He was ordered by the New York owners, who also hold a mortgage on the Red Sox, to send the three Boston players...." The *Boston Globe* had an article arguing that the only place to appeal was to Judge Landis.

Meanwhile, the other trade of the day resulted in upset. John "Stuffy" McInnis, being traded to Cleveland for Burns, Smith, and Harris, said he had a written no-trade agreement with Frazee. Smith didn't want to come to Boston and play for a second-division team. McInnis's agreement was apparently a separate agreement, and not part of the standard league form.
Burt Whitman in a special feature in the *Boston Herald* termed the trade "an insult to Boston fandom," while a *Boston American* editorial labeled it a "surrender of stars." Newspapers around the country were taken aback, to say the least. The *New York World* referred to the New York team as the "Boston Yankees." Sid Mercer of the *New York Journal* wrote, "They'll want to hang Frazee on Boston Common." (See also December 22 and 23.)

1918 The Red Sox trade outfielder Duffy Lewis and pitchers Dutch Leonard and Ernie Shore to the Yankees for pitchers Ray Caldwell and the wonderfully-named Slim Love, catcher Roxy Walters, outfielder Frank Gilhooley, and $15,000. The 195-pound Love had just been acquired from the Tigers and never played for the Red Sox. The prospect of being a Yankee in this era was perhaps too distressing to Leonard and he refused to report to New York; he wound up in Detroit.

TRANSACTIONS
1918: Traded Duffy Lewis, Dutch Leonard, and Ernie Shore to New York for
    Ray Caldwell, Frank Gilhooley, Slim Love, Roxy Walters, and cash.
1938: Traded Eric McNair to the Chicago White Sox for Boze Berger.
1995: Signed free agents Milt Cuyler and Tom Gordon, and ,
    granted free agency to Tim Van Egmond.
1998: Darren Bragg, Robinson Checo, and Keith Mitchell all released.
1999: The Red Sox granted free agency to Shea Hillenbrand, Butch Huskey, and Julio Santana.
2000: The Red Sox granted free agency to Israel Alcantara.
2001: The Red Sox signed free agent Johnny Damon, and granted free agency to Israel
    Alcantara, Todd Erdos, Allen McDill, Pokey Reese, and Chris Stynes.
2004: Released Lenny DiNardo to free agency (but re-signed him the very next day.)

BIRTHDATES
Freddie Muller 1907 (1933–1934); Bill Werle 1920 (1953–1954); Pete Charton 1942 (1964); Jim Wright 1950 (1978–1979); Dustin Hermanson 1972 (2002); Freddy Sanchez 1977 (2002–2003)

DEATHS
John Warner 1943; Walt Lynch 1976

December 22

1935 Jimmie Foxx won the award from the Atlantic City Tuna Club for catching a prize-winning tuna.

1921 Harry Frazee is "the champion wrecker of the baseball age," according to Ban Johnson, as quoted in an article on the recent trade that sent Everett Scott, Sad Sam Jones, and Bullet Joe Bush to join Babe Ruth and the Yankees. The Boston newspapers were livid. Paul Shannon of the *Boston Post* wrote that the 1922 team was now "bought and paid for;" his column was headlined AMERICAN LEAGUE PENNANT BOUGHT. The *Post*'s Neal O'Hara figured the trade guaranteed the Red Sox would end up in last place; he wrote, "Looks like Harry Frazee has given the Athletics seventh place for a Christmas present."

Indians ballplayer Elmer Smith spoke up, too. He was upset about being traded on the 20th. "Who wants to go to Boston, where the Sox are floundering down in the second division and the fans are sore at the team?" Smith said he was willing to go to any other city. In fact, by the middle of 1922, he ended up on the Yankees. (See also December 23 and 27.)

1910 Bill Carrigan rejected owner John I. Taylor's offer that he work in 1911 at a lower rate of pay, but be able to match his 1910 salary if he performed well. Taylor argued that Carrigan's play had slipped compared to 1909 (.249 instead of .296), declaring, "I am willing to pay as much as any man to a player who can deliver the goods, but will not pay fancy prices for ordinary work." Carrigan, who was in the tobacco business in Maine at the time, signed his 1911 contract on February 10.

TRANSACTIONS
1999: Free agent Jeff Fassero was signed.
2003: Re-signed Gabe Kapler to a one-year contract, one day after
    non-tendering him, making him a free agent.
2004: Signed Matt Clement as a free agent.

BIRTHDATES
Dave Schmidt 1956 (1981)

DEATHS
Ed Gallagher 1981

December 23

1986 Dave Stapleton, after spending his entire career with the Red Sox (his batting average declining every year for seven years), signs with Seattle as a free agent.

1938 Recently traded Sox infielder Eric McNair's brother Pat was at the wheel when the brand new car crashed into a horse and buggy, killing the horse and smashing the buggy. Neither the farmer driving the horse nor any people were injured.

1929 NEW GARTER FOR RED SOX read a headline in *The Sporting News*. Heinie Wagner took over from Bill Carrigan as manager of the Red Sox, in this era about as thankless an assignment as there was.

1921 The Boston papers kept up the drumbeat against Harry Frazee. On the recent trade, the *Post*'s O'Hara sarcastically suggested that Frazee was only acting in the Christmas spirit—"better to give than receive."

1916 Red Sox catcher Chester "Pinch" Thomas secretly wed Chicago cabaret dancer Miss Doxie Emerson (real name Doris Love.) "I'm going to quit dancing and go away out west and live with the cows and chickens," said Miss Thomas, speaking of her impending move to the Thomas farm in Medicine Lodge, Kansas.

TRANSACTIONS
1994: Tony Fossas and Chris Nabholz were both granted free agency.
1997: Darren Lewis signed as a free agent.
1999: Sang-Hoon Lee was signed as a free agent.
2003: Signed free agent Pokey Reese.
2004: Signed free agent Wade Miller.
2005: Welcome home! Boston signed former Yankees catcher John Flaherty, who'd been with the Sox before doing time with New York.

BIRTHDATES
Doc Gessler 1880 (1908–1909); George Whiteman 1882 (1907–1918); Tommy Thomas 1899 (1937); Hanley Ramirez 1983 (2005)

DEATHS
None yet

December 24

2004 Jason Varitek signs a contract extension with the Red Sox; the highly-regarded catcher is named the first team captain since Jim Rice. The signing caps a three-day stretch in which the Sox signed pitchers Matt Clement and Wade Miller on December 22 and 23.

1998 On the day before Christmas, Mayor Thomas Menino announced that pushcart vendors will indeed be allowed to continue to sell outside Fenway during games (see December 16, 1998.) "Fenway Park without peanut and sausage vendors is like Christmas without snow," declared the mayor. "It's the best Christmas present I ever got," crowed third-generation peanut vendor Nick Jacobs. The Red Sox backpedaled, saying their concern had been with safety. CEO John Harrington promised plans for a new ballpark in early 1999.

1967 Red Sox star Jim Lonborg falls while skiing and injures his knee. The 1967 Cy Young Award winner, 22–9 this past season, will fall to 6–10 in 1968.

1944 Tom Yawkey married Jean Hiller in a civil ceremony in Georgetown, South Carolina. Jean Yawkey is Tom's second wife.

TRANSACTIONS
1954: Sold Charlie Maxwell to the Baltimore Orioles.
2002: Signed free agent Chad Fox.

BIRTHDATES
None yet

DEATHS
Pinch Thomas 1953; Johnnie Heving 1968; Bill Rodgers 1978

December 25

2004 Legions of Red Sox fans wake up on Christmas morning and still can't believe that the Red Sox won the World Series.

1955 Dateline, December 25. The Boston chapter of the BBWAA named Billy Klaus as Rookie of the Year.

1954 The Christmas Day edition of the *Chicago Defender* reported that the Dodgers had rejected what the Red Sox called a "substantial offer" for "Negro second baseman" Charley Neal. The offer was thought to be $100,000.

1953 Former Sox manager Patsy Donovan died in Lawrence, MA. His friendship with one of the Xaverian brothers at the order's Baltimore orphanage helped the Red Sox sign Babe Ruth.

1915 A lengthy *Washington Post* story detailed how Sox president Joseph Lannin was a frequent backer of checkers players, and "the financial mainstay of the historic team match between Great Britain and this country in 1905." The question was posed whether Lannin had now topped Christy Mathewson as the best checker player in baseball.

1910 Manager Patsy Donovan and Mrs. Donovan returned to Boston after their honeymoon in Europe, which they largely spent in London and Paris. "Baseball and the signing of players was forgotten for a time," read the December 25 datelined story in the *Boston Globe*.

TRANSACTIONS
1970: Signed amateur free agent Bo Diaz. Really? On Christmas Day?

BIRTHDATES
Ted Lewis 1872 (1901); Herb Hunter 1896 (1920); Lloyd Brown 1904 (1933); Ben Chapman 1908 (1937–1938); Rickey Henderson 1958 (2002)

DEATHS
Doc Gessler 1924; Patsy Donovan 1953

December 26

2005 Jeff Reardon saved 367 major league ballgames, but had he not enough of the estimated $11,500,000 salary he was paid over 16 years of play? The day after Christmas, Reardon was arrested after entering Hamilton Jewelers at the Gardens Mall in Palm Beach Gardens, Florida with a note claiming he had a gun and was robbing the store. Would a jewelry store have cash? Had he forgotten to eat first? Shortly after fleeing the store with a grand total of $170, he was arrested at a nearby restaurant and charged with armed robbery even though he had not had a gun. Reardon's attorney said he was on five antidepression medications; he had found it extremely difficult to get over the death of his son Shane, who had overdosed on drugs in February 2004. And Reardon himself had just undergone angioplasty the day of December 23.

2002 Red Sox president Larry Lucchino ignites a bit of a firestorm by tweaking George Steinbrenner, declaring, "The Evil Empire extends its tentacles even into Latin America." Lucchino tweaked because he was piqued: the Red Sox had put on a full-court press to sign Cuban exile Jose Contreras and thought they had the inside track, only to be scooped by New York. (See also December 29, 2002.)

1995 A lucrative television deal with a syndicator crumbled and fell apart, leaving the Red Sox without a TV contract for 1996 and beyond.

1967 Just a little over two months after completing his Cy Young season, it was announced that Jim Lonborg would have to undergo surgery because of a torn ligament in his left knee, suffered in a skiing accident. There was no clause in his contract prohibiting skiing.

1944 Former Red Sox outfielder Si Rosenthal is reported under treatment in a U. S. Navy hospital for wounds suffered in the European theater when the ship on which he was serving exploded. His son Erwin was a Marine killed in action the previous year.

1919 In a Christmas present, the Red Sox formally sell Babe Ruth to the Yankees, though the deal is not announced until January 3, 1920. The actual agreement was for $125,000. A side deal included a loan of $350,000 to Harry Frazee from the Yankees owners, who took out a mortgage on Fenway Park as collateral.

1908 Never again would the team wear the famous red stocking insignia with the words "Red Sox" on their breast, according to team secretary McBreen. It would be replaced with the word "Boston."

BIRTHDATES
Doc Farrell 1901 (1935); Carlton Fisk 1947 (1969–1980); Dave Rader 1948 (1980); Jeff Stone 1960 (1989–1990); Esteban Beltre 1967 (1996); Carlos Valdez 1971 (1998)

DEATHS
Clyde Engle 1939; Jack Stansbury 1970; Tom McBride 2001

December 27

1945 Frank H. Baer of Brookline sued the Red Sox for $50,000 after being hit by a foul ball more than five years earlier. He alleged that his temporary box seat in the aisle was positioned in such a way that he was unable to duck out of the way of the foul and suffered six stitches and compromised vision for several months. Mary Walsh, a Red Sox secretary, testified that the park was largely empty, in that there were only 3,055 spectators at the June 6, 1940 game, and only 240 of the park's 1,376 box seats had been sold that day.

1921 Sox owner Harry Frazee "must pay for the mischief he has wrought," said AL President Ban Johnson. The battle raged on.

1917 Boston owner Frazee says he had been trying to sign Ed Barrow since June, and adds that when the American League magnates next meet, he will move to outlaw the spitball and other "queer" deliveries.

1909 Red Sox ownership arranged a 25-year lease from Harvard University for property in Forest Hills for a new ballpark to replace the Huntington Avenue Grounds when the lease expired after the 1911 season. As it transpired, the Sox built Fenway Park and not Forest Hills Park.

TRANSACTIONS
1977: Signed free agent Dick Drago.

BIRTHDATES
John Shea 1904 (1928); Phil Gagliano 1941 (1971–1972); Jim Leyritz 1963 (1998)

DEATHS
Hob Hiller 1956; Paul Lehner 1967; Oscar Judd 1995; Ivan Calderon 2003

December 28

1963 Dick Stuart of the Red Sox won the Comeback Player of the Year Award, fueled by his 42 homers and 118 RBI.

1942 Working to cooperate with the wartime Office of Defense Transportation, the Red Sox announced they would hold 1943 spring training indoors, at Tufts College in Medford, Massachusetts. From 1943–1945, most major league clubs trained much closer to home, to free up the trains for essential wartime deliveries.

1918 Harry Frazee announces Ed Barrow would manage the Red Sox in 1919.

1917 Red Sox owner Frazee spoke out against granting furloughs to baseball players in the military so that they could play baseball during the 1918 season.

1905 Pres. John I. Taylor denied any friction between himself and team captain Jimmy Collins. He also denied plans to sell the team, announced the team would be training in Macon, Georgia in the springtime, and said that they would have the services of pitcher Ralph Glaze over whom there had been a dispute with the Savannah ball club. (See also January 10, 1906.)

BIRTHDATES
Leslie Aulds 1920 (1947); Bill Lee 1946 (1969–1978); Zane Smith 1960 (1995); Benny Agbayani 1971 (2002)

DEATHS
Bill Pertica 1967; John Bischoff 1981

December 29

2002 Yankees owner George Steinbrenner fired back at Larry Lucchino (see December 26), saying that the Sox offered more than the Yankees had, and that clearly Contreras simply preferred to play for the Yankees. Other Yankees officials said that Contreras had been offended by Boston's attempt to cut him off from other teams by, for instance, booking all the rooms in the hotel where the pitcher was staying. It was implied that the Sox had Contreras tailed, too. Steinbrenner said of Lucchino's "Evil Empire" characterization, "That's how a sick person thinks," and went on to label Lucchino "baseball's foremost chameleon of all time." The invective reached such a peak that the Commissioner urged both parties to cool it. Contreras went just 7–2 for the Yankees, and was traded away after the 2003 season.

1973 Theo Epstein's birthday. If you wonder who Theo Epstein is, you're reading the wrong book.

1945 Bob Johnson and Dolph Camilli are both released, as the Sox prepare to welcome home pre-war stars now being mustered out of military service. Camilli had chosen to play with Boston because he'd wanted to play with Joe Cronin; he'd played with Joe on the playground when both were kids in San Francisco.

TRANSACTIONS
2002: Signed free agent Ramiro Mendoza.

BIRTHDATES
Bill Sweeney 1904 (1930–1931); Craig Grebeck 1964 (2001)

DEATHS
Gus Niarhos 2004

December 30

1920 Per an article in the December 30 *Sporting News*, Harry Frazee said all the stories surfacing every day that he was thinking of selling the Red Sox were "becoming annoying." He said that, as a businessman, the team had been for sale since the day he bought it, but that no one had approached his terms. Boston critics argued that he raised the price any time anyone showed serious interest; these same critics hoped some Boston group would move to buy the ball club back from Frazee.

1915 Red Sox owner Joseph Lannin said that player-manager Bill Carrigan would not continue as catcher in 1916, but would confine his work to managing alone. Carrigan felt otherwise as the season got underway, and appeared in 33 games, batting .270. He was 2-for-3 with one RBI in the 1916 World Series.

TRANSACTIONS
1993: Dave Valle signed as a free agent.

BIRTHDATES
Dick Porter 1901 (1934); Tom Murphy 1945 (1976–1977); Keith MacWhorter 1955 (1980)

DEATHS
None yet

December 31

2004   Not to belabor a point, but December 31 was the last day of the year in which the Red Sox finally won the World Series after 86 long years. Data subsequently released by SportScanINFO indicated that over three million Red Sox caps were sold in calendar year 2004.

2002   Ron "Papa Jack" Jackson is named as the fourth new Red Sox hitting coach in four years, following Dwight Evans, Rick Down, and Jim Rice.

1921   CANADIANS ASK FOR PRICE ON RED SOX—*Boston Globe*. A syndicate based in Toronto was reportedly exploring the purchase of the Red Sox, and wondered what the reaction would be from people in Boston.

1914   At 4:18 P.M. on New Year's Eve, the New York Yankees were sold by William S. Devery and Frank J. Farrell to a "colonel" and a "captain"—Col. Jacob Ruppert and Capt. Tillinghast Huston. The sale had—no surprise—League president Ban Johnson's fingerprints on it, and was one designed to make for a stronger New York franchise.

1909   Within minutes after Harry Lord's signed contract arrived at team offices, new manager Patsy Donovan named Lord to captain the 1910 Red Sox.

EVERY YEAR   Red Sox fans fervently hope for another World Championship.

TRANSACTIONS
1970: Sold Chuck Hartenstein to the White Sox.
2002: Named Ron Jackson major league hitting coach.

BIRTHDATES
Aleck Smith 1871 (1903); Loyd Christopher 1919 (1945); Rick Aguilera 1961 (1995)

DEATHS
Red Rollings 1964; Harry Dorish 2000

APPENDIX

PLAYER	BIRTH	DEATH	SOX DEBUT	YEARS ON RED SOX
AASE, Don	9/8/1954		7/26/1977	1977
ABAD, Andy	8/25/1972		9/5/2003	2003
ADAIR, Jerry	12/17/1936	5/31/1987	6/6/1967	1967–1968
ADAMS, Bob	7/24/1901	10/17/1996	9/22/1925	1925
ADAMS, Terry	3/6/1973		7/25/2004	2004
ADKINS, Doc	8/5/1872	2/21/1934	6/24/1902	1902
AGBAYANI, Benny	12/28/1971		9/6/2002	2002
AGGANIS, Harry	4/20/1929	6/27/1955	4/13/1954	1954–1955
AGNEW, Sam	4/12/1887	7/19/1951	4/13/1916	1916–1918
AGUILERA, Rick	12/31/1961		7/7/1995	1995
ALCANTARA, Israel	5/6/1973		6/25/2000	2000–2001
ALEXANDER, Dale	4/26/1903	3/2/1979	6/15/1932	1932–1933
ALEXANDER, Manny	3/20/1971		4/5/2000	2000
ALICEA, Luis	7/29/1965		4/26/1995	1995
ALLENSON, Gary	2/4/1955		4/8/1979	1979–1984
ALMADA, Mel	2/7/1913	8/13/1988	9/8/1933	1933–1937
ALMONTE, Hector	10/17/1975		6/4/2003	2003
ALTROCK, Nick	9/15/1876	1/20/1965	9/17/1902	1902–1903
ALVARADO, Luis	1/15/1949		9/13/1968	1968–1970
ALVAREZ, Abe	10/17/1982		7/22/2004	2004–2005
ANDERSEN, Larry	5/6/1953		9/2/1990	1990
ANDERSON, Brady	1/18/1964		4/4/1988	1988
ANDERSON, Fred	12/11/1885	11/8/1957	9/25/1909	1909, 1913
ANDERSON, Jimmy	1/22/1976		7/4/2004	2004
ANDRES, Ernie	1/11/1918		4/16/1946	1946
ANDREW, Kim	11/14/1953		4/16/1975	1975
ANDREWS, Ivy	5/6/1907	11/24/1970	6/11/1932	1932–1933
ANDREWS, Mike	7/9/1943		9/18/1966	1966–1970
ANDREWS, Shane	8/28/1971		9/7/2002	2002
APARICIO, Luis	4/29/1934		4/6/1971	1971–1973
APONTE, Luis	6/14/1953		9/4/1980	1980–1983
APPLETON, Pete	(See JABLONOWSKI, Pete)			
ARELLANES, Frank	1/28/1882	12/13/1918	7/28/1908	1908–1910
ARMAS, Tony	7/2/1953		4/5/1983	1983–1986
ARMBRUSTER, Charlie	8/30/1880	10/7/1964	7/17/1905	1905–1907
ARROJO, Rolando	7/18/1968		7/30/2000	2000–2002
ARROYO, Bronson	2/24/1977		8/25/2003	2003–2005
ASBJORNSON, Casper	6/19/1909	1/21/1970	9/17/1928	1928–1929
ASHLEY, Billy	7/11/1970		6/22/1998	1998
ASPROMONTE, Ken	9/22/1931		9/2/1957	1957–1958
ASTACIO, Pedro	11/28/1969		9/8/2004	2004
ATKINS, James	3/10/1921		9/29/1950	1950–1952
AUKER, Elden	9/21/1910		4/23/1939	1939
AULDS, Tex	12/28/1920		5/25/1947	1947
AVERY, Steve	4/14/1970		4/5/1997	1997–1998
AVILA, Bobby	4/2/1924	10/26/2004	5/24/1959	1959
AVILES, Ramon	1/22/1952		7/10/1977	1977
AZCUE, Joe	8/18/1939		4/23/1969	1969

PLAYER	BIRTH	DEATH	SOX DEBUT	YEARS ON RED SOX
BADER, Lore	4/27/1888	6/2/1973	5/17/1917	1917–1918
BAERGA, Carlos	11/4/1968		4/7/2002	2002
BAGBY, Jim Jr.	9/8/1916	9/2/1988	4/18/1938	1938–1940, 1946
BAILEY, Bob	10/13/1942		9/28/1977	1977–1978
BAILEY, Cory	1/24/1971		9/1/1993	1993–1994
BAILEY, Gene	11/25/1893	11/14/1973	7/5/1920	1920
BAKER, Al	2/28/1906	11/6/1982	8/20/1938	1938
BAKER, Floyd	10/10/1916	11/16/2004	5/14/1953	1953–1954
BAKER, Jack	5/4/1950		9/11/1976	1976–1977
BAKER, Tracy	11/7/1891	3/14/1975	6/19/1911	1911
BALL, Neal	4/22/1881	10/15/1957	6/29/1912	1912–1913
BANKHEAD, Scott	7/31/1963		4/8/1993	1993–1994
BANKS, Willie	2/27/1969		9/25/2001	2001–2002
BARBARE, Walter	8/11/1891	10/28/1965	7/3/1918	1918
BARBERICH, Frank	2/3/1882	5/1/1965	5/6/1910	1910
BARK, Brian	8/26/1968		7/6/1995	1995
BARKLEY, Brian	12/8/1975		5/28/1998	1998
BARNA, Babe	3/2/1915	5/18/1972	6/16/1943	1943
BARR, Steve	9/8/1951		10/1/1974	1974–1975
BARRETT, Bill	5/28/1900	1/26/1951	4/18/1929	1929–1930
BARRETT, Bob	1/27/1899	1/18/1982	5/23/1929	1929
BARRETT, Frank	7/1/1913	3/6/1998	6/14/1944	1944–1945
BARRETT, Jimmy	3/28/1875	10/24/1921	5/29/1907	1907–1908
BARRETT, Marty	6/23/1958		9/6/1982	1982–1990
BARRETT, Tom	4/2/1960		8/14/1992	1992
BARRY, Ed	10/2/1882	6/19/1920	8/21/1905	1905–1907
BARRY, Jack	4/26/1887	4/23/1961	7/3/1915	1915–1917, 1919
BATTS, Matt	10/16/1921		9/10/1947	1947–1951
BAUMANN, Frank	7/1/1933		7/31/1955	1955–1959
BAYLOR, Don	6/28/1949		4/7/1986	1986–1987
BAYNE, Bill	4/18/1899	5/22/1981	4/20/1929	1929–1930
BECK, Rod	8/3/1968		9/1/1999	1999–2001
BEDIENT, Hugh	10/23/1889	7/21/1965	4/26/1912	1912–1914
BELINDA, Stan	8/6/1966		5/6/1995	1995–1996
BELL, Gary	11/17/1936		6/8/1967	1967–1968
BELL, Juan	3/29/1968		6/27/1995	1995
BELLHORN, Mark	8/23/1974		4/4/2004	2004
BELTRE, Esteban	12/26/1967		4/5/1996	1996
BENIQUEZ, Juan	5/13/1950		9/4/1971	1971–1972, 1974–1975
BENJAMIN, Mike	11/22/1965		5/21/1997	1997–1998
BENNETT, Dennis	10/5/1939		5/4/1965	1965–1967
BENNETT, Frank	10/27/1904	3/18/1966	9/17/1927	1927–1928
BENTON, Al	3/18/1911	4/14/1968	7/1/1952	1952
BENZINGER, Todd	2/11/1963		6/21/1987	1987–1988
BERBERET, Lou	11/20/1929	4/6/2004	5/4/1958	1958
BERG, Moe	3/2/1902	5/29/1972	4/26/1935	1935–1939
BERGER, Boze	5/13/1910	11/3/1992	6/14/1939	1939
BERRY, Charlie	10/18/1902	9/6/1972	4/11/1928	1928–1932
BERRY, Sean	3/22/1966		7/24/2000	2000
BERRYHILL, Damon	12/3/1963		4/4/1994	1994
BEVAN, Hal	11/15/1930	10/5/1968	4/24/1952	1952
BEVILLE, Ben	8/28/1877	1/5/1937	5/24/1901	1901
BICHETTE, Dante	11/18/1963		9/1/2000	2000–2001

PLAYER	BIRTH	DEATH	SOX DEBUT	YEARS ON RED SOX
BIGELOW, Elliot	10/13/1897	8/10/1933	4/18/1929	1929
BILLINGHAM, Jack	2/21/1943		5/15/1980	1980
BIRD, Doug	3/5/1950		4/9/1983	1983
BISCHOFF, John	10/28/1894	12/28/1981	4/18/1925	1925–1926
BISHOP, Max	9/5/1899	2/24/1962	4/17/1934	1934–1935
BLACK, Dave	4/19/1892	10/27/1936	5/4/1923	1923
BLACKWELL, Tim	8/19/1952		7/3/1974	1974–1975
BLETHEN, Clarence	7/11/1893	4/11/1973	9/17/1923	1923
BLOSSER, Greg	6/26/1971		9/5/1993	1993–1994
BLUHM, Red	6/27/1894	5/7/1952	7/3/1918	1918
BODDICKER, Mike	8/23/1957		7/31/1988	1988–1990
BOERNER, Larry	1/21/1905	10/16/1969	6/30/1932	1932
BOGGS, Wade	6/15/1958		4/10/1982	1982–1992
BOLIN, Bobby	1/29/1939		9/12/1970	1970–1973
BOLLING, Milt	8/9/1930		9/10/1952	1952–1956
BOLTON, Tom	5/6/1962		5/17/1987	1987–1992
BOONE, Ike	2/17/1897	8/1/1958	9/18/1923	1923–1925
BOONE, Ray	7/27/1923		5/20/1960	1960
BORLAND, Toby	5/29/1969		5/13/1997	1997
BORLAND, Tom	2/14/1933		5/15/1960	1960–1961
BOUDREAU, Lou	7/17/1917	8/10/2001	4/17/1951	1951–1954
BOWEN, Sam	9/18/1952		8/25/1977	1977–1978, 1980
BOWERS, Stew	2/26/1915	12/14/2005	8/5/1935	1935–1936
BOWMAN, Joe	6/17/1910	11/22/1990	4/22/1944	1944–1945
BOWSFIELD, Ted	1/10/1935		7/20/1958	1958–1960
BOYD, Oil Can	10/6/1959		9/13/1982	1982–1989
BRADFORD, Chad	9/14/1974		7/14/2005	2005
BRADLEY, Herb	1/3/1903	10/16/1959	5/9/1927	1927–1929
BRADLEY, Hugh	5/23/1885	1/26/1949	4/25/1910	1910–1912
BRADY, Cliff	3/6/1897	9/25/1974	8/8/1920	1920
BRADY, King	5/28/1881	8/21/1947	10/5/1908	1908
BRAGG, Darren	9/7/1969		7/31/1996	1996–1998
BRANDENBURG, Mark	7/14/1970		8/1/1996	1996–1997
BRANDON, Darrell	9/11/1936		4/19/1966	1966–1968
BRATSCHI, Fred	1/16/1892	1/10/1962	4/13/1926	1926
BRESSOUD, Eddie	5/2/1932		4/10/1962	1962–1965
BRETT, Ken	9/18/1948	11/18/2003	9/27/1967	1967, 1969–1971
BREWER, Tom	9/3/1931		4/18/1954	1954–1961
BRICKNER, Ralph	5/2/1925	5/9/1994	5/4/1952	1952
BRILLHEART, Jim	9/28/1903	9/2/1972	4/15/1931	1931
BRODOWSKI, Dick	7/26/1932		6/15/1952	1952, 1955
BROGNA, Rico	4/18/1970		8/4/2000	2000
BROHAMER, Jack	2/26/1950		4/17/1978	1978–1980
BROWN, Adrian	2/7/1974		9/15/2003	2003
BROWN, Hal	12/11/1924		4/16/1953	1953–1955
BROWN, Jamie	3/31/1977		5/20/2004	2004
BROWN, Kevin	4/21/1973		9/10/2002	2002
BROWN, Lloyd	12/25/1904	1/14/1974	5/16/1933	1933
BROWN, Mace	5/21/1909	3/24/2002	4/25/1942	1942–1943, 1946
BROWN, Mike	3/4/1959		9/16/1982	1982–1986
BRUMLEY, Mike	4/9/1963		5/23/1991	1991
BRUNANSKY, Tom	8/20/1960		5/6/1990	1990–1992, 1994
BUCHER, Jim	3/11/1911	10/21/2004	5/30/1944	1944–1945

PLAYER	BIRTH	DEATH	SOX DEBUT	YEARS ON RED SOX
BUCKNER, Bill	12/14/1949		5/26/1984	1984–1987, 1990
BUDDIN, Don	5/5/1934		4/17/1956	1956, 1958–1961
BUFORD, Damon	6/12/1970		4/2/1998	1998–1999
BULLINGER, Kirk	10/28/1969		6/13/1999	1999
BURCHELL, Fred	7/14/1879	11/20/1951	9/26/1907	1907–1909
BURDA, Bob	7/16/1938		4/17/1972	1972
BURGMEIER, Tom	8/2/1943		4/12/1978	1978–1982
BURKETT, Jesse	12/4/1868	5/27/1953	4/14/1905	1905
BURKETT, John	11/28/1964		4/21/2002	2002–2003
BURKHART, Morgan	1/29/1972		6/27/2000	2000–2001
BURKS, Ellis	9/11/1964		4/30/1987	1987–1992, 2004
BURLESON, Rick	4/29/1951		5/4/1974	1974–1980
BURNS, George	1/31/1893	1/7/1978	4/12/1922	1922–1923
BURTON, Jim	10/27/1949		6/10/1975	1975–1977
BUSBY, Jim	1/8/1927	7/8/1996	4/12/1959	1959–1960
BUSH, Joe	11/27/1892	11/1/1974	4/23/1918	1918–1921
BUSHELMAN, Jack	8/29/1885	10/26/1955	9/11/1911	1911–1912
BUSHEY, Frank	8/1/1906	3/18/1972	9/17/1927	1927, 1930
BUTLAND, Bill	3/22/1918	9/19/1997	5/29/1940	1940, 1942, 1946–1947
BYERLY, Bud	10/26/1920		7/19/1958	1958
BYRD, Jim	10/3/1968		5/31/1993	1993
CABRERA, Orlando	11/2/1974		8/1/2004	2004
CADY, Hick	1/26/1886	3/3/1946	4/26/1912	1912–1917
CALDERON, Ivan	3/19/1962	12/27/2003	4/5/1993	1993
CALDWELL, Earl	4/9/1905	9/15/1981	7/31/1948	1948
CALDWELL, Ray	4/26/1888	8/17/1967	5/2/1919	1919
CAMILLI, Dolph	4/23/1907	10/21/1997	6/27/1945	1945
CAMPBELL, Bill	8/9/1948		4/7/1977	1977–1981
CAMPBELL, Paul	9/1/1917		4/15/1941	1941–1942, 1946
CANSECO, Jose	7/2/1964		4/26/1995	1995–1996
CARBO, Bernie	8/5/1947		4/5/1974	1974–1978
CAREY, Tom	10/11/1906	2/21/1970	4/25/1939	1939–1942, 1946
CARLISLE, Walter	7/6/1883	5/27/1945	5/8/1908	1908
CARLSTROM, Swede	10/26/1886	4/23/1935	9/13/1911	1911
CARLYLE, Cleo	9/7/1902	11/12/1967	5/16/1927	1927
CARLYLE, Roy	12/10/1900	11/22/1956	4/16/1925	1925–1926
CARRASCO, Hector	10/22/1969		9/12/2000	2000
CARRIGAN, Bill	10/22/1883	7/8/1969	7/7/1906	1906, 1908–1916
CARROLL, Ed	7/27/1907	10/13/1984	5/1/1929	1929
CASALE, Jerry	9/27/1933		9/14/1958	1958–1960
CASCARELLA, Joe	6/28/1907		7/4/1935	1935–1936
CASSIDY, Scott	10/3/1975		7/9/2005	2005
CASTILLO, Carlos	4/21/1975		7/8/2001	2001
CASTILLO, Frank	4/1/1969		4/5/2001	2001–2002, 2004
CATER, Danny	2/25/1940		4/15/1972	1972–1974
CECIL, Rex	10/8/1916	10/30/1966	8/13/1944	1944–1945
CEPEDA, Orlando	9/17/1937		4/6/1973	1973
CERONE, Rick	5/19/1954		4/16/1988	1988–1989
CHADBOURNE, Chet	10/28/1884	6/21/1943	9/17/1906	1906–1907
CHAKALES, Bob	8/10/1927		5/1/1957	1957
CHAMBERLAIN, Wes	4/13/1966		6/1/1994	1994–1995
CHANEY, Esty	1/29/1891	2/5/1952	8/2/1913	1913

PLAYER	BIRTH	DEATH	SOX DEBUT	YEARS ON RED SOX
CHAPLIN, Ed	9/25/1893	8/15/1978	9/4/1920	1920–1922
CHAPMAN, Ben	12/25/1908	7/9/1993	6/11/1937	1937–1938
CHARTON, Pete	12/21/1942		4/19/1964	1964
CHASE, Ken	10/6/1913	1/16/1985	4/26/1942	1942–1943
CHECH, Charlie	4/27/1878	1/31/1938	4/13/1909	1909
CHECO, Robinson	9/9/1971		9/16/1997	1997–1998
CHEN, Bruce	6/19/1977		5/11/2003	2003
CHESBRO, Jack	6/5/1874	11/6/1931	10/2/1909	1909
CHITTUM, Nelson	3/25/1933		8/1/1959	1959–1960
CHO, Jin Ho	8/16/1975		7/4/1998	1998–1999
CHRISTOPHER, Joe	12/13/1935		4/13/1966	1966
CHRISTOPHER, Loyd	12/31/1919	9/5/1991	4/20/1945	1945
CICERO, Joe	11/18/1910	3/30/1983	9/20/1929	1929–1930
CICOTTE, Eddie	6/19/1884	5/5/1969	4/17/1908	1908–1912
CISCO, Galen	3/7/1936		6/11/1961	1961–1962, 1967
CISSELL, Bill	1/3/1904	3/15/1949	4/19/1934	1934
CLARK, Danny	1/18/1894	5/23/1937	4/21/1924	1924
CLARK, Jack	11/10/1955		4/8/1991	1991–1992
CLARK, Otey	5/22/1918		4/17/1945	1945
CLARK, Phil	5/6/1968		4/27/1996	1996
CLARK, Tony	6/15/1972		4/1/2002	2002
CLEAR, Mark	5/27/1956		4/12/1981	1981–1985
CLEMENS, Roger	8/4/1962		5/15/1984	1984–1996
CLEMENT, Matt	8/12/1974		4/5/2005	2005
CLEMONS, Lance	7/6/1947		4/18/1974	1974
CLEVELAND, Reggie	5/23/1948		4/6/1974	1974–1978
CLEVENGER, Tex	7/9/1932		4/18/1954	1954
CLINTON, Lou	10/13/1937	12/6/1997	4/22/1960	1960–1964
CLOWERS, Bill	8/14/1898	1/13/1978	7/20/1926	1926
COCHRAN, George	2/12/1889	5/21/1960	7/29/1918	1918
COFFEY, Jack	1/28/1887	2/14/1966	8/14/1918	1918
COLE, Alex	8/17/1965		4/22/1996	1996
COLEMAN, Dave	10/26/1950		4/13/1977	1977
COLEMAN, Michael	8/16/1975		9/1/1997	1997, 1999
COLLIER, Lou	8/21/1973		7/29/2003	2003
COLLINS, Jimmy	1/16/1870	3/6/1943	4/26/1901	1901–1907
COLLINS, Ray	2/11/1887	1/9/1970	7/19/1909	1909–1915
COLLINS, Rip	2/26/1896	5/27/1968	4/23/1922	1922
COLLINS, Shano	12/4/1885	9/10/1955	4/13/1921	1921–1925
COMBS, Merrill	12/11/1919	7/8/1981	9/12/1947	1947, 1949–1950
COMSTOCK, Ralph	11/24/1890	9/13/1966	4/22/1915	1915
CONE, David	1/2/1963		5/17/2001	2001
CONGALTON, Bunk	1/24/1875	8/16/1937	5/21/1907	1907
CONIGLIARO, Billy	8/15/1947		4/11/1969	1969–1971
CONIGLIARO, Tony	1/7/1945	2/24/1990	4/16/1964	1964–1967, 1969–1970, 1975
CONLEY, Gene	11/10/1930		4/25/1961	1961–1963
CONNOLLY, Bud	5/25/1901	6/12/1964	5/3/1925	1925
CONNOLLY, Ed Sr.	7/17/1908	11/12/1963	9/20/1929	1929–1932
CONNOLLY, Ed Jr.	12/3/1939	7/1/1998	4/19/1964	1964
CONNOLLY, Joe	6/4/1896	3/30/1960	4/24/1924	1924
CONROY, Bill	2/26/1915	11/13/1997	4/14/1942	1942–1944
CONSOLO, Billy	8/18/1934		4/20/1953	1953–1959

PLAYER	BIRTH	DEATH	SOX DEBUT	YEARS ON RED SOX
COOKE, Dusty	6/23/1907	11/21/1987	5/16/1933	1933–1936
COONEY, Jimmy	8/24/1894	8/7/1991	9/22/1917	1917
COOPER, Cecil	12/20/1949		9/8/1971	1971–1976
COOPER, Guy	1/28/1893	8/2/1951	5/2/1914	1914–1915
COOPER, Scott	10/13/1967		9/5/1990	1990–1994
CORA, Alex	10/18/1975		7/7/2005	2005
CORDERO, Wil	10/3/1971		4/1/1996	1996–1997
CORMIER, Rheal	4/23/1967		4/28/1995	1995, 1999–2000
CORRELL, Vic	2/5/1946		10/4/1972	1972
CORSI, Jim	9/9/1961		4/11/1997	1997–1999
COUGHTRY, Marlan	9/11/1934		9/2/1960	1960
COUMBE, Fritz	12/13/1889	3/21/1978	4/22/1914	1914
COX, Ted	1/24/1955		9/18/1977	1977
CRAMER, Doc	7/22/1905	9/9/1990	4/14/1936	1936–1940
CRAVATH, Gavvy	3/23/1881	5/23/1963	4/18/1908	1908
CRAWFORD, Paxton	8/4/1977		7/1/2000	2000–2001
CRAWFORD, Steve	4/29/1958		9/2/1980	1980–1982, 1984–1987
CREEDEN, Pat	5/23/1906	4/20/1992	4/14/1931	1931
CREMINS, Bob	2/15/1906	3/27/2004	8/17/1927	1927
CRESPO, Cesar	5/23/1979		4/4/2004	2004
CRIGER, Lou	2/3/1872	5/14/1934	4/26/1901	1901–1908
CRONIN, Joe	10/12/1906	9/7/1984	4/16/1935	1935–1945
CROUCH, Zach	10/26/1965		6/4/1988	1988
CROUSHORE, Rich	8/7/1970		9/13/2000	2000
CRUZ, Jose	4/19/1974		8/3/2005	2005
CULBERSON, Leon	8/6/1919	9/17/1989	5/16/1943	1943–1947
CULP, Ray	8/6/1941		4/16/1968	1968–1973
CUMMINGS, Midre	10/14/1971		4/2/1998	1998, 2000
CUPPY, Nig	7/3/1869	7/27/1922	4/29/1901	1901
CURRY, Steve	9/13/1965		7/10/1988	1988
CURTIS, John	3/9/1948		8/13/1970	1970–1973
CUYLER, Milt	10/7/1968		4/5/1996	1996
DAHLGREN, Babe	6/15/1912	9/4/1996	4/16/1935	1935–1936
DALEY, Pete	1/14/1930		5/3/1955	1955–1959
DALESSANDRO, Dom	10/3/1913	4/29/1988	4/24/1937	1937
DAMON, Johnny	11/5/1973		4/1/2002	2002–2005
DANZIG, Babe	4/30/1887	7/14/1931	4/12/1909	1909
DARWIN, Bobby	2/16/1943		6/4/1976	1976–1977
DARWIN, Danny	10/25/1955		4/11/1991	1991–1994
DAUBACH, Brian	2/11/1972		4/9/1999	1999–2002, 2004
DAUGHTERS, Bob	8/5/1914	8/22/1988	4/24/1937	1937
DAWSON, Andre	7/10/1954		4/5/1993	1993–1994
DEAL, Cot	1/23/1923		9/11/1947	1947–1948
DEER, Rob	9/29/1960		8/22/1993	1993
DEININGER, Pep	10/10/1877	9/25/1950	4/26/1902	1902
DELCARMEN, Manny	2/16/1982		7/26/2005	2005
DELGADO, Alex	1/11/1971		4/4/1996	1996
DELOCK, Ike	11/11/1929		4/17/1952	1952–1953, 1955–1963
DEMETER, Don	6/25/1935		6/17/1966	1966–1967
DENMAN, Brian	2/12/1956		8/22/1982	1982
DENTE, Sam	4/26/1922	5/5/2002	7/10/1947	1947
DERRICK, Mike	9/19/1943		4/9/1970	1970

PLAYER	BIRTH	DEATH	SOX DEBUT	YEARS ON RED SOX
DESAUTELS, Gene	6/13/1907	11/5/1994	5/10/1937	1937–1940
DEUTSCH, Mel	7/26/1915		4/21/1946	1946
DEVINE, Mickey	5/9/1892	10/1/1937	4/17/1920	1920
DEVINEY, Hal	4/11/1893	1/4/1933	7/30/1920	1920
DEVORMER, Al	8/19/1891	8/29/1966	4/18/1923	1923
DIAZ, Bo	3/23/1953	11/23/1990	9/6/1977	1977
DIAZ, Juan	2/19/1976		6/12/2002	2002
DICKEY, George	7/10/1915	7/16/1976	9/21/1935	1935–1936
DICKMAN, Emerson	11/12/1914	4/27/1981	6/27/1936	1936, 1938–1941
DIDIER, Bob	2/16/1949		4/19/1974	1974
DILLARD, Steve	2/8/1951		9/28/1975	1975–1977
DIMAGGIO, Dom	2/12/1917		4/16/1940	1940–1942, 1946–1953
DINARDO, Lenny	9/19/1979		4/23/2004	2004–2005
DINNEEN, Bill	4/5/1876	1/13/1955	4/23/1902	1902–1907
DIPIETRO, Bob	9/1/1927		9/23/1951	1951
DOBENS, Ray	7/28/1906	4/21/1980	7/7/1929	1929
DOBSON, Joe	1/20/1917	6/23/1994	4/21/1941	1941–1943, 1946–1950, 1954
DODGE, Sam	12/9/1889	4/5/1966	9/24/1921	1921–1922
DODSON, Pat	10/11/1959		9/5/1986	1986–1988
DOERR, Bobby	4/7/1918		4/20/1937	1937–1944, 1946–1951
DOHERTY, John	6/11/1967		4/4/1996	1996
DOMINIQUE, Andy	10/30/1975		5/25/2004	2004
DONAHUE, John	4/19/1894	10/3/1949	9/25/1923	1923
DONAHUE, Pat	11/8/1884	1/31/1966	5/29/1908	1908–1910
DONNELS, Chris	4/21/1966		6/11/1995	1995
DONOHUE, Pete	11/5/1900	2/23/1988	4/29/1932	1932
DOPSON, John	7/14/1963		4/9/1989	1989–1993
DORAN, Tom	12/2/1880	6/22/1910	4/19/1904	1904–1906
DORISH, Harry	7/13/1921		4/15/1947	1947–1949, 1956
DORSEY, Jim	8/2/1955		9/20/1984	1984–1985
DOUGHERTY, Patsy	10/27/1876	4/30/1940	4/19/1902	1902–1904
DOWD, Tommy	4/20/1869	7/2/1933	4/26/1901	1901
DOYLE, Danny	1/24/1917	12/14/2004	9/14/1943	1943
DOYLE, Denny	1/17/1944		6/14/1975	1975–1977
DRAGO, Dick	6/25/1945		4/11/1974	1974–1975, 1978–1980
DREISEWERD, Clem	1/24/1916		8/29/1944	1944–1946
DROPO, Walt	1/30/1923		4/19/1949	1949–1952
DUBUC, Jean	9/15/1888	8/28/1958	7/28/1918	1918
DUFFY, Frank	10/14/1946		4/18/1978	1978–1979
DUGAN, Joe	5/12/1897	7/7/1982	4/12/1922	1922
DULIBA, Bob	1/9/1935		5/30/1965	1965
DUMONT, George	11/13/1895	10/13/1956	4/29/1919	1919
DURHAM, Ed	8/17/1908	4/27/1976	4/19/1929	1929–1932
DURST, Cedric	8/23/1896	2/16/1971	5/8/1930	1930
DWYER, Jim	1/3/1950		4/8/1979	1979–1980
EARLEY, Arnold	6/4/1933	9/29/1999	9/27/1960	1960–1965
EASLER, Mike	11/29/1950		4/2/1984	1984–1985
ECKERSLEY, Dennis	10/3/1954		4/8/1978	1978–1984, 1998
EGGERT, Elmer	1/29/1902	4/9/1971	4/27/1927	1927
EHMKE, Howard	4/24/1894	3/17/1959	4/23/1923	1923–1926
EIBEL, Hack	12/6/1893	10/16/1945	4/17/1920	1920

PLAYER	BIRTH	DEATH	SOX DEBUT	YEARS ON RED SOX
ELLSWORTH, Dick	3/22/1940		4/10/1968	1968–1969
ELLSWORTH, Steve	7/30/1960		4/7/1988	1988
EMBREE, Alan	1/23/1970		6/25/2002	2002–2005
ENGLE, Clyde	3/19/1884	12/26/1939	5/14/1910	1910–1914
ERDOS, Todd	11/21/1973		8/20/2001	2001
ESASKY, Nick	2/24/1960		4/3/1989	1989
ESHELMAN, Vaughn	5/22/1969		5/2/1995	1995–1997
EVANS, Al	9/28/1916	4/6/1979	7/21/1951	1951
EVANS, Bill	3/25/1919	11/30/1983	5/15/1951	1951
EVANS, Dwight	11/3/1951		9/16/1972	1972–1990
EVERETT, Carl	6/3/1970		4/4/2000	2000–2001
EVERS, Hoot	2/8/1921	1/25/1991	6/4/1952	1952–1954
EZZELL, Homer	2/28/1896	8/3/1976	4/26/1924	1924–1925
FANZONE, Carmen	8/30/1943		7/21/1970	1970
FARR, Steve	12/12/1956		7/10/1994	1994
FARRELL, Doc	12/26/1901	12/20/1966	4/29/1935	1935
FARRELL, Duke	8/31/1866	2/15/1925	4/20/1903	1903–1905
FASSERO, Jeff	1/5/1963		4/6/2000	2000
FERGUSON, Alex	2/16/1897	4/26/1976	4/14/1922	1922–1925
FERRELL, Rick	10/12/1905	7/27/1995	5/11/1933	1933–1937
FERRELL, Wes	2/2/1908	12/9/1976	5/30/1934	1934–1937
FERRIS, Hobe	12/7/1877	3/18/1938	4/26/1901	1901–1907
FERRISS, Boo	12/5/1921		4/29/1945	1945–1950
FEWSTER, Chick	11/10/1895	4/16/1945	7/30/1922	1922–1923
FINCH, Joel	8/20/1956		6/12/1979	1979
FINE, Tommy	10/10/1914	1/10/2005	4/26/1947	1947
FINNEY, Lou	8/13/1910	4/22/1966	5/11/1939	1939–1942, 1944–1945
FINNVOLD, Gar	3/11/1968		5/10/1994	1994
FIORE, Mike	10/11/1944		5/31/1970	1970–1971
FISCHER, Hank	1/11/1940		8/21/1966	1966–1967
FISK, Carlton	12/26/1947		9/18/1969	1969, 1971–1980
FITZGERALD, Howie	5/16/1902	2/27/1959	6/6/1926	1926
FLAGSTEAD, Ira	9/22/1893	3/13/1940	5/12/1923	1923–1929
FLAHERTY, John	10/21/1967		4/12/1992	1992–1993
FLAIR, Al	7/24/1916	7/25/1988	9/6/1941	1941
FLEMING, Bill	7/31/1913		8/21/1940	1940–1941
FLETCHER, Scott	7/30/1958		4/5/1993	1993–1994
FLORIE, Bryce	5/21/1970		8/3/1999	1999–2001
FLOWERS, Ben	6/15/1927		9/29/1951	1951, 1953
FLOYD, Cliff	12/5/1972		8/1/2002	2002
FONVILLE, Chad	3/5/1971		7/7/1999	1999
FOREMAN, Frank	5/1/1863	11/19/1957	5/3/1901	1901
FOREMAN, Happy	7/20/1897	2/13/1953	6/9/1926	1926
FORNIELES, Mike	1/18/1932		6/16/1957	1957–1963
FORTUNE, Gary	10/11/1894	9/23/1955	5/1/1920	1920
FOSSAS, Tony	9/23/1957		4/9/1991	1991–1994
FOSSUM, Casey	1/9/1978		7/28/2001	2001–2003
FOSTER, Eddie	2/13/1887	1/15/1937	4/15/1920	1920–1922
FOSTER, Rube	1/5/1888	3/1/1976	4/10/1913	1913–1917
FOTHERGILL, Bob	8/16/1897	3/20/1938	4/13/1933	1933
FOULKE, Keith	10/19/1972		4/6/2004	2004–2005
FOWLER, Boob	11/11/1900	10/8/1988	5/4/1926	1926

PLAYER	BIRTH	DEATH	SOX DEBUT	YEARS ON RED SOX
Fox, Chad	9/3/1970		3/31/2003	2003
Fox, Pete	3/8/1909	7/5/1966	4/15/1941	1941–1945
Foxx, Jimmie	10/22/1907	7/21/1967	4/14/1936	1936–1942
Foy, Joe	2/21/1943	10/12/1989	4/13/1966	1966–1968
Francis, Ray	3/8/1893	7/6/1934	5/9/1925	1925
Freeman, Buck	10/30/1871	6/25/1949	4/26/1901	1901–1907
Freeman, Hersh	7/1/1928	1/17/2004	9/10/1952	1952–1953, 1955
Freeman, John	1/24/1901	4/14/1958	6/17/1927	1927
French, Charlie	10/12/1883	3/30/1962	5/23/1909	1909–1910
Friberg, Bernie	8/18/1899	12/8/1958	4/13/1933	1933
Friend, Owen	3/21/1927		4/17/1955	1955
Frohwirth, Todd	9/28/1962		5/4/1994	1994
Frye, Jeff	8/31/1966		6/6/1996	1996–1997, 1999–2000
Fuhr, Oscar	8/22/1893	3/27/1975	4/23/1924	1924–1925
Fuller, Frank	1/1/1893	10/29/1965	9/21/1923	1923
Fullerton, Curt	9/13/1898	1/2/1975	4/14/1921	1921–1925, 1933
Gaetti, Gary	8/19/1958		4/4/2000	2000
Gaffke, Fabian	8/5/1913	2/8/1992	9/9/1936	1936–1938
Gagliano, Phil	12/27/1941		4/19/1971	1971–1972
Gainer, Del	11/10/1886	1/29/1947	5/26/1914	1914–1917, 1919
Gale, Rich	1/19/1954		6/10/1984	1984
Galehouse, Denny	12/7/1911		4/23/1939	1939–1940, 1947–1949
Gallagher, Bob	7/7/1948		5/17/1972	1972
Gallagher, Ed	11/28/1910	12/22/1981	7/8/1932	1932
Galvin, Jim	8/11/1907	9/30/1969	9/27/1930	1930
Garbark, Bob	11/13/1909	8/15/1990	4/26/1945	1945
Garces, Rich	5/18/1971		4/24/1996	1996–2002
Garciaparra, Nomar	7/23/1973		8/31/1996	1996–2004
Gardiner, Mike	10/19/1965		5/31/1991	1991–1992
Gardner, Billy	7/19/1927		6/14/1962	1962–1963
Gardner, Larry	5/13/1886	3/11/1976	6/25/1908	1908–1917
Gardner, Wes	4/29/1961		4/13/1986	1986–1990
Garman, Mike	9/16/1949		9/22/1969	1969, 1971–1973
Garrison, Cliff	8/13/1906	8/25/1994	4/16/1928	1928
Garrison, Ford	8/29/1915		4/22/1943	1943–1944
Gaston, Alex	3/12/1893	2/8/1976	4/13/1926	1926, 1929
Gaston, Milt	1/27/1896	4/26/1996	4/18/1929	1929–1931
Gedman, Rich	9/26/1959		9/7/1980	1980–1990
Geiger, Gary	4/4/1937	4/24/1996	4/12/1959	1959–1965
Gelbert, Charlie	4/27/1878	1/13/1967	8/21/1940	1940
Gerber, Wally	8/18/1891	6/19/1951	4/30/1928	1928–1929
Gernert, Dick	9/28/1928		4/16/1952	1952–1959
Gessler, Doc	12/23/1880	12/25/1924	4/14/1908	1908–1909
Geygan, Chappie	6/3/1903	3/15/1966	7/16/1924	1924–1926
Giambi, Jeremy	9/30/1974		3/31/2003	2003
Giannini, Joe	9/8/1888	9/26/1942	8/7/1911	1911
Gibson, Norwood	3/11/1877	7/7/1959	4/29/1903	1903–1906
Gibson, Russ	5/6/1939		4/14/1967	1967–1969
Gilbert, Andy	7/18/1914	8/29/1992	9/14/1942	1942, 1946
Gile, Don	4/19/1935		9/25/1959	1959–1962
Gilhooley, Frank	6/10/1892	7/11/1959	5/1/1919	1919
Gilkey, Bernard	9/24/1966		7/4/2000	2000

PLAYER	BIRTH	DEATH	SOX DEBUT	YEARS ON RED SOX
GILLESPIE, Bob	10/8/1918		5/11/1950	1950
GILLIS, Grant	1/24/1901	2/4/1981	5/1/1929	1929
GINSBERG, Joe	10/11/1926		6/4/1961	1961
GLAZE, Ralph	3/13/1882	10/31/1968	6/1/1906	1906–1908
GLEASON, Harry	3/28/1875	10/21/1961	9/27/1901	1901–1903
GLENN, Joe	11/19/1908	5/6/1985	5/20/1940	1940
GODWIN, John	3/10/1877	5/5/1956	8/14/1905	1905–1906
GOGGIN, Chuck	7/7/1945		9/21/1974	1974
GOMES, Wayne	1/15/1973		7/3/2002	2002
GONZALES, Joe	3/19/1915	11/16/1996	8/28/1937	1937
GONZALEZ, Eusebio	7/13/1892	2/14/1976	7/26/1918	1918
GONZALEZ, Jeremi	1/8/1975		5/2/2005	2005
GOOCH, Johnny	11/9/1897	3/15/1975	4/14/1933	1933
GOODMAN, Billy	3/22/1926	10/1/1984	4/19/1947	1947–1956
GORDON, Tom	11/18/1967		4/3/1996	1996–1999
GOSGER, Jim	11/6/1942		5/4/1963	1963, 1965–1966
GRAFFANINO, Tony	6/6/1972		7/20/2005	2005
GRAHAM, Charlie	4/24/1878	8/29/1948	4/16/1906	1906
GRAHAM, Lee	9/22/1959		9/3/1983	1983
GRAHAM, Skinny	8/12/1909	7/10/1967	9/14/1934	
GRAY, Dave	1/7/1943		6/14/1964	1964
GRAY, Jeff	4/10/1963		6/10/1990	1990–1991
GREBECK, Craig	12/29/1964		4/2/2001	2001
GREEN, Lenny	1/6/1933		4/12/1965	1965–1966
GREEN, Pumpsie	10/27/1933		7/21/1959	1959–1962
GREENWELL, Mike	7/18/1963		9/5/1985	1985–1996
GREGG, Vean	4/13/1885	7/29/1964	7/29/1914	1914–1916
GRIFFIN, Doug	6/4/1947		4/6/1971	1971–1977
GRIFFIN, Marty	9/2/1901	11/19/1951	7/25/1928	1928
GRILLI, Guido	1/9/1939		4/12/1966	1966
GRIMES, Ray	9/11/1893	5/25/1953	9/24/1920	1920
GRIMSHAW, Myron	11/30/1875	12/11/1936	4/25/1905	1905–1907
GRISSOM, Marv	3/31/1918	9/19/2005	4/21/1953	1953
GROSS, Kip	8/24/1964		4/11/1999	1999
GROSS, Turkey	2/21/1896	1/11/1936	4/14/1925	1925
GROVE, Lefty	3/6/1900	5/22/1975	5/5/1934	1934–1941
GRUNDT, Ken	8/26/1969		8/8/1996	1996–1997
GUBANICH, Creighton	3/27/1972		4/16/1999	1999
GUERRA, Mike	10/11/1912	10/9/1992	4/21/1951	1951
GUERRERO, Mario	9/28/1949		4/8/1973	1973–1974
GUINDON, Bobby	9/4/1943		9/19/1964	1964
GUMPERT, Randy	1/23/1918		4/16/1952	1952
GUNDERSON, Eric	3/29/1966		8/25/1995	1995–1996
GUNNING, Hy	8/6/1888	3/28/1975	8/8/1911	1911
GUTHRIE, Mark	9/22/1965		4/7/1999	1999
GUTIERREZ, Jackie	6/27/1960		9/6/1983	1983–1985
GUTIERREZ, Ricky	5/23/1970		7/22/2004	2004
GUTTERIDGE, Don	6/19/1912		7/25/1946	1946–1947
HAGEMAN, Casey	5/12/1887	4/1/1964	9/18/1911	1911–1912
HALAMA, John	2/22/1972		4/3/2005	2005
HALE, Odell	8/10/1908	6/9/1980	4/24/1941	1941
HALEY, Ray	1/23/1891	10/8/1973	4/21/1915	1915–1916

PLAYER	BIRTH	DEATH	SOX DEBUT	YEARS ON RED SOX
HALL, Charley	7/27/1885	12/6/1943	8/9/1909	1909–1913
HAMMOND, Chris	1/21/1966		4/3/1997	1997
HANCOCK, Garry	1/23/1954		7/16/1978	1978, 1980–1982
HANCOCK, Josh	4/11/1978		9/10/2002	2002
HANEY, Chris	11/16/1968		6/5/2002	2002
HANEY, Fred	4/25/1898	11/9/1977	4/13/1926	1926–1927
HANSEN , Craig	11/15/1983		9/19/2005	2005
HANSON, Erik	5/18/1965		4/29/1995	1995
HARDY, Carroll	5/18/1933		6/15/1960	1960–1962
HARIKKALA, Tim	7/15/1971		4/21/1999	1999
HARPER, Harry	4/24/1895	4/23/1963	4/22/1920	1920
HARPER, Tommy	10/14/1940		4/15/1972	1972–1974
HARRELL, Billy	7/18/1928		4/15/1961	1961
HARRELSON, Ken	9/4/1941		8/29/1967	1967–1969
HARRIS, Bill	6/23/1900	8/21/1965	8/3/1938	1938
HARRIS, Joe	2/1/1882	4/12/1966	9/22/1905	1905–1907
HARRIS, Joe	5/20/1891	12/10/1959	4/12/1922	1922–1925
HARRIS, Greg	11/2/1955		8/7/1989	1989–1994
HARRIS, Mickey	1/30/1917	4/15/1971	4/23/1940	1940–1941, 1946–1949
HARRIS, Reggie	8/12/1968		8/30/1996	1996
HARRISS, Slim	12/11/1896	9/19/1963	6/29/1926	1926–1928
HARSHMAN, Jack	7/12/1927		6/18/1959	1959
HARTENSTEIN, Chuck	5/26/1942		7/25/1970	1970
HARTLEY, Grover	7/2/1888	10/19/1964	4/15/1927	1927
HARTLEY, Mike	8/31/1961		4/29/1995	1995
HARTMAN, Charlie	8/10/1888	10/22/1960	6/24/1908	1908
HARVILLE, Chad	9/16/1976		9/2/2005	2005
HASELMAN, Bill	5/25/1966		4/29/1995	1995–1997, 2003
HASH, Herb	2/13/1911		4/19/1940	1940–1941
HASSLER, Andy	10/18/1951		7/24/1978	1978–1979
HATCHER, Billy	10/4/1960		7/9/1992	1992–1994
HATFIELD, Fred	3/18/1925		8/31/1950	1950–1952
HATTEBERG, Scott	12/14/1969		9/8/1995	1995–2001
HATTON, Grady	10/7/1922		5/26/1954	1954–1955
HAUSMANN, Clem	8/17/1919	8/29/1972	4/28/1944	1944–1945
HAYDEN, Jack	10/21/1880	8/3/1942	6/7/1906	1906
HAYES, Frankie	10/13/1914	6/22/1955	4/20/1947	1947
HEARN, Ed	9/17/1888	9/8/1952	6/9/1910	1910
HEEP, Danny	7/3/1957		4/9/1989	1989–1990
HEFFNER, Bob	9/13/1938		6/19/1963	1963–1965
HEFLIN, Randy	9/11/1918	8/17/1999	6/9/1945	1945–1946
HEIMACH, Fred	1/27/1901	6/1/1973	6/20/1926	1926
HEISE, Bob	5/12/1947		4/9/1975	1975–1976
HELMS, Tommy	5/5/1941		6/23/1977	1977
HEMPHILL, Charlie	4/20/1876	6/22/1953	4/26/1901	1901
HENDERSON, Dave	7/21/1958		8/19/1986	1986–1987
HENDERSON, Rickey	12/25/1958		4/1/2002	2002
HENDRYX, Tim	1/31/1891	8/14/1957	4/15/1920	1920–1921
HENRIKSEN, Olaf	4/26/1888	10/17/1962	8/11/1911	1911–1916
HENRY, Bill	10/15/1927		4/17/1952	1952–1955
HENRY, Butch	10/7/1968		4/2/1997	1997–1998
HENRY, Jim	6/26/1910	8/15/1976	4/23/1936	1936–1937
HERMANSON, Dustin	12/21/1972		7/20/2002	2002

PLAYER	BIRTH	DEATH	SOX DEBUT	YEARS ON RED SOX
HERNANDEZ, Ramon	8/31/1940		6/3/1977	1977
HERRERA, Mike	12/19/1897	2/3/1978	9/22/1925	1925–1926
HERRIN, Tom	9/12/1929		4/13/1954	1954
HESKETH, Joe	2/15/1959		8/3/1990	1990–1994
HETZEL, Eric	9/25/1963		7/1/1989	1989–1990
HEVING, Joe	9/2/1900	4/11/1970	8/3/1938	1938–1940
HEVING, Johnnie	4/29/1896	12/24/1968	5/31/1924	1924–1925, 1928–1930
HICKMAN, Charlie	3/4/1876	4/19/1934	4/19/1902	1902
HIGGINS, Pinky	5/27/1909	3/21/1969	4/20/1937	1937–1938, 1946
HILLENBRAND, Shea	7/27/1975		4/2/2001	2001–2003
HILLER, Hob	5/12/1893	12/27/1956	4/22/1920	1920
HILLMAN, Dave	9/14/1927		4/21/1960	1960–1961
HINKLE, Gordie	4/3/1905	3/19/1972	4/19/1934	1934
HINRICHS, Paul	8/31/1925		5/16/1951	1951
HINSON, Paul	5/9/1904	9/23/1960	4/19/1928	1928
HISNER, Harley	11/6/1926		9/30/1951	1951
HITCHCOCK, Billy	7/31/1916		4/19/1948	1948–1949
HOBLITZELL, Dick	10/26/1888	11/14/1962	7/20/1914	1914–1918
HOBSON, Butch	8/17/1951		9/7/1975	1975–80, 1992–94
HOCKETTE, George	4/7/1908	1/20/1974	9/17/1934	1934–1935
HODAPP, Johnny	9/26/1905	6/14/1980	4/13/1933	1933
HODERLEIN, Mel	6/24/1923		8/16/1951	1951
HOEFT, Billy	5/17/1932		5/9/1959	1959
HOEY, Jack	11/10/1881	11/14/1947	6/27/1906	1906–1908
HOFFMAN, Glenn	7/7/1958		4/12/1980	1980–1987
HOFMANN, Fred	6/10/1894	11/19/1964	4/12/1927	1927–1928
HOLCOMBE, Ken	8/23/1918		4/16/1953	1953
HOLLINS, Dave	5/25/1966		7/26/1995	1995
HOLM, Billy	7/21/1912	7/27/1977	4/19/1945	1945
HOOPER, Harry	8/24/1887	12/18/1974	4/16/1909	1909–1920
HORN, Sam	11/2/1963		7/25/1987	1987–1989
HORTON, Tony	12/6/1944		7/31/1964	1964–1967
HOSEY, Dwayne	3/11/1967		9/1/1995	1995–1996
HOUSE, Tom	4/29/1947		4/10/1976	1976–1977
HOUSIE, Wayne	5/20/1965		9/17/1991	1991
HOWARD, Chris	11/18/1965		5/13/1994	1994
HOWARD, Elston	2/23/1929	12/14/1980	8/5/1967	1967–1968
HOWARD, Paul	5/20/1884	8/29/1968	9/16/1909	1909
HOWE, Les	8/24/1895	7/26/1976	8/18/1923	1923–1924
HOWRY, Bobby	8/4/1973		8/1/2002	2002–2003
HOY, Peter	6/29/1966		4/11/1992	1992
HOYT, Waite	9/9/1899	8/25/1984	7/31/1919	1919–1920
HUDSON, Joe	9/29/1970		6/10/1995	1995–1997
HUDSON, Sid	1/3/1915		6/14/1952	1952–1954
HUGHES, Ed	10/5/1880	10/11/1927	9/4/1905	1905–1906
HUGHES, Terry	5/13/1949		4/6/1974	1974
HUGHES, Tom	11/29/1878	2/8/1956	7/18/1902	1902–1903
HUGHSON, Tex	2/9/1916	8/6/1993	4/16/1941	1941–1944, 1946–1949
HUMPHREY, Bill	6/17/1911	2/13/1992	4/24/1938	1938
HUNT, Ben	11/10/1888	9/27/1927	8/24/1910	1910
HUNTER, Buddy	8/9/1947		7/1/1971	1971, 1973, 1975
HUNTER, Herb	12/25/1896	7/25/1970	5/6/1920	1920
HURD, Tom	5/27/1924	9/5/1982	7/30/1954	1954–1956

PLAYER	BIRTH	DEATH	SOX DEBUT	YEARS ON RED SOX
HURST, Bruce	3/24/1958		4/12/1980	1980–1988
HUSKEY, Butch	11/10/1971		7/27/1999	1999
HUSTING, Bert	3/6/1878	9/3/1948	4/25/1902	1902
HYZDU, Adam	12/6/1971		9/3/2004	2004–2005
IRVINE, Daryl	11/15/1964		4/28/1990	1990–1992
JABLONOWSKI, Pete	5/20/1904	1/18/1974	6/12/1932	1932
JACKSON, Damian	8/16/1973		4/1/2003	2003
JACKSON, Ron	10/22/1933		4/18/1960	1960
JACOBSON, Baby Doll	8/16/1890	1/16/1977	6/17/1926	1926–1927
JACOBSON, Beany	6/5/1881	1/31/1933	6/19/1907	1907
JAMERSON, Charlie	1/26/1900	8/4/1980	8/16/1924	1924
JAMES, Bill	1/20/1887	5/24/1942	5/30/1919	1919
JAMES, Chris	10/4/1962		8/16/1995	1995
JANVRIN, Hal	8/27/1892	3/1/1962	7/9/1911	1911–1917
JARVIS, Ray	5/10/1946		4/15/1969	1969–1970
JEFFERSON, Reggie	9/25/1968		4/30/1995	1995–1999
JENKINS, Fergie	12/13/1943		4/9/1976	1976–1977
JENKINS, Tom	4/10/1898	5/3/1979	9/15/1925	1925–1926
JENSEN, Jackie	3/9/1927	7/14/1982	4/13/1954	1954–1961
JENSEN, Marcus	12/14/1972		6/13/2001	2001
JOHNS, Keith	7/19/1971		5/23/1998	1998
JOHNSON, Bob	11/26/1906	7/6/1982	4/18/1944	1944–1945
JOHNSON, Deron	7/17/1938	4/23/1992	9/9/1974	1974–1976
JOHNSON, Earl	4/2/1919	12/3/1994	7/20/1940	1940–1941, 1946–1950
JOHNSON, Hank	5/21/1906	8/20/1982	4/17/1933	1933–1935
JOHNSON, John Henry	8/21/1956		4/5/1983	1983–1984
JOHNSON, Rankin	2/4/1888	7/2/1972	4/20/1914	1914
JOHNSON, Roy	2/23/1903	9/10/1973	6/15/1932	1932–1935
JOHNSON, Vic	8/3/1920	5/10/2005	5/3/1944	1944–1945
JOHNSTON, Joel	3/8/1967		5/1/1995	1995
JOLLEY, Smead	1/14/1902	11/17/1991	4/30/1932	1932–1933
JONES, Bobby	4/11/1972		4/7/2004	2004
JONES, Charlie	6/2/1876	4/2/1947	5/2/1901	1901
JONES, Dalton	12/10/1943		4/17/1964	1964–1969
JONES, Jake	11/23/1920		6/15/1947	1947–1948
JONES, Rick	4/16/1955		4/18/1976	1976
JONES, Sad Sam	7/26/1892	7/6/1966	4/21/1916	1916–1921
JONES, Todd	4/24/1968		7/4/2003	2003
JOOST, Eddie	6/5/1916		4/12/1955	1955
JOSEPHSON, Duane	6/3/1942	1/30/1997	4/6/1971	1971–1972
JUDD, Oscar	2/14/1908	12/27/1995	4/16/1941	1941–1945
JUDGE, Joe	5/25/1894	3/11/1963	8/3/1933	1933–1934
JURAK, Ed	10/24/1957		6/30/1982	1982–1985
KALLIO, Rudy	12/14/1892	4/6/1979	4/14/1925	1925
KAPLER, Gabe	8/31/1975		6/28/2003	2003–2005
KARGER, Ed	5/6/1883	9/9/1957	7/29/1909	1909–1911
KARL, Andy	4/8/1914	4/8/1989	4/24/1943	1943
KAROW, Marty	7/18/1904	4/27/1986	6/21/1927	1927
KARR, Benn	11/28/1893	12/8/1968	4/20/1920	1920–1922
KASKO, Eddie	6/27/1932		4/15/1966	1966

PLAYER	BIRTH	DEATH	SOX DEBUT	YEARS ON RED SOX
KELL, George	8/23/1922		6/4/1952	1952–1954
KELLETT, Al	10/30/1901	7/14/1960	8/30/1924	1924
KELLETT, Red	7/15/1909	11/3/1970	7/2/1934	1934
KELLUM, Win	4/11/1876	8/10/1951	4/26/1901	1901
KELLY, Ed	12/10/1888	11/4/1928	4/14/1914	1914
KELTNER, Ken	10/31/1916	12/12/1991	4/23/1950	1950
KEMMERER, Russ	11/1/1931		6/27/1954	1954–1955, 1957
KENDALL, Fred	1/31/1949		4/23/1978	1978
KENNEDY, Bill	3/14/1921	4/9/1983	4/20/1953	1953
KENNEDY, John	5/29/1941		7/5/1970	1970–1974
KEOUGH, Marty	4/14/1935		4/21/1956	1956–1960
KIECKER, Dana	2/25/1961		4/12/1990	1990–1991
KIEFER, Joe	7/19/1899	7/5/1975	9/19/1925	1925–1926
KIELY, Leo	11/30/1929	1/18/1984	6/27/1951	1951, 1954–1956, 1958–1959
KILLILAY, Jack	5/24/1887	10/21/1968	5/13/1911	1911
KIM, Byung–Hyun	1/21/1979		6/1/2003	2003–2004
KIM, Sun–Woo	9/4/1977		6/15/2001	2001–2002
KINDER, Ellis	7/26/1914	10/16/1968	5/5/1948	1948–1955
KINNEY, Walt	9/9/1893	7/1/1971	7/26/1918	1918
KISON, Bruce	2/18/1950		4/14/1985	1985
KLAUS, Billy	12/9/1928		4/17/1955	1955–1958
KLEINOW, Red	7/20/1879	10/9/1929	5/30/1910	1910–1911
KLINE, Bob	12/9/1909	3/16/1987	9/17/1930	1930–1933
KLINE, Ron	3/9/1932	6/22/2002	7/9/1969	1969
KLINGER, Bob	6/4/1908	8/19/1977	5/23/1946	1946–1947
KNACKERT, Brent	8/1/1969		5/9/1996	1996
KNIGHT, John	10/6/1885	12/19/1965	6/8/1907	1907
KOLSTAD, Hal	6/1/1935		4/22/1962	1962–1963
KOONCE, Cal	11/18/1940	10/28/1993	6/10/1970	1970–1971
KOSCO, Andy	10/5/1941		8/17/1972	1972
KRAMER, Jack	1/5/1918	5/18/1995	5/1/1948	1948–1949
KRAUSSE, Lew	4/25/1943		4/17/1972	1972
KREUGER, Rick	11/3/1948		9/6/1975	1975–1977
KROH, Rube	8/25/1886	3/17/1944	9/30/1906	1906–1907
KRONER, John	11/13/1908	4/26/1968	9/29/1935	1935–1936
KRUG, Marty	9/10/1888	6/27/1966	5/29/1912	1912
KUTCHER, Randy	4/20/1960		6/10/1998	1988–1990
LACHANCE, Candy	2/15/1870	8/18/1932	4/19/1902	1902–1905
LACY, Kerry	8/7/1972		8/16/1996	1996–1997
LAFOREST, Ty	4/18/1917	5/5/1947	8/4/1945	1945
LAFRANCOIS, Roger	8/2/1954		5/27/1982	1982
LAHOUD, Joe	4/14/1947		4/10/1968	1968–1971
LAKE, Eddie	3/18/1916	6/7/1995	4/22/1943	1943–1945
LAMABE, Jack	10/3/1936		4/9/1963	1963–1965
LAMAR, Bill	3/21/1897	5/24/1970	6/16/1919	1919
LAMP, Dennis	9/23/1952		4/6/1988	1988–1991
LANCELLOTTI, Rick	7/5/1956		8/10/1990	1990
LANDIS, Bill	10/8/1942		4/16/1967	1967–1969
LANDIS, Jim	3/9/1934		8/23/1967	1967
LANGFORD, Sam	5/21/1899	7/31/1993	4/13/1926	1926
LANSFORD, Carney	2/7/1957		4/10/1981	1981–1982

Lansing, Mike	4/3/1968		7/29/2000	2000–2001
LaPorte, Frank	2/6/1880	9/25/1939	4/14/1908	1908
LaRose, John	10/25/1951		9/20/1978	1978
Lary, Lyn	1/28/1906	1/9/1973	5/17/1934	1934
Lazor, Johnny	9/9/1912		4/22/1943	1943–1946
Lee, Bill	12/28/1946		6/25/1969	1969–1978
Lee, Dud	8/22/1899	1/7/1971	4/15/1924	1924–1926
Lee, Sang–Hoon	3/11/1971		6/29/2000	2000
Lefebvre, Bill	11/11/1915		6/10/1938	1938–1939
Legett, Lou	6/1/1901	3/6/1988	7/5/1933	1933–1934
Leheny, Regis	1/5/1908	11/2/1976	5/21/1932	1932
Lehner, Paul	7/1/1920	12/27/1967	6/27/1952	1952
Leibold, Nemo	2/17/1892	2/4/1977	4/13/1921	1921–1923
Leister, John	1/3/1961		5/28/1987	1987, 1990
Lemke, Mark	8/13/1965		4/10/1998	1998
Lenhardt, Don	10/4/1922		4/15/1952	1952, 1954
Leonard, Dutch	4/16/1892	7/11/1952	4/12/1913	1913–1918
Lepcio, Ted	7/28/1930		4/15/1952	1952–1959
Lerchen, Dutch	4/4/1889	1/7/1962	8/14/1910	1910
LeRoy, Louis	2/18/1879	10/10/1944	4/20/1910	1910
Leskanic, Curt	4/2/1968		6/25/2004	2004
Lewis, Darren	8/28/1967		4/1/1998	1998–2001
Lewis, Duffy	4/18/1888	6/17/1979	4/16/1910	1910–1917
Lewis, Jack	2/14/1884	2/25/1956	9/16/1911	1911
Lewis, Ted	12/25/1872	5/24/1936	5/2/1901	1901
Leyritz, Jim	12/27/1963		4/1/1998	1998
Lickert, John	4/4/1960		9/19/1981	1981
Lilliquist, Derek	2/20/1966		4/28/1995	1995
Lipon, Johnny	11/10/1922		6/7/1952	1952–1953
Lisenbee, Hod	9/23/1898	11/14/1987	7/17/1929	1929–1932
Littlefield, Dick	3/18/1926	11/20/1997	7/7/1950	1950
Litton, Greg	7/13/1964		5/26/1994	1994
Lock, Don	7/27/1936		5/11/1969	1969
Lockwood, Skip	8/17/1946		4/17/1980	1980
Loepp, George	9/11/1901	9/4/1967	8/29/1928	1928
Lofton, James	3/6/1974		9/19/2001	2001
Lollar, Tim	3/17/1956		7/22/1985	1985–1986
Lomasney, Steve	8/29/1977		10/3/1999	1999
Lonborg, Jim	4/16/1942		4/23/1965	1965–1971
Lonergan, Walter	9/22/1885	1/23/1958	8/17/1911	1911
Looney, Brian	9/26/1969		5/5/1995	1995
Lord, Harry	3/8/1882	8/9/1948	9/25/1907	1907–1910
Lowe, Derek	6/1/1973		9/1/1997	1997–2004
Lucas, Johnny	2/10/1903	10/31/1970	4/15/1931	1931
Lucey, Joe	3/27/1897	7/30/1980	4/23/1925	1925
Lucier, Lou	3/23/1918		4/23/1943	1943–1944
Lundgren, Del	9/21/1899	10/19/1984	4/13/1926	1926–1927
Lupien, Tony	4/23/1917	7/9/2004	9/12/1940	1940, 1942–1943
Lyle, Sparky	7/22/1944		7/4/1967	1967–1971
Lynch, Walt	4/15/1897	12/21/1976	7/8/1922	1922
Lynn, Fred	2/3/1952		9/5/1974	1974–1980
Lyon, Brandon	8/10/1979		4/1/2003	2003
Lyons, Steve	6/3/1960		4/15/1985	1985–1986, 1991–1993

PLAYER	BIRTH	DEATH	SOX DEBUT	YEARS ON RED SOX
Macfarlane, Mike	4/12/1964		4/26/1995	1995
MacFayden, Danny	6/10/1905	8/26/1972	8/25/1926	1926–1932
Machado, Alejandro	4/26/1982		9/2/2005	2005
Mack, Shane	12/7/1963		4/2/1997	1997
MacLeod, Billy	5/13/1942		9/13/1962	1962
Macwhorter, Keith	12/30/1955		5/10/1980	1980
Madden, Bunny	9/14/1882	1/20/1954	6/3/1909	1909–1911
Maddux, Mike	8/27/1961		5/31/1995	1995–1996
Magrini, Pete	6/8/1942		4/13/1966	1966
Mahay, Ron	6/28/1971		5/21/1995	1995, 1997–1998
Mahomes, Pat	8/9/1970		8/30/1996	1996–1997
Mahoney, Chris	6/11/1885	7/15/1954	7/12/1910	1910
Mahoney, Jim	5/26/1934		7/28/1959	1959
Malaska, Mark	1/17/1978		4/9/2004	2004
Malave, Jose	5/31/1971		5/23/1996	1996–1997
Mallett, Jerry	9/18/1935		9/19/1959	1959
Maloy, Paul	6/4/1892	3/18/197	7/11/1913	1913
Malzone, Frank	2/28/1930		9/17/1955	1955–1965
Mantei, Matt	7/7/1973		4/3/2005	2005
Mantilla, Felix	7/29/1934		4/17/1963	1963–1965
Manto, Jeff	8/23/1964		5/22/1996	1996
Manush, Heinie	7/20/1901	5/12/1971	4/14/1936	1936
Manzanillo, Josias	10/16/1967		10/5/1991	1991
Marchildon, Phil	10/25/1913	1/10/1997	7/16/1950	1950
Marcum, Johnny	9/9/1909	9/10/1984	5/6/1936	1936–1938
Marichal, Juan	10/20/1937		4/14/1974	1974
Marquardt, Ollie	9/22/1902	2/7/1968	4/14/1931	1931
Marshall, Bill	2/14/1911	5/5/1977	6/20/1931	1931
Marshall, Mike	1/12/1960		8/20/1990	1990–1991
Martin, Babe	3/28/1920		5/25/1948	1948–1949
Martinez, Anastacio	11/3/1978		5/22/2004	2004
Martinez, Pedro	10/25/1971		4/1/1998	1998–2004
Martinez, Ramon	3/22/1968		9/2/1999	1999–2000
Martinez, Sandy	10/3/1970		9/8/2004	2004
Marzano, John	2/14/1963		7/31/1987	1987–1992
Masterson, Walt	6/22/1920		6/15/1949	1949–1952
Matchick, Tom	9/7/1943		4/12/1970	1970
Matthews, William	1/12/1878		8/28/1909	1909
Mauch, Gene	11/18/1925	8/8/2005	9/14/1956	1956–1957
Maxwell, Charlie	4/8/1927		9/20/1950	1950–1952, 1954
Mayer, Wally	7/8/1890	11/18/1951	9/28/1917	1917–1918
Maynard, Chick	11/2/1896	1/31/1957	6/27/1922	1922
Mays, Carl	11/12/1891	4/4/1971	4/15/1915	1915–1919
McAuliffe, Dick	11/29/1939		4/6/1974	1974–1975
McBride, Tom	11/2/1914	12/26/2001	4/23/1943	1943–1947
McCabe, Dick	2/21/1896	4/11/1950	5/30/1918	1918
McCall, Windy	7/18/1925		4/25/1948	1948–1949
McCann, Emmett	3/4/1902	4/15/1937	4/13/1926	1926
McCarthy, Tom	6/18/1961		7/5/1985	1985
McCarty, David	11/23/1969		8/5/2003	2003–2004
McCarver, Tim	10/16/1941		9/4/1974	1974–1975
McConnell, Amby	4/29/1883	5/20/1942	4/17/1908	1908–1910
McDermott, Mickey	8/29/1928	8/7/2003	4/24/1948	1948–1953

PLAYER	BIRTH	DEATH	SOX DEBUT	YEARS ON RED SOX
McDILL, Allen	8/23/1971		8/14/2001	2001
McDONALD, Jim	5/17/1927		7/27/1950	1950
McFARLAND, Ed	8/3/1874	11/28/1959	8/26/1908	1908
McGAH, Eddie	9/30/1921		4/26/1946	1946–1947
McGEE, Willie	11/2/1958		7/5/1995	1995
McGLOTHEN, Lynn	3/27/1950	8/14/1984	6/25/1972	1972–1973
McGOVERN, Art	2/27/1882	11/14/1915	4/21/1905	1905
McGRAW, Bob	4/10/1895	6/2/1978	8/2/1919	1919
McGUIRE, Deacon	11/18/1863	10/31/1936	6/29/1907	1907–1908
McHALE, Jim	12/17/1875	6/17/1959	4/14/1908	1908
McHALE, Marty	10/30/1888	5/7/1979	9/28/1910	1910–1911, 1916
McINNIS, Stuffy	9/19/1890	2/16/1960	4/15/1918	1918–1921
McKAIN, Archie	5/12/1911	5/21/1985	4/25/1937	1937–1938
McKEEL, Walt	1/17/1972		9/14/1996	1996–1997
McLAUGHLIN, Jud	3/24/1912	9/27/1964	6/23/1931	1931–1933
McLEAN, Larry	7/18/1881	3/24/1921	4/26/1901	1901
McMAHON, Doc	12/19/1886	12/11/1929	10/6/1908	1908
McMAHON, Don	1/4/1930	7/22/1987	6/4/1966	1966–1967
McMANUS, Marty	3/14/1900	2/18/1966	9/1/1931	1931–1933
McMILLAN, Norm	10/5/1895	9/28/1969	4/18/1923	1923
McNAIR, Eric	4/12/1909	3/11/1949	4/14/1936	1936–1938
McNALLY, Mike	9/9/1892	5/29/1965	4/21/1915	1915–1917, 1919–1920
McNAUGHTON, Gordon	7/31/1910	8/6/1942	8/13/1932	1932
McNEELY, Jeff	10/18/1969		9/5/1993	1993
McNEIL, Norm	10/22/1892	4/11/1942	6/21/1919	1919
McWILLIAMS, Bill	11/28/1910	1/21/1997	7/8/1931	1931
MEJIAS, Roman	8/9/1930		4/9/1963	1963–1964
MELE, Sam	1/21/1923		4/15/1947	1947–1949, 1954–1955
MELENDEZ, Jose	9/?/1965		5/29/1993	1993–1994
MELILLO, Ski	8/4/1899	11/14/1963	5/28/1935	1935–1937
MELVIN, Bob	10/28/1961		4/8/1993	1993
MENDOZA, Ramiro	6/15/1972		3/31/2003	2003–2004
MENOSKY, Mike	10/16/1894	4/11/1983	4/15/1920	1920–1923
MEOLA, Mike	10/19/1905	9/1/1976	4/24/1933	1933, 1936
MERCED, Orlando	11/2/1966		8/3/1998	1998
MERCHANT, Andy	8/30/1950		9/28/1975	1975–1976
MERCKER, Kent	2/1/1968		8/27/1999	1999
MEREDITH, Cla	6/4/1983		5/8/2005	2005
MERENA, Spike	11/18/1909	3/9/1977	9/16/1934	1934
MERLONI, Lou	4/6/1971		5/10/1998	1998–2003
MERSON, Jack	1/17/1922		4/24/1953	1953
METKOVICH, Catfish	10/8/1920	5/17/1995	7/16/1943	1943–1946
MEYER, Russ	10/25/1923	11/16/1997	4/24/1957	1957
MICHAELS, John	7/10/1907	11/18/1996	4/16/1932	1932
MIDKIFF, Dick	9/28/1914	10/30/1956	4/24/1938	1938
MIENTKIEWICZ, Doug	6/19/1974		8/3/2004	2004
MILES, Dee	2/15/1909	11/2/1976	4/24/1943	1943
MILLAR, Kevin	9/24/1971		3/31/2003	2003–2005
MILLER, Bing	8/30/1894	5/7/1966	4/17/1935	1935–1936
MILLER, Elmer	7/28/1890	11/28/1944	7/26/1922	1922
MILLER, Hack	1/1/1894	9/17/1971	8/7/1918	1918
MILLER, Otto	2/2/1901	7/26/1959	4/14/1930	1930–1931
MILLER, Rick	4/19/1948		9/4/1971	1971–1977, 1981–1985

PLAYER	BIRTH	DEATH	SOX DEBUT	YEARS ON RED SOX
MILLER, Wade	9/13/1976		5/8/2005	2005
MILLS, Buster	9/16/1908	12/1/1991	4/20/1937	1937
MILLS, Dick	1/29/1945		9/7/1970	1970
MINARCIN, Rudy	3/25/1930		9/15/1956	1956–1957
MINCHEY, Nate	8/31/1969		9/12/1993	1993–1994, 1996
MIRABELLI, Doug	10/18/1970		6/14/2001	2001–2005
MITCHELL, Charlie	6/24/1962		8/9/1984	1984–1985
MITCHELL, Fred	6/5/1878	10/13/1970	4/27/1901	1901–1902
MITCHELL, Johnny	8/9/1894	11/4/1965	7/25/1922	1922–1923
MITCHELL, Keith	8/6/1969		7/19/1998	1998
MITCHELL, Kevin	1/13/1962		4/5/1996	1996
MOFORD, Herb	8/6/1928	12/3/2005	4/21/1959	1959
MOLYNEAUX, Vince	8/17/1888	5/4/1950	5/30/1918	1918
MONBOUQUETTE, Bill	8/11/1936		7/18/1958	1958–1965
MONCEWICZ, Freddie	9/1/1903	4/23/1969	6/19/1928	1928
MONTGOMERY, Bob	4/16/1944		9/6/1970	1970–1979
MOORE, Bill	12/12/1903	5/24/1972	9/7/1926	1926–1927
MOORE, Wilcy	5/20/1897	3/29/1963	4/14/1931	1931–1932
MOREHEAD, Dave	9/5/1942		4/13/1963	1963–1968
MORET, Roger	9/16/1949		9/13/1970	1970–1975
MORGAN, Cy	11/10/1878	6/28/1962	8/6/1907	1907–1909
MORGAN, Ed	5/22/1904	4/9/1980	4/19/1934	1934
MORGAN, Red	10/6/1883	3/25/1981	6/20/1906	1906
MORRIS, Ed	12/7/1899	3/3/1932	4/11/1928	1928–1931
MORRISSEY, Frank	5/5/1876	2/22/1939	7/13/1901	1901
MORTON, Guy "Moose"	11/4/1930		9/17/1954	1954
MORTON, Kevin	8/3/1968		7/5/1991	1991
MOSELEY, Earl	9/7/1884	7/1/1963	6/17/1913	1913
MOSER, Walter	2/27/1881	12/10/1946	6/30/1911	1911
MOSES, Jerry	8/9/1946		5/9/1965	1965, 1968–1970
MOSES, Wally	10/8/1910	10/10/1990	7/26/1946	1946–1948
MOSKIMAN, Doc	12/20/1879	1/11/1953	8/23/1910	1910
MOSS, Les	5/14/1925		5/18/1951	1951
MOYER, Jamie	11/18/1962		4/3/1996	1996
MUELLER, Bill	3/17/1971		3/31/2003	2003–2005
MUELLER, Gordie	12/10/1922		4/19/1950	1950
MUFFETT, Billy	9/21/1930		6/25/1960	1960–1962
MULLEAVY, Greg	9/25/1905	2/1/1980	4/13/1933	1933
MULLER, Freddie	12/21/1907	10/20/1976	7/8/1933	1933–1934
MULLIGAN, Joe	7/31/1913	6/5/1986	6/28/1934	1934
MULRONEY, Frank	4/8/1903	11/11/1985	4/15/1930	1930
MUNDY, Bill	6/28/1889	9/23/1958	8/17/1913	1913
MURPHY, Johnny	7/14/1908	1/14/1970	4/26/1947	1947
MURPHY, Rob	5/26/1960		4/3/1989	1989–1990
MURPHY, Tom	12/30/1945		6/8/1976	1976–1977
MURPHY, Walter	9/27/1907	5/23/1976	4/19/1931	1931
MURRAY, George	9/23/1898	10/18/1955	4/19/1923	1923–1924
MURRAY, Matt	9/26/1970		8/12/1995	1995
MUSER, Tony	8/1/1947		9/14/1969	1969
MUSSER, Paul	6/24/1889	7/7/1973	7/22/1918	1919
MUSTAIKIS, Alex	3/26/1909	1/17/1970	7/7/1940	1940
MYER, Buddy	3/16/1904	10/31/1974	5/3/1927	1927–1928
MYERS, Elmer	3/2/1894	7/29/1976	8/6/1920	1920–1922

PLAYER	BIRTH	DEATH	SOX DEBUT	YEARS ON RED SOX
MYERS, Hap	4/8/1888	6/30/1967	4/16/1910	1910–1911
MYERS, Mike	6/26/1969		8/10/2004	2004–2005
NABHOLZ, Chris	1/5/1967		7/3/1994	1994
NAEHRING, Tim	2/1/1967		7/15/1990	1990–1997
NAGLE, Judge	3/10/1880	5/26/1971	4/26/1911	1911
NAGY, Mike	3/25/1948		4/21/1969	1969–1972
NARLESKI, Bill	6/9/1899	7/22/1964	4/18/1929	1929–1930
NEAL, Blaine	4/6/1978		4/3/2005	2005
NEITZKE, Ernie	11/13/1894	4/27/1977	6/2/1921	1921
NELSON, Bry	1/27/1974		5/14/2002	2002
NELSON, Joe	10/25/1974		7/10/2004	2004
NEUBAUER, Hal	5/13/1902	9/9/1949	6/12/1925	1925
NEWHAUSER, Don	11/7/1947		6/15/1972	1972–1974
NEWMAN, Jeff	9/11/1948		4/13/1983	1983–1984
NEWSOM, Bobo	8/11/1907	12/7/1962	6/12/1937	1937
NEWSOME, Dick	12/13/1909	12/15/1965	4/25/1941	1941–1943
NEWSOME, Skeeter	10/18/1910	8/31/1989	4/20/1941	1941–1945
NIARHOS, Gus	12/6/1920	12/29/2004	4/15/1952	1952–1953
NICHOLS, Chet	2/22/1931	3/27/1995	9/2/1960	1960–1963
NICHOLS, Reid	8/5/1958		9/16/1980	1980–1985
NIEMIEC, Al	5/18/1911	10/29/1995	9/19/1934	1934
NILES, Harry	9/10/1880	4/18/1953	8/22/1908	1908–1910
NIPPER, Al	4/2/1959		9/6/1983	1983–1987
NIPPERT, Merlin	9/1/1938		9/12/1962	1962
NIXON, Otis	1/9/1959		4/4/1994	1994
NIXON, Russ	2/19/1935		6/14/1960	1960–1965, 1968
NIXON, Trot	4/11/1974		9/21/1996	1996, 1998–2005
NIXON, Willard	6/17/1928		7/7/1950	1950–1958
NOMO, Hideo	8/31/1968		4/4/2001	2001
NONNENKAMP, Red	7/7/1910	12/3/2000	4/18/1938	1938–1939
NOURSE, Chet	8/7/1887	4/20/1958	7/27/1909	1909
NUNAMAKER, Les	1/25/1889	11/14/1938	4/28/1911	1911–1914
NUNNALLY, Jon	11/9/1971		9/2/1999	1999
OBERLIN, Frank	3/29/1876	1/6/1952	9/20/1906	1906–1907
O'BRIEN, Buck	5/9/1882	7/25/1959	9/9/1911	1911–1913
O'BRIEN, Jack	2/5/1873	6/10/1933	4/23/1903	1903
O'BERRY, Mike	4/20/1954		4/8/1979	1979
O'BRIEN, Syd	12/18/1944		4/15/1969	1969
O'BRIEN, Tommy	12/19/1918	11/5/1978	4/19/1949	1949–1950
O'DOUL, Lefty	3/4/1897	12/7/1969	4/19/1923	1923
OFFERMAN, Jose	11/8/1968		4/5/1999	1999–2002
OGLIVIE, Ben	2/11/1949		9/4/1971	1971–1973
OHKA, Tomokazu	3/18/1976		7/19/1999	1999–2001
OJEDA, Bob	12/17/1957		7/13/1980	1980–1985
OKRIE, Len	7/16/1923		4/16/1952	1952
O'LEARY, Troy	8/4/1969		4/30/1995	1995–2001
OLERUD, John	8/5/1968		5/28/2005	2005
OLIVER, Darren	10/6/1970		4/1/2002	2002
OLIVER, Gene	3/22/1935		4/18/1968	1968
OLIVER, Joe	7/24/1965		9/2/2001	2001
OLIVER, Tom	1/15/1903	12/26/2001	4/14/1930	1930–1933

PLAYER	BIRTH	DEATH	SOX DEBUT	YEARS ON RED SOX
OLMSTED, Hank	1/12/1879	1/6/1969	7/15/1905	1905
OLSON, Karl	7/6/1930		6/30/1951	1951, 1953–1955
OLSON, Marv	5/28/1907	2/5/1998	9/13/1931	1931–1933
OLSON, Ted	8/27/1912	12/9/1980	6/21/1936	1936–1938
O'NEILL, Bill	1/22/1880	7/20/1920	5/7/1904	1904
O'NEILL, Emmett	1/13/1918	10/11/1993	8/3/1943	1943–1945
O'NEILL, Steve	7/6/1891	1/26/1962	4/15/1924	1924
ONTIVEROS, Steve	3/5/1961		9/16/2000	2000
ORME, George	9/16/1891	3/16/1962	9/14/1920	1920
ORME, George	9/16/1891		9/14/1920	1920
O'ROURKE, Frank	11/28/1894	5/14/1986	4/12/1922	1922
ORTIZ, David	11/18/1975		4/1/2003	2003–2004
ORTIZ, Luis	5/25/1970		8/31/1993	1993–1994
OSINSKI, Dan	11/17/1933		4/12/1966	1966–1967
OSTDIEK, Harry	4/12/1881	5/6/1956	10/7/1908	1908
OSTERMUELLER, Fritz	9/15/1907	12/17/1957	4/21/1934	1934–1940
OSTROWSKI, Johnny	10/17/1917	11/13/1992	4/19/1948	1948
OWEN, Marv	3/22/1906	6/22/1991	5/30/1940	1940
OWEN, Mickey	4/4/1916		4/18/1954	1954
OWEN, Spike	4/19/1961		8/19/1986	1986–1988
OWENS, Frank	1/26/1886	7/2/1958	9/11/1905	1905
PAGLIARONI, Jim	12/8/1937		8/13/1955	1955, 1960–1962
PALM, Mike	2/13/1925		7/11/1948	1948
PANKOVITS, Jim	8/6/1955		9/16/1990	1990
PAPAI, Al	5/7/1917	9/7/1995	4/18/1950	1950
PAPE, Larry	7/21/1883	7/21/1918	7/6/1909	1909, 1911–1912
PAPELBON, Jonathan	11/23/1980		7/31/2005	2005
PAPI, Stan	2/4/1951		5/27/1999	1979–1980
PARENT, Freddy	11/25/1875	11/2/1972	4/26/1901	1901–1907
PARNELL, Mel	6/13/1922		4/20/1947	1947–1956
PARRISH, Larry	11/10/1953		7/18/1988	1988
PARTEE, Roy	9/7/1917		4/23/1943	1943–1944, 1946–1947
PARTENHEIMER, Stan	10/21/1922	1/28/1989	5/27/1944	1944
PASCHAL, Ben	10/13/1895	11/10/1974	9/13/1920	1920
PATTEN, Casey	5/7/1876	5/31/1935	6/18/1908	1908
PATTERSON, Hank	7/17/1907	9/30/1970	9/5/1932	1932
PATTIN, Marty	4/6/1943		4/15/1972	1972–1973
PAVLETICH, Don	7/13/1938		4/18/1970	1970–1971
PAXTON, Mike	9/3/1953		5/25/1977	1977
PAYTON, Jay	11/22/1972		4/3/2005	2005
PEACOCK, Johnny	1/10/1910	10/17/1981	9/23/1937	1937–1944
PELLAGRINI, Eddie	3/13/1918		4/22/1946	1946–1947
PEMBERTON, Rudy	12/17/1969		9/2/1996	1996–1997
PENA, Alejandro	6/25/1959		4/26/1995	1995
PENA, Jesus	3/8/1975		9/21/2000	2000
PENA, Juan	6/27/1977		5/8/1999	1999
PENA, Tony	6/4/1957		4/9/1990	1990–1993
PENNINGTON, Brad	4/14/1969		4/3/1996	1996
PENNOCK, Herb	2/10/1894	1/30/1948	6/9/1915	1915–1917, 1919–1922, 1934
PEREZ, Tony	5/14/1942		4/10/1980	1980–1982
PERISHO, Matt	6/8/1975		9/2/2005	2005

PLAYER	BIRTH	DEATH	SOX DEBUT	YEARS ON RED SOX
Perrin, John	2/4/1898	6/24/1969	7/11/1921	1921
Person, Robert	10/6/1969		5/14/2003	2003
Pertica, Bill	3/5/1897	12/28/1967	8/7/1918	1918
Pesky, Johnny	9/27/1919		4/14/1942	1942, 1946–1952
Petagine, Roberto	6/7/1971		8/4/2005	2005
Peters, Gary	4/21/1937		4/7/1970	1970–1972
Peterson, Bob	7/16/1884	11/27/1962	4/18/1906	1906–1907
Petrocelli, Rico	6/27/1943		9/21/1963	1963, 1965–1976
Petry, Dan	11/13/1958		8/21/1991	1991
Philley, Dave	5/16/1920		4/10/1962	1962
Phillips, Ed	9/20/1944		4/9/1970	1970
Pichardo, Hipolito	8/22/1969		5/31/2000	2000–2001
Picinich, Val	9/8/1896	12/5/1942	4/25/1923	1923–1925
Pickering, Calvin	9/29/1976		9/9/2001	2001
Pickering, Urbane	6/3/1899	5/13/1970	4/18/1931	1931–1932
Pierce, Jeff	6/7/1969		4/26/1995	1995
Piercy, Bill	5/2/1896	8/28/1951	5/20/1922	1922–1924
Piersall, Jim	11/14/1929		9/7/1950	1950, 1952–1958
Pipgras, George	12/20/1899	10/19/1986	5/17/1933	1933–1935
Pirkl, Greg	8/7/1970		8/8/1996	1996
Pittenger, Pinky	2/24/1899	11/4/1977	4/15/1921	1921–1923
Pizarro, Juan	2/7/1937		6/29/1968	1968–1969
Plantier, Phil	1/27/1969		8/21/1990	1990–1992
Plews, Herb	6/14/1928		6/12/1959	1959
Plympton, Jeff	11/24/1965		6/15/1991	1991
Poindexter, Jennings	9/30/1910	3/3/1983	9/15/1936	1936
Pole, Dick	10/13/1950		8/3/1973	1973–1976
Polly, Nick	4/18/1917	1/17/1993	4/19/1945	1945
Pond, Ralph	5/4/1888	9/8/1947	6/8/1910	1910
Poquette, Tom	10/30/1951		6/13/1979	1979, 1981
Porter, Dick	12/30/1901	9/24/1974	5/25/1934	1934
Porterfield, Bob	8/10/1923	4/28/1980	4/18/1956	1956–1958
Portugal, Mark	10/30/1962		4/9/1999	1999
Potter, Nels	8/23/1911	9/30/1990	7/1/1941	1941
Poulsen, Ken	8/4/1947		7/3/1967	1967
Pozo, Arquimedez	8/24/1973		7/25/1996	1996–1997
Pratt, Del	1/10/1888	9/30/1977	4/15/1921	1921–1922
Pratt, Larry	10/8/1886	1/8/1969	9/19/1914	1914
Prentiss, George	6/10/1876	9/8/1902	9/23/1901	1901–1902
Price, Joe	11/29/1956		5/8/1989	1989
Pride, Curtis	12/17/1968		9/19/1997	1997, 2000
Prothro, Doc	7/16/1893	10/14/1971	4/14/1925	1925
Pruiett, Tex	4/10/1883	3/6/1953	4/26/1907	1907–1908
Pulsipher, Bill	10/9/1973		6/28/2001	2001
Purtell, Billy	1/6/1886	3/17/1962	8/13/1910	1910–1911
Pytlak, Frankie	7/30/1908	5/8/1977	4/15/1941	1941, 1945–1946
Quantrill, Paul	11/3/1968		7/20/1992	1992–1994
Quinn, Frank	11/27/1927	1/11/1993	5/29/1949	1949–1950
Quinn, Jack	7/5/1883	4/17/1946	4/12/1922	1922–1925
Quinones, Rey	11/11/1963		5/17/1986	1986
Quintana, Carlos	8/26/1965		9/16/1988	1988–1991, 1993

PLAYER	BIRTH	DEATH	SOX DEBUT	YEARS ON RED SOX
RADATZ, Dick	4/2/1937	3/16/2005	4/10/1962	1962–1966
RADER, Dave	12/26/1948		4/10/1980	1980
RAINEY, Chuck	7/14/1954		4/8/1979	1979–1982
RAMIREZ, Hanley	12/23/1983		9/20/2005	2005
RAMIREZ, Manny	5/30/1972		4/2/2001	2001–2005
RAPP, Pat	7/13/1967		4/11/1999	1999
REARDON, Jeff	10/1/1955		4/17/1990	1990–1992
REDER, Johnny	9/24/1909	4/12/1990	4/16/1932	1932
REED, Jerry	10/8/1955		5/4/1990	1990
REED, Jody	7/26/1962		9/12/1987	1987–1992
REESE, Pokey	6/10/1973		4/4/2004	2004
REEVES, Bobby	6/24/1904	6/4/1993	4/18/1929	1929–1931
REGAN, Bill	1/23/1899	6/11/1968	6/2/1926	1926–1930
REHG, Wally	8/31/1888	4/5/1946	8/26/1913	1913–1915
REICHLE, Dick	11/23/1896	6/13/1967	9/19/1922	1922–1923
REMLINGER, Mike	3/23/1966		8/9/2005	2005
REMMERSWAAL, Win	3/8/1954		8/3/1979	1979–1980
REMY, Jerry	11/8/1952		4/7/1978	1978–1984
RENKO, Steve	12/10/1944		4/18/1979	1979–1980
RENNA, Bill	10/14/1924		4/21/1958	1958–1959
RENTERIA, Edgar	8/7/1976		4/3/2005	2005
REPULSKI, Rip	10/4/1927	2/10/1993	5/10/1960	1960–1961
REYES, Carlos	4/4/1969		6/23/1998	1998
REYNOLDS, Carl	2/1/1903	5/29/1978	4/17/1934	1934–1935
RHODES, Gordon	8/11/1907	3/24/1960	8/4/1932	1932–1935
RHODES, Karl	8/21/1968		5/27/1995	1995
RHYNE, Hal	3/30/1899	1/7/1971	4/18/1929	1929–1932
RICE, Jim	3/8/1953		8/19/1974	1974–1989
RICH, Woody	3/9/1916	4/18/1983	4/22/1939	1939–1941
RICHARDSON, Jeff	8/26/1965		4/9/1993	1993
RICHTER, Al	2/7/1927		9/23/1951	1951–1953
RIGGERT, Joe	12/11/1886	12/10/1973	5/12/1911	1911
RIGNEY, Topper	1/7/1897	6/6/1972	4/16/1926	1926–1927
RILES, Ernest	10/2/1960		4/9/1993	1993
RIPLEY, Allen	10/18/1952		4/10/1978	1978–1979
RIPLEY, Walt	11/26/1916	10/7/1990	8/17/1935	1935
RISING, Pop	1/2/1872	1/28/1938	8/10/1905	1905
RITCHIE, Jay	11/20/1936		8/4/1964	1964–1965
RIVERA, Luis	1/3/1964		6/6/1989	1989–1993
ROBERTS, Dave	5/31/1972		8/3/2004	2004
ROBIDOUX, Billy Jo	1/13/1964		4/9/1990	1990
ROBINSON, Aaron	6/23/1915	3/9/1966	8/8/1951	1951
ROBINSON, Floyd	5/9/1936		8/3/1968	1968
ROBINSON, Jack	2/20/1921		5/4/1949	1949
ROCHFORD, Mike	3/14/1963		9/3/1988	1988–1990
RODGERS, Bill	4/18/1887	12/24/1978	4/15/1915	1915
RODRIGUEZ, Carlos	11/1/1967		5/7/1994	1994–1995
RODRIGUEZ, Frankie	12/11/1972		4/26/1995	1995
RODRIGUEZ, Steve	11/29/1970		4/30/1995	1995
RODRIGUEZ, Tony	8/15/1970		7/6/1996	1996
ROGELL, Billy	11/24/1904	8/9/2003	4/14/1925	1925, 1927–1928
ROGERS, Lee	10/8/1913	11/23/1995	4/27/1938	1938
ROGGENBURK, Garry	4/16/1940		9/18/1966	1966, 1968–1969

PLAYER	BIRTH	DEATH	SOX DEBUT	YEARS ON RED SOX
ROHR, Billy	7/1/1945		4/14/1967	1967
ROLLINGS, Red	3/21/1904	12/31/1964	4/17/1927	1927–1928
ROMERO, Ed	12/9/1957		4/9/1986	1986–1989
ROMERO, Mandy	10/29/1967		9/1/1998	1998
ROMINE, Kevin	5/23/1961		9/5/1985	1985–1991
ROMO, Vicente	4/12/1943		4/25/1969	1969–1970
ROSAR, Buddy	7/3/1914	3/13/1994	8/4/1950	1950–1951
ROSE, Brian	2/13/1976		7/25/1997	1997–2000
ROSENTHAL, Si	11/13/1903	4/7/1969	9/8/1925	1925–1926
ROSS, Buster	3/11/1903	4/24/1982	6/15/1924	1924–1926
ROTH, Braggo	8/28/1892	9/11/1936	6/28/1919	1919
ROTHROCK, Jack	3/14/1905	2/2/1980	7/28/1925	1925–1932
ROWLAND, Rich	2/25/1964		4/7/1994	1994–1995
ROYER, Stan	8/31/1967		7/16/1994	1994
RUDI, Joe	9/7/1946		4/10/1981	1981
RUEL, Muddy	2/20/1896	11/13/1963	4/13/1921	1921–1922, 1931
RUFFING, Red	5/3/1904	2/17/1986	5/31/1924	1924–1930
RUNNELS, Pete	1/28/1928	5/20/1991	4/14/1958	1958–1962, 1966
RUPE, Ryan	3/31/1975		6/13/2003	2003
RUSSELL, Allan	7/31/1893	10/20/1972	8/2/1919	1919–1922
RUSSELL, Jack	10/24/1905	11/3/1990	5/5/1926	1926–1932, 1936
RUSSELL, Jeff	9/2/1961		4/5/1993	1993–1994
RUSSELL, Rip	1/26/1915	9/26/1976	4/21/1946	1946–1947
RUTH, Babe	2/6/1895	8/16/1948	7/11/1914	1914–1919
RYAN, Jack	9/19/1884	10/16/1949	4/12/1909	1909
RYAN, Jack	5/5/1905	9/2/1967	6/18/1929	1929
RYAN, Ken	10/24/1968		8/31/1992	1992–1995
RYAN, Mike	11/25/1941		10/3/1964	1964–1967
RYBA, Mike	6/9/1903	12/13/1971	4/20/1941	1941–1946
RYE, Gene	11/15/1906	1/21/1980	4/22/1931	1931
SABERHAGEN, Bret	4/11/1964		8/22/1997	1997–2001
SADLER, Donnie	6/17/1975		4/1/1998	1998–2000
SADOWSKI, Bob	2/19/1938		4/17/1966	1966
SADOWSKI, Ed	1/19/1931	11/6/1993	4/20/1960	1960
SAMBITO, Joe	6/28/1952		4/7/1986	1986–1987
SANCHEZ, Freddy	12/21/1977		9/10/2002	2002–2003
SANCHEZ, Rey	10/5/1967		4/1/2002	2002
SANDERS, Ken	7/8/1941		4/13/1966	1966
SANTANA, Marino	5/10/1972		7/19/1999	1999
SANTIAGO, Jose	8/15/1940		4/19/1966	1966–1970
SANTOS, Angel	8/14/1979		9/8/2001	2001
SATRIANO, Tom	8/28/1940		6/17/1969	1969–1970
SAUERBECK, Scott	11/9/1971		7/23/2003	2003
SAX, Dave	9/22/1958		4/21/1985	1985–1987
SAYLES, Bill	7/27/1917	11/20/1996	7/17/1939	1939
SCARBOROUGH, Ray	7/23/1917	7/1/1982	4/20/1951	1951–1952
SCARRITT, Russ	1/14/1903	12/4/1994	4/18/1929	1929–1931
SCHANG, Wally	8/22/1889	3/6/1965	4/22/1918	1918–1920
SCHANZ, Charley	6/8/1919	5/22/1992	4/18/1950	1950
SCHERBARTH, Bob	1/18/1926		4/23/1950	1950
SCHILLING, Chuck	10/25/1937		4/11/1961	1961–1965
SCHILLING, Curt	11/14/1966		4/6/2004	2004–2005

PLAYER	BIRTH	DEATH	SOX DEBUT	YEARS ON RED SOX
SCHIRALDI, Calvin	6/16/1962		7/20/1986	1986–1987
SCHLESINGER, Bill	11/5/1941		5/4/1965	1965
SCHLITZER, Biff	12/4/1884	1/4/1948	6/11/1909	1909
SCHMEES, George	9/6/1924		4/15/1952	1952
SCHMIDT, Dave	12/22/1956		4/28/1981	1981
SCHMITZ, Johnny	11/27/1920		4/22/1956	1956
SCHOFIELD, Dick	1/7/1935		4/11/1969	1969–1970
SCHOUREK, Pete	5/10/1969		8/13/1998	1998, 2000–2001
SCHRECKENGOST, Ossee	4/11/1875	7/9/1914	5/1/1901	1901
SCHROLL, Al	3/22/1932		4/20/1958	1958–1959
SCHWALL, Don	3/2/1936		5/21/1961	1961–1962
SCOTT, Everett	11/19/1892	11/2/1960	4/14/1914	1914–1921
SCOTT, George	3/23/1944		4/12/1966	1966–1971, 1977–1979
SEANEZ, Rudy	10/20/1968		5/21/2003	2003
SEAVER, Tom	11/17/1944		7/1/1986	1986
SEEDS, Bob	2/24/1907	10/28/1993	4/13/1933	1933–1934
SEGUI, Diego	8/17/1937		4/5/1974	1974–1975
SEIBEL, Phil	1/28/1979		4/15/2004	2004
SELBACH, Kip	3/24/1872	2/17/1956	7/4/1904	1904–1906
SELBY, Bill	6/11/1970		4/19/1996	1996
SELE, Aaron	6/25/1970		6/23/1993	1993–1997
SELLERS, Jeff	5/11/1964		9/15/1985	1985–1988
SETTLEMIRE, Merle	1/19/1903	6/12/1988	4/13/1928	1928
SHANER, Wally	5/24/1900	11/13/1992	5/8/1926	1926–1927
SHANKS, Howie	7/21/1890	7/30/194	4/18/1923	1923–1924
SHANNON, Red	2/11/1897	4/12/1970	6/30/1919	1919
SHAW, Al	10/3/1874	3/25/1958	4/11/1907	1907
SHEA, John	12/27/1904	11/30/1956	6/30/1928	1928
SHEA, Merv	9/5/1900	1/27/1953	4/13/1933	1933
SHEAFFER, Danny	8/2/1961		4/9/1987	1987
SHEAN, Dave	7/9/1883	5/22/1963	4/15/1918	1918–1919
SHEETS, Andy	11/19/1971		4/16/2000	2000
SHELDON, Rollie	12/17/1936		6/16/1966	1966
SHEPHERD, Keith	1/21/1968		4/28/1995	1995
SHERIDAN, Neill	11/20/1921		9/19/1948	1948
SHIELDS, Ben	6/17/1903	1/24/1982	5/18/1930	1930
SHIELL, Jason	10/19/1976		4/19/2003	2003
SHOFNER, Strick	7/23/1919		4/19/1947	1947
SHOPPACH, Kelly	4/29/1980		5/28/2005	2005
SHORE, Ernie	3/24/1891	9/24/1980	7/14/1914	1914–1917
SHORT, Bill	11/27/1937		8/21/1966	1966
SHORTEN, Chick	4/19/1892	10/23/1965	9/22/1915	1915–1917
SHOUSE, Brian	9/26/1968		4/21/1998	1998
SHUMPERT, Terry	8/16/1966		4/30/1995	1995
SIEBERN, Norm	7/26/1933		7/21/1967	1967–1968
SIEBERT, Sonny	1/14/1937		4/23/1969	1969–1973
SIMMONS, Al	5/22/1902	5/26/1956	4/27/1943	1943
SIMMONS, Pat	11/29/1908	7/3/1968	4/18/1928	1928–1929
SISLER, Dave	10/16/1931		4/21/1956	1956–1959
SIZEMORE, Ted	4/15/1945		8/18/1979	1979–1980
SKINNER, Camp	6/25/1897	8/4/1944	4/18/1923	1923
SKOK, Craig	9/1/1947		5/4/1973	1973
SLATTERY, Jack	1/6/1878	7/17/1949	9/28/1901	1901

PLAYER	BIRTH	DEATH	SOX DEBUT	YEARS ON RED SOX
SLAYTON, Steve	4/26/1902	12/20/1984	7/21/1928	1928
SLOCUMB, Heathcliff	6/7/1966		4/4/1996	1996–1997
SMALL, Charlie	10/24/1905	1/14/1953	7/7/1930	1930
SMITH, Al	2/7/1928	1/3/2002	8/5/1964	1964
SMITH, Aleck	1871	7/9/1919	5/12/1903	1903
SMITH, Bob	2/1/1931		4/22/1958	1958
SMITH, Bob "Riverboat"	5/13/1927	6/23/2003	4/29/1955	1955
SMITH, Charlie	4/20/1880	1/3/1929	9/13/1909	1909–1911
SMITH, Dan	9/15/1975		6/3/2000	2000
SMITH, Doug	5/25/1892	9/18/1973	7/10/1912	1912
SMITH, Eddie	12/14/1913	1/2/1994	8/15/1947	1947
SMITH, Elmer	9/21/1892	8/3/1984	4/12/1922	1922
SMITH, Frank	10/28/1879	11/3/1952	8/31/1910	1910–1911
SMITH, George	10/27/1901	5/26/1981	4/14/1930	1930
SMITH, George	7/7/1937	6/15/1987	4/12/1966	1966
SMITH, John	9/27/1906	5/9/1982	9/17/1931	1931
SMITH, Lee	12/4/1957		4/4/1988	1988–1990
SMITH, Paddy	5/16/1894	12/2/1990	7/6/1920	1920
SMITH, Pete	3/19/1940		9/13/1962	1962–1963
SMITH, Reggie	4/2/1945		9/18/1966	1966–1973
SMITH, Zane	12/28/1960		5/14/1995	1995
SMITHSON, Mike	1/21/1955		4/7/1988	1988–1989
SNELL, Wally	5/19/1889	7/23/1980	8/1/1913	1913
SNOPEK, Chris	9/20/1970		9/2/1998	1998
SNYDER, Earl	5/6/1976		4/18/2004	2004
SOLTERS, Moose	3/22/1906	9/28/1975	4/17/1934	1934–1935
SOMMERS, Rudy	10/30/1886	3/18/1949	4/13/1926	1926–1927
SOTHORON, Allen	4/27/1893	6/17/1939	5/29/1921	1921
SPANSWICK, Bill	7/8/1938		4/18/1964	1964
SPARKS, Tully	12/12/1874	7/15/1937	7/25/1902	1902
SPEAKER, Tris	4/4/1888	12/8/1958	9/14/1907	1907–1915
SPENCE, Stan	3/20/1915	1/9/1983	6/8/1940	1940–1941, 1948–1949
SPENCER, Tubby	1/26/1884	2/1/1945	4/17/1909	1909
SPOGNARDI, Andy	10/18/1908	1/1/2000	9/2/1932	1932
SPRAGUE, Ed	7/25/1967		7/1/2000	2000
SPRING, Jack	3/11/1933		5/22/1957	1957
SPROWL, Bobby	4/14/1956		9/5/1978	1978
STAHL, Chick	1/10/1873	3/28/1907	4/26/1901	1901–1906
STAHL, Jake	4/13/1879	9/18/1922	4/20/1903	1903, 1908–1910, 1912–1913
STAIRS, Matt	2/27/1968		6/23/1995	1995
STALLARD, Tracy	8/31/1937		9/24/1960	1960–1962
STANDAERT, Jerry	11/2/1901	8/4/1964	4/18/1929	1929
STANGE, Lee	10/27/1936		6/3/1966	1966–1970
STANIFER, Rob	3/10/1972		4/11/2000	2000
STANLEY, Bob	11/10/1954		4/16/1977	1977–1989
STANLEY, Mike	6/25/1963		4/1/1996	1996–2000
STANSBURY, Jack	12/6/1885	12/26/1970	6/30/1918	1918
STANTON, Mike	6/2/1967		8/1/1995	1995–1996, 2005
STAPLETON, Dave	1/16/1954		5/30/1980	1980–1986
STATZ, Jigger	10/20/1897	3/16/1988	6/12/1920	1920
STEELE, Elmer	5/17/1886	3/9/1966	9/12/1907	1907–1909
STEINER, Ben	7/28/1921	10/27/1988	4/17/1945	1945–1946

PLAYER	BIRTH	DEATH	SOX DEBUT	YEARS ON RED SOX
STEINER, Red	1/7/1915		5/11/1945	1945
STENHOUSE, Mike	5/29/1958		5/18/1986	1986
STEPHENS, Gene	1/20/1933		4/16/1952	1952–1953, 1955–1960
STEPHENS, Vern	10/23/1920	11/3/1968	4/19/1948	1948–1952
STEPHENSON, Jerry	10/6/1943		4/14/1963	1963, 1965–1968
STERN, Adam	2/12/1980		7/7/2005	2005
STEWART, Sammy	10/28/1954		4/7/1986	1986
STIGMAN, Dick	1/24/1936		4/16/1966	1966
STIMSON, Carl	7/18/1894	11/9/1936	6/6/1923	1923
STOBBS, Chuck	7/2/1929		9/15/1947	1947–1951
STOKES, Al	1/1/1900	12/19/1986	5/10/1925	1925–1926
STONE, Dean	9/1/1930		5/8/1957	1957
STONE, George	9/3/1877	1/3/1945	4/20/1903	1903
STONE, Jeff	12/26/1960		9/9/1989	1989–1990
STORIE, Howie	5/15/1911	7/27/1968	9/7/1931	1931–1932
STRINGER, Lou	5/13/1917		9/20/1948	1948–1950
STRUNK, Amos	1/22/1889	7/22/1979	4/15/1918	1918–1919
STUART, Dick	11/7/1932	12/18/2003	4/9/1963	1963–1964
STUMPF, George	12/15/1910	3/6/1993	9/19/1931	1931–1933
STURDIVANT, Tom	4/28/1930		4/18/1960	1960
STYNES, Chris	1/19/1973		4/2/2001	2001
SUCHECKI, Jim	8/25/1926	7/20/2000	5/20/1950	1950
SULLIVAN, Denny	9/28/1882	6/2/1956	4/11/1907	1907–1908
SULLIVAN, Frank	1/23/1930		7/31/1953	1953–1960
SULLIVAN, Haywood	12/15/1930	2/12/2003	9/20/1955	1955, 1957, 1959–1960
SULLIVAN, Marc	7/25/1958		10/1/1982	1982, 1984–1987
SUMNER, Carl	9/28/1908	2/8/1999	7/28/1928	1928
SUPPAN, Jeff	1/2/1975		7/17/1995	1995–1997, 2003
SUSCE, George	9/13/1931		4/15/1955	1955–1958
SWANSON, Bill	10/12/1888	10/14/1954	9/2/1914	1914
SWEENEY, Bill	12/29/1904	4/18/1957	4/14/1930	1930–1931
SWINDELL, Greg	1/2/1965		8/2/1998	1998
SWORMSTEDT, Len	10/6/1878	7/19/1964	9/28/1906	1906
TABOR, Jim	11/5/1916	8/22/1953	8/2/1938	1938–1944
TAITT, Doug	8/3/1902	12/12/1970	4/10/1928	1928–1929
TANANA, Frank	7/3/1953		4/12/1981	1981
TANNEHILL, Jesse	7/14/1874	9/22/1956	4/18/1904	1904–1908
TARBERT, Arlie	9/10/1904	11/27/1946	6/18/1927	1927–1928
TARTABULL, Jose	11/27/1938		6/16/1966	1966–1968
TARVER, LaSchelle	1/30/1959		7/12/1986	1986
TASBY, Willie	1/8/1933		6/12/1960	1960
TATE, Bennie	12/3/1901	10/27/1973	4/30/1932	1932
TATUM, Jim	10/9/1967		4/16/1996	1996
TATUM, Ken	4/25/1944		4/8/1971	1971–1973
TAVAREZ, Jesus	3/26/1971		6/17/1997	1997
TAYLOR, Harry	5/20/1919		9/23/1950	1950–1952
TAYLOR, Scott	8/2/1967		9/17/1992	1992–1993
TEBBETTS, Birdie	11/10/1912		5/23/1947	1947–1950
TERRY, Yank	2/11/1911	11/4/1979	8/3/1940	1940, 1942–1945
THIELMAN, Jake	5/20/1879	1/28/1928	8/9/1908	1908
THOMAS, Blaine	8/1888	8/21/1915	8/25/1911	1911
THOMAS, Fred	12/19/1892	1/15/1986	4/22/1918	1918

PLAYER	BIRTH	DEATH	SOX DEBUT	YEARS ON RED SOX
THOMAS, George	11/29/1937		4/12/1966	1966–1971
THOMAS, Lee	2/5/1936		6/5/1964	1964–1965
THOMAS, Pinch	1/24/1888	12/24/1953	4/24/1912	1912–1917
THOMAS, Tommy	12/23/1899	4/27/1988	7/19/1937	1937
THOMSON, Bobby	10/25/1923		4/19/1960	1960
THONEY, Jack	12/8/1879	10/24/1948	4/14/1908	1908–1909, 1911
THORMAHLEN, Hank	7/5/1896	2/6/1955	4/16/1921	1921
THRONEBERRY, Faye	6/22/1931		4/15/1952	1952, 1955–1957
TIANT, Luis	11/23/1940		6/11/1971	1971–1978
TILLMAN, Bob	3/24/1937	6/21/2000	4/15/1962	1962–1967
TIMLIN, Mike	3/10/1966		4/1/2003	2003–2005
TINSLEY, Lee	3/4/1969		4/6/1994	1994–1996
TOBIN, Jack	5/4/1892	12/10/1969	8/3/1926	1926–1927
TOBIN, Johnny	1/8/1921	1/18/1982	4/20/1945	1945
TODT, Phil	8/9/1901	11/15/1973	4/25/1924	1924–1930
TOLAR, Kevin	1/28/1971		4/16/2003	2003
TOMBERLIN, Andy	11/7/1966		5/11/1994	1994
TONNEMAN, Tony	9/10/1881	8/7/1951	9/19/1911	1911
TORREZ, Mike	8/28/1946		4/7/1978	1978–1982
TRAUTWEIN, John	8/7/1962		4/7/1988	1988
TRIMBLE, Joe	10/12/1930		4/29/1955	1955
TRLICEK, Ricky	4/26/1969		4/6/1994	1994, 1997
TROUT, Dizzy	6/29/1915	2/28/1972	6/4/1952	1952
TRUESDALE, Frank	3/31/1884	8/27/1943	6/11/1918	1918
TRUJILLO, Mike	1/12/1960		4/14/1985	1985–1986
TUDOR, John	2/2/1954		8/16/1979	1979–1983
TURLEY, Bob	9/19/1930		7/26/1963	1963
UMPHLETT, Tom	5/12/1930		4/16/1953	1953
UNGLAUB, Bob	7/31/1881	11/29/1916	4/15/1904	1904–1905, 1907–1908
URBINA, Ugueth	2/15/1974		8/1/2001	2001–2002
VACHE, Tex	11/17/1894	6/11/1953	4/16/1925	1925
VALDEZ, Carlos	12/26/1971		9/19/1998	1998
VALDEZ, Julio	6/3/1956		9/2/1980	1980–1983
VALDEZ, Sergio	9/7/1964		6/16/1994	1994
VALENTIN, John	2/18/1967		7/27/1992	1992–2001
VALLE, Dave	10/30/1960		4/4/1994	1994
VAN CAMP, Al	9/7/1903	2/2/1981	4/15/1931	1931–1932
VAN DYKE, Ben	8/15/1888	10/22/1973	9/15/1912	1912
VAN EGMOND, Tim	5/31/1969		6/26/1994	1994–1995
VANDENBERG, Hy	3/17/1906	7/31/1994	6/8/1935	1935
VARITEK, Jason	4/11/1972		9/24/1997	1997–2005
VAUGHN, Mo	12/15/1967		6/27/1991	1991–1998
VAZQUEZ, Ramon	8/21/1976		4/9/2005	2005
VEACH, Bobby	6/29/1888	8/7/1945	4/15/1924	1924–1925
VEALE, Bob	10/28/1935		9/10/1972	1972–1974
VERAS, Dario	3/13/1973		7/1/1998	1998
VERAS, Wilton	1/19/1978		7/1/1999	1999–2000
VERNON, Mickey	4/22/1918		4/17/1956	1956–1957
VICK, Sammy	4/12/1895	8/17/1986	6/2/1921	1921
VIOLA, Frank	4/19/1960		4/9/1992	1992–1994
VITT, Ossie	1/4/1890	1/31/1963	4/23/1919	1919–1921

PLAYER	BIRTH	DEATH	SOX DEBUT	YEARS ON RED SOX
VOLLMER, Clyde	9/24/1921		5/11/1950	1950–1952
VOLZ, Jake	4/4/1878	8/11/1962	9/28/1901	1901
VOSMIK, Joe	4/4/1910	1/27/1962	4/18/1938	1938–1939
WADE, Jake	4/1/1912		4/24/1939	1939
WAGNER, Charlie	12/3/1912		4/19/1938	1938–1942, 1946
WAGNER, Gary	6/28/1940		9/10/1969	1969–1970
WAGNER, Hal	7/2/1915	8/4/1979	5/10/1944	1944, 1946–1947
WAGNER, Heinie	9/23/1880	3/20/1943	9/26/1906	1906–1913, 1915–1916, 1918
WAKEFIELD, Tim	8/2/1966		5/27/1995	1995–2005
WALBERG, Rube	7/27/1896	10/27/1978	4/19/1934	1934–1937
WALKER, Chico	11/25/1957		9/2/1980	1980–1981, 1983–1984
WALKER, Tillie	9/4/1887	9/21/1959	4/12/1916	1916–1917
WALKER, Todd	5/25/1973		3/31/2003	2003
WALL, Murray	9/19/1926	10/8/1971	8/4/1957	1957–1959
WALSH, Jimmy	9/22/1885	7/3/1962	9/1/1916	1916–1917
WALTERS, Bucky	4/19/1909		7/9/1933	1933–1934
WALTERS, Fred	9/4/1912	2/1/1980	4/17/1945	1945
WALTERS, Roxy	11/5/1892	6/3/1956	4/27/1919	1919–1923
WAMBSGANSS, Bill	3/19/1894	12/8/1985	4/15/1924	1924–1925
WANNINGER, Pee–Wee	12/12/1902	3/7/1981	4/12/1927	1927
WARNER, John	8/15/1872	12/21/1943	4/19/1902	1902
WARSTLER, Rabbit	9/13/1903	5/31/1964	7/24/1930	1930–1933
WASDIN, John	8/5/1972		4/6/1997	1997–2000
WASLEWSKI, Gary	7/21/1941		6/11/1967	1967–1968
WATSON, Bob	4/10/1946		6/15/1979	1979
WATWOOD, Johnny	8/17/1905	3/1/1980	4/30/1932	1932–1933
WEAVER, Monte	6/15/1906	6/14/1994	4/24/1939	1939
WEBB, Earl	9/17/1897	5/23/1965	4/27/1930	1930–1932
WEBSTER, Lenny	2/10/1965		7/30/1999	1999
WEBSTER, Ray	11/15/1937		4/21/1960	1960
WEDGE, Eric	1/27/1968		10/5/1991	1991–1992, 1994
WEILAND, Bob	12/14/1905	11/9/1988	4/16/1932	1932–1934
WELCH, Frank	8/10/1897	7/25/1957	7/15/1927	1927
WELCH, Herb	10/19/1898	4/13/1967	9/15/1925	1925
WELCH, Johnny	12/2/1906	9/2/1940	7/26/1932	1932–1936
WELLS, David	5/20/1963		4/3/2005	2005
WELZER, Tony	4/5/1899	3/18/1971	4/13/1926	1926–1927
WENZ, Fred	8/26/1941		6/4/1968	1968–1969
WERBER, Billy	6/20/1908		5/14/1933	1933–1936
WERLE, Bill	12/21/1920		4/19/1953	1953–1954
WERTZ, Vic	2/9/1925	7/7/1983	4/12/1959	1959–1961
WEST, David	9/1/1964		7/24/1998	1998
WHITE, Matt	8/19/1977		5/27/2003	2003
WHITE, Sammy	7/7/1928	8/5/1991	9/26/1951	1951–1959
WHITEMAN, George	12/23/1882	2/10/1947	9/13/1907	1907, 1918
WHITEN, Mark	11/25/1966		4/26/1995	1995
WHITT, Ernie	6/13/1952		9/12/1976	1976
WIDMAR, Al	3/20/1925	10/15/2005	4/25/1947	1947
WIGHT, Bill	4/12/1922		4/17/1951	1951–1952
WILBER, Del	2/24/1919	7/18/2002	5/13/1952	1952–1954
WILHOIT, Joe	12/20/1885	9/25/1930	9/18/1919	1919

PLAYER	BIRTH	DEATH	SOX DEBUT	YEARS ON RED SOX
WILLIAMS, Dana	3/20/1963		6/21/1989	1989
WILLIAMS, Dave	2/7/1881	4/25/1918	7/2/1902	1902
WILLIAMS, Denny	12/13/1899	3/23/1929	4/23/1924	1924–1925, 1928
WILLIAMS, Dib	1/19/1910	4/2/1992	5/4/1935	1935
WILLIAMS, Dick	5/7/1929		4/17/1963	1963–1964
WILLIAMS, Ken	6/28/1890	1/22/1959	4/10/1928	1928–1929
WILLIAMS, Rip	1/31/1882	7/23/1933	4/12/1911	1911
WILLIAMS, Stan	9/14/1936		7/23/1972	1972
WILLIAMS, Ted	8/30/1918	7/5/2002	4/20/1939	1939–1942, 1946–1960
WILLIAMSON, Scott	2/17/1976		8/1/2003	2003–2004
WILLOUGHBY, Jim	1/31/1949		7/6/1975	1975–1977
WILLS, Ted	2/9/1934		5/24/1959	1959–1962
WILSON, Archie	11/25/1923		6/11/1952	1952
WILSON, Duane	6/29/1934		7/3/1958	1958
WILSON, Earl	10/2/1934	4/23/2005	7/28/1959	1959–1960, 1962–1966
WILSON, Gary	1/12/1877	5/1/1969	9/27/1902	1902
WILSON, Jack	4/12/1912	4/19/1995	4/29/1935	1935–1941
WILSON, Jim	2/20/1922	9/2/1986	4/18/1945	1945–1946
WILSON, John	4/25/1903	8/27/1980	5/9/1927	1927–1928
WILSON, Les	7/17/1885	4/4/1969	7/15/1911	1911
WILSON, Squanto	3/29/1889	3/26/1967	4/22/1914	1914
WILTSE, Hal	8/6/1903	11/2/1983	4/13/1926	1926–1928
WINGFIELD, Ted	8/7/1899	7/18/1975	9/13/1924	1924–1927
WINN, George	10/26/1897	11/1/1969	4/29/1919	1919
WINNINGHAM, Herm	12/1/1961		4/11/1992	1992
WINSETT, Tom	11/24/1909	7/20/1987	4/20/1930	1930–1931, 1933
WINTER, George	4/27/1878	5/26/1951	6/15/1901	1901–1908
WINTERS, Clarence	9/7/1898	6/29/1945	8/28/1924	1924
WISE, Rick	9/13/1945		4/13/1974	1974–1977
WITTIG, Johnnie	6/16/1914	2/24/1999	6/22/1949	1949
WOLCOTT, Bob	9/8/1973		6/17/1999	1999
WOLFE, Larry	3/2/1953		4/7/1979	1979–1980
WOLTER, Harry	7/11/1884	7/7/1970	4/17/1909	1909
WOOD, Ken	7/1/1924		4/16/1952	1952
WOOD, Joe	5/20/1916		5/1/1944	1944
WOOD, Smoky Joe	10/25/1889	7/27/1985	8/24/1908	1908–1915
WOOD, Wilbur	10/22/1941		6/30/1961	1961–1964
WOODARD, Steve	5/15/1975		4/1/2003	2003
WOODS, John	1/18/1898	10/4/1946	9/16/1924	1924
WOODS, Pinky	5/22/1915	10/30/1982	6/20/1943	1943–1945
WOODWARD, Rob	9/28/1962		9/5/1985	1985–1988
WOOTEN, Shawn	7/24/1972		5/26/2005	2005
WORKMAN, Hoge	9/25/1899	5/20/1972	6/27/1924	1924
WORTHINGTON, Al	2/5/1929		4/18/1960	1960
WRIGHT, Jim	12/21/1950		4/15/1978	1978–1979
WRIGHT, Tom	9/22/1923		4/23/1950	1950–1951
WYATT, John	4/19/1935	4/6/1998	6/14/1966	1966–1968
WYCKOFF, Weldon	2/19/1892	5/8/1961	6/27/1916	1916–1918
YASTRZEMSKI, Carl	8/22/1939		4/11/1961	1961–1983
YERKES, Steve	5/15/1888	1/31/1971	9/29/1909	1909, 1911–1914
YORK, Rudy	8/17/1913	2/5/1970	4/16/1946	1946–1947
YOUKILIS, Kevin	3/15/1979		5/15/2004	2004–2005
YOUNG, Cy	3/29/1867	11/4/1955	4/27/1901	1901–1908

PLAYER	BIRTH	DEATH	SOX DEBUT	YEARS ON RED SOX
Young, Matt	8/9/1958		4/10/1991	1991–1992
Young, Tim	10/15/1973		5/9/2000	2000
Zahniser, Paul	9/6/1896	9/26/1964	5/9/1925	1925–1926
Zarilla, Al	5/1/1919	9/4/1996	5/8/1949	1949–1950, 1952–1953
Zauchin, Norm	11/17/1929		9/23/1951	1951, 1955–1957
Zeiser, Matt	9/25/1888	6/10/1942	4/27/1914	1914
Zuber, Bill	3/26/1913	11/2/1982	6/23/1946	1946–1947
Zupcic, Bob	8/18/1966	8/18/1966	9/7/1991	1991–1994

Note: Two players have imprecise birthdates. Broadway Aleck Smith was born in 1871. Precisely when in 1871 seems to be unknown. Blaine Thomas was born in August 1888. What date in August remains unknown.

Acknowledgments

All events in this book, including known births, deaths, game items, and transactions are complete through December 31, 2005.

Information contained in the current book drew, first of all, on *The Baseball Chronology* provided on www.baseballlibrary.com, which was then supplemented by cross-reference to Ed Walton's 1978 book *This Date in Red Sox History* and a number of other books. Many other sources were consulted as well, and considerable time was spent simply scanning newspapers of the day over the century-plus of Red Sox history. A great deal of double-checking was done by comparing previously published information with contemporary game accounts available online through SABR. Members of SABR (the Society for American Baseball Research) all receive free online access to the ProQuest's historical newspapers of the *Atlanta Journal-Constitution, Boston Globe, Chicago Defender, Chicago Tribune, Los Angeles Times, New York Times*, and *Washington Post*. This access alone is easily worth the price of membership to any historian—not just baseball historians.

SABR members also receive a discount on subscriptions to Paper of Record, which offers online reading of *The Sporting News* (and scores of other historical publications.)

Literally a couple of hundred errors were found in previously published works, and those have been corrected here. Needless to say, this book may contain at least some errors as well, and we would very much appreciate having errors found by readers brought to our attention.

A note on spelling. Some names are found spelled more than one way in various books. Almost every book spells Clarence Walker's nickname as "Tilly", but Walker himself spelled it "Tillie" (see his signature in SABR's *Deadball Stars of the American League*, for example.) This book uses "Tillie". Spellings of Bill Dinneen's surname were uniformly and consistently spelled with two of the letter "n" during his playing career. In his years as umpire, it was often rendered as Dinneen. In the course of researching this book, we found a news story about how frustrated he been that sportswriters always left out the third "n"—so we have adopted Dinneen. "Nuf-Ced" McGreevy's name is often spelled McGreevey—even on the outside of the saloon he owned, but Royal Rooters chronicler Peter Nash reports: "All legal documents as well as his signature on those documents use the 'McGreevy' name."

Transactions: Most of the transaction information used here was obtained free of charge from, and is copyrighted by, Retrosheet. Any baseball researcher, or even casual fan, hoping to learn about events that might have occurred on a particular day or with a particular player should visit their free website located at: www.retrosheet.org.

We have not included each and every transaction in Red Sox baseball history, in part because in recent years there is such rapid turnover of player personnel that it would become cumbersome. There is no way to include every signing of every prospect, most of whom never make the team. We have gone through the 105 years of Red Sox history and selected out those transactions that include players whose names might be recognizable or who at least played for the Red Sox. Included in this volume are 80-90% of all the transactions listed on Retrosheet.

Special thanks to Patrick Brennick, who did the lion's share of the work compiling the list of Red Sox debuts, and to Brad San Martin for valiant proofreading and database work.

Thanks also to Bill Carle, Paul R. Carroll Jr., Jim Charlton, Jon Daly, Ted Fischer, Mark Halfon, Tom Hufford, Terry Kitchen, Sean Lahman, Bill Lee, John Lewis, Phil Lowry, Peter J. Nash, Bill Nowlin, Sr., Jim Prime, Brad San Martin, Wayne McElreavy, Steve Netsky, John Rickert, Tom Ruane, Johnny Siever, Lee Sinins, Frank Solensky, Lyle Spatz, Bob Timmerman, and Cecilia Tan.

Supplementary Web Log

Maybe this book seems long enough, but in editing, we pulled out hundreds of entries, simply to get the book down to a more manageable level. If you want to know of even more things that happened in Red Sox history, please check the Day By Day supplementary web log on the Rounder Books website at www.rounderbooks.com.

Have you got a good story we missed?

We would also like to hear from readers who have additional suggestions of items we might have overlooked but which would be worthy of inclusion in future editions. There are so many great stories. If you know of an interesting occurrence, event, or factoid that you think we should add to make this a more comprehensive book, please contact the author, Bill Nowlin, via e-mail at **bnowlin@rounder.com**. Thank you!

Did you spot an error?

If you think you spot an error, please contact us. We would like to be sure to have the most accurate listing we can, and would like to be able to correct any future editions.

Bill Nowlin, born 3.9 miles from Fenway Park in Jamaica Plain, has been following Red Sox history on a daily basis since the last few years of Ted Williams' career. He has written more than a dozen books and over 100 articles on the Red Sox, and still has a few ideas in mind for future efforts. Bill is the vice president of the Society for American Baseball Research, and one of the founders of Rounder Records. He currently lives in Cambridge, Massachusetts, still less than five miles from Fenway.